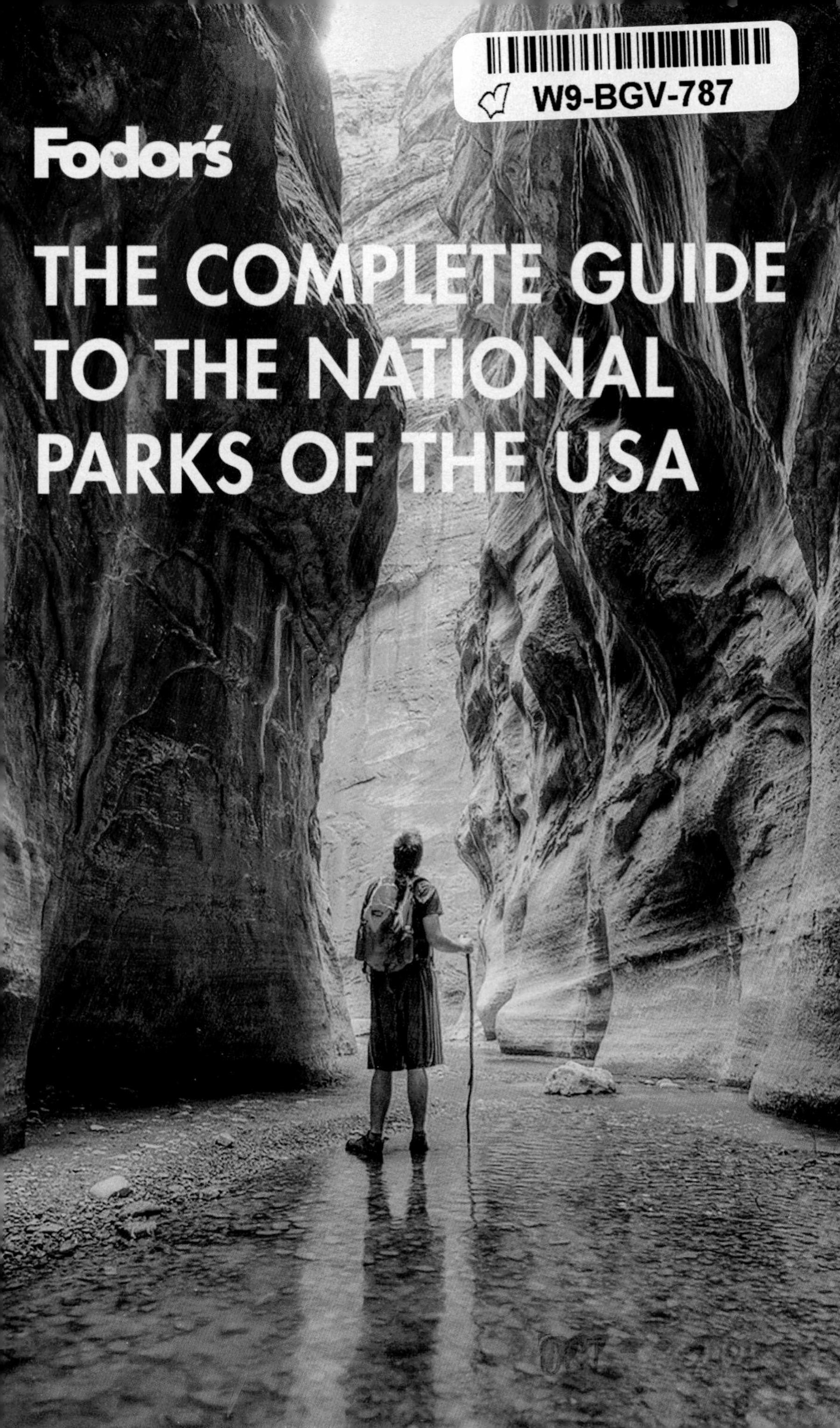
W9-BGV-787
Fodor's
THE COMPLETE GUIDE
TO THE NATIONAL
PARKS OF THE USA

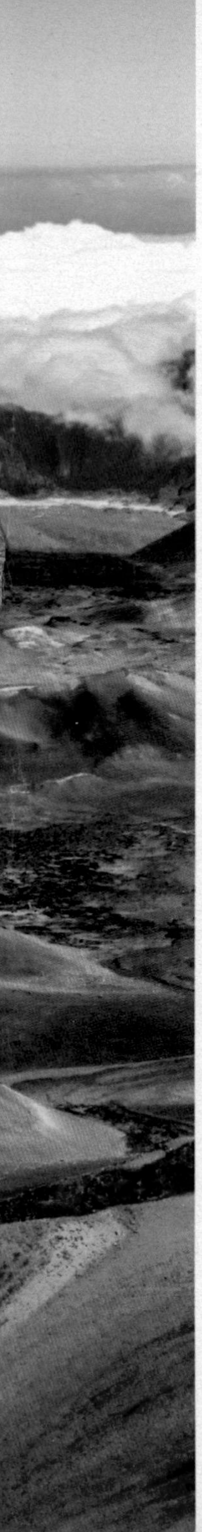

Welcome to the National Parks of the USA

Visits to America's national parks invite you to reconnect with nature on grand adventures. Raft waters in the Grand Canyon or New River Gorge. Watch Yellowstone geysers erupt, Glacier Bay ice calve, and Hawaii volcanoes smoke. Spot bison in the Badlands and gators in the Everglades. Explore Mammoth's caves or Carlsbad's caverns. Uncover history in Mesa Verde, Cuyahoga, and the Gateway Arch. See the Milky Way in Joshua Tree and the northern lights in Isle Royale. As you plan your travels, please confirm that places are still open, and let us know when we need to make updates at editors@fodors.com.

TOP REASONS TO GO

★ **Wildlife:** From bison to bald eagles to bears, the parks shelter amazing species.

★ **Hiking:** Countless scenic trails for all levels inspire and challenge walkers.

★ **Geology:** Unique formations like Utah's Arches and Kentucky's caves astound.

★ **Great Views:** Mountain peaks and scenic overlooks reward climbers and drivers alike.

★ **History:** Monuments and outposts tell the American story—from east to west.

★ **Luxury Lodges:** Famous hotels pair old-school grandeur with splendid surroundings.

Contents

Contents

Contents

Contents

Contents

MAPS

Chapter 1

EXPERIENCE THE NATIONAL PARKS OF THE USA

63 ULTIMATE EXPERIENCES

The National Parks of the USA offers terrific experiences that should be on every traveler's list. Here are Fodor's top picks for a memorable trip.

1 Day climb in the Tetons

Grand Teton National Park, Wyoming. Known for having some of the country's best rock climbing, the gold standard here is a trip 13,776 feet up the Grand Teton. It's open to beginners but better suited for experienced climbers. *(Ch. 27)*

2 Witness the beauty of the Big Room

Carlsbad Caverns National Park, New Mexico. The cavern's most beautiful section is a softly lit ballroom of sparkling speleothems called the Big Room. *(Ch. 13)*

3 Visit four dramatic landscapes

Canyonlands National Park, Utah. The Green and Colorado Rivers divide the park into districts of canyons, mesas, arches, and hoodoos. *(Ch. 11)*

4 See unusual boxwork cave formations

Wind Cave National Park, South Dakota. This is the seventh-longest cave system in the world, with roughly 150 surveyed miles of underground passageways. It's the densest "maze cave" on Earth. *(Ch. 60)*

5 See Delicate Arch and the Windows Section

Arches National Park, Utah. The sandstone arches here, famous symbols of the American Southwest, have been carved by thousands of years of wind, water, and ice. *(Ch. 5)*

6 Discover extinct creatures

Badlands National Park, South Dakota. This landscape of eroded rock formations preserves the remains of mammals 33 million years old. See replicas of some of the fossils discovered here. *(Ch. 6)*

7 Ogle General Sherman

Sequoia National Park, California. The General Sherman tree is the largest living tree in the world, at 275 feet tall and 36 feet in diameter at its roots. *(Ch. 54)*

8 Hike Half Dome

Yosemite National Park, California. The 16-mile round-trip trail to the top of Half Dome climbs nearly 5,000 feet. Hikers are rewarded with unparalleled views of the Yosemite Valley. *(Ch. 63)*

9 Investigate coastal tide pools

Olympic National Park, Washington. Along the park's rocky coastal outcroppings are tidepools full of giant green anemone, sea stars, and other intertidal species. *(Ch. 48)*

10 Hike into the Canyon

Grand Canyon National Park, Arizona. Views along the well-maintained, 12-mile (round-trip) Bright Angel Trail are unforgettable, whether you go the distance or just do a segment. *(Ch. 26)*

11 Drive the Going-to-the-Sun Road

Glacier National Park, Montana. Construction began in 1921 on the 50-mile-long road, which spans the width of the park. See the park's most famous features and wildlife. *(Ch. 24)*

12 Hike to the Santa Elena Canyon

Big Bend National Park, Texas. The sheer cliffs of the dramatic Santa Elena Canyon flank the Rio Grande, forming the boundary between Mexico and Texas in the park. *(Ch. 7)*

13 See volcanic erosion

Pinnacles National Park, California. This moonscape of eroded volcanic detritus is frequented by roughly 200 condors. See them at High Peaks or from the Peaks View scenic overlook. *(Ch. 50)*

14 Explore Wizard Island

Crater Lake National Park, Oregon. At the west end of Crater Lake, Wizard Island is a 763-foot cinder cone capped with a 100-foot-deep crater *(Ch. 16)*

15 Look into the past

Petrified Forest National Park, Arizona. Thousands of years of human history are on display in this desert landscape; over 600 archaeological and petroglyph sites have been found. *(Ch. 49)*

16 See one of the world's oldest organisms

Great Basin National Park, Nevada. Pine trees make up Nevada's ancient forest. The Bristlecone pine is the world's longest-living tree and likely its oldest living organism. *(Ch. 28)*

17 Watch hoodoos change color

Bryce Canyon National Park, Utah. Bryce Canyon has the largest concentration of hoodoos in the world. At sunset they are ablaze with pinks, oranges, yellows, and reds. *(Ch. 10)*

18 See the country's largest cactus

Saguaro National Park, Arizona. The Saguaro cactus, the largest succulent in the United States, grows in abundance in this slice of the Sonoran Desert. The plants can grow up to 40 feet. *(Ch. 53)*

19 See the South Rim Drive's 12 unique views

Black Canyon of the Gunnison National Park, Colorado. The 7-mile South Rim Drive has 12 separate overlooks, each offering a different view of the park's famous gorge. *(Ch. 9)*

20 Explore a geologic wrinkle in the Earth

Capitol Reef National Park, Utah. Utah's Waterpocket Fold is a geological wrinkle in the Earth's crust where shifting tectonic plates sent sedimentary rocks upward into a spiny plateau. *(Ch. 12)*

21 Trek to the summit of the Lassen Peak

Lassen Volcanic National Park, California. Lassen Peak is the world's largest "plug dome" volcano. Though dormant, it's the southernmost active volcano in the Cascade Range. *(Ch. 41)*

22 Hike one of the most dangerous volcanoes

Mount Rainier National Park, Washington. Mt. Rainier is considered one of the most dangerous volcanoes in the world due to its large film of glacial ice. *(Ch. 44)*

23 Explore desertscapes and ghost towns

Death Valley National Park, California. Mining towns sprang up in Death Valley when there was gold in the Panamint Mountains but were abandoned once the riches ran out in the late 1800s. *(Ch. 18)*

24 Kayak around Santa Cruz Island

Channel Islands National Park, California. Due to thousands of years of isolation, these islands are inhabited by plants and animals found nowhere else on Earth. Rent a kayak and explore. *(Ch. 14)*

25 Explore Cliff Palace

Mesa Verde National Park, Colorado. Cliff Palace was inhabited by 100 people for over a century before it was abandoned during 13th-century droughts. *(Ch. 43)*

26 Watch the goings on at Prairie Dog Town

Theodore Roosevelt National Park, North Dakota. The official "Prairie Dog Town" is less than a mile down the Buckhorn Trail from the Caprock Coulee Trailhead. *(Ch. 56)*

27 Hike the Pacific Crest Trail

Kings Canyon National Park, California. Through the High Sierra, a landscape of steep peaks and deep valleys, the trail hits its formidable highest point at Forester Pass, 13,153 feet above sea level. *(Ch. 54)*

28 Ascend the East Coast's highest mountain

Acadia National Park, Maine. At the first national park established east of the Mississippi, you can hike or drive to the 1,530-foot granite summit of Mount Desert Island's Cadillac Mountain. *(Ch. 4)*

29 Climb the Boca Chita Key lighthouse

Biscayne National Park, Florida. Take a boat trip to this 110-acre island, go for a hike, and ascend to the 65-foot lighthouse observation deck for a dramatic view of the ocean and Miami's skyline. *(Ch. 8)*

30 Swim around Fort Jefferson

Dry Tortugas National Park, Florida. Admire brightly colored tropical fish and thriving coral reefs as you swim and snorkel around the moat wall that surrounds Fort Jefferson. *(Ch. 20)*

31 Paddle the Turner River Canoe Trail

Everglades National Park, Florida. Keep an eye out for alligators, blue heron, hawks, and other wildlife as you kayak through mangroves and past imposing cypress trees on this 10-mile trek. *(Ch. 21)*

32 Go Canoeing in Cedar Creek

Congaree National Park, South Carolina. Watch for alligators, river otters, and wading birds as you canoe or kayak along a 15-mile waterway amid verdant old-growth forest. *(Ch. 15)*

33 Admire Denali's summit from Thorofare Ridge

Denali National Park, Alaska. From the sleek LEED-certified Eielson Visitor Center, hike the wildflower-strewn trail up to this ridge for views of Denali's 20,310-foot summit. *(Ch. 19)*

34 Fly over the Brooks Range

Gates of the Arctic National Park, Alaska. In this utterly remote 8.4-million-square-acre park, flightseeing trips carry visitors to pristine lakes for wilderness hikes and scenic paddles. *(Ch. 22)*

35 Bike to Brandywine Falls

Cuyahoga Valley National Park, Ohio. You can pedal or hike along the picturesque 1.5-mile Brandywine Gorge Trail to reach a boardwalk overlooking this majestic 60-foot cascade. *(Ch. 17)*

36 Paddle across Rainy Lake

Voyageurs National Park, Minnesota. Paddle the historic route of fur traders and indigenous inhabitants of pristine Rainy Lake aboard a 26-foot canoe. *(Ch. 58)*

37 Hike Saint John Island's Reef Trail

Virgin Islands National Park. The steep and lush Reef Trail passes under towering bay rum trees past petroglyphs and the ruins of a Dutch sugar plantation. *(Ch. 57)*

38 Set foot on the white ice of Root Glacier

Wrangell-St. Elias National Park, Alaska. In America's largest national park, spend a day hiking through Kennecott Mill Town, then traverse Root Glacier. *(Ch. 61)*

39 View massive glaciers

Glacier Bay National Park, Alaska. Whether on a massive cruise ship, a smaller day-tour boat, or a sea kayak, explore the waters and glaciers of this Alaska wonderland. *(Ch. 25)*

40 Descend into Kilaeua Iki Crater

Hawaii Volcanoes National Park, Hawaii. Follow the Devastation Trail into this crater by way of Thurston Lava Tube, a lush rain forest, and trek across a striking lakebed of hardened lava. *(Ch. 33)*

41 Watch the sunrise from Maui's highest peak

Haleakala National Park, Hawaii. Get up early, dress warmly, and drive to the park's Summit District to watch the breathtaking sunrise from the peak of Haleakala. *(Ch. 32)*

42 Drive stunning Newfound Gap Road

Great Smoky Mountains National Park, Tennessee and North Carolina. Enjoy alpine views and stop for a hike along the Appalachian Trail on this route that climbs more than 3,500 feet. *(Ch. 30)*

43 Ride to the top of an iconic 630-foot arch

Gateway Arch National Park, Missouri. Hop into a unique tram and ascend to the observation area atop the striking, Eero Saarinen–designed Arch for spectacular views of St. Louis and beyond. *(Ch. 23)*

44 Enjoy a day on (and around) West Beach

Indiana Dunes National Park, Indiana. The park's most popular beach not only has the most amenities but also a three-loop trail system with views of the dunes, Lake Michigan, and the Chicago skyline. *(Ch. 35)*

45 Scamper over 100-foot Arctic sand dunes

Kobuk Valley National Park, Alaska. Explore the Great Kobuk Sand Dunes, a 25-square-mile tract of shifting mounds of golden sand in this isolated wilderness in northwestern Alaska. *(Ch. 22)*

46 Soak in the springs at Buckstaff Bathhouse

Hot Springs National Park, Arkansas. Saunter along Bathhouse Row, then soak your bones during a mineral bath inside one of only two historic park bathhouses still operating today. *(Ch. 34)*

47 Paddle in Washington Harbor and Creek

Isle Royale National Park, Michigan. Make your way by canoe or kayak, keeping an eye out for moose, on the tranquil harbor and creek on the west end of this secluded, stunning island. *(Ch. 36)*

48 Fly over two active volcanoes

Lake Clark National Park, Alaska. Book a flightseeing tour for a view of the park's two active volcanoes and countless glaciers, then go for a bear-watching excursion along the water. *(Ch. 40)*

49 Snorkel in stunning South Pacific waters

National Park of American Samoa. At Ofu Beach, one of the most secluded stretches of white sand in the South Pacific, swim and snorkel along an isolated coral reef. *(Ch. 45)*

50 View bears at Brooks Falls

Katmai National Park, Alaska. Book an air taxi over the Alaska Range to historic Brooks Lodge and watch these hulking beasts fish for salmon swimming upriver at Brooks Falls. *(Ch. 38)*

51 Motor along scenic Skyline Drive

Shenandoah National Park, Virginia. Soak up breathtaking views of fall foliage or spring wildflowers as you make your way along this 105-mile ribbon of asphalt through the Blue Ridge Mountains. *(Ch. 55)*

52 Shoot the whitewater rapids of a gorge

New River Gorge National Park, West Virginia. Both relaxing rafting excursions and exhilarating runs over eye-popping Class IV and V rapids are offered in America's newest national park. *(Ch. 46)*

53 Kayak among glaciers

Kenai Fjords National Park, Alaska. Embark on a wildlife cruise through this dramatic fjord, spotting orca and humpback whales, then kayak through the icebergs to Aialik Glacier. *(Ch. 39)*

54 Explore the cave's Historic Entrance

Mammoth Cave National Park, Kentucky. Enter the world's longest-known cave system via the Historic Entrance on a self-guided walk along famous Broadway Avenue and through the Rotunda. *(Ch. 42)*

55 Ascend to the "Top of Texas"

Guadalupe Mountains National Park, Texas. Guadalupe Peak is the highest point in the state of Texas at 8,751 feet above sea level. If you're game enough to make it to the top, you'll climb 3,000 feet. *(Ch. 31)*

56 Hike The Narrows

Zion National Park, Utah. The only way to pass through The Narrows, a gorge so slim that it's less than 30 feet wide at some points, is by walking in the Virgin River. *(Ch. 64)*

57 Backpack beneath mountain glaciers

North Cascades National Park, Washington. Envisioned as an undeveloped backcountry, 94% of the park remains untouched, dotted with alpine lakes, forests, and 300 glaciers. *(Ch. 47)*

58 See the desert in bloom

Joshua Tree National Park, California. This rocky park is known for its unusual Joshua tree, a tall, stately yucca plant. In the springtime, cacti, succulents, and the Joshua trees are in full bloom. *(Ch. 37)*

59 Wander beneath soaring redwoods

Redwood National and State Parks, California. Hike beneath the world's tallest trees and explore the lush walls of 325-million-year-old Fern Canyon. *(Ch. 51)*

60 Sand sled down dunes

Great Sand Dunes National Park, Colorado. The sand dunes, the steepest in North America, are made up of 5 billion cubic meters of sand once found at the bottom of mountain lakes. *(Ch. 29)*

61 Drive through the dunes

White Sands National Park, New Mexico. As you curve around one set of towering white dunes after another, it feels as though you're driving through a snowy winter wonderland. *(Ch. 59)*

62 See the Grand Prismatic

Yellowstone National Park, Wyoming. Grand Prismatic Spring is the largest hot spring in the United States and the third largest in the world. *(Ch. 62)*

63 Ride across the park on horseback

Rocky Mountain National Park, Colorado. Ride on horseback through 415 square miles of incredible alpine beauty. Two stables offer guided tours in the summer. *(Ch. 52)*

CANADA
North Cascades National Park
Olympic National Park
Waterton Lakes National Park
Mount Rainier National Park
Glacier National Park
Washington
Montana
North Dakota
Theodore Roosevelt National Park
Oregon
Yellowstone National Park
Crater Lake National Park
Idaho
Wind Cave National Park
South Dakot
Redwood National Park
Grand Teton National Park
Badlands National Park
Lassen Volcanic National Park
Wyoming
Nevada
California
Nebraska
Yosemite National Park
Great Basin National Park
Arches National Park
Rocky Mountain National Park
Utah
Colorado
Kings Canyon National Park
Capitol Reef National Park
Black Canyon of the Gunnison National Park
Zion National Park
Pinnacles National Park
Sequoia National Park
Bryce Canyon National Park
Canyonlands National Park
Kansas
Great Sand Dunes National Park
Death Valley National Park
Mesa Verde National Park
Grand Canyon National Park
Channel Islands National Park
Petrified Forest National Park
Joshua Tree National Park
Arizona
New Mexico
Oklahoma
Saguaro National Park
White Sands National Park
Carlsbad Caverns National Park
Guadalupe Mountains National Park
Texas
Big Bend National Park
MEXICO
Alaska
NORTH SLOPE
Kobuk Valley National Park
Gates of the Arctic National Park
BROOKS RANGE
SEWARD PENINSULA
Fairbanks
Denali National Park
Yukon
CANADA
Denali (Mount McKinley)
ALASKA RANGE
Lake Clark National Park
Anchorage
Wrangell-Saint Elias National Park
Mount St Elias
Katmai National Park
Bristol Bay
Kenai Fjords National Park
Glacier Bay National Park
Juneau
ALASKA PENINSULA
GULF OF ALASKA
American Samoa
OLOSEGA
OFU
TA'Ū
TUTUILA
National Park of American Samoa
Pago Pago
South Pacific Ocean

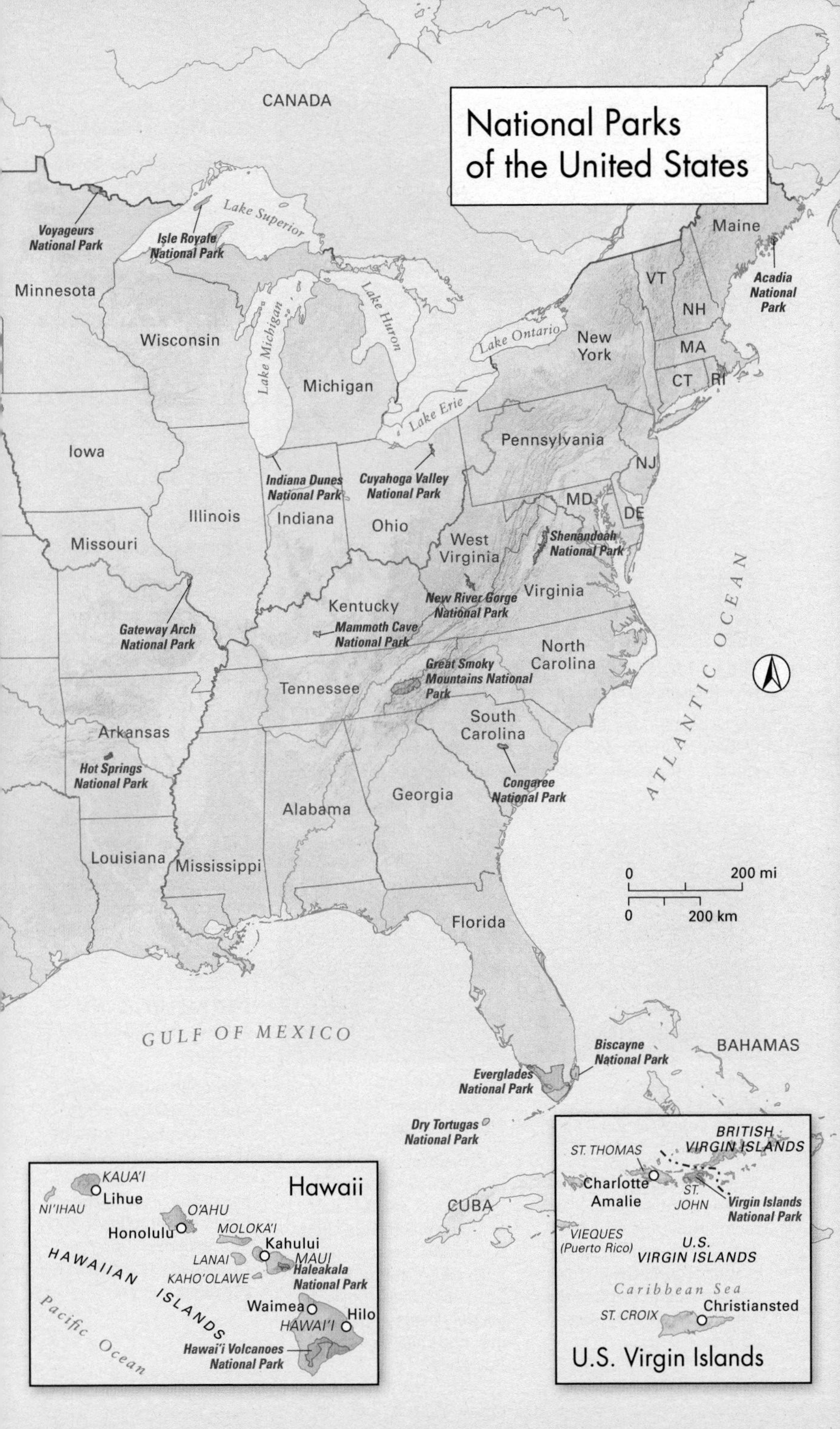
National Parks of the United States
CANADA
Lake Superior
Voyageurs National Park
Isle Royale National Park
Minnesota
Wisconsin
Lake Michigan
Lake Huron
Michigan
Lake Ontario
Lake Erie
Maine
Acadia National Park
VT
NH
MA
CT
RI
New York
Pennsylvania
NJ
MD
DE
Iowa
Indiana Dunes National Park
Cuyahoga Valley National Park
Illinois
Indiana
Ohio
Missouri
West Virginia
Shenandoah National Park
Virginia
New River Gorge National Park
Kentucky
Mammoth Cave National Park
Gateway Arch National Park
North Carolina
Great Smoky Mountains National Park
Tennessee
South Carolina
Arkansas
Hot Springs National Park
Congaree National Park
Georgia
Alabama
Louisiana
Mississippi
Florida
ATLANTIC OCEAN
0
200 mi
0
200 km
GULF OF MEXICO
Biscayne National Park
BAHAMAS
Everglades National Park
Dry Tortugas National Park
CUBA
Hawaii
KAUA'I
Lihue
NI'IHAU
O'AHU
Honolulu
MOLOKA'I
Kahului
LANAI
MAUI
KAHO'OLAWE
Haleakala National Park
HAWAIIAN ISLANDS
Pacific Ocean
Waimea
Hilo
HAWAI'I
Hawai'i Volcanoes National Park
BRITISH VIRGIN ISLANDS
ST. THOMAS
Charlotte Amalie
ST. JOHN
Virgin Islands National Park
VIEQUES (Puerto Rico)
U.S. VIRGIN ISLANDS
Caribbean Sea
ST. CROIX
Christiansted
U.S. Virgin Islands

The Best National Park Lodges

JENNY LAKE LODGE
Grand Teton National Park, Wyoming

East Coast "dudes" began this homestead in 1922. Hiking trails offer views of Grand Teton and Mt. Moran, and guests can ride horses and cruiser-style bikes around the grounds.

THE INN AT DEATH VALLEY
Death Valley National Park, California

This 1927 Spanish Mission–style inn underwent renovations and reopened in 2018 with luxurious new casitas around the historic Oasis Gardens. Explore the winding trails of Mosaic Canyon.

PARADISE INN
Mount Rainier National Park, Washington

Visitors began staying at the timber-frame inn here in 1917, and it hasn't changed much since then. A restaurant complete with park views and a cozy fireplace serves appropriately hearty fare like mac and cheese or bison Bolognese.

ZION LODGE
Zion National Park, Utah

The only place to stay in the park, this 1920s-era lodge is framed by lofty sandstone cliffs. Rustic cabins offer porches with incredible views and stone fireplaces. Bonus: at night, you can watch deer grazing on the lawn in the moonlight.

THE AHWAHNEE HOTEL
Yosemite National Park, California

Built in 1927, the hotel blends art deco and Native American design elements—some of which inspired the fictional Overlook Hotel in *The Shining*. Stay in a main lodge room for classic decor, or a cozy cottage with a fireplace.

EL TOVAR HOTEL
Grand Canyon National Park, Arizona

Situated a short stroll from the Grand Canyon's famed South Rim, it's all about location at El Tovar. The canyon empties of tourists after sunset, so you'll have the place all to yourself.

OLD FAITHFUL INN
Yellowstone National Park, Wyoming

The lobby, built in 1904 and flanked by gigantic stone fireplaces, is one of the biggest log structures in the world. In the 1950s, a printing press in the basement supplied nightly dinner menus. Comfortably furnished rooms here face the famous geyser.

The Ahwahnee Hotel, Yosemite

MANY GLACIER HOTEL
Glacier National Park, Montana

Glacial peaks provide a grand backdrop for this rustic lodge beside Swiftcurrent Lake in Glacier National Park's northeastern section. The series of Swiss chalet–style buildings house modestly decorated guest rooms.

KALALOCH LODGE
Olympic National Park, Washington

Come to this serene ocean-front setting to explore rain forests, glaciers, and protected coastline. Spend a day at Ruby Beach or Lake Crescent, before enjoying sustainable seafood and Washington State wines at Creekside Restaurant back at the lodge.

SKYLAND
Shenandoah National Park, Virginia

It's all about the view at this lodge with motel-style rooms and cabins that sit atop this 3,680-foot ridge. You can gaze from your room's deck and from the hotel's dining room.

CRATER LAKE LODGE
Crater Lake National Park, Oregon

Gaze on the deepest lake in the U.S. from this rustic lodge perched on the southwest rim of the caldera. The vivid blue water is due to the lake's depth—nearly 2,000 feet—and the surrounding volcanic peaks only add to the dramatic beauty.

VOLCANO HOUSE
Hawaii Volcanoes National Park, Hawaii

As recently as 2020, guests staying in this simple red-clapboard 1870s lodge perched on the rim of a caldera have been able to look out from the grounds and the dining room to see the orange-pink glow of lava bubbling within Halema'uma'u crater.

Wildlife in the Parks

BISON
Yellowstone is the only place in the country where bison have lived continuously since prehistoric times; currently, the park's two herds have about 4,700 animals. Bison can also be seen at Badlands, Grand Teton, Great Sand Dunes, Theodore Roosevelt, and Wind Cave.

GRAY WOLF
Listed as endangered in some parts of the country, these formidable canines communicate with each other through body language, barks, and howls. Wolves are wary of humans, but you might spot one at Denali, Grand Teton, Isle Royale, Voyageurs, and Yellowstone.

MOOSE
Feeding on fir, willows, and aspens, the moose is the largest member of the deer family: the most impressive bulls stand 7 feet tall at the shoulders and weigh up to 1,600 pounds. Look for them in Acadia, Glacier, Grand Teton, Isle Royale, Rocky Mountain, Voyageurs, and Yellowstone.

RAPTORS
Raptor species thrive across the country, including golden and bald eagles. Once-extinct California condors—with their amazing 9.5-foot wingspan—now fly over Pinnacles, while snowy owls are sometimes seen, or heard, in Acadia. In warmer climes, watch for snow-tailed kites in the Everglades and ʻio (Hawaiian hawks) above Hawaii Volcanoes.

BIGHORN SHEEP
Found on rocky ledges, they fascinate with their rutting during autumn mating season and their ability to travel where the rest of us can't. In winter, the docile herd animals descend to lower elevations. Found in many western national parks, their cousins, Dall sheep, are common in Denali and elsewhere in Alaska.

BEARS
Male grizzlies, also known as brown bears, can weigh 700 pounds and reach a height of 8 feet when standing on their hind legs—they're common to Alaska, Montana, and Wyoming parks. Black bears are about half the size and range as far as Acadia, the Everglades, and Saguaro. Bear sightings can cause trail closures.

ELK
These ungulates congregate where forest meets meadows, and are found in many national parks, including Redwood, Great Smoky Mountains, and Rocky Mountain. In September and October, bulls attract mating partners by bugling, a loud whistling. Their smaller white-necked cousins, caribou, can be seen in Denali and other Alaska parks.

COYOTE
As big as mid-size dogs, coyotes thrive in many national parks, especially in the West but increasingly throughout the country. Most often alone or in pairs, they occasionally form small packs for hunting. Commonly about half the size, their cousins the fox are also frequent park residents.

MOUNTAIN GOAT
Not really goats at all (they're actually related to antelope), these woolly mountaineers live in high elevations throughout the northwestern United States. Look for them in Glacier, Glacier Bay, Kenai Fjords, Mount Rainier, North Cascades, and Yellowstone.

MOUNTAIN LION
Although these enormous carnivores, which can be 8 feet long and weigh up to 200 pounds, live throughout western North America, you won't see them in most parks due to their elusive nature. Also known as cougars and—in their one eastern habit, the Everglades—panthers, they're capable of taking down an elk.

Wildlife in the Parks

WHALES
Alaska's waters are prime for black-and-white orcas, humpback, gray, and occasionally blue whales. A variety of these massive sea mammals can also be seen off the coasts of Acadia, American Samoa, Channel Islands, Haleakala, Hawaii Volcanoes, Olympic, and Redwood national parks.

AQUATIC BIRDS
Birdwatching—especially for aquatic species—is a popular park activity. Look for cormorants, harlequin ducks, and marbled murrelets in Olympic and Alaska's coastal parks, and flamingoes and roseate spoonbills in the Everglades. Listen for the eerie call of common loons in Acadia, Voyageurs, and Isle Royale.

ALLIGATORS AND CROCODILES
These cold-blooded reptiles inhabit the Everglades and Biscayne, which are the northernmost habitats for crocodiles (freshwater and saltwater), and the southernmost habitats for alligators (freshwater and some brackish wetlands), which are also found in Congaree.

BATS
Nearly 50 species of these flying mammals have been identified in national parks. Most prominently seen in Carlsbad Caverns and Mammoth Cave, bats also thrive in Wind Cave, Great Smoky Mountains, and Virgin Islands. The "flying fox" bats of American Samoa are the islands' only native mammals.

SNAKES AND LIZARDS
Cold-blooded vertebrate reptiles, including snakes and lizards, are a common presence in most national parks. Keep an eye out for rattlesnakes in the lower 48, as well as copperheads in the Southeast, and colorful coral snakes in the Southwest, Texas, and Florida. You may see iguanas, geckos, and other lizards in the Virgin Islands, Florida, and desert parks.

SEA TURTLES
On the shore of Hawaii Volcanoes, from June through October, you may be lucky enough to see nesting honuea (or hawksbill turtles), which weigh up to 150 pounds and lay more than 150 eggs. Hawksbill and a few other types of sea turtles can also be seen in American Samoa, Virgin Islands, and Florida's three national parks.

MANATEES
These gentle, lumbering aquatic mammals—downlisted from endangered to threatened in 2017 thanks to aggressive conservation efforts—are often seen, especially during the cooler months, during tours in the mangrove swamps of the Everglades and occasionally in Biscayne.

TERRESTRIAL BIRDS
There are countless types of land birds in the national park system, from chatty songbirds in Alaska to golden-fronted woodpeckers and Mexican jays in Big Bend to scarlet tanagers and indigo buntings in Shenandoah. The Hawaiian nene goose is found in Haleakala and Hawaii Volcanoes.

TROPICAL FISH
All of those warm-seas parks popular for snorkeling and diving—American Samoa, Dry Tortugas, Biscayne, and Virgin Islands—are excellent places to view colorful fish, including raccoon butterflyfish, stingrays, queen angels, spotlight parrotfish, and checkered puffers.

SEALS AND SEA LIONS
Playful harbor seals are a favorite sight along the rocky shores of Kenai Fjords, Acadia, and Olympic national parks. Sea lions, their gregarious so-called second cousins, are noisier, have ear flaps, spend more time ashore, and proliferate along the Pacific Coast at Channel Islands, Glacier Bay, and Redwood.

The Diversity of America's National Parks

Apostle Islands National Lakeshore, WI

TYPES OF NPS UNITS
The most common NPS designations include national monuments (85), national historic sites (73), and national historic parks (61), but the network also includes national battlefields, preserves, memorials, seashores, lakeshores, recreation areas, and more. Here are 12 of our favorite units.

APOSTLE ISLANDS NATIONAL LAKESHORE, WI
This 22-island archipelago in Lake Superior is a wonderland for kayaking through dramatic sea caves and relaxing hikes through groves of pine and aspen. You'll find no fewer than eight lighthouses, and Stockton Island is famed for its thriving black-bear population. If you'd rather not paddle, book a scenic cruise.

CANYON DE CHELLY NATIONAL MONUMENT, AZ
Comprising two long, 1,000-foot canyons, Canyon de Chelly lies entirely within the Navajo Nation. You can only venture into the canyons with an authorized Navajo guide, but it's easy to enjoy the astounding views from the several observation points along two park roads that snake along the canyon rims.

CAPE COD NATIONAL SEASHORE, MA
Extending 30 miles from Chatham to Provincetown and encompassing Cape Cod's outer "hook," this 43,000-acre swatch of superb beaches, undulating dunes, marshes and wetlands, and pitch-pine and scrub-oak forest is laced with walking, biking, and horseback trails.

CATOCTIN MOUNTAIN PARK, MD
Just a 90-minute drive outside Washington, DC and home to the storied American presidential retreat, Camp David, this 6,000-acre tract of Blue Ridge Mountains wilderness consists of dense woodlands, rocky lodges, and rustic cabins that were developed by the Works Progress Administration in the 1930s.

CHACO CULTURE NATIONAL HISTORIC SITE, NM
Reached by remote, rutted, unpaved roads, this archaeological treasure 150 miles northwest of Albuquerque takes some effort to reach, but the rewards are many. Excavations have uncovered what was from 850 to 1250 AD a vast network of commerce and culture. Several of the ancient structures—such as an immense Great Kiva, Casa Rinconada, or Pueblo Bonito—are simply astounding.

CRATERS OF THE MOON NATIONAL MONUMENT, ID
This impressive 750,000-acre monument and preserve is a font of otherworldly geothermal features, including boiling mud pools, steaming vents, and large craters. A marked walkway snakes for 2 miles through the belching, sulfurous landscape, past boiling pits and hissing crevices.

Canyon de Chelly National Monument, Az

DEVILS TOWER NATIONAL MONUMENT, WY
This rocky, grooved butte juts upward 1,280 feet above the plain of the Belle Fourche River and was designated America's first national monument in 1906. The tower was a tourist magnet long before a spaceship landed here in the movie *Close Encounters of the Third Kind.* It's popular among expert climbers, but even casual visitors can make the hike around its base.

JEAN LAFITTE NATIONAL HISTORIC PARK & PRESERVE, LA
A collection of sites devoted to preserving southern Louisiana's distinct Cajun culture, Jean Lafitte comprises six different sites as well as a headquarters in New Orleans. The park encompasses outstanding museums and cultural centers as well as trails and canoe routes through hardwood forests and dense swamps.

KALUAPAPA NATIONAL HISTORIC PARK, HI
Part of what's memorable about visiting this historic park where those who suffered from Hansen's disease, or leprosy, were once exiled is hiking the steep trail that switchbacks down a 1,700-foot sea cliff to this isolated coastal strip on Molokai's remote north coast (you can also fly in). It's a fascinating site that commemorates a tragic legacy.

MOUNT ST. HELENS NATIONAL VOLCANIC MONUMENT, WA
One of the most prominent peaks in the Northwest's rugged Cascade Range, Mount St. Helens National Volcanic Monument affords visitors an up-close look at the site of the most destructive volcanic blast in U.S. history. A modern, scenic highway carries travelers near the summit, which offers thrilling opportunities for climbing, hiking, and learning about volcanology.

NATCHEZ TRACE NATIONAL SCENIC TRAIL, MS–AL–TN
Among a handful of linear NPS units, this 444-mile scenic parkway winds through lush pine and hardwood forests, accessing ancient Native American mounds, historic homes, Civil War sites, lush waterfalls, and cypress swamps.

POINT REYES NATIONAL SEASHORE, CA
The West Coast's only national seashore, this 71,000-acre spot encompasses hiking trails, secluded beaches, and rugged grasslands, and sheer bluffs from which you can often spy whales, sea lions, and other marine life.

Buffalo Soldiers and the Early National Park Service

Throughout the American Indian Wars of 1866 through 1892, the U.S. government enlisted vast numbers of black soldiers to serve in its cavalry and infantry divisions, many of them among the 180,000 black veterans of the Civil War. Those who signed on were confined to all-black regiments led by white officers, and were treated as third-rate citizens. Despite many hardships—including poor rations, racism, mounts sometimes described as "old and half-dead," and having to serve in harsh and desolate areas of the western frontier—many troops thrived, and they collectively became known as Buffalo Soldiers.

Explanations vary as to how these brave men (and one barely documented woman) received their unique moniker. Some say the Native Americans they fought—and sometimes protected—named them out of respect for their courage and fortitude, traits associated with buffalo. Many national park units where these valiant cavalrymen served now commemorate and interpret their legacy, including Fort Davis National Historic Site and Big Bend National Park in Texas, Fort Larned National Historic Site in Kansas, Fort Vancouver National Historic Site in Washington, Hawaii Volcanoes National Park, Chiricahua National Monument in Arizona, and Klondike Gold Rush National Historical Park in Skagway, Alaska—here the men enforced order among the unruly throngs of prospectors who descended on the area in 1899. One of the best places to learn about their history is the Charles Young Buffalo Soldiers National Monument in Xenia, Ohio, which was established in 2013 to honor the life of one of the greatest leaders—and Civil Rights pioneers—among the ranks of these soldiers.

Another state in which Buffalo Soldiers played a vital role is California. In the early 1900s, they spent winters at what's now San Francisco's Golden Gate National Recreation, and at Sequoia, Kings Canyon, and Yosemite national parks, troops from the 24th Infantry and 9th Cavalry spent summers patrolling and protecting against poachers, illegal loggers, and other ill-doers, in this capacity acting as precursors to today's park rangers. In Sequoia, Buffalo Soldiers helped develop the park's infrastructure, constructing park roads through treacherous terrain and carving out the first trail to the Lower 48's highest peak, 14,494-foot Mount Whitney. And in Yosemite, the troops built the first museum in a national park, an arboretum (no longer in existence) near the banks of the Merced River, near the Wawona Hotel.

For more on the legacy of Buffalo Soldiers in the national park service, visit 🌐 *nps.gov/subjects/buffalosoldiers*.

Chapter 2

PLANNING YOUR VISIT

Updated by
Andrew Collins

Know Before You Go

When is the best time to visit? What are the must-see sights? What do I need to plan ahead for? Do I need to reserve campsites? What should I bring? Can I bring my pet to the parks? Is traveling with kids a good idea? We've got answers and a few tips to help you make the most of your visit.

SEASONS AND WEATHER WORK DIFFERENTLY

National parks are places of extremes—extreme beauty and extreme weather. In May, for example, you'll see snow at Yellowstone and North Cascades; while down at Guadalupe Mountains on the Texas/ New Mexico border, the unrelenting sun has already dried out the landscape; and in the humid Everglades, average highs are already in the low 90s. No matter which park you visit, prepare for both excessive heat and brutal cold.

PLAN AHEAD FOR THE MOST ADVENTUROUS PARK EXPERIENCES

National park rangers protect the parks' ecologies from the millions of tourists who visit annually. This means that for some of the most popular adventures in the park—kayaking up-bay at Glacier Bay or exploring Cleaveland Avenue in Mammoth Cave—there are only a handful of spots open and they often fill up well in advance, so be sure to reserve early on the park's website. In some places, like at Yosemite's Half Dome, the required permit is accessible only via a lottery system, with just 300 winners a day.

LEAVE NO TRACE

Anything you bring into the park must be carried back out or put in the appropriate garbage or recycling receptacle. Don't pick up any rocks or artifacts or fossils; don't collect flowers or firewood; and never touch or interact with a wild animal.

SOME CAMPSITES ARE RESERVED FOR WALK-UPS

Most parks reserve campsites for first-come, first-served walk-ups. As long as you get there as early in the morning as possible, you're likely to get a spot, even on weekends. They aren't always the most desirable campgrounds in the park, though—at Yosemite, for example, most of the walk-up sites are located in high country and not in the Yosemite Valley—but it's much better than staying home.

RECOGNIZE AND RESPECT THE PARK'S INDIGENOUS HISTORY

For many centuries, the only visitors to this nation's wilderness were the indigenous peoples of North America. Evidence of settlement and exploration by Native Americans in the national parks dates back more than 10,000 years. Thanks to a mandate that enforces management of cultural and ecological resources in the parks, artifacts left behind have been well preserved. For some of the best insight into Native American history, plan a visit to Haleakalā, Olympic, Mesa Verde, the Grand Canyon, Badlands, or the Utah triad—Arches, Zion, and Canyonlands. If you find an artifact while hiking or backpacking in a national park, never pick it up; artifacts are useless to archaeologists unless they are discovered in situ.

FIRES ARE A HUGE CONCERN

Although wildfires have always been an issue, particularly during June and July, in recent years, hot, dry conditions, overgrown forests, and unhealthy trees have turned the West into a tinderbox, and wildfires have ravaged the landscape year-round, In 2017, more than 12,000 acres of Glacier National Park were destroyed by the Howe Ridge Fire; in 2018, Yosemite closed for the first time since 1990 due to the nearby Ferguson Fire; and in 2020, it seemed as if all of California was ablaze. It's critical that you be mindful of fire alerts and that you follow fire-prevention protocols. Most parks still allow campfires in designated fire pits, while others have charcoal grills. Outside of these designated areas, fires are both illegal and incredibly dangerous. If you plan to camp in the backcountry and need fire for cooking, bring a small camp stove or propane burner.

DON'T SKIP THE VISITOR CENTER

At most national parks, the visitor center is more than just a place to get information on the best hiking trails. Here you'll often find museum-quality displays on the park's ecology, geology, and biology; some even have archaeological artifacts on view.

TAKE WARNING SIGNS AND RANGER ADVICE SERIOUSLY

National parks are among the few remaining places in the United States that have not been entirely engineered for your safety; in some cases the only thing that stands between you and certain death is a sign. Visitors die every year in climbing, hiking, and swimming accidents and animal encounters in America's national parks. Always take precautionary signs and ranger advice seriously.

FIND BEAUTY AND SOLITUDE AWAY FROM THE FAMOUS SITES

It's kind of a catch-22: you go to a national park to experience the beauty and solitude of the natural world only to discover that everyone else had the same plan. Rather than visiting the most popular sites, hit the trails (or water), particularly routes that are longer than 3 miles and can't be traversed by baby carriages and large tour groups. They may not be listed as the park's must-see locations, but they're almost guaranteed to be just as spectacular, yet apart from the crowds.

GET A GOOD LOOK AT WHAT WE COULD LOSE AS CLIMATE CHANGE PROGRESSES

National parks are ground zero for the environmental havoc wrought by climate change. These extreme environments are seeing rapid change as glaciers melt (Glacier Bay), wildfires rage (Yosemite and Glacier), and tides rise (Biscayne, Dry Tortugas, and the Everglades). While this is devastating to watch, visiting the national parks reminds us what we have to lose.

PETS IN THE PARK

Generally, pets are allowed only in developed areas of the national parks, including drive-in campgrounds and picnic areas. They must be kept on a leash at all times. With the exception of guide dogs, pets are not allowed inside buildings, on most trails, on beaches, or in the backcountry. They also may be prohibited in areas controlled by concessionaires, such as restaurants. Some national parks have kennels; call ahead to learn the details and to see if there's availability. Some of the national forests (🌐 *www.fs.fed.us*) surrounding the parks have camping and are more lenient with pets, although you should not plan to leave your pet unattended at the campsite.

TRAVELING WITH KIDS

If you plan to travel with kids, check out these websites before heading out for ways to entertain and educate. 🌐 *smokeybear.com/en/smokey-for-kids*; 🌐 *www.nationalparks.org/our-work/programs/npf-kids*; 🌐 *www.nps.gov/kids/junior-ranger-online.htm*; 🌐 *www.doi.gov/public/teachandlearn*

VIEW THE WORK OF KEN BURNS

Watch the amazing 12-hour PBS miniseries or read the follow-up book, *The National Parks: America's Best Idea*, produced by the legendary documentary maker Ken Burns. These mesmerizing, beautifully filmed and photographed works detail national park system's establishment and stewardship from the mid-19th century to the present.

USE MAPS

If you plan to do a lot of hiking or mountaineering, especially in the backcountry, invest in detailed maps and a compass. Topographical maps are sold in well-equipped outdoor stores (REI and Cabela's, for example). Maps in different scales are available from the U.S. Geological Survey. To order, go to 🌐 *www.usgs.gov/pubprod/maps.html* or call ☎ *888/275–8747*.

Park Passes

NATIONWIDE PASSES

Although not all national parks charge admission—and children under age 16 always enter free—many do. If you're visiting even a few of the most expensive American national parks in one vacation or over the course of a year, you can save money with one of the America the Beautiful (all called Interagency) passes, which generally cover the cardholder and all others in a single vehicle (or the cardholder and up to three other passengers age 16 and older at places that charge per person).

What's more, the passes are valid for entry to more than 2,000 federal recreation sites managed by six participating agencies. These include the NPS as well as the Bureau of Land Management, Bureau of Reclamation, Fish and Wildlife Service, U.S. Army Corps of Engineers, and USDA Forest Service.

Although the NPS (🌐 *www.nps.gov/planyourvisit/passes.htm*) has pass details, the easiest strategy is to buy a pass in person—they're sold at every national park as well as many other federal recreation sites that collects fees, and you can pay in cash or with a credit card.

Additionally, you can buy passes online or by phone (there's a $5 or $10 handling charge) from the United States Geological Survey (USGS, ☎ *888/275–8747, Option 2* 🌐 *store.usgs.gov/pass* or Recreation.gov (☎ *877/444–6777* reservations, ☎ *606/515–6777* international 🌐 *www.recreation.gov*). Keep in mind, though, that annual passes are good for a year from the month of purchase, so if you buy one online, you may want to avoid placing your order more than a few weeks before your intended first use.

All passes are nontransferable and nonrefundable (lost or stolen passes must be repurchased), and you must show photo ID with your pass at entrances.

Access Pass. United States citizens or permanent residents with disabilities medically determined to be permanent (documentation required) can acquire this free lifetime pass. At some locations, it might also allow for discounts on camping, tours, and other amenities.

Annual Pass. Available to anyone age 16 or older, this pass costs $80. It can be shared by two "owners," who need not be related or married (both must sign the back of the pass). It's also good for you and all of your passengers in a noncommercial vehicle at parks that charge per vehicle, or you and four adults at parks with per-person fees.

Every Kid Outdoors Pass. This free pass (🌐 *everykidoutdoors.gov*) is available to U.S. students in their fourth-grade school year (i.e., it's valid Sept.–Aug.) and covers three accompanying family members or friends.

Senior Pass. If you're 62 or older and are a U.S. citizen or permanent resident, you can buy an annual $20 pass or a lifetime $80 pass. At some sites, this pass might also allow for discounts on some amenities and services such as camping and guided tours; discounts vary from park to park. In addition, senior citizens can acquire passes via a mail-in application (🌐 *store.usgs.gov/s3fs-public/senior_pass_application.pdf*); additional fees apply.

Volunteer Pass. Look into this free, annual pass if you've logged 250 volunteer hours at recreation sites or lands overseen by one of the six federal pass-program agencies.

Military Pass. This pass is free to current members (and members' dependents) of the Army, Navy, Air Force, Marines, and Coast Guard, as well as the Reserves and National Guard.

■ TIP→ The Golden Eagle, Golden Age, and Golden Access passes have been discontinued. These passes can be used for park entrance if they are still valid according to the pass's original provisions.

INDIVIDUAL PARK PASSES

Most national parks offer individual annual passes. Prices vary but hover around $35 to $70 (🌐 *www.nps.gov/aboutus/entrance-fee-prices.htm*). In a few cases these passes include admission to two sites (say, a national park and a national monument, recreation area, or forest) that are near each other. If you might visit a particular park more than once in a year, look into its annual pass, but remember that $80 America the Beautiful pass costs only a little more than some individual park passes and may be a better value if you're visiting a few parks in a year. On the other hand, sometimes there's only a small difference between a single day's and a year's admission. For example, Bryce Canyon charges $35 per vehicle for a seven-day permit but only $5 more for the annual pass, meaning a $30 savings if you return to the park within the year.

In other cases, the entrance fee to one park includes admission to other federally managed sites nearby: a $55 Southeast Utah Parks Pass gets you into Arches and Canyonlands, plus Natural Bridges National Monument, for a year; any paid entrance to Sequoia and Kings Canyon includes access to the Hume Lake District of Sequoia National Forest/Giant Sequoia National Monument; and for an extra $5, you can add unlimited access to Arapahoe National Recreation Area to your $70 Rocky Mountain NP annual pass.

FREE ADMISSION

Each year, the national parks designate a handful of "Free Entrance Days" (check the NPS website, 🌐 *www.nps.gov/findapark/feefreeparks.htm*, for the most updated list). In addition, many parks—315 of the 423 NPS properties—never charge an admission fee. They include:

- Biscayne
- Channel Islands*
- Congaree
- Cuyahoga Valley
- Gates of the Arctic
- Great Basin*
- Great Smoky Mountains
- Hot Springs
- Kenai Fjords
- Kobuk Valley
- Lake Clark
- New River Gorge
- North Cascades
- Redwood
- Voyageurs
- Wind Cave*
- Wrangell–St. Elias

**There is a fee for transportation to Channel Islands; cave tours at Great Basin and Wind Cave have a fee.*

Family Fun

TOP 5 TIPS

1. Plan ahead. At many parks, rooms and campsites fill up fast, so make your reservations as early as you can. Many parks will have every room and campsite booked several months in advance (weekends are especially popular). We recommend booking at least six months ahead, and more if you plan to visit one of the more popular parks, such as Grand Canyon, Grand Teton, Great Smoky Mountains, Yellowstone, or Yosemite. If you plan on staying outside the park, check with the hotels you're considering as far ahead as you can, as these places can fill up fast as well. You can also go online. All the national parks have websites—links to all of them are at the National Park Service page (🌐 *www.nps.gov*).

2. Get the kids involved. It might seem easier to do the planning yourself, but you'll probably have a better time—and your kids definitely will—if you involve them. No matter how old they are, children ought to have a good idea of where you're going and what you're about to experience. It will help get them excited beforehand and will likely make them feel like they have a say and a stake in the trip. Discuss the park's attractions and give your kids a choice of two or three options (that are all amenable to you, of course). Many of the parks' sites have links with advice on family travel or info on children's activities.

3. Know your children. Consider your child's interests. This will help you plan a vacation that's both safe and memorable (for all the right reasons). For starters, if you have kids under four, be honest with yourself about whether the national park itself is an appropriate destination. Parents are notorious for projecting their awe for majestic scenery and overall enthusiasm for sightseeing on their younger kids, who might be more interested in cataloging the snacks in the hotel room's minibar. Likewise, be realistic about your child's stamina and ability. If your children have never been hiking, don't expect them to be able to do a long hike at a higher altitude than they are used to. Remember: Children's first experience hiking can make them a lover or a hater of the activity, so start off slowly and try some practice hikes near home.

4. Pack wisely. Be sure you're bringing kid-size versions of the necessities you'll pack for yourself. Depending on the park you're visiting (and the activities you're planning), that will probably include sturdy sandals or hiking shoes, sunglasses, sunscreen, and insect repellent. You'll almost certainly need a few layers of clothing and plenty of water and snacks. In terms of hydration, the American Academy of Pediatrics recommends giving children ages 9 to 12 about 3 to 8 ounces of water or another beverage every 20 minutes during strenuous exercise; adolescents should drink 34 to 50 ounces every hour.

5. Develop a Plan B. National parks are natural places, meaning they change dramatically with the seasons and the weather, so you should plan on alternate activities if Mother Nature isn't cooperative. And if you've already talked with your kids about your options, you can pick a new plan that appeals to everyone.

BUDGETING YOUR TRIP

Like most vacations, a trip to a national park can be as frugal, or as fancy, as you like. Here are a few things to consider:

Getting in. Admission varies by park, ranging from free to $35 per vehicle (or $10–$15 per person and $15–$30 per motorcycle). You also can buy an America the Beautiful Pass for $80 (⇨ *see Park Passes for more information*).

Sleeping. Fewer than half of the parks charge for camping; the cost is typically less than $25 per night. In many parks, you also can stay at a lodge, where prices run from $120 to $500 a night. Most parks have several accommodation options outside the park, as well.

Eating. In each of the parks, all the in-park concessions are run by companies under contract with the National Park Service, meaning their prices are set by the government. Generally speaking, prices are a bit higher than what you'd pay outside the park, but not significantly so. You also can bring in your own food and eat at one of the park's picnic areas.

Entertainment. Just looking at the wonders of the park is entertainment enough for many youngsters, but the many sports and outdoor activities—from hiking and bicycling to horseback riding and cave touring, depending on the park—help children stay active while exploring. Many park visitor centers also have films; some parks, such as Grand Canyon and Zion, even have IMAX movies. Cost for these offerings varies, ranging from free to a couple hundred dollars for more involved programs, such as a white-water rafting trip.

Souvenirs. All the parks have gift shops, and many stock items that are actually useful. For example, you'll find things like kid-size binoculars, fanny packs, and magnifying glasses, all of which can make your child's visit even more enjoyable. Budget $10 or $15 to cover one item (maybe something you might have bought for your child anyway, like a new sun hat).

KIDS' PROGRAMS

Roughly two-thirds of the 423 U.S. National Park Service units (national parks as well as historic sites, national monuments, preserves, and other significant places) are part of the Junior Ranger Program, which offers kids the opportunity to learn about individual parks by filling out a short workbook or participating in an activity such as taking a hike with a park ranger. After completing the program, kids get a badge (or a pin or patch, depending on the park). For availability, check with the ranger station or visitor center when you arrive; you can also check online ahead of time (🌐 *www.nps.gov/kids/parks-with-junior-ranger-programs.htm*). Kids can also complete Junior Ranger activities online (🌐 *www.nps.gov/kids/junior-ranger-online.htm*).

In addition to the Junior Ranger Program, kids can find a variety of activities in the parks designed just for them. Some parks, such as Olympic, loan "Discovery Backpacks" filled with kid-friendly tools like magnifying glasses (check ahead for availability). Other parks, like Grand Teton, have smartphone apps with information on park sites, current events, and history, as well as photo-editing features that allow for creative social-media sharing.

Many ongoing general-interest or park-specific programs—stargazing in Bryce Canyon, say, or ranger-led wildlife and wildflower walks through Shenandoah's meadows—will also be of interest to kids.

■ TIP→ **If your child is in the fourth grade, don't forget to get the free Every Kid Outdoors Pass. For more details visit everykid-outdoors.gov.**

Best Paired With...

Wondering what National Parks to pair together to make the perfect road trip? Here's a list of National Parks and their "Best Paired With" nearby parks or other NPS units.

Acadia: Katahdin Woods and Waters National Monument or Cape Cod National Seashore

American Samoa: Haleakala and Hawaii Volcanoes

Arches: Canyonlands, Capitol Reef, and Colorado National Monument

Badlands: Wind Cave and Devils Tower National Monument

Big Bend: Guadalupe Mountains and Fort Davis National Historic Site

Biscayne: Dry Tortugas or Everglades and Big Cypress National Preserve

Black Canyon of the Gunnison: Colorado National Monument, Curecanti National Recreation Area, and Mesa Verde

Bryce Canyon: Capitol Reef, Zion, and Grand Staircase–Escalante National Monument

Canyonlands: Arches, Capitol Reef, and Natural Bridges National Monument

Capitol Reef: Bryce Canyon, Zion, and Grand Staircase–Escalante National Monument

Carlsbad Caverns: Guadalupe Mountains and White Sands

Channel Islands: Carrizo Plain National Monument and Santa Monica Mountains National Monument

Congaree: Fort Sumter and Fort Moultrie National Historic Park or Chattahoochee River National Recreation Area

Crater Lake: Oregon Caves National Monument, Lava Beds National Monument, Lassen Volcanic, or Redwoods

Cuyahoga Valley: Indiana Dunes and River Raisin National Battlefield Park

Death Valley: Joshua Tree or Sequoia and Kings Canyon

Denali: Wrangell–St. Elias

Dry Tortugas: Everglades and Biscayne

Everglades: Biscayne and Dry Tortugas or Big Cypress National Preserve

Gates of the Arctic: Kobuk Valley and Noatak National Preserve

Gateway Arch: Mammoth Cave or Ozark National Scenic Riverway

Glacier: Yellowstone

Glacier Bay: Wrangell–St. Elias or Klondike Gold Rush National Historic Park and Sitka National Historic Park

Grand Canyon: Zion or Petrified Forest and Canyon de Chelly National Monument

Grand Teton: Yellowstone or Craters of the Moon National Monument

Great Basin: Zion, Bryce Canyon, and Capitol Reef

Great Sand Dunes: Rio Grande del Norte National Monument or Browns Canyon National Monument

Great Smoky Mountains: Mammoth Cave or New River Gorge and Shenandoah

Guadalupe Mountains: Big Bend or Carlsbad Caverns and White Sands

Haleakala: Hawaii Volcanoes or Kalaupapa National Historic Park

Hawaii Volcanoes: Haleakala or Pu'uhonua O Honaunau National Historic Park and Kaloko-Honokohau National Historic Park

Hot Springs: Fort Smith National Historic Site and Chickasaw National Recreation Area

Indiana Dunes: River Raisin National Battlefield Park and Cuyahoga Valley

Isle Royale: Keweenaw National Historic Park, Apostle Islands National Lakeshore, and Voyageurs

Joshua Tree: Death Valley and Mojave National Preserve

Katmai: Lake Clark, Kenai Fjords, and Aniakchak National Monument

Kenai Fjords: Lake Clark and Katmai or Wrangell–St. Elias

Kobuk Valley: Gates of the Arctic, Noatak National Preserve, and Cape Krusenstern National Monument

Lake Clark: Katmai and Kenai Fjords

Lassen Volcanic: Whiskeytown–Shasta–Trinity National Recreation Area, Redwood, and Crater Lake

Mammoth: Gateway Arch or Great Smoky Mountains and New River Gorge

Mesa Verde: Aztec Ruins National Monument and Chaco National Historic Park or Hovenweep National Monument and Canyonlands

Mount Rainier: North Cascades, Olympic, and Mount St. Helens National Volcanic Monument

New River Gorge: Shenandoah and Great Smoky Mountains or Mammoth Cave

North Cascades: Lake Chelan National Recreation Area, Mount Rainier, and Olympic

Olympic: San Juan Islands National Historic Park, Mount Rainier, and North Cascades

Petrified Forest: Grand Canyon, Canyon de Chelly National Monument, and Hubbell Trading Post National Historic Site

Pinnacles: Yosemite, or Golden Gate National Recreation Area, Muir Woods National Monument, and Point Reyes National Seashore

Redwood: Lassen Volcanic or Oregon Caves National Monument and Crater Lake

Rocky Mountain: Browns Canyon National Monument, Colorado National Monument, or Dinosaur National Monument

Saguaro: Casa Grande Ruins National Monument and Organ Pipe Cactus National Monument

Sequoia and Kings Canyon: Yosemite or Death Valley

Shenandoah: New River Gorge and Great Smoky Mountains or Harpers Ferry National Historic Park

Theodore Roosevelt: Devils Tower National Monument or Badlands and Wind Cave

Virgin Islands: Virgin Islands Coral Reef National Monument, Salt Bay River National Historic Park, and San Juan National Historic Site

Voyageurs: Grand Portage National Monument, Apostle Islands National Lakeshore, and Isle Royale

White Sands: Organ Mountains–Desert Peaks National Monument or Carlsbad Caverns and Guadalupe Mountains

Wind Cave: Badlands, Jewel Cave National Monument, and Mount Rushmore National Memorial

Wrangell–St. Elias: Glacier Bay, Kenai Fjords, or Denali

Yellowstone: Grand Teton or Glacier

Yosemite: Sequoia and Kings Canyon and Devils Postpile National Monument

Zion: Bryce Canyon and Grand Canyon or Great Basin

BEST BETS

Fodor's writers and editors have chosen our favorites to help you plan. Search individual chapters for details, and also see Chapter 1 for our favorite park lodges.

BEST SUNRISES
Acadia (Cadillac Mountain)
Bryce Canyon (Sunrise Point)
Death Valley (Zabriskie Point)
Grand Canyon (Yaki Point)
Great Sand Dunes (Star Dune)
Haleakala (Red Hill Observatory)
Voyageurs National Park (Kabetogama Lake)

BEST SUNSETS
Arches (Delicate Arch)
Big Bend (Window View Trail)
Badlands (Pinnacles Overlook)
Olympic (Ruby Beach)
Saguaro (Gates Pass)
Shenandoah (Stony Man Summit)
Yosemite (Olmsted Point)

BEST NORTHERN LIGHTS VIEWING
Acadia
All of Alaska's parks
Glacier
Isle Royale
North Cascades
Theodore Roosevelt
Voyageurs

BEST FOR STARGAZING
All Northern Lights parks
Black Canyon of the Gunnison
Canyonlands
Crater Lake
Dry Tortugas
Great Basin
Great Sand Dunes
Guadalupe Mountains

BEST FOR SOLITUDE
All of Alaska's parks
American Samoa
Black Canyon of the Gunnison
Congaree
Great Basin
Guadalupe Mountains
Isle Royale
North Cascades
Voyageurs

BEST FOR WILDFLOWERS
Big Bend
Glacier
Grand Teton
Great Smoky Mountains
Joshua Tree
Mount Rainier
Shenandoah

BEST FOR FALL FOLIAGE
Acadia
Cuyahoga Valley
Grand Teton
Great Smoky Mountains
Rocky Mountain
Shenandoah
Yosemite

BEST ISLAND ADVENTURES
Acadia
American Samoa
Channel Islands
Crater Lake (Wizard Island)
Dry Tortugas
Isle Royale
Virgin Islands

BEST FOR BEACHES
American Samoa
Dry Tortugas
Indiana Dunes
Olympic
Redwood
Virgin Islands

BEST FOR WATERFALLS
Cuyahoga Valley
Great Smoky Mountains
Haleakala
Katmai National Park
Mount Rainier
Olympic
Shenandoah
Yellowstone
Yosemite

BEST FOR DRAMATIC ROCK FORMATIONS
Arches and Canyonlands
Badlands
Bryce
Capitol Reef
Carlsbad Caverns
Death Valley
Grand Canyon
Joshua Tree
Lassen Volcanic
Mammoth Cave
Petrified Forest
Pinnacles
Yosemite
Zion

BEST FOR GEOTHERMAL AND VOLCANIC FEATURES
Channel Islands
Crater Lake
Haleakala

Hawaii Volcanoes
Hot Springs
Katmai National Park
Lake Clark
Lassen Volcanic
Mount Rainier
Wrangell–St. Elias
Yellowstone

BEST TO VISIT BY TRAIN
Channel Islands
Cuyahoga
Denali
Gateway Arch
Glacier
Grand Canyon
Indiana Dunes
Kenai Fjords
New River Gorge
Saguaro

BEST SCENIC DRIVES
Arches
(Arches Scenic Drive)
Badlands (Badlands Loop)
Big Bend (Ross Maxwell Scenic Drive)
Black Canyon of the Gunnison
(South Rim Drive)
Crater Lake (Rim Drive)
Glacier (Going to the Sun Road)
Denali (Park Road)
Great Smoky Mountains
(Newfound Gap Road)
Petrified Forest (Petrified Forest Road)
Redwood (Coastal Drive)
Saguaro
(Cactus Forest Loop)
Shenandoah
(Skyline Drive)
Theodore Roosevelt
(Scenic Loop Drive)
White Sands
(Dunes Drive)
Zion (Zion Canyon Scenic Drive)

BEST NIGHTTIME EXPERIENCES
Bryce Canyon
(full moon hike)
Carlsbad Caverns
(bat flight program)
Congaree (synchronous firefly viewing)
Everglades
(full moon bike ride)
Great Basin (Annual Astronomy Festival)
Hawaii Volcanoes
(night lava viewing tours)
Pinnacles National Park
(night hikes)
White Sands
(full moon hike)

BEST HIKES FOR ALL ABILITIES
Canyonlands (Grand View Point Overlook)
Everglades
(Anhinga Trail)
Grand Teton (Inspiration Point, *via ferry)*
Great Sand Dunes
(Montville Nature Trail)
Hawaii Volcanoes
(Thurston Lava Tube)
Indiana Dunes (Dune Succession Trail)
Lassen (Bumpass Hell)
Redwood (Big Tree Loop)
Sequoia (Moro Rock Trail)
Wind Cave (Rankin Ridge)
Zion (Canyon Overlook)

BEST MULTIDAY HIKES
Big Bend
(Outer Mountain Park)
Crater Lake
(Pacific Crest Trail)
Gates of the Arctic
(Oolah Pass)
Grand Canyon
(Rim-to-Rim)
Great Smoky Mountains
(Appalachian Trail)
Isle Royale
(Greenstone Ridge)
Olympic National Park
(Hoh River to Blue Glacier)
Redwood (Coastal Trail)

BEST FOR CLIMBING
Arches
Grand Teton
Joshua Tree
New River Gorge
North Cascades
Rocky Mountain
Sequoia and Kings Canyon
Wrangell–St. Elias
Yosemite
Zion

BEST FOR CAVING
Carlsbad Caverns
Great Basin
Hawaii Volcanoes
Mammoth Cave
Pinnacles
Sequoia and Kings Canyon
Wind Cave

BEST BIRD-WATCHING
Big Bend
Carlsbad Caverns
Death Valley
Everglades
Grand Teton
Haleakala
Indiana Dunes
Katmai
Kenai Fjords

BEST OVERALL WILDLIFE VIEWING
All of Alaska's parks
Big Bend
Channel Islands
Everglades
Isle Royale
Olympic
Rocky Mountain
Theodore Roosevelt
Virgin Islands
Yellowstone

BEST FOR BOATING
Acadia
Biscayne
Channel Islands
Everglades
Glacier Bay
Isle Royale
New River Gorge
Voyageurs

BEST FOR SNORKELING AND DIVING
American Samoa
Biscayne
Channel Islands
Dry Tortuga
Kenai Fjords
Virgin Islands

BEST FOR HORSEBACK RIDING
Acadia
Big Bend
Bryce Canyon
Cuyahoga Valley
Great Smoky Mountains
Lassen Volcanic
Rocky Mountain
Shenandoah

BEST IN THE SNOW
Acadia
All of Alaska's parks
Crater Lake
Grand Teton
Mesa Verde
Mount Rainier
Olympic
Rocky Mountain
Yellowstone
Yosemite

BEST CAMPGROUNDS
Acadia (Seawall)
Big Bend (Chisos Basin)
Capitol Reef (Fruita)
Denali (Savage River)
Dry Tortugas (Garden Key)
Grand Canyon (North Rim)
Great Smoky Mountains (Elkmont)
Kings Canyon (Azalea)
Mount Rainier (White River)

BEST RESTAURANT VIEWS
Acadia (Jordan Pond House)
Crater Lake (Crater Lake Lodge)
Grand Canyon (Grand Canyon Lodge)
Grand Teton (Jenny Lake Lodge)
Hawaii Volcanoes (The Rim at Volcano House)
Mesa Verde (Metate Room)
Olympic National Park (Creekside Restaurant)
Shenandoah (Pollock Dining Room)
Yosemite (Mountain Room)
Zion (Red Rock Grill)

BEST GATEWAY TOWNS
Acadia (Bar Harbor)
Arches and Canyonlands (Moab)
Grand Teton (Jackson)
Great Smoky Mountains (Gatlinburg)
Hawaii Volcanoes (Volcano)
Kenai Fjords (Seward)
Rocky Mountain (Estes Park)
Theodore Roosevelt (Medora)
Zion (Springdale)

BEST HISTORICAL SITES
Big Bend (Mariscal Mine)
Capitol Reef (Fruita Historic District)
Death Valley (Harmony Borax Works)
Dry Tortugas (Fort Jefferson)
Guadalupe Mountain (Frijole Ranch)
Lake Clark (Dick Proenneke's Cabin)
Mammoth Cave (churches)
Virgin Islands (Catherineberg Sugar Mill Ruins)
Wrangell–St. Elias (Kennecott Mines)

BEST ARCHITECTURE
Cuyahoga Valley
Gateway Arch
Glacier
Grand Canyon
Hot Springs
Mount Rainier
Petrified Forest
White Sands
Yellowstone
Yosemite

BEST MUSEUMS
Carlsbad Caverns (Visitor Center)
Channel Islands (Visitor Center)
Gateway Arch (Old Courthouse)
Great Smoky Mountains (Mountain Farm Museum)
Mesa Verde (Chapin Mesa Archeological Museum)
Mount Rainier (Henry M. Jackson Visitor Center)
Sequoia (Giant Forest Museum)
Zion (Zion Human History Museum)

BEST FOR INDIGENOUS CULTURE
All of Alaska's parks
Badlands
Canyonlands
Capitol Reef
Glacier
Mesa Verde
Olympic
Redwood
Virgin Islands
Wind Cave

Chapter 3

GREAT ITINERARIES

Updated by
Andrew Collins

Vast wilderness and endless recreation opportunities make it easy to spend an entire vacation exploring just one national park. But with these adventure-packed road-trip itineraries, you can easily explore more than just one.

Each itinerary is meant to inspire a road trip that you can tailor to your interests and your travel style. Each is also geared to summer travel. If visiting at another time of year, check with the park(s) about road conditions and seasonal road and other closures.

Washington State National Parks, 8 Days

A trip to Washington's three national parks—plus a visit to Mount St. Helen's National Volcanic Monument—takes you through rugged Pacific coastline and high alpine terrain as well as lush temperate rain forest, glaciers, waterfalls, and some of the largest remnants of ancient forests in the U.S.

DAY 1: STARTING OUT

For those coming from out of state, the nearest airport is **Seattle-Tacoma International,** where you can start your journey by picking up a rental car. Depending on when your flight gets in, you can rest up at a nearby hotel for the night or make the 85-mile, 1½-hour drive to **Sedro-Woolley,** Washington, where you can spend the night.

DAY 2: NORTH CASCADES

46 miles or about an hour drive from Sedro-Woolley.

From Sedro-Woolley, drive east for 46 miles along Route 20, also known as the North Cascades Highway, to the entrance of **North Cascades National Park.** Take your first stroll through an old-growth forest on the Skagit River Loop (1.8 miles), which starts at the visitor center near the town of Newhalem, about 9 miles from the entrance, then devote the rest of the day to driving through the park on Route 20, stopping at various overlooks. Exit the park and continue through the scenic Methow Valley and on to **Chelan** (about 190 miles from the park's western boundary) to stay the night.

DAYS 3–4: MOUNT RAINIER

205 miles or a 3-hour, 45-minute drive from Chelan; 136 miles or a 2-hour, 45-minute drive from Arlington.

From Chelan, get an early start to drive to Ohanapecosh, the southeastern entrance to **Mount Rainier National Park.** When you arrive, take a drive on the spectacular Sunrise Road (about 30 miles round-trip), which reveals the "back" (northeast) side of Rainier. Book a room in nearby **Ashford** (about 19 miles east of the park's Nisqually entrance) and make that your base for the next two nights.

The next day, energetic hikers will want to tackle one of the four- to six-hour trails that scale the park's many peaks. Less ambitious visitors can take one of the shorter hikes in the Paradise Inn area or join a ranger-led walk through wildflower

meadows. Another option is to hike to Panorama Point (a strenuous 4-mile round-trip), near the foot of the Muir Snowfield, for breathtaking views of the glaciers and high ridges of Rainier. Finish your day with dinner at the Paradise Inn, where you can watch the sunset on the peak.

DAY 5: MOUNT ST. HELENS AND THE OLYMPIC FOOTHILLS

120 miles or a 2½-hour drive from Mount Rainier; 245 miles or a 4½-hour drive north from Mount St. Helens to Port Angeles.

Today, drive south to spend the day visiting the **Mount St. Helens National Volcanic Monument,** where you can enter from the west side via Route 504 and see the destruction caused by the 1980 eruption. After leaving the monument, follow Route 504 back to Interstate 5 and head north to Olympia, winding through scenic Puget Sound countryside, skirting the Olympic foothills, and periodically dipping down to the waterfront en route to **Port Angeles,** where you'll spend the night.

DAYS 6–7: OLYMPIC

19½ miles (40 minutes) south from Port Angeles to Hurricane Ridge; 69 miles (1½ hours) southwest from Port Angeles to La Push; 72 miles (1 hour, 40 minutes) south from Hoh Rain Forest to Lake Quinault.

The next morning, launch into a full day at **Olympic National Park.** From the Port Angeles entrance, drive south to Hurricane Ridge, where you'll find several trails taking you through meadows and subalpine forest. The Hurricane Hill Trail (3.2 miles round-trip) delivers panoramic views of the mountains and ocean. Afterward, head back to Port Angeles for the night.

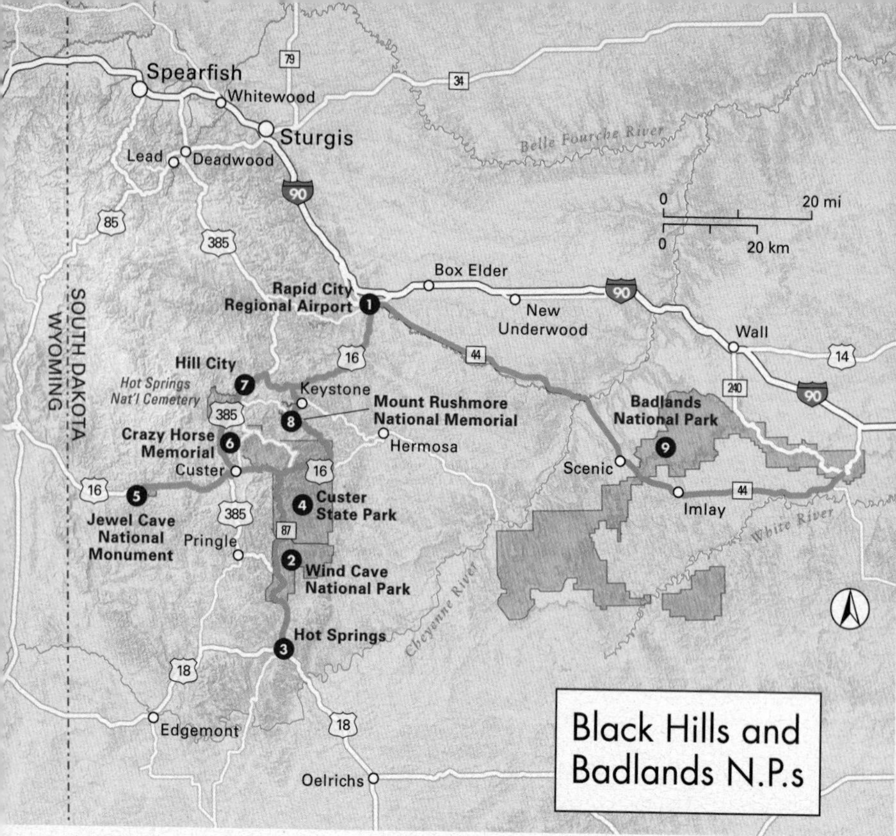

On Day 7, follow U.S. 101 west to **La Push,** a skinny satellite of coastal land that's part of the national park. From La Push, hike 1.4 miles to Third Beach for a taste of the wild Pacific coastline. Back on U.S. 101, head south to the town of Forks and then east to the **Hoh Rain Forest,** also part of Olympic National Park. Explore the moss-covered alders and big-leaf maples, then follow a circular route on U.S. 101 to **Lake Quinault,** winding west toward the coast, then back to the lake and the national park. Check into the Lake Quinault Lodge, then drive up the river to access one of several trails—the Graves Creek Trail is a popular choice—through the lush Quinault Valley.

DAY 8: HEADING HOME

Catch your flight back home from Seattle–Tacoma International, about 130 miles (a 2½-hour drive) from Olympic via I–5.

The Black Hills and Badlands National Parks, 6 Days

The national parks of southwestern South Dakota—along with the state park and two national memorials nearby—deliver a surprising variety of sights: the swaying grasses and abundant wildlife of one of the country's few remaining intact prairies, the complex labyrinth of passages and unique geologic formations in one of the world's longest caves, and some of the richest fossil beds on Earth.

DAY 1: WIND CAVE

The closest commercial airport is **Rapid City Regional Airport,** about 70 miles northeast from Wind Cave. Arrive in the morning to pick up your rental car and make the 1½-hour drive to **Wind Cave National Park,** with more than 33,000 acres of wildlife habitat above ground (home to bison, elk, pronghorn, and coyotes) and one of the world's longest caves below. Take an afternoon cave tour and a short drive through the park. Spend the night in **Hot Springs,** about 10 miles from the park's southern boundary.

DAY 2: CUSTER STATE PARK

36 miles or a 45-minute drive northeast from Hot Springs.

Spend today at **Custer State Park,** which is adjacent to Wind Cave. The 71,000-acre park has exceptional drives, lots of wildlife (including a herd of 1,400 bison), and fingerlike granite spires rising from the forest floor (they're the reason this is called the Needles region of South Dakota). While you're in the park, be sure to visit Limber Pine Natural Area, a National Natural Landmark containing spectacular ridges of granite. If you have time, check out the Cathedral Spires trail, 3 miles round-trip. Overnight in one of five mountain lodges at the Custer State Park Resort.

DAY 3: JEWEL CAVE NATIONAL MONUMENT AND CRAZY HORSE MEMORIAL

About 28 miles (40 minutes) west from Custer State Park to Jewel Cave, 20 miles northeast from Jewel Cave to Crazy Horse Memorial.

Today, venture down U.S. 16 to **Jewel Cave National Monument,** 13 miles west of the town of Custer, an underground wilderness where you can see beautiful nailhead and dogtooth spar crystals lining its more than 195 miles of passageways. After visiting Jewel Cave, head back to Custer and take U.S. 16/385 to **Crazy Horse Memorial** (about 7 miles north of Custer), home to a colossal mountain carving of the legendary Lakota leader and the Indian Museum of North America. Afterward, head 12 miles north to the former gold and tin mining town of **Hill City,** where you'll spend the night.

DAY 4: MOUNT RUSHMORE

12 miles or about a 30-minute drive northwest from Hill City.

This morning, travel to **Mount Rushmore National Memorial,** where you can view the huge carved renderings of presidents Washington, Jefferson, Theodore Roosevelt, and Lincoln. Afterward, head northwest for 23 miles back to **Rapid City,** the eastern gateway to the Black Hills. Spend the night here.

DAY 5: BADLANDS

62 miles or a 1-hour drive southeast from Rapid City to the northeast entrance of Badlands.

Begin your day early and drive east (via Interstate 90) to **Badlands National Park,** a 244,000-acre geologic wonderland. The Badlands Highway Loop Road (Highway 240) wiggles through the moonlike landscape of the park's north unit for 32 miles. Stop in at Ben Reifel Visitor Center, at the far eastern edge of the park, to pick up a trail map and head out on a hike. The Notch Trail, 1½ miles round-trip, offers spectacular views of the White River Valley, but is definitely not for anyone with a fear of heights. The Cliff Shelf trail, ½ mile round-trip, is a more mellow option that showcases rock formations and juniper forest, as well as occasional wildlife sightings.

After you leave the park, head back to Rapid City to spend the night.

DAY 6: HEADING HOME

The airport in Rapid City is about 10 minutes southeast of town.

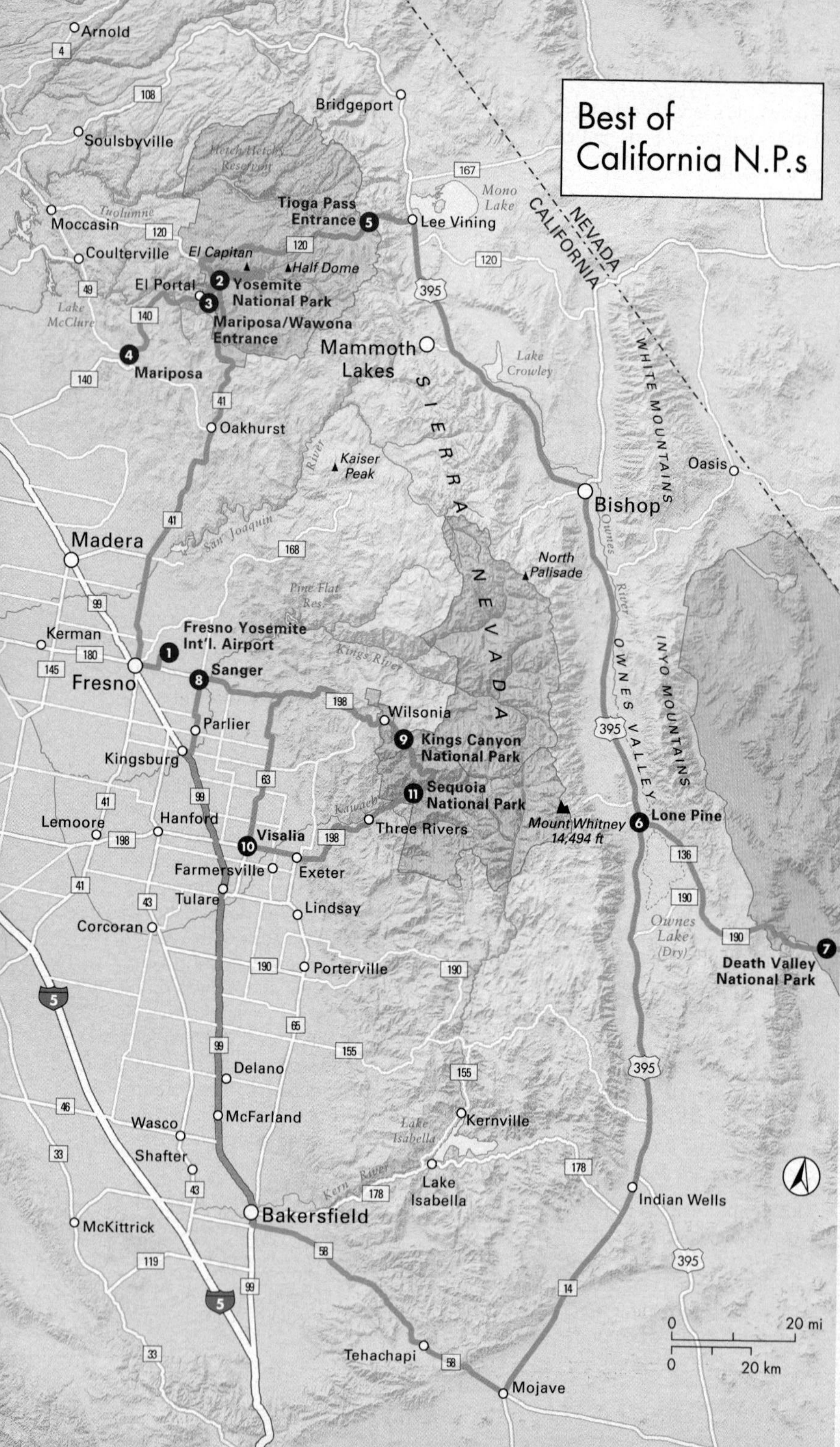

Best of California N.P.s
Arnold
Bridgeport
Soulsbyville
Hetch Hetchy Reservoir
Mono Lake
Tioga Pass Entrance
Lee Vining
Moccasin
Tuolumne
Coulterville
El Capitan
Half Dome
El Portal
Yosemite National Park
Mariposa/Wawona Entrance
Lake McClure
Mariposa
Mammoth Lakes
Lake Crowley
NEVADA
CALIFORNIA
WHITE MOUNTAINS
SIERRA NEVADA
Oakhurst
Kaiser Peak
River
Oasis
Bishop
San Joaquin
Madera
North Palisade
Owens River
Pine Flat Res.
Kerman
Fresno Yosemite Int'l. Airport
Fresno
Sanger
Kings River
INYO MOUNTAINS
OWENS VALLEY
Wilsonia
Parlier
Kings Canyon National Park
Kingsburg
Sequoia National Park
Lemoore
Hanford
Kaweah
Mount Whitney 14,494 ft
Lone Pine
Three Rivers
Visalia
Farmersville
Exeter
Tulare
Lindsay
Corcoran
Owens Lake (Dry)
Death Valley National Park
Porterville
Delano
Kernville
Lake Isabella
Wasco
McFarland
Shafter
Kern River
Indian Wells
Bakersfield
McKittrick
Tehachapi
Mojave
0 20 mi
0 20 km

California National Parks, 9 Days

This trip takes you to California's most popular national parks. Yosemite is a nearly 1,200-square-mile expanse in the western Sierras filled with meadows, waterfalls, and spectacular granite domes and canyons. Nearby Sequoia and Kings Canyon national parks deliver spectacular alpine scenery along with the world's largest trees. And Death Valley is a land of extremes, with its impossibly dry (and hot) below-sea-level basin alongside high mountain peaks and diverse wildlife.

DAY 1: STARTING OUT

If you're planning to start this trip with a flight, your best bet would be to arrive at **Fresno Yosemite International Airport,** which is about 70 miles from the southern entrance to Yosemite (your first stop) and 80 miles from the northern entrance to Sequoia and Kings Canyon (your last).

From the airport, head north toward **Yosemite National Park** and its **Mariposa/Wawona Entrance,** following Highway 41. Depending on how much time you've got, either do some exploring (head for the Yosemite Valley Visitor Center, about 32 miles from the Wawona entrance) or look for lodging. You can stay in the park (there are several options, from primitive camping to luxury rooms at the Ahwahnee Hotel) or in **Mariposa,** about 43 miles (1 hour) west of the Wawona Entrance on Route 140.

DAYS 2–4: YOSEMITE

126 miles, a 2-hour drive, southeast from Yosemite's Tioga Pass Entrance to Lone Pine.

Early in the morning of Day 2, head into Yosemite Valley, near the center of the park, and take a hike on Lower Yosemite Fall Trail, an easy 1.1-mile loop. If you've got more time and ambition, continue on for the first mile of the Upper Fall Trail to Columbia Rock, where you'll be rewarded with spectacular views of both the upper and lower sections of the highest waterfall in North America. Afterward, stop in at the historic Ahwahnee Hotel, then attend one of the ranger programs or a presentation at Yosemite Theater.

On your second day in the park, head back to the Yosemite Valley area, and take an easy hike around Mirror Lake (5 miles round-trip) or a more strenuous trek to Vernal Fall (2.5 miles round-trip), then drop in at the Yosemite Museum (next to the visitor center) and the nearby reconstructed Indian Village. Drive up to Glacier Point for a valley-wide view, timing your arrival for sunset.

On your last day in the park, head east to Tuolumne Meadows, where you can stretch your legs with a hike (an easy option is the 1½-mile round-trip trail to Soda Springs and historic Parsons Lodge). Then take a drive on Tioga Road (check ahead to make sure it is not closed), a 59-mile stretch through the high country that takes you over Tioga Pass (9,941 feet) and along the highest stretch of road in California. Leave the park through the **Tioga Pass Entrance,** then drive to the town of **Lone Pine,** where you'll spend the night.

DAYS 5–6: DEATH VALLEY

53 miles or a 60-minute drive southwest from Lone Pine to the park's western Panamint entrance; 280 miles (about 4½ hours) northwest from Panamint entrance to Sanger.

On Day 5, drive to **Death Valley National Park,** known as the lowest, driest, and hottest place in North America. Covering more than 5,300 square miles, it's also the biggest national park in the lower 48, with vast expanses of desert and mountain ranges extending as far as the eye can see. **■ TIP→ The best time to hike Death Valley is November–March, as hiking in the summer heat can be hazardous.**

Begin in the Furnace Creek area, roughly in the middle of the park. If you're getting an early start, hike into Golden Canyon by taking the 1-mile-long interpretive trail, which starts 2 miles south of Highway 190 on Badwater Road. From there, head to Devil's Golf Course (11 miles south of Furnace Creek) to see millions of tiny salt pinnacles and, if you get up close, a mass of perfectly round holes. Badwater Basin, 8 miles farther south, has expansive saltwater flats and the lowest point in the park, which is 282 feet below sea level. Then go to the highest spot—Dante's View, 5,000 feet above the valley floor—for the best views and blessedly cooler temperatures (the lookout is about 20 miles southeast of Furnace Creek). If you want to hike, there's a trail leading from the parking area onto Dante's Ridge that offers even more spectacular vistas (it's ½ mile to the first summit, then another 4 miles to Mt. Perry).

On your second day in Death Valley, explore the northern section of the park, by driving about 53 miles north of Furnace Creek on Ubehebe Crater Road to its namesake crater. From there, if your car has high clearance and good tires, you can drive 27 miles southwest on a rough dirt road to the Racetrack, a phenomenal dry lake bed famous for its mysterious moving rocks (to see the rocks, drive 2 miles past the Grandstand parking area).

Leave the park via the western (Panamint) entrance and head southwest toward Sequoia and Kings Canyon. Stop in **Sanger** to spend the night.

DAYS 7–8: SEQUOIA AND KINGS CANYON

41 miles or a 50-minute drive east from Sanger to Kings Canyon; 35 miles or a 40-minute drive southwest from Sequoia to Visalia.

From Sanger, drive east to the Big Stump Entrance of **Kings Canyon National Park.** Inside the park, head to Grant Grove Village and stop at the visitor center there, then take the Kings Canyon Scenic Byway (Route 180) along the Kings River and its giant granite canyon that is well over a mile deep at some points. Stop along the way at pull-outs for long vistas of some of the highest mountains in the United States. Hike the Zumwalt Meadow Trail (1½ miles), which starts just before the end of the road, 4½ miles from Cedar Grove Village, for gorgeous views of the park's largest meadow, plus high granite walls, talus, and the river below. At the end of the day, follow Route 180 back to Grant Grove Village and take Generals Highway south into Sequoia National Park. Leave through the Ash Mountain Entrance and head to the nearby town of **Visalia** for the night.

Spend the next day exploring **Sequoia National Park,** where some of the world's oldest and largest trees stand. Driving the winding, 40-mile-long Generals Highway takes about two hours. Be sure to stop at the Redwood Mountain Overlook, just outside Cedar Grove Village, for terrific views of the world's largest sequoia grove. Take a hike on the Congress Trail (2 miles), which starts at the General Sherman Tree, the world's largest tree, just off the Generals Highway near Wolverton Road. At the end of the day, head back to Sanger for the night.

DAY 9: HEADING HOME

From Sanger, it's a short 13-mile drive (about 20 minutes) to the Fresno airport.

Utah and Arizona National Parks, 9 Days

This itinerary takes you through Zion's massive sandstone cliffs and narrow slot canyons, the hoodoos (odd-shape pillars of rock left by erosion) of Bryce Canyon, and the overwhelming majesty of the Grand Canyon, close to 300 river miles long, 18 miles wide, and a mile deep.

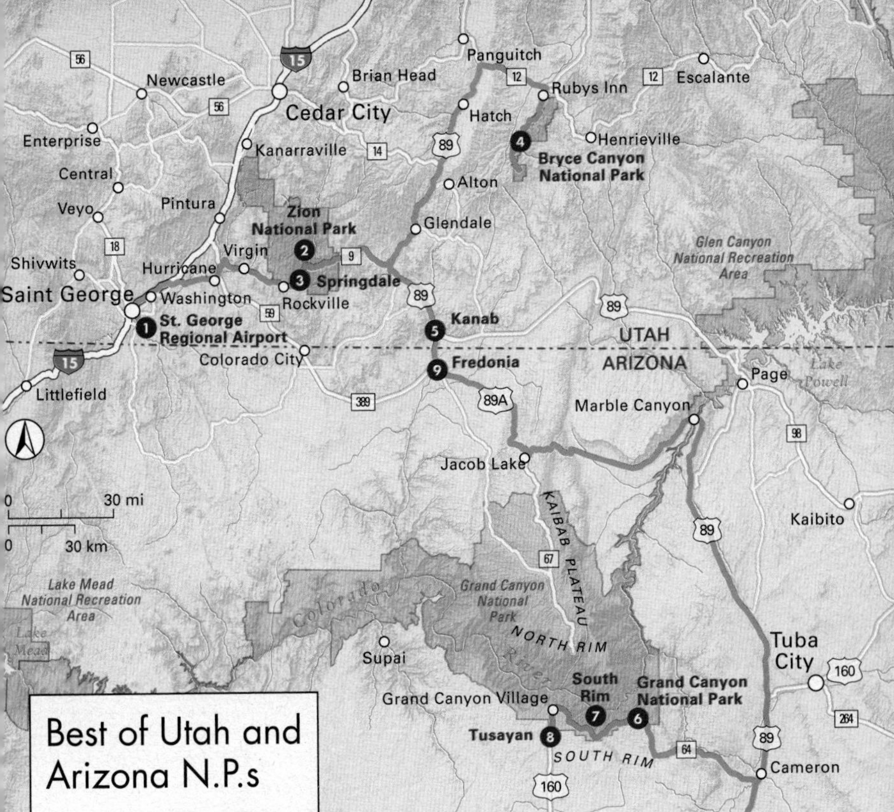

DAY 1: STARTING OUT

45 miles or about a 50-minute drive northeast from St. George airport to the south entrance of Zion National Park.

Plan to fly into and out of **St. George Regional Airport** in St. George, Utah. It's close to all three parks, with Zion a little more than an hour away.

From the airport, head east toward **Zion National Park,** about 46 miles. Depending on how much daylight you've got, you can start exploring the park—enter at the south entrance and head to the Zion Canyon Visitor Center—or find a room for the next three nights in **Springdale,** the bustling town just outside the park (1.1 miles from the south entrance).

DAYS 2–3: ZION

74 miles or about a 1-hour, 25-minute drive northeast from the east entrance of Zion to Bryce Canyon.

Start your day at the visitor center, just inside the south entrance, south of the junction of the Zion–Mount Carmel Highway and the Zion Canyon Scenic Drive. Then explore the scenic drive, either in your own vehicle (January through early February only) or via the park's shuttle, which costs $1 per person per day (though there might be same-day "walk-up" availability, tickets should be purchased in advance through Recreation.gov as they are not sold in the park). Shuttles typically run every five minutes from 7 am to 5 pm mid-February through Thanksgiving and over the year-end holiday season, and a round-trip ride takes about 80 minutes. Intrepid hikers will want to tackle the Narrows, Zion's famous 16-mile-long gorge cut by the Virgin River, which requires hikers to spend more than half of their time walking, wading, or swimming in the fast-flowing river. For everyone else, Zion offers plenty of other hiking options. The Emerald Pool trails (about 1 mile each) take you on a fairly easy hike from Zion Lodge, about 3 miles from Canyon Junction, to Lower and Upper Emerald Pool and waterfalls.

Spend the next day exploring the Kolob Canyons, in the northwestern corner of the park about 40 miles from Canyon Junction. Take the Kolob Canyons Road 5 miles to its end at the Kolob Canyons Viewpoint, where you'll get fabulous views of the surrounding red rock canyons. For a spectacular 5-mile hike, drive about 2 miles back on the Kolob Canyons Road to the Taylor Creek Trail, which takes you past historic homesteaders' cabins and through a narrow box canyon to the Double Arch Alcove, a large arched grotto.

At the end of the day, leave the park via the beautiful Zion–Mount Carmel Highway and its historic mile-long tunnel. You'll pass through slickrock country, with huge, petrified sandstone dunes etched by ancient waters, and head to Bryce Canyon, where you'll spend the night (you've got a few lodging options, both inside and just outside the park in the town of Bryce Canyon).

DAY 4: BRYCE CANYON

75 miles or about a 1-hour, 30-minute drive southwest from Bryce Canyon to Kanab.

Start your tour of **Bryce Canyon National Park** at the visitor center, about 1 mile past the park entrance. Central to your tour of Bryce Canyon is the 18-mile-long main park road, where numerous scenic turnouts reveal vistas of bright red-orange rock. **■TIP→ If you're visiting from mid-April to late October, the free Bryce Canyon Shuttle will take you to many of the park's most popular attractions.** Trails worth exploring include the 1-mile Bristlecone Loop Trail and the 1.3-mile Navajo Loop Trail, both of which will get you into the heart of the park.

At the end of the day, leave the park and head toward **Kanab** to spend the night en route to the Grand Canyon.

DAY 5: EN ROUTE TO THE GRAND CANYON

294 miles or a 5-hour drive south from Kanab to the South Rim of the Grand Canyon.

Today, you'll drive from Kanab to **Grand Canyon National Park.** Check into a hotel in Grand Canyon Village on the **South Rim** or in **Tusayan,** a few miles to the south, for the next two nights. If you've got time, hike (or take the shuttle) to Yavapai Point, just west of the visitor center in the South Rim Village, to catch the sunset.

DAYS 6–8: GRAND CANYON

284 miles or about a 4-hour, 40-minute drive north from the South Rim to Fredonia.

If you didn't make it yesterday, begin today's tour with a stop at the Grand Canyon Visitor Center, near Mather Point in the South Rim Village, for the latest maps and information. While you're there, check out the Historic District, with its early-19th-century train depot and other buildings, many built by the Santa Fe Railroad. Get your bearings with a drive (or, if you're visiting early spring–late fall, a free shuttle ride on the red line) on the 7-mile-long Hermit Road. Hike the Rim Trail, a nearly flat path (much of which is paved) that hugs the edge of the canyon from the Village to Hermit's Rest, 2.8 miles to the west.

On your second day in the park, tackle the upper section of one of the "Corridor Trails"—South Kaibab or Bright Angel—which start at the South Rim and meet in the Bright Angel Campground at the bottom of the canyon (the third Corridor

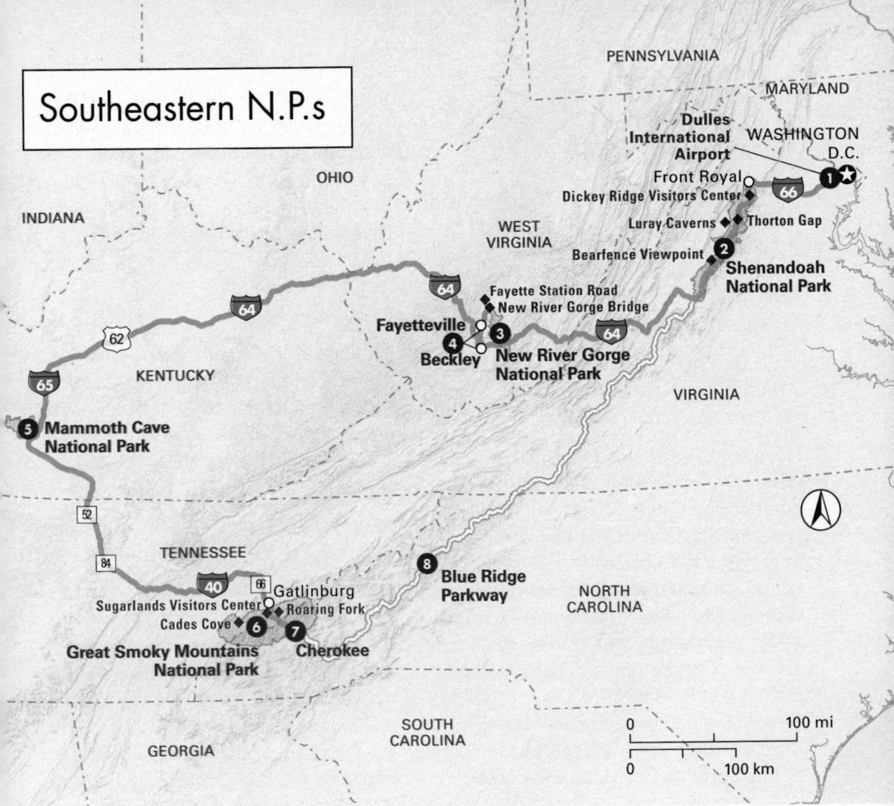

Trail, North Kaibab, connects the bottom of the canyon to the North Rim). Bright Angel, the easier of the two, is one of the most scenic paths into the canyon; the trailhead is near Kolb Studio, at the western end of the Village.

For your last day in the park, sign up for an interpretive ranger-led program; they cover a wide variety of subjects, including geology, history, and wildlife, so pick up a list at the Grand Canyon Visitor Center. Afterward, you can spend the night in (or near) the park again, or start your drive back toward the airport in St. George. The town of **Fredonia, Arizona,** would be a good stopping point for the night.

DAY 9: HEADING HOME

The St. George Regional Airport is 77 miles (1 hour, 20 minutes) northwest of Fredonia.

Southeastern National Parks, 9 Days

This verdant and vertiginous adventure takes you through some of the Appalachian region's highest mountains and most riveting scenery, including Shenandoah and Great Smoky Mountains national parks, which are connected by the dramatic Blue Ridge Parkway. Elevated to full national park status in 2021, New River Gorge is the deepest and longest gorge in the Appalachian Mountains, and southwestern Kentucky's Mammoth Cave National Park preserves the world's longest cave system.

DAY 1: STARTING OUT

60 miles west of Dulles International Airport to Front Royal, VA.

From Washington, D.C., make the 90-minute drive to Front Royal—which has plenty of hotels and restaurants—at the northern end of **Shenandoah National Park.** Stop at the Dickey Ridge Visitor Center to see exhibits and pick up maps and trail brochures.

DAY 2: SHENANDOAH

40 miles south of Front Royal.

Head south early along Skyline Drive, which stretches 105 miles along the crest of Blue Ridge Mountains. This linear park that's seldom wider than 5 miles offers countless places to pull off and set up a picnic blanket—or set out on a well-marked hike. For a rewarding side adventure, detour west 9 miles from the Thornton Gap Entrance to explore Virginia's biggest cave system, Luray Caverns. Back in the park, spend your second night either at Skyland Resort or 10 miles farther south at Big Meadows Lodge.

DAYS 3–5: NEW RIVER GORGE TO MAMMOTH CAVE

210 miles or a 4-hour drive west from Harry F. Byrd Sr. Visitor Center to Fayetteville, WV; 365 miles or about a 6-hour drive west from Fayetteville to Cave City, KY.

Continue south along Skyline Drive, stopping for a short hike to Bearfence Viewpoint or Blackrock Summit before heading west on I–64 to **New River Gorge National Park,** a rugged 70,000-acre wilderness bisected by one of the world's oldest rivers. From its Canyon Rim Visitor Center, follow the short boardwalk to a stunning overlook, and then drive the spectacular 8-mile Fayette Station Road. Spend the night in nearby Fayetteville or Beckley (20 miles south).

To fully grasp the wonder of New River Gorge, on Day 4, book a three- to four-hour whitewater rafting adventure from one of the park's licensed outfitters. In the afternoon, drive west to **Mammoth Cave National Park,** where you can stay in the park's Lodge at Mammoth Cave or nearby in Cave City.

On Day 5, explore the most dramatic sections of the 400-mile-long cave system, either on a ranger-led tour or the self-guided Extended Historic Tour, which showcases such geological wonders as Broadway Avenue and Giant's Coffin.

DAYS 6–8: GREAT SMOKY MOUNTAINS

240 miles or a 4½-hour drive southeast to Gatlinburg, TN.

On Day 6, drive to rollicking Gatlinburg, the northern gateway to **Great Smoky Mountains National Park** and a colorful, family-friendly repository of quirky motels and lodges. The next morning, stop by the Sugarlands Visitor Center before exploring the northern highlights of this 814-square-mile park, which has more than 16 peaks exceeding 6,000 feet. Must-do drives include the Roaring Fork Motor Trail and Cades Cove Loop Road.

On Day 8, gradually make your way south, visiting the observation tower atop 6,643-foot Clingmans Dome, hiking a stretch of the Appalachian Trail, and touring the engaging Mountain Farm Museum. Spend the night outside the park's southern entrance in Cherokee, North Carolina.

DAY 9: HEADING HOME

It's 420-mile drive back to Shenandoah National Park along interstate highways. But if you have the time, we recommend driving the gorgeous Blue Ridge Parkway, following it all 469 miles back to Shenandoah.

Chapter 4

ACADIA NATIONAL PARK

4

Updated by
John Blodgett

Camping	Hotels	Activities	Scenery	Crowds
★★★☆☆	★★★★☆	★★★★★	★★★★★	★★★★☆

WELCOME TO ACADIA NATIONAL PARK

TOP REASONS TO GO

★ **Unforgettable vistas:** Whether from the air, trail, boat, or road, your gaze is bound to fall on an astounding sight of rugged natural beauty.

★ **Unique roadways:** Forty-five miles of finely crafted stone roads built and gifted by a famed philanthropic family can be enjoyed via two feet, two wheels, or horse-drawn carriage.

★ **First light:** Anyone who climbs Cadillac Mountain in time for sunrise can claim to be the first in the country to watch the sun come up.

★ **The parting sea:** For about three hours a day, low tide exposes a land bridge between Bar Harbor and Bar Island—and a hiking experience unlike most any other.

★ **Four flavors:** Visit the park on both halves of Mount Desert Island, the tip of Schoodic Peninsula, and roughly half of tiny and remote Isle au Haut, and you won't feel you're repeating yourself.

1 **East Side of Mount Desert Island.** The most visited part of Acadia National Park contains the amenities hub of Bar Harbor and some of the park's best-known attractions, including the carriage roads and Cadillac Mountain.

2 **West Side of Mount Desert Island.** The quieter side of Acadia National Park on Mount Desert Island is no less rewarding to visit, and includes the warmer of the park's two swimming beaches, the iconic Bass Harbor Head Light, and hiking to the landmark Beech Mountain fire lookout tower.

3 **Schoodic Peninsula.** Visitors here enjoy all the grandeur of Mount Desert Island with a more secluded feel. Highlights include a loop road, bike paths, hiking trails, and the Schoodic Institute, an educational facility on the grounds of a former Navy base.

4 **Isle au Haut.** The park's smallest and most remote and primitive campground is here, as is a network of gravel roads for mountain biking and trails for hiking. Amenities are meager.

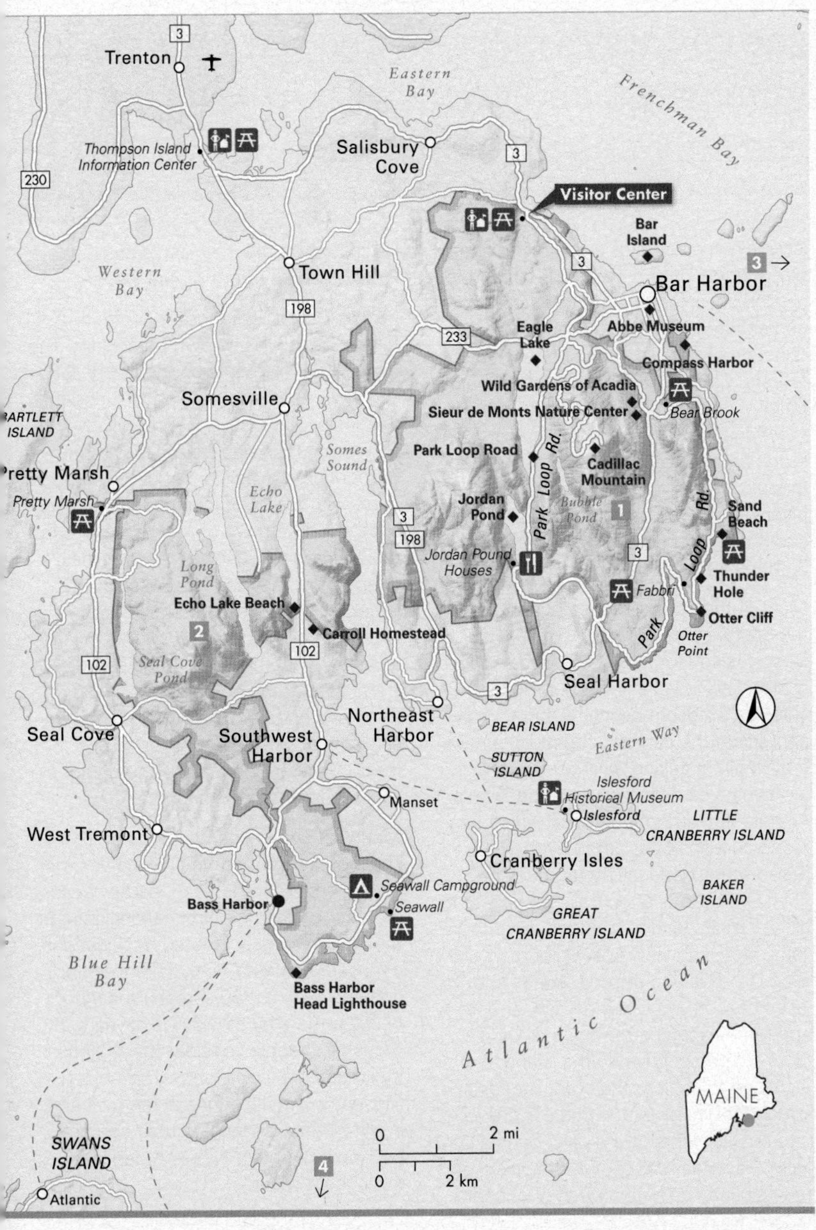

Trenton
Eastern Bay
Frenchman Bay
Thompson Island Information Center
Salisbury Cove
Visitor Center
Bar Island
Bar Harbor
Western Bay
Town Hill
Eagle Lake
Abbe Museum
Compass Harbor
Wild Gardens of Acadia
Sieur de Monts Nature Center
Bear Brook
Somesville
BARTLETT ISLAND
Park Loop Road
Park Loop Rd.
Cadillac Mountain
Somes Sound
Pretty Marsh
Echo Lake
Jordan Pond
Bubble Pond
Sand Beach
Jordan Pound Houses
Long Pond
Fabbri
Thunder Hole
Echo Lake Beach
Otter Cliff
Carroll Homestead
Otter Point
Seal Cove Pond
Seal Harbor
Northeast Harbor
Seal Cove
Southwest Harbor
BEAR ISLAND
Eastern Way
SUTTON ISLAND
Islesford Historical Museum
Manset
Islesford
LITTLE CRANBERRY ISLAND
West Tremont
Cranberry Isles
Seawall Campground
BAKER ISLAND
Bass Harbor
Seawall
GREAT CRANBERRY ISLAND
Blue Hill Bay
Bass Harbor Head Lighthouse
Atlantic Ocean
MAINE
SWANS ISLAND
Atlantic
0 2 mi
0 2 km

With about 48,000 acres of protected forests, beaches, mountains, and rocky coastline, Acadia National Park is one of the country's most visited national parks (almost 3.5 million visitors in 2019) and the only one in Maine.

Acadia holds some of the most spectacular scenery on the Eastern Seaboard: a rugged coastline of surf-pounded granite and an interior graced by sculpted mountains, quiet ponds, and lush, deciduous forests. Cadillac Mountain—the highest point of land on the East Coast—dominates the park. The park also has graceful stone bridges, miles of carriage roads (popular with walkers, runners, and bikers as well as horse-drawn carriages), and the Jordan Pond House restaurant (famous for its popovers).

Most of the park comprises the bulk of the approximately 12- by 15-mile Mount Desert Island (pronounced "dessert" by locals). The 27-mile Park Loop Road provides an excellent overview, but to truly appreciate the park you must experience it by walking, hiking, biking, sea kayaking, or taking a carriage ride—the latter on a 45-mile network of finely crafted stone roads built and later gifted by the late philanthropist and part-time resident John D. Rockefeller Jr. Trails for hikers of all skill levels lead to rounded mountaintops, providing views of Frenchman and Blue Hill bays and beyond. Ponds and lakes beckon you to swim, fish, or boat, and ferries and charter boats provide a different perspective on the island and a chance to explore the outer islands or watch for whales and puffins. There are two smaller parts of the park: on Isle au Haut, 15 miles away out in the ocean and reachable by ferry, and on the Schoodic Peninsula, on the mainland across Frenchman Bay from Mount Desert.

Mount Desert Island has four different towns, each with its own personality. The town of Bar Harbor is on the northeastern corner of the island and includes the villages of Hulls Cove, Salisbury Cove, and Town Hill. Aside from Acadia, Bar Harbor is the major tourist destination here, with plenty of lodging, dining, and shopping. The town of Mount Desert, in the middle of the island, has four main villages: Somesville, Seal Harbor, Otter Creek, and Northeast Harbor. Southwest Harbor includes the smaller village of Manset south of the village center. Tremont is at the southernmost tip of the island and stretches up the western shore. It includes the villages of Bass Harbor (with its frequently photographed lighthouse), Bernard, and Seal Cove.

Mount Desert Island was once a preserve of summer homes for the very rich (and still is for some), and, partly because of this, Acadia is the first national park in the country largely created by donations of private land (the Rockefellers alone donated over 11,000 acres). Predating white settlers by thousands of years, the Wabanaki people consider these lands their ancestral homelands. The Abbe Museum, with locations in the park and in Bar Harbor, celebrates their heritage and the heritage of Native Americans throughout Maine.

AVERAGE HIGH/LOW TEMPERATURES					
JAN.	**FEB.**	**MAR.**	**APR.**	**MAY**	**JUNE**
31/14	35/17	42/25	53/35	65/45	74/54
JULY	**AUG.**	**SEPT.**	**OCT.**	**NOV.**	**DEC.**
79/59	78/59	71/52	59/42	48/33	37/21

Planning

When to Go

Peak visitation is June through August and early September. Parking can be a challenge (and traffic congested) during the high season, when parking lots at many popular areas fill quickly. Autumn attracts leaf peepers seeking to view Maine's famous fall foliage. For hardy souls winter can be a wonderful time to visit, with far fewer visitors and many opportunities to cross-country ski or snowshoe—just know that many paved park roads, including all but two short sections of the Park Loop Road, close from December 1 to mid-April (unpaved roads are closed mid-November to mid-May), and many dining and lodging facilities are hibernating. Consider visiting in the spring, when temperatures start to rise but crowds haven't yet formed.

Getting Here and Around

AIR

Bangor International Airport (BGR) in Bangor is the closest major airport to Acadia National Park. Driving distance from here to Mount Desert Island is approximately 50 miles; drive Route 1A to Ellsworth, then take Route 3 to Mount Desert Island and then continue to Bar Harbor. Taxi, bus, and shuttle services are also available.

Farther south along the coast, Portland International Airport (PWM) is approximately 3 hours to the Mount Desert Island area. Renting a car is your best bet for getting to Acadia National Park from here; take I–295 to I–95 (a toll highway) to Bangor, then follow Route 1A to Route 3 in Ellsworth and continue to Mount Desert Island.

The small regional Hancock County-Bar Harbor Airport (BHB) is located in Trenton minutes away from the bridge to Mount Desert Island. Cape Air and JetBlue both offer flights to and from Logan International Airport (BOS) in Boston. Car rentals and taxi service are both available here.

CAR

Route 3 leads to Mount Desert Island and Bar Harbor from Ellsworth and circles the eastern part of the island. Route 102 is the major road on the west side.

FERRY

Isle au Haut Boat Services provides a daily mail-boat ferry service out of Stonington to Isle au Haut. During the summer season, trips increase from two to five Monday–Saturday and from one to two on Sunday. From mid-June until late September, the boat also stops at Duck Harbor, in the island section of Acadia National Park (it will not unload bicycles, kayaks, or canoes at the Park Landing, but will at the Town Landing). Ferry service is scaled back in the fall, then returns to the regular or "winter" schedule.

From Bass Harbor, the Maine State Ferry Service operates the *Captain Henry Lee,* carrying both passengers and vehicles to Swans Island (40 minutes; $17.50 per adult round-trip, $38.50 per car with driver) and Frenchboro (50 minutes; $17.50 per adult round-trip, $38.50 per car with driver). Round-trip service to Frenchboro on the car ferry is available every Thursday and Sunday and the first and third Wednesday; a round-trip passenger-only service to Frenchboro on a smaller boat is offered Friday April–November with trips departing Bass Harbor at 8 am and 5:15 pm with returns at 9 am and 6 pm.

CONTACTS Isle au Haut Boat Services. ✉ *37 Seabreeze Ave., Stonington* ☎ *207/367–5193* 🌐 *isleauhaut.com.* **Maine State Ferry Service.** ✉ *45 Granville Rd., Bass Harbor* ☎ *207/244–3254* 🌐 *www.maine.gov/mdot/ferry.*

SHUTTLE

Island Explorer buses, which serve the park and island villages late June–Columbus Day, offer transportation to and around the park. In addition to regularly scheduled stops, they also pick up and drop off passengers anywhere in the park it is safe to stop.

On the Schoodic Peninsula, with bus service from Prospect Harbor, Birch Harbor, and Winter Harbor to anywhere in the Schoodic Peninsula section of the park that's safe to stop. The bus also connects with the Winter Harbor ferry terminal, where you can take a ferry back to Bar Harbor.

CONTACTS Island Explorer. ☎ *207/667–5796* 🌐 *www.exploreacadia.com.*

Inspiration

In *Granite, Fire, and Fog: The Natural and Cultural History of Acadia,* ecologist and naturalist Tom Wessels intimately examines how nature, time and weather, and the humanity they attracted and influenced, all have interacted to create "a landscape that can be found nowhere else in the United States." In closing the book Wessels takes readers along on a favorite hike to help illustrate the natural and human history he related in previous chapters.

Who better than John D. Rockefeller, Jr.'s granddaughter to tell the story about the famed carriage roads that he created and whose stone pathways have since delighted millions of Acadia National Park visitors? In *Mr. Rockefeller's Roads: The Untold Story of Acadia's Carriage Roads,* Ann Rockefeller Roberts relies on her family connection and her own personal enjoyment of the carriage roads, stemming from childhood, to relate their history from behind the scenes.

The 1999 film *The Cider House Rules,* based on a 1985 novel of the same name by John Irving and starring Tobey Maguire, Charlize Theron, and Michael Caine, is primarily set in a fictitious Maine orphanage. While many scenes were filmed in New Hampshire and Massachusetts, some were shot in or near Acadia National Park, including at Sand Beach and in Bass Harbor.

Park Essentials

ACCESSIBILITY

Many Acadia National Park sights, amenities, and information sources are at least partly accessible to people facing accessibility challenges. Island Explorer shuttle buses are wheelchair accessible, as are most major visitor and information centers and many picnic sites. Parking, restroom and changing areas at Echo Lake Beach and Sand Beach are wheelchair accessible, though stairs to the water at Sand Beach prevent water access. Wheelchair access to hiking trails, scenic overlooks, and carriage roads vary. Download an Accessibility Guide from the park website or pick up a copy at one of the visitor centers for more information.

PARK FEES AND PERMITS

A user fee is required May–October. The per-vehicle fee is $30 ($25 for motorcycles) for a seven-consecutive-day pass; you can walk or bike in on a $15 individual pass (also good for seven days); or you can use your National Park America the Beautiful Pass, which allows entrance to any national park in the United States. There are also a few fee-free days throughout the year.

PARK HOURS

The park is open 24 hours a day, year-round, but roads are closed December–mid-April, except for the Ocean Drive section of Park Loop Road and a small part of the road with access to Jordan Pond.

CELL PHONE RECEPTION

Cell phone coverage can be spotty outside of the Bar Harbor area, especially on the west side of Mount Desert Island and Isle au Haut.

Hotels

Lodging is not available within Acadia National Park. Bar Harbor has the greatest variety and number of nearby lodging facilities, with some towns and villages on Mount Desert Island having at least one or two smaller options worth looking into. With short notice in the high season the Ellsworth area might be your best bet.

Restaurants

The Jordan Pond House Restaurant is the only dining option within the park, serving lunch, tea, and dinner mid-May to late October. A number of restaurants serving a variety of cuisines are located in Bar Harbor, while smaller coastal communities usually have at least one or two small eateries.

HOTEL AND RESTAURANT PRICES

Hotel prices in the reviews are the lowest cost of a standard double room in high season. Restaurant prices in the reviews are the average cost of a main course at dinner, or if dinner is not served, at lunch.

What It Costs

	$	$$	$$$	$$$$
RESTAURANTS	under $18	$18–$24	$25–$35	over $35
HOTELS	under $200	$200–$299	$300–$399	over $399

Tours

Bar Harbor Whale Watch Co.
BOAT TOURS | FAMILY | This company has six boats, one of them a 130-foot jet-propelled double-hulled catamaran with spacious decks. The company offers lighthouse, lobstering, sunset, and seal-, puffin-, and whale-watching cruises, as well as a trip to Acadia National Park's Baker Island and a nine-hour tour that passes 18 lighthouses, including seven in Canada. ✉ *1 West St., Bar Harbor* ☎ *207/288–2386, 888/942–5374* 🌐 *www.barharborwhales.com.*

Coastal Kayaking Tours
GUIDED TOURS | FAMILY | This outfitter has been leading trips in the scenic waters off Mount Desert Island since 1982. Trips are limited to no more than 12 people. The season is mid-May–mid-October. ✉ *48 Cottage St., Bar Harbor* ☎ *207/288–9605* 🌐 *www.acadiafun.com.*

Downeast Sailing Adventures
BOAT TOURS | FAMILY | Take two-hour sailing trips and sunset cruises for $50 per person with six passengers, or hire a private charter starting at $125 per hour. Boats depart the Upper Town Dock in Southwest Harbor and several other locations. ✉ *Eagle Lake Rd., Bar Harbor* ☎ *207/288–2216* 🌐 *www.downeastsail.com.*

Margaret Todd
BOAT TOURS | FAMILY | The 151-foot four-masted schooner *Margaret Todd* operates 1½- to 2-hour trips three times daily among the islands of Frenchman

Bay. The sunset sail has live folk music, and the 2 pm trip is sometimes narrated by an Acadia National Park ranger. Trips are $42–$48 and depart mid-May–mid-October. ✉ *Bar Harbor Inn pier, 7 Newport Dr., Bar Harbor* ☎ *207/288–4585* 🌐 *www.downeastwindjammer.com.*

★ **Scenic Flights of Acadia**

AIR EXCURSIONS | Air tours of the Acadia National Park area range from a 15-minute quickie of Bar Harbor ($49 per person) to a 35-minute overview that encircles Mount Desert island for $129 per person. ✉ *1044 Bar Harbor Rd., Rte. 3, Trenton* ☎ *207/667–6527* 🌐 *www.scenicflightsofacadia.com.*

Visitor Information

CONTACTS Acadia National Park. ☎ *207/288–3338* 🌐 *www.nps.gov/acad.* **Mount Desert Chamber of Commerce.** ☎ *207/276–5040* 🌐 *mtdesertchamber.org.* **Mount Desert Island Information Center at Thompson Island.** ☎ *207/288–3338* 🌐 *www.nps.gov/acad/planyourvisit/hours.htm.*

East Side of Mount Desert Island

10 miles south of Ellsworth via Rte. 3.

Many of Acadia National Parks best-loved features, including all of its carriage roads, Sand Beach, and Cadillac Mountain, are on this side of Mount Desert Island. So, too, is Bar Harbor, the island's largest town and your best bet for finding lodging and dining.

Sights

BEACHES

Sand Beach

BEACH—SIGHT | This pocket beach is hugged by two picturesque rocky outcroppings, and the combination of the crashing waves and the chilly water (peaking at around 55°F) keeps most people on the beach. You'll find some swimmers at the height of summer, but the rest of the year this is a place for strolling and snapping photos. In the shoulder season, you'll have the place to yourself. **Amenities:** lifeguards; parking; toilets. **Best for:** solitude; sunrise; walking. ✉ *Ocean Dr. section of Park Loop Rd., 3 miles south of Rte. 3, Acadia National Park.*

GEOLOGICAL FORMATIONS

Thunder Hole

CAVE | When conditions are just so at this popular visitor attraction, the force of pounding surf being squeezed into a narrow slot of cliffside pink granite causes a boom that sounds like thunder and often sends ocean spray up to 40 feet into the air—soaking observers standing nearby behind safety railings. Time your visit within two hours of high tide for the best chance to observe the phenomenon, located along the Park Loop Road about 1 mile south of Sand Beach and 10 miles from Hulls Cove Visitor Center. ✉ *Bar Harbor* ✥ *About 1 mile south of Sand Beach* ☎ *207/288–3338* 🌐 *nps.gov/acad.*

HISTORIC SIGHTS

★ **Abbe Museum**

MUSEUM | **FAMILY** | This important museum dedicated to Maine's indigenous tribes—collectively known as the Wabanaki—is the state's only Smithsonian-affiliated facility and one of the few places in Maine to experience Native culture as interpreted by Native peoples themselves. The year-round archaeology exhibit displays spear points, bone tools, and other artifacts found around Mount Desert Island and exhibits often feature contemporary Native American art, and there are frequent demonstrations of everything from boatbuilding to basket weaving. Call on rainy days for impromptu children's activities. A second location, inside the park at Sieur de Monts Spring, open only during the summer, features artifacts from the earliest digs around the island. ✉ *26 Mount Desert St., Bar Harbor* ☎ *207/288–3519* 🌐 *www.abbemuseum.org* 🎫 *$10.*

SCENIC DRIVES

★ Park Loop Road

SCENIC DRIVE | FAMILY | This 27-mile road provides a perfect introduction to the park. You can drive it in an hour, but allow at least half a day, so that you can explore the many sites along the way. The route is also served by the free Island Explorer buses, which also pick up and drop off passengers anywhere it is safe to stop along the route. Traveling south on Park Loop Road toward Sand Beach, you'll reach a small ticket booth, where, if you haven't already, you will need to pay the park entrance fee (May–October). Traffic is one-way from the Route 233 entrance to the Stanley Brook Road entrance south of the Jordan Pond House. The section known as Ocean Drive is open year-round, as is a small section that provides access to Jordan Pond from Seal Harbor. ✉ *Acadia National Park.*

SCENIC STOPS

Bar Island

ISLAND | FAMILY | Offering one of Acadia National Park's more unique experiences, Bar Island is only accessible by foot and during a three-hour window when low tide exposes a ½-mile gravel bar connecting Bar Island to Bar Harbor. The entire Bar Island trail offers an easy 1.9 mile round trip hike; once on the island you can enjoy views of Bar Harbor and Frenchman Bay. Make sure to check the tide charts before setting out, because once covered by rising tidal waters it'll be another 9 hours before the land bridge is once again exposed. ✉ *Bar Harbor* ✣ *Access via West St. then Bridge St.* ☎ *207/288–3338* 🌐 *nps.gov/acad.*

The Early Bird Gets the Sun

During your visit to Mount Desert, pick a day when you are willing to get up very early, around 4:30 or 5 am. Drive with a friend, or a camera with a timer, to the top of Cadillac Mountain in Acadia National Park, and stand on the highest rock you can find and wait for the sun to come up. When it does, have your friend, or your camera, take a photo of you looking at it and label the photo something like, "The first person in the country to see the sun come up today."

★ Cadillac Mountain

MOUNTAIN—SIGHT | FAMILY | At 1,530 feet, this is one of the first places in the United States to see the sun's rays at daybreak. Named after a Frenchman who explored here in the late 1600s and who later founded Detroit, this is the highest mountain on the Eastern Seaboard north of Brazil. Hundreds of visitors make the trek to see the sunrise or—for those less inclined to get up so early—sunset. From the smooth summit you have a stunning 360-degree view of the jagged coastline that runs around the island. The road up the mountain is closed December–mid-May. ✉ *Cadillac Summit Rd., Acadia National Park* 🌐 *www.nps.gov/acad.*

Compass Harbor

LOCAL INTEREST | This easy 0.8-mile trail to the shore passes through land once owned by George B. Dorr—Acadia National Park's first superintendent and a key player in the park's creation. In addition to views of Frenchman Bay, the trail offers glimpses of his former estate, including the foundation of his cottage and gardens including apple trees. ✉ *399 Main St., Bar Harbor* ☎ *207/288–3338* 🌐 *nps.gov/acad.*

Eagle Lake

BODY OF WATER | Located just east of Acadia National Park headquarters, 425-acre Eagle Lake is the largest freshwater lake on Mountain Desert Island. Swimming is not allowed, but kayaking and fishing are and the encircling 6.1-mile carriage road invites walkers and cyclists. ✉ *Eagle Lake Rd., Bar Harbor* ✣ *½ mile east of Acadia National Park headquarters* ☎ *207/288–3338* 🌐 *nps.gov/acad.*

Jordan Pond

BODY OF WATER | Iconic mountain views abound at this body of water known as a tarn for having been formed by retreating glaciers. Listen for the call of common loons and watch for cliff-nesting peregrine falcons while hiking the 3.3 mile loop trail. A boat launch area serves kayakers, but because it's a public water supply swimming is not allowed. Parking is available off Park Loop Road at the historic Jordan Pond House, where a restaurant serves popular popovers and tea and other goodies from late April to late October. ✉ *2928 Park Loop Rd.* ☎ *207/288–3338* 🌐 *nps.gov/acad.*

Otter Cliff

NATURE SITE | The terminus of the popular Ocean Path walking trail, which starts 2 miles north at the Sand Beach parking lot, Otter Cliff looms 110 feet above the crashing surf of the North Atlantic. Don't fret if you're not up for the walk, for you can still enjoy the view from the overlook off Park Loop Road, where you can often watch rock climbers crawling on the cliff face. Nearby on the shore are thousands of round boulders of various sizes that have been smoothed into shape by many thousands of years of wave action. ✉ *Park Loop Rd., Bar Harbor* ✣ *About ¾ mile south of Thunder Hole on Park Loop Rd.* ☎ *207/288–3338* 🌐 *nps.gov/acad.*

Book a Carriage Ride

Riding down one of the park's scenic carriage roads in a horse-drawn carriage is a truly unique way to experience Acadia. You can book a reservation for a ride, late May–mid-October, with Wildwood Stables, located next to Park Loop Road (☎ 877/276–3622). One of the carriages can accommodate wheelchairs.

Sieur de Monts Nature Center

INFO CENTER | This visitor and information center is the first major stop along the Park Loop Road. It's in an area known as the "Heart of Acadia," which memorializes George Dorr, Acadia National Park's first superintendent, and includes Sieur de Monts Spring, Wild Gardens of Acadia, one of the park's two Abbe Museum facilities honoring the area's Native American heritage, and walking paths. The nature center is typically open from May through Columbus Day. ✉ *Park Loop Rd., Bar Harbor* ☎ *207/288–3338* 🌐 *nps.gov/acad.*

Wild Gardens of Acadia

GARDEN | A variety of park habitats including meadows, bogs, and mountaintops are simulated at this facility, which includes numerous plants native to Acadia National Park. All are labeled to ease identification while you're out exploring. It sits on land purchased and eventually donated to the park by George Dorr, who would serve as the first Acadia National Park superintendent. ✉ *Park Loop Rd., Bar Harbor* ☎ *207/288–3338* 🌐 *nps.gov/acad.*

TRAILS

Cadillac Mountain North Ridge Trail

TRAIL | You can easily drive to the summit of Cadillac Mountain (except in winter), but this mostly exposed, 4.4-mile out and back hike rewards hikers with expansive views of Bar Harbor, Frenchman Bay, and the Schoodic Peninsula at most every step. The trail is worth undertaking at either sunrise or sunset (or both!). Because parking can be limited especially in the high season, park officials recommend taking the Island Explorer bus for access via a 0.1-mile section of the Kebo Brook Trail. *Moderate.* ✉ *Park Loop Rd., Bar Harbor* ✣ *Trailhead: Access is via Park Loop Rd. near where one-way travel to Sand Beach starts* ☎ *207/288–3338* 🌐 *nps.gov/acad.*

★ Ocean Path Trail

TRAIL | This easily accessible 4.4-mile round-trip trail runs parallel to the Ocean Drive section of the Park Loop Road from Sand Beach to Otter Point. It has some of the best scenery in Maine: cliffs and boulders of pink granite at the ocean's edge, twisted branches of dwarf jack pines, and ocean views that stretch to the horizon. Be sure to save time to stop at **Thunder Hole,** named for the sound the waves make as they thrash through a narrow opening in the granite cliffs, into a sea cave, and whoosh up and out. Approximately halfway between Sand Beach and Otter Cliff, steps lead down to the water, where you can watch the wave action close up. Use caution as you descend (access may be limited due to storms), and also if you venture onto the outer cliffs along this walk. *Easy.* ✉ *Ocean Dr. section of Park Loop Rd., Acadia National Park* ✣ *Trailhead: Upper parking lot of Sand Beach.*

VISITOR CENTERS

Hulls Cove Visitor Center

INFO CENTER | FAMILY | This is a great spot to get your bearings. A large 3D relief map of Mount Desert Island gives you the lay of the land, and a free 15-minute video about everything the park has to offer plays every half hour. You can pick up guidebooks, maps of hiking trails and carriage roads, and recordings for drive-it-yourself tours—don't forget to grab a schedule of ranger-led programs, which includes guided hikes and other interpretive events. Junior-ranger programs for kids, nature hikes, photography walks, tide-pool explorations, and evening talks are all popular. The Acadia National Park Headquarters, off Route 233 near the north end of Eagle Lake, serves as the park's visitor center during the off-season. ✉ *25 Visitor Center Rd., Bar Harbor* ☎ *207/288–3338* 🌐 *www.nps.gov/acad.*

Village Green Information Center

INFO CENTER | This small information center doubles as a facility for the Island Explorer shuttle bus service and is staffed from 8 am–5 pm from June to Columbus Day. Park entrance passes can be purchased here, as well as some maps and brochures. ✉ *19 Firefly La., Bar Harbor* ☎ *207/288–3338* 🌐 *www.nps.gov/acad.*

Restaurants

★ Burning Tree

$$$ | SEAFOOD | One of the top restaurants in Maine, this easy-to-miss gem with a festive dining room is on Route 3, not far from Bar Harbor in the village of Otter Creek. The seasonal menu emphasizes freshly caught seafood, and half a dozen or so species of fish are offered virtually every day—all from the Gulf of Maine. **Known for:** farm to table cuisine; made onsite to-go food items; regionally sourced ingredients like fresh local seafood. 💲 *Average main: $30* ✉ *69 Otter Creek Dr., Otter Creek* ✣ *5 miles from Bar Harbor, 7 miles from Northeast Harbor* ☎ *207/288–9331* ⏲ *Closed mid-Oct.–mid-June. No lunch.*

★ **Havana**

$$$ | **CUBAN** | A lively yet intimate spot, Havana serves Latin-inspired dishes paired with robust wines right in the middle of downtown Bar Harbor. In the summer, have a bite on "the Parrilla" (the informal, no-reservations patio); year round, dine in a pleasant indoor space with a modern aesthetic, featuring clean lines and cheery colors. **Known for:** Lobster Moqueca (a Brazilian seafood stew); a lively atmosphere fueled by craft cocktails like mojitos and caipairinhas; the Havana Paella. *Average main: $34 318 Main St., Bar Harbor 207/288–2822 www.havanamaine.com No lunch.*

Coffee and Quick Bites

Lompoc Cafe and Books

$ | **AMERICAN** | This shop is nestled beside a shaded patio just a quick walk from the downtown Bar Harbor bustle. Stop in for a quiet respite for relaxing with a coffee or beer while noshing on a bagel or artisanal pizza and perusing a book. **Known for:** banh mi sandwich in breakfast and lunch versions; eclectic selection of books; located next to public parking lot. *Average main: $11 36 Rodick St., Bar Harbor 207/901–0004 www.lompoc-cafe.com Closed Mon.*

Hotels

Bar Harbor Inn and Spa

$$$ | **HOTEL** | Originally established in the late 1800s as a men's social club, this waterfront inn has rooms spread among three buildings on well-landscaped grounds. **Pros:** bay and ocean views; proximity to downtown and Acadia National Park; shore path along the waterfront from the hotel. **Cons:** spotty cell phone service; views often include cruise ships in port; dining reservations recommended. *Rooms from: $350 1 Newport Dr., Bar Harbor 207/288–3351, 800/248–3351 www.barharborinn.com Closed late Nov.–mid-Mar. 153 rooms Free breakfast.*

Island Place

$ | **HOTEL** | **FAMILY** | This motel's clean rooms and central location make it a good base for exploring the Bar Harbor area. **Pros:** centrally located; microwave and refrigerator available for guests in lobby; free parking. **Cons:** two-night minimum in high season; basic rooms; renovated motel-style lodgings are not for everyone. *Rooms from: $188 51 Holland Ave., Bar Harbor 207/288–3771 www.islandplacebh.com 10 rooms No meals.*

★ **West Street Hotel**

$$$$ | **RESORT** | Maine has some pretty phenomenal resort destinations in the Kennebunks and on the Mid-Coast, but to enjoy the state's premiere resort experience you'll do best to make the trek Down East to Bar Harbor to stay at the West Street Hotel, where resort culture truly shines. **Pros:** all the expected luxuries of a resort and then some; each floor is equipped with guest pantries filled with snacks and goodies; one of the most tastefully decorated resorts in Maine. **Cons:** it's a trek to get Down East; $25 daily resort fee; dogs allowed, but for an additional $75 per dog per night (two-dog limit). *Rooms from: $479 50 West St., Bar Harbor 207/288–0825 www.theweststreethotel.com 85 rooms Free breakfast.*

West Side of Mount Desert Island

7 miles east of Bar Harbor via Rte. 233 and Rte. 3.

This side of Acadia National Park might seem removed due to its distance from the population and amenities center of Bar Harbor, but there's plenty worth exploring on this side of Somes Sound. Echo Lake Beach, one of the park's two swimming beaches and the one with the warmest water, is over here, as is Bass Harbor Head Light, one of Maine's most photographed lighthouses. Some of the park's most popular hiking trails adorn Acadia and Beech mountains.

Sights

BEACHES

Echo Lake Beach

BEACH—SIGHT | FAMILY | A quiet lake surrounded by woods in the shadow of Beech Mountain, Echo Lake draws swimmers to its sandy southern shore. The lake bottom is a bit muckier than the ocean beaches nearby, but the water is considerably warmer. The surrounding trail network skirts the lake and ascends the mountain. The beach is 2 miles north of Southwest Harbor. **Amenities:** lifeguards; toilets. **Best for:** swimming. ✉ *Echo Lake Beach Rd., off Rte. 102, Acadia National Park.*

HISTORIC SIGHTS

★ **Bass Harbor Head Light**

LIGHTHOUSE | Built in 1858, this lighthouse is one of the most photographed lights in Maine. Now automated, it marks the entrance to Bass Harbor and Blue Hill Bay. You can't actually go inside—the grounds and residence are Coast Guard property—but two trails around the facility have excellent views. It's within Acadia National Park, and there is parking. **TIP→ The best place to take a picture is from the rocks below—but watch your step, as they can be slippery.** ✉ *Lighthouse Rd., off Rte. 102A, Bass Harbor* ☎ *207/244–9753* *Free.*

Carroll Homestead

BUILDING | For almost a century beginning in the early 1800s, three generations of the Carroll family homesteaded at this small-scale farm that was donated to the park in 1982. The weathered farmhouse still stands and is occasionally opened to ranger-led tours; check the park calendar for details. ✉ *Southwest Harbor* ✣ *About 30 minutes from Hulls Cove Visitor Center* ☎ *207/288–3338* 🌐 *nps.gov/acad.*

SCENIC STOPS

Bass Harbor

TOWN | FAMILY | This tiny lobstering village with a relaxed atmosphere and a few accommodations and restaurants. If you're looking to get away from the crowds, consider using this hardworking community as your base. Although Bass Harbor does not draw as many tourists as other villages, the Bass Harbor Head Light in Acadia National Park is one of the region's most popular attractions and is undoubtedly one of the most photographed lighthouses in Maine. From Bass Harbor, you can hike the Ship Harbor Nature Trail or take a ferry to Frenchboro or Swans Island.

TRAILS

★ **Acadia Mountain Trail**

TRAIL | If you're up for a challenge, this is one of the area's best trails. The 2.5-mile round-trip climb up Acadia Mountain is a steep and strenuous 700-foot climb, but the payoff views of Somes Sound are grand. If you want a guided trip, look into ranger-led hikes for this trail. This is the only mountain on Mount Desert Island that lies east–west rather than north–south. *Difficult.* ✉ *Rte. 102, Acadia National Park* ✣ *Trailhead: 1 mile north of Echo Lake Rd. on Rte. 102* ☎ *207/288–3338* 🌐 *www.nps.gov/acad.*

Beech Mountain

TRAIL | This relatively short loop trail—1.2 miles round-trip—has a unique payoff: a fire lookout tower with views of Somes Sound, Echo Lake, Acadia Mountain and beyond from its accessible platform. The forested and rocky trail is popular with sunset seekers, who are reminded to carry appropriate clothing and headlamps for the descent. *Moderate.* ✉ *Park Loop Rd., Bar Harbor* ✣ *Trailhead: 4 miles south of Somesville on Beech Hill Rd. off Rte. 102* ☎ *207/288–3338* 🌐 *nps.gov/acad.*

Ship Harbor Nature Trail

TRAIL | This 1.3-mile, figure-8 trail is popular with families and especially birders. About half the trail loops through woods, while the remainder is alongside a sheltered cove where great blue herons feed in the mudflats during low tide. *Easy.* ✉ *Rte. 102A, Southwest Harbor* ✥ *Trailhead: 1.3 miles west of Seawall picnic area on Rte. 102A* ☎ *207/288–3338* 🌐 *nps.gov/acad.*

VISITOR CENTER

Seawall Ranger Station

INFO CENTER | This small information center is located at Acadia National Park's Seawall Campground, approximately 18 miles from Bar Harbor on Mount Desert Island's west side. The station is typically open 9 am–8 pm from about Memorial Day until Columbus Day, but hours may vary. ✉ *378 Seawall Rd., Southwest Harbor* ☎ *207/288–3338* 🌐 *www.nps.gov/acad.*

Restaurants

Thurston's Lobster Pound

$$ | SEAFOOD | Right on Bass Harbor, looking across to the village, Thurston's is easy to spot because of its bright yellow awning. You can order everything from a grilled-cheese crab sandwich, haddock chowder, or hamburger to a boiled lobster served with clams or mussels and dine at covered outdoor tables, or you can buy fresh lobsters to go. **Known for:** family-friendly environment; lobster fresh off the boat; good place to watch sunsets. [$] *Average main: $20* ✉ *Steamboat Wharf, 9 Thurston Rd., Bernard* ☎ *207/244–7600* 🌐 *www.thurstonforlobster.com* ⏲ *Closed mid-Oct.–Memorial Day.*

Schoodic Peninsula

25 miles east of Ellsworth via U.S. 1 and Rte. 186.

The only section of Acadia National Park that sits on the mainland is at the southern end of the Schoodic Peninsula in the town of Winter Harbor. The landscape of Schoodic Peninsula's craggy coastline, towering evergreens, and views over Frenchman Bay are breathtaking yearround—and less crowded than over on Mount Desert Island.

During the summer season you can take a passenger ferry ($15 one-way, $30 round-trip) from Bar Harbor to Winter Harbor, where you can catch the free Island Explorer bus, which stops throughout this section of the park. Don't forget: you'll need to take the ferry to get back to Bar Harbor.

Sights

HISTORIC SIGHTS

Schoodic Institute

COLLEGE | In the Schoodic Peninsula section of Acadia National Park, this center offers lectures, workshops, and kid-friendly events about nature. It's worth a drive-by just to see the Rockefeller Building, a massive 1935 French Eclectic and Renaissance-style structure with a stone-and-half-timber facade that served as naval offices and housing. The building now acts as a visitor center after an extensive renovation. ✉ *9 Atterbury Circle, Winter Harbor* ☎ *207/288–1310* 🌐 *www.schoodicinstitute.org.*

Did You Know?

The Somesville Bridge, found on the West Side of Mount Desert Island, is a popular stop for a photo op.

SCENIC DRIVES

Schoodic Loop Road

SCENIC DRIVE | The park maintains this scenic 6-mile loop that edges along the coast, yielding views of Grindstone Neck, Winter Harbor, Winter Harbor Lighthouse, and, across the water, Cadillac Mountain. Parking lots along its length provide access to the Alder Trail and Anvil Trail. At the tip of Schoodic Point, just beyond the Schoodic Institute, huge slabs of pink granite lie jumbled along the shore, thrashed unmercifully by the crashing surf, and jack pines cling to life amid the rocks. ✉ *Schoodic Loop Rd., Winter Harbor* ⊕ *½ mile east of Newman St. and Main St. in Winter Harbor* ☎ *207/288–3338* 🌐 *nps.gov/acad.*

SCENIC STOPS

Blueberry Hill

SCENIC DRIVE | The parking area here, about 1 mile east of Schoodic Point, offers scenic views of nearby Little Moose and Schoodic islands and the ocean beyond. It's also where to park if you're planning to hike a loop consisting of the Alder and Anvil trails across the road from the parking lot. ✉ *Winter Harbor* ⊕ *About 1 mile east of Schoodic Point* ☎ *207/288–3338* 🌐 *nps.gov/acad.*

Frazer Point

MARINA | The only boat pier maintained by Acadia National Park is here, serving kayakers and canoeists who wish to explore Frenchman Bay. There's also a picnic area and parking lot. ✉ *Schoodic Loop Rd., Winter Harbor* ☎ *207/288–3338* 🌐 *nps.gov/acad.*

Schoodic Point

SCENIC DRIVE | Located at the end of Avey Cove Road, where there's a sizable parking lot, Schoodic Point is where the dramatic granite shoreline meets crashing waves. Look east for a close view of Little Moose Island; a bit farther away to the west is a sidelong view of Mount Desert Island. To the south is an inspiring view of the open ocean. ✉ *Arey Cove Rd., Winter Harbor* ☎ *207/288–3338* 🌐 *nps.gov/acad.*

TRAILS

Alder Trail

TRAIL | Popular with birders, this easy 1.2-mile out-and-back trail is usually begun from the trailhead across from the Blueberry Hill parking area. You can turn around at the ranger cabin, or walk a bit farther to add the Schoodic Head Trail to your jaunt. *Easy.* ✉ *Schoodic Loop Rd.* ⊕ *Trailhead: 1 mile east of Schoodic Point parking area on Schoodic Loop Rd.* ☎ *207/288–3338* 🌐 *nps.gov/acad.*

Anvil Trail

TRAIL | The longest trail on the Schoodic Peninsula—2.2 miles out and back—gradually climbs to tree-covered and boulder-strewn Schoodic Head, at 440 feet the highest point on the Schoodic Peninsula. On the way there, keep an eye out for the sign pointing you to The Anvil, a rock overlook with views of Schoodic Point. *Difficult.* ✉ *Acadia National Park* ⊕ *Trailhead: A short walk east of Blueberry Hill parking lot on the loop road* ☎ *207/288–3338* 🌐 *nps.gov/acad.*

Schoodic Head Trail

TRAIL | This 1.2-mile out and back trail ascends to the 440-foot summit of Schoodic Head, which affords views of surrounding mountains, forests, and the ocean. It's commonly hiked in conjunction with the nearby Alder Trail. *Moderate.* ✉ *Schoodic Loop Rd.* ⊕ *Trailhead: ½ mile east of Schoodic Loop Rd. off Mountain Rd. and Ranger Cabin Rd.* ☎ *207/288–3338* 🌐 *nps.gov/acad.*

VISITOR CENTERS

Rockefeller Welcome Center

INFO CENTER | This facility offers information on the park as well as the old Navy base that now comprises the Schoodic Institute campus. ✉ *1 Atterbury Circle, Winter Harbor* ☎ *207/288–3338* 🌐 *nps.gov/acad.*

Schoodic Woods Campground Ranger Station

INFO CENTER | This ranger station serves triple duty as campground host, information center, and Island Explorer bus stop. ✉ *54 Farview Dr., Winter Harbor* ☎ *207/288–3338* 🌐 *nps.gov/acad.*

Restaurants

Chase's Restaurant

$ | **SEAFOOD** | **FAMILY** | This family restaurant has a reputation for serving good, basic fare—and in this region that means a whole lot of fresh fish. There are large and small fried seafood dinners, as well as several more expensive seafood platters. **Known for:** family-friendly dining; classic Maine fare; no-frills atmosphere. *Average main: $14* ✉ *193 Main St., Winter Harbor* ☎ *207/963–7171.*

Hotels

Acadia's Oceanside Meadows Inn

$ | **B&B/INN** | **FAMILY** | A must for nature lovers, this lodging sits on a 200-acre preserve dotted with woods, streams, salt marshes, and ponds; it's home to the Oceanside Meadows Innstitute for the Arts and Sciences, which holds lectures, musical performances, art exhibits, and other events in the restored barn. **Pros:** one of the region's few sand beaches; staff share info about the area over tea; most rooms have water views. **Cons:** need to cross road to beach; only serves breakfast. *Rooms from: $185* ✉ *Rte. 195 Prospect Harbor Rd., Prospect Harbor* ☎ *207/963–5557* 🌐 *www.oceaninn.com* *Closed mid-Oct.–late May* *15 rooms* *Free breakfast.*

Isle Au Haut

6 miles south of Stonington via ferry.

French explorer Samuel D. Champlain discovered Isle au Haut—or "High Island"—in 1604, but heaps of shells suggest that native populations lived on or visited the island prior to his arrival. The island is accessible only by passenger-only mail boat, but the 45-minute journey is well worth the effort. Acadia National Park extends to cover part of the island, with miles of trails, and the boat will drop visitors off there in peak season. The island has some seasonal rentals but no inns and only three stores. There's one main road here: partly paved and partly unpaved, it circles the island and goes through the Acadia National Park section.

Sights

SCENIC STOPS

Duck Harbor

ISLAND | Acadia National Park's most primitive (and therefore secluded) campground is located here, as is a dock for the passenger-only ferry that serves Isle au Haut from Stonington on the mainland. Note that the ferry only stops here from June through late-September; in the off-season or if you miss the boat, it's a hike of about 4 miles back to the main dock at Isle au Haut Town Landing. ✉ *Duck Harbor, Isle Au Haut* ☎ *207/288–3338* 🌐 *nps.gov/acad.*

Western Head

ISLAND | Located at the southern tip of Isle au Haut, Western Head is accessible by foot or bicycle from Town Landing on gravel roads. Once here, you have a few hiking trails to choose from (bicycles not allowed). ✉ *Isle Au Haut* ☎ *207/288–3338* 🌐 *nps.gov/acad.*

TRAILS

Western Head Trail

TRAIL | Dramatic coastal cliff views are your reward for visiting perhaps the most remote corner of Acadia National Park. This is most commonly hiked as a loop that also includes Western Head Road and Cliff Trail. Once off the wooded road, the trail alternates between forest and granite clifftop, with opportunities to go off-course and explore the rocky shoreline. Access is via the Duck Harbor mailboat pier; total distance is approximately 3.3 miles. There are no amenities available, so be sure to pack plenty of water and snacks. *Moderate. ✉ Isle Au Haut ✣ Trailhead: Near Duck Harbor Campground ☎ 207/288–3338 🌐 nps.gov/acad.*

Restaurants

Maine Lobster Lady

$ | **SEAFOOD** | Come summer, this former island innkeeper sells yummy and quick eats, many of them made with fish from local waters and her own organic garden produce. Her "food truck" (actually a tow trailer) is parked in the Island Store parking lot on Isle au Haut. **Known for:** everything prepared in-the-truck; traditional Maine lobster rolls; whoopie pies. *$ Average main: $17 ✉ Off Main Rd., Isle Au Haut ☎ 207/335–5141 in summer, 207/669–2751 🌐 www.mainelobsterlady.com.*

Activities

The best way to see Acadia National Park is to get out of your vehicle and explore on foot or by bicycle or boat. There are more than 45 miles of carriage roads that are perfect for walking and biking in the warmer months and for cross-country skiing and snowshoeing in winter. There are more than 150 miles of trails for hiking, numerous ponds and lakes for canoeing or kayaking, two beaches for swimming, and steep cliffs for rock climbing.

BIKING

Exploring Acadia National Park on a bike can be heavenly. There are a variety of surfaces from paved to gravel, inland to seaside, so best to keep that in mind. A park entrance pass is required to ride anywhere within park boundaries; be sure to carry your pass or leave it in view in your parked car. On carriage roads, bicyclists must yield to everyone, including horses, and not exceed 20 mph; in winter, bikes are not permitted on carriage roads groomed for cross-country skiing. The Park Loop Road is open to cyclists, but the road is narrow, often congested and has no shoulders; biking the road is discouraged during peak hours, and cyclists must ride with the flow of traffic where the road is one-way. Island Explorer buses have at least two and sometimes four racks to give riders a rest or a shuttle ride from one spot to another. Pick up a free biking map at any visitor center or download it from the park's website.

Acadia Bike

BICYCLING | **FAMILY** | Rent mountain bikes and hybrids at Acadia Bike, both good models for negotiating the carriage roads in Acadia National Park. *✉ 48 Cottage St., Bar Harbor ☎ 207/288–9605, 800/526–8615 🌐 www.acadiabike.com.*

Bar Harbor Bicycle Shop

BICYCLING | Rent bikes for anywhere from four hours to a full week at the Bar Harbor Bicycle Shop. *✉ 141 Cottage St., Bar Harbor ☎ 207/288–3886 🌐 www.barharborbike.com.*

BIRD-WATCHING

Acadia National Park is for the birds—much to the enjoyment of birders of a feather from all corners. Famed avian illustrator Roger Tory Peterson is known to have deemed Mount Desert Island as "the warbler capital of the world" for being home to more than 20 species of the energetic and colorful songbirds. According to the National Park Service, approximately 308 species altogether have been encountered in or near the park. The park's website outlines a dozen areas rich in birdwatching opportunities. Come fall, park rangers lead hawkwatches from the summit of Cadillac Mountain, counting hundreds and even thousands of migrating raptors. In addition to its namesake tours, Bar Harbor Whale Watch Co. offers cruises that seek out the comically colorful seabird known as the puffin.

CAMPING

Acadia National Park's two main campgrounds, Seawall and Blackwoods, don't have water views, but the price is right and the ocean is just a 10-minute walk from each. The park's other two campgrounds—Schoodic Woods and Duck Harbor—are located in the Schoodic Peninsula and Isle au Haut sections, respectively.

Blackwoods Campground. Located only 5 miles from Bar Harbor, this is Acadia's most popular campground. It is open early May to mid-October and well served by the Island Explorer bus system. ✉ *Rte. 3, 5 miles south of Bar Harbor* ☎ *877/444–6777 for reservations* 🌐 *www.recreation.gov.*

Mount Desert Campground. Located outside the park, this campground's 150 sites are all tucked in the woods and many are on the waterfront. Vehicles longer than 20 feet are not allowed. Canoes and kayaks are available for rent. It is open mid-June to mid-September. ✉ *Somesville* ☎ *207/244–3710* 🌐 *www.mountdesert-campground.com.*

Seawall Campground. On the quiet western side of the island, Seawall is open late May–mid-October. ✉ *Rte. 102A, 4 miles south of Southwest Harbor* ☎ *877/444–6777 for reservations* 🌐 *www.recreation.gov.*

EDUCATIONAL PROGRAMS

The National Park Service offers a variety of ranger-led programming and tours, including the popular Junior Ranger Program for kids and, unique to Acadia National Park, citizen science opportunities at the Schoodic Institute. Visit the parks website for more information.

HIKING

Acadia National Park maintains more than 150 miles of hiking trails, from easy strolls around lakes and ponds to rigorous treks with climbs up rock faces and scrambles along cliffs. Although hiking trails are concentrated on the east side of the island, the west side also has some scenic trails. For those wishing for a longer trek, try the trails leading up Cadillac Mountain or Dorr Mountain; you may also try Parkman, Sargeant, and Penobscot mountains. Most hiking is done mid-May–mid-November; snow falls early in Maine, so from as early as late November to the end of March, cross-country skiing and snowshoeing replace hiking. Volunteers groom most of the carriage roads if there's been 4 inches of snow or more. ■ **TIP→ Every few years, someone falls off one of the park's trails or cliffs and is swept out to sea. There is a lot of loose, rocky gravel along the shoreline, and sea rocks can often be slippery—so watch your step.**

MULTISPORT OUTFITTERS

Name just about any popular sporting activity—kayaking, cycling, rock climbing, cross-country skiing, and snowshoeing, to say nothing of hiking—and chances are you can do it at Acadia National Park. Cadillac Mountain Sports serves all of them, and their staff will be happy to answer your questions and offer advice for where to go to exert yourself.

Cadillac Mountain Sports

HIKING/WALKING | One of the best sporting-goods stores in the state, Cadillac Mountain Sports has developed a following of locals and visitors alike. Here you'll find top-quality climbing, hiking, boating, paddling, and camping equipment, and in winter you can rent cross-country skis, ice skates, and snowshoes. ✉ *26 Cottage St., Bar Harbor* ☎ *207/288–4532* 🌐 *www.cadillacsports.com.*

SCENIC FLIGHTS

Viewing the Acadia National Park region from above is a great way to get your bearings for your on-the-ground (and on-the-water) explorations, and perhaps the easiest way to wrap your arms around the sheer variety of scenery and attractions. For $129 per person, Scenic Flights of Acadia (⇨ *see Tours section of the chapter planner*) offers a 35-minute tour encompassing the Mount Desert Island areas of the park.

SWIMMING

The park has two swimming beaches, Sand Beach and Echo Lake Beach. Sand Beach, along Park Loop Road, has changing rooms, restrooms, and a lifeguard on duty Memorial Day–Labor Day.

What's Nearby

No matter where you're coming from or what section of Acadia National Park you're going to, you'd have to go out of your way not to pass through the gateway of **Ellsworth.** This small city of approximately 8,000 is the largest town closest to the park and houses a variety of big-box retailers to make stocking up on food and other items a snap. In the high season and especially at the last minute, you'll have a better chance of finding lodging here. From Ellsworth it's about a 30-minute drive to Bar Harbor and the park's center, an hour's drive to Stonington for the ferry to Isle au Haut, and 35 minutes to Winter Harbor just atop the Schoodic Peninsula. All three can be considered park gateways, though only Bar Harbor approaches the amenities of Ellsworth; the latter two towns are tiny, with only a relatively few dining and lodging options apiece.

A resort town since the 19th century, Bar Harbor is the artistic, culinary, and social center of Mount Desert Island, and it serves visitors to Acadia National Park with inns, motels, and restaurants. Shops are clustered along Main, Mount Desert, and Cottage streets; take a stroll down West Street, a National Historic District, where you can see some fine old houses.

Chapter 5

ARCHES NATIONAL PARK

Updated by
Stina Sieg

Camping ★★☆☆☆ | Hotels ★★★★☆ | Activities ★★★☆☆ | Scenery ★★★★★ | Crowds ★★★★★

WELCOME TO ARCHES NATIONAL PARK

TOP REASONS TO GO

★ **Arch appeal:** Nowhere in the world has as large an array or quantity of natural arches.

★ **Legendary landscape:** A photographer's dream—no wonder it's been the chosen backdrop for many Hollywood films.

★ **Treasures hanging in the balance:** Landscape Arch and Balanced Rock look like they might topple any day. And they could—the features in this park erode and evolve constantly.

★ **Fins and needles:** Fins are thin, parallel walls of eroding rock that slowly disintegrate into towerlike "needles." The spaces around and between them will carve their way into your memories like the wind and water that formed them.

1 **Devils Garden.** Eighteen miles from the visitor center, this is the end of the paved road in Arches. It has the park's only campground, a picnic area, and access to drinking water. Trails in Devils Garden lead to Landscape Arch and several other noteworthy formations.

2 **Fiery Furnace.** About 14 miles from the visitor center this area is so labeled because its orange spires of rock look much like tongues of flame. Reservations are required, and can be made up to six months in advance, to join the twice-daily ranger-guided treks. Or you can obtain a permit to visit Fiery Furnace on your own, but only experienced, well-prepared hikers should attempt this option.

3 **Delicate Arch/Wolfe Ranch.** A spur road about 11.7 miles from the visitor center leads to the moderately strenuous 3-mile round-trip trail and viewpoints for the park's most famous feature—Delicate Arch. To see it from below, follow the road to the viewpoint, then walk to either easily accessible viewing area.

4 **The Windows.** Reached on a spur 9.2 miles from the visitor center, here you can see many of the park's natural arches from your car or on an easy rolling trail.

5 **Balanced Rock.** This giant rock teeters atop a pedestal, creating a 128-foot formation of red rock grandeur right along the roadside, about 9 miles from the visitor center.

6 **Petrified Dunes.** Just a tiny pull-out about 5 miles from the visitor center, stop here for pictures of acres and acres of petrified sand dunes.

7 **Courthouse Towers.** The Three Gossips, Sheep Rock, and Tower of Babel are all here. Enter this section of the park 3 miles past the visitor center. The Park Avenue Trail winds through the area.

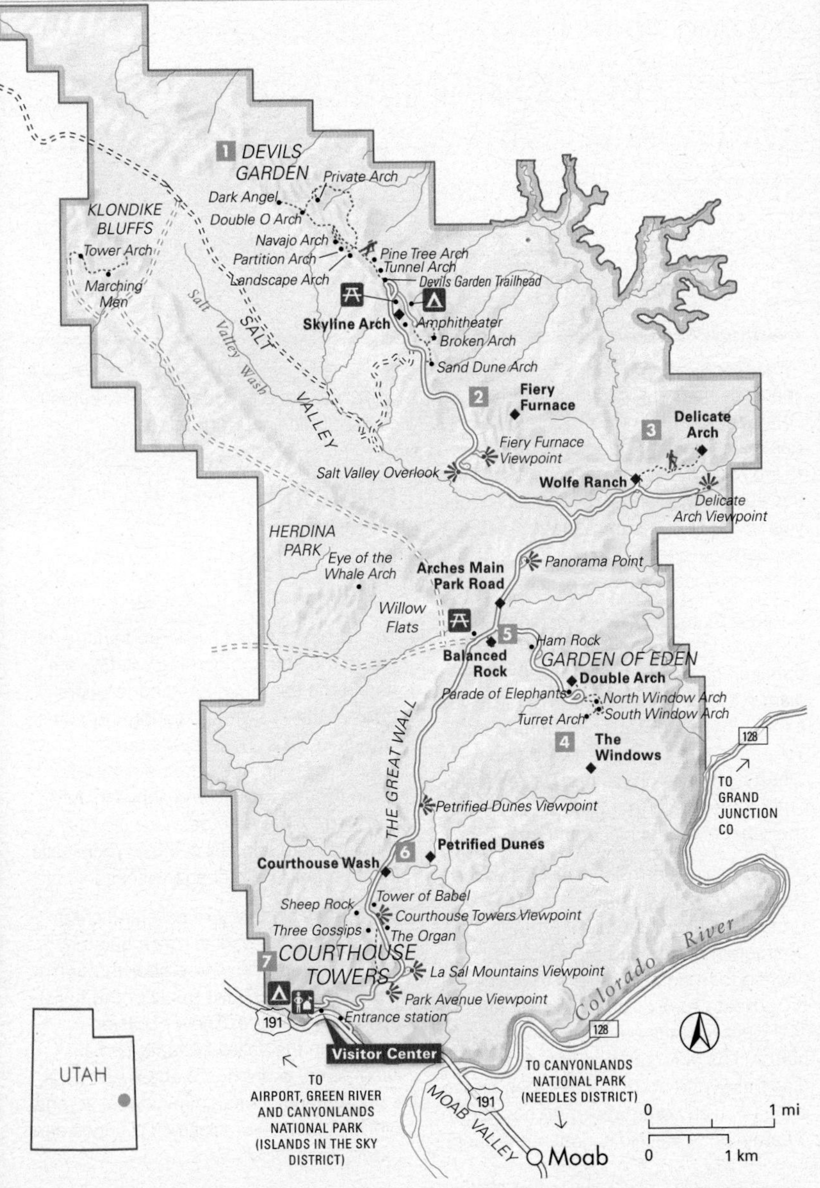
1 DEVILS GARDEN
Private Arch
Dark Angel
Double O Arch
Navajo Arch
Partition Arch
Landscape Arch
Pine Tree Arch
Tunnel Arch
Devils Garden Trailhead
Skyline Arch
Amphitheater
Broken Arch
Sand Dune Arch
KLONDIKE BLUFFS
Tower Arch
Marching Men
Salt Valley Wash
SALT VALLEY
2 Fiery Furnace
Fiery Furnace Viewpoint
Salt Valley Overlook
3 Delicate Arch
Wolfe Ranch
Delicate Arch Viewpoint
HERDINA PARK
Eye of the Whale Arch
Arches Main Park Road
Panorama Point
Willow Flats
5
Ham Rock
Balanced Rock
GARDEN OF EDEN
Double Arch
Parade of Elephants
North Window Arch
South Window Arch
Turret Arch
4 The Windows
THE GREAT WALL
Petrified Dunes Viewpoint
6 Petrified Dunes
Courthouse Wash
Tower of Babel
Sheep Rock
Courthouse Towers Viewpoint
Three Gossips
The Organ
7 COURTHOUSE TOWERS
La Sal Mountains Viewpoint
Park Avenue Viewpoint
Entrance station
Visitor Center
191
128
TO GRAND JUNCTION CO
Colorado River
UTAH
TO AIRPORT, GREEN RIVER AND CANYONLANDS NATIONAL PARK (ISLANDS IN THE SKY DISTRICT)
MOAB VALLEY
TO CANYONLANDS NATIONAL PARK (NEEDLES DISTRICT)
Moab
0
1 mi
0
1 km

More than 1.5 million visitors come to Arches annually, drawn by the red rock landscape and its wind- and water-carved rock formations. The park is named for the 2,000-plus sandstone arches that frame horizons, cast precious shade, and are in a perpetual state of gradual transformation, the result of constant erosion.

Fancifully named attractions like Three Penguins, Queen Nefertiti, and Tower of Babel stir curiosity, beckoning visitors to stop and marvel. Immerse yourself in this spectacular landscape, but don't lose yourself entirely—summer temperatures frequently exceed 100°F, and water is hard to come by inside the park boundaries.

It's easy to spot some of the arches from your car, but take the time to step outside and walk beneath the spans and giant walls of orange rock. This gives you a much better idea of their proportion. You may feel as writer Edward Abbey did when he awoke on his first day as a park ranger in Arches: that you're walking in the most beautiful place on Earth.

It's especially worthwhile to visit as the sun goes down. At sunset, the rock formations glow, and you'll often find photographers behind their tripods waiting for magnificent rays to descend on Delicate Arch or other popular sites. The Fiery Furnace earns its name as its narrow fins glow red just before the sun dips below the horizon. Full-moon nights are particularly dramatic in Arches as the creamy white Navajo sandstone reflects light, and eerie silhouettes are created by towering fins and formations.

Planning

When to Go

The busiest times of year are spring and fall. In the spring blooming wildflowers herald the end of winter, and temperatures in the 70s and 80s bring the year's largest crowds. The crowds remain steady in summer as the thermostat often exceeds 100°F and above in July and August. Sudden dramatic cloudbursts create rainfalls over red rock walls in late-summer "monsoon" season.

Fall means clear, warm days and crisp, cool nights. The park is much quieter in winter, and from December through February you can hike many of the trails in relative solitude. Snow occasionally falls in the valley beneath La Sal Mountains, and when it does, Arches is a photographer's paradise, with a serene white dusting over slickrock mounds and natural rock windows.

AVERAGE HIGH/LOW TEMPERATURES					
JAN.	**FEB.**	**MAR.**	**APR.**	**MAY**	**JUNE**
44/22	52/28	64/35	71/42	82/51	93/60
JULY	**AUG.**	**SEPT.**	**OCT.**	**NOV.**	**DEC.**
100/67	97/66	88/55	74/42	56/30	45/23

Getting Here and Around

AIR

Moab is served by tiny Canyonlands Field Airport, which has daily service to Denver on United Airlines and a couple of car rental agencies. The nearest midsize airport is Grand Junction Regional Airport in Grand Junction, Colorado, which is approximately 110 miles from Moab and is served by several major airlines.

CAR

The park entrance is just off U.S. 191 on the north side of downtown Moab, 28 miles south of Interstate 70 and 130 miles north of the Arizona border. Arches is also about 30 miles from the Island in the Sky section and 80 miles from the Needles District of Canyonlands National Park. If you're driving to Arches from points east on Interstate 70, consider taking Exit 214 in Utah (about 50 miles west of Grand Junction), and continuing south on picturesque Highway 128, the Colorado River Scenic Byway, about 50 miles to Moab. Bear in mind that services can be sparse on even major roads in these parts.

Branching off the main 18-mile park road—officially known as Arches Scenic Road—are two spurs, one 2½ miles to the Windows section and one 1.6 miles to Delicate Arch trailhead and viewpoint. There are several four-wheel-drive roads in the park; always check at the visitor center for conditions before attempting to traverse them. The entrance road into the park can back up mid-morning to early afternoon during busy periods. You'll encounter less traffic early in the morning or at sunset.

TRAIN

The *California Zephyr*, operated by Amtrak (☎ *800/872–7245*), stops daily in Green River, about 50 miles northwest of Moab.

Inspiration

127 Hours: Between a Rock and a Hard Place by Aron Ralston. This true story—made into a movie of the same name starring James Franco—took place southeast of Arches and is a modern-day survivor story of solitary man in nature.

Canyon Country Wildflowers, by Damian Fagan, can help you name the colorful blossoms you see during wildflower season (spring and early summer). *Desert Solitaire*. Eminent naturalist Edward Abbey's first ranger assignment was Arches; this classic is a must-read.

Park Essentials

ACCESSIBILITY

Not all park facilities meet federally mandated accessibility standards, but as visitation to Arches increases, the park continues efforts to increase accessibility. Visitors with mobility impairments can access the visitor center, all park restrooms, and two campsites at the Devils Garden Campground (4H is first-come, first served, while site 7 can be reserved up to six months in advance March–October). The Park Avenue Viewpoint is a paved path with a slight decline near the end, and both Delicate Arch and Balanced Rock viewpoints are partially hard-surfaced. For those with visual disabilities, visitor center exhibits include audio recordings and some tactile elements. You can also request an audio version of the park brochure (or listen to it on the park website 🌐 *www.nps.gov/arch*). Large-print and braille versions of park information are also available at the visitor center.

PARK FEES AND PERMITS

Admission to the park is $30 per vehicle, $25 per motorcycle, and $15 per person entering on foot or bicycle, valid for seven days. To encourage visitation to the park during less busy times, a $50 local park pass grants you admission to both Arches and Canyonlands parks as well as Natural Bridges and Hovenweep national monuments for one year.

PARK HOURS

Arches National Park is open year-round, seven days a week, around the clock. It's in the Mountain time zone.

CELL PHONE RECEPTION

Cell phone reception is spotty in the park and in general is strongest whenever the La Sal mountains are visible. There are pay phones outside the visitor center.

Hotels

Though there are no hotels or cabins in the park itself, in the surrounding area every type of lodging is available, from economy chain motels to B&Bs and high-end, high-adventure resorts. It's important to know when popular events are held, however, as accommodations can, and do, fill up weeks ahead of time.

Restaurants

In the park itself, there are no dining facilities and no snack bars. Supermarkets, bakeries, and delis in downtown Moab will be happy to make you food to go. If you bring a packed lunch, there are several picnic areas from which to choose.

Visitor Information

PARK CONTACT INFORMATION Arches National Park. ✉ *N. U.S. 191, Arches National Park* ☎ *435/719–2299* 🌐 *www.nps.gov/arch.*

Devils Garden

18 miles north of the visitor center.

At the end of the paved road in Arches, Devils Garden is the most developed area of the park, with the park's only campground and drinking water. It's also the site of the busiest trailheads.

Sights

GEOLOGICAL FORMATIONS

Skyline Arch

NATURE SITE | FAMILY | A quick walk from the parking lot at Skyline Arch, 16½ miles from the park entrance, gives you closer views and better photos. The short trail is less than a ½ mile round-trip and takes only a few minutes to travel. ✉ *Devils Garden Rd., Arches National Park.*

SCENIC DRIVES

★ **Arches Main Park Road**

SCENIC DRIVE | The main park road and its two short spurs are extremely scenic and allow you to enjoy many park sights from your car. The main road leads through Courthouse Towers, where you can see Sheep Rock and the Three Gossips, then alongside the Great Wall, the Petrified Dunes, and Balanced Rock. A drive to the Windows section takes you to attractions like Double Arch, and you can see Skyline Arch along the roadside as you approach the Devils Garden campground. The road to Delicate Arch allows hiking access to one of the park's main features. Allow about two hours to drive the 45-mile round-trip, more if you explore the spurs and their features and stop at viewpoints along the way. ✉ *Arches National Park.*

TRAILS

Broken Arch Trail

TRAIL | An easy walk across open grassland, this loop trail passes Broken Arch, which is also visible from the road. The arch gets its name because it appears to be cracked in the middle, but it's not really broken. The trail is 1¼ miles round-trip, but you can extend your adventure to about 2 miles round-trip by continuing north past Tapestry Arch and through Devils Garden Campground. *Easy.* ✉ *Arches National Park* ✣ *Trailhead: Off Devils Garden Rd., 16½ miles from park entrance.*

★ Devils Garden Trail

TRAIL | Landscape Arch is a highlight of this trail but is just one of several arches within reach, depending on your ambitions. It's an easy ¾-mile one-way (mostly gravel, relatively flat) trip to Landscape Arch, one of the longest stone spans in the world. Beyond Landscape Arch the scenery changes dramatically and the hike becomes more strenuous, as you must climb and straddle slickrock fins and negotiate some short, steep inclines. Finally, around a sharp bend, the stacked spans that compose Double O Arch come suddenly into view. Allow up to three hours for this round-trip hike of just over 4 miles. For a still longer (about a 7-mile round-trip) and more rigorous trek, venture on to see a formation called Dark Angel and then return to the trailhead on the primitive loop, making the short side hike to Private Arch. The hike to Dark Angel is a difficult route through fins. Other possible (and worthwhile) detours lead to Navajo Arch, Partition Arch, Tunnel Arch, and Pine Tree Arch. Allow about five hours for this adventure, take plenty of water, and watch your route carefully. Pick up the park's useful guide to Devils Garden, or download it from the website before you go. *Moderate–Difficult.* ✉ *Arches National Park* ✣ *Trailhead: On Devils Garden Rd., end of main road, 18 miles from park entrance.*

Landscape Arch

TRAIL | This natural rock opening, which measures 306 feet from base to base and looks like a delicate ribbon of rock bending over the horizon, is the longest geologic span in North America. In 1991, a slab of rock about 60 feet long, 11 feet wide, and 4 feet thick fell from the underside, leaving it even thinner. You reach it via a rolling, gravel, 1.6-mile-long trail. *Easy–Moderate.* ✉ *Arches National Park* ✣ *Trailhead: At Devils Garden Rd., at end of main road, 18 miles north of park entrance.*

Tower Arch Trail

TRAIL | Check with park rangers before attempting the dirt road through Salt Valley to Klondike Bluffs parking area. If rains haven't washed out the road, a trip to this seldom-visited area provides a solitude-filled hike culminating in a giant rock opening. Allow from two to three hours for this 3½-mile round-trip hike, not including the drive. *Moderate.* ✉ *Arches National Park* ✣ *Trailhead: At Klondike Bluffs parking area, 24½ miles from park entrance, 7¾ miles off main road.*

Fiery Furnace

14 miles north of the park entrance.

Fewer than 10% of the park's visitors ever descend into the chasms and washes of Fiery Furnace (a permit or a ranger-led hike is the only way to go), but you can gain an appreciation for this twisted, unyielding landscape from the Overlook. At sunset, the rocks glow a vibrant flamelike red, which gives the formation its daunting moniker.

Sights

TRAILS

Fiery Furnace

TRAIL | This area of the park has taken on a near-mythical lure for park visitors, who are drawn to challenging yet breathtaking terrain. Rangers strongly discourage inexperienced hikers from entering here—in fact, you can't enter without watching a video about how to help protect this very special section of the park and obtaining a permit ($6). Reservations can be made up to six months in advance to get a spot on the 2-mile round-trip ranger-led hikes ($16), offered mid-April–September, through this unique formation. A hike through these rugged rocks and sandy washes is challenging but fascinating. Hikers will need to use their hands at times to scramble up and through narrow cracks and along vertigo-inducing ledges above drop-offs, and there are no trail markings. If you're not familiar with the Furnace you can easily get lost or cause damage, so watch your step and use great caution. For information about reservations, see Ranger Programs Overview above. The less intrepid can view Fiery Furnace from the Overlook off the main road. *Difficult.* ✉ *Arches National Park* ✣ *Trailhead: Off main road, about 14 miles from park entrance.*

Sand Dune Arch Trail

TRAIL | **FAMILY** | You may return to the car with shoes full of bright red sand from this giant sandbox in the desert—it's fun exploring in and around the rock. Set aside five minutes for this shady, 530-yard walk and plenty of time if you have kids, who will love playing amid this dramatic landscape. Never climb on this or any other arch in the park, no matter how tempting—it's illegal, and it could result in damage to the fragile geology or personal injury. The trail intersects with the Broken Arch Trail—you can visit both arches with an easy 1½-mile round-trip walk. *Easy.* ✉ *Arches National Park* ✣ *Trailhead: Off Arches Scenic Dr., about 16½ miles from park entrance.*

Delicate Arch/ Wolfe Ranch

13 miles north of the park entrance.

The iconic symbol of the park and the state (it appears on many of Utah's license plates), Delicate Arch is tall and prominent compared with many of the spans in the park—it's big enough that it could shelter a four-story building. The arch is a remnant of an Entrada Sandstone fin; the rest of the rock has eroded and it now frames La Sal Mountains in the background. Drive 2.2 miles off the main road to the viewpoint to see the arch from a distance, or hike right up to it from the trailhead that starts near Wolfe Ranch. The trail, 1.2 miles off the main road, is a moderately strenuous 3-mile round-trip hike with no shade or access to water. It's especially picturesque shortly after sunrise or before sunset.

HISTORIC SIGHTS

Wolfe Ranch

HISTORIC SITE | Civil War veteran John Wesley Wolfe and his son started a small ranch here in 1888. He added a cabin in 1906 when his daughter Esther and her family came west to live. Built out of Fremont cottonwoods, the rustic one-room cabin still stands on the site. Look for remains of a root cellar and a corral as well. Even older than these structures is the nearby Ute rock-art panel by the Delicate Arch trailhead. About 150 feet past the footbridge and before the trail starts to climb, you can see images of bighorn sheep and figures on horseback, as well as some smaller images believed to be dogs. ✉ *Off Delicate Arch Rd., Arches National Park.*

A hike in "The Windows" is 1-mile round-trip.

TRAILS

★ Delicate Arch Trail

TRAIL | To see the park's most famous freestanding arch up close takes effort and won't offer you much solitude—but it's worth every step. The 3-mile round-trip trail ascends via steep slickrock, sandy paths, and along one narrow ledge (at the very end) that might give pause to anyone afraid of heights. Plus, there's almost no shade. First-timers should start early to avoid the midday heat in summer. Still, at sunrise, sunset, and every hour in between, it's the park's busiest trail. Bring plenty of water, especially in the warmer months, as heatstroke and dehydration are very real possibilities. Allow two to three hours, depending on your fitness level and how long you care to linger at the arch. If you go at sunset or sunrise, bring a headlamp or flashlight. Don't miss Wolfe Ranch and some ancient rock art near the trailhead. *Moderate–Difficult.* ✉ *Arches National Park* ✥ *Trailhead: On Delicate Arch Rd., 13 miles from park entrance.*

The Windows

11¾ miles north of the park entrance.

As you head north from the park entrance, turn right at Balanced Rock to find this concentration of natural windows, caves, and needles. Stretch your legs on the easy paths that wind between the arches and soak in a variety of geological formations.

Sights

GEOLOGICAL FORMATIONS

Double Arch

NATURE SITE | In the Windows section of the park, 11¾ miles from the park entrance, Double Arch has appeared in several Hollywood movies, including *Indiana Jones and the Last Crusade.* From the parking lot you can also take the short and easy Window Trail to view North Window, South Window, and Turret Arch. ✉ *The Windows Rd., Arches National Park.*

TRAILS

Double Arch Trail

TRAIL | FAMILY | If it's not too hot, it's a simple walk to here from Windows Trail. This relatively flat trek leads to two massive arches that make for great photo opportunities. The ½-mile round-trip gives you a good taste of desert flora and fauna. *Easy.* ✉ *Arches National Park* ✢ *Trailhead: 2½ miles from main road, on Windows Section spur road.*

The Windows

TRAIL | FAMILY | An early stop for many visitors to the park, a trek through the Windows gives you an opportunity to get out and enjoy the desert air. Here you'll see three giant openings in the rock and walk on a trail that leads right through the holes. Allow about an hour on this gently inclined, 1-mile round-trip hike. As most visitors don't follow the "primitive" trail around the backside of the two windows, take advantage if you want some desert solitude. The primitive trail adds an extra half hour to the hike. *Easy.* ✉ *Arches National Park* ✢ *Trailhead: On the Windows Rd., 12 miles from park entrance.*

Balanced Rock

9¼ miles north of the park entrance.

One of the park's favorite sights, this rock is visible for several minutes as you approach—and just gets more impressive and mysterious as you get closer. The formation's total height is 128 feet, with the huge balanced rock rising 55 feet above the pedestal. Be sure to hop out of the car and walk the short (⅓-mile) loop around the base.

Sights

TRAILS

Balanced Rock Trail

TRAIL | FAMILY | You'll want to stop at Balanced Rock for photo ops, so you may as well walk the easy, partially paved trail around the famous landmark. This is one of the most accessible trails in the park and is suitable even for small children. The 15-minute stroll is only about ⅓ mile round-trip. *Easy.* ✉ *Arches National Park* ✢ *Trailhead: Approximately 9¼ miles from park entrance.*

Park Avenue Trail

TRAIL | The first named trail that park visitors encounter, this is a relatively easy, 2-mile round-trip walk (with only one small hill but a somewhat steep descent into the canyon) amid walls and towers that vaguely resemble a New York City skyline. You'll walk under the gaze of Queen Nefertiti, a giant rock formation that some observers think has Egyptian-looking features. If you are traveling with companions, make it a one-way, 1-mile downhill trek by having them pick you up at the Courthouse Towers Viewpoint. Allow about 45 minutes for the one-way journey. *Easy–Moderate.* ✉ *Arches National Park* ✢ *Trailhead: 2 miles from park entrance on main park road.*

VISITOR CENTERS

Arches Visitor Center

INFO CENTER | FAMILY | With well-designed hands-on exhibits about the park's geology, wildlife, and history; helpful rangers; a water station; and a bookstore; the center is a great way to start your park visit. It also has picnic tables and something that's rare in the park: cell service for many carriers. ✉ *N. U.S. 191, Arches National Park* ☎ *435/719–2299* 🌐 *nps.gov/arch.*

Petrified Dunes

5 miles north of the visitor center.

Sights

SCENIC STOPS

Petrified Dunes

NATURE SITE | FAMILY | Just a tiny pull-out, this memorable stop features acres upon acres of reddish-gold, petrified sand dunes. There's no trail here, so roam as you like while keeping track of where you are. If you do lose your way, heading west will take you back to the main road. ✉ *Arches National Park* ✥ *6 miles from park entrance.*

Courthouse Towers

3 miles north of the visitor center.

This collection of towering rock formations looks unreal from a distance and even more breathtaking up close. The Three Gossips does indeed resemble a gaggle of wildly tall people sharing some kind of secret. Sheep Rock is right below, with the massive Tower of Babel just a bit north. Enter this section of the park 3 miles past the visitor center. The extremely popular Park Avenue Trail winds through the area.

Sights

SCENIC STOPS

Courthouse Wash

NATURE SITE | Although this rock-art panel fell victim to an unusual case of vandalism in 1980, when someone scoured the petroglyphs and pictographs that had been left by four cultures, you can still see ancient images if you take a short walk from the parking area on the left-hand side of the road, heading south. ✉ *U.S. 191, about 2 miles south of Arches entrance, Arches National Park.*

Activities

BIRD-WATCHING

Within the park you'll definitely see plenty of the big, black, beautiful ravens. Look for them perched on top of a picturesque juniper branch or balancing on the bald knob of a rock. Noisy black-billed magpies populate the park, as do the more melodic canyon and rock wrens. Lucky visitors may spot a red-tailed hawk and hear its distinctive call. Serious birders will have more fun visiting the Nature Conservancy's Scott and Norma Matheson Wetlands Preserve, 5 miles south of the park. The wetlands is home to more than 200 species of birds including the wood duck, western screech owl, indigo bunting, and plumbeous vireo.

CAMPING

Devils Garden Campground. This campground is one of the most unusual—and gorgeous—in the West, and in the national park system, for that matter. ✉ *End of main road, 18 miles from park entrance* ☎ *435/719–2299, 877/444–6777 for reservations* 🌐 *www.recreation.gov.*

EDUCATIONAL PROGRAMS

Junior Ranger Program

NATIONAL/STATE PARK | FAMILY | Kids of all ages can pick up a Junior Ranger booklet at the visitor center. It's full of activities, word games, drawings, and thought-provoking material about the park and the wildlife. To earn your Junior Ranger badge, you must complete several activities in the booklet, attend a ranger program, or watch the park film and pick up some trash in the park. ✉ *Arches National Park.*

Red Rock Explorer Pack

NATIONAL/STATE PARK | FAMILY | Families can check out a youth backpack filled with tools for learning about both Arches and Canyonlands national parks. A guide for naturalists, a three-ring binder of activities, hand lens magnifier, and binoculars are just some of the loaner items. Backpacks can be returned to either Arches or Island in the Sky visitor center. Use of the backpack is free. ✉ *Arches National Park.*

HIKING

Getting out on any one of the park trails will surely cause you to fall in love with this Mars-like landscape. But remember, you are hiking in a desert environment and approximately 1 mile above sea level. Many people succumb to heat and dehydration because they do not drink enough water. Park rangers recommend a gallon of water per day per person, plus electrolytes.

★ Fiery Furnace Walk

HIKING/WALKING | Join a park ranger on a 2½-hour scramble through a labyrinth of rock fins and narrow sandstone canyons. You'll see arches and other eye-popping formations that can't be viewed from the road. You should be very fit and not afraid of heights or confined spaces for this moderately strenuous experience. Wear sturdy hiking shoes, sunscreen, and a hat, and bring at least a liter of water. Guided walks into the Fiery Furnace are offered mid-April through September, usually a few times a day (hours vary), and leave from Fiery Furnace Viewpoint, about 15 miles from the park visitor center. Tickets for the morning walks must be reserved (at 🌐 *www.recreation.gov*) and are available beginning six months in advance and up to four days before the day of the tour. Tickets for afternoon Fiery Furnace walks must be purchased in person at the park visitor center, ideally as soon as you arrive in Moab and as far ahead as seven days before your hike. Children ages 5–12 are charged half price; kids under 5 are not allowed. Book early as the program usually fills months prior to each walk. ✉ *Arches National Park* ✣ *Trailhead: On Arches Scenic Dr.* 🎫 *$16* ⏲ *Guided hikes not offered Oct.–mid-April.*

ROCK CLIMBING AND CANYONEERING

Desert Highlights

CLIMBING/MOUNTAINEERING | This guide company takes adventurous types on descents and ascents through canyons (with the help of ropes), including those found in the Fiery Furnace at Arches National Park. Full-day and multiday canyoneering treks are available to destinations both in and near the national parks. ✉ *16 S. 100 E, Moab* ☎ *435/259–4433* 🌐 *www.deserthighlights.com* 🎫 *From $105.*

What's Nearby

Moab is the primary gateway to both Arches and Canyonlands national parks. Don't let its outsize image and status as Grand County seat fool you: only about 5,200 people live here year-round—compared with the 1.5 million who visit annually. Near the Colorado River in a beautiful valley between red rock cliffs, Moab is an interesting, eclectic place to visit, and it's home to a mix of both super-casual and hip restaurants, plus Southwestern-inspired souvenirs, art galleries, tour operators, recreation outfitters, and a selection of lodging options.

The next-closest town to Arches, about 50 miles to the northwest, is **Green River,** a fairly sleepy little town with some less expensive—but also less noteworthy—dining and lodging options and the excellent John Wesley Powell River History Museum. Each September the fragrance of fresh cantaloupe, watermelon, and honeydew fills the air, especially during Melon Days, a family-fun harvest celebration on the third weekend of September. As Moab hotels have become more expensive and crowded spring through fall, many park visitors have taken to staying farther south in the small southeastern Utah towns of **Monticello, Blanding,** and **Bluff,** and even 110 miles away up in **Grand Junction, Colorado,** a lively and attractive small city of about 62,000 with a bustling historic downtown and some great, reasonably priced dining and lodging options and close proximity to gorgeous Colorado National Monument.

Chapter 6

BADLANDS NATIONAL PARK

Updated by
Carson Walker

Camping	Hotels	Activities	Scenery	Crowds
★★★☆☆	★★★☆☆	★★★☆☆	★★★★★	★★★★☆

WELCOME TO BADLANDS NATIONAL PARK

TOP REASONS TO GO

★ **Fossils:** From the mid-1800s, the fossil-rich Badlands area has welcomed paleontologists, research institutions, and fossil hunters who have discovered the fossil remnants of numerous species from ancient days.

★ **A world of wildlife:** Badlands National Park is home to a wide array of wildlife: bison, pronghorn, deer, black-footed ferrets, prairie dogs, rabbits, coyotes, foxes, and badgers.

★ **Missiles:** The Minuteman Missile National Historic Site, north of the entrance to the park, represents the only remaining intact components of a nuclear missile.

★ **Stars aplenty:** Due to its remote location and vastly open country, Badlands National Park contains some of the clearest and cleanest air in the country, which makes it perfect for viewing the night sky.

★ **Moonscape:** With hundreds of square miles of ragged ridgelines and sawtooth spires, Badlands National Park touts a landscape that is otherworldly.

1 **North Unit.** This is the most accessible unit and includes the Badlands Wilderness Area.

2 **Palmer Creek Unit.** This is the most isolated section of the park—no recognized roads pass through its borders. You must obtain permission from private landowners to pass through their property (contact the White River Visitor Center). Allot one day to hike in and one day to hike out.

3 **Stronghold Unit.** This was used as a gunnery range for the United States Air Force and the South Dakota National Guard from 1942 until the late 1960s. Discarded remnants and unexploded ordnance make this area potentially dangerous. Do not handle fragments; report the location to a ranger instead.

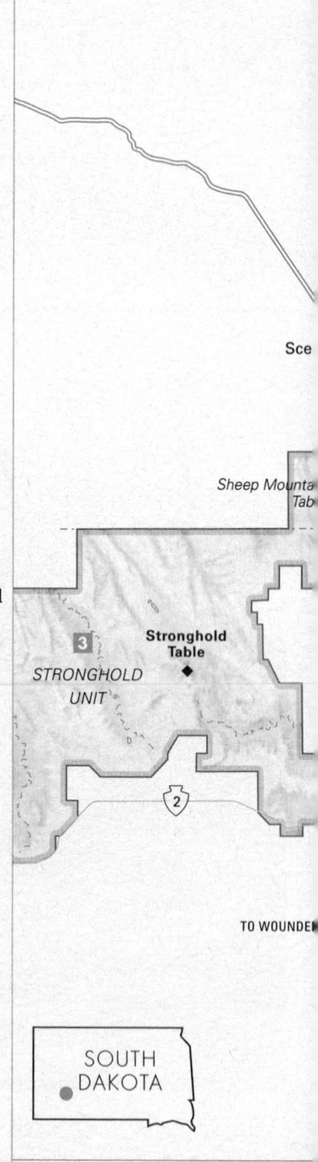

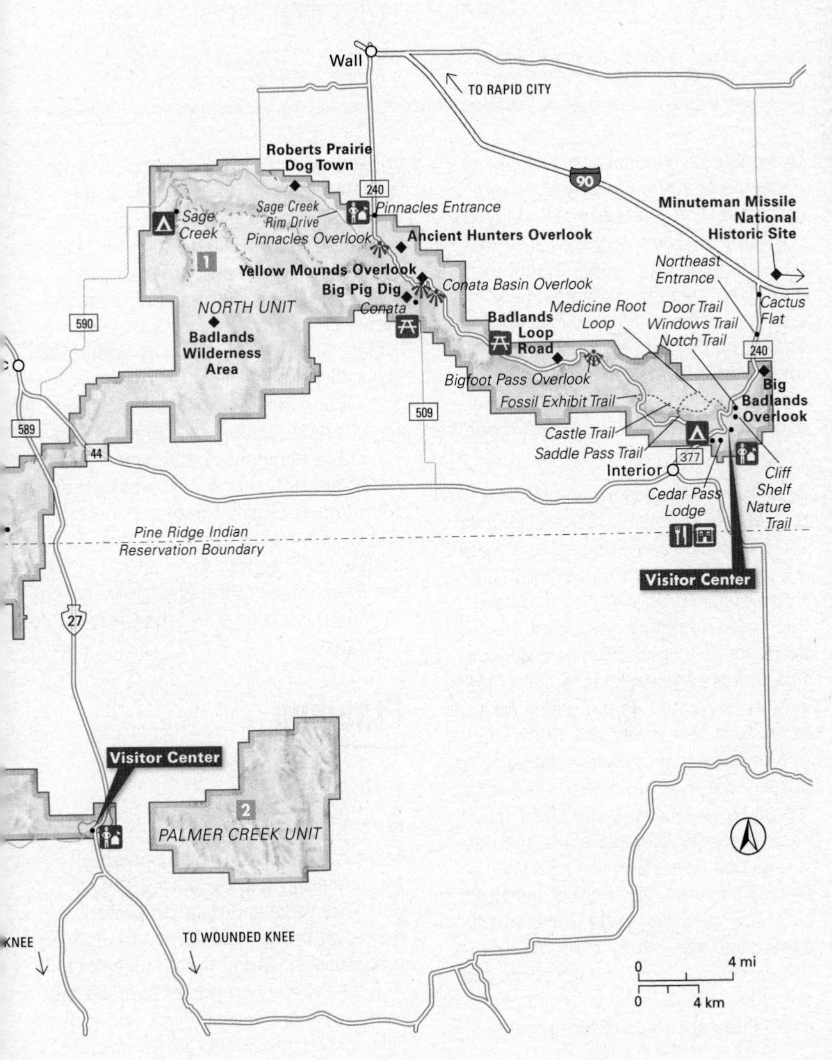
Wall
TO RAPID CITY
90
Roberts Prairie Dog Town
240
Sage Creek Rim Drive
Pinnacles Entrance
Sage Creek
Pinnacles Overlook
Ancient Hunters Overlook
Minuteman Missile National Historic Site
1
Yellow Mounds Overlook
Conata Basin Overlook
Big Pig Dig
Conata
NORTH UNIT
Badlands Wilderness Area
590
Badlands Loop Road
Medicine Root Loop
Door Trail
Windows Trail
Notch Trail
Northeast Entrance
Cactus Flat
240
Big Badlands Overlook
Bigfoot Pass Overlook
Fossil Exhibit Trail
509
589
Castle Trail
Saddle Pass Trail
44
377
Interior
Cedar Pass Lodge
Cliff Shelf Nature Trail
Pine Ridge Indian Reservation Boundary
Visitor Center
27
Visitor Center
2
PALMER CREEK UNIT
KNEE
TO WOUNDED KNEE
0
4 mi
0
4 km

Ravaged over time by wind and rain, the 380 square miles of chiseled spires, ragged ridge lines, and deep ravines of South Dakota's Badlands continue to erode and evolve.

Designated a national park in 1978, Badlands features the largest mixed-grass prairie in the National Park System. It's home to prairie dog towns as well as bison, bighorn sheep, pronghorn antelope, mule deer, coyotes, jackrabbits, the endangered black-footed ferret, and numerous bird species. There's also fossil evidence of prehistoric creatures, including the three-toed horse, camel, sabre-toothed cat, and an ancestor of the rhinoceros.

Despite its vastness, most of the park is relatively accessible. Several shorter trails are wheelchair-friendly, and visitors are allowed to walk through formations made of sand, silt, and clay that have been cemented into solid form. Though there are only about 20 miles of formal trails, hikers and backpackers are free to explore and camp off the paths because of an open-hike policy. The North Unit, one of three that comprise the park, attracts the most visitors. It's home to the park headquarters and offers the easiest access by vehicle over the Badlands Loop Road. Buffalo Gap National Grassland surrounds most of the North Unit. The other two units to the south, Stronghold and Palmer Creek, lie within the Pine Ridge Indian Reservation, and the Oglala Sioux Tribe can limit access, so check the park website for updates.

The area around Badlands National Park is rich in Native American and Cold War history. In the 1890s, Sioux warriors performed the Ghost Dance rituals on what is now the Stronghold Unit. When they refused to end the practice, the U.S. Army was called in. On Dec. 29, 1890, soldiers shot and killed 150 to 300 Lakota men, women and children at nearby Wounded Knee, the last confrontation between Native Americans and the United States Army. If you do venture to the park's southern districts, you can visit the Wounded Knee Massacre Memorial, which marks the mass grave and is a somber reminder of that part of our nation's history. North of the park, the Minuteman Missile National Historic Site is a decommissioned nuclear missile site with a visitor center. An hour's drive west are Rapid City and the Black Hills, home to Mount Rushmore and the Crazy Horse Memorial.

Planning

When to Go

Most visitors see the park between Memorial Day and Labor Day. The park's vast size and isolation prevent it from ever being too packed—though it is usually crowded the first week of August, when hundreds of thousands of motorcycle enthusiasts flock to the Black Hills for the annual Sturgis Motorcycle Rally (⇨ *see Wind Cave chapter for more info*). In summer, temperatures typically hover around 90°F—though it can get as hot as 116°F—and sudden mid-afternoon

AVERAGE HIGH/LOW TEMPERATURES					
JAN.	**FEB.**	**MAR.**	**APR.**	**MAY**	**JUNE**
34/11	40/16	48/24	62/33	72/44	82/56
JULY	**AUG.**	**SEPT.**	**OCT.**	**NOV.**	**DEC.**
91/60	92/55	81/46	65/34	48/21	39/17

thunderstorms are not unusual. Storms put on a spectacular show of thunder and lightning, but it rarely rains for more than 10 or 15 minutes (the average annual rainfall is 16 inches). Autumn weather is generally sunny and warm. Snow usually appears by late October. Winter temperatures can be as low as –40°F. Early spring is often wet, cold, and unpredictable. By May the weather usually stabilizes, bringing pleasant 70°F days.

Getting Here and Around

CAR

The North Unit of Badlands National Park is 75 miles east of Rapid City (with a regional airport) and about 140 miles northeast of Wind Cave National Park in western South Dakota. It's accessed via Exit 110 or 131 off I–90, or Route 44 east to Route 377. Few roads, paved or otherwise, pass within the park. Badlands Loop Road (Route 240) is the most traveled and the only one that intersects I–90. It's well maintained and rarely crowded. Parts of Route 44 and Route 27 run at the fringes of the badlands, connecting the visitor centers and Rapid City. Unpaved roads should be traveled with care when wet. Sheep Mountain Table Road, the only public road into the Stronghold Unit, is impassable when wet, with deep ruts—sometimes only high-clearance vehicles can get through. Off-road driving is prohibited. There's free parking at visitor centers, overlooks, and trailheads.

Inspiration

Badlands National Park, by Jan Cerney and part of the Images of America Series, uses historical photography to help shed light on a ruggedly surreal landscape that has, over the centuries, been traversed by Native Americans, fur traders, cattlemen, homesteaders, and fossil hunters.

Mount Rushmore, Badlands, Wind Cave: Going Underground, by Mike Graf, with illustrations by Marjorie Leggitt, takes kids on national park learning adventures with the Parker family.

Several movies have featured scenes from South Dakota's badlands, including *Nomadland, Dances With Wolves, Starship Troopers, Armageddon, How the West Was Won, Thunderheart,* and *Badlands.*

Park Essentials

ACCESSIBILITY

Cedar Pass Lodge, the visitor centers, and most overlooks are wheelchair accessible. The Fossil Exhibit Trail and the Window Trail have reserved parking and are accessible by ramp, although they are quite steep in places. The Door and Cliff Shelf trails are accessible by boardwalk. Cedar Pass Campground has two fully accessible sites, plus many other sites that are sculpted and easily negotiated by wheelchair users; its office and amphitheater also are accessible. The Bigfoot Picnic Area has reserved parking, ramps, and an accessible pit toilet. Other areas can be difficult or impossible to navigate by those with limited mobility.

PARK FEES AND PERMITS

The entrance fee is $12 per person or $25 per vehicle, and is good for seven days. An annual park pass is $50. A backcountry permit isn't required for hiking or camping in Badlands National Park, but check in at park headquarters before setting out on a backcountry journey. Backpackers may set up camps anywhere except within a half mile of roads or trails. Open fires are prohibited.

PARK HOURS

The park is open 24/7 year-round and is in the Mountain time zone. Ranger programs are offered late May to early September. For offerings and times, check at the Ben Reifel Visitor Center and the Cedar Pass Lodge; a schedule might also be posted at the Cedar Pass Campground kiosk.

CELL PHONE RECEPTION

Cell phone service has improved measurably over the last decade in western South Dakota, but you may not get a signal in much of the park. The closest pay phone you'll find will likely be in Wall.

Hotels

If you're determined to bed down within park boundaries, you have only one choice: Cedar Pass Lodge. Though rustic, it's comfortable, inexpensive, and has eco-friendly cabins.

The rustic-but-comfy formula is repeated by the area's few motels, hotels, and inns. Most are chain hotels grouped around the interstate. Whether you stay inside or outside the park, you shouldn't have to worry about making reservations very far in advance, except during the first full week of August, when the entire region is inundated with motorcyclists for the annual Sturgis Motorcycle Rally. Rooms for miles around book up more than a year in advance. *Hotel reviews have been shortened. For full information, visit Fodors.com.*

What It Costs

	$	$$	$$$	$$$$
RESTAURANTS	under $13	$13–$20	$21–$30	over $30
HOTELS	under $101	$101–$150	$151–$200	over $200

Restaurants

Dining on the prairies of South Dakota has always been a casual and family-oriented experience, and in that sense little has changed in the past century. Even the fare, which consists largely of steak and potatoes, has stayed consistent (in fact, in some towns, "vegetarian" can be a dirty word). But for its lack of comparative sophistication, the grub in the restaurants surrounding Badlands National Park is typically very good. You'll probably never have a better steak—beef or buffalo—outside this area. You should also try cuisine influenced by Native American cooking. In the park itself there's only one restaurant. The food is quite good, but don't hesitate to explore other options farther afield. *Restaurant reviews have been shortened. For full information, visit Fodors.com.*

Tours

Affordable Adventures Badlands and Wall Drug Tour

GUIDED TOURS | Take a seven-hour narrated tour through the park and surrounding badlands, with a stop at the famous Wall Drug Store for lunch (not included in the fee), the Minuteman II Missile Museum, and the Prairie Homestead Sod House Historical Site. Tours can easily be customized and are available year-round; there's hotel pickup in Rapid City. ✉ *5542 Meteor St., Rapid City* ☎ *605/342–7691, 888/888–8249* 🌐 *www.affordableadventuresbh.com* 🎟 *$145.*

Visitor Information

A free park newspaper, *Badlands Visitor Guide,* is available at the park's visitor centers and by request. Several park brochures on such topics as geology, photography, and horseback riding in the park are free at the visitor centers and from 🌐 *www.nps.gov/badl.*

PARK CONTACT INFORMATION Badlands National Park. ☎ *605/433–5361* 🌐 *www.nps.gov/badl.* **Black Hills Visitor Information Center.** ✉ *1851 Discovery Circle, Rapid City* ☎ *605/355–3700 information center, 888/945–7676 booking information* 🌐 *www.blackhillsbadlands.com.*

North Unit

34 miles from Wall (northeast entrance).

The North Unit hosts most of the major attractions and is most accessible from Interstate 90. The Badlands Loop Road has numerous overlooks that offer varying views as well as the park's formal hiking trails. Ben Reifel Visitor Center is a must-stop with museum exhibits, a fossil preparation lab, a film about the park, and bookstore.

While not technically part of the Badlands National Park, Minuteman Missile National Historic Site and Visitor Center is a prominent fixture close to the northeast park entrance road and definitely worth a stop to learn about the area's prominent role in the Cold War.

Sights

HISTORIC SITES

Big Pig Dig

ARCHAEOLOGICAL SITE | Until 2008, paleontologists dug for fossils at this site near the Conata Picnic Area. It was named for a large fossil originally thought to be of a prehistoric pig (it turned out to be a small, hornless rhinoceros). Wayside signs and exhibits, including a mural, provide context on the area and its fossils. ✉ *Badlands National Park* ⊕ *17 miles northwest of Ben Reifel Visitor Center.*

Minuteman Missile National Historic Site

HISTORIC SITE | This remote piece of United States history just north of Badlands National Park gives visitors the opportunity to tour a decommissioned Minuteman II intercontinental ballistic missile (ICBM) site, the first national park in the world dedicated to the Cold War. Start at the visitor center at I–90 Exit 131 to watch a film and view informative exhibits. The second site is the Delta 01-Lanch Control Facility at Exit 127. It's open only to visitors with tickets to the ranger-led tour that are available at the visitor center on a first-come, first-served basis. The next stop west, at Exit 116, is the Delta-09 missile silo, which has exhibits and a self-guided cell phone tour that describe the site and give visitors a view down into the silo. ✉ *I–90 Exit 126* ☎ *605/433–5552* 🌐 *nps.gov/mimi.*

SCENIC DRIVES

For the average visitor, a casual drive is the essential means by which to see Badlands National Park. To do the scenery justice, drive slowly, and don't hesitate to get out and explore on foot when the occasion calls for it.

★ Badlands Loop Road

SCENIC DRIVE | The simplest drive is on two-lane Badlands Loop Road (Route/Highway 240). The drive circles from Exit 110 off I–90 through the park and back to the interstate at Exit 131. Start from either end and make your way around to the various overlooks along the way. Pinnacles and Yellow Mounds overlooks are outstanding places to examine the sandy pink- and brown-toned ridges and spires distinctive to the badlands. The landscape flattens out slightly to the north, revealing spectacular views of mixed-grass prairies. The Cedar Pass area of the drive has some of the park's best

The two-lane Badlands Loop Road has more than a dozen scenic overlooks that provide amazing views of the spires and ridges that make the Badlands so distinct.

trails. ✉ *I–90, Exit 110, Badlands National Park* 🌐 *www.nps.gov/badl.*

SCENIC STOPS

★ Badlands Wilderness Area

NATURE PRESERVE | Covering about a quarter of the park, this 100-square-mile area is part of the country's largest prairie wilderness. About two-thirds of the Sage Creek region is mixed-grass prairie, making it the ideal grazing grounds for bison, pronghorn, and other native animals. The Hay Butte Overlook (2 miles northwest on Sage Creek Rim Road) and the Pinnacles Overlook (1 mile south of the Pinnacles entrance) are the best places to get an overview of the wilderness area. Feel free to park at an overlook and hike your own route into the untamed, unmarked prairie. ✉ *Badlands National Park* ⊕ *25 miles northwest of Ben Reifel Visitor Center* 🌐 *www.nps.gov/badl.*

Big Badlands Overlook

VIEWPOINT | From this spot just south of the park's northeast entrance, the vast majority of the park's 1 million annual visitors get their first views of the White River Badlands. ✉ *Badlands National Park* ⊕ *5 miles northeast of the Ben Reifel Visitor Center.*

Roberts Prairie Dog Town

NATURE PRESERVE | **FAMILY** | Once a homestead, the site today contains one of the country's largest (if not the largest) colonies of black-tailed prairie dogs. ✉ *Sage Creek Rim Rd., Badlands National Park* ⊕ *5 miles west of Badlands Loop Rd.*

Yellow Mounds Overlook

VIEWPOINT | Contrasting sharply with the whites, grays, and browns of the Badlands' pinnacles, the mounds viewed from here greet you with soft yet vivid yellows, reds, and purples. ✉ *Badlands National Park* ⊕ *16 miles northwest of Ben Reifel Visitor Center.*

TRAILS

If you want a challenge, you might consider trekking this 100-square-mile parcel of grassy steppes and rocky canyons east of the highway and south of Sage Creek Rim Road, near the Pinnacles entrance. There are no services here and very few visitors, even in summer. Before venturing out, check in with park staff at one of the visitor centers.

Cliff Shelf Nature Trail

TRAIL | This ½-mile loop winds through a wooded prairie oasis in the middle of dry, rocky ridges and climbs 200 feet to a peak above White River Valley for an incomparable view. Look for chipmunks, squirrels, and red-winged blackbirds in the wet wood, and eagles, hawks, and vultures at hilltop. Even casual hikers can complete this trail in far less than an hour, but if you want to observe the true diversity of wildlife present here, stay longer. *Moderate.* ✉ *Badlands National Park* ✣ *Trailhead: 1 mile east of Ben Reifel Visitor Center, off Hwy. 240.*

★ **Fossil Exhibit Trail**

TRAIL | **FAMILY** | The trail, in place since 1964, has fossil replicas of early mammals displayed at wayside exhibits along its ¼-mile length, which is completely wheelchair accessible. Give yourself at least an hour to fully enjoy this popular hike. *Easy.* ✉ *Badlands National Park* ✣ *Trailhead: 5 miles northwest of Ben Reifel Visitor Center, off Hwy. 240.*

Window Trail

TRAIL | This ¼-mile round-trip trail ends at a natural hole, or window, in a rock wall. You'll see more of the distinctive badlands pinnacles and spires. *Easy.* ✉ *Badlands National Park* ✣ *Trailhead: 2 miles north of Ben Reifel Visitor Center, off Hwy. 240.*

VISITOR CENTERS

Ben Reifel Visitor Center

INFO CENTER | Open year-round, the park's main information hub has brochures, maps, and information on ranger programs. Check out exhibits on geology and wildlife, and watch paleontologists at work in the Fossil Prep Lab (June–September). View the film, *Land of Stone and Light,* in the 95-seat theater, and shop in the Badlands Natural History Association Bookstore. The facility is named for a Sioux activist and the first Lakota to serve in Congress. Born on the nearby Rosebud Indian Reservation, Ben Reifel also served in the Army during World War II. ✉ *Badlands National Park* ✣ *Badlands Loop Rd., near Hwy. 377 junction, 8 miles from northeast entrance* ☎ *605/433–5361.*

Minuteman Missile Visitors Center

HISTORIC SITE | This modern visitor center is full of Cold War history. If you were alive during the Cold War era (or are a fan of *War Games*), it's a must-see trip back in time, with immersive displays that capture the history of the United States' nuclear standoff with the former Soviet Union. For children and grandchildren, the site does a great job explaining this not-too-distant piece of history that gives context to the country's relationship with the USSR. While the visitor center (and two accompanying sites) aren't in Badlands National Park, it's less than 10 minutes from the northeast entrance, making it a perfect stop before or after your park visit. ✣ *I–90 Exit 131* ☎ *605/433–5552* 🌐 *www.nps.gov/mimi.*

Restaurants

Cedar Pass Lodge Restaurant

$ | **AMERICAN** | **FAMILY** | Cool off within dark, knotty-pine walls under an exposed-beam ceiling, and enjoy a hearty meal of steak or tacos and fry bread. **Known for:** locally sourced fish, meat, and produce; fresh fry bread; decent selection of vegetarian and gluten-free dishes. [$] *Average main: $9* ✉ *20681 Hwy. 240, Interior* ☎ *605/433–5460* 🌐 *www.cedarpasslodge.com* ⏲ *Closed Nov.–mid-Apr.*

Hotels

Cedar Pass Lodge

$$$ | **HOTEL** | Besides impressive views of the badlands, these cabins include modern touches like flat-screen TVs and Wi-Fi connections. **Pros:** new cabins; the best stargazing in South Dakota; pine deck chairs to enjoy the scenery. **Cons:** remote location; long drive to other restaurants; pricey. *Rooms from: $176* ✉ *20681 Hwy. 240, Interior* ☎ *605/433–5460, 877/386–4383* 🌐 *www.cedarpasslodge.com* ⏲ *Closed Nov.–mid-Apr.* *26 cabins* *No meals.*

Palmer Creek Unit

26 miles from Kyle.

This is a very remote part of the park and accessible only with permission to cross private land. Backcountry camping is allowed, but you have to hike in and follow all rules and regulations.

Stronghold Unit

4 miles from Scenic and 34 miles from Ben Reifel Visitor Center in the North Unit.

With few paved roads and no campgrounds, the park's southwest section is difficult to access without a four-wheel-drive vehicle. If you're willing to trek, its isolation provides a rare opportunity to explore the Badlands rock formations and prairies completely undisturbed. From 1942 to 1968, the U.S. Air Force and South Dakota National Guard used much of the area as a gunnery range. Hundreds of fossils were destroyed by bomber pilots, who frequently targeted the large fossil remains of an elephant-size titanothere (an extinct relative of the rhinoceros). Beware of unexploded bombs, shells, rockets, and other hazardous materials. Steer clear of it and find another route.

Sights

SCENIC STOPS

Stronghold Table

HISTORIC SITE | Within the Stronghold Unit, the Stronghold Table, a 3-mile-long plateau, can be reached only by crossing a narrow land bridge just wide enough to let a wagon pass. It was here, just before the Massacre at Wounded Knee in 1890, that some 600 Sioux gathered to perform one of the last known Ghost Dances, a ritual in which the Sioux wore white shirts that they believed would protect them from bullets. ✉ *Badlands National Park* ✣ *North and west of White River Visitor Center; entrance off Hwy. 27* 🌐 *www.nps.gov/badl.*

TRAILS

Sheep Mountain Table Road

TRAIL | This 7-mile dirt road in the Stronghold Unit is ideal for mountain biking, but should be attempted only when dry, and riders must stay on the road. The terrain is level for the first 3 miles, then it climbs and levels out again. At the top you can take in great views of the area. ✉ *Badlands National Park* ✣ *About 14 miles north of White River Visitor Center.*

VISITOR CENTER

White River Visitor Center

INFO CENTER | Open in summer, this small center serves almost exclusively serious hikers and campers venturing into the Stronghold or Palmer unit. If that's you, stop here for maps and details about road and trail conditions. The center is on the Pine Ridge Indian Reservation. While you're here you can see fossils and Lakota artifacts, and learn about Sioux culture. ✉ *Badlands National Park* ✣ *25 miles south of Hwy. 44 via Hwy. 27* ☎ *605/455–2878* 🌐 *www.nps.gov/badl.*

Activities

BIKING

Bicycles are permitted only on designated roads, which may be paved or unpaved. They are prohibited from closed roads, trails, and the backcountry. Flat-resistant tires are recommended.

Two Wheeler Dealer Cycle and Fitness

BICYCLING | Family-owned and-operated Two Wheeler Dealer Cycle and Fitness, based in Spearfish, stocks hundreds of bikes for sale and plenty of them to rent. The service is exceptional. ✉ *305 Main St. Suite 1, Spearfish* ☎ *605/642–7545* 🌐 *www.twowheelerdealer.com.*

BIRD-WATCHING

Especially around sunset, get set to watch the badlands come to life. More than 215 bird species have been recorded in the area, including herons, pelicans, cormorants, egrets, swans, geese, hawks, golden and bald eagles, falcons, vultures, cranes, doves, and cuckoos. Established roads and trails are the best places from which to watch for nesting species. The Cliff Shelf Nature Trail and the Castle Trail, which both traverse areas with surprisingly thick vegetation, are especially good locations. You may even catch sight of a rare burrowing owl at the Roberts Prairie Dog Town.

CAMPING

Pitching a tent and sleeping under the stars is one of the greatest ways to fully experience the sheer isolation and unadulterated empty spaces of Badlands National Park. You'll find two relatively easy-access campgrounds within park boundaries, but only one has any sort of amenities. The second is little more than a flat patch of ground with some signs. Unless you desperately need a flush toilet to have an enjoyable camping experience, you're just as well off hiking into the wilderness and choosing your own campsite. You can set up camp anywhere that's at least a half mile from a road or trail and is not visible from any road or trail.

Cedar Pass Campground. With tent sites and 20 RV sites as well as coin-operated showers, this is the most developed campground in the park, and it's near Ben Reifel Visitor Center, Cedar Pass Lodge, and a half-dozen hiking trails. ✉ *Rte. 377, ¼ mile south of Badlands Loop Rd.* ☎ *605/433–5361* 🌐 *www.cedarpasslodge.com.*

EDUCATIONAL PROGRAMS

Evening Program and Night Sky Viewing

TOUR—SIGHT | Watch a 45-minute presentation on the wildlife, natural history, paleontology, or another aspect of the Badlands. Shows typically begin around 9 pm. Stick around afterward for the Night Sky Viewing, a stargazing interpretive program complete with telescopes. ✉ *Cedar Pass Campground amphitheater, 20681 Hwy. 240, Badlands National Park* 🌐 *www.nps.gov/badl.*

Fossil Talk

TOUR—SIGHT | What were the Badlands like many years ago? This 20-minute talk about protected fossil exhibits will inspire and answer all your questions. It's usually held at 10:30 am and 1:30 pm daily at the Fossil Exhibit Trail. ✉ *Badlands National Park* ✣ *Fossil Exhibit Trail, Badlands Loop Rd., 5 miles northwest of Ben Reifel Visitor Center* 🌐 *www.nps.gov/badl.*

Geology Walk

TOUR—SIGHT | Learn the geologic story of the White River Badlands in a 45-minute walk, generally departing from the Door Trailhead daily at 8:30 am. The terrain can be rough in places, so be sure to wear hiking boots or sneakers. A hat is a good idea, too. ✉ *Badlands National Park* ✣ *Door and Window trails parking area, Badlands Loop Rd., 2 miles south of the northeast entrance* 🌐 *www.nps.gov/badl.*

Junior Ranger Program

TOUR—SIGHT | **FAMILY** | Children ages 7–12 can join in this daily, 30-minute adventure, typically a short hike, game, or other hands-on activity focused on badlands wildlife, geology, or fossils. Parents are welcome. Meet at the visitor center at 11 am, and wear closed-toe shoes. ✉ *Ben Reifel Visitor Center, 25216 Hwy. 240, Badlands National Park* ☎ *605/433–5361* 🌐 *www.nps.gov/badl.*

HIKING

The otherworldliness of the badlands is best appreciated with a walk through them. Take time to examine the dusty rock beneath your feet, and be on the lookout for fossils and animals. Fossil Exhibit Trail and Cliff Shelf Nature Trail are must-dos, but even these popular trails tend to be primitive. You'll find bathrooms at Fossil Exhibit Trail. Both trails feature boardwalks, so you won't be shuffling through dirt and gravel. Door Trail and Window Trail are also short, easy, and easily accessible treks on the east end of the North Unit. Notch Trail is nearby but is more of a strenuous hike that offers an awesome view of the White River Valley. Castle Trail, the park's longest, takes you deep into the badlands. Extend your hike by connecting with Medicine Root Trail or Saddle Pass Trail. Thanks to Badlands National Park's open-hike policy, you can also venture off the trails. One area to consider is the Sage Creek Wilderness Area where the park's bison live.

Because the weather here can be so variable, be prepared for anything. Wear sunglasses, a hat, and long pants, and have rain gear available. It's illegal to interfere with park resources, which include everything from rocks and fossils to plants and artifacts. Stay at least 100 yards away from wildlife. Due to the dry climate, open fires are never allowed. Tell friends, relatives, and the park rangers if you're going to embark on a multiday expedition. Assume that your cell phone, if you've brought one, won't get a signal in the park. But most important of all, be sure to bring your own water. Sources of water in the park are few and far between, and none of them are drinkable. All water in the park is contaminated by minerals and sediment, and park authorities warn that it's untreatable. If you're backpacking into the wilderness, bring at least a gallon of water per person per day. For day hikes, rangers suggest you drink at least a quart per person per hour.

OUTFITTERS

Scheels All Sport

HIKING/WALKING | In the Rushmore Crossing Mall, off I–90 at the East-North Street or Lacrosse Street exit, this enormous shop carries a wide selection of all-weather hiking gear, footwear, and clothes as well as binoculars suitable for bird-watchers. ✉ *1225 Eglin St., Rapid City* ☎ *605/342–9033* 🌐 *www.scheels.com.*

What's Nearby

Located off I–90, 50 miles east of the edge of the Black Hills (and **Rapid City**, the largest community on this side of the state), Badlands National Park allows travelers a unique stop in a highly dense area of national parks, monuments, and memorials including Mount Rushmore National Memorial, Wind Cave National Park, Jewel Cave National Monument, Devils Tower National Monument, and Custer State Park. The Black Hills provide a wonderful backdrop for the dry canyon and dusty buttes of the badlands. Park entrances along I–90 are near the towns of **Wall** on the west (home to the famous Wall Drug) and **Kadoka** on the east, which have lodging, restaurants, gas and auto repair, and other support services.

Called the "City of Presidents" because of the life-size bronze statues of U.S. presidents that adorn virtually every downtown street corner, **Rapid City** is the largest urban center in a 350-mile radius. The city is an excellent base from which to explore the treasures of the state's southwestern corner, including Mount Rushmore (25 miles south) and Wind Cave National Park (50 miles south).

Chapter 7

BIG BEND NATIONAL PARK

Updated by Andrew Collins

Camping	Hotels	Activities	Scenery	Crowds
★★★★☆	★★★★☆	★★★★★	★★★★★	★★★★☆

WELCOME TO BIG BEND NATIONAL PARK

TOP REASONS TO GO

★ **Varied terrain:** Visit a desert of prickly cacti, a fabled international-border river, bird-abundant woods, and mountain spirals all in the same day.

★ **Wonderful wildlife:** Catch sight of the park's extremely diverse animals, including fuzzy tarantulas, bands of swarthy javelinas, reclusive mountain lions, and lumbering black bears.

★ **Bird-watching:** Spy a pied-billed grebe or another member of the park's more than 450 bird species, including the Lucifer hummingbird and the unique-to-this-area *pato mexicano* (Mexican duck).

★ **Hot spots:** Dip into the natural hot springs (105°F) near Rio Grande Village.

★ **Mile-high mountains:** Lace up your hiking boots and climb the Chisos Mountains, reaching almost 8,000 feet skyward in some places and remaining relatively cool except May–October, when temperatures reach into the upper 90s even at high elevations.

1 **Chisos Basin.** This bowl-shape canyon amid the Chisos Mountains—along with nearby Panther Junction—is at the heart of Big Bend. It's a base for numerous hikes and a prime place to watch a sunset through a "fracture" in the bowl known as the Window.

2 **Castolon.** Just east of Santa Elena Canyon, this cluster of adobe dwellings, once used by ranchers and the U.S. military, anchors the park's west side.

3 **Rio Grande Village.** Tall, shady cottonwoods highlight the park's eastern fringe along the Mexican border and Rio Grande. It's popular with bird-watching and camping enthusiasts.

4 **Persimmon Gap.** The park's engaging Fossil Discovery Exhibit is a highlight of this arid northern portion of the park that includes the Persimmon Gap entrance and several remote back roads where nomadic warriors once traveled to Mexico via the Comanche Trail.

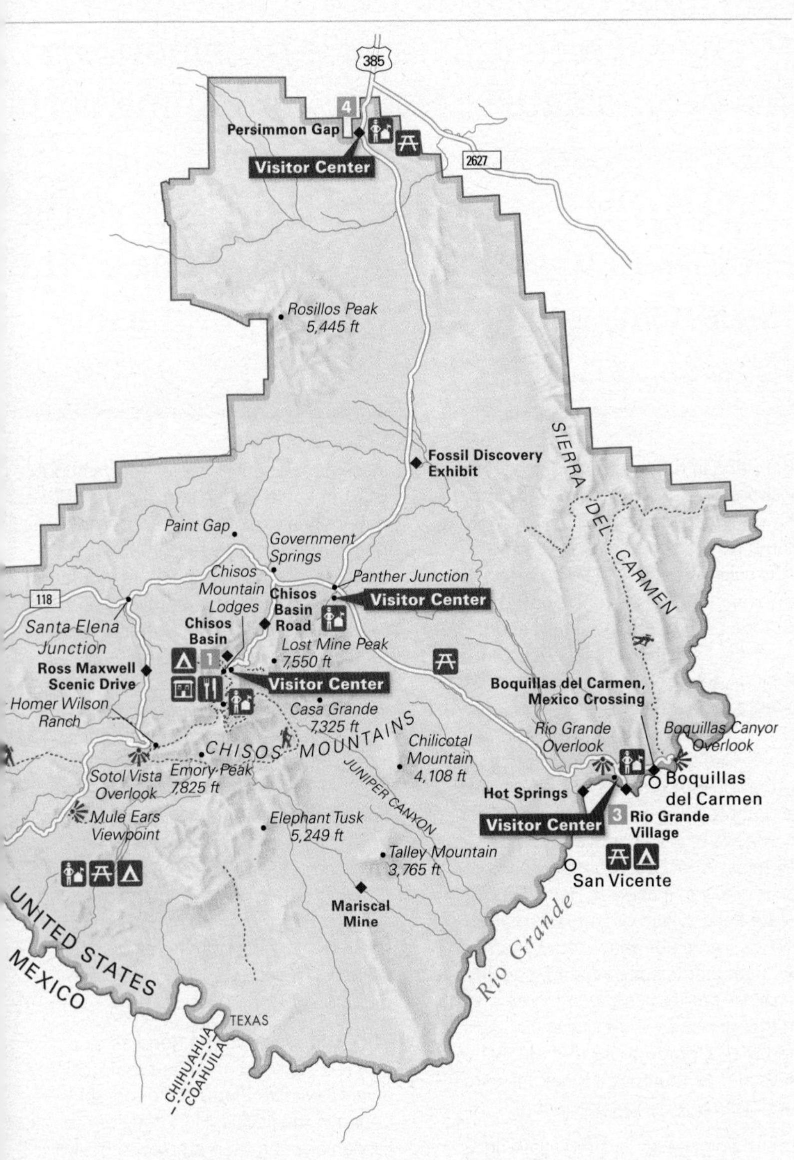
385
4
Persimmon Gap
Visitor Center
2627
Rosillos Peak
5,445 ft
SIERRA DEL CARMEN
Fossil Discovery Exhibit
Paint Gap
Government Springs
Chisos Mountain Lodges
Chisos Basin Road
Panther Junction
Visitor Center
118
Santa Elena Junction
Chisos Basin
1
Lost Mine Peak
7,550 ft
Ross Maxwell Scenic Drive
Visitor Center
Homer Wilson Ranch
Casa Grande
7,325 ft
CHISOS MOUNTAINS
Chilicotal Mountain
4,108 ft
JUNIPER CANYON
Boquillas del Carmen, Mexico Crossing
Rio Grande Overlook
Boquillas Canyon Overlook
Sotol Vista Overlook
Emory Peak
7,825 ft
Boquillas del Carmen
Hot Springs
Mule Ears Viewpoint
Elephant Tusk
5,249 ft
Visitor Center
3
Rio Grande Village
Talley Mountain
3,765 ft
San Vicente
Mariscal Mine
Rio Grande
UNITED STATES
MEXICO
TEXAS
CHIHUAHUA
COAHUILA

Cradled in the southwestern elbow of Texas, this 801,163-acre park hugs a wild and undeveloped 118-mile span of the Rio Grande, which separates it from northern Mexico's isolated deserts. Containing both the craggy, forested Chisos Mountains and the flat, starkly beautiful plains of the Chihuahuan Desert, Big Bend is one of the nation's largest and most geographically diverse parks.

Big Bend is the kind of park that rewards visitors almost exponentially the more time they spend here. There's simply too much to see and explore to fully appreciate the park in a day or two. Start by exploring the canyons along the Rio Grande at the park's western and eastern reaches, and you'll come away with an entirely different sense of Big Bend than if you spend a day trekking through the alpine forests of the Chisos Mountains, which rise some 6,200 feet above the river. This part of Texas is incredibly vast and untouched, even as you travel for hundreds of miles outside the park—just 15 miles west of the national park, for example, you'll find Big Bend Ranch State Park, which preserves another 311,000 acres of unspoiled wilderness. With its grand scale in mind, and keeping in mind that there's much to see and do in the nearby town of Marathon, Alpine, and Marfa, do try to budget at least three days and as much as a week for a truly satisfying Big Bend experience.

The region has always felt vast and untamed. Although archaeological evidence documents the presence of local human activity as far back as 6500 BC, the harsh terrain and climate helped deter significant development. The Spaniards who arrived in 1535 encountered several bands of nomadic hunters whom they dubbed the Chisos, and both Mescalero Apache and Comanche tribes regularly passed through the region en route to Mexico's interior until well into the 19th century, but large-scale permanent settlements were never established in this land the Spaniards referred to as El Despoblado, or The Uninhabitable. The first nonnatives to take any real interest in Big Bend began arriving in the mid-19th century, and they engaged in two principle activities: mining and ranching. You can find remnants of both endeavors in many parts of the park, including Mariscal Mine, Sam Nail Ranch, and the Castolon Historic District.

Efforts to preserve Big Bend as a park—in recognition of its breathtakingly diverse wildlife, flora, and geography—began in the 1930s. Hundreds of mostly Hispanic young men employed by the Civilian Conservation Corps (CCC) carved out trails, built visitor facilities, and

AVERAGE HIGH/LOW TEMPERATURES					
JAN.	**FEB.**	**MAR.**	**APR.**	**MAY**	**JUNE**
62/38	68/42	75/48	84/56	89/63	95/70
JULY	**AUG.**	**SEPT.**	**OCT.**	**NOV.**	**DEC.**
93/71	92/71	86/65	81/57	71/47	63/39

constructed what remains one of Big Bend's signature features, the curving 7-mile road that climbs from the high desert near Panther Junction up into the crisp-aired peaks of the Chisos Basin. The Texas state government purchased more than 600,000 acres of private land in the early 1940s, and on June 12, 1944, Big Bend National Park welcomed its first visitors. Although the park enjoys a devoted following, its remoteness also helps to keep it from feeling overrun. Fewer than a half-million visitors pass through this massive preserve each year, a tiny fraction of the number of who visit much smaller parks in the West. This fact may not offer you much comfort when Chisos Mountains Lodge is fully booked, or you can't snag a parking space at the Lost Mine Trailhead. But take heart—if you're willing to venture out into Big Bend's more remote backcountry, the promise of solitude and spectacular natural beauty await, even during the busiest times.

Planning

When to Go

There is never a bad time to make a Big Bend foray—but during Thanksgiving, Christmas, and spring break, be aware that competition for rooms at Chisos Mountains Lodge, campsites, and nearby hotels is fierce—with reservations needed up to a year in advance.

Depending on the season—and sometimes even the day—Big Bend can be hot, dry, cold, or rainy. Many shun the park in late spring and summer, because temperatures skyrocket (up to 120°F down along the river) from May through August, and the Rio Grande lowers. In winter, temperatures rarely dip below 30°F. During those few times the mercury takes a dive, visitors might be rewarded with a rare snowfall at upper elevations. The mountains routinely are 5 to 20 degrees cooler than the rest of the park, while the sweltering stretches of the Rio Grande are 5 to 10 degrees warmer.

Getting Here and Around

AIR

The nearest major airport is in Midland, four hours north of the park, but many visitors fly into El Paso, five hours northwest, which is served by more flights and airlines.

CAR

It can take 90 minutes to cross this huge park, but you'll be treated to gorgeous scenery. Big Bend's northern entrance is 39 miles south of Marathon via U.S. 385, but it's another 45 minutes drive to reach central Chisos Basin. To the western entrance, it's 80 miles from Alpine via Highway 118 and 70 miles from Presidio on Highway FM 170. Paved park roads have twists and turns, some very extreme in higher elevations; if you have an RV longer than 24 feet or a trailer longer than 20 feet, you should avoid Chisos Basin Road into higher terrain in the park's center. Four-wheel-drive vehicles are needed for many backcountry roads.

Inspiration

Naturalist's Big Bend, by Roland H. Wauer and Carl M. Fleming, paints a picture of the park's diverse plants and animals.

Big Bend: The Story Behind the Scenery, by Carol E. Sperling, is rife with colorful photos illustrating the park's history and geology.

For gleeful and awestruck thoughts on the Big Bend wilderness, check out *God's Country or Devil's Playground,* which collects the writing of nearly 60 authors.

The Natural History Association's *Backcountry Road Guide* gives in-depth information on the web of paved and improved dirt roads running through the park—and the views you can see from them. Find it on sale at park visitor centers.

Although not many movies have filmed directly in the park, several have been shot in and around Marfa, to the north. The most famous is *Giant,* the epic 1956 James Dean and Elizabeth Taylor epic, but the town and surrounding region has appeared prominently in *No Country for Old Men* and *There Will Be Blood,* both produced in 2007, and *Fandango* in 1985.

Park Essentials

ACCESSIBILITY

Visitor centers and some campsites at Rio Grande Village and Chisos Basin are wheelchair accessible. The Founder's Walk and Panther Path at Panther Junction, Window View Trail at Chisos Basin, and Rio Grande Village Nature Trail boardwalk are wheelchair-accessible trails. The Rio Grande and Chisos Basin amphitheaters also are accessible.

PARK FEES AND PERMITS

It costs $30 to enter at the gate by car, and your pass is good for seven days. Entry on foot, bicycle, or commercial vehicle is $15; entry by motorcycle is $25. Camping fees in developed campgrounds are $16 per night, while backcountry camping is $10 for up to 14 days. Mandatory backcountry camping, boating, and fishing permits are available at visitor centers.

PARK HOURS

Big Bend National Park never closes. Visitor centers at Rio Grande Village, Persimmon Gap, and the Castolon Historic District close in summer. The park is in the Central time zone.

CELL PHONE RECEPTION

Cell phone reception is spotty in much of the park, though service is generally more reliable near the visitor centers and on some of the higher-elevation trails in the Chisos Mountains.

Hotels

At the Chisos Mountains Lodge, the only hotel in the park, you can select from a freestanding stone cottage or a motel-style room, both within a pace or two of popular trailheads and spectacular views—Chisos sunsets and sunrises are not to be missed. The region flanking Big Bend retains its grand historic hotels, such as the glamorous Hotel Paisano in Marfa (which now competes with some very hip design hotels), the Gage Hotel in Marathon, and the Holland Hotel in Alpine. But you'll also find the well-outfitted Lajitas Golf Resort and some distinctive—some spendy, some not—options near the park in Terlingua. *Hotel reviews have been shortened. For full information, visit Fodors.com.*

What It Costs

$	$$	$$$	$$$$
RESTAURANTS			
under $16	$16–$22	$23–$30	over $30
HOTELS			
under $120	$120–$180	$181–$240	over $240

Restaurants

Although the park itself has just one no-frills restaurant, albeit with stunning Chisos Basin views, little Terlingua—just outside the park entrance, has a few more interesting options. And the towns along the U.S. 90 corridor north of the park, including Marathon, Alpine, and Marfa, have a mix of noteworthy eateries, ranging from historic steak-focused hotel dining rooms to hip Austin-style contemporary bistros and mod coffeehouses. *Restaurant reviews have been shortened. For full information, visit Fodors.com.*

Visitor Information

There are five visitor centers in Big Bend: Panther Junction, considered park headquarters, at the intersection of Western Entrance Road (which Highway 118 becomes) and Persimmon Road (which U.S. 385 becomes); Persimmon Gap at the park's northern entrance at U.S. 385; Rio Grande Village, on the eastern border near Boquillas Canyon and Mexico; the Castolon Historic District on Ross Maxwell Scenic Drive, near Santa Elena Canyon in the southwestern corner of the park; and up high in Chisos Basin, by Chisos Mountains Lodge. Rio Grande Village, Castolon, and Persimmon Gap are closed May–October.

CONTACTS Big Bend National Park. ☎ *432/477–2251* 🌐 *www.nps.gov/bibe.*

Chisos Basin

30 miles east of Terlingua, 68 miles south of Marathon, 103 miles southeast of Alpine.

The geographical heart of this enormous park, and the best place to begin your explorations, also encompasses its highest points—the mountains surrounding the Chisos Basin. It's here that you'll find the park's only lodging and restaurant and some of its most rewarding hikes and scenery. There's a small visitor center in Chisos Basin as well, and 10 miles north at the junction of the park's main roads you can visit Big Bend's main visitor center at Panther Junction and stock up on fuel and basic snacks at an adjacent gas station.

Sights

SCENIC DRIVES

★ Chisos Basin Road

MOUNTAIN—SIGHT | This 7-mile road climbs majestically from Chisos Basin Junction to Chisos Mountains Lodge, with a spur leading to a campground. In these higher elevations you're slightly more likely to spot mountain lions and bears as well as white-tailed deer amid juniper and pinyon pines. You'll also see smooth, red-barked Texas madrone along with some Chisos oaks and Douglas fir trees. Roadside exhibits explain the various ecosystems. Because of sharp curves and switchbacks, this drive is not suitable for RVs longer than 24 feet. ✉ *Big Bend National Park* ⊕ *3 miles west of Panther Junction.*

SCENIC STOPS

★ Chisos Basin

NATURE SITE | Panoramic vistas, a restaurant with an up-close view of jagged mountain peaks, and glimpses of the Colima warbler (which summers in Big Bend) await in the forested Chisos Basin. The spiritual heart of Big Bend, at an elevation of 5,400 feet, it's ringed by taller peaks and has a lodge, a campground, a grocery store, an amphitheater, a visitor center, and access to some of the park's best hiking trails. Winter sometimes brings snow, but in summer this is where you can find relief from the desert heat below. ✉ *Big Bend National Park* ✣ *End of Chisos Mountain Rd.*

TRAILS

Chihuahuan Desert Nature Trail

TRAIL | FAMILY | A windmill and spring form a desert oasis, a refreshing backdrop to a ½-mile round-trip, hot and flat nature trail; wild doves are abundant, the hike is pleasant, and kids will do just fine. Keep an eye out for the elf owl, one of the sought-after birds in the park. *Easy.* ✉ *Big Bend National Park* ✣ *Trailhead: Dugout Wells, 6 miles southeast of Panther Junction.*

Chisos Basin Loop Trail

TRAIL | FAMILY | This forested 2-mile round-trip romp that begins at 5,400-foot elevation affords sweeping views of the lower desert and distant volcanic mountains. The loop intersects with a few longer trails but offers a good sense of the basin if you have only an hour or so. *Easy–moderate, elevation gain 500 feet.* ✉ *Big Bend National Park* ✣ *Trailhead: West end of Chisos Basin parking lot.*

★ Emory Peak Trail

TRAIL | Give yourself about seven hours to complete this rugged 10½-mile round-trip alpine trek to the park's highest peak, at 7,832 feet. The initial 3½-mile stretch follows the Pinnacles Trail, which eventually leads to the South Rim—a rewarding 12- to 14½-mile round-trip adventure that can be done in a very long full day but is more easily managed with a night of camping. For Emory Peak, you pick up a 1-mile spur that affords some dazzling vistas as it zigzags up to the summit. Note there's a bit of scrambling over rocks the final 25 feet, but the panoramic views are worth the effort. *Difficult, 2,400-foot elevation gain.* ✉ *Big Bend National Park* ✣ *Trailhead: West end of Chisos Basin parking lot.*

★ Grapevine Hills Trail to Balanced Rock

TRAIL | FAMILY | This memorable ramble to one of the park's most distinctive rock formations begins with a 6½-mile drive along a maintained but slightly rough dirt road across a yucca and sagebrush desert north of Chisos Mountains Basin Junction. From the parking area, a relatively flat and easy 2.2-mile round-trip trail leads to a wonderland of igneous *laccolith* rock spires and boulders. Near the end of the trail, you'll scramble a bit up a rocky slope to balanced rock, a giant stone wedged rather improbably across vertical rock piles, creating a "window" through which you can see across the park's southeastern reaches. Although the drive can be managed in a standard car, it's easier with a high-clearance vehicle, especially during wet conditions. *Easy.* ✉ *Big Bend National Park* ✣ *Trailhead: Mile 6.4 of Grapevine Hills Rd.*

★ Lost Mine Trail

TRAIL | Set aside about three hours to explore the nature of the Chisos Mountains along this 4.8-mile round-trip trail. It starts at 5,700 feet and climbs 1,100 feet to an even loftier vantage point that takes in spectacular, soaring peaks and colorful rock formations. There's a breathtaking view at marker 10, about a mile up—a nice photo op if you haven't time for the full hike. Try to get here early, as the parking lot is small and often fills up quickly. *Moderate–difficult.* ✉ *Big Bend National Park* ✣ *Trailhead: Mile marker 5, Chisos Basin Rd.*

Window View Nature Trail

TRAIL | FAMILY | This 0.3-mile round-trip paved nature trail is wheelchair accessible and also great for little ones. Take in the beautiful, craggy-sided Chisos and look through the V-shape rock-sided "Window" framing the desert below (you can hike to this very point via the quite rewarding, moderately difficult 5.6-mile round-trip Window Trail, which is accessed from the same trailhead). This self-guided trail, which is especially captivating at sunset, is easily accomplished in 20 minutes. Be on the lookout for wild javelina, which occasionally root through here. They're not normally aggressive, but give them a respectful distance. *Easy.* ✉ *Big Bend National Park* ✣ *Trailhead: West end of Chisos Basin parking lot.*

VISITOR CENTERS

Chisos Basin Visitor Center

INFO CENTER | The small but informative center, by the park's only lodge, is one of the better equipped, with an interactive computer exhibit and a bookstore. An adjacent general store has camping supplies and basic groceries. There are nods to the wild, with natural resource and geology exhibits, a map of bear and mountain lion sightings, and a larger-than-life representation of a mountain lion. The center sponsors educational activities here and at the nearby Chisos Basin Amphitheater. ✉ *End of Chisos Basin Rd.* ☎ *432/477–2251* 🌐 *www.nps.gov/bibe.*

★ **Panther Junction Visitor Center**

INFO CENTER | **FAMILY** | The park's main visitor center, near the base of the Chisos Mountains, contains a bookstore and impressive exhibits on the park's mountain, river, and desert environments. An elegantly produced 22-minute film detailing the wonders of the park shows every half-hour in the theater, and there's a sprawling replica of the park's topographical folds. Nearby, a gas station offers limited groceries. ✉ *1 Panther Junction Dr.* ☎ *432/477–2251* 🌐 *www.nps.gov/bibe.*

Restaurants

Chisos Mountains Lodge Restaurant

$$ | **AMERICAN** | **FAMILY** | The star attraction here, whether you dine inside or on the gracious patio, is the signature view through three walls of windows that bring the craggy Chisos Mountains to your table. They serve decent, tried-and-true American food, with a few Mexican specialties; the staff is friendly and efficient. **Known for:** astounding views from dining room and patio; nice selection of Texas craft beers; tasty soups of the day. $ *Average main: $16* ✉ *End of Chisos Mountain Rd.* ☎ *432/477–2291* 🌐 *www.chisosmountainslodge.com.*

Hotels

★ **Chisos Mountains Lodge**

$$ | **HOTEL** | **FAMILY** | With ranger talks just next door at the visitor center, miles of hiking trails to suit all levels of fitness, and plenty of wildlife nearby, these comfortable no-frills rooms—some of which have been nicely remodeled—are a great place for families. **Pros:** sweeping mountain views from many rooms; steps from numerous hikes; reasonable rates for the dramatic setting. **Cons:** no phones or TVs; Wi-Fi is weak or nonexistent in many rooms; small, basic bathrooms. $ *Rooms from: $155* ✉ *End of Chisos Basin Rd.* ☎ *432/477–2291 desk, 877/386–4383 Forever Resorts* 🌐 *www.chisosmountainslodge.com* *72 rooms* *No meals.*

Castolon

35 miles southwest of Panther Junction and Chisos Basin, 40 miles south of Terlingua.

Big Bend's southwestern section, which includes the spectacular viewpoints and hiking trails along Ross Maxwell Scenic Drive as well as the breathtaking views of Santa Elena Canyon, is anchored by the Castolon Historic District, with its visitor center and general store. The area from Castolon west to Santa Elena Canyon, along a pretty stretch of the Rio Grande, is quite a bit warmer than the rest of the park and more enjoyable to visit fall through spring (the visitor center is closed in summer, too).

Sights

HISTORIC SITES

Castolon Historic District

HISTORIC SITE | Adobe buildings and wooden shacks serve as reminders of the farming and military community of Castolon, near the banks of the Rio Grande. Although a 2019 wildfire caused significant damage to the district, including the destruction of the building that housed the Castolon Visitor Center and La Harmonia general store, firefighters saved many artifacts and buildings, including the Magdalena House, which contains historical exhibits. The old Officer's Quarters building now temporarily houses the visitor center, and a temporary building contains the general store. Eventual plans call for relocating these operations permanently inside the historic Garlick House. ✉ *Big Bend National Park* ✥ *Ross Maxwell Scenic Dr.*

SCENIC DRIVES

★ **Ross Maxwell Scenic Drive**

FARM/RANCH | **FAMILY** | Although it extends only 30 miles, you can easily spend a full day on this winding ribbon of blacktop soaking up soaring alpine views, exploring historic sites, taking short hikes, and earning a true Big Bend education. There are scenic overlooks, a magnificent western perspective of the Chisos Mountains, informative exhibit signs, and the ruins of old homesteads. Top waysides along this route that don't take more than a half-hour or so to explore include Sam Nail Ranch, the remains of an adobe homestead in a shady grove with a creek that draws myriad birdlife; Sotol Vista Overlook, a grand promontory with sweeping views of the southwestern side of the park (including Santa Elena Canyon); and Tuff Canyon, a striking steep-walled volcanic-rock canyon. Slightly longer but highly worthwhile excursions include the 1-mile round-trip hike into a green valley to Blue Creek Ranch (aka Homer Wilson Ranch), and the 1-mile round-trip ramble to Lower Burro Mesa Pouroff, a sheer box canyon reached via a 1½-mile side road. Mile Ears Viewpoint, which entails a 4-mile round-trip hike to a gurgling desert spring, is another intriguing side adventure. If you have plenty of time and don't mind driving on a bumpy, washboard gravel road, you can make this drive a loop by reconnecting with West Entrance Road (near Highway 118) from Santa Elena Canyon via unpaved Old Maverick Road for 14 miles—allow an hour for this road, and avoid it if you're driving an RV or there's been a lot of rain. ✉ *Big Bend National Park* ✥ *Off West Entrance Rd., 12 miles west of Panther Junction.*

TRAILS

★ **Santa Elena Canyon Trail**

TRAIL | **FAMILY** | A 1.7-mile round-trip crosses marshy Terlingua Creek, scales a rocky staircase, and deposits you on the banks of the Rio Grande for a cathedral-like view of stunning 1,500-foot cliff walls boxing in the river. Try to visit near sunset, when the sun stains the cliffs a rich red-brown chestnut. In clear weather, an overlook on the Ross Maxwell Scenic Drive affords a panoramic view into the canyon. Summer can feel like a sauna, but you might have this secluded place to yourself, and the trail sometimes closes due to mud and flooding following heavy rains. *Easy–moderate.* ✉ *Big Bend National Park* ✥ *Trailhead: End of Ross Maxwell Scenic Dr.*

VISITOR CENTER

Castolon Visitor Center

HISTORIC SITE | **FAMILY** | Temporarily housed in the old Officer's Quarters building following its destruction during a 2019 wildfire, this visitor center in the Castolon Historic District contains hands-on exhibits of fossils, plants, and implements used by the farmers and miners who settled here in the 1800s and early 1900s. There's also an old adobe gallery displaying poster boards explaining the U.S.–Mexico "transparent border." ✉ *Ross Maxwell Scenic Dr.* ☎ *432/477–2251* 🌐 *www.nps.gov/bibe* 🕙 *Closed May–Oct.*

West Texas fauna include prairie dogs, jackrabbits, and roadrunners, while its flora include yuccas.

Rio Grande Village

21 miles southeast of Panther Junction, 89 miles southeast of Marathon.

As with the Castolon area, Rio Grande Village is the base for exploring a long stretch of the river for which it's named—and from here you can access a number of interesting sites in the park's southeastern quadrant, including Boquillas Canyon, a natural hot springs, and the eerily abandoned Mariscal Mine. Despite the name, Rio Grande Village isn't a village per se so much as a cluster of services that include RV and tent campgrounds, an amphitheater, a boat launch, a summer-only visitor center, and a gas station and small grocery store. A grove of giant cottonwood trees alongside the river makes for cooling shadows in this area of the park that can be unbearably hot in summer, and the grassy picnic area is highly recommended for bird-watching. Just east of the village, you can cross into Boquillas del Carmen, Mexico, by row boat through the only official U.S. Customs port of entry in the park.

Sights

HISTORIC SITES

Boquillas del Carmen, Mexico Crossing
NATIONAL/STATE PARK | If you have a valid passport, you can use this crossing, about 2 miles east of Rio Grande Village, to visit the village of Boquillas del Carmen. Check the park website for current hours, but generally the crossing is open May–October from 9 am to 6 pm, Friday through Monday, and the rest of the year from 8 am to 5 pm, Wednesday through Sunday. Once a mining boomtown that fed off rich minerals and silver, Boquillas has shrunk to a small village, but there is a restaurant and bar along with a few shops. U.S. citizens can bring back up to $200 in merchandise duty-free. To get across, you can access a $5 round-trip row boat across the river and a $3 entrance fee to enter the Mexican Protected Area that the village is located in.

The remaining ¾-mile to the village can be made on foot, by donkey ($5 round-trip), pickup truck ($5), or horseback ($8). ⚠ **If you do not return to the border in time, you may be stuck in Mexico for two or three days.** ✥ *Off Boquillas Canyon Rd.*

★ Hot Springs

HOT SPRINGS | **FAMILY** | Follow this 1-mile loop trail to soak in 105°F waters alongside the Rio Grande (bring a swimsuit), where petroglyphs coat the canyon walls nearby. The remains of a post office, motel, and bathhouse point to the old commercial establishment operating here in the early 1900s. Along the hike, you can hear the Rio Grande at every turn, and low trees occasionally shelter the walkway. The 1.6-mile dirt road leading to the Hot Springs trailhead from Rio Grande Village Road cannot accommodate RVs and is best avoided after rainstorms. Also, don't leave valuables in your car, especially during the slow season. Temperatures can soar to 120°F, so hike in the morning or during cooler months. You can also hike to the springs via the more challenging 6-mile Hot Springs Canyon Trail, the trailhead of which is at Daniel's Ranch, on the west side of Rio Grande Village ✉ *End of Hot Springs Rd.*

Mariscal Mine

MINE | Hard-working men and women once coaxed cinnabar, or mercury ore, from the Mariscal Mine, located at the north end of Mariscal Mountain, in the southern reaches of the park. The mines and surrounding stone buildings were abandoned in the 1940s. If you visit, take care not to touch the timeworn stones, as they may contain poisonous mercury residue. You need a high-clearance vehicle to navigate the 20-mile road, which begins 5 miles west of Rio Grande Village; check with park rangers for current road conditions, and allow a half-day for this fascinating but remote adventure. ✉ *End of River Rd. E.*

TRAILS

★ Boquillas Canyon Trail

TRAIL | After climbing over a rocky bluff with sweeping views of the Rio Grande and the desert in Mexico beyond it, this picturesque 1.4-mile round-trip trek drops into a lush sandy canyon and parallels the river. Soaring cliffs rise on either side, and the trail ends at a scenic point where the canyon narrows dramatically. *Easy–Moderate.* ✉ *Big Bend National Park* ✥ *Trailhead: Parking lot at end of Boquillas Canyon Spur Rd.*

Rio Grande Village Nature Trail

TRAIL | **FAMILY** | Down by the Rio Grande, this short, ¾-mile loop trail packs a powerful wildlife punch. The village is one of the best spots in the park to see rare birds, and other wildlife isn't in short supply either. Keep a lookout for coyotes, javelinas (they look like wild pigs), and other mammals. This is a good trail for kids, so expect higher traffic. Restrooms are nearby, and the trail can be done in less than an hour. The first ¼ mile is wheelchair accessible. *Easy.* ✉ *Big Bend National Park* ✥ *Trailhead: Site #18 of Rio Grande Village Campground.*

VISITOR CENTER

Rio Grande Village Visitor Center

INFO CENTER | At this seasonal center you take in the videos of Big Bend's geological and natural features at the minitheater and view exhibits on the Rio Grande. ✉ *End of Rio Grande Village Rd.* ☎ *432/477–2251* 🌐 *www.nps.gov/bibe* ⏲ *Closed May–Oct.*

Persimmon Gap

27 miles north of Panther Junction, 41 miles south of Marathon.

With few services and not too many trails or formal sites, Big Bend's northern section—which contains the Persimmon Gap entrance as well as a small summer-only visitor center—offers a quieter and more introspective sense of the park. Flanked by the North Rosillos, Santiago, and Sierra Del Carmen mountains, the area is bisected by the main park road from Marathon along with a few rough but picturesque unpaved roads that are best tackled with a high-clearance vehicle. The area's must-see is the Fossil Discovery Exhibit, just off the main park road.

Sights

HISTORIC SITES

★ Fossil Discovery Exhibit

ARCHAEOLOGICAL SITE | FAMILY | This covered, open-air building with a beautiful contemporary design contains renderings, infographic displays, and touch-friendly models of the dinosaur fossils that have been discovered here just off the road between Persimmon Gap and Panther Junction. The imaginatively presented exhibits clearly explain Big Bend's ancient geological history, dating back some 130 million years to when a vast, shallow inland sea covered the area. Scientists have recovered fossils of sharks, sea urchins, and oysters as well as of the dinosaurs and giant alligators who roamed the landscape after the sea receded. Kids can climb on fossil-inspired structures beside the exhibit space, where you'll also find a shaded picnic area and a short nature trail that leads to a sweeping overlook of Big Bend's key geological features. The exhibit area is open dawn to dusk. ✉ *Off Park Rd.* ✣ *18 miles south of Persimmon Gap.*

VISITOR CENTER

Persimmon Gap Visitor Center

INFO CENTER | Complete with exhibits and a bookstore, this seasonal visitor center is the northern gateway into miles of flatlands that surround the more scenic heart of Big Bend. ✉ *Big Bend National Park* ✣ *On Main Park Rd. (U.S. 385)* ☎ *432/477–2251* 🌐 *www.nps.gov/bibe* ⏲ *Closed May–Oct.*

Activities

Spectacular and varied scenery plus more than 300 miles of roads spell adventure for hikers, bikers, horseback riders, or those simply seeking a ramble on foot or by Jeep. A web of dusty, unpaved roads lures adventuresome drivers and experienced hikers deep into the backcountry, while paved roads lead to most of the park's better-known and more established trails and scenic overlooks. Because the park has nearly half of the bird species in North America, birding ranks high. Boating is popular along the Rio Grande, where you can view some of the park's most striking features.

BIKING

Mountain biking the backcountry roads can be so solitary that you're unlikely to encounter another human being; note that bikes are not permitted off-road or on trails. The solitude also means you should prepare for the unexpected with ample supplies, especially water and sun protection (summer heat is brutal, and shade is scarce). Biking is recommended only during the cooler months (October–April).

On paved roads, a regular road bike should suffice, but you'll have to bring your own—outfitters in the area tend to rent only mountain bikes. For an easy ride on mostly level ground, try the 14-mile (one-way) unpaved **Old Maverick Road** on the west side of the park, connecting Santa Elena Canyon Road and West Entrance roads. For a challenge, take the unpaved **Old Ore Road** for 27 miles from the park's northern reaches to near Rio Grande Village on the east side.

BIRD-WATCHING

Situated on north–south migratory pathways, Big Bend attracts approximately 450 species of birds—more than any other national park. In fact, the birds that flit, waddle, soar, and swim in the park represent more than half the bird species in North America, including the Colima warbler, found nowhere else in the United States. To glimpse darting Lucifer hummingbirds, turkey vultures, golden eagles, and the famous Colima, look to the Chisos Mountains. To spy woodpeckers and scaled quail (distinctive for dangling crests), look to the desert scrub. And for cuckoos, cardinals, and screech owls, you must prowl along the river, especially around Rio Grande Village, where you might spy summer tanagers and vermilion flycatchers. Rangers often lead birding talks.

BOATING AND RAFTING

The watery pathway that is the Rio Grande is one of Big Bend's most spectacular "trails" of a sort. The river's 118 miles that border the park form its backbone, defining the vegetation, landforms, and animals found at the park's southern rim. By turns shallow and deep, the river flows through stunning canyons and picks up speed over small and large rapids.

Alternately soothing and exciting (Class II and III rapids develop here, particularly after the summer rains), the river can be traversed in several ways, from guided rafting tours to more strenuous kayak and canoe expeditions. In general, rafting trips spell smoother sailing for families, though thrills are inherent when soaring over the river's meringue-like tips and troughs.

You can bring your own raft to the boat launch at the Rio Grande, but you must obtain a river-use permit (free for day-use, $10 if you plan to camp overnight along the river) from a visitor center, where you should also check with staff to make sure river levels are appropriate for an outing (neither too low nor too high). No motorized craft are allowed on the Rio Grande. For less fuss, go with a tour guide or outfitter—most of these are just outside the park around Terlingua and Lajitas. Guided trips can last from a few hours to several days (these longer adventures can cost thousands of dollars). Most outfitters also rent rafts, canoes, kayaks, and inflatable kayaks (nicknamed "duckies") for when the river is low. Personalized river tours are available all year, and they might include gourmet rafting tours that end with filet mignon and live country music.

CAMPING

The park's copious campsites are separated, roughly, into two categories—frontcountry and backcountry. Each of its four frontcountry sites, except Rio Grande Village RV Campground, has toilet facilities at a minimum. Inside the park, rates are $16 for tent sites and $36 for the RV sites at Rio Grande Village. Far more numerous are the primitive backcountry sites, which require $10 permits from the visitor center. Primitive campsites with spectacular views are accessed via River Road, Glenn Springs, Old Ore Road, Paint Gap, Old Maverick Road, Grapevine Hills, Pine Canyon, and Croton Springs.

Chisos Basin Campground. Scenic views and cool shade are the highlights here, as well as access to some of the best alpine hiking in the park. About half of these sites can be reserved. ✉ *End of Chisos Basin Rd.* ☎ *877/444–6777* 🌐 *www.recreation.gov.*

Cottonwood Campground. This 24-site, first-come, first-served spot near Castolon Visitor Center is popular for bird-watching near the Rio Grande. ✉ *Off Ross Maxwell Scenic Dr.* ☎ *877/444–6777* 🌐 *www.recreation.gov*

Rio Grande Village Campground. This shady oasis is a popular birding spot. It's also a great site for kids and seniors, due to the ease of accessing facilities. There are 100 campsites with coin-operated showers, restrooms, and laundry. ✉ *End of Rio Grande Village Rd.* ☎ *877/444–6777* 🌐 *www.recreation.gov.*

Rio Grande Village RV Park. Often full during holidays, this is one of the best sites for families because of the minitheater and proximity to the hot spring, which is fun to soak in at night. There are 25

RV sites with full hookups. ✉ *End of Rio Grande Village Rd.* ☎ *432/477–2293.*

EDUCATIONAL PROGRAMS

★ Interpretive Activities

INFO CENTER | FAMILY | Ranger-guided activities are held throughout the park, indoors and outdoors, and include slideshows, talks, and walks on cultural and natural history, including wildlife and birds. Check visitor centers and campground bulletin boards for event postings, which are usually updated every two weeks. ✉ *Big Bend National Park.*

Junior Ranger Program

INFO CENTER | FAMILY | This self-guided program for kids of all ages is taught through a free booklet of nature-based activities (available at visitor centers). Upon completion of the course, kids are given a Junior Ranger badge or patch. ✉ *Big Bend National Park.*

HIKING

Each of the park's zones has a wealth of intriguing trails. The east side offers rigorous mountain hikes, border canyons, limestone aplenty, and sandy washes with neat geographic formations. West-side trails access the striking scenery of Santa Elena Canyon and venture out through volcanic rock formations and past abandoned ranches along Ross Maxwell Scenic Drive. The heart of the park has abandoned mines, pine-topped vistas, scrub vegetation around the Chisos, and vast deserts with massive boulders and colorful cacti lying just north of the Chisos Mountains, out in the Grapevine Hills. **■ TIP→ Carry enough drinking water—a gallon per person daily (more when extremely hot).**

While Big Bend certainly has "expedition level" trails to test the most veteran backpacker, many are very demanding and potentially dangerous—attempt these only if you're quite experienced. The trails we've included in this chapter are best suited to moderately active hikers, but a few easy ones are appropriate even for novices and young kids.

HORSEBACK RIDING

At Big Bend, you can bring your own horses or book a guided excursion, which can last from two hours to several days, through an outfitter. The going might be slow in some parts, as horses aren't allowed on paved roads. If you're bringing your own horses for the day, you must obtain a free backcountry permit from a visitor. You may camp with your horse at any of the park's primitive campsites, but not in the developed areas. There's a primitive campsite with corrals for eight horses about 5 miles north of Panther Junction at Hannold Draw; it can be reserved up to 180 days in advance at ☎ *432/477–1158* 🌐 *www.recreation.gov*; the cost is $10 per night.

Big Bend & Lajitas Stables

HORSEBACK RIDING | FAMILY | This outfitter with locations at Lajitas Resort and in Study Butte offers trail rides on the western edge of the national park and the eastern edge of Big Bend Ranch State Park. Rides range from one to five hours with lunch. ✉ *Hwy. 118 at FM 170, Study Butte* ☎ *432/371–3064, 800/887–4331* 🌐 *www.lajitasstables.com* 🎫 *From $47.*

JEEP TOURS

Wheeled traffic is welcome in the park, up to a point. RVs, trucks, cars, and Jeeps are allowed on designated paved and dirt roads, though personal ATV use is prohibited. Jeep rental isn't available inside the park, but Jeep, SUV, and ATV tours just outside the park are possible through outfitters. Jeep tours can cost as little as about $85 for a three-hour tour, while ATV tours start at about $180.

MULTISPORT OUTFITTERS

Angell Expeditions

TOUR—SPORTS | A smaller outfitter based between Lajitas and Presidio in tiny Redford, Angell customizes river- (kayaking and rafting) and land-based (jeep and hiking) tours at both Big Bend National Park and

Big Bend Ranch State Park—or at regional destinations beyond park boundaries. ✉ *Redford* ☎ *432/384–2307* 🌐 *www.angell-expeditions.com* 🎟 *From $140.*

★ Big Bend River Tours

TOUR—SPORTS | FAMILY | Exploring the Rio Grande is this outfitter's specialty. Custom tours can be half a day up to 10 days and include rafting, canoeing, and hiking and horseback trips combined with a river float. ✉ *23331 FM 170, Terlingua* ☎ *800/545–4240, 432/371–3033* 🌐 *www.bigbendrivertours.com* 🎟 *From $82.*

Desert Sports

TOUR—SPORTS | From rentals—mountain bikes, boats, and inflatable kayaks—to experienced guides for multiday mountain-bike touring, boating, and hiking, this outfitter has it covered. The company prides itself on its small size and personal touch. ✉ *22937 FM 170, Terlingua* ☎ *432/371–2727* 🌐 *www.desertsportstx.com* 🎟 *From $150.*

Far Flung Outdoor Center

TOUR—SPORTS | FAMILY | Call these pros for personalized nature, historical, and geological trips via rafts, ATVs, and 4X4s. Trips include gourmet rafting tours with cheese and wine served on checkered tablecloths alongside the river, and sometimes spectacular star viewing at night. The property also offers overnight casitas with kitchenettes and a full range of amenities. ✉ *23310 FM 170, Terlingua* ☎ *432/371–2633* 🌐 *www.bigbendfarflung.com* 🎟 *From $84.*

What's Nearby

The handful of towns nearest (and just west of) the park are quite tiny and include a now defunct quicksilver mining town **Terlingua** and its neighbor **Study Butte,** which contain a smattering of places to stay and eat as well as several local tour operators. The combined Terlingua–Study Butte population is about 190, many of them iconoclasts and big-city refugees. Follow FM 170 west from Terlingua for 13 miles to the flat-rock formations of tiny **Lajitas,** an erstwhile U.S. Cavalry outpost that's been converted into a sprawling golf and equestrian resort. Lajitas and the border town of **Presidio,** 65 miles to the west, are gateways to enormous Big Bend Ranch State Park.

Although they're 45 minutes to a couple of hours from the park, the historic West Texas towns along U.S. 90 are extremely popular with visitors to Big Bend, in part because each of these communities has its own rich history and distinctive personality—and this area abounds with intriguing dining and lodging options. **Marathon,** just a 45-minute drive from the northern entrance, is the closest of these to the park's northern (Persimmon Gap) entrance and has a fun Old West railroad vibe and the iconic Gage Hotel. A half-hour west, **Alpine** sits amid the Davis Mountains, some 80 miles north of the park's western entrance. It's known for Sul Ross State University, with its excellent Museum of the Big Bend, and you'll find a few notable eateries, galleries, and hotels. Another half-hour west is **Marfa,** a middle-of-nowhere West Texas hamlet with a world-renowned contemporary arts scene and an increasingly hip and stylish clutch of restaurants, art galleries, hotels, and boutiques. Its spooky, unexplained "Marfa lights" are attributed to everything from atmospheric disturbances to imagination. From Marfa and Alpine, it's about a half-hour north to **Fort Davis,** a scenic and historic town in the Davis Mountains that's also home to several worthwhile attractions and historic lodgings.

Chapter 8

BISCAYNE NATIONAL PARK

Updated by
Gary McKechnie

Camping ★★☆☆☆ | Hotels ★☆☆☆☆ | Activities ★★★★★ | Scenery ★★★★☆ | Crowds ★★☆☆☆

WELCOME TO BISCAYNE NATIONAL PARK

TOP REASONS TO GO

★ **Solitude:** Privacy is plentiful as you navigate your way across this watery, 173,000-acre wonderland.

★ **Nature:** Populating the northernmost of the Florida Keys is an incredibly diverse collection of wildlife including wading birds, tropical fish, curious dolphins, gentle manatees, and undersea life ranging from colorful reefs to fluffy sponges.

★ **History:** Biscayne's past inhabitants have included 19th-century pioneers and 20th-century industrialists. For divers, the area's shipwrecks are a historical highlight.

★ **Enlightening recreation:** With ranger talks, tours, films, and museum exhibits—not to mention activities like boating, fishing, shelling, and snorkeling or diving—it's impossible to visit Biscayne without learning something about its ecosystems.

1 **Homestead.** Situated between Biscayne and Everglades national parks—edged by Biscayne Bay to the east and Florida City and the Redlands district's farms and fields to the west—Homestead makes an ideal base for exploring the area. It's home to the Biscayne's Dante Fascell Visitor Center, and it has plenty of hotels, restaurants, and stores, many of them chains.

2 **Biscayne Bay and the Upper Keys.** Just four of this park's 44 islands—Elliott, Boca Chita, Adams, and Sands keys—are open to visitors. These and other islands are part of a strand known as the Upper Keys, which are sprinkled for about 18 nautical miles north to south throughout the extremely wide and very shallow (average depth is 4 feet) Biscayne Bay. Peer into the bay's clear waters, and you'll see vase sponges, corals, and sea grass. Look north to the horizon to see the modern profiles of Miami and Miami Beach, roughly 30 miles away.

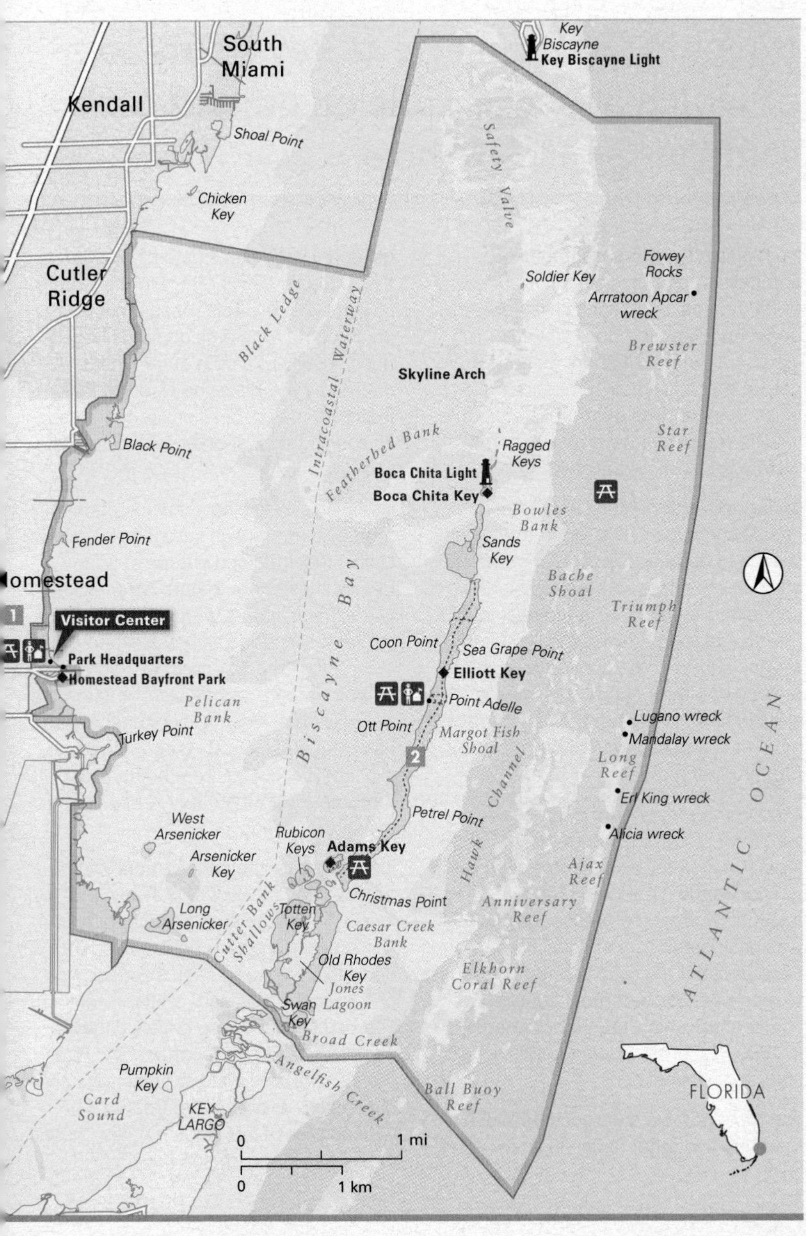
South Miami
Kendall
Shoal Point
Chicken Key
Cutler Ridge
Key Biscayne
Key Biscayne Light
Safety Valve
Soldier Key
Fowey Rocks
Arrratoon Apcar wreck
Brewster Reef
Black Ledge
Intracoastal Waterway
Skyline Arch
Featherbed Bank
Black Point
Ragged Keys
Boca Chita Light
Boca Chita Key
Star Reef
Bowles Bank
Sands Key
Fender Point
Homestead
Bache Shoal
Triumph Reef
Visitor Center
Park Headquarters
Homestead Bayfront Park
Biscayne Bay
Coon Point
Sea Grape Point
Elliott Key
Point Adelle
Pelican Bank
Turkey Point
Ott Point
Margot Fish Shoal
Lugano wreck
Mandalay wreck
Long Reef
Hawk Channel
Erl King wreck
West Arsenicker
Petrel Point
Alicia wreck
Rubicon Keys
Adams Key
Arsenicker Key
Ajax Reef
Christmas Point
Anniversary Reef
Long Arsenicker
Cutter Bank Shallows
Totten Key
Caesar Creek Bank
Old Rhodes Key
Jones Lagoon
Elkhorn Coral Reef
Swan Key
Broad Creek
ATLANTIC OCEAN
Angelfish Creek
Pumpkin Key
Card Sound
KEY LARGO
Ball Buoy Reef
FLORIDA
0
1 mi
0
1 km

Some 500,000 annual visitors make a deliberate choice, to visit this park, most often as a day trip from nearby Miami. Its main draws are its 44 keys, only four of which are accessible on guided park tours or by private boat.

No mainland commercial transportation travels to accessible Elliott, Boca Chita, Adams, and Sands keys (located between Elliott and Boca Chita), which are about 8 miles offshore amid an archipelago that stretches 18 nautical miles north to south. The other 40 islets are wildlife refuges or have rocky shores or waters too shallow for boats.

In the mid-20th century, some business leaders pushed to open the larger islands to commercial development via a series of bridges; others envisioned a shoreline framed by oil refineries, with massive tankers arriving through dredged channels. It took the concentrated and prolonged efforts of environmentalists and politicians to resist these commercial pressures and secure this bay realm for future generations.

Among the proponents of preservation was then-Congressman Dante B. Fascell, who arranged for the federal government to acquire the islands and Biscayne Bay. In 1968, most of the present-day park was designated as a national monument. Six years later it was expanded south to reach the northernmost boundary of John Pennekamp Coral Reef State Park. In 1980, Congress upgraded Biscayne's status to national park.

The most notable difference between Biscayne and other national parks is that, beyond a shoreline swath of mangrove trees, roughly 95% of it is in the waters of Biscayne Bay. This means that your enjoyment of the park depends largely upon access to a boat or on what's offered by the Biscayne National Park Institute, the concessionaire that arranges scenic tours, snorkeling excursions, and dive trips.

Camping and fishing are also options, though swimming is surprisingly limited. Unlike the soft-sand shores of Miami Beach, those here feature hard-packed, shell-strewn sands with waters containing mud flats and sea grass. There is one swimming area just north of Elliott Key's harbor, though you can also swim on the key's eastern, Atlantic side (neither site has lifeguards). Most visitors, however, slip into the waters from boats. (Just remember to put out a dive flag before taking the plunge.)

Nevertheless, the park attracts visitors from around the world. They join the locals who climb aboard their boats and sail south from metropolitan Miami for an enjoyable weekend at bucolic Biscayne. The appeal of this park is literally natural. The barrier islands are largely undeveloped, so wildlife is abundant, and, with the clarity of the waters, coral reefs and wrecks are easily visible. Best of all, with an area of 270 square miles, there's plenty peace, quiet, and privacy.

AVERAGE HIGH/LOW TEMPERATURES					
JAN.	**FEB.**	**MAR.**	**APR.**	**MAY**	**JUNE**
76/61	77/62	80/66	83/69	86/73	88/76
JULY	**AUG.**	**SEPT.**	**OCT.**	**NOV.**	**DEC.**
89/78	89/78	88/77	85/74	81/69	77/64

Planning

When to Go

Although it's too chilly for snorkeling in November and December, mosquitoes are nearly nonexistent, which makes a visit then refreshingly pest-free. In April, conditions are good for paddling and diving. Summer is the best time to explore the reefs, as well as the shipwrecks along the underwater Biscayne Maritime Heritage Trail. The waters are warm, the colors are vibrant, and, aside from afternoon storms, the seas are calm. That said, summer is when the park gets most of its 60 inches of annual precipitation; the season is also hot and humid, with lots of mosquitoes and the threat of hurricanes. Regardless of when you come, bring water, sunscreen, and insect repellent.

Getting Here and Around

AIR

Miami International Airport is the closest commercial air gateway. There are car-rental agencies in and around the airport, which is about an hour's drive from Biscayne National Park.

CAR

Heading east from Homestead, or even Everglades National Park (approximately 20- and 30-minute drives, respectively), the routes are straightforward and easy to navigate. The drive south from Miami, however, involves a tangle of routes that may include I–95, I–195, U.S. 1, U.S. 41, the Florida Turnpike, and toll roads.

■ TIP→ **When using GPS to reach the park, it's best to type "Dante Fascell Visitor Center" in as the destination.** Typing in "Key Biscayne National Park" works nearly as well, but plugging in just "Key Biscayne" will take you to a barrier island about 30 miles north.

Inspiration

Biscayne: The Story Behind the Scenery, by L. Wayne Landrum, the park's former chief ranger, provides beautiful pictures and adequate descriptions of the principal zones of interest, although it overlooks the story of how the park was saved for the public.

Park Essentials

ACCESSIBILITY

Ramps and elevators make the second-level visitor center gift shop and museum easily accessible, and a level boardwalk as well as a hard-packed, crushed-shell path that extends to the end of the jetty can also be traveled by wheelchairs and motorized scooters. Some boating trips, such as the Biscayne Heritage Tour, can accommodate wheelchairs, with access to boats via a ramp. As smaller vessels might not have ramp access, ask when booking an excursion.

PARK FEES AND PERMITS

There's no fee to enter Biscayne National Park or to access its keys. If you plan to stay overnight at Elliott Key or Boca Chita, however, there's a $25 camping fee that's remitted at the kiosk, with a ranger checking to see if every camper has paid up. The only other fees are for scenic tours and diving excursions offered by the Biscayne National Park Institute.

PARK HOURS

The park is open year-round. Hours are 9 to 5 daily for the visitor center, 7:30 to 5:30 daily for the grounds, and 24/7 for the surrounding park waters.

CELL PHONE RECEPTION

Cell phone coverage is fine at Convoy Point's Dante Fascell Visitor Center, but not so good several miles offshore and beyond the barrier islands.

Hotels

Aside from primitive camping, there is no in-park lodging. The nearest commercial accommodations are about 10 miles to the west in the heart of Homestead. Miami and its suburbs have plenty of urban resorts, boutique hotels, inns, and Airbnb properties.

Restaurants

Aside from the limited selection of chips, drinks, cookies, candies, and refrigerated sandwiches that are sold in the bookstore/gift shop, there's no food service within park boundaries. South of the visitor center, Homestead Bayfront Park has restaurants and a full-service marina.

Tours

★ **Biscayne National Park Institute**

BOAT TOURS | One of the most enriching ways to experience the national park is on a Biscayne National Park Institute boat tour or diving excursion. Although adventures vary in length, all of them put you in the knowledgeable hands of a park staffer, who will teach you about this Florida ecosystem and its history.

Among the offerings are the naturalist-led Paddle the Mangroves & Seagrass Meadows kayak tour (1.5 hours, $39); the Snorkel Experience/Island Visit (3.5 hours, $99), which explores a reef, a shipwreck, or mangrove sites and is limited to 12 or fewer people; and the Heritage of Biscayne Cruise (3.5 hours, $79), a guided pontoon-boat cruise that covers the natural and human history of the major islands, with a leisurely stop on Boca Chita. Tours can be booked online in advance; check-in and departure is from the Dante Fascell Visitor Center. ✉ *Dante Fascell Visitor Center, 9700 S.W. 328th St., Sir Lancelot Jones Way, Homestead* ☎ *786/335–3644* 🌐 *biscaynenationalparkinstitute.org.*

Visitor Information

CONTACTS Biscayne National Park. ✉ *9700 S.W. 328th St., Sir Lancelot Jones Way, Homestead* ☎ *305/230–1144* 🌐 *www.nps.gov/bisc.*

In the Park

30 miles south of Miami, 18 miles northeast of Everglades National Park.

Roughly 95% of this aquatic park is found on keys in Biscayne Bay east of the mainland community of Homestead, where Convoy Point is the site of the park's Dante Fascell Visitor Center and the departure point for tours and excursions conducted by the Biscayne National Park Institute. A jetty beside the visitor center extends a few hundred yards into the water, its shaded walkway providing spots to fish or simply sit on a bench to enjoy the bay views.

Sights

SCENIC STOPS

Adams Key

ISLAND | FAMILY | A stone's throw from the western tip of Elliott Key and 9 miles southeast of Convoy Point, Adams Key is open for day use. It was once the site of the Cocolobo Club, a retreat known

You can explore mangroves as well as the bay on tours offered by the Biscayne National Park Institute.

for hosting Presidents Harding, Hoover, Johnson, and Nixon, as well as other famous and infamous characters. Hurricane Andrew blew away what remained of club facilities in 1992. The island has picnic areas with grills, restrooms, dockage, and a short trail running along the shore through a hardwood hammock. Rangers live on-island. Access is by private boat, with no pets or overnight docking allowed. ✉ *Biscayne National Park* ✣ *9 miles west of Convoy Point* 🌐 *www.nps.gov/bisc/planyourvisit/adamskey.htm.*

Boca Chita Key

ISLAND | FAMILY | Echoes of the past ring across Boca Chita, which is listed on the National Register of Historic Places for its 10 historic structures. The island once was owned by the late Mark C. Honeywell, former president of Honeywell Company. A half-mile hiking trail curves around the island's south side. Climb the 65-foot-high lighthouse (by ranger tour only) for a panoramic view of Miami, or check out the cannon from the HMS Fowey. There's no freshwater, access is by private boat only, and no pets are allowed. Only portable toilets are on-site, with no sinks or showers. A $25 fee for overnight docking (6 pm to 6 am) covers a campsite. ✉ *Biscayne National Park* 🌐 *www.nps.gov/bisc/planyourvisit/bocachita.htm.*

Elliott Key

ISLAND | FAMILY | The largest of the islands, 9 miles east of Convoy Point, Elliott Key has a mile-long hiking trail on the bay side at the north end of the campground. Another trail called Spite Highway runs approximately 6 miles down the center of the island. Boaters may dock at any of 33 slips; the $25 fee for staying overnight includes use of a tent area for up to six people in two tents. Facilities include restrooms, picnic tables, fresh drinking water, cold showers, grills, and a campground. Leashed pets are allowed in developed areas only, not on trails. A 30-foot-wide sandy shoreline about a mile north of the harbor on the west (bay) side of the key is the only one in the national park, and boaters like to anchor off here to swim. The beach, fun for families, is for day use only; it has picnic areas and a short trail. ✉ *Biscayne National Park* 🌐 *www.nps.gov/bisc/planyourvisit/elliottkey.htm.*

TRAILS

Adams Key Trail

TRAIL | FAMILY | Starting (or ending) near the home used by park rangers, and ending (or starting) by the sign that marks Adams Key, this ½-mile cleared path runs through the woods, so there are no water views. Hard-packed with dirt, leaves, and grass, the trail takes only 15 minutes to complete—faster if you're trying to outpace mosquitoes. *Easy.* ✉ *Adams Key, Biscayne National Park* 🌐 *www.nps.gov/bisc.*

Boca Chita Trail

TRAIL | FAMILY | This horseshoe-shape trail starts near the harbor, just between the two stone columns that once marked the entrance into Mark Honeywell's island retreat. Roughly ½-mile long, the trail is wide (likely because it was once a road) and signs along the way explain historical aspects of the island. Portions of the trail lead through the woods; other stretches reveal the shoreline, where views can open to Sands Key or a nice photo op of the ornamental lighthouse. *Easy.* ✉ *Boca Chita Key, Biscayne National Park* 🌐 *www.nps.gov/bisc.*

Elliott Loop Trail

TRAIL | FAMILY | This trail will take you all the way from Biscayne Bay to the Straits of Florida—in just about 20 minutes. The U-shape, 1.1-mile route has two trailheads, one at each side of the harbor, and covers the width of Elliott Key before circling back to the bayside. It's an enjoyable, 45-minute, round-trip hike that includes a stretch of boardwalk with views of the rocky shoreline. Although the trail can be sandy, dirty, and rocky, overall it's a pleasant excursion. *Moderate.* ✉ *Elliott Key, Biscayne National Park* 🌐 *www.nps.gov/bisc.*

Maritime Heritage Trail

TRAIL | FAMILY | Like the keys, the coral reefs of Biscayne Bay are very popular park attractions. In addition to various corals, sponges, and brilliant sea life, the fragile ecosystems here contain a half-dozen wrecks (dating from 1878 to 1968) that can be found along the Maritime Heritage Trail. The wrecks are in various stages of decay; can easily be seen when snorkeling, though some require a deeper dive with scuba equipment; and are roughly in a line, starting near the northernmost key with a gap of several miles before a concentrated collection of them. Most visitors access the reef and wrecks aboard scheduled tours departing from the visitor center. ✉ *Biscayne National Park* 🌐 *www.nps.gov/bisc/learn/historyculture/maritime-heritage-trail.htm.*

Spite Highway

TRAIL | FAMILY | It's usually annoying when a road reduces from six lanes to one, but here the advantage is that the six-lane highway developers cleaved down the middle of Elliott Key has been overtaken by time and nature to leave this one-lane hiking trail. The trailhead branches off the Elliott Key Trail to begin the longest hike in the park, one that does not include any water views. If you go the distance, you'll have completed a round-trip of roughly 14 miles on a level, and often canopied, trail. *Moderate.* ✉ *Elliott Key, Biscayne National Park* 🌐 *www.nps.gov/bisc.*

VISITOR CENTERS

★ Dante Fascell Visitor Center

INFO CENTER | FAMILY | At what is a great starting point for every land-based visit, you can get a good sense of the park just by soaking up views of mangroves and Biscayne Bay as seen from the wide veranda. The compact but very informative collection in the small museum offers insights into the park's natural, geological, and human history. The visitor center is also where you'll sign up for tours, snorkeling excursions, and ranger programs. Restrooms with showers, a gift shop, picnic tables, grills, and children's activities are also found here. ✉ *Convoy Point, 9700 S.W. 328th St., Sir Lancelot Jones Way, Homestead* ☎ *305/230–1144* 🌐 *www.nps.gov/bisc/index.htm* 🎫 *Free.*

Activities

BOATING

Although the park's concessionaire can get you to islands and dive sites, you'll have more latitude (and longitude) if you know how to handle a boat—and know where to rent one.

Club Nautico

BOATING | Situated at the Crandon Park Marina on Key Biscayne, Club Nautico rents speedboats, whalers, and yachts. Prices are available on request. ✉ *4000 Crandon Park Blvd., Key Biscayne* ☎ *786/266–6037* 🌐 *www.clubnauticomiami.com.*

Herbert Hoover Marina

BOATING | **FAMILY** | Just south of Biscayne National Park, Miami-Dade County operates this marina, which has 174 boat slips (accommodating vessels up to 50 feet long), a bait and tackle shop, boat ramps, freshwater hookups, fuel, showers, a marine store, and various other services. ✉ *Homestead Bayfront Park, 9698 S.W. 328th St., Homestead* ☎ *305/230–3033* 🌐 *www.miamidade.gov/parks/homestead-bayfront.asp.*

Sailing on Biscayne Bay

BOATING | With this outfit, charters lasting from two hours to a full day are aboard a 40-foot yacht with stops at sand bars and islands. Call ahead for prices. ☎ *305/323–0783* 🌐 *www.sailingonbiscaynebay.com.*

BIRD-WATCHING

Located along the **Great Florida Birding and Wildlife Trail** (🌐 *www.floridabirdingtrail.com*), the park is a significant sanctuary, with more than 170 species sighted around the islands.

Brown pelicans patrol the bay, suddenly rising and then plunging beak first to capture prey in their baggy pouches, and white ibis probe exposed mud flats for small fish and crustaceans.

More rarely seen are American peregrine falcons, which migrate through the park; bald eagles, which can sometimes be spotted in coastal or inland areas; and wood stork, a large, white, wading bird with a black head and black wing linings.

CAMPING

Boca Chita Key Campground. This primitive camping area has no designated sites; just find a spot in the open field, and put down stakes. Saltwater toilets, picnic tables, grills, and a modest nature trail are among the facilities. There's no fresh water. You can visit the nonworking lighthouse, which is open periodically—usually on weekends. There's a small harbor and a sea wall with places to tie up your boat ($25 per-night docking fee includes camping). ✉ *Boca Chita Key, 8 miles off shore from the park's visitor center* ☎ *305/230–7275* 🌐 *www.recreation.gov.*

Elliott Key Campground. Rather than designated sites at this island campground, there's an open camping area for you to pitch your tent. Since you can only reach the island by boat, this campground is never full. You can hike the short nature trails, swim, sunbathe on the small beach, and watch an automated audiovisual program about the ecosystem. Facilities include drinking water, restrooms, cold showers, picnic tables, a ranger station, and a boat harbor with 33 slips ($25 per-night docking/camping fee). ✉ *Elliott Key, 7 miles off shore from the park's visitor center* ☎ *305/230–7275* 🌐 *www.recreation.gov.*

DIVING AND SNORKELING

Diving, one of the park's major draws, is great year-round, but it's best in the summer when sunshine mingled with calmer winds and seas result in enhanced viewing opportunities. Most visitors dive or snorkel as part of an excursion offered by the Biscayne National Park Institute.

Reef life ranges from soft, flagellant fans, plumes, and whips found chiefly in shallow patch reefs to hard brain corals, elkhorn, and staghorn forms that can withstand depths and heavier shoreline wave action. A diverse population of colorful fish—angelfish, gobies, grunts, parrot fish, pork fish, wrasses, and many more—inhabits the reefs.

FISHING

Although no fishing charters depart from the park, more than 100 fishing charters depart from Key Biscayne, Miami, and Miami Beach, and you can find an extensive list of them on 🌐 *www.fishingbooker.com*. Rates range from $450 to around $800, and often the only thing you need to bring is you. Charter-boat captains will provide rods, reels, tackle, live bait, lures, drinks, and fishing licenses. Chances are, they'll also clean and fillet your fish when you've returned to the marina.

Although captains will (hopefully) lead you to the best spots, on the flats, bonefish and tarpon are available year-round, as are reef fish like snapper, grouper, and grunt. Deepwater catches include billfish, bluefish, mackerel, and sailfish—all migratory and typically found in winter—as well as dolphinfish, typically found in summer and ranging from schoolies to 60 or 70 pounders.

HIKING

The best land exploring is on Elliott Key, which has free slips for 33 boats and offers campsites, drinking fountains, restrooms with freshwater showers, and a swimming area with marker buoys north of the harbor. Elliott is the largest of the keys (more than 7 miles long), with a trail running nearly its whole length and a shorter loop trail, with a boardwalk, of slightly more than a mile from bay to ocean and around.

What's Nearby

Few national parks enjoy such an ideal location. Although it appears remote when you're skimming across the waters or exploring life below the surface, the park is within view of the **Miami** and **Miami Beach** skylines. To be sure, most visitors base themselves in either of these cities or nearby **Homestead** and make Biscayne a day trip.

Chapter 9

BLACK CANYON OF THE GUNNISON NATIONAL PARK

Updated by
Kellee Katagi

Camping	Hotels	Activities	Scenery	Crowds
★★★★☆	★★☆☆☆	★★★☆☆	★★★★★	★★☆☆☆

WELCOME TO BLACK CANYON OF THE GUNNISON NATIONAL PARK

TOP REASONS TO GO

★ **Sheer of heights:** Play it safe, but edge as close to the canyon rim as you dare and peer over into an abyss that's more than 2,700 feet deep in some places.

★ **Rapids transit:** Experienced paddlers can tackle Class V rapids and 50°F water with the occasional portage past untamable sections of the Gunnison River.

★ **Fine fishing:** Fish the rare Gold Medal Waters of the Gunnison. Of the 27,000 miles of trout streams in Colorado, only 329 miles have this "gold medal" distinction.

★ **Triple-park action:** Check out Curecanti National Recreation Area and Gunnison Gorge National Conservation Area, which bookend Black Canyon.

★ **Cliff-hangers:** Watch experts climb the Painted Wall—Colorado's tallest vertical wall at 2,250 feet—and other challenging rock faces.

1 **East Portal.** The only way you can get down to the river via automobile in Black Canyon is on the steep East Portal Road. There's a campground and picnic area here, as well as fishing and trail access. Check the park website before you go, however; a repaving project will be closing the road for an extended time.

2 **North Rim.** If you want to access this side of the canyon from the South Rim, you will have to leave the park and wend around it to either the west (through Montrose and Delta) or to the east (via Highway 92); expect a drive of at least two hours. The area's remoteness and difficult location mean the North Rim is rarely crowded; the road is partially unpaved and closes in the winter. There's also a small ranger station here.

3 **South Rim.** This is the main area of the park. The park's only visitor center is here, along with a campground, a few picnic areas, and many hiking trails. The South Rim Road closes at Gunnison Point in the winter, when skiers and snowshoers take over.

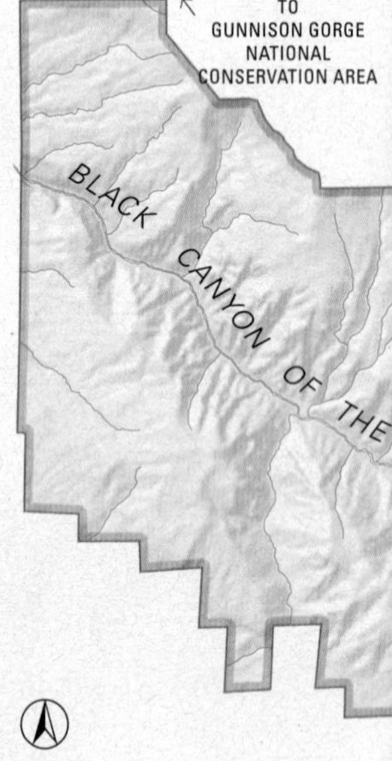

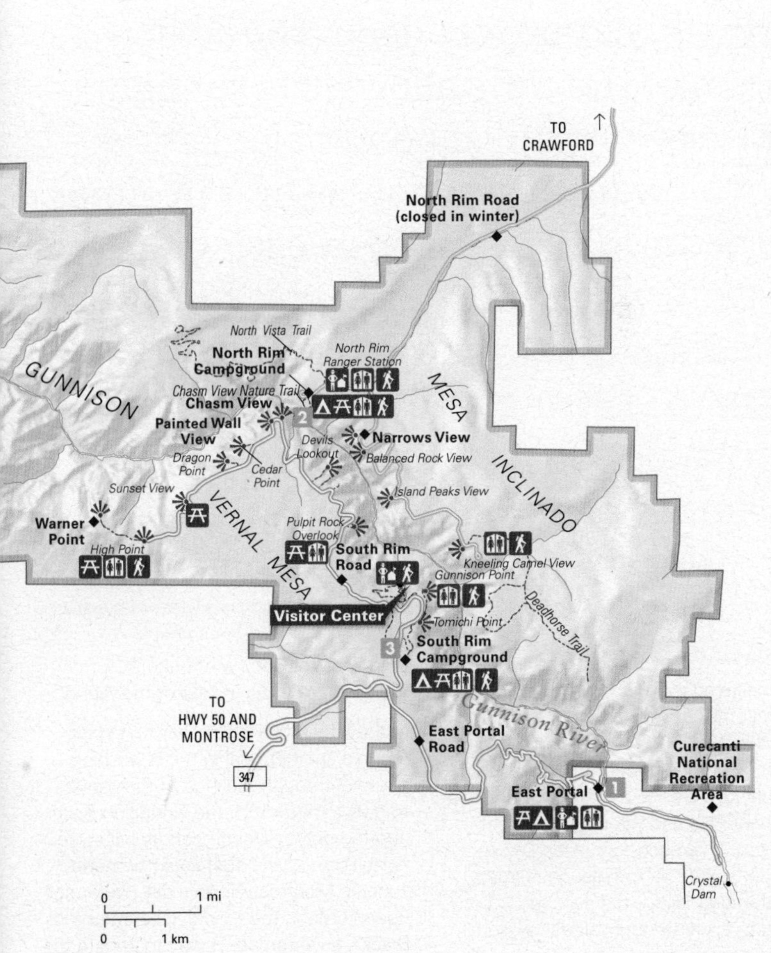
TO
CRAWFORD
North Rim Road
(closed in winter)
North Vista Trail
North Rim
Campground
North Rim
Ranger Station
Chasm View Nature Trail
Chasm View
GUNNISON
MESA
Painted Wall
View
Narrows View
Devils
Lookout
Balanced Rock View
Dragon
Point
Cedar
Point
INCLINADO
Sunset View
Island Peaks View
VERNAL
Warner
Point
Pulpit Rock
Overlook
High Point
South Rim
Road
Kneeling Camel View
MESA
Gunnison Point
Deadhorse Trail
Visitor Center
Tomichi Point
South Rim
Campground
TO
HWY 50 AND
MONTROSE
Gunnison River
East Portal
Road
Curecanti
National
Recreation
Area
347
East Portal
Crystal
Dam
0
1 mi
0
1 km

The Black Canyon of the Gunnison River is one of Colorado's most awe-inspiring places—a vivid testament to the powers of erosion, the canyon is roughly 2,000 feet deep. The steep angles of the cliffs allow little sunlight, and ever-present shadows blanket the canyon walls, leaving some of it in almost perpetual darkness and inspiring the canyon's name. And while this dramatic landscape makes the gorge a remarkable place to visit, it also has prevented any permanent occupation—there's no evidence that humans have ever taken up residence within the canyon's walls.

Spanish explorers encountered the formidable chasm in 1765 and 1776, and several other expeditions surveyed it from the mid-1800s to the early 1900s. The early groups hoped to find a route suitable for trains to transport the West's rich resources and the people extracting them. One such train—the Denver and Rio Grande narrow-gauge railroad, completed in 1882—did succeed in constructing a line through the far eastern reaches of the canyon, from Gunnison to Cimmaron, but ultimately concluded that the steepest and deepest part of the canyon, which is now the national park, was "impenetrable." Even so, the rail line's views were majestic enough and the passages narrow enough to earn it the moniker "Scenic Line of the World."

In the late 1800s Black Canyon explorers had another goal in mind: building a tunnel through the side of the canyon to divert water from the Gunnison River into the nearby Uncompahgre Valley, to nurture crops and sustain settlements, such as Montrose. To this day, water still flows through the tunnel, located at the Black Canyon's East Portal, to irrigate the valley's rich farmland.

Once the tunnel was complete, the focus shifted from esteeming the canyon for its resources to appreciating its aesthetic and recreational value. In 1933, Black Canyon of the Gunnison was

AVERAGE HIGH/LOW TEMPERATURES

JAN.	FEB.	MAR.	APR.	MAY	JUNE
37/14	42/16	50/18	47/23	67/37	75/44
JULY	**AUG.**	**SEPT.**	**OCT.**	**NOV.**	**DEC.**
84/51	81/50	72/42	62/31	48/23	37/12

designated a national monument, and from 1933 to 1935, Civilian Conservation Corps crews built the North Rim Road, under the direction of the National Park Service. More than 60 years later, in 1999, the canyon was redesignated as a national park. Today, the canyon is far enough removed from civilization that its unspoiled depths continue, as an 1883 explorer wrote, to "arouse the wondering and reverent amazement of one's being."

Planning

When to Go

Summer is the busiest season, with July experiencing the greatest crowds. However, a spring or fall visit gives you two advantages: fewer people and cooler temperatures. In summer, especially in years with little rainfall, daytime temperatures can reach into the 90s. Winter brings even more solitude, as all but one section of campsites are shut down and only about 2 miles of South Rim Road, the park's main road, are plowed.

November through March is when the snow hits, with an average of about 3 to 8 inches of it monthly. March through April and July and August are the rainiest, with about an inch of precipitation each month. June is generally the driest month. Temperatures at the bottom of the canyon are about 8 degrees warmer than at the rim.

Getting Here and Around

AIR

The Black Canyon of the Gunnison lies between the cities of Gunnison and Montrose, both with small regional airports.

CAR

The park has three roads. South Rim Road, reached by Route 347, is the primary thoroughfare and winds along the canyon's South Rim. From about late November to early April, the road is not plowed past the visitor center at Gunnison Point. North Rim Road, reached by Route 92, is usually open from April through Thanksgiving; in winter, the road is unplowed. On the park's south side, the serpentine East Portal Road descends abruptly to the Gunnison River below. The road is usually open from April through the end of November. Because of the grade, vehicles or vehicle-trailer combinations longer than 22 feet are not permitted. The park has no public transportation.

Inspiration

The Gunnison Country, by Duane Vandenbusche, contains nearly 500 pages of historical photographs and essays on the park.

The Essential Guide to Black Canyon of the Gunnison National Park, by John Jenkins, is one of the definitive guides to the park.

The *South Rim Driving Tour Guide* is enlivened by David Halpern's evocative black-and-white images.

A Kid's Guide to Exploring Black Canyon of the Gunnison National Park, by Renee Skelton, is perfect for the 6–12 set.

Park Essentials

ACCESSIBILITY

South Rim Visitor Center is accessible to people with mobility impairments, as are most of the sites at South Rim Campground. Drive-to overlooks on the South Rim include Tomichi Point, the alternate gravel viewpoint at Pulpit Rock (the main one is not accessible), Chasm View (gravel), Sunset View, and High Point. Balanced Rock (gravel) is the only drive-to viewpoint on the North Rim. None of the park's hiking trails are accessible by car.

PARK FEES AND PERMITS

Entrance fees are $25 per week per vehicle. Visitors entering on bicycle, motorcycle, or on foot pay $15 for a weekly pass. To access the inner canyon, you must pick up a wilderness permit (no fee).

PARK HOURS

The park is open 24/7 year-round. It's in the Mountain time zone.

CELL PHONE RECEPTION

Cell phone reception in the park is unreliable and sporadic, but the most common spot for visitors to find a cell signal is at High Point, near the end of the South Rim Road, 6 miles from the visitor center.

Hotels

Black Canyon is devoid of hotels. Smaller hotels and rustic lodges are nearby, as are a few of the larger chains.

Restaurants

The park itself has no eateries, but nearby towns have choices ranging from traditional American to an eclectic café and bakery. There are, however, a variety of picnic areas in the park, all with pit toilets; all are closed when it snows.

Visitor Information

PARK CONTACT INFORMATION Black Canyon of the Gunnison National Park. ⊕ *7 miles north of U.S. 50 on CO Hwy. 347* ☎ *970/641–2337* 🌐 *www.nps.gov/blca.*

East Portal

15 miles from Montrose, 7 miles from the South Rim Visitor Center.

This area of the park offers the only opportunity for visitors to experience the bottom of the canyon, without attempting a highly technical rock scramble or tackling Class V rapids. A steep, 5-mile road—to the right immediately past the park's south entrance—leads down to the Gunnison River, where you'll find picnic areas, a campground, a short riverside trail, and world-class fishing.

Sights

SCENIC DRIVES

East Portal Road

SCENIC DRIVE | The only way to access the Gunnison River from the park by car is via this paved route, which drops approximately 2,000 feet down to the water in only 5 miles, giving it an extremely steep grade. Vehicles longer than 22 feet are not allowed on the road. If you're towing a trailer, you can unhitch it near the entrance to South Rim campground. The bottom of the road is actually in the adjacent Curecanti National Recreation Area. There you'll find a picnic area, a campground, a primitive riverside trail, and beautiful scenery. A tour of East Portal Road, with a brief stop at the bottom, takes about 45 minutes. Immediately after arrival through the park's South entrance, take a right on East Portal Road. ⏲ *Closed mid-Nov.–mid.-Apr.*

SCENIC STOPS

Curecanti National Recreation Area

BODY OF WATER | This recreation area, part of the National Park Service, encompasses three reservoirs along 40 miles of the Gunnison River and can be accessed at the bottom of the East Portal Road. Blue Mesa, nearly 20 miles long, is the largest body of water in Colorado; Morrow Point and Crystal are fjordlike reservoirs set in the upper Black Canyon of the Gunnison. All three reservoirs provide water-based recreational opportunities, including fishing, boating, and paddling, but only Blue Mesa offers boat ramps. Excellent fly-fishing can be found upstream (east) of Blue Mesa Reservoir along the Gunnison River. A variety of camping and hiking opportunities are also available. The Elk Creek Visitor Center on U.S. 50 is available year-round for trip-planning assistance. ✉ *102 Elk Creek, Gunnison* ☎ *970/641–2337* 🌐 *www.nps.gov/cure* 🎫 *Free.*

North Rim

27 miles south of Paonia, 77 miles from South Rim Visitor Center.

Black Canyon's North Rim is much less frequented, but no less spectacular—the walls here are nearly vertical—than the South Rim. To reach the 15½-mile-long North Rim Road, take the signed turnoff from Route 92 about 3 miles south of Crawford. The road is paved for about the first 4 miles; the rest is gravel. After 11 miles, turn left at the intersection (the North Rim Campground is to the right). There are six overlooks along the road as it snakes along the rim's edge. Kneeling Camel, at the road's east end, provides the broadest view of the canyon. Set aside about two hours for a tour of the North Rim.

Sights

SCENIC STOPS

Narrows View

VIEWPOINT | Look upriver from this North Rim viewing spot and you'll be able to see into the canyon's narrowest section, just a slot really, with only 40 feet between the walls at the bottom. The canyon is also taller (1,725 feet) here than it is wide at the rim (1,150 feet). ✉ *North Rim Rd., first overlook along the left fork of the North Rim Rd., Black Canyon of the Gunnison National Park.*

TRAILS

Chasm View Nature Trail

TRAIL | The park's shortest trail (0.3 mile round-trip) starts at North Rim Campground and offers an impressive 50-yard walk right along the canyon rim as well as an eye-popping view of Painted Wall and Serpent Point. This is also an excellent place to spot raptors, swifts, and other birds. *Moderate.* ✉ *Black Canyon of the Gunnison National Park* ✣ *Trailhead: At North Rim Campground, 11¼ miles from Rte. 92.*

Deadhorse Trail

TRAIL | Despite its name, the 6-mile Deadhorse Trail is actually a pleasant hike, starting on an old service road from the Kneeling Camel view on the North Rim Road. The trail's farthest point provides the park's easternmost viewpoint. From this overlook, the canyon is much more open, with pinnacles and spires rising along its sides. *Easy.* ✉ *Black Canyon of the Gunnison National Park* ✣ *Trailhead: At the southernmost end of North Rim Rd.*

North Vista Trail

TRAIL | The round-trip hike to Exclamation Point is 3 miles; a more difficult foray to the top of 8,563-foot Green Mountain (a mesa, really) is 7 miles. The trail leads you along the North Rim; keep an eye out for especially gnarled pinyon pines—the North Rim is the site of some of the oldest groves of pinyons in North America, between 700 and 900 years old. *Moderate.* ✉ *Black Canyon of the Gunnison National Park* ✣ *Trailhead: at North Rim ranger station, off North Rim Rd., 11 miles from Rte. 92 turnoff.*

VISITOR CENTER

North Rim Ranger Station

INFO CENTER | This small facility on the park's North Rim is open sporadically and only in summer. Rangers can provide information and assistance and can issue permits for wilderness use and rock climbing. If rangers are out in the field, which they often are, guests can find directions for obtaining permits posted in the station. ✉ *North Rim Rd., 11 miles from Rte. 92 turnoff, Black Canyon of the Gunnison National Park* ☎ *970/641–2337.*

South Rim

15 miles from Montrose.

The South Rim is the hub of the park, a 7-mile stretch that houses the visitor center; 12 canyon overlooks; a campground; multiple hiking trails; and opportunities for ranger-led talks, hikes, and kids programs.

Sights

SCENIC DRIVES

South Rim Road

SCENIC DRIVE | This paved 7-mile stretch from Tomichi Point to High Point is the park's main road. The drive follows the canyon's level South Rim; 12 overlooks are accessible from the road, most via short gravel trails. Several short hikes along the rim also begin roadside. Allow between two and three hours round-trip.

SCENIC STOPS

Chasm and Painted Wall Views

VIEWPOINT | At the heart-in-your-throat Chasm viewpoint, the canyon walls plummet 1,820 feet to the river, but are only 1,100 feet apart at the top. As you peer down into the depths, keep in mind that this section is where the Gunnison River descends at its steepest rate, dropping 240 feet within the span of a mile. A few hundred yards farther is the best place from which to see Painted Wall, Colorado's tallest cliff. Pinkish swaths of pegmatite (a crystalline, granitelike rock) give the wall its colorful, marbled appearance. ✉ *Black Canyon of the Gunnison National Park* ✣ *Approximately 3½ miles from the visitor center on South Rim Rd.*

Warner Point

NATURE SITE | This viewpoint, at the end of the Warner Point Nature Trail, delivers awesome views of the canyon's deepest point (2,722 feet), plus the nearby San Juan and West Elk mountain ranges. ✉ *End of Warner Point Nature Trail, westernmost end of South Rim Rd., Black Canyon of the Gunnison National Park.*

TRAILS

Cedar Point Overlook Trail

TRAIL | **FAMILY** | This 0.4-mile round-trip interpretive trail leads out from South Rim Road to two overlooks. It's an easy stroll, and signs along the way detail the surrounding plants. *Easy.* ✉ *Black Canyon of the Gunnison National Park* ✣ *Trailhead: Off South Rim Rd., 4¼ miles from South Rim Visitor Center.*

Oak Flat Loop Trail

TRAIL | This 2-mile loop is the most demanding of the South Rim hikes, as it brings you about 400 feet below the canyon rim. In places, the trail is narrow and crosses some steep slopes, but you won't have to navigate any steep drop-offs. Oak Flat is the shadiest of all the South Rim trails; small groves of aspen and thick stands of Douglas fir along the loop offer some respite from the sun. *Difficult.* ✉ *Black Canyon of the Gunnison National Park* ✣ *Trailhead: Just west of the South Rim Visitor Center.*

Rim Rock Nature Trail

TRAIL | The terrain on this 1-mile round-trip trail is primarily flat and exposed to the sun, with a bird's-eye view into the canyon. The trail connects the visitor center and the campground. There's an interpretive pamphlet, which corresponds to markers along the route, available at both destinations. *Moderate.* ✉ *Black Canyon of the Gunnison National Park* ✣ *Trailheads: At Tomichi Point overlook or Loop C in South Rim Campground.*

★ **Warner Point Nature Trail**

TRAIL | The 1½-mile round-trip hike starts from High Point. It provides fabulous vistas of the San Juan and West Elk mountains and Uncompahgre Valley. Warner Point, at trail's end, has the steepest drop-off from rim to river: a dizzying 2,722 feet. *Moderate.* ✉ *Black Canyon of the Gunnison National Park* ✣ *Trailhead: At the end of South Rim Rd.*

VISITOR CENTER

South Rim Visitor Center

INFO CENTER | The park's only visitor center offers interactive exhibits and an introductory film detailing the park's geology and wildlife. Inquire at the center about free informational ranger programs. ✉ *Black Canyon of the Gunnison National Park* ✣ *1½ mile from the entrance station on South Rim Rd.* ☎ *970/249–1914.*

Activities

BIKING

Bikes are not permitted on any of the trails, but cycling along the South Rim or North Rim Road is a great way to view the park. **■ TIP→ Be careful: the roads are fairly narrow.**

BIRD-WATCHING

The sheer cliffs of Black Canyon, though not suited for human habitation, provide a great habitat for birds. Peregrine falcons, white-throated swifts, and other cliff-dwelling birds revel in the dizzying heights, while at river level you'll find American dippers foraging for food in the rushing waters. Canyon wrens, which nest in the cliffs, are more often heard than seen, but their hauntingly beautiful songs are unforgettable. Dusky grouse are common in the sagebrush areas above the canyon, and red-tailed and Cooper's hawks and turkey vultures frequent the canyon rims. The best times for birding are spring and early summer.

BOATING AND KAYAKING

With Class V rapids, the Gunnison River is one of the premier kayak challenges in North America. The spectacular 14-mile stretch of the river that passes through the park is so narrow in some sections that the rim seems to be closing up above your head. Once you're downstream from the rapids (and out of the park), the canyon opens up into what is called the Gunnison Gorge National Conservation Area. The rapids ease considerably, and the trip becomes more of a quiet float on Class I to Class IV water. Access to the Gunnison Gorge is only by foot or horseback. However, several outfitters offer guided raft and kayak trips in the Gunnison Gorge and other sections of the Gunnison River.

Kayaking the river through the park requires a wilderness use permit (and lots of expertise); rafting is not allowed. You can, however, take a guided pontoon-boat trip into the eastern end of the canyon via Morrow Point Boat Tours, which launch from the Curecanti National Recreation Area, east of the park.

Dvorak Expeditions

WHITE-WATER RAFTING | The outfitter offers rafting trips through the Gunnison Gorge, just northwest of the Black Canyon. Excursions last from one to three days and can be combined with fishing- or photography-focused excursions. ✉ *17921 U.S. 285, Nathrop* ☎ *719/539–6851, 800/824–3795* 🌐 *www.dvorakexpeditions.com* 🎫 *From $229.*

Lake Fork Marina

BOATING | Located on the western end of Blue Mesa Reservoir off U.S. 92, the Lake Fork Marina rents all types of boats. If you have your own, there's a ramp at the marina and slips for rent. Guided fishing excursions can also be booked here. ✉ *Off U.S. 92, near Lake Fork Campground, Gunnison* ☎ *970/641–3048* 🌐 *www.thebluemesa.com.*

Morrow Point Boat Tours

BOATING | Starting in neighboring Curecanti National Recreation Area, these guided tours run twice daily (except Tuesday) in the summer, at 10 am and 1 pm. Morrow Point Boat Tours take passengers on a 90-minute trip into the Black Canyon via pontoon boat. Passengers must walk 1 mile in each direction to and from the boat dock (includes quite a few stairs), and reservations are required. ✉ *Pine Creek Trail and Boat Dock, U.S. 50, milepost 130, 25 miles west of Gunnison, Gunnison* ☎ *970/641–2337* 🌐 *www.nps.gov/cure* 🎫 *$25* ⏲ *Closed mid-Sept.–May.*

Wilderness Aware Rafting

KAYAKING | Wilderness Aware Rafting takes visitors on single- or multiday trips through the Gunnison Gorge (there is no commercial rafting in the Black Canyon). ✉ *12600 U.S. Hwy. 285, Buena Vista* ☎ *800/462–7238, 719/395–2112* 🌐 *www.inaraft.com* 🎫 *From $274.*

CAMPING

There are three campgrounds in Black Canyon national park. The small North Rim Campground is first come, first served, and is closed in the winter. Vehicles longer than 35 feet are discouraged from this campground. South Rim Campground is considerably larger and has a loop that's open year-round. Reservations are accepted in South Rim Loops A and B. Power hookups exist only in Loop B. The East Portal campground is at the bottom of the steep East Portal Road and is open whenever the road is open. It offers 15 first-come, first-served tent sites in a pretty, riverside setting. Water has to be trucked up to the campgrounds, so use it in moderation; it's shut off in mid-to-late September. Generators are not allowed at the South Rim and are highly discouraged on the North Rim.

EDUCATIONAL OFFERINGS

Junior Ranger Program. Kids of all ages can participate in this program with an activities booklet to fill in while exploring the park. Inquire at the South Rim Visitor Center.

FISHING

The three dams built upriver from the park in Curecanti National Recreation Area have created prime trout fishing in the waters below. Certain restrictions apply: Only artificial flies and lures are permitted, and a Colorado fishing license is required for people ages 16 and older. Rainbow trout are catch-and-release only, and there are size and possession limits on brown trout (check at the visitor center). Most anglers access the river from the bottom of East Portal Road; an undeveloped trail goes along the riverbank for about ¾ of a mile.

HIKING

All trails can be hot in summer and most don't receive much shade, so bring water, a hat, and plenty of sunscreen. Dogs are permitted, on leash, on Rim Rock, Cedar Point Nature, and Chasm View Nature trails, and at any overlook. Venturing into the inner canyon, while doable, is not for the faint of heart—or slight of step. Six named routes lead down to the river, but they are not maintained or marked, and they require a wilderness permit. In fact, the park staff won't even call them trails; they refer to them as "Class III scrambles" These supersteep, rocky routes vary in one-way distance from 1 to 2¾ miles, and the descent can be anywhere from 1,800 to 2,722 feet. Your reward, of course, is a rare look at the bottom of the canyon and the fast-flowing Gunnison. ■ **TIP→ Don't attempt an inner-canyon excursion without plenty of water (the park's recommendation is one gallon per person, per day).** For descriptions of the routes and the necessary permit to hike them, stop at the visitor center at the South Rim or the North Rim ranger station. Dogs are not permitted in the inner canyon.

Did You Know?

Though you won't likely see them, coyotes live in the canyon. The size of medium dogs, coyotes are largely nocturnal; listen for their distinctive howls and high-pitched yelps, which you can usually hear in the early evening. Coyotes also bark when protecting their dens or food.

WINTER ACTIVITIES

From late November to early April, South Rim Road is not plowed past the visitor center, offering park guests a unique opportunity to cross-country ski or snowshoe on the road. The Park Service also grooms a cross-country ski trail and marks a snowshoe trail through the woods, both starting at the visitor center. It's possible to ski or snowshoe on the unplowed North Rim Road, too, but it's about 4 miles from where the road closes, through sagebrush flats, to the canyon rim.

What's Nearby

The primary gateway to Black Canyon is **Montrose,** 15 miles west of the park. The legendary Ute chief, Ouray, and his wife, Chipeta, lived near here in the late 1800s. Today, Montrose straddles the important agricultural and mining regions along the Uncompahgre River, and is the area's main shopping hub. Northeast on Route 92 (20 miles) is **Paonia,** a unique and charming blend of the old and new West. About 60 miles to the east, along Highway 50, lies the town of **Gunnison,** home to Western Colorado University and a low-key hub for outdoor enthusiasts. Black Canyon visitors coming from Denver often stop off for a day or two in Gunnison and the skiing and mountain biking paradise that is **Crested Butte.**

Chapter 10

BRYCE CANYON NATIONAL PARK

Updated by
Shelley Arenas

Camping ★★★☆☆

Hotels ★★★☆☆

Activities ★★★☆☆

Scenery ★★★★★

Crowds ★★★★☆

WELCOME TO BRYCE CANYON NATIONAL PARK

TOP REASONS TO GO

★ **Hoodoo heaven:** The boldly colored, gravity-defying limestone tentacles reaching skyward—called hoodoos—are Bryce Canyon's most recognizable attraction.

★ **Famous fresh air:** With some of the clearest skies in the nation, the park offers views that, on a clear day, can extend more than 100 miles and into three states.

★ **Spectacular sunrises and sunsets:** The deep orange and crimson hues of the park's hoodoos are intensified by the light of the sun at either end of the day.

★ **Dramatically different zones:** From the highest point of the rim to the canyon base, the park spans 2,000 feet, so you can explore three unique climatic zones: spruce-fir forest, ponderosa-pine forest, and pinyon pine-juniper forest.

★ **Snowy fun:** Bryce gets an average of 87 inches of snowfall a year, and is a popular destination for skiers and snowshoe enthusiasts.

1 **Bryce Canyon North.** Bryce Amphitheater is the heart of the park. From here you can access the historic Bryce Canyon Lodge as well as Sunrise, Sunset, and Inspiration points. Walk to Bryce Point at sunrise to view the mesmerizing collection of massive hoodoos known as Silent City. The 23-mile Under-the-Rim Trail is the best way to reach Bryce Canyon backcountry. It can be a challenging three-day adventure or half day of fun via one of the four access points from the main road. Several primitive campgrounds line the route.

2 **Bryce Canyon South.** Rainbow and Yovimpa Points are at the end of the scenic road, but not of the scenery. Here you can hike a trail to see some ancient bristlecone pines and look south into Grand Staircase-Escalante National Monument.

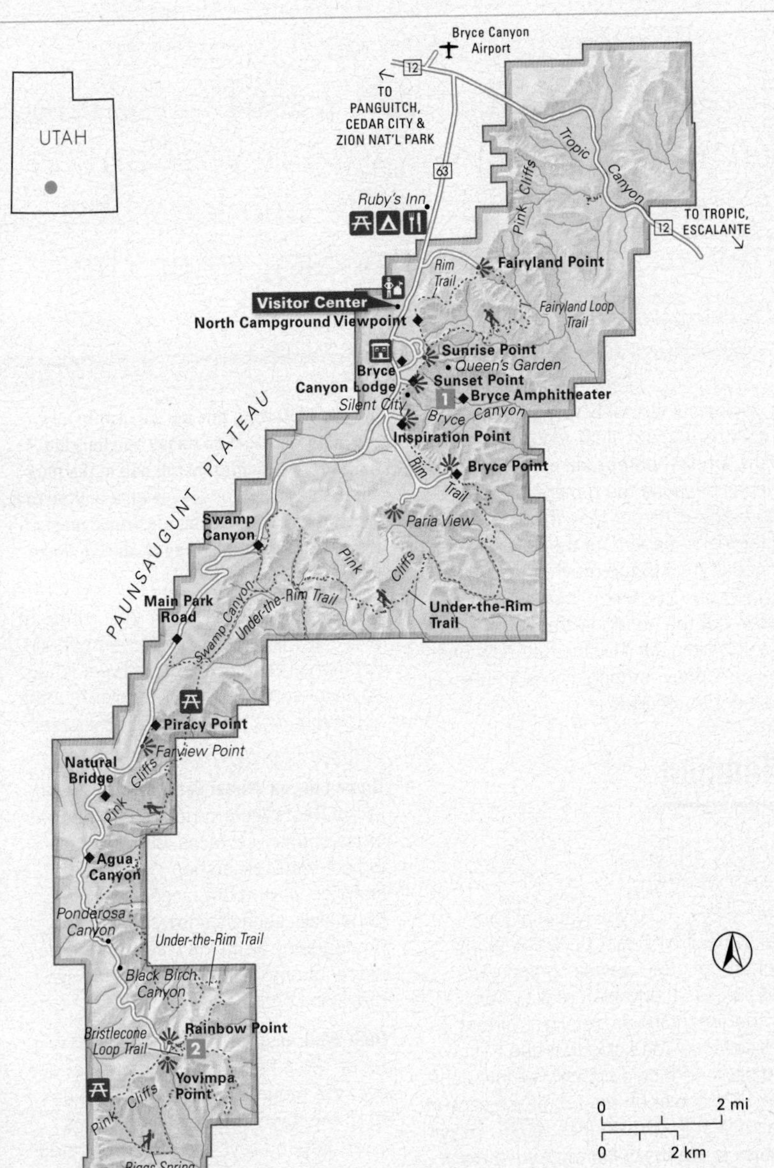
UTAH
Bryce Canyon Airport
12
TO PANGUITCH, CEDAR CITY & ZION NAT'L PARK
63
Ruby's Inn
Tropic Canyon
Pink Cliffs
TO TROPIC, ESCALANTE
Rim Trail
Fairyland Point
Visitor Center
Fairyland Loop Trail
North Campground Viewpoint
Sunrise Point
Queen's Garden
Bryce Canyon Lodge
Sunset Point
1
Bryce Amphitheater
Silent City
Bryce Canyon
Inspiration Point
PAUNSAUGUNT PLATEAU
Rim Trail
Bryce Point
Swamp Canyon
Paria View
Pink Cliffs
Main Park Road
Swamp Canyon
Under-the-Rim Trail
Under-the-Rim Trail
Piracy Point
Fairview Point
Natural Bridge
Pink Cliffs
Agua Canyon
Ponderosa Canyon
Under-the-Rim Trail
Black Birch Canyon
Bristlecone Loop Trail
Rainbow Point
2
Yovimpa Point
Pink Cliffs
Riggs Spring Trail
0
2 mi
0
2 km

A land that captures the imagination and the heart, Bryce is a favorite among the Southwest's national parks. Although its splendor had been well known for decades, Bryce Canyon wasn't designated a national park until 1928. Bryce Canyon is famous for its fanciful hoodoos, best viewed at sunrise or sunset, when the light plays off the red rock.

In geological terms, Bryce is actually an amphitheater, not a canyon. The hoodoos in the amphitheater took on their unusual shapes because the top layer of rock—cap rock—is harder than the layers below it. If erosion undercuts the soft rock beneath the cap too much, the hoodoo will tumble. Bryce continues to evolve today, but the hoodoos are a permanent feature; old ones may die, but new ones are constantly forming as the amphitheater rim recedes.

Planning

When to Go

Around Bryce Canyon National Park and the nearby Cedar Breaks National Monument area, elevations approach and surpass 9,000 feet, making for temperamental weather, intermittent and seasonal road closures due to snow, and downright cold nights well into June. The air is cooler on the rim of the canyon than it is at lower altitudes. ■ **TIP→ If you choose to see Bryce Canyon April through October, you'll be visiting with the rest of the world. During this period, traffic on the main road can be heavy and parking limited, so consider taking one of the park shuttle buses. RV access is also limited to a handful of lots and camping areas, most of them near the park entrance, during these months.**

If it's solitude you're looking for, come to Bryce any time between November and February. The park is open all year long, so if you come during the cooler months you might just have a trail all to yourself.

FESTIVALS AND EVENTS

Bryce Canyon Winter Festival. This event at the Best Western Ruby's Inn features cross-country ski races, snow-sculpting contests, ski archery, ice-skating, and kids' snow boot races. Clinics to hone skills such as snowshoeing and photography also take place, and there's plenty of entertainment, too. 🌐 *www.rubysinn.com.*

Quilt Walk Festival. During the bitter winter of 1864, Panguitch residents set out over the mountains to fetch provisions from the town of Parowan, 40 miles away. Legend says the men, frustrated and ready to turn back, laid a quilt on the snow and knelt to pray. Soon they

AVERAGE HIGH/LOW TEMPERATURES					
JAN.	FEB.	MAR.	APR.	MAY	JUNE
37/15	38/17	45/23	54/29	64/37	75/45
JULY	AUG.	SEPT.	OCT.	NOV.	DEC.
80/53	77/50	70/42	58/32	45/23	36/15

realized the quilt had kept them from sinking into the snow. Spreading quilts before them as they walked, leapfrog style, the men traveled to Parowan and back. This four-day event in June commemorates the event with quilting classes, a tour of pioneer homes, tractor pull, dinner-theater, and other events. 🌐 *www.quiltwalk.org.*

Getting Here and Around

AIR

The nearest commercial airport to Bryce Canyon, Cedar City Regional Airport is 80 miles west and has daily direct flights from Salt Lake City. The airports in Salt Lake City and Las Vegas are the closest major ones to the park—each is about a four-hour drive.

BUS

A shuttle bus system operates in Bryce Canyon from mid-April through mid-October. Buses start at 8 am and run every 10 to 15 minutes until 8 pm in summer and 6 pm in early spring and October; they're free once you pay park admission. The route begins at the Shuttle Station north of the park, where parking is available (visitors can also park at Ruby's Inn or Ruby's Campground outside the park entrance and catch the shuttle there). It stops at the visitor center, lodge, campgrounds, and all the main overlooks and trailheads.

CAR

The closest major cities to Bryce Canyon are Salt Lake City and Las Vegas, each about 270 miles away. You reach the park via Highway 63, just off of Highway 12, which connects U.S. 89 just south of Panguitch with Torrey, near Capitol Reef National Park. You can see the park's highlights by driving along the well-maintained road running the length of the main scenic area. Bryce has no restrictions on automobiles on the main road, but from spring through fall you may encounter heavy traffic and full parking lots—it's advisable to take the shuttle bus at this time.

Inspiration

Bryce Canyon Auto and Hiking Guide, available from the Bryce Canyon Natural History Association, has info on the geology and history of the area.

Park Essentials

ACCESSIBILITY

Most park facilities were constructed between 1930 and 1960. Some have been upgraded for wheelchair accessibility, while others can be used with some assistance. The Sunset campground offers two sites with wheelchair access. Few of the trails, however, can be managed in a standard wheelchair due to the sandy, rocky, or uneven terrain. The section of the Rim Trail between Sunrise and Inspiration points is wheelchair accessible. The 1-mile Bristlecone Loop Trail at Rainbow Point has a hard surface and could be used with assistance, but several grades do not meet accessibility standards. Accessible parking is marked at all overlooks and public facilities.

PARK FEES

The entrance fee is $35 per vehicle for a seven-day pass and $20 for pedestrians or bicyclists, and includes unlimited use of the park shuttle. An annual Bryce Canyon park pass, good for one year from the date of purchase, costs $40. If you leave your private vehicle outside the park at the shuttle staging area or Ruby's Inn or Campground, the one-time entrance fee is $35 per party and includes transportation on the shuttle.

A $5 backcountry permit, available from the visitor center, is required for camping in the park's interior, allowed only on Under-the-Rim Trail and Rigg's Spring Loop, both south of Bryce Point. Campfires are not permitted.

PARK HOURS

The park is open 24/7, year-round. It's in the Mountain time zone.

CELL PHONE RECEPTION

Cell phone reception is hit-or-miss in the park, with some of the higher points along the main road your best bet. The lodge and visitor center have limited (it can be slow during busy periods) Wi-Fi, and there are pay phones at a few key spots in the park, but these are gradually being removed.

Hotels

Lodgings in and around Bryce Canyon include both rustic and modern options, but all fill up fast in summer. Bryce Canyon Lodge is the only hotel inside the park, but there are a number of options in Bryce Canyon City, just north of the park's entrance. Nearby Panguitch and Tropic, and Escalante a bit farther away, are small towns with a number of additional budget and mid-range hotels, and these places tend to have more last-minute availability.

Restaurants

Dining options in the park proper are limited to a few options in or near Bryce Canyon Lodge; you'll also find a handful of restaurants serving mostly standard American fare within a few miles of the park entrance, in Bryce Canyon City. Venture farther afield—to Tropic and Escalante to the east, and Panguitch and Hatch to the west—and the diversity of culinary offerings increases a bit.

Hotel and restaurant reviews have been shortened. For full information visit Fodors.com. Hotel prices are the lowest cost of a standard double room in high season. Restaurant prices are the average cost of a main course at dinner, or if dinner is not served, at lunch.

What It Costs

$	$$	$$$	$$$$
RESTAURANTS			
under $16	$16–$22	$23–$30	over $30
HOTELS			
under $125	$125–$175	$176–$225	over $225

Tours

Bryce Canyon Airlines & Helicopters
AIR EXCURSIONS | For a bird's-eye view of Bryce Canyon National Park, take a dramatic helicopter ride or airplane tour over the fantastic sandstone formations. Longer full-canyon tours and added excursions to sites such as the Grand Canyon, Monument Valley, and Zion are also offered. Flights last from 35 minutes to four hours. ☎ *435/834–8060* 🌐 *www.rubysinn.com/scenic-flights* 🎫 *From $110.*

Visitor Information

PARK CONTACT INFORMATION Bryce Canyon National Park. ☎ *435/834–5322* 🌐 *www.nps.gov/brca.*

Bryce Canyon North

Bryce Ampitheater is the central part of the park. Here you'll find the visitor center, lodge, campgrounds, and many of the most popular trails and viewpoints. A convenient free shuttle runs a loop through this area, stopping at eight main spots where you can get out and explore. It also runs through the nearby town of Bryce Canyon City, so you don't need to bring your vehicle if you're staying at one of the hotels just outside the park.

Bryce Canyon's longest trail leads backpackers under the rim of the park's plateau that edges the natural amphitheater. Hiking the full 23-mile Under the Rim Trail will require an overnight stay, though there are some shorter trails to access parts of this area on day hikes. On clear nights, the stargazing can be amazing.

Sights

HISTORICAL SIGHTS

Bryce Canyon Lodge

BUILDING | The lodge's architect, Gilbert Stanley Underwood, was a national park specialist, having designed lodges at Zion and the Grand Canyon before turning his T square to Bryce in 1924. The results are worth a visit as this National Historic Landmark has been faithfully restored, right down to the lobby's huge limestone fireplace and log and wrought-iron chandelier. Inside the historic building, the only remaining hotel built by the Grand Circle Utah Parks Company, are a restaurant and gift shop, as well as information on park activities. The lodge operation includes several historic log cabins and two motels nearby on the wooded grounds, just a short walk from the rim trail. Everything but the Sunset Lodge (which is open early March–early January) shuts down from early November through late March. ✉ *Off Hwy. 63, Bryce Canyon National Park* ☎ *435/834–8700* 🌐 *www.brycecanyonforever.com.*

SCENIC DRIVES

★ Main Park Road

SCENIC DRIVE | Following miles of canyon rim, this thoroughfare gives access to more than a dozen scenic overlooks between the park entrance and Rainbow Point. Major overlooks are rarely more than a few minutes' walk from the parking areas, and many let you see more than 100 miles on clear days. Remember that all overlooks lie east of the road. To keep things simple, proceed to the southern end of the park and stop at the overlooks on your northbound return; they will all be on the right side of the road. Allow two to three hours to travel the entire 36-mile round-trip. The road is open year-round, but may close temporarily after heavy snowfalls. Keep your eyes open for wildlife as you drive. Trailers are not allowed at Bryce Point and Paria View, but you can park them at the parking lot across the road from the visitor center. RVs can drive throughout the park (with limited parking options spring through fall), but vehicles longer than 25 feet are not allowed at Paria View. ✉ *Bryce Canyon National Park.*

SCENIC STOPS

Agua Canyon

VIEWPOINT | This overlook in the southern section of the park, 12 miles south of the park entrance, has a nice view of several standout hoodoos. Look for the top-heavy formation called the Hunter, which actually has a few small hardy trees growing on its cap. As the rock erodes, the park evolves; snap a picture because the Hunter may look different the next time you visit. ✉ *Bryce Canyon National Park* 🌐 *www.nps.gov/brca/planyourvisit/aguacanyon.htm.*

Bryce Point

VIEWPOINT | After absorbing views of the Black Mountains and Navajo Mountain, you can follow the Under-the-Rim Trail and go exploring beyond Bryce Amphitheater to the cluster of top-heavy hoodoos known collectively as the Hat Shop. Or, take a left off the Under-the-Rim Trail and hike the challenging Peekaboo Loop Trail with its geological highlight, the Wall of Windows. Openings carved into a wall of rock illustrate the drama of erosion that formed Bryce Canyon. ✉ *Inspiration Point Rd., 5½ miles south of park entrance, Bryce Canyon National Park.*

Fairyland Point

VIEWPOINT | Best visited as you exit the park, this scenic overlook adjacent to Boat Mesa, ½ mile north of the visitor center and a mile off the main park road, has splendid views of Fairyland Amphitheater and its delicate, fanciful forms. The Sinking Ship and other formations stand before the grand backdrop of the Aquarius Plateau and distant Navajo Mountain. Nearby is the Fairyland Loop trailhead—it's a stunning five-hour hike in summer and a favorite of snowshoers in winter. ✉ *Off Hwy. 63, Bryce Canyon National Park.*

★ **Inspiration Point**

VIEWPOINT | Not far (1½ miles) east along the Rim Trail from Bryce Point is Inspiration Point, site of a wonderful vista on the main amphitheater and one of the best places in the park to see the sunset. (You will have plenty of company and hear a variety of languages as the sun goes down.) ✉ *Inspiration Point Rd., Bryce Canyon National Park* 🌐 *www.nps.gov/brca/planyourvisit/inspiration.htm.*

Natural Bridge

VIEWPOINT | Formed over millions of years by wind, water, and chemical erosion, this 85-foot rusty-orange arch formation—one of several rock arches in the park—is an essential photo op. Beyond the parking lot lies a rare stand of aspen trees, their leaves twinkling in the wind. Watch out for distracted drivers at this stunning viewpoint. ✉ *Main park road, 11 miles south of park entrance, Bryce Canyon National Park* 🌐 *www.nps.gov/brca/planyourvisit/naturalbridge.htm.*

North Campground Viewpoint

VIEWPOINT | **FAMILY** | Across the road and slightly east of the Bryce Canyon Visitor Center, this popular campground has a couple of scenic picnic areas plus a general store and easy trail access. ✉ *Main park road, Bryce Canyon National Park* ✣ *½ mile south of visitor center.*

Piracy Point

VIEWPOINT | A gallery of views, this primitive picnic area lies ¼ mile north of Farview Point, slightly off the main road. ✉ *About 8 miles south of the park entrance on the main park road, Bryce Canyon National Park* ⛵ *Reservations not accepted.*

★ **Sunrise Point**

VIEWPOINT | Named for its stunning views at dawn, this overlook a short walk from Bryce Canyon Lodge is one of the park's most popular stops. It's also the trailhead for the Queen's Garden Trail and the Fairyland Loop Trail. You have to descend the Queen's Garden Trail to get a glimpse of the regal Queen Victoria, a hoodoo that appears to sport a crown and glorious full skirt. The trail is popular and marked clearly, but a bit challenging with 350 feet of elevation change. ✉ *Off Hwy. 63, Bryce Canyon National Park.*

Sunset Point

VIEWPOINT | Watch the late-day sun paint the hoodoos here. You can see Thor's Hammer, a delicate formation similar to a balanced rock, from the rim, but when you hike 550 feet down into the amphitheater on the Navajo Loop Trail, you can walk through the famous and very popular Wall Street—a deep, shady "slot" canyon. The point is near Bryce Canyon Lodge. ✉ *Bryce Canyon National Park* 🌐 *www.nps.gov/brca/planyourvisit/sunset.htm.*

TRAILS

Fairyland Loop Trail

TRAIL | Hike into whimsical Fairyland Canyon on this trail that gets more strenuous and less crowded as you progress along its 8 miles. It winds around hoodoos, across trickles of water, and finally to a natural window in the rock at Tower Bridge, 1½ miles from Sunrise Point and 4 miles from Fairyland Point. The pink-and-white badlands and hoodoos surround you the whole way. Don't feel like you have to go the whole distance to make it worthwhile. But if you do, allow at least five hours round-trip with 1,700 feet of elevation change. *Difficult.* ✉ *Bryce Canyon National Park* ✣ *Trailheads: At Fairyland Point and Sunrise Point* 🌐 *www.nps.gov/brca/planyourvisit/fairylandloop.htm.*

Hat Shop Trail

TRAIL | The sedimentary haberdashery sits 2 miles from the trailhead. Hard gray caps balance precariously atop narrow pedestals of softer, rust-color rock. Allow three to four hours to travel this somewhat strenuous but rewarding 4-mile round-trip trail, the first part of the longer Under-the-Rim Trail. *Moderate.* ✉ *Bryce Canyon National Park* ✣ *Trailhead: At Bryce Point, 5½ miles south of park entrance* 🌐 *www.nps.gov/brca/planyourvisit/hatshop.htm.*

Navajo Loop Trail

TRAIL | **FAMILY** | One of Bryce's most popular and dramatic attractions is this steep descent via a series of switchbacks leading to Wall Street, a slightly claustrophobic hallway of rock only 20 feet wide in places, with walls 100 feet high. After a walk through the Silent City, the northern end of the trail brings Thor's Hammer into view. A well-marked intersection offers a shorter way back via Two Bridges Trail or continuing on the Queen's Garden Trail to Sunrise Point. For the short version allow at least an hour on this 1½-mile trail with 550 feet of elevation change. *Moderate.* ✉ *Bryce Canyon National Park* ✣ *Trailhead: At Sunset Point, near Bryce Canyon Lodge* 🌐 *www.nps.gov/brca/planyourvisit/navajotrail.htm.*

★ Navajo/Queen's Garden Combination Loop

TRAIL | **FAMILY** | By walking this extended 3-mile loop, you can see some of the best of Bryce; it takes a little more than two hours. The route passes fantastic formations and an open forest of pine and juniper on the amphitheater floor. Descend into the amphitheater from Sunrise Point on the Queen's Garden Trail and ascend via the Navajo Loop Trail; return to your starting point via the Rim Trail. *Moderate.* ✉ *Bryce Canyon National Park* ✣ *Trailheads: At Sunset and Sunrise Points, 2 miles south of park entrance* 🌐 *www.nps.gov/brca/planyourvisit/qgnavajocombo.htm.*

★ Peekaboo Loop Trail

TRAIL | The reward of this steep trail is the Wall of Windows and the Three Wise Men. Horses use this trail in spring, summer, and fall and have the right-of-way. Start at Bryce, Sunrise, or Sunset Point and allow four to five hours to hike the 5-mile trail or 7-mile double-loop. *Difficult.* ✉ *Bryce Canyon National Park* ✣ *Trailheads: At Bryce Point, 5½ miles south of park entrance; Sunrise and Sunset Points, near Bryce Canyon Lodge.*

★ Queen's Garden Trail

TRAIL | **FAMILY** | This hike is the easiest way down into the amphitheater, with 350 feet of elevation change leading to a short tunnel, quirky hoodoos, and lots of like-minded hikers. It's the essential Bryce "sampler." Allow two hours total to hike the 1½-mile trail plus the ½-mile rim-side path and back. *Easy.* ✉ *Bryce Canyon National Park* ✣ *Trailhead: At Sunrise Point, 2 miles south of park entrance* 🌐 *www.nps.gov/brca/planyourvisit/queensgarden.htm.*

Tower Bridge

TRAIL | This short, less-crowded hike on the Fairyland Loop Trail takes you to a natural bridge deep in the amphitheater. Walk through pink and white badlands with hoodoos all around on this 3-mile trip that takes two to three hours and has 800 feet of elevation change. It is not in itself a loop trail if you start and return to Sunrise Point rather than continue on the Fairyland Loop. *Moderate.* ✉ *Bryce Canyon National Park* ✣ *Trailhead: At Sunrise Point, 1 mile off main park road, south of park entrance* 🌐 *www.nps.gov/brca/planyourvisit/towerbridge.htm.*

Under-the-Rim Trail

TRAIL | Starting at Bryce Point, the trail travels 23 miles to Rainbow Point, passing through the Pink Cliffs, traversing Agua Canyon and Ponderosa Canyon, and taking you by several springs. Most of the hike is on the amphitheater floor, characterized by up-and-down terrain among stands of ponderosa pine; the elevation change totals about 1,500 feet. It's the park's longest trail, but four trailheads along the main park road allow you to connect to the Under-the-Rim Trail and cover its length as a series of day hikes. Allow at least two days to hike the route in its entirety, and although it's not a hoodoo-heavy hike, there's plenty to see to make it a more leisurely three-day affair. *Difficult.* ✉ *Bryce Canyon National Park* ✣ *Trailheads: At Bryce Point, Swamp Canyon, Ponderosa Canyon, and Rainbow Point.*

VISITOR CENTERS

★ **Bryce Canyon Visitor Center**

INFO CENTER | **FAMILY** | Even if you're anxious to hit the hoodoos, the visitor center—just to your right after the park entrance station—is the best place to start if you want to know what you're looking at and how it got there. Rangers staff a counter where you can ask questions or let them map out an itinerary of "must-sees" based on your time and physical abilities. There are also multimedia exhibits, Wi-Fi, books, maps, backcountry camping permits for sale, and the Bryce Canyon Natural History Association gift shop, whose proceeds help to support park programs and conservation. ✉ *Hwy. 63, Bryce Canyon National Park* ☎ *435/834–5322* 🌐 *www.nps.gov/brca.*

Restaurants

★ **Bryce Canyon Lodge Restaurant**

$$$ | **AMERICAN** | With a high-beam ceiling, tall windows, and a massive stone fireplace, the dining room at this historic lodge set among towering pines abounds with rustic western charm. The kitchen serves three meals a day (reservations aren't accepted, so be prepared for a wait), and the dishes—highlights of which include buffalo sirloin steak, burgundy-braised bison stew, and almond-and-panko-crusted trout—feature organic or sustainable ingredients whenever possible. **Known for:** good selection of local craft beers; delicious desserts, including a fudge-brownie sundae and six-layer carrot cake; hearty breakfasts. [$] *Average main: $28* ✉ *Off Hwy. 63, Bryce Canyon National Park* ☎ *435/834–8700* 🌐 *www.brycecanyonforever.com/dining* ⏲ *Closed early Nov.–late Mar.*

Valhalla Pizzeria & Coffee Shop

$ | **PIZZA** | **FAMILY** | A quick and casual 40-seat eatery across the parking lot from Bryce Canyon Lodge, this pizzeria and coffee shop is a good bet for an inexpensive meal, especially when the lodge dining room is too crowded. Coffee shop choices include an espresso bar, house-made pastries, and fresh fruit, or kick back on the tranquil patio in the evening and enjoy fresh pizza or salad. **Known for:** convenient and casual; decent beer and wine selection; filling pizzas. [$] *Average main: $13* ✉ *Off Hwy. 63, Bryce Canyon National Park* ☎ *435/834–8709* 🌐 *www.brycecanyonforever.com/pizza* ⏲ *Closed mid-Sept.–mid-May.*

Hotels

★ Bryce Canyon Lodge
$$$ | **HOTEL** | This historic, rugged stone-and-wood lodge close to the amphitheater's rim offers western-style rooms with semi-private balconies or porches in two motel buildings; suites in the historic inn; and cozy, beautifully designed lodgepole pine-and-stone cabins, some with cathedral ceilings and gas fireplaces. **Pros:** close to canyon rim and trails; lodge is steeped in history and has loads of personality; cabins have fireplaces and exude rustic charm. **Cons:** closed in winter; books up fast; no TVs or air-conditioning. *Rooms from: $223* *Off Hwy. 63, Bryce Canyon National Park* *435/834–8700, 877/386–4383* *www.brycecanyonforever.com* *Closed Jan.–early Mar.* *113 rooms* *No meals.*

Shopping

Bryce Canyon Lodge Gift Shop
CONVENIENCE/GENERAL STORES | Here you can buy Native American and Southwestern crafts, such as pottery and jewelry, along with T-shirts, jackets, dolls, and books. *Bryce Canyon Lodge, Hwy. 63, 2 miles south of park entrance, Bryce Canyon National Park* *435/834–8700* *www.brycecanyonforever.com/bryce-canyon-shopping* *Closed mid-Nov.–late Mar.*

Bryce Canyon General Store
CONVENIENCE/GENERAL STORES | Buy groceries, T-shirts, hats, books, postcards, and camping items that you might have left behind, as well as snacks, drinks, juices, and quick meals at this multipurpose facility at Sunrise Point near the North Campground. Picnic tables under pine trees offer a shady break. *Bryce Canyon National Park* *About ½ mile off the main park road, 2 miles south of the park entrance* *www.brycecanyonforever.com/bryce-canyon-shopping* *Closed Nov.–mid-Mar.*

Visitor Center Bookstore
BOOKS/STATIONERY | The Bryce Canyon Natural History Association runs a bookstore inside the park visitor center where you can find maps, books, videos, stuffed animals, DVDs, clothing, and postcards. *Bryce Canyon Visitor Center, 1 mile south of park entrance, Bryce Canyon National Park* *888/362–2642* *www.shop.brycecanyon.org.*

Bryce Canyon South

Heading south from park entrance, this is as far as you can drive on the 18-mile park road. The area includes a short, easy trail through the forest as well as a longer difficult trail. The viewpoints at Rainbow and Yovimpa look to the north and south, so you'll want to visit both. Many visitors like to drive to this part of the park first, then drive back north.

Sights

SCENIC DRIVES AND OVERLOOKS

★ Rainbow and Yovimpa Points
VIEWPOINT | Separated by less than half a mile, Rainbow and Yovimpa points offer two fine panoramas facing opposite directions. Rainbow Point's best view is to the north overlooking the southern rim of the amphitheater and giving a glimpse of Grand Staircase–Escalante National Monument; Yovimpa Point's vista spreads out to the south. On an especially clear day you can see all the way to Arizona's highest point, Humphreys Peak, 150 miles away. Yovimpa Point also has a shady and quiet picnic area with tables and restrooms. You can hike between them on the easy Bristlecone Loop Trail or tackle the more strenuous 9-mile Riggs Spring Loop Trail, which passes the tallest point in the park. This is the outermost auto stop on the main road, so visitors often drive here first and make it their starting point, then work their way back to the park entrance. *End*

Yovimpa Point looks to the south of Bryce Canyon, offering a spectacular view.

of main park road, 18 miles south of park entrance, Bryce Canyon National Park.

TRAILS

Bristlecone Loop Trail

TRAIL | This 1-mile trail with a modest 200 feet of elevation gain lets you see the park from its highest points of more than 9,000 feet, alternating between spruce and fir forest and wide-open vistas out over Grand Staircase–Escalante National Monument and beyond. You might see yellow-bellied marmots and dusky grouse, critters not found at lower elevations in the park. Plan on 45 minutes to an hour. *Easy.* ✉ *Bryce Canyon National Park* ✣ *Trailhead: At Rainbow Point parking lot, 18 miles south of park entrance* 🌐 *www.nps.gov/brca/planyourvisit/bristleconeloop.htm.*

Riggs Spring Loop Trail

TRAIL | One of the park's two true backpacker trails, this rigorous 9-mile path has overnight options at three campsites along the way. You'll journey past groves of twinkling aspen trees and the eponymous spring close to the campsite. Start at either Yovimpa or Rainbow Point and be prepared for 1,500 feet of elevation change. Campers need to check in at the visitor center ahead of time for backcountry permits. *Difficult.* ✉ *Bryce Canyon National Park* ✣ *Trailheads: At Yovimpa and Rainbow points, 18 miles south of park entrance* 🌐 *www.nps.gov/brca/planyourvisit/riggsspringloop.htm.*

Activities

BIRD-WATCHING

More than 210 bird species have been identified in Bryce. Violet-green swallows and white-throated swifts are common, as are Steller's jays, American coots, rufous hummingbirds, and mountain bluebirds. Lucky bird-watchers will see golden eagles floating across the skies above the pink rocks of the amphitheater, and experienced birders might spot an osprey nest high in the canyon wall. The best time in the park for avian variety is from May through July.

CAMPING

North Campground. A cool, shady retreat in a forest of ponderosa pines, this is a great home base for campers visiting Bryce Canyon. You're near the general store, The Lodge, trailheads, and the visitor center. Reservations are accepted for some RV sites; for the rest it's first-come, first-served, and the campground usually fills by early afternoon in July, August, and September. Just be aware that some sites feel crowded and not private. ✉ *Main park road, ½ mile south of visitor center* ☎ *435/834–5322.*

Sunset Campground. This serene alpine campground is within walking distance of Bryce Canyon Lodge and many trailheads. Most of the 100 or so sites are filled on a first-come, first-served basis, but 20 tent sites can be reserved up to six months in advance. The campground fills by early afternoon in July though September, so secure your campsite before you sightsee. Reservations are required for the group site. As one of the most accessible hiking areas of the park, it can be crowded. ✉ *Main park road, 2 miles south of visitor center* ☎ *435/834–5322.*

EDUCATIONAL PROGRAMS

RANGER PROGRAMS

Campfire and Auditorium Programs. Bryce Canyon's natural diversity comes alive in the park's North Campground amphitheater, the Visitor Center Theater, or in the Bryce Canyon Lodge Auditorium. Ranger talks, multimedia programs, and guided walks introduce you to geology, astronomy, wildlife, history, and many other topics related to Bryce Canyon and the West. 🌐 *www.nps.gov/brca/planyourvisit/ranger-programs.htm.*

Geology Talks. Rangers host free 20-minute discussions twice a day about the long geological history of Bryce Canyon. These interesting talks are held at Sunset Point and no reservations are needed. 🌐 *www.nps.gov/brca/planyourvisit/ranger-programs.htm.*

Junior Ranger Program. Kids can sign up to be Junior Rangers at the Bryce Canyon Visitor Center. They have to complete several activities in their free Junior Ranger booklet and attend a ranger program, visit the park museum, or watch the park movie. Allow three to six hours total to earn the park's Junior Ranger badge. Ask a ranger about each day's schedule of events and topics, or look for postings at the visitor center, Bryce Canyon Lodge, and campground bulletin boards. 🌐 *www.nps.gov/brca/learn/kidsyouth/beajuniorranger.htm.*

Telescopes Program. City folk are lucky to see 2,500 stars in their artificially illuminated skies, but out here among the hoodoos you see three times as many. The 90-minute program at the visitor center includes low-key ranger talks on astronomy, followed by telescope viewing (weather permitting). The program is typically offered on Thursday–Saturday nights at 10 pm from Memorial Day through Labor Day weekends and some Saturdays during the rest of the year. Check the visitor center for details. 🌐 *www.nps.gov/brca/planyourvisit/ranger-programs.htm.*

HIKING

To get up close and personal with the park's hoodoos, set aside a half day to hike into the amphitheater. Remember that the air gets warmer the lower you go, and the altitude will have you huffing and puffing unless you're very fit. The uneven terrain calls for lace-up shoes on even the well-trodden, high-traffic trails and sturdy hiking boots for the more challenging ones. No below-rim trails are paved. Bathrooms are at most trailheads but not down in the amphitheater.

RANGER-LED HIKES

★ Full Moon Hike

WALKING TOURS | Rangers lead guided hikes on the nights around each full moon (two per month). You must wear heavy-traction shoes and reserve a spot on the day of the hike. In peak season the tickets are distributed through a lottery system. Schedules are posted at the visitor center and on the park's website. No flashlights or head lamps are allowed, and children must be at least 8 years old. In winter, when there's at least 16 inches of snow, the hike is by snowshoe. ✉ *Bryce Canyon National Park* ☎ *435/834–5322* 🌐 *www.nps.gov/brca/planyourvisit/fullmoonhikes.htm.*

Rim Walk

WALKING TOURS | Join a park ranger for a ½-mile, 75-minute-long stroll along the gorgeous rim of Bryce Canyon starting at the Sunset Point overlook. Reservations are not required for the walk, which is offered twice daily from Memorial Day through Labor Day weekends, then usually daily the rest of the year. In winter, when snow levels allow, this becomes a snowshoe hike (for ages 8 and up only). Check with the visitor center or the park website for details. ✉ *Bryce Canyon National Park* 🌐 *www.nps.gov/brca/planyourvisit/ranger-programs.htm.*

HORSEBACK RIDING

Canyon Trail Rides

HORSEBACK RIDING | **FAMILY** | Descend to the floor of the Bryce Canyon Amphitheater via horse or mule—most visitors have no riding experience, so don't hesitate to join in. A two-hour ride (children as young as 7 can participate) ambles along the amphitheater floor through the Queen's Garden before returning to Sunrise Point. The three-hour expedition (children must be at least 10 years old) follows Peekaboo Loop Trail, winds past the Fairy Castle, and passes the Wall of Windows before returning to Sunrise Point. For either ride, the weight limit is 220 pounds. Two rides a day of each type leave in the morning and early afternoon. There are no rides from November through March. ✉ *Bryce Canyon Lodge, Off Hwy. 63, Bryce Canyon National Park* ☎ *435/679–8665, 435/834–5500 Bryce Canyon reservations* 🌐 *www.canyonrides.com* 🎫 *From $65.*

Ruby's Horseback Adventures

HORSEBACK RIDING | **FAMILY** | Ride to the rim of Bryce Canyon, venture through narrow slot canyons in Grand Staircase–Escalante National Monument, or even retrace the trails taken by outlaw Butch Cassidy more than a century ago. Rides last from 90 minutes to all day. Kids must be 7 or older to ride, in some cases 10. Wagon rides to the rim of Bryce Canyon are available for all ages, as are sleigh rides in winter. ✉ *Bryce Canyon National Park* ☎ *866/782–0002* 🌐 *www.horserides.net* 🎫 *From $68.*

What's Nearby

Just a few miles from the visitor center and right on the shuttle route, **Bryce Canyon City** was incorporated in 2007 by the owners of the Ruby's Inn nearly a century after it first began welcoming guests. Though there are less than 200 year-round residents, thousands of tourists stay here each year to explore the adjacent park and partake in events like the town's winter festival.

The small town of **Panguitch** is 25 miles northwest of Bryce Canyon. It has restaurants, motels, gas stations, and trinket shops. You'll find a few more eateries and other businesses in tiny **Hatch,** 15 miles south of Panguitch. Just 10 miles east of the park, little **Tropic** has a handful of noteworthy lodgings and eateries. Continue about 37 miles northeast to reach **Escalante,** a western gateway to the Grand Staircase–Escalante National Monument with several good places to stay and eat. From Interstate 15, **Cedar City** is where you exit to Bryce (it's a 90-minute drive). With a population of 31,200, it's the region's largest city and the home of Southern Utah University and the Utah Shakespeare Festival, which draws theater buffs from all over.

Chapter 11

CANYONLANDS NATIONAL PARK

Updated by
Stina Sieg

Camping	Hotels	Activities	Scenery	Crowds
★★☆☆☆	★★★☆☆	★★★★☆	★★★★☆	★★★★☆

WELCOME TO CANYONLANDS NATIONAL PARK

TOP REASONS TO GO

★ **Endless vistas:** The view from Island in the Sky stretches for miles as you look out over millennia of sculpting by wind and rain.

★ **Seeking solitude:** Needles, an astoundingly beautiful part of the park to explore on foot, sees very few visitors—it can sometimes feel like you have it all to yourself.

★ **Radical rides:** The Cataract Canyon rapids and the White Rim Trail are world-class adventures by boat or bike.

★ **Native American artifacts:** View rock art and Ancestral Pueblo dwellings in the park.

★ **Wonderful wilderness:** Some of the country's most untouched landscapes are within the park's boundaries, and they're worth the extra effort needed to get there.

★ **The night skies:** Far away from city lights, Canyonlands is ideal for stargazing.

1 **Island in the Sky.** From any of the overlooks here you can see for miles and look down thousands of feet to canyon floors. Chocolate-brown canyons are capped by white rock, and deep-red monuments rise nearby.

2 **Needles.** Pink, orange, and red rock is layered with white rock and stands in spires and pinnacles around grassy meadows. Extravagantly red mesas and buttes interrupt the horizon as in a picture postcard of the Old West.

3 **The Maze.** Only the most intrepid adventurers explore this incredibly remote mosaic of rock formations. There's a reason Butch Cassidy hid out here.

4 **Horseshoe Canyon.** Plan on several hours of dirt-road driving to get here, but the famous rock-art panel "Great Gallery" is a grand reward at the end of a long hike.

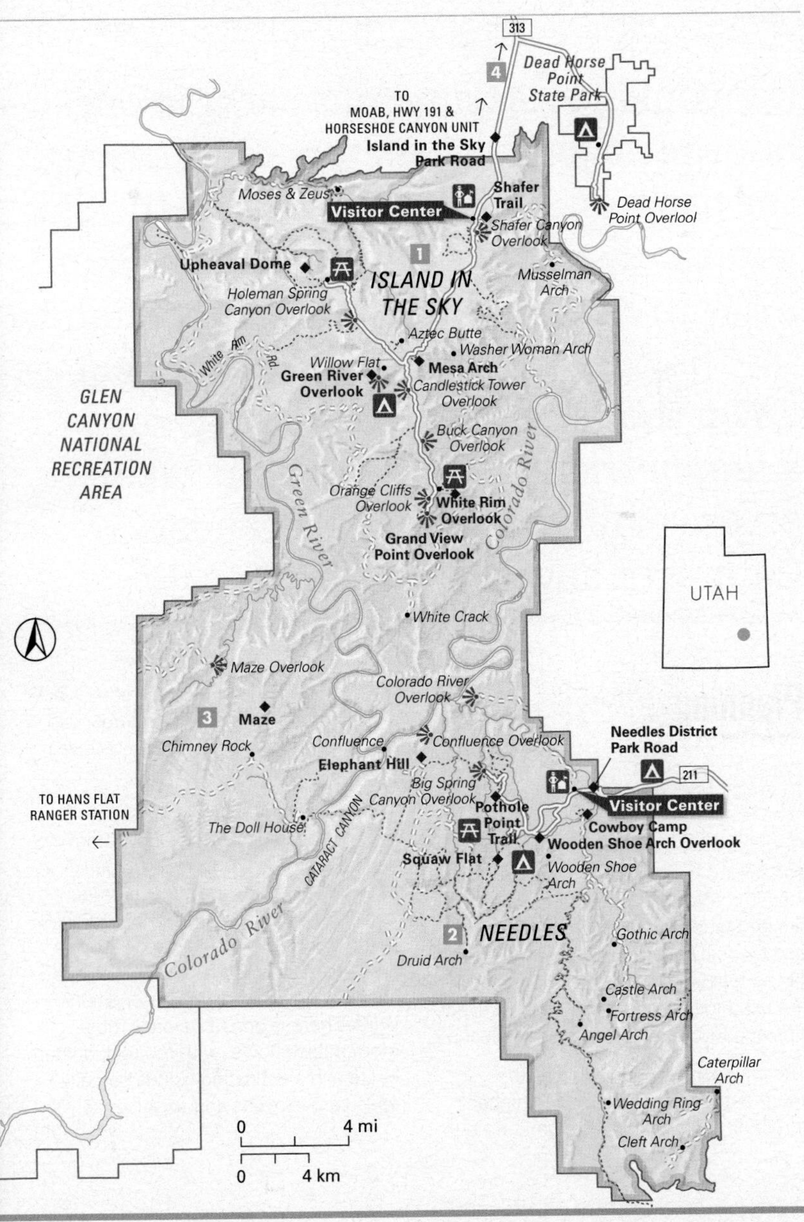
313
Dead Horse Point State Park
TO MOAB, HWY 191 & HORSESHOE CANYON UNIT
Island in the Sky Park Road
Shafer Trail
Visitor Center
Moses & Zeus
Dead Horse Point Overlool
Shafer Canyon Overlook
Upheaval Dome
ISLAND IN THE SKY
Holeman Spring Canyon Overlook
Musselman Arch
Aztec Butte
Washer Woman Arch
White Rim Rd.
Willow Flat
Mesa Arch
Green River Overlook
Candlestick Tower Overlook
GLEN CANYON NATIONAL RECREATION AREA
Buck Canyon Overlook
Green River
Colorado River
Orange Cliffs Overlook
White Rim Overlook
Grand View Point Overlook
UTAH
White Crack
Maze Overlook
Colorado River Overlook
Maze
Chimney Rock
Confluence
Confluence Overlook
Needles District Park Road
Elephant Hill
211
Big Spring Canyon Overlook
Visitor Center
TO HANS FLAT RANGER STATION
Pothole Point Trail
The Doll House
CATARACT CANYON
Cowboy Camp
Wooden Shoe Arch Overlook
Squaw Flat
Wooden Shoe Arch
NEEDLES
Gothic Arch
Colorado River
Druid Arch
Castle Arch
Fortress Arch
Angel Arch
Caterpillar Arch
Wedding Ring Arch
Cleft Arch
0 4 mi
0 4 km

AVERAGE HIGH/LOW TEMPERATURES					
JAN.	FEB.	MAR.	APR.	MAY	JUNE
44/22	52/28	64/35	71/42	82/51	93/60
JULY	AUG.	SEPT.	OCT.	NOV.	DEC.
100/67	97/66	88/55	74/42	56/30	45/23

Canyonlands is truly four parks in one, but the majority of visitors drive through the panoramic vistas of Island in the Sky and barely venture anywhere else. Plan a day to explore the Needles district and see the park from the bottom up. Float down the Green and Colorado rivers on a family-friendly rafting trip, or take on the white water in the legendary Cataract Canyon.

Planning

When to Go

Gorgeous weather means that spring and fall are most popular. Canyonlands is seldom crowded, but in spring backpackers and four-wheelers populate the trails and roads. During Easter week, some of the four-wheel-drive trails in the park are used for Jeep Safari, an annual event drawing thousands of visitors to Moab.

The crowds thin out by July as the thermostat reaches 100°F and higher for about four weeks. It's a great time to get out on the Colorado or Green River winding through the park. October can be a little rainy, but the region receives only 8 inches of rain annually.

The well-kept secret is that winter, except during occasional snow storms, can be a great time to tour the park. Crowds are gone, snowcapped mountains stand in the background, and key roads in Island in the Sky and Needles are well-maintained (although it's wise to check the park website for conditions). Winter here is one of nature's most memorable shows, with red rock dusted white and low-floating clouds partially obscuring canyons and towers.

Getting Here and Around

AIR

Moab is served by tiny Canyonlands Field Airport, which has daily service to Denver on SkyWest/United Airlines and a couple of car rental agencies. The nearest mid-sized airport is Grand Junction Regional Airport in Grand Junction, Colorado, which is approximately 110 miles from Moab and is served by most major airlines.

CAR

Off U.S. 191, Canyonlands' Island in the Sky Visitor Center is 29 miles from Arches National Park and 32 miles from Moab on Highway 313 west of U.S. 191; the Needles District is 80 miles from Moab and reached via Highway 211, 34 miles west of U.S. 191.

Before starting a journey to any of Canyonlands' three districts, make sure your gas tank is topped off, as there are no services inside the large park. The Maze is especially remote, 135 miles from Moab, and actually a bit closer (100 miles) to Capitol Reef National Park. In the Island in the Sky District, it's about 12 miles from the entrance station to Grand View Point, with a 5-mile spur to Upheaval Dome. The Needles scenic drive is 10 miles from the entrance station, with two spurs, about 3 miles each. Roads in the Maze—suitable only for high-clearance, four-wheel-drive vehicles—wind for hundreds of miles through the rugged canyons. Within the parks, it's critical that you park only in designated pull-outs or parking areas.

Park Essentials

ACCESSIBILITY

There are currently no trails in Canyonlands accessible to people in wheelchairs, but Grand View Point, Buck Canyon Overlook, and Green River Overlook at Island in the Sky are wheelchair accessible. In Needles, the visitor center, restrooms, Squaw Flat Campground, and Wooden Shoe Overlook are wheelchair accessible. The visitor centers at the Island in the Sky and Needles districts are also accessible, and the park's pit toilets are accessible with some assistance.

PARK FEES AND PERMITS

Admission is $30 per vehicle, $15 per person on foot or bicycle, and $25 per motorcycle, good for seven days. Your Canyonlands pass is good for all the park's districts. There's no entrance fee to the Maze District of Canyonlands. A $55 local park pass grants you admission to both Arches and Canyonlands as well as Natural Bridges and Hovenweep national monuments for one year.

You need a permit for overnight backpacking, four-wheel-drive camping, river trips, and mountain-bike camping. Online reservations can be made four months in advance on the park website (🌐 *www.nps.gov/cany*). Four-wheel-drive day use in Salt, Horse, and Lavender canyons and all motorized vehicles and bicycles on the Elephant Hill and White Rim trails also require a permit, which you can obtain online up to 24 hours before your trip or in person at visitor centers.

PARK HOURS

Canyonlands National Park is open 24 hours a day, seven days a week, year-round. It is in the Mountain time zone.

CELL PHONE RECEPTION

Cell phone reception may be available in some parts of the park, but not reliably so. Public telephones are at the park's visitor centers.

Restaurants

There are no dining facilities in the park, although Needles Outpost campground, a mile from Needles Visitor Center, has a small solar-powered store with snacks and drinks. Moab has a multitude of dining options, and there are a few very casual restaurants in Blanding (in Blanding, restaurants don't serve alcohol and are typically closed Sunday), plus a couple of excellent eateries a bit farther south in Bluff.

Hotels

There is no lodging in the park. Most visitors—especially those focused on Island in the Sky—stay in Moab or perhaps Green River, but the small towns of Blanding and Bluff—which have a smattering of motels and inns—are also convenient for exploring the Needles District.

Tours

Redtail Air Adventures

AIR EXCURSIONS | This company's daily, regional tours give you an eagle's-eye view of the park, and you'll walk away with new respect and understanding of the word "wilderness." The Canyonlands Tour, one of several flightseeing options, lasts for one hour. A two-person minimum applies. ✉ *Canyonlands Field Airport, 94 W. Aviation Way, Moab* ✣ *Off U.S. 191* ☎ *435/259–7421* 🌐 *flyredtail.com* 🎫 *From $184 per person.*

Visitor Information

PARK CONTACT INFORMATION Canyonlands National Park. ☎ *435/719–2313* 🌐 *www.nps.gov/cany.*

Island in the Sky

Standing at one of the overlooks at Island in the Sky, it's hard to fully take in what looks like an oil painting a thousand feet below. Rivers and rain have eroded the desert floor for millennia, creating mesas, towers, and the park's famously deep canyons, all with an earthy red hue. While the view alone is worth the trip, getting onto one of the district's hiking trails or four-wheel roads will get you up close with its rough beauty. While it's still a shade over 30 miles from Moab, this is the most accessible—and far most visited—section of the park.

Sights

SCENIC DRIVES

Island in the Sky Park Road

SCENIC DRIVE | This 12-mile-long main road inside the park is bisected by a 5-mile side road to the Upheaval Dome area. To enjoy dramatic views, including the Green and Colorado river basins, stop at the overlooks and take the short walks. Once you get to the park, allow at least two hours—and ideally four—to explore. ✉ *Island in the Sky.*

SCENIC STOPS

Green River Overlook

VIEWPOINT | From the road it's just 100 yards to this stunning view of the Green River to the south and west. It's not far from Island in the Sky (Willow Flat) campground. ✉ *About 1 mile off Upheaval Dome Rd., Island in the Sky* ✣ *7 miles from visitor center.*

White Rim Overlook Trail

VIEWPOINT | The cliffs fall away on three sides at the end of this 1-mile level hike until you get a dramatic view of the White Rim and Monument Basin. There are restrooms at the trailhead. ✉ *Grand View Point, Island in the Sky.*

TRAILS

Aztec Butte Trail

TRAIL | The highlight of the 2-mile round-trip hike is the chance to see Ancestral Pueblo granaries. The view into Taylor Canyon is also nice. *Moderate.* ✉ *Island in the Sky* ✣ *Trailhead: Upheaval Dome Rd., about 7 miles from visitor center.*

★ Grand View Point Trail

TRAIL | This 360-degree view is the main event for many visitors to Island in the Sky. Look down on the deep canyons of the Colorado and Green rivers, which have been carved by water and erosion over the millennia. Many people just stop at the paved overlook and drive on, but you'll gain breathtaking perspective by strolling along this 2-mile round-trip, flat cliffside trail. On a clear day you can see up to 100 miles to the Maze and Needles districts of the park and each of Utah's major laccolithic mountain ranges: the Henrys, Abajos, and La Sals. *Easy.* ✉ *End of main park road, Island in the Sky* ⊕ *12 miles from visitor center.*

★ Mesa Arch Trail

TRAIL | If you don't have time for the 2,000 arches in nearby Arches National Park, you should take the easy, ½-mile round-trip walk to Mesa Arch. After the overlooks this is the most popular trail in the park. The arch is above a cliff that drops 800 feet to the canyon bottom. Through the arch, views of Washerwoman Arch and surrounding buttes, spires, and canyons make this a favorite photo opportunity. *Easy.* ✉ *Off main park road, Island in the Sky* ⊕ *6 miles from visitor center.*

Shafer Trail

TRAIL | This rough trek that leads to the 100-mile White Rim Road was probably first established by ancient Native Americans, but in the early 1900s ranchers used it to drive cattle into the canyon. Originally narrow and rugged, it was upgraded during the uranium boom, when miners hauled ore by truck from the canyon floor. Check out the road's winding route down canyon walls from Shafer Canyon Overlook before you drive it to see why it's mostly used by daring four-wheelers and energetic mountain bikers. Off the main road, less than 1 mile from the park entrance, it descends 1,400 feet to the White Rim. Check with the visitor center about road conditions before driving the Shafer Trail. It's often impassable after rain or snow. ✉ *Island in the Sky.*

★ Upheaval Dome Trail

TRAIL | This mysterious crater is one of the wonders of Island in the Sky. Some geologists believe it's an eroded salt dome, but others think it was made by a meteorite. Either way, it's worth the steep hike to see it and decide for yourself. The moderate hike to the first overlook is about a ½-mile; energetic visitors can continue another ½-mile to the second overlook for an even better perspective. The trail is steeper and rougher after the first overlook. Round-trip to the second overlook is 2 miles. The trailhead has restrooms and a picnic area. *Moderate.* ✉ *End of Upheaval Dome Rd., Island in the Sky* ⊕ *11 miles from visitor center.*

Whale Rock Trail

TRAIL | If you've been hankering to walk across some of that pavement-smooth stuff they call slickrock, the hike to Whale Rock will make your feet happy. This 1-mile round-trip adventure, which culminates with a tough final 100-foot climb and features some potentially dangerous dropoffs, takes you to the very top of the whale's back. Once you get there, you are rewarded with great views of Upheaval Dome and Trail Canyon. *Moderate.* ✉ *Island in the Sky* ⊕ *Trailhead: Upheaval Dome Rd., 10 miles from visitor center.*

VISITOR CENTER

★ Island in the Sky Visitor Center

INFO CENTER | The gateway to the world-famous White Rim Trail, this visitor center 21 miles from U.S. 191 draws a mix of mountain bikers, hikers, and tourists. Enjoy the orientation film, then browse the bookstore for information about the region. Exhibits help explain animal adaptations as well as some of the history of the park. Check the website or at the center for a daily schedule of ranger-led programs. ✉ *Off Hwy. 313, Island in the Sky* ☎ *435/259–4712* ⏲ *Closed late Dec.–early Mar.*

Sandstone spires and Native American rock art are among the draws in the Needles district.

Needles

Lower in elevation than Island in the Sky, Needles is more about on-the-ground exploration than far-off vistas, but it's an especially good area for long-distance hiking, mountain biking, and four-wheel driving. The district is named for its massive sandstone spires, with hundreds of the formations poking up toward the sky. There are also several striking examples of Native American rock art here, well worth the hikes to reach them. With relatively few visitors, Needles makes for a quiet place to set up camp and recharge for a few days before returning to busy nearby Moab.

Sights

HISTORIC SIGHTS

Cowboy Camp

HISTORIC SITE | **FAMILY** | This fascinating stop on the 0.6-mile round-trip **Cave Spring Trail** is an authentic example of cowboy life more than a century ago. You do not need to complete the entire trail (which includes two short ladders and some rocky hiking) to see the 19th-century artifacts at Cowboy Camp. ✉ *End of Cave Springs Rd., Needles* ✥ *2.3 miles from visitor center.*

SCENIC DRIVES

Needles District Park Road

SCENIC DRIVE | You'll feel like you've driven into a Hollywood Western as you roll along the park road in the Needles District. Red mesas and buttes rise against the horizon, blue mountain ranges interrupt the rangelands, and the colorful red-and-white needles stand like soldiers on the far side of grassy meadows. Definitely hop out of the car at a few of the marked roadside stops, including both overlooks at Pothole Point. Allow at least two hours in this less-traveled section of the park. ✉ *Needles.*

SCENIC STOPS

Wooden Shoe Arch Overlook

VIEWPOINT | **FAMILY** | Kids enjoy looking for the tiny window in the rock that looks like a wooden shoe with a turned-up toe. If you can't find it on your own, there's a marker to help you. ✉ *Off main park road, Needles* ✣ *2 miles from visitor center.*

TRAILS

★ Cave Spring Trail

TRAIL | One of the best, most interesting trails in the park takes you past a historic cowboy camp, precontact rock art, and great views. Two wooden ladders and one short, steep stretch may make this a little daunting for the extremely young or old, but it's also a short hike (0.6 mile round-trip), features some shade, and has many notable features. *Moderate.* ✉ *Needles* ✣ *Trailhead: End of Cave Springs Rd., 2.3 miles from visitor center.*

★ Joint Trail

TRAIL | Part of the Chesler Park Loop, this trail follows a series of deep, narrow fractures in the rock. A shady spot in summer, it will give you good views of the Needles formations for which the district is named. The loop travels briefly along a four-wheel-drive road and is 11 miles round-trip; allow at least five hours to complete it. *Difficult.* ✉ *Needles* ✣ *Trailhead: Elephant Hill parking lot, 6 miles from visitor center.*

Pothole Point Trail

TRAIL | Microscopic creatures lie dormant in pools that fill only after rare rainstorms. When the rains do come, some eggs hatch within hours and life becomes visible. If you're lucky, you'll hit Pothole Point after a storm. The dramatic views of the Needles and Six Shooter Peak make this easy, 0.6-mile round-trip worthwhile. Plan for about 45 minutes. There's no shade, so wear a hat and take plenty of water. ✉ *Off main road, Needles* ✣ *5 miles from visitor center.*

Slickrock Trail

TRAIL | Wear a hat and carry plenty of water if you're on this trail—you won't find any shade along the 2.4-mile round-trip trek. This is the rare frontcountry site where you might spot one of the few remaining native herds of bighorn sheep in the national park system. Nice panoramic views. *Easy.* ✉ *Needles* ✣ *Trailhead: Main park road, 6 miles from visitor center.*

VISITOR CENTER

Needles District Visitor Center

INFO CENTER | This gorgeous building is 34 miles from U.S. 191 via Highway 211, near the park entrance. Needles is remote, so it's worth stopping to inquire about road, weather, and park conditions. You can also watch the interesting orientation film, refill water bottles, and get books, trail maps, and other information. ✉ *Off Hwy. 211, Needles* ☎ *435/259–4711* ⏲ *Closed late Nov.–early Mar.*

Maze

The most remote district of the park, the Maze is hours away from any town and is accessible only via high-clearance, four-wheel-drive vehicles. A trip here should not be taken lightly. Many of the hikes are considered some of the most dangerous in the world, and self-sufficiency is critical. But the few who do choose to visit this wild tangle of rock and desert are handsomely rewarded with unforgettable views and a silent solitude that's hard to find anywhere else. Plan to spend at least several days here, and bring all the water, food, and gas you'll need.

Sights

VISITOR CENTER

Hans Flat Ranger Station

INFO CENTER | Only experienced and intrepid visitors will likely ever visit this remote outpost—on a dirt road 46 miles east of Highway 24 in Hanksville. The office is a trove of books, maps, and other documents about the unforgiving Maze District of Canyonlands, but rangers will strongly dissuade any inexperienced off-road drivers and backpackers to proceed into this truly rugged wilderness. There's a pit toilet, but no water, food, or services of any kind. If you're headed for the backcountry, permits cost $30 per group for up to 14 days. Rangers offer guided hikes in Horseshoe Canyon on most weekends in spring and fall. ■ TIP→ **Call the ranger station for road conditions leading to Horseshoe Canyon/ Hans Flat, as rain can make travel difficult.** ✉ *Jct. of Recreation Rds. 777 and 633, Maze* ☎ *435/259–2652.*

Horseshoe Canyon

Remote Horseshoe Canyon is not contiguous with the rest of Canyonlands National Park. Added to the park in 1971, it has what may be America's most significant surviving examples of rock art. While the canyon can usually be accessed by two-wheel drive vehicles via a graded dirt road, it's still 2½ hours from Moab. And the road conditions can change abruptly, so visitors without a four-wheel drive vehicle should always consult the park's road conditions hotline before departing. Rangers lead hikes here in the spring and fall.

Sights

Horseshoe Canyon Trail
TRAIL | This remote region of the park is accessible by dirt road, and only in good weather. Park at the lip of the canyon and hike 7 miles round trip to the Great Gallery, considered by some to be the most significant rock-art panel in North America. Ghostly life-size figures in the Barrier Canyon style populate the amazing panel. The hike is moderately strenuous, with a 700-foot descent. Allow at least six hours for the trip and take a gallon of water per person. There's no camping allowed in the canyon, although you can camp on top near the parking lot. *Difficult.* ■ TIP→ **Call Hans Flat Ranger Station before heading out, because rain can make the access road a muddy mess.** ✉ *Horseshoe Canyon* ✣ *Trailhead: 32 miles east of Hwy. 24.*

Activities

BIKING

Mountain bikers from all over the world like to brag that they've conquered the 100 miles of White Rim Road. The trail's fame is well deserved: it traverses steep roads, broken rock, and dramatic ledges, as well as long stretches that wind through the canyons and look down onto others. If you're biking White Rim without an outfitter, you'll need careful planning, vehicle support, and much sought-after backcountry reservations. Permits are available no more than four months, and no less than two days, prior to permit start date. There is a 15-person, three-vehicle limit for groups. Day-use permits are also required and can be obtained at the Island in the Sky visitor center or reserved 24 hours in advance through the park's website. Follow the turn-off about 1 mile from the entrance, then 11 miles further along Shafer Trail in Island in the Sky.

In addition to the company listed below, **Rim Tours** and **Western Spirit Cycling Adventures** offer tours in both Arches and Canyonlands.

Magpie Cycling
BICYCLING | Professional guides and mountain biking instructors lead groups (or lone riders) on daylong and multiday bike trips exploring the Moab region's most memorable terrain, including the White Rim, Needles, and the Maze. If you need to rent a bike, Magpie can meet you at its preferred shop, Poison Spider Bicycles (☎ *800/635–1792* 🌐 *poisonspiderbicycles.com*). ✉ *Moab* ☎ *435/259–4464* 🌐 *www.magpiecycling.com* 🎫 *Day tours from $150, multiday from $875.*

BOATING AND RAFTING

In Labyrinth Canyon, north of the park boundary, and in Stillwater Canyon, in the Island in the Sky District, the river is quiet and calm and there's plenty of shoreside camping. The Island in the Sky leg of the Colorado River, from Moab to its confluence with the Green River and downstream a few more miles to Spanish Bottom, is ideal for both canoeing and for rides with an outfitter in a large, stable jet boat. If you want to take a self-guided flat-water float trip in the park you must obtain a $30 permit, which you have to request by mail or fax. Make your upstream travel arrangements with a shuttle company before you request a permit. For permits, contact the reservation office at park headquarters (☎ *435/259–4351*).

Oars
WHITE-WATER RAFTING | FAMILY | This well-regarded outfitter can take you for several days of rafting the Colorado, Green, and San Juan rivers. Hiking/interpretive trips are available in Canyonlands and Arches. ✉ *Moab* ☎ *435/259–5865, 800/346–6277* 🌐 *www.oars.com/utah* *From $109.*

Sheri Griffith Expeditions
BOATING | FAMILY | In addition to trips through the white water of Cataract, Westwater, and Desolation canyons, on the Colorado and Green rivers, this company also offers specialty expeditions for women, writers, photographers, and families. One of their more luxurious expeditions features dinners cooked by a professional chef and served on linen-covered tables. Cots and other sleeping amenities also make roughing it a little more comfortable. ✉ *2231 S. U.S. 191, Moab* ☎ *435/259–8229, 800/332–2439* 🌐 *www.griffithexp.com* *From $185.*

CAMPING

Canyonlands campgrounds are some of the most beautiful in the national park system. At the Needles District, campers will enjoy fairly private campsites tucked against red rock walls and dotted with pinyon and juniper trees. At Island in the Sky, starry nights and spectacular vistas make the small campground an intimate treasure. Hookups are not available in either of the park's campgrounds; however, some sites are long enough to accommodate units up to 28 feet long.

Needles Campground. The defining features of the camp sites at Squaw Flat are house-size red rock formations, which provide some shade, offer privacy from adjacent campers, and make this one of the more unique campgrounds in the national park system. ✉ *Off main road, about 3 miles from park entrance, Needles* ☎ *435/259–4711*.

Willow Flat Campground. From this little campground on a mesa top, you can walk to spectacular views of the Green River. Most sites have a bit of shade from juniper trees. ✉ *Off main park road, about 7 miles from park entrance, Island in the Sky* ☎ *435/259–4712*.

EDUCATIONAL PROGRAMS

Just like borrowing a book from a library, kids can check out an **Explorer Pack** filled with tools for learning. The sturdy backpack includes binoculars, a magnifying glass, and a three-ring binder full of activities. These are available at Needles and Island in the Sky visitor centers.

Kids of all ages can also pick up a **Junior Ranger** booklet at the visitor centers. It's full of puzzles, word games, and fun facts about the park and its wildlife. To earn the Junior Ranger badge, they must complete several activities in the booklet.

Grand View Point Overlook Talk
ORIENTATION | FAMILY | Spring through fall, rangers present interpretive programs at Grand View Point about the geology that created Utah's Canyonlands. ✉ *Grand View Point, Island in the Sky*.

FOUR-WHEELING

Nearly 200 miles of challenging back-country roads lead to campsites, trailheads, and natural and cultural features in Canyonlands. All of the roads require high-clearance, four-wheel-drive vehicles, and many are inappropriate for inexperienced drivers. The 100-mile White Rim Trail, for example, can be extremely challenging, so make sure that your four-wheel-drive skills are well honed and that you are capable of making basic vehicle repairs. Carry at least one full-size spare tire, extra gas, extra water, a shovel, a high-lift jack, and—October through April—chains for all four tires. Double-check to see that your vehicle is in top-notch condition, for you definitely don't want to break down in the interior of the park: towing expenses can exceed $1,000.

Day-use permits, available at the park visitor centers or 24 hours in advance through the park website, are required for motorized and bicycle trips on the Elephant Hill and White Rim trails. For overnight four-wheeling trips, you must purchase a $30 permit, which you can reserve no more than four months and no fewer than two days in advance by contacting the Backcountry Reservations Office (☎ *435/259–4351*). Cyclists share all roads, so be aware and cautious of their presence. Vehicular traffic traveling uphill has the right-of-way. Check at the visitor center for current road conditions before taking off into the backcountry. You must carry a washable, reusable toilet with you in the Maze District and carry out all waste.

HIKING

At Canyonlands National Park you can immerse yourself in the intoxicating colors, smells, and textures of the desert. ⚠ **Make sure to bring water and electrolytes, as dehydration is the number-one cause of search-and-rescue calls here.**

What's Nearby

Moab, the major gateway to both Arches and Canyonlands national parks, abounds with outfitters, shops, restaurants, and lodging options—see the Arches National Park chapter for more on this bustling, free-spirited hub of outdoor recreation. A handful of smaller communities south of Moab along U.S. 191 are closer than Moab to the Needles District and contain a smattering of amenities.

Roughly 55 miles south of Moab, **Monticello** is less than an hour from the Needles District and lies at 7,000 feet elevation, making it a cool summer refuge from desert heat. In winter it gets downright cold and sometimes receives heavy snow; the Abajo Mountains rise to 11,360 feet to the west of town. Monticello has a few basic motels and restaurants and is a good halfway point between Moab and Colorado's Mesa Verde National Park. Tiny **Blanding,** 20 miles south of Monticello, has a few bare-bones motels and prides itself on old-fashioned conservative values—it's a dry town, so alcohol sales are prohibited. It's the gateway to Edge of the Cedars State Park, Hovenweep National Monument, Natural Bridges Natural Monument, Grand Gulch, and the eastern end of Lake Powell. About 25 miles south of Blanding, tiny **Bluff** has a couple of the region's most appealing lodging and dining options and is an excellent gateway for Hovenweep, exploring the San Juan River, and visiting Monument Valley and the northern edge of the Navajo Nation.

Chapter 12

CAPITOL REEF NATIONAL PARK

Updated by
Shelley Arenas

Camping	Hotels	Activities	Scenery	Crowds
★★☆☆☆	★★☆☆☆	★★★★☆	★★★★★	★★☆☆☆

WELCOME TO CAPITOL REEF NATIONAL PARK

TOP REASONS TO GO

★ **The Waterpocket Fold:** See an excellent example of a monocline—a fold in the Earth's crust with one very steep side in an area that is otherwise horizontal. This one's almost 100 miles long.

★ **Fewer crowds:** Although visitation has nearly doubled (to more than 1.2 million per year) since 2011, Capitol Reef is less crowded than nearby parks, such as Zion and Bryce Canyon.

★ **Fresh fruit:** Pick apples, pears, apricots, and peaches in season at the pioneer-planted orchards at historic Fruita. These trees still produce plenty of fruit.

★ **Rock art:** View pictographs and petroglyphs left by Native Americans who lived in this area from AD 300 to 1300.

★ **Pioneer artifacts:** Buy tools and utensils similar to those used by Mormon pioneers at the Gifford Homestead.

1 **Fruita.** This historic pioneer village is at the heart of what most people see of Capitol Reef. The one and only park visitor center nearby is the place to get travel and weather information and maps. Scenic Drive, through Capitol Gorge, provides a view of the Golden Throne.

2 **Scenic Drive.** Winding 8 miles through the park, this aptly named road is the best way to get an overview of Capitol Reef's highlights, and it's the most accessible for all vehicles. It takes about 90 minutes to drive to the end and back, but you'll want to take your time with so many interesting sights to see along the way.

3 **Cathedral Valley.** The views are stunning and the silence deafening in the park's remote northern section. High-clearance vehicles are required, as is crossing the Fremont River. Driving in this valley is next to impossible when the Cathedral Valley Road is wet, so ask at the visitor center about current weather and road conditions.

4 **Muley Twist Canyon.** At the southern reaches of the park, this canyon is accessed via Notom-Bullfrog Road from the north, and Burr Trail Road from the west and southeast. High-clearance vehicles are required for Upper Muley and Strike Valley Overlook.

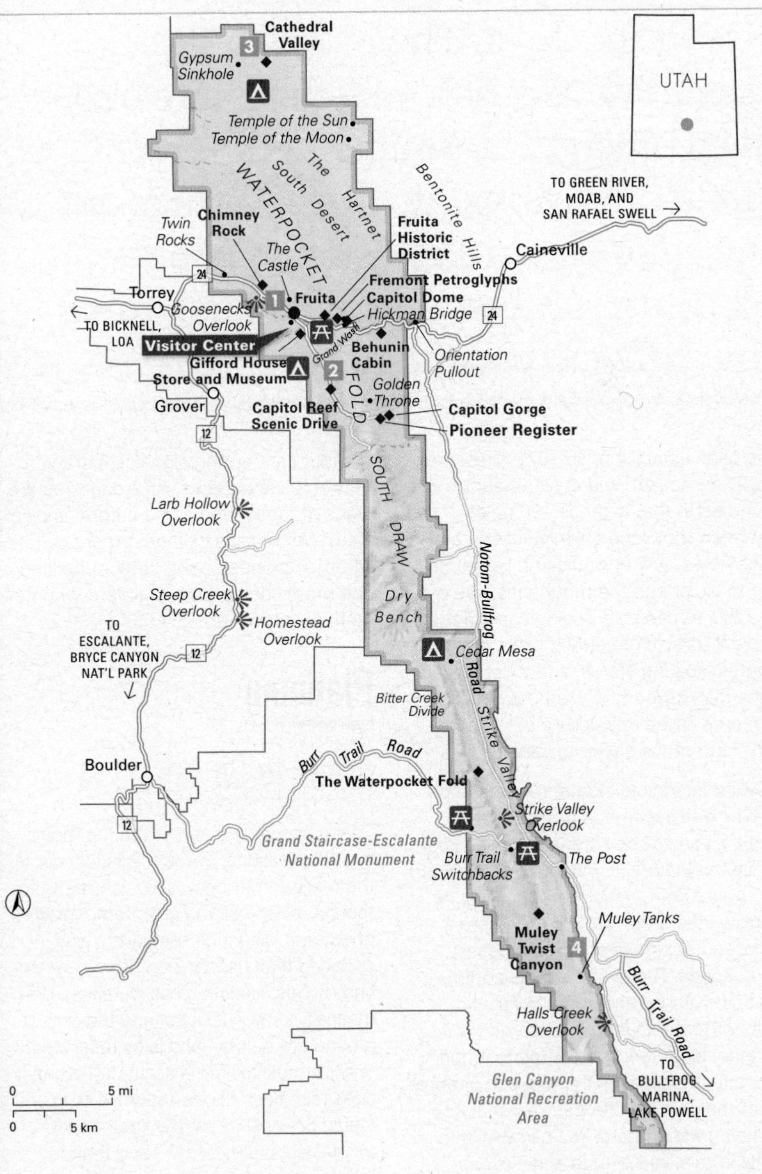
Cathedral Valley
3
Gypsum Sinkhole
Temple of the Sun
Temple of the Moon
The South Desert
The Hartnet
WATERPOCKET
Bentonite Hills
UTAH
TO GREEN RIVER, MOAB, AND SAN RAFAEL SWELL
Twin Rocks
Chimney Rock
The Castle
Fruita Historic District
Caineville
24
Fremont Petroglyphs
Torrey
1
Fruita
Capitol Dome
Goosenecks Overlook
Hickman Bridge
TO BICKNELL, LOA
Visitor Center
Grand Wash
Behunin Cabin
Orientation Pullout
Gifford House Store and Museum
2
FOLD
Golden Throne
Grover
Capitol Reef Scenic Drive
Capitol Gorge
Pioneer Register
12
SOUTH DRAW
Larb Hollow Overlook
Notom-Bullfrog Road
Steep Creek Overlook
Homestead Overlook
Dry Bench
TO ESCALANTE, BRYCE CANYON NAT'L PARK
Cedar Mesa
Bitter Creek Divide
Strike Valley
Burr Trail Road
Boulder
The Waterpocket Fold
Strike Valley Overlook
Grand Staircase-Escalante National Monument
Burr Trail Switchbacks
The Post
Muley Tanks
Muley Twist Canyon
4
Burr Trail Road
Halls Creek Overlook
TO BULLFROG MARINA, LAKE POWELL
Glen Canyon National Recreation Area
0 5 mi
0 5 km

Capitol Reef National Park is a natural kaleidoscopic feast for the eyes, with colors more dramatic than anywhere else in the West. The Moenkopi rock formation is a rich, red-chocolate hue; deep blue-green juniper and pinyon stand out against it. Sunset brings out the colors in an explosion of copper, platinum, and orange, then dusk turns the cliffs purple and blue.

The park, established in 1971, preserves the Waterpocket Fold, a giant wrinkle in the earth that extends 100 miles between Thousand Lake Mountain and Lake Powell. When you climb high onto the rocks or into the mountains, you can see this remarkable geologic wonder and the jumble of colorful cliffs, massive domes, soaring spires, and twisting canyons that surround it. It's no wonder early pioneers called this part of the country the "land of the sleeping rainbow."

Beyond incredible sights, the fragrance of pine and sage rises from the earth, and canyon wrens serenade you as you sit by the water. Flowing across the heart of Capitol Reef is the Fremont River, a narrow little creek that can turn into a swollen, raging torrent during desert flash floods. The river sustains cottonwoods, wildlife, and verdant valleys rich with fruit. During the harvest, your sensory experience is complete when you bite into a perfect ripe peach or apple from the park's orchards. Your soul, too, will be gratified here. You can walk the trails in relative solitude and—except during busier periods—enjoy the beauty without confronting significant crowds on the roads or paths. All around you are signs of those who came before: ancient Native Americans of the Fremont culture, Mormon pioneers who settled the land, and other courageous explorers who traveled the canyons.

Planning

When to Go

Spring and early summer are the most bustling seasons. Some folks clear out in the midsummer heat, and then return for the apple harvest and crisp temperatures of autumn. Although the park is less crowded than nearby Zion, Bryce Canyon, and Arches, visitation has increased dramatically in recent years, and the campground fills quickly (and is by reservation only). Annual rainfall is scant, but when it does rain, flash floods can wipe out park roads. Snowfall is usually light. Sudden, short-lived snowstorms—and thunderstorms—are not uncommon in the spring.

AVERAGE HIGH/LOW TEMPERATURES					
JAN.	**FEB.**	**MAR.**	**APR.**	**MAY**	**JUNE**
41/20	47/26	58/34	66/40	75/48	87/59
JULY	**AUG.**	**SEPT.**	**OCT.**	**NOV.**	**DEC.**
91/65	88/63	80/55	66/44	51/31	41/21

FESTIVALS AND EVENTS

Harvest Time Scarecrow Festival. Events for this month-long celebration marking the end of another busy season are held throughout Wayne County. In addition to a scarecrow contest, there are plenty of family-friendly events, including live music, arts and crafts, pumpkin carving, and a Halloween party. 🌐 *www.entradainstitute.org.*

Wayne County Fair. The great American county fair tradition is at its finest in Loa in mid-August. A demolition derby, rodeo, horse shows, and a parade are all part of the fun. You'll also find crafts such as handmade quilts, agricultural exhibits, children's games, and plenty of good food. 🌐 *waynecountyutah.org.*

Getting Here and Around

AIR

The nearest major airports are in Salt Lake City and Las Vegas, about 3½ and 5½ hours away by car, respectively. St. George Regional Airport (3½ hours away) is a handy, smaller airport with direct flights from several major cities in the West, Cedar City Municipal Airport (2¾ hours) has direct daily service on Delta from Salt Lake City, and Canyonlands Field Airport in Moab (2 hours away) has direct daily service on United Airlines from Denver.

CAR

You can approach Capitol Reef country from several routes, including highways 24 and 72 from Interstate 70 (and Moab), Highway 12 from Bryce Canyon National Park, and Highway 20 to U.S. 89 to Highway 62 from Interstate 15. All are well-maintained, safe roads that bisect rich agricultural communities steeped in Mormon history (especially in the nearby towns of Bicknell and Loa). Highway 24 runs across the middle of Capitol Reef National Park, offering scenic views the entire way.

Inspiration

The Capitol Reef Reader, edited by Stephen Trimble, shares writings about the park by almost 50 authors, and nearly 100 photos, many taken by the editor during dacades of hiking Capitol Reef's trails.

Capitol Reef: Canyon Country Eden, by Rose Houk, is an award-winning collection of photographs and lyrical essays on the park.

Dwellers of the Rainbow: Fremont Culture in Capitol Reef National Park, by Rose Houk, offers a brief background of the Fremont culture in Capitol Reef.

Red Rock Eden, by George Davidson, tells the story of historic Fruita, its settlements, and its orchards.

Park Essentials

ACCESSIBILITY

Capitol Reef doesn't have many trails that are accessible to people in wheelchairs. The visitor center, museum, film, and restrooms are all accessible, as is the campground amphitheater where evening programs are held. The Fruita Campground Loop C restroom is accessible; so is the boardwalk to the petroglyph panel on Highway 24, 1.2 miles east of the visitor center.

PARK FEES AND PERMITS

There is no fee to enter the park, but it's $20 per vehicle (or $10 per bicycle and $15 per motorcycle) to travel on Scenic Drive beyond Fruita Campground; this fee is good for one week, paid via the "honor system" at a drop box versus a staffed entry gate. Backcountry camping permits are free; pick them up at the visitor center. An annual pass that allows unlimited access to Scenic Drive is $35.

PARK HOURS

The park is open 24/7 year-round. It's in the Mountain time zone.

CELL PHONE RECEPTION

Cell phone reception is nearly nonexistent in the park, although you may pick up a weak signal in a few spots. Pay phones are at the visitor center and at Fruita Campground.

Hotels

There are no lodging options within Capitol Reef, but clean and comfortable accommodations for all budgets exist just west in nearby Torrey, and not far beyond in Bicknell and Loa. There are also a couple of options east of the park, in Hanksville. Book well ahead if visiting March through October.

Restaurants

Inside Capitol Reef you won't find any restaurants, though in summer there's a small store selling baked goods and ice cream. More dining options exist close by in Torrey, where you can find everything from creative Southwestern fusion cuisine to basic hamburger joints serving consistently good food.

Visitor Information

PARK CONTACT INFORMATION Capitol Reef National Park. ✉ *Off Hwy. 24* ☎ *435/425–3791* 🌐 *www.nps.gov/care.*

Fruita

In the 1880s, Nels Johnson became the first homesteader in the Fremont River Valley, building his home near the confluence of Sulphur Creek and the Fremont River. Other Mormon settlers followed and established small farms and orchards, creating the village of Junction. The orchards thrived, and by 1900 the name was changed to Fruita. The orchards, less than a mile from the visitor center, are preserved and protected as a Rural Historic District.

GEOLOGICAL LANDMARKS

Capitol Dome

NATURE SITE | One of the rock formations that gave the park its name, this giant sandstone dome is visible in the vicinity of the Hickman Bridge trailhead, 1.9 miles east of the visitor center. ✉ *Hwy. 24, Capitol Reef National Park.*

Chimney Rock

NATURE SITE | Even in a landscape of spires, cliffs, and knobs, this deep-red landform, 3.9 miles west of the visitor center, is unmistakable. ✉ *Hwy. 24, Capitol Reef National Park.*

HISTORIC SIGHTS

Behunin Cabin

BUILDING | FAMILY | Elijah Cutler Behunin used blocks of sandstone to build this cabin in 1882. Floods in the lowlands made life too difficult, and he moved before the turn of that century. The house, 5.9 miles east of the visitor center, is empty, but you can peek through the window to see the interior. ✉ *Hwy. 24, Capitol Reef National Park.*

Fremont Petroglyphs

NATIVE SITE | Between AD 300 and 1300, the Capitol Reef area was occupied by Native Americans who were eventually referred to by archaeologists as the Fremont, named after the Fremont River

Did You Know?

The 3.5-mile round-trip trek up to Chimney Rock has some steep switch-backs, but the journey yields panoramic views. The trailhead is 3 miles from the park visitor center, near the entrance. It is forbidden to rock climb on it.

that flows through the park. A nice stroll along a boardwalk bridge, 1.1 miles east of the visitor center, allows close-up views of ancient rock art, which can be identified by the large trapezoidal figures often depicted wearing headdresses and ear baubles. ✉ *Hwy. 24, Capitol Reef National Park.*

TRAILS

★ Chimney Rock Trail

TRAIL | You're almost sure to see ravens drifting on thermal winds around the deep-red Mummy Cliff that rings the base of this trail. This loop trail begins with a steep climb to a rim above dramatic Chimney Rock. The trail is 3.6 miles round-trip, with a 590-foot elevation change. No shade. Use caution during monsoon storms due to lightning hazards. Allow three to four hours. *Moderate–Difficult.* ✉ *Capitol Reef National Park* ✣ *Trailhead: Hwy. 24, about 3 miles west of visitor center.*

Fremont River Trail

TRAIL | What starts as a quiet little stroll beside the river turns into an adventure. The first ½ mile of the trail wanders past orchards next to the Fremont River. After you pass through a narrow gate, the trail changes personality and you're in for a steep climb on an exposed ledge with drop-offs. The views at the top of the 480-foot ascent are worth it. It's 2 miles round-trip; allow two hours. *Moderate.* ✉ *Capitol Reef National Park* ✣ *Trailhead: Near amphitheater off Loop C of Fruita Campground, about 1 mile from visitor center.*

Golden Throne Trail

TRAIL | As you hike to the base of the Golden Throne, you may be lucky enough to see one of the park's elusive desert bighorn sheep, but you're more likely to spot their split-hoof tracks. The trail is about 2 miles of gradual rise with some steps and drop-offs. The Golden Throne is hidden until you near the end of the trail, then suddenly you see the huge sandstone monolith. If you hike near sundown, the throne burns gold. The round-trip hike is 4 miles and takes two to three hours. *Difficult.* ✉ *Capitol Reef National Park* ✣ *Trailhead: At end of Capitol Gorge Rd., 10 miles south of visitor center.*

Goosenecks Trail

TRAIL | This nice little walk gives you a good introduction to the land surrounding Capitol Reef. You'll enjoy the dizzying views from the overlook. It's only 0.2 miles round-trip to the overlook and a very easy walk. *Easy.* ✉ *Hwy. 24, about 3 miles west of visitor center, Capitol Reef National Park.*

Hickman Bridge Trail

TRAIL | This trail leads to a natural bridge of Kayenta sandstone, with a 133-foot opening carved by intermittent flash floods. Early on, the route climbs a set of steps along the Fremont River. The trail splits, leading along the right-hand branch to a strenuous uphill climb to the Rim Overlook and Navajo Knobs. Stay to your left to see the bridge, and you'll encounter a moderate up-and-down trail. Up the wash on your way to the bridge is a Fremont granary on the right side of the small canyon. Allow about two hours for the 1.8-mile round-trip. Expect lots of company. *Moderate.* ✉ *Capitol Reef National Park* ✣ *Trailhead: Hwy. 24, 2 miles east of visitor center.*

Sunset Point Trail

TRAIL | The trail starts from the same parking lot as the Goosenecks Trail, on your way into the park about 3.3 miles west of the visitor center. Benches along this easy, 0.8-mile round-trip invite you to sit and meditate surrounded by the colorful desert. At the trail's end, you will be rewarded with broad vistas into the park; it's even better at sunset. *Easy.* ✉ *Hwy. 24, Capitol Reef National Park.*

SCENIC DRIVES

★ Utah Scenic Byway 24

SCENIC DRIVE | For 75 miles between Loa and Hanksville, you'll cut right through Capitol Reef National Park. Colorful rock formations in all their hues of red, cream, pink, gold, and deep purple extend from one end of the route to the other. The closer you get to the park the more colorful the landscape becomes. The vibrant rock finally gives way to lush green hills and the mountains west of Loa.

VISITOR CENTERS

Capitol Reef Visitor Center

INFO CENTER | FAMILY | Watch a park movie, talk with rangers, or peruse the many books, maps, and materials for sale in the bookstore. Towering over the center (11 miles east of Torrey) is the Castle, one of the park's most prominent rock formations. ✉ *Scenic Dr. at Hwy. 24, Capitol Reef National Park* ☎ *435/425–3791* 🌐 *www.nps.gov/care.*

Scenic Drive

This 8-mile road, simply called Scenic Drive, starts at the visitor center and winds its way through the Fruita Historic District and colorful sandstone cliffs into Capitol Gorge; a side road, Grand Wash Road, provides access into the canyon. At Capitol Gorge, the canyon walls become steep and impressive but the route becomes unpaved for about the last 2 miles, and road conditions may vary due to weather and usage. Check with the visitor center before setting out.

Sights

GEOLOGICAL LANDMARKS

The Waterpocket Fold

NATURE SITE | A giant wrinkle in the earth extends almost 100 miles between Thousand Lake Mountain and Lake Powell. You can glimpse the fold by driving south on Scenic Drive after it branches off Highway 24, past the Fruita Historic District. For complete immersion enter the park via the 36-mile Burr Trail from Boulder. Roads through the southernmost reaches of the park are largely unpaved. The area is accessible to most vehicles during dry weather, but check with the visitor center for current road conditions. ✉ *Capitol Reef National Park.*

HISTORIC SIGHTS

Gifford House Store and Museum

NATIONAL/STATE PARK | One mile south of the visitor center in a grassy meadow with the Fremont River flowing by, this is an idyllic shady spot in the Fruita Historic District for a sack lunch, complete with tables, drinking water, grills, and a convenient restroom. The store sells reproductions of pioneer tools and items made by local craftspeople; there's also locally made fruit pies and ice cream to enjoy with your picnic. ✉ *Scenic Dr., Capitol Reef National Park.*

Pioneer Register

HISTORIC SITE | Travelers passing through Capitol Gorge in the 19th and early 20th centuries etched the canyon wall with their names and the date. Directly across the canyon from the Pioneer Register and about 50 feet up are signatures etched into the canyon wall by an early United States Geologic Survey crew. Though it's illegal to write or scratch on the canyon walls today, plenty of damage has been done by vandals over the years. You can reach the register via an easy hike from the sheltered trailhead at the end of Capitol Gorge Road, 10.3 miles south of the visitor center; the register is about 10 minutes along the hike to the sandstone "tanks." ✉ *Off Scenic Dr., Capitol Reef National Park.*

SCENIC DRIVES

★ Capitol Gorge

SCENIC DRIVE | Eight miles south of the visitor center, Scenic Drive ends, at which point you can drive an unpaved spur road into Capitol Gorge. The narrow, twisting road on the floor of the gorge was a route for pioneer wagons traversing this part of Utah starting in the 1860s. After every flash flood, pioneers would laboriously clear the route so wagons could continue to go through. The gorge became the main automobile route in the area until 1962, when Highway 24 was built. The short drive to the end of the road has striking views of the surrounding cliffs and leads to one of the park's most popular walks: the hiking trail to the water-holding "tanks" eroded into the sandstone. ✉ *Scenic Dr., Capitol Reef National Park.*

TRAILS

★ Capitol Gorge Trail and the Tanks

NATIONAL/STATE PARK | Starting at the Pioneer Register, about a ½ mile from the Capitol Gorge parking lot, is a ½-mile trail that climbs to the Tanks—holes in the sandstone, formed by erosion, that hold water after it rains. After a scramble up about ¼ mile of steep trail with cliff drop-offs, you can look down into the Tanks and see a natural bridge below the lower tank. Including the walk to the Pioneer Register, allow an hour or more for this interesting hike, one of the park's most popular. *Moderate.* ✉ *Capitol Reef National Park* ✣ *Trailhead: At end of Scenic Dr., 10 miles south of visitor center.*

Cohab Canyon Trail

TRAIL | Find rock wrens and Western pipistrelles (canyon bats) on this trail. One end is directly across from the Fruita Campground on Scenic Drive; the other is across from the Hickman Bridge parking lot. The first ¼ mile from Fruita is strenuous, but the walk becomes easier except for turnoffs to the overlooks, which are short. You'll find miniature arches, skinny side canyons, and honeycombed patterns on canyon walls where the wrens make nests. The trail is 3.2 miles round-trip to the Hickman Bridge parking lot (two to three hours). The Overlook Trail adds 1 mile. Allow two hours to overlooks and back. *Moderate.* ✉ *Capitol Reef National Park* ✣ *Trailheads: Scenic Dr., about 1 mile south of visitor center, or Hwy. 24, about 2 miles east of visitor center.*

Grand Wash Trail

TRAIL | At the end of unpaved Grand Wash Road you can continue on foot through the canyon to its end at Highway 24. This flat hike takes you through a wide wash between canyon walls, and is an excellent place to study the geology up close. The round-trip hike is 4.4 miles; allow two to three hours for your walk. Check at the ranger station for flash-flood warnings before entering the wash. *Easy.* ✉ *Capitol Reef National Park* ✣ *Trailhead: At Hwy. 24, east of Hickman Bridge parking lot, or at end of Grand Wash Rd., off Scenic Dr. about 5 miles from visitor center.*

Cathedral Valley

This primitive, rugged area was named for its sandstone geological features that are reminiscent of Gothic cathedrals. Visiting is quite the backroad adventure, so not many people make the effort to drive on roads that some have called brutal. But if you have the right vehicle and an adventurous spirit, the rewards of seeing ancient natural wonders should be worth it. The selenite crystals of Glass Mountain attract rockhounds for a closer look, but no collecting is allowed. Sunset and sunrise at the Temple of the Sun and Temple of the Moon monoliths are especially colorful and photogenic.

Sights

SCENIC DRIVES

Cathedral Valley/North District Loop

TRAIL | The north end of Capitol Reef, along this backcountry road, is filled with towering monoliths, panoramic vistas, water crossings, and a stark desert landscape. The area is remote and the road through it unpaved, so do not enter without a suitable mountain bike or high-clearance vehicle, some planning, and a cell phone (although reception is virtually nonexistent). The trail through the valley is a 58-mile loop that you can begin at River Ford Road, 11¾ miles east of the visitor center off Highway 24; allow half a day. If your time is limited, you can tour only the Caineville Wash Road, which takes about two hours by ATV or four-wheel drive vehicle. If you are planning a multiday trip, there's a primitive campground about halfway through the loop. Pick up a self-guided tour brochure at the visitor center. ✉ *River Ford Rd., off Hwy. 24, Capitol Reef National Park.*

Muley Twist Canyon

This long canyon runs 12 miles north to south at the south end of park. It was used as a pass by pioneers traveling by wagon through the Waterpocket Fold and got its name because it was so narrow that it could "twist a mule." Park visitors typically explore Lower Muley Twist Canyon on long day hikes or overnight (a permit is required for overnight camping). Upper Muley Twist Canyon has some shorter trails, including a one-mile hike to an overlook. Trails are not maintained, so bring a map, along with plenty of water as the area is quite hot in summer. High-clearance vehicles are necessary for most of the roads.

Activities

BIKING

Bicycles are allowed only on established roads in the park. Highway 24 is a state highway and receives a substantial amount of through traffic, so it's not the best place to pedal. Scenic Drive is better, but the road is narrow, and you have to contend with drivers dazed by the beautiful surroundings. In fact, it's a good idea to traverse it in the morning or evening when traffic is reduced, or in the off-season. Four-wheel-drive roads are certainly less traveled, but they are often sandy, rocky, and steep. The Cathedral Valley/North District Loop is popular with mountain bikers (but also with four-wheelers). You cannot ride your bicycle in washes or on hiking trails.

South Draw Road

BICYCLING | This is a very strenuous but picturesque ride that traverses dirt, sand, and rocky surfaces, and crosses several creeks that may be muddy. It's not recommended in winter or spring because of deep snow at higher elevations. The route starts at an elevation of 8,500 feet on Boulder Mountain, 13 miles south of Torrey, and ends 15¾ miles later at 5,500 feet in the Pleasant Creek parking area at the end of Scenic Drive. ✉ *Bowns Reservoir Rd. and Hwy. 12, Capitol Reef National Park.*

CAMPING

Campgrounds—both the highly convenient Fruita Campground and the backcountry sites—in Capitol Reef fill up fast between March and October. Most of the area's state parks have camping facilities, and the region's two national forests offer many wonderful sites.

Cathedral Valley Campground. This small (just six sites), basic (no water, pit toilet), no-fee campground in the park's remote northern district touts sprawling views, but the bumpy road there is hard to navigate. ✉ *Hartnet Junction, on Caineville Wash Rd.* ☎ *435/425–3791.*

Cedar Mesa Campground. Wonderful views of the Waterpocket Fold and Henry Mountains surround this primitive (pit toilet, no water), no-fee campground with five sites in the park's southern district. ✉ *Notom-Bullfrog Rd., 22 miles south of Hwy. 24* ☎ *435/425–3791.*

Fruita Campground. Near the orchards and the Fremont River, the park's developed (flush toilets, running water), shady campground is a great place to call home for a few days. The sites require a $20 nightly fee, and those nearest the Fremont River or the orchards are the most coveted. ✉ *Scenic Dr., about 1 mile south of visitor center* ☎ *435/425–3791* 🌐 *www.recreation.gov.*

EDUCATIONAL PROGRAMS

RANGER PROGRAMS

In summer, ranger programs are offered at no charge. You can obtain current information about ranger talks and other park events at the visitor center or campground bulletin boards.

Evening Program. Learn about Capitol Reef's geology, Native American cultures, wildlife, and more at the campground amphitheater about a mile from the visitor center. Programs typically begin around sunset. See the schedule at the visitor center. 🌐 *www.nps.gov/care/planyourvisit/ranger-programs.htm.*

Junior Ranger Program. Each child who participates in this self-guided, year-round program completes a combination of activities in the Junior Ranger booklet and attends a ranger program or watches the park movie. 🌐 *www.nps.gov/care/planyourvisit/ranger-programs.htm.*

Ranger Talks. Typically, the park offers a daily morning geology talk at the visitor center and a daily afternoon petroglyph-panel talk. Occasional geology hikes, history tours, and moon and stargazing tours are also sometimes offered. Times vary. 🌐 *www.nps.gov/care/planyourvisit/ranger-programs.htm.*

FOUR-WHEELING

You can explore Capitol Reef in a 4X4 on a number of exciting backcountry routes, but note that all vehicles must remain on designated roadways. Road conditions can vary greatly depending on recent weather patterns. The Cathedral Valley/North District Loop is popular with four-wheelers (and also with mountain bikers).

HIKING

Many park trails in Capitol Reef include steep climbs, but there are a few easy-to-moderate hikes. A short drive from the visitor center takes you to a dozen trails near the Fruita Historic District, but there are more challenging hikes in the other areas.

HORSEBACK RIDING

Many areas in the park are closed to horses and pack animals, so it's a good idea to check with the visitor center before you set out with your animals. Day use does not require a permit, but you need to get one for overnight camping with horses and pack animals.

Hondoo Rivers & Trails in Torrey runs horseback tours into the national park. Unless you ride with a park-licensed outfitter, you have to bring your own horse, as no rentals are available.

What's Nearby

The best home base for exploring Capitol Reef, the pretty town of **Torrey,** just west of the park, has lots of personality. Giant old cottonwood trees make it a shady, cool place to stay, and the townspeople are friendly and accommodating. A little farther west on Highway 24, tiny **Teasdale** is a charming settlement cradled in a cove of the Aquarius Plateau. The homes look out onto brilliantly colored cliffs and green fields. Quiet **Bicknell** lies another few miles west of Torrey. The Wayne County seat of **Loa,** 10 miles west of Torrey, was settled by pioneers in the 1870s. If you head south from Torrey instead of west, you can take a spectacular 32-mile drive along Highway 12 to **Boulder,** a town so remote that its mail was carried on horseback until 1940. Nearby is Anasazi State Park. In the opposite direction, 51 miles east, **Hanksville** is a place to stop for food and fuel—the small wayside en route to Moab also has a couple of decent budget motels.

Chapter 13

CARLSBAD CAVERNS NATIONAL PARK

Updated by
Andrew Collins

Camping ★☆☆☆☆
Hotels ★★☆☆☆
Activities ★★★☆☆
Scenery ★★★★☆
Crowds ★★★★★

WELCOME TO CARLSBAD CAVERNS NATIONAL PARK

TOP REASONS TO GO

★ **400,000 hungry bats:** From mid-May to late October, bats wing to and from the caverns in a swirling, visible tornado.

★ **Take a self-guided tour through the underworld:** Plummet 75 stories underground and step into enormous caves hung with stalactites and bristling with stalagmites.

★ **Hike through the high desert:** Several relatively uncrowded trails, including the dramatic Rattlesnake Canyon Trail, provide views of the park's stunning above-ground desert scenery.

★ **Birding at Rattlesnake Springs:** Nine-tenths of the park's 357 bird species, including roadrunners, golden eagles, and acrobatic cave swallows, visit this green desert oasis with a shaded picnic area.

★ **Living Desert Zoo and Gardens:** More preserve than zoo, this 1,500-acre state park in the nearby city of Carlsbad houses scores of rare species, including black bears, Bolson tortoises, and endangered Mexican wolves.

1 Carlsbad Cavern Aboveground. The first place to experience the park is the visitor center (and excellent museum) above the cavern, this part of the park also features scenic drives and hikes through a dramatic Chihuahuan desertscape.

2 Carlsbad Cavern Belowground. Travel 75 stories below the surface to visit the main cavern's Big Room, where you can traipse beneath a 230-foot-tall ceiling and take in immense and eerie cave formations.

3 Rattlesnake Springs and Slaughter Canyon. Reached via a different entrance, these less-visited but rewarding areas in the western half of the park are notable for their rugged canyon hikes and outstanding bird-watching.

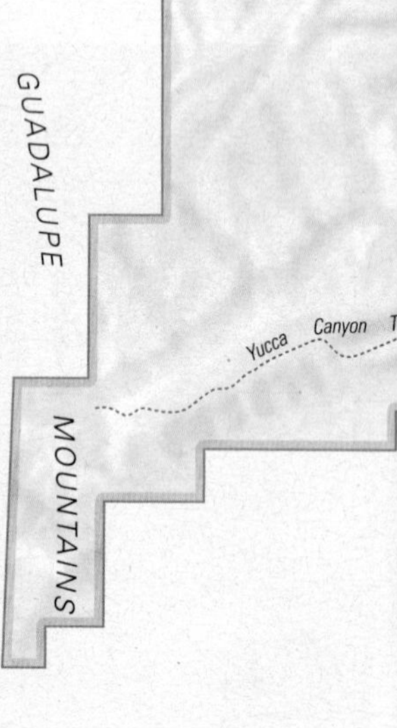

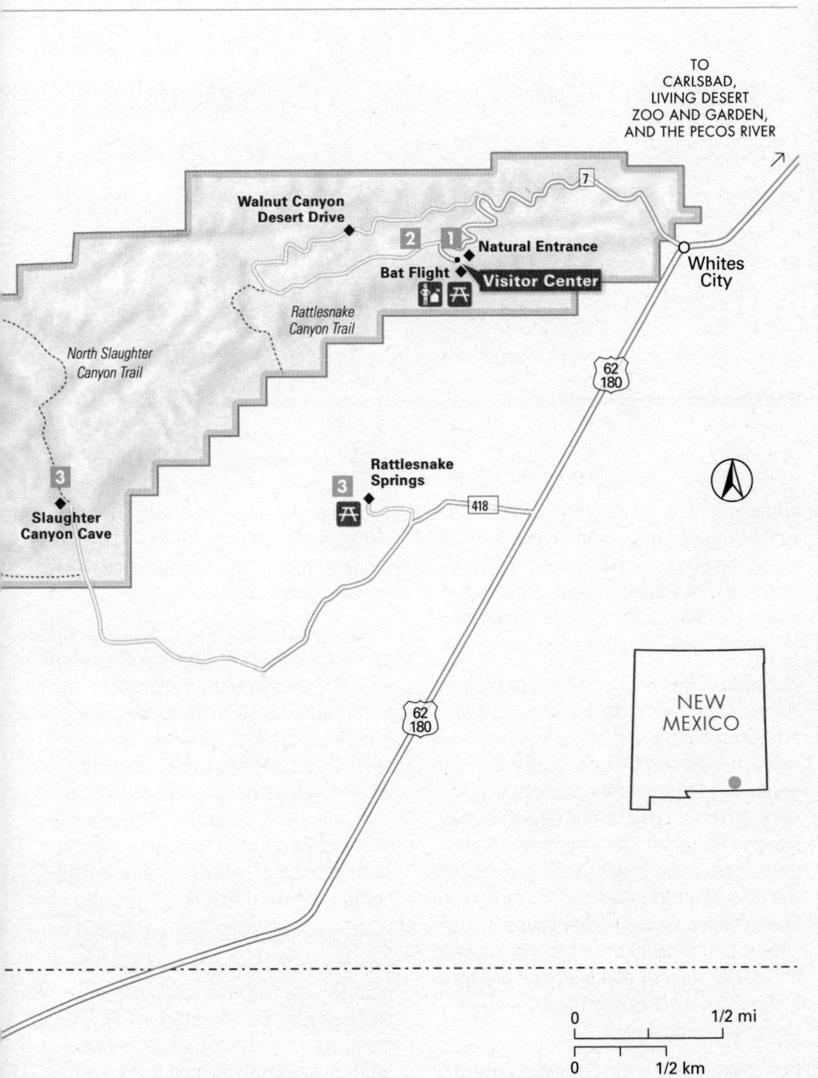
TO
CARLSBAD,
LIVING DESERT
ZOO AND GARDEN,
AND THE PECOS RIVER
7
Walnut Canyon
Desert Drive
2
1
Natural Entrance
Bat Flight
Visitor Center
Whites
City
Rattlesnake
Canyon Trail
North Slaughter
Canyon Trail
62
180
Rattlesnake
Springs
3
418
3
Slaughter
Canyon Cave
NEW
MEXICO
62
180
0
1/2 mi
0
1/2 km

On the surface, Carlsbad Caverns National Park looks deceptively like the rest of southeastern New Mexico's high desert—but all bets are off once visitors set foot in the elevator, which plunges 75 stories underground into a massive cavern, part of a network of formations located within a massive reef that formed 265 million years ago when this area was covered by a vast inland sea.

Wherever you go within the park's 46,766 acres, whether driving or hiking aboveground or touring subterranean areas open to visitors, it's impossible to fully grasp the sheer wonder and immensity of the area's unique geology. You'll never see more than a tiny fraction of the park from any given vantage point.

Carlsbad Cavern, whose 14-acre Big Room is the park's definitive must-see attraction, and one that you'll want to set aside at least three hours to explore. This eerie world beneath the surface is part silky darkness, part subterranean hallucination—its hundreds of formations alternately resemble cakes, ocean waves, and the face of a mountain troll. Explorer Jim White began exploring the caves in the 1890s, and in 1930 both the main cavern and a vast tract of aboveground canyons and mesas were designated Carlsbad Caverns National Park.

Remarkably, the main Carlsbad Cavern is but one of more than 110 limestone caves that have been identified within the park's boundaries. Most of them, including the largest and deepest (at 1,604 feet belowground), Lechuguilla, aren't open to the general public. Scientists only discovered Lechuguilla's huge network of rooms in 1986. So far they've mapped more than 145 miles of passages—and their work continues.

If you spend most of your first visit to the park exploring its subterranean caverns, you may be surprised to learn how much terrain there is to cover aboveground. Hikers can trek for miles across cactus-studded ridges and through wildlife-rich canyons—there's even a lush little oasis of cottonwood trees, Rattlesnake Springs, in the park's western section, which you reach by taking an entirely different road into the park.

Carlsbad Caverns is also one of two exceptional national parks within the vicinity. Just over the Texas border, a picturesque 45-minute drive to the southwest, you can investigate Guadalupe Mountains National Park, home to the highest peaks in the Lone Star State and miles of rugged trails.

AVERAGE HIGH/LOW TEMPERATURES					
JAN.	FEB.	MAR.	APR.	MAY	JUNE
56/33	60/36	66/42	75/50	83/58	91/64
JULY	AUG.	SEPT.	OCT.	NOV.	DEC.
91/66	89/65	83/60	75/52	64/42	58/35

Planning

When to Go

While the desert above may alternately bake or freeze, the caverns remain in the mid-50s. If you're coming to see the Brazilian free-tailed bat, arrive between spring and mid-fall, keeping in mind that hiking the park's aboveground trails can be uncomfortably hot in summer.

FESTIVAL AND EVENTS

Dawn of the Bats. The third Saturday in July each year, early risers gather at the cave's entrance to watch tens of thousands of bats return home from their nocturnal search for food. Nature walks and other special ranger programs are offered as well during this free event. 🌐 *www.nps.gov/cave.*

Getting Here and Around

AIR

The nearest full-service airports are in the Texas cities of El Paso (150 miles away) and Midland (160 miles away). Cavern City Air Terminal, between Carlsbad and the park, is served by a small regional carrier, Boutique Air, with regularly scheduled service to both Albuquerque and Dallas/Fort Worth.

CAR

The park entrance is 21 miles southwest of Carlsbad, New Mexico, and 32 miles north of Guadalupe Mountains National Park via U.S. 62/180. The ascending 7-mile Carlsbad Cavern Highway from the turnoff at Whites City (which has a gas station) is paved with pull-outs that allow scenic vistas. Be alert for wildlife crossing roadways, especially in the early morning and at night.

Inspiration

Jim White's Own Story, by early explorer Jim White, tells of this cowboy's exploits into the heart of Carlsbad Caverns before it was developed as a national park.

Edward J. Greene's *Carlsbad Caverns: The Story Behind the Scenery* provides a fascinating account of the geological story behind this strange and magical landscape.

If many of the underground scenes in the classic 1959 adventure film *Journey to the Center of the Earth* look familiar, it's because they were shot inside the Big Room deep inside Carlsbad Caverns National Park.

Park Essentials

ACCESSIBILITY

Though the park covers a huge expanse aboveground (with key areas reached by paved roads), most of the parts you'll want to see are below the surface. Trails through the most-visited portion of the main cavern are paved and well maintained, and portions of the paved Big Room trail in Carlsbad Cavern is accessible to wheelchairs. Individuals who have difficulty walking should access the Big Room via elevator. Strollers are not permitted on any trails.

PARK FEES AND PERMITS

No fee is charged to enter the aboveground portion of the park. It costs $15 to descend into Carlsbad Caverns either by elevator or through the Natural Entrance (admission is free for kids 15 and under). Costs for guided tours of other parts of the main cavern or the other cavern in the park, Slaughter Canyon Cave, range from $7 to $20 plus general admission. For guided-tour reservations go to 🌐 *www.recreation.gov* or call ☎ *877/444–6777*.

Those planning overnight hikes must obtain a free backcountry permit, and all hikers are advised to stop at the visitor center information desk for trail and park road conditions. Trails are marked by cairns (rock piles) and in some places can be tricky to follow; download or carry a good topographic map. Dogs are not allowed in the park, but a kennel is available at the park visitor center for a fee.

PARK HOURS

The park is open year-round, except Christmas Day, New Year's Day, and Thanksgiving. From Memorial Day weekend through Labor Day, access to the cavern is from 8:30 to 5; entrance tickets are sold until 4:45, with the last entry via the Natural Entrance at 4. After Labor Day until Memorial Day weekend, cavern access is from 8:30 to 3:30; entrance tickets are sold until 3:15, and the last entry via the Natural Entrance is at 2:30. Last-ticket times do sometimes change throughout the year due to maintenance and other causes—always confirm hours on the website before you arrive. Carlsbad Caverns is in the Mountain time zone.

CELL PHONE RECEPTION

Cell phone service is spotty in the park. It works best in the parking lots outside the visitor center. There's no Wi-Fi or cell service inside any caverns. Note that your cell phone may pick up a signal from towers in the adjacent Central time zone, giving you the incorrect impression that you're an hour ahead.

Restaurants

Inside the park there are just two dining options—the surface-level dining room and the underground snack bar near the elevator. Everything is reasonably priced, but food quality at the park restaurants is nothing to write home about. Outside the park, skip the mediocre eatery in nearby Whites City and drive into Carlsbad, which has plenty of good options. *Restaurant reviews have been shortened. For full information, visit Fodors.com.*

Hotels

Camping in the backcountry, at least a half mile from any trail, is your only lodging option in the park. You must obtain a backcountry camping permit at the visitor center.

Outside the park your options expand, but rates in the immediate vicinity can be steep at times due to demand by workers in the booming nearby oil-field industry—even cookie-cutter chain hotels in Carlsbad sometimes run more than $250 a night. Whites City, just outside the park's main entrance, has a very basic and affordable motel. You can often find comparable lodgings for at least 50% less than Carlsbad prices farther afield, in Artesia (an hour away) and even Roswell (a little less than two hours).

Tours

Carlsbad Caverns is famous for the beauty and breadth of its inky depths, as well as for the accessibility of some of its largest caves. All cave tours, except for the self-guided Natural Entrance and Big Room, are ranger-led, so you can count on a safe experience, even in remote caves. Depending on the difficulty of your cave selection (the Hall of the White Giant cavern is hardest to navigate), you'll need sturdy pants, hiking boots with ankle support, and some water. The fee for the Natural Entrance and Big Room is $15 and is good for three days. Guided tours have an additional fee of $7 to $20.

Ranger-Led Tours

GUIDED TOURS | FAMILY | Cavers who wish to explore both developed and wild caves can go on ranger-led tours, all of which require three AA batteries for headlamps (which will be supplied). Reservations for the five different tours (Hall of the White Giant, Lower Cave, Slaughter Canyon Cave, Left-Hand Tunnel, and King's Palace) are generally required at least a day in advance. Payment is by credit card over the phone or online. ✉ *Carlsbad Caverns National Park* ☎ *877/444–6777 for reservations* 🌐 *www.nps.gov/cave* 🎫 *From $7.*

Visitor Information

PARK CONTACT INFORMATION Carlsbad Caverns National Park. ✉ *Park Visitor Center, 727 Carlsbad Caverns Hwy., Carlsbad* ☎ *575/785–2232, 575/875–3012 bat flight schedule* 🌐 *www.nps.gov/cave.*

Carlsbad Cavern Aboveground

7 miles west of White City, 25 miles southwest of Carlsbad.

The eastern half of Carlsbad Caverns National Park, reached from U.S. 62/180 at Whites City via Carlsbad Caverns Highway, is where you'll find most of the key attractions, including the visitor center, which sits directly above the main cavern for which the park is named. This section of the park also contains several worthwhile hiking trails, some accessed from the visitor center and others from Walnut Canyon Desert Drive, a scenic unpaved loop road with several overlooks.

Sights

SCENIC DRIVES

Walnut Canyon Desert Drive

SCENIC DRIVE | This scenic drive (labeled as Reef Top Cir. on some maps) begins a ½ mile from the visitor center and travels 9½ miles along the top of a ridge to the edge of Rattlesnake Canyon—which you can access via a marked trail—and sinks back down through upper Walnut Canyon to the main entrance road. The backcountry scenery on this one-way gravel loop is stunning; go late in the afternoon or early in the morning to enjoy the full spectrum of changing light and dancing colors. Along the way, you'll see Big Hill Seep's trickling water, the tall, flowing ridges of the Guadalupe mountain range, and maybe even some robust mule deer. The scenic road is not for RVs or trailers. ✉ *Off Carlsbad Caverns Hwy., Carlsbad Caverns National Park* ✣ *Just before entrance to visitor center parking lot.*

SCENIC STOPS

Bat Flight

CAVE | The 400,000-member Brazilian free-tailed bat colony here snatches up 3 tons of bugs a night. Watch them leave at dusk from the park amphitheater at the Natural Entrance, where a ranger discusses these intriguing creatures. The bats aren't on any predictable schedule, so times can be a little iffy. Ideally, viewers will first hear the bats preparing to exit, followed by a vortex of black specks swirling out of the cave mouth in search of dinner against the darkening sky. When conditions are favorable, hundreds of thousands of bats will soar off over the span of half an hour or longer. ✉ *727 Carlsbad Caverns Hwy., Carlsbad Caverns National Park.*

TRAILS

Chihuahuan Desert Nature Trail

TRAIL | FAMILY | While waiting for the evening bat-flight program, take this ½-mile self-guided loop hike that begins just east of the visitor center. The tagged and identified flowers and plants make this a good place to get acquainted with local desert flora. Part of the trail is an easy stroll even for the littlest ones, and part is wheelchair accessible. The payoff is great for everyone, too: a sweeping, vivid view of the desert basin. *Easy.* ✉ *Carlsbad Caverns National Park* ✣ *Trailhead: Just east of visitor center.*

Guadalupe Ridge Trail

TRAIL | This long, winding trail extends for some 100 miles through the Chihuahuan Desert in southern New Mexico and western Texas and can be hiked from Carlsbad Caverns through to the Guadalupe Mountains. Within Carlsbad Caverns National Park, the most interesting portion runs for about 12 miles one-way from the western side of Walnut Canyon Desert Drive to the park's western boundary with Lincoln National Forest. If you hike all 12 miles and back, an overnight stay in the backcountry is strongly recommended. The hike may be long, but for serious hikers the up-close-and-personal views into Rattlesnake and Slaughter canyons are more than worth it—not to mention the serenity of being miles away from civilization. *Difficult.* ✉ *Carlsbad Caverns National Park* ✣ *Trailhead: Junction of Walnut Canyon Desert Dr. and Ridge Rd.*

Old Guano Road Trail

TRAIL | Meandering a little more than 3½ miles one-way on steadily descending terrain (elevation gain is about 750 feet), the trail dips sharply toward its end at Whites City campground. Give yourself two to three hours to complete the walk. The high desert sun can make this hike a bit taxing any time of year, especially in summer. *Moderate.* ✉ *Carlsbad Caverns National Park* ✣ *Trailhead: Bat Flight Amphitheater.*

★ Rattlesnake Canyon Trail

TRAIL | Small cairns guide you along this picturesque trail, which winds 600 feet into the canyon—it's especially lush with greenery from spring through fall. Allow half a day to trek down into the canyon and make the somewhat strenuous climb out; the total trip is about 6 miles. For a look into the canyon, you can make the ¼-mile stroll to an overlook. *Moderate.* ✉ *Carlsbad Caverns National Park* ✣ *Trailhead: Interpretive marker 9, Walnut Canyon Desert Dr.*

VISITOR CENTERS

★ Carlsbad Caverns Visitor Center

INFO CENTER | FAMILY | Within this spacious, modern facility at the top of an escarpment, a 75-seat theater offers engrossing films and ranger programs about the different types of caves. Exhibits offer a primer on bats, geology, wildlife, and the early tribes and settlers who once lived in and passed through the area. There's also an excellent exhibit on Lechuguilla, the country's deepest limestone cave, which scientists began mapping in 1986 and have located some 145 miles (it's on the park's northern border and isn't open to the general public). Friendly rangers staff an information desk, where maps are distributed and cavern tickets are sold. There's also an extensive gift shop and bookstore, and restaurant. ✉ *727 Carlsbad Caverns Hwy., Carlsbad Caverns National Park* ☎ *575/785–2232* 🌐 *www.nps.gov/cave.*

Restaurants

Carlsbad Caverns Restaurant

$ | AMERICAN | This comfy, cafeteria-style restaurant in the visitor center serves basic food—hamburgers, sandwiches, some Mexican dishes—and is fine in a pinch. There are also packaged takeout items. **Known for:** close proximity to the main cavern; no alcohol; takeout options. [$] *Average main: $9* ✉ *727 Carlsbad Caverns Hwy., Carlsbad Caverns National Park* ☎ *575/785–2281* 🌐 *www.carlsbadcavernstradingco.com* ⊙ *No dinner.*

Carlsbad Cavern Belowground

Directly beneath Carlsbad Caverns Visitor Center.

With a floor space equal to about 14 football fields, this subterranean focal point of Carlsbad Cavern clues visitors in to just how large the cavern really is. The White House could fit in one corner of the Big Room, and wouldn't come close to grazing the 230-foot ceiling. Once you buy a $15 ticket at the visitor center, you can enter the cavern by elevator or through the Natural Entrance via a 1¼-mile descending trail. Either way, at 750 feet below the surface you will connect with the self-guided 1¼-mile Big Room loop. Even in summer, long pants and long-sleeved shirts are advised for cave temperatures in the mid-50s. The main cavern also accesses the King's Palace, Left Hand Tunnel, and Hall of the White Giant caves, which can be visited only by guided tour (these all depart from the visitor center). As of this writing, tentative plans are underway to renovate and redesign some of the cavern's trails. These projects may result in the temporary closure of some portions of the cavern; check the park website for the latest advisories.

Sights

GEOLOGICAL SITES

★ The Big Room

CAVE | FAMILY | A relatively level (it has some steps), paved pathway leads through these almost hallucinatory wonders of various formations and decorations. Exhibits and signage also provide a layman's lesson on how the cavern was carved (for even more details, rent an audio guide from the visitor center for $5). ✉ *Visitor Center, Carlsbad Caverns National Park* 🎫 *$15.*

Hall of the White Giant

SPELUNKING | Plan to squirm—and even crawl on your belly—through some tight passages for long distances to access a very remote chamber, where you'll see towering, glistening white formations that explain the name. This strenuous, ranger-led tour lasts about four hours. Steep climbs and sharp drop-offs might elate you—or make you queasy. Wear sturdy hiking shoes. No kids under 12. ✉ *Carlsbad Caverns National Park* ☎ *877/444–6777 reservations* 🌐 *www.recreation.gov* 🎫 *$20* ✍ *Reservations essential.*

★ King's Palace

SPELUNKING | FAMILY | Throughout this regal room, stunningly handsome and indeed fit for a king, you'll see leggy "soda straws" large enough for a giant to sip, plus bizarre formations that defy reality. The tour also winds through the Queen's Chamber, dressed in ladylike, multitiered curtains of stone. The mile-long walk is on a paved trail, but there's one steep hill toward the end. This ranger-guided tour lasts about 1½ hours and gives you a "look" at the natural essence of a cave—a complete blackout, when artificial lights (and sound) are extinguished. While advance reservations are highly recommended, this is the one tour you might be able to sign up for on the spot. Children younger than four aren't permitted. ✉ *Carlsbad Caverns National Park* ☎ *877/444–6777 reservations* 🌐 *www.recreation.gov* 🎫 *$8.*

Left Hand Tunnel

SPELUNKING | FAMILY | Lantern light illuminates the easy ½-mile walk on this detour in the main Carlsbad Cavern, which leads to Permian Age fossils—indicating that these caves were hollowed from the Permian Reef that still underlies the Guadalupe Mountain range above. The guided tour over a packed dirt trail lasts about two hours. It's a moderate trek that older kids can easily negotiate, but children under six aren't allowed. ✉ *Carlsbad Caverns National Park*

The Big Room is a limestone chamber in the cavern.

☎ *877/444–6777 reservations* 🌐 *www.recreation.gov* 🎫 *$7.*

Lower Cave

SPELUNKING | Fifty-foot vertical ladders and a dirt path lead you into undeveloped portions of Carlsbad Cavern. It takes about three hours to negotiate this moderately strenuous side trip led by a knowledgeable ranger. No children under 12. ✉ *Carlsbad Caverns National Park* ☎ *877/444–6777 reservations* 🌐 *www.recreation.gov* 🎫 *$20* ✍ *Reservations essential.*

★ Natural Entrance

CAVE | FAMILY | As natural daylight recedes, a self-guided, paved trail twists and turns downward from the yawning mouth of the main cavern, about 100 yards east of the visitor center. The route is winding and sometimes slick from water seepage aboveground. A steep descent of about 750 feet, much of it secured by hand rails, takes you about a mile through the main corridor and past dramatic features such as the Bat Cave and the Boneyard. (Despite its eerie name, the formations here don't look much like femurs and fibulae; they're more like spongy bone insides.) Iceberg Rock is a massive boulder that dropped from the cave ceiling millennia ago. After about a mile, you'll link up underground with the Big Room Trail and can return to the surface via elevator or by hiking back out. Footware with a good grip is recommended. ✉ *727 Carlsbad Cavern Hwy., Carlsbad Caverns National Park* 🎫 *$15.*

Restaurants

Underground Lunchroom

$ | FAST FOOD | At 750 feet underground, near the elevator and entrance to the Big Room, you can grab a snack, soft drink, or club sandwich at this handy snack bar. Service is quick, even when there's a crowd, and although the food doesn't stand out, it's fun dining in this otherworldly setting. **Known for:** unusual cavern setting; quick service; convenience. [$] *Average main: $7* ✉ *727 Carlsbad Caverns Hwy., Carlsbad Caverns National Park* ☎ *575/785–2232* 🌐 *www.carlsbadcavernstradingco.com* 🕒 *No dinner.*

Rattlesnake Springs and Slaughter Canyon

16 miles south of Carlsbad Caverns Visitor Center, 29 miles southwest of Carlsbad.

Accessed from U.S. 62/180 via Highway 418, the secluded western half of the park contains a handful of notable wilderness features, including the lush and small Rattlesnake Springs area and the visually striking Slaughter Canyon, which contains some terrific hiking trails and a popular but challenging cave accessible only by guided tour. Enormous cottonwood trees shade Rattlesnake Springs, a cool, tranquil oasis near the Black River. The rare desert wetland harbors butterflies, mammals, and reptiles, as well as 90% of the park's 357 bird species. This oasis also has a shaded picnic area, potable water, and permanent toilets, but camping and overnight parking are not allowed.

Sights

GEOLOGICAL SITES

Slaughter Canyon Cave

CAVE | Discovered in the 1930s by a local goatherd, this cave is one of the most popular secondary sites in the park, about a 40-minute drive southwest of the visitor center (you'll follow a ranger in your own vehicle to get there). Both the hike to the cave mouth and the tour will take about half a day, but it's worth it to view the deep cavern darkness as it's penetrated only by flashlights and sometimes headlamps. From the Slaughter Canyon parking area, it takes about 45 minutes to make the steep ½-mile climb up a trail leading to the mouth of the cave. You'll find that the cave consists primarily of a single corridor, 1,140 feet long, with numerous side passages.

You can take some worthwhile pictures of this cave. Wear hiking shoes with ankle support, and carry plenty of water. No kids under eight. It's a great adventure if you're in shape and love caving. ✉ *End of Hwy. 418, Carlsbad Caverns National Park* ☎ *877/444–6777 reservations* 🌐 *www.recreation.gov* 🎫 *$15* ✍ *Reservations essential.*

SCENIC SPOTS

★ Rattlesnake Springs

NATURE PRESERVE | FAMILY | Enormous old-growth cottonwood trees shade the recreation area at this cool, secluded oasis near Black River. The rare desert wetland harbors butterflies, mammals, and reptiles, as well as 90% of the park's 357 bird species. Because southern New Mexico is in the northernmost region of the Chihuahuan Desert, you're likely to see birds largely unseen anywhere else in the United States outside extreme southern Texas and Arizona. If you see a flash of crimson, you might have spotted a vermilion flycatcher. Wild turkeys also flap around this oasis. Don't let the name scare you; there may be rattlesnakes here, but no more than at any similar site in the Southwest. Restroom facilities are available, but camping and overnight parking are not allowed. ✉ *Hwy. 418, Carlsbad Caverns National Park* ✣ *8½ miles southwest of Whites City.*

TRAILS

Slaughter Canyon Trail

TRAIL | Beginning at the Slaughter Canyon Cave parking lot (four-wheel-drive or high-clearance vehicles are recommended; check with visitor center for road conditions before setting out), the trail traverses a heavily vegetated canyon bottom into a remote part of the park. As you begin hiking, look off to the east (to your right) to see the dun-colored ridges and wrinkles of the Elephant Back formation, the first of many dramatic limestone formations visible from the trail. The route travels 5½ miles one-way, the last 3 miles steeply climbing onto a limestone ridge escarpment. Allow a full day for the round-trip, and prepare for an elevation gain of 1,850 feet. *Difficult.* ✉ *Carlsbad Caverns National Park* ✣ *Trailhead: At Slaughter Canyon Cave parking lot, Hwy. 418, 10 miles west of U.S. 62/180.*

★ **Yucca Canyon Trail**

TRAIL | Sweeping views of the Guadalupe Mountains and El Capitan give allure to this challenging but beautiful trail. Drive past Rattlesnake Springs and stop at the park boundary before reaching the Slaughter Canyon Cave parking lot (four-wheel-drive or high-clearance vehicles are recommended; check with visitor center for road conditions before setting out). Turn west along the boundary fence line to the trailhead. The 7½-mile round-trip begins at the mouth of Yucca Canyon and climbs nearly 1,500 feet up to the top of the escarpment for a panoramic view. *Difficult.* ✉ *Carlsbad Caverns National Park* ✣ *Trailhead: At Slaughter Canyon Cave parking lot, Hwy. 418, 10 miles west of U.S. 62/180.*

Activities

BIRD-WATCHING

From redheaded turkey vultures to golden eagles, 357 species of birds have been identified in Carlsbad Caverns National Park. The park's Rattlesnake Springs area is the best for this activity. Ask for a checklist at the visitor center and then start looking for greater roadrunners, red-winged blackbirds, white-throated swifts, northern flickers, and pygmy nuthatches. Because southern New Mexico is in the northernmost region of the Chihuahuan Desert, you're likely to see birds largely unseen anywhere else in the United States outside extreme southern Texas and Arizona. If you see a flash of crimson, you might have spotted a vermilion flycatcher. Wild turkeys also flap around this oasis.

CAMPING

Backcountry camping is by permit only. No campfires are allowed in the park, and all camping is hike-to. There are commercial campgrounds in Whites City and Carlsbad, and nearby Guadalupe Mountains National Park has both designated campgrounds and backcountry sites.

HIKING

Deep, dark, and mysterious, the Carlsbad Caverns are such a park focal point that the 46,766-plus acres of wilderness above them have gone largely undeveloped, perfect for those looking for solitude—and there's no fee for accessing the park's aboveground areas. Rudimentary trails crisscross the dry, textured terrain and lead up to elevations of 6,000 feet or more. These routes often take a half day or more to travel; Guadalupe Ridge Trail is long enough that it calls for camping overnight. Walkers who just want a little dusty taste of desert flowers and wildlife should try the Chihuahuan Desert Nature Walk.

What's Nearby

On the Pecos River—with 3 miles of beaches, lawns, and picturesque riverside pathways—**Carlsbad** is the best base for lodging and dining near the park. At the park's main entrance road, about 7 miles from the visitor center, **Whites City** is a tiny privately owned village with a basic motel, restaurant, and gas station.

Chapter 14

CHANNEL ISLANDS NATIONAL PARK

Updated by
Cheryl Crabtree

Camping ★★★★☆ | Hotels ★★★☆☆ | Activities ★★★★★ | Scenery ★★★★☆ | Crowds ★★☆☆☆

WELCOME TO CHANNEL ISLANDS NATIONAL PARK

TOP REASONS TO GO

★ **Rare flora and fauna:** The Channel Islands are home to 145 species of terrestrial plants and animals found nowhere else on Earth.

★ **Time travel:** With no cars, phones, or services and away from hectic modern life, these undeveloped islands provide a glimpse of what California was like hundreds of years ago.

★ **Underwater adventures:** The incredibly healthy channel waters rank among the top 10 diving destinations on the planet—but you can also visit the kelp forest virtually via Channel Islands Live, a live underwater program.

★ **Marvelous marine mammals:** More than 30 species of seals, sea lions, whales, and other marine mammals ply the park's waters at various times of year.

★ **Sea-cave kayaking:** Paddle around otherwise inaccessible portions of the park's 175 miles of gorgeous coastline—including one of the world's largest sea caves.

1 **Anacapa.** Tiny Anacapa is a 5-mile stretch of three islets, with towering cliffs, caves, natural bridges, and rich kelp forests.

2 **San Miguel.** The park's westernmost island (access permit required), has an ancient caliche forest and hundreds of archaeological sites chronicling the Native Americans' 13,000-year history on the islands. More than 30,000 pinnipeds (seals and sea lions) hang out on the island's beaches during certain times of year.

3 **Santa Barbara.** More than 5 miles of trails crisscross this tiny island, known for its wildlife viewing and native plants. It's a favorite destination for diving, snorkeling, and kayaking.

4 **Santa Cruz.** The park's largest island offers some of the best hikes and kayaking opportunities, as well as one of the world's largest and deepest sea caves.

5 **Santa Rosa.** Campers love to stay on Santa Rosa, with its myriad hiking opportunities, stunning white-sand beaches, and rare grove of Torrey pines. It's also the only island accessible by plane.

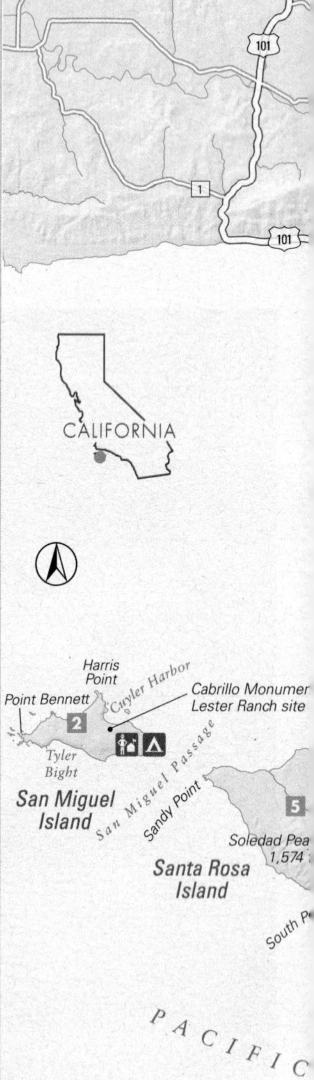

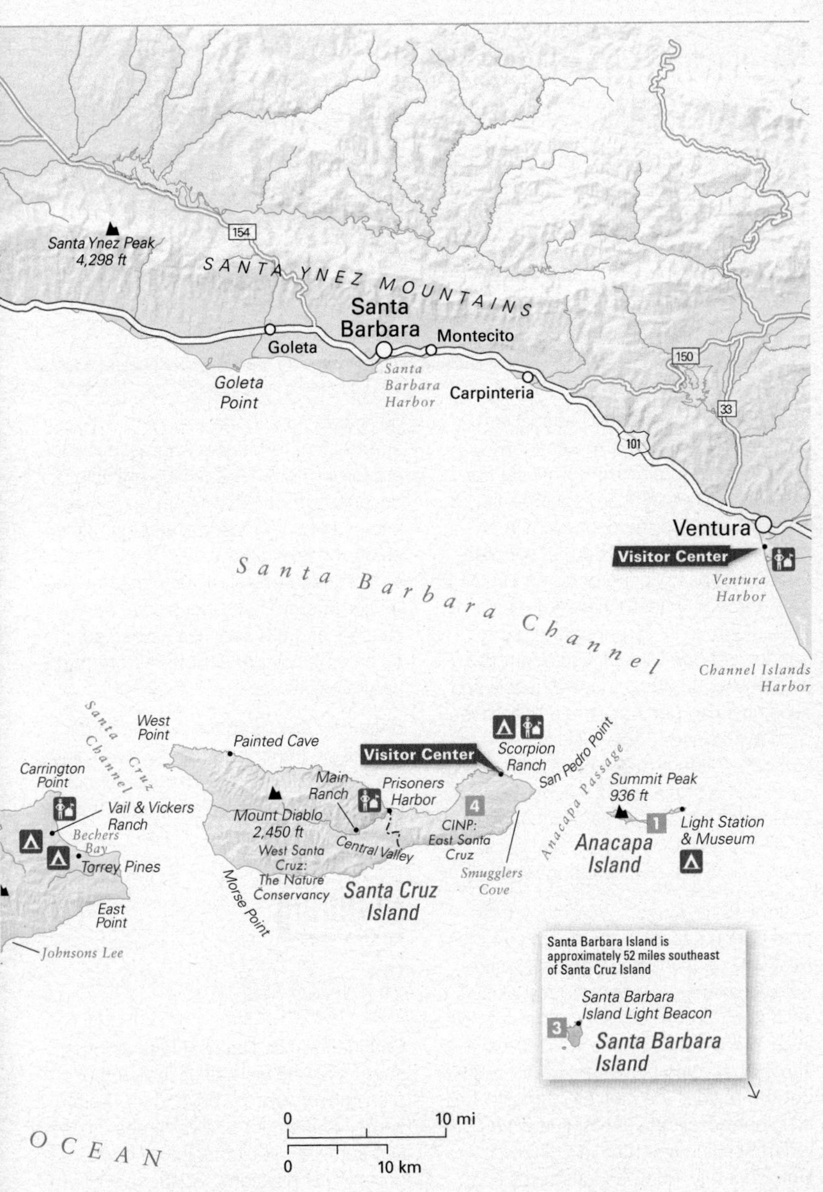
Santa Ynez Peak
4,298 ft
SANTA YNEZ MOUNTAINS
154
Santa Barbara
Goleta
Montecito
Goleta Point
Santa Barbara Harbor
Carpinteria
150
33
101
Ventura
Visitor Center
Ventura Harbor
Santa Barbara Channel
Channel Islands Harbor
Santa Cruz Channel
West Point
Painted Cave
Visitor Center
Scorpion Ranch
San Pedro Point
Anacapa Passage
Carrington Point
Main Ranch
Prisoners Harbor
Summit Peak
936 ft
Vail & Vickers Ranch
Mount Diablo
2,450 ft
4
CINP: East Santa Cruz
1
Light Station & Museum
Bechers Bay
West Santa Cruz: The Nature Conservancy
Central Valley
Anacapa Island
Torrey Pines
Morse Point
Smugglers Cove
Santa Cruz Island
East Point
Johnsons Lee
Santa Barbara Island is approximately 52 miles southeast of Santa Cruz Island
Santa Barbara Island Light Beacon
3
Santa Barbara Island
0
10 mi
0
10 km
OCEAN

On crystal-clear days, the craggy peaks of Channel Islands are easy to see from the mainland, jutting from the Pacific in sharp detail. Sometimes called the North American Galápagos, they form a magnificent nature preserve, home to many native plants, land animals, and marine creatures—some found nowhere else on the planet.

Established in 1980, the national park includes five of the eight Channel Islands—ranging in size from 1-square-mile Santa Barbara to 96-square-mile Santa Cruz—and the nautical mile of ocean that surrounds them. If you visit East Anacapa in spring or summer, you'll walk through a nesting area of western gulls. If you're lucky enough to get to windswept San Miguel, you might see as many as 30,000 pinnipeds (seals and sea lions) camped out on the beach. You can kayak close to the seals (as long as you don't disturb them) or snorkel or dive amid some of the world's richest kelp forests. Even traveling on an excursion boat gives you a chance to view sea lions, brown pelicans, and spouting whales.

Scientists have uncovered many treasures during decades of research on these relatively undeveloped islands. Archaeological evidence at Santa Rosa Island's Arlington Springs site shows that people lived in coastal California 13,000 years ago and traveled by watercraft throughout the region. The native Chumash lived on the islands until the late 1700s, when Spaniards settled in California. Unfortunately, European diseases and the demise of the trade-based economy devastated the indigenous population, and the few remaining Chumash islanders left in 1816–17. Over the ensuing decades, other humans set up fishing and otter hunting camps and built ranches on the islands; the U.S. Navy also established several military installations. All commercial operations have now ceased, and the park has embarked on an ambitious project to restore the natural habitats.

Relatively few people travel out to the park. If you're among the few who do make the effort, know that a splendid land-and-sea wilderness—minus the crowds—awaits.

Planning

When to Go

Channel Islands National Park records about 410,000 visitors each year, but many never venture beyond the visitor center. During the busiest times (holidays and summer weekends) book transportation and accommodations well in advance.

The warm, dry summer and fall months are the best time to go camping. Humpback and blue whales arrive to feed from late June through early fall. The rains usually come December through March—but this is also the best time to spot gray whales and get hotel discounts. In the late spring, thousands of migratory birds descend on the islands to hatch their young, and wildflowers carpet the slopes. The water temperature is nearly always cool, so bring a wet suit if you plan to spend time in the ocean, even in the summer. Fog, high winds, and rough seas can happen any time of the year.

Getting Here and Around

AIR

You can arrange charter service to Santa Rosa and San Miguel islands. Flights depart from the Camarillo Airport, south of Ventura, or the Santa Barbara Airport.

CONTACTS Channel Islands Aviation. ✉ *305 Durley Ave., Camarillo* ☎ *805/987–1301* 🌐 *www.flycia.com.*

BOAT

The visitor center for Channel Islands National Park is on California's mainland, in the town of Ventura, off U.S. 101. From the harbors at Ventura, Santa Barbara, and Oxnard you can board a boat to one of the islands. If you have your own boat, you can land at any of the park islands without a permit, but you should visit the park website for instructions and information on restricted areas. A permit is required to land on the Nature Conservancy property on Santa Cruz Island. Boaters landing at San Miguel must contact the park ranger beforehand.

CONTACTS Island Packers. ✉ *3550 Harbor Blvd., Oxnard* ☎ *805/642–1393* 🌐 *islandpackers.com.*

CAR

To reach the Ventura harbor, exit U.S. 101 in Ventura at Seaward Boulevard or Victoria Avenue, and follow the signs to Ventura Harbor/Spinnaker Drive. To access Channel Islands Harbor in Oxnard, exit U.S. 101 at Victoria Avenue, and head south approximately 7 miles to Channel Islands Boulevard. To access dive and whale-watching boats in Santa Barbara, exit U.S. 101 at Castillo Street, and head south to Cabrillo Boulevard, then turn right for the harbor entrance. Private vehicles are not permitted on the islands. Pets are also not allowed in the park.

Transit Times to the Islands

Island	Distance and Time by Boat	Cost (per hiker/ camper)
Anacapa Island	14 miles/1 hr from Oxnard	$59/$79
San Miguel Island	58 miles/3 hrs from Ventura	$105/$147
Santa Barbara Island	55 miles/2½–3 hrs from Ventura	$82/$114
Santa Cruz Island	20 miles/1 hr from Ventura	$59/$79
Santa Rosa Island	46 miles/2 hrs from Ventura	$82/$114

TRAIN

Amtrak makes stops in Santa Barbara, Ventura, and Oxnard; from the Amtrak station, just take a taxi, rideshare service, or waterfront shuttle bus to the harbor.

Inspiration

California's Channel Islands: A History is an extensive cultural, geologic, and historical account of all eight Channel Islands by Frederic Caire Chiles, whose pioneering great-grandfather settled Santa Cruz Island in the 1800s.

Channel Islands National Park and National Marine Sanctuary—California's Galapagos is a visual overview with more than 140 images by photographer Tim Hauf.

AVERAGE HIGH/LOW TEMPERATURES					
JAN.	**FEB.**	**MAR.**	**APR.**	**MAY**	**JUNE**
66/44	66/45	66/46	68/48	69/51	71/55
JULY	**AUG.**	**SEPT.**	**OCT.**	**NOV.**	**DEC.**
74/57	75/59	75/57	74/53	70/48	66/44

Diary of a Sea Captain's Wife: Tales of Santa Cruz Island is by Margaret H. Eaton, who, along with her husband, ran a camp-resort at Pelican Bay on Santa Cruz Island in the early 1900s.

Island of the Blue Dolphins , a legendary novel by Scott O'Dell that's great for kids, tells the tale of 12-year-old Karana, a native Chumash girl who must fend for herself for years after she's abandoned on one of the Channel Islands.

North America's Galapagos: The Historic Channel Islands Biological Survey , by Corinne Heyning Laverty, is a tale of the 33-member research team that chronicled the islands' history and evolution in the 1930s.

When the Killing's Done , a novel by T. Coraghessan Boyle, dives deep into the conflict between efforts to protect native wildlife by ridding the islands of invasive species and people who oppose any purposeful killing of animals.

Park Essentials

ACCESSIBILITY

The Channel Islands National Park Robert J. Lagomarsino Visitor Center is fully accessible. The islands themselves have few facilities and are not easy to navigate by individuals in wheelchairs or those with limited mobility. Limited wheelchair access is available on Santa Rosa Island via air transportation.

PARK FEES AND PERMITS

There is no fee to enter Channel Islands National Park, but unless you have your own boat, you will pay $40 or more per person for a ride with a boat operator. The cost of taking a boat to the park varies depending on which operator you choose. Also, there is a $15-per-day fee for staying in one of the islands' campgrounds.

If you take your own boat, landing permits are not required to visit islands administered by the National Park Service. However, boaters who want to land on the Nature Conservancy preserve on Santa Cruz Island must have a permit. Visit 🌐 *www.nature.org/cruzpermit* for permit information; allow 10 business days to process and return your permit application. If you anchor in a nearby cove at any island, at least one person should remain aboard the boat at all times. San Miguel Island is property of the U.S. Navy. To visit it, you must obtain an access permit, which is available at the boat and air concession offices and at a self-registration station on the island. To hike beyond the ranger station on San Miguel, you need a reservation and permit; call ☎ *805/658–5700* to be matched up with a ranger, who must accompany you. Anglers must have a state fishing license; for details, call the California Department of Fish and Wildlife at ☎ *916/653–7664* or visit 🌐 *wildlifeca.gov*. More than a dozen Marine Protected Areas (MPAs) with special regulations surround the islands, so read the guidelines carefully before you depart.

PARK HOURS

The islands are open every day of the year. The visitor center in Ventura is closed on Thanksgiving and Christmas. Channel Islands National Park is in the Pacific time zone.

CELL PHONE RECEPTION

Reception is spotty and varies by location and service provider. Public telephones are available on the mainland near the visitor center but not on the islands.

Hotels

In the park, your only option is sleeping in a tent at a no-frills campground. If you hanker for more creature comforts, you can splurge on a bunk and meals on a dive boat.

Restaurants

Out on the islands, there are no restaurants, no snack bars, and in some cases, no potable water. Instead, pack a fancy picnic or a simple sandwich. For a quick meal before or after your island trip, each of the harbors has a number of decent eateries nearby.

Visitor Information

CONTACTS Channel Islands National Park Robert J. Lagomarsino Visitor Center. ✉ *1901 Spinnaker Dr., Ventura* ☎ *805/658–5730* 🌐 *www.nps.gov/chis.* **Outdoors Santa Barbara Visitor Center.** ✉ *113 Harbor Way, Santa Barbara* ☎ *805/456–8752* 🌐 *outdoorsb.sbmm.org.*

Anacapa Island

14 miles from Channel Islands Harbor in Oxnard.

Anacapa is actually comprised of three narrow islets. Although the tips of these volcanic formations nearly touch, the islets are inaccessible from one another except by boat. All three have towering cliffs, isolated sea caves, and natural bridges; Arch Rock, on East Anacapa, is one of the park's best-known symbols. Wildlife viewing is the main activity on East Anacapa, particularly in summer when seagull chicks are newly hatched and sea lions and seals lounge on the beaches. Exhibits at East Anacapa's compact **museum** include the original lead-crystal Fresnel lens from the 1932 lighthouse. There are picnic tables at the island's visitor center.

On West Anacapa, depending on the season, boats travel to **Frenchy's Cove.** On a voyage here you might see anemones, limpets, barnacles, mussel beds, and colorful marine algae in the pristine tide pools. The rest of West Anacapa is closed to protect nesting brown pelicans.

Sights

TRAILS

Inspiration Point Trail

TRAIL | FAMILY | This 1½-mile hike along flat terrain takes in most of East Anacapa. There are great views from Inspiration Point and Cathedral Cove. *Easy.* ✉ *Trailhead: At Landing Cove, Anacapa Island.*

San Miguel Island

58 miles from Ventura.

The westernmost of the Channel Islands, San Miguel Island is often battered by storms sweeping across the North Pacific. The 15-square-mile island's wild windswept landscape is lush with vegetation. Point Bennett, at the western tip, offers one of the world's most spectacular wildlife displays when more than 30,000 pinnipeds hit its beach. Explorer Juan Rodríguez Cabrillo was the first European to visit this island; he claimed it for Spain in 1542. Legend holds that Cabrillo died on one of the Channel Islands—no one knows where he's buried, but there's a memorial to him on a bluff above Cuyler Harbor. Unlike the other islands in the park, there are no picnic tables here, but there is an isolated campground.

Inspiration point on Anacapa Island

Sights

TRAILS

Cuyler Harbor Beach Trail

TRAIL | This easy walk takes you along a 2-mile-long white sand beach on San Miguel. The eastern section is occasionally cut off by high tides. An access permit is required. *Easy.* ✉ *Trailhead: At San Miguel Campground, San Miguel Island.*

Lester Ranch Trail

TRAIL | This short but strenuous 2-mile hike leads up a spectacular canyon filled with waterfalls and lush native plants. At the end of a steep climb to the top of a peak, views of the historic Lester Ranch and the Cabrillo Monument await. If you plan to hike beyond the Lester Ranch, you'll need a hiking permit in addition to an island-access permit; call or visit the park website for details. *Difficult.* ✉ *Trailhead: At San Miguel Campground, San Miguel Island* ☎ *805/658–5730.*

Point Bennett Trail

TRAIL | Rangers conduct 15-mile hikes across San Miguel to Point Bennett, where more than 30,000 pinnipeds (three different species) can be seen. An access permit is required. *Difficult.* ✉ *Trailhead: At San Miguel Campground, San Miguel Island.*

Santa Barbara Island

55 miles from Ventura.

At about 1 square mile, Santa Barbara Island is the smallest of the Channel Islands and nearly 35 miles south of the others. Triangular in shape, Santa Barbara's steep cliffs—which offer a perfect nesting spot for the Scripps's murrelet, a rare seabird—are topped by twin peaks. In spring you can enjoy a brilliant display of yellow coreopsis. Learn about the wildlife on and around the islands at the island's small **museum**.

Although the island is open to the public, access to it is difficult. Its dock was damaged in major storms, and it's uncertain when it will be repaired. In the interim, when conditions allow (i.e., the swells aren't too high and the tide is right), boats can land only at a rocky ledge near the damaged dock. Check with the park for weather conditions and updates on the dock and island landings.

Sights

TRAILS

Elephant Seal Cove Trail

TRAIL | This moderate-to-strenuous, 2½-mile, round-trip walk takes you across Santa Barbara to a point where you can view magnificent elephant seals from steep cliffs. *Moderate.* ✉ *Trailhead: At Landing Cove, Santa Barbara Island.*

Santa Cruz Island

20 miles from Ventura.

Five miles west of Anacapa, 96-square-mile Santa Cruz Island is the largest of the Channel Islands. The National Park Service manages the easternmost 24% of it; the rest is owned by the Nature Conservancy, which requires a permit to land. When your boat drops you off on a portion of the 70 miles of craggy coastline, you see two rugged mountain ranges with peaks soaring to 2,500 feet and deep canyons traversed by streams. This landscape is the habitat of a remarkable variety of flora and fauna—more than 600 types of plants, 140 kinds of land birds, 11 mammal species, five varieties of reptiles, and three amphibian species live here. Bird-watchers may want to look for the endemic island scrub jay, which is found nowhere else in the world.

One of the largest and deepest sea caves in the world, Painted Cave, lies along the northwest coast of Santa Cruz. Named for the colorful lichen and algae that cover its walls, the cave is nearly ¼ mile long and 100 feet wide. In spring, a waterfall cascades over the entrance. Kayakers may see seals or sea lions cruising beside their boats in the cave.

The Channel Islands hold some of the richest archaeological resources in North America, and all artifacts are protected within the park. On Santa Cruz, you can see remnants of a dozen Chumash villages, the largest of which is at the island's eastern end in the area now called Scorpion Ranch. The Chumash mined the island's extensive chert deposits for tools to produce shell-bead money, which they traded with people on the mainland. You can learn about Chumash history and view artifacts, tools, and exhibits on native plant and wildlife at the interpretive visitor center near the landing dock. You can also explore remnants of the early-1900s ranching era in the restored historic adobe and outbuildings.

Sights

TRAILS

Cavern Point Trail

TRAIL | **FAMILY** | This moderate 2-mile hike takes you to the bluffs northwest of Scorpion harbor on Santa Cruz, where there are magnificent coastal views and pods of migrating gray whales from December through March. *Moderate.* ✉ *Trailhead: At Scorpion Ranch Campground, Santa Cruz Island.*

Historic Ranch Trail

TRAIL | **FAMILY** | This easy ½-mile walk on Santa Cruz Island takes you to a historic ranch where you can visit an interpretive center in an 1800s adobe and see remnants of a cattle ranch. *Easy.* ✉ *Trailhead: At Scorpion Beach, Santa Cruz Island.*

★ **Prisoners Harbor/Pelican Cove Trail**

TRAIL | Taking in quite a bit of Santa Cruz, this moderate to strenuous 3-mile trail one-way to Pelican Cove is one of the best hikes in the park. You must be accompanied by an Island Packers naturalist or secure a permit (visit 🌐 *www.*

nature.org/cruzpermit; allow 10 to 15 business days to process and return your application), as the hike takes you through Nature Conservancy property. *Moderate.* ✉ *Trailhead: At Prisoners Harbor, Santa Cruz Island.*

Santa Rosa Island

46 miles from Ventura.

Between Santa Cruz and San Miguel, Santa Rosa is the second largest of the Channel Islands. The terrain along the coast varies from broad, sandy beaches to sheer cliffs—a central mountain range, rising to 1,589 feet, breaks the island's low profile. Santa Rosa is home to about 500 species of plants, including the rare Torrey pine, and three unusual mammals: the island fox, the spotted skunk, and the deer mouse. They hardly compare, though, to their predecessors: a nearly complete skeleton of a 6-foot-tall pygmy mammoth was unearthed in 1994.

From 1901 to 1998, cattle were raised at the island's **Vail & Vickers Ranch.** The route from Santa Rosa's landing dock to the campground passes by the historic ranch buildings, barns, equipment, and the wooden pier where cattle were brought onto the island. There are picnic tables behind the ranch house here as well as at Water Canyon Beach.

Sights

TRAILS

East Point Trail

TRAIL | This strenuous 12-mile hike along beautiful white-sand beaches yields the opportunity to see rare Torrey pines. Some beaches are closed between March and September, so you have to remain on the road for portions of this hike. *Difficult.* ✉ *Trailhead: At Santa Rosa Campground, Santa Rosa Island.*

Torrey Pines Trail

TRAIL | This moderate 5-mile loop climbs up to Santa Rosa's grove of rare Torrey pines and offers stellar views of Becher's Bay and the channel. *Moderate.* ✉ *Trailhead: At Santa Rosa Campground, Santa Rosa Island.*

Water Canyon Trail

TRAIL | Starting at Santa Rosa Campground, this 2-mile walk along a white-sand beach features some exceptional beachcombing. Frequent strong winds can turn this easy hike into a fairly strenuous excursion, though. You can extend your walk by following animal paths to Water Canyon, which is full of native vegetation. *Easy.* ✉ *Trailhead: At Santa Rosa Campground, Santa Rosa Island.*

Activities

CAMPING

Camping is the best way to experience the natural beauty and isolation of Channel Islands National Park. Unrestricted by tour schedules, you have plenty of time to explore mountain trails, snorkel in the kelp forests, or kayak into sea caves. Campsites are primitive, with no water (except on Santa Rosa and Santa Cruz) or electricity. Campfires are not allowed on the islands, though you may use enclosed camp stoves. Use bear boxes for storing your food. You must carry all your gear and pack out all trash. Campers must arrange transportation to the islands before reserving a campsite (and yes, park personnel do check).

National Park Service Reservation System

You can get specifics on each campground and reserve a campsite ($15 per night) by contacting the National Park Service Reservation System up to six months in advance. ☎ *877/444–6777* 🌐 *www.recreation.gov.*

DIVING

Island waters offer some of the world's best dives. In the relatively warm water around Anacapa and eastern Santa Cruz, you can get great photographs of rarely seen giant black bass swimming among the kelp forests. Here you also find a reef covered with red brittle starfish. If you're an experienced diver, you might swim among five species of seals and sea lions, or try your hand at spearing rockfish or halibut near San Miguel and Santa Rosa. The best time to scuba dive is in summer and fall, when the water is often clear up to a 100-foot depth.

Peace Dive Boat

SCUBA DIVING | Ventura Harbor–based Peace Dive Boat runs single-day diving adventures near all the Channel Islands. ✉ *1691 Spinnaker Dr., Dock E, Ventura* ☎ *949/247–1106* 🌐 *www.peaceboat.com* 🎫 *From $145.*

Raptor Dive Boat

SCUBA DIVING | The *Raptor*, a 46-foot custom boat, takes divers on two- and three-tank trips to Anacapa and Santa Cruz islands and is available for private charters. ✉ *Ventura* ☎ *805/650–7700* 🌐 *www.raptordive.com* 🎫 *From $140.*

Spectre Dive Boat

SCUBA DIVING | This boat runs single-day diving trips to Anacapa and Santa Cruz. Fees include three dives, air, and food. ✉ *1575 Spinnaker Dr., Dock D, Ventura* ☎ *805/486–1166* 🌐 *www.spectreboat.com* 🎫 *From $135.*

EDUCATIONAL PROGRAMS

RANGER PROGRAMS

Ranger programs are held at the Channel Islands National Park Robert J. Lagomarsino Visitor Center in Ventura.

Channel Islands Live Program

NATIONAL/STATE PARK | **FAMILY** | Want a cool sneak preview of the islands and the colorful sea life below? Experience them virtually through the Channel Islands Live Program, which takes you on interactive tours of the park. In the Live Dive Program, divers armed with video cameras explore the undersea world of the kelp forest off Anacapa Island. Images are transmitted to monitors located on the dock at Landing Cove, in the mainland visitor center, and online. The Live Hike Program takes you on a similar interactive virtual tour of Anacapa Island. Live webcams also connect you 24/7 with panoramic views of Anacapa Island, bald eagle and peregrine falcon nests, and Santa Cruz Island (from Mt. Diablo, the island's highest peak). 🌐 *www.nps.gov/chis/planyourvisit/channel-islands-live-nps.htm* 🎫 *Free.*

Tidepool Talk

TOUR—SIGHT | **FAMILY** | Explore the area's marine habitat without getting your feet wet. Rangers at the Channel Islands Visitor Center demonstrate how animals and plants adapt to the harsh conditions found in tidal pools of the Channel Islands. The talks generally take place at 11 am and 3 pm on weekends and most holidays. ✉ *Channel Islands National Park Visitor Center, 1901 Spinnaker Rd., Ventura* ☎ *805/658–5730* 🌐 *www.nps.gov/chis/planyourvisit/programs.htm* 🎫 *Free.*

KAYAKING

The most remote parts of the Channel Islands are accessible only by a sea kayak. Some of the best kayaking in the park can be found on Anacapa, Santa Barbara, and the eastern tip of Santa Cruz. Anacapa has plenty of sea caves, tidal pools, and even natural bridges you can paddle beneath. Santa Cruz has plenty of secluded beaches to explore, as well as seabird nesting sites and seal and sea lion rookeries. One of the world's largest colonies of Scripps's murrelets resides here, and brown pelicans, cormorants, and storm petrels nest in Santa Barbara's steep cliffs.

It's too far to kayak from the mainland out to the islands, but outfitters can take you to them year-round, though high seas may cause tour cancellations between December and March. ■ **TIP→ Channel waters can be unpredictable and challenging. Don't venture out alone unless you are**

an experienced kayaker; guided trips are highly recommended. All kayakers should carry proper safety gear and equipment and be prepared for sudden strong winds and weather changes. Also refrain from disturbing wildlife. Visit the park website for kayaking rules and tips.

The operator listed here holds permits from the National Park Service to conduct kayak tours; if you choose a different company, verify that it holds the proper permits.

Channel Islands Adventure Company
KAYAKING | Full-service outfitter Channel Islands Adventure Company (an arm of Santa Barbara Adventure Company) conducts guided kayaking and snorkeling day trips from its storefront at Scorpion Anchorage on Santa Cruz Island. The company also offers chartered single- and multiday excursions to the Channel Islands. All trips depart from Ventura Harbor and include equipment, guides, and paddling lessons. There's an additional fee for transportation with an Island Packers boat. ✉ *32 E. Haley St., Santa Barbara* ☎ *805/884–9283* 🌐 *islandkayaking.com* *From $112 plus $59 ferry.*

WHALE-WATCHING

About a third of the world's cetacean species (27 to be exact) can be seen in the Santa Barbara Channel. In July and August, humpback and blue whales feed off the north shore of Santa Rosa. From late December through March, up to 10,000 gray whales pass through the Santa Barbara Channel on their way from Alaska to Mexico and back again, and on a whale-watching trip during this time frame, you should see one or more of them. Though fewer in number, other types of whales swim the channel June through August.

Island Packers
WHALE-WATCHING | Depending on the season, you can take a three-hour tour or an all-day excursion from either Ventura or Channel Islands harbors with Island Packers. From January through March you're almost guaranteed to see gray whales in the channel. ✉ *1691 Spinnaker Dr., Ventura* ☎ *805/642–1393* 🌐 *www.islandpackers.com* *From $38.*

What's Nearby

With a population of nearly 110,000, **Ventura** is the main gateway to Channel Islands National Park. It's a classic California beach town filled with interesting restaurants, shops, galleries, a wide range of accommodations, and miles of clean, white beaches. South of Ventura is **Oxnard,** a community of 208,000 boasting a busy harbor and uncrowded beaches. Known for its Spanish ambience, **Santa Barbara** has a beautiful waterfront set against a backdrop of towering mountains—plus glistening palm-lined beaches, whitewashed adobe structures with red-tile roofs, and a downtown/waterfront area with a hip, youthful vibe.

Chapter 15

CONGAREE NATIONAL PARK

Updated by
Stratton Lawrence

Camping ★★☆☆☆

Hotels ★☆☆☆☆

Activities ★★★★☆

Scenery ★★★☆☆

Crowds ★★☆☆☆

WELCOME TO CONGAREE NATIONAL PARK

TOP REASONS TO GO

★ **Primeval paddle:** Canoe or kayak through an ancient forest of old growth cypress trees.

★ **Hike through a swamp:** Miles of elevated boardwalks grant access to an otherwise impenetrable ecosystem.

★ **Watch for woodpeckers:** Pileated woodpeckers abound in this birding paradise that's also a rich duck habitat.

★ **Camp under the canopy:** Most of the park is open to backcountry camping and ripe for multiday exploration.

★ **See the glow:** Each May, the park's fireflies put on a synchronous show that draws thousands of visitors.

1 **Cedar Creek.** Paddle a meandering stream through the heart of the largest intact bottomland forest in the southeastern U.S. Three put-in spots allow for day trips or longer overnights.

2 **Boardwalk Trail.** This 2.6-mile, wheelchair-accessible loop carries you deep into the heart of the swamp, without getting your shoes muddy.

3 **Kingsnake and River Trail.** More than 20 miles of trails allow for loops and self-supported overnights deep into the swampy woods.

4 **East Congaree.** The park's still-developing east end has two short trails, including one with river access. Adventurous kayakers will find some of the world's biggest cypress trees deep in these watery woods.

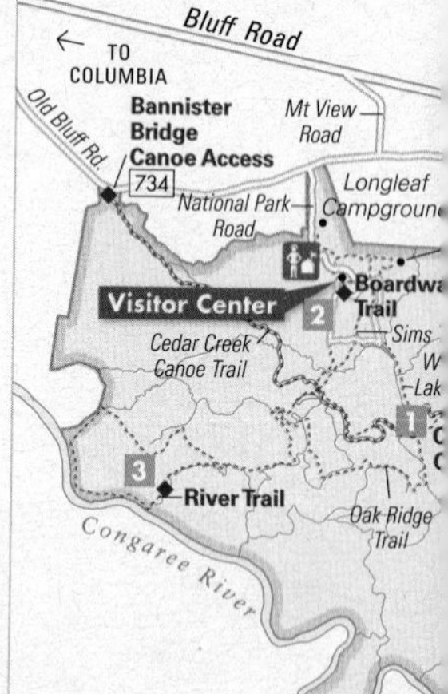

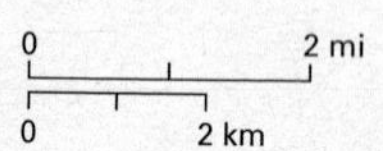

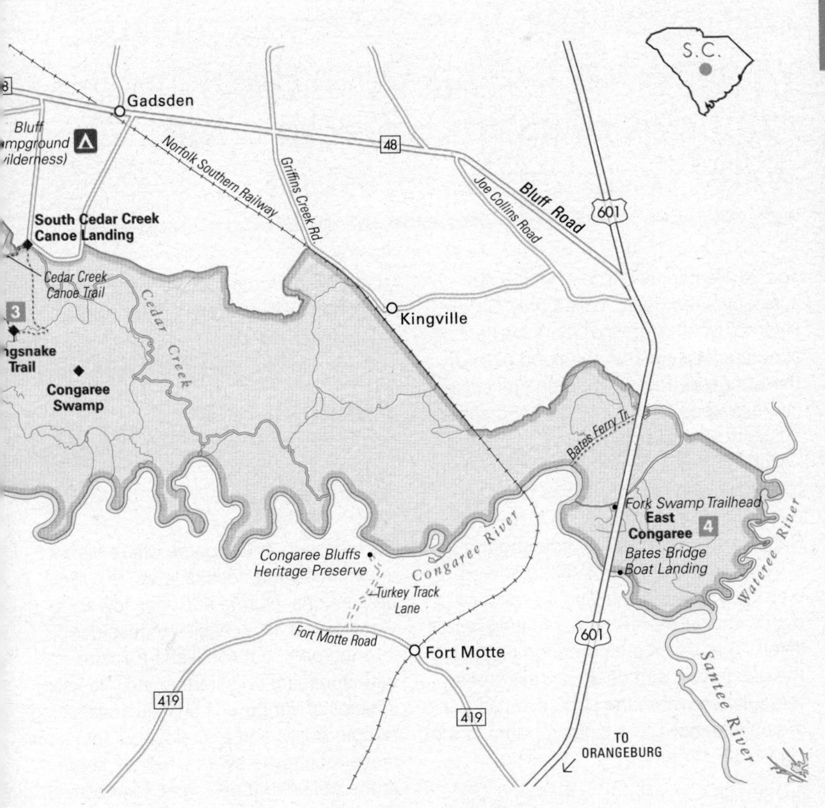
S.C.
Gadsden
Bluff
48
Norfolk Southern Railway
Griffins Creek Rd
Joe Collins Road
Bluff Road
601
South Cedar Creek
Canoe Landing
Cedar Creek
Canoe Trail
3
Trail
Congaree
Swamp
Cedar Creek
Kingville
Bates Ferry Tr.
Fork Swamp Trailhead
East
Congaree
4
Bates Bridge
Boat Landing
Congaree Bluffs
Heritage Preserve
Congaree River
Turkey Track
Lane
Wateree River
Fort Motte Road
Fort Motte
601
419
419
Santee River
TO
ORANGEBURG

Close your eyes deep within the swamp at Congaree National Park and you'll hear a vibrant soundscape—wind rustling in the cypress trees, a pileated woodpecker calling. Open them and see rainbows of natural oil across the still water covering the forest floor.

The whole park is part of the 315,000-acre Cowasee Basin, called the "Green Heart of South Carolina." Park borders lie almost entirely within the flood plain of the Congaree River, protecting its ancient cypress trees from logging by the sheer difficulty of accessing them. During the American Revolution, this forbidding forest allowed patriot militias to disappear and retreat to relative safety—the British army didn't dare wade into the swamp. In the centuries that followed, attempts to settle the land were foiled by the Congaree River's fluctuating water levels. That same phenomenon protected the old growth stands of cypress trees that survive within the park, even as the region experienced a logging boom in the early 20th century.

In 1976, in the wake of renewed logging interest, local preservation groups (led by visitor center namesake, Harry Hampton) succeeded in protecting the land as the Congaree Swamp National Monument. It became a National Park—South Carolina's first—in 2003.

When the Congaree overflows its banks (which occurs throughout the year, but most often in the fall through early spring), only the Boardwalk Trail and Bluff Trail are accessible without a canoe or kayak. Congaree is a place that nature intended to leave for the animals and plants. Park infrastructure like the Boardwalk Trail gives visitors a glimpse of this enchanting world.

Planning

When to Go

Each season at Congaree offers distinct advantages and necessitates its own precautions. During summer, lower water levels allow easier access deep into the park, but you'll share space with abundant wildlife that includes six species of venomous snakes, sweltering temperatures and a mosquito population that's monitored by an informal gauge at the trailhead (peaking at "war zone"). During winter, when temperatures average in the 50s, you're unlikely to contend with bugs or snakes, but trails are more likely to be underwater or muddy. Outside of the easily accessible Boardwalk Trail—and only then on Saturdays and holidays—Congaree is largely a quiet, solitary experience. The exception is on May evenings, when the synchronous fireflies put on their show and the small parking lot exceeds capacity.

AVERAGE HIGH/LOW TEMPERATURES					
JAN.	**FEB.**	**MAR.**	**APR.**	**MAY**	**JUNE**
56/33	59/35	68/44	75/50	81/59	89/68
JULY	**AUG.**	**SEPT.**	**OCT.**	**NOV.**	**DEC.**
91/71	91/71	85/65	75/52	67/41	58/34

FESTIVALS AND EVENTS

Congaree SwampFest. On the grounds of the nearby historic Harriet Barber house, this private annual event (tickets are $25 per person) offers an authentic taste of life in the Carolina lowlands, including local barbecue and live R&B music.

Fireflies Festival. The fireflies in Congaree exhibit a rare phenomenon—during their two-week mating season each spring (fluctuating between mid-May and mid-June), they glow in sync with one another, lighting the forest with a dazzling natural glow. During this brief time period, Congaree National Park's visitor center remains open until 10 pm, with special parking, hiking, and camping restrictions to prevent overcrowding. Shuttles from Columbia are also available.

Getting Here and Around

AIR

Columbia Metropolitan Airport (CAE) is 30 minutes from the park. The park is also accessible from Charleston International Airport (CHS) in just under two hours driving time (about 100 miles).

CAR

Despite its relative proximity to Columbia, Congaree feels remote. The nearby small towns are little more than intersections with a convenience store. Visitors not camping in the park make the half-hour drive from Columbia on the rural two-lane Highway 48. From Columbia, head south on 48. After passing Interstate 77, it's a straight shot until turning right at the park entrance road.

Visitors from Charleston have the option of approaching via the east. From Interstate 95 in Santee, take U.S.-301 for three miles to SC-267. This road parallels Lake Marion as it heads north (Lone Star BBQ near Elloree is an excellent lunch stop) until intersection U.S.-601, which crosses the Congaree River and offers access to the east end of the park. From 601, travel west on Highway 48 to the park entrance.

TRAIN

Amtrak's Silver Star train stops in Columbia. From there, a private vehicle is needed to reach the park.

Inspiration

Congaree was only recently discovered by most travelers. Its difficult-to-access interior means that prior to national park infrastructure, few people ventured into the swamp. That's reflected in the lack of literature and film about the park. One exception is Mark Kinzer's *Nature's Return: An Environmental History of Congaree National Park,* which explores the logging industry's role in transforming the swamp, and reveals the indicators visitors can look for to see signs of a recovering ecosystem.

19th-century novelist, William Gilmore Simms, set one of his novels in the swamp. *The Scout: Or, the Black Riders of Congaree* takes place in the 1780s, during the American Revolution.

Park Essentials

ACCESSIBILITY

The Boardwalk Trail is suitable for wheelchairs and strollers; it's filled with families on weekends. There are two wheelchairs with big inflatable tires that can be borrowed at the visitor center, enabling access to the flat and wide Sims Trail.

PARK FEES AND PERMITS

There are no entrance fees at Congaree. Overnight camping is $20 per site at Longleaf Campground and $5 per site at Bluff Campground. Backcountry camping is free—obtain a permit at the visitor center. Fishing requires a South Carolina freshwater fishing license.

PARK HOURS

The park, which is in the Eastern time zone, is open 24/7. The Harry Hampton Visitor Center is open from 9 am to 4 pm daily, and until 10 pm during the two-week Fireflies Festival.

CELL PHONE RECEPTION

LTE service is strong at the visitor center and Boardwalk Trail. Signals become weaker—but are still generally available—on trails in the southern half of the park.

Hotels

There are no hotels within the Congaree National Park borders, but there are two primitive campgrounds within its borders. For more refined lodging, visitors must travel to Columbia, half an hour away, where there are plenty of chain and boutique hotel options.

Restaurants

There are no concessions in the park, and dining options near Congaree are limited. The visitor center has a limited selection of snacks and drinks for sale. Most day-trippers bring a picnic. Plan on dinner in Columbia, where a few spots like Motor Supply Company Bistro and Publico rival the fare in Charleston. However, if you find yourself in need of nearby sustenance, there are two restaurants within 10 minutes of the park entrance.

Tours

Local outfitters run regular day trips and overnight excursions on Cedar Creek, and several offer kayak and canoe rentals.

Park rangers lead regular guided walks and paddles in the park, including Discovery Walks along the Boardwalk Trail that inform visitors about the hardwood forest's history and importance. Numbered stations along the trail also facilitate a self-guided tour—free informative pamphlets are available at the Harry Hampton Visitor Center. Other occasional tours include the Owl Prowl, an evening walk focused on bird calls and nocturnal animals. Available tours are posted to the calendar on the website.

Carolina Outdoor Adventures

ECOTOURISM | FAMILY | Naturalist guides lead paddlers on a three-hour out-and-back kayak tour, departing from South Cedar Creek Canoe Landing. Tours are available on weekends during winter and throughout the week during spring and fall. If you visit on a full moon, their night paddles offer an otherworldly experience into the blackwater swamp ✉ *Hopkins* ☎ *803/381–2293* 🌐 *carolinaoutdooradventures.com* 🎫 *$75.*

Discovery Walks

WALKING TOURS | Volunteer naturalists lead these free, leisurely two-hour walks on Saturday (typically at 9:30, but call because they vary) that explore the animal and plant life around the Boardwalk Trail. The biggest values are in identifying bird calls (and locating the birds) and finding small animals like salamanders and crawfish that are difficult to spot without expert guidance. Families are welcome. ✉ *Harry Hampton Visitor Center, 100*

National Park Rd. ☎ *803/776–4396* 🌐 *www.nps.gov/cong* 🎫 *Free.*

JK Adventure Guides

ECOTOURISM | FAMILY | Early birds and weekday visitors appreciate the 9 am tours offered by this local outfitter. Many birds are still active in the late morning, especially during winter. These two- to three-hour tours leave from South Cedar Creek Canoe Landing. ✉ *Hopkins* ☎ *803/397–0000* 🌐 *jkadventureguides.com* 🎫 *$80.*

Owl Prowl

WALKING TOURS | FAMILY | When the sun sets in Congaree Swamp, a symphony of nocturnal birds and animals begin their day. A park ranger or volunteer naturalist leads these two-hour guided walks along the Boardwalk Trail that begin at dusk on weekend evenings (call first to confirm). Guests frequently hear and spot owls along the trail, including the Great Horned Owl. **■ TIP→ Bring a flashlight with a red light mode so that lights don't disturb the animal life. Red cellophane is available from rangers to cover flashlights without this feature.** ✉ *Harry Hampton Visitor Center, 100 National Park Rd.* ☎ *803/776–4396* 🌐 *www.nps.gov/cong.*

Palmetto Outdoors

ECOTOURISM | FAMILY | During spring and fall, Palmetto offers guided three-hour tours at 11 am on weekends from South Cedar Creek Canoe Landing. There are shuttles from Columbia. ✉ *Hopkins* ☎ *803/404–8254* 🌐 *palmettooutdoor.com* 🎫 *$80.*

River Runner Outdoor Center

ECOTOURISM | FAMILY | This outfitter has led tours in Congaree since before it was a national park, and their guides are top-notch. The three-tours depart at 1 pm on Saturday between February through May and in October and November. For unguided trips, River Runner rents kayaks and canoes and offers shuttles. ✉ *Hopkins* ☎ *803/776–4396* 🌐 *shopriverrunner.com* 🎫 *$60.*

Wilderness Guided Canoe Tours

ECOTOURISM | FAMILY | In addition to the daily tours led by local outfitters (see "Canoeing and Kayaking"), park rangers offer guided canoe trips through the swamp. Tours are three hours and are typically offered during spring and fall. All equipment is provided. Children over six are welcome but must know how to swim. Fees may apply, and reservations are available at 🌐 *recreation.gov* when these tours become available. ✉ *100 National Park Rd., Hopkins* ☎ *803/776–4396* 🌐 *www.nps.gov/cong.*

Visitor Information

CONTACTS Congaree National Park. ✉ *100 National Park Rd., Hopkins* ☎ *803/776–4396* 🌐 *www.nps.gov/cong.*

The Swamp

19 miles from downtown Columbia.

The drive from Columbia and entrance road into the park give glimpses of the bottomland forest that forms the Congaree River's floodplain, but seconds from the Harry Hampton Visitor Center on the Boardwalk Trail, hikers enter another world. The elevated 2-mile Boardwalk Trail transports visitors into a magical, primordial world of towering cypress trees whose distinctive knees (above-ground root protrusions) break the surface of the muddy, flooded forest.

Sights

SCENIC STOPS

Bannister Bridge Canoe Access

BODY OF WATER | FAMILY | Even if you're not planning a paddle trip, it's worth a stop to see Cedar Creek at this landing on Old Bluff Road, 2 miles before the park entrance. A 100-yard trail from the parking area leads to a high bank along the creek that's a perfect place to stop for a snack or picnic. ✉ *183 Roger Myers Rd.*

South Cedar Creek Canoe Landing

BODY OF WATER | Paddlers planning a one-way canoe day trip from Bannister Bridge Canoe Access will take out here, and it's also the primary access point for out-and-back paddles into the swamp. A bridge crosses Cedar Creek here at an endpoint of the Kingsnake Trail. ✉ *Congaree National Park* ✣ *Exiting the park, take a right and travel 2.6 miles on Old Bluff Rd. to South Cedar Creek Rd. Take a right and continue 1.8 miles to the landing.*

TRAILS

Bates Ferry Trail

TRAIL | **FAMILY** | From U.S.-601 in the east section of the park, this 19th-century road—once the route to a ferry across the river—offers the easiest access to the Congaree River in the park. A few sections of the 1.1-mile path can be soggy, but it's manageable any time of year. In the summer, low water levels often reveal a wide sandbar along the riverbank that's perfect for a picnic. *Easy.* ■ TIP→ **The General Greene Tree—Congaree's largest bald cypress tree at 30 feet in circumference—is along this trail.** ✉ *Congaree National Park* ✣ *Trailhead: A brown National Park sign marks the trail along U.S.-601, exactly 2 miles south of the intersection of 601 and SC-48.*

Bluff Trail

TRAIL | **FAMILY** | New growth loblolly pines form the canopy over this 1.8-mile trail that passes through a dramatically different habitat than the lowland swamp. The trail loops past both campgrounds. When high water levels prevent a deeper exploration of the swamp, the Bluff Trail is a pleasant alternative. *Easy.* ✉ *Congaree National Park* ✣ *Trailhead: Start this loop from the Harry Hampton Visitor Center or the Longleaf Campground.*

★ **Boardwalk Trail**

TRAIL | **FAMILY** | Most visitors to Congaree come to walk this easy 2.6-mile loop. The elevated boardwalk lets you experience perennially flooded areas of the forest that are otherwise difficult to access. Bring binoculars to spy on woodpeckers, and look out for otters at the Weston Lake overlook. ■ TIP→ **Benches built into the handrails offer idyllic spots to stop for a picnic along your walk.** *Easy.* ✉ *Congaree National Park* ✣ *Trailhead: Harry Hampton Visitor Center.*

Kingsnake Trail

TRAIL | This narrow 6-mile path offers the easiest trail access to the most remote parts of the park, but requires a shuttle to be walked as a one-way. The trail spurs off of the Weston Lake Loop and parallels Cedar Creek before jutting south, and then turns to rejoin the creek at the South Cedar Creek Canoe Landing. *Moderate.* ■ TIP→ **This trail is not a loop, so either drop a car for a shuttle or plan an out-and-back hike.** ✉ *Congaree National Park* ✣ *Trailhead: South Cedar Creek Canoe Landing or the Harry Hampton Visitor Center, via the Weston Lake Trail.*

Sims Trail

TRAIL | **FAMILY** | Bisecting the Boardwalk Trail loop, the wide Sims Trail runs a straight line through the swamp on an elevated causeway that was once a hunting road. It's a pleasant walk that sees fewer crowds than the Boardwalk loop on busy weekend days, and it's the fastest route to access the wilderness trails deeper in the park. *Easy.* ✉ *Congaree National Park* ✣ *Trailhead: Harry Hampton Visitor Center.*

★ **Weston Lake Loop Trail**

TRAIL | **FAMILY** | Visitors wanting to see a bit more than the Boardwalk, but who want to keep their feet (relatively) clean, can tackle this 4.4-mile loop that passes its namesake lake deep in the forest. The southern edge of the trail parallels Cedar Creek, where you'll see much of the same scenery (including wood ducks) that you'd experience via a paddle trip. *Easy.* ✉ *Congaree National Park* ✣ *Trailhead: Harry Hampton Visitor Center, via the Boardwalk Trail.*

Called bald cypress knees, these formations can be found all over the swamp; their purpose is unknown.

VISITOR CENTER

Harry Hampton Visitor Center

MUSEUM | FAMILY | Nearly all of the park's trails, including the Boardwalk Trail, begin and end at this small but thoughtful visitor center. Inside, you'll find a gift shop; exhibits about the park's animals, trees, and flora; and a theater with a short video on the park's history. Volunteer docents staff the trailhead to provide updated info on conditions and recent wildlife sightings. **■ TIP→ If you forgot bug spray or didn't pack enough water, stop into the gift shop before your hike for critical supplies.** Adjacent to the visitor center, a covered pavilion includes picnic tables and trashcans. ✉ *100 National Park Rd.* ☎ *803/776–4396* 🌐 *nps.gov/cong.*

Activities

BIRD-WATCHING

The soundscape at Congaree is almost as stunning as the visual spectacle. Close your eyes, and apart from wind rustling in the cypress trees far overhead, you'll hear songbirds, the screeches of pileated woodpeckers, and the calls of owls. Nearly 200 bird species call Congaree home at some point during the year, including abundant wild turkey, barred owls, wood ducks and several species of woodpecker. Winter months offer clear vistas across the swamp, offering incredible vantage points of woodpeckers and warblers hunting their prey. Even visitors typically not interested in birding will be grateful to have binoculars on hand.

CANOEING AND KAYAKING

Cedar Creek is a blackwater stream that runs through the heart of Congaree; the Cedar Creek Canoe Trail follows approximately 15 miles of the river, starting at Bannister's Bridge and going all the way to the Congaree River. Local outfitters and park rangers offer canoe trips and rentals. Self-supported paddlers can drop a car at South Cedar Creek Canoe Landing to paddle the 6½ miles (3–5 hours) from Bannister Bridge Landing as a day trip, or obtain a backcountry camping permit to tackle the 21 miles to Bates Bridge Landing, through the most remote sections of the park. Be aware of water levels and forecasts, and for longer trips, be prepared to portage around downed trees through muddy banks where snakes are common during warmer months.

EDUCATIONAL PROGRAMS

Park rangers lead regular guided walks and paddles in the park; available tours are posted to the calendar on the park's website. ⇨ *See the Tours section in the chapter planner for more information.*

Families can pick up a free Junior Ranger program booklet at the visitor center. These activity packets help to keep younger visitors engaged with their surroundings through scavenger hunts and interactive games. Kids earn a badge or patch for participating.

FISHING

The hike-in nature of fishing within Congaree equals low pressure and healthy populations of striped bass, yellow perch, bluegill, and catfish, among others. A South Carolina freshwater license is required ($11 for a 14-day license, available at 🌐 *dnr.sc.gov*). Weston Lake is the most popular and easily accessible spot (1½ miles from the visitor center). Note that fishing from footbridges is not permitted within the park. Bait and tackle are for sale (and the local knowledge is free) at Smooth Quick Stop Convenience Store (✉ *6045 Bluff Rd.*), five miles west of the park entrance on Highway 48.

HIKING

Exploring Congaree on foot ranges from the easy Boardwalk Trail loop to rugged, long-distance adventures in the backcountry that require wading through flooded areas. Nearly every trail in the park begins and ends at the Harry Hampton Visitor Center. To escape Saturday crowds on the boardwalk, add the Sims Trail or the Weston Lake Loop Trail to your itinerary. The truly adventurous can tackle the Oakridge Trail, the River Trail and the Kingsnake Trail (a one-way trail from the visitor center to the South Cedar Creek Canoe Landing). The still-developing east end of the park includes the short Fork Swamp Trail loop and the Bates Ferry Trail, notable for its easy access to the Congaree River (as opposed to the 10-mile River Trail loop).

What's Nearby

The area around Congaree Swamp is rural and undeveloped, but there are a few amenities available to park visitors. Driving west from the park (3.8 miles from the entrance), the small town of **Gadsden** has a gas station and two restaurants, Big T's BBQ and JD's Place.

Columbia, South Carolina's capital city, is also a college town (the University of South Carolina dominates much of downtown), making it an excellent base for exploring Congaree National Park. For visitors not camping within the park, it's also the most practical place to stay. In addition to the usual array of recognizable chains, several boutique hotels offer attractive options like the Graduate Columbia and Hotel Trundle. Plan on dinner in Columbia, where a few spots like Motor Supply Company Bistro and Publico rival the fare in Charleston.

En route from Columbia, 5 miles before the park entrance, Smooth Quick Stop Convenience Store (✉ *6045 Bluff Rd.*), sells drinks, snacks, and fishing supplies.

Chapter 16

CRATER LAKE NATIONAL PARK

Updated by
Andrew Collins

Camping	Hotels	Activities	Scenery	Crowds
★★★☆☆	★★★☆☆	★★★★☆	★★★★★	★★★★★

WELCOME TO CRATER LAKE NATIONAL PARK

TOP REASONS TO GO

★ **The lake:** Cruise inside the caldera basin and gaze into the extraordinary sapphire-blue water of the country's deepest lake, stopping for a ramble around Wizard Island.

★ **Native land:** Enjoy the rare luxury of interacting with totally unspoiled terrain.

★ **The night sky:** Billions of stars glisten in the pitch-black darkness of an unpolluted sky.

★ **Splendid hikes:** Accessible trails spool off the main roads and wind past colorful bursts of wildflowers and cascading waterfalls.

★ **Lake-rim lodging:** Spend the night perched on the lake rim at the rustic yet stately Crater Lake Lodge.

1 **Rim Village.** Situated about 900 feet above the lake's south shore, this is the point from which most visitors first lay eyes on the lake. Home to historic Crater Lake Lodge, a gift shop, café, and visitor center, it's the only area along the rim with year-round access.

2 **Rim Drive.** This 33-mile scenic road encircles the lake and connects with Rim Village, the North Entrance road, and Cleetwood Cove's trailhead as well as some of the most popular overlooks and hikes in the park.

3 **Cleetwood Cove and Wizard Island.** A steep 1.1-mile trail leads down to Cleetwood Cove, which offers visitors the only access to the lake's edge; boat tours leave from the dock and circle the lake and, in some cases, ferry passengers to Wizard Island, a volcanic cinder cone on the west side of the lake.

4 **Mazama Village.** About 5 miles south of Rim Village and adjacent to the only year-round entrance (Annie Springs), this cluster of services is a good place to stock up on snacks, beverages, and fuel and contains the park's only other lodging.

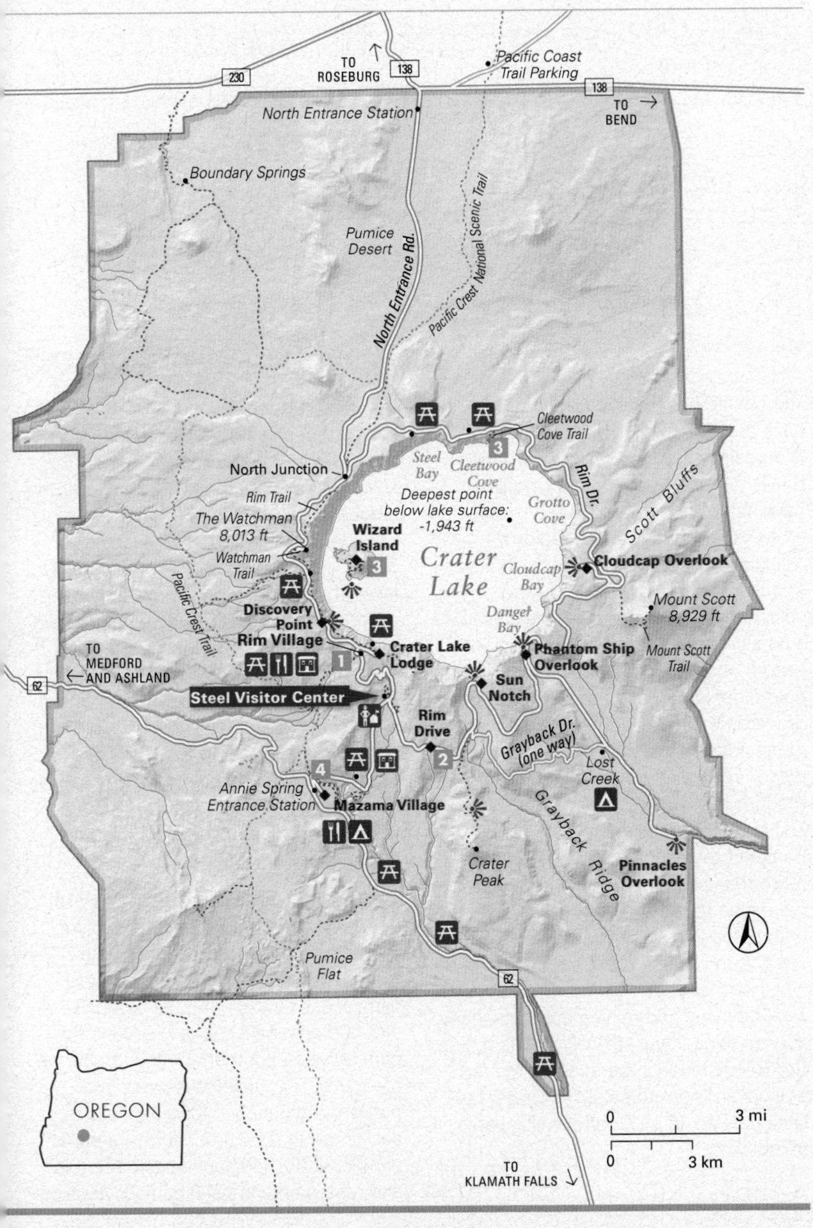
TO ROSEBURG
230
138
Pacific Coast Trail Parking
138
TO BEND
North Entrance Station
Boundary Springs
Pumice Desert
North Entrance Rd.
Pacific Crest National Scenic Trail
Cleetwood Cove Trail
North Junction
Steel Bay
Cleetwood Cove
Deepest point below lake surface: -1,943 ft
Grotto Cove
Rim Dr.
Scott Bluffs
Rim Trail
The Watchman 8,013 ft
Wizard Island
Crater Lake
Cloudcap Bay
Cloudcap Overlook
Watchman Trail
Pacific Crest Trail
Discovery Point
Danger Bay
Mount Scott 8,929 ft
Rim Village
Crater Lake Lodge
Phantom Ship Overlook
Mount Scott Trail
TO MEDFORD AND ASHLAND
62
Steel Visitor Center
Sun Notch
Rim Drive
Grayback Dr. (one way)
Lost Creek
Annie Spring Entrance Station
Mazama Village
Grayback Ridge
Crater Peak
Pinnacles Overlook
Pumice Flat
62
OREGON
0
3 mi
0
3 km
TO KLAMATH FALLS

The pure, crystalline blue of Crater Lake astounds visitors at first sight. More than 5 miles wide and ringed by cliffs almost 2,000 feet high, the 400-foot-deep lake was created approximately 7,700 years ago, following Mt. Mazama's fiery explosion. Today, it's both the clearest and deepest lake in the United States—and the ninth deepest in the world.

Human life has thrived around Crater Lake and the surrounding Cascade Mountains since the massive eruption of Mt. Mazama—park archaeologists have actually unearthed human-made artifacts, attributed to the region's Makalak (today's Klamath tribe) indigenous inhabitants, beneath layers of volcanic debris. Europeans, specifically a small band of ragtag prospectors in search of a fabled (and never to be found) goldmine, laid eyes on this ethereal body of water in 1853. Over the next couple of decades, more visitors arrived and a wagon road that would become today's modern Highway 62 was constructed just south of the lake en route from Prospect to Fort Klamath. Using nothing more than pipe and piano wire, surveyors were able to determine the lake's depth with surprising accuracy in 1886—they were found much more recently to be off by a mere 53 feet. Against the wishes of local ranching and mining interests, early conservation advocate William Gladstone Steel succeeded in persuading the federal government to establish Crater Lake National Park in 1902, after many years of lobbying.

For most of today's visitors, the park's star attractions are the lake itself and the breathtakingly situated Crater Lake Lodge, which was built 12 years after the establishment of the park. The terrace outside the lodge is a particularly memorable spot to gaze out at this immense lake, but you can view it from dozens of other spots along Rim Drive, the 33-mile paved road that encircles it. A favorite overlook affords a clear view down to Phantom Ship, which vaguely resembles a ghost ship with its several vertical rock pillars. From high atop the lake's rim, Phantom Ship also looks tiny. In fact, it's the height of a 14-story building. Though it takes some effort to reach, Wizard Island is another outstanding draw.

There's more to this park than the lake, however. Other park highlights include the natural, unspoiled beauty of the forest and the geological marvels you can access by exploring the extensive 183,000-acre backcountry. Beyond the park borders, southern Oregon's charms are many, from wildlife refuges and outdoor recreation in Klamath Falls to acclaimed theater productions, a super wine country, and sophisticated hotels and restaurants in Ashland and Medford.

AVERAGE HIGH/LOW TEMPERATURES					
JAN.	**FEB.**	**MAR.**	**APR.**	**MAY**	**JUNE**
34/18	35/18	37/19	42/23	50/28	58/34
JULY	**AUG.**	**SEPT.**	**OCT.**	**NOV.**	**DEC.**
68/41	69/41	63/37	52/31	40/23	34/19

Planning

When to Go

The park's high season is July and August. September and early October are also popular but tend to draw smaller crowds. By mid-October until well into June, most of the park closes due to heavy snowfall. The road is kept open just from the South Entrance to Rim Village in winter, except during severe weather. Early summer snowmelt often creates watery breeding areas for mosquitoes. Bring lots of insect repellent in June and July to help fend off mosquito swarms in the early morning and at sunset. You might even consider a hat with mosquito netting.

Getting Here and Around

AIR

Rogue Valley International–Medford Airport (MFR) is the nearest commercial airport. About 75 miles southwest of the park, it's served by Alaska, Allegiant, American, Delta, and United Airlines and has rental car agencies. Amtrak trains stop in downtown Klamath Falls, 50 miles south of the park; car rentals are available there, too.

CAR

Crater Lake National Park's South (aka Annie Spring) Entrance, open year-round, is off southern Oregon's Highway 62, which runs northeast from Interstate 5 in Medford and northwest from U.S. 97 in Klamath Falls. From Portland, allow from 5½ to 6 hours to reach the park's South Entrance (via Interstate 5 to Medford). In summer, when the North Entrance is open, the drive from Portland takes just 4½ hours via Interstate 5 to Roseberg and then Highway 138.

Most of the park is accessible only from late June or early July through mid-October. The rest of the year, snow blocks park roadways and entrances except Highway 62 and the road from Mazama Village to Rim Village. Also in winter, no gasoline is available in the park, so be sure to top off your tank before you arrive. Beware that you may encounter icy conditions any time of year, particularly in the early morning.

Inspiration

Crater Lake National Park: A Global Treasure, by former park rangers Ann and Myron Sutton, celebrates the park's first 100 years with stunning photography, charts, and drawings.

*Crater Lake: The Story Behind the Scenery,*by Ronald G. Warfield, Lee Juillerat, Larry Smith, and Peter C. Howorth, creates an overview of Crater Lake's history and physical features with large photos and detailed captions that accompany the text.

*Wild,*the acclaimed 2014 film starring Reese Witherspoon and based on Cheryl Strayed's memoir about hiking the entire Pacific Crest Trail, contains some gorgeous scenes filmed at Crater Lake.

Park Essentials

ACCESSIBILITY

All the overlooks along Rim Drive are accessible to those with impaired mobility, as are Crater Lake Lodge, the facilities at Rim Village (with the exception of Sinnott Memorial Overlook), and Steel Visitor Center. A half-dozen accessible campsites are available at Mazama Campground.

PARK FEES AND PERMITS

Admission to the park is $30 per vehicle in summer, $20 in winter, good for seven days. For overnight trips, backcountry campers and hikers must obtain a free wilderness permit at Canfield Ranger Station, adjacent to Steel Visitor Center and open daily 9–5 from mid-April through early November, and 10–4 the rest of the year.

PARK HOURS

Crater Lake National Park is open 24 hours a day year-round; however, snow closes most park roadways from October to June. Lodging and most dining facilities are open usually from late May to mid-October (Rim Village Café the one year-round dining option). The park is in the Pacific time zone.

CELL PHONE RECEPTION

Cell phone reception in the park is spotty, although it's reasonably strong in Rim Village and Mazama Village.

Hotels

Crater Lake's summer season is relatively brief, and Crater Lake Lodge, the park's main accommodation, generally books up a year in advance, but it's worth checking even on short notice, as last-minute cancellations do happen on occasion. The other in-park option, the Cabins at Mazama Village, also books up early in summer. Outside the park there are a few spots in small towns near the park, like Prospect and Union Creek, and you'll find numerous lodgings in Klamath Falls, Medford, Ashland, and—worth considering if you're visiting the park via the North Entrance—Roseburg. Even Bend is an option, as it's just a two-hour drive from North Entrance, which is only slightly longer than the drive from Ashland to the South Entrance. *Hotel reviews have been shortened. For full information, visit Fodors.com.*

Restaurants

There are just a few casual eateries and convenience stores within the park, all in Rim Village or Mazama Village. For a memorable meal on the caldera's rim, book a meal at Crater Lake Lodge. Outside the park, Klamath Falls has a smattering of good restaurants, and both Medford and Ashland abound with first-rate eateries serving farm-to-table cuisine and local Rogue Valley wines. *Restaurant reviews have been shortened. For full information visit Fodors.com.*

What It Costs

	$	$$	$$$	$$$$
RESTAURANTS				
	under $16	$16–$22	$23–$30	over $30
HOTELS				
	under $150	$150–$200	$201–$250	over $250

Tours

★ Boat Tours

BOAT TOURS | FAMILY | The most popular way to tour Crater Lake itself is on a two-hour ranger-led excursion aboard a 37-passenger launch. The first narrated tour leaves the dock at 9:30 am; the last departs at 3:45 pm. Several of the 10 daily boats stop at Wizard Island, where you can get off and reboard three or six hours later. Some of these trips act as shuttles, with no ranger narration. They're perfect if you just want to get to Wizard Island to hike. The shuttles leave at 8:30 and 11:30 and return to Cleetwood Cove at 12:15, 3:05, and 4:35. To get to the dock you must hike down Cleetwood Cove Trail, a strenuous 1.1-mile walk that descends 700 feet in elevation along the way; only those in excellent physical shape should attempt the hike. Bring adequate water with you. Purchase boat-tour tickets at Crater Lake Lodge, Annie Creek Restaurant and gift shop, the top of the trail, and through reservations. Restrooms are available at the top and bottom of the trail. ✉ *Crater Lake National Park* ✣ *Access Cleetwood Cove Trail off Rim Dr., 11 miles north of Rim Village* ☎ *866/292–6720* 🌐 *www.travelcraterlake.com* 🎫 *From $28.*

Visitor Information

PARK CONTACT INFORMATION Crater Lake National Park. ☎ *541/594–3000* 🌐 *www.nps.gov/crla.*

Rim Village

7 miles north of Mazama Village and South Entrance, 15 miles south of North Entrance, 80 miles northeast of Medford.

The park's most famous man-made attraction, Crater Lake Lodge, is the centerpiece of this small cluster of buildings located just off Rim Drive and offering stupendous views of the lake. A paved promenade some 900 feet above the lake's surface runs west from the lodge past a seasonal (summer only) visitor center, Sinnott Memorial Overlook, and the Rim Village Cafe and Gift Shop, which is the only restaurant and retailer in the park open in winter. The paved walkway continues for a short distance east of the lodge before connecting to the popular Garfield Peak Trail.

Sights

HISTORIC SITES

★ Crater Lake Lodge

HOTEL—SIGHT | Built in 1915, this regal log-and-stone structure was designed in the classic style of western national park lodges, and the original lodgepole-pine pillars, beams, and stone fireplaces are still intact. The lobby, fondly referred to as the Great Hall, serves as a warm, welcoming gathering place where you can play games, socialize with a cocktail, or gaze out of the many windows to view spectacular sunrises and sunsets by a crackling fire. Exhibits off the lobby contain historic photographs and memorabilia from throughout the park's history. ✉ *Rim Village* 🌐 *www.travelcraterlake.com.*

TRAILS

★ Garfield Peak Trail

TRAIL | Part of the fun of this dramatic 3.6-mile round-trip scramble to a rocky summit with dazzling lake views is that the hike begins and ends along the paved walkway by Crater Lake Lodge. Keep an eye out for pikas and marmots near the summit, and when you finish, congratulate your efforts after making this 1,010-foot ascent by celebrating with a drink on the terrace of the lodge. *Difficult.* ✉ *Crater Lake National Park* ✣ *Trailhead: Crater Lake Lodge.*

VISITOR CENTER

Rim Visitor Center

INFO CENTER | Stop here in summer for park information and to visit the neighboring Sinnott Memorial Overlook, which has a small museum with geology exhibits and a covered observation terrace 900 feet above the lake. Ranger talks take place several times a day, and although it's closed in winter, snowshoe walks leave from outside the visitor center on weekends. ✉ *Rim Dr.* ✣ *7 miles north of Annie Spring entrance station* ☎ *541/594–3000* 🌐 *www.nps.gov/crla* ⏲ *Closed Oct.–mid-May.*

Restaurants

★ **Crater Lake Lodge Dining Room**

$$$ | PACIFIC NORTHWEST | The only upscale restaurant option inside the park (dinner reservations are essential), the dining room is magnificent, with a large stone fireplace and views of Crater Lake's clear-blue waters. Breakfast and lunch are enjoyable here, but the dinner is the main attraction, with tempting dishes that emphasize local produce and Pacific Northwest seafood—think wild mushroom–and–caramelized onion flatbread and pan-seared wild salmon with seasonal veggies. **Known for:** nice selection of Oregon wines; Oregon berry cobbler; views of the lake. *$ Average main: $29 ✉ Crater Lake Lodge, 1 Lodge Loop Rd. ☎ 541/594–2255 🌐 www.craterlakelodges.com ⏲ Closed mid-Oct.–mid-May.*

Hotels

★ **Crater Lake Lodge**

$$$ | HOTEL | The period feel of this 1915 lodge on the caldera's rim is reflected in its lodgepole-pine columns, gleaming wood floors, and stone fireplaces in the common areas, and the simple guest rooms. **Pros:** ideal location for watching sunrise and sunset reflected on the lake; exudes rustic charm; excellent restaurant. **Cons:** books up far in advance; rooms are small and have tubs only, no shower; no air-conditioning, phone, or TV in rooms. *$ Rooms from: $209 ✉ 1 Lodge Loop Rd. ✥ Rim Village, east of Rim Visitor Center ☎ 541/594–2255, 866/292–6720 🌐 www.travelcraterlake.com ⏲ Closed mid-Oct.–mid-May 71 rooms No meals.*

Rim Drive

Access points are 4 miles north of Mazama Village and South Entrance, and 8 miles south of North Entrance.

There are few more scenic drives in the West than this 33-mile paved loop that encircles the rim of the lake. As you make your way around Rim Drive, you'll find pulloffs for some of Crater Lake's most exhilarating overlooks and hikes, including the parking area for Cleetwood Cove's boat cruises and the side road to dramatic Pinnacles Overlook. Keep in mind that Rim Drive (except for the short stretch connecting Rim Village to the South Entrance) is closed due to snow from late fall to late spring.

Sights

SCENIC DRIVES

★ **Rim Drive**

SCENIC DRIVE | Take this 33-mile scenic loop for views of the lake and its cliffs from every conceivable angle. The drive takes two hours not counting frequent stops at overlooks and short hikes that can easily stretch this to a half day. Rim Drive is typically closed due to heavy snowfall from late fall to late spring. *✉ Crater Lake National Park ✥ Access points are 4 miles north of South Entrance and 8 miles south of North Entrance.*

SCENIC STOPS

Cloudcap Overlook

VIEWPOINT | The highest road-access overlook on the Crater Lake rim, Cloudcap has a westward view (best enjoyed in the morning) across the lake to Wizard Island and an eastward view of Mt. Scott, the volcanic cone that is the park's highest point. *✉ Crater Lake National Park ✥ 1 mile off Rim Dr.*

Discovery Point

VIEWPOINT | This overlook marks the spot at which prospectors first spied the lake in 1853. Wizard Island is just northeast, close to shore. ✉ *West Rim Dr.* ✣ *1½ miles north of Rim Village.*

Phantom Ship Overlook

VIEWPOINT | From this point you can get a close look at Phantom Ship, a rock formation that resembles a schooner with furled masts and looks ghostly in fog. ✉ *East Rim Dr.*

★ Pinnacles Overlook

VIEWPOINT | Ascending from the banks of Sand and Wheeler creeks, unearthly spires of eroded ash resemble the peaks of fairy-tale castles. Once upon a time, the road continued east to a former entrance. A path now replaces the old road and follows the rim of Sand Creek (affording more views of pinnacles) to where the entrance sign still stands. ✉ *End of Pinnacles Rd.* ✣ *6 miles from Rim Rd.*

Sun Notch

VIEWPOINT | It's a relatively easy ½-mile loop hike through wildflowers and dry meadow to this overlook, which has views of Crater Lake and Phantom Ship. Mind the cliff edges. ✉ *East Rim Dr.*

TRAILS

★ Castle Crest Wildflower Trail

TRAIL | This picturesque 1-mile round-trip trek passes through a spring-fed meadow and is one of the park's flatter hikes. Wildflowers burst into full bloom here in July. You can also access Castle Crest via a similarly easy ½-mile loop trail from East Rim Drive. *Easy.* ✉ *Crater Lake National Park* ✣ *Trailhead: E. Rim Dr., across road from Steel Visitor Center.*

★ Mt. Scott Trail

TRAIL | This strenuous 4½-mile round-trip trail takes you to the park's highest point—the top of Mt. Scott, the oldest volcanic cone of Mt. Mazama, at 8,929 feet. At a leisurely pace, give yourself about two hours to make the steep uphill trek—and about 60 minutes to get down. The trail starts at an elevation of about 7,679 feet, so the climb is not extreme, but the trail is steep in spots. The views of the lake and the broad Klamath Basin are spectacular. *Difficult.* ✉ *Crater Lake National Park* ✣ *Trailhead: Rim Dr., across from road to Cloudcap Overlook.*

Pacific Crest Trail

TRAIL | You can hike a portion of the Pacific Crest Trail, which extends from Mexico to Canada and winds through the park for 33 miles. For this prime backcountry experience, catch the trail off Highway 138 about a mile east of the North Entrance, where it heads south and then toward the west rim of the lake and circles it for about 6 miles, then descends down Dutton Creek to the Mazama Village area. You'll need a detailed map for this hike; check online or with the PCT association. *Difficult.* ✉ *Crater Lake National Park* ✣ *Trailhead: At Pacific Crest Trail parking lot, off Hwy. 138, 1 mile east of North Entrance* 🌐 *www.pcta.org.*

★ Watchman Peak Trail

TRAIL | This is one of the park's best and most easily accessed hikes. Though it's just more than 1½ miles round-trip, the trail climbs more than 400 feet—not counting the steps up to the actual lookout, which has great views of Wizard Island and the lake. *Moderate.* ✉ *Crater Lake National Park* ✣ *Trailhead: At Watchman Overlook, Rim Dr., about 4 miles northwest of Rim Village.*

VISITOR CENTER

Steel Visitor Center

INFO CENTER | Open year-round, the center, part of the park's headquarters, has restrooms, a small post office, and a shop that sells books, maps, and postcards. There are fewer exhibits than at comparable national park visitor centers, but you can view an engaging 22-minute film that describes the lake's formation and geology and examines the area's cultural history. ✉ *Rim Dr.* ✣ *4 miles north of Annie Spring entrance station* ☎ *541/594–3000* 🌐 *www.nps.gov/crla.*

The sunsets, and sunrises, over Crater Lake are quite spectacular, especially when the light hits Wizard Island.

Cleetwood Cove and Wizard Island

11 miles north of Rim Visitor Center, 13 miles southeast of North Entrance.

Offering the only permissible way to access the lake, Cleetwood Cove and its boat dock are reached by hiking down a 1.1-mile switchback trail—it's an easy ramble down, but getting back up to the trailhead can be challenging if you're not in good shape or unused to high elevations. Boat cruises around the lake and out to Wizard Island, a craggy volcanic cinder cone that's great fun to explore, depart from the cove.

Sights

SCENIC STOPS

★ Wizard Island

BODY OF WATER | The volcanic eruption that led to the creation of Crater Lake resulted in the formation of this magical island a ¼ mile off the lake's western shore. The views at its summit—reached on a somewhat challenging 2-mile hike—are stupendous.

Getting to the island requires a strenuous 1-mile hike down (and later back up) the steep Cleetwood Cove Trail to the cove's dock. There, board either the shuttle boat to Wizard Island or a Crater Lake narrated tour boat that includes a stop on the island. If you opt for the latter, you can explore Wizard Island a bit and reboard a later boat to resume the lake tour.

The hike to Wizard Summit, 763 feet above the lake's surface, begins at the island's boat dock and steeply ascends over rock-strewn terrain; a path at the top circles the 90-foot-deep crater's rim. More moderate is the 1¾-mile hike on a rocky trail along the shore of Wizard Island, so called because William Steel, an early Crater Lake booster, thought its shape resembled a wizard's hat. ✉ *Crater Lake National Park* ✣ *Boats launch from foot of Cleetwood Cove Trail, off Rim Dr.* ☎ *541/594–2255,*

866/292–6720 ⊕ www.travelcraterlake.com ⊟ Shuttle boat $28, tour boat $55.

TRAILS

Cleetwood Cove Trail

TRAIL | This strenuous 2¼-mile round-trip hike descends 700 feet down nearly vertical cliffs along the lake to the boat dock. Be in very good shape before you tackle this well-maintained trail—it's the hike back up that catches some visitors unprepared. Bring along plenty of water. *Difficult. ⊠ Crater Lake National Park ✣ Trailhead: On E. Rim Dr., 4½ miles east of North Entrance Rd.*

Mazama Village

7 miles south of Rim Village, 21 miles south of North Entrance, 73 miles northeast of Medford.

Adjacent to the South (Annie Spring) Entrance and offering the only park services outside of Rim Village, this quiet, shaded area contains a summer-only campground, cabin-style motel, restaurant, convenience store with a water bottle filling station, amphitheater, and gas station.

Sights

TRAILS

Annie Creek Canyon Trail

TRAIL | This somewhat challenging 1.7-mile hike loops through a deep stream-cut canyon, providing views of the narrow cleft scarred by volcanic activity. This is a good area to look for flowers and deer. *Moderate. ⊠ Mazama Campground, Mazama Village Rd. ✣ Trailhead: Behind amphitheater between D and E campground loops.*

Godfrey Glen Trail

TRAIL | This 1.1-mile loop trail is an easy stroll through an old-growth forest with canyon views. Its dirt path is accessible to wheelchairs with assistance. *Easy. ⊠ Crater Lake National Park ✣ Trailhead: Munson Valley Rd., 2½ miles south of Steel Visitor Center.*

Restaurants

Annie Creek Restaurant

$ | AMERICAN | FAMILY | This family-friendly dining spot in Mazama Village serves hearty if unmemorable comfort fare, and service can be hit or miss. Blue cheese–bacon burgers, Cobb salads, sandwiches, meat loaf, and a tofu stir-fry are all on the menu, and American standards are served at breakfast. **Known for:** pine-shaded outdoor seating area; convenient to lake and the park's southern hiking trails; several varieties of burgers. *[$] Average main: $13 ⊠ Mazama Village Rd. and Ave. C ✣ Near Annie Spring entrance station ☎ 541/594–2255 ⊕ www.travelcraterlake.com ⊙ Closed late Sept.–late May.*

Hotels

The Cabins at Mazama Village

$$ | HOTEL | In a wooded area 7 miles south of the lake, this complex is made up of several A-frame buildings and has modest rooms with two queen beds and a private bath. **Pros:** clean and well-kept facility; very close to the lake and plenty of hiking trails; most affordable of the park lodgings. **Cons:** lots of traffic into adjacent campground; no a/c, TVs, or phones in rooms; not actually on Crater Lake (but a short drive away). *[$] Rooms from: $172 ⊠ Mazama Village ✣ Near Annie Spring entrance station ☎ 541/594–2255, 866/292–6720 ⊕ www.travelcraterlake.com ⊙ Closed late Sept.–late May ⊟ 40 rooms ⊚ No meals.*

Activities

BIKING

Circling the lake via 33-mile Rim Drive on a bicycle is a highly rewarding experience, so much so that the park holds a Ride the Rim bike event on two Saturdays each September. During this event the park closes a 24-mile portion of East Rim Drive to motor-vehicle traffic. Bikes are never permitted on park trails. The nearest place to the park to rent bikes is Diamond Lake Resort, 5 miles north of the park's North Entrance.

CAMPING

Tent campers and RV enthusiasts alike enjoy the heavily wooded and well-equipped setting of Mazama Campground. Lost Creek is much smaller, with minimal amenities and a more "rustic" Crater Lake experience. Pack bug repellent and patience if camping in the snowmelt season.

Mazama Campground. This campground open from mid-June through late September is set well below the lake caldera in the pine and fir forest of the Cascades not far from the main access road (Highway 62). Drinking water, showers, and laundry facilities help ensure that you don't have to rough it too much. About half the 214 spaces are pull-throughs, some with electricity and a few with hookups. The best tent spots are on some of the outer loops above Annie Creek Canyon. Tent sites cost $21, RV ones $31–$42. ✉ *Mazama Village, near Annie Spring entrance station* ☎ *541/594–2255, 866/292–6720* 🌐 *www.craterlakelodges.com.*

EDUCATIONAL OFFERINGS

Junior Ranger Program

TOUR—SIGHT | **FAMILY** | Kids ages 6–12 learn about Crater Lake while earning a Junior Ranger patch in daily activities in summer at the Rim Visitor Center, and year-round they can earn a badge by completing the Junior Ranger Activity Book, which can be picked up at either visitor center.

SKIING

Cross-country skiing is quite popular at Rim Village, along a portion of West Rim Drive going toward Wizard Island Overlook, and on East Rim Drive to Vidae Falls. Check the winter edition of the park newspaper (it's available online at 🌐 *www.nps.gov/crla*) for a map with descriptions of trails. The road is plowed to Rim Village, but it can be closed temporarily due to severe storms. There are no maintained alpine ski trails in the park, although some backcountry trails are marked with blue diamonds or snow poles—only experts should consider downhill skiing in the park. Snow tires and chains are essential when visiting in winter.

What's Nearby

About 30 miles south of the main Annie Spring (South) Entrance, tiny **Prospect** is the nearest town to the park—it contains a small hotel as well as a gas station and a few basic eateries, and just about 10 miles beyond you'll find the best nearby dining option, Beckie's Cafe. The main gateways to the park's year-round South Entrance are Klamath Falls (due south) and the Ashland-Medford area (southwest), and for the summer-only North Entrance, Roseburg is a good base camp. **Klamath Falls** is an easygoing center of outdoor recreation that's close to some impressive wildlife refuges and has a handful of places to stay and eat. Although a bit farther away, both the city of **Medford,** which has the region's largest airport, and the artsy and outdoorsy university town of **Ashland** offer the greatest variety of attractions in this part of the state, from a fast-growing crop of exceptional wineries to acclaimed theater. These are also good bases if planning a visit to Oregon Caves National Monument, about 75 miles west of Medford. **Roseburg's** location at the edge of the southern Cascades led to its status as a timber-industry center—still the heart of the town's economy—but its setting along the Umpqua River also draws fishing, rafting, and hiking enthusiasts. The drive from Roseburg to Crater Lake's North Entrance takes a little under two hours.

Chapter 17

CUYAHOGA VALLEY NATIONAL PARK

Updated by
Kristan Schiller

Camping ★☆☆☆☆

Hotels ★★☆☆☆

Activities ★★★★★

Scenery ★★★★★

Crowds ★★★★☆

WELCOME TO CUYAHOGA VALLEY NATIONAL PARK

TOP REASONS TO GO

★ **Hike a historic trade route:** Explore a restored section of the Ohio and Erie Canal Towpath, originally used for mules pulling canal boats that transported goods on the Ohio River.

★ **Enjoy the view:** Observe the Cuyahoga Valley from an overlook atop sandstone ledges carved by glaciers. See ancient petroglyphs or ascend a giant rock staircase.

★ **Ski the slopes:** Ski or snowboard at Boston Mills and Brandywine Ski Resorts. Enjoy apres ski around a crackling fire in a cozy alpine lodge.

★ **Take a Farm Crawl:** Visit any one of the 11 working farms that are part of the Countryside Initiative, a partnership allowing smallholders practicing sustainable agriculture to lease land within the national park.

★ **Board a scenic train ride:** Journey through the striking scenery and varied wildlife of the Cuyahoga Valley aboard a Class III railroad

1 **North.** Here you'll find some of the park's most picturesque trails including a 40-mile section of the Buckeye Trail, which encircles the entire state of Ohio. You'll also find the northern trailheads of the park's popular Towpath Trail, which follows the historic Ohio & Erie Canal, the cascading Brandywine Falls, and the Boston Mill Visitor Center, a converted 1905 general store. If it's winter, make your way to nearby Boston Mills or Brandywine Ski Resort. Spring, summer or fall, outfit yourself with a kayak and glide along the Cuyahoga River, which winds its way past the Federal-style Frazee House, the Greek Revival–style Stanford House, and the National Register of Historic Places–listed Station Road Bridge.

2 **South.** Anchored by the northern suburbs of Akron, the park's southern half contains a tapestry of historic sites, modern attractions, and pristine wilderness as well as being home of the Cuyahoga Valley Scenic Railroad, Sarah's Vineyard, and Blossom Music Center, the summer home of the world-renowned Cleveland Orchestra. Head to Howe Meadow to browse the stalls at the Countryside Farmer's Market, or make your way east to Hale Farm & Village, a living history museum that illustrates what everyday life was like on a 19th-century working farm. There's also Beaver Marsh Boardwalk which teems with wildlife.

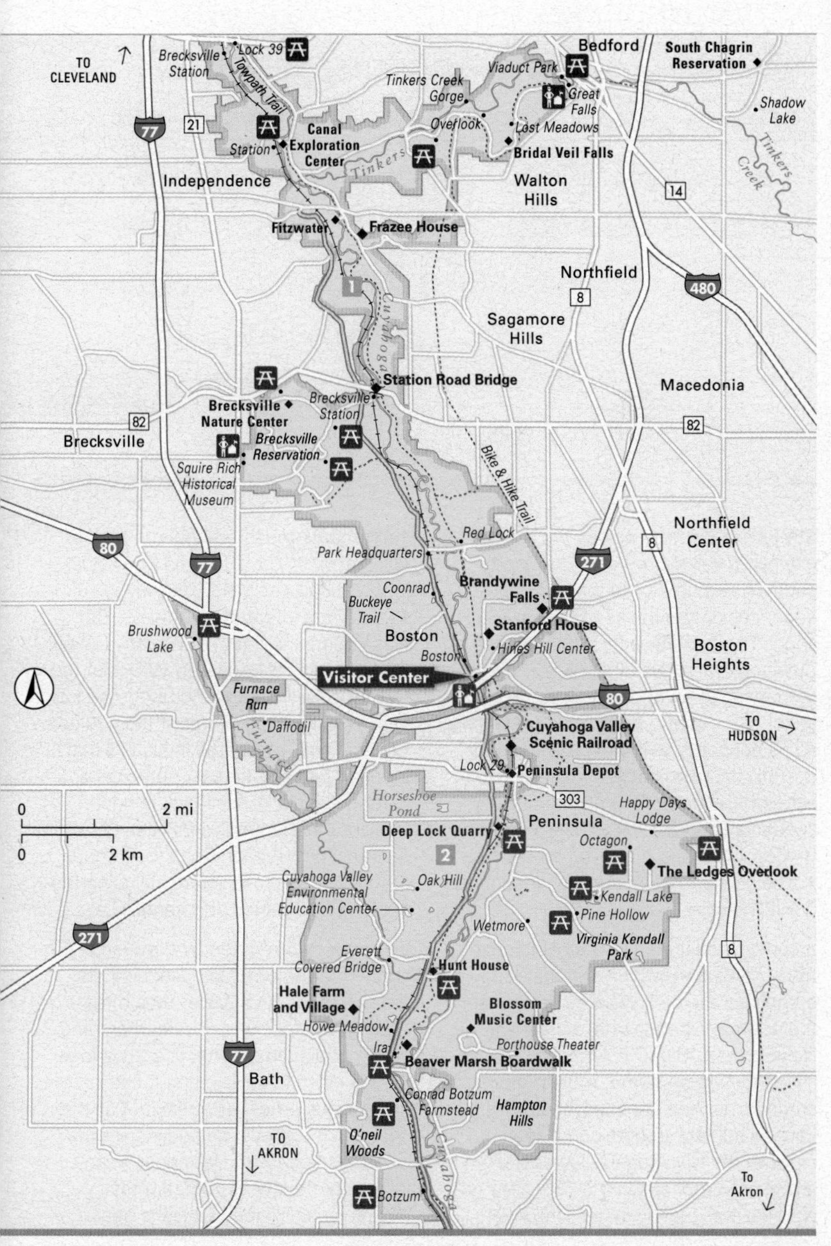
TO CLEVELAND
Brecksville Station
Lock 39
Towpath Trail
Bedford
South Chagrin Reservation
Viaduct Park
Tinkers Creek Gorge
Great Falls
Shadow Lake
Canal Exploration Center
Station
Overlook
Lost Meadows
Bridal Veil Falls
Tinkers
Tinkers Creek
Independence
Walton Hills
Fitzwater
Frazee House
Northfield
Sagamore Hills
Cuyahoga
Station Road Bridge
Macedonia
Brecksville Nature Center
Brecksville Station
Brecksville
Brecksville Reservation
Squire Rich Historical Museum
Bike & Hike Trail
Northfield Center
Red Lock
Park Headquarters
Coonrad
Buckeye Trail
Brandywine Falls
Brushwood Lake
Boston
Stanford House
Hines Hill Center
Boston Heights
Visitor Center
Furnace Run
Daffodil
Furnace
Cuyahoga Valley Scenic Railroad
TO HUDSON
Lock 29
Peninsula Depot
Horseshoe Pond
Happy Days Lodge
Peninsula
Deep Lock Quarry
Octagon
The Ledges Overlook
0
2 mi
0
2 km
Cuyahoga Valley Environmental Education Center
Oak Hill
Kendall Lake
Pine Hollow
Wetmore
Virginia Kendall Park
Everett Covered Bridge
Hunt House
Hale Farm and Village
Blossom Music Center
Howe Meadow
Ira
Porthouse Theater
Beaver Marsh Boardwalk
Bath
Conrad Botzum Farmstead
Hampton Hills
TO AKRON
O'neil Woods
Cuyahoga
To Akron
Botzum
21
14
8
480
82
80
271
303
77

Covering 51 square miles, Cuyahoga Valley is one of America's smallest national parks, but it's also among the most-visited, drawing more than 2.4 million people annually. Truth be told, the park's untidiness is its greatest asset. For here you can kayak a river, hop on a scenic railway, see a world-renowned orchestra play live, and hike amidst ancient sandstone ledges, all in the space of a single day if you so choose.

Stretching 20 miles across the forested, elongated valley between Cleveland's southern suburbs to Akron's northern edge, beside the banks of the Cuyahoga River and bisected by highways, Cuyahoga Valley National Park (CVNP) is something of an anomaly. A conglomerate of city, county, state, and federal park areas peppered with private attractions, this still fledgling national park is an altogether different animal than the seemingly endless wilderness of Zion, Bryce, or the Grand Canyon whose soaring heights and open spaces far surpass CVNP in scale.

It could be said that early inhabitants of the sprawling swath of land that today comprises the park were as diverse as the activities that now take place there. No less than 10 native American tribes called the region home, most prominent among them the Lenape Nation. The Lenape hunted, traded, and planted crops in the Cuyahoga Valley until the arrival of Europeans in the 18th century. What was just a cluster of frontier settlements mushroomed into towns, spurred on by the Ohio and Erie Canal in the 1830s, the Valley Railway in 1880, and in time, interstate highways. But it wasn't until the death of wealthy Clevelander Hayward Kendall in 1927 that the Cuyahoga Valley began to be turned into park land. Kendall, owner of the 430-acre Ritchie Farm, stipulated in his will that the land be used for park purposes and named Virginia Kendall Park in honor of his mother. A few years later, FDR's Civilian Conservation Corps built much of the park's infrastructure including the shelters at Octagon and Kendall Lake.

While partly protected by Cleveland and Akron metropolitan park districts, the Cuyahoga River Valley was threatened by encroaching development and rapid population growth. The Cuyahoga River's claim to fame—that it had caught fire, several times, as a result of all the pollution it carried—helped inspire the country's first Earth Day and it wasn't long after the river's 1969 fire that conservation-minded Ohioans began

AVERAGE HIGH/LOW TEMPERATURES					
JAN.	**FEB.**	**MAR.**	**APR.**	**MAY**	**JUNE**
34/20	37/21	46/29	59/39	70/49	79/59
JULY	**AUG.**	**SEPT.**	**OCT.**	**NOV.**	**DEC.**
83/63	81/62	74/55	62/45	50/35	39/26

fighting to save both the waterway and the valley that surrounds it. Then rookie Democratic Congressman John Seiberling from Akron, a dedicated environmentalist who went on to serve seven terms, galvanized public support and in 1974, Congress passed a bill creating a National Recreation Area, administered by the National Park Service. The park then started acquiring private land and securing cooperative agreements with developments already in place within the designated 33,000-acre area. More than 25 years later, on October 11, 2000, the region was designated a national park by Congress.

Planning

When to Go

Each season in the park has its own advantages. Fall foliage often peaks in mid-October so autumn is considered the best time to visit by many, given the stunning tapestry of vivid yellows, reds, and oranges in the forested sections of the park and along the river. Temperatures during the fall range from low 70s in daytime to freezing at night. Winter is also beautiful and brings with it opportunities for downhill and cross-country skiing, snowshoeing, sledding, and winter hiking. Weather rapidly changes during wintertime in Northeast Ohio due to the lake effect snow from Lake Erie, with temperatures ranging from mid-30s to below zero. Spring's rain and warmer climes create a canvas of blooming wildflowers in the park, with hikers hitting the trails in droves. During summer temperatures range from 49°F to 95°F and can be humid.

Getting Here and Around

AIR

The nearest airport to Cuyahoga Valley National Park is Cleveland Hopkins International Airport (CLE), which is 17 miles away and a 20-minute drive from the northern end of the park. Cleveland Hopkins offers daily flights to the area from major carriers including American Airlines, and United, as well as frequent flights on Frontier, JetBlue, Southwest Airlines, Allegiant, and Spirit.

Akron-Canton Airport (CAK) is just 25 miles from the park, or a 30-minute drive, with daily flights from American Airlines, Delta, United, and Spirit.

Car rentals are available at both airports.

BUS

Greater Cleveland Regional Transit Authority bus lines 51 A, B, and C offer routes from downtown Cleveland to the northern end of the park, which take about 45 minutes.

CONTACTS Greater Cleveland Regional Transit Authority. 🌐 *www.riderta.com.*

CAR

Freeways and roads cut directly through Cuyahoga Valley National Park so it's easy to access the park and everything inside it. Interstate 271 bisects the park at an angle, running from just north of center in the northeast corner to just south of center in the south west corner, while I–80 bisects the park at its center. Both of these major thoroughfares, which can be accessed from points east and west, lead into smaller byways that lead into the park grounds. Interstate 77, meanwhile, runs north–south just outside the western edge of the park. If you're traveling from Cleveland or Akron and points south, hop on I–77 to get to the park.

TRAIN

The nearest train station to the park is the Amtrak (🌐 *www.amtrak.com*) station in downtown Cleveland.

Inspiration

The book called simply *Cuyahoga Valley,* released by Arcadia Publishing, the Cuyahoga Valley Historical Museum, and the Cuyahoga Valley National Park Association and comprised mainly of archival photographs and historical accounts of the valley from the arrival of settlers from New England in 1795 through to the present day.

Cuyahoga Valley National Park Handbook: Revised and Updated offers a brief history of the park and the politics that led to its formation, with a forward by late Ohio Congressman John Seiberling, a dedicated conservationist whose efforts were instrumental in this process. History buffs may wish to delve into Seiberling's autobiography, *A Passion for the Land: John F. Seiberling and the Environmental Movement.*

PBS Western Reserve produced the one-hour documentary *Generations: Cuyahoga Valley National Park* in 2009 as a companion production to Ken Burns' six-part documentary series *The National Parks: America's Best Idea.*

Park Essentials

ACCESSIBILITY

All visitor centers in the park are accessible as are many of the park's picnic shelters and most popular attractions including the Ohio & Erie Canal Towpath Trail, Beaver Marsh Boardwalk, Canal Exploration Center, and Brandywine Falls (upper boardwalk). The Cuyahoga Valley Scenic Railroad within the park has a lift for wheelchair-bound passengers and Stanford House offers an accessible room for overnight lodging. To plan visits for guests with accessibility concerns call ☎ *440/546–5992* and ask for the park's accessibility coordinator.

PARK FEES AND PERMITS

Admission to the park is free. The use of picnic shelters throughout the park is also free, with the exception of The Ledges and Octagon Shelters in the Virginia Kendall Area, which can be reserved at 🌐 *www.recreation.gov* for $110 on weekends and holidays and $80 on weekdays.

There are private venues within the park, which will, of course, charge an entrance fee such as Boston Mills Brandywine Ski Resort and Blossom Music Center, to name just a few.

Certain activities inside the park require a special use permit. These include many types of organized gatherings and distribution of printed material and other public expressions of opinion. Weddings and commercial filming also require special use permits. Contact the Permit Coordinator at ☎ *440/546–5991* for cost of special use permits and to purchase.

PARK HOURS

Cuyahoga Valley National Park is open every day of the year, 24 hours a day, with the exception of the following areas, which are closed from dusk until morning opening: Brandywine Falls, The Ledges, Octagon Shelter, Kendall Lake, Happy Days South Parking Area, and Kendall Hill Area on Quick Road. In addition, Indigo Lake and Kendall Lake in Cuyahoga Valley National Park are closed to swimming.

CELL PHONE RECEPTION

While Wi-Fi is not provided, cellular service can be accessed throughout the park.

Hotels

The only two lodgings within the grounds of Cuyahoga Valley National Park are the bed and breakfast Inn at Brandywine Falls and the historic Stanford House. The former is a beautifully renovated Greek Revival, six-bedroom inn with modern amenities, built in 1848, which overlooks scenic Brandywine Falls while the latter is a rustic nine-bedroom farmhouse dating to 1806, adjacent to the Towpath Trail. Nearby Richfield, just outside the park, has the Cuyahoga Valley Inn and there are numerous major hotel chains in Akron and Cleveland as well as the smaller towns and cities surrounding the park.

Restaurants

Inside park grounds there is one restaurant, Sarah's Vineyard, which serves soups, salads, sandwiches, pastas, and wood-fired pizzas. Sarah's is also a vineyard and winery, as the name suggests, where you can taste up to 10 wines made from locally grown grapes. While Sarah's is the only restaurant inside the park, there are plenty of dining opportunities just outside park borders. Peninsula offers The Winking Lizard and Fisher's Café & Pub in the middle of the park just off the Towpath Trail and Merriman Valley in Akron has restaurants near the Towpath Trail south of the park. Valley View, north of the park, also has restaurants near the Towpath Trail. Of course, the city of Cleveland, just a short drive to the north of the park, also offers oodles of eateries from casual to fine dining.

Tours

The Adventure Center at Kent State University

ADVENTURE TOURS | The Adventure Center at nearby Kent State University runs adventure trips throughout Ohio that range from just a few hours to multiple days or nights, some of which take place in the park. Past trips include snowshoe hikes, mountain biking, and kayaking, the latter organized by Crooked River Adventures, a canoe and kayak livery in downtown Kent which runs 45 minute to 2½ hour trips on the Cuyahoga River on the weekends from the middle of May through the beginning of October ("Cuyahoga means Crooked River to the native American tribes who named it"). ☎ *330/672–2803* 🌐 *www.kent.edu/rec-services/adventure-trips* 🎫 *From $10.*

Cuyahoga Valley Environmental Education Center

GUIDED TOURS | Run by the Conservancy for Cuyahoga Valley National Park (not the national park itself), the center is on park grounds, but it's *only* open for people who have prebooked events and tours with them. Programs include guided night hikes, trail excursions, and pond explorations with knowledgeable instructors. ✉ *1403 W. Hines Hill Rd. , Peninsula* ☎ *330/657–2909* 🌐 *www.conservancy-forcvnp.org* 🎫 *Fees vary.*

Visitor Information

CONTACTS Cuyahoga Valley National Park Headquarters. ✉ *15610 Vaugn Rd., Brecksville* ☎ *440/717–3890* 🌐 *www.nps.gov/cuva.*

North

19 miles south of downtown Cleveland; 2 miles north of Canal Exploration Center; 32 miles north of Akron.

This section of the park, everything north of Interstate 271, contains many of the historical sights within the park as well as the two main visitor centers, Boston Mill Visitor Center and the Canal Exploration Center. The North section might also be described as the more active section of the park, as it contains many of the most popular trails. The North section is the

The 65-foot Brandywine Falls are one of the park's most popular attractions.

closest section to the city of Cleveland due north, the most populated city near the park and a gateway for visitors flying to the region from areas farther afield.

Sights

HISTORIC SIGHTS

Frazee House

HISTORIC SITE | One of the earliest brick houses in the Cuyahoga Valley, this Federal-style home built in 1827 on the banks of the Cuyahoga River belonged to Stephen and Mehitable Frazee, successful farmers who raised seven children in the home. The house, listed on the National Register of Historic Places, was constructed with clay from the back yard and lumber from the property's walnut, chestnut, and oak trees. Historical documents show that after the Ohio & Erie Canal opened in 1825, the home likely served as an inn and tavern for travelers passing through along the canal. ✉ *7733 Canal Rd., Valley View* ☎ *440/717–3890* 🌐 *www.nps.gov/cuva/planyourvisit/the-frazee-house.htm.*

Stanford House

HISTORIC SITE | **FAMILY** | A Greek Revival–style farmhouse on Stanford Road, just minutes from the Towpath Trail, Stanford House was built by George Stanford, son of James Stanford who settled the property in 1806 and was one of the original surveyors of Boston Township. During the late 19th century and into the turn of the 20th, the Stanford family farmed wheat, hay, cattle, and sheep, as well as cultivating lumber. One of the best-known early settlers of the region, George and his wife Catherine had eight children though only one—George Carter—outlived his parents. George and his son were active in local politics, holding several positions in public office. When the Ohio & Erie Canal was built alongside the river in front of Stanford House in 1827, it connected the Stanfords to markets in Cleveland, Akron, and beyond, which ensured the continued prosperity of the family. Over time, George added several outlying structures including a barn, smokehouse, a springhouse, and granary. ✉ *6093 Stanford Rd., Peninsula*

☎ *330/657–2909* 🌐 *www.nps.gov/cuva/learn/historyculture/stanford-house.htm.*

Station Road Bridge

BRIDGE/TUNNEL | Listed on the National Register of Historic Places, Station Road Bridge was built in 1881 to link Station Road in Cuyahoga County to Pine Hill Road in Summit County. It's the oldest remaining metal truss bridge in the Cuyahoga Valley and is located at the narrowest part of the valley, built one year after Valley Railway began service at Brecksville Station just south of the bridge. Constructed of wrought iron by the local Massillon Bridge Company with a single span covering 124 feet, the bridge has been repaired twice: once in 1991, when it was disassembled and sent to Elmira, New York for repairs and the second time in November 2020, with repairs completing in spring of 2021. The second time around, repair work on the bridge was done entirely in place. It is unique that the bridge is made of iron; most bridges before this time were built of wood and most built after were built of steel. ✉ *13513 Station Rd., Brecksville* ☎ *440/717–3890* 🌐 *www.nps.gov/articles/000/preserving-the-station-road-bridge.htm.*

SCENIC STOPS

★ Brandywine Falls

NATIONAL/STATE PARK | **FAMILY** | The 65-foot Brandywine Falls, one of the park's most popular attractions, are named after the once booming mill town of Brandywine, which no longer exists. The first thing visitors will see when they enter the parking lot is a grouping of seven picnic tables (two of which are handicap accessible), an outdoor grill, and restrooms. To view the falls, head toward the forest and begin walking on a wooden boardwalk that borders a slate and sandstone cliff. You can either walk along a flat upper walkway to a lookout near the top of the falls, or you can take a stairway to a point about midway down the gorge where you'll come upon a wooden overlook with a perfect view of the falls. ✉ *8176 Brandywine Rd., Sagamore Hills* ☎ *440/717–3890* 🌐 *www.nps.gov/cuva/learn/historyculture/brandywine-falls.htm.*

TRAILS

Blue Hen Falls Trail

TRAIL | **FAMILY** | The trail to 15-foot Blue Hen Falls is a favorite of many of the park's own rangers. Hikers can park at Boston Mill Visitor Center, follow the Buckeye Trail uphill, cross Boston Mills Road, and then hike half a mile down a steep incline; don't miss the beautiful little waterfall. The 3-mile hike requires an unmarked road crossing so be extra cautious during this stretch. Hiking boots for this trail are highly recommended as the trail can get extremely muddy. *Moderate.* ✉ *Cuyahoga Valley National Park* ✣ *Trailhead: 2001 Boston Mills Rd.* ☎ *440/717–3890* 🌐 *www.nps.gov/cuva.*

The Buckeye Trail

TRAIL | **FAMILY** | A 40-mile section of Ohio's 1,444 mile Buckeye Trail, which loops around the entire state, passes through the park. The park section of the trail weaves its way in a narrow, single track through pine, oak, and hemlock forests, across streams, through ravines, and even alongside highways. It's not an easy trail and can be rocky: you should be prepared to get dirty and wet. There are blue blazes that mark the Buckeye Trail so finding your way should not be a problem. Currently, the road portions of the trail are being relocated into trail areas. *Moderate.* ✉ *Cuyahoga Valley National Park* ✣ *Trailhead: On Gorge Pkwy 0.4 miles northwest of Egbert Rd. in Bedford Reservation* ☎ *440/717–3890* 🌐 *www.nps.gov/cuva/backpacking.htm.*

★ Ohio & Erie Canal Towpath Trail

TRAIL | Constructed by the State of Ohio between 1825 and 1832, the Ohio & Erie Canal was an inland waterway made up of a series of sandstone locks connecting Lake Erie in Cleveland with the Ohio River in Portsmouth. The canal boats—pulled by mules on the towpath beside the water—made it possible to ship goods from Lake Erie to the Gulf of Mexico by way of the Ohio and Mississippi rivers. When railroads were introduced in 1876, the canal's significance declined and after the flood of 1913, less than 100 years after the canal opened, it was abandoned. Neglected for decades, the Ohio & Erie Canal Towpath Trail was refurbished and is now the key walking, running, and biking route and stretches over 90 miles across four counties and through the length of Cuyahoga Valley National Park. Work on the trail is ongoing; it will be 101 miles long when complete. *Easy.* ✉ *8000 Rockside Rd., Independence* ✣ *Trailhead: Lock 39 Trailhead, the northernmost trailhead within CVNP* ☎ *440/717–3890* 🌐 *www.nps.gov/cuva/planyourvisit/ohio-and-erie-canal-towpath-trail.htm.*

VISITOR CENTERS

Boston Mill Visitor Center

BUILDING | FAMILY | The main visitor center for the park, the Boston Mill Visitor Center, is located in a restored 1905 building; to be precise, it's in the reimagined former company store of the now defunct Cleveland-Akron Bag Company, a hub where workers would go for supplies. The center is an excellent launching pad for park visitors, who can meet staff, plan their itinerary, and explore exhibits before setting off into the park. The south room has a tabletop model of the Cuyahoga Valley flanked by murals depicting Cleveland to the north and Akron to the south. There's also a gift shop selling souvenirs and park-related books. ✉ *6947 Riverview Rd., Peninsula* ☎ *440/717–3890* 🌐 *www.nps.gov/cuva/boston-mill-visitor-center.htm.*

Canal Exploration Center

HISTORIC SITE | FAMILY | Located in a canal-era building that once served passengers waiting to pass through Canal Lock 38, the center houses a variety of exhibits that illustrate life along the Ohio and Erie Canal in Cuyahoga Valley. You can read the diary of a teenage canal worker, listen to a free African American recount his experiences as a canal boat captain, and try on the daily attire of boatmen and captains who worked along the canal. You'll meet volunteers and rangers and have the opportunity to explore interactive maps, games, and an on-site bookstore. Lock demonstrations are conducted seasonally and on weekends. ✉ *7104 Canal Rd., Valley View* ☎ *440/717–3890* 🌐 *www.nps.gov/cuva/learn/historyculture/canal-exploration-center.htm* ⏲ *Canal Exploration Center closed Dec.–Apr. and May weekdays.*

Hotels

The Inn at Brandywine Falls

$$$ | B&B/INN | Overlooking the 67-foot Brandywine Falls within the park, this 1848-built Greek Revival–style bed-and-breakfast has been updated with modern amenities for travelers seeking a comfortable sleep inside park grounds. **Pros:** free Wi-Fi; easy access to hiking and biking trails; breakfast served as early as 7 am with prior request. **Cons:** staircase can be tricky for those with mobility issues; old plumbing; some rooms outdated. [$] *Rooms from: $225* ✉ *8230 Brandywine Rd., Sagamore Hills* ☎ *888/306–3381, 330/467–1812* 🌐 *www.innatbrandywinefalls.com* 🛏 *6 rooms* 🍽 *Free breakfast.*

South

8½ miles north of downtown Akron; 1 mile south of Boston Mill Visitor Center; 25 miles south of Cleveland.

This section of the park, everything south of Interstate 271, offers an astonishing array of activities for park visitors. It's home to two of the region's top draws for children as well as history buffs: the popular Cuyahoga Valley Scenic Railroad, a beautifully restored railway giving themed rides throughout the park, and Hale Farm & Village, a living history museum set on a former 19th-century homestead. There's also Sarah's Vineyard, the first alcohol-producing establishment inside any national park, and the Blossom Music Center, where you can see the Cleveland Orchestra perform during summer. The South section is also where you'll encounter some of the park's best wildlife spotting and scenic vistas: Beaver Marsh Boardwalk, the Ledges Overlook, and Wetmore Bridle Trail. The South section is also the closest section to the city of Akron, a gateway for visitors and also the hometown of the late Ohio Congressman John Sieberling, who was instrumental in the park's creation.

Sights

HISTORIC SIGHTS

★ Cuyahoga Valley Scenic Railroad

HISTORIC SITE | FAMILY | Gaze out your window at deer, beavers and all manner of birdlife as well as the gurgling Cuyahoga River from the comfortable seat of a restored Class III railroad car. The Cuyahoga Valley Line which dates back to 1880, went into steep decline with the advent of automobiles and trucks in the 20th century. In 1972, community leaders create a non-profit that restored the railway and eventually began offering rides through the park. The route allows passengers to hop on or off at any of nine stations to explore the park; it also runs alongside several miles of the Ohio and Erie Canal Towpath Trail. For just $5, you can put your bike on the train, ride a few stops, then bike back to your car (called "Bike Aboard.") Or, for a more leisurely experience, book a nonstop trip aboard the Fall Flyer for a 2½-hour ride dedicated to viewing fall foliage. Other excursions include trips themed around wine and beer-tasting, a chef-prepared four-course meal, and murder mysteries. There's even a train-theme car for children, with a miniature train set, maps, toys, and other train-related items for kids to play with. ✉ *1664 Main St., Peninsula* ☎ *330/439–5708* 🌐 *www.cvsr.org.*

Hale Farm and Village

BUILDING | FAMILY | Comprised of 32 historic buildings spread out over 100 acres, Hale Farm and Village is a living history museum that illustrates what life was like in the Cuyahoga Valley for early white settlers. The farm, listed on the National Register of Historic Places in 1973, was the original homestead of Jonathan Hale, a Connecticut farmer who migrated in 1810 to the Cuyahoga Valley region known then as the Western Reserve. Many of the buildings are open for self-guided experiences, while craft demonstrations of various 19th-century trades such as candle-making, glass blowing, blacksmithing, and pottery take place regularly. The Gatehouse Welcome Center at Hale Farm has an on-site gift shop and a lovely restaurant, Cafe 1810, which sources its produce from Hale's gardens and farm. ✉ *2686 Oak Hill Rd., Bath* ☎ *216/721–5722* 🌐 *halefarm.org* 🎫 *$12.*

SCENIC STOPS

★ Beaver Marsh Boardwalk

DAM | FAMILY | Just north of the Ira Trailhead on the Towpath Trail, this former junkyard-turned-boardwalk is one of the top wildlife-viewing locations in the park. Thirty years ago, the area was littered with broken-down automobiles; today, it teems with over 200 bird species and other wildlife, mainly beavers, who've made a comfortable home of the surrounding marshlands. Designated as an Important Bird Area by the National Audubon Society, Beaver Marsh Boardwalk is an ideal spot for hikers and trail runners looking to take in the view. Waterfowl, wrens, sparrows, orioles, frogs, water snakes, and even the occasional otter make appearances here. ✉ *3801 Riverview Rd., Peninsula* ☎ *440/717–3890* 🌐 *www.nps.gov/cuva/planyourvisit/the-beaver-marsh.htm.*

The Ledges Overlook

FOREST | FAMILY | Easily the most popular overlook in the park, this sandstone outcrop affords visitors an unobstructed, west-facing view across the vast Cuyahoga Valley which is particularly beautiful at sunset. A series of stone "shelves," the Ledges are often called the "Ritchie Ledges" by locals. William Ritchie was a farmer who owned the land in the 19th century, then sold it in 1913 to wealthy Cleveland industrialist Hayward Kendall, who used it as a hunting retreat. The Ledges connect to a 2.2. mile loop and larger trail network in the historic Virginia Kendall Area, named after Hayward's mother. From the parking lot, walk to the southwest corner of the nearby grass field to get there. ✉ *701 Truxell Rd., Peninsula* ☎ *440/717–3890* 🌐 *www.nps.gov/cuva/the-ledges.htm.*

TRAILS

Tree Farm Trail

TRAIL | The trail loops through forests and across a large open field next to a neighborhood Christmas tree farm. Considered to be an easier hike at just under 3 miles, ramblers will see an abundance of wildlife including deer, fox, coyote, and several bird species on this well-trodden trail, which begins and ends at the northeast edge of Horseshoe Pond trailhead. Visitors are asked to be respectful of private property lines when walking along the trail, which also provides access to a fishing pier at Horseshoe Pond. Near the pond, you'll find a restroom and a picnic pavilion with tables and grills. *Easy.* ✉ *2075 Major Rd., Peninsula* ✥ *Trailhead: Horseshoe Pond trailhead* ☎ *440/717–3890* 🌐 *www.nps.gov/cuva/planyourvisit/family-hikes.htm.*

Wetmore Trail

TRAIL | West of the Virginia Kendall Area, the 4.7 mile Wetmore Trail, made up of old farmers paths and logging roads, now serves as a corridor for horseback riding, hiking, and dog-walking (dogs must be kept on a leash). Part of a larger trail network that includes Tabletop Trail and Langes Run Trail, the trail is at its peak in the spring, summer, and fall. In 2003, heavy flood damage closed about a mile of the trail but a detailed plan by the Conservancy for Cuyahoga Valley National Park restored it in 2020. *Moderate.* ✉ *Peninsula* ✥ *Trailhead: 4653 Wetmore Rd.* ☎ *440/717–3890* 🌐 *www.nps.gov/cuva/planyourvisit/horse-trails.htm.*

VISITOR CENTER

Hunt House Visitor Center

INFO CENTER | FAMILY | About 50 yards from the Ohio and Erie Canal Towpath Trail, the visitor center offers child-friendly nature exhibits as well as puppets, coloring books, and other toys. It's also a convenient rest stop for bikers and hikers along the Towpath Trail, given its proximity. It's staffed only on occasion with park volunteers as it's not the park's main visitor center, but it is open daily during the summer. ✉ *2054 Bolanz Rd., Peninsula* ☎ *440/717–3890* 🌐 *www.nps.gov/cuva/planyourvisit/hours.htm* ⏲ *Closed Labor Day–Mar. and weekdays Apr.–Memorial Day.*

Restaurants

Sarah's Vineyard

$ | AMERICAN | FAMILY | Just inside the southeast corner of the park and across from Blossom Music Center, this family owned and operated winery and wine bar serves wood-fired pizzas, pasta, salads, and burgers as well as a broad selection of wines from Ohio. There are two outdoor pavilions, a fireplace, and pet-friendly garden seating as well as a gallery that sells crafts made by local artists. **Known for:** Ohio white wines made from grapes grown on property; wood-fired pizzas; festive outdoor seating. $ *Average main: $13* ✉ *1204 W. Steels Corners Rd.* ☎ *330/929–8057* 🌐 *www.sarahsvineyardwinery.com* ⏲ *Closed Mon.–Thurs. No lunch.*

Farming Land to Protect It

What sets Cuyahoga Valley apart from any other national park is a cluster of working farms inside the park's boundaries. And what makes this possible is the Countryside Initiative (*countrysidefoodandfarms.org/countryside-initiative/*).

Launched in 1999, the nonprofit organization strives to protect the CVNP's land and build a sustainable food culture throughout the region by partnering with 10 family farms who applied for—and received—60-year leases within the park. The nonprofit also runs a series of farmers markets to help sell the yield from these farms including one on Saturday, May through October in the park's Howe Meadow. When it began, the program was the first of its kind in the country, incorporating sustainable agriculture into a national park's conservation efforts. Since then, a handful of other parks have initiated similar partnerships, using Countryside as their model The participating farms must provide detailed sustainability plans each year as well as follow certain guidelines, though the park gives them some flexibility in what types of sustainable practices they use. For example, one farm uses permaculture as their primary management system while another uses rotational animal grazing. The farms are also required to welcome visitors and educate them on sustainable agriculture.

Most of the farms are within minutes of each other, so grab a tote bag and farm-hop. At Greenfield Berry Farm, for example, you can pick blueberries to put in your cereal the next morning while at Sarah's Vineyard you'll taste wines grown from grapes grown on the property to accompany your lunch or dinner order. And at Spice Acres, stock up on asparagus and mushrooms for that quiche recipe you've been meaning to tackle.

Performing Arts

★ Blossom Music Center

ARTS CENTERS | FAMILY | The summer home of the Cleveland Orchestra, Blossom Music Center has become something of a Cleveland institution since it opened in 1968. Set inside the park's grounds on more than 500 wooded acres, the striking, triangular pavilion seats 5,700 people with room for 13,500 more on a sweeping green lawn that fans out from the pavilion in the shape of a seashell. In addition to hosting regular summer performances by the orchestra, Blossom has welcomed international rock bands, country musicians, and other dance and musical acts throughout the decades. It's a rite of passage for most Northeast Ohioans to bring a blanket and make themselves comfortable on the lawn underneath the stars for a live performance at Blossom. **■ TIP→ Grab dinner at Sarah's Vineyard before the show, then mosey over to Blossom with plenty of time to get that perfect spot on the lawn before the night's entertainment begins.** ✉ *1145 W. Steels Corners Rd.* ☎ *330/920–8040* 🌐 *www.clevelandamphitheater.com.*

Activities

BIKING

There are a handful of trails for cyclists in the park, the best being the Ohio & Erie Canal Towpath Trail (20 miles of which is inside the park while the remaining 80 extends beyond it). The Towpath trail also offers the Bike Aboard program where you can bike the trail in one direction and hop on the Cuyahoga Valley Scenic Railroad and ride back to your car ($5 per person one-way). In addition, 16 miles of the Summit Metro Parks Bike & Hike Trail border the national park, connecting to the Towpath Trail near Holzhauer Road south of State Route 82; there are also more than 60 miles of paved cycling paths in Brecksville and Bedford Reservations, some of the most scenic being inside the national park. Mountain bikers will want to hit the East Rim Trail System, accessed by taking Route 8 to Boston Mills Road, heading west past Olde 8, and parking at the Bike & Hike Trailhead parking lot. You'll cycle north on the Bike & Hike Trail a short while before reaching the access point for East Rim Trail. Century Cycles in Peninsula rents bikes.

Century Cycles

BICYCLING | ✉ *1621 Main St., Peninsula* ☎ *330/657–2209* 🌐 *www.centurycycles.com.*

BIRD-WATCHING

The forested wetlands, rivers, and native plants in the park offer a welcome habitat for as many as 250 bird species which is why Audubon has designated the park an Important Bird Area. Birdwatchers will be privy to sightings of Baltimore Oriole, Eastern Bluebird, Red-tailed Hawk, Great Horned Owl, Great Blue Heron and Bald Eagle, the latter two returning to the park recently after decades away. One of the best places to see these birds is Beaver Marsh Boardwalk, especially in March and November during the waterfowl migrations. Don't forget your binoculars!

CAMPING

Cuyahoga Valley no longer offers camping within the park, however, park officials are said to be exploring options and plans to establish a public input process.

CANOEING AND KAYAKING

The Cuyahoga River, or "crooked" river, is a popular waterway for kayakers and canoers, and 22 of its 100 miles run through the park. Paddlers should be aware that it can get rough in spots and should check water levels and weather conditions before heading out. The river can be accessed by paddlers at five spots within the park: Lock 29 Trailhead parking lot in Peninsula, Boston Store Trailhead in the Village of Boston, the south side of Vaughn Road bridge near Red Lock Trailhead in Northfield, Station Road Bridge Trailhead in Brecksville, and Lock 39 Trailhead in Valley View. ■ **TIP→ Burning River Adventures offers kayak and canoe rentals for one to three hour excursions along the river.**

Burning River Adventures

CANOEING/ROWING/SKULLING | ✉ *Cuyahoga Falls* ☎ *330/969–2628* 🌐 *www.paddletheriver.com.*

CROSS-COUNTRY SKIING AND SNOWSHOEING

Cross-country skiing and snowshoeing in the park are practiced on most trails with the exception of The Ledges and Brandywine Falls trails, which are not suitable (or safe) for either. A few of the best trails for cross-country skiing and snowshoeing are Oak Hill Trail, Tree Farm Trail, and Cross Country Trail. Snowshoes are available to rent in the Boston Mills area.

EDUCATIONAL PROGRAMS

Programs for Kids. Ranger-led activities include hiking while looking for signs of animals, bird identification lessons, and learning outdoor survival skills. Kids can also participate in the Junior Ranger program where they receive a badge for completing activity books, available at the park's visitor centers. 🌐 *www.nps.gov/cuva/learn/kidsyouth/beajuniorranger.htm.*

Questing. Modeled after the British practice of letterboxing, the park's "questing" experience (🌐 *www.ohioanderiecanalway.com/activities/questing*) runs mid-April to mid-November. Maps, available at the park's visitor centers, guide questers from one park "treasure box" to the next, where you leave your mark in a ledger, collect a stamp, and re-hide the box for other questers to discover.

Ranger-led Programs. Park rangers lead talks on everything from the founding of the Cuyahoga Valley Scenic Railroad to the behavior of animals who call the park home. Check schedules at the visitor centers or visit the park's online calendar at 🌐 *www.nps.gov/cuva/planyourvisit/calendar.htm* for more information.

FISHING

In addition to the Cuyahoga River itself, there are dozens of ponds and lakes in which you can cast your line inside the park. Visitors are asked to practice catch-and-release fishing, so as not to deplete the fish population. An Ohio fishing license is required and park rangers do make routine checks. A 3-Day Nonresident License costs $19.

HIKING

The most reliable way to get a sense of the Cuyahoga Valley's pioneer past, as well as the diversity of terrain within the park, is on foot. The park has more than 125 miles of hiking trails ranging from easy to difficult, many of which are wheelchair-accessible. The most famous trail is the Towpath Trail which follows the historic route of the Ohio and Erie Canal, 20 miles of which falls within the park. A portion of Ohio's statewide Buckeye Trail also passes through the park. There are also several off-the-beaten path hikes where you can ramble across streams, along bridges, and through woodlands, blending in with the wildlife who call the park home.

SKIING, SNOWBOARDING, AND SNOW TUBING

Downhill skiing and snow boarding are offered inside the park at Boston Mills and Brandywine Resorts, two "sister" ski areas owned and operated by Vail Resorts. Polar Blast Snow Tubing Park at Brandywine, accessible by way of the same driveway entrance, offers snow tubing. All three locations offer equipment rental, and Boston Mills and Brandywine also offer instruction. Boston Mills is the main resort with 18 runs and 79 acres of skiable landscape.

Boston Mills Ski Resort

SKIING/SNOWBOARDING | **FAMILY** | While it may be the only ski resort in the world located in a valley instead of in the mountains, Boston Mills (sister ski resort to Brandywine a mile away) offers seven ski runs suitable for all experience levels and five chair lifts on 40 skiable acres. This no-frills, family-friendly resort is inside Cuyahoga Valley National Park, however, the resort is privately owned and managed. There's a fireplace in the center of the lodge and a basic menu with sandwiches and pizza for après ski as well as a selection of local beers. Many Ohioans consider it a great place to learn to ski, but keep in mind that this is Northeast Ohio, not Aspen or Zermatt. Rent equipment or bring your own; lift tickets start at $25. ✉ *7100 Riverview Rd., Peninsula* ☎ *330/657–2334, 800/875–4241* 🌐 *www.bmbw.com.*

Brandywine Ski Resort

SKIING/SNOWBOARDING | **FAMILY** | Sister resort to Boston Mills a mile up the road, Brandywine—while family-friendly—caters to a slightly younger, hipper crowd of snowboarders and college kids. Brandywine has 11 runs, 5 lifts, and a slightly newer ski lodge and there's late night skiing on weekends from 8 pm until 1 am; tickets start at $25. A little-known fact about Brandywine is that Olympic Gold Medalist Red Gerard began his snowboarding career on the slopes of Brandywine while living in Rocky River, an upscale Cleveland suburb. ✉ *1146 W. Highland Rd., Sagamore Hills* ☎ *800/875–4241* 🌐 *www.bmbw.com.*

Polar Blast Tubing Park

SNOW SPORTS | **FAMILY** | With 20 lanes of various terrain from which to choose, this tubing park provides a fun and relatively effortless adrenaline rush for kids and adults. The park also has conveyor lifts so tubers don't have to walk back to the top of the hill. Tubes are provided for a two-hour session ($25). ✉ *Brandywine Ski Resort, 1146 W. Highland Rd., Sagamore Hills* ☎ *800/875–4241* 🌐 *www.bmbw.com.*

What's Nearby

Northeast Ohio's largest city is **Cleveland,** set along the southern shore of Lake Erie, population 385,000 and the Cuyahoga County seat. About a 15-minute drive from the northern border of the park, Cleveland has the IM Pei–designed Rock and Roll Hall of Fame, the West Side Market, the Cleveland Museum of Art, and Playhouse Square, which holds regular performances of Broadway shows. Cleveland also has an impressive array of restaurants serving multicultural cuisine and the region's largest choice of hotels from major chains (there's a Ritz Carlton downtown) to historic inns.

At the center of Cuyahoga Valley National Park, in a pocket of nonpark land a few minutes east of the Ohio and Erie Canal Towpath, lies the little town of **Peninsula** (population 565), a historic village that linked the region to the eastern trade routes when the canal opened. Once a hub of stone quarrying and boat building, Peninsula's main street is now lined with art galleries, specialty shops, and restaurants (there are two: The Winking Lizard Tavern and Fisher's Café & Pub). It's the perfect place to stop off for lunch or refreshments while hiking, biking, or skiing the Towpath Trail.

The affluent city of **Hudson,** 10 minutes east of CVNP, has a similar small-town feel though Hudson is much larger than Peninsula. The town's downtown shopping district on Main Street has a delightful bookstore, The Learned Owl, and several good restaurants. One-time home of abolitionist John Brown, Hudson was a stop along the Underground Railroad, and you can visit several historic homes and churches that once housed fugitive slaves trying to reach freedom in Canada.

Just 10 minutes south of the park is **Akron,** a rust belt city with a handful of chain hotels and one elegant bed and breakfast, O'Neil House. The Akron Art Museum has some interesting works and the city itself offers a lively music scene (don't forget, Akron is hometown of Chrissie Hynde, Devo, and the Black Keys). Larger venues such as Akron Civic Theatre and EJ Thomas Performing Arts Hall host big names while the city's back streets house a handful of live music clubs like Blu Jazz and Musica. Akron is also the hometown of John Sieberling, the Congressman who helped establish Cuyahoga Valley National Park. You can tour his family's ancestral home, The Stan Hywet Hall and Gardens (🌐 *www.stanhywet.org*), a 65-room Tudor Revival mansion built by his grandfather, Goodyear Tire & Rubber Company co-founder F.A. Seiberling.

Chapter 18

DEATH VALLEY NATIONAL PARK

Updated by
Cheryl Crabtree

Camping	Hotels	Activities	Scenery	Crowds
★★★☆☆	★★★★☆	★★★☆☆	★★★★★	★★☆☆☆

WELCOME TO DEATH VALLEY NATIONAL PARK

TOP REASONS TO GO

★ **Roving rocks:** Death Valley's Racetrack is home to moving boulders, a rare phenomenon that until recently had scientists baffled.

★ **Lowest spot on the continent:** Stand on the lowest spot on the continent at Badwater, 282 feet below sea level.

★ **Wildflower explosion:** In spring, this desert landscape is ablaze with greenery and colorful flowers, especially between Badwater and Ashford Mill.

★ **Ghost towns:** Death Valley is renowned for its Wild West heritage and is home to dozens of crumbling settlements including Chloride City, Greenwater, Harrisburg, Keeler, Leadfield, Panamint City, and Skidoo, as well as nearby Ballarat and Rhyolite.

★ **Naturally amazing:** From canyons to sand dunes to salt flats and dry lake beds, Death Valley serves up plenty of geological treasures.

1 Central Death Valley. Furnace Creek sits in the heart of Death Valley—if you have only a short time in the park, head here. You can visit gorgeous Golden Canyon, Zabriskie Point, the Salt Creek Interpretive Trail, and Artists Drive, among other popular points of interest.

2 Northern Death Valley. This region is uphill from Furnace Creek, which means marginally cooler temperatures. Be sure to stop by Rhyolite Ghost Town on Highway 374 before entering the park and exploring colorful Titus Canyon and jaw-dropping Ubehebe Crater.

3 Southern Death Valley. This is a desolate area, but there are plenty of sights that help convey Death Valley's rich history. Don't miss the Dublin Gulch Caves.

4 Western Death Valley. Panamint Springs Resort is a nice place to grab a meal and get your bearings before moving on to quaint Darwin Falls, smooth rolling sand dunes, beehive-shape Wildrose Charcoal Kilns, and historic Stovepipe Wells Village.

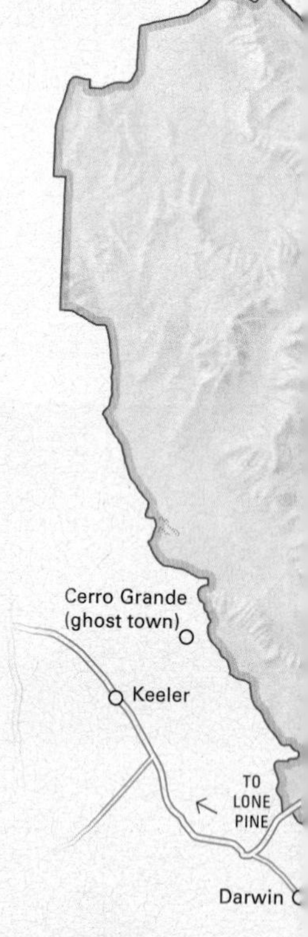

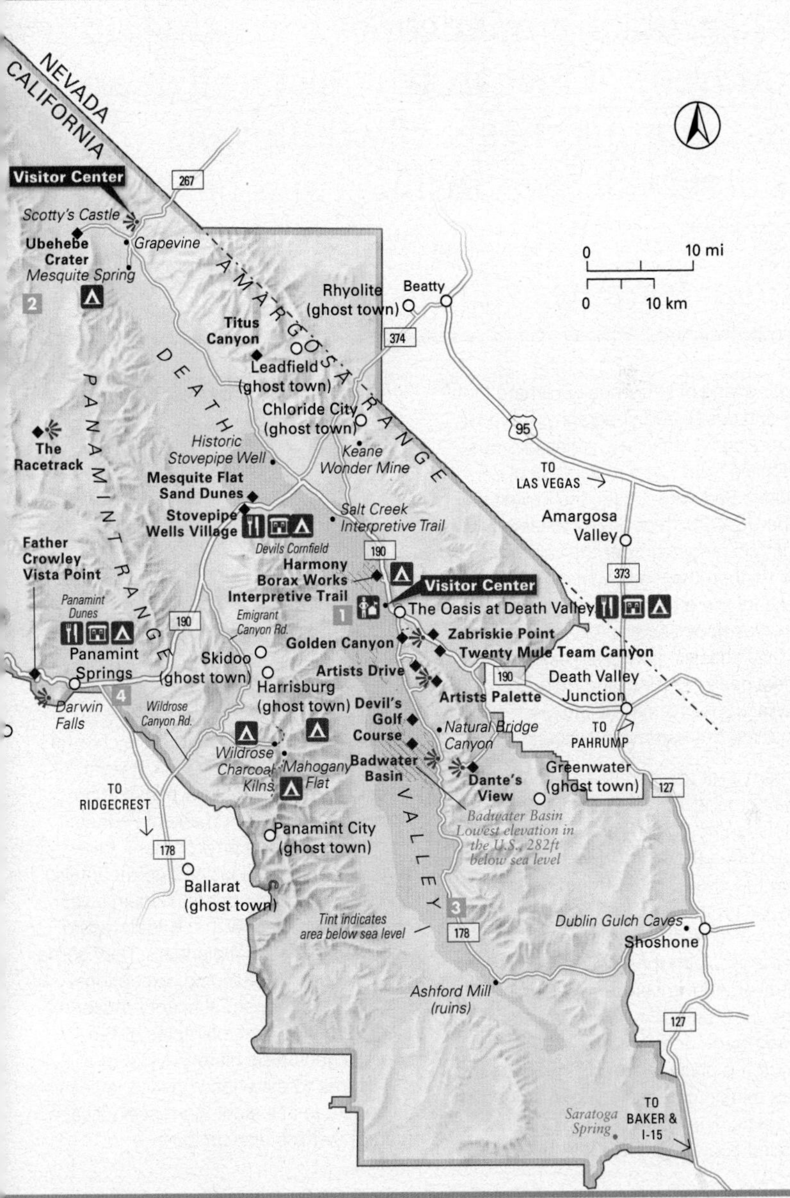
NEVADA
CALIFORNIA
Visitor Center
267
Scotty's Castle
Ubehebe Crater
Grapevine
Mesquite Spring
2
AMARGOSA RANGE
DEATH
PANAMINT RANGE
Titus Canyon
Leadfield (ghost town)
Rhyolite (ghost town)
Beatty
374
0
10 mi
0
10 km
Chloride City (ghost town)
95
The Racetrack
Historic Stovepipe Well
Keane Wonder Mine
Mesquite Flat Sand Dunes
TO LAS VEGAS
Stovepipe Wells Village
Salt Creek Interpretive Trail
Amargosa Valley
Father Crowley Vista Point
Devils Cornfield
190
Harmony Borax Works Interpretive Trail
373
Visitor Center
1
The Oasis at Death Valley
Panamint Dunes
190
Emigrant Canyon Rd.
Zabriskie Point
Golden Canyon
Twenty Mule Team Canyon
Panamint Springs
Skidoo (ghost town)
Artists Drive
190
Death Valley Junction
Harrisburg (ghost town)
Artists Palette
4
Darwin Falls
Wildrose Canyon Rd.
Devil's Golf Course
Natural Bridge Canyon
TO PAHRUMP
Wildrose Charcoal Kilns
Mahogany Flat
Badwater Basin
Dante's View
Greenwater (ghost town)
127
TO RIDGECREST
VALLEY
Badwater Basin Lowest elevation in the U.S., 282ft below sea level
178
Panamint City (ghost town)
Ballarat (ghost town)
3
Tint indicates area below sea level
178
Dublin Gulch Caves
Shoshone
Ashford Mill (ruins)
127
Saratoga Spring
TO BAKER & I-15

The natural riches of Death Valley—the largest national park outside Alaska—are overwhelming: rolling waves of sand dunes, black cinder cones thrusting up hundreds of feet from a blistered desert floor, riotous sheets of wildflowers, bizarrely shaped Joshua trees basking in the orange glow of a sunset, tiny pupfish, and a dramatic silence.

This is a land of extremes of climate (hottest and driest) and geography. The park centers on Death Valley, which extends 156 miles from north to south and includes Badwater Basin, the lowest point in the USA (282 feet below sea level). Two mountain ranges border the valley: the Panamint on the west, where Telescope Peak juts more than 11,000 feet up from the valley floor, and the Amargosa in the east. Salt basins, spring-fed oases, sand dunes, deep canyons, and more than a thousand miles of paved and dirt roads punctuate the barren landscapes.

Humans first roamed this once-lush region around 10,000 years ago. The Timbisha Shoshone have lived here for more than a thousand years, originally along the shores of a 30-foot-deep lake. They called the area Timbisha for the red-hued rocks in the hillsides. Gold-rush pioneers looking for a shortcut to California traversed the barren expanse in 1849; some met their demise in the harsh environment, and those who survived named the place Death Valley. Silver and borax mining companies soon arrived on the scene. They didn't last long (most had stopped operations by 1910), but they left ghost towns and ramshackle mines as evidence of their dreams.

In 1933, President Herbert Hoover proclaimed the area a national monument to protect both its natural beauty and its scientific importance. In 1994, Congress passed the California Desert Protection Act, adding 1.3 million acres and designating the region a national park. Today, Death Valley National Park encompasses nearly 3.5 million acres, 93 percent of which is designated wilderness.

Despite its moniker, Death Valley teems with life. More than a million visitors a year come here to view plants and animals that reveal remarkable adaptations to the desert environment, hike through deep canyons and up mountain trails, gaze at planets and stars in a vast night sky, and follow in the footsteps of ancient cultures and pioneers. They come to explore an outstanding, exceptionally diverse outdoor natural history museum, filled with excellent examples of the planet's geological history. Most of all, they come to experience peace, quiet, and solitude in a stark, surreal landscape found nowhere else on Earth.

AVERAGE HIGH/LOW TEMPERATURES					
JAN.	**FEB.**	**MAR.**	**APR.**	**MAY**	**JUNE**
65/39	72/46	80/53	90/62	99/71	109/80
JULY	**AUG.**	**SEPT.**	**OCT.**	**NOV.**	**DEC.**
115/88	113/85	106/75	92/62	76/48	65/39

Planning

When to Go

Most of the park's 1.7 million annual visitors come between late fall and early spring, taking advantage of moderate temperatures and the lack of rainfall. During these cooler months, you will need to book a room in advance, but don't worry: the park never feels crowded. If you visit in summer, believe everything you've ever heard about desert heat—it can be brutal, with temperatures often topping 120°F. The dry air wicks moisture from the body without causing a sweat, so drink plenty of water. Bring sunglasses, a hat, and sufficient clothing to block the sun's rays and the wind. Flash floods are fairly common; sections of roadway can be flooded or washed away, as they were after a major flood in 2015. The wettest month is February, when the park receives an average of 0.3 inch of rain.

FESTIVALS AND EVENTS

Bishop Mule Days. Entertainment at this five-day festival over the Memorial Day weekend includes top country-music stars, an arts-and-crafts fair, barbecues, country dances, the longest-running nonmotorized parade in the United States, and more than 700 mules competing in 181 events. Admission is free. 🌐 *www.muledays.org*

Death Valley Dark Sky Festival. A full weekend program, held in late February or early March, celebrates Death Valley's celestial distinctions with guided hikes, ranger talks, a night-sky photo session, family events, and a star party. 🌐 *www.nps.gov/deva/planyourvisit/death-valley-dark-sky-festival.htm*

Getting Here and Around

AIR

The closest airport to the park with commercial service, Las Vegas McCarren International Airport, is 130 miles away, so you'll still need to drive a couple of hours to reach the park. Roughly 160 miles to the west, Burbank's Bob Hope Airport is the second-closest airport.

CAR

It can take more than three hours to cross from one side of the park to another, so it's important to choose an entrance point that makes sense for what you want to see. If you're driving from Los Angeles, enter through the western portion along Highway 395; from Las Vegas, enter from the north at Beatty, Nevada, or via the central entrance at Death Valley Junction. Travelers from Orange County, San Diego, and the Inland Empire should access the park via Interstate 15 North at Baker.

Distances can be deceiving: what seems close can be very far away. Much of the park can be viewed on regularly scheduled bus tours, but these often don't allow time for hikes to sites not seen from the road, such as Salt Creek, Golden Canyon, and Natural Bridge. The best option is to drive to a number of the sites, get out of the car, and walk.

When driving in Death Valley, reliable maps are important, as signage is often limited or, in a few places, nonexistent. Bring a phone, but don't rely on cell coverage exclusively in every remote area, and pack plenty of food and water (3 gallons per person per day is recommended). Cars, especially in summer, should be prepared for the hot, dry weather, too. Some of the park's most spectacular canyons are accessible only via four-wheel-drive vehicles, but make sure the trip is well planned and use a backcountry map. Be aware of possible winter closures or driving restrictions because of snow. The National Park Service's website (🌐 *nps.gov/deva*) stays up-to-date on road closures during the wet (and popular) months. ⚠ **One of the park's signature landmarks, Scotty's Castle, and the 8-mile road connecting it to the park border may be closed until 2022 due to damage from a 2015 flood.**

CONTACTS California Highway Patrol. ☎ *800/427–7623 recorded info from CalTrans, 760/872–5900 live dispatcher at Bishop Communications Center* 🌐 *www.chp.ca.gov.*

Inspiration

Hiking Death Valley: A Guide to Its Wonders and Mining Past, by Michel Dragonnet, offers detailed information on 57 day hikes and backpacking trips.

Survival Arts of the Primitive Paiutes, a bestseller by Margaret M. Wheat, describes how the Paiutes developed ways to survive in the harsh climate of the Death Valley and Nevada region.

Park Essentials

ACCESSIBILITY

All of Death Valley's visitor centers, contact stations, and museums are accessible to all visitors. The campgrounds at Furnace Creek, Sunset, and Stovepipe Wells have wheelchair-accessible sites. Highway 190, Badwater Road, and paved roads to Dante's View and Wildrose provide access to the major scenic viewpoints and historic points of interest.

PARK FEES AND PERMITS

The entrance fee is $30 per vehicle, $25 for motorcycles, and $15 for those entering on foot or bike. The payment, valid for seven consecutive days, is collected at the park's ranger stations, self-serve fee stations, and the visitor center at Furnace Creek. Annual park passes, valid only at Death Valley, are $55.

A permit is not required for groups of 14 or fewer, but if you're planning an overnight visit to the backcountry, complete a registration form at the Furnace Creek Visitor Center. Backcountry camping is allowed in areas that are at least 2 miles from maintained campgrounds and the main paved or unpaved roads and ¼ mile from water sources. Most abandoned mining areas are restricted to day use.

PARK HOURS

The park is open day or night year-round. Most facilities operate daily 8–6.

CELL PHONE RECEPTION

Results vary, but in general you should be able to get fairly good reception on the valley floor. In the surrounding mountains, however, don't count on it.

Hotels

It's difficult to find lodging anywhere in Death Valley that doesn't have breathtaking views of the park and surrounding mountains. Most accommodations, aside from the Inn at Death Valley, are homey and rustic. Rooms fill up quickly during the fall and spring seasons, and reservations are required about three months in advance for the prime weekends.

Restaurants

Inside the park, if you're looking for a special evening out, head to the Inn at Death Valley Dining Room, which is also a great spot to start the day with a hearty gourmet breakfast. Most other eateries within the park are mom-and-pop-type places with basic American fare.

Hotel and restaurant reviews have been shortened. For full information visit Fodors.com. Hotel prices are the lowest cost of a standard double room in high season. Restaurant prices are the average cost of a main course at dinner, or if dinner is not served, at lunch.

What It Costs

$	$$	$$$	$$$$
RESTAURANTS			
under $12	$12–$20	$21–$30	over $30
HOTELS			
under $100	$100–$150	$151–$200	over $200

Tours

Furnace Creek Visitor Center programs
GUIDED TOURS | This center has many programs, including ranger-led hikes that explore natural wonders such as Golden Canyon, nighttime stargazing parties with telescopes, and evening ranger talks. ✉ *Furnace Creek Visitor Center, Rte. 190, 30 miles northwest of Death Valley Junction, Death Valley* ☎ *760/786–2331* 🌐 *www.nps.gov/deva/planyourvisit/tours.htm* 🎫 *Free.*

Visitor Information

CONTACTS Death Valley National Park. ☎ *760/786–3200* 🌐 *www.nps.gov/deva.*

Central Death Valley

12 miles west of the Death Valley National Park Highway 190 entrance.

Furnace Creek village (194 feet below sea level) was once the center of mining operations for the Pacific Coast Borax Company. Today, it's the hub of Death Valley National Park, home to park headquarters and visitor center; the Timbisha Indian Village; and the Oasis at Death Valley hotels, golf course, restaurants, and market. Many major park sites are a short drive from here, including Artists Drive, Badwater Basin, Dante's View, and Zabriskie Point. Stovepipe Wells Village (where you will want to fill up at the gas station) lies 25 miles northwest of Furnace Creek.

Sights

HISTORIC SIGHTS

Harmony Borax Works
HISTORIC SITE | Death Valley's mule teams hauled borax from here to the railroad town of Mojave, 165 miles away. The teams plied the route until 1889, when the railroad finally arrived in Zabriskie. Constructed in 1883, one of the oldest buildings in Death Valley houses the Borax Museum, 2 miles south of the borax works at the Ranch at the Oasis at Death Valley (between the restaurants and the post office). Originally a miners' bunkhouse, the building once stood in Twenty Mule Team Canyon. Now it displays mining machinery and historical exhibits. The adjacent structure is the original mule-team barn. ✉ *Harmony Borax Works Rd., west of Hwy. 190 at Ranch at Death Valley* 🌐 *www.nps.gov/deva/historyculture/harmony.htm.*

SCENIC DRIVE

Artists Drive
SCENIC DRIVE | This 9-mile, one-way route skirts the foothills of the Black Mountains and provides intimate views of the changing landscape. Once inside the palette, the valley's expanses are replaced

by the small-scale natural beauty of pigments created by volcanic deposits or sedimentary layers. It's a quiet, lonely drive, and shouldn't be rushed. Reach Artists Palette by heading south on Badwater Road from its intersection with Route 190. ✉ *Death Valley National Park.*

SCENIC STOPS

Artists Palette

NATURE SITE | So called for the contrasting colors of its volcanic deposits and sedimentary layers, this is one of the signature sights of Death Valley. Artists Drive, the approach to the area, is one-way heading north off Badwater Road, so if you're visiting Badwater from Furnace Creek, come here on the way back. The drive winds through foothills of sedimentary and volcanic rocks. About 4 miles along, a short side road veers right to a parking lot that's a few hundred feet before the "palette," whose natural colors include shades of green, gold, and pink. ✉ *Off Badwater Rd., Death Valley ✣ 11 miles south of Furnace Creek.*

Badwater Basin

NATURE SITE | At 282 feet below sea level, Badwater is the lowest spot of land in North America—and also one of the hottest. Stairs and wheelchair ramps descend from the parking lot to a wooden platform that overlooks a sodium chloride pool, a small but remarkably persistent reminder that the valley floor used to contain a lake. You can continue past the platform on a broad, white path that peters out after a ½ mile or so. Badwater is one of the most popular and easily accessible sites within the park. From this lowest point, be sure to look across to Telescope Peak, which towers more than 2 miles above the valley floor. ✉ *Badwater Rd., Death Valley ✣ 19 miles south of Furnace Creek.*

Devil's Golf Course

NATURE SITE | Thousands of miniature salt pinnacles carved into surreal shapes by the desert wind dot this wildly varied landscape. The salt was pushed up to the surface by pressure created as underground salt- and water-bearing gravel crystallized. Get out of your vehicle, and take a closer look; you may see perfectly round holes descending into the ground. ✉ *Badwater Rd., Death Valley ✣ 13 miles south of Furnace Creek. Turn right onto dirt road and drive 1 mile.*

Golden Canyon

NATURE SITE | Just south of Furnace Creek, these glimmering mountains are perhaps best known for their role in the original *Star Wars*. The canyon is also a fine hiking spot, with gorgeous views of the Panamint Mountains, ancient dry lake beds, and alluvial fans. ✉ *Hwy. 178, Death Valley ✣ From Furnace Creek Visitor Center, drive 2 miles south on Hwy. 190, then 2 miles south on Hwy. 178 to parking area; the lot has kiosk with trail guides.*

Mesquite Flat Sand Dunes

NATURE SITE | These dunes, made up of minute pieces of quartz and other rock, are ever-changing products of the wind-rippled hills, with curving crests and a sun-bleached hue. The dunes are the most photographed destination in the park, and you can see them at their best at sunrise and sunset. Keep your eyes open for animal tracks—you may even spot a coyote or fox. Bring plenty of water, and note where you parked your car: it's easy to become disoriented in this ocean of sand. If you lose your bearings, climb to the top of a dune, and scan the horizon for the parking lot. ✉ *Death Valley ✣ 19 miles north of Hwy. 190, northeast of Stovepipe Wells Village.*

Zabriskie Point

VIEWPOINT | Although only about 710 feet in elevation, this is one of the park's most scenic spots, overlooking a striking panorama of wrinkled, multicolor hills. It's a great place to watch the sunrise, but it can be bustling any time of day. Pair it with a drive out to magnificent Dante's View. ✉ *Hwy. 190, Death Valley ✣ 5 miles south of Furnace Creek.*

The Mesquite Flat Sand Dunes

TRAILS

Keane Wonder Mine Trail

TRAIL | This fascinating relic of Death Valley's gold-mining past, built in 1907, reopened in November 2017 after nine years of repair work. Its most unique feature is the mile-long tramway that descends 1,000 vertical feet, which once carried gold ore and still has the original cables attached. From here, a network of trails leads to other old mines. A climb to the uppermost tramway terminal is rewarded by expansive views of the valley. ✉ *Access road off Beatty Cutoff Rd., 17½ miles north of Furnace Creek, Death Valley.*

Mosaic Canyon Trail

TRAIL | **FAMILY** | A gradual uphill trail (4 miles round-trip) winds through the smoothly polished, marbleized limestone walls of this narrow canyon. There are dry falls to climb at the upper end. *Moderate.* ✉ *Death Valley* ✣ *Trailhead: Access road off Hwy. 190, ½ mile west of Stovepipe Wells Village.*

Natural Bridge Canyon Trail

TRAIL | A rough 2-mile access road from Badwater Road leads to a trailhead. From there, set off to see interesting geological features in addition to the bridge, which is a ½ mile away. The one-way trail continues for a few hundred yards, but scenic returns diminish quickly, and eventually you're confronted with climbing boulders. *Easy.* ✉ *Death Valley* ✣ *Trailhead: Access road off Badwater Rd., 15 miles south of Furnace Creek.*

Salt Creek Interpretive Trail

TRAIL | **FAMILY** | This trail, a ½-mile boardwalk circuit, loops through a spring-fed wash. The nearby hills are brown and gray, but the floor of the wash is alive with aquatic plants such as pickleweed and salt grass. The stream and ponds here are among the few places in the park to see the rare pupfish, the only native fish species in Death Valley. They're most easily seen during their spawning season in February and March. Animals such as bobcats, foxes, coyotes, and snakes visit the spring, and you may also see ravens, common snipes, killdeer, and great blue herons. *Easy.* ✉ *Death Valley* ✢ *Trailhead: Off Hwy. 190, 14 miles north of Furnace Creek.*

VISITOR CENTERS

Furnace Creek Visitor Center and Museum
INFO CENTER | The exhibits and artifacts here provide a broad overview of how Death Valley formed; you can pick up maps at the bookstore run by the Death Valley Natural History Association. This is also the place to find out about ranger programs (available November through April) or check out a live presentation about the valley's cultural and natural history. The helpful center offers regular showings of a 20-minute film about the park, and this is the place for children to get their free Junior Ranger booklet, packed with games and information about the park and its critters. ✉ *Hwy. 190, Death Valley* ✢ *30 miles northwest of Death Valley Junction* ☎ *760/786–3200* 🌐 *www.nps.gov/deva.*

Restaurants

★ Inn at the Oasis at Death Valley Dining Room
$$$$ | **AMERICAN** | Fireplaces, beamed ceilings, and spectacular views provide a visual feast to match this fine-dining restaurant's ambitious menu. Dinner entrées include salmon, free-range chicken, and filet mignon, and there's a seasonal menu of vegetarian dishes. **Known for:** views of surrounding desert; old-school charm; can be pricey. $ *Average main: $42* ✉ *Inn at the Oasis at Death Valley, Hwy. 190, Furnace Creek* ☎ *760/786–3385* 🌐 *www.oasisatdeathvalley.com.*

Last Kind Words Saloon
$$$ | **AMERICAN** | Swing through wooden doors into a spacious dining room that recreates an authentic Old West saloon, decked out with a wooden bar and furniture, mounted animal heads, fugitive wanted fliers, film posters, and other memorabilia. The traditional steak house menu also includes crab cakes and other seafood, along with pastas, flatbreads, and vegan and gluten-free options. **Known for:** hefty steaks, ribs, and seasonal game dishes; extensive drinks menu, from local craft beer to whiskeys and wines; outdoor patio with fireplace. $ *Average main: $29* ✉ *The Ranch at the Oasis at Death Valley, Hwy. 190, Furnace Creek* ☎ *760/786–3335* 🌐 *www.oasisatdeathvalley.com/dine/last-kind-words-saloon.*

Hotels

★ The Inn at the Oasis at Death Valley
$$$$ | **HOTEL** | Built in 1927, this adobe-brick-and-stone lodge in one of the park's greenest oases reopened in 2018 after a $100 million renovation, offering Death Valley's most luxurious accommodations, including 22 brand-new one- and two-bedroom casitas. **Pros:** refined; comfortable; great views. **Cons:** services reduced during low season (July and August); expensive; resort fee. $ *Rooms from: $499* ✉ *Furnace Creek Village, near intersection of Hwy. 190 and Badwater Rd., Death Valley* ☎ *760/786–2345* 🌐 *www.oasisatdeathvalley.com* *88 rooms* *No meals.*

The Ranch at the Oasis at Death Valley
$$$$ | **RESORT** | **FAMILY** | Originally the crew headquarters for the Pacific Coast Borax Company, the four buildings here have motel-style rooms that are a great option for families. **Pros:** good family atmosphere; central location; walk to the golf course. **Cons:** rooms can get hot in summer despite a/c; resort fee; thin walls and ceilings in some rooms. $ *Rooms from: $279* ✉ *Hwy. 190, Furnace Creek* ☎ *760/786–2345* 🌐 *www.oasisatdeathvalley.com* *224 rooms* *No meals.*

Stovepipe Wells Village Hotel
$$ | **HOTEL** | If you prefer quiet nights and an unfettered view of the night sky and nearby Mesquite Flat Sand Dunes and Mosaic Canyon, this property is for

you. **Pros:** intimate, relaxed; no big-time partying; authentic desert-community ambience. **Cons:** isolated; cheapest patio rooms very small; limited Wi-Fi access. *$ Rooms from: $144 ✉ 51880 Hwy. 190, Stovepipe Wells ☎ 760/786–7090 🌐 www.deathvalleyhotels.com 83 rooms No meals.*

Northern Death Valley

6 miles west of Beatty, Nevada, via Nevada Hwy. 374, and 54 miles north of Furnace Creek via Hwy. 190 and Scotty's Castle Rd.

Venture into the remote northern region of the park to travel along the 27-mile Titus Canyon scenic drive, visit Racetrack and Ubehebe Crater, and hike along Fall Canyon and Titus Canyon Trails. Scotty's Castle, one of the park's main sights, and the 8-mile road that connects it to the park border, is currently closed to repair damage from a 2015 flood; it's expected to reopen in 2022. Check the park website for updates before you visit.

Sights

SCENIC DRIVES

Titus Canyon

SCENIC DRIVE | This popular, one-way, 27-mile drive starts at Nevada Highway 374 (Daylight Pass Road), 2 miles from the park's boundary. Highlights include the Leadville Ghost Town and the spectacular limestone and dolomite narrows. Toward the end, a two-way section of gravel road leads you into the mouth of the canyon from Scotty's Castle Road (closed until at least 2022). This drive is steep, bumpy, and narrow. High-clearance vehicles are strongly recommended. *✉ Death Valley National Park ✣ Access road off Nevada Hwy. 374, 6 miles west of Beatty, NV.*

SCENIC STOPS

Racetrack

NATURE SITE | Getting here involves a 28-mile journey over a washboard dirt road, but the reward is well worth the trip. Where else in the world do rocks move on their own? This mysterious phenomenon, which baffled scientists for years, now appears to have been "settled." Research has shown that the movement merely involves a rare confluence of conditions: rain and then cold to create a layer of ice that becomes a sail, thus enabling gusty winds to readily push the rocks along—sometimes for several hundred yards. When the mud dries, a telltale trail remains. The trek to the Racetrack can be made in a truck or SUV with thick tires (including spares) and high clearance; other types of vehicles aren't recommended as sharp rocks can slash tires. *✉ Death Valley ✣ 27 miles west of Ubehebe Crater via rough dirt road.*

Ubehebe Crater

VOLCANO | At 500 feet deep and ½ mile across, this crater resulted from underground steam and gas explosions, some as recently as 300 years ago. Volcanic ash spreads out over most of the area, and the cinders lie as deep as 150 feet near the crater's rim. Trek down to the crater's floor or walk around it on a fairly level path. Either way, you need about an hour and will be treated to fantastic views. The hike from the floor can be strenuous. *✉ N. Death Valley Hwy., Death Valley ✣ 8 miles northwest of Scotty's Castle.*

TRAILS

Fall Canyon Trail

TRAIL | This is a 3-mile, one-way hike from the Titus canyon parking area. First, walk ½ mile north along the base of the mountains to a large wash, then go 2½ miles up the canyon to a 35-foot dry fall. You can continue by climbing around to the falls on the south side. *Moderate. ✉ Death Valley National Park ✣ Trailhead: Access road off Scotty's Castle Rd., 33 miles northwest of Furnace Creek.*

Titus Canyon Trail

TRAIL | The narrow floor of Titus Canyon is made of hard-packed gravel and dirt, and it's a constant, moderate, uphill walk (3-mile round-trip is the trail's most popular tack). Klare Spring and some petroglyphs are 5½ miles from the western mouth of the canyon, but you can get a feeling for the area on a shorter walk. *Easy.* ✉ *Death Valley National Park.*

Southern Death Valley

Entrance on Hwy. 178, 1 mile west of Shoshone and 73 miles southeast of Furnace Creek.

Highway 178 traverses Death Valley from its southern border near Shoshone, through Badwater Basin, and up to Furnace Creek.

Sights

SCENIC STOPS

★ Dante's View

VIEWPOINT | This lookout is 5,450 feet above sea level in the Black Mountains. In the dry desert air you can see across most of 160-mile-long Death Valley. The view is astounding. Take a 10-minute, mildly strenuous walk from the parking lot toward a series of rocky overlooks, where, with binoculars, you can spot some signature sites. A few interpretive signs point out the highlights below in the valley and across in the Sierra. Getting here from Furnace Creek takes about an hour—time well invested. ✉ *Dante's View Rd., Death Valley* ✣ *Off Hwy. 190, 35 miles from Badwater, 20 miles south of Twenty Mule Team Canyon.*

Western Death Valley

Panamint Springs is on Hwy. 190, 30 miles southwest of Stovepipe Wells and 50 miles east of Lone Pine and Hwy. 395.

Panamint Springs, a tiny burg with a rustic resort, market, and gas station, anchors the western portion of the park and is a good base for hiking several trails. Pull over at Father Crowley Vista Point for exceptional views of the Panamint Valley and the high Sierra on Highway 190 if you're traveling between Lone Pine and Panamint Springs.

Sights

SCENIC STOPS

Father Crowley Vista Point

VIEWPOINT | Pull off Highway 190 in Western Death Valley into the vista point parking lot to gaze at the remnants of eerie volcanic flows down to Rainbow Canyon. Stroll a short distance to catch a sweeping overview of northern Panamint Valley. This is also an excellent site for stargazing. ✉ *Death Valley National Park.*

TRAILS

★ Darwin Falls

TRAIL | **FAMILY** | This lovely, 2-mile round-trip hike rewards you with a refreshing year-round waterfall surrounded by thick vegetation and a rocky gorge. No swimming or bathing is allowed, but it's a beautiful place for a picnic. Adventurous hikers can scramble higher toward more rewarding views of the falls. ⚠ **Some sections of the trail are not passable for those with mobility issues.** *Easy.* ✉ *Death Valley National Park* ✣ *Trailhead: Access the 2-mile graded dirt road and parking area off Hwy. 190, 1 mile west of Panamint Springs Resort.*

★ **Telescope Peak Trail**

TRAIL | The 14-mile round-trip (with 3,000 feet of elevation gain) trail begins at Mahogany Flat Campground, which is accessible by a rough dirt road. The steep and at some points treacherous trail winds through pinyon, juniper, and bristlecone pines, with excellent views of Death Valley and Panamint Valley. Ice axes and crampons may be necessary in winter—check at the Furnace Creek Visitor Center. It takes a minimum of six grueling hours to hike to the top of the 11,049-foot peak and then return. *Difficult.* ✉ *Death Valley* ✢ *Trailhead: Off Wildrose Rd., south of Charcoal Kilns.*

Restaurants

Panamint Springs Resort Restaurant

$$ | **AMERICAN** | This is a great place for steak and a beer—choose from more than 150 different beers and ales—or pasta and a salad. In summer, evening meals are served outdoors on the porch, which has spectacular views of Panamint Valley. **Known for:** good burgers; extensive beer selection; great views from the porch. $ *Average main: $15* ✉ *Hwy. 190, Death Valley* ✢ *31 miles west of Stovepipe Wells* ☎ *775/482–7680* 🌐 *www.panamintsprings.com/services/dining-bar.*

Activities

BIKING

Mountain biking is permitted on any of the back roads and roadways open to the public (bikes aren't permitted on hiking trails). Visit 🌐 *www.nps.gov/deva/planyourvisit/bikingandmtbiking.htm* for a list of suggested routes for all levels of ability.

Escape Adventures (*Escape Adventures*)

BICYCLING | Ride into the heart of Death Valley on the Death Valley & Red Rock Mountain Bike Tour, a five-day trip through the national park. A customizable two-day journey (on single-track trails and jeep roads) includes accommodations (both camping and inns). Bikes, tents, and other gear may be rented for an additional price. Tours are available February–April and October only. ✉ *Death Valley National Park* ☎ *800/596–2953, 702/596–2953* 🌐 *www.escapeadventures.com* 🎫 *From $1950.*

BIRD-WATCHING

Approximately 350 bird species have been identified in Death Valley. You can download a complete park bird checklist, divided by season, at 🌐 *www.nps.gov/deva/learn/nature/upload/death-valley-bird-checklist.pdf.* Rangers at Furnace Creek Visitor Center often lead birding walks through various locations between November and March.

CAMPING

Camping is prohibited in historic sites and day-use spots. You'll need a high-clearance or 4X4 vehicle to reach campgrounds. For backcountry camping information, visit 🌐 *www.nps.gov/deva/planyourvisit/camping.htm.*

Fires are permitted only in metal grates and may be restricted in summer. Wood gathering is prohibited at all campgrounds, and it's best to bring your own. Firewood is expensive and limited in supply at general stores in Furnace Creek and Stovepipe Wells.

Furnace Creek. This campground, 196 feet below sea level, has some shaded tent sites and is open all year. ✉ *Hwy. 190, Furnace Creek* ☎ *760/786–2441.*

Panamint Springs Resort. Part of a complex that includes a motel and cabin, this campground is surrounded by cottonwoods. The daily fee includes use of the showers and restrooms. ✉ *Hwy. 190, 28 miles west of Stovepipe Wells* ☎ *775/482–7680.*

Sunset Campground. This first-come, first-served campground is a gravel-and-asphalt RV city. Closed mid-April to mid-October. ✉ *Sunset Campground Rd., 1 mile north of Furnace Creek* ☎ *800/365–2267.*

EDUCATIONAL PROGRAMS

Junior Ranger Program

TOUR—SIGHT | FAMILY | Children can pick up a workbook and complete activities to earn a souvenir badge. ✉ *Death Valley National Park.*

FOUR-WHEELING

Butte Valley

TOUR—SPORTS | A high-clearance, four-wheel-drive vehicle and nerves of steel are required to tackle this 21-mile road in the southwest part of the park. It climbs from 200 feet below sea level to an elevation of 4,700 feet, and the geological formations along the way reveal the development of Death Valley. It also travels through Butte Valley, passing the Warm Springs talc mine, to Geologist's Cabin, a charming and cheery little structure where you can spend the night, if nobody else beats you to it. The cabin, which sits under a cottonwood tree, has a fireplace, table and chairs, and a sink. Farther up the road, Stella's Cabin and Russell Camp are also open for public use. Keep the historic cabins clean, and restock any items that you use. The road is even rougher if you continue over Mengel Pass. Check road conditions before heading out. ✉ *Trailhead on Warm Spring Canyon Rd., Death Valley* ✣ *50 miles south of Furnace Creek Visitor Center.*

GOLF

Furnace Creek Golf Course at the Oasis at Death Valley

GOLF | Golfers rave about how their drives carry at altitude, so what happens on the lowest golf course in the world (214 feet below sea level)? Its improbably green fairways are lined with date palms and tamarisk trees, and its level of difficulty is rated surprisingly high. You can rent clubs and carts, and there are golf packages available for resort guests. In fall and winter, reservations are essential. ✉ *Hwy. 190, Furnace Creek* ☎ *760/786–3373* 🌐 *www.oasisatdeathvalley.com* 🎫 *From $48* ⛳ *18 holes, 6215 yards, par 70.*

HIKING

Plan to hike before or after midday in the spring, summer, or fall, unless you're in the mood for a masochistic baking. Carry plenty of water, wear protective clothing, and keep an eye out for black widows, scorpions, snakes, and other potentially dangerous creatures.

HORSEBACK AND CARRIAGE RIDES

Furnace Creek Stables

HORSEBACK RIDING | FAMILY | Set off on a one- or two-hour guided horseback, carriage, or hay wagon ride from Furnace Creek Stables. The rides traverse trails with views of the surrounding mountains, where multicolor volcanic rock and alluvial fans form a background for date palms and other vegetation. Evening carriage rides take passengers around the golf course and the Ranch at Death Valley. The stables are open October–May only. ✉ *Hwy. 190, Furnace Creek* ☎ *760/614–1018* 🌐 *www.oasisatdeathvalley.com/plan/horseback-wagon-rides* 🎫 *From $60.*

What's Nearby

Founded at the turn of the 20th century, **Beatty** sits 16 miles east of the California–Nevada border on Death Valley's northern side. **Lone Pine,** named for a single pine tree found at the bottom of the canyon of the same name, is on the park's west side. The nearby Alabama Hills have been used in many movies and TV scenes, including segments in *The Lone Ranger.* **Independence ,** a well-preserved outpost that dates from the 1860s, lies 16 miles north of Lone Pine on Highway 395. At the park's southern edge, tiny, unincorporated **Shoshone** started out as a mining town.

Chapter 19

DENALI NATIONAL PARK AND PRESERVE

Updated by
David Cannamore

Camping ★★★★★ | Hotels ★★★☆☆ | Activities ★★★★★ | Scenery ★★★★★ | Crowds ★★★★☆

WELCOME TO DENALI NATIONAL PARK AND PRESERVE

TOP REASONS TO GO

★ **Backcountry hiking:** Getting off the road system and into the park's managed units allows for a true wilderness experience, limited only by time and the strength of your legs. For on-trail hiking try Savage River or Mt. Healy Overlook Trail.

★ **Denali flightseeing:** Soar over river valleys and up glaciers to the slopes of Denali to see the continent's wildest scenery. Some tours also offer landings on Ruth Glacier.

★ **Sled-dog demonstrations:** Watch half-hour demonstrations at the nation's oldest working dogsled kennel. Since the 1920s, sled dogs have been hauling rangers and workers to Denali's interior.

★ **Rafting:** Experience Denali in its wild rapids or serene flat water.

★ **Wonder Lake:** It takes all day to get to Wonder Lake via bus, but your chances of spotting wildlife are excellent. And from Wonder Lake the view of the massive slopes of Denali is something you'll never forget.

1 The Entrance. Just outside the park you'll find a strip of hotels, restaurants, and shops; just inside the park are the official visitor center, the least scenic campsites in Denali, and a level of chaos—at least in high season—that does not reflect the park's beauty.

2 Eielson Visitor Center. Deep in the heart of the park, near a favored caribou trail, Eielson offers great mountain views and sweeping vistas of the glaciated landscape. If you can't make it all the way to Wonder Lake, at least make it here.

3 The Mountain. Call it Denali or just "the Mountain." It's the highest spot on the continent, a double-edged peak that draws more than 1,000 climbers a year. Fewer than half make it to the top, but that's okay: it's easy enough to enjoy the view from below.

4 Wonder Lake. The end of the road for most vehicles, the lake is a full day's ride on one of the park buses. For your time, when the weather allows, you get the best view of the mountain anywhere in the park. And even when the mountain is hiding in the clouds, this is one of the prettiest stretches of landscape in the world.

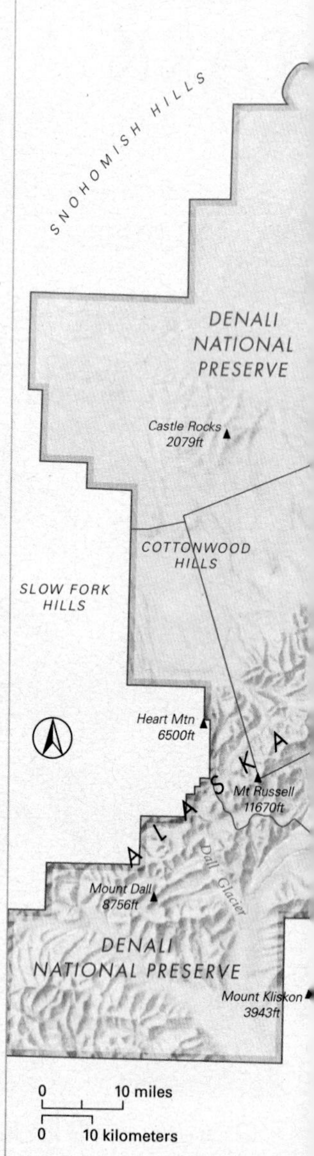

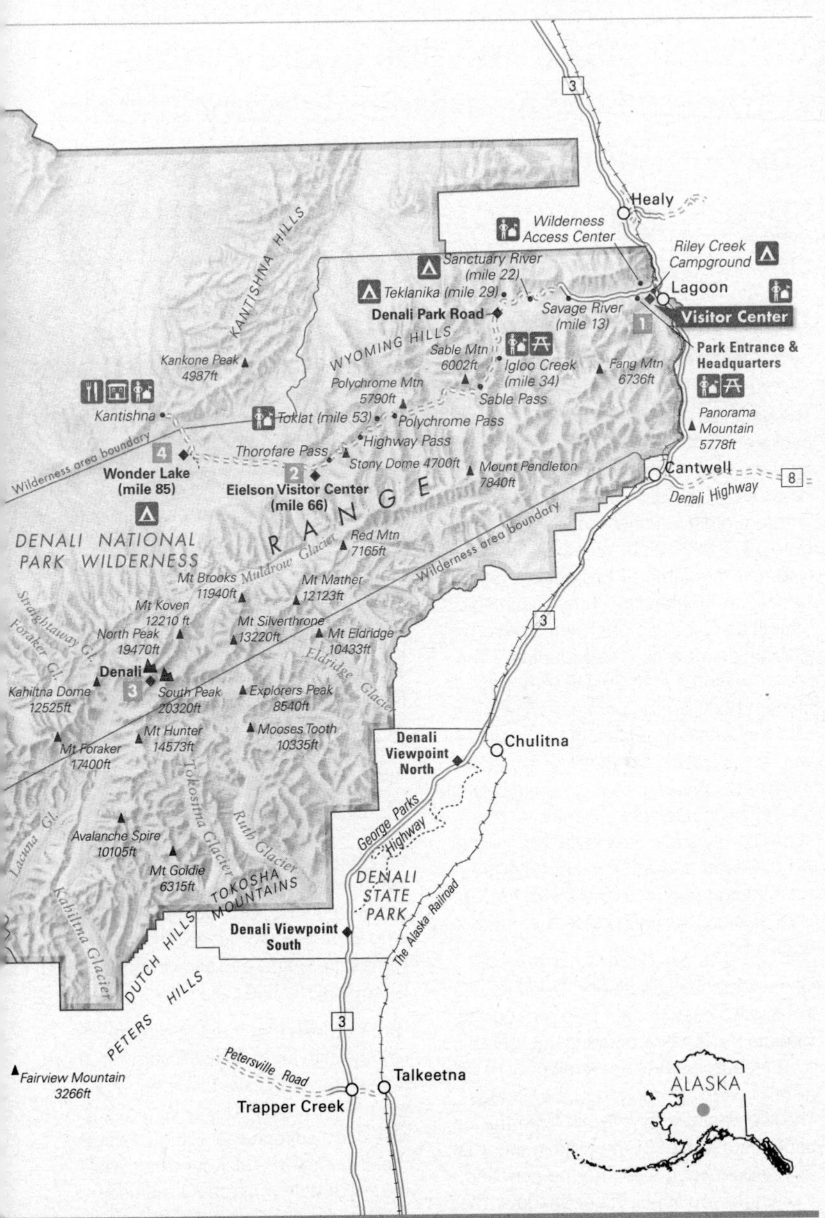
Healy
Wilderness Access Center
Riley Creek Campground
Sanctuary River (mile 22)
Teklanika (mile 29)
Lagoon
Visitor Center
Denali Park Road
Savage River (mile 13)
Park Entrance & Headquarters
KANTISHNA HILLS
WYOMING HILLS
Sable Mtn 6002ft
Igloo Creek (mile 34)
Fang Mtn 6736ft
Kankone Peak 4987ft
Polychrome Mtn 5790ft
Sable Pass
Kantishna
Toklat (mile 53)
Polychrome Pass
Panorama Mountain 5778ft
Highway Pass
Wilderness area boundary
Thorofare Pass
Stony Dome 4700ft
Mount Pendleton 7840ft
Cantwell
Wonder Lake (mile 85)
Eielson Visitor Center (mile 66)
Denali Highway
RANGE
Red Mtn 7165ft
DENALI NATIONAL PARK WILDERNESS
Muldrow Glacier
Mt Brooks 11940ft
Mt Mather 12123ft
Mt Koven 12210 ft
Straightaway Gl.
Foraker Gl.
North Peak 19470ft
Mt Silverthrone 13220ft
Mt Eldridge 10433ft
Eldridge Glacier
Denali
Kahiltna Dome 12525ft
South Peak 20320ft
Explorers Peak 8540ft
Mt Hunter 14573ft
Mooses Tooth 10335ft
Mt Foraker 17400ft
Denali Viewpoint North
Chulitna
Tokositna Glacier
Ruth Glacier
Lacuna Gl.
Avalanche Spire 10105ft
Mt Goldie 6315ft
George Parks Highway
TOKOSHA MOUNTAINS
DENALI STATE PARK
The Alaska Railroad
Kahiltna Glacier
DUTCH HILLS
Denali Viewpoint South
PETERS HILLS
Petersville Road
Fairview Mountain 3266ft
Talkeetna
Trapper Creek
ALASKA
3
8

Denali National Park and Preserve is Alaska's most visited attraction for many reasons. The most accessible of Alaska's national parks and one of only three connected to the state's highway system, the 6-million-acre wilderness offers spectacular mountain views, a variety of wildlife, striking vegetation, and unforgettable landscapes.

The park lies 120 miles south of Fairbanks and 240 miles north of Anchorage on the George Parks Highway. The keystone of the park is Mt. Denali itself. The mountain was named Mt. McKinley from 1917 to 2015, but President Obama changed the name of this peak back to Denali, an Athabascan name meaning "the High One." It's often referred to by Alaskans simply as "the Mountain." The peak measures in at 20,310 feet, the highest point on the continent. Denali is also the tallest mountain in the world—yes, Mt. Everest is higher, but it sits on the Tibetan plateau, as if it was standing on a chair to rise above Denali, which starts barely above sea level. Mt. Hunter (14,573 feet) and Mt. Foraker (17,400 feet) stand sentinel to the south of Denali with glaciers flowing across the entire Alaska Range.

Despite its dizzying height, Denali is not always easy to see. Like most great mountains, it has a tendency to create its own weather, which for a majority of the time involves a large amount of clouds. The mountain is only visible from the park about a third of the time in summer. The deeper you travel into the park and the longer you linger in her shadow, the better the odds are that the cloudy veil will be lifted.

While you wait to catch a glimpse of Denali, there's plenty more to look for. Dozens of mammal species populate the park, including the "Big Five" of Alaskan animals: the moose, grizzly bear, wolf, Dall sheep, and caribou. Snowshoe hare and arctic ground squirrels watch with suspicious eyes from the roadside, and the sky is filled with the calls of willow ptarmigan and eagles. Tundra and spruce-laden Taiga forests lead to the rocky foothills of the Alaska Range, populated by lichens and small grasses favored by caribou. There are also the harsh glaciers and sharp peaks of the mountains themselves, but be aware that mountaineering in this region is not a casual endeavor. Only about half of those who attempt to summit North America's highest peak succeed and careful planning is required months in advance.

But for those that would prefer not to risk the thin air of Denali's summit, there are still several ways to experience the park, from half-day excursions to weeklong adventures. Hiking trails dot the area near the visitor center while the more bold might try a multiday

AVERAGE HIGH/LOW TEMPERATURES					
JAN.	**FEB.**	**MAR.**	**APR.**	**MAY**	**JUNE**
11/-5	17/-2	26/1	39/16	54/31	65/41
JULY	**AUG.**	**SEPT.**	**OCT.**	**NOV.**	**DEC.**
67/45	61/40	50/31	32/14	17/1	15/-1

backpacking trip through the tundra. Tour buses cover the length of the park road, with six campgrounds available along it. The buses feature informative and keen-eyed drivers, who are constantly looking to spot wildlife. Flightseeing tours are offered from the nearby community of Healy, which, barring bad weather, will get you up close to the mountains (Denali included), and many even include a glacier walk.

Planning

When to Go

Denali's main season runs mid-May through early September. About 90% of travelers come in these months, and with good reason: warmish weather, long days, and all the facilities are open. Shoulder seasons (early May and late September) can be incredibly beautiful in the park, with few people around; plus, you can often drive your own car a fair way down the park road, since the buses don't run. Exact opening and closing dates for seasonal properties tend to vary year to year, and when traveling close to shoulder season, it's best to inquire directly before your visit to ensure a place is open. In winter the only way into the park is on skis or snowshoes or by dog-sled. You'll have the place almost entirely to yourself—most of the businesses at the park entrance are closed—and if you're comfortable in deep snow and freezing weather, there is no better time to see Denali.

No matter how much time you have, plan ahead. Bus and campsite reservations are available for the summer season beginning December 1. **TIP→ Reserve tickets for buses ahead of time; call the numbers provided here or log on to www.reservedenali.com.** Although you can often just walk up and get on something, it may not be the experience you're after. Advance planning makes for the best trips.

Getting Here and Around

AIR

Fairbanks International Airport (FAI), the closest international airport to Fairbanks, is 120 miles to the north. Bush planes fly into the community of Healy just north of the park entrance or Talkeetna 150 miles to the south. These two smaller strips are where the majority of the flight seeing tours for Denali depart from.

CAR

The park is 120 miles south of Fairbanks, or 240 miles north of Anchorage, on the George Parks Highway, which is the most common access route.

There is a second, seldom-used road to the park: the Denali Highway leads from Paxon, which is accessible from the Richardson Highway (it connects Fairbanks and Valdez) to Cantwell, coming out just south of the park entrance. This 134-mile road is mostly unpaved, with few services. Only people with high-clearance cars should try it. The Denali Highway is closed in winter.

Unless you are staying at the Teklanika Campground at mile 29 (a three-day minimum stay is required), personal vehicles are only allowed along the first 15 miles of the Denali road. There is a road lottery for a day in September (the exact date varies every year) where you can drive your personal vehicle into the park, but these days are often crowded and traffic-filled even if you come sans-vehicle.

SHUTTLE

Only one road penetrates Denali's expansive wilderness: the 92-mile Denali Park Road, which winds from the park entrance to Wonder Lake (as far as the regular buses go) and on the inholding of Kantishna, the historic mining district in the heart of the park, where there are a couple of private lodges. The first 15 miles of the road are paved and open to all vehicles. During the summer months, the road beyond the checkpoint at Savage River is limited to tour buses, special permit holders, and the community members of Kantishna. To get around the park, you need to get on one of the buses or start hiking.

TRAIN

For those who don't want to drive, Denali National Park is a regular stop on the Alaska Railroad's Anchorage–Fairbanks route. The railway sells packages that combine train travel with hotels and trips into the park. There are great views along the way, especially when crossing the Hurricane Gulch Bridge, and the train is a lovely, comfortable way to travel. The final approach to the park is much prettier by train than via car.

Inspiration

A story that has captured the imagination of some and the frustration of others, Jon Krakauer's book *Into the Wild* (and subsequent 2007 movie directed by Sean Penn) follows the mysterious journey of Chris McCandless from the east coast to the wilds of Alaska. The iconic bus along the Stampede Trail where his body was discovered has been the site of much frustration for search-and-rescue crew ever since as backpackers and sightseers attempt to reach it. The bus has since been removed although you can still see the model used in the film at the nearby 49th State Brewing Company in Healy.

One of the most recognized and important naturalists of the 20th century, Adolph Murie will be forever remembered for his work within Denali National Park. Well researched but condensed and easy to read, you don't need to be a PhD-carrying scientist to appreciate the wealth of knowledge and history of the area in *A Naturalist in Alaska*.

It isn't necessary to stand on the highest peak in North America to appreciate Art Davidson's vivid descriptions in *Minus 148*. The book details the first winter ascent of the mountain and is best enjoyed next to a roaring fire with a hot beverage of your choice.

Denali National Park, Alaska Guide to Hiking, Photography, and Camping is an intensive look at the park's geography and a must for backpackers. Ike Waits keeps updating this guidebook, the most recent one highlights more than 40 hikes and backpacking trips through the park's tundra.

Park Essentials

ACCESSIBILITY

While many of the wilderness areas are impossible to reach for those with disabilities, the park has done a good job of configuring several areas to make them accessible for the majority of visitors. All campground talks and theater programs take place in wheelchair accessible areas. When possible, ASL translations of ranger programs can be made available. Since Denali is such a remote setting, the earlier you can make this request, the more likely the park will be able to provide this service.

Most trails in the park have a base of native vegetation punctuated by rocks and roots, but several trails around the park entrance like the Bike Loop and Horseshoe Lake Trails are made of compacted gravel and are the easiest for a wheelchair to navigate.

All campgrounds that admit vehicles have some level of accessibility, the best of which is Riley Creek campground. Here you'll find specific campsites that have been surfaced with compact gravel and are located close to the mercantile.

Some of the tour buses have a wheelchair lift. Like the ASL translation option, the sooner that you can request one of these specific buses for your tour the better. The same service is available to reach the sled dog kennels 1.5 miles from the entrance. The kennel amphitheater has limited seating, so it's best to show up early to ensure a spot.

Two wheelchairs are available at the Denali Visitor Center, which are available on a first-come, first-served basis.

PARK FEES AND PERMITS

Admission to Denali is $15 per person for a seven-day entrance permit.

PARK HOURS

The park never closes. There may not be anybody around to accept the admission fee in deep winter, but the gates are always open.

CELL PHONE RECEPTION

Don't count on cell-phone reception past the first mile or two beyond the visitor center.

Hotels

There are plenty of options right outside the park entrance, but don't expect to find anything open in winter. Year-round lodgings can be found in Healy.

Restaurants

There's a small grill-style restaurant near the park's visitor center, but otherwise there are no traditional restaurants or grocery stores inside the park so you'll need to carry in your food. Just outside the park entrance, in the area known as Glitter Gulch, you'll find dozens of restaurants open during the summer only. Year-round grocery stores are found 10 miles north of the entrance in the town of Healy.

Restaurant and hotel reviews have been shortened. For full information, visit Fodors.com. Restaurant prices are the average cost of a main course at dinner or, if dinner is not served, at lunch. Hotel prices are the lowest cost of a standard double room in high season

What It Costs

	$	$$	$$$	$$$$
RESTAURANTS				
	under $14	$14–$22	$23–$32	over $32
HOTELS				
	under $100	$100–$175	$176–$250	over $250

Tours

Don't be alarmed by the crowded park entrance; that gets left behind very quickly. After the chaos of private businesses that line the George Parks Highway and the throngs at the visitor center, there's pretty much nothing else in the park but wilderness. From the bus you'll have the opportunity to see Denali's wildlife in natural settings, as the animals are habituated to the road and vehicles, and go about their daily routine with little bother. In fact, the animals really like the road: it's easier for them to walk along it than to work through the tundra and tussocks.

Bus trips take time. The maximum speed limit is 35 mph, and the buses don't hit that very often. Add in rest stops, wildlife sightings, and slowdowns for passing, and it's an 8- to 11-hour day to reach the heart of the park and the best Denali views from miles 62–85. Buses run from May 20 to September 13, although if you're running up close against one of those dates, call to make sure. **TIP→ If you decide to tour the park by bus, you have two choices: a sightseeing bus tour or a ride on the shuttle bus. The differences between the two are significant.**

BUSES AND SHUTTLES

Camper Buses

BUS TOURS | These buses serve permitted backpackers and those staying in campgrounds along the road. Seats in the back of the bus are removed for gear storage and there is room for two bikes (the bike spaces must be reserved ahead of time). While there is no formal narration, bus drivers aren't likely to let you miss anything important. The $60 pass includes transportation anywhere down the road as far as Wonder Lake for the length of the backpacker's stay; kids under 15 are free. Tell the driver ahead of time where you'd like to get out. ✉ *Denali National Park* ☎ *800/622–7275* 🌐 *www.reservedenali.com* 🎫 *$60* 🕒 *Closed mid-Sept.–mid-May.*

Shuttle Buses

BUS TOURS | The park's shuttle and transit buses are a more informal, cheaper, and independent way to experience Denali. These buses are green-painted, converted school buses while the formally narrated tour buses are tan. While these trips are not formally narrated, the majority of bus drivers enjoy sharing information with riders, and the buses are equipped with speakers. Transit buses offer the freedom to disembark virtually anywhere along the road system and explore the park for yourself. Catching a ride back is as simple as returning to the road and waiting for the next transit bus to come by. Note that full buses will not stop, so it's possible to wait for an hour or more for your ride back. Like the narrated tours, transit buses are operated by Doyon/Aramark and bookings are made through the concessionaire. Reservations are not required, and about a quarter of the seats are saved for walk-ons. But if you're visiting during peak season, it's best to make reservations ahead of time to ensure availability. Schedules can be found on the National Park Service's Denali website; departure times are relatively reliable although they can fluctuate during the summer. ✉ *Denali National Park* ☎ *800/622–7275* 🌐 *www.reservedenali.com* 🎫 *Free–$60* 🕒 *Closed mid-Sept.–mid-May.*

Tour Buses

BUS TOURS | Guided bus tours offer the most informative introduction to the park. Each trip is led by a trained naturalist who drives the bus and gives a full narration. All tours include rest stops approximately every 90 minutes. Unlike the transit buses, you are not allowed to wander off on your own. The shortest is the five-hour Natural History Tour that travels to Teklanika at mile 27. Besides moose and the occasional caribou, chances of seeing the park's large mammals are limited on this route, and glimpses of Denali are possible but not probable. The next longest option is the seven to eight-hour Tundra Wilderness Tour that reaches Stony Brook at mile 62; this is the best choice for wildlife and photography enthusiasts. The longest narrated tour is the Kantishna Experience, a 12-hour extravaganza that runs the full 92 miles of park road to the old mining town of Kantishna. Advance reservations are required for all bus tours, and they can be made starting on December 1, with exact departure times fluctuating depending on demand and time of year. It's best to consult Doyon/Aramark for an exact schedule as departure times are often not set until a few days before. ✉ *Denali National Park* ☎ *800/622–7275* 🌐 *www.reservedenali.com* 🎫 *From $102* 🕒 *Closed mid-Sept.–mid-May.*

Visitor Information

CONTACTS Denali National Park Headquarters. ☎ *907/683–2294 information* 🌐 *www.nps.gov/dena.*

In the Park

With a landmass larger than Massachusetts, Denali National Park and Preserve has too much area for even the most dedicated vacationer to explore in one go. In fact, several of Denali's most spectacular landforms are found deep within the park, but are still visible from the park road. The multicolor volcanic rocks at Cathedral Mountain and Polychrome Pass reflect the vivid hues of the American Southwest. The braided channels of glacially fed streams such as the Teklanika, Toklat, and McKinley rivers serve as highway routes for both animals and hikers. The debris- and tundra-covered ice of the Muldrow Glacier, one of the largest glaciers to flow out of Denali National Park's high mountains, is visible from Eielson Visitor Center, at mile 66 of the park road. Wonder Lake, a narrow kettle pond that's a remnant from Alaska's ice ages, lies at mile 85, just a few miles from the former gold-boom camp of Kantishna.

When planning your trip, consider whether you want to strike out on your own as a backcountry traveler or to stay at a lodge nearby and enjoy Denali as a day hiker with the help of a tour or shuttle bus. Both options require some advance planning, for bus tickets or backcountry permits. But both options also offer a magnificent experience. It's important to reserve tickets for narrated bus tours ahead of time; ⇨ *see the Denali Planner for contact information* or log on to 🌐 *www.reservedenali.com.*

Sights

GEOLOGICAL FORMATIONS

★ Denali

MOUNTAIN—SIGHT | In the heart of mainland Alaska, within 6-million-acre Denali National Park and Preserve, the continent's most majestic peak rises into the heavens. Formerly known as Mt. McKinley, this 20,310-foot massif of ice, snow, and rock has been renamed to honor its Alaska Native name, Denali, or "the High One." Some simply call it "the Mountain." One thing is certain: it's a giant among giants, and the most dominant feature in a land of extremes and superlatives. Those who have walked Denali's slopes know it to be a wild, desolate place. As the highest peak in North America, Denali is a target of mountaineers who aspire to ascend the "seven summits"—the tallest mountains on each continent. A foreboding and mysterious place, it was terra incognita—unclimbed and unknown to most people—as recently as the late 1890s. Among Athabascan tribes, however, the mountain was a revered landmark; many generations regarded it as a holy place and a point of reference. The mountain's vertical rise is the highest in the world. This means that at 18,000 feet over the lowlands (which are some 2,000 feet above sea level), Denali's vertical rise is even greater than that of Mt. Everest, at 29,035-feet (which sits 12,000 feet above the Tibetan plateau, some 17,000 feet above sea level). Denali's awesome height and its subarctic location make it one of the coldest mountains on Earth, if not *the* coldest. Primarily made of granite, Denali undergoes continual shifting and uplift thanks to plate tectonics (the Pacific Plate pushing against the North American Plate); it grows about 1 millimeter per year. ✉ *Denali National Park.*

SCENIC DRIVES

If you're camping nearby and have your own vehicle, a drive to Savage River at first light or sunset is a good way to avoid the crowds. Wildlife tends to be more active during these quiet hours, especially if the forecast has been hot and dry.

Denali Park Road

LOCAL INTEREST | No matter whether you visit on foot, bike, or bus, you'll want to utilize the Denali road system as much as possible. Personal vehicles are only allowed the first 15 miles of the 92-mile long road, and most of the best potential views and wildlife are beyond this 15-mile marker. The view from the Eielson Visitor Center and Wonder Lake are the park's most iconic and these are located at miles 66 and 85, respectively.

But amazing views of the rolling tundra, foothills, and grizzly bears can be had almost anywhere. Take your time and if possible, spend multiple days either taking bus tours, hiking, or biking through the park to give yourself the best chance of an unforgettable view or wildlife encounter.

While the park is never technically closed, much of the road is snowed in during the winter months. Depending on the snowfall, travel along the park road can be hampered in spring and fall as well. The road is generally open up to Mountain Vista (mile 13) by mid-February. ⊠ *Denali National Park* ⊕ *www.nps.gov/dena/planyourvisit/visiting-denali.htm* ⊙ *Weather-dependent in spring, fall, and winter. Generally open to mile 13 by mid-Feb.*

SCENIC STOPS

Private vehicles are unable to access Stony Hill, Polychrome, or any of the other iconic stops in the park like Eielson Visitor Center and Wonder Lake. However, most bus tours make stops at most of them.

TRAILS

McKinley Station Trail

TRAIL | The Station trail begins at the visitor center and follows a winding path down toward the Riley and Hines Creeks. While the trail drops more than 100 feet during its 1½-mile-long path, the grade is never very steep and the trail is made of compacted gravel for easy walking. *Easy.* ⊠ *Denali National Park* ✣ *Trailhead: A one-way trail with access points at the Denali Visitor Center and Riley Creek Campground* ⊕ *www.nps.gov/dena/planyourvisit/dayhiking.htm.*

Rock Creek Trail

TRAIL | After following the Taiga Trail for a short time, the Rock Creek Trail splits to the west and offers a steeper, challenging, and quieter journey through the woods. Farther from the road than many of the trails near the park entrance, this 30" wide trail can have a steep grade at times of up to 15%. All together the trail runs about 2.5 miles one-way, ending at the Sled Dog Kennels. *Moderate* ⊠ *Denali National Park* ✣ *Trailhead: One-way trail with access from the Denali Visitor Center and Sled Dog Kennels* ⊕ *www.nps.gov/dena/planyourvisit/dayhiking.htm.*

Taiga Loop Trail

TRAIL | A simple forested trail that winds around the Denali Visitor Center and other buildings and connects with the bus and train depot. The trail is made of gravel with minimal grade, most explorers should be able to complete the loop in less than an hour. **■ TIP→ Access may be limited by snowfall in winter.** *Easy.* ⊠ *Denali National Park* ✣ *Trailhead: Looped trail with access from the visitor center and bus depot* ⊕ *www.nps.gov/dena/planyourvisit/dayhiking.htm.*

Savage Alpine Trail

TRAIL | Running about 4 miles, this trail system connects the Savage River pullout and campground areas. You can use the Savage River Shuttle to access the trailhead or your personal vehicle. Note that if you're using your own vehicle, the trail spits you out about 2 miles down the road system. **■ TIP→ The trail isn't accessible for most of the winter.** *Moderate.* ⊠ *Denali National Park* ✣ *Trailhead: Located at the Savage River and Mountain Vista Picnic Areas.*

Savage River Loop

TRAIL | True to its name, the River Loop follows the Savage River up the valley carved between Mount Margaret and Healy Ridge for about a mile. The trail crosses a bridge before traveling down the valley and reconnecting with the Savage River Picnic Area. **■ TIP→ The trail is inaccessible during winter months.** *Moderate.* ✉ *Denali National Park* ✣ *Trailhead: Savage River Picnic Area* 🌐 *www.nps.gov/dena/planyourvisit/savagecanyon.htm.*

VISITOR CENTERS

Denali Education Center

COLLEGE | FAMILY | Situated on 10 acres of forest across from Denali National Park, this nonprofit offers intensive learning experiences that range from a variety of all-inclusive weeklong Road Scholar programs to weeklong youth programs, including hands-on research in conjunction with the National Park Service or backpacking trips for high schoolers. Public events as well as day and evening dinner programs are offered at intervals throughout the summer months. On the first weekend of August the center sponsors the Fundraising Auction, which draws in hundreds of people and thousands of articles for sale, all for a fantastic cause. ✉ *Parks Hwy., Box 212, Denali National Park* ✣ *Mile 231* ☎ *907/683–2597* 🌐 *www.denali.org* ⏲ *Closed mid-Sept.–mid-May.*

Denali Visitor Center

INFO CENTER | Open from mid-May through mid-September, the center is 1½ miles beyond the park's entrance, and includes two floors' worth of displays detailing the park's natural and cultural history along with several life-size representations of the park's largest animals. A theater on the main floor plays the 20-minute film *The Heartbeats of Denali* twice an hour. The center is the starting point for most interpretive ranger hikes and several other trails you can explore independently. This is also the place to go for your backcountry camping permits (permits aren't necessary for day hikes). Nearby facilities include the railroad and bus depots, the Morino Grill, and the Alaska Geographic bookstore. ✉ *Denali National Park Rd., Denali National Park* ☎ *907/683–9532* 🌐 *www.nps.gov/dena* ⏲ *Closed mid-Sept.–mid-May.*

Eielson Visitor Center

INFO CENTER | Famous for its views of Denali, the Eielson Visitor Center is found at mile 66 of the park road. Park rangers are present throughout the day either leading presentations or hikes such as the leisurely Eielson Stroll. While there is a small gallery of Denali-inspired art here, this visitor center is all about the view, dominated, with a little luck, by the mountain itself. The center opens on June 1 and closes on the second Thursday after Labor Day; it's open daily 9–5:30. It's accessible by any of the shuttle buses that pass mile 66, excluding the Kantishna Experience tour. For backpackers, the bathrooms remain unlocked 24-hours a day during the summer. ✉ *Park Rd., Denali National Park* ✣ *Mile 66* 🌐 *www.nps.gov/dena/planyourvisit/the-eielson-visitor-center.htm* ⏲ *Closed early Sept.–May.*

Murie Science and Learning Center

COLLEGE | Next to the Denali Visitor Center, Murie Science and Learning Center is the foundation of the park's science-based education programs, and also serves as the winter visitor center when the Denali Visitor Center is closed. Hours during the summer vary, and the center usually opens only for special presentations. During off-season camping at the Riley Campground, it's the go-to spot for ranger information and, yes, bathrooms with running water. ✉ *Park Rd., Denali National Park* ✣ *Mile 1.5* ☎ *907/683–6432* 🌐 *www.nps.gov/rlc/murie.*

Wilderness Access Center

INFO CENTER | Also known as the Bus Depot, this center just inside the park entrance is where you can reserve campgrounds and bus trips into the park. For those that arrive after 7 pm, campground reservations can be made at the Riley Creek Mercantile until 11 pm. There's also a coffee stand—your last chance for a cup of joe unless you bring the makings for campsite coffee with you. ✉ *Park Rd., Denali National Park* ✣ *Mile 0.5* ☎ *907/683–9532* 🌐 *www.nps.gov/dena/planyourvisit/wildernessaccesscenter.htm* ⏲ *Closed mid-Sept.–mid-May.*

Restaurants

The Denali Doghouse

$ | **AMERICAN** | It's all about the dog at this casual, dog-decorated and hot dog–theme joint whose menu includes hot dogs topped with gourmet bacon, cheese, kraut, slaw, or chili. The owners are locals and rely on made-in-Alaska products so all quarter-pound burger patties are hand-pressed while fries and onion rings are fresh. **Known for:** quick lunch and dinners; reindeer hot dogs; one of the cheaper (and most filling) options in Glitter Gulch. $ *Average main: $9* ✉ *Parks Hwy., Denali National Park* ✣ *Mile 238.6* ☎ *907/683–3647* 🌐 *www.denalidoghouse.com* ⏲ *Closed mid-Sept.–mid-May.*

Denali Park Salmon Bake

$$ | **SEAFOOD** | Affectionately known as "The Bake," this upbeat and lively spot does everything it can to make every night a party: from frequent live music events, to karaoke, to cramming every holiday into the summer season, there's always something happening. While salmon and other Alaska seafood is on the menu, there is no traditional all-you-can-eat salmon buffet. **Known for:** live music (by local musicians) and dancing; Alaska-sourced elk burger; Alaska beers on tap. $ *Average main: $18* ✉ *Parks Hwy., Denali National Park* ✣ *Mile 238.5* ☎ *907/683–2733* 🌐 *www.denaliparksalmonbake.com* ⏲ *Closed late Sept.–early May.*

Moose-AKa's

$$ | **EASTERN EUROPEAN** | Just as unique as its name, Moose-AKa's brings something different to the table for those in Glitter Gulch. Specializing in authentic European items, they offer crepes, stuffed peppers, and, of course, moussaka. **Known for:** fantastic European-inspired menu where you'd least expect it; Serbian-inspired tempura fried crepes; cozy atmosphere. $ *Average main: $19* ✉ *George Parks Hwy., Denali National Park* ✣ *Mile 238.9* ☎ *907/687–0003* 🌐 *www.moose-akas.com* ⏲ *Closed mid-Sept.–mid-May.*

★ **Prospector's Historic Pizzeria and Ale House**

$$ | **AMERICAN** | **FAMILY** | Built to have an old-time-saloon feel, this restaurant serves a seemingly endless selection of handcrafted pizzas, as well as salad, soup, pastas, and brick-oven sandwiches. Farm-to-table ingredients are used whenever possible and include locally grown greens, Alaska raised meat, and seafood. **Known for:** Deadliest Catch pizza that comes with a pound of king crab legs; largest and most diverse beer selection around; wide-ranging menu that includes gluten-free, vegetarian, and vegan options. $ *Average main: $20* ✉ *Parks Hwy., Denali National Park* ✣ *Mile 238.9* ☎ *907/683–7437* 🌐 *www.prospectorspizza.com* ⏲ *Closed late Sept.–early May.*

Hotels

If you can afford it, stay at a wilderness lodge within Denali, like Camp Denali and North Face Lodge or the Kantishna Roadhouse.

★ **Camp Denali and North Face Lodge**

$$$$ | **RESORT** | The legendary, family-owned and-operated Camp Denali and North Face Lodge both offer stunning views of Denali and active learning experiences deep within Denali National Park, at mile 89 on the park road. **Pros:** only in-park lodge with a view of Denali; knowledgeable and attentive staff; strong

In the fall, the mountains of Denali National Park are surrounded by brilliant orange and red foliage.

emphasis on learning. **Cons:** credit cards not accepted; steep rates and three-night minimum stay; alcohol is BYO. 💲 *Rooms from: $1310* ✉ *Denali Park Rd., Denali National Park* ✣ *Mile 89* ☎ *907/683–2290* 🌐 *www.campdenali.com* 💳 *No credit cards* 🕓 *Closed mid-Sept.–late May* 🛏 *18 cabins (Camp Denali), 15 rooms (North Face Lodge)* 🍴 *All-inclusive.*

Kantishna Roadhouse

$$$$ | **RESORT** | Run by the Athabascan Doyon Tourism, this establishment at mile 95 on the park road offers an enriching wilderness getaway. **Pros:** guided hikes with naturalists; home to the only saloon in the Denali backcountry; transport from the train station is provided. **Cons:** no connection to the outside world besides a phone booth; lacks a direct view of Denali; two-night minimum stay. 💲 *Rooms from: $1135* ✉ *Denali Park Rd., Denali National Park* ✣ *Mile 92* ☎ *800/942–7420, 907/374–3041* 🌐 *www.kantishnaroadhouse.com* 🕓 *Closed mid-Sept.–early June* 🛏 *32 rooms* 🍴 *All-inclusive.*

Activities

BIKING

Mountain biking is allowed along the entire park road, and no permit is required for day trips. Bikes can be transported for free on the park's shuttle buses, though space is limited and available on a first-come, first-served basis. Before heading out, you should check with the park rangers at the visitor center; if there has been a wolf kill or a lot of bear sightings by the road, bike access might be limited. Bring proper gear including a bike repair kit.

The road is unpaved after the first 15 miles. Beyond the Savage River checkpoint the road is dirt and gravel, and during the day the road is busy with the park buses, which can leave bikers choking on dust. The road can get really sloppy in the rain, too. The best time to bike is late evening, when the midnight sun is shining and buses have stopped shuttling passengers for the day. When biking on the road, you need to be aware of your surroundings and observe park rules. Do not try to outride bears, moose, or wolves as it's a race you won't win. Off-road riding is forbidden, and some sensitive wildlife areas are closed to hiking and biking. The Sable Pass area is always closed to off-road excursions on foot or bike because of the high bear population, and other sites are closed due to denning activity or recent signs of carcass scavenging.

To bike deep in the park, take a transit shuttle to Eielson Visitor Center at mile 66, one of the highest points along the park road. From here you can ride downhill to Wonder Lake at mile 85, and then catch another bus to the top of the hill. Private vehicles aren't allowed this far into the park, minimizing dust and traffic.

Bike Denali rents mountain bikes and all the necessary gear you'll need for biking the park road whether you plan on being out of the afternoon or days at a time.

Bike Denali

BICYCLING | Locally owned and situated in Glitter Gulch just outside the park entrance, Bike Denali specializes in rentals instead of tours. You get more than just a bike with your rental though, as the basic packages include everything you need for a day on Denali's road system including a lock, tire repair kit, high visibility day pannier (special bags that attach to the bike frame), and bear spray with a holster. Even cargo and child trailers are available. Longer rentals extending more than a week are also possible for those that want to experience the park in this unique style. Additional gear is available to help make bike camping possible. 24-hour bike rentals start at $75. ✉ *Parks Hwy., Denali National Park* ✣ *Mile 238.5* ☎ *907/378–2107* 🌐 *bikedenali.com.*

BOATING AND RAFTING

Several privately owned raft and tour companies operate along the Parks Highway near the entrance to Denali, and they schedule daily rafting, both in the fairly placid areas on the Nenana and through the 10-mile-long Nenana River canyon, which has stretches of Class IV–V rapids—enough to make you think you're on a very wet roller coaster. The Nenana is Alaska's most accessible white water, and if you don't mind getting a little chilly, a river trip is not just a lot of fun, it's also a fantastic way to see a different side of the landscape. Most outfitters lend out dry suits for river trips; it takes a few minutes to get used to wearing one (they feel tight around the neck) but they're essential gear to keep you safe if you fall into the water.

Denali Raft Adventures

WHITE-WATER RAFTING | This outfitter launches its rafts several times daily on two- and four-hour scenic and white-water trips on the Nenana River. GORE-TEX dry suits are provided. Guests under the age of 18 must have a release waiver signed by a parent or guardian. Contact the company for copies before the trip. Courtesy pickup at hotels and the train depot is available within a 7-mile radius of their location. Two-hour, half-day, and full-day tours are available, starting at $102 per person. ✉ *Mile 238.6, Parks Hwy., Denali National Park* ☎ *907/683–2234, 888/683–2234* 🌐 *www.denaliraft.com* ⏲ *June–mid-Sept.*

CAMPING

If you want to camp in the park, either in a tent or an RV, there are six campgrounds, with varying levels of access and facilities. Two of the campgrounds—Riley Creek (near the park entrance, essentially no scenery at all) and Savage River (mile 13; on a very clear day, you might be able to see the mountain from here, but not much of it)—have spaces that accommodate tents, RVs, and campers. Visitors with private vehicles can also drive to the Teklanika campsite (mile 29; a three-night minimum stay helps keep the traffic down), but they must first obtain park-road travel permits. Sanctuary River (mile 22, the smallest campground in the park, ideal if you want to be alone but can't backpack), Igloo Creek (mile 43, comparable to Sanctuary River), and Wonder Lake (mile 85, the cream of the crop in Denali camping—best views of the mountain and great easy hikes) have tent spaces only. The camper buses offer the only access to these sites. Riley Creek is the only campground open year-round, but does not have potable water during the winter and other amenities may not be available. Visit 🌐 *www.reservedenali.com* for details.

Visitors to the Sanctuary and Igloo Creek campsites should come prepared: both campgrounds lack treated drinking water. All campgrounds have vault toilets and food lockers. Individual sites are beyond sight of the park road, though within easy walking distance.

Fees for individual sites range from $15 to $30 per night (higher rates are for the RV sites); Wonder Lake has an additional one-time reservation fee of $6.50. Campsites can be reserved in advance online, through the Denali National Park website (🌐 *www.reservedenali.com*). Reservations can also be made in person at the park. It's best to visit Denali's website before making reservations, both to see the reservation form and to learn whether any changes in the reservation system have been made.

Igloo Creek. Another small, tent-only campground, Igloo Creek has seven sites that are first-come, first-served. There's no potable water or staff on-site, and open fires aren't permitted so bring a cook stove for your meals. ✉ *35 miles inside park* 🌐 *www.nps.gov/dena/planyourvisit/campgrounds.htm.*

Riley Creek. A wooded campground with plenty of amenities, Riley Creek serves as a staging area for deeper forays into the park and is the only campground open year round. There is still cell phone reception here, and while there aren't any electrical hookups, all the conveniences of Glitter Gulch are a short drive away. There's a small camp store near the campground with ice and firewood available for purchase. ✉ *1/4 mile inside park* 🌐 *www.nps.gov/dena/planyourvisit/campgrounds.htm.*

Sanctuary River. While a lot of the area around the campground is brushy, if you're willing to push through the foliage you'll have access to the nearby mountains and the memorable hiking that can be found close to Sanctuary River's seven campsites. It's a tent-only sight (no RVs), and there are no reservations, so it's first-come, first-served; there also isn't potable water or staff. Open fires are not permitted so bring a cookstove for your meals. ✉ *22 miles inside park* 🌐 *www.nps.gov/dena/planyourvisit/campgrounds.htm.*

Savage River. Nestled within a spruce forest, many of the campsites are a short walk from the Savage River, a beautiful braided stream where glimpses of Denali can be had on clear days. This is the first campground where you lose cell phone service. Potable water and staff are available on site and there are spots for both tents and RVs. ✉ *14 miles inside park* 🌐 *www.nps.gov/dena/planyourvisit/campgrounds.htm.*

Teklanika River. The only way to drive your personal vehicle more than 15 miles into the park is by reserving a three-night stay at Teklanika. Once you've arrived, your vehicle must remain in the campground for the duration of your stay, though it's easy to catch rides on the camper or tour buses that pass by daily. Potable water and park rangers are both on site. ✉ *29 miles inside park* 🌐 *www.nps.gov/dena/planyourvisit/campgrounds.htm.*

Wonder Lake. The furthest campsite in the park, Wonder Lake has 28 tent-only spots. The area is favored for its incredible views of the Mountain when weather allows. Amenities are rudimentary but flush toilets are available seasonally as

Moose and Bear Safety

Moose

Commonly underestimated by visitors and locals alike, moose can pose a threat despite their lack of claws and sharp teeth. They may look gangly, but are fast moving and will charge when threatened. Per park guidelines, moose should be enjoyed from a respectable distance of at least 25 yards. If the animal's behavior changes, you're too close. Give mother moose and their calves extra distance as they can be especially unpredictable. If a moose charges, seek shelter in a thick stand of trees or behind any large object that it can't get through. Remember: moose can kick with either their front *or* back hooves.

Bears

Most visitors seek the Goldilocks bear encounter: not too far, not too close, but just right. But bears are capable of reaching speeds of 35 miles per hour, which can turn "just right" into "oh no!" in a heartbeat. The best method is to prevent bad bear encounters before they happen. This means giving bears lots of space, making plenty of noise while hiking, and keeping a clean camp with food stored properly in bear cans away from your tent. Park-issued, bear-proof containers come in two sizes that weigh three and seven pounds, respectively. Small containers hold 3–5 days worth of food for one person. Bigger ones can hold enough food for 7–10 days. Some personal bear containers are also accepted; check the park website for other approved containers. If you do come across a bear at close range, do not run as a bear perceives anything that runs as food. Speak calmly to the bear. Make yourself appear as big as possible (i.e., open up your jacket, spread your legs, or if in a group, stand together to form a "super creature") and back away slowly in the direction from which you came. Scan the surrounding area for cubs or a moose kill, both of which a bear will defend passionately.

Bears that choose to approach or stand on their hind legs are not necessarily aggressive. Most are simply curious and want a better look at you. A bear standing sideways to show its full profile, huffing, or jaw-popping are signs of potential aggression. Should a bear charge, stand your ground and deploy bear spray at a close distance. Most charges are simply bluffs. Play dead as a last resort by falling to the ground, curling in a ball, and wrapping your hands around your neck to protect it. Signs are peppered across the park with additional bear safety tips and park rangers are well-versed in bear safety.

is an amphitheater. Be prepared with bug nets and spray, the mosquitoes can be brutal at times. ✉ *85 miles inside park* 🌐 *www.nps.gov/dena/planyourvisit/campgrounds.htm.*

HIKING

There are few places in the world wilder and more beautiful to hike than Denali's wilderness regions. It's easy to get lost in the beauty and the desire to climb just one more ridge, but know your limits and consult park staff before you head out. Also be sure to follow "Leave No Trace" etiquette, be prepared for bear encounters, and bring all necessary equipment.

With the exception of the trails near the entrance and at the Savage River checkpoint, the park is essentially trail-less. Distances may look attainable from a distance, with foothills off the side of the road appearing no more than an hour away. Be wary of such predictions. Distances in the tundra are farther than they appear and while it may look smooth, bogs, willows, alder, and other obstacles can quickly hinder the best-laid plans. Be conservative with your goals, take your time, and leave a hike plan with someone that includes your intended destination and when to expect to hear from you. Once you finalize this plan, do not deviate from it.

GUIDED HIKES

In addition to exploring the park on your own, you can take free ranger-guided discovery hikes and learn more about the park's natural and human history. Rangers lead daily hikes throughout summer. Inquire at the visitor center. You can also tour with privately operated outfitters.

Rangers will talk about the area's plants, animals, and geological features. Before heading into the wilderness, even on a short hike, check in at the Backcountry Information Center located in the visitor center. Rangers will update you on conditions and make route suggestions. Because this is bear country, the Park Service provides backpackers with bear-proof food containers. These containers are mandatory if you're staying overnight in the backcountry.

MOUNTAIN CLIMBING

Alaska Mountaineering School

CLIMBING/MOUNTAINEERING | This outfitter leads backpacking trips in wilderness areas near Talkeetna and elsewhere in the state, including the Brooks Range, and glacier treks that can include overnighting on the ice. It also conducts mountaineering courses that run from 6 to 12 days, expeditions to Denali (figure on at least three weeks; prices from $11,000) and other peaks in the Alaska Range, and climbs for all levels of expertise. A weeklong novice course, which should be enough to get you comfortable in the mountains, runs about $2,900. Custom trips, backpacking, and workshops are also offered throughout the summer ranging from day courses to weeklong adventures. While you're in Talkeetna, check out the AMS mountain and gear shop on F Street. ✉ *13765 3rd St., Talkeetna* ☎ *907/733–1016* 🌐 *www.climbalaska.org.*

SCENIC FLIGHTS

A flightseeing tour of the park is one of the best ways to get a sense of the Alaska Range's size and scope. Flightseeing is also the best way to get close-up views of Denali and its neighboring giants, and maybe even stand on a glacier, all without the hassle of days of hiking and lugging food and gear.

Most Denali flightseeing is done out of Talkeetna, a small end-of-the-road town between Anchorage and Denali, and the operators will offer several tours, including a quick fly-by, a summit tour, a glacier landing—something for everybody. But there are a few outfitters nearer to the park that fly either from McKinley Park airstrip or the small airfield in Healy, 20 miles north. It's best to take the longest, most detailed tour you can afford, so you don't go back home wishing you'd had a chance to see more.

Fly Denali

AIR EXCURSIONS | This is the only flightseeing company based in Healy with a permit to land on the glaciers of Denali. Prices are $599 for adults, and include more than 100 minutes of flight time and 20–30 minutes on the Ruth Glacier and its amphitheater. ✉ *Healy Airport, Healy Rd., Healy* ✣ *Turn right off George Parks Highway at mile 238.7 and follow 2 miles* ☎ *907/683–2359, 877/770–2359* 🌐 *www.flydenali.com.*

WINTER SPORTS

Snowshoers and skiers generally arrive with their own gear and park or camp at the Riley Creek Campground at the park entrance. The Park Service does keep some loaner snowshoes on hand; check at the Murie Science and Learning Center (which doubles as the winter visitor center). Dog mushing can also be done with your own team, or you can contact one of the park concessionaires that run single-day or multiday trips.

Denali Dog Sled Expeditions
LOCAL SPORTS | Owned by the couple behind Earthsong Lodge, Denali Dog Sled Expeditions is the only dogsledding company that has the National Park Service okay to run trips in Denali National Park. And, midwinter, the park will feel as if it's all yours. The company specializes in multiday trips of 2 to 10 days (starting at $2,775 per person). Early in the season and between trips, they also offer day trips of one to four hours (from $140); call ahead to check availability. Denali Dog Sled Expeditions also offers cross-country skiers and mountaineers dogsled team support for multiday winter cabin and hut trips in the park. ✉ *Mile 4, Stampede Rd., Healy* ✢ *17 miles northwest of Denali National Park* ☎ *907/683–2863* 🌐 *www.earthsonglodge.com* 🎟 *From $140.*

Ruth Glacier

Even the shortest flightseeing trips usually include a passage through the Great Gorge of **Ruth Glacier,** one of the major glaciers flowing off Denali's south side. Bordered by gray granite walls and gigantic spires, this spectacular chasm is North America's deepest gorge. Leaving the area, flightseers enter the immense, mountain-encircled glacial basins of Ruth Glacier's Don Sheldon Amphitheater. Among the enclosing peaks are some of the range's most rugged and descriptively named peaks, including Moose's Tooth and Rooster Comb. Truly, it's one of the most beautiful places on the planet.

What's Nearby

There are two areas near the park entrance with a variety of amenities and accommodations within 15 miles of the park entrance. The nearest of these is **"Glitter Gulch,"** which contains a long strip of hotels, guide shops, and restaurants. The Gulch is predominately seasonal, so don't expect to find any businesses open in winter. While there's no shortage of restaurants ranging from sit-down to grab-and-go selections, you won't find grocery stores or anything of that nature.

A little farther north along the road system is the community of **Healy**. This town of almost 1,000 people provides some more substantial offerings as it also supports the nearby mining sites along with serving as a jumping off point for independent travelers. Here you'll find year round accommodations from cozy B&Bs like the Dome Home to more traditional inns like the Aurora Denali Lodge. The 49th State Brewery, one of the area's best restaurants, offers an excellent range of in-house beer as well as several locally grown dishes.

To the south is **Denali State Park.** A little ways north of Talkeetna, this protected wilderness encompasses almost 300,000 acres including foothills, mountains, streams, glaciers, and lakes. Camping, hiking, and canoeing are popular activities within the state park. Fishing is also possible with all five species of salmon spawning within the park along with numerous types of trout and dolly varden.

Chapter 20

DRY TORTUGAS NATIONAL PARK

Updated by
Gary McKechnie

Camping	Hotels	Activities	Scenery	Crowds
★★★☆☆	★☆☆☆☆	★★★★☆	★★★★☆	★★★☆☆

WELCOME TO DRY TORTUGAS NATIONAL PARK

TOP REASONS TO GO

★ **Sea plus:** Land accounts for just 1% of the park, but its brilliant blue waters, pelagic birds, coral reefs, and colorful fish make nature photography, snorkeling, and scuba diving unforgettable experiences.

★ **It's far out:** With a location 70 miles west of Key West, visits here feel like adventures. Boaters can further explore the park's 100 square miles, dropping anchor wherever the fish are biting or where a reef or a wreck needs investigating.

★ **The stars are the stars:** There's very little light pollution in this remote location, so the stars in the night sky are brilliantly bright.

★ **History happened here:** Within the walls of Fort Jefferson, the western hemisphere's largest brick structure, soldiers were sheltered and convicts confined—including the infamous Dr. Samuel Mudd, who aided in the escape of Lincoln's assassin.

1 Garden Key. With the imposing Fort Jefferson historic site, the park headquarters and visitor center, and campgrounds, Garden Key is considered "park central."

2 Bush Key. In late fall and early winter, sooty terns, brown noddies, and other birds return to this undeveloped 16-acre island just east of Garden Key. Their journey across the waters may be easier than that of humans: waves tend to wash away the land bridge that extends from the neighboring island, in which case access is via canoe or kayak. Visits during nesting season are prohibited; at other times, a mile-long hike along a shoreline trail is a pleasant experience.

3 Loggerhead Key. When Juan Ponce de Leon dubbed these islands "torutugas" (Spanish for "turtles") he may have been referring to the loggerhead sea turtles found on this 42-acre island, the archipelago's largest. Wildlife is rich on this key, which has a swimming area on its northwest side.

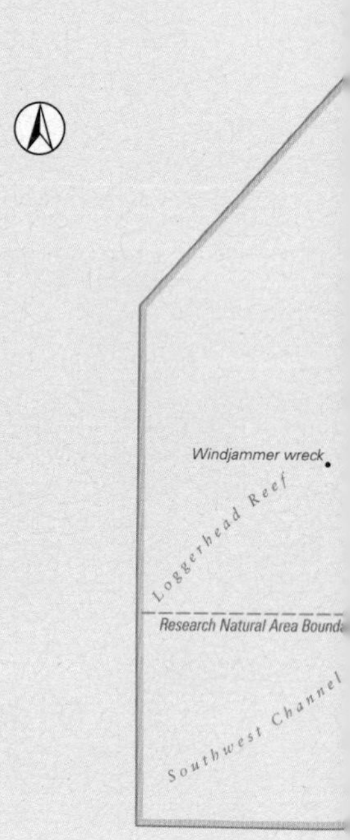

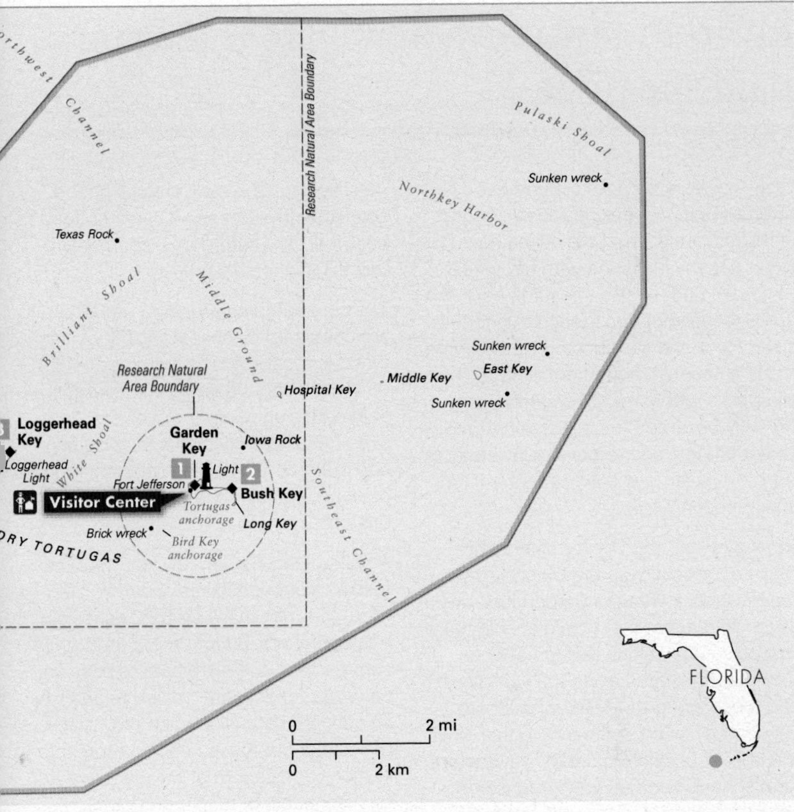
Channel
Research Natural Area Boundary
Pulaski Shoal
Sunken wreck
Northkey Harbor
Texas Rock
Brilliant Shoal
Middle Ground
Sunken wreck
East Key
Middle Key
Research Natural
Area Boundary
Hospital Key
Sunken wreck
Loggerhead
Key
Garden
Key
Iowa Rock
White Shoal
Loggerhead
Light
Light
Fort Jefferson
1
2
Bush Key
Visitor Center
Tortugas
anchorage
Long Key
Southeast Channel
Brick wreck
Bird Key
anchorage
DRY TORTUGAS
0
2 mi
0
2 km
FLORIDA

The coral reefs and islands of the Dry Tortugas were quite familiar to the region's early sailing ships. Those that failed to cautiously navigate the waters paid the price.

Over the years, wrecks occurred as often as once a week, leaving a fortune in historic artifacts on the ocean floor. Don't get any ideas. As with the wealth of natural underwater treasures here, the policy is look but don't touch. When the seven keys and surrounding waters were made a national monument in 1935, all wrecks within its 100-square-miles officially became the possession of the United States, and removing any artifacts from them can result in forfeiture, fines, and imprisonment.

What elevated the Dry Tortugas to historic importance was the Union Army's realization that 42-acre Garden Key was a strategic outpost that would enable them to block enemy ships sailing between Confederate states along the Gulf Coast and those along the Atlantic seaboard. Garden Key's Fort Jefferson, to this day the largest brick structure in the western hemisphere, became the "American Gibraltar." Following the war, the fort became an inescapable prison—in essence, a precursor to Alcatraz.

Then, as now, it requires effort to reach this park, which is accessible only by seaplane or boat. It takes the fast ferry a little more than two hours to make the 70-mile voyage from Key West to Garden Key, where day-trippers tour Fort Jefferson and congregate on the sandy beach to relax in the sun, enjoy picnics, and go snorkeling. Some camp overnight on Garden Key to experience a therapeutic absence of noise, lights, and civilization. Also lacking, however, are cell phone coverage, Internet service, water, food, boat fuel, and bathrooms (composting toilets have to suffice).

The coral reefs surrounding Garden Key are populated by snapper, grouper, and wrasse, most them accustomed to the flotilla of visitors floating in their midst. For serious snorkelers and divers, however, the prized destinations, including one of the few surviving concentrations of elkhorn coral in the Keys, are farther offshore.

A self-guided Garden Key land tour that follows signposts takes about 45 minutes, although many visitors, especially photographers, budget more time since some scenic shots are hard to pass up. Ferry passengers are treated to a talk by an onboard naturalist when they reach the island, but those needing more information can check in at the visitor center for a schedule of ranger programs.

Planning

When to Go

When choosing a time to visit, remember that Florida's hurricane season runs between June 1 and November 30, and summer also features blazing heat in a park with few air-conditioned shelters. Between December and March, temperatures are generally still high enough

AVERAGE HIGH/LOW TEMPERATURES					
JAN.	**FEB.**	**MAR.**	**APR.**	**MAY**	**JUNE**
74/64	75/64	78/67	81/70	86/74	90/76
JULY	**AUG.**	**SEPT.**	**OCT.**	**NOV.**	**DEC.**
91/78	92/78	90/77	85/75	79/71	76/66

to enjoy swimming, diving, fishing, and nature hikes. If visiting during this period, call ahead to reserve your seat on the fast ferry, to book a seaplane flight, or to rent a boat.

Getting Here and Around

AIR

Key West Seaplane Adventures has half- and full-day trips that depart from the Key West airport. Although it's on the high end for most travelers, this is the only way to get to the islands by plane.

BOAT

The *Yankee Freedom III*, a high-speed enclosed catamaran, departs from a marina in Key West's Old Town on a two-hour (plus) voyage for day trips to Garden Key. Private boats are also allowed to dock.

Inspiration

In his book *America's Fortress: A History of Fort Jefferson, Dry Tortugas, Florida,* Thomas Reid covers the architectural, military, environmental, and political history of the fort. *Dry Tortugas National Park (Images of America)* by James A. Kushlan and Kirsten Hines, contains insightful commentary on and intriguing archival images of not only the fort but also of the islands, including their wildlife and offshore shipwrecks.

Park Essentials

ACCESSIBILITY

Fort Jefferson's ground level and walking trail are accessible to those using wheelchairs and motorized scooters, but the upper two levels of the 19th-century structure are not. A ramp at the Fort Jefferson dock accommodates wheelchairs and scooters disembarking from the *Yankee Freedom III* and charter vessels.

PARK FEES AND PERMITS

Park admission is $15 for all visitors 16 and older and is valid for seven days. Camping costs an additional $15 for individual sites or $30 for group sites per night. Camping fees are paid at a self-service site in the campground, although digital passes can be purchased in advance at 🌐 *recreation.gov*. Guests arriving by personal vessel must pay the entrance fee and acquire a free boat permit at Garden Key. ⚠ **The park does not accept credit or debit cards—fees are paid with cash or check only.**

PARK HOURS

The park is open 24/7, with Fort Jefferson accessible between sunrise and sunset. Bush Key is closed during the sooty tern nesting season between mid-January and mid-October. Some remote islands—such as East, Middle, Hospital, and Long keys—may also be closed occasionally to protect wildlife.

CELL PHONE RECEPTION

There's no cell phone coverage or Wi-Fi within the park.

Hotels

Although you can stay overnight in a primitive campsite, there are no hotels in the Dry Tortugas. The closest accommodations are in Key West.

Restaurants

There's no food service of any kind in the Dry Tortugas, nor is there drinking water available for day or overnight visitors.

Tours

Key West Seaplane Adventures

AIR EXCURSIONS | Twice daily, 40-minute flights to the Dry Tortugas skim above the trademark cystalline waters of the Florida Keys. If you opt for the morning trip, you'll beat the ferries to the island and have things to yourself for a while. This comes at a cost: the flights offered by this company—the only one allowed to offer scheduled service to the park—are not cheap. On four-hour excursions ($361 per person) you'll spend 2½ hours on the island; full-day outings ($634) allow for 6½ hours ashore. Complimentary water, soft drinks, and snorkeling equipment (mask, fins, floatation vests) are provided. ✉ *3471 S. Roosevelt Blvd., New Town* ☎ *305/615–7429* 🌐 *keywestseaplanecharters.com.*

Yankee Freedom III

BOAT TOURS | The most popular way to reach Dry Tortugas National park is aboard this sleek, 110-foot catamaran, which races from Key West across 70 miles of the Gulf of Mexico in about 2¼ hours. Getting to the park is half the fun thanks to a wide-open sundeck; an air-conditioned lower deck with complimentary breakfast snacks, restrooms, and freshwater rinse showers; and an upper-deck with a cocktail bar. When you reach the island, you can join the ferry's guide for a 45-minute nature tour before enjoying the box lunch that's provided. In the afternoon, you're free to swim, snorkel (gear is included), and explore the shore and adjacent Bush Key. Day trips cost $190 per person, camping trips are $210, and park admission is included in the fee. Trips depart from the ferry terminal at 100 Grinnell Street in the Historic Seaport. ✉ *Ticket booth, 240 Margaret St., Old Town* ☎ *305/294–7009, 800/634–0939* 🌐 *www.drytortugas.com.*

Visitor Information

CONTACTS Dry Tortugas National Park. ☎ *305/242–7700* 🌐 *www.nps.gov/drto.*

In the Park

Garden Key is 70 miles west of Key West.

Water makes up about 99% of Dry Tortugas, which encompasses a handful of keys amid 100 square miles in the Gulf of Mexico. Most people arrive via a fast ferry or a chartered seaplane for visits of four or eight hours.

Sights

BEACHES

East Beach

BEACH—SIGHT | **FAMILY** | Bush Key projects off the east side of Garden Key, and if you walk along its north or south shores, the waterfront is laced with white sands and plenty of room for privacy. At the end of the line at Long Key, this beach is the most remote in this area of the park, with small waves rolling in on its easternmost shore. **Amenities:** none. **Best for:** solitude; swimming; walking. ✉ *Dry Tortugas National Park, Garden Key* ☎ *305/242–7700* 🌐 *www.nps.gov/drto.*

Loggerhead Key Beach

BEACH—SIGHT | Few visitors make it to the beach on uninhabited Loggerhead Key, several miles west of Garden Key and accessible only by private boat. If

The moat alongside Fort Jefferson is a great place to stroll (or snorkel!).

you do get here, you'll likely be the only one relaxing on soft sands that border clear-as-glass waters. A lighthouse, an abandoned home, walking trails, and wildlife are part of its appeal. **Amenities:** none. **Best for:** snorkeling; solitude. ✉ *Dry Tortugas National Park, Loggerhead Key* ☎ *305/242–7700* 🌐 *www.nps.gov/drto.*

North Beach

BEACH—SIGHT | **FAMILY** | After stepping ashore on Garden Key, walk to the right, and, a short distance away, you'll come to this white sand beach. Its proximity to the ruins of a coal dock makes it popular for snorkeling, although stronger currents and sea breezes can make both snorkeling and swimming a tad more difficult than elsewhere. **Amenities:** none. **Best for:** snorkeling; walking. ✉ *Dry Tortugas National Park, Garden Key* ☎ *305/242–7700* 🌐 *www.nps.gov/drto.*

South Beach

BEACH—SIGHT | **FAMILY** | Upon landing at Garden Key's pier, walk to your left, and, just beyond the camping area, you'll arrive at the shores of tranquil South Beach. Here the white sands are ideal for sunbathing, and the clear, calm waters are just right for snorkeling—especially by the old coal docks, which attract plenty of active and colorful marine life. **Amenities:** none. **Best for:** snorkeling; sunset; swimming; walking. ✉ *Dry Tortugas National Park, Garden Key* ☎ *305/242–7700* 🌐 *www.nps.gov/drto.*

HISTORIC SIGHTS

Fort Jefferson

HISTORIC SITE | **FAMILY** | Although there are hundreds of historic sites within Dry Tortugas National Park, most are shipwrecks hidden beneath the waves. One structure, though, is visible in nearly every promotional image of the park: Fort Jefferson.

In 1846, construction began on what was to be an "advance post"—for ships patrolling the Florida Straits between the Gulf and the Atlantic—and safe harbor for repairs, supplies, and shelter. When the Civil War exploded, the fort became even more strategically important as it could either provide the Union with a staging area for an invasion, or it could serve as a base for the Confederacy and its privateers. Ultimately, however, Fort Jefferson was never completed nor fully armed, and its imposing presence alone may have discouraged takeover attempts.

After 1865, the fort was used as a prison for deserters; in 1874, it was abandoned, though it served as a refueling stop for warships. In limbo for decades, it fell into disrepair until President Roosevelt declared the Dry Tortugas a national monument in 1935. Today, as you wander the sprawling parade ground, you'll be surrounded by the largest brick structure in the western hemisphere, one that required more than 16 million bricks to cover an area of over 16 acres. ✉ *Dry Tortugas National Park, Garden Key* ☎ *305/242–7700* 🌐 *www.nps.gov/drto.*

Tortugas Harbor Lighthouse

LIGHTHOUSE | FAMILY | Centuries of shipwrecks in the waters surrounding Dry Tortugas made a lighthouse a good investment. The first was installed on the eastern shore of Garden Key in 1826, but it had flaws in its design and operation. After decades of bureaucratic back and forth, a second lighthouse was constructed on Loggerhead Key—the Dry Torutugas Light—in 1858 (it's still going strong today), and repairs were ultimately made to the Tortugas Harbor Lighthouse. Then, back-to-back hurricanes put it out of commission, prompting construction of a new lighthouse amid the bastions of Fort Jefferson. In 2020, the park launched a $4.5 million restoration project to preserve this historic structure for the next 100-plus years. ✉ *Dry Tortugas National Park, Garden Key* ☎ *305/242–7700* 🌐 *www.nps.gov/drto.*

UNDERWATER SIGHTS

Historic Coaling Pier Pilings

REEF | FAMILY | Far removed from civilization, Fort Jefferson was an oasis for ships and crew—especially steamships that needed a load of coal. When the warehouses that held the coal were wiped out by a hurricane, all that remained were pilings near North and South beaches. Over time, they've become a popular gathering place for grouper, tarpon, barracudas, colorful corals—and snorkelers. ✉ *Dry Tortugas National Park, Garden Key* ☎ *305/242–7700* 🌐 *www.nps.gov/drto.*

The Moat Wall

REEF | FAMILY | Historically, the moat wall served double duty, protecting Fort Jefferson from amphibious assault and keeping the gulf's rough waters at bay. Today, it serves as a snorkeling site, with swimmers following the exterior of the moat between the north end of South Beach and the south end of North Beach. Over time, sections of the wall, anchor chains, and cement barrels have fallen into the waters to create artificial reefs that attract squid, nurse sharks, hogfish, barracuda, and butterfly fish. ✉ *Dry Tortugas National Park, Garden Key* ☎ *305/242–7700* 🌐 *www.nps.gov/drto.*

VISITOR CENTERS

Garden Key Visitor Center

INFO CENTER | FAMILY | The main visitor center inside Fort Jefferson features artifacts from the mid-1800s, historical documents and images, underwater video of the surrounding reefs, and natural history exhibits. When you arrive at Garden Key, check on the schedule of free ranger-led programs, including Fort Jefferson history tours, ecological moat walks, living-history demonstrations, and special events. ✉ *Dry Tortugas National Park, Garden Key* ☎ *305/242–7700* 🌐 *www.nps.gov/drto.*

Activities

BIRD-WATCHING

Although Dry Tortugas is a premier year-round destination for ornithologists, nature gives the park an extra boost each spring, when migrating species cross the seas and blend in with the approximately 300 types of birds that have been spotted here. Two of the most popular sightings are of the magnificent frigate

Since 1846, Fort Jefferson has played many roles—advance post, safe harbor, and lighthouse station among them.

birds that soar over the ocean, skimming fish from the surface, and the huge colonies of sooty terns that return each year to Bush Key, their only nesting site in the entire United States.

Wildside Nature Tours

BIRD WATCHING | With trip prices starting at $1,600 per person, this operator's offerings are geared toward serious birders. Its multiday trips include lodging and meals (seafood is a specialty) aboard the 88-foot boat *Makai*, which sails to the Dry Tortugas. No more than a dozen passengers have three days to see and photograph sooty terns, brown noddies, masked boobies, and magnificent frigatebirds, with professional guides helping to spot these and dozens of other species. ☎ *888/875–9453* 🌐 *wildsidenaturetours.com/wildside-tour/birding-dry-tortugas.*

BOATING AND SAILING

There are no rental services or outfitters in the park, so if you plan to paddle, you must transport your kayak or canoe here aboard the fast ferry. When booking your ferry trip, be sure to ask if there will be room for your equipment. A handful of companies based in Key West offer Dry Tortugas sailing charters.

Tortugas Sailing Adventures

SAILING | This company's 42-foot foot catamaran accommodates only four guests on its multiday excursions. Traveling at an average speed of 8 knots, the first overnight finds you at anchor beside an uninhabited island before reaching Dry Tortugas National Park to explore Fort Jefferson and, later, Loggerhead Key, which not even seaplanes or the fast ferry can reach. The crew is skilled at assisting guests with snorkeling, diving, fishing, bird-watching, and historic tours of Fort Jefferson. A two-day/one-night experience starts at $1,675 per person, with a minimum two-guest occupancy. ✉ *7005 Shrimp Rd., Dock A-6, Key West* ☎ *305/896–2477* 🌐 *tortugasailingadventures.com.*

CAMPING

Garden Key Campground. Only one island is open to overnight guests, and it's Garden Key, where a primitive campground has individual, first-come, first-served sites accommodating three two-person tents. Amenities are limited to picnic tables, elevated grills, and composting toilets—there's no available food or water, showers, electricity, cell service, or Internet access—so you must bring in all supplies, including ice and charcoal (gas cannisters aren't allowed on the ferry). Rangers recommend bringing at least two gallons of water per day per person as well as an extra day's worth of food in the event weather delays the ferry. ✉ *Dry Tortugas National Park, Garden Key* 🌐 *www.recreation.gov.*

DIVING AND SNORKELING

Diving and snorkeling are the park's most popular activities—and for good reason. The waters are always clear and usually calm, and there's plenty to see, including shipwrecks that occurred within park boundaries. Some are in shallow waters and readily visible with snorkeling equipment; others are more remote, reachable only by boat and requiring scuba gear. Most visitors arrive via the fast ferry, and the fee includes use of snorkeling gear (mask, fins, floatation vest), which is all that's needed to explore the waters and reefs off Garden Key.

Finz Dive Center

DIVING/SNORKELING | Possessing one of the few permits for dive trips within Dry Tortugas National Park, Finz takes certified scuba divers on full-day excursions to assorted dive sites, where the waters are crystal clear, the corals are brilliant, and the schools of colorful tropical fish mingle with exotic marine life. Lasting up to 12 hours, the tour also includes lunch, snacks, and time at Fort Jefferson. Check your balance before booking, though: the three-tank trip is just over $2,000 per person—plus rental equipment. ✉ *5130 Overseas Hwy., Key West* ☎ *305/395–0880* 🌐 *www.finzdivecenter.com.*

FISHING

★ Key West Pro Guides

FISHING | **FAMILY** | This outfitter offers four-, five-, six-, or eight-hour private charters, and you can choose from more than a dozen captains. Trips include flats, backcountry, reef, offshore fishing, and specialty excursions to the Dry Tortugas. Whatever your fishing pleasure, the captains will hook you up. ✉ *31 Miriam St., Stock Island* ☎ *866/259–4205* 🌐 *www.keywestproguides.com* 💵 *From $500.*

HIKING

The trail system here isn't very extensive, with most of the routes on Garden Key. All are level, easy, and designed primarily to let you explore a bit of the island without disturbing sensitive wildlife areas. Of course, there's plenty of "hiking" to be done along the shoreline.

What's Nearby

With little development in Dry Tortugas, **Key West** is the nearest place for the amenities of civilization. America's southernmost city achieved legendary status for its extraordinary history, which brims with tales of pirates and immigrants and features such characters as Henry Flagler (and his Overseas Railway), Ernest Hemingway, and Harry Truman.

Chapter 21

EVERGLADES NATIONAL PARK

Updated by
Gary McKechnie

Camping ★★★★★ | Hotels ★★★★☆ | Activities ★★★★☆ | Scenery ★★★★★ | Crowds ★★★☆☆

WELCOME TO EVERGLADES NATIONAL PARK

TOP REASONS TO GO

★ **Alligators all around:** If you've come to Florida to see an alligator, you've come to the right place. The Everglades is one place where alligators and their crocodile cousins co-exist.

★ **Water ways:** There are numerous kayak trails within the park (including the monumental 99-mile Wilderness Waterway).

★ **More backwater boating:** To really experience the park's intricate ecology, explore the environment on a guided tour of its bays, or rent a houseboat for an extended self-guided experience.

★ **For the birds:** The Everglades encompasses several prime sites found along the famed Great Florida Birding & Wildlife Trail (🌐 *www.floridabirdingtrail.com*), with opportunities to see hundreds of indigenous and migrating species.

★ **Edible Everglades:** This unique environment inspired unique dishes, giving you the chance to taste items such as alligator tail, frogs' legs, and swamp cabbage made from hearts of palm.

1 **Ernest F. Coe Visitor Center.** The park's main entrance, and home of its primary visitor center, is where the scenic 38-mile drive to Flamingo begins..

2 **Royal Palm.** This is the starting point for ranger talks and self-guided tours along the Gumbo Limbo and Anhinga Trails. It's also where the Nike Missile Base is located.

3 **Shark Valley.** The Observation Tower is one of the area's focal points, as is a visitor center, recreational trail, and tram tours (in the dry season).

4 **Flamingo.** Drive as far south as you can go on the Florida mainland to arrive in Flamingo, which is in essence, the park's downtown. There's an RV and tent campground, new-in-2021 hotels, a marina, and concessionaires that provide guided tours, fishing charters, and houseboat rentals.

5 **Everglades City and the Gulf Coast.** The western entrance into the park is the gateway to the Ten Thousand Islands, an expanse of mangrove islands and maze-like waterways. Interpretive nature tours depart from the visitor center, andguided canoe or kayak excursions are available, as are canoe or kayak rentals.

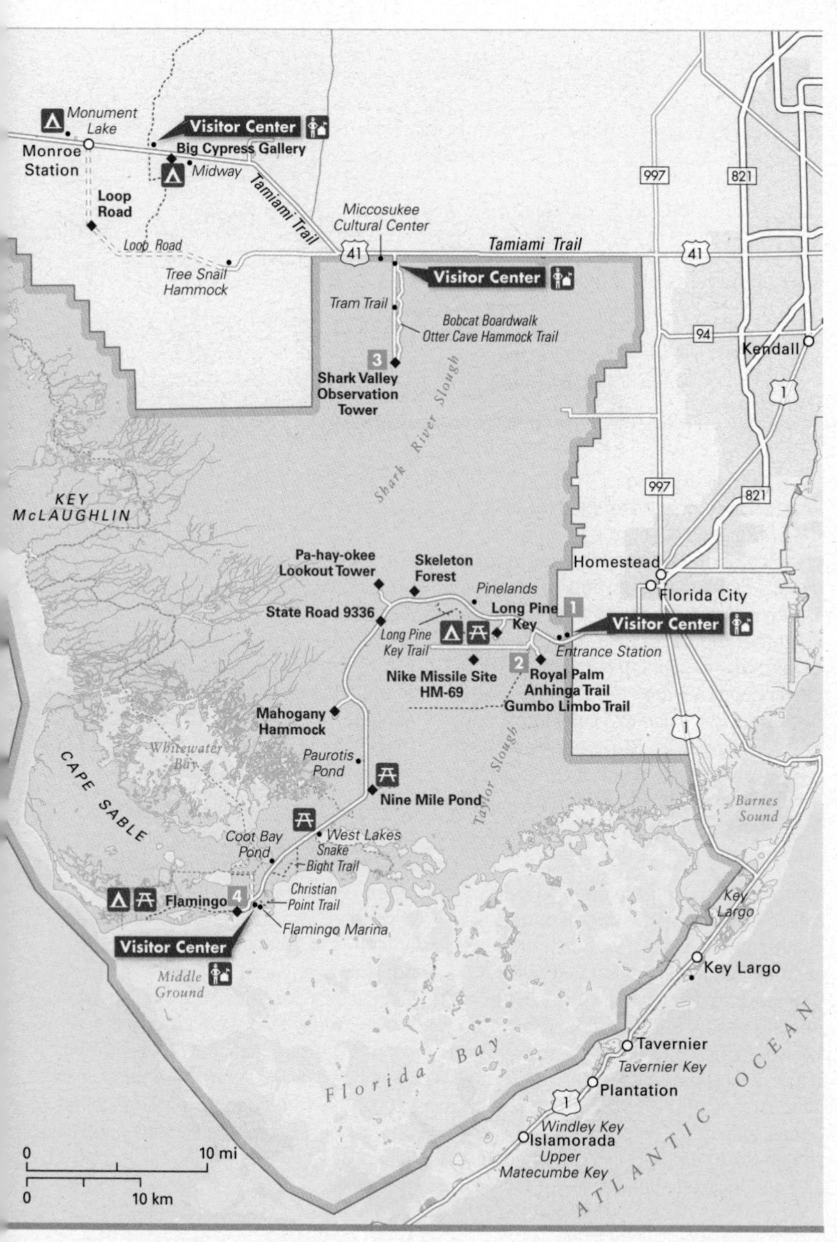
Monument Lake
Visitor Center
Monroe Station
Big Cypress Gallery
Midway
Loop Road
Tamiami Trail
Loop Road
Tree Snail Hammock
Miccosukee Cultural Center
41
Tamiami Trail
Visitor Center
Tram Trail
Bobcat Boardwalk
Otter Cave Hammock Trail
3
Shark Valley Observation Tower
Shark River Slough
997
821
94
Kendall
1
KEY McLAUGHLIN
Pa-hay-okee Lookout Tower
Skeleton Forest
Pinelands
Long Pine Key
1
State Road 9336
Long Pine Key Trail
Visitor Center
Entrance Station
Homestead
Florida City
2
Nike Missile Site HM-69
Royal Palm
Anhinga Trail
Gumbo Limbo Trail
Mahogany Hammock
Whitewater Bay
Paurotis Pond
CAPE SABLE
Nine Mile Pond
Taylor Slough
Barnes Sound
West Lakes
Coot Bay Pond
Snake Bight Trail
Christian Point Trail
Flamingo
4
Flamingo Marina
Visitor Center
Middle Ground
Key Largo
Key Largo
Florida Bay
Tavernier
Tavernier Key
Plantation
ATLANTIC OCEAN
Windley Key
Islamorada
Upper Matecumbe Key
0
10 mi
0
10 km

An elusive mystery to early settlers, the general consensus of speculators and developers was that the Everglades was a useless swampland. It took decades for people to realize that the Everglades were, in the immortal description of naturalist Marjory Stoneman Douglas, an essential facet in a "River of Grass" that flowed over vast amounts of the lower Florida peninsula.

On a journey that begins in Shingle Creek near Orlando, this watershed (of which the Everglades is only a part) covers a distance of more than 200 miles across a slope of only 20 feet. Along the way, it gathers from the Kissimmee River and other tributaries as it moves slowly toward Miami, fanning out from Lake Okeechobee before creeping into and over the Everglades to empty into Florida Bay and the Gulf of Mexico. Where the fresh water mingles with the salt waters, the brackish soup acts as a coastal nursery, sloshing into bays to bathe life in the mangroves and the coral reefs.

Visitors can move from open saw-grass prairie to dense hardwood hammock. Watery sloughs teem with fish, freshwater marshes are sprinkled with wildflowers, and coastal mangroves harbor nesting birds and sea turtles. The 100 keys of Florida Bay are home to pelicans, ospreys, and bald eagles; the Ten Thousand Islands of the Gulf Coast, to the gentle manatee. The park is also a last refuge for 14 officially listed threatened and endangered species.

Ancient Calusa shell mounds in the backcountry bear silent witness to the importance of the Glades in the lives of early Native Americans. Some canoe trails might date from the Seminole Wars (1818–55), when the U.S. government tried to forcibly relocate the region's Native Americans. Today, some members of the Miccosukee tribes still live as their ancestors did on the hardwood hammocks in the Glades; the Seminoles have a reservation north of the park.

After thousands of birds were killed for their plumage and alligators were poached nearly to extinction for their hides, conservationists pushed efforts to save the Everglades and their inhabitants. In 1947 the southeastern corner became Everglades National Park; the Ten Thousand Islands area was added in 1957. Today Everglades is one of the country's largest national parks and is recognized by the world community as a Wetland of International Importance, an International Biosphere Reserve, and a World Heritage Site.

AVERAGE HIGH/LOW TEMPERATURES					
JAN.	**FEB.**	**MAR.**	**APR.**	**MAY**	**JUNE**
78/54	80/56	82/58	85/61	88/66	90/71
JULY	**AUG.**	**SEPT.**	**OCT.**	**NOV.**	**DEC.**
91/73	92/73	91/73	87/70	83/63	79/67

Planning

When to Go

Winter is the best, and busiest, time to visit the Everglades (although "busy" is relative in a region covering 2,400 square miles, or more than two Rhode Islands). From November to March, temperatures and mosquito activity are more tolerable, while low water levels concentrate the resident wildlife and migratory birds settle in for the season. Ranger-led programs are widely available this time of year.

It's around April when the weather begins to turn humid and rainy, and tours and facilities are less crowded. Migratory birds depart, and you may have to look a little harder to see wildlife. Summer brings intense sun and afternoon rainstorms. Water levels rise and mosquitoes abound, making outdoor activity virtually unbearable, although insect repellent is a necessity any time of year.

Getting Here and Around

AIR

Miami International Airport (MIA) is 34 miles from Homestead and 47 miles from the eastern access to Everglades National Park. Shuttles run between MIA and Homestead. Southwest Florida International Airport (RSW), in Fort Myers, a little more than an hour's drive from Everglades City, is the closest major airport to the Everglades' western entrance.

CAR

Since there is no public transportation into the Everglades, you should arrange to arrive by car. Although ride share services like Lyft and Uber do operate in the major cities of South Florida, riders will find it hard to secure a return trip from this remote area. Rental cars, scheduled shuttles, and taxis are safer bets.

Although the national park is larger than the state of Delaware, the fact that only two roads: SR 9336 leading in from Homestead and Florida City and reaching the end of the Florida mainland in Flamingo, and U.S. 41 crossing the state between Miami and Naples, make navigating the park relatively easy. Indeed, with a park map that details these highways and side roads that dip deeper into hammocks, meadows, overlooks, and visitor centers you have nearly all you need to find your way around.

Inspiration

The 1947 classic, *Everglades: River of Grass,* by conservationist Marjory Stoneman Douglas is a must-read.

Everglades, by Jean Craighead George, illustrates the park's natural history in a children's book.

Swamplandia!, by Karen Russell, brings readers into the swamp by telling the story of a family's gator-wrestling theme park near Everglades City.

The 2019 PBS documentary *The Swamp* chronicles attempts to convert the Everglades into an agricultural and urban paradise.

Park Essentials

ACCESSIBILITY

All visitor centers are equipped for travelers with disabilities. Detailed information on handicapped-accessible ranger talks, sight and hearing accessibility, policies related to service animals, and accommodations for boat, tram, and other concession tours can be found at 🌐 *www.nps.gov/ever/planyourvisit/accessibility.htm.*

Everglades trails and hammocks that accommodate wheelchairs and scooters are the Anhinga Trail, Gumbo Limbo Trail, Pineland Trail, Pa-hay-okee Overlook, the Mahogany Hammock Trail, West Lake Trail, and Bobcat Hammock. Each of these have firm and stable surfaces that are either paved or a boardwalk, and are less than ¾ of a mile in distance.

PARK FEES AND PERMITS

The fee is $30 per vehicle; $25 per motorcycle; and $15 per pedestrian or cyclist. Payable online or at the gates, admission is good for seven consecutive days at all park entrances. Annual passes are $55.

Fees for camping vary on the campground and type of camping you choose, that is, RV or an eco-tent or backcountry. For the most up-to-date seasonal rates, availability, and schedules (some may close due to flooding) visit 🌐 *www.flamingoeverglades.com/camping* or call ☎ *855/708–2207.*

PARK HOURS

The park is open daily, year-round. Both the main entrance near Florida City and Homestead and the Gulf Coast entrance are open 24/7. The Shark Valley entrance is open 8:30 am to 6 pm.

CELL PHONE RECEPTION

You can expect to receive good to excellent cell phone coverage when in the vicinity of the visitor centers at Ernest F. Coe, Shark Valley, and Everglades City, as well as in Flamingo complex. Naturally, quality drops when traveling the remote stretches between these points and when exploring the back waters of the Ten Thousand Islands.

Hotels

Aside from the campground, eco-tents, and RV park at Flamingo, as well as a second campground at Long Pine Key near the Homestead entrance, there are no lodging options within the park. That is scheduled to change in late 2021 with the premiere of a 24-room hotel being created at the epicenter of the Flamingo community.

Restaurants

With the opening of a new waterfront hotel at Flamingo (scheduled for late 2021) will come the hotel's indoor/outdoor restaurant overlooking Florida Bay. For now, the stores at the Ernest F. Coe Visitor Center, Royal Palm Visitor Center, Gulf Coast Visitor Center, and the Flamingo marina offer a limited variety of snack foods and beverages. Adjacent to the Everglades Guest Services building in Flamingo, a food truck is open Wednesday through Sunday from 11:30 am–4 pm.

Tours

The often-hidden beauty of Everglades National Park can be revealed by joining free ranger-led hikes, bicycle tours, bird-watching tours, and canoe trips. The number and variety of these excursions are greatest from mid-December through Easter, while some (such as the canoe trips) are not offered in summer. Among the more popular excursions are a 50-minute walk around the Taylor Slough (departing from the Royal Palm Visitor Center); a 15-mile, two-hour tram tour focusing on the wildlife of Shark Valley;

and 30-minute evening presentations. From the Royal Palm Visitor Center and Shark Valley Information Center, you can get your feet wet on "Slough Slogs" through the sawgrass marshes (■ **TIP→ Be sure to wear long pants and lace-up shoes.**). For a list of available tours in the park, visit 🌐 *www.nps.gov/ever/planyourvisit/guidedtours.htm*.

Another option is tuning into the audio driving tour; a free podcast that will guide you through various areas of the park. You can find that at 🌐 *www.nps.gov/ever/learn/photosmultimedia/podcast.htm*.

Boat tours, which include commentary from a naturalist, also depart from Flamingo, including the Everglades Backcountry Boat Tour through Flamingo Adventures. Later in the afternoon Flamingo Adventures also offers the Florida Bay Sundown Boat Tour, which heads into the open waters of the bay on a double-deck catamaran where you'll have chance to catch glimpses of ospreys, wading birds, manatees, sea turtles, dolphins … and sunsets. For self-guided tours, canoes and kayaks can be rented at Flamingo's Marina Store (✉ *1 Flamingo Lodge Hwy. Homestead* ☎ *239/695–1095*). At the Gulf Coast Visitor Center in Everglades City, a 90-minute excursion ventures across Chokoloskee Bay, into Indian Key Pass, and through the mangrove islands to explore the Ten Thousand Islands.

Coopertown Air Boats

GUIDED TOURS | Having zipped across the Everglades since 1945, this company in small Coopertown (pop. 8) has had plenty of time to know the Everglades and will introduce you to its intricate environment on a nine-mile tour through open spans of sawgrass and into hardwood hammocks to see "gator holes" and other wildlife including Purple Gallanule, the endangered Everglade Snail Kite, and the plentiful herons, grackles, turtles, and raccoons that thrive in this world. Afterward, take some time at their educational center before grabbing a bite of gator tail and frogs' legs at the on-site restaurant. ✉ *22700 S.W. 8th St., Miami* ☎ *305/226–6048* 🌐 *coopertownairboats.com*.

Everglades Backcountry Boat Tour

GUIDED TOURS | **FAMILY** | Everglades National Park's official concessionaire, generically known as Guest Services, Inc., operates two similar, but separate operations, with Flamingo Adventures based in Flamingo on Florida Bay, and Everglades Adventures based in Everglades City on the Gulf Coast. The marina in Flamingo runs boat tours in addition to renting canoes, kayaks, and bikes. A 90-minute backcountry cruise up Buttonwood Canal through Coot Bay and Tarpon Creek into Whitewater Bay winds under a heavy canopy of mangroves to reveal abundant wildlife—from alligators, crocodiles, and turtles to herons, hawks, and egrets. Tickets can be purchased at the marina or online. ✉ *1 Flamingo Lodge Hwy., on Buttonwood Canal, Flamingo* ☎ *855/708–2207* 🌐 *flamingoeverglades.com/boat-tours* 🎟 *$40*.

Everglades Florida Adventures Boat Tours

BOAT TOURS | **FAMILY** | The same concessionaire that operates boat tours and watercraft rentals in Flamingo is the same that sets sail on excursions into the Ten Thousand Islands National Wildlife Refuge. Adventure seekers often see dolphins, manatees, bald eagles, and roseate spoonbills in the saltwater portion of the Everglades. Mangrove wilderness tours on smaller boats (up to six passengers) embark on shorter trips through the swampy, brackish areas. This is the best option to see alligators, bobcats, mangrove fox squirrels, and birds, including the mangrove cuckoo. ✉ *Gulf Coast Visitor Center, 815 Oyster Bar La., Everglades City* ☎ *855/793–5542* 🌐 *evergladesfloridaadventures.com* 🎟 *Tours from $40*.

Everglades Safari Park

GUIDED TOURS | Consolidating a gift shop, café, nature show (alligator wrestling a specialty), and airboat service at this single location, the highlight is the 40-minute airboat ride. Tours, priced at $27 for adults, depart roughly every 20–30 minutes, with longer (and more expensive) airboat tours available. Discounts are offered when buying online (an additional discount applies if you carry a National Parks annual pass). ✉ *26700 S.W. 8 St., Miami* ☎ *305/226–6923* 🌐 *www.evergladessafaripark.com.*

Gator Park

BOAT TOURS | This outfitter offers group as well as private airboat tours. Guides will point out some of the estimated 200,000 alligators that call this area home, along with their American crocodile cousins. Also plentiful are racoons, deer, wild boar, endangered birds, turtles, fish species from largemouth bass to bluegill and catfish, and a variety of snakes that are completely content in the surrounding woods and waters. Tickets start at $24.99. **■ TIP→ If needed, you can arrange round-trip transportation from Miami starting at $25 per person.** ✉ *24050 S.W. 8th St. (U.S. 41), Miami* ☎ *305/559–2255* 🌐 *www.gatorpark.com.*

Shark Valley Tram Tours

GUIDED TOURS | FAMILY | Provided Shark Valley isn't closed due to flooding (call in advance), these popular two-hour, narrated tours aboard B99 bio-diesel trams (they basically run on a vegetable oil) depart from the Shark Valley Visitor Center on a 15-mile loop into the interior, stopping at the wheelchair-accessible observation tower along the way to give all guests access to a panoramic look at the vastness of the Everglades. Reservations are recommended, and you'll want to bring your own water. Reservations are recommended December through April. ✉ *Shark Valley Visitor Center, 36000 S.W. 8th St., Miami* ☎ *305/221–8455* 🌐 *www.sharkvalleytramtours.com* *$27.*

Visitor Information

CONTACTS Everglades National Park. ☎ *305/242–7700* 🌐 *www.nps.gov/ever.*

Ernest F. Coe Visitor Center to Flamingo Visitor Center

About 50 miles southwest of Miami.

Driving southwest from Miami you'll reach the twin communities of Homestead and Florida City. Continue driving southwest on State Road 9336 through the farming community of Redlands and you'll soon reach Everglades National Park's most utilized entrance. Once you've reached the Ernest F. Coe Visitor Center, it's a 38-mile drive to Flamingo, the park's southernmost headquarters. What enhances this pleasingly tranquil drive is that State Road 9336 transverses sections of the park's ecosystems—hardwood hammock, freshwater prairie, pinelands, freshwater slough, cypress, coastal prairie, mangrove, and marine-estuarine. With all this in mind, don't race to Flamingo. Take your time to explore the roads that lead to hammocks and meadows and marshes and estuaries; put in a kayak and paddle among the mangroves; or simply pull over beside a limitless prairie, turn off the car, and soak in the all-encompassing silence. **■ TIP→ Once at Flamingo, Mrazek and Coot Bay ponds are the best spots to observe wading birds feeding early in the morning or later in the afternoon.**

Sights

HISTORIC SIGHTS

Nike Missile Site HM-69

MILITARY SITE | A relic from a chilling time, the Nike Missile Site was in use between 1966 and 1979; a line of defense (or offense) in the Cold War between the

Airboat tours are a popular way to see the Everglades, but due to environmental concerns, only three companies are authorized within the park: Coopertown, Everglades Safari Park, and Gator Park.

United States and Cuba. Open between early December and late March, you can visit the missile barns and assembly building on a self-guided or ranger-led tour. ✉ *Everglades National Park* ⏲ *Closed Apr.–Nov.*

SCENIC DRIVES

State Road 9336

LOCAL INTEREST | What makes this drive scenic is its singularity: This is the only road that crosses through the southern region of the park, stretching from west of Homestead all the way to the Ernest F. Coe Visitor Center by the main entrance and reaching the end of the line at Flamingo, a small community 38 miles away. En route you'll experience the rare sensation of witnessing a vast and quiet land; one that becomes especially impactful when you stop, turn off the engine, and realize that from horizon to horizon, there is often no one in sight but you and nothing to hear but nature. For a closer look at the land, consider taking one of several paved roads that lead deeper into backcountry regions or taking a break at any of the marked scenic stops or tranquil ponds found adjacent to the main road. ✉ *Everglades National Park.*

SCENIC STOPS

Mahogany Hammock

FOREST | A simple boardwalk found off a spur road midway between the park entrance and Flamingo is a natural gateway into a jungle setting. Trees and vegetation that includes gumbo limbo trees and air plants border the boardwalk, wrap around it, and often enclose the view overhead to provide a curiously comforting sensation. Note the word "hammock" is a term for a stand of trees that form an unique ecological island within an ecosystem. ■ **TIP→ America's largest living mahogany tree is within this hammock.** ✉ *Everglades National Park.*

Pa-hay-okee Lookout Tower

VIEWPOINT | For expansive views of the "River of Grass" and a chance to glimpse Everglades wildlife, walk the short Pa-hay-okee Overlook Trail, which ends at a covered observation tower. While at first glance it may appear you're looking at plenty of nothing, just take your time, look around, and tune into the silence of this immense landscape. It's really something. ✉ *Everglades National Park* ✣ *13 miles from Ernest F. Coe Visitor Center* ☎ *305/242–7700* 🌐 *www.nps.gov/ever.*

Skeleton Forest

FOREST | While the name evokes images of a sprawling, haunted woodland, this is actually far more understated. Still, this condensed stand of dwarf cypress trees along the roadside a few miles east of the Pa-Hay-Okee Overlook is worth a short stop as you drive south on Route 9336. Their growth stunted and their foliage bleached by the shallow waters and thin soil where they're rooted, the result is a ghostly vision of a forest ... that's not quite a forest. ✉ *Everglades National Park.*

TRAILS

★ Anhinga Trail

TRAIL | One of the most popular trails in the Everglades, Anhinga is known for its ample wildlife viewing opportunities. The 0.8-mile, wheelchair-accessible trail cuts through sawgrass marsh and allows you to see alligators, egrets, and herons, and, of course, the trail's namesake waterbirds: anhingas. It also provides close encounters (sometimes too close) with alligators that find it pleasing to sun themselves just feet from the walkways. *Easy.* ✉ *Royal Palm Information Center, Everglades National Park* ✣ *Trailhead: 4 miles from main park entrance at Ernest F. Coe Visitor Center* ☎ *305/242–7700* 🌐 *nps.gov/ever.*

Gumbo Limbo Trail

TRAIL | Just steps away from the Anhinga Trail, this nature trail through a jungle-like blend of air plants, royal palms, ferns and, appropriately, gumbo limbo trees is less than a half-mile round-trip. Much of the trail is shaded by the thick jungle-like canopy, which makes this one of the easiest ways to get a taste of the Everglades' environment. *Easy.* ✉ *Everglades National Park* ✣ *Trailhead: Opposite the Royal Palm Visitor Center.*

Long Pine Key Nature Trail

TRAIL | Unique in its composition, this trail is actually comprised of several independent, yet connected, trails that stretch for more than 22 miles. Some of the trailheads start near the Long Pine Key Campground, located 7 miles from the main park entrance, although you'll also spot access to trails where they meet paved roads (just pull over, put on your hiking boots, and head out). Although these wooded trails are not wheelchair accessible, they're perfect for a walk—and absolutely appealing to bicyclists. *Moderate.* ✉ *Everglades National Park* ✣ *Trailheads: Many trails start by the Long Pine Key Campground, 7 miles from the main park entrance/Ernest Coe Visitor Center. Some trails can be joined where they meet paved roads.*

Mahogany Hammock Trail

TRAIL | **FAMILY** | This half-mile, handicapped-accessible boardwalk trail takes you through a hardwood hammock where the lush vegetation includes gumbo-limbo trees and air plants. This thick canopy forest is typical of South Florida and also happens to be home to America's largest mahogany tree. Along the way, listen for the call of birds which are hidden within the thick forest. *Easy.* ✉ *Royal Palm Information Center, Everglades National Park* ✣ *Trailhead: 20 miles from main park entrance at Ernest F. Coe Visitor Center* ☎ *305/242–7700* 🌐 *nps.gov/ever.*

Pa-hay-okee Overlook Trail

TRAIL | Located 13 miles from the entrance, this is a trail in name only; a 0.16-mile U-shaped boardwalk where, at its farthest point, you arrive at an elevated and covered observation deck. The short walk belies what you find—this is the perfect place to pause for a time and take in the unlimited landscape that stretches out before you. Wheelchair-accessible, this is perhaps the easiest trail in the Everglades. *Easy.* ✉ *Everglades National Park* ✣ *Trailhead: Easily seen at the end of the parking area.*

Pineland Trail

TRAIL | A familiar sight to most Floridians, the saw palmettos, wildflowers, and pine trees scattered across the sand scrub can still seem exotic to visitors who will see all of this in abundance on the half-mile, round-trip trail. It's wheelchair accessible, although tree roots can present a challenge. *Easy.* ✉ *Everglades National Park* ✣ *Trailhead: Just beside the parking area.*

VISITOR CENTERS

Ernest F. Coe Visitor Center

INFO CENTER | FAMILY | The park's main visitor center is named after the Connecticut landscape designer, Ernest F. Coe, who moved to Miami at the age of 60 where he was at first intrigued by, and then fell in love with, the Everglades. It was Coe who became the leading proponent to turn this region into a national park; he raised funds, generated support, and worked out ways visitors could see the Everglades with minimal impact on the environment. This is a convenient first stop to pick up a map, watch an introductory film providing an overview of Everglades, and view exhibits that reveal the nature of the park. ■ **TIP→ The visitor center is outside park gates, so you can stop in without paying park admission (and use the restrooms). Also, due to the remoteness of this location, visitors arriving via ride-sharing services (Uber, Lyft) should plan for return transportation before starting their adventure. There's no public transportation to this site.** ✉ *40001 State Rd. 9336, Homestead* ☎ *305/242–7700* 🌐 *www.nps.gov/ever/planyourvisit/coedirections.htm* 🎫 *Free.*

Royal Palm Information Station and Bookstore

INFO CENTER | FAMILY | Just a few miles past the park entrance, this is an ideal stop if you have limited time to visit the Everglades. When you arrive, note the medallion attached to the building's wall which pays tribute to members of the Florida Federation of Women's Clubs who donated the 4,000 surrounding acres in 1916. At the small bookstore, you'll find nature guidebooks along with a limited inventory souvenirs and snack items, while just outside in a covered pavilion, rangers present talks on the park's history and wildlife. The park's Pine Island Trails (Anhinga Trail, Gumbo Limbo Trail, Lone Pine Key Trails, Pineland Trail, Pahayokee Overlook, and Mahogany Hammock Trail) are also around the visitor center. As always, arm yourself with insect repellent. ✉ *Everglades National Park* ✣ *A little over a mile away from Ernest F. Coe Visitor Center* ☎ *305/242–7237* 🌐 *www.nps.gov/ever/planyourvisit/royal-palm.htm.*

Everglades City and the Gulf Coast.

About 86 miles west of Miami, 37 miles southeast of Naples.

The park's western gateway is the most convenient entrance for travelers coming from Southwest Florida. From Naples, take U.S./Highway 41 east for 37 miles, and turn right onto State Road 29. To reach the Gulf Coast entrance from Miami, take U.S./Highway 41 (Tamiami Trail) west for about 90 miles, turn left (south) onto State Road 29, and travel another 3 miles through Everglades City to the Gulf Coast Ranger Station.

Sights

SCENIC STOPS

Ten Thousand Islands

NATURE PRESERVE | A surreal landscape by any measure, Ten Thousand Islands is a 35,000-acre chain of islands and smaller mangrove islets south of Marco Island. This National Wildlife Refuge is a magnet for kayakers, naturalists, birdwatchers, and photographers thanks to the refuge's proliferation of fish, birds, and other wildlife. Finding your way through the islands can be confusing, so the NPS recommends visitors consult NOAA

Charts #11430 and 11432 to find their way. While the northern islands lie in the national refuge, the lower islands lie within Everglades National Park and are best accessed by boat tours leaving from the Gulf Coast Visitor Center. If you're driving from Naples, you can also park at Marsh Trail, the best spot for accessing trails. Kayaking and hiking are popular activities for day visitors, who may spot endangered species such as Florida manatees, peregrine falcons, and Atlantic loggerheads. ✉ *815 Oyster Bar La., Everglades City* ☎ *239/657–8001* 🌐 *www.fws.gov.*

TRAILS

Kayakers and canoers can access miles of Gulf Coast Water Trails along or near the park's southern and western coasts.

VISITOR CENTERS

Gulf Coast Visitor Center

INFO CENTER | **FAMILY** | The best place to start exploring Everglades National Park's watery western side is at this visitor center just south of Everglades City (5 miles south of U.S./Highway 41/Tamiami Trail), where rangers can give you the park lowdown and provide you with informational brochures and backcountry permits. The Gulf Coast Visitor Center serves as the gateway for exploring the Ten Thousand Islands, a maze of mangrove islands and waterways that extends to Flamingo and Florida Bay and are accessible only by boat in this region. Naturalist-led boat trips are handled by Everglades Florida Adventures of Guest Services, Inc., the concessioner that also rents canoes and kayaks. ✉ *815 Oyster Bar La., Everglades City* ☎ *239/695–3311* 🌐 *www.nps.gov/ever/planyourvisit/gcdirections.htm.*

Restaurants

Camellia Street Grill

$ | **SEAFOOD** | The grill features a waterfront deck and prides itself on fresh seafood and southern cooking including sautéed gator, Seminole Indian fry bread, fried green tomatoes, and stone crab. This spot is pure Old Florida goodness. **Known for:** Old Florida vibe; classic Florida dishes (stone crab, gator bites, Key lime pie); waterfront setting. $ *Average main: $15* ✉ *202 Camellia St. W, Everglades City* ☎ *239/695–2003* 🌐 *www.camelliastreetgrill.com.*

Island Cafe

$$ | **AMERICAN** | Just up the block from the Gulf Coast Visitor Center, the café is a convenient stop for frogs' legs and gator nuggets. If you're looking for more traditional fare, they've got that, too, including full breakfasts, salads, a variety of sandwiches, and seafood including oysters, crab cakes, shrimp, and scallops gathered from the waters next door. **Known for:** specialty sandwiches (gator burgers and crab cake reubens); favorite among locals; large breakfasts. $ *Average main: $19* ✉ *305 Collier Ave., Everglades City* ☎ *239/695–0003* 🌐 *www.islandcafeecity.com.*

Hotels

The Rod and Gun Club

$ | **HOTEL** | This Old Florida lodge, which still retains its distinct sportsman vibe with guests embarking on Everglades excursions, has guest rooms that include a screened-in private porch and standard amenities like flat-screen TVs, mini-refrigerators, and free Wi-Fi. **Pros:** history around every corner; casual elegance; Old Florida traditions. **Cons:** remote location; few rooms; may be too antiquated for some guests. $ *Rooms from: $149* ✉ *200 W. Broadway, Everglades City* ☎ *239/695–2101* 🌐 *rodandguneverglades.com* *17 rooms* *No meals.*

Shopping

In the small downtown area of Everglades City, just north of the Visitor Center, you'll find bait and tackle stores, outdoors outfitters, assorted independent businesses, and Right Choice Supermarket, which is the perfect spot to stock up on picnic items, snacks, ice, and camping essentials.

Flamingo

38 miles from the Ernest F. Coe Visitor Center, 48 miles from Homestead, 56 miles from Biscayne National Park, 80 miles from Miami International Airport, 85 miles from Miami, 89 miles from Miami Beach.

At the southernmost point of the park's main road to the Flamingo community, you'll find a visitor center, marina store (with beverages, snacks, and a gift shop), public boat ramp, and campground with nearby hiking and nature trails. This is where you'll go for backcountry permits. Despite the name, you probably won't find any flamingos here. To try to get a glimpse of the flamboyant pink birds with toothpick legs, check out Snake Bight Trail, starting about 5 miles from the Flamingo outpost. But they are a rare sight indeed. Visitors can pitch tents or bring RVs to the campground, where amenities include solar-heated showers and electricity for RV sites. Be sure to make a reservation during winter, and note that during the summer wet season, portions of the campgrounds are closed due to flooding.

Sights

SCENIC STOPS

Nine Mile Pond

BODY OF WATER | Located just off the park's main road 11 miles north of Flamingo, this marked kayak trail leads through freshwater marsh and mangrove tunnels that make it a favorite spot for paddlers. You can rent a kayak or canoe at the Flamingo Marina or go on a ranger-led tour from Flamingo Visitor Center. Don't be shocked if you see an alligator or two swimming nearby. In fact, be surprised if you don't. ✉ *Flamingo Visitor Center, 1 Flamingo Lodge Hwy., Everglades National Park* ☎ *239/695–2945* 🌐 *nps.gov/ever.*

TRAILS

Guy Bradley Trail

TRAIL | This 1-mile-long path is a scenic shortcut from the Flamingo Visitor Center to the Flamingo Campground. Bradley, the trail's namesake, was an Audubon warden who was killed by poachers in 1905. *Easy.* ✉ *Everglades National Park* ✥ *Trailhead: Southwest parking area by Flamingo Visitor Center; beside Amphitheatre by tent camping area.*

Snake Bight Trail

TRAIL | On the Snake Bight Trail (in this case, "bight" meaning a curve in the coastline), you'll be able to walk through a tropical hardwood hammock, see a variety of tropical tree species, and cap it off on a boardwalk that overlooks the bay. Birdwatching reaches its peak at high tide. Note the trail is 1.6 miles one-way, but in order to protect the habitat of an endangered bird species, it's not being maintained. *Moderate.* ✉ *Everglades National Park* ✥ *Trailhead: 4 miles north of the Flamingo visitor center on the main road.*

VISITOR CENTER

Flamingo Visitor Center

INFO CENTER | FAMILY | Flamingo features a visitor center where you can consult with rangers and join walking tours, and it's also where you'll find a well-stocked marina store with beverages, snacks, camping provisions, and a gift shop. There are also boat rentals, guided boat tours, walking trails, an RV and tent campground, and a collection of "eco-tents" on the shores of Florida Bay that lean towards "glamping." The winter season is traditionally the busiest, so be sure to arrive with reservations in hand, while during the hot and rainy summer season, portions of the campground may be closed due to flooding. Note that significant changes came to the park's southernmost point in 2021, including a new-in-2021 hotel and restaurant.

The 50-foot-tall Shark Valley Observation Tower has a wheelchair-accessible ramp to the top.

✉ 1 Flamingo Lodge Hwy., Homestead ☎ 239/695–2945 🌐 www.nps.gov/ever/planyourvisit/flamdirections.htm.

 Nightlife

The Ten Thousand Islands archipelago is one of the few dark sky regions in southwest Florida, making this one of the best spots for stargazing and viewing the Milky Way in all its magnificence. Astronomers cite Pavilion Key, located 11 miles south of Everglades City as a prime location for photographing the night sky.

 Shopping

The small marina store is fairly well stocked with snacks and drinks, Everglades souvenirs, t-shirts, baseball caps, flip-flops, guidebooks, sunscreen, insect repellent, fishing, kayaking, and camping supplies.

Shark Valley

23½ miles west of Florida's Turnpike, off Tamiami Trail. About an hour west of Miami.

Unlike the western United States where towering mountain chains create valleys, here the elevation of the western coastal ridge is only about 15 feet and the Atlantic ridge just a few feet higher. But that's enough to create Shark Valley (Elevation: 7 feet). The Shark Valley entrance on U.S./Highway 41 (Tamiami Trail) is 40 miles west of Miami or, coming from the Gulf Coast, 72 miles east of Naples. No matter how you reach it, when you arrive you'll discover another vast area of the Everglades.

To cover the most ground, hop aboard a two-hour tram tour with a naturalist guide. It stops halfway for a trip to the top of the 45-foot-tall Shark Valley Observation Tower via a sloping ramp. Prefer to do the trail on foot? It takes nerve to walk the 15-mile loop in Shark Valley, because in the winter months alligators sunbathe along the road. Most, however, do move out of the way when they see you coming. You can also ride a bicycle (the folks who operate the tram tours rent well-used bikes daily from 8:30 am to 4 pm for $20 per bike with helmets available). Near the bike-rental area, a short boardwalk trail meanders through sawgrass, and another courses through a tropical hardwood hammock. **TIP→ Pets are allowed in parking lots and campgrounds, but not on trails or in wilderness areas.**

Sights

SCENIC STOPS

Shark Valley Observation Tower

VIEWPOINT | FAMILY | At the halfway point of the Shark Valley loop or tram tour, you'll see (and likely be persuaded to scale) the Observation Tower, which, at 50 feet, is the highest accessible point in Everglades National Park. From the summit you'll be able to see roughly 20 miles in any direction; do the math and that's 1,600 square miles of Everglades goodness. As you take in the River of Grass in all its subtle glory, observe waterbirds as well as alligators and maybe even river otters crossing the road. The tower has a wheelchair-accessible ramp to the top. If you don't want to take the tram from the Shark Valley Visitor Center, you can either hike or bike in, but private cars are not allowed. ✉ *Shark Valley Tram Tours, 36000 S.W. 8th St., Miami* 🌐 *www.sharkvalleytramtours.com.*

TRAILS

Bobcat Boardwalk

TRAIL | At 1 mile round-trip, the handicapped-accessible boardwalk clips across a short section of a sawgrass slough and tropical hardwood forest. If you don't have time for the longer tram tour or cycling the Loop Road, this will give you a small taste of this area of the Everglades. *Easy.* ✉ *Everglades National Park* ✣ *Trailhead: About 100 yards east of the Shark Valley Visitor Center off the Shark Valley Loop Rd.*

Otter Cave Hammock Trail

TRAIL | If the Bobcat Boardwalk whetted your appetite, this half-mile round-trip trek takes hikers through a tropical hardwood forest, with a small footbridges crossing a small stream. A narrow, sandy trail disappears into the hammock, a heavily wooded eco-island, immersing you in the incredibly diverse natural tapestry of the Everglades. *Easy.* ✉ *Everglades National Park* ✣ *Trailhead: Due south of the visitor center on the West Rd.*

VISITOR CENTER

Shark Valley Visitor Center

INFO CENTER | FAMILY | If Flamingo feels too far away, Shark Valley can provide an idea of the Everglades through educational displays, a park video, and informational brochures. Books and other goods, such as hats, sunscreen, insect repellent, and postcards are available, along with restrooms. Park rangers are also available, ready for your questions. Provided the valley isn't flooded, this is where you'll find the two-hour tram tour and Observation Tower. ✉ *36000 S.W. 8th St., Miami* ✣ *23½ miles west of Florida's Turnpike, off Tamiami Trail* ☎ *305/221–8776* 🌐 *www.nps.gov/ever/planyourvisit/svdirections.htm.*

Activities

BIKING

Aside from tram tours and hiking a few trails, the most popular way to experience Shark Valley is by bike, which puts you closer to the wildlife and wilderness. If you're traveling without your own bike, rentals of single-speed bikes for children and adults are available for $20 (helmets included). Completing the paved 15-mile loop usually takes between two and three hours depending on how many stops you make for photographs. Before setting out, make sure you're hydrated and ready to replenish fluids along the way as there's no water on the trail. Also be prepared with sunscreen, insect repellent, and an eye on the weather. In the summertime, not only is it blazing hot, you can count on afternoon thunderstorms.

Shark Valley Bicycle Rentals

BICYCLING | **FAMILY** | The single-speed bikes come with baskets and helmets, along with child seats for kids under 35 pounds. The fleet also includes a few 20-inch junior models. You'll need a driver's license or other ID for a deposit. ✉ *Shark Valley Visitor Center, 36000 S.W. 8th St., Shark Valley* ☎ *305/221–8455* 🌐 *www.sharkvalleytramtours.com/everglades-bicycle-tours* 💵 *$20 per bike.*

BIRD-WATCHING

Some of South Florida's best birding is in Everglades National Park, especially the Flamingo area.

Tropical Audubon Society

The Tropical Audubon Society is where South Florida's most enthusiastic birders flock together to conserve local ecosystems while ensuring birds and their habitats are safe. This chapter of the National Audubon Society is extremely active year-round, and its birding field trips are fun and educational. Visit the website for the calendar of events and other valuable birding resources. ✉ *5530 Sunset Dr., Miami* ☎ *305/667–7337* 🌐 *www.tropicaudubon.org.*

BOATING

Gliding over the swamp in an airboat, a flat-bottomed boat propelled by a huge fan, used to be a very popular way to tour the Everglades. But due to environmental concerns, they've been curbed. The National Park Service currently authorizes just three airboat tour companies inside Everglades National Park boundaries: Coopertown, Everglades Safari Park, and Gator Park—all of which are located just east of the Shark Valley Visitor Center on U.S. 41. The rest operate outside the boundaries of the park, even if they may advertise "Everglades." If you're concerned about your footprint, why not rent a kayak or hike the trails instead?

CAMPING

Flamingo Campground. The park's most popular camping location offers an unforgettable year-round experience on a beautiful open field with a refreshing breeze fueled by the winds of the Florida Bay. There are 38 walk-in sites by the bay, and 54 additional tent sites in the "A-Loop" near the RV area, which offers 61 sites, 41 of them equipped with 41 electrical hook-ups. Campgrounds have solar-heated showers, two dump stations, picnic tables, grills, and an amphitheater for winter programs. For an evening of glamping, check out the wonderfully cushy eco-tents (🌐 *flamingoeverglades.com/camping*). Overlooking the shores of Florida Bay, they start at $50 and come equipped with electricity, fans, and lamps. With just 20 eco-tents available, be sure to make a reservation during winter, and note that during the summer wet season, portions of the campgrounds are closed due to flooding. A short distance from the campground is the Marina Store, which has a gift shop and sells beverages and snacks, as well as rents houseboats for an extended stay on the water.

Long Pine Key Campground. Like Flamingo Campground, this camping area is accessible from the Homestead entrance to the park and has spaces for tents (26 sites) and RVs (81 sites). It's near popular trails including Long Pine Key Trail and just a few miles from Anhinga Trail at the Royal Palm Center. Amenities include fresh water, cold showers, and restrooms. Rates start at $25 per night. Reserve at ☎ *855/708–2207* 🌐 *flamingoeverglades.com.*

CANOEING AND KAYAKING

The 99-mile inland **Wilderness Waterway** between Flamingo and Everglades City is open to motorboats as well as canoes, although, depending on water levels, powerboats may have trouble navigating above Whitewater Bay. Flat-water canoeing and kayaking are best in winter, when temperatures are moderate, rainfall diminishes, and mosquitoes back off—a little, anyway. This activity is for the experienced and adventurous; most paddlers take eight days to complete the trail. But you can also do a day trip. The Flamingo area has well-marked water trails, but be sure to tell someone where you're going and when you expect to return. Getting lost is easy, and spending the night without proper gear can be unpleasant, if not dangerous. A company known as Guest Services, Inc. is the authorized concessioner for Flamingo, and they handle all reservations and rentals.

★ **Everglades Adventures**

KAYAKING | Everglades Adventure can arrange canoe and kayak rentals as well as guided 90-minute tours of the Ten Thousand Islands. Highlights include bird and gator sightings, mangrove forests, and spectacular sunsets, depending on the time of your tour. ✉ *815 Oyster Bay La., Everglades City* ☎ *855/793–5542* 🌐 *www.evergladesfloridaadventures.com* 🎫 *Canoe rentals from $25; kayak rentals from $30.*

EDUCATIONAL PROGRAMS

There are multiple programs offered throughout the park by rangers and concessionaires; the park's website (🌐 *www.nps.gov/ever/planyourvisit/events.htm*) provides the best and most current listing of scheduled events at various locations. There you'll find programs such as nature walks ranging from mild to muddy, guided bicycle tours, special trips to the Nike missile site, moonlight walks, early morning hikes, full moon bicycle treks, ranger talks, and full-day ranger-led tours.

Each visitor center has their own programs which are posted daily at each visitor center. At Royal Palm, the ranger-led programs include The Anhinga Amble (a 50-minute stroll brings you close to alligators, wading birds, and other wildlife) and Glades Glimpse (a 20-minute talk in the shade), which are offered year-round, including the summer months.

FISHING

Much of the Everglades is covered with water, which makes fishing—in freshwater, saltwater, or brackish water—a popular recreational activity. In the waters of Florida Bay and the Ten Thousand Islands you can cast for snapper, sea trout, redfish, bass, bluegill and much more. There are boat ramps and a marina store in Flamingo, with bait and tackle shops, outfitters, and fishing guides available in and around the western entrance to the park at Everglades City. Freshwater and saltwater fishing require separate Florida fishing licenses. For in-depth information on fishing in Florida, visit the **Florida Fish and Wildlife Conservation Commission** (🌐 *myfwc.com/fishing/*).

HIKING

Several short trails between the Ernest F. Coe Visitor Center and the Flamingo Visitor Center each take less than an hour to walk. A few miles from the park entrance at Royal Palm the jungle-like Gumbo Limbo and the wide-open Anhinga are each easy trails that are wheelchair-accessible; a few miles west the Pinelands Trail is where you can see the park's limestone bedrock; and the Snake Bight Trail where you can walk through a tropical hardwood hammock. For a complete list of trails (there are well over a dozen, along with canoe trails) visit 🌐 *www.nps.gov/ever/planyourvisit/hiking-trails.htm.* **■ TIP→ Before heading out on the trails, check the weather and stock up on bug repellent, sunscreen, and water.**

The Flamingo section has numerous short interpretive trails including the West Lake Trail, Snake Bight Trail, Rowdy Bend Trail, Christian Point Trail, Bear Lake

Trail, Eco Pond Trail, Guy Bradley Trail, Bayshore Trail, and Coastal Prairie Trail. The Hells Bay and Nine Mile Pond canoe trails are also here.

MULTISPORT OUTFITTERS

In Flamingo, Flamingo Everglades rents canoes, kayaks, and houseboats, but at the western entrance to the park there are numerous outfitters, guides, stores, and services near the visitor center who can help you prepare for a fishing excursion or the more demanding experience of paddling the Wilderness Waterway.

Flamingo Everglades

KAYAKING | At Flamingo, the community located on the southernmost point of the Florida mainland, Flamingo Everglades handles the campground, canoeing, kayaking, and houseboat rentals, the Marina Store, and guided tour operations. ✉ *1 Flamingo Lodge Hwy., Everglades National Park* ☎ *855/708–2207* 🌐 *flamingoeverglades.com.*

What's Nearby

Although Everglades National Park is renowned for its vast expanses wilderness, it's also sandwiched between the Gulf of Mexico and the Atlantic Ocean where coastal communities are a constant and growing presence. While their insatiable need for the waters of the Everglades is a distinct challenge, their presence can be a relief for visitors who may tolerate nature for a day or two, but soon long for the creature comforts of an air conditioned hotel room, a table-service restaurant, and unlimited access to the Internet.

Approximately 10 miles from the eastern entrance of the park, the closest communities are **Homestead** and **Florida City,** each of which provide all of the familiar stores, restaurants, and hotels a traveler may need. Just east of these towns is **Biscayne National Park,** which, like the Everglades, is nearly all water. Farther north are the fashionable cities of **Coconut Grove, Coral Gables, Key Biscayne, Miami,** and cosmopolitan **Miami Beach.**

On the western edge of the park on the shores of the Gulf of Mexico is the resort community of **Marco Island** and, to the north, **Naples,** known for its tony vibe, upscale shopping, and trendy restaurants.

Established in 1974 as the nation's first national preserve, **Big Cypress National Preserve** includes more than 729,000 acres along the northern border of the Everglades National Park. Compared with the park, the preserve is less developed and hosts fewer visitors, and that makes it ideal for naturalists, birders, and hikers. Several scenic drives branch out from Tamiami Trail; a few lead to camping areas and roadside picnic spots. Aside from the Oasis Visitor Center, a popular springboard for viewing alligators, the newer Big Cypress Swamp Welcome Center features a platform for watching manatees. Both centers, along Tamiami Trail between Miami and Naples, feature a 25-minute film on Big Cypress. Hiking, hunting, and off-road vehicles (airboat, swamp buggy, four-wheel drive) are allowed—in limited areas—by permit.

Chapter 22

22

GATES OF THE ARCTIC AND KOBUK VALLEY NATIONAL PARKS

Updated by
Dawnell Smith

Camping	Hotels	Activities	Scenery	Crowds
★☆☆☆☆	★☆☆☆☆	★★★☆☆	★★★★★	★☆☆☆☆

WELCOME TO GATES OF THE ARCTIC AND KOBUK VALLEY NATIONAL PARKS

TOP REASONS TO GO

★ **Arctic adventure:** Take a flightseeing trip that lands in both national parks. Hike the Kobuk sand dunes. Backpack into Arrigetch Peaks. Paddle one of Gates of the Arctic's six National Wild and Scenic Rivers. Chill out under the midnight sun or amid the northern lights.

★ **Arctic animals:** The parks nourish wildlife like grizzlies, wolves, musk oxen, moose, Dall sheep, wolverines, and smaller mammals and birds. Indeed, the western Arctic caribou herd—the largest in the United States—passes north in the spring and south in the fall, crossing Kobuk Valley on the way.

★ **Arctic ways of life:** Gates of the Arctic and Kobuk Valley provide incredible opportunities for seeing a place where Iñupiat, Koyukon Athabascan, and Gwich'in peoples have lived for thousands of years, and learning about their history, culture, and contemporary life.

1 Gates of the Arctic National Park and Preserve. The country's least visited national park envelopes 8.4 million acres that includes the headwaters of six National Wild and Scenic Rivers, along with the central Brooks Range, a 700-mile stretch of mountains that continues east to the Arctic National Wildlife Refuge and into Canada.

2 Kobuk Valley National Park. Kobuk Valley's 1.79 million acres of massive sand dunes, tundra, woodlands, mountains, and rivers are about 100 miles east of Kotzebue—called Qikiktagruk in Iñupiaq—the largest community on Alaska's northwestern coast.

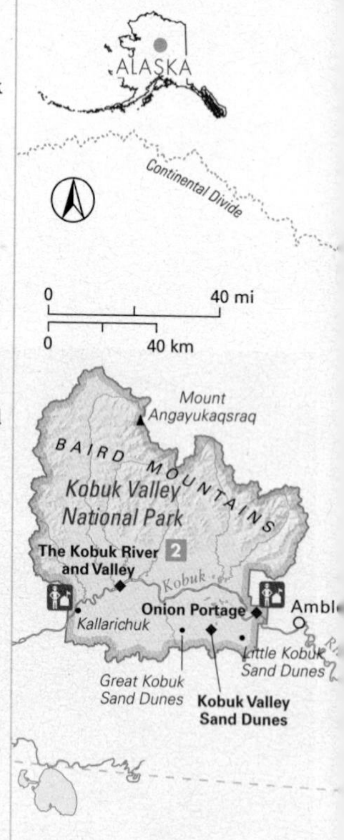

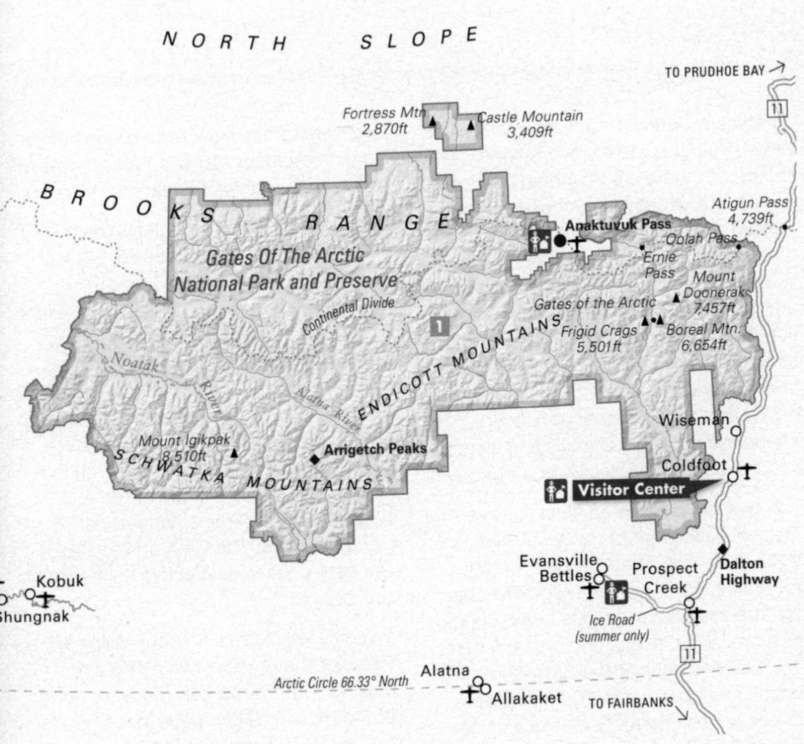
NORTH SLOPE
TO PRUDHOE BAY
11
Fortress Mtn
2,870ft
Castle Mountain
3,409ft
BROOKS RANGE
Gates Of The Arctic
National Park and Preserve
Anaktuvuk Pass
Atigun Pass
4,739ft
Oolah Pass
Ernie
Pass
Mount
Doonerak
7,457ft
Gates of the Arctic
Continental Divide
1
Frigid Crags
5,501ft
Boreal Mtn.
6,654ft
ENDICOTT MOUNTAINS
Noatak
River
Alatna River
Wiseman
Mount Igikpak
8,510ft
Arrigetch Peaks
SCHWATKA MOUNTAINS
Coldfoot
Visitor Center
Evansville
Bettles
Prospect
Creek
Dalton
Highway
Kobuk
Shungnak
Ice Road
(summer only)
11
Alatna
Arctic Circle 66.33° North
Allakaket
TO FAIRBANKS

Known for migrating caribou herds, scenic rivers, enormous dune fields, dramatic peaks, and zero crowds, these two parks offer remarkable Arctic experiences.

Combined, Gates of the Arctic and Kobuk Valley could hold nearly five Yellowstones, yet there are no lodges, no roads, and no latte stops inside these parks. Instead, you'll find the small plants of the tundra, bird sounds in the forest, and, if you're in the right place at the right time, the clicking of caribou on their migration. These Arctic landscapes continue to sustain Arctic ways of life, and draw photographers, birders, backpackers, packrafters, and national park lovers interested in seeing animals and learning about the region's geology and ecology.

The two parks make up an expansive Arctic landscape west of the Arctic National Wildlife Refuge. These lands together form an integrated Arctic region known for treeless tundra speckled with ponds, lakes, lagoons, rivers, and boreal forest. The tree line ends at the Brooks Range, which stretches some 700 miles west to east across northern Alaska and into Canada's Yukon Territory. Considered a subrange of the Rocky Mountains, the range is the continent's northernmost; it's also the highest one above the Arctic Circle, with peaks of nearly 9,000 feet. Gates of the Arctic, Kobuk Valley, and Noatak National Preserve all lie within it.

The whole region sustains the largest caribou herds in the country, along with hundreds of species of birds, as well as human communities with long histories and connections with the land. The people whose ancestors have lived in the region for thousands of years continue their ways of life here, with dozens of villages throughout Alaska's Arctic, some of which are jumping off points for travelers.

In the 1930s, Robert Marshall, the principal founder of the Wilderness Society, traveled with local guides into the area now included in Gates of the Arctic. Like many of those who explored Alaska, he gave English names to park features, including Frigid Crag and Boreal Mountain, two peaks on either side of the North Fork of the Koyukuk River. These were the original "gates" for which the park is named. Like Gates of the Arctic, Kobuk Valley became a national park in December 1980. Its Great Kobuk Sand Dunes are the largest active dunes in the Arctic.

The only way to reach Kobuk Valley or Gates of the Arctic is by small plane, boat, or foot. The Dalton Highway—one of the most isolated roads in the country—can get you closer to Gates of the Arctic, but you'll still have to fly or hike in. Flightseeing trips offer a bird's-eye view and a visceral sense of the scope of this region, but the best way to experience these Arctic parks requires getting on the ground, perhaps walking on the Kobuk sand dunes, trekking into the Arrigetch Peaks, camping along the Kobuk River, or paddling one of the many waterways.

AVERAGE HIGH/LOW TEMPERATURES IN BETTLES					
JAN.	FEB.	MAR.	APR.	MAY	JUNE
-7/-23	4/-16	15/-14	36/9	54/29	67/41
JULY	AUG.	SEPT.	OCT.	NOV.	DEC.
67/43	63/38	45/27	26/12	2/-12	-3/-18

Planning

When to Go

They call it the land of midnight sun for a reason. On a clear day above the Arctic Circle, the sun appears to move left to right rather than down, which means you can keep hiking, paddling, or otherwise exploring long past your usual bedtime. Most people visit Gates of the Arctic and Kobuk Valley from June to August to take advantage of higher temperatures as well as those long days. Even in this season, though, the weather can be unpredictable and extreme—hot and sticky or cold, wet, and windy. Mosquitoes and other insects are an elemental force, too, so bring protective clothes and bug spray.

Wildflowers can bloom as early as mid-June, and August brings ripe berries and autumn colors. Expect wet ground conditions after spring snowmelts, and much colder temperatures in late August and September.

■ **TIP→ For most people, the best way to visit these parks is on daylong flightseeing excursions or multiday guided trips organized through outfitters or lodges.** Outfitters tend to offer trips from May to August. In other months, though, more of them are offering custom options and packages with activities like dog sledding, skiing, snow machining, and Aurora Borealis viewing. Area lodges tend to stay open beyond August—some even remain open in winter.

Getting Here and Around

AIR

Fairbanks International is the nearest major airport to Kobuk Valley and Gates of the Arctic, but that still leaves hundreds of miles to go. Most people access both parks via small planes on scheduled flights or prearranged drop-offs/pick-ups. There are direct scheduled flights from Anchorage or Fairbanks to Kotzebue, as well as from Fairbanks to Anaktuvuk Pass (the only village in Gates of the Arctic), Coldfoot, and Bettles. Scheduled flights out of Kotzebue head to dozens of villages, including Ambler, where air taxis can take you the last legs into these parks.

■ **TIP→ In addition to companies that specialize in scenic flights to both parks, several air-taxi services offer flightseeing excursions.**

Bering Air
This airline with hubs in Kotzebue and Nome makes scheduled flights to 27 communities in the northwest Arctic, including Ambler, outside the southeast boundary of Kobuk Valley National Park. ✉ *Kotzebue* ☎ *907/442–3943 Kotzebue, 907/443–5464 Nome* 🌐 *www.beringair.com.*

Wright Air
This small airline provides scheduled passenger service from Fairbanks to Anaktuvuk Pass, Bettles, and Coldfoot. ✉ *Fairbanks* ☎ *907/474–0502* 🌐 *www.wrightairservice.com.*

CAR

You can't drive into either park, but you can get close to Gates of the Arctic by heading north from Fairbanks on the Dalton Highway, a two-way gravel industrial road along the park's eastern boundary. There are no amenities on this road until Coldfoot, which has a few nearby lodges and travel services. From Coldfoot, you can hike or catch a flight into the park.

Companies that will rent cars for this rough, remote drive include Arctic Outfitters (🌐 *www.arctic-outfitters.com*), Alaska Auto Rental (🌐 *alaskaautorental.com*), and Go North Alaska (🌐 *gonorth-alaska.com*). In addition, Dalton Highway Express (🌐 *www.daltonhighwayexpress.com*) offers June-to-August bus service from Fairbanks to Coldfoot.

Inspiration

Arctic Voices, edited by photographer and writer Subhankar Banerjee, contains compelling first-person narratives from prominent writers, artists, activists, researchers, and thinkers addressing human rights, the climate crisis, and the extraction of resources in the Arctic.

Two Old Women is a retelling of a tribal legend that author Velma Wallis heard as a child. It focuses on two elders who were left behind by their tribe during a famine and had to survive a harsh winter on their own.

Park Essentials

ACCESSIBILITY

There are no facilities or trails—ADA compliant or otherwise—in either Gates of the Arctic or Kobuk Valley national parks.

PARK FEES AND PERMITS

Neither Gates of the Arctic nor Kobuk Valley charges an entrance fee or requires a permit. It is requested that visitors to either park check in at a visitor center for a backcountry orientation.

PARK HOURS

Both parks are open 24/7 year-round.

CELL PHONE RECEPTION

There is no cell phone reception in either Gates of the Arctic or Kobuk Valley.

Hotels

Small Arctic communities en route to Kobuk Valley and Gates of the Arctic usually have one or more basic hotels or lodges, where guests might share bathroom and/or kitchen facilities. Some lodges offer packages that cover meals, activities, and transportation (or some combination of them); always inquire about what's included when booking. Note, too, that some cabins can accommodate more than two people, and there might be minimum-stay requirements. Rooms fill up quickly, so book ahead. It never hurts to carry a tent as backup!

Restaurants

Many Arctic communities have at least a few eateries with a range of fare, sometimes made with local seafood and produce. You won't need reservations, but you should confirm business hours. All food prices, including those at small grocery stores, reflect the high cost of transporting goods to the region. A burger with no extras can cost $10, large pizzas with one topping more than $30. Lodges might offer inclusive rates that cover meals. Some also serve beer, wine, and a limited range of cocktails.

Tours

Alaska Alpine Adventures

ADVENTURE TOURS | This family-friendly company offers paddling, backpacking, and combination trips throughout Alaska. Options include 10 days of hiking in Arrigetch Peaks in Gates of the Arctic and 12 days of rafting the Noatak River and hiking the sand dunes in Kobuk Valley. ✉ *Anchorage* ☎ *877/525–2577* 🌐 *www.alaskaalpineadventures.com* 🎫 *From $5195.*

Arctic Backcountry Flying Service

AIR EXCURSIONS | This Kotzebue air service offers flightseeing and air-taxi drop-offs and pick-ups throughout the Arctic. A Kobuk Valley and Gates of the Arctic half-day flightseeing trip that lands in both parks costs about $530 per person if the five-seater Cessna is full. ✉ *Kotzebue* ☎ *907/442–3200* 🌐 *www.arcticbackcountry.com.*

Arctic Treks

GUIDED TOURS | The 7- to 12-day trips offered by this outfitter include hiking in the Arrigetch Peaks, fall caribou-viewing in Gates of the Arctic, and hiking and camping trips that go to both parks. ✉ *Fairbanks* ☎ *907/455–6502* 🌐 *www.arctictreksadventures.com* 🎫 *From $4700.*

★ **Arctic Wild**

ADVENTURE TOURS | Small-group trips throughout the Arctic and Alaska cater to those looking for a range of experiences, from mountain backpacking and packrafting to canoeing, whitewater rafting, birding, and viewing or photographing terrestrial and marine animals. ✉ *Fairbanks* ☎ *907/479–8203* 🌐 *arcticwild.com* 🎫 *From $5100.*

Coyote Air

AIR EXCURSIONS | Coyote offers airtaxi service and custom and flightseeing trips, including drop-offs at Long Lake in Gates of the Arctic for a day hike and scenic flights around the massive rock faces of the Arrigetch Peaks ($700 per person, two-person minimum). The daylong Gates of the Arctic and Kobuk Valley combo trip can be extended to include Arrigetch Peaks. ✉ *Coldfoot* ☎ *907/678–5995 summer contact number, 907/687–3993 winter contact number* 🌐 *flycoyote.com.*

Dalton Highway Express

BUS TOURS | This local business specializes in June-to-August transportation on Alaska's Dalton Highway, which winds through the Yukon-Tanana uplands, travels along the Yukon River, and crosses the Arctic Circle through Atigun Pass and the Brooks Range, ending at the Arctic Ocean. Travelers can take the bus from Fairbanks to Coldfoot, about 20 miles south of Gates of the Arctic, and arrange air taxi service into either park from there. ✉ *Fairbanks* ☎ *907/474–3555 Fairbanks* 🌐 *www.daltonhighwayexpress.com.*

Expeditions Alaska

ADVENTURE TOURS | Although this company specializes in backpacking and photo tours, it also offers an array of paddling, hiking, and camping trips. Arctic options include backpacking in the Arrigetch Peaks and a shorter two- to four-day Alatna River packrafting trip. ✉ *Anchorage* ☎ *770/952–4549* 🌐 *www.expeditionsalaska.com* 🎫 *From $2600.*

Golden Eagle Outfitters Air Taxi

AIR EXCURSIONS | This company flies out of Kotzebue and offers flightseeing trips, including tours that feature multiple national parks, as well as air-taxi services in the Arctic. ✉ *Kotzebue* ☎ *907/388–5968* 🌐 *alaskawildernessexpeditions.com.*

Northern Alaska Tour Company

ADVENTURE TOURS | This company arranges shorter trips out of Fairbanks, including flightseeing excursions above the Arctic Circle and an evening flight tour that offers views of the Brooks Range before stopping at Anaktuvuk Pass. ✉ *Fairbanks* ☎ *907/474–8600, 800/474–1986* 🌐 *www.northernalaska.com* 🎫 *From $599.*

Onion Portage Adventures

ADVENTURE TOURS | This company, which also has several lodging options, offers Kobuk Valley rafting, fishing, hiking, and camping trips. Boat tours to the sand dunes include a night of camping.

Stunning vistas like this one showcase the diverse ecosystems of these two parks.

907/445–5195 www.onionportage-alaska.com From $1700 for full-boat (6 people) tour and overnight at Kobuk Valley sand dunes.

Visitor Information

CONTACTS Gates of the Arctic National Park and Preserve. *907/459–3730 Fairbanks Alaska Public Lands Info Center (year-round), 907/661–3520 Anaktuvuk Pass (Apr.–Sept.), 907/678–5209 Arctic Interagency Visitor Center (Coldfoot; July–Sept.), 907/692–5494 Bettles (July–Sept.) www.nps.gov/gaar.* **Kobuk Valley National Park.** *907/442–3890 www.nps.gov/kova.*

Gates of the Arctic National Park and Preserve

Coldfoot is 420 air miles north of Anchorage and 250 air miles northwest of Fairbanks.

The northernmost national park in the United States stands apart, with 8.4 million acres of truly epic scenery featuring endless, cragged peaks (once part of an ancient seabed), stunning river valleys, and 6 of Alaska's 13 Wild and Scenic Rivers: the Alatna, John, Kobuk, Noatak, North Fork Koyukuk, and Tinayguk. With a scant 10,000 visitors a year, Gates of the Arctic promises solitude.

On foot, the contours of the land will take you into terrain pockmarked with blue- and green-hued ponds and huge glacial lakes. For a fully immersive experience (and bragging rights), hike the famed and arduous Anaktuvuk Pass, or backpack into the Arrigetch Peaks, massive granite pinnacles that rise thousands of feet.

Sights

GEOLOGICAL FORMATIONS

Arrigetch Peaks

MOUNTAIN—SIGHT | The showpiece of the Brooks Range and a designated National Natural Landmark, these peaks draw hikers, flightseers, and even climbers intrepid enough to scale granite walls that rise thousands of feet. "Arrigetch" means "fingers of the outstretched hand" in the Iñupiaq language, and the name truly conveys the sense of awe experienced by many who visit them. ✉ *Gates of the Arctic National Park and Preserve.*

SCENIC DRIVES

The Dalton Highway

SCENIC DRIVE | One of the nation's most isolated roads, Alaska Route 11 consists mostly of loose-packed dirt and gravel that can put wear and tear on your vehicle—and your spine. It can also take you on a sublime road trip. The Dalton was built to support construction of the Trans-Alaska Pipeline, which parallels the road, and the north slope oil fields, but the spellbinding scenery includes boreal forest, the Brooks Range, Arctic foothills, and coastal plain tundra. The 400-plus-mile "haul road" starts 80 miles north of Fairbanks in Livengood (population: a baker's dozen, more or less). A few miles short of the Arctic Ocean, it ends in Deadhorse, a place named exactly how it feels. The drive can be treacherous, with hazards ranging from speeding 18-wheelers to fog, snow, rain, potholes, steep grades, and only a few services along the way. Plan ahead (spare tires, provisions, etc.), and take your time.

SCENIC STOPS

Anaktuvuk Pass

TOWN | Anaktuvuk Pass lies on a divide between the Anaktuvuk and John rivers in the central Brooks Range. A small Nunamuit Iñupiaq village of the same name sits atop this 2,000-foot pass. The economy and traditions here center on the caribou herds that supply residents with most of their meat. Surrounded by mountains, rivers, and lakes, this is one of the north slope's most scenic spots. Daily flights from Fairbanks travel to the village, and you can walk from there into the park. You can also do backbacking trips that start or end at the pass. As elsewhere, some of the terrain here is on private or Native Corporation land, so inquire at the ranger station about where it's best to hike and camp—and whether or not you need permission to do so. ✉ *Gates of the Arctic National Park and Preserve* ☎ *907/661–3520 Anaktuvuk Pass Ranger Station (Apr.–Sept.).*

National Wild and Scenic Rivers

BODY OF WATER | The Alatna, John, Kobuk, Noatak, North Fork, Koyukuk, and Tinayguk rivers make up 6 of the 13 National Wild and Scenic Rivers in Gates of the Arctic National Park. They have been byways for people and animals for thousands of years, and they support each summer's explosion of life. They're also navigable, with a variety of access points. Most people use inflatable canoes, packrafts, or other collapsible boats, as air taxis don't haul rigid vessels. Although the waters are generally Class I and II rapids, a few sections include Class II–IV rapids. The water is cold, and conditions constantly change, but when the going is good, boating can beat walking through thick tussocks and boggy ground. ✉ *Gates of the Arctic National Park and Preserve* ☎ *907/459–3730 National Park Service in Fairbanks* 🌐 *www.nps.gov/gaar/learn/nature/wildandscenicrivers.htm.*

VISITOR CENTERS

Gates of the Arctic National Park Visitor Centers

INFO CENTER | Information is available at visitor centers in Fairbanks (year-round), Bettles, Coldfoot, and Anaktuvuk Pass. ☎ *907/459–3730 Fairbanks Alaska Public Lands Info Center (year-round),*

The tundra—backed by breathtaking formations—in the fall.

907/692–5494 Bettles Ranger Station (July–Sept. only), 907/678–5209 Arctic Interagency Visitor Center (Coldfoot; July–Sept.), 907/661–3520 Anaktuvuk Pass (Apr.–Sept.) www.nps.gov/gaar.

Hotels

Bettles Lodge
$$$$ | **B&B/INN** | Open year round and offering an array of all-inclusive packages, the historic Bettles and its more modern Aurora Lodge together make a comfortable base camp for northern-lights viewing or trips to Gates of the Arctic and Kobuk Valley national parks. **Pros:** lots of on-site services and amenities; tasty meals and to-die-for hot cocoa; sometimes accessible from Dalton Highway via ice road in winter. **Cons:** shared baths; weather and shoulder seasons may limit activities; pricey for fairly basic accommodations. *Rooms from: $1090 1 Airline Dr. Short walk from the airport or Bettles Ranger Station 907/692–5111 bettleslodge.com 14 rooms All-inclusive Transportation from Fairbanks, local tours, and other extras included in packages.*

Iniakuk Lake Wilderness Lodge
$$$$ | **ALL-INCLUSIVE** | Just 6 miles south of Gates of the Arctic and west of Bettles, the Iniakuk Lake lodge offers packages with meals and guided tours; three lodge rooms with shared baths, 24-hour electricity, and satellite internet; and two more-remote dry cabins where the views make up for the lack of amenities. **Pros:** year-round activities and spellbinding scenery; superb meals and snacks; solar power and satellite Internet at the lodge. **Cons:** very expensive and very remote; BYOB; small, so booking ahead is essential. *Rooms from: $6925 877/479–6354 gofarnorth.com Closed Oct.–Jan. and May (except by special request) 5 units All-inclusive.*

What's Nearby

Anuktuvuk Pass, on the north side of the park in the Brooks Range, is the only village in Gates of the Arctic. The community of about 250 people has a grocery store, lodging, camping, dining, ranger station, post office, health clinic, and the Simon Paneak Memorial Museum. Many visitors do one-day trips to the village from Fairbanks, while others organize multiweek trips that start or end in the village.

On the park's southeastern edge, along the Koyukuk River, **Bettles** has a ranger station and visitor center, eateries, tour operators, and air-taxi service. The Bettles Lodge caters to visitors all year, with summer Gates of the Arctic trips and winter Aurora Borealis packages. Bettles is off the road system for most of the year (though there's sometimes ice-road access from the Dalton Highway in winter), but many people access Gates of the Arctic through it, as it's served by scheduled commercial flights from Fairbanks.

Originally a mining camp, **Coldfoot** now mainly serves as a truck stop on the Dalton Highway (Alaska Route 11). The town of fewer than a dozen people has eateries, lodging, the Arctic Interagency Visitor Center, and travel services. From here you can catch a flightseeing trip or air taxi into Gates of the Arctic.

Kobuk Valley National Park

Kotzebue is 440 air miles northwest of Fairbanks, 550 air miles northwest of Anchorage, and 335 air miles west of Coldfoot.

Half a million caribou leave tracks on the vast Kobuk dunes every year, tracing their migration in the sandy remnants of retreating glaciers from the Pleistocene epoch. These dunes appear as a rivuleted sand sprawl in a park with broad wetlands, meandering rivers, boreal forests, and mountains rising from wide and wooded valleys. The Kobuk River bisects the park, with dunes situated in the lower reaches and rivers valleys and the Baird Mountains to the north. The boreal forest reaches its most northern limits in the valley, giving way to upland areas of tundra and scree. The Western Arctic caribou herd—the largest in the United States—passes north in the spring and south in the fall, crossing Kobuk on the way.

Sights

GEOLOGICAL FORMATIONS

Kobuk Valley Sand Dunes

NATURE SITE | South of the Kobuk River, the Great Kobuk (the largest active, high-altitude dune field on Earth), Little Kobuk, and Hunt River sand dunes—stabilized by small trees, shrubs, and the lichen that's typical of the tundra—cover much of southern Kobuk Valley. They formed when glaciers slowly pulverized mountain rock into sand that washed into the valley during the last ice age. Of note, a flowering herb called the Kobuk Locoweed is only found on the slopes of the Great Kobuk Sand Dunes. Most outfitters and air taxis that operate in the Arctic will take visitors to the sand dunes. ✉ *Kobuk Valley National Park.*

SCENIC STOPS

The Kobuk River and Valley

BODY OF WATER | Kobuk Valley provides a glimpse into what the thousand-mile-wide grassland of Beringia, the land connecting Asia and North America during the last ice age, looked like. The Kobuk River bisects the national park, with dunes to the south, and broad wetlands leading to the Baird Mountains to the north. Running hundreds of miles (60 of them in the national park) from the Endicott Mountains to Kotzebue Sound, the generally wide river has been used for transportation for thousands of years. It also sustains large population of sheefish, a large predatory whitefish in the salmon family that spawns in the river's upper reaches every fall. A portion of the vast Western Arctic caribou herd uses the Kobuk River valley as a winter range, and the boreal forest reaches its northernmost limits here. ✉ *Kobuk Valley National Park.*

Onion Portage

BODY OF WATER | Near the park's southeastern boundary, the Kobuk River makes a wide bend that creates a long, narrow peninsula. Locals call it Paatitaaq, or Onion Portage, for the wild onions that grow along the banks here. Twice a year, the western Arctic caribou herd crosses the tundra and down the slopes into the Kobuk River on their migration across the Brooks Range. Although the changing climate has made it harder to predict when the herd will cross, Inupiat hunters continue to use these crossings to bring food to their communities. The area also has an archeological site with artifacts, campsites, and house ruins and is an Archeological District National Historic Landmark. There's easy access by boat from Ambler, a community to the east, and by air taxi. ✉ *Kobuk Valley National Park.*

VISITOR CENTERS

The Northwest Arctic Heritage Center

INFO CENTER | This facility in Kotzebue serves as the visitor center for Kobuk Valley National Park, Cape Krusenstern National Monument, and Noatak National Preserve. Here you can find information and borrow bear-resistant containers on a first-come, first-served basis. ✉ *Kobuk Valley National Park, Kotzebue* ☎ *907/442–3890* 🌐 *www.nps.gov/kova.*

Hotels

Kobuk River Lodge

$ | **B&B/INN** | Located in Ambler, east of Kobuk Valley National Park, this lodge offers rooms for rent with meals included, as well as supplies, guided tours, and river transport services into the park on the Kobuk River. **Pros:** easy access to hiking, fishing, sightseeing on the Kobuk River and in the valley; laundry facilities; Wi-Fi and satellite TV. **Cons:** tight quarters; limited room amenities; only one room has a double bed. $ *Rooms from: $200* ✉ *11 Ambler Ave.* ☎ *907/445–5235 tours and lodging reservations, 907/445–2166 store and restaurant* 🌐 *www.kobukriverlodge.com* *3 rooms* *All-inclusive.*

Onion Portage Adventures

$ | **B&B/INN** | This travel outfitter offers accommodations in Ambler, with three rooms in a house, two in a remodeled Atco trailer, two remote cabins, and an Onion Portage campsite where it has erected several dome shelters for summer or winter use. **Pros:** varied options in Ambler or Kobuk Valley; all-seasons in-park option; easy access to Onion Portage and sand dunes. **Cons:** limited amenities; access for some lodging requires boat or snow machine; no meal options yet. $ *Rooms from: $150* ☎ *907/445–5195 reservations* 🌐 *www.onionportagealaska.com* *9 units* *No meals.*

What's Nearby

Kotzebue, also known as Qikiktagruk in Iñupiaq, sits on a flat gravel spit at the end of the Baldwin Peninsula in the Kotzebue Sound. As it's where multiple rivers meet with the Chukchi Sea, the city of about 3,000 people is a regional transportation hub and a starting point for fishing, paddling, hiking trips. The town has travel and tour services; a handful of places to eat and stay; the Northwest Arctic Heritage Centre, with information about the national park, area natural history, and Iñupiat cultures; and the Sulianich Art Center, which sells jewelry, baskets, carvings, and other crafts.

From Kotzebue or Fairbanks you can also grab an air taxi to **Ambler,** or Ivisaappaat in Iñupiaq, a village of just under 300 people right on the Kobuk River. Lodging options here include Kobuk River Lodge and Onion Portage Adventures. There are also eateries, stores, and other services, plus easy access to Kobuk Valley by boat.

Chapter 23

GATEWAY ARCH NATIONAL PARK

Updated by
Mary McHugh

MO

Camping
★☆☆☆☆

Hotels
★★★★★

Activities
★★★★★

Scenery
★★★★★

Crowds
★★★★☆

WELCOME TO GATEWAY ARCH NATIONAL PARK

TOP REASONS TO GO

★ **Immerse yourself in the Arch:** Ride the tram 63 stories to its top, and sway (up to 18 inches in 150 mph winds) along with it in the observation deck. Take in its sky-high, 30-mile views to the east and west of the Mississippi River. Stand at the bottom of one of its legs, and look up. Post your pics to the Arch's popular and humorous Twitter feed: @GatewayArchSTL.

★ **Cruise Old Muddy:** Sail through history along the Mississippi River aboard the *Tom Sawyer* or the *Becky Thatcher,* replica 19th-century paddlewheelers. First brought here in 1964 to take sightseers out to view construction of the Arch, both continue to entertain with dinner and other specialty cruises.

★ **Time travel:** At the on-site museum, touch bison fur, sit inside a pirogue (dugout canoe), walk inside a replica colonial house. Experience still more history—over 200 years of it—with interactive maps, jumbo video screens, and re-created soundtracks of life in various time periods.

1 In the Park. Set at the edge of downtown St. Louis, along the winding contours of the mighty Mississippi, Gateway Arch National Park puts visitors at the epicenter of exploration with an explosive array of sensory experiences both inside and out. The Arch, its underground museum, and the surrounding riverside landscape make this an urban oasis for outdoor enthusiasts, history buffs, and anyone with a camera. Just a short stroll west across a beautifully landscaped pedestrian walkway from the Arch grounds, more history awaits at the Old Courthouse.

2 Elsewhere in Downtown St. Louis. Within and just beyond its 1-square-mile footprint, which begins with the reflection of the Gateway Arch on the banks of the Mighty Mississippi, downtown St. Louis has many architectural wonders and other attractions; an abundance of greenspace; and plenty of restaurants, nightspots, and hotels.

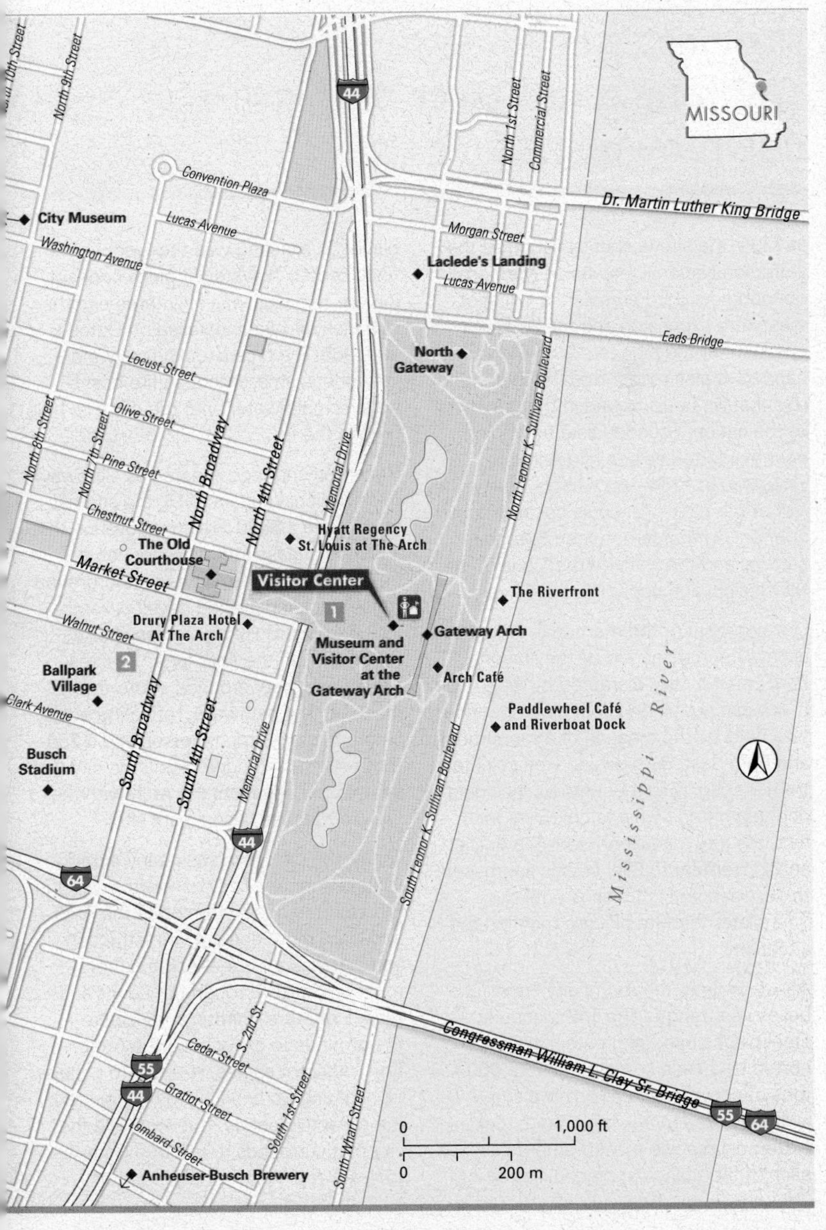
MISSOURI
North 10th Street
North 9th Street
Convention Plaza
City Museum
Lucas Avenue
Washington Avenue
North 1st Street
Commercial Street
Dr. Martin Luther King Bridge
Morgan Street
Laclede's Landing
Lucas Avenue
Eads Bridge
North Gateway
Locust Street
Olive Street
North 8th Street
North 7th Street
Pine Street
North Broadway
North 4th Street
Memorial Drive
North Leonor K. Sullivan Boulevard
Chestnut Street
Hyatt Regency St. Louis at The Arch
The Old Courthouse
Market Street
Visitor Center
The Riverfront
Drury Plaza Hotel At The Arch
Walnut Street
Museum and Visitor Center at the Gateway Arch
Gateway Arch
Arch Café
Ballpark Village
Clark Avenue
Paddlewheel Café and Riverboat Dock
Busch Stadium
South Broadway
South 4th Street
Memorial Drive
South Leonor K. Sullivan Boulevard
Mississippi River
Congressman William L. Clay Sr. Bridge
Cedar Street
S. 2nd St.
Gratiot Street
South 1st Street
Lombard Street
South Wharf Street
Anheuser-Busch Brewery
0
1,000 ft
0
200 m
44
64
55
1
2

Ironically, the nation's tallest man-made monument sits within the smallest national park. Eero Saarinen's 630-foot, stainless-steel Gateway Arch is the stunning centerpiece of this 91-acre downtown St. Louis site.

In 1935, the site was established as the Jefferson National Expansion Memorial, honoring our third president's vision of westward expansion and the adventurous spirit of the pioneers who made it happen. It also recognized the important role that St. Louis played in the growth of the nation. Founded as a fur-trading post by Pierre Laclede and Auguste Chouteau in 1764—on what is, today, the site of the park—St. Louis became a vital hub for commerce between European settlers and the Native Americans of the Mississippi and upper Missouri rivers.

Development of the memorial, which has always been managed by the National Park Service, was disrupted by World War II. It wasn't until 1947 that a competition was held for the creation of a monument and Eero Saarinen's design was selected from among 171 other entries, including one submitted by his father, Eliel. In fact, the jury mistakenly sent the finalist announcement to Eliel (it was addressed to "E. Saarinen"). It wasn't until two hours later that the officials rectified the situation.

Above ground, the Arch's airy curve belies its strength. The 142 triangular steel pieces used to create it are supported by a base comprised of 26,000 tons of concrete that is firmly planted in limestone bedrock. Engineers took extremely precise measurements as each of the triangular pieces was fit into place. So exacting was the work, that the final, center, "keystone" piece connecting the two legs was only three-eighths of a inch off when installed on October 28, 1965. The crowd looked skyward in hypnotic amazement as fire hoses sprayed cold water onto the piece to help finalize the fit.

Renamed and redesignated as Gateway Arch National Park in 2018, the site has undergone a $380 million renovation that included a glass-atrium visitor center entrance and a re-imagined underground museum. Landscaping developments included the museum's grassy berm roof between the Arch legs, 11 acres of stunning new grounds, more than 5 miles of new pathways, reflecting pools, a natural grass amphitheater, and a 250-foot pedestrian bridge facing the city that seamlessly connects the Arch with the Old Courthouse, also a park site.

Today, the park receives nearly 4 million visitors annually. They come from around the world to ride to the top of the Arch and learn more about its construction and America's pioneer spirit in the museum; stroll through the Lewis and Clark Explorers' Garden and explore the grounds to experience the Arch from different angles, see the 16 panels highlighting St. Louis history, or picnic by the reflective ponds. The Arch, like the city that surrounds it, is a true Gateway to the West.

AVERAGE HIGH/LOW TEMPERATURES					
JAN.	**FEB.**	**MAR.**	**APR.**	**MAY**	**JUNE**
40/23	45/27	56/38	67/48	77/58	86/67
JULY	**AUG.**	**SEPT.**	**OCT.**	**NOV.**	**DEC.**
90/71	88/69	81/61	70/50	57/39	44/29

Planning

When to Go

Typically, summers in St. Louis are hot and humid, with several days in July and August reaching the 100°F mark. Winters (December through February) are cold, with occasional snow. However, as various fronts move in, a 60°F day in January is not out of the ordinary. The best time to visit is between May and October, when the city has a full calendar of activities, including sporting events and festivals, and provides ample opportunities for families on a budget.

FESTIVALS AND EVENTS

Fair Saint Louis. The Arch grounds host one of the country's best Fourth of July weekend celebrations. The three-day party includes family-friendly activities, an air show, concerts by chart-topping entertainers, and spectacular fireworks over the Mississippi River each night. Best of all: everything is free.

Blues at the Arch. Bring a blanket or lawn chair and listen to the storied blues as performed by hometown artists at this free concert series, held at the park's grassy amphitheater every Friday in August.

Getting Here and Around

The park is set in the heart of St. Louis, a city that is itself set in the heart of the Midwest and has two of the world's greatest rivers (the Mississippi and the Missouri) flowing through it. Travel here from most places is easy and convenient—by plane, train, or automobile. In addition to a well-served airport and four interstates, St. Louis has Amtrak, MetroLink light rail, and MetroBus service. With good public transit and numerous bike- and pedestrian-friendly pathways, you don't need a car to explore the park and the surrounding downtown area. Note, though, that parking is readily available in high-rise garages, lots, and metered curbside spaces.

AIR

The region's main St. Louis Lambert International Airport (STL) is about 30 minutes northwest of the park on Interstate I–70. There is access to the MetroLink light rail system at each terminal. Airport Express shuttle vans provide transportation between the airport and downtown hotels.

CAR

Four major interstates (I–44, I–55, I–64, and I–70) make it easy to drive to St. Louis, which you can do in a day or less from numerous cities. Four interstate linkages (I–255, I–170, I–270, and I–370) facilitate driving throughout the city, and four bridges link downtown St. Louis with Illinois in the east.

Broadway and Jefferson avenues are the major north–south thoroughfares through downtown. Market Street and Washington Avenue run east–west. Leonor K. Sullivan Boulevard follows along the riverfront.

SHUTTLE

The city's excellent public transit system can get you right to the park. On the MetroLink train, you can exit at Laclede's Landing Station and walk south through the park to the museum's west entrance, which faces Fourth Street and the Old Courthouse. Alternatively, exit at the 8th and Pine Station and head east to the Old Courthouse. Signage and painted markings on the sidewalk will guide you. MetroBuses also stop near the park.

CONTACTS Metro St. Louis. ✉ *1 Metropolitan Sq., 211 N. Broadway, Suite 700, Downtown* ☎ *314/231–2345* 🌐 *www.metrostlouis.org.*

TRAIN

The St. Louis Gateway Transportation Center, a state-of-the-art facility right in downtown St. Louis, serves **Amtrak** (☎ *800/872–7245* 🌐 *www.amtrak.com*), MetroLink light rail, and intercity and local buses.

CONTACTS St. Louis Gateway Transportation Center. ✉ *430 S. 15th St., Downtown.*

Inspiration

Jim Merkel's fascinating *The Making of an Icon: The Dreamers, the Schemers, and the Hard Hats Who Built the Gateway Arch,* and *The Construction of the Gateway Arch,* a paperback pictorial essay from the Jefferson National Parks Association, are both good nonfiction reads. Two popular children's books are *To the Top: A Gateway Arch Story* by Amanda E. Doyle and *The Most Awesome Arch* by Joe Johans.

Park Essentials

ACCESSIBILITY

Other than the Tram Ride to the Top of the Arch, the main Gateway Arch complex and surrounding grounds are fully accessible. This includes the visitor center lobby, museum, theater, cafés, and store. Those with mobility, spatial, or even height issues can experience what's going on 630 feet above them via the Keystone replica—an exact, 17-foot-wide reproduction of the Arch's top piece with four monitors providing livestream views from on high.

Two ramps provide access between the Arch grounds and the boulevard, located along the riverfront. Accessible ramps are also located at the Broadway and 4th Street entrances to the Old Courthouse. Most of its first floor is wheelchair accessible; the upper floors are currently reachable only by stairs, though renovations are slated to bring an elevator to the second floor.

Sign-language interpretation for live programs is available with one-week advanced notice. Accessible metered parking is available (first-come, first-served) on most downtown streets.

PARK FEES AND PERMITS

Entrance to Gateway Arch National Park grounds, museum, and visitor center is free. There are fees for the Tram Ride to the Top, the 28-minute documentary, *Monument to the Dream* in the visitor center's Tucker Theater, and riverboat cruises (combo tickets are available). Although helicopter rides, which also cost extra, are considered part of the Arch experience, they are handled by an independent operator.

Tickets: You can buy tickets in person at the Gateway Arch Visitor Center or online (☎ *877/982–1410* 🌐 *www.gatewayarch.com/buy-tickets*). During the peak summer season, tickets frequently sell out, so advanced purchase is strongly recommended. ■ **TIP→ Tram rides that don't depart at the top of the hour often have more available space.** Also, be sure to arrive at least 30 minutes prior to your tram ride to allow time for going through airport-style security (shoes are not removed, though).

PARK HOURS

Gateway Arch National Park, Gateway Arch, and the Old Courthouse are open year-round. Longer summer hours begin on the Saturday before Memorial Day and continue through Labor Day weekend.

CELL PHONE RECEPTION

Free public Wi-Fi is available throughout Gateway Arch National Park, including at the top of the Arch. So, post and Tweet away.

Hotels

Although there aren't any hotels within the park, the Drury Plaza Hotel St. Louis at the Arch and the Hyatt Regency at the Arch are both directly across the street from the site and offer Arch discount packages. Just a short distance away is an assortment of chain and boutique hotels, one just steps from Busch Stadium. Some offer rooftop skyline, stadium, and Arch views; others are in renovated, architecturally significant buildings.

Restaurants

Both the Arch Café, in the lobby of the park's visitor center, and the riverfront Paddlewheel Café offer unique dishes, some them themed and many of them made with locally sourced ingredients. Mere blocks away, downtown options include both fine-dining and family-friendly restaurants, as well as fantastic food trucks and authentic ethnic eateries. Ballpark Village, Laclede's Landing, and Washington Avenue, all just blocks from the park, teem with restaurants and brewpubs.

Hotel and restaurant reviews have been shortened. For full information, visit Fodor's.com. Hotel prices are the lowest cost of a standard double room in high season. Restaurant prices are the average cost of a main course at dinner, or if dinner is not served, at lunch.

What It Costs

	$	$$	$$$	$$$$
RESTAURANTS	under $10	$10–$20	$21–$30	over $30
HOTELS	under $125	$125–$150	$151–$175	over $175

Tours

Gateway Arch Ranger Tours and Programs
GUIDED TOURS | FAMILY | Schedule a group tour of the museum and visitor center or join one of the free ranger-led tours that depart on the hour from the entrance lobby. There's also a variety of other free park service programs offered throughout the year, including ranger talks, guest lectures, and special themed events. ✉ *St. Louis* ☎ *314/655–1600* 🌐 *www.nps.gov/jeff.*

Gateway Helicopter Tours
AIR EXCURSIONS | FAMILY | Check out an aerial view of the Arch with this independent operator's helicopter rides offered daily (weather permitting) between 11 am and 5 pm from April through November. Four tours accommodate parties of two or three and range in duration from 2 to 3 minutes for the Riverfront Experience ($43 per person) to 18 to 20 minutes for the St. Louis Deluxe Experience ($169 per person). ✉ *50 N. Leonor K. Sullivan Blvd., Downtown* ☎ *314/496–4494* 🌐 *www.gatewayhelicoptertours.com.*

★ **Riverboats at the Gateway Arch**
BOAT TOURS | FAMILY | Between March and November, cruise along the Mighty Mississippi aboard one of two magnificent, replica, 19th-century riverboats: the *Tom Sawyer* or the *Becky Thatcher*. In addition to incredible views (especially from the top deck), you'll enjoy entertaining narrations and the swishing sound of the paddlewheel in the water. Though schedules vary, there are regular daily departures

for the one-hour Riverfront Cruises ($21), and you can grab a bite to eat or a drink at the dockside Paddlewheel Café before or after your trip. If it's Friday or Saturday, though, consider booking a two-hour Skyline Dinner Cruise ($51), which boards at 7 pm and includes a three-course meal (kids menus are available). ✉ *50 S. Leonor K. Sullivan Blvd., Downtown* ☎ *877/982–1410* 🌐 *www.gatewayarch.com/riverboats.*

Visitor Information

CONTACTS Gateway Arch National Park. ✉ *11 N. 4th St., #1810, Downtown* ☎ *314/655–1600* 🌐 *www.nps.gov/jeff.*

In the Park

Gateway Arch National Park includes not only its iconic namesake structure but also a 150,000-square-foot underground museum and visitor center with an airy glass atrium and a grassy berm roof (situated between the Arch legs), as well as 11 acres of stunning grounds laced by more than 5 miles of paths (all stroller and wheelchair-accessible). Kick off your shoes and picnic beside one of the reflecting pools, stroll through the Explorers' Garden, and enjoy an event at the natural grass amphitheater. Don't forget to visit the Old Courthouse, which is seamlessly connected to the Arch grounds and the river via a 250-foot grassy land bridge.

Sights

HISTORIC SIGHTS

★ The Gateway Arch

BUILDING | FAMILY | The Gateway Arch is a truly a sky-high experience. Not only is this marvel of design and engineering as tall (63 stories or 630 feet) as it is wide, but it's also 75 feet higher than the Washington Monument and twice the height of the Statue of Liberty. People come from around the world to enjoy the Arch from every angle—looking down from the top (where the sway can be up to 18 inches in 150 mph winds) or looking up from the bottom; from above in a helicopter or from below aboard a riverboat. Those uncomfortable with heights can skip the ride up and watch livestream video of topside views inside the Keystone replica. The Tram Ride to the Top experience includes an interactive, preboarding exhibit covering the decade in which the Arch was constructed. You then board one of eight, five-person tram capsules that travel at about 5 miles per hour. The ride takes four minutes up and three minutes down. Although the average visit takes 45 to 60 minutes, including transit time, you can stay in the observation deck to enjoy the views (both east and west) for as long as you like. Please note, though, that there are no amenities, including restrooms, at the top, so plan accordingly. Also, come prepared for incredible Instagram moments, and be sure to tag photos to the Arch's humorous and popular twitter account: @GatewayArchSTL. ✉ *Gateway Arch National Park, 11 N. 4th St., Downtown* ☎ *877/982–1410, 314/655–1600* 🌐 *www.gatewayarch.com.*

★ Museum and Visitor Center at the Gateway Arch

MUSEUM | FAMILY | The Arch's west entrance, facing Fourth Street and the Old Courthouse, is flooded with bright natural light. From this glass atrium, you can access the visitor center, the underground museum, the lobby for the Tram Ride to the Top, the Tucker Theater, the Arch Café, and the Arch Store. The museum showcases more than 200 years of history, from the founding of St. Louis by French fur traders Pierre Laclede and Auguste Chouteau in 1764 to the completion of the Arch in 1965. Huge digital maps, oversize murals, wall-size video screens, authentic soundscapes, interactive touch screens, and inclusive narratives bring all this history

The Arch towers over St. Louis, its artful, soaring curve mirrored in the Mississippi as it flows beside the park's eastern edge.

to life in six themed galleries: Jefferson's Vision, Colonial St. Louis, The Riverfront Era, Manifest Destiny, Building the Arch, and New Frontiers. In the Tucker Theater, watch in awe as the last piece of the Arch is lowered into position in the 28-minute documentary, *Monument to the Dream*, produced by Charles E. Guggenheim and nominated for an Academy Award in 1967. The tram lobby features not only a replica tram car but also an exact 17-foot-wide replica of the Arch's top piece, the Keystone, with livestream video from the observation deck 630 feet above. Be sure to exit the visitor center via the north or south doors, so you can look up for a jaw-dropping view of the Arch towering overhead. ✉ *Gateway Arch National Park, 11 N. 4th St., Downtown* ☎ *877/982–1410, 314/655–1600* 🌐 *www.gatewayarch.com.*

★ North Gateway

PROMENADE | **FAMILY** | Wide concrete pathways loop through and around this 7.5-acre section of the national park, where a natural grass amphitheater is the site of concerts and other events throughout the year, including August's Blues at the Arch Friday night music series. The north section is also home to the Explorers' Garden, which is planted with flora that Meriwether Lewis and William Clark encountered on their journey west and features paths scaled for children. Enjoy incredible views of the Arch, the city skyline, and Eads Bridge, which was completed in 1874, making it not only the world's first all-steel span but also the oldest bridge over the Mississippi River. ✉ *Gateway Arch National Park, 11 N. 4th St., Downtown* ☎ *314/655–1600* 🌐 *www.nps.gov/jeff.*

★ The Old Courthouse

HISTORIC SITE | **FAMILY** | Built in the early 1800s and part of the park service's National Underground Railroad Network to Freedom, the 192-foot-tall, green-domed Old Courthouse is a neoclassical masterpiece situated across a 250-foot grassy pedestrian bridge from the national park visitor center. A life-size sculpture of Dred and Harriett Scott outside the courthouse entrance serves as a poignant reminder of the determination it takes to change the course of history. Inside, it's humbling to stand in the exact spot where history did, indeed, change. The courtrooms here served as center stage for two landmark 19th-century cases: when two slaves, Dred and Harriet Scott (*Dred Scott v. Sanford*), sued for their freedom and when suffragist Virginia Minor fought for women's right to vote (*Minor v. Happersett*). The gorgeous, three-tiered rotunda is modeled after the dome in Rome's St. Peter's Basilica, and four murals painted by Carl Wimar highlight significant moments in St. Louis history. In addition to visiting two of the original courtrooms, you can participate in ranger-led tours; experience trial reenactments and other special events throughout the year; and see the 17-minute film, *Slavery on Trial: The Dred Scott Decision*, and the 10-minute film, *Lewis and Clark, Preparation for the Expedition*. Note that ongoing courthouse renovations have caused closures, so check ahead. Regardless, be sure to snap a photo of the courthouse framed by the Gateway Arch—a quintessential St. Louis shot. ✉ *Gateway Arch National Park, 11 N. 4th St., Downtown* ☎ *314/655–1600* 🌐 *www.nps.gov/jeff.*

TRAILS

★ The Riverfront

PROMENADE | From the base of Gateway Arch National Park's Grand Staircase enjoy strolls along Leonor K. Sullivan Boulevard, the 1.5-mile riverfront promenade that stretches from the landing for the riverboats at the south end to the Laclede's Landing historic site at the north end. The promenade hosts outdoor activities and events throughout the year and is the hub not only for the seasonal riverboat cruises but also Arch helicopter rides. A bike path along the riverfront promenade serves as the hub of the River Ring, a network of trails developed by **Great Rivers Greenway** (🌐 *greatriversgreenway.org*). To the north, the Mississippi Greenway provides a 12.5-mile trail, connecting downtown St. Louis to the Old Chain of Rocks Bridge, a historic Route 66 landmark. ✉ *S. Leonor K. Sullivan Blvd., Downtown* 🌐 *www.archpark.org.*

Restaurants

Arch Café

$$ | **AMERICAN** | **FAMILY** | Load up on the city's signature dishes—toasted ravioli, perhaps, or dry-rubbed barbecue ribs—made using locally sourced ingredients at this café in the national park's visitor center. Options also include Junior Meals for younger patrons and the Beast Burger for more adventurous eaters. **Known for:** farm-to-table fare; vegetarian and vegan choices; lunchbox options. Ⓢ *Average main: $10* ✉ *Gateway Arch National Park, 11 N. 4th St., Downtown* ☎ *314/300–8710* 🌐 *www.cafearch.com.*

Paddlewheel Café

$ | **AMERICAN** | **FAMILY** | For an intimate riverfront feel, stop by the city's only waterfront dining destination, located at the paddlewheeler dock on the levee near the national park. Try the smashed double burger, Nashville hot chicken sandwich, or fingerling catfish. **Known for:** craft brews and cocktails; Mississippi River views; lunchbox options. Ⓢ *Average main: $7* ✉ *Riverboats at the Gateway Arch, 50 S. Leonor K. Sullivan Blvd., Downtown* ☎ *877/982–1410* 🌐 *www.gatewayarch.com* ⏲ *Closed Nov.–Mar.*

Elsewhere in Downtown St. Louis

Downtown is very walkable, with wide sidewalks and an easy-to-follow grid of numbered, east–west streets. It also has eight MetroLink stations located near key attractions. A mile-long greenspace starts at the Gateway Arch National park and heads west along Market Street to

Union Station, home to, among other things, a 200-foot-high observation wheel and a 250,000-gallon aquarium. Nestled along side streets are numerous other attractions including Busch Stadium, restaurants, and hotels.

Sights

Anheuser-Busch Brewery
WINERY/DISTILLERY | Built in 1852, the 142-acre Anheuser-Busch site consists of nearly 150 structures, many of them brick and done in an elaborate, Germanic Romanesque–style. The Clydesdale Stables, the six-story, stone Brewhouse, and the Administration Building (the former Lyon's Schoolhouse) are all on the National Register of Historic Places. Take a tour, sample Anheuser-Busch beers, and snap photos of the world-famous Budweiser Clydesdales. ✉ *12th and Lynch Sts., Soulard* ☎ *314/577–2626* 🌐 *www.budweisertours.com* 🎫 *Free.*

★ **Ballpark Village**
LOCAL INTEREST | **FAMILY** | Adjacent to Busch Stadium and just one block south of the Old Courthouse, this dining-and-entertainment district is very much a hot spot when Cardinals fans converge on downtown before and after games. But it's also a great place to hang out, grab a bite, and watch sports at other times, too. There's plenty of parking nearby. ✉ *601 Clark Ave., Downtown* ☎ *314/797–7530* 🌐 *www.stlballparkvillage.com.*

★ **Busch Stadium**
SPORTS VENUE | **FAMILY** | Two blocks south of the Old Courthouse, this 46,000-seat, retro-style stadium is home to the city's beloved Major League Baseball team. The St. Louis Cardinals have won 11 World Series Championships and 19 National League pennants, so remember to wear your red! Stadium tours, which begin at Gate 3 on Eighth Street, are offered year-round and include views from the Radio Broadcast Booth, Cardinals Club, and Redbird Club. See the World Series trophies in the Champions Club, and get a player's perspective from the Cardinals Dugout. ✉ *700 Clark Ave., Downtown* ☎ *314/345–9600, 314/345–9000 for tours* 🌐 *www.mlb.com/cardinals/ballpark.*

★ **City Museum**
MUSEUM | **FAMILY** | Expect the unexpected at this insanely fun, award-winning museum that's truly a playhouse for adults and kids alike. It's housed in a 100-year-old, 600,000-square-foot warehouse (the former International Shoe Building) that incorporates repurposed architectural and industrial objects to create features like metal walkways (miles of them), slides, caves, tunnels, and secret passages. There's also a rooftop school bus and a Ferris wheel. Oh, and a circus and a train. ✉ *750 N. 16th St., Downtown* ☎ *314/231–2489* 🌐 *www.citymuseum.org* 🎫 *$12* 🕓 *Closed Mon. and Tues.*

Laclede's Landing
HISTORIC SITE | **FAMILY** | Just one block from Gateway National Park's north entrance, this nine-block district is complete with cobblestone streets, 17 historic buildings, seven restaurants, and one great view of the river. Arch parking is available here, and the MetroLink light rail stops at this location, too. ✉ *Bordered by I–70, Martin Luther King Bridge, and the historic Eads Bridge, 710 N. 2nd St., Downtown* ☎ *314/241–5875* 🌐 *www.lacledeslanding.com.*

Restaurants

Bailey's Range
$$ | **AMERICAN** | **FAMILY** | Belly up to the long, high-top, community table for a burger made using 100% grass-fed, American-range beef served on a house-made bun and accompanied by house-made ketchups. Wash it down with a lemonade (or something a bit stronger). **Known for:** lots of local beers on tap; boozy shakes; vegan ice cream. 💲 *Average main: $10* ✉ *920 Olive St., Downtown* ☎ *314/241–8121* 🌐 *www.baileysrange.com.*

Broadway Oyster Bar

$$ | **CAJUN** | **FAMILY** | Just three blocks south of the Old Courthouse, be transported to the heart of Bourbon Street upon walking through the door of this restaurant, where every inch of space is decorated with twinkling lights, humorous signs, Mardi Gras beads—you name it. If the aromas of jambalaya and étouffée don't grab you, then the music will: for more than 30 years, patrons have grooved daily to local and national bands performing jazz, blues, roots, bluegrass, reggae, or rock. **Known for:** Gulf oysters; Cajun and Creole dishes; zesty cocktails. *Average main: $16 736 S. Broadway, Downtown 314/621–8811 www.broadwayoysterbar.com.*

Coffee and Quick Bites

Crown Candy Kitchen

$ | **AMERICAN** | In business since 1913, Crown Candy Kitchen is a bit of a time capsule thanks to its Coca-Cola collectibles, vintage jukebox, and classic soda fountain. Enjoy house-made chocolates and other sweets; thickly stacked sandwiches, jumbo franks, or chili; and butterscotch malteds, chocolate phosphates, or deluxe sundaes. **Known for:** family operated for four generations; 1930s feel; classic local eatery. *Average main: $8 1401 St. Louis Ave., Downtown 314/621–9650 www.crowncandykitchen.net Closed Sun.*

Hotels

Drury Plaza Hotel at the Arch

$$ | **HOTEL** | **FAMILY** | Three buildings on the National Register of Historic Places were carefully renovated and transformed into this hotel just across the street from Gateway Arch National Park. **Pros:** family and pet friendly; stunning design details; Arch-visit packages. **Cons:** underground hotel parking challenging for large vehicles; crowded during peak season; some rooms have interior windows facing hallways. *Rooms from: $130 2 S. 4th St., Downtown 314/231–3003 www.druryhotels.com 353 rooms Free breakfast.*

Hilton St. Louis at the Ballpark

$$$ | **HOTEL** | **FAMILY** | Located one block from Ballpark Village and two blocks from Busch Stadium, the Hilton features rooms with incredible views of the Gateway Arch, Old Courthouse, and the ballpark; an indoor pool; a fitness center; and the award-winning 360 rooftop bar with fire pits and still more city panoramas. **Pros:** great for families; close to many attractions; rooftop bar with a 360-degree skyline view. **Cons:** crowded during Cardinal games; no on-site parking; needs updating. *Rooms from: $164 1 S. Broadway, Downtown 314/421–1776 www.hilton.com 675 rooms No meals.*

Hyatt Regency St. Louis at the Arch

$ | **HOTEL** | **FAMILY** | Directly across the street from Gateway Arch National Park and within two blocks of Busch Stadium and Ballpark Village, the Hyatt has spectacular views of not only the Arch and the Mississippi River but also of the St. Louis skyline. **Pros:** luxury at a great price; good for families; Arch-visit packages. **Cons:** no on-site self-parking; valet only; needs updates; bedding is less than sumptuous. *Rooms from: $104 315 Chestnut St., Downtown 314/655–1234 www.hyatt.com 910 rooms No meals.*

Chapter 24

GLACIER AND WATERTON LAKES NATIONAL PARKS

Updated by
Debbie Olsen

Camping ★★★★★ | Hotels ★★★☆☆ | Activities ★★★★★ | Scenery ★★★★☆ | Crowds ★★☆☆☆

WELCOME TO GLACIER AND WATERTON LAKES NATIONAL PARKS

TOP REASONS TO GO

★ **Witness the Divide:** The rugged mountains that weave their way through Glacier and Waterton along the Continental Divide seem to have glaciers in every hollow melting into tiny streams, raging rivers, and icy-cold mountain lakes.

★ **Just hike it:** Hundreds of miles of trails of all levels of difficulty lace the park, from flat and easy half-hour strolls to steep, strenuous all-day hikes.

★ **Go to the sun:** Crossing the Continental Divide at the 6,646-foot-high Logan Pass, Glacier's Going-to-the-Sun Road is a spectacular drive.

★ **View the wildlife:** This is one of the few places in North America where all native carnivores, including grizzlies, black bears, coyotes, and wolves, still survive.

★ **See glaciers while you still can:** Approximately 150 glaciers were present in Glacier National Park in 1850; by 2010, there were only 25 left.

1 **Western Glacier National Park.** Known to the Kootenai people as "sacred dancing lake," Lake McDonald is the largest glacial water basin lake in Glacier National Park and a highlight of its western reaches.

2 **Along the Going-to-the-Sun Road.** At 6,646 feet, Logan Pass is the highest point on, and very much a highlight of, Glacier National Park's famous (and famously beautiful) Going-to-the-Sun Road. From mid-June to mid-October, a 1½-mile boardwalk leads to an overlook that crosses an area filled with lush meadows and wildflowers.

3 **Eastern Glacier National Park.** St. Mary Lake and Many Glacier are the major highlights of the eastern side of Glacier National Park. Grinnell Glacier, the most accessible glacier in the park, is reached via a hike that begins near Swiftcurrent Lake in the Many Glacier region.

4 **Waterton Lakes National Park.** The Canadian national park is the meeting of two worlds: the flatlands of the prairie and the abrupt upthrust of the mountains. The park is also home to a vast array of wildlife, spectacular scenery, and wonderful hiking trails.

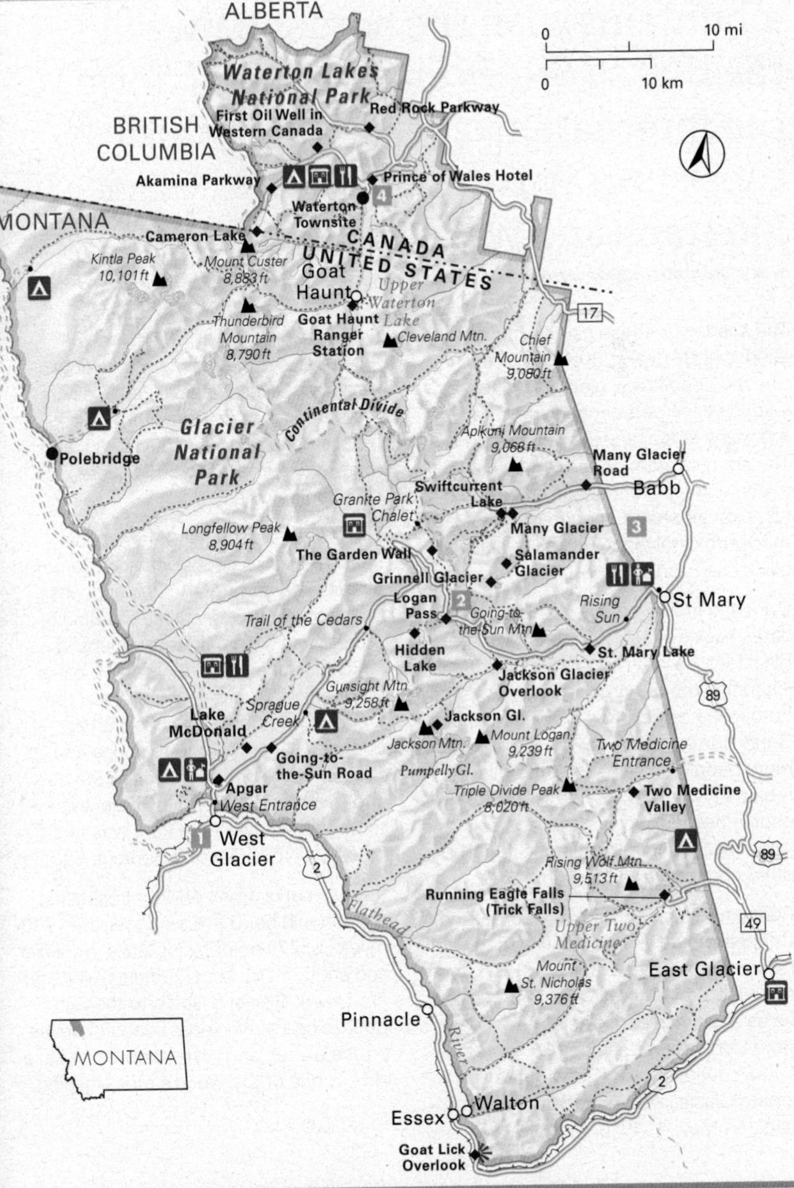
ALBERTA
BRITISH COLUMBIA
MONTANA
Waterton Lakes National Park
First Oil Well in Western Canada
Red Rock Parkway
Akamina Parkway
Prince of Wales Hotel
Waterton Townsite
Cameron Lake
CANADA
UNITED STATES
Kintla Peak 10,101 ft
Mount Custer 8,883 ft
Goat Haunt
Upper Waterton Lake
Thunderbird Mountain 8,790 ft
Goat Haunt Ranger Station
Cleveland Mtn.
Chief Mountain 9,080 ft
Continental Divide
Glacier National Park
Polebridge
Apikuni Mountain 9,068 ft
Many Glacier Road
Babb
Swiftcurrent Lake
Granite Park Chalet
Many Glacier
Longfellow Peak 8,904 ft
The Garden Wall
Salamander Glacier
Grinnell Glacier
Logan Pass
Rising Sun
St Mary
Going-to-the-Sun Mtn.
Trail of the Cedars
Hidden Lake
St. Mary Lake
Jackson Glacier Overlook
Gunsight Mtn. 9,258 ft
Sprague Creek
Lake McDonald
Jackson Gl.
Jackson Mtn.
Mount Logan 9,239 ft
Two Medicine Entrance
Going-to-the-Sun Road
Pumpelly Gl.
Apgar
West Entrance
Triple Divide Peak 8,020 ft
Two Medicine Valley
West Glacier
Rising Wolf Mtn. 9,513 ft
Running Eagle Falls (Trick Falls)
Flathead
Upper Two Medicine
Mount St. Nicholas 9,376 ft
East Glacier
Pinnacle
River
MONTANA
Walton
Essex
Goat Lick Overlook
0 10 mi
0 10 km
1
2
3
4
17
89
2
49

The astonishing landscapes at the crown of the continent know no boundaries. Here, the rugged, glacier-carved mountains span the border between the United States and Canada to form the International Peace Park, which consists of two national parks: Glacier in Montana and Waterton Lakes in Alberta.

The scenery in these parks is unparalleled: craggy peaks, thick coniferous forests, deep lakes, gleaming glaciers, wildflower-carpeted meadows, and too many stunning waterfalls to count. The animals roaming the terrain include everything from ungulates such as deer, elk, bighorn sheep, mountain goats, and moose to carnivores like mountain lions, black bears, and grizzlies.

Evidence of human use in this area dates back over 10,000 years, with the Blackfeet, Salish, and Kootenai peoples inhabiting the region long before the first Europeans came. The completion of the Great Northern Railway in 1891 allowed more people to visit and settle this region of Montana. By the late 1800s, people began to realize the land had value far beyond mining, agricultural, or other commercial endeavors.

Renowned conservationist George Bird Grinnell and other influential leaders lobbied for nearly a decade to have the so-called Crown of the Continent protected as a national park. Their efforts were rewarded when President Taft set aside 1,583 square miles (4,100 square km) to create Glacier, America's 10th national park, on May 11, 1910.

On May 30, 1895, a 140-square-km (54-square-mile) area of what is now Waterton Lakes National Park was first protected as a Dominion Forest Park. It became a national park in 1930, and today it encompasses 505 square km (195 square miles).

The idea of creating an International Peace Park was conceived and promoted by the Cardston Rotary Club and was unanimously endorsed in a meeting of Alberta and Montana Rotary clubs in 1931. On June 18, 1932, the two parks were officially united, establishing the world's first International Peace Park—an enduring symbol of the harmony and friendship between the United States and Canada. In 1995, the Glacier-Waterton International Peace Park was designated a UNESCO World Heritage Site.

If these parks aren't on your bucket list, they should be. There are more than 700 miles (1,127 km) of hiking trails in Glacier and another 200 km (120 miles) in Waterton Lakes. Glacier's Going-to-the-Sun Road is one of the most beautiful drives on the planet, and Waterton's Crypt Lake Hike is one of the world's most thrilling.

GLACIER AVERAGE HIGH/LOW TEMPERATURES IN FAHRENHEIT					
JAN.	**FEB.**	**MAR.**	**APR.**	**MAY**	**JUNE**
28/15	35/19	42/23	53/30	64/37	71/44
JULY	**AUG.**	**SEPT.**	**OCT.**	**NOV.**	**DEC.**
79/47	78/46	67/39	53/32	37/25	30/18

WATERTON AVERAGE HIGH/LOW TEMPERATURES IN CELSIUS					
JAN.	**FEB.**	**MAR.**	**APR.**	**MAY**	**JUNE**
0/-11	1/-10	6/-6	10/-2	15/3	19/6
JULY	**AUG.**	**SEPT.**	**OCT.**	**NOV.**	**DEC.**
23/8	22/7	17/3	12/1	3/-6	1/-9

Planning

When to Go

Of the 2 million annual visitors to Glacier and 400,000 to Waterton, most come between July and mid-September, when the streams are flowing, wildlife is roaming, and naturalist programs are fully underway. Snow removal on the alpine portion of Going-to-the-Sun Road is usually completed by mid-June; the opening of Logan Pass at the road's summit marks the summer opening of Glacier. Canada's Victoria Day in late May marks the beginning of the season in Waterton. Spring and fall are quieter.

Getting Here and Around

AIR

The nearest airports to Glacier are in Kalispell (25 miles) and Great Falls (157 miles), both in Montana. The nearest airport to Waterton Lakes is in Calgary (271 km [168 miles]).

CONTACTS Glacier Park International Airport. ✉ *4170 Hwy. 2 E, Kalispell* ☎ *406/257–5994* 🌐 *iflyglacier.com.*

BUS

Glacier National Park operates a free hop-on, hop-off shuttle along the Going-to-the-Sun Road from July through early September. The shuttle runs from Apgar to St. Mary Visitor Center; park visitor centers have departure information.

CAR

On the western side of Glacier National Park, U.S. 2 goes to West Glacier. At the park's northwestern edge, North Fork Road connects to Polebridge. On the park's east side, U.S. 2 goes to East Glacier and Highway 49 reaches to Two Medicine. U.S. 89 accesses St. Mary, and U.S. Route 3 connects to Many Glacier. Take the Chief Mountain Highway (Highway 17) to access Waterton Lakes in summer or U.S. 89 to Alberta Highway 2 through Cardston and then west via Highway 5 any time of the year.

In both parks, repeated freezing and thawing can cause roads—either gravel or paved—to deteriorate, so drive slowly. In summer, road reconstruction is part of the park experience as crews take advantage of the few warm months to complete projects. At any time of the year, anticipate that rocks and wildlife may be just around the bend. Gasoline is available along most paved roads, and scenic pull-outs are frequent. Most development and services center on Lake McDonald in the west and St. Mary Lake in the east.

BORDER CROSSINGS

A passport is required of everyone crossing the Canadian–U.S. border. When you arrive at the border crossing, customs officers will ask for information such as where you are going and where you are from. You and your vehicle are subject to random search. Firearms are prohibited, except hunting rifles, which require permission (obtained in advance). Soil, seeds, meat, and many fruits are also prohibited. Kids traveling with only one parent need a notarized letter from the other parent giving permission to enter Canada or the United States. If you are traveling with pets, you need proof of up-to-date immunizations to cross in either direction. Citizens from most countries (Canada, Mexico, and Bermuda are exceptions) entering the United States from Canada must pay $6 (cash only) at the border for a required I–94 or I–94W Arrival-Departure Record form, to be returned to border officials when leaving the United States. Contact United States Customs (☎ *406/335–2611* 🌐 *www.cbp.gov*) or the Canada Border Services Agency (☎ *403/344–3767* 🌐 *www.cbsa-asfc.gc.ca*) for more information.

TRAIN

Montana's Amtrak stations are all on the *Empire Builder* route that connects Glacier National Park with Chicago and Portland/Seattle. The main stops near the park are at East Glacier Park Village, West Glacier, Essex, and Whitefish. From the stations, you can rent a car.

Inspiration

Fools Crow, by James Welch and first published in 1986, is a fictional but fascinating look at what life was like for Native Americans living in this region of Montana before Glacier became a national park.

The Melting World: A Journey Across America's Vanishing Glaciers, is by Christopher White, who traveled to Montana to chronicle the work of Dan Fagre, a climate scientist and ecologist, who has spent years monitoring ice sheets in Glacier National Park.

Park Essentials

ACCESSIBILITY

All visitor centers are wheelchair accessible, and most of the campgrounds and picnic areas are paved, with extended-length picnic tables and accessible restrooms. Three of Glacier's nature trails are wheelchair accessible: the Trail of the Cedars, Running Eagle Falls, and the Oberlin Bend Trail, just west of Logan Pass. In Waterton, the Linnet Lake Trail, Waterton Townsite Trail, Cameron Lake day-use area, and the International Peace Park Pavilion are wheelchair accessible.

PARK FEES AND PERMITS

Entrance fees for Glacier are $35 per vehicle in summer and $25 per vehicle in winter. The fee for motorcycles is $30 in peak season and $15 November 1–April 30. Entrance fees are good for seven days, or you can buy a Glacier National Park annual pass for $70. A day pass to Waterton Lakes is C$7.90 for an individual or C$16 per seven people per vehicle. *Passes to Glacier and Waterton must be purchased separately.*

At Glacier, the required backcountry permit is $7 per person per day from the Apgar Backcountry Permit Center after mid-April for the upcoming summer. Reservations cost $40. Waterton requires backcountry camping permits, with reservations available up to 90 days ahead at the visitor reception center. The fee is C$10.02 per person per night. A nonrefundable reservation fee of $11.96 is also charged.

PARK HOURS

The parks are open year-round, but many roads and facilities close from October through May. The parks are in the Mountain time zone.

CELL PHONE RECEPTION

Cell coverage is improving, but, in mountainous terrain, poor reception is common. Service is best in West Glacier or St. Mary in Glacier National Park and in the Waterton Townsite in Waterton Lakes National Park.

Hotels

Lodgings in the parks tend to be rustic and simple, though there are a few grand lodges. Some modern accommodations have pools, hot tubs, boat rentals, guided excursions, and fine dining.

Restaurants

Steak houses serving certified Angus beef are typical of the region; in recent years, resort communities have diversified their menus to include bison, venison, elk, moose, trout, and gluten-free and vegetarian options. Casual attire is the norm.

Hotel and restaurant reviews have been shortened. For full information visit Fodors.com. Hotel prices are the lowest cost of a standard double room in high season. Restaurant prices are the average cost of a main course at dinner, or if dinner is not served, at lunch.

What It Costs in U.S. Dollars

$	$$	$$$	$$$$
RESTAURANTS			
under $13	$13–$20	$21–$30	over $30
HOTELS			
under $100	$100–$150	$151–$200	over $200

What It Costs in Canadian Dollars

$	$$	$$$	$$$$
RESTAURANTS			
under C$15	C$15–C$20	C$21–C$25	over C$25
HOTELS			
under C$150	C$150–C$200	C$201–C$250	over C$250

Tours

Dark Sky Guides

GUIDED TOURS | A Night Sky Discovery Tour is the most popular offering from this tour company. Hike to a viewing spot, and learn about the legends associated wth constellations from a knowledgeable guide. See stars close up with powerful telescopes. The company also conducts twilight wildlife walks and starry skies strolls. ✉ *Box 56, Waterton Lakes National Park* 🌐 *darkskyguides.ca* 🎫 *From C$20 per person.*

Red Bus Tours

BUS TOURS | Glacier National Park Lodges operates driver-narrated bus tours that cover most areas of the park that are accessible by road. The tour of Going-to-the-Sun Road, a favorite, is conducted in vintage, 1936, red buses with roll-back tops—photo opportunities are plentiful. In addition to tours, which last from a few hours to a full day, hiker shuttles and transfers from the West Glacier train station to Lake McDonald Lodge or the Village Inn are available. You can catch your tour from the doorstep of Glacier Park Lodge or a few steps from Apgar Village Lodge, West Glacier Village, Motel Lake McDonald, and St. Mary Village. Reservations are essential. ☎ *855/733–4522, 303/265–7010* 🌐 *www.glaciernationalparklodges.com/red-bus-tours* 🎫 *Tours from $55; shuttles from $6.*

Sun Tours

BUS TOURS | Tour the park in an air-conditioned coach, and learn from Native American guides who concentrate on how Glacier's features are relevant to the Blackfeet Nation, past and present. These tours depart from East Glacier and the St. Mary Visitor Center. *29 Glacier Ave., East Glacier Park* *406/732–9220, 800/786–9220* *www.glaciersuntours.com* *From $50.*

Visitor Information

PARK CONTACT INFORMATION Glacier Country Montana. *140 N. Higgens Ave., Suite 204, Missoula* *800/338–5072* *www.glaciermt.com.* **Glacier National Park.** *406/888–7800* *www.nps.gov/glac.* **Waterton Lakes Chamber of Commerce.** *www.mywaterton.ca.* **Waterton Lakes National Park.** *403/859–5133, 403/859–2224 year-round* *www.pc.gc.ca/waterton.*

Glacier National Park

The massive peaks of the Continental Divide in northwest Montana are the backbone of Glacier National Park and its sister park in Canada, Waterton Lakes, which together make up the International Peace Park. From their slopes, melting snow and alpine glaciers yield the headwaters of rivers that flow west to the Pacific Ocean, north to the Arctic Ocean, and southeast to the Atlantic Ocean via the Gulf of Mexico. Coniferous forests, thickly vegetated stream bottoms, and green-carpeted meadows provide homes and sustenance for all kinds of wildlife.

Western Glacier National Park

35 miles northeast from Kalispell to the Apgar Visitor Center via U.S. Route 2.

The western side of the park is closest to the airport in the city of Kalispell and has the most amenities. Highlights include the bustling village of West Glacier, Apgar Village, Lake McDonald, and the tiny community of Polebridge. West Glacier Village is just over 2 miles from the Apgar Visitor Center.

Sights

HISTORIC SIGHTS

Apgar

TOWN | **FAMILY** | On the southwest end of Lake McDonald, this tiny village has a few stores, an ice-cream shop, motels, ranger buildings, a campground, and a historic schoolhouse. A store called the Montana House is open year-round, but except for the weekend-only visitor center, no other services remain open from November to mid-May. Across the street from the visitor center, **Apgar Discovery Cabin** is filled with animal posters, kids' activities, and maps. *2 miles north of west entrance, Glacier National Park* *406/888–7939.*

SCENIC DRIVES

Apgar Village to Polebridge (Camas Road and North Fork Road)

SCENIC DRIVE | The 25-mile journey to the tiny community of Polebridge involves travel along a gravel road that has a few potholes, but the scenery along the north fork of the Flathead River makes up for the bumpy ride. Be on the lookout for wildlife, and be sure to stop for a snack at the Polebridge Mercantile and Bakery.

West Glacier Village to East Glacier Park Village (US-2 E)

SCENIC DRIVE | A paved, 57-mile, two-lane highway follows the middle fork of the Flathead River and connects West Glacier with East Glacier. Enjoy lovely mountain views, stop at Goat Lick to look for mountain goats, or consider having lunch at the Izaak Walton Inn in Essex.

SCENIC STOPS

Goat Lick Overlook

VIEWPOINT | Mountain goats frequent this natural salt lick on a cliff above the middle fork of the Flathead River. Watch the wildlife from an observation stand. ✉ *U.S. 2, 29 miles southeast of West Glacier Village, Glacier National Park.*

Lake McDonald

BODY OF WATER | This beautiful, 10-mile-long lake, the parks' largest, is accessible year-round from Going-to-the-Sun Road. Cruise to the middle for a view of the surrounding glacier-clad mountains. You can fish and horseback ride at either end, and in winter, snowshoe and cross-country ski. ✉ *2 miles north of west entrance, Glacier National Park.*

Polebridge

TOWN | On the banks of the North Fork of the Flathead River on Glacier National Park's western edge, this tiny community (population 25) has just one store, one restaurant and saloon, one camp store, and one hostel, yet it is a gem in the wilderness. You can see where a massive wildfire burned up to some of the buildings in 1988 and how quickly new growth has advanced. The entrance station, staffed in summer only, is the gateway to Bowman and Kintla lakes, as well as Logging and Quartz lakes, which are in the backcountry and accessible only by hiking trails. The bakery at the Polebridge Mercantile store is amazing, with huckleberry macaroons or bear claws and hot, gooey cinnamon buns. ✉ *Polebridge.*

TRAILS

Rocky Point Nature Trail

TRAIL | Enjoy fantastic mountain and lake views on this family-friendly, 1.9-mile trail along the western shore of Lake McDonald. *Easy.* ✥ *Trailhead: near Fish Creek Campground.*

VISITOR CENTERS

Apgar Visitor Center

INFO CENTER | **FAMILY** | This is a great first stop if you're entering the park from the west. Here you can get all kinds of information, including maps, permits, books, and the *Junior Ranger* newspaper, and you can check out displays that will help you plan your tour of the park. There is a variety of ranger-led programs including free snowshoe walks in winter. Snowshoes can be rented for $2 at the visitor center. ✉ *2 miles north of West Glacier in Apgar Village, Glacier National Park* ☎ *406/888–7800.*

Travel Alberta West Glacier Information Center

INFO CENTER | Plan your visit to the Canadian side of the International Peace Park with the help of travel experts at this visitor center in West Glacier. You'll find maps, pamphlets, displays, and bathroom facilities here. ✉ *125 Going-to-the-Sun Rd., West Glacier* ☎ *406/888–5743* ⏲ *Mid-Sept.–mid-May.*

Restaurants

Lake McDonald Lodge Restaurants

$$$ | **AMERICAN** | In Russell's Fireside Dining Room, take in a great view of the lake while enjoying standards such as pasta, steak, wild game, and salmon; delicious salads; or local favorites like the huckleberry elk burger or the Montana rainbow trout. Many ingredients are locally sourced, and there is a nice selection of cocktails, wine, and craft beer. **Known for:** incredible views of Lake McDonald; hearty regional fare at main restaurant, pizza and burgers at smaller eateries; breakfast and (on request) box lunches in main restaurant. Ⓢ *Average main: $22* ✉ *Glacier National Park* ✣ *Going-to-the-Sun Rd., 10 miles north of Apgar* ☎ *406/888–5431, 406/892–2525* 🌐 *www.glaciernationalparklodges.com/dining/lake-mcdonald-lodge* ⏲ *Closed early Oct.–early June.*

Hotels

★ Lake McDonald Lodge

$$$ | HOTEL | On the shores of Lake McDonald, near Apgar and West Glacier, this historic lodge—where public spaces feature massive timbers, stone fireplaces, and animal trophies—is an ideal base for exploring the park's western side. **Pros:** lakeside setting; historic property; close to Apgar, West Glacier, and Going-to-the-Sun Road. **Cons:** rustic; no TV (except in suites) and limited Wi-Fi; small bathrooms. Ⓢ *Rooms from: $200* ✉ *Going-to-the-Sun Rd., Glacier National Park* ☎ *855/733–4522, 406/888–5431* 🌐 *www.glaciernationalparklodges.com* *80 units* *No meals.*

Village Inn

$$$ | HOTEL | Listen to waves gently lap the shores of beautiful Lake McDonald at this motel, which is on the National Register of Historic Places and was fully renovated in recent years, so all its rooms have Wi-Fi, new beds, and furnishings that fit with the historic style. **Pros:** great views; convenient Apgar village location; kitchenettes in some rooms. **Cons:** rustic motel; no a/c; no in-room phones. Ⓢ *Rooms from: $165* ✉ *Apgar Village, Glacier National Park* ☎ *855/733–4522* 🌐 *www.glaciernationalparklodges.com* ⏲ *Closed Oct. 2–late May* *36 rooms* *No meals.*

Along the Going-to-the-Sun Road

50 miles between Glacier National Park's western and eastern reaches.

The Going-to-the-Sun Road, one of the nation's most beautiful drives, connects Lake McDonald on the western side of Glacier with St. Mary Lake on the east. Turnoffs provide views of the high country and glacier-carved valleys. Consider making the ride in one of the vintage red buses operated by Glacier National Park Lodges (☎ *844/868–7474*). Drivers double as guides, and they can roll back the tops of the vehicles for better views. Logan Pass, elevation 6,646 feet (2,026 meters), sits at the Continental Divide, the highest point on the Going-to-the-Sun Road.

Sights

SCENIC STOPS

The Garden Wall

NATURE SITE | An abrupt and jagged wall of rock juts above the road and is visible for about 10 miles as it follows Logan Creek from just past Avalanche Creek Campground to Logan Pass. ✉ *Going-to-the-Sun Rd., 24–34 miles northeast of West Glacier, Glacier National Park.*

Jackson Glacier Overlook

VIEWPOINT | On the eastern side of the Continental Divide, you come into view of Jackson Glacier looming in a rocky pass across the upper St. Mary River valley. If it isn't covered with snow, you'll see sharp peaks of ice. The glacier is shrinking and may disappear in another 100 years. ✉ *5 miles east of Logan Pass, Glacier National Park.*

The 50-mile Going-to-the-Sun Road takes about two hours to drive, depending on how often you stop.

Logan Pass

SCENIC DRIVE | At 6,646 feet, this is the park's highest point accessible by motor vehicle. Crowded in July and August, it offers unparalleled views of both sides of the Continental Divide. Mountain goats, bighorn sheep, and grizzly bears frequent the area. The Logan Pass Visitor Center is just east of the pass. ✉ *34 miles east of West Glacier, 18 miles west of St. Mary, Glacier National Park.*

TRAILS

Avalanche Lake Trail

TRAIL | From Avalanche Creek Campground, take this 3-mile trail leading to mountain-ringed Avalanche Lake. The walk is only moderately difficult (it ascends 730 feet), making this one of the park's most accessible backcountry lakes. Crowds fill the parking area and trail during July and August and on sunny weekends in May and June. *Moderate.* ✉ *Glacier National Park* ✣ *Trailhead: across from Avalanche Creek Campground, 15 miles north of Apgar on Going-to-the-Sun Rd.*

Baring Falls

TRAIL | **FAMILY** | For a nice family hike, try the 1.3-mile path from the Sun Point parking area. It leads to a spruce and Douglas fir woods; cross a log bridge over Baring Creek and you arrive at the base of gushing Baring Falls. *Easy.* ✉ *Glacier National Park* ✣ *Trailhead 11 miles east of Logan Pass on Going-to-the-Sun Rd., at Sun Point parking area.*

Hidden Lake Nature Trail

TRAIL | Hidden Lake Overlook is an easy, 1½-mile hike from the Logan Pass Visitor Center. Along the way, you'll pass through beautiful alpine meadows known as the Hanging Gardens. Enjoy incredible views of Hidden Lake, Bearhat Mountain, Mt. Cannon, Fusillade Mountain, Gunsight Mountain, and Sperry Glacier. It's common to see mountain goats near the overlook. If you want a challenge, continue hiking all the way down to the edge of the lake—a moderate 5.4-mile round-trip hike. *Easy to moderate.* ✉ *Glacier National Park* ✣ *Trailhead: behind Logan Pass Visitor Center.*

★ **Highline Trail**

TRAIL | From the Logan Pass parking lot, hike north along the Garden Wall and just below the craggy Continental Divide. Wildflowers dominate the 7.6 miles to Granite Park Chalet, a National Historic Landmark, where hikers with reservations can overnight. Return to Logan Pass along the same trail or hike down 4½ miles (a 2,500-foot descent) on the Loop Trail. *Moderate.* ✉ *Glacier National Park* ✣ *Trailhead: at Logan Pass Visitor Center.*

Trail of the Cedars

TRAIL | **FAMILY** | This ½-mile boardwalk loop through an ancient cedar and hemlock forest is a favorite of families with small children and people with disabilities (it's wheelchair accessible). Interpretive signs describe the habitat and natural history. *Easy.* ✉ *Glacier National Park* ✣ *Trailhead: across from Avalanche Creek Campground, 15 miles north of Apgar on Going-to-the-Sun Rd.*

VISITOR CENTERS

Logan Pass Visitor Center

INFO CENTER | Built of stone, this center stands sturdy against the severe weather that forces it to close in winter. When it's open, rangers give 10-minute talks on the alpine environment and offer a variety of activities including guided hikes. You can get advice from them and buy books and maps. ✉ *Going-to-the-Sun Rd., Glacier National Park* ✣ *34 miles east of West Glacier, 18 miles west of St. Mary* ☎ *406/888–7800.*

Hotels

Granite Park Chalet

$$ | **B&B/INN** | Early tourists used to ride horses 7 to 9 miles through the park each day and stay at a different chalet each night; today, the only way to reach the Granite Park, one of two such chalets that's still standing (Sperry is the other), is via hiking trails. **Pros:** beautiful scenery; secluded; historic lodging. **Cons:** difficult to access; rustic; far from services (and you must bring your own food and water). $ *Rooms from: $115* ✉ *Going-to-the-Sun Rd., Glacier National Park* ✣ *7.6 miles south of Logan Pass* ☎ *888/345–2649* 🌐 *www.graniteparkchalet.com* ⏲ *Closed mid-Sept.–late June* *12 rooms* 🍽 *No meals.*

Eastern Glacier National Park

Via U.S. routes 2 and 89, St. Mary is 130 miles northeast of Kalispell and 97 miles northeast of Apgar; via the Going-to-the-Sun Road, it's roughly 50 miles between Apgar and St. Mary.

The park's eastern end has historical and cultural significance to the Blackfeet Nation, and much of this region is on tribal lands. East Glacier Park Village is the hub with shops, restaurants, and hotels. Two Medicine Lake, St. Mary Lake, and Swiftcurrent Lake are scenic highlights of this area. The eastern end of the Going-to-the-Sun Road is near the tiny community of St. Mary on the western border of the Blackfeet Indian Reservation.

Sights

SCENIC DRIVES

East Glacier Park Village to Two Medicine Lake and Saint Mary Lake

SCENIC DRIVE | You'll see the striking contrast of prairies and mountains as you travel northwest from East Glacier Park Village to Two Medicine Lake on MT-49. Once you turn onto Two Medicine Road, you'll be heading straight toward snowcapped peaks and lovely Two Medicine Lake. From there, head back out to MT-49 and then to US-89 North to make your way to the town of St. Mary and then onto the Going-to-the-Sun Road to reach St. Mary Lake, the park's second largest. The entire route is 49 miles one-way. End the drive with an additional stop at Swiftcurrent

Lake, and you'll cover about 75 miles total. ✉ *Glacier National Park.*

SCENIC STOPS

Running Eagle Falls (Trick Falls)

BODY OF WATER | Cascading near Two Medicine, these are actually two different waterfalls from two different sources. In spring, when the water level is high, the upper falls join the lower falls for a 40-foot drop into Two Medicine River; in summer, the upper falls dry up, revealing the lower 20-foot falls that start midway down the precipice. ✉ *2 miles east of Two Medicine entrance, Glacier National Park.*

St. Mary Lake

BODY OF WATER | When the breezes calm, the park's second-largest lake mirrors the snowcapped granite peaks that line the St. Mary Valley. To get a good look at the beautiful scenery, follow the Sun Point Nature Trail (closed for renovation in 2016) along the lake's shore. The hike is 1 mile each way. ✉ *1 mile west of St. Mary, Glacier National Park.*

Swiftcurrent Lake

BODY OF WATER | The Many Glacier Hotel is perched on the shores of Swiftcurrent Lake. The views here are some of the park's prettiest, taking in the mountains that rise more than 3,000 feet immediately west of the lake. Scenic boat tours ply the waters and transport hikers to trails that lead to other lakes and glaciers in the park's Many Glacier region.

Two Medicine Valley

NATURE SITE | Rugged, often windy, and always beautiful, the valley is a remote 9-mile drive from Highway 49 and is surrounded by some of the park's most stark, rocky peaks. Near the valley's lake you can rent a canoe, take a narrated boat tour, camp, and hike. Bears frequent the area. The road is closed from late October through late May. ✉ *Two Medicine entrance, 9 miles east of Hwy. 49, Glacier National Park* ☎ *406/888–7800, 406/257–2426 boat tours.*

TRAILS

Grinnell Glacier Trail

TRAIL | In 1926, one giant ice mass broke apart to create the Salamander and Grinnell glaciers, which have been shrinking ever since. The 5½-mile trail to Grinnell Glacier, the park's most accessible, is marked by several spectacular viewpoints. You start at Swiftcurrent Lake's picnic area, climb a moraine to Lake Josephine, then climb to the Grinnell Glacier overlook. Halfway up, turn around to see the prairie land to the northeast. You can cut about 2 miles (each way) off the hike by taking scenic boat rides across Swiftcurrent Lake and Lake Josephine. From July to mid-September, a ranger-led hike departs from the Many Glacier Hotel boat dock on most mornings at 8:30. *Difficult.* ✉ *Glacier National Park* ✣ *Trailheads: Swiftcurrent Lake picnic area or Lake Josephine boat dock.*

Iceberg Lake Trail

TRAIL | This moderately strenuous, 9-mile, round-trip hike passes the gushing Ptarmigan Falls, then climbs to its namesake, where icebergs bob in the chilly mountain loch. Mountain goats hang out on sheer cliffs above, bighorn sheep graze in the high mountain meadows, and grizzly bears dig for glacier lily bulbs, grubs, and other delicacies. Rangers lead hikes here almost daily in summer, leaving at 8:30 am. *Moderate.* ✉ *Glacier National Park* ✣ *Trailhead: at Swiftcurrent Inn parking lot, off Many Glacier Rd.*

Sun Point Nature Trail

TRAIL | A stunning waterfall awaits at the end of this well-groomed, 1.3-mile trail along the cliffs and shores of picturesque St. Mary Lake. You can hike one-way and take a boat transfer back. *Easy.* ✉ *Glacier National Park* ✣ *Trailhead: 11 miles east of Logan Pass on Going-to-the-Sun Rd., at Sun Point parking area.*

VISITOR CENTERS

St. Mary Visitor Center

INFO CENTER | Glacier's largest visitor complex has a huge relief map of the park's peaks and valleys and screens a 15-minute orientation video. Exhibits help visitors understand the park from the perspective of its original inhabitants—the Blackfeet, Salish, Kootenai, and Pend d'Orielle peoples. Rangers conduct evening presentations in summer, and the auditorium hosts Native America Speaks programs. The center also has books and maps for sale, backcountry camping permits, and large viewing windows facing the 10-mile-long St. Mary Lake. ✉ *Going-to-the-Sun Rd., off U.S. 89, Glacier National Park* ☎ *406/732–7750.*

Restaurants

Ptarmigan Dining Room

$$$ | **AMERICAN** | The picturesque Ptarmigan's massive windows afford stunning views of Grinnell Point over Swiftcurrent Lake. Known for using regional, sustainably sourced ingredients, the restaurant specializes in dishes such as house-smoked Montana trout, braised bison short ribs, and roasted duck with Flathead cherry chutney. **Known for:** exceptional views; gluten-free and vegetarian options amid the regional fish-and-game mix; huckleberry cobbler (and margaritas!). *$ Average main: $28* ✉ *Many Glacier Rd., Glacier National Park* ☎ *303/265–7010* 🌐 *www.glaciernationalparklodges.com* ⏲ *Closed late Sept.–early June.*

Hotels

Many Glacier Hotel

$$$$ | **HOTEL** | On Swiftcurrent Lake in the park's northeastern section, this is the most isolated of the grand hotels, and—especially if you are able to book a lake-view balcony room—among the most scenic. **Pros:** stunning views from lodge; secluded; good hiking trails nearby. **Cons:** rustic rooms; no TV, limited Internet; the road leading to the lodge is very rough. *$ Rooms from: $207* ✉ *Many Glacier Rd., Glacier National Park* ⊕ *12 miles west of Babb* ☎ *855/733–4522, 406/732–4411* 🌐 *www.glaciernationalparklodges.com* ⏲ *Closed mid-Sept.–mid-June* *214 rooms* *No meals.*

Activities

AIR TOURS

OUTFITTERS AND EXPEDITIONS

Glacier Aviation Services

TOUR—SPORTS | Get a bird's-eye view of the mountains and glaciers inside Glacier National Park on a 30- to 60-minute tour aboard a state-of-the-art, eco-friendly helicopter. ✉ *1761 E. 2nd St., Whitefish* ☎ *406/387–4141, 877/811–1142* 🌐 *glacieraviationservices.com* *From $187.*

BIKING

Glacier Cyclery

BICYCLING | Daily and weekly bike rentals of touring, road, and mountain bikes for all ages and skill levels are available here. The shop also sells bikes, equipment, and attire, and does repairs. Information about local trails is available on its website and in the store. ✉ *326 2nd St. E, Whitefish* ☎ *406/862–6446* 🌐 *www.glaciercyclery.com* *From $30.*

Great Northern Cycle & Ski

BICYCLING | You can rent road and mountain bikes from this outfitter, which also services and repairs bikes and sells cycling and skiing attire and gear. ✉ *328 Central Ave., Whitefish* ☎ *406/862–5321* 🌐 *www.gncycleski.com* *From $75.*

BOATING AND RAFTING

Glacier Park Boat Company

BOATING | This company conducts 45- to 90-minute tours of five lakes. A Lake McDonald cruise takes you from the dock at Lake McDonald Lodge to the middle of the lake for an unparalleled view of the Continental Divide's Garden Wall. The Many Glacier tours on Swiftcurrent

Lake and Lake Josephine depart from Many Glacier Hotel and provide views of the Continental Divide. Two Medicine Lake cruises leave from the dock near the ranger station and lead to several trails. St. Mary Lake cruises leave from the launch near the Rising Sun Campground and head to Red Eagle Mountain and other spots. You can also rent small watercraft at Apgar, Lake McDonald, Two Medicine, and Many Glacier. ☎ *406/257–2426* 🌐 *www.glacierparkboats.com* 🎫 *Tours from $22.25, rentals from $15.*

Great Northern Whitewater

BOATING | Sign up for daylong or multiday white-water, kayaking, and fishing trips, or look into the outfitter's River School, where you can learn how to paddleboard, kayak, or even become a rafting guide. This company also rents Swiss-style chalets with views of Glacier's peaks. ✉ *12127 U.S. 2 E, Glacier National Park* ✥ *1 mile south of West Glacier* ☎ *406/387–5340, 800/735–7897* 🌐 *www.greatnorthernresort.com* 🎫 *From $60.*

Wild River Adventures

BOATING | Brave the white water in an inflatable kayak or a traditional raft or enjoy a scenic float with these guys, who will paddle you over the Middle Fork of the Flathead, and peddle you tall tales all the while. They also conduct trail rides and scenic fishing trips on rivers around Glacier National Park. ✉ *11900 U.S. 2 E, 1 mile west of West Glacier, Glacier National Park* ☎ *406/387–9453, 800/700–7056* 🌐 *www.riverwild.com* 🎫 *From $58.*

CAMPING

Apgar Campground. This popular and large campground on the southern shore of Lake McDonald in the park's western reaches has many activities and services. ✉ *Apgar Rd.* ☎ *406/888–7800.*

Avalanche Creek Campground. This peaceful campground on Going-to-the-Sun Road is shaded by huge red cedars and bordered by Avalanche Creek. ✉ *15.7 miles from west entrance on Going-to-the-Sun Rd.* ☎ *406/888–7800.*

Many Glacier Campground. One of the most beautiful spots in the park is also a favorite for bears. ✉ *Next to Swiftcurrent Motor Inn on Many Glacier Rd.*

Sprague Creek Campground. This sometimes noisy roadside campground for tents, RVs, and truck campers (no towed units) offers spectacular views of the lake and sunsets, and there's fishing from shore. ✉ *Going-to-the-Sun Rd., 1 mile south of Lake McDonald Lodge* ☎ *406/888–7800.*

EDUCATIONAL PROGRAMS

Glacier Institute

TOUR—SIGHT | **FAMILY** | Based near West Glacier at the Field Camp and on the remote western boundary at the Big Creek Outdoor Education Center, this learning institute offers an array of field courses for kids and adults. Year-round, experts in wildlife biology, native plants, and river ecology lead treks into Glacier's backcountry on daylong and multiday programs. The Youth Adventure Series for children ages 6 to 11 features one-day naturalist courses; preteens and teens can take weeklong trips. Three-day family camps for ages seven and up are also on offer. ✉ *137 Main St., Kalispell* ☎ *406/755–1211, 406/755–7154* 🌐 *www.glacierinstitute.org* 🎫 *From $70.*

FISHING

Within Glacier there's an almost unlimited range of fishing possibilities, with catch-and-release encouraged. You can fish in most waters of the park, but the best fishing is generally in the least accessible spots. A license is not required inside the park, but you must stop by a park office to pick up a copy of the regulations. The season runs from the third Saturday in May through November. Several companies offer guided fishing trips. ■ TIP→ **Fishing on both the North Fork and the Middle Fork of the Flathead River requires a Montana conservation**

license ($10), an AIS Prevention Pass ($15), and a Montana fishing license ($25 for two consecutive days or $86 for a season). They are available at most convenience stores, sports shops, and from the Montana Department of Fish, Wildlife, and Parks (☎ *406/752–5501* 🌐 *www.fwp.mt.gov*).

HIKING

Glacier Guides

HIKING/WALKING | The exclusive backpacking guide service in Glacier National Park can arrange guided full- or multiday hikes. All are customized to match the skill level of the hikers, and they include stops to identify plants, animals, and habitats. ✉ *11970 U.S. 2 E, West Glacier* ☎ *406/387–5555, 800/521–7238* 🌐 *www.glacierguides.com* 🎫 *From $53.*

HORSEBACK RIDING

Glacier Gateway Trailrides

HORSEBACK RIDING | On this East Glacier company's trips, a Blackfoot cowboy guides riders on Blackfeet Nation land adjacent to the Two Medicine area of Glacier National Park. Rides, from an hour to all day, climb through aspen groves to high-country views of Dancing Lady and Bison mountains. Special cattle-drive rides are also offered. Riders must be seven or older, and reservations are essential. ✉ *520 3rd Ave. Hwy 49, East Glacier Park* ☎ *406/226–4408 in season, 406/338–5560 off season, 406/226–4409 fax* 🎫 *From $70.*

Swan Mountain Outfitters

HORSEBACK RIDING | The only outfitter that offers horseback riding inside the park, Swan begins its treks at Apgar, Lake McDonald, Many Glacier, and West Glacier. Trips for beginning to advanced riders cover both flat and mountainous terrain. Fishing can also be included, and this operator also offers one- or multiday llama pack trips. Riders must be seven or older and weigh less than 250 pounds. Reservations are essential. ✉ *Coram* ☎ *877/888–5557 central reservations, 406/387–4405 Apgar Corral* 🌐 *www.swanmountainglacier.com* 🎫 *From $50.*

MULTISPORT OUTFITTERS

Glacier Guides and Montana Raft Company

WHITE-WATER RAFTING | Take a raft trip through the Wild-and-Scenic–designated white water of the Middle Fork of the Flathead and combine it with a hike, horseback ride, or barbecue. Other offerings include guided hikes and bike rides, fly-fishing trips, and multiday adventures. The company also offers bike (including e-bike) rentals and fly-fishing lessons. ✉ *11970 U.S. 2 E, 1 mile west of West Glacier, Glacier National Park* ☎ *406/387–5555, 800/521–7238* 🌐 *www.glacierguides.com* 🎫 *From $53.*

Glacier Raft Company and Outdoor Center

BOATING | In addition to running fishing trips, family float rides, saddle-and-paddle adventures, kayak trips, and high-adrenaline white-water adventure rafting excursions, this outfitter will set you up with camping, backpacking, and fishing gear. There's also a full-service fly-fishing shop and outdoor store. You can stay in one of 13 log cabins or a glacier-view home. ✉ *12400 U.S 2 E, West Glacier* ☎ *406/888–5454, 800/235–6781* 🌐 *www.glacierraftco.com* 🎫 *From $65.*

Waterton Lakes National Park

A World Heritage Site, Waterton Lakes National Park represents the meeting of two worlds—the flatlands of the prairie and the abrupt upthrust of the mountains—squeezing an unusual mix of wildlife, flora, and climate zones into its 505 square km (200 square miles). The quaint alpine town of Waterton lies just off the shore of Upper Waterton Lake, and the historic Prince of Wales Hotel sits high on a hill overlooking it all. The park is quieter than most of the other Rocky Mountain parks, but it is just as beautiful and diverse. Visitors coming from Glacier National Park typically reach Waterton via the seasonal Chief Mountain Highway border crossing, 67 miles northwest of East Glacier Park Village. It's also possible to access the park via the border crossing at Carway, which is open year-round.

In September 2017, the Kenow Wildfire burned 19,303 hectares (47,698 acres) of parkland, greatly affecting park infrastructure, including more than 80% of its hiking trail network. Check the website to learn the status of trails before heading out.

Sights

SCENIC DRIVES

Akamina Parkway

BODY OF WATER | Take this winding, 16-km (10-mile) road up to Cameron Lake, but drive slowly and watch for wildlife: it's common to see bears along the way. At the lake you will find a relatively flat, paved, 1.6-km (1-mile) trail that hugs the western shore and makes a nice walk. Bring your binoculars. Grizzly bears are often spotted on the lower slopes of the mountains at the far end of the lake. ✉ *Waterton Lakes National Park.*

Red Rock Parkway

SCENIC DRIVE | The 15-km (9-mile) route takes you from the prairie up the Blakiston Valley to Red Rock Canyon, where water has cut through the earth, exposing red sedimentary rock. It's common to see bears just off the road, especially in autumn, when the berries are ripe. ✉ *Waterton Lakes National Park.*

SCENIC STOPS

Cameron Lake

BODY OF WATER | The jewel of Waterton, Cameron Lake sits in a land of glacially carved cirques (steep-walled basins). In summer, hundreds of varieties of alpine wildflowers fill the area, including 22 kinds of wild orchids. Canoes, rowboats, kayaks, and fishing gear can be rented here. ✉ *Akamina Pkwy., 13 km (8 miles) southwest of Waterton Townsite, Waterton Lakes National Park.*

Goat Haunt Ranger Station

NATURE PRESERVE | Reached only by foot trail, private boat, or tour boat from Waterton Townsite, this spot on the U.S. end of Waterton Lake is the stomping ground for mountain goats, moose, grizzlies, and black bears. It is also the official border crossing for the U.S.side of Waterton Lake. In recent years, the crossing has not been staffed by U.S. Customs personnel, and, consequently, tour boats do not allow passengers to disembark at Goat Haunt as they once did. If you want to explore the trails on this end of the lake, you will need to hike or paddle in on your own. Check in before arrival by using the CBP ROAM app. Visitors to this area must carry their passports and proof of ROAM trip approval.The hikes on the U.S. side of the lake were unaffected by the wildfires of recent years. ✉ *Southern end of Waterton Lake, Waterton Lakes National Park* ☎ *403/859–2362* 🌐 *www.watertoncruise.com* 🎫 *Tour boat C$51.*

Waterton Townsite

TOWN | In roughly the park's geographic center, this low-key townsite swells with tourists in summer, and restaurants and shops open to serve them. In winter only a few motels are open, and services are limited. ✉ *Waterton Townsite.*

TRAILS

Bear's Hump Trail

TRAIL | This steep, 2.8-km (1.4-mile) trail climbs to an overlook with a great view of Upper Waterton Lake and the townsite. *Moderate.* ✉ *Waterton Lakes National Park* ✣ *Trailhead: across from Prince of Wales access road. Behind site of old visitor information center.*

Bertha Lake Trail

TRAIL | This 11.4-km (7.1-mile) round-trip trail leads from Waterton Townsite through a Douglas fir forest to a beautiful overlook of Upper Waterton Lake, and on to Lower Bertha Falls. From there, a steeper climb takes you past Upper Bertha Falls to Bertha Lake. In June, the wildflowers along the trail are stunning. *Moderate.* ✉ *Waterton Lakes National Park* ✣ *Trailhead: at parking lot off Evergreen Ave., west of Townsite Campground.*

Blakiston Falls

TRAIL | A 2-km (1.2-mi) round-trip hike will take you from Red Rock Canyon to Blakiston Falls. Several viewpoints overlook the falls. *Easy* ✉ *Waterton Lakes National Park* ✣ *Trailhead: at Red Rock Canyon lower parking lot. Cross the bridge over Red Rock Creek, then turn left across the bridge over Bauerman Creek, and turn right to follow the trail.*

Cameron Lake Shore Trail

TRAIL | **FAMILY** | Relatively flat and paved, this 1.6-km (1-mile) one-way trail offers a peaceful hike. Look for wildflowers along the shoreline and grizzlies on the lower slopes of the mountains at the far end of the lake. *Easy.* ✉ *Waterton Lakes National Park* ✣ *Trailhead: at lakeshore in front of parking lot, 13 km (8 miles) southwest of Waterton Townsite.*

Crandell Lake Trail

TRAIL | This 2½-km (1½-mile) trail winds through fragrant pine forest, ending at a popular mountain lake. *Easy.* ✉ *Waterton Lakes National Park* ✣ *Trailhead: about halfway up Akamina Pkwy.*

★ **Crypt Lake Trail**

TRAIL | Awe-inspiring and strenuous, this 17.2-km (11-mile) round-trip trail is one of the most stunning hikes in the Canadian Rockies. Conquering the trail involves taking a boat taxi across Waterton Lake, climbing 700 meters (2,300 feet), crawling through a tunnel nearly 30 meters (100 feet) long, and scrambling across a sheer rock face. The reward, and well worth it: views of a 183-meter (600-foot) cascading waterfall and the turquoise waters of Crypt Lake. This hike was completely untouched by the wildfires of recent years. *Difficult.* ✉ *Waterton Lakes National Park* ✣ *Trailhead: at Crypt Landing, accessed by ferry from Waterton Townsite.*

VISITOR CENTERS

Waterton Information Centre

INFO CENTER | The original Waterton Information Centre was destroyed by the Kenow Wildfire in 2017, and a new building is under construction. Until it's finished, the visitor center is in the Lion's Hall in the Waterton Townsite. Stop in to pick up brochures, maps, and books. You can also pick up the booklet for the free Xplorer Program for kids between ages 6 and 11. Park interpreters are on hand to answer questions and give directions. ✉ *Waterton Rd., before townsite, Waterton Lakes National Park* ☎ *403/859–5133.*

Restaurants

Lakeside Chophouse

$$$$ | **STEAKHOUSE** | Grab a window seat or a spot on the patio to enjoy the spectacular view from Waterton's only lakefront restaurant. This is the place in the park for a steak dinner—locally produced Alberta beef plays a starring role on the globally inspired menu. **Known for:** great steaks; lakefront views; all-day service. [$] *Average main: C$29* ✉ *Bayshore Inn, 111 Waterton Ave., Waterton Townsite* ☎ *888/527–9555, 403/859–2211* 🌐 *www.bayshoreinn.com.*

Thirsty Bear Kitchen & Bar

$$ | **AMERICAN** | Waterton's only gastropub is the place for live music most weekends and casual eats anytime. The nachos here are the best in town, and there's a wide selection of burgers, sandwiches, and wraps—all served with salad or fries. **Known for:** live music and a dance floor; great casual dining; fun atmosphere with big-screen TVs, pool tables, and foosball. [$] *Average main: C$20* ✉ *111 Waterton Ave., Waterton Townsite* ☎ *403/859–2211 Ext. 309* 🌐 *www.thirstybearwaterton.com* ⏲ *Closed mid-Oct.–mid-May.*

Hotels

Bayshore Inn
$$$$ | **HOTEL** | Right in town and on the shores of Waterton Lake, this inn has a lot going for it: lovely views, the only on-site spa in Waterton, multiple dining options, and easy access to many services. **Pros:** only lakefront accommodation in Waterton; plenty of on-site amenities; great townsite location. **Cons:** older-style hotel; rustic motor inn; can sometimes hear noise between rooms. *Rooms from: C$269* *111 Waterton Ave., Waterton Townsite* *888/527–9555, 403/859–2211* *www.bayshoreinn.com* *Closed mid-Oct.–Apr.* *70 rooms* *No meals.*

Bear Mountain Motel
$ | **HOTEL** | This classic, 1960s motel offers a variety of affordable accommodations that have painted cinder-block walls, wood-beam ceilings, and small bathrooms with shower stalls. **Pros:** most affordable accommodation in Waterton; clean, comfortable, and very basic; family-run motel right in townsite. **Cons:** noise can be an issue with the old cinder-block construction; closed in winter; no in-room coffee or tea (available in main office). *Rooms from: C$149* *208 Mount View Rd., Waterton Townsite* *403/859–2366* *bearmountainmotel.com* *Closed Oct.–Apr.* *36 rooms* *No meals.*

Prince of Wales Hotel
$$$$ | **HOTEL** | A high steeple crowns this iconic, 1920s hotel, which is fantastically ornamented with eaves, balconies, and turrets; is perched between two lakes with a high-mountain backdrop; and has a lobby where two-story windows capture the views. **Pros:** spectacular valley and townsite views; historic property; bellmen wear kilts. **Cons:** very rustic rooms; no TVs; no a/c. *Rooms from: C$259* *Off Hwy. 5, Waterton Lakes National Park* *Turn left at marked access road at top of hill just before village* *844/868–7474, 403/859–2231* *www.glacierparkcollection.com/lodging/prince-of-wales-hotel* *Closed late Sept.–mid-May* *86 rooms* *No meals.*

Waterton Glacier Suites
$$$$ | **HOTEL** | In the heart of the townsite, this all-suite property is within walking distance of restaurants, shopping, and the dock on beautiful Waterton Lake. **Pros:** modern suites with mini-refrigerators and a/c; open year-round; convenient location. **Cons:** no views; pullout sofas uncomfortable; no on-site breakfast. *Rooms from: C$319* *107 Wildflower Ave., Waterton Townsite* *403/859–2004, 866/621–3330* *www.watertonsuites.com* *26 rooms* *No meals.*

Activities

BIKING

Blakiston and Company
BICYCLING | Rent electric bikes, canoes, kayaks, and stand-up paddleboards through this company. *102 Mountain Rd., Waterton Townsite* *800/456–0772* *www.blakistonandcompany.com.*

Pat's Waterton
BICYCLING | **FAMILY** | Choose from surrey, mountain, and e-bikes or motorized scooters at Pat's, which also rents tennis rackets, strollers, coolers, life jackets, hiking poles, bear spray, and binoculars. *224 Mt. View Rd., Waterton Townsite* *403/859–2266* *www.patswaterton.com* *From $15.*

BOATING

Cameron Lake Boat Rentals
BOATING | Rent canoes, kayaks, rowboats, pedal boats, and stand-up paddleboards right at the docks on Cameron Lake. You can also buy tackle and rent fishing rods. *Waterton Lakes National Park* *At the boat docks at Cameron Lake, 16 km (10 miles) southwest of the townsite* *403/627–6443* *www.cameronlakeboatrentals.com.*

Waterton Inter-Nation Shoreline Cruise Co.
BOATING | This company's two-hour round-trip boat tour along Upper Waterton Lake from Waterton Townsite to Goat Haunt Ranger Station is one of the most popular activities in Waterton. The narrated tour passes scenic bays, sheer cliffs, and snow-clad peaks. This company also offers a shuttle service for the Crypt Lake and Vimy Peak hikes. ✉ *Waterton Townsite Marina, northwest corner of Waterton Lake near Bayshore Inn, Waterton Lakes National Park* ☎ *403/859–2362, 403/859–2362* 🌐 *www.watertoncruise.com* 🎫 *C$55.*

CAMPING

Visitors can prebook campsites for a fee of C$11 online or C$13.50 by phone. The reservation service is available at 🌐 *www.reservation.parkscanada.gc.ca* or by phone at ☎ *877/737–3783.*

Waterton Townsite Campground. Though the campground is busy and windy, sites here are grassy and flat with access to kitchen shelters and have views down the lake into the U.S. part of the Peace Park. ✉ *Waterton and Vimy Aves.* ☎ *877/737–3783.*

HORSEBACK RIDING

Alpine Stables
HORSEBACK RIDING | At these family-owned stables you can arrange hour-long trail rides and full-day guided excursions within the park, as well as multiday pack trips through the Rockies and foothills. They are open May through September. ✉ *Waterton Lakes National Park* ☎ *403/859–2462, 403/653–2449* 🌐 *www.alpinestables.com* 🎫 *From C$45.*

What's Nearby

You could easily spend a week exploring Waterton and Glacier, but you may wish to take advantage of hotels, restaurants, sights, and outfitters in nearby towns. Outside Glacier National Park's western reaches and 2½ miles south of the Apgar Visitor Center is the gateway community of **West Glacier;** 27 miles to its southeast is **Essex.** Slightly farther afield to the southwest of West Glacier are **Columbia Falls** and **Whitefish.** Just over 40 miles southeast of the St. Mary Visitor Center on the east side of the park is the gateway of **East Glacier Park Village.** To the northeast, roughly midway between the visitor center and East Glacier, is the interesting town of **Browning.** Note that there are Amtrak stations in Whitefish, West Glacier, Essex, East Glacier Park Village, and Browning.

Chapter 25

GLACIER BAY NATIONAL PARK AND PRESERVE

Updated by
David Cannamore

Camping ★★★★★

Hotels ★☆☆☆☆

Activities ★★★★☆

Scenery ★★★★★

Crowds ★★★★★

WELCOME TO GLACIER BAY NATIONAL PARK AND PRESERVE

TOP REASONS TO GO

★ **Paddling in paradise:** Several wilderness areas and countless pocket beaches are accessible only by kayak. As you glide along, the only sounds will likely be those of the water dripping off your paddle and the breath of humpback whales.

★ **Birds, whales, and bears galore:** Puffins and other sea birds can be found in the mid- and upper portions of Glacier Bay, which also has more sea otters than California's entire coast. The humpback whale population is so robust that a study has been conducted here every summer since the 1970s, with individuals identified by unique markings on the underside of their flukes. Brown, black, and the mysterious Glacier bears wander the tidelines, turning over boulders as if they were basketballs.

★ **A living, breathing science lesson:** Glaciers are constantly reshaping the geography of the bay, making it the perfect place to study glacial succession and how plants, animals, and the land are affected by these frigid and powerful sculptors.

1 Bartlett Cove. The park's nerve center is the jumping off point for most trips, including the tour boat that runs every day in peak season.

2 West Arm of Glacier Bay. Glacier Bay is shaped like a big "Y," with Bartlett Cove near its base and glaciers in each of its two "arms." The most famous and accessible tidewater glaciers—including the Margerie—are in the West Arm, making it the most "crowded" area. The park's day boat travels up the West Arm from Bartlett Cove, serving as both a tour boat and a water taxi for backcountry campers and kayakers.

3 East Arm of Glacier Bay. The wild, remote East Arm has abundant wildlife and excellent views, but only one of its glaciers, the McBride, is tidewater—and it's retreating rapidly. It's also hard to reach owing to strong tides and icebergs.

4 Outer Coast and Surrounding Waters. Although some fishing and whale-watching excursions visit the Icy Strait and Point Adolphus, near the entrance to Glacier Bay, most visitors see the outer coast while passing by on a cruise ship or passing overhead on a flightseeing excursion.

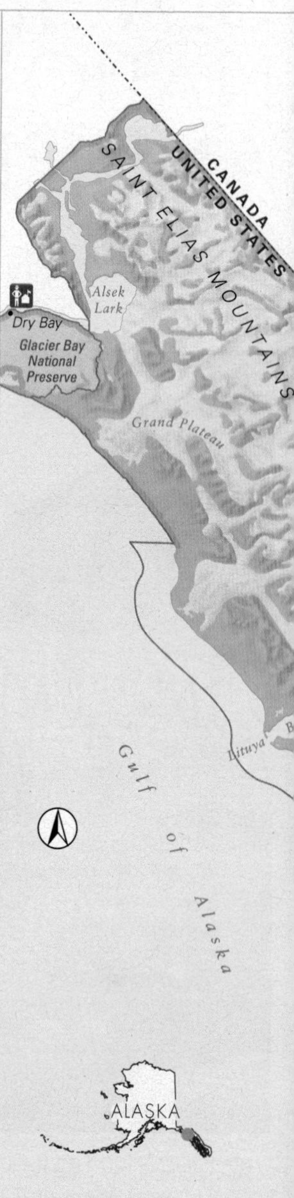

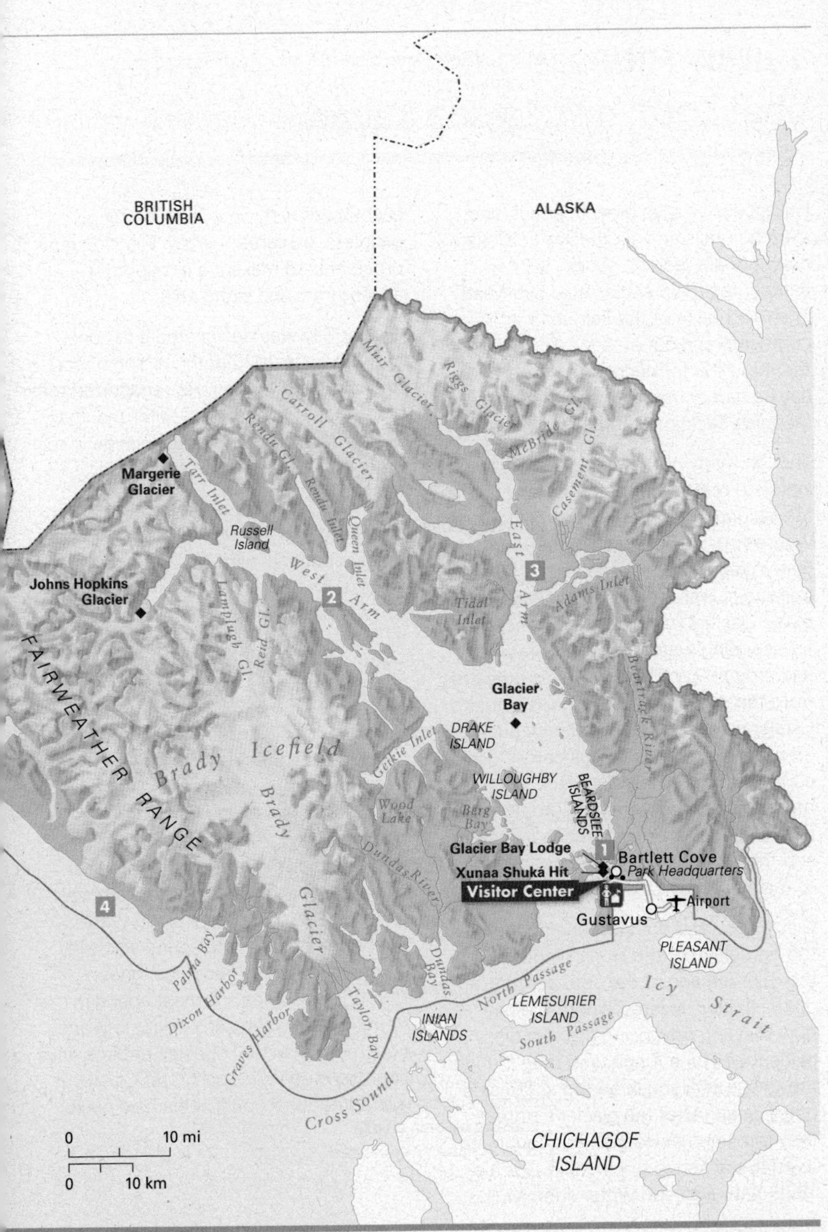
BRITISH COLUMBIA
ALASKA
Muir Glacier
Riggs Glacier
McBride Gl.
Carroll Glacier
Rendu Gl.
Rendu Inlet
Casement Gl.
Margerie Glacier
Tarr Inlet
Russell Island
Queen Inlet
East Arm
West Arm
Johns Hopkins Glacier
Lamplugh Gl.
Reid Gl.
Tidal Inlet
Adams Inlet
FAIRWEATHER RANGE
Glacier Bay
Beartrack River
DRAKE ISLAND
Brady Icefield
Geikie Inlet
WILLOUGHBY ISLAND
BEARDSLEE ISLANDS
Brady Glacier
Wood Lake
Berg Bay
Glacier Bay Lodge
Xunaa Shuká Hit
Visitor Center
Bartlett Cove
Park Headquarters
Dundas River
Airport
Gustavus
Palma Bay
Dixon Harbor
Graves Harbor
Taylor Bay
Dundas Bay
North Passage
PLEASANT ISLAND
LEMESURIER ISLAND
Icy Strait
INIAN ISLANDS
South Passage
Cross Sound
CHICHAGOF ISLAND
0 10 mi
0 10 km

Glacier Bay is a wild, magical place that rewards nature lovers of all persuasions, particularly those who get out on the water—aboard a cruise ship, on a day-boat tour, or in a sea kayak.

Humpback whales breach, spout, and slap their tails against the water. Coastal brown bears feed on sedge, salmon, and berries. Bald eagles soar overhead. The mountains of the Fairweather Range come into and out of view. And then there are the formations that give the bay its name. Indeed, coming here is like stepping back into the Little Ice Age.

Though many of the estimated 1,000 glaciers are remote terrestrial or lakewater formations, this is one of the few places where you can approach massive tidewater glaciers. Bergs the size of 10-story buildings crash from the "snouts" of these glaciers, reverberating like cannon fire, sending water and spray skyward, and propelling mini–tidal waves outward from the point of impact. Johns Hopkins Glacier calves so often and with such volume that large cruise ships can seldom come within 2 miles of its face. Although most glaciers are retreating, some—such as the Johns Hopkins, despite its calving, and the Marjorie—receive enough snow to maintain their size or even grow.

Glacier Bay and the surrounding area is the homeland of the Huna Tlingit. Before the mini–ice age of the 18th century, an outwash plain existed where the bay now resides. Advancing glaciers displaced the Huna Tlingit, and they founded the village of Hoonah on the south side of Icy Strait. After the glacier's retreat, they remained in Hoonah but continued to hunt and fish in the area. In October 1879, naturalist and writer John Muir, accompanied by several Huna Tlingit paddlers, explored the bay. His eloquent prose helped make it a hot spot for adventurers and sightseers.

Glacier Bay was designated a national monument in 1925 at the urging of scientist William Cooper. He recognized the area's unique opportunities for the study of plant succession after glaciation in real time, and his work continues today.

Over time, the size of the protected area increased and, in 1980, Glacier Bay was made a national park. For most of today's visitors, two or three days in Bartlett Cove is plenty of time to have a rewarding park experience. Those planning to camp in the backcountry or do a lot of kayaking probably need at least a week.

Because of all its glacial activity, the bay itself is a still-forming body of water that supports a variety of wildlife and ecosystems, including lush spruce-and-hemlock rain forest. Be on the lookout for the region's rare Glacier bears (aka blue bears), a variation of the black bear, which is also found here along with the brown bear. In late spring and early summer, watch for mountain goats. Humpback whales are most abundant from June through early August. In addition, more than 200 species of birds have been spotted in the park, and it's all but guaranteed that you'll see a bald eagle.

AVERAGE HIGH/LOW TEMPERATURES

JAN.	FEB.	MAR.	APR.	MAY	JUNE
32/22	36/23	39/25	49/32	56/38	61/45
JULY	**AUG.**	**SEPT.**	**OCT.**	**NOV.**	**DEC.**
63/49	63/48	57/43	48/36	39/28	33/24

Planning

When to Go

Summers can be temperate, with lush, green forest (you won't see glaciers from the visitor center in Bartlett Cove—the closest are 55 miles up the bay). It's important to note that temperatures near the glaciers can be highly variable; even in summer they can drop below freezing in localized areas. The best (and driest) weather is in May and June.

Getting Here and Around

Although Glacier Bay and the nearby community of Gustavus are technically on the mainland, there is no road connecting them to Juneau. The only way to get the area is by plane or the ferry system, which does offer car transport.

AIR

Flights from Juneau to Gustavus are 30 minutes. Alaska Airlines has daily service in the summer, as do other smaller, light-aircraft companies (some of them year-round).

CONTACTS Alaska Sea Planes. ✉ *1873 Shell Simmons Dr., Juneau* ✣ *1st entrance in Juneau Terminal as you're pulling in* ☎ *907/789–3331* 🌐 *flyalaska-seaplanes.com.*

BOAT

As Glacier Bay is best experienced from the water, it's fitting to arrive in the park by sea. Although its schedule can vary and winter service can be sporadic, the Alaska Marine Highway ferry generally sails from Juneau to Gustavus once or twice a week in summer. From there, it's a 10-mile shuttle/car ride to the park.

Although two cruise ships per day can enter the park in summer, there is no port of call for them. Nor do they anchor in area waters. They simply sail through the region—with passengers enjoying the scenery from the deck—as part of a greater Alaska itinerary that might also pass along the park's outer coast.

For most visitors, the best way to see the park's shoreline woodlands, marine life, and key tidewater glaciers is aboard the day boat.

Alaska Marine Highway
The 49-mile, six-hour journey from Juneau to Gustavus is scenic, with views of multiple glaciers and the Fairweather Mountain Range on clear days. Diner-style food is available for purchase, and there's a large stern deck that's perfect for taking in the scenery. Although there are generally two sailings a week in summer, it might be weeks between trips in winter. Reserve early for vehicle transport. Costs for this are dependent on vehicle length (RVs can be no more than 48 feet) and the time of year. ✉ *13485 Glacier Hwy., Juneau* ☎ *907/465–3941, 800/642–0066* 🌐 *dot.alaska.gov/amhs.*

Glacier Bay Day Boat
Each day in summer, a high-speed, 150-passenger catamaran leaves at 7:30 am (boarding is at 7) from the dock at Bartlett Cove for sails up the bay's West Arm to the Margerie Glacier. Operated by Glacier Bay Lodge and Tours, the eight-hour excursion is narrated by a park

ranger and includes a light lunch. Campers and sea kayakers heading up the bay ride the same boat. ✉ *179 Bartlett Cove Rd., Bartlett Cove* ☎ *888/229–8687* 🌐 *www.visitglacierbay.com* 🎫 *$228.*

CAR

It's a 20-minute drive from the ferry dock or airport in Gustavus to Bartlett Cove, home to Glacier Bay Lodge and the park's visitor center and visitor information station.

SHUTTLE

The Glacier Bay Lodge offers guests free shuttle service, which is generally correlated with the departures and arrivals of flights, ferries, and tours. If there's space, most shuttle drivers will let you ride to and from Gustavus to explore the town or pick up supplies. Many Gustavus B&Bs also provide free ferry dock and airport shuttle service.

TAXI

There are a couple of locally owned taxi services in Gustavus, and a run between Bartlett Cove and Gustavus costs around $15 per person each way.

CONTACTS TLC Taxi. ☎ *907/697–2239* 🌐 *www.glacierbaytravel.com/tlctaxi.htm.*

Inspiration

The Only Kayak: A Journey into the Heart of Alaska is Kim Heacox's love letter to Glacier Bay and conservation and a modern-day ode to John Muir, following his career from park ranger to photographer to activist and writer. Starting with Muir's first visit, the book covers key moments on the area's path to federal protection along with Muir's personal connection to Gustavus and Glacier Bay.

Although John Muir's classic *Travels in Alaska* was written more than 100 years ago, it remains inherently readable and is filled with spectacular anecdotes and stories. The highlight is Muir's first exploration of Glacier Bay in October of 1879 and his journey up to the foot of the Grand Pacific Glacier. Many of the geographic points described are still visible today.

Park Essentials

ACCESSIBILITY

The Forest Loop trail in Bartlett Cove is ADA accessible, complete with ramps and boardwalks through a spruce and hemlock forest. Vehicles that provide service to and from the airport are accessible to people using wheelchairs, as is one room in the Glacier Bay Lodge. The Bartlett Cove dock is outfitted with a floating ramp that connects it to shore.

PARK FEES AND PERMITS

There is no fee to enter Glacier Bay National Park. The Bartlett Cove Campground and backcountry permits are also free.

PARK HOURS

The park is open year-round, though most amenities are open only seasonally. The visitor information station (VIS) is open from early May through late September. The tour boats and Glacier Bay Lodge, which is home to the park visitor center, start to ramp up on Memorial Day and cease operations around Labor Day.

CELL PHONE RECEPTION

There's no cell phone service in the park. A public phone for local calls is outside the VIS. Free Wi-Fi is available at the picnic tables near the VIS and in public areas of the Glacier Bay Lodge.

Hotels

The Glacier Bay Lodge, home to the park visitor center, is the only hotel. Rooms are in cabin-style complexes connected to the main building via boardwalks that weave through the rain forest. Some rooms have a view of Bartlett Cove.

Restaurants

The Fairweather Dining Room in the Glacier Bay Lodge is open to nonguests, serves all three meals, and has a full bar. There's also a deck with outdoor dining and a view of the cove.

Hotel and restaurant reviews have been shortened. For full information visit Fodors.com. Hotel prices are the lowest cost of a standard double room in high season. Restaurant prices are the average cost of a main course at dinner, or if dinner is not served, at lunch.

What It Costs

	$	$$	$$$	$$$$
RESTAURANTS	under $14	$14–$22	$22–$30	over $30
HOTELS	under $100	$100–$200	$201–$300	over $300

Tours

Gustavus Water Taxi

BOAT TOURS | FAMILY | Local kayak operators often use this company, which specializes in kayak drop-offs and pick-ups. It also offers private tours, including whale-watching excursions, and custom sightseeing packages, with forays to the outer coast and nearby Inian Islands. No more than six passengers are allowed on the company's vessel, the *Taurus*, and prices start at $300. ✉ *1508 Glacier Ave., Juneau* ☎ *907/209–9833* 🌐 *gustavuswatertaxi.com.*

Visitor Information

CONTACTS Glacier Bay National Park. ☎ *907/697–2230* 🌐 *www.nps.gov/glba.*

In the Park

Gustavus is 48 air miles west of Juneau; Bartlett Cove is 10 miles northwest of Gustavus.

Near the northern end of the Inside Passage in southeastern Alaska, Glacier Bay National Park and Preserve is aptly named, preserving, among other things, an estimated 1,000 glaciers in its boundaries. Many are very remote terrestrial or lakewater formations, but several massive tidewater glaciers are readily visible from the water.

Ferries and planes travel between Juneau and the tiny community of Gustavus. One road from there leads to Bartlett Cove, home to the park visitor center and visitor information station (VIS); its only hotel, restaurant, and campground; the dock for the daily tour boat; and a few maintained trails.

Sights

HISTORIC SIGHTS

Xunaa Shuká Hít (*Huna Tribal House*)

NATIVE SITE | FAMILY | This 2,500-square-foot, re-created, cedar post-and-plank clan house, dedicated in 2016, is a space for the Huna Tlingit clans—whose ancestral homeland is Glacier Bay—to gather for meetings and ceremonies. It's also a place where visitors can learn about traditional food, art, crafts, dance, and other aspects of Tlingit culture. ✉ *Glacier Bay National Park* ✣ *Just south of Glacier Bay Lodge* ☎ *907/697–2230* 🌐 *www.nps.gov/glba.*

SCENIC STOPS

Johns Hopkins Glacier

NATURE SITE | The inlet to Johns Hopkins cuts deep into the Fairweather Mountain range, making it another of the lucky few glaciers that have remained stable in recent years. Although it is tidewater, it isn't visited as often as Margerie Glacier because it takes longer to travel down

Paddling a kayak through icy waters and inlets is one of the best ways to explore Glacier Bay.

the inlet to it. Further, this inlet is closed to motorized traffic for the first half of the summer as it's a critical habitat for pupping harbor seals. ✉ *Glacier Bay National Park* ✣ *Johns Hopkins Inlet, West Arm of upper Glacier Bay, 63 nautical miles northwest of Bartlett Cove.*

Margerie Glacier

NATURE SITE | The final destination for most tour vessels and cruise ships, charismatic Margerie frequently calves large chunks of ice off its 350-foot face. Unlike most of the world's glaciers, the Margerie has maintained a relatively stable position over the past several years thanks to high precipitation levels in the Fairweather Mountains where it originates. ✉ *Glacier Bay National Park* ✣ *West Arm of upper Glacier Bay, 55 nautical miles northwest of Bartlett Cove.*

TRAILS

Bartlett Lake Trail

TRAIL | The longest of the Bartlett Cove trails is an offshoot of the Bartlett River Trail. Look for the trailhead about a mile down the river trail on your right. After climbing a moraine, you weave through the woods for approximately 4 miles before reaching the lake. The serenity and the views make the total 12-mile journey—a seven- to eight-hour, out-and-back endeavor—worth the effort. *Moderate–Difficult.* ✉ *Glacier Bay National Park* ✣ *Trailhead: Off Bartlett River Trail* 🌐 *www.nps.gov/glba.*

Bartlett River Trail

TRAIL | This 5-mile, round-trip route borders an intertidal lagoon, runs alongside an old glacial moraine, zigzags through the woods, and spits you out in a designated wilderness area at the Bartlett River estuary. From the trailhead, located a short walk from the Glacier Bay Lodge, it's about 2 miles to the river, and although this portion can be muddy and slippery, the park service does maintain it. The stretch that continues along the riverbank for a couple more miles isn't maintained, and segments of it can be difficult to navigate, depending on the tide or recent rainfall. Bear sightings are common here, especially when the salmon are running. *Moderate–Difficult.* ✉ *Glacier Bay National Park* ✣ *Trailhead: East of Glacier Bay Lodge in Bartlett Cove* 🌐 *www.nps.gov/glba.*

Forest Loop Trail

TRAIL | FAMILY | Of the handful of trails in the Bartlett Cove area, this is the shortest and easiest. It's a 1-mile round-trip route that starts just across the road from the Glacier Bay Lodge and travels through the rain forest and along the beach. Boardwalks make up the first half of the trail, allowing those using wheelchairs to access the two viewing platforms that overlook a pond where moose can sometimes be spotted. *Easy.* ✉ *Glacier Bay National Park* ✣ *Trailhead: Across from Glacier Bay Lodge in Bartlett Cove* 🌐 *www.nps.gov/glba.*

Tlingit Trail

TRAIL | FAMILY | Following Bartlett Cove's tideline, this ½-mile (one-way), grated-gravel route has several interpretive sights, including a humpback-whale skeleton, a traditional Tlingit canoe, and the tribal clanhouse. The trail ends on the park road, so you can make a full loop back to the lodge, just ¼ mile away. *Easy.* ✉ *Glacier Bay National Park* ✣ *Trailhead: Glacier Bay Lodge or the VIS* 🌐 *www.nps.gov/glba.*

Towers Trail

TRAIL | If you want to see the lake and don't have all day to hike, the Towers Trail, which is open to bikes along its first 1.7 miles, provides quicker access. Named for an old tower beacon for the airport, the 3-mile route arrives at the lake in roughly the same spot as the Bartlett Lake Trail and has similar views. The trailhead is just outside of the park, about 3 miles closer to Gustavus. *Moderate.* ✉ *Glacier Bay National Park* ✣ *Trailhead: Take 1st left after "Welcome to Glacier Bay" sign and continue ½ mile* 🌐 *www.nps.gov/glba.*

VISITOR CENTERS

The visitor center is on the second floor of the Glacier Park Lodge. ■ **TIP→ Don't confuse the visitor center with the visitor information station (referred to locally as the "VIS"), which is in a park building down by the dock next to the covered picnic tables.** Staffed by park rangers and open sporadically, the VIS is where you go to get camping permits and camping, boating, and backcountry orientations.

Glacier Bay National Park Visitor Center

INFO CENTER | FAMILY | Located on the second floor of the lodge, the visitor center has a small theater where the 30-minute film, *Beneath the Reflections,* showcases park highlights. A few basic and somewhat dated exhibits outside the theater provide details on some of the bay's flora, fauna, and glaciers in the bay. A small kiosk sells books on the area, including a couple by local authors. ✉ *Glacier Bay Lodge, 179 Bartlett Cove Rd., Bartlett Cove* ☎ *907/ 697–2627* 🌐 *www.nps.gov/glba.*

Glacier Bay National Park Visitor Information Station (*VIS*)

INFO CENTER | At this building down by the dock, next to the sheltered picnic tables, park rangers provide camping permits, backcountry or boating orientations, and updates on weather and other current conditions. ✉ *Bartlett Cove* ✣ *By the dock* ☎ *907/697–2627* 🌐 *www.nps.gov/glba.*

Restaurants

Fairweather Dining Room

$$ | AMERICAN | FAMILY | The menu at the restaurant in the Glacier Bay Lodge, which serves three meals a day and is open to both nonguests and guests, has a decent selection sandwiches, salads, burgers, and other American fare as well as pasta, steak, and seafood entrées. Sometimes, the indoor dining room requires reservations, but there's almost always room on the sheltered outdoor deck, which has better views of Bartlett

Cove and the Fairweather Mountains. **Known for:** the only restaurant in the park; fresh Alaskan seafood; both buffet and à la carte breakfasts. *Average main: $22* *Glacier Bay National Park, 179 Bartlett Cove Rd., Glacier Bay Lodge, Bartlett Cove* *907/697–4000* *www.visitglacierbay.com* *Closed post–Labor Day weekend until Memorial Day weekend.*

Hotels

Glacier Bay Lodge

$$$ | **HOTEL** | Built of massive timbers and blending well with the surrounding rain forest, the only accommodation in the national park has rustic rooms (accessible by boardwalk); a large porch overlooking Glacier Bay; and a roster of activities that includes whale-watching excursions, kayaking trips, guided hikes, and boat tours of the bay. **Pros:** ample hiking trails nearby; good local seafood at restaurant; packages include meal, transfers, and boat tour of Glacier Bay. **Cons:** dining options within the park are all on the property; location is somewhat remote; dated decor. *Rooms from: $225* *Glacier Bay National Park, 179 Bartlett Cove Rd., Bartlett Cove* *888/229–8687 reservations, 907/697–4000* *www.visitglacierbay.com* *Closed post–Labor Day weekend until Memorial Day weekend* *49 rooms* *Free breakfast.*

Activities

BIKING

Biking in the park is limited to the short stretch to the Towers Trail and the primary 10-mile road between Bartlett Cove and Gustavus. This road is mostly flat, but it has no shoulder or sidewalk. Be mindful not only of any approaching vehicles but also of wildlife. Biking can be a nice way to explore Gustavus, which is small but spread out. Glacier Bay Lodge and several Gustavus accommodations have bikes available for guests to use, sometimes for free (check when booking).

BIRD-WATCHING

The park provides several pamphlets to help visitors identify its vibrant and diverse species of land and terrestrial birds. The most sought after of these winged residents are the tufted and horned puffins, famous for their bright orange bills. They're commonly sighted near South Marble Island (tour boats linger here for opportunities to spot this and other marine species) and farther up near the glaciers.

Marbled murrelets, tiny seabirds no bigger than a rubber duckie, are often seen bobbing in pairs all over the bay. They require old-growth forests for their nests, and mated pairs will travel dozens of miles to fish the rich waters.

No discussion of Alaska birdlife would be complete without mentioning the bald eagle. Watch for them riding the thermals, divebombing for fish, or roosting in trees—their distinctive white, "ping-pong" heads sharply contrasting with the forest's dark green foliage.

CAMPING

The one maintained campground in Glacier Bay National Park has many amenities and is free. **TIP→ Although the National Park Service has considered expanding the Bartlett Cove amenities to include an RV park, at this time there is no dedicated RV parking anywhere in Bartlett Cove or Gustavus.**

Backcountry camping requires a permit (free), which you can organize at the dockside VIS. You'll be asked to provide basic information (e.g., the number of people in your party, a description of your tents and other gear) as well as a trip itinerary. The day boat makes two designated backcountry stops to pick up and drop off campers on its daily tour of the bay. Bear in mind that Glacier Bay is a "paddler's park" with no backpacking trails; the best way to experience these wild areas really is by kayak rather than on foot.

Bartlett Cove Campground. Sites are just inside the treeline at this free, well-maintained, tents-only campground, which is about ½ mile from the VIS. Securing a tent-site is rarely an issue, so reservations aren't required. Before your first night, you must, however, attend an hour-long orientation at the VIS. Afterward, you can use one of the available wheelbarrows to haul your gear to the campground along a groomed path. Amenities include a fire pit and firewood near the shore, a warming hut for drying clothes, and multiple bear-proof food caches. (Wildlife is common in this area, so take proper bear-safety precautions.) For a fee, you can take a hot shower or use the laundry facilities at the Glacier Bay Lodge, a 10-minute walk away. ✉ *Glacier Bay National Park, Bartlett Cove* ☎ *907/697–4000* 🌐 *www.nps.gov/glba/planyourvisit/campground.htm.*

EDUCATIONAL PROGRAMS

In the park's peak summer season, rangers lead daily, low-intensity interpretive walks (times vary) along maintained trails or the shoreline. They usually begin in the lobby of the Glacier Bay Lodge and focus on the region's natural and indigenous history. The lodge is also where the park service sometimes offers nighttime presentations by scientists or rangers on a wide range of topics.

One of the newest additions to the park is the waterside Xunaa Shuká Hít (Huna Tribal House), which was constructed in 2016 and features authentic totem poles created by Huna Tlingit carvers. The house is open daily on a limited basis for talks and presentations during the summertime.

FISHING

Beginning in midsummer, all five salmon species start returning to their native rivers to spawn. Sockeye or "red salmon" are the first to come back in late June, with a peak the first or second week of July. Coho or "silver" salmon arrive in late August with an extended run that can last through September.

Fishing access is up the Bartlett River Trail, which isn't maintained beyond the mouth of the river. Tidal fluctuations and heavy rain can cause portions of the trail to become swampy or washout entirely, so sturdy, waterproof boots and rain gear are recommended. Both black and brown bears are common guests at this buffet. Always fish with a partner, carry bear spray, and make plenty of noise.

If you'd prefer to get out on a boat, there are several sport-fishing companies and lodges in Gustavus. Although reservations usually aren't necessary, they're still a good idea.

Glacier Bay Sportfishing

FISHING | Locally owned and operated, Glacier Bay Sportfishing is also one of the most established outfits in Gustavus. The company doesn't have a permit to fish in the park, but some of the best fishing is found outside the park anyway, so you'll have a chance to catch both salmon and halibut while soaking up Icy Strait vistas. Full-day fishing trips start at $1,700 for four passengers. Whale-watching tours are also available, with trips starting at $900 for six people. Lunch isn't provided with either package. ✉ *Gustavus* ☎ *907/697–3038* 🌐 *glacierbaysportfishing.com.*

HIKING

Several short, maintained trails begin near the Glacier Bay Lodge. The first half of the Forest Loop trail can be walked in an hour. The Bartlett Lake and River trails can take an entire day, depending on your pace. Whales and other marine mammals like sea otters, harbor seals, and sea lions are common cove visitors. Both black and brown bears traverse the area regularly, as do moose and, on the rare occasion, wolves and coyotes.

KAYAKING

The park's day boat transports kayakers to select spots of the bay each day between late May and Labor Day. Unless you're an expert kayaker, it's best arrange a guided tour.

Alaska Mountain Guides

KAYAKING | Take day kayaking trips for whale watching at Point Adolphus, a premier humpback gathering spot, as well as multiday sea-kayaking expeditions next to tidewater glaciers in Glacier Bay National Park with Alaska Mountain Guides. ✉ *Gustavus* ☎ *907/313–4422, 800/766–3396* 🌐 *www.alaskamountainguides.com* 🎫 *Day trips from $200.*

★ Glacier Bay Sea Kayaks

KAYAKING | Kayak rentals and single- and multiday trips with knowledgeable guides can be arranged in Bartlett Cove with this official park concessionaire. You will be given instructions on handling the craft plus camping and routing suggestions. ✉ *Bartlett Cove* ☎ *907/697–2257* 🌐 *www.glacierbayseakayaks.com* 🎫 *Guided day trips from $95.*

★ Spirit Walker Expeditions

KAYAKING | Spirit Walker's single- and multiday kayak trips (from $150) travel through the Icy Strait region and focus on the marine mammal hotbed at Point Adolphus. Trips to Glacier Bay and other remote areas of southeastern Alaska are also offered. ✉ *Gustavus* ☎ *800/529–2537* 🌐 *www.seakayakalaska.com.*

SCENIC FLIGHTS

Ward Air

TOUR—SPORTS | Take flightseeing trips to Glacier Bay, the Juneau Icefield, Elfin Cove, Tracy Arm, and Pack Creek with Ward Air. Charter flights to Gustavus and Bartlett Cove are also available on request. ✉ *8991 Yandukin Dr., Juneau* ☎ *907/789–9150* 🌐 *www.wardair.com.*

WHALE-WATCHING

The TAZ Whale Watching Tours

WHALE-WATCHING | Step aboard the M/V *TAZ* and check out the Icy Strait and Point Adolphus, near the entrance to Glacier Bay, for awesome views of humpback whales and many other marine mammals. All tours out of Gustavus include binoculars, snacks, and hot beverages. Half-day tours and custom charters accommodating up to 28 passengers are offered. ✉ *Gustavus* ☎ *907/321–2302, 888/698–2726* 🌐 *www.tazwhalewatching.com* 🎫 *From $123.*

What's Nearby

The hamlet of **Gustavus** is the jumping off point for Bartlett Cove and an alternative base of operations for visits to Glacier Bay. About 500-people call this old homesteader haven—where folks still wave at passing vehicles and pedestrians—home year-round. The community has a rich and unique frontier flavor.

A general store sells food, camping equipment, fishing gear, and anything else you might have forgotten at home. Gustavus also has several B&Bs and small lodges. Most are happy to prebook trip packages for you and will provide shuttle service to and from the park or the Gustavus airport and dock. Although the town is small, it's spread out, so some accommodations have bikes that guests can borrow or rent.

Sit-down restaurants are hard to come by in Gustavus. Lodges, such as the Annie Mae and the Beartrack, serve meals to the general public (reservations advised). Local seafood (including halibut and river salmon) appears on most menus, and you can often get a burger or steak, too. Look for seasonal dishes made with local berries. Several varieties flourish here, including wild strawberries, which dominate sandy shorelines.

Chapter 26

GRAND CANYON NATIONAL PARK

Updated by
Mara Levin

Camping	Hotels	Activities	Scenery	Crowds
★★★★★	★★★★★	★★★★★	★★★★★	★★★★★

WELCOME TO GRAND CANYON NATIONAL PARK

TOP REASONS TO GO

★ **Its status:** This is one of those places about which you really want to say, "Been there, done that!"

★ **Awesome vistas:** The Painted Desert, sandstone canyon walls, pine and fir forests, mesas, plateaus, volcanic features, the Colorado River, streams, and waterfalls make for some jaw-dropping moments.

★ **Year-round adventure:** Outdoors enthusiasts can bike, boat, camp, fish, hike, ride mules, white-water raft, watch birds and wildlife, cross-country ski, and snowshoe.

★ **Continuing education:** Adults and kids can have fun learning, thanks to free park-sponsored nature walks and interpretive programs.

★ **Sky-high and river-low experiences:** Experience the canyon via plane, train, and automobile, as well as by helicopter, row- or motorboat, bike, mule, or foot.

1 **South Rim.** The South Rim is where the action is: Grand Canyon Village's lodging, camping, eateries, stores, and museums, plus plenty of trailheads into the canyon. Four free shuttle routes cover more than 35 stops, and visitors who'd rather relax than rough it can treat themselves to comfy hotel rooms and elegant restaurant meals (lodging and camping reservations are essential).

2 **North Rim.** Of the nearly 5 million people who visit the park annually, 90% enter at the South Rim, but many consider the North Rim even more gorgeous—and worth the extra effort. Open only from mid-May to the end of October (or the first good snowfall), the North Rim has legitimate bragging rights: at more than 8,000 feet above sea level (1,000 feet higher than the South Rim), it has precious solitude and seven developed viewpoints. Rather than staring into the canyon's depths, you get a true sense of its expanse.

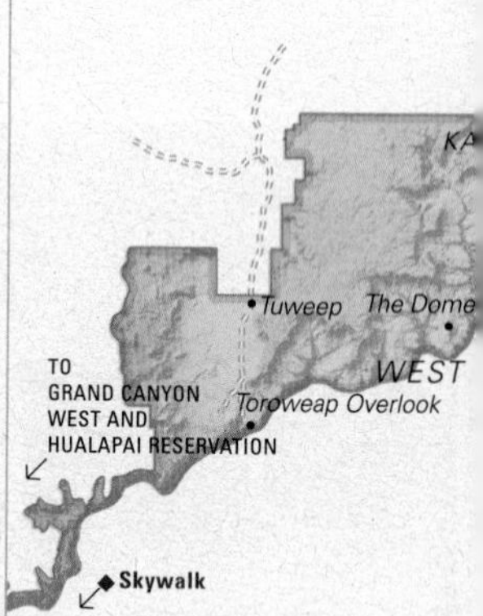

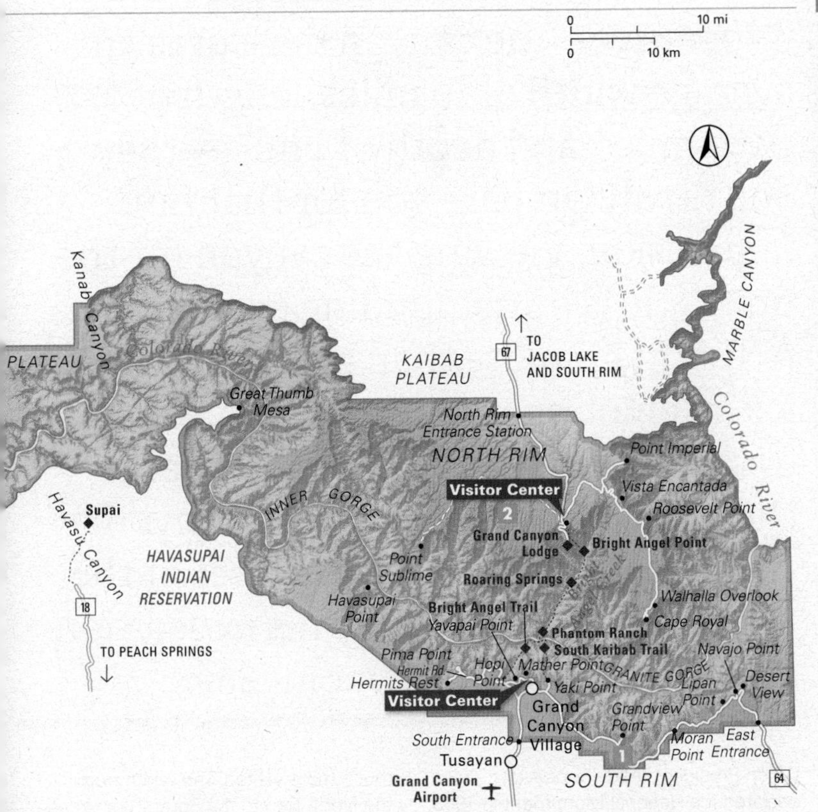
0
10 mi
0
10 km
MARBLE CANYON
Colorado River
TO
JACOB LAKE
AND SOUTH RIM
67
KAIBAB
PLATEAU
Kanab Canyon
PLATEAU
Colorado River
Great Thumb
Mesa
North Rim
Entrance Station
NORTH RIM
Point Imperial
Vista Encantada
Roosevelt Point
Visitor Center
2
INNER GORGE
Supai
Havasu Canyon
HAVASUPAI
INDIAN
RESERVATION
18
TO PEACH SPRINGS
Point
Sublime
Grand Canyon
Lodge
Bright Angel Point
Roaring Springs
Bright Angel Creek
Walhalla Overlook
Havasupai
Point
Bright Angel Trail
Yavapai Point
Cape Royal
Phantom Ranch
South Kaibab Trail
Navajo Point
Pima Point
Hermit Rd.
Hermits Rest
Hopi
Point
Mather Point
GRANITE GORGE
Yaki Point
Lipan
Point
Desert
View
Visitor Center
Grand
Canyon
Village
Grandview
Point
South Entrance
Moran
Point
East
Entrance
1
Tusayan
SOUTH RIM
64
Grand Canyon
Airport

When it comes to the Grand Canyon, there are statistics, and there are sensations. While the former are impressive—the canyon measures an average width of 10 miles, length of 277 river miles, and depth of 1 mile—they don't truly prepare you for that first impression. Viewing the canyon for the first time is an astounding experience. Actually, it's more than an experience: it's an emotion, one that only just begins to be captured with the word "Grand," the name bestowed upon the canyon by John Wesley Powell, an explorer of the American West, as he led his expedition down the Colorado River in 1869.

When President Teddy Roosevelt declared it a National Monument in 1908, he called it "the one great sight every American should see." Though many visitors do just that—stand at the rim and marvel in awe—there are manifold ways to soak up the canyon's magnificence. Hike or ride a trusty mule down into the canyon, bike or ramble along its rim, fly over, or raft through on the Colorado River.

Roughly 6 million visitors come to the park each year. You can access the canyon via two main points—the South Rim and the North Rim—but the South Rim is much easier to get to and therefore much more visited. The width from the North Rim to the South Rim varies from 600 feet to 18 miles, but traveling between rims by road requires a 215-mile drive. Hiking arduous trails from rim to rim is a steep and strenuous trek of at least 21 miles, but it's well worth the effort. You'll travel through five of North America's seven life zones. (To do this any other way, you'd have to journey from the Mexican desert to the Canadian woods.) West of Grand Canyon National Park, the tribal lands of the Hualapai and the Havasupai lie along the so-called West Rim of the canyon, where you'll find the impressive glass Skywalk.

SOUTH RIM AVERAGE HIGH/LOW TEMPERATURES					
JAN.	**FEB.**	**MAR.**	**APR.**	**MAY**	**JUNE**
41/18	45/21	51/25	60/32	70/39	81/47
JULY	**AUG.**	**SEPT.**	**OCT.**	**NOV.**	**DEC.**
84/54	82/53	76/47	65/36	52/27	43/20

NORTH RIM AVERAGE HIGH/LOW TEMPERATURES					
JAN.	**FEB.**	**MAR.**	**APR.**	**MAY**	**JUNE**
37/16	39/18	44/21	53/29	62/34	73/40
JULY	**AUG.**	**SEPT.**	**OCT.**	**NOV.**	**DEC.**
77/46	75/45	69/39	59/31	46/24	40/20

INNER CANYON AVERAGE HIGH/LOW TEMPERATURES					
JAN.	**FEB.**	**MAR.**	**APR.**	**MAY**	**JUNE**
56/36	62/42	71/48	82/56	92/63	101/72
JULY	**AUG.**	**SEPT.**	**OCT.**	**NOV.**	**DEC.**
106/78	103/75	97/69	84/58	68/46	57/37

Planning

When to Go

There's no bad time to visit the canyon, though the busiest times of year are summer and spring break. Visiting the South Rim during these peak seasons, as well as holidays, requires patience and a tolerance for crowds. If you plan to hike into the canyon, be aware that temperatures rise as you descend; summer daytime highs at the bottom are often over 100° F. Fall and winter at the South Rim are spectacular and far less crowded. Note that weather changes on a whim in this exposed high-desert region. The North Rim shuts down mid-October through mid-May due to weather conditions and related road closures.

Planning Your Time

Plan ahead: Mule rides require at least a six-month advance reservation—longer for the busy season (most can be reserved up to 13 months in advance). Multiday rafting trips should be reserved at least a year in advance.

Once you arrive, pick up the free *Pocket Map and Services Guide,* a brochure with a detailed map and schedule of free programs, at the entrance gate or at any of the visitor centers. The free *Grand Canyon Accessibility Guide* is also available.

The park is most crowded on the South Rim, especially near the Visitor Center/Mather Point and in Grand Canyon Village, as well as on the scenic drives.

Getting Here and Around

SOUTH RIM

CAR

The best route into the park from the east or south is from Flagstaff. Take U.S. 180 northwest to the park's southern entrance and Grand Canyon Visitor Center. From the west on Interstate 40, the most direct route to the South Rim is taking Highway 64 from Williams to U.S. 180.

PARK SHUTTLE

The South Rim is open to car traffic year-round, though access to Hermits Rest is limited to shuttle buses during summer months. There are four free shuttle routes that run from one hour before sunrise until one hour after sunset, every 15 to 30 minutes: the **Hermits Rest Route** operates March through November, between Grand Canyon Village and Hermits Rest. The **Village Route** operates year-round in the village area, stopping at lodgings, the general store, and the Grand Canyon Visitor Center. The **Kaibab Rim Route** goes from the visitor center to five viewpoints, including the Yavapai Geology Museum and Yaki Point (where cars are not permitted). The **Tusayan Route** travels between the village and the town of Tusayan from March through September. A fifth route, the **Hiker's Express,** shuttles hikers from the village to the South Kaibab Trailhead twice each morning. ■ **TIP→ In summer, South Rim roads are congested and it's easier, and sometimes required, to park your car and take the free shuttle.**

TAXI AND SHUTTLE

Although there's no public transportation into the Grand Canyon, you can hire a taxi to take you to or from the Grand Canyon Village or any of the Tusayan hotels. Groome Transportation has frequent shuttle service between Flagstaff, Williams, Tusayan, and Grand Canyon Village (at Maswik Lodge); they also have connecting service from Phoenix and Sedona.

TAXI AND SHUTTLE CONTACTS Groome Transportation. ☎ *928/226–8060, 800/888–2749* 🌐 *www.groometransportation.com.* **Xanterra.** ☎ *928/638–2822, 888/297–2757* 🌐 *www.xanterra.com.*

TRAIN

Grand Canyon Railway

TRAIN TOURS | FAMILY | There's no need to deal with all of the other drivers racing to the South Rim. Sit back and relax in the comfy train cars of the Grand Canyon Railway. Live music, storytelling, and a pretend train robbery enliven the trip as you journey past the landscape through prairie, ranch, and national park land to the log-cabin train station in Grand Canyon Village. You won't see the Grand Canyon from the train, but you can walk (¼ mile) or catch the shuttle at the restored, historic Grand Canyon Railway Station. The vintage train departs from the Williams Depot every morning and makes the 65-mile journey in 2¼ hours. You can do the round-trip in a single day; however, it's a more relaxing and enjoyable strategy to stay for a night or two at the South Rim before returning to Williams. ☎ *800/843–8724* 🌐 *www.thetrain.com* 💵 *$82–$219 round-trip; Rates do not include $35 park entry fee (for up to 9 persons).*

NORTH RIM

AIR

The nearest airport to the North Rim is **St. George Regional Airport** (☎ *435/627–4080* 🌐 *www.flysgu.com*) in Utah, 164 miles north, with regular service provided by American, Delta, and United airlines.

CAR

To reach the North Rim by car, take U.S. 89 north from Flagstaff past Cameron, turning left onto U.S. 89A at Bitter Springs. At Jacob Lake, take Highway 67 directly to the Grand Canyon North Rim. You can drive yourself to the scenic viewpoints and trailheads; the only transportation offered in the park is a shuttle twice each morning that brings eager hikers from Grand Canyon Lodge to the North

Kaibab Trailhead (a 2-mile trip). Note that services on the North Rim shut down in mid-October, and the road closes after the first major snowfall (usually the end of October); Highway 67 south of Jacob Lake is closed.

SHUTTLE

From mid-May to mid-October, the **Trans Canyon Shuttle** (☎ *928/638–2820* 🌐 *www.trans-canyonshuttle.com*) travels daily between the South and North rims—the ride takes 4½ hours each way. The fare is $90 each way and reservations are required.

Inspiration

ARIZONA DOCUMENTARIES. Whether you want to learn about the Grand Canyon, Arizona's efforts to manage its water, or famous national figures such as Barry Goldwater or Sandra Day O'Connor, Arizona PBS has a collection well worth navigating 🌐 *wazpbs.org/tv/arizonacollection*.

Park Essentials

PARK FEES AND PERMITS

A fee of $35 per vehicle or $20 per person for pedestrians and cyclists is good for one week's access at both rims.

The $70 Grand Canyon Pass gives unlimited access to the park for 12 months. The annual America the Beautiful **National Parks and Recreational Land Pass** (☎ *888/275–8747* 🌐 *store.usgs.gov/pass, $80*) provides unlimited access to all national parks and federal recreation areas for 12 months.

No permits are needed for day hikers, but **backcountry permits** (☎ *928/638–7875* 🌐 *www.nps.gov/grca, $10, plus $8 per person per night*) are necessary for overnight hikers camping below the rim. Permits are limited, so make your reservation as far in advance as possible—they're taken by fax (☎ *928/638–2125*), by mail (✉ *1824 S. Thompson St., Suite 201, Flagstaff, AZ 86001*), or in person at the Backcountry Information centers (in the village on the South Rim and near the visitor center on the North Rim) up to four months prior to your arrival. A limited number of last-minute permits are available for Indian Garden, Bright Angel, and Cottonwood campgrounds each day. Camping on the North Rim and the South Rim is restricted to designated campgrounds (☎ *877/444–6777* 🌐 *www.recreation.gov*).

PARK HOURS

The South Rim is open continuously every day of the year (weather permitting), while the North Rim is open mid-May through October. Because Arizona does not observe daylight saving time, the park is in the same time zone as California and Nevada from mid-March to early November, and in the Mountain time zone the rest of the year. Just to the east of the park, the Navajo Nation observes daylight saving time.

CELL PHONE RECEPTION

Cell phone coverage can be spotty at both the South Rim and North Rim—though Verizon customers report better reception at the South Rim. Don't expect a strong signal anywhere in the park, but Grand Canyon Village is usually the best bet.

Hotels

The park's accommodations include three "historic-rustic" facilities and four motel-style lodges, all of which have undergone significant upgrades over the past decade. Of the 922 rooms, cabins, and suites, only 203 are at the North Rim, all at the Grand Canyon Lodge. Outside El Tovar Hotel, the canyon's architectural highlight, accommodations are relatively basic but comfortable, and the most sought-after rooms have canyon views. Rates vary widely, but most rooms fall in the $175 to $250 range, though the most basic units on the South

Rim go for just $125. Yavapai Lodge, on the South Rim, is the only hotel in the park that allows pets.

Reservations are a must, especially during the busy summer season. **■ TIP→ If you want to get your first choice (especially Bright Angel Lodge or El Tovar), make reservations as far in advance as possible; they're taken up to 13 months ahead. You might find a last-minute cancellation, but you shouldn't count on it.** Although lodging at the South Rim will keep you close to the action, the frenetic activity and crowded facilities are off-putting to some. With short notice, the best time to find a room on the South Rim is in winter. And though the North Rim is less crowded than the South Rim, the only lodging available is at Grand Canyon Lodge.

Just south of the South Rim park boundary, Tusayan's hotels are in a convenient location but without bargains, while Williams (about an hour's drive) and Flagstaff (about 90 minutes away) can provide price breaks on food and lodging, as well as a respite from the crowds. Extra amenities (e.g., swimming pools and gyms) are also more abundant. Even outside the park, reservations are always a good idea.

LODGING CONTACTS Xanterra Parks & Resorts. ☎ *888/297–2757* 🌐 *www.grandcanyonlodges.com.* **Delaware North.** ☎ *877/404–4611* 🌐 *www.visitgrandcanyon.com.*

Restaurants

Within the park on the South Rim, you can find everything from cafeteria food to casual café fare to creatively prepared, Western- and Southwestern-inspired American cuisine—there's even a coffeehouse with organic joe. Reservations are accepted (and recommended) only for dinner at El Tovar Dining Room; they can be made up to six months in advance with El Tovar room reservations, 30 days in advance without. You should also make dinner reservations at the Grand Canyon Lodge Dining Room on the North Rim—as the only "upscale" dining option, the restaurant fills up quickly at dinner throughout the season (the other choice on the North Rim is a deli). The dress code is casual across the board, but El Tovar is your best option if you're looking to dress up a bit and thumb through an extensive wine list. Options for picnic supplies at the South Rim include the general store in Market Plaza and healthy grab-and-go fare at Bright Angel Bicycles' café next to the Visitor Center. Drinking water and restrooms are available only at some picnic spots.

Bring your picnic basket and enjoy dining alfresco surrounded by some of the most beautiful backdrops in the country. Be sure to bring water, as it's unavailable at many of these spots, as are restrooms. **Buggeln,** 15 miles east of Grand Canyon Village on Desert View Drive, has some secluded, shady spots. **Grandview Point** has, as the name implies, grand vistas; it's 12 miles east of the village on Desert View Drive. **Cape Royal,** 23 miles south of the North Rim Visitor Center, at the end of Cape Royal Road, is the most popular designated picnic area on the North Rim due to its panoramic views. **Point Imperial,** 11 miles northeast of the North Rim Visitor Center, has shade and some privacy.

Eateries outside the park generally range from mediocre to terrible—you didn't come all the way to the Grand Canyon for the food, did you? Our selections highlight your best options. Of towns near the park, Flagstaff definitely has the leg up on culinary variety and quality, with Tusayan (near the South Rim) and Jacob Lake (the closest town to the North Rim) offering mostly either fast food or merely adequate sit-down restaurants. Near the park, even the priciest places welcome casual dress. On the Hualapai and Havasupai reservations in Havasu Canyon and on the West Rim, dining is limited and basic.

Hotel and restaurant reviews have been shortened. For full information, visit Fodors.com.

What It Costs

	$	$$	$$$	$$$$
RESTAURANTS	under $12	$12–$20	$21–$30	Over $30
HOTELS	under $120	$120–$175	$176–$250	Over $250

Tours

Grand Canyon Conservancy Field Institute

GUIDED TOURS | Instructors lead guided educational tours, hikes around the canyon, and weekend programs at the South Rim. With more than 200 classes a year, tour topics include everything from archaeology and backcountry medicine to photography and natural history. Contact GCC for a schedule and price list. Private hikes can be arranged. Discounted classes are available for members; annual dues are $35. ✉ *GCA Warehouse, 2–B Albright Ave., Grand Canyon Village* ☎ *928/638–7035, 866/471–4435* 🌐 *www.grandcanyon.org/fieldinstitute* 🎫 *From $235.*

Xanterra Motorcoach Tours

GUIDED TOURS | Narrated by knowledgeable guides, tours include the Hermits Rest Tour, which travels along the old wagon road built by the Santa Fe Railway; the Desert View Tour, which glimpses the Colorado River's rapids and stops at Lipan Point; Sunrise and Sunset Tours; and combination tours. ☎ *303/297–2757, 888/297–2757* 🌐 *www.grandcanyonlodges.com* 🎫 *From $40.*

Visitor Information

CONTACTS Grand Canyon National Park. ☎ *928/638–7888* 🌐 *www.nps.gov/grca.*

Grand Canyon South Rim

Visitors to the canyon converge mostly on the South Rim, and mostly in summer. Grand Canyon Village is here, with a majority of the park's lodging and camping, trailheads, restaurants, stores, and museums, along with a nearby airport and railroad depot. Believe it or not, the average stay in the park is a mere half day or so; this is not advised! You need to spend several days to truly appreciate this marvelous place, but at the very least, give it a full day. Hike down into the canyon, or along the rim, to get away from the crowds and experience nature at its finest.

Sights

HISTORIC SIGHTS

Tusayan Ruin and Museum

ARCHAEOLOGICAL SITE | This museum offers a quick orientation to the prehistoric and modern indigenous populations of the Grand Canyon and the Colorado Plateau, including an excavation of an 800-year-old Pueblo site. Of special interest are split-twig figurines dating back 2,000 to 4,000 years and other artifacts left behind by ancient cultures. A ranger leads daily interpretive tours of the Ancestral Pueblo village. ✉ *Grand Canyon National Park* ✣ *About 20 miles east of Grand Canyon Village on E. Rim Dr.* ☎ *928/638–7888* 🎫 *Free.*

SCENIC DRIVES

Desert View Drive

SCENIC DRIVE | This heavily traveled 25-mile stretch of road follows the rim from the east entrance to Grand Canyon Village. Starting from the less-congested entry near Desert View, road warriors can get their first glimpse of the canyon from the 70-foot-tall watchtower, the top of which provides the highest viewpoint on the South Rim. Six developed canyon viewpoints in addition to unmarked pullouts, the remains of an Ancestral

Puebloan dwelling at the Tusayan Ruin and Museum, and the secluded and lovely Buggeln picnic area make for great stops along the South Rim. The Kaibab Rim Route shuttle bus travels a short section of Desert View Drive and takes 50 minutes to ride round-trip without getting off at any of the stops: Grand Canyon Visitor Center, South Kaibab Trailhead, Yaki Point, Pipe Creek Vista, Mather Point, and Yavapai Geology Museum. ✉ *Grand Canyon National Park.*

Hermit Road

SCENIC DRIVE | The Santa Fe Company built Hermit Road, formerly known as West Rim Drive, in 1912 as a scenic tour route. Nine overlooks dot this 7-mile stretch, each worth a visit. The road is filled with hairpin turns, so make sure you adhere to posted speed limits. A 1½-mile Greenway trail offers easy access to cyclists looking to enjoy the original 1912 Hermit Rim Road. From March through November, Hermit Road is closed to private auto traffic because of congestion; during this period, a free shuttle bus carries visitors to all the overlooks. Riding the bus round-trip without getting off at any of the viewpoints takes 80 minutes; the return trip stops only at Hermits Rest, Pima, Mohave, and Powell points. ✉ *Grand Canyon National Park.*

SCENIC STOPS

The Abyss

VIEWPOINT | At an elevation of 6,720 feet, the Abyss is one of the most awesome stops on Hermit Road, revealing a sheer drop of 3,000 feet to the Tonto Platform, a wide terrace of Tapeats sandstone about two-thirds of the way down the canyon. From the Abyss you'll also see several isolated sandstone columns, the largest of which is called the Monument. ✉ *Grand Canyon National Park* ✣ *About 5 miles west of Hermit Rd. Junction on Hermit Rd.*

Desert View and Watchtower

VIEWPOINT | From the top of the 70-foot stone-and-mortar watchtower with its 360-degree views, even the muted hues of the distant Painted Desert to the east and the Vermilion Cliffs rising from a high plateau near the Utah border are visible. In the chasm below, angling to the north toward Marble Canyon, an imposing stretch of the Colorado River reveals itself. Up several flights of stairs, the watchtower houses a glass-enclosed observatory with telescopes. ✉ *Grand Canyon National Park* ✣ *Just north of East Entrance Station on Desert View Dr.* ☎ *928/638–7888* 🌐 *www.nps.gov/grca* 🎫 *Free.*

Grandview Point

VIEWPOINT | At an elevation of 7,399 feet, the view from here is one of the finest in the canyon. To the northeast is a group of dominant buttes, including Krishna Shrine, Vishnu Temple, Rama Shrine, and Sheba Temple. A short stretch of the Colorado River is also visible. Directly below the point, and accessible by the steep and rugged Grandview Trail, is Horseshoe Mesa, where you can see remnants of Last Chance Copper Mine. ✉ *Grand Canyon National Park* ✣ *About 12 miles east of Grand Canyon Village on Desert View Dr.*

Hermits Rest

VIEWPOINT | This westernmost viewpoint and Hermit Trail, which descends from it, were named for "hermit" Louis Boucher, a 19th-century French-Canadian prospector who had a number of mining claims and a roughly built home down in the canyon. The trail served as the original mule ride down to Hermit Camp beginning in 1914. Views from here include Hermit Rapids and the towering cliffs of the Supai and Redwall formations. You can buy curios and snacks in the stone building at Hermits Rest. ✉ *Grand Canyon National Park* ✣ *About 8 miles west of Hermit Rd. Junction on Hermit Rd.*

★ Hopi Point

VIEWPOINT | From this elevation of 7,071 feet, you can see a large section of the Colorado River; although it appears as a thin line, the river is nearly 350 feet wide. The overlook extends farther into the canyon than any other point on Hermit Road. The incredible unobstructed views make this a popular place to watch the sunset.

Across the canyon to the north is Shiva Temple. In 1937 Harold Anthony of the American Museum of Natural History led an expedition to the rock formation in the belief that it supported life that had been cut off from the rest of the canyon. Imagine the expedition members' surprise when they found an empty Kodak film box on top of the temple—it had been left behind by Emery Kolb, who felt slighted for not having been invited to join Anthony's tour.

Directly below Hopi Point lies Dana Butte, named for a prominent 19th-century geologist. In 1919 an entrepreneur proposed connecting Hopi Point, Dana Butte, and the Tower of Set across the river with an aerial tramway, a technically feasible plan that fortunately has not been realized. ✉ *Grand Canyon National Park* ✢ *About 4 miles west of Hermit Rd. Junction on Hermit Rd.*

Lipan Point

VIEWPOINT | Here, at the canyon's widest point, you can get an astonishing visual profile of the gorge's geologic history, with a view of every eroded layer of the canyon and one of the longest visible stretches of Colorado River. The spacious panorama stretches to the Vermilion Cliffs on the northeastern horizon and features a multitude of imaginatively named spires, buttes, and temples—intriguing rock formations named after their resemblance to ancient pyramids. You can also see Unkar Delta, where a creek joins the Colorado to form powerful rapids and a broad beach. Ancestral Pueblo farmers worked the Unkar Delta for hundreds of years, growing corn, beans, and melons. ✉ *Grand Canyon National Park* ✢ *About 25 miles east of Grand Canyon Village on Desert View Dr.*

★ Mather Point

VIEWPOINT | You'll likely get your first glimpse of the canyon from this viewpoint, one of the most impressive and accessible (next to the main visitor center plaza) on the South Rim. Named for the National Park Service's first director, Stephen Mather, this spot yields extraordinary views of the Grand Canyon, including deep into the inner gorge and numerous buttes: Wotans Throne, Brahma Temple, and Zoroaster Temple, among others. The Grand Canyon Lodge, on the North Rim, is almost directly north from Mather Point and only 10 miles away—yet you have to drive 215 miles to get from one spot to the other. ✉ *Near Grand Canyon Visitor Center, Grand Canyon National Park* ☎ *928/638–7888* 🌐 *www.nps.gov/grca.*

Moran Point

VIEWPOINT | This point was named for American landscape artist Thomas Moran, who was especially fond of the play of light and shadows from this location. He first visited the canyon with John Wesley Powell in 1873. "Thomas Moran's name, more than any other, with the possible exception of Major Powell's, is to be associated with the Grand Canyon," wrote noted canyon photographer Ellsworth Kolb. It's fitting that Moran Point is a favorite spot of photographers and painters. ✉ *Grand Canyon National Park* ✢ *About 17 miles east of Grand Canyon Village on Desert View Dr.*

Trailview Overlook

VIEWPOINT | Look down on a dramatic view of the Bright Angel and Plateau Point trails as they zigzag down the canyon. In the deep gorge to the north flows Bright Angel Creek, one of the region's few permanent tributary streams of the Colorado River. Toward the south is an unobstructed view of the distant San Francisco Peaks, as well as Bill Williams

Mountain (on the horizon) and Red Butte (about 15 miles south of the canyon rim). ✉ *Grand Canyon National Park* ✣ *About 2 miles west of Hermit Rd. Junction on Hermit Rd.*

Yaki Point

VIEWPOINT | Stop here for an exceptional view of Wotans Throne, a flat-top butte named by François Matthes, a U.S. Geological Survey scientist who developed the first topographical map of the Grand Canyon. The overlook juts out over the canyon, providing unobstructed views of inner-canyon rock formations, South Rim cliffs, and Clear Creek canyon. About a mile south of Yaki Point is the trailhead for the South Kaibab Trail. **TIP→ The point is one of the best places on the South Rim to watch the sunrise and the sunset.** ✉ *Grand Canyon National Park* ✣ *2 miles east of Grand Canyon Village on Desert View Dr.*

★ **Yavapai Point**

MUSEUM | Dominated by the Yavapai Geology Museum and Observation Station, this point displays panoramic views of the mighty gorge through a wall of windows. Exhibits at the museum include videos of the canyon floor and the Colorado River, a scaled diorama of the canyon with national park boundaries, fossils, and rock fragments used to re-create the complex layers of the canyon walls, and a display on the natural forces used to carve the chasm. Dig even deeper into Grand Canyon geology with free daily ranger programs. This point is also a good location to watch the sunset. ✉ *Grand Canyon Village* ✣ *1 mile east of Market Plaza.*

TRAILS

★ **Bright Angel Trail**

TRAIL | This well-maintained trail is one of the most scenic (and busiest) hiking paths from the South Rim to the bottom of the canyon (9.6 miles each way). Rest houses are equipped with water at the 1½- and 3-mile points from May through September, and at Indian Garden (4 miles) year-round. Water is also available at Bright Angel Campground, 9¼ miles below the trailhead. Plateau Point, on a spur trail about 1½ miles below Indian Garden, is as far as you should attempt to go on a day hike; the round-trip will take six to nine hours.

Bright Angel Trail is the easiest of all the footpaths into the canyon, but because the climb out from the bottom is an ascent of 5,510 feet, the trip should be attempted only by those in good physical condition and should be avoided in midsummer due to extreme heat. The top of the trail can be icy in winter. Originally a bighorn sheep path and later used by the Havasupai, the trail was widened late in the 19th century for prospectors and is now used for both mule and foot traffic. Also note that mule trains have the right-of-way—and sometimes leave unpleasant surprises in your path. *Moderate.* ✉ *Grand Canyon National Park* ✣ *Trailhead: Kolb Studio, Hermit Rd.*

★ **Rim Trail**

TRAIL | The South Rim's most popular walking path is the 12-mile (one-way) Rim Trail, which runs along the edge of the canyon from Pipe Creek Vista (the first overlook on Desert View Drive) to Hermits Rest. This walk, which is paved to Maricopa Point and for the last 1½ miles to Hermits Rest, visits several of the South Rim's historic landmarks. Allow anywhere from 15 minutes to a full day, depending on how much of the trail you want to cover; the Rim Trail is an ideal day hike, as it varies only a few hundred feet in elevation from Mather Point (7,120 feet) to the trailhead at Hermits Rest (6,650 feet). The trail also can be accessed from several spots in Grand Canyon Village and from the major viewpoints along Hermit Road, which are serviced by shuttle buses during the busy summer months. On the Rim Trail, water is available only in the Grand Canyon Village area and at Hermits Rest. *Easy.* ✉ *Grand Canyon National Park.*

South Kaibab Trail

TRAIL | This trail starts near Yaki Point, 4 miles east of Grand Canyon Village, and is accessible via the free shuttle bus.

Because the route is so steep (and sometimes icy in winter)—descending from the trailhead at 7,260 feet down to 2,480 feet at the Colorado River—and has no water, many hikers take this trail down, then ascend via the less-demanding Bright Angel Trail. Allow four to six hours to reach the Colorado River on this 6.4-mile trek. At the river, the trail crosses a suspension bridge and runs on to Phantom Ranch. Along the trail there is no water and little shade. There are no campgrounds, though there are portable toilets at Cedar Ridge (6,320 feet), 1½ miles from the trailhead. An emergency phone is available at the Tipoff, 4.6 miles down the trail (3 miles past Cedar Ridge). The trail corkscrews down through some spectacular geology. Look for (but don't remove) fossils in the limestone when taking water breaks. *Difficult.* ✉ *Grand Canyon National Park* ✣ *Trailhead: Yaki Point Rd., off Desert View Dr.*

VISITOR CENTERS

Desert View Information Center

Near the watchtower, at Desert View Point, this nonprofit Grand Canyon Association store and information center has a nice selection of books, park pamphlets, gifts, and educational materials. It's also a handy place to pick up maps and info if you enter the park at the Eastern entrance. All sales from the association stores go to support the park programs. ✉ *Eastern entrance, Grand Canyon National Park* ☎ *800/858–2808, 928/638–7888.*

Grand Canyon Verkamp's Visitor Center

This small visitor center is named for the Verkamp family, who operated a curios shop on the South Rim for more than a hundred years. The building serves as an official visitor center, ranger station (get your Junior Ranger badges here), bookstore, and museum, with compelling exhibits on the Verkamps and other pioneers in this region. ✉ *Desert View Dr., Grand Canyon Village* ✣ *Across from El Tovar Hotel* ☎ *928/638–7146.*

Grand Canyon Visitor Center

INFO CENTER | The park's main orientation center provides pamphlets and resources to help plan your visit. It also holds engaging interpretive exhibits on the park. Rangers are on hand to answer questions and aid in planning canyon excursions. A daily schedule of ranger-led hikes and evening lectures is available, and a 20-minute film about the history, geology, and wildlife of the canyon plays every 30 minutes in the theater. The bicycle rental office, a small café, and a huge gift store are also in this complex. It's a short walk from here to Mather Point, or a short ride on the shuttle bus, which can take you into Grand Canyon Village. The visitor center is also accessible from the village via a leisurely 1-mile walk on the Greenway Trail, a paved pathway that meanders through the forest. ✉ *East side of Grand Canyon Village, 450 Hwy. 64, Grand Canyon* ☎ *928/638–7888* 🌐 *www.explorethecanyon.com.*

Yavapai Geology Museum

Learn about the geology of the canyon at this Grand Canyon Association museum and bookstore. You can also catch the park shuttle bus or pick up information for the Rim Trail here. The views of the canyon and Phantom Ranch from inside this historic building are stupendous. ✉ *1 mile east of Market Plaza, Grand Canyon Village* ☎ *928/638–7888.*

Restaurants

Arizona Steakhouse

$$$ | **STEAKHOUSE** | The canyon views from this casual Southwestern-style steak house are the best of any restaurant at the South Rim. The dinner menu leans toward steak-house dishes, while lunch is primarily salads and sandwiches with a Southwestern twist. **Known for:** views of the Grand Canyon; Southwest fare; local craft beers and wines. $ *Average main: $28* ✉ *Bright Angel Lodge, Desert View Dr., Grand Canyon Village* ☎ *928/638–2631* 🌐 *www.grandcanyonlodges.com.*

★ El Tovar Dining Room

$$$ | SOUTHWESTERN | Even at the edge of the Grand Canyon it's possible to find gourmet dining. This cozy room of dark wood beams and stone, nestled in the historic El Tovar Lodge, dates to 1905. **Known for:** historic setting with canyon views; local and organic ingredients; fine dining that's worth the splurge. $ *Average main: $28* ✉ *El Tovar Hotel, Desert View Dr., Grand Canyon Village* ☎ *928/638–2631* 🌐 *www.grandcanyonlodges.com.*

Fred Harvey Burger

$$ | SOUTHWESTERN | FAMILY | Open for breakfast, lunch, and dinner, this casual café at Bright Angel Lodge serves basics like pancakes, salads, sandwiches, pastas, burgers, and steaks. Or you can step it up a notch and order some of the same selections straight from the neighboring Arizona Steakhouse's menu, including prime rib, baby back ribs, and wild salmon. **Known for:** reasonably priced American fare; family-friendly menu and setting; some vegetarian and gluten-free options. $ *Average main: $14* ✉ *Bright Angel Lodge, Desert View Dr., Grand Canyon Village* ☎ *928/638–2631* 🌐 *www.grandcanyonlodges.com.*

Maswik Food Court

$ | AMERICAN | FAMILY | You can get a burger, hot sandwich, pasta, or Mexican fare at this food court, as well as pizza by the slice and wine and beer in the adjacent Maswik Pizza Pub. This casual eatery is in Maswik Lodge, ¼ mile from the rim, and the Pizza Pub stays open until 11 pm (you can also order pizza to take out). **Known for:** good selection (something for everyone); later hours; pizza to go. $ *Average main: $10* ✉ *Maswik Lodge, Desert View Dr., Grand Canyon Village* 🌐 *www.grandcanyonlodges.com.*

Yavapai Lodge Restaurant and Tavern

$$ | AMERICAN | If you don't have time for full-service, the restaurant in Yavapai Lodge offers cafeteria-style dining for breakfast, lunch, and dinner, including hot and cold sandwiches, pizza, barbecue ribs, and rotisserie chicken. Wine and beer, including craft brews from nearby Flagstaff, are also on the menu; or enjoy drinks on the patio at the adjacent Yavapai Tavern. **Known for:** quick bites or hearty meals; convenient dining in Market Plaza; patio with firepit at Yavapai Tavern. $ *Average main: $19* ✉ *Yavapai Lodge, Desert View Dr., Grand Canyon Village* ☎ *928/638–4001* 🌐 *www.visitgrandcanyon.com.*

Hotels

Bright Angel Lodge

$ | HOTEL | Famed architect Mary Jane Colter designed this 1935 log-and-stone structure, which sits within a few yards of the canyon rim and blends superbly with the canyon walls; its location is similar to El Tovar's but for about half the price. **Pros:** good value for the amazing location; charming rooms and cabins steps from the rim; on-site Internet kiosks and transportation desk for the mule ride. **Cons:** popular lobby is always packed; parking is a bit of a hike; only some rooms have canyon views. $ *Rooms from: $104* ✉ *Desert View Dr., Grand Canyon Village* ☎ *888/297–2757 reservations only, 928/638–2631* 🌐 *www.grandcanyonlodges.com* *105 units* 🍽 *No meals.*

★ El Tovar Hotel

$$$$ | HOTEL | The hotel's proximity to all of the canyon's facilities, European hunting-lodge atmosphere, attractively updated rooms and tile baths, and renowned dining room make it the best place to stay on the South Rim. A registered National Historic Landmark, the "architectural crown jewel of the Grand Canyon" was built in 1905 of Oregon pine logs and native stone. **Pros:** historic lodging just steps from the South Rim; fabulous lounge with outdoor seating and canyon views; best in-park dining on-site. **Cons:** books up quickly; priciest lodging in the park; rooms are comfortable, not luxurious. *Rooms from: $275 Desert View Dr., Grand Canyon Village 888/297–2757 reservations only, 928/638–2631 www.grandcanyonlodges.com 78 rooms No meals.*

Kachina Lodge

$$$ | **HOTEL** | The well-appointed rooms at this motel-style lodge in Grand Canyon Village on the South Rim are a good bet for families and are within easy walking distance of dining facilities at nearby lodges. **Pros:** partial canyon views in half the rooms; family-friendly; steps from the best restaurants in the park. **Cons:** check-in at nearby El Tovar Hotel; limited parking; no air conditioning. *Rooms from: $232 Desert View Dr., Grand Canyon Village 888/297–2757 reservations only, 928/638–2631 www.grandcanyonlodges.com 49 rooms No meals.*

Maswik Lodge

$$ | **HOTEL** | **FAMILY** | Far from the noisy crowds, Maswik accommodations are in two-story, contemporary motel-style buildings nestled in a shady ponderosa pine forest. **Pros:** units are modern, spacious, and well equipped; good for families; affordable dining options. **Cons:** rooms lack historic charm; tucked away from the rim in the forest; no elevators for second-floor rooms. *Rooms from: $159 Grand Canyon Village 888/297–2757 reservations only, 928/638–2631 www.grandcanyonlodges.com 278 rooms No meals.*

Phantom Ranch

$ | **B&B/INN** | In a grove of cottonwood trees on the canyon floor, Phantom Ranch is accessible only to hikers, river rafters, and mule trekkers; there are 40 dormitory bunk beds and 14 beds in cabins, all with shared baths (though cabins have toilets and sinks). **Pros:** only inner-canyon lodging option; fabulous canyon views; remote access limits crowds. **Cons:** reservations are booked up to a year in advance; few amenities; shared bathrooms. *Rooms from: $65 On canyon floor, Grand Canyon National Park At intersection of Bright Angel and Kaibab trails 303/297–2757, 888/297–2757 www.grandcanyonlodges.com 54 beds No meals.*

Thunderbird Lodge

$$$$ | **HOTEL** | This motel with comfortable, simple rooms and partial canyon views has all the modern amenities you'd expect at a typical mid-price chain hotel—even pod coffeemakers. **Pros:** canyon views in some rooms; family-friendly; convenient to dining and activities in Grand Canyon Village. **Cons:** check-in at nearby Bright Angel Lodge; limited parking nearby; no air conditioning (but some rooms have effective evaporative coolers). *Rooms from: $264 Desert View Dr., Grand Canyon Village 888/297–2757 reservations only, 928/638–2631 www.grandcanyonlodges.com 55 rooms No meals.*

Yavapai Lodge

$$ | **HOTEL** | The largest motel-style lodge in the park is tucked in a pinyon-pine and juniper forest at the eastern end of Grand Canyon Village, across from Market Plaza. **Pros:** transportation-activities desk in the lobby; walk to Market Plaza in Grand Canyon Village; only pet-friendly lodging at South Rim. **Cons:** farthest lodging in park from the rim (1 mile); generic appearance. *Rooms from: $154 10 Yavapai Lodge Rd., Grand Canyon Village 877/404–4611 reservations only www.visitgrandcanyon.com 358 rooms No meals.*

Activities

BOATING AND RAFTING

The National Park Service restricts the number of visitors allowed on the Colorado River each season, and seats fill up fast. Due to the limited availability, reservations for multiday trips should be made a year or two in advance. Lots of people book trips for summer's peak period: June through August. If you're flexible, take advantage of the Arizona weather; May to early June and September are ideal rafting times in the Grand Canyon.

Most trips begin at Lees Ferry, a few miles below the Glen Canyon Dam near Page. There are tranquil half- and full-day float trips from the Glen Canyon Dam to Lees Ferry, as well as raft trips that run from 3 to 18 days. For outfitters, see the boating and rafting listings under Lees Ferry in ⇨ *Nearby Towns* of this chapter. The shorter three- and four-day voyages either begin or end at Phantom Ranch at the bottom of the Grand Canyon at river mile 87. On the longer trips, you'll encounter the best of the canyon's white water along the way, including Lava Falls, listed in the *Guinness Book of World Records* as "the fastest navigable white water stretch in North America." Life jackets, beverages, tents, sheets, tarps, sleeping bags, dry bags, first aid, and food are provided—but you'll still need to plan ahead by packing clothing, a rain suit, hats, sunscreen, toiletries, and other sundries. Commercial outfitters allow each river runner two waterproof bags to store items during the day. Just keep in mind that one of the bags will be filled up with the provided sleeping bag and tarp, which leaves only one for your personal belongings.

CAMPING

Within the national park, there are two developed campgrounds on the South Rim and one on the North Rim. All campgrounds charge nightly camping fees in addition to the general park entrance fee; some accept reservations up to six months in advance (☎ *877/444–6777* 🌐 *www.recreation.gov*) and others are first-come, first-served.

Camping anywhere outside a developed rim campground, including in the canyon, requires a permit from the Backcountry Information Center, which also serves as your reservation. Permits can be requested by mail or fax only; applying well in advance is recommended. Call ☎ *928/638–7875* between 1 pm and 5 pm weekdays for information.

CROSS-COUNTRY SKIING

Tusayan Ranger District

SKIING/SNOWBOARDING | Although you can't schuss down into the Grand Canyon, you can cross-country ski in the woods near the rim when there's enough snow, usually mid-December through early March. The ungroomed trails, suitable for beginner and intermediate skiers, begin at the Grandview Lookout and travel through the Kaibab National Forest. For details, contact the Tusayan Ranger District. ✉ *176 Lincoln Log Loop, Grand Canyon* ☎ *928/638–2443* 🌐 *www.fs.usda.gov/kaibab.*

Arranging Tours

Transportation-services desks are maintained at Bright Angel, Maswik Lodge, and Yavapai Lodge (closed in winter) in Grand Canyon Village. The desks provide information and handle bookings for sightseeing tours, taxi and bus services, and mule rides (but don't count on last-minute availability). There's also a concierge at El Tovar that can arrange most tours, with the exception of mule rides. On the North Rim, Grand Canyon Lodge has general information about local services.

HIKING

Although permits are not required for day hikes, you must have a backcountry permit for longer trips (⇨ *see Park Fees and Permits*). Some of the more popular trails are listed under ⇨ *Sights*, including **Bright Angel Trail, Rim Trail,** and **South Kaibab Trail**; more detailed information and maps can be obtained from the Backcountry Information centers. Also, rangers can help design a trip to suit your abilities.

Remember that the canyon has significant elevation changes and, in summer, extreme temperature ranges, which can pose problems for people who aren't in good shape or who have heart or respiratory problems. ■ TIP→ **Carry plenty of water and energy foods.** Listen to the podcast *Hiking Smart* on the Park's website to prepare for your trip. The majority of each year's 400 search-and-rescue incidents result from hikers underestimating the size of the canyon, hiking beyond their abilities, or not packing sufficient food and water.

■ TIP→ **Under no circumstances should you attempt a day hike from the rim to the river and back.** Remember that when it's 85°F on the South Rim, it's 110°F on the canyon floor. Allow two to four days if you want to hike rim to rim (it's easier to descend from the North Rim, as it's more than 1,000 feet higher than the South Rim). Hiking steep trails from rim to rim is a strenuous trek of at least 21 miles and should be attempted only by experienced canyon hikers.

HORSEBACK RIDING

Mule rides provide an intimate glimpse into the canyon for those who have the time, but not the stamina, to see the canyon on foot. ■ TIP→ **Reservations are essential and are accepted up to 13 months in advance.**

These trips have been conducted since the early 1900s. A comforting fact as you ride the narrow trail: no one's ever been killed while riding a mule that fell off a cliff. (Nevertheless, the treks are not for the faint of heart or people in questionable health.)

★ Xanterra Parks & Resorts Mule Rides
TOUR—SPORTS | These trips delve either into the canyon from the South Rim to Phantom Ranch, or east along the canyon's rim. Riders must be at least nine years old and 57 inches tall, weigh less than 200 pounds for the Phantom Ranch ride or less than 225 pounds for the rim ride, and understand English. Children under 18 must be accompanied by an adult. Riders must be in fairly good physical condition, and pregnant women are advised not to take these trips.

The two-hour ride along the rim costs $153. An overnight mule ride with a stay in a cabin at Phantom Ranch at the bottom of the canyon, with meals included, is $693 ($1,205 for two riders). Package prices vary since a cabin at Phantom Ranch can accommodate up to four people. From November through February, you can stay for up to two nights at Phantom Ranch. Reservations are a must, but you can check at the Bright Angel Transportation Desk to see if there's last-minute availability. ☎ *888/297–2757, 303/297–2757* 🌐 *www.grandcanyonlodges.com* ⛵ *Reservations essential.*

JEEP TOURS

Jeep rides can be rough; if you have had back injuries, check with your doctor before taking a 4X4 tour. It's a good idea to book a week or two ahead, and even longer if you're visiting in summer or on busy weekends.

Buck Wild Hummer Tours
DRIVING TOURS | With this tour company, you can see majestic rim views in Grand Canyon National Park and learn about the history, geology, and wildlife of the canyon from the comfort of a 13-passenger Hummer. Daily tours run either in the morning or at sunset. ✉ *469 AZ 64, Grand Canyon* ☎ *928/362–5940* 🌐 *buckwildhummertours.com* 🎫 *From $99.*

Did You Know?

Sure-footed mules take riders along the rim for half-day trips and down into the canyon for longer excursions. Two-day trips include an overnight stay at Phantom Ranch on the canyon floor.

Grand Canyon Custom Tours

TOUR—SPORTS | This tour company offers a full-day off-road adventure to the bottom of the Grand Canyon West (rather than Grand Canyon National Park) year-round in comfortable cruisers (small luxury vans with heating and air-conditioning) rather than jeeps. Tours leave from either Flagstaff or Williams. ✉ *Williams* ☎ *928/779–3163* 🌐 *grandcanyoncustomtours.com* 🎫 *From $269.*

Grand Canyon Jeep Tours & Safaris

TOUR—SPORTS | If you'd like to get off the pavement and see parts of the park that are accessible only by dirt road, a jeep tour can be just the ticket. From March through November, this tour operator leads daily three-hour off-road tours within the park, as well as jeep tours to a petroglyph site in Kaibab National Forest. Sunset tours to the canyon rim and combo tours adding helicopter or plane flights are also available. ✉ *Grand Canyon National Park* ☎ *928/638–5337* 🌐 *grandcanyonjeeptours.com* 🎫 *From $79.*

SCENIC FLIGHTS

Flights by plane and helicopter over the canyon are offered by a number of companies, departing from the Grand Canyon Airport at the south end of Tusayan. Though the noise and disruption of so many aircraft buzzing around the canyon is controversial, flightseeing remains a popular, if expensive, option. You'll have more visibility from a helicopter, but they're louder and more expensive than the fixed-wing planes. Prices and lengths of tours vary, but you can expect to pay about $159 per adult for short plane trips and approximately $300 for helicopter tours (and about $550 for combination plane and helicopter tours leaving from Vegas). These companies often have significant discounts in winter—check the company websites to find the best deals.

Grand Canyon Airlines

FLYING/SKYDIVING/SOARING | This company offers a variety of plane tours, from a 45-minute fixed-wing tour of the eastern edge of the Grand Canyon, the North Rim, and the Kaibab Plateau to an all-day tour that combines "flightseeing" with four-wheel-drive tours of Antelope Canyon and float trips on the Colorado River. They also schedule combination tours that leave from Las Vegas (plane flight from Las Vegas to Grand Canyon Airport, then helicopter flight into the canyon). ✉ *Grand Canyon Airport, Tusayan* ☎ *702/835–8484, 866/235–9422* 🌐 *www.grandcanyonairlines.com* 🎫 *From $159.*

Maverick Helicopters

FLYING/SKYDIVING/SOARING | This company offers 45-minute tours of the South Rim, North Rim, and Dragon Corridor of the Grand Canyon, as well as tours to the canyon out of Las Vegas. A landing tour option for those flying from Las Vegas to the West Rim sets you down in the canyon for champagne and a snack below the rim. ✉ *Grand Canyon Airport, Grand Canyon* ☎ *928/638–2622* 🌐 *www.maverickhelicopter.com* 🎫 *From $299.*

Grand Canyon North Rim

The North Rim stands 1,000 feet higher than the South Rim and has a more alpine climate, with twice as much annual precipitation. Here, in the deep forests of the Kaibab Plateau, the crowds are thinner, the facilities fewer, and the views even more spectacular. Due to snow, the North Rim is off-limits in winter. The buildings and concessions are closed mid-October through mid-May. The road and entrance gate close when the snow makes them impassable—usually by the end of November.

Lodgings are limited in this more remote park, with only one historic lodge (with cabins and hotel-type rooms as well as a restaurant) and a single campground. Dining options have opened up a little with a deli and a coffeehouse/saloon next door to the lodge. Your best bet may be to pack your camping gear and hiking boots and take several days to explore the lush Kaibab Forest. The canyon's highest, most dramatic rim views can also be enjoyed on two wheels (via primitive dirt access roads) and on four legs (courtesy of a trusty mule).

HISTORIC SIGHTS

Grand Canyon Lodge

HISTORIC SITE | Built in 1937 by the Union Pacific Railroad (replacing the original 1928 building, which burned in a fire), this massive stone structure is listed on the National Register of Historic Places. Its huge sunroom has hardwood floors, high-beamed ceilings, and a marvelous view of the canyon through plate-glass windows. On warm days, visitors sit in the sun and drink in the surrounding beauty on an outdoor viewing deck, where National Park Service employees deliver free lectures on geology and history. The dining room serves breakfast, lunch, and dinner; the Roughrider Saloon is a bar by night and a coffee shop in the morning. ✉ *Grand Canyon National Park* ✣ *Off Hwy. 67 near Bright Angel Point* ☎ *928/638–2611 May.–Oct.* 🌐 *www.grandcanyonforever.com* ⊗ *Closed Nov.–mid-May.*

SCENIC DRIVE

★ Highway 67

SCENIC DRIVE | Open mid-May to roughly mid-November (or the first big snowfall), this two-lane paved road climbs 1,400 feet in elevation as it passes through the Kaibab National Forest. Also called the North Rim Parkway, this scenic route crosses the limestone-capped Kaibab Plateau—passing broad meadows, sun-dappled forests, and small lakes and springs—before abruptly falling away at the abyss of the Grand Canyon. Wildlife abounds in the thick ponderosa pine forests and lush mountain meadows. It's common to see deer, turkeys, and coyotes as you drive through such a remote region. Point Imperial and Cape Royal branch off this scenic drive, which runs from Jacob Lake to Bright Angel Point. ✉ *Hwy. 67, Grand Canyon National Park.*

SCENIC STOPS

★ Bright Angel Point

TRAIL | This trail, which leads to one of the most awe-inspiring overlooks on either rim, starts on the grounds of the Grand Canyon Lodge and runs along the crest of a point of rocks that juts into the canyon for several hundred yards. The walk is only ½ mile round-trip, but it's an exciting trek accented by sheer drops on each side of the trail. In a few spots where the route is extremely narrow, metal railings ensure visitors' safety. The temptation to clamber out on precarious perches to have your picture taken should be resisted at all costs. ✉ *North Rim Dr., Grand Canyon National Park* ✣ *Near Grand Canyon Lodge.*

Cape Royal

TRAIL | A popular sunset destination, Cape Royal showcases the canyon's jagged landscape; you'll also get a glimpse of the Colorado River, framed by a natural stone arch called Angels Window. In autumn, the aspens turn a beautiful gold, adding even more color to an already magnificent scene of the forested surroundings. The easy and rewarding 1-mile round-trip hike along **Cliff Springs Trail** starts here; it takes you through a forested ravine and terminates at Cliff Springs, where the forest opens to another impressive view of the canyon walls. ✉ *Cape Royal Scenic Dr., Grand Canyon National Park* ✣ *23 miles southeast of Grand Canyon Lodge.*

Point Imperial

VIEWPOINT | At 8,803 feet, Point Imperial has the highest vista point at either rim; it offers magnificent views of both the canyon and the distant country: the Vermilion Cliffs to the north, the 10,000-foot Navajo Mountain to the northeast in Utah, the Painted Desert to the east, and the Little Colorado River canyon to the southeast. Other prominent points of interest include views of Mt. Hayden, Saddle Mountain, and Marble Canyon. ✉ *Point Imperial Rd., Grand Canyon National Park* ✣ *11 miles northeast of Grand Canyon Lodge.*

★ Point Sublime

VIEWPOINT | You can camp within feet of the canyon's edge at this awe-inspiring site. Sunrises and sunsets are spectacular. The winding road, through gorgeous high country, is only 17 miles, but it will take you at least two hours one-way. The road is intended only for vehicles with high road clearance (pickups and four-wheel-drive vehicles). It is also necessary to be properly equipped for wilderness road travel. Check with a park ranger or at the information desk at Grand Canyon Lodge before taking this journey. You may camp here only with a permit from the Backcountry Information Center. ✉ *North Rim Dr., Grand Canyon National Park* ✣ *About 20 miles west of North Rim Visitor Center.*

Roosevelt Point

VIEWPOINT | Named after the president who gave the Grand Canyon its national monument status in 1908 (it was upgraded to national park status in 1919), Roosevelt Point is the best place to see the confluence of the Little Colorado River and the Grand Canyon. The cliffs above the Colorado River south of the junction are known as the Palisades of the Desert. A short woodland loop trail leads to this eastern viewpoint. ✉ *Cape Royal Rd., Grand Canyon National Park* ✣ *18 miles east of Grand Canyon Lodge.*

Vista Encantada

VIEWPOINT | This point on the Walhalla Plateau offers views of the upper drainage of Nankoweap Creek, a rock pinnacle known as Brady Peak, and the Painted Desert to the east. This is an enchanting place for a picnic lunch. ✉ *Cape Royal Rd., Grand Canyon National Park* ✣ *16 miles southeast of Grand Canyon Lodge.*

Walhalla Overlook

VIEWPOINT | One of the lowest elevations on the North Rim, this overlook has views of the Unkar Delta, a fertile region used by Ancestral Pueblo as farmland. These ancient people also gathered food and hunted game on the North Rim. A flat path leads to the remains of the Walhalla Glades Pueblo, which was inhabited from 1050 to 1150. ✉ *Cape Royal Rd., Grand Canyon National Park* ✣ *22½ miles southeast of Grand Canyon Lodge.*

TRAILS

Cape Final Trail

TRAIL | This 4-mile (round-trip) gravel path follows an old jeep trail through a ponderosa pine forest to the canyon overlook at Cape Final with panoramic views of the northern canyon, the Palisades of the Desert, and the impressive spectacle of Juno Temple. *Easy.* ✉ *Grand Canyon National Park* ✣ *Trailhead: dirt parking lot 5 miles south of Roosevelt Point on Cape Royal Rd.*

Ken Patrick Trail

TRAIL | This primitive trail, one of the longest on the North Rim, travels 10 miles one-way (allow six hours each way) from the trailhead at 8,250 feet to Point Imperial at 8,803 feet. It crosses drainages and occasionally detours around fallen trees. The end of the road, at Point Imperial, brings the highest views from either rim. Note that there is no water along this trail. *Difficult.* ✉ *Grand Canyon National Park* ✣ *Trailhead: east side of North Kaibab trailhead parking lot.*

North Kaibab Trail

TRAIL | At 8,241 feet, this trail leads into the canyon and down to Phantom Ranch. It is recommended for experienced hikers only, who should allow four days for the round-trip hike. The long, steep path drops 5,840 feet over a distance of 14½ miles to Phantom Ranch and the Colorado River, so the National Park Service suggests that day hikers not go farther than Roaring Springs (5,020 feet) before turning to hike back up out of the canyon.

After about 7 miles, Cottonwood Campground (4,080 feet) has drinking water in summer, restrooms, shade trees, and a ranger. *Difficult.* ■ **TIP→ A free shuttle takes hikers to the North Kaibab trailhead twice daily from Grand Canyon Lodge; reserve a spot the day before.** ✉ *Grand Canyon National Park* ✣ *Trailhead: about 2 miles north of Grand Canyon Lodge.*

Roosevelt Point Trail

TRAIL | FAMILY | This easy 0.2-mile round-trip trail loops through the forest to the scenic viewpoint. Allow 20 minutes for this relaxed, secluded hike. *Easy.* ✉ *Grand Canyon National Park* ✣ *Trailhead: Cape Royal Rd.*

Transept Trail

TRAIL | FAMILY | This 3-mile-round-trip, 1½-hour trail begins near the Grand Canyon Lodge at 8,255 feet. Well maintained and well marked, it has little elevation change, sticking near the rim before reaching a dramatic view of a large stream through Bright Angel Canyon. The trail leads to Transept Canyon, which geologist Clarence Dutton named in 1882, declaring it "far grander than Yosemite." Check the posted schedule to find a ranger talk along this trail; it's also a great place to view fall foliage. Flash floods can occur any time of the year, especially June through September when thunderstorms develop rapidly. *Easy.* ✉ *Grand Canyon National Park* ✣ *Trailhead: near Grand Canyon Lodge east patio.*

Uncle Jim Trail

TRAIL | This 5-mile, three-hour loop starts at 8,300 feet and winds south through the forest, past Roaring Springs and Bright Angel canyons. The highlight of this rim hike is Uncle Jim Point, which, at 8,244 feet, overlooks the upper sections of the North Kaibab Trail. *Moderate.* ✉ *Grand Canyon National Park* ✣ *Trailhead: North Kaibab Trail parking lot.*

Widforss Trail

TRAIL | Round-trip, Widforss Trail is 9.8 miles, with an elevation change of only 200 feet. Allow five to six hours for the hike, which starts at 8,080 feet and passes through shady forests of pine, spruce, fir, and aspen on its way to Widforss Point, at 7,900 feet. Here you'll have good views of five temples: Zoroaster, Brahma, and Deva to the southeast, and Buddha and Manu to the southwest. You are likely to see wildflowers in summer, and this is a good trail for viewing fall foliage. It's named in honor of artist Gunnar M. Widforss, renowned for his paintings of national park landscapes. *Moderate.* ✉ *Grand Canyon National Park* ✣ *Trailhead: off dirt road about 2 miles north of Grand Canyon Lodge.*

VISITOR CENTER

North Rim Visitor Center

INFO CENTER | View exhibits, peruse the bookstore, and pick up useful maps and brochures at this visitor center. Interpretive programs are often scheduled in summer. If you're craving refreshments, it's a short walk from here to the Roughrider Saloon at the Grand Canyon Lodge. ✉ *Near Grand Canyon Lodge at North Rim, Grand Canyon National Park* ☎ *928/638–7864* 🌐 *www.nps.gov/grca.*

Restaurants

Deli in the Pines

$ | AMERICAN | Dining choices are limited on the North Rim, but this deli next to the lodge is your best bet for a meal on a budget or grabbing a premade sandwich on the go. Selections also include pizza (gluten-free or standard crust), salads, custom-made sandwiches, and soft-serve ice cream. **Known for:** convenient quick bite; sandwiches to take on the trail; outdoor seating. $ *Average main: $9* ✉ *Grand Canyon Lodge, Bright Angel Point, North Rim* ☎ *928/638–2611* 🌐 *www.grandcanyonforever.com* ⏲ *Closed mid-Oct.–mid-May.*

★ **Grand Canyon Lodge Dining Room**

$$$ | **SOUTHWESTERN** | The high wood-beamed ceilings, stone walls, and spectacular views in this spacious, historic room are perhaps the biggest draw for the lodge's main restaurant. Dinner includes Southwestern steakhouse fare that would make any cowboy feel at home, including selections such as bison and elk. **Known for:** incredible views; charming, historic room; steaks, fish, game, and vegetarian selections. *Average main: $25 Grand Canyon Lodge, Bright Angel Point, North Rim 928/638–2611 www.grandcanyonforever.com Closed mid-Oct.–mid-May.*

Duffel Service: Lighten Your Load

Hikers staying at either Phantom Ranch or Bright Angel Campground can take advantage of the ranch's duffel service: bags or packs weighing 30 pounds or less can be transported to or from the ranch by mule for a fee of $81 each way. As is true for many desirable things at the canyon, reservations are a must. *303/297–2757 www.grandcanyonlodges.com.*

Hotels

★ **Grand Canyon Lodge**

$$ | **HOTEL** | This historic property, constructed mainly in the 1920s and '30s, is the only lodging on the North Rim. The main building has locally quarried limestone walls and timbered ceilings. **Pros:** steps away from gorgeous North Rim views; close to several easy hiking trails; historic lodge building a national landmark. **Cons:** fills up fast; limited amenities; most cabins far from main lodge building. *Rooms from: $146 Hwy. 67, North Rim 877/386–4383 reservations, 928/638–2611 May–Oct. www.grandcanyonforever.com Closed mid-Oct.–mid-May 218 rooms No meals.*

Activities

BIKING

Mountain bikers can test the many dirt access roads found in this remote area. The 17-mile trek to Point Sublime is, well, sublime; though you'll share this road with high-clearance vehicles, it's rare to spot other people on most of these primitive pathways.

Bicycles and leashed pets are allowed on the well-maintained 1.2-mile (one-way) **Bridle Trail,** which follows the road from Grand Canyon Lodge to the North Kaibab Trailhead. A 12-mile section of the **Arizona Trail** is also open to bicycles; it passes through pine forests within the park and continues north into Kaibab National Forest. Bikes are prohibited on all other national park trails.

CAMPING

North Rim Campground. The only designated campground at the North Rim of Grand Canyon National Park sits in a pine forest 3 miles north of the rim, and has 84 RV and tent sites (no hookups). Reserve in advance. *Hwy. 67, North Rim 877/444–6777 www.recreation.gov.*

EDUCATIONAL PROGRAMS

Interpretive Ranger Programs

TOUR—SIGHT | Daily guided hikes and talks may focus on any aspect of the canyon—from geology and flora and fauna to history and the canyon's early inhabitants. Schedules are available online. *928/638–7967 www.nps.gov/grca Free.*

Junior Ranger Program

TOUR—SIGHT | **FAMILY** | In summer, children ages four and up can take part in hands-on educational programs and earn a Junior Ranger certificate and badge. Sign up at the North Rim Visitor Center for these independent and ranger-led activities. *928/638–7967 www.nps.gov/grca Free.*

HORSEBACK RIDING

Canyon Trail Rides

TOUR—SPORTS | FAMILY | This company leads mule rides along the easier trails of the North Rim. Options include one- and three-hour rides along the rim or a three-hour ride down into the canyon (minimum age 7 for one-hour rides, 10 for three-hour rides). The one-hour ride is $45, and the three-hour rides are $90. Weight limits are 200 pounds for canyon rides and 220 pounds for the rim rides. Available daily from May 15 to October 15, these excursions are popular, so make reservations in advance. ☎ *435/679–8665* 🌐 *www.canyonrides.com* 🎫 *From $45.*

What's Nearby

The northwest section of Arizona is geographically fascinating. In addition to the Grand Canyon, it's home to national forests, national monuments, and national recreation areas. Towns, however, are small and scattered. Many of them cater to visiting adventurers, and Native American reservations dot the map. Apart from **Tusayan**, located 2 miles from the South Rim, the closest town to the canyon's South Rim is **Williams**, the "Gateway to the Grand Canyon," 58 miles south.

The communities closest to the North Rim—all of them tiny and with limited services—include **Fredonia**, 76 miles north; **Marble Canyon,** 80 miles northeast; **Lees Ferry,** 85 miles east; and **Jacob Lake,** 45 miles north.

The Hualapai Reservation encompasses a million acres in the Grand Canyon, along 108 miles of the Colorado River, with two main areas open to tourists. The **West Rim** has the Skywalk, a glass walkway suspended 70 feet over the edge of the canyon rim; Hualapai cultural exhibits and dancing; horseback riding; ziplining; and helicopter rides. **Peach Springs**, a two-hour drive from the West Rim on historic Route 66, is the tribal capital and the launch site for raft trips on this stretch of the river. Lodging is available both on the rim, at Hualapai Ranch, and in Peach Springs, at the Hualapai Lodge. Although increasingly popular, the West Rim is still relatively remote and visited by far fewer people than the South Rim—keep in mind that it's more than 120 miles away from the nearest interstate highways.

Chapter 27

GRAND TETON NATIONAL PARK

Updated by
Andrew Collins

Camping ★★★★★ | Hotels ★★★★★ | Activities ★★★★☆ | Scenery ★★★★★ | Crowds ★★★★☆

WELCOME TO GRAND TETON NATIONAL PARK

TOP REASONS TO GO

★ **Heavenward hikes:** Trek where grizzled frontiersmen roamed. Jackson Hole got its name from mountain man Davey Jackson; now there are hundreds of trails for you to explore.

★ **Wildlife big and small:** Keep an eye out for little fellows like short-tailed weasels and beaver, as well as bison, elk, moose, wolves, and both black and grizzly bears.

★ **Waves to make:** Float the Snake River or take a canoe, kayak, or stand-up paddleboard onto Jackson Lake or Jenny Lake.

★ **Homesteader history:** Visit the 1890s barns and ranch buildings of Mormon Row or Menor's Ferry.

★ **Cycling paradise:** Safely pedal your way to and through Grand Teton on miles of pathways and rural roads.

★ **Trout trophies:** Grab your rod and slither over to the Snake River, where cutthroat trout are an angler's delight.

1 **Moose.** Anchoring the southern end of the park, Moose is home to the Craig Thomas Discovery and Visitor Center, Dornan's lodgings and other services, the Menor's Ferry and Mormon Row historic districts, and Laurance S. Rockefeller Preserve. Grand Teton's nearest section to Jackson and Jackson Hole Ski Resort is laced with bike paths and both gentle and rigorous hiking trails, with mountain peaks looming on the west side and sagebrush-covered open range to the east, across the Snake River and around Antelope Flats.

2 **Jenny Lake.** The Teton Range reflects in this small (1,191-acre) but spectacular lake in the middle of the park that has visitor services on its developed east shore and pristine trails on its west shore—you can take a boat ride across the lake or hike entirely around it.

3 **Jackson Lake.** Most adventures in the northern end of the park revolve around this large alpine lake, which offers several lodging and dining options as well as marinas where you can launch or rent boats. The Snake River passes through the north end of the lake and back out to the south through Jackson Lake Dam around Oxbow Bend, a famously scenic spot for watching wildlife.

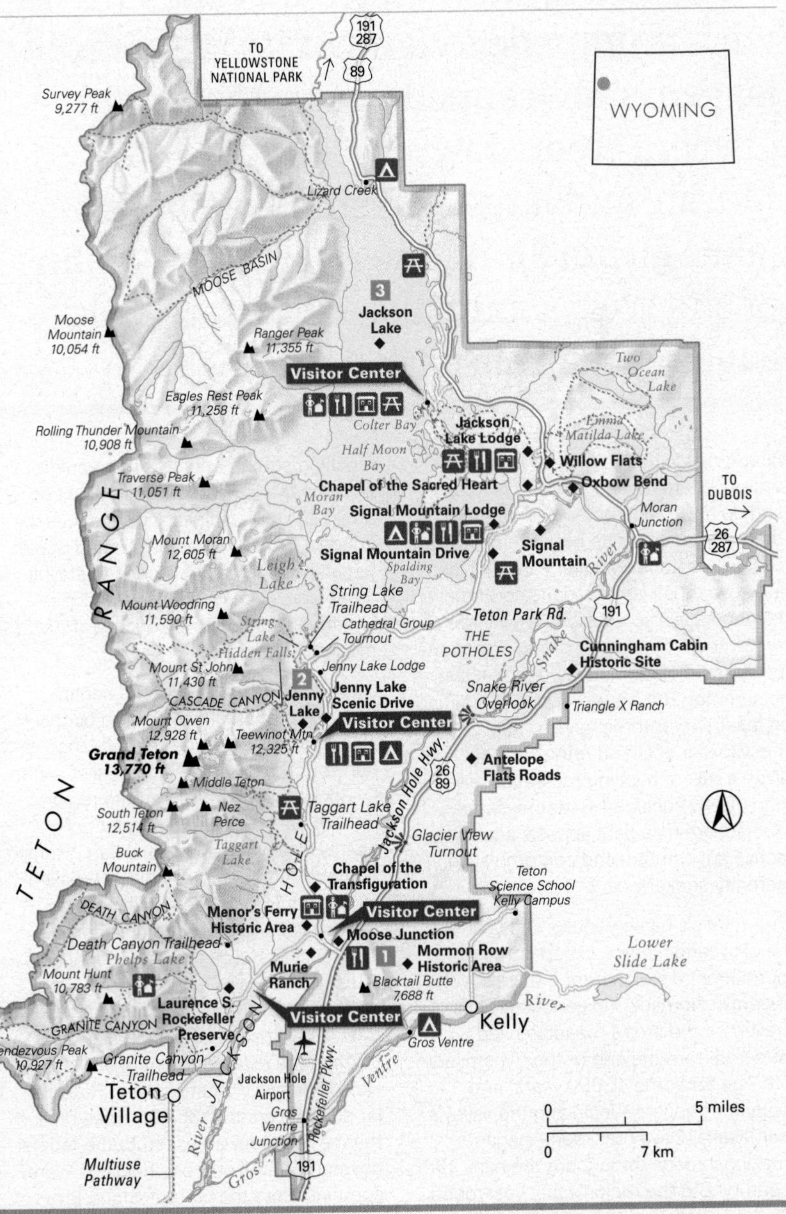
TO
YELLOWSTONE
NATIONAL PARK
191
287
89
WYOMING
Survey Peak
9,277 ft
Lizard Creek
MOOSE BASIN
3
Jackson
Lake
Moose
Mountain
10,054 ft
Ranger Peak
11,355 ft
Visitor Center
Eagles Rest Peak
11,258 ft
Colter Bay
Rolling Thunder Mountain
10,908 ft
Half Moon
Bay
Jackson
Lake Lodge
Two
Ocean
Lake
Emma
Matilda Lake
Willow Flats
Oxbow Bend
Traverse Peak
11,051 ft
Chapel of the Sacred Heart
Moran
Bay
Signal Mountain Lodge
TO
DUBOIS
Moran
Junction
26
287
Mount Moran
12,605 ft
Signal Mountain Drive
Signal
Mountain
Spalding
Bay
River
Leigh
Lake
String Lake
Trailhead
Mount Woodring
11,590 ft
String
Lake
Cathedral Group
Turnout
Teton Park Rd.
191
THE
POTHOLES
Snake
Hidden Falls
Cunningham Cabin
Historic Site
Mount St John
11,430 ft
Jenny Lake Lodge
2
Jenny
Lake
Jenny Lake
Scenic Drive
Snake River
Overlook
CASCADE CANYON
Triangle X Ranch
Mount Owen
12,928 ft
Visitor Center
Teewinot Mtn
12,325 ft
Grand Teton
13,770 ft
Antelope
Flats Roads
26
89
Jackson Hole Hwy.
Middle Teton
TETON RANGE
South Teton
12,514 ft
Nez
Perce
Taggart Lake
Trailhead
Taggart
Lake
Glacier View
Turnout
Buck
Mountain
Chapel of the
Transfiguration
Teton
Science School
Kelly Campus
JACKSON HOLE
DEATH CANYON
Menor's Ferry
Historic Area
Visitor Center
Moose Junction
Death Canyon Trailhead
Lower
Slide Lake
1
Mormon Row
Historic Area
Phelps Lake
Murie
Ranch
Mount Hunt
10,783 ft
Blacktail Butte
7,688 ft
River
Laurence S.
Rockefeller
Preserve
Kelly
GRANITE CANYON
Visitor Center
Gros Ventre
Rendezvous Peak
10,927 ft
Granite Canyon
Trailhead
Ventre
Teton
Village
Jackson Hole
Airport
Rockefeller Pkwy.
Gros
Ventre
Junction
River
0
5 miles
0
7 km
Multiuse
Pathway
191
Gros

The Teton Range—dominated by the 13,770-foot Grand Teton—rises more than a mile above Jackson Hole's valley floor, with unimpeded views of its magnificent, jagged, snowcapped peaks. Mountain glaciers creep down 12,605-foot Mt. Moran, and large and small piedmont lakes gleam along the range's base. Many of the West's animals—elk, bears, bald eagles—call this park home.

First-time visitors to Grand Teton sometimes underestimate all there is to see and do here, visiting the park briefly as a detour from either its northern neighbor, Yellowstone National Park—which is seven times larger—or its southern neighbor, Jackson, a swanky year-round resort town famous for skiing and snowboarding in winter and a host of activities in summer. But it's well worth budgeting at least two or three days to fully grasp the wonder of Grand Teton National Park. With a mix of bustling recreation areas and utterly secluded wilderness, this 485-square-mile park appeals equally to active adventurers and contemplative serenity seekers.

The region's harsh winters and challenging terrain helped keep it free of permanent development until relatively recently. Nomadic indigenous groups traversed the area's meadows and streams from the end of the Pleistocene Ice Age for some 11,000 years, and early fur trappers—including the valley's namesake, Davey Jackson—began making inroads throughout the early 19th century. But the region's first year-round ranching settlements in what would become the town of Jackson didn't occur until 1894. It wasn't long before wealthy "dudes" from the eastern United States began paying gobs of money to stay at these sprawling, scenic compounds, and thus was born the concept of the modern "dude ranch."

Jackson Hole and the Tetons began to develop at breakneck speed by the 1920s, drawing the interest of conservationists, too, including industrialist John D. Rockefeller, who toured the region in 1926 with the Superintendent of nearby Yellowstone National Park, Horace Albright. Although many locals recoiled at the thought of federal intervention, Rockefeller and other preservationists led a successful campaign for congress to establish Grand Teton National Park in 1929. Over the next 20 years, Franklin D. Roosevelt set aside additional land through the establishment of Jackson Hole National Monument, and Rockefeller donated another 35,000 acres of land that he'd steadily amassed to the federal government. All of these holdings were combined into the current Grand Teton

AVERAGE HIGH/LOW TEMPERATURES					
JAN.	FEB.	MAR.	APR.	MAY	JUNE
28/5	33/8	43/17	53/24	63/31	74/37
JULY	AUG.	SEPT.	OCT.	NOV.	DEC.
82/41	81/39	71/31	59/23	40/16	28/6

National Park in 1950. Throughout the park's evolution, Rockefeller also helped to spur its commercial and recreational development by establishing Jenny Lake and Jackson Lake lodges, along with smaller compounds of cabins and campgrounds throughout the park. And in 2001, his son donated the family's last piece of land in the area, 1,106-acre Laurance S. Rockefeller Preserve.

Although it receives the most recognition for its hulking mountain peaks, this is as much a park of scenic bodies of water and sweeping wildlife-rich meadows as it is an alpine destination. Boating, fishing, and lakeside camping are every bit as popular as hiking and climbing in the peaks, and photographers flock here from all over the world for the chance to see rare birds, lumbering moose and elk, and formidable wolves and black and grizzly bears. Some of the best terrain in the park can be accessed from well-maintained park roads and relatively short trails, but opportunities for rugged treks through miles of pristine back-country also abound. Grand Teton offers splendid activities for a range of abilities and interests.

Planning

When to Go

In July and August all the roads, trails, and visitor centers are open, and the Snake River's float season is in full swing. You can expect smaller crowds and often lower rates in spring and fall, but some services and roads are limited. Grand Teton Lodge Company, the park's major concessionaire, winds down its activities in late September, and most of Teton Park Road closes from November through April (U.S. 26/191/89 stays open all winter). In spring and fall, Teton Park Road is open to pedestrians, cyclists, and in-line skaters; in winter, it's transformed into a cross-country ski trail.

Getting Here and Around

AIR

Five major airlines offer service to Jackson Hole Airport (JAC), the only commercial airport inside a national park (it was established before the park opened).

CAR

Jackson Hole's main highway (U.S. 89/191) runs the length of the park, from Jackson to Yellowstone National Park's south entrance. This highway also joins with U.S. 26 south of Moran Junction and U.S. 287 north of Moran Junction. This road is open all year from Jackson to Moran Junction and north to Flagg Ranch, 2 miles south of Yellowstone. From Jackson, it's about 20-minutes to the park's southern (Moose) entrance. Coming from the north, it's about a 10-minute drive to the park's northern boundary.

Two scenic back-road entrances to Grand Teton are closed by snow from November through mid-May and can be heavily rutted through June. Moose-Wilson Road (Hwy. 390) starts at Highway 22 in Wilson and travels 7 miles north past Teton Village to the Granite Canyon entrance station. Of the 9 miles from here to Moose, 1½ are gravel and can be a little bumpy; high-clearance vehicles are best, but you can manage this route with a regular passenger car if you take it slow. This route is closed to large trucks, trailers, and RVs. Even rougher is 60-mile Grassy Lake Road, which heads east from Highway 32 in Ashton, Idaho, through Targhee National Forest. It connects with the John D. Rockefeller, Jr. Memorial Parkway span of U.S. 89/191/287, between Grand Teton and Yellowstone.

Inspiration

A Field Guide to Yellowstone and Grand Teton National Parks, by Kurt F. Johnson, provides a comprehensive compilation of the flora and fauna of the greater Yellowstone area, including more than 1,200 color photographs.

Robert W. Righter's *Peaks, Politics, and Passion: Grand Teton National Park Comes of Age* gives the fascinating backstory behind the park's evolution since its establishment in 1950.

Park Essentials

ACCESSIBILITY

The frontcountry portions of Grand Teton are largely accessible to people using wheelchairs. There's designated parking at most sites, and some interpretive trails and campgrounds are easily accessible. There are accessible restrooms at visitor centers. The visitor centers also distribute an *Accessibility* brochure, which you can download from the park website.

PARK FEES AND PERMITS

Park entrance costs $35 for autos; $30 for motorcycles; and $20 per person on foot or bicycle, good for seven days in Grand Teton. The winter day-use fee is $15.

PARK HOURS

The park is open 24/7 year-round. It's in the Mountain time zone.

CELL PHONE RECEPTION

Cell phones work in most developed areas and occasionally on trails, especially at higher elevations in the park's frontcountry.

Hotels

For a park its size, Grand Teton has a tremendous variety of lodging options, from simple campgrounds, cabins, and standard motel rooms to fancier (and quite pricey) suites in historic lodges.

Restaurants

The park has some good restaurants that are especially strong on local game, fowl, and fish dishes. It's getting easier to find tasty, often seasonal, vegetarian fare, too. Casual is the word for most places.

Hotel and restaurant reviews have been shortened. For full information visit Fodors.com. Hotel prices are the lowest cost of a standard double room in high season. Restaurant prices are the average cost of a main course at dinner, or if dinner is not served, at lunch.

What It Costs

$	$$	$$$	$$$$
RESTAURANTS			
under $16	$16–$22	$22–$30	over $30
HOTELS			
under $150	$151–$225	$226–$300	over $300

Tours

Grand Teton Lodge Company Bus Tours

BUS TOURS | **FAMILY** | Half-day tours depart from Jackson Lake Lodge and include visits to scenic viewpoints, visitor centers, and other park sites. Guides provide information about park geology, history, wildlife, and ecosystems. Full-day tours continue into Yellowstone. ✉ *Grand Teton National Park* ☎ *307/543–3100* 🌐 *www.gtlc.com* 🎟 *From $90.*

Jackson Hole Wildlife Safaris

GUIDED TOURS | Run by a staff of world-class photographers, this Jackson company offers half-, full-, and multiday tours in summer and winter that bring guests to some of the best places in Grand Teton to view elk, bison, big-horn sheep, coyotes, foxes, and other wildlife that thrives in the park. Tours to Yellowstone are offered, too. ✉ *Jackson* ☎ *307/690–6402* 🌐 *www.jacksonholewildlifesafaris.com* 🎟 *Tours from $275.*

★ **Jackson Lake Cruises**

BOAT TOURS | **FAMILY** | Grand Teton Lodge Company runs 1½-hour Jackson Lake cruises from Colter Bay Village Marina throughout the day, as well as breakfast, lunch, and dinner cruises. Guides explain how forest fires and glaciers have shaped the Grand Teton landscape. ✉ *Grand Teton National Park* ☎ *307/543–3100* 🌐 *www.gtlc.com* 🎟 *From $40.*

Teton Science School

SPECIAL-INTEREST | **FAMILY** | The school conducts guided wildlife expeditions in Grand Teton, Yellowstone, and surrounding forests—participants see and learn about wolves, bears, bighorn sheep, and other animals. Full-day and half-day excursions are offered, as well as custom trips. The bear and wolf expedition is a thrilling three-day, two-night field adventure during spring and fall. ✉ *700 Coyote Canyon Rd., Jackson* ☎ *307/733–1313* 🌐 *www.tetonscience.org* 🎟 *Tours from $165.*

★ **Teton Wagon Train and Horse Adventures**

ADVENTURE TOURS | **FAMILY** | Unforgettable four- and seven-day covered wagon rides and horseback trips follow Grassy Lake Road on the "back side" of the Tetons. You can combine the trip with a river trip and a tour of Yellowstone and Grand Teton. ✉ *Jackson* ☎ *307/734–6101, 888/734–6101* 🌐 *www.tetonwagontrain.com* 🎟 *From $1,095.*

Visitor Information

CONTACTS Grand Teton National Park. ☎ *307/739–3300* 🌐 *www.nps.gov/grte.* **Jackson Hole and Greater Yellowstone Visitor Center.** ✉ *532 N. Cache St., Jackson* ☎ *307/733–3316* 🌐 *www.fws.gov.*

Moose

13 miles north of Jackson, 65 miles south of Yellowstone's Grant Village.

Most visitors to Grand Teton spend a good bit of time, and often begin their adventures, in and around Moose, which is the hub for exploring the southern end of the park (nearest to Jackson). The striking, contemporary Craig Thomas and Laurance S. Rockefeller Preserve visitor centers are excellent places to learn about the park's natural history and conservation efforts, and there's easy and more challenging hiking near both. Also near Moose is Dornan's service complex, with dining, lodging, gas, and a market.

Sights

HISTORIC SITES

Chapel of the Transfiguration

RELIGIOUS SITE | This tiny chapel built in 1925 on land donated by Maud Noble is still a functioning Episcopal church. Couples come here to exchange vows with the Tetons as a backdrop, and tourists snap photos of the small church with its awe-inspiring view. ✉ *End of Menors Ferry Rd., ½ mile off Teton Park Rd., Moose* ☎ *307/733–2603* 🌐 *www.stjohns-jackson.org/chapel-of-the-transfiguration* ⏲ *Closed Sept.–late May.*

The Chapel of the Transfiguration is still a functioning Episcopal church.

Menor's Ferry Historic Area

HISTORIC SITE | FAMILY | Down a path from the Chapel of the Transfiguration, the ferry on display here is not the original, but it's an accurate re-creation of the double-pontoon craft built by Bill Menor in 1894. That was how people crossed the Snake River before bridges were installed. While the replica ferry is no longer in operation, it's fun to see. In the cluster of turn-of-the-20th-century buildings there are displays on historical transportation methods. Pick up a pamphlet for a self-guided tour. ✉ *End of Menors Ferry Rd.* ✣ *¼ mile off Teton Park Rd.*

Mormon Row Historic Area

HISTORIC SITE | Settled by homesteaders between 1896 and 1907, this area received its name because many of them were members of the Church of Jesus Christ of Latter-day Saints, also known as Mormons. The remaining barns, homes, and outbuildings are representative of early homesteading in the West. You can wander around, hike the row, and take photographs. The century-old T.A. Moulton Barn is said to be the most-photographed barn in the state. ✉ *Grand Teton National Park* ✣ *Off Antelope Flats Rd., 2 miles north of Moose Junction.*

Murie Ranch

HISTORIC SITE | FAMILY | Set on a former 1930s dude ranch, this complex of historic log buildings is sometimes credited as being the home of America's conservation movement—the work of its former owners, the Muries, led to passage of the 1964 Wilderness Act. You can hike the grounds and view interpretive signs on an easy 1-mile round-trip stroll from the nearby Craig Thomas Discovery and Visitor Center. Part of the property is used as a satellite campus of the superb Teton Science School, which offers conservation and educational programs about the park. ✉ *Moose* ✣ *Trailhead: Craig Thomas Discovery and Visitor Center.*

SCENIC DRIVES

Antelope Flats Road

SCENIC DRIVE | Off U.S. 191/26/89, about 2 miles north of Moose Junction, this narrow road wanders eastward over sagebrush flats, intersecting with the gravel lane to the Mormon Row Historic District. Less than 2 miles past here is a three-way intersection where you can turn right to loop around past the tiny hamlet of Kelly and Gros Ventre campground and rejoin the main highway at Gros Ventre Junction. Keep an eye out for abundant and swift pronghorn, along with bison, foxes, raptors, and more than a few cyclists. ✉ *Grand Teton National Park* ⊙ *Closed winter.*

SCENIC STOPS

Laurance S. Rockefeller Preserve

NATURE PRESERVE | **FAMILY** | This immense 1,106-acre preserve devoted to conversation includes miles of trails. You can access it via the Valley Trail, 1¾ miles north of the Granite Canyon trailhead and ½ mile south of the Death Canyon turnoff. Hikers can admire the Phelps Lake shoreline from a loop trail beginning at the preserve's sleek, contemporary interpretive center, or climb a ridgeline with beautiful views of aspens, wildflowers, and regional birds. ✉ *Off Moose-Wilson Rd.*

TRAILS

Lake Creek–Woodland Trail Loop

TRAIL | This relaxing, mostly level ramble alongside Lake Creek leads through a verdant forest to the southern shore of Phelps Lake, where you're rewarded with grand views up into Death Canyon. *Easy.* ✉ *Moose* ✣ *Trailhead: Laurence S. Rockefeller Preserve Center.*

★ Phelps Lake Overlook and Loop Trail

TRAIL | The quickest way to view this stunning lake, this 2-mile round-trip Phelps Lake Overlook Trail takes you from the Death Canyon trailhead up conifer- and aspen-lined glacial moraine to a view that's accessible only on foot. Expect abundant bird life: Western tanagers, northern flickers, and ruby-crowned kinglets thrive in the bordering woods, and hummingbirds feed on scarlet gilia beneath the overlook. From here, if you're up for a longer, enjoyable adventure, continue along the steep trail down to the north shore of the lake, where you can pick up the Phelps Loop Trail and follow it around the lake or all the way to Rockefeller Preserve. Hiking just to the overlook and back takes just over an hour, but allow four to five hours if continuing on to the Phelps Loop Trail. *Moderate–Difficult.* ✉ *Grand Teton National Park* ✣ *Trailhead: End of White-grass Ranch Rd., off Moose-Wilson Rd.*

Taggart Lake Trail

TRAIL | Hike 1½ miles from the trailhead to the lake and then, optionally, you can extend your trek by continuing on a 4-mile route around the lake where the terrain becomes steeper near Beaver Creek, or making the 5-mile loop trail around Bradley Lake, just to the north. There are views of Avalanche Canyon and areas where you might see moose. Allow an hour to get to the lake and back and another two to three hours to make it around one or both lakes. *Moderate.* ✉ *Grand Teton National Park* ✣ *Trailhead: Teton Park Rd., 4.8 miles south of Jenny Lake Visitor Center.*

VISITOR CENTERS

Craig Thomas Discovery and Visitor Center

INFO CENTER | This strikingly designed contemporary building contains interactive and interpretive exhibits dedicated to themes of preservation, mountaineering, and local wildlife. There's also a 3D map of the park and streaming video along a footpath showing the area's intricate natural features. Dozens of Native American artifacts from the David T. Vernon Collection are housed here. A plush, 155-seat theater shows a nature documentary every half hour. ✉ *Teton Park Rd., Moose* ☎ *307/739–3399* 🌐 *www.nps.gov/grte* ⊙ *Closed Nov.–late Mar.*

★ **Laurance S. Rockefeller Preserve Center**
INFO CENTER | **FAMILY** | This contemporary structure feels more like an art gallery than an interpretive facility. The elegant, eco-friendly building is more than just eye candy—you can experience the sounds of the park in a cylindrical audio chamber, and laminated maps in the reading room are great for trip planning. Rangers here promote "contemplative hiking" and are well informed about the many birds around the center's trailheads. It's best to get here in the early morning or late evening because the small parking area fills quickly. A ranger leads a hike to the lake every morning. ✉ *End of LSR Preserve Entrance Rd.* ☎ *307/739–3300* 🌐 *www.nps.gov/grte* ⏲ *Closed late Sept.–May.*

Restaurants

Dornan's Pizza & Pasta Company
$$ | **PIZZA** | Simple but hearty pizzas and pastas are the draw here, but you'll also find generous margaritas, a diverse wine list, and occasional live music. Place your order at the front counter, then head to a table inside, on the side deck, or upstairs on the roof, which has stunning mountain views. **Known for:** well-priced food; great wine shop next door (and no corkage fee); spectacular mountain views. $ *Average main: $17* ✉ *12170 Dornan's Rd.* ☎ *307/733–2415* 🌐 *www.dornans.com.*

Hotels

★ **Dornan's Spur Ranch Cabins**
$$$ | **RENTAL** | **FAMILY** | The lodging component of Dornan's shopping, dining, and recreation development in Moose, at the south end of the park, offers one- and two-bedroom cabins with fully stocked kitchens and great views of meadows, the peaks of the Tetons, or the Snake River. **Pros:** simple, clean cabins with good Wi-Fi; great for families; you may see wildlife out your window. **Cons:** not much privacy; rustic interiors not for everyone; no pets. $ *Rooms from: $275* ✉ *12170 Dornan's Rd., Moose* ☎ *307/733–2415* 🌐 *www.dornans.com* ⏲ *Closed Nov. and Apr.* *12 cabins* *No meals.*

Jenny Lake

7 miles north of Moose, 12 miles southwest of Jackson Lake Junction.

Framed to the west by Teton's magnificent peaks, Jenny Lake is one of the most picturesque—and indeed photographed—bodies of water in the Rockies. It's also the main developed area in the park's mid-section, home to a luxurious and historic lodge as well as a visitor center and ranger station, and a very popular campground. From the lake's eastern shore, you can access miles of hiking trails into the mountains across the lake, either by taking the short boat ride to the western shore or hiking there via the trail that encircles the lake. Trails also lead nearby to similarly stunning but undeveloped Leigh Lake, which is popular for paddle-sports enthusiasts and hikers.

Sights

SCENIC DRIVES

★ **Jenny Lake Scenic Drive**
SCENIC DRIVE | This 4-mile, one-way loop provides the park's best roadside close-ups of the Tetons and the eastern shore of Jenny Lake as it winds south through groves of lodgepole pine and open meadows. Roughly 1½ miles off Teton Park Road, the Cathedral Group Turnout faces 13,770-foot Grand Teton (the range's highest peak), flanked by 12,928-foot Mt. Owen and 12,325-foot Mt. Teewinot. ✉ *Jenny Lake.*

TRAILS

★ Cascade Canyon–Hidden Falls–Inspiration Point Trail

TRAIL | FAMILY | Take Jenny Lake Boating's 20-minute boat ride or the 2¼-mile (each way) Jenny Loop Trail around the south side of the lake from the Jenny Lake Visitor Center to the start of a gentle, ½-mile climb to 200-foot Hidden Falls, the park's most popular (though crowded) hiking destination. Listen for the distinctive bleating of the rabbitlike pikas among the glacial boulders and pines. The trail continues half a mile to Inspiration Point over a moderately steep, rocky path with sweeping lake views. From here, continue west another 1½ miles into the heart of Cascade Canyon, with its dramatic views through the mountains and out toward Petersen Glacier. With the 10-minute boat shuttle ($18 round-trip), plan on a couple of hours to experience this trail—add another two hours if you hike the whole way, which is your only option from October through mid-May, when the shuttle doesn't run. *Easy–Moderate.* ✉ *Grand Teton National Park* ✥ *Trailhead: Jenny Lake Visitor Center* 🌐 *www.jennylakeboating.com.*

Jenny Lake Loop Trail

TRAIL | FAMILY | You can walk to Hidden Falls from Jenny Lake Visitor Center by following the mostly level trail around the south shore of the lake to Cascade Canyon Trail. Jenny Lake Trail continues around the lake for a total of 6½ miles. It's an easily managed though somewhat long trail hike if you circumnavigate the whole lake—allow three hours, not counting any forays into Cascade Canyon on the west side of the lake. You'll walk through a lodgepole-pine forest, have expansive views of the lake and the land to the east, and hug the shoulder of the massive Teton range itself. Along the way you may see elk, foxes, pikas, golden-mantled ground squirrels, and a variety of ducks and water birds. *Moderate.* ✉ *Grand Teton National Park* ✥ *Trailhead: Jenny Lake Visitor Center.*

★ Leigh Lake Trail

TRAIL | This flat trail follows String Lake's northeastern shore to Leigh Lake's southern shore, covering 2 miles in a round-trip of about an hour. You can extend your hike into a moderate 7½-mile, four-hour round-trip by following the forested east shore of Leigh Lake to tiny but pretty Bearpaw Lake. Along the way you'll have views of Mt. Moran across the lake, and you may be lucky enough to spot a moose or a bear. Another option from Leigh Lake's southern shore is the 13-mile round-trip hike into Paintbrush Canyon to Holly Lake. *Moderate.* ✉ *Grand Teton National Park* ✥ *Trailhead: String Lake Picnic Area.*

String Lake Trail

TRAIL | The 3½-mile loop around String Lake lies in the shadows of 11,144-foot Rockchuck Peak and 11,430-foot Mt. Saint John. This is also a good place to see moose and elk, hear songbirds, and view wildflowers. The hike, which takes about three hours, is a bit less crowded than others in the vicinity. *Easy–Moderate.* ✉ *Grand Teton National Park* ✥ *Trailhead: off Jenny Lake Rd.*

VISITOR CENTER

★ Jenny Lake Visitor Center and Ranger Station

INFO CENTER | Located steps from one another inside historic 1920s cabins by the Jenny Lake parking area, trailhead, and shuttle boat dock, these two ranger-staffed information centers serve different functions. The visitor center is inside a building that was once used as a studio by the park's first official park photographer, Harrison Crandall. Today it's filled with exhibits on the history of art and artists in the park. It also contains a bookstore and information about daily ranger programs. The smaller ranger station occupies a 1925 cabin that once held the park's first museum and is now a one-stop for backcountry and mountaineering advice and permits as well as boat permits. ✉ *Off Teton Park Rd., Jenny*

Lake ☎ *307/739–3392* 🌐 *www.nps.gov/grte* ⏲ *Closed early Sept.–late May.*

Restaurants

★ **Jenny Lake Lodge Dining Room**

$$$$ | MODERN AMERICAN | Elegant yet rustic, Grand Teton's finest dining space is highly ambitious for a national park restaurant. For dinner, the prix-fixe, five-course menu features locally sourced ingredients and an inventive, thoughtfully assembled wine list. **Known for:** jackets encouraged for men and reservations a must; regional meats and fish, like bison, bass, and duck; lovely mountain views. $ *Average main: $98* ✉ *Jenny Lake Rd.* ☎ *307/543–3100* 🌐 *www.gtlc.com* ⏲ *Closed early Oct.–May.*

Hotels

★ **Jenny Lake Lodge**

$$$$ | RESORT | This 1920s lodge resort, the most expensive and arguably the most elegant in any national park, is nestled off the scenic Jenny Lake Loop Road and bordering a wildflower meadow. **Pros:** ultracushy digs in a pristine setting; easy stroll from Jenny Lake trails; homey touches, like hand-made furniture and quilts. **Cons:** very expensive; not suitable for kids; often booked up months in advance. $ *Rooms from: $555* ✉ *Jenny Lake Rd.* ☎ *307/543–3100* 🌐 *www.gtlc.com* ⏲ *Closed early Oct.–May* *37 cabins* *No meals.*

Jackson Lake

24 miles north of Moose, 45 miles south of Yellowstone's Grant Village.

The biggest of Grand Teton's glacier-carved lakes (it's more than 22 times the size of equally famous Jenny Lake), this body of water in the park's northern reaches was enlarged by the 1906 construction of the Jackson Lake Dam, an impressive structure that you can view from Teton Park Road just south of Jackson Lake Junction. You can fish, sail, and water-ski here—three marinas (Colter Bay, Leeks, and Signal Mountain) provide access for boaters. Several picnic areas, campgrounds, and lodges overlook the lake, and vista points like Oxbow Bend, the summit of Signal Mountain, and Willow Flats are excellent places to take in the park's geological and wildlife scenery.

Sights

HISTORIC SITES

Cunningham Cabin Historic Site

HISTORIC SITE | At the end of a gravel spur road, an easy ¾-mile trail runs through sagebrush around Pierce Cunningham's low-slung 1888 log-cabin homestead. Although you can peer inside, the building has no furnishings or displays. Watch for badgers, coyotes, and Uinta ground squirrels in the area. ✉ *Antelope Flats* ✣ *½ mile off U.S. 26/89/191, 5 miles south of Moran Junction.*

SCENIC DRIVES

Signal Mountain Summit

SCENIC DRIVE | FAMILY | This popular 4-mile drive climbs 700 feet along a winding forest road that offers glimpses of Jackson Lake and Mt. Moran. At the top, park and follow the well-marked path to one of the park's best panoramas. From 7,593 feet above sea level your gaze can sweep over all of Jackson Hole and the 40-mile Teton Range. The views are particularly dramatic at sunset. The road is not appropriate for long trailers and is closed in winter. ✉ *Off Teton Park Rd.* ⏲ *Closed Nov.–May.*

SCENIC STOPS

Chapel of the Sacred Heart

RELIGIOUS SITE | This small log Catholic chapel sits in the pine forest with a view of Jackson Lake. It's open only for services, but you can enjoy the view anytime, and the grounds are nice for a picnic. ✉ *Grand Teton National Park* ✣ *Off Teton Park Rd., ¼ mile east of Signal*

Mountain Lodge ☎ 🌐 *www.olmcatholic.org* ⏲ *Closed Oct.–June.*

★ Oxbow Bend

VIEWPOINT | This peaceful spot overlooks a quiet backwater left by the Snake River when it cut a new southern channel. White pelicans stop here on their spring migration (many stay on through summer), sandhill cranes and trumpeter swans visit frequently, osprey nest nearby, and great blue herons nest amid the cottonwoods along the river. Use binoculars to search for bald eagles, moose, beaver, and otter. The Oxbow is known for the reflection of Mt. Moran that marks its calm waters in early morning. ✉ *Grand Teton National Park* ✣ *U.S. 89/191/287, 2½ miles east of Jackson Lake Junction.*

Willow Flats

NATURE PRESERVE | You'll often see moose grazing in this marshy area, in part because of its flourishing willow bushes, where moose both eat and hide. Elk also graze here, and you'll occasionally see grizzly bears and wolves pursue their calves at the start of summer. This is also a good place to see birds and waterfowl, and the short Lunch Tree Hill Trail heads from the overlook parking area past beaver ponds to some vibrant bird-watching terrain. ✉ *Grand Teton National Park* ✣ *U.S. 89/191/287, 1 mile north of Jackson Lake Junction.*

TRAILS

★ Colter Bay Lakeshore Trail

TRAIL | **FAMILY** | This easy, wonderfully picturesque 1¾-mile round-trip excursion treats you to views of Jackson Lake and the Tetons. As you follow the level trail along the rocky shore and forest's edge, you may see moose and bald eagles. Allow two hours to complete the walk. *Easy.* ✉ *Grand Teton National Park* ✣ *Trailhead: on the beach just north of Colter Bay Visitor Center.*

Grand View Point Trail

TRAIL | Give yourself about four hours, which allows time for relaxing and soaking up dramatic views of back toward Jackson Lake and the Teton Range, to complete this moderately challenging 5.6-mile round-trip trek that starts at Jackson Lake Lodge. The trail curves around tiny Christian Pond and along the western shore of the much larger Emma Matilda Lake before climbing nearly 1,000 feet in elevation to this lovely viewpoint. ✉ *Moran* ✣ *Trailhead: Jackson Lake Lodge.*

VISITOR CENTERS

Colter Bay Visitor Center

INFO CENTER | At this useful center near the shore of Jackson Lake, a small display shows off items from the park's collection of Native American artifacts. (Hundreds more are being conserved and stored for future displays.) In summer, rangers lead daily hikes from here. Nightly ranger talks on various topics are also offered. ✉ *Colter Bay Marina Rd., Colter Bay* ☎ *307/739–3594* 🌐 *www.nps.gov/grte* ⏲ *Closed early Oct.–mid-May.*

Flagg Ranch Information Station

INFO CENTER | This small seasonal visitor center with exhibits on John D. Rockefeller and the region's natural history is the first place you'll come to if driving south from Yellowstone. It's in the same village as Headwaters Lodge, along with a convenience store, restaurant, and gas station. ✉ *100 Grassy Lakes Rd., Moran* ✣ *20 miles north of Jackson Lake Lodge* ☎ *307/543–2372* 🌐 *www.nps.gov/grte* ⏲ *Closed early Sept.–early June.*

Restaurants

Cafe Court Pizzeria

$ | **AMERICAN** | **FAMILY** | Quick and cheap is the name of the game at this no-frills cafeteria at Colter Bay Village. The menu features pizzas, salads, and toasted subs. **Known for:** big, simple meals to eat in or take out; pizza offered by the slice or whole pie; closes later than many other options. $ *Average main: $11* ✉ *Colter Bay Village Rd.* ☎ *307/543–2811* 🌐 *www.gtlc.com* ⏲ *Closed late Sept.–late May.*

Jackson Lake Lodge Mural Room

$$$$ | **AMERICAN** | One of the park's most picturesque restaurants gets its name from a 700-square-foot mural painted by the Western artist Carl Roters that details a Wyoming mountain man rendezvous. The menu showcases lavishly presented American fare, such as chilled prawns with a bloody Mary vinaigrette, seared King salmon with toasted-almond couscous, and grilled elk rib eye with a cherry compote. **Known for:** sumptuous mountain views; upscale lunches, dinners, and buffet breakfasts; regional favorites like bison, elk, and trout. $ *Average main: $35* ✉ *100 Jackson Lake Lodge Rd.* ☎ *307/543–2811* 🌐 *www.gtlc.com* ⏲ *Closed early Oct.–mid-May.*

★ **Peaks Restaurant**

$$$ | **MODERN AMERICAN** | At Signal Mountain Lodge, this casual Western-style bistro offers up delectable fish and meat dishes, as well as views of Jackson Lake and the Tetons. The Trapper Grill next door also serves lunch, the adjacent Deadman's Bar is a fun spot for nachos and huckleberry margaritas, and about 10 miles north, the same concessionaire operates the popular Leek's Pizzeria, overlooking the marina of the same name. **Known for:** menu focuses on seasonal, regional ingredients; among the park's more reasonably priced restaurants; nice lake views. $ *Average main: $27* ✉ *Signal Mountain Lodge Rd.* ☎ *307/543–2831* 🌐 *www.signalmountainlodge.com* ⏲ *Closed mid-Oct.–mid-May.*

Pioneer Grill at Jackson Lake Lodge

$$ | **AMERICAN** | With an old-fashioned soda fountain, friendly service, and seats along a winding counter, this eatery recalls a 1950s-era luncheonette. Tuck into Cobb salads, apple-cheddar burgers, banana splits, and other classic American fare. **Known for:** quick, reasonably priced food; seating is along a 200-foot-long counter; huckleberry pancakes and milkshakes. $ *Average main: $17* ✉ *100 Jackson Lake Lodge Rd.* ☎ *307/543–2811* 🌐 *www.gtlc.com* ⏲ *Closed early Oct.–mid-May.*

Ranch House at Colter Bay Village

$$ | **AMERICAN** | The casual Ranch House offers friendly service and moderate prices, making it a good choice for travelers on a budget or families who can't take another cafeteria meal. Western-style meals—pulled pork sandwiches, smoked spare ribs, rotisserie chicken—dominate the menu. **Known for:** traditional barbecue fare; hearty pasta dishes; gluten-free, vegetarian, and vegan. $ *Average main: $20* ✉ *Colter Bay Village Rd., Colter Bay* ☎ *307/543–2811* 🌐 *www.gtlc.com* ⏲ *Closed late Sept.–late May.*

Hotels

Colter Bay Village

$$$ | **HOTEL** | **FAMILY** | A stroll from Jackson Lake, this cluster of Western-style one- and two-room cabins is close to trails, dining options, a visitor center, and plenty of other activities. **Pros:** good value; many nearby facilities; close to lake and hiking trails. **Cons:** not much privacy; no TVs or phones, and unreliable Wi-Fi; rustic feel won't appeal to everyone. $ *Rooms from: $200* ✉ *Colter Bay Village Rd., Colter Bay* ☎ *307/543–3100* 🌐 *www.gtlc.com* ⏲ *Closed late Sept.–late May* 🛏 *232 cabins* 🍽 *No meals.*

Headwaters Lodge & Cabins at Flagg Ranch

$$$ | **HOTEL** | Set along the scenic connecting road between the north boundary of Grand Teton and the South Entrance of Yellowstone, this secluded compound offers both upscale cabins with patios, handcrafted furniture, and private baths, and less-expensive rustic camping cabins that share a common bathhouse with the campground and RV park. **Pros:** good base between Grand Teton and Yellowstone; tranquil setting; mix of upscale

and budget accommodations. **Cons:** no Wi-Fi; limited dining options; remote location. *Rooms from: $248* *100 Grassy Lake Rd., Moran* *307/543–2861* *www.gtlc.com* *Closed Oct.–May* *92 rooms* *No meals.*

★ Jackson Lake Lodge

$$$$ | **HOTEL** | This sprawling resort with its distinctive mid-century modern features was designed by renowned architect Gilbert Stanley Underwood and stands on a bluff with spectacular views across Jackson Lake to the Tetons. **Pros:** in center of Grand Teton; heated outdoor pool; great restaurants. **Cons:** some rooms don't have great views; very pricey; spotty Wi-Fi. *Rooms from: $346* *100 Jackson Lake Lodge Rd.* *307/543–3100* *www.gtlc.com* *Closed early Oct.–mid-May* *385 rooms* *No meals.*

★ Signal Mountain Lodge

$$$ | **HOTEL** | The main building of this lodge on Jackson Lake's southern shoreline has a cozy lounge and a grand pine deck overlooking the lake; stay in a traditional lodge room or a rustic cabin, some with sleek kitchens. **Pros:** excellent restaurants and bar; great lakefront location; some rooms have fireplaces. **Cons:** rustic, simple decor; not all rooms have water views; lakefront rooms are expensive. *Rooms from: $287* *Signal Mountain Lodge Rd.* *307/543–2831* *www.signalmountainlodge.com* *Closed mid-Oct.–mid-May* *79 rooms* *No meals.*

Activities

BIKING

Since the first paved pathways were completed in Jackson Hole in 1996, the valley has become a cyclist's paradise. Almost 60 miles of paved pathways thread through Jackson Hole, with more in the works. Note that bicycles aren't allowed on trails or in the backcountry.

Hoback Sports

BICYCLING | **FAMILY** | Get your own bike tuned up or rent one: road, mountain, hybrid, kids', and trailers. The shop also sells bikes, clothing, and mountain sporting accessories, as well as ski rentals and other winter-sports equipment. *520 W. Broadway, Suite 3, Jackson* *307/733–5335* *www.hobacksports.com.*

Teton Mountain Bike Tours

BICYCLING | Mountain bikers of all skill levels can take this company's guided half-, full-, or multiday tours into Grand Teton and Yellowstone national parks, as well as winter tours of Jackson Hole on snow bikes with fat, studded tires. The outfit also rents bikes. *545 N. Cache St., Jackson* *307/733–0712* *www.tetonmtbike.com* *Tours from $80.*

BIRD-WATCHING

With more than 300 species of birds, the Tetons make excellent bird-watching country. Here you might spot both the calliope hummingbird (the smallest North American hummingbird) and the trumpeter swan (the world's largest waterfowl). Birds of prey circle around Antelope Flats Road—the surrounding fields are good hunting turf for red-tailed hawks and prairie falcons, and Oxbow Bend, which draws white pelicans during their spring northerly migration along with bald eagles and great blue herons. At Taggart Lake and Phelps Lake you might see woodpeckers, bluebirds, and hummingbirds. Look for songbirds, such as pine and evening grosbeaks and Cassin's finches, in surrounding open pine and aspen forests.

BOATING

Before launching on any of the state's waters, including those in the park, you must purchase a seasonal permit ($40 for motorized boats, $12 for nonmotorized, including SUPs), available year-round at Craig Thomas and Colter Bay visitor centers, where you can also check with rangers about current conditions. You also must go through an AIS (Aquatic

Invasive Species) inspection, which costs $30 for motorized boats and $15 for nonmotorized; the nearest inspection sites are at the Moose and Moran park entrance stations.

★ Barker-Ewing Scenic Float Trips
BOATING | FAMILY | Float along a peaceful 10-mile stretch of the Snake River within the park and look for wildlife as knowledgeable guides talk about area history, geology, plants, and animals. Private custom trips can also be arranged. ✉ *Moose* ☎ *307/733–1800, 800/365–1800* 🌐 *www.barkerewing.com* *From $80.*

★ Colter Bay Village Marina
BOATING | FAMILY | You can rent motorboats, kayaks, and canoes at Colter Bay from Grand Teton Lodge Company. Guided fishing trips are also available. ✉ *Colter Bay Village Rd.* ✣ *Off U.S. 89/191/287* ☎ *307/543–3100* 🌐 *www.gtlc.com.*

Dave Hansen Whitewater & Scenic Trips
WHITE-WATER RAFTING | Going strong since 1967, this highly respected outfit offers both rip-roaring white-water trips down class II–III Snake River rapids and more relaxing floats on calmer stretches. ✉ *Jackson* ☎ *307/733–6295* 🌐 *www.davehansenwhitewater.com* ☞ *From $87.*

Leek's Marina
BOATING | At this Signal Mountain Lodge–operated marina on the northern end of Jackson Lake, there are boat rentals, nightly buoys, an excellent pizza restaurant, and parking for boat trailers and other vehicles for up to three nights. ✉ *U.S. 89/191/287, 6 miles north of Jackson Lake Junction* ☎ *307/543–2831* 🌐 *www.signalmountainlodge.com.*

★ National Park Float Trips
BOATING | FAMILY | The knowledgeable and charismatic Triangle X guides will row you down 10 miles of the Snake River through pristine riparian habitat in Grand Teton National Park. For the best wildlife viewing, book a dawn or evening dinner float. ✉ *Moose* ☎ *307/733–5500* 🌐 *nationalparkfloattrips.com* *From $82.*

★ Rendezvous River Sports
BOATING | FAMILY | However you'd like to hit the water, the river rats at Rendezvous are here to help. They offer instruction for stand-up paddleboarding and kayaking, as well as guided trips on area rivers and lakes. Or you could choose a backcountry adventure in the national parks. The shop rents kayaks, canoes, rafts, and paddleboards. ✉ *945 W. Broadway, Jackson* ☎ *307/733–2471* 🌐 *www.jacksonholekayak.com* *From $205.*

Signal Mountain Lodge Marina
BOATING | This Jackson Lake marina rents pontoon boats, deck cruisers, motorboats, kayaks, and canoes by the hour or all day. ✉ *Signal Mountain Lodge Rd.* ☎ *307/543–2831* 🌐 *www.signalmountainlodge.com.*

CAMPING

You'll find a variety of campgrounds, from small areas where only tents are allowed (starting from $11 nightly) to full RV parks with all services (from $64 nightly for full hookups). All developed campgrounds have toilets and water; plan to bring your own firewood. Check in at National Park Service campsites as early as possible—sites are assigned on a first-come, first-served basis.

You can reserve a backcountry campsite between early January and mid-May for a $45 nonrefundable fee using the online reservation system. Two-thirds of all sites are set aside for in-person, walk-in permits ($35), so you can also take a chance on securing a site when you arrive.

Colter Bay Campground and RV Park. Big, busy, noisy, and filled by noon, this centrally located campground has tent and trailer or RV sites. ☎ *307/543–2811 for tent campground, 307/543–3100 for RV Park.*

Gros Ventre. The park's second biggest campground is set in an open, grassy area on the bank of the Gros Ventre River, away from the mountains but not far from the village of Kelly, on park's southeastern edge. ☎ *307/734–4431*.

Headwaters Campground at Flagg Ranch. In a shady pine grove overlooking the headwaters of the Snake River, these sites set just north of the park border along John D. Rockefeller, Jr. Memorial Parkway provide a great base for exploring Grand Teton or Yellowstone. The showers and laundry facilities are a bonus, and camper cabins are available. ☎ *307/543–2861*.

Jenny Lake. Wooded sites and Teton views make this tent-only spot the most desirable campground in the park, and it fills early. ☎ *307/543–3390*.

Lizard Creek. Views of Jackson Lake's north end, wooded sites, and the relative isolation of this campground make it a relaxing choice. ☎ *307/543–2831*.

Signal Mountain. This campground in a hilly setting on Jackson Lake has boat access to the lake. ☎ *307/543–2831*.

CLIMBING

Exum Mountain Guides

CLIMBING/MOUNTAINEERING | FAMILY | The climbing experiences offered by the oldest guide service in North America include one-day mountain climbs, shorter and easier adventures geared toward beginners, weeklong clinics culminating in a two-day ascent of the Grand Teton, and backcountry adventures on skis and snowboards. ✉ *Grand Teton National Park* ☎ *307/733–2297* 🌐 *www.exumguides.com* 🎫 *From $180.*

EDUCATIONAL PROGRAMS

Check visitor centers and the park newspaper for locations and times of the park's many ranger programs.

Campfire Programs

TOUR—SIGHT | FAMILY | In summer, park rangers give free slide-show presentations, usually at Colter Bay. ✉ *Grand Teton National Park* 🌐 *www.nps.gov/grte.*

Junior Ranger Program

TOUR—SIGHT | FAMILY | Children and even adults can earn a Junior Ranger badge or patch by picking up a Junior Ranger booklet at any park visitor center. ✉ *Grand Teton National Park* 🌐 *www.nps.gov/grte.*

Nature Explorer's Backpack Program

INFO CENTER | FAMILY | Rangers at the Laurance S. Rockefeller Preserve Center lend a nature journal and a backpack full of activities to children ages 6 –12 before sending them out along the trails at the Rockefeller Preserve. ✉ *Grand Teton National Park* ☎ *307/739–3654*.

FISHING

Rainbow, brook, lake, and native cutthroat trout inhabit the park's waters. The Snake's 75 miles of river and tributary are world-renowned for their fishing. To fish in the park, you need a Wyoming fishing license, which you can purchase from the state game and fish department or at Colter Bay Village Marina, Dornan's, Signal Mountain Lodge, and area sporting-goods stores. A day permit for nonresidents costs $14, and an annual permit costs $102 plus $12.50 for a conservation stamp.

Grand Teton Lodge Company Fishing Trips

FISHING | The park's major concessionaire operates guided fishing trips on Jackson Lake and guided fly-fishing trips on the Snake River. ✉ *Grand Teton National Park* ☎ *307/543–3100* 🌐 *www.gtlc.com* 🎫 *From $115.*

Signal Mountain Lodge

FISHING | Hourly and half-day Jackson Lake guided fishing trips depart from the marina at Signal Mountain Lodge, weather permitting. The rates include equipment and tackle. ✉ *Signal Mountain Rd.* ☎ *307/543–2831* 🌐 *www.signalmountainlodge.com* 💳 *From $139.*

HIKING

The Hole Hiking Experience

HIKING/WALKING | For more than three decades, guides have led hikes and wildlife tours for all ages and ability levels in the Greater Yellowstone Ecosystem. The trips have an interpretive focus,with information about the history, geology, and ecology of the area. Many excursions incorporate yoga or have a holistic bent. In winter, cross-country ski and snowshoe tours in are offered in the park. ✉ *Jackson* ☎ *307/690–4453* 🌐 *www.holehike.com* ☞ *From $150.*

HORSEBACK RIDING

Grand Teton Lodge Company Horseback Rides

HORSEBACK RIDING | **FAMILY** | Rides start at Jackson Lake Lodge, Colter Bay Village, Headwaters Lodge, and Jenny Lake Lodge corrals. One- and two-hour trips are available, and beginners are welcome, with pony rides for small children. ✉ *Grand Teton National Park* ☎ *307/543–3100* 🌐 *www.gtlc.com* ☞ *From $50.*

Triangle X Ranch

HORSEBACK RIDING | **FAMILY** | This classic dude ranch just south of Moran Junction on the eastern edge of the park offers day horseback trips as well as multiday experiences that include comfy cabin accommodations, meals, rides, and lots of other fun activities. ✉ *2 Triangle X Ranch Rd., Moose* ☎ *307/733–2183* 🌐 *www.trianglex.com.*

What's Nearby

The major gateway to Grand Teton National Park is the famously beautiful and beautiful-peopled town of **Jackson,** along with its neighbors **Teton Village**—popular among skiers and snowboarders from all over the world as the home of Jackson Hole Mountain Resort—and the small, unincorporated community of **Wilson.** These three communities form a triangle surrounded by greater Jackson Hole, with Teton Village at the northern tip and sharing a border with the south end of the national park, and Jackson and Wilson forming the two southern points. For a small town, Jackson has an extensive array of hotels and inns, restaurants and bars, and galleries and shops. Steadily growing Wilson has a handful of additional options, while Teton Village has hundreds of hotel rooms and condos, plus several restaurants, but it's really a self-contained resort community that while close to the park doesn't have the inviting small-town character that you'll find in Jackson.

Chapter 28

GREAT BASIN NATIONAL PARK

Updated by
Stina Sieg

Camping ★★☆☆☆

Hotels ★☆☆☆☆

Activities ★★★☆☆

Scenery ★★★★☆

Crowds ★☆☆☆☆

WELCOME TO GREAT BASIN NATIONAL PARK

TOP REASONS TO GO

★ **Ancient trees:** The twisting, windswept bristlecone pines in Great Basin can live to be thousands of years old.

★ **Desert skyscraper:** Wheeler Peak rises out of the desert basin with summit temperatures often 20–30 degrees below that of the visitor center.

★ **Rare shields:** Look for hundreds of these unique disk-shape formations inside Lehman Caves.

★ **Gather your pine nuts while you may:** Come in the fall and go a little nutty, as you can gather up to three gunnysacks of pinyon pine nuts, found in abundance throughout the park. They're great on salads.

★ **Celestial show:** Pitch-dark nights make for dazzling stars. Gaze on your own or attend a seasonal nighttime talk, led by a park ranger.

1 **Lehman Caves.** Highlighted by the limestone caverns, this is the primary destination for many Great Basin visitors. It's located next to a popular visitor center and just past the start of Wheeler Peak Scenic Drive.

2 **Wheeler Peak.** This 13,063-footer is the park's centerpiece, and is especially stunning when capped with snow. Hikers can climb the mountain via strenuous, day-use-only trails, which also lead to small alpine lakes, a glacier, and some ancient bristlecone pines.

3 **Snake Creek Canyon.** This is the less crowded, more remote part of an already remote park. Trails follow creeks and cross meadows in the southern parts of the park, and six primitive campgrounds line Snake Creek. A bristlecone pine grove is nearby, though far off any beaten path.

4 **Arch Canyon.** A high-clearance, four-wheel-drive vehicle is recommended, and sturdy boots and sun protection are critical if you want to get to Lexington Arch, which is unusual in that it is formed of limestone, not sandstone as most arches are. This is a day-use-only area.

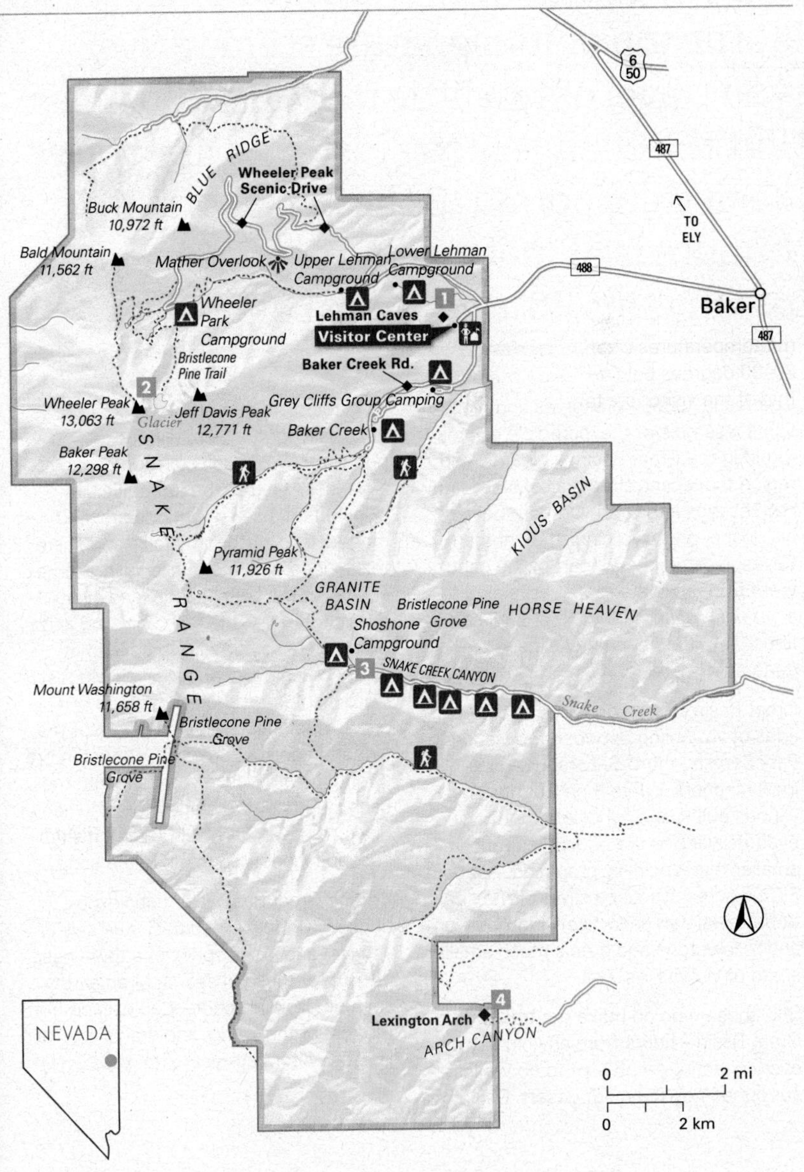
6
50
487
TO ELY
488
Baker
487
BLUE RIDGE
Wheeler Peak Scenic Drive
Buck Mountain 10,972 ft
Bald Mountain 11,562 ft
Mather Overlook
Upper Lehman Campground
Lower Lehman Campground
1
Wheeler Park Campground
Lehman Caves
Visitor Center
Bristlecone Pine Trail
Baker Creek Rd.
2
Wheeler Peak 13,063 ft
Glacier
Jeff Davis Peak 12,771 ft
Grey Cliffs Group Camping
Baker Creek
Baker Peak 12,298 ft
SNAKE RANGE
KIOUS BASIN
Pyramid Peak 11,926 ft
GRANITE BASIN
Bristlecone Pine Grove
HORSE HEAVEN
Shoshone Campground
3
SNAKE CREEK CANYON
Snake Creek
Mount Washington 11,658 ft
Bristlecone Pine Grove
Bristlecone Pine Grove
4
Lexington Arch
ARCH CANYON
NEVADA
0
2 mi
0
2 km

As you drive from the vast, sagebrush-dotted desert near Great Basin National Park's entrance into the cool alpine forests at the top of its signature scenic drive, you travel only a little more than 10 miles. But the change is so drastic it's like you've been transported to the Rocky Mountains, hundreds of miles away. That's a big part of why this little gem of a park exists.

Created in 1986, it preserves and highlights a sample of the incredible diversity found in the Great Basin, a gigantic arid region that spans almost all of Nevada and reaches into Utah, Oregon, California, Idaho, and Wyoming. The Lehman Caves, located in the heart of the park, went from a private tourist attraction to a national monument in 1922 until being folded into the new national park a few generations later.

Great Basin's founding came after decades of wrangling between the National Park Service, the U.S. Forest Service, local ranchers, White Pine County, and various politicians, whose compromises eventually led to the park being much smaller than originally proposed. At about 77,000 acres, it's just a sliver of the size of better-known parks like Grand Canyon and Yellowstone and gets a much smaller share of visitors, as well.

Still, those who do make the trek to Great Basin—hours from any big city in every direction—find a lot to do while surrounded by the quiet desert. Daily cave tours are one of the biggest draws, especially for families, with tickets so popular they can sell out months in advance. At night, the famously dark skies offset a sea of bright stars, and rangers lead astronomy talks and share telescopes with the public several times a week in the high season (and even host a festival in the fall). Camping and hiking are also huge, with trails to fit pretty much every ability level. Modest walks can get you to alpine lakes or a grove of bristlecone pines, some of the oldest organisms on earth. Longer, more strenuous hikes take you deep into the backcountry or the craggy top of Wheeler Peak. At more than 13,000 feet, it's the second-highest mountain in the state.

Visiting Great Basin is a rustic experience, with few amenities, little cell service, and just a speck of a town nearby. But for those in search of an earthy solitude, it's a much-needed escape from the rest of the world, and draws a certain kind of visitor back year after year.

AVERAGE HIGH/LOW TEMPERATURES					
JAN.	**FEB.**	**MAR.**	**APR.**	**MAY**	**JUNE**
41/18	44/21	48/24	56/31	66/40	76/48
JULY	**AUG.**	**SEPT.**	**OCT.**	**NOV.**	**DEC.**
86/57	83/56	75/47	62/47	49/26	42/20

Planning

When to Go

Summer is when you'll find the most amenities open and also the most visitors. While Great Basin doesn't get crowded to the extent of larger parks, it has been somewhat "discovered" in recent years, leading to hard-to-find parking and camping spots between around Memorial Day and Labor Day, and sometimes beyond. In these warmer months, you should be comfortable in shorts and T-shirts during the day—though temperatures drop at night, and get colder the higher up you climb, so bring light jackets and pants. Fall and spring can be lovely times to visit, though you should plan for lower temperatures at night and fewer businesses open in Baker, the small town near the park.

A winter visit can be sublime in its solitude, but the hardy visitor must be prepared for the elements, especially if the backcountry is a destination. With temperatures hovering in the low teens, heavy coats, boots, and other appropriate winter gear are necessary. Some roads might be impassable in inclement weather; check ahead with a park ranger. No dining or groceries are available in the park during the winter, and the closest option is several miles away at the year-round Border Inn.

FESTIVALS AND EVENTS

Great Basin Astronomy Festival. In 2016, Great Basin was named a Dark Sky Park by the International Dark Skies Assocation. This festival, spread out over a few days every fall, is a chance to experience these famous nighttime skies, with talks, workshops, and, of course, looks at the stars through park telescopes. Be sure to snag a reservation, as it can fill up fast. 🌐 *www.nps.gov/grba/planyourvisit/great-basin-astronomy-festival.htm.*

Silver State Classic Challenge. Twice a year, car enthusiasts of all stripes close a state highway for the country's largest (and most venerable) open-road race for amateur fast-car drivers. The event occurs the third weekend of May and the third weekend of September south of Ely on Route 318, from Lund to Hiko, and is open to just about any four-wheeled vehicle. 🌐 *www.sscc.us.*

White Pine County Fair. Livestock, flower, and vegetable competitions, plus horse races, food booths, dancing, and a barbecue dinner make this fair, held at the White Pine County Fairgrounds in Ely, the real thing. The dates fluctuate every August. 🌐 *www.wpcfair.com.*

Getting Here and Around

AIR

The nearest airport is in Cedar City (142 miles) but will likely be pricey. Salt Lake City (239 miles) and Las Vegas (303 miles) are better bets, though you'll probably get the cheapest fares (and might have the most fun) flying into Vegas.

CAR

The entrance to Great Basin is on Route 488, 5 miles west of its junction with Route 487. From Ely, take U.S. 6/50 to Route 487. From Salt Lake City or Cedar City, Utah, take Interstate 15 South to

U.S. 6/50 West; from Las Vegas, drive north on Interstate 15 and then north on Route 93 to access U.S. 6/50. ⚠ **Don't rely on GPS to get to the park, as sometimes it sends people up remote dirt roads. The turnoff to the main section of the park is well marked in the center of Baker.**

In the park, Baker Creek Road and portions of Wheeler Peak Scenic Drive, above Upper Lehman Creek, are closed from November to June. The road to the visitor center and the roads to the developed campgrounds are paved, but two-wheel-drive cars don't do well in winter storms. RVs and trailers over 24 feet aren't allowed above Upper Lehman Creek. With an 8% grade, the road to Wheeler Peak is steep and curvy, but not dangerous if you take it slow. Motorcyclists should watch for gravel on the road's surface.

There are two gas stations located nearby. The tiny Baker Sinclair station is just outside the park entrance, while about 7½ miles farther, the Border Inn has a Phillips 66 station, open 24/7.

Inspiration

Hiking Great Basin National Park, by Bruce Grubbs, will get your Great Basin trip off on the right foot.

Trails to Explore in Great Basin National Park, by Rose Houk, is all about hiking in the park.

Geology of the Great Basin, by Bill Fiero, and *Basin and Range,* by John McPhee, present geological tours of the Great Basin.

Park Essentials

ACCESSIBILITY

Designated accessibility parking spaces are available at both visitor centers. The centers themselves are both on one level, fully accessible to those with impaired mobility, with accessible bathrooms. The park slide show is captioned. The park has two ADA-compliant trails, though both are unpaved: the Island Forest Trail (0.4 mile) at the top of Wheeler Peak Drive and the Shoshone Trail (0.1 mile) at Snake Creek. Baker Creek Campground, Upper Lehman Creek Campground, and Wheeler Peak Campground are accessible, though the restroom access ramp at Upper Lehman Creek Campground is steep.

PARK FEES AND PERMITS

Admission to the park is free, but if you want to tour Lehman Caves there's a fee ($9–$11, depending on tour length). To fish in Great Basin National Park, those 12 and older need a state fishing license from the Nevada Department of Wildlife (🌐 *www.ndow.org*). The one-day nonresident license is $18, plus $7 for each additional day at time of purchase ($80 for a year). Backcountry hikers do not need permits, but for your own safety you should fill out a form at the visitor center before setting out.

PARK HOURS

The park is open 24/7 year-round; May–August, visitor center hours are 8–4:30; hours may vary from year to year. It's in the Pacific time zone.

CELL PHONE RECEPTION

There's decent coverage close to Lehman Caves; the more remote you get, the spottier it becomes. Some service is available higher portions of the Wheeler Peak hike.

SHOPS AND GROCERS

While the closest full-service grocery store is an hour away in Ely, the Stargazer Inn in Baker has a small market with some basics, including snacks, beer, and wine. Similar supplies can be found a few miles outside of town at the Border Inn's grocery section.

Hotels

There is no lodging in the park, so plan to arrive early to snag one of its coveted first-come, first-served campsites, or expect to camp in the backcountry. There is a handful motels in nearby Baker and many more to choose from about an hour away in Ely.

Restaurants

Dining in the park itself is limited to basic but tasty breakfast and lunch fare at the Lehman Caves Cafe and Gift Shop. About 5 miles away in Baker, a town of less than 100 people, there are a few good options. Fire grates are available at each campsite in the park's four developed campgrounds for barbecuing.

Visitor Information

PARK CONTACT INFORMATION Great Basin National Park. ✉ *Rte. 488, Baker* ☎ *775/234–7331* 🌐 *www.nps.gov/grba.*

Lehman Caves

5½ miles from Baker.

Essentially the gateway to this small park, this area contains an in-depth visitor center and fun gift shop, the park's only restaurant (seasonal), hiking trails, and campgrounds. Perhaps most important, it's home to the Lehman Caves, the park's most well-known attraction. This is a good corner of the park to plan out your adventures or relax with a glass of wine after a day of hiking.

Sights

SCENIC DRIVES

Baker Creek Road

SCENIC DRIVE | Though less popular than the Wheeler Peak Scenic Drive, this gravel road affords gorgeous views of Wheeler Peak, the Baker Creek Drainage, and Snake Valley. Beautiful wildflowers are an extra treat in spring and early summer. The road is closed in the winter, and there are no pull-outs or scenic overlooks. *½ mile inside park boundary off Rte. 488* *Closed Nov.–May.*

SCENIC STOPS

★ Lehman Caves

CAVE | FAMILY | While Indigenous people were the first to explore and use the caves, rancher and miner Absalom Lehman is credited with discovering this underground wonder in 1885. The single limestone and marble cavern is 2½ miles long, with stalactites, stalagmites, helictites, flowstone, popcorn, and other bizarre mineral formations that cover almost every surface. Lehman Caves is one of the best places to see rare shield formations, created when calcite-rich water is forced from tiny cracks in a cave wall, ceiling, or floor. Year-round the cave maintains a constant, damp temperature of 50°F, so wear a light jacket and nonskid shoes. Go for the full 90-minute tour if you have time; during summer, it's offered several times a day, as is the 60-minute tour. Expect daily tours during the winter. Children under age five are not allowed on the 90-minute tours, except during the winter; those under 16 must be accompanied by an adult. Take the 0.3-mile Mountain View Nature Trail beforehand to see the original cave entrance and **Rhodes Cabin,** where black-and-white photographs of the park's earlier days line the walls. ⚠ **Get tickets as far in advance as possible at recreation.gov. Tours can sell out months in advance.** ✉ *Lehman Caves Visitor Center, Great Basin National Park* ☎ *775/234–7331* *From $9.*

TRAILS

Mountain View Nature Trail

TRAIL | FAMILY | Just past the Rhodes Cabin on the right side of the visitor center, this short and easy trail (0.3 mile) through pinyon pine and juniper trees is marked with signs describing the plants. The path passes the original entrance to Lehman Caves and loops back to the visitor center. It's a great way to spend a half hour or so while you wait for your cave tour to start. *Easy.* ✉ *Great Basin National Park* ✣ *Trailhead: At Lehman Caves Visitor Center.*

VISITOR CENTERS

Great Basin Visitor Center

INFO CENTER | FAMILY | Here you can see exhibits on the flora, fauna, and geology of the park, or ask a ranger to suggest a favorite hike. Books, videos, and souvenirs are for sale. Water is available. ✉ *Rte. 487 , just north of Baker, Great Basin National Park* ☎ *775/234–7520* ⏲ *Closed Oct.–late Apr.*

Lehman Caves Visitor Center

INFO CENTER | FAMILY | Regularly scheduled cave tours lasting 60 or 90 minutes depart from here. Mountain View Nature Trail encircles the visitor center and includes Rhodes Cabin and the historic cave entrance. Buy gifts for friends and family back home at the bookstore, or just take in the view with a glass of wine at the adjacent café. There's also a replica of the park's famed caves you can walk through. ✉ *Rte. 488 , ½ mile inside park boundary, Great Basin National Park* ☎ *775/234–7331.*

Restaurants

Lehman Caves Cafe and Gift Shop

$ | AMERICAN | This casual spot is a great place to soak in the vast desert view and offers simple breakfasts and lunches. The sandwiches, filled with meats smoked by the owner, are especially good. **Known for:** a nice place to unwind with a beer or glass of wine into the late afternoon; the only restaurant in the park; delicious cookies and other treats, baked by a local pastry chef. $ *Average main: $10* ✉ *Next to visitor center, Great Basin National Park* ☎ *775/234–7200* ⏲ *Closed Nov.–May. No dinner.*

Wheeler Peak

12 miles from the Lehman Caves Visitor Center.

You'll find some of the most dramatic scenery, including panoramic desert views, in this high-elevation section of the park. Here, hiking trails take you to some of Great Basin's most photographed spots: clear alpine lakes, a grove of bristlecone pines, and the top of Nevada's second-highest peak. This area's sole camping area, Wheeler Peak Campground, is one of the most beautiful in the park. The scenic drive that transports you from the desert to the forest is an attraction in itself but, like the campground in this prized section, is open only seasonally.

Sights

SCENIC DRIVES

★ **Wheeler Peak Scenic Drive**

SCENIC DRIVE | When this stunning seasonable road is open, it's a must for Great Basin visitors. Less than a mile from the visitor center off Route 488, turn onto this paved road that winds its way up to elevations of 10,000 feet. You'll go past pinyon-juniper forest in lower elevations; as you climb, the air cools as much as 20–30 degrees. Along the way, pull off at overlooks for awe-inspiring glimpses of the peaks of the South Snake Range. A short interpretive trail leads to a ditch that once carried water to the historic Osceola mining site. Turn off at Mather Overlook, elevation 9,000 feet, for the best photo ops. Wheeler Overlook is the best place to see Wheeler Peak, as well as fall colors. Allow 1½ hours for the

Lehman Caves: It's amazing what a little water and air can do to a room.

24-mile round-trip, not including hikes. ✉ *Baker* ✣ *Just inside park boundary, off Rte. 488 about 5 miles west of Baker* 🌐 *www.nps.gov/grba/planyourvisit/wheeler-peak-scenic-drive.htm* ⊙ *Closed Nov.–June.*

TRAILS

Alpine Lakes Trail

TRAIL | This moderate, 2.7-mile trek loops past the beautiful Stella and Teresa lakes from the trailhead near Wheeler Peak Campground. You'll rise and fall about 600 feet in elevation as you pass through subalpine and alpine forest. The views of Wheeler Peak, amid wildflowers (in summer), white fir, shimmering aspens, and towering ponderosa pines, make this a memorable hike. The trailhead is at nearly 10,000 feet, so make sure you're adjusted to the altitude and prepared for changing weather. Allow three hours. *Moderate.* ✉ *Great Basin National Park* ✣ *Trailhead: At Bristlecone parking area, near end of Wheeler Peak Scenic Dr.*

★ Bristlecone Pine Trail

TRAIL | **FAMILY** | Though the park has several bristlecone pine groves, the only way to see the gnarled, ancient trees up close is to hike this trail. From the parking area to the grove, it's a moderate 2.8-mile hike that takes about an hour each way. Rangers offer informative talks in season; inquire at the visitor center. The Bristlecone Pine Trail also leads to the **Glacier Trail,** which skirts the southernmost permanent ice field on the continent and ends with a view of a small rock glacier, the only one in Nevada. It's less than 3 miles back to the parking lot. Allow three hours for the moderate hike and remember the trailhead is at 9,800 feet above sea level. *Moderate.* ✉ *Great Basin National Park* ✣ *Trailhead: Summit Trail parking area, Wheeler Peak Scenic Dr., 12 miles from Lehman Caves Visitor Center.*

Osceola Ditch Trail

TRAIL | FAMILY | In 1890, at a cost of $108,223, the Osceola Gravel Mining Company constructed an 18-mile-long trench. The ditch was part of an attempt to glean gold from the South Snake Range, but water shortages and the company's failure to find much gold forced the mining operation to shut down in 1905. You can reach portions of the eastern section of the ditch on foot via the Osceola Ditch Trail, which passes through pine and fir trees and has interpretive signs along the way. Allow 30 minutes for this easy 0.3-mile round-trip hike. *Easy.* ✉ *Great Basin National Park* ✣ *Trailhead: Wheeler Peak Scenic Dr.*

★ **Wheeler Peak Summit Trail**

TRAIL | Begin this full-day, 8.6-mile hike early in the day so as to minimize exposure to afternoon storms. Depart and return to Summit Trailhead near the end of Wheeler Peak Scenic Drive. Most of the route follows a ridge up the mountain to the summit. Elevation gain is 2,900 feet to 13,063 feet above sea level, so hikers should have good stamina and watch for altitude sickness and/or hypothermia due to drastic temperature and weather changes. The trail becomes especially steep and challenging, with lots of loose rocks, toward the summit. *Difficult.* ✉ *Great Basin National Park* ✣ *Trailhead: Wheeler Peak Scenic Dr., Summit Trail parking area.*

Snake Creek Canyon

11 miles from Baker.

Great Basin is already far from pretty much everything, but for those who want to go just a little bit farther, Snake Creek offers true solitude. Free, primitive campsites are shaded by trees, with fire rings and picnic tables but no water or bathrooms. Snake Creek Road is open year-round, but can become snowy or muddy in the winter and spring. High-clearance vehicles are recommended, while RVs and trailers are not. A cluster of trails are at the end of the road, including routes to Johnson and Baker lakes.

Sights

SCENIC SIGHTS

Lexington Arch

NATURE SITE | Tucked far away in the rugged backcountry, Lexington Arch is six stories high, looming over Lexington Creek. While most arches are made of sandstone, this arch is limestone, more often associated with caves. That leads some to believe it was once a passage in a cave system. The 5.4-mile (round-trip) hike to the arch is challenging, with little to no shade. Hiking boots, sunscreen, water, and snacks are essential. It's one of the few trails in the park where leashed pets are allowed. The arch is actually located south of Snake Creek, outside of the small town of Garrison, Utah. Only high-clearance, four-wheel-drive vehicles are recommended on the dirt road leading to it. ⚠ **Traveling to the arch can be dangerous, as the road becomes rougher the closer you get to the trailhead. Make sure to stop driving before you get in trouble and walk the rest of the way.** ✉ *Baker* ✣ *Drive south from Baker on Rte. 487 until it becomes Utah 21. Pass through Garrison, then past Pruess Lake. Turn right at the sign for Lexington Arch, and take that dirt road about 7 miles until you reach a washed-out section. Take the south fork to reach the trailhead for the arch. Due to road damage, parking will be ½ to 1 mile away from the trailhead.*

Activities

Great Basin National Park is a great place for experienced outdoor adventurers. The closest outdoor store is an hour away in Ely, so bring everything you might need, and be prepared to go it alone. Permits are not required to go off the beaten path, but if you're planning a multiday hike, register with a ranger just in case. The effort is worth it, as the backcountry is pristine and not at all crowded, no matter the time of year. As is the case in all national parks, bicycling is restricted to existing roads, which can get busy with cars, especially Wheeler Peak Scenic Drive. Always be cautious, and consider biking on less popular roads.

BIRD-WATCHING

An impressive list of bird species have been sighted here—238, according to the National Park Service checklist. Some, such as the common raven and American robin, can be seen at most locations. Others, such as the red-naped sapsucker, are more commonly seen near Lehman Creek. In the higher elevations, listen for the loud shriek of Clark's nutcracker, storing nuts.

CAMPING

Great Basin has four developed campgrounds, all easily accessible by car, but only the Lower Lehman Creek Campground is open year-round. All are first come, first served, and can be paid for on-site with cash, check, or credit card. The campgrounds do fill up, so try to snag your spot early.

Primitive campsites around Snake and Strawberry creeks are open year-round and are free; however, snow and rain can make access to the sites difficult. RVs and trailers are not recommended.

Baker Creek Campground. The turnoff is just past the park entrance, on the left as you approach the Lehman Caves Visitor Center. ✉ *2½ miles south of Rte. 488, 3 miles from visitor center in the Lehman Caves section of the park.*

Lower Lehman Creek Campground. Other than Great Basin's primitive sites, this is the only campground in the park that is open year-round. It's the first turnoff past the Lehman Caves Visitor Center. ✉ *2½ miles from visitor center on Wheeler Peak Scenic Dr. in the Lehman Caves section of the park.*

Upper Lehman Creek Campground. About a mile past the Lower Lehman Creek turnoff, this camp fills up quickly in the summer. ✉ *4 miles from visitor center on Wheeler Peak Scenic Dr. in the Lehman Caves section of the park.*

Wheeler Peak Campground. This cool high-elevation campground at the end of Wheeler Peak Scenic Drive has stunning views and is near trailheads. Many consider it the nicest in the park. ✉ *13 miles from Lehman Caves Visitor Center on Wheeler Peak Scenic Dr. in the Wheeler Peak section of the park.*

CROSS-COUNTRY SKIING

Lehman Creek Trail

SKIING/SNOWBOARDING | In summer, descend 2,050 feet by hiking Lehman Creek Trail one-way (downhill) from Wheeler Peak campground to Upper Lehman Creek campground. In winter, it is the most popular cross-country skiing trail in the park. You may need snowshoes to reach the skiable upper section, with free rentals available at the Lehman Cave Visitor Center.

EDUCATIONAL OFFERINGS

Junior Ranger Program

TOUR—SIGHT | **FAMILY** | Youngsters answer questions and complete activities related to the park and then are sworn in as Junior Rangers and receive a Great Basin badge. ✉ *Great Basin National Park* ☎ *775/234–7331* 🌐 *www.nps.gov/grba.*

Weekly Astronomy Programs

OBSERVATORY | **FAMILY** | You'll find some of the country's darkest skies—and brightest stars—at Great Basin. Due to its low light pollution, it was even named a Dark Sky Park by the International Dark Sky Association in 2016. As astrotourism has grown, Great Basin has responded by building a brand-new amphitheatre for these ranger-led stargazing programs. Expect to be dazzled as you get a chance to see the wild blue yonder through a telescope. It's often crowded, especially during the summer, when the program is held several times a week. It drops down to once a week in shoulder seasons. ✉ *Lehman Caves Visitor Center, Baker* 🌐 *www.nps.gov/grba* ⊗ *Closed Nov.–Mar.*

HIKING

You'll witness beautiful views by driving along the Wheeler Peak Scenic Drive and other park roads, but hiking allows an in-depth experience that just can't be matched. Trails at Great Basin run the gamut from short, wheelchair-accessible paths to multiday backpacking excursions. Destinations include evergreen forest, flowering meadows and an extremely tall mountain peak. When you pick up a trail map at the visitor center, ask about trail conditions and bring appropriate clothing when you set out from any trailhead.

No matter the trail length, always carry water, and remember that the trails are at high elevations, so pace yourself accordingly. Never enter abandoned mineshafts or tunnels because they are unstable and dangerous. Those headed into the backcountry don't need to obtain a permit, but are encouraged to register at either of the two visitor centers. Regardless of the season, inquire about the weather, as it can be harsh and unpredictable. Since cell reception is spotty at best, a personal locator beacon can be a lifesaver when adventuring on remote trails.

What's Nearby

An hour's drive west of the park, at the intersection of three U.S. highways, **Ely** (population 4,000) is the largest town for hours in every direction. It grew up in the second wave of the early Nevada mining boom, right at the optimistic turn of the 20th century. For 70 years copper kept the town in business, but when it ran out in the early 1980s, Ely declined fast. Then, in 1986, the National Park Service designated Great Basin National Park, and the town got a boost. Ely has since been rebuilt and revitalized, though it's kept a quirky, faded feel. If you want to stay much closer to the park, tiny **Baker** (population roughly 75) has far fewer amenities but is slowly reawakening. The cluster of homes and small businesses on Route 487 is about 5 miles from the Lehman Caves Visitor Center.

Chapter 29

GREAT SAND DUNES NATIONAL PARK

Updated by
Whitney Bryen

Camping	Hotels	Activities	Scenery	Crowds
★★★☆☆	★☆☆☆☆	★★★★☆	★★★★☆	★★★☆☆

WELCOME TO GREAT SAND DUNES NATIONAL PARK

TOP REASONS TO GO

★ **Dune climbing:** Trek through the 30 square miles of main dunes in this landlocked dune field.

★ **Unrivaled diversity:** You can see eight completely different life zones in this park, ranging from salty wetlands and lush forests to parched sand sheet and frozen alpine peaks, all in a single day.

★ **Starry skies:** Gaze expansive views of the Milky Way staged above silouettes of the rolling dunes and jagged mountain peaks below.

★ **Aspens in autumn:** Take a hike—or, if you've got a high-clearance four-wheel-drive vehicle and good driving skills, take the rough road—up to Medano Pass during fall foliage season when the aspens turn gold.

★ **Vigorous hikes:** Pack a picnic lunch and climb up to High Dune, followed by the more strenuous stretch over to Star Dune. Or tackle the dramatic Music Pass Trail, which rewards you with two alpine lakes above the tree line if you can make the steep 4-mile climb.

1 **Main Use Area.** This relatively compact area contains all of the park's developed campgrounds, trails, and the visitor center.

2 **Sand Dunes.** The 30-square-mile field of sand has no designated trails. The highest dune in the park—and, in fact, in North America—is 750-foot-high Star Dune.

3 **Sangre de Cristo Mountains.** Named the "Blood of Christ" Mountains by Spanish explorers because of their ruddy color—especially at sunrise and sunset—the range contains 10 of Colorado's 54 Fourteeners (mountains taller than 14,000 feet); six within the preserve are more than 13,000 feet tall.

4 **Southern Grasslands.** Wildlife, such as elk and bison, feed on the park's grassy areas, primarily found in the park's southern area and the Great Sand Dunes National Preserve.

5 **Medano Creek Wetlands.** Popular with a variety of birds and amphibians, these seasonal wetlands form in the area around Medano Creek, where cottonwood and willow trees also thrive.

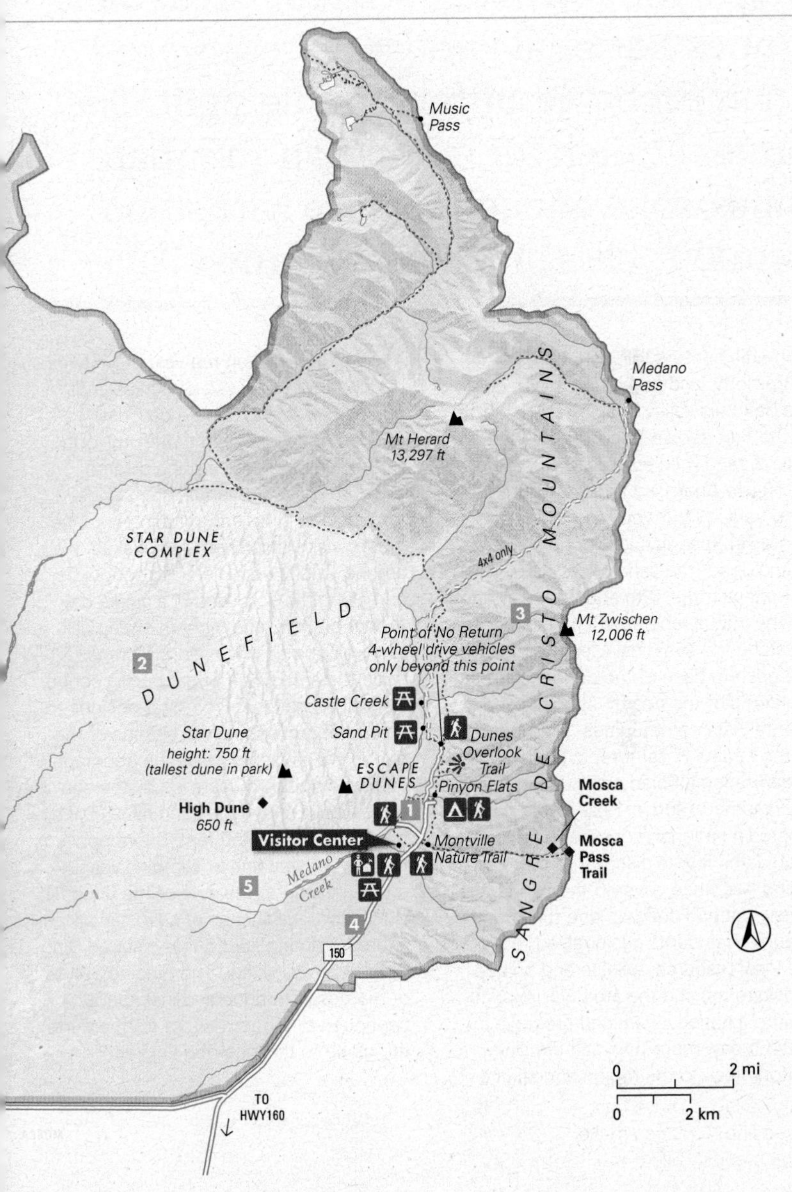
Music Pass
Medano Pass
SANGRE DE CRISTO MOUNTAINS
Mt Herard 13,297 ft
STAR DUNE COMPLEX
4x4 only
DUNEFIELD
3
Mt Zwischen 12,006 ft
Point of No Return 4-wheel drive vehicles only beyond this point
2
Castle Creek
Sand Pit
Dunes Overlook Trail
Star Dune height: 750 ft (tallest dune in park)
ESCAPE DUNES
Pinyon Flats
Mosca Creek
High Dune 650 ft
1
Visitor Center
Montville Nature Trail
Mosca Pass Trail
Medano Creek
5
4
150
0 2 mi
0 2 km
TO HWY160

Created by winds that sweep the San Luis Valley floor, the enormous sand dunes that form the heart of Great Sand Dunes National Park and Preserve are an improbable, unforgettable sight. The dunes stretch for more than 30 square miles, solid enough to have withstood 440,000 years of Mother Nature.

Nomadic hunters followed herds of mammoths and prehistoric bison into the San Luis Valley, making them some of the first people to visit the dunes. The hills of sand marked a common route for Native American tribes and explorers who traveled between the plains and Santa Fe. Speculation that gold was hiding under the sand attracted droves of miners in the 19th and 20th centuries. By the 1920s, operations had sprung up along the seasonal Medano Creek at the eastern base of the dunes, alarming residents of the nearby Alamosa and Monte Vista communities. Members of the Ladies Philanthropic Educational Organization lobbied politicians to protect the landmark, and in 1932 it was designated a national monument. Seventy years later, it was discovered that a large inland lake once covered the San Luis Valley, but had dried up due to climate change. Residents again rallied to protect the local resource, wildlife and unique ecosystems, and the area was expanded into a national park and preserve in 2004. Today, more than half a million visitors flock to the region annually to gawk at and play on the vast mountains of sand framed by the low grasslands and high-reaching Sangre de Cristo peaks. The tallest sand dunes in North America are nestled among diverse ecosystems of wetlands, grasslands, forests, and a towering mountain range where visitors can fish alpine lakes, walk among wildflowers, listen to songbirds, and climb the soft sand in a single day. Pronghorn, elk, and bighorn sheep call the area home, while sandhill cranes flood the area twice a year during spring and fall migrations. From star designs to sharp defined edges, the shapes of the dunes are as disparate as the geography surrounding them. Warmed by the sun or coated in snow, the sand hills, which tower as high as 750 feet, offer opportunities for sledding or climbing year-round. Adding to the awe of the unusual landscape, avalanches of sand can create a rare humming sound that inspired Bing Crosby's musical hit "The Singing Sands of Alamosa." Intrigue and inspiration continues to attract visitors from around the globe to this one-of-a-kind site.

Planning

When to Go

More than half a million visitors come to the park each year, most on summer weekends; they tend to congregate around the main parking area and Medano Creek. To avoid the crowds, hike away from the main area up to the High Dune. Or come in the winter, when the park is a place for contemplation and repose—as well as skiing and sledding.

Fall and spring are the prettiest times to visit, with the surrounding mountains still capped with snow in May, and leaves on the aspen trees turning gold in September and early October. In summer, the surface temperature of the sand can climb to 150°F in the afternoon, so climbing the dunes is best in the morning or late afternoon. Because of the high altitude—about 8,200 feet at the visitor center—the park's air temperatures remain in the 70s most of the summer.

Getting Here and Around

CAR

The park and preserve is about 240 miles from both Denver and Albuquerque, and roughly 180 miles from Colorado Springs and Santa Fe. The fastest route from Denver is Interstate 25 south to U.S. 160, heading west to just past Blanca, to Highway 150 north, which goes right to the park's main entrance. For a more scenic route, take U.S. 285 over Kenosha, Red Hill, and Poncha Passes, turn onto Highway 17 just south of Villa Grove, then take County Lane 6 to the park (watch for signs just south of Hooper). From Albuquerque, go north on Interstate 25 to Santa Fe, then north on U.S. 285 to Alamosa, then U.S. 160 east to Highway 150. From the west, Highway 17 and County Lane 6 take you to the park. The park entrance station is about 3 miles from the park boundary, and it's about a mile from there to the visitor center; the main parking lot is about a mile farther.

Park Essentials

ACCESSIBILITY

The park has two wheelchairs with balloon tires (for the sand) that can be borrowed; someone must push them. You can reserve one by calling the visitor center. Accessible campsites are available in the park's only campground.

PARK FEES AND PERMITS

Entrance fees are $25 per vehicle and are valid for one week from date of purchase. Pick up camping permits ($20 per night per site at Pinyon Flats Campground) and backpacking permits (free) online at 🌐 *www.recreation.gov.*

PARK HOURS

The park, open 24/7, is in the Mountain time zone.

Hotels

There are no hotels, motels, or lodges in the park. The nearest lodge is right outside the park entrance, and there are many hotels in Alamosa and a handful of them in other surrounding towns including Salida, Walsenburg, and Monte Vista.

Restaurants

The nearest restaurant is located just outside of the park entrance. There are no dining establishments in the park. In the visitor center and at the campground there are vending machines with drinks that are stocked mid-spring through mid-fall. There is one picnic area in the park situated along the edge of the dunes and the seasonal Medano Creek.

Visitor Information

CONTACTS Great Sand Dunes National Park and Preserve. ✉ *11999 Hwy. 150, Mosca* ☎ *719/378–6395* 🌐 *www.nps.gov/grsa.*

Main Use Area

There's one paved road in the park, and it goes to the park visitor center, the amphitheater, and about another mile to the Pinyon Flats Campground. Past the campground, you can take a regular car another mile on the Medano Pass Primitive Road to the Point of No Return. ⚠ **Beyond the Point of No Return, only four-wheel high-clearance vehicles are allowed.**

Sights

TRAILS

★ Mosca Pass Trail

TRAIL | This moderately challenging route follows the Montville Trail laid out centuries ago by Native Americans, which became the Mosca Pass toll road used in the late 1800s and early 1900s. This is a good afternoon hike, because the trail rises through the trees and subalpine meadows, often following Mosca Creek. Watch for grouse and turkey along the route and listen for songbirds and owls cooing at dusk. It is 3½ miles one way, with a 1,400-foot gain in elevation. Hiking time is about two hours each way. *Moderate.* ✉ *Great Sand Dunes National Park* ✥ *Trailhead: Lower end of trail begins at Montville Trailhead, just north of visitor center.*

VISITOR CENTER

Great Sand Dunes Visitor Center

INFO CENTER | View exhibits and artwork, browse in the bookstore, and watch a 20-minute film with an overview of the dunes. Rangers are on hand to answer questions. Facilities include restrooms and a vending machine stocked with soft drinks and snacks, but no other food. (The Great Sand Dunes Oasis, just outside the park boundary, has a café that is open generally late April through early October.) ✉ *Near the park entrance* ☎ *719/378–6395* 🌐 *www.nps.gov/grsa/planyourvisit/visitor-center.htm.*

Sand Dune Field

Seven types of sandy mounds decorate this ever-changing landscape shaped by wind and tucked into a pocket among the Sangre de Cristo mountains. The more than 30 square miles of big dunes in the heart of the park are the main attraction, although the surrounding sand sheet does have some smaller dunes. These mountains of sand range from a few feet to 750 feet into the sky, and all offer spectacular views of the dune field and the bordering peaks. You can start putting your feet in the sand 3 miles past the main park entrance.

Sights

SCENIC STOPS

High Dune

TRAIL | This isn't the park's highest dune, but it's high enough in the dune field to provide a view of all the dunes from its summit. It's on the first ridge of dunes you see from the main parking area. ✉ *Great Sand Dunes National Park.*

TRAILS

Hike to High Dune

TRAIL | **FAMILY** | Get a panoramic view of all the surrounding dunes from the top of High Dune. Since there's no formal path, the smartest approach is to zigzag up the dune ridgelines traversing about 2½ miles round-trip. High Dune is 699 feet high, and to get there and back takes about two hours, or longer if there's been no rain for some time and the sand is soft. If you add on the walk to the 750-foot Star Dune, plan on another two or three hours and a strenuous workout up and down the dunes. *Easy–Moderate.* ✉ *Great Sand Dunes National Park* ✥ *Start from main dune field.*

Near water in the park's grasslands area is where you might see elk, mule deer, and lizards.

Sangre de Cristo Mountains

Stretching from central Colorado to southeast New Mexico, the Sangre de Cristo mountains contains 10 peaks that tower more than 14,000 feet. Spanish for "the blood of Christ," the range is named for the red hues reflected during sunrise and sunset. The peaks offer hundreds of miles of alpine hiking, rock climbing, and skiing and provide a home to elk and bighorn sheep.

Southern Grasslands

The less explored grasslands of the park offer solitude from the busy sand dunes. Sunflowers coat the area in mid-August, adding a colorful layer to the panoramic views of sand hills and mountain peaks offered in the distance. Keep an eye out for miniature sand-color lizards, pronghorns and burrowing owls that live among the shrubs.

Medano Creek Wetlands

Colorado's only natural beach runs along the eastern base of the sand dunes, but it's only temporary. At the edge of the cottonwood trees, Medano Creek emerges in the spring and lingers into early summer as a result of run-off from winter snow melt. Ask a ranger where to find the hidden pools where birds can be seen chasing tadpoles—they appear in new places each year directed by the shifting sand.

Activities

BIRD-WATCHING

The San Luis Valley is famous for its migratory birds, many of which stop in the park. Great Sand Dunes also has many permanent feathered residents. In the wetlands, you might see American white pelicans and the American avocet. On the forested sections of the mountains there are goshawks, northern harriers, gray jays, and Steller's jays. And in the alpine tundra there are golden eagles, hawks, horned larks, and white-tailed ptarmigan.

CAMPING

Great Sand Dunes has one campground, open April through October. During weekends in the summer, it can fill up with RVs and tents by midafternoon. Black bears live in the preserve, so when camping there, keep your food, trash, and toiletries in the trunk of your car (or use bear-proof containers). There is one campground and RV park near the entrance to Great Sand Dunes, and several others in the area.

Pinyon Flats Campground. Set in a pine forest about a mile past the visitor center, this campground has a trail leading to the dunes. Sites must be reserved online; RVs are allowed, but there are no hookups. ✉ *On the main park road, near the visitor center* 🌐 *www.recreation.gov* ☎ *719/378–6399.*

EDUCATIONAL PROGRAMS

RANGER PROGRAMS

Interpretive Programs

TOUR—SIGHT | **FAMILY** | Family-friendly nature walks designed to help visitors learn more about the Great Sand Dunes National Park are scheduled most days from late May through September, and sporadically in April and October. Call or drop in to ask about sunset walks, afternoon weekend tours, and evening stargazing programs. The Junior Ranger program is a favorite for children ages 3 to 12, who can earn their badge by completing a booklet of activities. ✉ *Programs begin at the visitor center* ☎ *719/378–6395* 🎫 *Free.*

FISHING

Fly-fishermen can angle for Rio Grande cutthroat trout in the upper reaches of Medano Creek, which is accessible by four-wheel-drive vehicle. It's catch-and-release only, and a Colorado license is required (☎ *800/244–5613*). There's also fishing in Upper and Lower Sand Creek Lakes, but it's a very long hike (3 or 4 miles from the Music Pass trailhead, located on the far side of the park in the San Isabel National Forest).

HIKING

Visitors can walk just about anywhere on the sand dunes in the heart of the park. The best view of all the dunes is from the top of High Dune. There are no formal trails because the sand keeps shifting, but you don't really need them: It's extremely difficult to get lost out here. If you're hiking, carry plenty of water; if you're going into the backcountry to camp overnight, carry even more water and a water filtration system. A free permit is required to backpack in the park. Also, watch for weather changes. If there's a thunderstorm and lightning, get off the dunes or trail immediately, and seek shelter. Before hiking, leave word with someone indicating where you're going to hike and when you expect to be back. Tell that contact to call 911 if you don't show up when expected.

What's Nearby

The vast expanse one sees from the dunes is the San Luis Valley. Covering 8,000 square miles (and with an average altitude of 7,500 feet), the San Luis Valley is the world's largest alpine valley, sprawling on a broad, flat, dry plain between the San Juan Mountains to the west and the Sangre de Cristo range to the east, and extending south into northern New Mexico. The area is one of the state's major agricultural producers.

Alamosa, the San Luis Valley's major city, is 35 miles southwest of Great Sand Dunes via U.S. 160 and Highway 150. It's a casual, central base for exploring the park and the surrounding region. The rest of the area is dotted with tiny towns, including **Mosca, Blanca, Antonito,** and **Fort Garland,** to the south of the park, and **Monte Vista** and **Hooper** to the west. They are all within an hour's drive from the park.

Chapter 30

GREAT SMOKY MOUNTAINS NATIONAL PARK

Updated by
Cameron Roberts

Camping ★★★★★

Hotels ★☆☆☆☆

Activities ★★★★☆

Scenery ★★★★★

Crowds ★★★★☆

WELCOME TO GREAT SMOKY MOUNTAINS NATIONAL PARK

TOP REASONS TO GO

★ **Witness the wilderness:** This is one of the last remaining big chunks of wilderness in the East. Get away from civilization in more than 800 square miles of tranquillity, with old-growth forests, clear streams, 900 miles of hiking trails, wildflowers, and panoramic vistas from mile-high mountains.

★ **Get your endorphins going:** Outdoor junkies can bike, boat, camp, fish, hike, ride horses, white-water raft, watch birds and wildlife, and even cross-country ski.

★ **Experience mountain culture:** Visit restored mountain cabins and tour "ghost towns" in the park, with old frame and log buildings preserved much as they were 100 years ago.

★ **Spot wildlife:** Biologists estimate there are more than 1,600 bears, 6,000 deer, and 150 elk now in the park.

★ **It's free!:** It's one of the few major national parks in the country with no admission fee (though charges apply for campgrounds and a few activities).

1 Tennessee Side. If you're looking for a family-friendly vacation, the Tennessee side is your best bet. Just inside the main entrances at Gatlinburg and Townsend are easy-to-reach attractions like Cades Cove, with its scenic wide valley, pioneer buildings, and extensive wildlife—you might catch a glimpse of black bears.

2 North Carolina Side. A little quieter than the Tennessee side, the North Carolina side is home to the observation tower atop Clingmans Dome, the highest point east of the Rockies. Historical sites like Cataloochee are a ghostly reminder of the past. The park's main gateway, and location of the Oconaluftee Visitor Center, is at the bustling town of Cherokee, where numerous attractions tell the story of the Cherokee Nation.

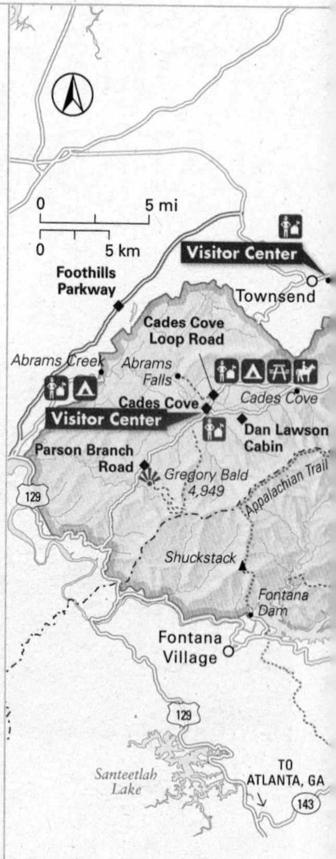

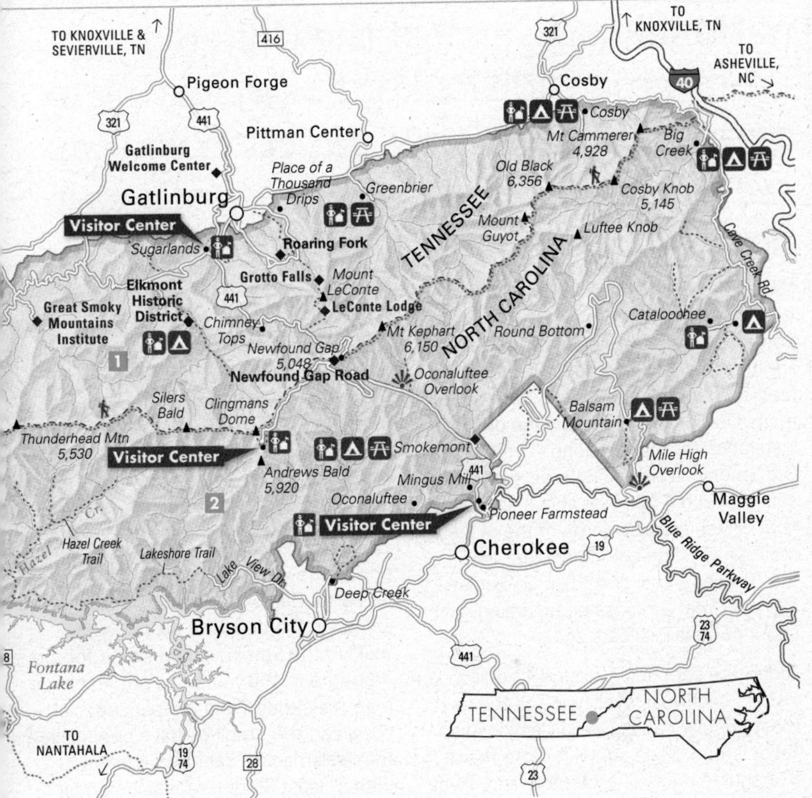
TO KNOXVILLE & SEVIERVILLE, TN
416
321
TO KNOXVILLE, TN
TO ASHEVILLE, NC
40
Pigeon Forge
Cosby
321
441
Pittman Center
Cosby
Mt Cammerer 4,928
Big Creek
Gatlinburg Welcome Center
Place of a Thousand Drips
Old Black 6,356
Gatlinburg
Greenbrier
Cosby Knob 5,145
Visitor Center
TENNESSEE
Mount Guyot
Luftee Knob
Sugarlands
Roaring Fork
Cove Creek Rd
Grotto Falls
Mount LeConte
Elkmont Historic District
LeConte Lodge
NORTH CAROLINA
441
Great Smoky Mountains Institute
Chimney Tops
Cataloochee
Mt Kephart 6,150
Round Bottom
Newfound Gap 5,048
Newfound Gap Road
Oconaluftee Overlook
Silers Bald
Clingmans Dome
Balsam Mountain
Thunderhead Mtn 5,530
Visitor Center
Smokemont
Mile High Overlook
Andrews Bald 5,920
441
Mingus Mill
Maggie Valley
Oconaluftee
Visitor Center
Pioneer Farmstead
Hazel Cr.
Hazel Creek Trail
Lakeshore Trail
Cherokee
19
Blue Ridge Parkway
Lake View Dr
Deep Creek
Bryson City
23 74
441
Fontana Lake
TENNESSEE
NORTH CAROLINA
TO NANTAHALA
19 74
28
23

Great Smoky Mountains National Park is one of the great wild areas of the eastern United States and the most visited national park in all of the United States. From a roadside lookout or a clearing in a trail, in every visible direction you can see the mountains march toward a vast horizon of wilderness.

Some of the tallest mountains in the East are here, including 16 peaks over 6,000 feet. The highest in the park, Clingmans Dome, was reputedly the original inspiration for the folk song "On Top of Old Smoky." It rises 6,643 feet above sea level and 4,503 feet above the valley floor. These are also some of the oldest mountains in the world, far older than the Rockies, Alps, or Andes. Geologists say the Great Smokies began being built about 480 million years ago.

Today, the park hosts around 12 million visitors each year, over twice as the next most popular parks, Grand Canyon and Yellowstone. Even so, with more than 814 square miles of protected land, if you get out of your car you can soon be in a remote cove where your closest neighbors are deer, bobcats, and black bears.

The Qualla Boundary, at the southeastern entrance to the park, belongs to the Eastern Band of Cherokees and represents a small part of their ancestral home. When you're in the Cherokee area, and the Smokies in general, respect the fact that this is sacred land. Take the time to learn about its fascinating history from places like the Cherokee Museum, and consider buying your souvenirs at shops like the Qualla Arts and Crafts Mutual. Some things are also a little different on Cherokee land: you'll see that signs posted in the Qualla Boundary include translations in the Cherokee language, and you need a special permit to fish here.

Due to a fortuitous combination of moderate climate and diverse geography, Great Smoky Mountains National Park is one of the most biologically rich spots on earth. Bears are the most famous animal in the park, but elk are also making the Smokies their home for the first time in 150 years. It's not just large mammals that make the park special, however; the Smokies have been called the "salamander capital of the world," with at least 30 different salamander species. It is also one of the few places on earth where, for a few evenings in June, you can see synchronous fireflies flashing in perfect unison.

The park offers extraordinary opportunities for other outdoor activities: it has world-class hiking, on nearly 900 miles of trails, ranging from easy half-hour nature walks to weeklong backpacking treks. Although backcountry hiking has its wonders, some of the most interesting sights in the park can be seen from the comfort of your car or motorcycle.

AVERAGE HIGH/LOW TEMPERATURES					
JAN.	**FEB.**	**MAR.**	**APR.**	**MAY**	**JUNE**
41/18	45/21	54/27	63/34	69/43	75/51
JULY	**AUG.**	**SEPT.**	**OCT.**	**NOV.**	**DEC.**
78/55	77/54	72/48	63/36	53/27	44/21

Planning

When to Go

High Season: There's no bad time to visit the Smokies. The biggest crowds in the park arrive mid-June to mid-August, and throughout the month of October for peak fall foliage viewing. Beat the crowds by coming on weekdays and also early in the day, before 10 am. By mid-June, haze, heat, and high humidity have arrived. In July, highs at the lower elevations average 88°F, but at Clingmans Dome (elevation 6,643 feet) the average high is just 65°F. In September a pattern of warm, sunny days and cool nights sets in.

Low Season: Winter in the park can be beautiful, especially when there's snow on the ground or frost on the tree limbs. The air is usually clearer in the winter, with less haze, and with leaves off the trees the visibility is excellent. Winters in the park see some snow, especially at the higher elevations. Many visitor centers, roads, campgrounds, and other services in and around the park close for the winter season. But on the other hand, January has just a sixth of the visitors you'd encounter in July.

Value Season: Late spring is a wonderful time to visit the park, as wildflowers are in bloom and it's before the heat, humidity, and crowds of summer. The weather in the park is highly changeable, especially in the spring. On one day it may be a balmy 70°F, and the next bitterly cold and snowy.

FESTIVALS AND EVENTS

Fall Heritage Festival and Old Timers' Day at Cades Cove. Visitors are invited to bring lawn chairs and a picnic along to Old Timers' Day at Cades Cove. Held in late September at the Cable Mill area of Cades Cove, Old Timers' Day allows former residents of Cades Cove and their descendants, along with the general public, to reminisce about the old days in the valley. The Cades Cove event is now part of a two-day Fall Heritage Festival at the Great Smoky Mountains Heritage Center in Townsend, just outside the park. At Townsend you can enjoy bluegrass music, clogging and square dancing, arts and crafts demonstrations, and mountain food. Both events are free, though there's a park fee at Townsend. 🌐 *www.smokymountains.org*

Spring Wildflower Pilgrimage. Each year in mid-to-late April, the Great Smoky Mountains National Park and the Great Smoky Mountains Association host the Spring Wildflower Pilgrimage. It attracts wildflower enthusiasts from all over the country for five days of wildflower and natural-history walks, seminars, classes, photography tours, and other events. Instructors include National Park Service staff, along with outside experts. Most of the activities are at various locations in the park, both on the North Carolina and Tennessee sides. Begun in 1951, the pilgrimage has grown to more than 150 different walks, classes, and events. Advance registration online begins in February of the year of the conference, and some events quickly sell out. Check the website for current details and dates. 🌐 *www.wildflowerpilgrimage.org*

Getting Here and Around

Although there are numerous entrances to the North Carolina side of the park, the main entrance is via U.S. Route 441 near Cherokee and the Oconaluftee Visitor Center.

Another, and much more pleasant (but slower), route to the Smokies is the Blue Ridge Parkway, which has its southern terminus in Cherokee.

You can enter the park by car at nine different places on the Tennessee side. Most of these entrances take you just a short distance into the park to a developed campground or picnic area. The two major entrances to the park on the western side are from Gatlinburg and Townsend.

AIR

The closest airport on the North Carolina side with national air service is Asheville Regional Airport (AVL), about 60 miles east of the Cherokee entrance. On the Tennessee side, the closest major airport is Knoxville McGhee Tyson Airport (TYS), about 45 miles west of the Sugarlands entrance.

AIRPORT INFORMATION Asheville Regional Airport. *(AVL)* ✉ *61 Terminal Dr., Fletcher* ✥ *Off I–26* 🌐 *www.flyavl.com.* **Knoxville McGhee Tyson Airport.** *(TYS)* ✉ *2025 Alcoa Hwy., Alcoa* ☎ *828/684–2226* 🌐 *www.flyknoxville.com.*

CAR

The nearest sizable city to the park in North Carolina is Asheville. This hip, liberal-minded city is about 50 miles east of Cherokee and the Oconaluftee Visitor Center. It takes a little more than an hour to get from Asheville to the Cherokee entrance of the park, via Interstate 40 and U.S. Routes 19 and 441. If you aren't pressed for time, however, we advise traveling via the Blue Ridge Parkway—it takes longer, but the scenery is worth it.

The closest sizable city to the park in Tennessee is Knoxville, about 40 miles west of the Sugarlands entrance, via U.S. Route 441.

Coming either from the east or west, Interstate 40 is the main interstate access route to the Great Smokies; from the north and south, Interstates 75, 81, and 26 are primary arteries.

U.S. Route 441, also called Newfound Gap Road, is the main road through the park, and the only paved road that goes all the way through. It travels 31 miles between Cherokee and Gatlinburg, crossing Newfound Gap at nearly a mile high. Once out of the park on the Tennessee side, avoid driving through Gatlinburg (take the bypass option instead), as even in the off-season, intense traffic means you can spend an hour crawling through this small and very touristy town.

Restaurants

Besides the park's numerous picnic areas, the only food service in the park is a camp store deli in Cades Cove on the Tennessee side.

Outside the park you'll find many more dining options, from fast food to fine dining, the latter especially in Asheville, North Carolina, which is known for its farm-to-table, locavore food culture. On the Tennessee side, both Gatlinburg and Pigeon Forge, which might just rank among the most touristy towns in the country, have myriad fast-food and family dining choices. Knoxville also has many good dining options.

Hotels and Campgrounds

The only accommodations actually in the park aside from the abundant and reasonably priced campgrounds are at LeConte Lodge. There are 939 tent and RV camping spaces at 10 developed campgrounds, two (Cades Cove and

Smokemont) open year-round, in addition to more than 100 backcountry campsites, shelters, and horse camps. The cost for camping ranges from $4 per person per site (backcountry sites and shelters, with a maximum of $20) to $18–$27 per night for front-country sites. All but one of the campgrounds accept RVs and trailers, though most have size limits. Immediately outside the park are many commercial campgrounds and RV parks. Permits are required for all backcountry camping. Sites at all developed campgrounds can be reserved up to 6 months in advance by calling ☎ *877/444–6777* or visiting 🌐 *www.recreation.gov*; reservations are *required* at all campgrounds.

Outside the park, you have a gargantuan selection of hotels of every ilk. On the Tennessee side, in Gatlinburg you'll see a street sign that says "2,000 Hotel Rooms" and points up the hill, and that's just in one section of town. On the North Carolina side, lodging is mostly more low-key, but you can choose from old mountain inns, bed-and-breakfasts, and motels in the small towns of Bryson City, Waynesville, and Robbinsville. A seemingly ever-expanding number of hotel towers are connected to the giant Harrah's casino in Cherokee. About 50 miles away, in and around Asheville, you can choose from among one of the largest collections of B&Bs in the Southeast, along with hip urban hotels and classic mountain resorts.

Inspiration

Asheville native Wayne Caldwell's 2007 novel, *Cataloochee*, tells the story of three generations of mountain families in Cataloochee Cove. As the government took steps to relocate the settlers out of Cataloochee to make room for the Great Smoky Mountain National Park, a tragic act of violence touches the families.

Park Essentials

ACCESSIBILITY

The three main visitor centers are wheelchair-accessible and have accessible parking spaces; the Cades Cove ampitheater is level and easily accessible. Three campgrounds (Cades Cove, Elkmount, and Smokemont) have wheelchair-accessible campsites. Only the Sugarland Valley Nature Trail is paved and wheelchair-accessible; most historic buildings throughout the park are not, but the walkways surrounding them are mostly hard-packed gravel that can be navigated by wheelchair users with some assistance.

PARK FEES AND PERMITS

Unlike at most other national parks, admission to the Great Smokies is free. Admission to all historical and natural sites within the park is also free. Picnicking is free. Frontcountry campgrounds charge a nightly fee, and backcountry camping requires a $4 nightly permit.

Camping and overnight hiking in the backcountry require a permit. General backcountry permits are $4 per night. To camp in the backcountry, you must complete a permit at one of the 14 self-registration stations in and near the park, which are available 24 hours a day, by telephone, or online. Your permit must designate the campsite or shelter at which you will stay for each night of your trip. Keep the permit with you and drop the top copy in the registration box. Download a park trail map or get the locations of all reserved and nonreserved backcountry campsites and shelters. Day hikes do not require a permit.

PARK HOURS

The park is open 24 hours a day, 365 days a year. Primary roads are always open (weather-permitting), but some secondary roads, campgrounds, and other visitor facilities close in winter.

CELL PHONE RECEPTION

Reception varies widely, but is generally not good. There are no towers within the park boundaries, so typically good reception is only available near park borders and around the three main visitor centers and in some areas of high elevation. Deeper within the park, you'll find almost no service, including at LeConte Lodge. The park service offers no public Wi-Fi service.

PETS

Pets are permitted in some areas of the park but are strictly prohibited in others. Dogs and other pets are allowed in most campgrounds, picnic areas, and along roads, but at all times they must be kept on a leash measuring no more than 6 feet. Pets are not allowed on park trails, except the Gatlinburg and the Oconaluftee River trails, and they are not permitted anywhere in the backcountry. Pet excrement must be immediately collected and disposed of in a trash can.

Visitor Information

There are three main visitor centers in the park: Oconaluftee Visitor Center near Cherokee (looking great after a $3 million renovation and expansion), Sugarlands Visitor Center near Gatlinburg (featuring extensive exhibits in a nature museum about the park's incredibly varied flora and fauna), and Cades Cove Visitor Center on the 11-mile Cades Cove Loop. Some of the best hiking trails fan out from these facilities, making then hard to pass up despite the crowds. In addition, there is a compact visitor contact station at Clingmans Dome.

There are five information centers in communities just outside the park (there's one in Bryson City on the North Carolina side, and on the Tennessee side one in Sevierville, one in Townsend, and two in Gatlinburg). All the gateway towns around the park entrances have their own visitor information centers with plenty of information about the park.

CONTACTS Great Smoky Mountains National Park. ☎ *865/436–1200* 🌐 *www.nps.gov/grsm/planyourvisit/index.htm.*

Tennessee Side

The Tennessee side of the Great Smokies get heavy action. Some 2 million people a year tour Cades Cove, and on a busy fall weekend the traffic on the Cades Cove Loop may remind you of midtown Manhattan. The Tennessee side also has the largest and busiest campgrounds and picnic areas.

If you prefer peace and quiet and natural beauty, all is not lost. With just a little bit of effort, you can find your way to lovely and little-visited parts of the Tennessee side of the park. Greenbrier, for example, is a picnicking paradise that's often virtually deserted. The Roaring Fork Motor Trail, a 5-mile winding road that passes historic buildings, old-growth forests, and waterfalls, is a delight, and the Foothills Parkway, a scenic, unfinished road along the western and southern edges of the park, is an undiscovered gem. Several of the best hiking trails in the park are also in Tennessee.

The Tennessee side is also the family-fun side particularly in the towns of Gatlinburg and Pigeon Forge. You can tour historical sites, treat the family to mini golf or go karts, tire the kids out at nearby theme parks, try a different restaurant at every meal, or enjoy some grown-up time at a bar or music theater.

HISTORIC SIGHTS

★ Cades Cove

HISTORIC SITE | FAMILY | A 6,800-acre valley surrounded by high mountains, Cades Cove has more historic buildings than any other area in the park. Driving, hiking, or biking the 11-mile Cades Cove Loop Road gives you access to three old

Cades Cove has a number of historical houses, log cabins, and barns.

churches (Methodist, Primitive Baptist, and Missionary Baptist), a working gristmill (Cable Mill), a number of log cabins and houses in a variety of styles, and many outbuildings, including cantilevered barns, which used balanced beams to support large overhangs. The Cherokee name for this valley is Tsiyahi, "place of otters," but today you're more likely to see bears, deer, coyotes, and wild turkeys. For hundreds of years the Cherokee People hunted in Cades Cove, but there is no evidence of major settlements. Under the terms of the Calhoun Treaty of 1819, the Cherokee lost their rights to Cades Cove, and the first white settlers came in the early 1820s. By the middle of the 19th century, well over 100 settler families were growing corn, wheat, oats, and vegetables. For a while, when government-licensed distilleries were allowed in Tennessee, corn whiskey was the major product of the valley. After the establishment of the park in the 1930s, many of the nearly 200 buildings were torn down to allow the land to revert to its natural state. More recently, the remaining farmsteads and other structures have been restored to depict life in Cades Cove as it was from around 1825 to 1900. Keep in mind that this route gets 2 million visitors per year; at peak times traffic in and out of here can be extremely slow. ✉ *Cades Cove Loop Rd., Great Smoky Mountains National Park* ☎ *865/436–1200* 🌐 *www.nps.gov/grsm/planyourvisit/cadescove.htm.*

Dan Lawson Cabin

HISTORIC SITE | **FAMILY** | From many points along the 11-mile Cades Cove Loop Road, you'll enjoy iconic views of the broad Cades Cove Valley. The Park Service keeps hayfields and pastures cleared, so you can see how the valley may have looked in the late 19th century when it was farmed by more than 100 families. Typical is the view across the valley from the front porch of the Dan Lawson Cabin, the original portion of which was built in 1856. ✉ *Cades Cove Loop Rd., Townsend* ☎ *865/436–1200* 🌐 *www.nps.gov/grsm.*

★ Elkmont Historic District

HISTORIC SITE | FAMILY | What began as a logging town in the early years of the 20th century evolved into a summer colony for wealthy families from Knoxville, Chattanooga, and elsewhere in Tennessee. Many prominent east Tennessee families bought land here and built vacation homes and the Wonderland Hotel. After the national park was established, parts of Elkmont were placed on the National Registry of Historic Places. Today, Elkmont is primarily a campground, although many of the original 74 cottages remain along Jakes Creek and Little River. Most of the cottages are at the far end of the campground—follow the Elkmont Nature Trail or drive along a separate paved road off Little River Road. In recent years, the Park Service has been stabilizing and restoring several homes along Jakes Creek. Four cabins were restored in 2017 and are open to the public. The Appalachian Clubhouse, built for a hunting and fishing club, has been restored to its 1930s appearance, complete with rocking chairs on the porch. ✉ *Little River Rd., Great Smoky Mountains National Park* ✣ *4½ miles west of Sugarlands Entrance* ☎ *865/436–1200* 🌐 *www.nps.gov/grsm/planyourvisit/elkmont.htm.*

Roaring Fork

NATIONAL/STATE PARK | FAMILY | Roaring Fork was settled by Europeans beginning in the 1830s. At its height around the turn of the 20th century, there were about two dozen families in the area. Most lived a simple, hardscrabble existence, trying to scrape out a living from the rough mountain land. The Noah "Bud" Ogle Self-Guided Nature Trail, on Orchard Road just before entering the one-way Roaring Fork Motor Nature Trail, offers a walking tour of an authentic mountain farmstead and surrounding hardwood forest. Highlights include a log cabin, barn, streamside mill, and a wooden flume system to bring water to the farm. Among the historic structures on the Motor Nature Trail, all open for you to explore, are the Jim Bales Cabin, the Ephraim Bales Cabin, and the Alfred Reagan House, one of the more "upscale" residences at Roaring Fork. ✉ *Orchard Rd., Great Smoky Mountains National Park* ☎ *865/436–1200* 🌐 *www.nps.gov/grsm/planyourvisit/roaringfork.htm* ⏲ *Closed late Nov.–Mar.*

SCENIC DRIVES

★ Cades Cove Loop Road

SCENIC DRIVE | FAMILY | This 11-mile loop through Cades Cove is the most popular route in the park and arguably the most scenic part of the Smoky Mountains. The one-way, one-lane paved road starts 7.3 miles from the national park's Townsend Entrance. Stop at the orientation shelter and pick up a tour booklet. The drive begins with views over wide pastures to the mountains at the crest of the Smokies. Few other places in the Appalachians offer such views across wide valleys with hayfields and wildflower meadows framed by split-rail fences and surrounded by tall mountains. Along the way, you'll pass three 19th-century churches and many restored houses and barns that are open for exploration. A highlight is the Cable Mill area, with a visitor center, working water-powered gristmill, and a restored farmstead. The Cades Cove Loop Road is also an excellent place to see wildlife, including black bears, white-tailed deer, and wild turkeys. Whenever you visit, even in winter, you can expect traffic delays, as passing points on the one-way road are few and far between. Allow at least two to three hours to drive the loop, longer if you want to stop and explore the historic buildings. If you get frustrated with delays, there are two points at which you can cut across the loop on improved gravel roads, exiting sooner. A campground and picnic area are open year-round. The road is closed from sunset to sunrise. ✉ *Cades Loop Rd. , off Laurel Creek Rd., Townsend* ☎ *865/436–1200* 🌐 *www.nps.gov/grsm/planyourvisit/cadescove.htm.*

Foothills Parkway

SCENIC DRIVE | FAMILY | A 72-mile scenic roadway, Foothills Parkway has long been planned to parallel the northern, western, and southwestern edges of the Great Smoky Mountains National Park, providing dramatic views of the Smokies. Construction began in the 1960s, but due to funding problems it still hasn't been completed. About 17 miles from U.S. Route 129 at Chilhowee Lake to U.S. Route 321 at Walland were completed in 1966. In late 2018, another 16-mile section of the parkway was opened, connecting with this original section and running to Wears Valley. A 5.6-mile section runs from Interstate 40 south to U.S. Route 321. In between these sections are more than 33 miles where construction has not even begun. Rights-of-way have been purchased, but there is no state or federal money to build it. Known as the "Tail of the Dragon," a serpentine section of U.S. Route 129 is popular with motorcycle and sports car enthusiasts; it connects with the end of the Foothills Parkway at Chilhowee. ✉ *Gatlinburg* ☎ *865/436–1200* 🌐 *www.nps.gov/places/foothills-parkway.htm.*

★ Newfound Gap Road

SCENIC DRIVE | FAMILY | In a little more than 14 miles, Newfound Gap Road climbs more than 3,500 feet, from Gatlinburg to the gap through the crest of the Smokies at 5,046 feet. It takes you through Southern cove hardwood, pine-oak, and Northern hardwood forests to the spruce-fir forest at Newfound Gap. Unlike other roads in the park, Newfound Gap Road has mile markers, starting at the park entrance near Gatlinburg. Sugarlands Visitor Center is at mile marker 1.7. At Newfound Gap (mile marker 14.7), you can straddle the Tennessee–North Carolina state line and also hike some of the Appalachian Trail. ✉ *U.S. Rte. 441 MM 14.7, Great Smoky Mountains National Park* ☎ *865/436–1200* 🌐 *www.nps.gov/grsm/planyourvisit/nfg.htm.*

Parson Branch Road

SCENIC DRIVE | FAMILY | Following a wagon track, this 8-mile unpaved road has been used for more than 150 years. Some believe that Parson Branch Road was named for ministers who held religious retreats nearby, but others believe they were named for Joshua Parson, an early settler in the area. The road begins at the southwestern edge of Cades Cove Loop Road just beyond the visitor center at Cable Mill. Although unpaved, it doesn't require four-wheel drive except after heavy rains, when a few sections may become flooded or muddy. It offers no scenic vistas, but it runs through old-growth forests, with huge poplars and hemlocks along the roadway. RVs are prohibited on this road. ✉ *Parson Branch Rd. , off Cades Cove Loop Rd., Townsend* ☎ *865/436–1200* 🌐 *www.nps.gov/grsm/planyourvisit/seasonalroads.htm* ⏲ *Closed mid-Nov.–mid-Mar.*

★ Roaring Fork Motor Nature Trail

SCENIC DRIVE | FAMILY | The 6-mile Roaring Fork offers a dramatic counterpoint to Cades Cove Loop Road, which meanders through a wide-open valley. Roaring Fork closes in, with the forest sometimes literally just inches from your fender. The one-way, paved road is so narrow in places that RVs, trailers, and buses are not permitted. The trail starts just beyond the Noah "Bud" Ogle Farmstead and the Rainbow Falls trailhead. Stop and pick up a Roaring Fork Auto Tour booklet at the information shelter. Numbered markers along the route are keyed to 16 stops highlighted in the booklet. Along the road are many opportunities to get closer to nature. A favorite sight is the old Alfred Reagan House, which is painted in the original blue, yellow, and cream, "all three colors that Sears and Roebuck had," according to a story attributed to Mr. Reagan. There are several good hiking trails starting along the road, including the Trillium Gap Trail to Mt. LeConte. The road follows Roaring Fork Creek a good part of the way, and the finale is a small waterfall called "The Place of a Thousand Drips," right beside the road. ✉ *Roaring Fork Motor Nature Tr., Gatlinburg ✥ To get to Roaring Fork from Gatlinburg from the parkway (U.S. 441), turn onto Historic Nature Trail at stoplight No. 8 in Gatlinburg and follow it to Cherokee Orchard entrance of park ☎ 865/436–1200 🌐 www.nps.gov/grsm/planyourvisit/roaringfork.htm ⊙ Closed Dec.–Mar.*

SCENIC STOPS

Campbell Overlook

VIEWPOINT | FAMILY | Named for Carlos Campbell, a conservationist who was instrumental in helping to establish the park, Campbell Overlook provides a good view up a valley to Bull Head peak and, farther up, to Balsam Point. An exhibit at the overlook explains the different types of forests within the park. ✉ *Newfound Gap Rd., MM 3.9, Great Smoky Mountains National Park 🌐 www.nps.gov/grsm.*

Chimney Tops Overlook

VIEWPOINT | FAMILY | From any of the three overlooks grouped together on Newfound Gap Road, you'll have a good view of the Chimney Tops—twin peaks that cap 2,000-foot-high cliffs. Sadly, you'll also see dozens of dead fir and spruce trees, victims of the invasive woolly adelgids. ✉ *Newfound Gap Rd., MM 7.1, Gatlinburg ☎ 865/436–1200 🌐 www.nps.gov/grsm.*

Gatlinburg Bypass Overlook

VIEWPOINT | This 4-mile roadway runs just north of Gatlinburg toward Pigeon Forge. It tracks around the side of Mt. Harrison. Take this route to avoid the stop-and-go traffic of downtown Gatlinburg when leaving or entering the park. The second overlook when headed out of the park toward Pigeon Forge has the best views of Gatlinburg and Mt. LeConte. ✉ *Gatlinburg Bypass ☎ 865/436–1200 🌐 www.nps.gov/grsm.*

Gregory Bald

VIEWPOINT | From almost 5,000 feet on Gregory Bald, you have a breathtaking view of Cades Cove and Rich Mountain to the north and the Nantahala and Yellow Creek mountains to the south. You can also see Fontana Lake to the southeast. Many colorful rhododendrons grow on and around the bald, blooming in late June. Gregory Bald is one of only two balds in the Smokies that are being kept cleared of tree growth by the Park Service. This is a view that just a few thousand people a year will see, as it's reachable only by a strenuous hike via the Gregory Ridge Trail of more than 11 miles round-trip. The trailhead is at the end of Forge Creek Road in Cades Cove. ✉ *Gregory Ridge Trail, off Forge Creek Rd., Townsend ☎ 865/436–1200 🌐 www.nps.gov/grsm.*

Look Rock

VIEWPOINT | FAMILY | The viewpoints looking east on the western section of the Foothills Parkway around Look Rock have remarkable vistas. This is also a great spot to enjoy the sunrise over the Smokies. Stargazers gather at the five overlooks south of the Look Rock exit because light pollution is especially low. ✉ *Foothills Pkwy., Great Smoky Mountains National Park ☎ 865/436–1200 🌐 www.nps.gov/grsm.*

Roaring Fork Motor Nature Trail Site Number 3

VIEWPOINT | FAMILY | While most of the Roaring Fork Motor Nature Trail takes you on a narrow and winding one-way road through forested areas where the views are limited, at the beginning of the drive the first and second overlooks present good views of the distant mountain ridges. The best scenery is from the second overlook, marked as the number 3 site on the Roaring Fork auto tour. ✉ *Roaring Fork Motor Tr. ☎ 865/436–1200 🌐 www.nps.gov/grsm ⊙ Closed late Nov.–Mar.*

TRAILS

★ Abrams Falls Trail

TRAIL | This 5-mile round-trip trail is one of the most popular in the Smokies, thanks to its trailhead location Cades Cove Loop Road. Beginning at the wooden bridge over Abrams Creek, the trail first follows a pleasant course through rhododendron, then becomes steeper at a couple of points, especially near Arbutus Ridge. The path then leads above Abrams Falls and down to Wilson Creek. Though only about 20 feet high, the falls are beautiful, with a large volume of water and a broad pool below. ⚠ **It is dangerous to climb, jump from, or swim near the falls.** *Moderate.* ✉ *Cades Cove Loop Rd., between signposts 10 and 11, Townsend* ☎ *865/436–1200* 🌐 *www.nps.gov/grsm/planyourvisit/abrams-falls.htm.*

★ Alum Cave Trail

TRAIL | One of the best and most popular hikes in the national park, the fairly short 2.3-mile one-way hike to Alum Cave Bluffs contains some of the most interesting geological formations in the Smokies. Arch Rock, a natural arch created by millions of years of freezing and thawing, and Alum Bluffs, a large overhanging rock ledge, are the highlights. This very well-known trail does not offer much solitude, especially on weekends. From the bluffs you can continue on another 2.8 miles to reach Mt. LeConte, passing awe-inspiring mountain vistas. Alum Cave Bluffs is the shortest of five trail routes to LeConte Lodge, but it is also the steepest, with an elevation gain of over 2,700 feet. *Moderate.* ✉ *Newfound Gap Rd. MM 10.4., Great Smoky Mountains National Park* ☎ *865/436–1200* 🌐 *www.nps.gov/grsm/planyourvisit/chimneys-alternative-alum-cave-bluffs.htm.*

Appalachian Trail at Newfound Gap

TRAIL | For those who want to say they hiked part of the Appalachian Trail, this 72-mile section through the Great Smokies is a great place to start. Park in the Newfound Gap Overlook parking lot and cross the road to the trail. From Newfound Gap to Indian Gap, the trail travels 1.7 miles through high-elevation spruce and fir forests, and in late spring and summer there are quite a few wildflowers. The total round-trip distance is 3.4 miles. *Easy.* ✉ *Newfound Gap Overlook, Newfound Gap Rd., Great Smoky Mountains National Park* ☎ *865/436–1200* 🌐 *www.nps.gov/grsm/planyourvisit/nfg.htm.*

Chimney Tops Trail

TRAIL | Pant, wheeze, and gasp. This is a fairly short yet steep trail that will take a lot out of you, but it gives back a lot, too. The payoff for the difficult climb is one of the best views in the Smokies. In places the trail has loose rock (hiking poles are recommended), and the elevation gain is 1,350 feet. Some sections have steep stairs. A new observation deck was built roughly ¼ mile from the summit, with views of Mt. LeConte and the pinnacles. The total distance round-trip is 3.6 miles. *Difficult.* ✉ *Newfound Gap Rd., 6.9 miles from Sugarlands Visitor Center, Gatlinburg* ☎ *865/436–1200* 🌐 *www.nps.gov/grsm/planyourvisit/chimney-tops.htm* 🎟 *Free.*

Elkmont Nature Trail

TRAIL | FAMILY | This 1-mile loop is good for families, especially if you're camping at Elkmont. It passes by many of the remaining buildings in the Elkmont Historic District. Pick up a self-guided brochure at the start of the trail. *Easy.* ✉ *Little River Rd., Great Smoky Mountains National Park* ✣ *Near Elkmont Campground* ☎ *865/436–1200* 🌐 *www.nps.gov/grsm/planyourvisit/elkmont.htm.*

Gatlinburg Trail

TRAIL | FAMILY | This is one of only two trails in the park where dogs and bicycles are permitted (the other one is Oconaluftee River Trail on the North Carolina side). Dogs must be on leashes. The 1.9-mile trail starts at Sugarlands Visitor Center and follows the Little Pigeon River. *Easy.* ✉ *Sugarlands Visitor Center, Newfound Gap Rd., Gatlinburg* ☎ *865/436–1200* 🌐 *www.nps.gov/grsm/planyourvisit/gatlinburg-trail.htm.*

Laurel Falls Trail

TRAIL | FAMILY | This paved trail is fairly easy. It takes you past a series of cascades to a 60-foot waterfall and a stand of old-growth forest. The trail is extremely popular in summer and on weekends almost anytime (trolleys from Gatlinburg stop here), so don't expect solitude. The 1.3-mile paved trail to the falls is wheelchair accessible. The total round-trip hike is 2.6 miles. *Easy.* ✉ *Little River Rd., between Sugarlands Visitor Center and Elkmont Campground, Gatlinburg* ☎ *865/436–1200* 🌐 *www.nps.gov/grsm.*

Little River Trail

TRAIL | This 5.1-mile loop (if Cucumber Gap and Jakes Creek trails are included) offers a little of everything—historical buildings, a waterfall, and wildflowers. The first part of the trail wanders past remnants of old logging operations and cottages that were once the summer homes of wealthy Tennesseans. Huskey Branch Falls appears at about 2 miles. The Little River Trail passes the junction with three other trails, offering the possibility for even longer hikes—Cucumber Gap at 2.3 miles, Huskey Gap at 2.7 miles, and Goshen Prong Trail at 3.7 miles. The trail is normally open even in winter. This is the habitat of the synchronous fireflies, which put on their light show on late May and June evenings. *Moderate* ✉ *Little River Rd. , near Elkmont Campground, Gatlinburg* ☎ *865/436–1200* 🌐 *www.nps.gov/grsm.*

Sugarlands Valley Trail

TRAIL | FAMILY | The easiest trail in the park, it's only a quarter mile, virtually level, and paved, so it's suitable for young children, strollers, and wheelchairs. A brochure available at the start explains the numbered exhibits and features of the trail. *Easy* ✉ *Newfound Gap Rd., south of Sugarlands Visitor Center, Gatlinburg* ☎ *865/436–1200* 🌐 *www.nps.gov/grsm.*

The Appalachian Trail

Each spring nearly 3,000 hikers set out to conquer the 2,190-mile Appalachian Trail. Most hike north from Springer Mountain, Georgia, toward Mt. Katahdin, Maine. By the time they get to the Great Smokies, 160 miles from the trailhead in Georgia, about half the hikers will already have dropped out. Typically, fewer than 800 hikers per year complete the entire AT, which takes an average of 165 days. At Newfound Gap Overlook, you can get on it for a short hike on the North Carolina–Tennessee line.

Trillium Gap Trail

TRAIL | FAMILY | Grotto Falls is the only waterfall in the park that you can walk behind. The Trillium Gap Trail, off the Roaring Fork Motor Nature Trail, takes you there through a hemlock forest. Only 1.3 miles long, with an easy slope, this trail is suitable for novice hikers and is one of the most popular in the park. The total round-trip distance to Grotto Falls is 2.6 miles. Trillium Gap Trail continues on to LeConte Lodge. It is a horse trail, and llamas resupplying the lodge also use it. *Easy* ✉ *Roaring Fork Motor Nature Tr., Gatlinburg* ☎ *865/436–1200* 🌐 *www.nps.gov/grsm.*

VISITOR CENTERS

Cades Cove Visitor Center

INFO CENTER | FAMILY | Located near the midway point on the highly popular 11-mile Cades Cove Loop, Cades Cove Visitor Center is especially worth visiting to see the Cable Mill, which operates spring through fall, and the Becky Cable House, a pioneer home with farm outbuildings. ✉ *Cades Cove Loop Rd., Great Smoky Mountains National Park* ☎ *865/436–1200* 🌐 *www.nps.gov/grsm/planyourvisit/visitorcenters.htm.*

Sugarlands Visitor Center
INFO CENTER | FAMILY | The main visitor center on the Tennessee side, Sugarlands features extensive exhibits in a nature museum about park flora and fauna, as well as a 20-minute film about the park. Ranger-led programs are held from spring to fall. There are hiking trails nearby. ✉ *1420 Fighting Creek Gap Rd.* ☎ *865/436–1200* 🌐 *www.nps.gov/grsm/planyourvisit/visitorcenters.htm.*

Hotels

★ **LeConte Lodge**
$$$$ | B&B/INN | FAMILY | Set at 6,360 feet near the summit of Mt. LeConte, this hike-in lodge is remote, rustic, and remarkable. **Pros:** unique setting high on Mt. LeConte; a true escape from civilization; breakfast and dinner included in rates. **Cons:** books up many months in advance; few modern conveniences; hike-in access only. $ *Rooms from: $303* ✉ *End of Trillium Gap Trail, Great Smoky Mountains National Park* ☎ *865/429–5704* 🌐 *www.lecontelodge.com* ⏲ *Closed mid-Nov.– late Mar.* *10 rooms* *Some meals.*

The Sugarlands, Townsend, and Cades Cove visitor centers have attractive gift shops and bookstores, with first-rate selections of books and maps on the Smokies and nearby mountain areas, as well as some souvenirs. There is a small convenience store with some picnic and camping items, along with a snack bar at the Cades Cove Campground. Firewood is available at Cades Cove Campground and Elkmont. For groceries, camping supplies, and other shopping items outside the national park, your best bet is Sevierville. Pigeon Forge, Townsend, and Gatlinburg also have grocery stores and other places to stock up.

Activities

BIKING

Tennessee requires that youth age 16 and under wear a helmet, though it's strongly recommended that all riders do so, regardless of age.

Cades Cove Loop Road. Arguably the best place to bike in the national park, this 11-mile loop is mostly level and takes you through some lovely scenery. Vehicle traffic can be heavy, especially on weekends in summer and fall. Serious cyclists come here from early May to late September, when the loop is closed to motor vehicles on Wednesday and Saturday morning until 10. Bicycles and helmets can be rented in summer and fall at Cades Cove Campground.

Foothills Parkway West. Parts of this scenic 72-mile road have light vehicular traffic, making it fairly safe place for bicycling.

Gatlinburg Trail. This is the only hiking trail on the Tennessee side where bikes are permitted. The trail takes you 1.9 miles from the Sugarlands Visitor Center to the outskirts of Gatlinburg. Pets on leashes are also allowed on this trail.

Parsons Branch Road. This narrow, unpaved back road twists and dips from near Cable Mill on the Cades Cove Loop Road to U.S. Route 129.

CAMPING

No matter your style of camping, there are plenty of campgrounds in the national park. Reservations for campgrounds on the Tennessee side can be made online or by phone up to six months in advance.

Backcountry permits are required for overnight camping, hiking, or backpacking, and generally cost $4 per night. Advance reservations are required for all backcountry campsites.

Abrams Creek Campground. Beside a meandering creek, this 16-site campground sits on the extreme western edge of the park, way off the beaten path. Although it sits at an elevation of 1,125 feet, summers can be hot and humid. Several excellent hiking trails, including Gold Mine, Cane Creek, Rabbit Creek, and Little Bottoms begin at or near the campground. It's closed late October through late April. The daily fee is $17.50. ✉ *Abrams Creek Campground Rd., off Happy Valley Rd.* ☎ *865/436–1200* 🌐 *www.nps.gov/grsm.*

Cades Cove Campground. One of the largest campgrounds in the Smokies, the 159-site Cades Cove Campground also has the most on-site services. It has a small general store with a snack bar, bike rentals, horse stables, and an amphitheater. In spring it's covered with wildflowers, while in the fall the maples turn vivid reds and yellows. I'ts one of just two campgrounds in the national park that are open year-round (the other is Smokemont on the North Carolina side). This is a popular campground and often fills up in summer and fall, and reservations can be made up to six months in advance. The fee is $25. ✉ *10042 Campground Dr., at entrance to Cades Cove Loop Rd.* ☎ *865/448–2472* 🌐 *www.recreation.gov.*

Cosby Campground. Set among poplars, hemlocks, and rhododendrons, Cosby Campground sits near Cosby and Rock creeks. Most of the campsites are reserved for tents, and RVs and trailers are limited to 25 feet. Bears are fairly common in the area, and several campsites may be temporarily closed due to bear activity. Nearby are the trailheads for Snake Den Ridge and Gabes Mountain Trails. This rarely busy campground nearly always has sites available. It's closed November through early April. The daily fee is $17.50. ✉ *127 Cosby Park Rd., off TN 32* ☎ *423/487–2683* 🌐 *www. recreation.gov.*

Elkmont Campground. Easy access to hiking trails and swimming in the Little River make Elkmont ideal for families with kids. Nearby is the Elkmont Historic District, which has old vacation cabins to explore. Even though Elkmont is the largest campground in the park, with 200 tent and RV sites available, it is often fully booked. Rates are $25 to $27. Spots can be made up to six months in advance. It's closed early November through late March. ✉ *434 Elkmont Rd.* ☎ *877/444–6777* 🌐 *www.recreation.gov.*

EDUCATIONAL OFFERINGS

Great Smoky Mountains Institute at Tremont
TOUR—SPORTS | **FAMILY** | Located within the national park at Tremont, this residential environmental education center offers a variety of programs year-round for student groups, teachers, and families. Programs include photography, crafts, and backpacking trips. Accommodations are in Caylor Lodge, a climate-controlled dormitory that sleeps up to 125 people, as well as in tents on platforms. Meals are served family style in a large dining hall. Some 5,000 students and adults attend programs each year. ✉ *9275 Tremont Rd., Townsend* ☎ *865/448–6709* 🌐 *www.gsmit.org.*

Smoky Mountain Field School
TOUR—SPORTS | **FAMILY** | The University of Tennessee's Smoky Mountain Field School offers noncredit workshops, hikes, and outdoor adventures for adults and families. Participants choose from among more than 30 weekend programs held at various locations within the park. Fees vary, ranging from around $69 for courses such as wildflower identification and wild food foraging to $249 for a hike and overnight stay at LeConte Lodge. ✉ *Knoxville* ☎ *865/974–0150* 🌐 *smfs.utk. edu* 🕒 *No classes mid-Nov.–Feb.*

FISHING

There are more than 200 miles of wild trout streams on the Tennessee side of the park. Trout streams are open to fishing year-round. Among the best trout streams on the Tennessee side are Little River, Abrams Creek, and Little Pigeon River.

Everyone over 15 must possess a valid fishing license or permit from Tennessee or North Carolina. Either state license is valid throughout the park, and no trout stamp is required. Fishing licenses are not available in the park but may be purchased in nearby towns and online from the Tennessee Wildlife Resource Agency (*www.nps.gov*).

For backcountry trips, you may want to hire a guide. Full-day fishing trips cost about $250–$300 for one angler, $250–$350 for two. Only guides approved by the National Park Service are permitted to take anglers into the backcountry.

Little River Outfitters

FISHING | This large fly-fishing shop and school has been in business since 1994. It specializes in fly tying and other skills. Although it does not offer guide services, it can hook you up with guides for fishing in the Smokies or elsewhere. *106 Town Square Dr., Townsend 865/448–9459 www.littleriveroutfitters.com.*

Smoky Mountain Angler

FISHING | This well-equipped fly-fishing shop offers equipment rentals, fishing licenses, and half-day and full-day fly- and spin-fishing trips with one of its half dozen guides. Full-day guided trout fishing trips in the park are around $275 for one person and $325 for two. *469 Brookside Village Way, Gatlinburg 865/436–8746 www.smokymountainangler.com.*

HIKING

The national park has more than 800 miles of hiking trails, about half of which are on the Tennessee side. The trails range from short nature walks to long, strenuous hikes that gain several thousand feet in elevation. Park trails are well maintained most of the year, but be prepared for erosion and washouts December through May.

Weather in the park is subject to rapid change. A day in spring or fall might start out warm and sunny, but by the time you reach a mile-high elevation the temperature may be near freezing. The higher elevations of the park can get up to 85 inches of rain and snow annually.

Although permits are not required for day hikes, you must have a backcountry permit for overnight trips.

HORSEBACK RIDING

Several hundred miles of backcountry trails on the Tennessee side are open to horseback riders.

Cades Cove Riding Stables

HORSEBACK RIDING | FAMILY | Along with horseback riding this park concessionaire offers hayrides, carriage rides, and guided trail rides. It's first-come, first-served, with no reservations except for large groups. Call the stables to find out times and dates of ranger-led hayrides. Horseback riders must be at least six years old and weigh no more than 250 pounds. *Cades Cove Campground, 10042 Campground Dr., at entrance to Cades Cove Loop Rd., Townsend 865/448–9009 www.cadescovestables.com Closed Dec.–early Mar. From $15.*

TUBING

Little River is the most popular tubing river on the west side of the Smokies. It's mostly flat water, with a few mild rapids. Several outfitters in Townsend rent tubes and life jackets and provide shuttle buses or vans that drop you off upstream. Expect to pay from $10 to $18 per person Outfitters are generally open May through September or October.

Smoky Mountain River Rat

WATER SPORTS | FAMILY | This outfitter, the best of the bunch in the Townsend area, offers tubing on the Little River during warmer months. Tube rental, life jacket, and a shuttle service is $18. *205 Wears Valley Rd., Townsend 865/448–8888 www.smokymtnriverrat.com Closed Nov.–Apr.*

North Carolina Side

The Great Smoky Mountains National Park may be headquartered in Tennessee, but more of the park is on the North Carolina side. The North Carolina Side boasts the highest mountain in the park—Clingmans Dome, elevation 6,643 feet—and four more of the 10 highest peaks: Mount Guyot, Mount Chapman, Old Black, and Luftee Knob. It's also home to Fontana Lake, which forms much of the park's southwestern boundary. The small towns along the edge of the park—including Robbinsville, Bryson City, Dillsboro, and Sylva—sometimes bill themselves as "the quiet side of the park," and with good reason.

But there's no reason for Carolinians and Tennesseans to get into a bragging match. Within the park itself, both sides are actually quite similar in terms of scenery, activities, flora and fauna, and historical sites. Indeed, you probably won't even know when you go from one side of the park to the other. ■ TIP→ **There are numerous picnic areas and campgrounds but no food service or lodging options on the North Carolina side of the park.**

Sights

GEOLOGICAL FORMATIONS

★ Clingmans Dome

MOUNTAIN—SIGHT | FAMILY | At an elevation of more than 6,600 feet, this is the third-highest peak east of the Rockies, only a few feet shorter than the tallest, Mt. Mitchell. From the parking lot (where there are restrooms) at the end of Clingmans Dome Road, walk up a paved, but steep, half-mile trail to the observation tower offering 360-degree views from the "top of Old Smoky." There's also a small visitor center and bookshop (open April to November). Temperatures here are usually 10 to 15 degrees lower than at the entrance to the park. Clingmans Dome Road is closed to vehicular traffic in winter, but if there's snow on the ground you can put on your snowshoes and hike up to the peak. ✉ *Clingmans Dome Rd., Great Smoky Mountains National Park* ✣ *7 miles from U.S. 441* ☎ *865/436–1200* 🌐 *www.nps.gov/grsm/planyourvisit/clingmansdome.htm* 🎫 *Free* ⏲ *Closed Dec.–Mar.*

HISTORIC SIGHTS

★ Cataloochee Valley

HISTORIC SITE | FAMILY | This is one of the most memorable and eeriest sites in all of the Smokies. At one time Cataloochee was a community of more than 1,200 people. After the land was annexed for the national park in 1934, the community dispersed. Although many of the original buildings are gone, more than a dozen houses, cabins, barns, and churches still stand. You can visit the Palmer Methodist Chapel, the Beech Grove School, and the Woody, Caldwell, and Messer homesteads. You have a good chance of spotting elk here, especially in the evening and early morning. You'll also likely see wild turkeys, deer, and perhaps bears. Cataloochee is one of the most remote parts of the Smokies reachable by car via a narrow, winding, gravel road. The novels of Asheville-area native Wayne Caldwell, *Cataloochee* and *Requiem by Fire,* depict Cataloochee before the coming of the park. ✉ *Cove Creek Rd., off Rte. 276, Great Smoky Mountains National Park* ☎ *865/436–1200* 🌐 *www.nps.gov/grsm* 🎫 *Free* ⏲ *Often closed in winter due to snow and ice.*

Mingus Mill

FACTORY | FAMILY | In the late 19th century this was a state-of-the-art gristmill, with two large grist stones powered by a store-bought turbine rather than a hand-built wheel. From mid-March to just after Thanksgiving, you can watch the miller make cornmeal and even buy a pound of it. ✉ *U.S. 441, Great Smoky Mountains National Park* ✣ *2 miles north of Cherokee* ☎ *865/436–1200* 🌐 *www.nps.*

gov/grsm/planyourvisit/mfm.htm 🎫 *Free* ⏲ *Closed late Nov.–mid-Mar.*

★ Mountain Farm Museum

MUSEUM VILLAGE | FAMILY | This is perhaps the best re-creation anywhere of an Appalachian mountain farmstead. The nine farm buildings, all dating from the late 19th century, were moved in the 1950s to this site next to the Oconaluftee Visitor Center from various locations within the park. Besides a furnished two-story chestnut log cabin, there is a barn, apple house, corncrib, smokehouse, bee gums, springhouse, chicken coop, and other outbuildings. In season, corn, tomatoes, pole beans, squash, and other mountain crops are grown in the garden, and the park staff sometimes puts on demonstrations of pioneer activities, such as making apple butter and molasses. Two easy 1½-mile walking trails begin near the museum. Dogs on leashes are allowed on the trail but not within the farm grounds. Elk are sometimes seen grazing in the pastures adjoining the farm, and occasionally you may see white-tailed deer and wild turkeys. ✉ *Oconaluftee Visitor Center, U.S. 441, Great Smoky Mountains National Park* ✥ *1½ miles from Cherokee* ☎ *865/436–1200* 🌐 *www.nps.gov/grsm/planyourvisit/mfm.htm* 🎫 *Free.*

Proctor

HISTORIC SITE | Once a thriving lumber and copper mining town on Hazel Creek, Proctor has mostly been taken over by nature. Among the structures remaining are the white-frame Calhoun House, probably built in the early 1900s; the foundations of a church and of several other buildings; and bridges over Hazel Creek. About half a mile away is the Proctor cemetery. Proctor is best reached by boat across Fontana Lake. After arriving on the north shore of the lake, it's a short walk to the site of the old town. Fontana Marina offers daily boat transport across the lake. ✉ *Great Smoky Mountains National Park* ☎ *828/498–2129* 🌐 *www.nps.gov/grsm/learn/historyculture/people.htm.*

Road to Nowhere

HISTORIC SITE | FAMILY | Lakeview Drive was originally proposed as a way for local communities to reach their family cemeteries, after being displaced from their homes for the Fontana Dam project in the 1940s. An environmental issue halted the construction of Lakeview Drive, earning its nickname as the "Road to Nowhere." Today, the road begins at the park's entrance from Fontana Road in Bryson City, and ends at a tunnel 6 miles into the park. The drive is quite scenic, with an overlook of Fontana Lake and a few trailheads along the way. A network of hiking trails (including a 3.2-mile loop) begin at the tunnel. ✉ *Lakeview Dr., Great Smoky Mountains National Park* ☎ *865/436–1200* 🌐 *www.nps.gov/grsm* 🎫 *Free.*

Smokemont Baptist Church

RELIGIOUS SITE | Also known as the Oconaluftee Baptist Church, Smokemont Baptist Church is all that remains of the once-thriving lumbering community of Smokemont. Founded in 1832, and rebuilt in 1916, the church was added to the National Register of Historic Places in 1976. To get to the graceful, white-frame church, turn off Newfound Gap Road at the Smokemont Campground, cross the Oconaluftee, and park in the area just past the bridge. The church is across the road and up the hill. An old cemetery, the Bradley Cemetery, is nearby. ✉ *Newfound Gap Rd., MM 17.2, Great Smoky Mountains National Park* ☎ *865/426–1200* 🌐 *www.nps.gov/grsm.*

PICNIC AREAS

Picnic areas, however, provide amenities such as restrooms—some with pit toilets and some with flush toilets, but not all have running water in the bathrooms (bring hand sanitizer) or potable drinking water. Most of the 11 developed picnic areas in the park have raised grills for cooking. Picnic grounds in the park are free, except for group pavilions at several grounds, which can be reserved in advance and charge from $12.50 to $80 per group. To avoid future problems with bears, clean your grill and picnic area thoroughly before leaving.

SCENIC DRIVES

Cove Creek Road

SCENIC DRIVE | **FAMILY** | This drive takes you to one of the most beautiful valleys in the Smokies and to one of its most interesting (and least visited) destinations. The first 7 miles of Cove Creek Road are on a mostly paved, winding, two-lane road through a scenic rural valley. As you enter the park, the road becomes gravel. Although in the park this is a two-way road, in places it is wide enough only for one vehicle, so you may have to pull over and let an oncoming vehicle pass. At points the curvy road hugs the mountainside, with steep drop-offs, making it unsuitable for larger vehicles. As you near the Cataloochee Valley, suddenly you're on a paved road again. Follow the paved road, as it is a shortcut to the historic buildings of Cataloochee. Keep a lookout for elk, wild turkey, deer, and other wildlife. Try to visit off-season, as you'll face less traffic on Cove Creek Road and the valley is so peaceful and relaxing. However, the road may close at times in winter. ✉ *Cove Creek Rd., Great Smoky Mountains National Park* ☎ *865/436–1200* 🌐 *www.nps.gov/grsm* 💵 *Free.*

Heintooga Ridge Road–Balsam Mountain Road

SCENIC DRIVE | Begin this drive near mile marker 458 of the Blue Ridge Parkway, about 11 miles from Cherokee. Travel about 8 miles along the paved Heintooga Ridge Road, a mile-high drive that is lined with evergreens. At this elevation, you're often literally in the clouds. Near the Heintooga Picnic Area, take the narrow, unpaved 18-mile Balsam Mountain Road, sometimes called Roundbottom Road. Although it's only one lane wide and with many sharp curves, Balsam Mountain Road is well maintained and does not require a four-wheel-drive vehicle. Travel trailers and other large vehicles are prohibited. The roadside scenery changes as you descend from the higher elevations with firs and hemlocks of Balsam Mountain to the lowlands toward Cherokee. There is a profusion of flowers along Balsam Mountain Road especially in the spring. If you tire of driving, there are plenty of nearby trails, including the 11-mile Balsam Mountain Trail and 3.3-mile Palmer Creek Trail. Another 12 miles on Big Cove Road, mostly through rural areas outside the park, gets you back to Cherokee. ✉ *Heintooga Ridge Rd., off Blue Ridge Pkwy., Great Smoky Mountains National Park.*

★ Newfound Gap Road

SCENIC DRIVE | **FAMILY** | Newfound Gap Road is by far the busiest road on the national park's North Carolina side, with more than a million vehicles making the 16-mile climb from an elevation of 2,000 feet near Cherokee to almost a mile at Newfound Gap (and then down to Gatlinburg on the Tennessee side). It's the only paved road that goes all the way through the center of the park, so you definitely won't escape from the crowds. The scenery is memorable, however. If you don't have time to explore the back roads, Newfound Gap Road will give you a flavor of the richness and variety of the Smokies. Unlike most other roads in the park, Newfound Gap Road has mile markers; however, the markers run backward (as far as North Carolinians are concerned), starting at 31.1 where it intersects with the Blue Ridge Parkway near Cherokee. Among the sites on the road are Oconaluftee Visitor Center and Mountain Farm Museum (mile marker 30.3); Mingus Mill (mile marker 29.9); Smokemont Campground and Nature Trail (mile marker 27.2); Web Overlook (mile marker 17.7), from which there's a good view almost due west of Clingmans Dome; and Newfound Gap (mile marker 14.7), the start of the 7-mile road to Clingmans Dome. The speed limit on Newfound Gap Road tops out at 45 mph. ✉ *Newfound Gap Rd., off Blue Ridge Pkwy., Great Smoky Mountains National Park* ☎ *865/436–1200* 🌐 *www.nps.gov/grsm/planyourvisit/nfg.htm* 🎫 *Free.*

SCENIC STOPS

Big Witch Overlook

VIEWPOINT | FAMILY | This overlook offers fine views into the eastern side of the Smokies, and in May and June the roadsides bloom with rosebay rhododendron. ✉ *Blue Ridge Pkwy. MM 461.9, Cherokee* ☎ *828/298–0398* 🌐 *www.nps.gov/blri* 🎫 *Free.*

Cataloochee Valley Overlook

VIEWPOINT | FAMILY | This is a great spot to take in the broad expanse of Cataloochee Valley. Cataloochee comes from a Cherokee word meaning "row upon row" or "standing in rows," and indeed you'll see rows of mountain ridges here. The overlook is well marked and has a split-rail fence. ✉ *Cataloochee Entrance Rd., Great Smoky Mountains National Park* ☎ *865/436–1200* 🌐 *www.nps.gov/grsm* 🎫 *Free.*

Heintooga Overlook

VIEWPOINT | FAMILY | One of the best spots to watch the sunset, Heintooga Overlook has sweeping views westward of the crest of the Great Smokies. ✉ *Heintooga Ridge Rd., Great Smoky Mountains National Park* ☎ *865/436–1200* 🌐 *www.nps.gov/grsm* 🎫 *Free* 🕑 *Closed Nov.–late May.*

★ Newfound Gap Overlook

VIEWPOINT | FAMILY | At 5,048 feet, Newfound Gap is a drivable pass through the top of the park and provides excellent views of a broad swath of the Smokies. The ridge at Newfound Gap marks the North Carolina–Tennessee state line. If you want to say you've been on the Appalachian Trail, it's a short and easy walk away from here. Franklin Delano Roosevelt officially dedicated the park at this site in 1940. ✉ *Newfound Gap Rd., MM 14.7* ☎ *865/436–1200* 🌐 *www.nps.gov/grsm.*

Oconaluftee Valley Overlook

VIEWPOINT | FAMILY | From atop the Thomas Divide, just a little below the crest of the Smokies, you can look down at winding Newfound Gap Road. This is also a good spot to view the sunrise in the Smokies. ✉ *Newfound Gap Rd., MM 15.4, Great Smoky Mountains National Park* ☎ *865/436–1200* 🌐 *www.nps.gov/grsm* 🎫 *Free.*

TRAILS

Clingmans Dome Trail

TRAIL | FAMILY | If you've been driving too long and want a place to stretch your legs, unbeatable views of the Smokies, and an ecological lesson, take the ½-mile (1-mile round-trip) trail from the Clingmans Dome Visitor Center parking lot to the observation tower at the top of Clingmans Dome, the highest peak in the Smokies. While paved, the trail is fairly steep, and at well over 6,000 feet elevation you'll probably be gasping for air. Many of the fir trees here are dead, killed by an alien invader, the balsam woolly adelgid. There's a small visitor information station on the trail. In the parking lot, often full in season, there are restrooms. *Easy* ✉ *Clingmans Dome Rd., Great Smoky Mountains National Park* ☎ *865/436–1200* 🌐 *www.nps.gov/grsm/planyourvisit/clingmansdome.htm* 🕑 *Clingmans Dome Rd. closed Dec.–Mar.*

Flat Creek Trail

TRAIL | FAMILY | This is one of the hidden gems in the park. It's little known, but it's a delightful hike, especially in summer when this higher elevation means respite from stifling temperatures. The 2.6-mile path stretches through pretty woodlands with evergreens, birch, rhododendron, and wildflowers. The elevation gain is about 570 feet. *Moderate* ✉ *Heintooga Ridge Rd., MM 5.4, Great Smoky Mountains National Park* ☎ *865/436–1200* 🌐 *www.nps.gov/grsm* ☞ *Heintooga Ridge Rd. closed Nov.–late May.*

Hazel Creek Trail

TRAIL | This hike begins with a boat ride across the lake from Fontana Resort Marina. Your captain will give you directions on how to get from the docking point to the trailhead. A half-mile on the Hazel Creek Trail (known on some park maps as Lakeshore Trail) will take you to the old lumber and mining town of Proctor. After about 5.1 miles, bear right onto the Jenkins Ridge Trail, which will take you to Bone Valley Trail. Bone Valley gets its name from the herd of cattle, moved here for summer pasture in 1888, that died in a spring snowstorm. This is an easy hike (as hikes go in the Smokies), mostly following an old road and railroad bed. However, it is also a long hike, but you could always do a shorter section. *Easy* ✉ *Great Smoky Mountains National Park* ✣ *Trailhead near Backcountry Campsite 86* ☎ *828/498–2129 boat reservations* 🌐 *www.nps.gov/grsm.*

Kephart Prong Trail

TRAIL | A 4.2-mile round-trip woodland trail, named for one of the early promoters of the park, wanders beside a stream to the remains of a Civilian Conservation Corps camp. Close by, the trail takes a moderate slope to Mt. Kephart, gaining over 900 feet in elevation. *Moderate* ✉ *Newfound Gap Rd., 5 miles north of Smokemont Campground, Great Smoky Mountains National Park* ☎ *865/436–1200* 🌐 *www.nps.gov/grsm.*

Little Cataloochee Trail

TRAIL | No other hike in the Smokies offers a cultural and historic experience quite like this one. In the early 20th century, Cataloochee Cove had the largest population of any place in the Smokies, around 1,200 people. Most of the original structures have been torn down or have succumbed to the elements, but a few historic frame buildings remain along this remote trail. Some have been restored by the park staff, such as the Cook Log Cabin near Davidson Gap, an apple house, and a church. You'll see several of these, along with rock walls and other artifacts, on the Little Cataloochee Trail. The trail is 6 miles each way, including a mile-long section of Pretty Hollow Gap Trail. Allow at least six hours for this hike. *Moderate* ✉ *Little Cataloochee Trailhead, Old Cataloochee Tpk., Great Smoky Mountains National Park* ☎ *865/436–1200* 🌐 *www.nps.gov/grsm/planyourvisit/cataloochee.htm.*

Smokemont Loop Trail

TRAIL | A 6.1-mile round-trip loop takes you by streams and, in spring and summer, lots of wildflowers, including trailing arbutus. At Smokemont Campground near Cherokee, this is an easy trail to access. The only downside is that there are no long-range views. *Moderate* ✉ *Smokemont Campground, Newfound Gap Rd., Great Smoky Mountains National Park* ☎ *865/436–1200* 🌐 *www.nps.gov/grsm.*

★ Three Waterfalls Loop

TRAIL | FAMILY | For the effort of a 2.4-mile hike at the Deep Creek entrance to the park near Bryson City, this trail will reward you with three pretty waterfalls: Tom Branch, Indian Creek, and Juney Whank, which you can see close-up from a 90-foot-long wooden bridge. *Moderate* ✉ *Deep Creek Rd., Great Smoky Mountains National Park* ✣ *Near Bryson City entrance* ☎ *865/436–1200* 🌐 *www.nps.gov/grsm* ⏲ *Campground closed Nov.–mid-Apr.*

VISITOR CENTERS

Clingmans Dome Visitor Contact Station

INFO CENTER | FAMILY | While not a full-fledged visitor information center, Clingmans Dome has a staffed information kiosk, along with a small park store and bookshop. There are restrooms in the Clingsmans Dome parking lot. ✉ *Clingmans Dome, Great Smoky Mountains National Park* ☎ *865/436–1200* 🌐 *www.nps.gov/grsm/planyourvisit/visitorcenters.htm* ⏲ *Closed Dec.–Mar.*

★ Oconaluftee Visitor Center

INFO CENTER | FAMILY | The park's main information center on the North Carolina side is looking great after a $3 million renovation and expansion. It is 1½ miles from Cherokee and offers interactive displays, a 20-minute film, a large book and gift shop, ranger-led programs, and assistance from helpful volunteers. There are restrooms and vending machines. Adjoining the visitor center, in a large level field next to the Oconaluftee River, is the Mountain Farm Museum, a reconstruction of an early 1900s mountain farmstead. Herds of elk are sometimes seen here. ✉ *Newfound Gap Rd., MM 30.3, Great Smoky Mountains National Park* ☎ *865/436–1200* 🌐 *www.nps.gov/grsm/planyourvisit/visitorcenters.htm.*

Activities

BIKING

The North Carolina side of the Smokies offers excellent cycling, and bicycles are permitted on most roads. Avoid Newfound Gap Road, which can be clogged with vehicular traffic. Instead, head to the (mostly) paved roads of Lakeview Drive—the so-called Road to Nowhere near Bryson City—and the Cataloochee Valley. Balsam Mountain Road and Cove Creek Road also offer pleasant biking with very little auto traffic. Since these roads are unpaved, with mostly gravel surfaces, you should use a mountain bike or an all-terrain hybrid. Helmets are not required in the park, but are strongly recommended.

BIKE RENTALS

Nantahala Outdoor Center Bike Shop

BICYCLING | FAMILY | Watch river rafters swoosh by on the Nantahala River as you get your bike tuned up or rent a bike at this friendly outfitter. Avid bikers on staff will give you tips on the best biking spots. All rentals include a helmet and a bike rack to transport the bike on your car. During busy periods you should reserve well in advance. This is the closest bike rental to the Tsali Recreation Area, famous for its mountain biking. ✉ *13077 U.S. 19 W, Bryson City* ☎ *828/785–4846* 🌐 *www.noc.com* ☞ *$40 a day.*

BOATING

★ Fontana Lake

BOATING | FAMILY | Covering around 12,000 acres, Fontana Lake borders the southern edge of the Great Smokies. Unlike most other nearby lakes, Fontana's shoreline is almost completely undeveloped, since about 90% of it is owned by the federal government. Fishing here is excellent, especially for smallmouth bass, muskie, and walleye. On the downside, the Tennessee Valley Authority generates power at Fontana Dam, sometimes lowering the water level. The dam, completed in 1944, at 480 feet is the highest concrete dam east of the Rockies. The dam's visitor center gets about 50,000 visitors a year. The Appalachian Trail crosses the top of the dam. ✉ *Fontana Dam Visitor Center, 71 Fontana Dam Rd., Great Smoky Mountains National Park* ✣ *3 miles from Fontana Village off NC 28* ☎ *865/498–2234* 🌐 *www.visitnc.com/listing/UHdY/fontana-dam-visitors-center* 🎫 *Free* ☞ *Visitor center closed Nov.–Mar.*

BOAT RENTALS

Fontana Marina

BOATING | FAMILY | Boat rentals—including kayaks, canoes, pontoon boats, and paddleboards—are available at Fontana Marina. The marina runs a shuttle service across the lake twice daily, and can drop hikers, anglers, and campers at Hazel Creek, Eagle Creek, Pilkey Creek, Kirkland Branch, and other north shore locations. ✉ *300 Woods Rd., Fontana Dam* ✣ *Off NC 28 N* ☎ *828/498–2129* 🌐 *www.fontanavillage.com/marina* ⏲ *Closed Nov.–Apr.* ☞ *Shuttles to Hazel Creek $50 per person.*

CAMPING

Four developed campgrounds—Balsam Mountain, Big Creek, Cataloochee, and Deep Creek—require reservations, and reservations are strongly recommended at Smokemont during high season. Only Smokemont is open year-round, and from November to April sites are first-come, first-served.

Balsam Mountain Campground. If you like camping among the evergreens, tent-only Balsam Mountain is for you. It's the highest campground in the park, at more than 5,300 feet. You may want to warm up in the evening with a campfire, even in summer. Due to its remote location off the Blue Ridge Parkway, the 64-site campground is rarely full, even on peak weekends. It's closed mid-October though late May. The camping fee is $17.50. ✉ *Near end of Heintooga Ridge Rd., Cherokee* ☎ *65/436–1200* 🌐 *www.nps.gov/grsm/planyourvisit/balsam-mountain.htm.*

Cataloochee Campground. The appeal of this small campground is its location in the beautiful and historical Cataloochee Valley. Reservations for all the 27 tent sites are required. Take care driving into the valley; the unpaved Cove Creek Road is narrow with sharp curves, and in some places you hug the mountainside. It's closed late October through late March. The camping fee is $25. ✉ *Cataloochee Valley, Cove Creek Rd., Waynesville* ☎ *877/444–6777* 🌐 *www.nps.gov/grsm/planyourvisit/cataloochee-campground.htm.*

Deep Creek Campground. This campground at the Bryson City entrance to the park is near the most popular tubing spot on the North Carolina side of the Smokies. There are also several swimming holes. Of the 92 sites here, 42 are for tents only. It's closed late October through late March. The camping fee is $25. ✉ *1912 E. Deep Creek Rd., Bryson City* ☎ *865/436–1200* 🌐 *www.nps. gov/grsm/planyourvisit/deep-creek-campground.htm.*

Smokemont Campground. With 142 sites (98 for tents and 44 for RVs), Smokemont is the largest campground on the North Carolina side of the park, and is year-round. Some of the campsites are a little too close together, but the sites themselves are spacious. The camping fee is $25. ✉ *Off Newfound Gap Rd., 6 miles north of Cherokee* ☎ *877/444–6777* 🌐 *www.nps.gov/grsm/planyourvisit/smokemont-campground.htm.*

EDUCATIONAL OFFERINGS

Discover the flora, fauna, and mountain culture of the Smokies with scheduled ranger programs and nature walks.

Interpretive Ranger Programs
TOUR—SPORTS | FAMILY | The National Park Service organizes all sorts of activities, such as daily guided hikes and talks, from spring to fall. The programs vary widely, from talks on mountain culture, blacksmithing, and old-time fiddle and banjo music to tours through historical areas of the park. Many of the programs are suitable for older children as well as for adults. Oconaluftee Visitor Center is a good place to learn about park events. ☎ *865/436–1200* 🌐 *www.nps.gov/grca/planyourvisit/ranger-program.htm.*

Junior Ranger Program
TOUR—SPORTS | FAMILY | Children ages 5 to 12 can take part in these hands-on educational programs. Kids can pick up a Junior Ranger booklet at the Oconaluftee Visitor Center. Spring through fall the park offers many age-appropriate demonstrations, classes, and programs, such as Stream Splashin', Critters and Crawlies, and—our favorite—Whose Poop's on My Boots? For kids 13 and older (including adults), look for events in the park's Not-So-Junior-Ranger Program. ☎ *865/436–1200* 🌐 *www.nps.gov/grsm/learn/kidsyouth/beajuniorranger.htm.*

FISHING

The North Carolina side of the Smokies has one of the best wild trout fisheries in the East. It has more than 1,000 miles of streams, and all are open to fishing year-round except Bear Creek where it meets Forney Creek. Native brook trout thrive in colder high-elevation streams, while brown and rainbow trout (not native but now widely present in the region) can live in somewhat warmer waters. Among the best trout streams on this side of the park are Deep Creek, Big Creek, Cataloochee Creek, Palmer Creek, Twentymile Creek, Raven Fork, Hazel Creek, and Noland Creek. Fishing licenses are available online at *www.ncwildlife.org.*

To fish in the Cherokee Reservation (Qualla Boundary), everyone over 12 needs a separate tribal permit, available at shops on the reservation.

HIKING

Great Smoky Mountains National Park has almost 900 miles of hiking trails, about equally divided between the North Carolina and Tennessee sides. The trails range from short nature walks to long, strenuous hikes that gain several thousand feet in elevation. The Little Cataloochee Trail is a favorite, but Flat Creek and Smokemont Loop are also extraordinary hikes.

Although permits are not required for day hikes, you must have a backcountry permit for overnight trips.

HORSEBACK RIDING

Get back to nature and away from the crowds with a horseback ride through the forest. Guided horseback rides are offered by one park concessionaire at Smokemont near Cherokee. Rides are at a walking pace, so they are suitable for even inexperienced riders.

Smokemont Riding Stable

HORSEBACK RIDING | FAMILY | The emphasis here is on a family-friendly horseback-riding experience, suitable even for novice riders. Choose either the one-hour trail ride or a 2½-hour waterfall ride. If you don't feel like saddling up, Smokemont also offers wagon rides. ✉ *135 Smokemont Riding Stable Rd., Cherokee* ✣ *Off U.S. 441* ☎ *828/497–2373* 🌐 *www.smokemontridingstable.com* ⏲ *Closed mid-Nov.–early Mar.* ☞ *1-hr rides $35.*

TUBING

On a hot summer's day there's nothing like hitting the water. On the North Carolina side, you can swim or go tubing on Deep Creek near Bryson City. The upper section is a little wild and woolly, with white water flowing from cold mountain springs. The lower section of Deep Creek is more suitable for kids. There are several tubing outfitters near the entrance of the park at Deep Creek. Some have changing rooms and showers. Wear a swimsuit and bring towels and dry clothes to change into. Most outfitters are open April through October.

Smoky Mountain Campground

WATER SPORTS | FAMILY | Just outside the Bryson City Entrance to the national park, look for this rustic structure with "TUBES" in huge red letters across the roof. This highly commercial operation rents tubes and sells camping supplies. It also has a campground and rental cabins. ✉ *1840 W. Deep Creek Rd., Bryson City* ☎ *828/488–9665* 🌐 *www.smokymtn-campground.com* ⏲ *Closed Nov.–Mar.*

What's Nearby

On the Tennessee side, or the western side of the park, the nearby gateway of **Gatlinburg** has an almost carnival-like atmosphere, with nearly every business—souvenir stores, fudge shops, oddities museums—focused entirely on the tourist market. On some days, more than 35,000 visitors stay in its chain hotels, pack its casual eateries, and crowd the main street that's less than a mile long. Rivaling it for popularity are the adjacent communities of **Pigeon Forge,** home to the fabulous Dollywood, and **Sevierville.** The nearby Townsend Entrance to the park is appealing if your destination is Cades Cove.

Adjoining the eastern side of the park in North Carolina is the Cherokee Indian Reservation, officially known as the Qualla Boundary. It consists of almost 57,000 acres, and the town of **Cherokee** is its capital. Truth be told, there are two Cherokees: There's the Cherokee with the often-tacky pop culture, with junky gift shops full of cheap plastic "Indian crafts." These are designed to appeal to the lowest common denominator of the tourist masses. But there's another Cherokee that's a window into the rich heritage of the tribe's Eastern Band. Although now relatively small in number—Eastern Band tribal enrollment is about 14,000—these Cherokee and their ancestors have been responsible for keeping alive the Cherokee culture. They are the descendants of those who hid in the Great Smoky Mountains to avoid the Trail of Tears, the forced removal of the Cherokee Nation to Oklahoma in the 19th century. They are survivors, extremely attached to the hiking, swimming, trout fishing, and natural beauty of their ancestral homeland. You'll note that due to tribal efforts, all official signs in the Qualla Boundary, and many private commercial ones, are in the Cherokee language as well as in English. The reservation is dry, with no alcohol sales, except at the huge Harrah's casino complex. This means that there are few upscale restaurants in the area (because they depend on wine and cocktail sales for much of their profits), just fast-food and mom-and-pop places. Near the town of Cherokee, the Blue Ridge Parkway begins its 469-mile meandering journey north through the North Carolina mountains to Virginia's Skyline Drive.

Waynesville is the seat of Haywood County and where the Blue Ridge Parkway meets the Great Smokies. About 40% of the county is occupied by Great Smoky Mountains National Park, Pisgah National Forest, and the Harmon Den Wildlife Management Area. The town of Waynesville is a rival of Blowing Rock and Highlands as a summer and vacation-home retreat for the well-to-do, though the atmosphere here is a bit more countrified. The compact downtown area is charming and walkable, and there are many small shops and restaurants, and every July, Folkmoot USA, a two-week international festival that began in Waynesville in 1984, brings music and dancing groups from around the world to various venues in Waynesville and elsewhere in western North Carolina.

A little more than an hour's drive from the national park's Oconaluftee Entrance, the city of Asheville is nationally known for its art galleries, hip downtown scene, eclectic restaurants, and varied lodgings, including one of the largest collections of B&Bs in the Southeast.

On the North Carolina side, **Bryson City** is a little mountain town on the Nantahala River, one of the lesser-known gateways to the Great Smokies. The town's most striking feature is the former city hall with a four-sided clock. Since becoming the depot and headquarters of the Great Smoky Mountains Railroad, the downtown area has been rejuvenated, mostly with gift shops, restaurants, craft breweries, and ice-cream stands.

If you truly want to get away from everything, head to the area around **Robbinsville** in the far southwest corner of North Carolina, a little south of the southern edge of the Great Smokies. The town of Robbinsville offers little, but the Snowbird Mountains, Lake Santeetlah, Fontana Lake, the rugged Joyce Kilmer–Slickrock Wilderness, and the Joyce Kilmer Memorial Forest, with its giant virgin poplars and sycamores, are definitely highlights of this part of North Carolina.

Chapter 31

GUADALUPE MOUNTAINS NATIONAL PARK

Updated by
Andrew Collins

Camping ★★★☆☆ | Hotels ★★☆☆☆ | Activities ★★★★☆ | Scenery ★★★★☆ | Crowds ★☆☆☆☆

WELCOME TO GUADALUPE MOUNTAINS NATIONAL PARK

TOP REASONS TO GO

★ **Tower over Texas:** This dramatic wilderness is home to 8,751-foot Guadalupe Peak, the state's highest point.

★ **Fall for fiery foliage:** Though surrounded by the arid Chihuahuan desert, the park has miles of beautiful foliage in McKittrick Canyon. In late October and early November, it bursts with flaming colors.

★ **Hike unhindered:** The main activity at the park is hiking its rugged, remote, and often challenging trails: 80 miles' worth that are nearly always free of crowds.

★ **Marvel at wildlife:** A variety of wildlife—including shaggy brown elk, furtive mountain lions, and shy black bears—traipse the mountains, woods, and desert here, and there's fantastic bird-watching, too.

★ **The Old West whispers:** Rock ruins and former homesteads—Frijole Ranch History Museum is a highlight—dot a hardscrabble landscape that pioneers worked hard to tame.

1 **Pine Springs.** The park's main visitor center, its most popular campground and trailheads, and historic sites like Frijole Ranch and the Pinery Butterfield Stage Station ruins are located in this most central unit of the park.

2 **McKittrick Canyon.** Beautiful year-round, the lush green foliage along McKittrick Canyon's trout-filled desert stream bursts into many hues in autumn.

3 **Dog Canyon.** Just over the New Mexico border, this tranquil, forested high-desert wilderness contains a scenic campground and trails, including the trek to 7,830-foot Lost Peak.

4 **Salt Basin Dunes.** This remote unit in the western end of the park access acres of powdery-white gypsum dunes.

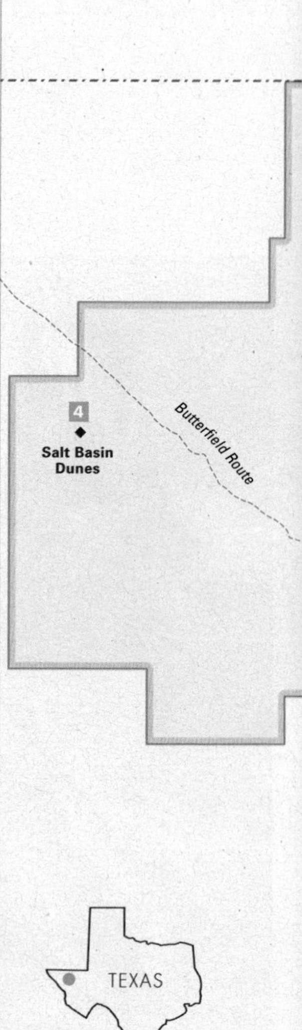

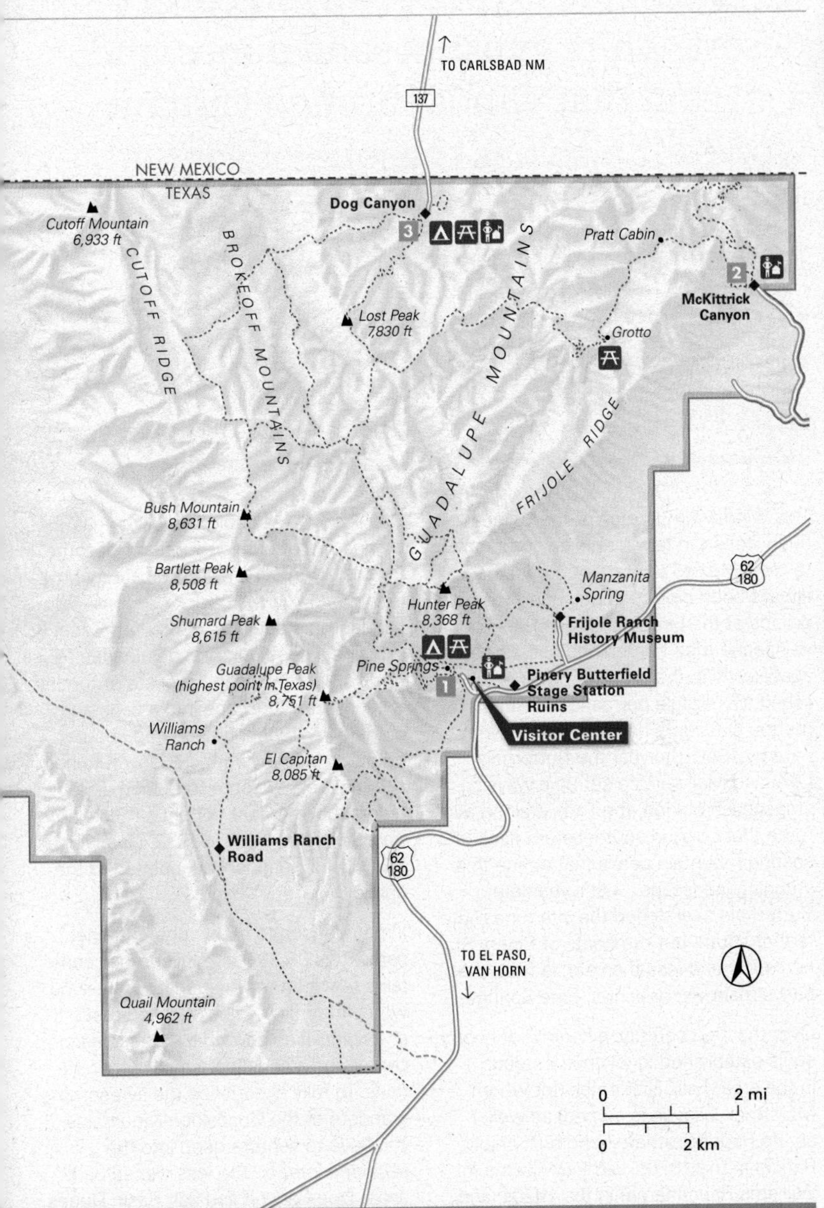

TO CARLSBAD NM
137
NEW MEXICO
TEXAS
Dog Canyon
3
Cutoff Mountain
6,933 ft
CUTOFF RIDGE
BROKEOFF MOUNTAINS
GUADALUPE MOUNTAINS
Pratt Cabin
2
McKittrick Canyon
Lost Peak
7,830 ft
Grotto
FRIJOLE RIDGE
Bush Mountain
8,631 ft
Bartlett Peak
8,508 ft
Manzanita Spring
62
180
Hunter Peak
8,368 ft
Shumard Peak
8,615 ft
Frijole Ranch History Museum
Guadalupe Peak
(highest point in Texas)
8,751 ft
Pine Springs
1
Pinery Butterfield Stage Station Ruins
Visitor Center
Williams Ranch
El Capitan
8,085 ft
Williams Ranch Road
62
180
TO EL PASO,
VAN HORN
Quail Mountain
4,962 ft
0
2 mi
0
2 km

Guadalupe Mountains National Park is a study in extremes: it has mountaintop forests but also rocky canyons, arid desert, white gypsum sand dunes, and a stream that winds through verdant woods. It also has the loftiest spot in Texas: 8,751-foot Guadalupe Peak. The mountain dominates the view from every approach, but it's just one part of a rugged landscape carved by wind, water, and time.

This windswept stretch of the Chihuahuan Desert in far West Texas, adjacent to New Mexico's southern border, has always been a place of solitude. Roaming groups of the peripatetic Mescalero-Apache tribe hunted and harvested agave cacti in the area but never established any sizable permanent settlements. Outsiders had scarcely set foot here by 1858, the year the Butterfield Overland Mail service set up a wayside stagecoach station, the Pinery, along a route that hugged southeastern flank of soaring mountain peaks that define this stunning landscape. Just a year later, Butterfield abandoned the site for a route farther south, but remnants of Pinery Station still stand less than a mile from the park's main visitor center, Pine Springs.

Over the next century, a handful of hearty souls established lonely homesteads in the area: Felix McKittrick (for whom McKittrick Canyon is named) as well as the Rader Brothers (who built Frijole Ranch) in the 1870s, James Williams (of Williams Ranch fame) in the 1920s, and Wallace Pratt, a geologist for the gas company that would eventually become Exxon, who built a pair of vacation homes in the 1930s in McKittrick Canyon—his handsome stone-and-wood Pratt Cabin remains a popular hiking destination to this day. Pratt was an advocate of turning this pristine landscape into a park, and in the early 1960s, he donated about 6,000 acres of McKittrick Canyon to help see his dreams come to fruition. The federal government bought a much larger tract soon after, and in 1972, Guadalupe Mountains National Park opened to the public.

In comparison to many other national parks, this 86,367-acre wilderness contains few features shaped by man—you won't find many miles of paved roads or any facilities beyond a modest visitor center and a couple of small ranger stations. To fully experience the awesome grandeur of the Guadalupe Mountains, you have to venture deep into the secluded interior. The less-visited park units, Dog Canyon and Salt Basin Dunes,

AVERAGE HIGH/LOW TEMPERATURES					
JAN.	FEB.	MAR.	APR.	MAY	JUNE
53/30	58/35	63/38	71/46	78/55	88/63
JULY	AUG.	SEPT.	OCT.	NOV.	DEC.
87/63	84/62	78/57	71/49	61/38	57/33

are an hour or two by car from the main visitor center. Unsurprisingly, the park is a favorite of long-distance hikers and backcountry campers.

That said, visitors with limited hiking experience or young kids in tow will find plenty within the park to keep them busy for at least a day, including a handful of easy nature trails and some historic buildings easily reached from U.S. 62/180, the highway that passes through the most accessible portions of the park. Head northeast on this highway, and in 45 minutes you'll reach New Mexico's Carlsbad Caverns National Park, which you might consider visiting in combination with Guadalupe Mountains. There's little else to see or do within an hour of this park, but the city of El Paso—less than two hours' drive west—has a growing art and culinary scene as well as some impressive parks and outdoor attractions.

Planning

When to Go

Trails here are rarely crowded, except in fall, when foliage changes colors in McKittrick Canyon, and during spring break in March. Still, this is a very remote area, and you probably won't find much congestion. Backcountry trails are best explored in spring and fall, when it's cooler but not too cold. Snow, not uncommon in winter, can linger in the higher elevations. The windy season is March through May, and the rainy months are July and August.

Getting Here and Around

AIR

Carlsbad's Cavern City Air Terminal, 55 miles northeast, is served by Boutique Air, with regular service from Albuquerque and Dallas/Fort Worth, but there's just one major car rental agency (Enterprise). More practical is El Paso International Airport, 100 miles west, which is served by all major air carriers and car rental companies.

CAR

Few roadways penetrate this rugged park that's primarily designated wilderness. Most sites are off U.S. 62/180, but reaching two remote park units entails long, circuitous drives: Salt Basin Dunes, on the park's western edge, is accessed from FM Road 1576 near Dell City, and Dog Canyon, on the north end of the park, is reached via Highway 137 from New Mexico.

Inspiration

The Pine Springs Visitor Center sells several excellent books on the Guadalupe Mountains' natural features and history, including the illustrated *The Guadalupes,* by Dan Murphy. Other good titles include *Trails of the Guadalupes,* by Don Kurtz and William D. Goran, and *Hiking Carlsbad Caverns and Guadalupe Mountains National Parks,* by Bill Schneider.

Park Essentials

ACCESSIBILITY

The wheelchair-accessible Pine Springs Visitor Center has a wheelchair available for use. The ¾-mile round-trip Pinery Trail from the visitor center to Butterfield Stage Ruins is wheelchair accessible, as is McKittrick Contact Station.

PARK FEES AND PERMITS

The $10 park fee is good for one week and payable at the visitor center and major trailheads. Camping is $15 nightly per site. For overnight backpacking trips, you must get a free permit from either the visitor center or Dog Canyon Office.

PARK HOURS

The park is open 24/7, year-round. It's in the Mountain time zone, but beware that your cell phone may pick up a signal from towers in the adjacent Central time zone, giving you the incorrect impression that you're an hour ahead.

CELL PHONE RECEPTION

Reception in the park is very spotty, but cell phones generally work around Pine Springs Visitor Center (which also has Wi-Fi) and Frijole Ranch.

Restaurants

Dining in the park is a do-it-yourself affair—bring a camp stove if you plan on cooking, as wood and charcoal fires aren't permitted anywhere. There are no restaurants, but the visitor center sells a few drink and snack items, and Whites City, New Mexico (35 miles), has an unremarkable restaurant and a convenience store. You'll find extensive dining options in Carlsbad, New Mexico (55 miles), and El Paso (100 miles).

Hotels

There are no hotels in or even very near the park. There's one no-frills motel in Whites City, New Mexico (35 miles), and several hotels in Carlsbad, New Mexico (55 miles), but these lodgings can be expensive because of demand by local oil-industry workers. Many visitors stay in Van Horn (60 miles), which has a cool, old historic lodging (Hotel El Capitan), and in El Paso, which is a fairly scenic 90- to 110-minute drive and has dozens of options.

Visitor Information

The park comprises four distinct sections, with the headquarters and main visitor center located in the Pine Springs area; it and the McKittrick Canyon unit (with a small ranger station) are easily reached off U.S. 62/180. Long back-country drives are required to reach the remote Dog Canyon (also with a small ranger station) and Salt Basin Dunes sections.

CONTACTS Guadalupe Mountains National Park. ✉ *Pine Springs Visitor Center, 400 Pine Canyon Dr.* ☎ *915/828–3251* 🌐 *www.nps.gov/gumo.*

Pine Springs

55 miles southwest of Carlsbad, NM, 100 miles east of El Paso.

You'll find the park's only visitor center and the majority of its key attractions in the Pine Springs area, which is just off U.S. 62/180 in the southeastern corner of the park—it's the best place to begin your explorations of this vast wilderness. From the visitor center, it's a ½-mile walk or drive to the popular Pine Springs Campground, which is also the trailhead for such hiking highlights as Guadalupe Peak, El Capitan and Salt Basin Overlook,

Devil's Hall, and the Bowl. Also nearby is Frijole Ranch and its desert springs and Williams Ranch Road.

HISTORIC SIGHTS

★ Frijole Ranch History Museum
COLLEGE | FAMILY | With its grassy, tree-shaded grounds, you could almost imagine this handsome and peaceful little 1876 ranch house somewhere other than the harsh Chihuahuan Desert. Inside what's believed to be the region's oldest intact structure, displays and photographs depict ranch life and early park history. Easy, family-friendly hiking trails lead to wildlife oases at Manzanita Spring and Smith Spring. Hours are sporadic, so check with the visitor center if you wish to go inside. Still, it's good fun just to explore the ranch grounds and outbuildings, orchard, and still-functioning irrigation system. ✉ *Frijole Ranch Rd.* ☎ *915/828–3251* 🌐 *www.nps.gov/gumo.*

Pinery Butterfield Stage Station Ruins
ARCHAEOLOGICAL SITE | FAMILY | In the mid-1800s passengers en route from St. Louis to California on the Butterfield Overland Mail stagecoach route stopped here for rest and refreshment. At more than a mile in elevation, the station was the highest on the journey, but it operated for only about a year. The ruins provide a peek into the past: the bare remains of a few buildings with rock walls (but no roofs) layered on the desert floor. Do not touch. You can drive here from U.S. 62/180, but it's more interesting to stroll over via the paved ¾-mile round-trip natural trail from the visitor center. ✉ *U.S. 62/180* ✣ *Just east of visitor center* 🌐 *www.nps.gov/gumo.*

SCENIC DRIVES

Williams Ranch Road
ARCHAEOLOGICAL SITE | Although this adventure isn't for the faint of heart—a high-clearance, four-wheel-drive vehicle is required—this rough but enjoyable 7¼-mile, one-way drive over what was once the Butterfield Overland Mail Stage Line passes by dramatic limestone cliffs and offers panoramic views. Access is from U.S. 62/180 at the park's southeast border, and you must get a key at the visitor center to unlock the gate. It takes about an hour to reach the old ranch house, at the base of a 3,000-foot cliff. This is a day-trip only; overnight parking is prohibited. ✣ *Off U.S. 62/180.*

TRAILS

★ The Bowl
TRAIL | Meandering through forests of pine and Douglas fir, this trail to an aptly named mountaintop valley is one of the most gorgeous in the park. The strenuous 9.1-mile round-trip has an elevation gain of 2,500 feet and can take up to 10 hours. It's where rangers go when they want to enjoy themselves. Bring lots of water. *Difficult.* ✉ *Guadalupe Mountains National Park* ✣ *Trailhead: Pine Springs Campground.*

★ Devil's Hall Trail
TRAIL | FAMILY | Wind through a Chihuahuan Desert habitat thick with spiked agave plants, prickly pear cacti, ponderosa pines, and a dry riverbed strewn with giant boulders to Devil's Hall, a narrow 10-foot-wide canyon with walls that soar to more than 100 feet. At a leisurely pace, this 4.2-mile round-trip jaunt will take three or four hours. *Moderate.* ✉ *Guadalupe Mountains National Park* ✣ *Trailhead: Pine Springs Campground.*

El Capitan/Salt Basin Overlook Trails
TRAIL | Several trails combine to form a popular loop through the low desert. El Capitan skirts the base of El Capitan peak for about 3.5 miles, leading to a junction with Salt Basin Overlook. The 4.7-mile Salt Basin Overlook trail begins at the Pine Springs Trailhead and has views of the stark white salt flat below and loops back onto the El Capitan Trail. The 11.3-mile round-trip is not recommended during the intense heat of summer, because there is absolutely no shade.

Moderate–Difficult. ✉ *Guadalupe Mountains National Park* ✣ *Trailhead: Pine Springs Campground.*

Frijole/Foothills Trail

TRAIL | FAMILY | Branching off the Frijole Ranch Trail, this relatively flat hike leads to Pine Springs Campground and Visitor Center. The 5½-mile round-trip through desert vistas takes about four hours. *Moderate.* ✉ *Guadalupe Mountains National Park* ✣ *Trailhead: Frijole Ranch Cultural Museum.*

★ Guadalupe Peak Trail

TRAIL | An 8.4-mile workout over a steep grade to the top of Texas pays off with a passage through several ecosystems and some great views. The round-trip hike takes six to eight hours, but the trail is clearly defined and doesn't require undue athleticism. The steepest climbs are in the beginning. In summer, start this hike in early morning to allow a descent before afternoon thunderstorms flare up. Lightning targets high peaks. Be alert to changing weather and head for lower ground if conditions worsen. Also, Guadalupe Peak is considered one of the windiest points in the U.S. *Difficult, elevation gain 3,000 feet.* ✉ *Guadalupe Mountains National Park* ✣ *Trailhead: Pine Springs Campground.*

★ Smith Spring Trail

TRAIL | FAMILY | Departing from the Frijole Ranch, the trail heads for a shady oasis where you may spot mule deer and elk drawn to the miracle of water in the desert. As a bonus, the route passes Manzanita Spring, another wildlife refuge only 0.2 mile past Frijole Ranch. Allow 1½ hours to complete the 2.3-mile round-trip walk. This is a good hike for older kids whose legs won't tire as easily, but it's not wheelchair accessible past Manzanita Spring. *Easy–Moderate.* ✉ *Guadalupe Mountains National Park* ✣ *Trailhead: Frijole Ranch.*

VISITOR CENTER

★ Pine Springs Visitor Center

INFO CENTER | You can pick up maps, brochures, and hiking permits here at the park's visitor center, just off U.S. 62/180. A slide show and a 12-minute movie provide a quick introduction to the park, half of which is protected as a designated wilderness area. Informative exhibits depict geological history, area wildlife, and flora ranging from lowland desert to forested mountaintop. You can access several trails and a lovely picnic area and campground a short ½-mile drive or stroll from the visitor center. ✉ *400 Pine Canyon Dr.* ☎ *915/828–3251* 🌐 *www.nps.gov/gumo.*

McKittrick Canyon

12 miles northeast of Pine Springs Visitor Center.

A desert creek flows through this verdant canyon, which is easily accessed from U.S. 62/180, a 20-minute drive from the Pine Springs Visitor Center. One of the most wondrous sights of West Texas, the canyon is lined with walnut, maple, and other trees that explode into brilliant hues each autumn, from late October into early November (check with the visitor center for foliage updates). You're likely to spot mule deer here seeking water. And you'll find trailheads for several great hiking trails, including Pratt Cabin and the Grotto. The small ranger station here is staffed only part time.

Sights

TRAILS

★ McKittrick Canyon to Pratt Cabin and Grotto

TRAIL | FAMILY | View stream and canyon woodlands along a 4.8-mile round-trip excursion that leads to the vacant Pratt Cabin (sometimes called Pratt Lodge), which was built of stone during the Great Depression in the "most beautiful spot in Texas," according to its original owner, Wallace Pratt. Perhaps he was enthralled by an oasis of running water carving through the canyon floor or a colorful riot of autumn foliage. Continue another mile each way to reach the Grotto, where you'll discover a picnic area overlooking a flowing stream and surface rock that resembles formations in an underground cave with jagged overhangs. Just beyond the Grotto is the historic Hunter Line Cabin. Allow two to three hours to visit Pratt Cabin and another hour or two if you go to the Grotto. *Moderate.* ✉ *Guadalupe Mountains National Park* ✥ *Trailhead: McKittrick Contact Station.*

McKittrick Canyon Nature Trail

TRAIL | **FAMILY** | Signs along this nearly 1-mile loop explain the geological and botanical history of the area, and the views, while not spectacular, are engaging enough to hold your interest. You can take the loop in either of two directions when you come to a fork in the trail. *Easy–Moderate.* ✉ *Guadalupe Mountains National Park* ✥ *Trailhead: McKittrick Contact Station.*

Permian Reef Trail

TRAIL | If you're in shape and have a serious geological bent, you may want to hike this approximately 8.5-mile round-trip climb. It heads through open, expansive desert country to a forested ridge with Douglas fir and ponderosa pines. Panoramic views of McKittrick Canyon and the surrounding mountain ranges allow you to observe many rock layers. A geology guidebook coordinated to trail makers is available at the Pine Springs Visitor Center. Set aside at least eight hours for this trek. *Difficult, elevation gain 2,000 feet.* ✉ *Guadalupe Mountains National Park* ✥ *Trailhead: McKittrick Canyon Trailhead.*

VISITOR CENTER

★ McKittrick Canyon Contact Station

ARCHAEOLOGICAL SITE | Poster-size illustrations on a shaded, outdoor patio of this intermittently staffed ranger station tell the geological story of the Guadalupe Mountains, believed to have been carved from an ancient sea. You can also hear the recorded memoirs of oilman Wallace Pratt, who donated his ranch and surrounding area to the federal government for preservation. Nearby trailheads access a 1-mile nature loop and lengthier hikes. ✉ *4 miles off U.S. 62/180* 🌐 *www.nps.gov/gumo.*

Dog Canyon

102 miles northwest of Pine Springs Visitor Center.

This tranquil, wooded alpine canyon sits at an elevation of 6,300 feet and is situated at the extreme north end of the park, a two-hour drive from Pine Springs Visitor Center. Because it's such a long way to go, many who visit Dog Canyon overnight at one of the several campsites near the entrance and small ranger station. The lovely, shaded campground also has a few picnic tables—it's common to see mule deer. Drinking water and restrooms are available. This unit also has trails—popular for hiking on foot or on horseback—to several majestic vistas and is especially pleasant in summer, as it remains much cooler than the lower desert sections of the park. You get here via Highway 137 off U.S. 285 (12 miles north of Carlsbad, New Mexico) or by Highway 408 off U.S. 62/180 (9 miles south of Carlsbad). Intrepid hikers with backcountry camping experience can get to Dog Canyon from McKittrick Canyon and Pine Springs on foot; however, depending on the trail, this adventure involves at least 15 miles of hiking and a few thousand feet of elevation gain each way—those who attempt it usually allow three or four days to do so.

TRAILS

Indian Meadow Nature Trail

TRAIL | FAMILY | This mostly level 0.6-mile round-trip hike crosses an arroyo into meadowlands and offers a relaxing way to savor Dog Canyon's peaceful countryside in less than an hour. *Easy.* ✉ *Guadalupe Mountains National Park* ✣ *Trailhead: Dog Canyon Office.*

Marcus Overlook

TRAIL | FAMILY | A 4½-mile round-trip with an 800-foot elevation gain rewards you with a panoramic view of West Dog Canyon. Set aside about half a day for it. *Moderate.* ✉ *Guadalupe Mountains National Park* ✣ *Trailhead: Dog Canyon Campground.*

VISITOR CENTER

Dog Canyon Office

INFO CENTER | With a helpful staff who can advise you on making the most of your time in Dog Canyon, this small ranger station acts as a gateway to the vast, dramatic high country in the remote northern section of the park. ✉ *Hwy. 137* ☎ *575/981–2418.*

Salt Basin Dunes

48 miles west of Pine Springs Visitor Center.

This little-explored unit in the remote far western edge of the park accesses stunning white gypsum dunes similar to those found about 90 miles northwest in New Mexico's White Sands National Park. But for some shaded picnic tables and pit toilets by the parking area, there are no facilities at Salt Basin Dunes, and it's about an hour's drive from Pine Springs Visitor Center via U.S. 62, FM Road 1576, and unpaved Williams Road; the nearby village of Dell City has a gas station and convenience store. This area is typically very hot in summer (and receives no shade), and fierce winds are possible in the spring, making late fall through winter the best time to go.

TRAILS

Salt Basin Dunes Trail

TRAIL | It's about a mile east of the trailhead to reach this eerily beautiful 2,000-acre expanse of gypsum sand dunes, the largest of which climbs to heights of 60 feet. Allow a couple of hours to walk 3 or 4 miles through this brilliant white-sand landscape, which also offers fine views east of the Guadalupe Mountains western escarpment. *Moderate.* ✉ *Guadalupe Mountains National Park* ✣ *Trailhead: End of Williams Rd.*

Activities

BIRD-WATCHING

More than 300 species of birds have been spotted in the park, including the ladder-backed woodpecker, Scott's oriole, Say's phoebe, and white-throated swift. Many migratory birds—such as fleeting hummingbirds and larger but less graceful turkey vultures—stop at Guadalupe during spring and fall migrations. **Manzanita Springs,** near the Frijole Ranch History Museum, is an excellent birding spot. There aren't any local guides, but park rangers can help you spot some native species.

Books on birding are available at the visitor center, and bird lovers will find the park's birding checklist especially helpful. It's easy to spot the larger birds of prey circling overhead, such as keen-beaked golden eagles and swift, red-tailed hawks. Watch for owls in the **Bowl** area and for swift-footed roadrunners in the desert areas (they're quick, but not as speedy as their cartoon counterpart).

The sun sets over the desert landscape of west Texas at Guadalupe Mountains National Park.

CAMPING

The park has two developed campgrounds—Dog Canyon and Paine Springs—that charge $15 nightly per site, and 10 designated primitive backcountry sites where you can camp for free (you must first obtain a permit at Pine Springs Visitor Center or Dog Canyon Office) and enjoy miles of unspoiled land. In the backcountry, no restrooms are provided; visitors may dig their own privies, but toilet paper and other waste should be packed out. Wood and charcoal fires are prohibited throughout the park, but you can use a camp stove at both developed and backcountry sites.

Dog Canyon Campground. This campground is remote, but well worth the effort. The very well-maintained camping area is in a cool, high-elevation coniferous forest, with nine tent sites and four RV sites (no hookups, 23-foot maximum). ✉ *Hwy. 137, just within park northern entrance* ☎ *575/981–2418.*

Pine Springs Campground. You'll be snuggled amid pinyon and juniper trees near the base of a tall mountain peak at this resting place a ½ mile from the Pine Springs Visitor Center. It has 20 tent sites, 19 RV sites (no hookups), one wheelchair-accessible site, and two group sites. ✉ *U.S. 62/180* ☎ *915/828–3251.*

EDUCATIONAL PROGRAMS

Junior Ranger Program

COLLEGE | **FAMILY** | The park offers a self-guided Junior Ranger Program: kids choose activities from a workbook—including nature hikes and answering questions based on park exhibits—and earn a badge once they've completed four. If they complete six, they earn an additional patch. Workbooks are available at the visitor center or at the park website. ✉ *Guadalupe Mountains National Park.*

HIKING

No matter which trail you select, pack wisely—the visitor center carries only very limited supplies. Bring a gallon of water per day per person (there are water-filling stations at the visitor center and ranger stations), as well as sunscreen, sturdy footwear, and hats. The area has a triple-whammy regarding sun ailments: it's very open, very sunny, and has a high altitude (which makes sunburns more likely).

What's Nearby

The Guadalupe Mountains border New Mexico to the north and are just a half-hour drive from **Whites City,** a tiny village with a few basic services that's by the entrance to Carlsbad Caverns National Park, and another 20 minutes from the small city of **Carlsbad,** which is a popular regional base but tends to have expensive lodgings; see Carlsbad Caverns National Park for more information. In Texas, although they're a bit farther away than Carlsbad, the town of **Van Horn** (an hour south) and the city of **El Paso** (90 minutes west) are handy bases. The drive from either place is picturesque and free of traffic. Van Horn is also a good stopover if making your way from Big Bend National park. El Paso, which is home to the region's major airport and has undergone an impressive downtown renaissance in recent years, offers much to see and do and is also convenient to visiting New Mexico's White Sands National Park.

Chapter 32

HALEAKALA NATIONAL PARK

Updated by
Lehia Apana

Camping	Hotels	Activities	Scenery	Crowds
★★★★★	★☆☆☆☆	★★★★★	★★★★★	★★★☆☆

WELCOME TO HALEAKALA NATIONAL PARK

TOP REASONS TO GO

★ **Unusual sightings:** Haleakala has the highest number of rare and endangered species of any national park in the United States, including its unofficial mascot: the eye-catching silversword that grows nowhere else on Earth.

★ **Spectacular sunrise:** Translated as "House of the Sun," Haleakala lives up to its name by offering dramatic and awe-inspiring vantages to welcome a new day.

★ **Happy campers:** From easy drive-up camping to backcountry cabins reached only by foot, there's a wilderness experience for all levels.

★ **Natural wonders:** Here you'll find some of the best—and certainly the most diverse—hiking trails on Maui. Explore a bamboo forest, volcanic landscapes, and lush jungle all within park boundaries.

★ **Hear the silence:** Dubbed "the quietest place on Earth," Haleakala's stark volcanic landscape is a peaceful respite from the constant buzz of everyday life.

1 Summit District. When most people think of Haleakala National Park, they have the Summit District in mind, home to the awe-inspiring 10,023-foot volcanic peak. Many come to view sunrise from this lofty perch, and this area is rich with exotic wilderness, diverse hiking trails, and epic back country camping.

2 Kipahulu District. This branch of Haleakala National Park runs down the mountain from the crater and reaches the sea (at Hana Highway mile marker 42), where a freshwater stream cascades from one pool to the next. A popular hiking trail winds through a bamboo forest and leads to a spectacular waterfall.

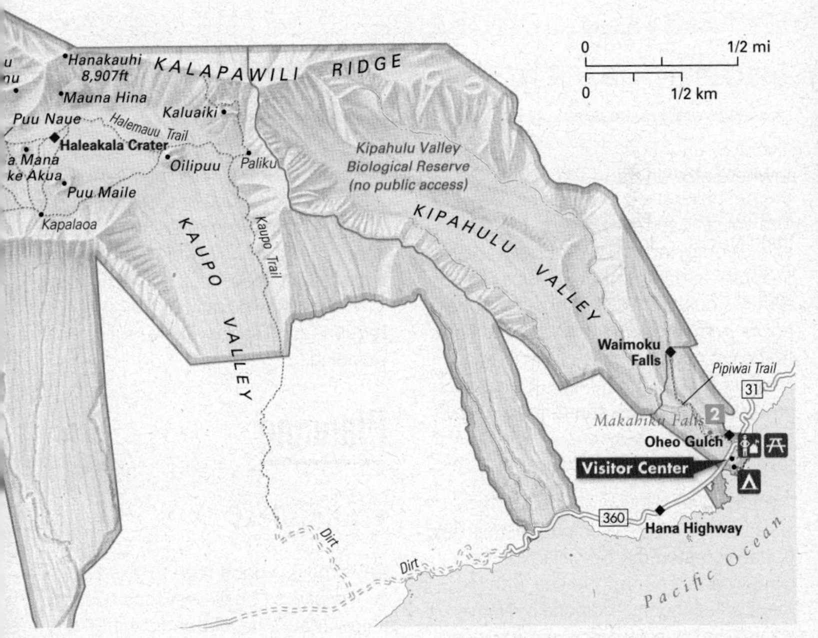

Hanakauhi
8,907ft
KALAPAWILI RIDGE
Mauna Hina
Kaluaiki
Puu Naue
Halemauu Trail
Haleakala Crater
Oilipuu
Paliku
Puu Maile
Kapalaoa
Kipahulu Valley
Biological Reserve
(no public access)
KIPAHULU VALLEY
KAUPO VALLEY
Kaupo Trail
Waimoku
Falls
Pipiwai Trail
31
Makahiku Falls
2
Oheo Gulch
Visitor Center
360
Hana Highway
Dirt
Dirt
Pacific Ocean
0
1/2 mi
0
1/2 km

Nowhere else on Earth can you drive from sea level to 10,023 feet in only 38 miles. And what's more shocking: in that short vertical ascent to the summit of the volcano Haleakala you'll journey from lush, tropical island landscape to the stark, moonlike basin of the volcano's enormous, otherworldly crater.

Exploring Haleakala Crater is one of the best hiking experiences on Maui. The volcanic terrain offers an impressive diversity of colors, textures, and shapes—almost as if the lava has been artfully sculpted. The barren landscape is home to many plants, insects, and birds that exist nowhere else on earth and have developed intriguing survival mechanisms, such as the sun-reflecting, hairy leaves of the silversword, which allow it to survive the intense climate.

Translated as "House of the Sun," Haleakala is where demigod Maui is said to have created the Hawaiian islands by pulling them from the sea with his magical fish hook. Additionally, Native Hawaiians consider the summit a wao akua, or "realm of the gods," akin to a temple or other place of worship. To this day, Haleakala remains a deeply cultural and spiritual place, and modern practitioners still perform ancient rituals here. Visitors are encouraged to be mindful of this sacred place by remaining on designated trails and treating this environment with the utmost respect.

Established in 1916, Haleakala National Park covers an astonishing 33,222 acres, with the Haleakala Crater as its centerpiece. There's terrific hiking, including trails for one-hour, four-hour, eight-hour, and overnight hikes, one of which goes through the Waikamoi Cloud Forest on Monday and Thursday only and requires reservations (call the park line no more than a week in advance). No other hikes require reservations. There is also on-site camping.

Planning

When to Go

Any time is a good time to visit Haleakala. The park's "busy" seasons typically follow Maui's travel trends, with many visitors arriving during winter (when it's freezing elsewhere), summer (popular for family travel), and during spring and fall breaks.

Sunrise at Haleakala is the busiest time, no matter the day. This early-morning experience became so popular that reservations are now required to enter the park between 3 and 7 am. Sunset also draws spectators, but it's not nearly as crowded, and reservations aren't necessary.

AVERAGE HIGH/LOW TEMPERATURES					
JAN.	FEB.	MAR.	APR.	MAY	JUNE
61/44	61/43	61/44	61/44	64/46	66/48
JULY	AUG.	SEPT.	OCT.	NOV.	DEC.
67/49	67/49	66/48	65/48	64/47	62/45

Before you head to the Summit District, call for the latest park weather conditions (☎ *866/944–5025*). Extreme gusty winds, heavy rain, and even snow in winter are not uncommon. Because of the high altitude, the mountaintop temperature is often as much as 30 degrees cooler than that at sea level. Be sure to bring a jacket. Also make sure you have a full tank of gas, as no service stations exist beyond Kula.

The Kipahulu District is closer to sea level, so the weather is mild compared to the summit. Daytime average temperatures range from 70°F to 80°F throughout the year, while night time averages 65°F to 70°F.

Getting Here and Around

AIR

Kahului Aiport (OGG) in Central Maui is the island's only major airport, so that's where you'll fly into and out of. Haleakala National Park is a nearly one-hour drive from the airport.

CONTACTS Kahului Airport (OGG). ✉ *1 Keolani Pl., Kahului* ☎ *808/872–3830* 🌐 *www.airports.hawaii.gov/ogg.*

CAR

To reach Haleakala National Park and the mountain's breathtaking summit, take Route 36 east of Kahului to the Haleakala Highway (Route 37). Head east, up the mountain to the unlikely intersection of Haleakala Highway and Haleakala Highway. If you continue straight the road's name changes to Kula Highway (still Route 37). Instead, turn left onto Haleakala Highway—this is now Route 377. After about 6 miles, make a left onto Crater Road (Route 378). After several long switchbacks (look out for downhill bikers), you'll come to the park entrance.

Park Essentials

ACCESSIBILITY

Wheelchair access within the park is mostly limited to the visitor centers and the summit building, which can be reached via a steep ramp. Wilderness trails are rugged and unpaved.

PARK FEES AND PERMITS

There's a $30-per-car fee to enter the park, good for three days. ■ **TIP→ Hold on to your receipt—it can also be used at both the Summit and Kipahulu districts.**

Reservations must be made at 🌐 *www.recreation.gov* to view the sunrise from the summit; $1 ticket per vehicle. This allows you to enter the summit area between 3 and 7 am. If you don't snag one of these coveted spots, consider visiting for sunset, which, on most days, offers equally stunning views.

Permits and reservations are required for the three backcountry cabins at Holua, Kapalaoa, and Paliku ($75 per night) and the wilderness tent-camping at Holua and Paliku ($8 per night) via 🌐 *www.recreation.gov.*

PARK HOURS

The Summit Area is open 24/7, 365 days a year. Note that you'll need a sunrise viewing reservation to enter the park between 3 and 7 am. The Kipahulu District is open from 9 am to 5 pm daily.

CELL PHONE RECEPTION

Cellular reception is generally good within the Summit District, depending on your service provider. Reception can be spotty at best within the remote Kipahulu District.

Hotels

The residential town of Kula sits just outside the park boundaries. There are a handful of dining options, but accommodations are limited, save for Kula Lodge and some B&Bs. Most park visitors stay overnight in the resort and condo areas in south or west Maui, then drive to the park. Staying at the park overnight is limited to camping.

Restaurants

There are no restaurants or snack shops within the park, so plan ahead. The nearest town to the Summit District is Kula, a quiet residential area that includes some restaurants, a few small markets, and a gas station. Grab provisions in town or at Pukalani on your way up the mountain.

The far-flung Kipahulu District is limited to roadside stands, and not much else. There are two general stores and a gas station in Hana, which is 10 miles away.

Safety

Always call the National Weather Service to check the weather conditions (☎ *866/944–5025*) before hiking Haleakala National Park, as winds, heavy rain, and snow may occur.

Tours

Explore Maui Nature

ECOTOURISM | Maui's only bird-watching tour runs Tuesday and/or Thursday, and includes stops at Haleakala National Park and Kealia Pond National Wildlife Refuge. A certified guide leads the search for native forest birds and coastal species unique to these islands. There are also hiking-only excursions that explore Haleakala's Summit District, and custom private tours are available. Tours run six- to eight hours and start at $225 per person. ✉ *Haleakala National Park* ☎ *844/550–6284* 🌐 *www.exploremauinature.com.*

Maui Stargazing

GUIDED TOURS | The "House of the Sun" is also a world-class spot to observe the night sky. The experience begins with sunset at the summit, followed by a one-hour tour of the cosmos. Peer through the largest portable telescope on the mountain and learn about the various nebulae, star clusters, and galaxies you're seeing. Hot beverages, snacks, and winter outerwear are provided. ✉ *Kula Lodge, 15200 Haleakala Hwy., Kula* ☎ *808/298–8254* 🌐 *www.mauistargazing.com.*

Roberts Hawaii

GUIDED TOURS | Locally owned and operated since 1941, Roberts has become one of the largest tour companies in the state. Haleakala-focused excursions are limited to 12 guests per guide and include a sunrise trip ($187), and sunset-stargazing combo ($219). There's also a multi-stop tour that includes Haleakala National Park ($173). ✉ *70 E. Kaahumanu Ave., Kahului* ☎ *808/539–9400* 🌐 *www.robertshawaii.com.*

Exploring the interior of the Haleakala Crater might be the closest most people get to walking on the moon.

Visitor Information

CONTACTS Haleakala National Park. *808/572–4400* *www.nps.gov/hale.*

Summit District

14 miles from Kula.

At Haleakala's Summit District, nature rules. Even better, there's something for every kind of outdoor enthusiast—from backcountry camping to easy day hikes, spectacular sunrises to mesmerizing stargazing, and the chance to spot rare native birds and Hawaiian plants found nowhere else in the world.

Sights

GEOLOGICAL FORMATIONS

★ Haleakala Crater

NATURE SITE | The park's main attraction is the eroded depression found at the Summit District known as Haleakala Crater. And, undoubtedly, the island's best hiking is found here. If you're in shape, do a day hike descending from the summit along **Keoneheehee Trail** (aka Sliding Sands Trail) to the crater floor. You might also consider spending several days here amid the cinder cones, lava flows, and all that loud silence. Entering the crater is like landing on a different planet. In the early 1960s, NASA actually brought moon-suited astronauts here to practice what it would be like to "walk on the moon." Tent camping and cabins are available with permits. On the 30 miles of trails you can traverse black sand and wild lava formations, follow the trail of blooming *ahinahina* (silverswords), and take in tremendous views of big sky and burned-red cliffs.

The best time to go into the crater is in summer, when the conditions are generally more predictable. Be sure to bring layered clothing—and plenty of warm clothes if you're staying overnight. It may be scorching hot during the day, but it gets mighty chilly after dark. Bring your own drinking water, as potable water is available only at the two visitor centers. Overnight visitors must get a permit at park headquarters before entering the crater. ✉ *Haleakala Crater Rd.* ☎ *808/572–4400* 🌐 *www.nps.gov/hale* 💵 *$30 park entrance fee per vehicle (good for 3 days).*

Haleakala Volcano

VOLCANO | The park's main geological feature is the volcano itself, which spans much of east Maui from summit to sea. This dormant volcano has experienced at least 10 eruptions in the past thousand years; though unlikely, it's possible that it will erupt again in this lifetime. ✉ *Haleakala National Park.*

SCENIC DRIVES

Haleakala Highway

SCENIC DRIVE | Also known as Crater Road, this serpentine roadway leads skyward to Haleakala's Summit District. It offers panoramic views of Maui's central valley, the island's western mountain range, and both coastlines. On clear days, neighboring islands are visible in the distance. ✉ *Haleakala Hwy., Kula.*

SCENIC STOPS

Kalahaku Overlook

VIEWPOINT | The view here offers a different perspective of the crater, and at this elevation the famous silversword plant grows amid the cinders. This odd, endangered beauty grows only at the summit of Haleakala. It begins life as a silver, spiny-leaf rosette and is the sole home of a variety of native insects (it's the only shelter around). The silversword reaches maturity between 7 and 17 years, when it sends forth a 3- to 8-foot-tall stalk with several hundred tiny sunflowers. It blooms once, then dies. ✉ *Haleakala National Park.*

Leleiwi Overlook

VIEWPOINT | Located at about the 8,800-foot level, the Leleiwi Overlook offers your first awe-inspiring view of the crater. The small hills in the basin are cinder cones (*puu* in Hawaiian). If you're here in the late afternoon, it's possible you'll see yourself reflected on the clouds and encircled by a rainbow—a phenomenon called the Brocken Specter. Don't wait long for this, because it's not a daily occurrence. ✉ *Off Haleakala Hwy., Makawao.*

Puu Ulaula Overlook

VIEWPOINT | The highest point on Maui is this 10,023-foot summit, where a glass-enclosed lookout provides a 360-degree view. The building is open 24 hours a day, and this is where many visitors gather to view sunrise. Bring jackets, warm layers, hats, and blankets to stay warm on the cold and windy summit. On a clear day you can see the islands of Molokai, Lanai, Kahoolawe, and Hawaii Island; on a *really* clear day you can even spot Oahu glimmering in the distance. ✉ *Makawao.*

TRAILS

Halemauu Trail

TRAIL | Two half-day hikes involve descending into the crater and returning the way you came. The first, Halemauu Trail, is 2¼ miles round-trip. The cliffside, snaking switchbacks of this trail offer views stretching across the crater floor to its far walls. On clear days you can peer through the Koolau Gap to Hana. Native flowers and shrubs grow along the rail, which is typically misty and cool (though still exposed to the sun). When you reach the gate at the bottom, head back up. ■ **TIP→ For those who want a less strenuous hike, turn around at the natural land bridge known as "Rainbow Bridge," to avoid the steep switchbacks.** *Difficult.* ✉ *Haleakala National Park* ✣ *Trailhead: Off Hwy. 378, between mile markers 14 and 15.*

Hosmer Grove Loop Trail

TRAIL | Just as you enter the park, Hosmer Grove offers a short 10-minute hike and an hour-long, ½-mile loop trail that will give you insight into Hawaii's fragile ecology. Anyone can go on these hikes, whereas a longer trail through the

Waikamoi Cloud Forest is accessible only with park ranger-guided hikes. Call park headquarters for the schedule. Facilities here include six campsites (no permit needed, available on a first-come, first-served basis), pit toilets, drinking water, and cooking shelters. *Easy.* ⊠ *Haleakala National Park* ✣ *Trailhead: Near the Hosmer Grove Campground.*

Keoneheehee Trail (*Sliding Sands Trail*)
TRAIL | This 5-mile round-trip hike descends Keoneheehee Trail (aka Sliding Sands) into an alien landscape of reddish black cinders, lava bombs, and silverswords. It's easy to imagine life before humans in the solitude and silence of this place. *Difficult.* ⊠ *Haleakala National Park* ✣ *Trailhead: Haleakala Visitor Center.*

Pa Ka'oao Trail
TRAIL | Just past the Haleakala Visitors Center, this 0.4-mile out-and-back trail (aka. White Hill) offers expansive crater views for relatively little effort. Climbing just 100 feet elevation, this well-maintained trail is perfect for those short on time. *Easy.* ⊠ *Haleakala National Park* ✣ *Trailhead: Haleakala Visitors Center.*

Supply Trail
TRAIL | This single-track trail begins near the park entrance and Hosmer Grove, and climbs about 1,000 feet elevation through native shrubland and gentle switchbacks. There are a handful of parking spots at the trailhead, or park at Hosmer Grove. This hike ends where it meets the Halemauu Trail, and the two can be combined into a longer journey. *Moderate.* ⊠ *Haleakala National Park* ✣ *Trailhead: Near Hosmer Grove.*

VISITOR CENTERS

Haleakala Visitor Center
INFO CENTER | Located at the crater summit, the visitor center has exhibits inside and a trail that leads to Pa Kaoao (White Hill)—a short, easy walk with even better views of the valley. ⊠ *Haleakala Hwy., Makawao* 🌐 *www.nps.gov/hale.*

Park Headquarters Visitor Center
INFO CENTER | Just past the Summit District entrance is the Park Headquarters Visitor Center, where you'll find trail maps and displays about geology, Hawaiian culture, and endangered species protected within the park. Hikers and campers should check-in here before heading up the mountain. Maps, posters, and other memorabilia are available at the gift shop. ⊠ *Haleakala Hwy.* ☎ *808/572–4400* 🌐 *www.nps.gov/hale.*

Kipahulu District

12 miles from Hana.

The Kipahulu section of Haleakala National Park, also known as the backside of Haleakala, is rich with greenery, waterfalls, ocean vistas, ancient archaeological sites, and a variety of hikes.

Sights

SCENIC DRIVES

Hana Highway
SCENIC DRIVE | Also known as The Road to Hana (Highways 36 and 360), this famed drive is a destination in itself: 52 miles of snaking roads, single-lane bridges, and enough blind turns to give you chicken skin. The route from Central Maui to Hana may seem short—and those in a rush can make this drive within two to three hours. But if you do it right, it could take all day. Along the way you'll see waterfalls, tropical forests, eclectic roadside stands, and enough Pacific Ocean panoramas to fill your camera's memory card. ⊠ *Hana.*

SCENIC STOPS

★ **Oheo Gulch**
BODY OF WATER | One branch of Haleakala National Park runs down the mountain from the crater and reaches the sea here, 12 miles past Hana at mile marker 42 on the Hana Highway, where a basalt-lined stream cascades from one pool to

the next. Some tour guides still incorrectly call this area Seven Sacred Pools, but in truth there are more than seven, and they've never been considered sacred. ⚠ **While you may be tempted to take a dip, know that the pools are often closed because of landslides and flash flooding. If you see a closure notice, take it seriously, as people have died here.** The place gets crowded, as most people who drive the Hana Highway make this their last stop. It's best to get here early to soak up the solace of these waterfalls. **TIP→ The $30 entrance fee per car is good for three days and includes entry to Haleakala's Summit District.** *✉ Hana Hwy., 12 miles south of Hana, Hana 🌐 www.nps.gov/hale.*

Waimoku Falls

BODY OF WATER | If you enjoy hiking, go up the stream from the pools on the 2-mile hike to Waimoku Falls via Pipiwai Trail. The trail crosses a spectacular gorge, then turns into a boardwalk that takes you through an amazing bamboo forest. The hike also includes a giant banyan tree, views of Makahiku Falls, and forests of tropical plant life. Guided ranger hikes are offered through the National Park Service at 10 am on Sundays. After returning from your hike you can pitch a tent in the grassy campground down by the sea. *✉ Hana ☎ 808/248–7375 🌐 www.nps.gov/hale.*

TRAILS

Kahakai Trail

TRAIL | This quarter-mile hike (more like a walk) stretches between Kuloa Point and the Kipahulu campground. It provides rugged shoreline views, and there are places where you can stop to gaze at the surging waves below. *Easy. ✉ Hana ✢ Trailhead: Kuloa Point 🌐 www.nps.gov/hale 🎟 $30 park entrance fee per vehicle (good for 3 days).*

Kuloa Point Trail

TRAIL | A half-mile walk, this trail takes you from the Kipahulu Visitor Center down to the pools of Oheo at Kuloa Point, where the fresh water pools and ocean meet. On the trail you pass native trees and precontact Hawaiian sites. **TIP→ Tempting as it is, swimming in the ocean is strongly discouraged. While it may seem calm near sea level, unpredictable conditions at higher elevations cause flash flooding and other dangers.** *Easy. ✉ Hana Hwy., Hana ✢ Trailhead: Kipahulu Visitor Center 🌐 www.nps.gov/hale 🎟 $30 park entrance fee per vehicle (good for 3 days).*

★ Pipiwai Trail

TRAIL | This popular 2-mile trek upstream reveals two magnificent waterfalls: Makahiku Falls at about 0.5 miles in, and the grand finale 400-foot Waimoku Falls, pounding down in all its power and glory. Following signs from the parking lot, head across the road and uphill into the forest. The trail borders a sensational gorge and passes onto a boardwalk through a mystifying forest of giant bamboo that's known as the "bamboo forest." This stomp through muddy and rocky terrain takes around three hours to fully enjoy. Although this trail is never truly crowded, it's best done early in the morning before the tours arrive. Be sure to bring mosquito repellent. *Moderate. ✉ Hana Hwy., Hana ✢ Trailhead: Near mile marker 42 🌐 www.nps.gov/hale 🎟 $30 park entrance fee per vehicle (good for 3 days).*

The Ohia Tree

Found only on the Hawaiian islands, the ohia tree is currently endangered. If you're visiting from one of the other islands (Hawaii Island in particular) and plan to hike, be sure to clean any dirt from your shoes and clothing (and equipment if applicable) so that the fungus that kills the tree won't spread.

VISITOR CENTERS

Hale Halawai

BUILDING | Translated as "Meeting House," this open-air thatched building is a modern example of ancient building practices. It was erected in 2010 by park staff under the direction of a local craftsman who specializes in traditional Hawaiian architecture. The hale is oceanside of the visitor center, where the Pipiwai and Kuloa Point trails meet. ✉ *Hana Hwy.*

Kipahulu Visitor Center

INFO CENTER | This oceanside information center offers historical and cultural displays, plus daily ranger presentations. ✉ *Hana Hwy., Kipahulu* ☎ *808/248–7375* 🌐 *www.nps.gov/hale.*

Activities

BIKING

Several companies offer guided bike tours down Haleakala. This activity is a great way to enjoy an easy, gravity-induced bike ride, but isn't for those not confident on a bike. The ride is inherently dangerous due to the slope, sharp turns, and the fact that you're riding down an actual road with cars on it. That said, the guided bike companies take every safety precaution. A few companies offer unguided (or, as they like to say, "self-guided") tours where they provide you with the bike and transportation to the mountain and then you're free to descend at your own pace. Most companies offer discounts for online bookings.

Haleakala National Park no longer allows commercial downhill bicycle rides within the park's boundaries. As a result, tour amenities and routes differ by company. Ask about sunrise viewing from the Haleakala summit (be prepared to leave *very* early in the morning), if this is an important feature for you. Some lower-price tours begin at the 6,500-foot elevation just outside the national park boundaries, where you will be unable to view the sunrise over the crater. Weather conditions on Haleakala vary greatly, so a visible sunrise can never be guaranteed. Sunrise is downright cold at the summit, so be sure to dress in layers and wear closed-toe shoes.

Each company has age and weight restrictions, and pregnant women are discouraged from participating, although they are generally welcome in the escort van. Reconsider this activity if you have difficulty with high altitudes, have recently been scuba diving, or are taking medications that may cause drowsiness.

Bike Maui

BICYCLING | If biking down the side of Haleakala sounds like fun, Bike Maui is ready to pick you up at your resort, shuttle you to the mountain, help you onto a bike, and follow you as you coast down through clouds and gorgeous scenery into the town of Pukalani. There are also private or self-guided rides, and a combination bike and zipline tour that features ocean and treetop views of Maui's north shore. Enjoy stunning bicoastal views of the island as you descend the 21 switchbacks from the 6,500-foot elevation down to either Pukalani or Haliimaile. A postride breakfast is offered on some tours. ■ **TIP→ Book online for substantial discounts.** ✉ *810 Haiku Rd. , #120, Haiku-Pauwela* ☎ *808/575–9575* 🌐 *www.bikemaui.com.*

★ **Cruiser Phil's Volcano Riders**

BICYCLING | In the downhill bicycle industry since 1983, "Cruiser" Phil Feliciano offers both group and private tours that include hotel transfers, coffee and snacks, and a guided 23-mile ride down the mountain. Participants should be older than 12, at least 5 feet tall, weigh less than 280 pounds, and have ridden a bike in the past year. Feliciano also offers structured independent bike tours ($150), van-only tours, and packages that include a ziplining experience. Discounts are available for online bookings. ✉ *810 Haiku Rd. #120, Haiku-Pauwela* ☎ *808/575–9575* 🌐 *www.cruiserphils.com.*

Go Cycling Maui

BICYCLING | Serious cyclists can join an exhilarating group ride with Donnie Arnoult, a fixture on the Maui cycling scene since 1999. Routes include Haiku to Keanae, Kula to Kahikinui, and the ultimate Maui cycling challenge: Paia to the top of Haleakala crater. One-day rides are $185 per person ($215 to go to the crater). You bring your own cycling shoes, pedals, and clothes, and Donnie provides the bicycle, helmet, gloves, water bottle, snacks, and energy drinks. His shop is also a full-service cycling store offering sales, rentals, and repairs. ✉ *99 Hana Hwy., Unit A, Paia* ☎ *808/579–9009* 🌐 *www.gocyclingmaui.com.*

Maui Mountain Cruisers

BICYCLING | This partially guided bike tour begins at the company's Paia shop, where you'll be outfitted before being shuttled 6,500 feet to the Haleakala National Park entrance. Once there, you're free to "cruise" the approximately 26 miles downhill to your starting point, stopping at the many shops, eateries, and historic sites along the way. Cost is $80. ✉ *381 Baldwin Ave. #C, Paia* ☎ *808/871–6014* 🌐 *www.mauimountaincruisers.com.*

CAMPING

There are three ways to stay overnight at Haleakala: drive-up camping, wilderness tents, and backcountry cabins. The easiest options are the Kipahulu and Hosmer Grove campgrounds; tent camping at Holua and Paliku and the three highly coveted backcountry cabins at Holua, Kapalaoa, and Paliku require hiking into the crater. Overnight stays in the park are limited to three nights in a 30-day period. Cabin and wilderness campsite reservations can be made at 🌐 *Recreation.gov.*

Hosmer Grove Campground. This drive-up camping spot is located near the entrance to Haleakala's Summit District. No permit is needed, but it's on a first-come, first-served basis. Campers pitch a tent on an open grassy area that sits next to a forest and nature hike. There are picnic tables, BBQ grills, drinking water, and pit toilets. ✉ *Summit District.*

Kipahulu Campground. This drive-up campground sits 12 miles past Hana, and is located next to the Kipahulu Visitor Center. Set in a sprawling field next to the ocean, it includes picnic tables, BBQ grills, and pit toilets. Drinking water and restrooms are available at the visitor center. No permit is needed, and it's on a first come, first served basis. ✉ *Kipahulu District.*

EDUCATIONAL PROGRAMS

A variety of programs are available including cultural demonstrations, informational talks, and ranger-guided walks. Check the website for dates and times.

HIKING

Hikes on Maui include treks along coastal seashore, verdant rain forest, and alpine desert. Orchids, hibiscus, ginger, heliconia, and anthuriums grow wild on many trails, and exotic fruits like mountain apple, *lilikoi* (passion fruit), and strawberry guava provide refreshing snacks for hikers. ■ **TIP→ Hawaii possesses some of the world's rarest plants, insects, and birds. Pocket field guides are available at most grocery or drug stores and can really illuminate your walk.**

★ **Friends of Haleakala National Park**

HIKING/WALKING | This nonprofit offers overnight trips into the volcanic crater. The purpose of your trip, the service work itself, isn't too much—mostly native planting, removing invasive plants, and light cabin maintenance. But participants are asked to check the website to learn more about the trip and certify readiness for service work. A knowledgeable guide accompanies each trip, taking you to places you'd otherwise miss and teaching you about the native flora and fauna. ☎ *808/876–1673* 🌐 *www.fhnp.org.*

★ **Hike Maui**

HIKING/WALKING | Started in 1983, the area's oldest hiking company remains extremely well regarded for its hikes led by enthusiastic, highly trained guides who weave botany, geology, ethnobotany, culture, and history into the outdoor experience. The seven-hour Haleakala tour ($199) includes two hikes, each revealing vastly different environments that make up this national park. The 11-hour Hana excursion ($219) takes you to the park's remote eastern edge, where you'll explore a bamboo forest that leads to a stunning 400-foot waterfall, among other stops. Hike Maui supplies day packs, rain gear, mosquito repellent, first-aid supplies, bottled water, snacks, lunch, and transportation to and from the site. ✉ *Kahului* ☎ *808/784–7982* 🌐 *www.hikemaui.com.*

Holo Holo Maui Tours

HIKING/WALKING | Run by a Native Hawaiian family, these private excursions highlight the cultural significance of Maui's most beloved sights. The five-hour Haleakala tour ($189, plus park admission) begins near sea level and traverses varied landscapes and microclimates until arriving at the crater. Short hikes and scenic stops are included, and guides cater to the pace and interests of each group. Tours run mornings and afternoons, and water and snacks are provided. ✉ *Hwy. 380, Kahului* ⊕ *South of S. Puunene Ave.* ☎ *808/298–5562* 🌐 *www.holoholomauitours.com.*

Kipahulu 'Ohana

HIKING/WALKING | Native Hawaiian guides from this nonprofit organization lead cultural interpretive hikes and taro patch tours at Kipahulu near Hana through a cooperative agreement with Haleakala National Park. The two-hour hike ($49) takes you to scenic overlooks and past remnants from the sugar-cane industry, culminating at an ancient taro farm that has been restored to active production. A three-hour hike ($79) includes a side trip to 400-foot Waimoku Falls. You can park at Kipahulu Visitor Center ($30 per car) and meet your guide at the Hale Kuai, the traditional thatched house near the center. ✉ *Hana* ☎ *808/248–8558* 🌐 *www.kipahulu.org.*

Sierra Club

HIKING/WALKING | One great avenue into the island's untrammeled wilderness is Maui's chapter of the Sierra Club. Join one of the club's hikes into pristine forests, along ancient coastal paths, to historic sites, and to Haleakala Crater. Some outings require volunteer service, but most are just for fun. Bring your own food and water, rain gear, sunscreen, sturdy shoes, and a suggested donation of $5 for hikers over age 14 ($3 for Sierra Club members). This is a true bargain. 🌐 *www.mauisierraclub.org.*

SCENIC FLIGHTS

Helicopter flight-seeing excursions can take you over the West Maui Mountains, Haleakala Crater, or the island of Molokai. This is a beautiful, thrilling way to see the island, and the *only* way to see some of its most dramatic areas and waterfalls. Tour prices usually include a digital video of your trip so you can relive the experience at home. Prices run from about $210 for a half-hour flight to more than $350 for a 75-minute tour with an ocean or cliffside landing. Discounts may be available online or, if you're willing to chance it, by calling at the last minute.

Tour operators come under sharp scrutiny for passenger safety and equipment maintenance. Don't be shy; ask about a company's safety record, flight paths, age of equipment, and level of operator experience. Generally, though, if it's still in business, it's doing something right.

Air Maui Helicopters

TOUR—SPORTS | Priding itself on a perfect safety record, Air Maui provides 45-minute flights covering Haleakala Crater and Hana ($229). A deluxe package ($268) includes a cliffside landing. Discounts are available online. Charter flights are also available. ✉ *1 Kahului Airport Rd., Hangar 110, Kahului* ☎ *877/238–4942, 808/877–7005* 🌐 *www.airmaui.com.*

Blue Hawaiian Helicopters

TOUR—SPORTS | Since 1985, this company has provided aerial adventures in Hawaii and has been integral in some of the filming Hollywood has done on Maui. Complete island tours start at 65 minutes and include views of lush valleys, waterfalls, rain forests and Haleakala crater ($399), with a bonus option to land at a remote location along the Haleakala slopes. Its A-Star and Eco-Star helicopters are air-conditioned and have Bose noise-blocking headsets for all passengers. Charter flights are also available. ✉ *1 Lelepio Pl., Hangar 105, Kahului* ☎ *808/871–8844, 800/745–2583* 🌐 *www.bluehawaiian.com.*

Sunshine Helicopters

TOUR—SPORTS | The 45-minute Hana–Haleakala tour ($234) soars past Haleakala National Park, revealing its many faces, including the arid moonlike crater and lush eastern edge dripping with waterfalls and rain forests. First-class seating is available for an additional fee. Charter flights can be arranged. A pilot-narrated digital record of your actual flight is available for purchase. ✉ *Kahului Airport Rd. , Hangar 107, Kahului* ☎ *808/270–3999, 866/501–7738* 🌐 *www.sunshinehelicopters.com.*

ZIPLINES

Skyline Eco Adventures

ZIP LINING | The first company to open a zipline course in the United States, Skyline has expanded to offer Haleakala Sunrise tours ($160) that are followed by breakfast at picturesque Kula Lodge. The Haleakala Sunrise & Zip Tour ($230) adds on a ziplining adventure that leads you across an Indiana Jones-style swinging bridge. Tours include hotel pick-up/drop-off. ✉ *Kula* ☎ *808/878–8037* 🌐 *www.skylinehawaii.com.*

What's Nearby

On the broad shoulder of Haleakala is the bucolic town of **Kula.** From this lofty vantage, Central Maui unfolds before you as a blend of farmland and modern civilization bookended by the island's northern and southern shores. While Kula is beloved by locals for its cool weather and country vistas, it remains somewhat off-the-beaten path for visitors seeking golden shores and salty seas. As the gateway to Haleakala National Park, the town sees its share of rental vehicles and tour vans, but mostly as they whiz through headed for higher ground. Accommodation options are mostly limited to **Kula Lodge** and B&Bs, so most visitors stay elsewhere on the island and make a day trip to Haleakala. Dining options are limited, but there are a handful of superb options including **Kula Bistro** and **Kula Lodge.** As you're headed to Haleakala, another great option is the **Kulamalu Food Trucks** (technically in the town of Pukalani), where you'll find everything from Thai food to pizza, burgers to barbecue.

Many visitors experience the Kipahulu District as a day trip, as accommodation and dining options here are virtually nonexistent. Unless you're camping at the park itself, those who remain in the area overnight will likely stay in **Hana,** a sleepy rural town in its own right. Luxurious **Hana-Maui Resort** is the sole hotel, and there are plenty of vacation rentals and B&Bs. There are a few restaurants in town, although your best bet is to stop at one of the roadside eateries or food trucks. **Thai Food By Pranee** and **Chow Wagon** are favorites among locals and visitors, and Hana Farms dishes up satisfying wood-fired pizzas.

Chapter 33

HAWAII VOLCANOES NATIONAL PARK

Updated by
Karen Anderson

Camping ★★★☆☆

Hotels ★★★★☆

Activities ★★★★★

Scenery ★★★★★

Crowds ★★★☆☆

WELCOME TO HAWAII VOLCANOES NATIONAL PARK

TOP REASONS TO GO

★ **Lava viewing:** There is the potential to witness molten lava from an active volcano.

★ **Scenic hiking:** Easy-to-moderate trails unveil rainforests, steam vents, lava tubes, craters, and calderas.

★ **Driving adventures:** From the summit to the sea, Chain of Craters Road descends past intriguing geological features and remote terrain.

★ **Rare ecosystems:** The park teems with native birds, nene geese, and threatened and/or endangered flora and fauna.

★ **Historic accommodations:** Perched above the Summit Caldera, the historic Volcano House hotel features a lobby with enormous picture windows and a wood-burning fireplace.

1 Kilauea Summit Area. The park's star attractions are located at the summit including the Steam Vents; Sulphur Banks; Kilauea Iki Crater; Thurston Lava Tube; Devastation Trail; the Summit Caldera; Halemaumau Crater; Kilauea Visitor Center; Volcano House; and a campground.

2 Greater Park Area. Drive beyond the summit area to such phenomenal sights as a series of pit craters along the 38-mile Chain of Craters Road, the dramatic Mauna Ulu lava flows, the Puu Loa petroglyphs, and thespectacular sites at sea level including the Holei Sea Arch and the Puu Loa petroglyphs. More than 123,000 acres of wilderness provide abundant backcountry destinations at high elevations and along the coast. The park also stretches to the Ka'u Desert, a rugged landscape replete with ancient footprints imprinted in hardened layers of ash from a devastating eruption in 1790.

3 The Kahuku Unit. Located near South Point on the southwest side of the island, the park's newest section unveils a 116,000-acre pastoral landscape on the slopes of Mauna Loa.

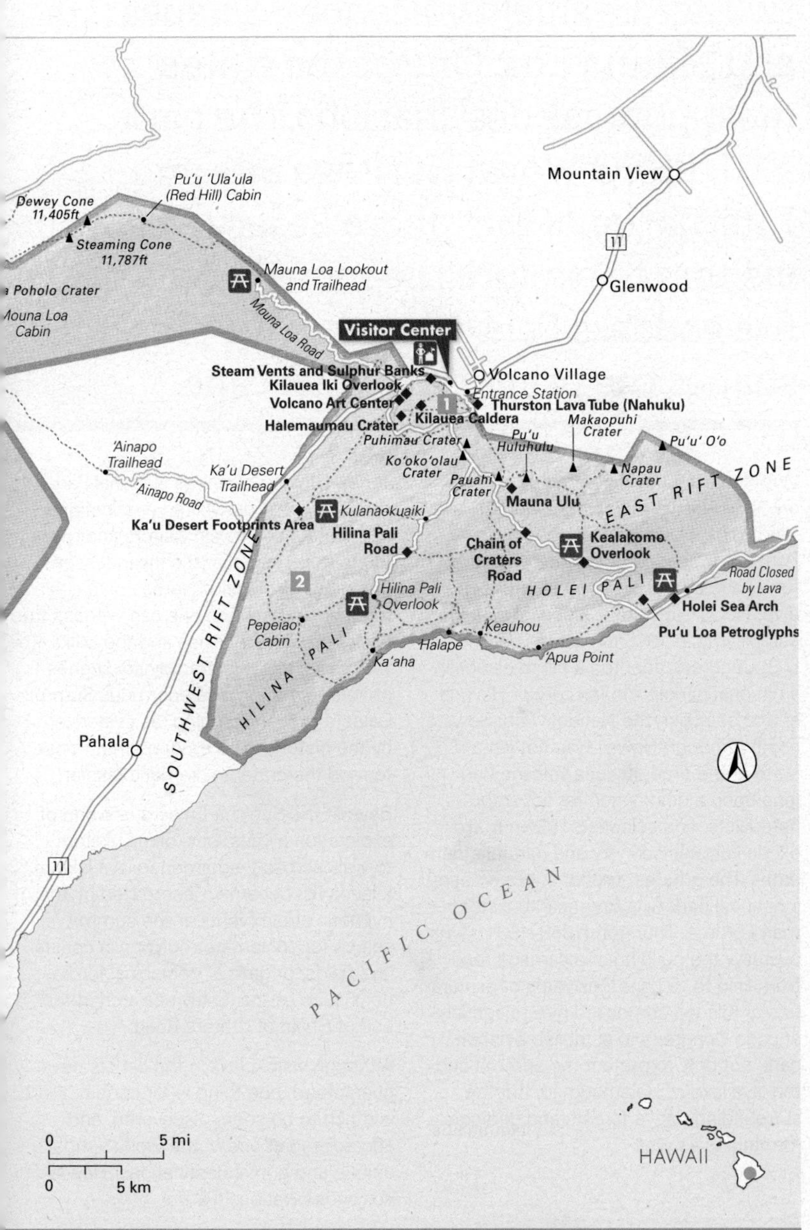
Mountain View
11
Glenwood
Pu'u 'Ula'ula
(Red Hill) Cabin
Dewey Cone
11,405ft
Steaming Cone
11,787ft
Mauna Loa Lookout
and Trailhead
Poholo Crater
Mouna Loa
Cabin
Mouna Loa Road
Visitor Center
Steam Vents and Sulphur Banks
Kilauea Iki Overlook
Volcano Art Center
Halemaumau Crater
Volcano Village
Entrance Station
Thurston Lava Tube (Nahuku)
Kilauea Caldera
Makaopuhi
Crater
Pu'u
Huluhulu
Pu'u' O'o
Puhimau Crater
Ko'oko'olau
Crater
Pauahi
Crater
Napau
Crater
'Ainapo
Trailhead
Ainapo Road
Ka'u Desert
Trailhead
Ka'u Desert Footprints Area
Kulanaokuaiki
Hilina Pali
Road
Mauna Ulu
EAST RIFT ZONE
Chain of
Craters
Road
Kealakomo
Overlook
HOLEI PALI
Road Closed
by Lava
Holei Sea Arch
Pu'u Loa Petroglyphs
Hilina Pali
Overlook
Pepeiao
Cabin
Ka'aha
Halape
Keauhou
'Apua Point
HILINA PALI
SOUTHWEST RIFT ZONE
Pahala
PACIFIC OCEAN
0
5 mi
0
5 km
HAWAII

Hawaii Volcanoes National Park encompasses 333,308 acres across two active shield volcanoes: Kilauea and Mauna Loa. One of the state's most popular destinations, the park, a UNESCO World Heritage Site and International Biosphere Reserve, beckons visitors to explore the sacred home of the fire goddess Pele, whose active presence shapes the primordial landscape.

With forested trails, steaming ground cracks, massive pit craters, and prehistoric vibes, Hawaii Volcanoes National Park is a must-see destination whether for a half-day trek or a weeklong deep dive. Hawaii Volcanoes National Park was established in 1916 the same year the U.S. Congress adopted a bill to establish a national park in the Territory of Hawaii, and to establish the National Park Service itself. Although Hawaii was not yet a state at the time, Kilauea Volcano had long been a destination for adventurers, naturalists, and scientists drawn to the exotic volcanic scenery and natural steam baths. The greatest proponent of creating a national park was American businessman Lorrin A. Thurston (1858–1931), who oversaw the building of a carriage road from Hilo to Volcano. His years of exploration at Kilauea compelled him to actively engage Congress to establish a national park, not only to protect the summit and the lava lake of Halemaumau, but the surrounding native forests and geological formations as well.

Today, Hawaii Volcanoes National Park is one of the most visited destinations in the state of Hawaii. Visitors and residents alike marvel at the incandescent orange glow of Halemaumau on a clear, moonlit nights when one can witness the backdrop of starry skies and the Milky Way rising above extraordinary scenes of Pele's creation. The enormous Summit Caldera is ever changing, as evidenced by the historic 2018 eruption that transformed the crater in dramatic fashion.

Beyond the Summit Caldera, a world of exploration awaits, beckoning visitors to walk across the hardened lava lake of Kilauea Iki, become mesmerized by the hypnotic steam vents at the summit, search for ancient petroglyphs in coastal lava fields, or gaze at geological formations such as the lonely sea arch at the end of Chain of Craters Road.

Although visible lava in the park is never guaranteed, one thing is for certain: there is much to be seen, discovered, and appreciated at one of the world's most unique and primal destinations, Hawaii Volcanoes National Park.

Recent Events at the Summit

The park has recovered from the damaging events of the infamous 2018 Kilauea eruption that rocked the summit caldera for several months and also destroyed residential subdivisions in the distant town of Pahoa. It all began in early May 2018 when the famed lava lake at Halemaumau, which wowed visitors for an entire decade prior, suddenly drained from view after the catastrophic collapse of the Puu Oo Vent in the lower East Rift Zone a week prior. Over the course of the next few months, dramatic changes took place at Halemaumau Crater, which dropped to 1,600 feet deep and more than doubled its size. Damaged beyond repair at the edge of the caldera, the Jaggar Museum and the Hawaii Volcano Observatory are now closed permanently, but most of the park's favorite attractions, however, survived intact including Thurston Lava Tube, Halemaumau Trail, and Kilauea Iki Trail.

The Kilauea eruption came to an end on September 4, 2018, followed by two years of quiet with no visible lava. Just when it seemed there might be a long-term hiatus from live-lava drama at Kilauea, an unexpected eruption took place within Halemaumau Crater beginning on December 20, 2020. Cascading from vents inside the crater, lava vaporized an enormous lake of water that had formed the year prior. Within a month, a new lava lake had risen 700 feet high and counting. The nighttime glow returned to the summit, but it's unknown whether the crater will continue to erupt long term or whether this latest eruption will be short-lived. Even when there is no visible lava, Hawaii Volcanoes National Park provides abundant diversions and a plethora of dramatic sights for hikers, cyclists, bird-watchers, campers and picnickers.

Planning

When to Go

Any time of year is an ideal time to visit Hawaii Volcanoes National Park, where mild temperatures are the norm and sunny skies compete with clouds, rain and mist on any given day. If there is active eruption going on inside Halemaumau Crater, crowds flock to witness Pele's fiery glow at night when the glow is most prominent and transforms the night sky. The Kilauea Visitor Center and the park's official website provide tips on where to park, including overflow parking if necessary. Kilauea's summit is located at the 4,000-foot elevation, with temperatures at the summit averaging 12- to 15-degrees cooler than at sea level. Wet weather is always a possibility, so bring a light hooded rain jacket, long pants, and an umbrella, in addition to bringing a pair shorts for potential hot weather. At the volcano, you never know when a surprise rain shower, blazing sun, or wet windy conditions might take place throughout the day.

FESTIVALS AND EVENTS

Held in July, **The Hawaii Volcanoes National Park Cultural Festival** has been an annual event for more than 40 years. Highlights include ranger-led tours, workshops with cultural practitioners, Hawaiian crafts, musical performers, hula halau, and storytelling. Hands-on demonstrations perpetuate Hawaiian traditions such as poi pounding or tapa-cloth making.

AVERAGE HIGH/LOW TEMPERATURES					
JAN.	**FEB.**	**MAR.**	**APR.**	**MAY**	**JUNE**
68/49	67/49	67/50	68/51	68/51	71/54
JULY	**AUG.**	**SEPT.**	**OCT.**	**NOV.**	**DEC.**
72/55	73/55	73/55	73/55	70/53	68/51

A two-day festival in July, **Experience Volcano Festival** celebrates arts, food, culture, and activities in the town of Volcano Village just outside the park.

Every August, **the Kilauea Cultural Festival and BioBlitz** takes place over a two-day period in the park with hula performances, live music, and cultural demonstrations. Informational kiosks highlight environmental and science-related topics. The BioBliz invites volunteers, students, and visitors to identify and tally plant, insect, and animal species in the park.

After Dark in the Park happens on select Tuesday evenings at Kilauea Visitor Center auditorium, with presentations by scientists, artists, and experts on Hawaiian cultural topics.

Getting Here and Around

AIR

If your primary goal for visiting the Big Island is to visit Hawaii Volcanoes National Park, then fly into Hilo International Airport (ITO) if you can as it's only about 45 minutes to the Park Headquarters at Kilauea Visitor Center. It's a long drive from Kona International Airport (KOA; about 2½ hours) to Volcano.

CAR

You'll need a car to adequately explore the park, but there's no need to rent a four-wheel drive. There are two main roads inside the park: Crater Rim Drive, which is at the summit, and Chain of Craters Road, which leads all the way down to the coast. It's easy to plan a driving itinerary within the park's boundaries.

Speed limits in the park are enforced for a reason. Not only is the region highly visited, the park strives to maintain visitor safety for all, as well as provide protection for the endangered Hawaiian nene goose that roam the area.

Inspiration

While serving as a correspondent for a prominent Sacramento newspaper in 1866, the famed author visited Kilauea almost 50 years before the national park was established. His dispatches, compiled as *Mark Twain in Hawaii: Roughing It in the Sandwich Islands,* features compelling accounts of the erupting Kilauea Volcano and its boiling cauldron of lava. Twain stayed at Volcano House, which at the time was perched on the caldera rim at a different spot than it is today. He wrote: "The surprise of finding a good hotel in such an outlandish spot startled me considerably more than the volcano did."

Published in 1875, *Six Months in the Sandwich Islands,* a legendary travelogue by British explorer Isabella Bird, recounts her dangerous trek across the Kilauea caldera to reach the edge of the molten Halemaumau Crater. Traveling by horseback, Bird also completed an expedition of the active Mauna Loa volcano in addition to other Big Island journeys.

The late Big Island artist Herb Kawainui Kane is known for his iconic paintings of early Hawaii and the myths and legends surrounding the fire goddess Pele. Kane's popular book, *Pele: Goddess of Hawaii's Volcanoes,* is illustrated with reproductions of his color paintings.

Park Essentials

ACCESSIBILITY

Wheelchair-accessible facilities at the park include Kilauea Visitor Center, Volcano House, and Volcano Art Center, as well as the restrooms at the Kipukapuaulu picnic grounds, Mauna Ulu trailhead, Kilauea Iki parking lot, and the end of Chain of Craters Road. Most of the Sulphur Banks trail can be traversed by wheelchair providing you begin at the Steam Vents parking lot. It's also possible for wheelchairs to cross the short gravel path leading from the Steam Vents parking lot to the Steaming Bluff overlook above the Kilauea Caldera. Kilauea Visitor Center offers a limited number of wheelchairs for use. American Sign Language interpretative services should be booked at least two weeks in advance.

PARK FEES AND PERMITS

Valid for 7 days, entrance passes are $30 per private vehicle (15 passengers or less); $25 per motorcycle; and $15 for walk-ins and cyclists. A good deal for frequent park visitors, the annual Tri-Park pass is $55 and provides entry to three parks: Hawaii Volcanoes National Park; Puuhonua o Honaunau National Historical Park (in South Kona); and Haleakala National Park (on Maui). Free admission is given to active-duty military, veterans, and Gold Star Families. Lifetime passes are available to seniors 62 and older for $80. Credit cards are preferred payment method at the manned entrance station. Park entrance fees are waived on select holidays. The primary campground in the park costs $15 per night. Camping fees in the backcountry cost $10 per trip. For a $150 application fee, special permits can be obtained for small private weddings; $25 for scattering of ashes.

PARK HOURS

The park is open 24 hours a day, 7 days a week including on holidays. Kilauea Visitor Center is open daily from 10 am to 5 pm. The Kahuku Unit is generally open from 9 am to 4 pm Wednesday through Sunday, although these days and times can be subject to change depending on staffing availability.

CELL PHONE RECEPTION

For the most part, cell reception is good throughout the park with the exception of some remote areas in the backcountry. Depending on your carrier, coverage could be spotty near Mauna Ulu on Chain of Craters Road, and at sea level.

Hotels

If you visit Hawaii Volcanoes National Park, plan to spend at least one night in Volcano Village. This allows you time to explore additional hiking trails and park attractions, as well as to see the village with its art galleries, cafés, restaurants, and shops. There are plenty of places to stay in Volcano Village, and many are both charming and reasonably priced. The park has one hotel, the famous Volcano House. (Kilauea Military Camp inside the park offers lodging in 90 vintage cottages only for military members/veterans and their families.) Volcano Village has just enough dining and art destinations to satisfy you for a day or two.

Restaurants

Inside the park, a restaurant and lounge (The Rim) inside Volcano House serves breakfast, lunch, and dinner overlooking the summit from the rim of Kilauea Caldera. There are also casual public eateries at Kilauea Military Camp within the park. You'll find a handful of dining options, several general stores, and a gas station in Volcano Village. If you can't find what you're looking for, Hilo is about a 35-minute drive away, and the Keaau grocery store and fast-food joints are 25 minutes away.

Safety

When visiting Hawaii Volcanoes National Park, don't venture off marked trails or into closed areas, and don't get too close to open steam vents, ground cracks, or steep cliffsides. Many hikes in the park are on rugged, open lava fields where winds, rain, and searing sun can happen at a moment's notice. Wear plenty of sunscreen and a hat or hooded, light jacket and close-toed shoes; always carry plenty of water with you. Volcanic fumes can be hazardous. Heed any air-quality warnings that are posted at the Kilauea Visitor Center and throughout the park. Down along the coast, strong winds, and high surf are possible.

Tours

★ Friends of Hawaii Volcanoes National Park

GUIDED TOURS | The park's official philanthropic organization, this nonprofit group offers fantastic, private tours of Hawaii Volcanoes National Park led by renowned geologists, volcanologists, retired rangers, biologists, botanists, or nature photographers. Visitors have the chance to get connected with the park on a deeper level and hone in on specific topics like biology, botany, culture, landscape photography, birding, and more. These four-, six-, or eight-hour customized excursions are priced at flat rates for one- to six people. Multiday treks are also available. Proceeds support projects and programs at Hawaii Volcanoes National Park. ✉ *Volcano* ☎ *808/985–7373* 🌐 *www.fhvnp.org.*

Hawaii Forest & Trails

ADVENTURE TOURS | **FAMILY** | Tour packages showcase both popular and off-the-beaten-path destinations in the park. For the "Volcano Unveiled" tour, an expert certified guide leads 2–3 miles of moderate hikes showcasing the natural, geological, and cultural resources of the park. Snacks, beverages, and deli-style lunch are included. Available gear includes walking sticks, flashlights, and rain ponchos. Pickup locations are based in the Waikoloa Beach Resort area. ✉ *735–593 Olowalu St., Suite #A, Kailua-Kona* ☎ *808/331–8505* 🌐 *www.hawaii-forest.com.*

KapohoKine Adventures

ADVENTURE TOURS | **FAMILY** | Departing from Hilo, this outfitter's "Hilo, Hawaii Volcano Hike" starts with a journey to the Puna Coast, site of the historic 2018 eruption that decimated parts of the area. Visitors can check out recent lava flows that have dramatically altered the coastline near a newly formed black sand beach. Lunch is served at Isaac Hale Beach Park, which was miraculously spared by the 2018 flows. Next stop is Hawaii Volcanoes National Park for a hike along the Kilauea Iki Overlook trail and to other sites at the summit before descending into the outer floor of the Kileaua Caldera via the Halemaumau Trail. This outfitter also offers volcano tours that depart from Kailua-Kona and Kohala. ✉ *Grand Naniloa DoubleTree by Hilton, 93 Banyan Dr., Hilo* ☎ *808/964–1000* 🌐 *www.kapohokine.com.*

Ranger-Led Guided Hikes

WALKING TOURS | **FAMILY** | Park rangers at Kilauea Visitor Center lead at least one or two free guided hikes per day limited to approximately 20 people each. The 90-minute Sulphur Banks and Steam Vents tour is an easy 1.5-mile round-trip stroll from the visitor center, while the "Explore the Summit" tour offers a 45-minute walk to sights near Volcano House. Other specific tours are featured depending on the availability of rangers. "A Walk into the Past," a living-history tour led by a volunteer dressed in period costume, takes visitors to an underground lab with equipment used by Thomas A. Jaggar, founder of Hawaii Volcanoes Observatory in 1912. ✉ *1 Crater Rim Dr.* ☎ *808/985–6011* 🌐 *www.nps.gov/havo.*

Visitor Information

Home base for the park's rangers, Kilauea Visitor Center offers informational displays, trail guides, maps, and ranger-led talks. The park's official government website presents comprehensive resources about destinations at the park, while the park's social media accounts on Twitter and Facebook also keep followers informed about the latest happenings.

The official monitoring organization for all of Hawaii's volcanoes, Hawaii Volcano Observatory (HVO) provides a wealth of educational information about Kilauea and Mauna Loa. Its weekly "Volcano Watch" articles keep readers informed of anything and everything related to Big Island volcanoes. Check out the website for real-time webcams, informative videos, image galleries, up-to-the-minute monitoring data, and an extensive database of academic publications, geologic maps, fact sheets, journal articles, books, and more.

CONTACTS Hawaii Volcanoes National Park. ☎ *808/985–6011* 🌐 *www.nps.gov/havo.* **Hawaii Volcano Observatory Website.** 🌐 *www.usgs.gov/observatories/hawaiian-volcano-observatory.*

Kilauea Summit Area

30 miles southwest of Hilo, 96 miles southeast of Kailua-Kona

In the heart of Hawaii Volcanoes National Park, a primeval landscape unfolds at the summit of Kilauea Volcano, where steam rises continuously from cracks in the earth and volcanic gases create malodorous sulfur banks. Here, Halemaumau Crater has doubled in diameter from the seismic events of the 2018 Kilauea eruption. In addition to the many geological sights, the summit area of the park includes Kilauea Visitor Center, Volcano Art Center Gallery, and Volcano House, a landmark hotel perched above the rim of the massive Kilauea Caldera. This is a good area to begin your visit to the park.

Sights

GEOLOGICAL FORMATIONS

Kilauea Caldera

NATURE SITE | Measuring 7.8 miles in circumference with walls up to 400 feet, the massive Kilauea Caldera contains within it Halemaumau Crater, a large pit crater that has been erupting off and on for centuries. At one time encircling the entire caldera prior to the 2008 eruption when a portion of the road was cut off, Crater Rim Drive offers many scenic lookouts for viewing the caldera and Halemaumau Crater. Visitors can also hike down into the edge of the caldera via Halemaumau Trail or Byron Ledge Trail. ✉ *Crater Rim Dr.* ☎ *808/985–6011* 🌐 *www.nps.gov/havo.*

Kilauea Iki Crater

NATURE SITE | Whether you hike across the floor of this massive pit crater or take in the views from above, Kilauea Iki Crater is one of the park's star attractions you won't want to miss. Measuring a mile across and 400 feet deep, Kilauea Iki Crater is located adjacent to the main summit caldera. The floor of the crater is actually a hardened lava lake that formed during a dramatic five-week eruption of the crater in 1959. Lava fountains reached 1,900 feet high creating the large cinder cone at one end of the crater and sending fragments of molten lava through the air in a southwesterly direction where Devastation Trail is now. Visitors can view the crater from various lookout points along the rim, or take a switchback trail that descends to the crater floor. ✉ *1 Crater Rim Dr.* ✣ *3.2 miles from the visitor center via Crater Rim Dr.* ☎ *808/985–6011* 🌐 *www.nps.gov/havo.*

To reach the entrance to the Thurston Lava Tube, visitors must climb down a series of stairs surrounded by lush foliage

Thurston Lava Tube (Nahuku)

NATURE SITE | FAMILY | One of the star attractions in the park, the Thurston Lava Tube (named "Nahuku" in Hawaiian) spans 600 feet underground. The massive cavelike tube, discovered in 1913, was formed by hot molten lava traveling through the channel. To reach the entrance of the tube, visitors descend a series of stairs surrounded by lush foliage and the sounds of native birds. The Kilauea eruption of 2018 resulted in an almost two-year closure of the Thurston Lava Tube as engineers surveyed for potential structural damage. Long-term safety monitoring of the cave resulted in an "all clear" from engineers and specialists in March 2020. During the closure, the drainage system was improved to reduce standing water on the cave's floor, and electrical lines were replaced. Visitors should not touch the walls or delicate tree root systems that grow down through the ceiling. **■TIP→ Parking is limited near the tube; if the lot is full, you can park at the Kilauea Iki Overlook parking lot a ½ mile away.** ✉ *Crater Rim Dr.* ✣ *1½ miles from the park entrance* ☎ *808/985–6101* 🌐 *www.nps.gov/havo.*

HISTORIC SIGHTS

Volcano Art Center

ARTS VENUE | Built in 1877 as the Volcano House Hotel, the charming building that now houses Volcano Art Center boasts a fascinating history. Originally situated overlooking Kilauea crater, the inn was built of native ohia wood and other native hardwoods, and it featured a fireplace, porch, and six guest rooms. Through the years as more rooms and wings were added, the original structure was relocated to where it sits today. Its location near active steam vents almost led to its demise before being rescued in 1976. ✉ *1 Crater Rim Dr.* ✣ *Within walking distance of Kilauea Visitor Center* ☎ *808/967–7565* 🌐 *www.volcanoartcenter.org.*

SCENIC STOPS

★ **Halemaumau Crater**

VOLCANO | For native Hawaiians, Halemaumau Crater is the sacred home of Pele, the fire goddess; for scientists at the Hawaiian Volcano Observatory, this mighty pit crater within the massive Kilauea Caldera is an ever-changing force to be reckoned with. Prior to Kilauea's 2018 eruption, Halemaumau's visible lava lake awed visitors for 10 years. Then Puu Oo Vent, which had been erupting in the East Rift Zone for 35 years, collapsed in April 2018. As lava from the distant vent drained away, so did the lava lake at Halemaumau Crater. A relentless series of seismic events at the summit followed, doubling the diameter of Halemaumau Crater and deepening it by 1,300 feet. A year after the eruption ended in August 2018, a lake of water began forming, eventually growing to 160 feet deep. Then on December 20, 2020, an unexpected eruption within the crater instantly vaporized the water lake, sending molten lava cascading into the crater from vents within the walls and commencing the return of an active lava lake to Halemaumau as of February 2021. Although the lookout point at the Jaggar Museum has permanently closed due to earthquake damage, there are many places in the park to view the magnificent crater, including at the Steaming Bluff Overlook and at Volcano House hotel. ✉ *Crater Rim Dr.* ☎ *808/985–6101* 🌐 *www.nps.gov/havo.*

Kilauea Iki Overlook

TRAIL | Gaze across at the massive, mile-long Kilauea Iki Crater from this scenic overlook. Steam still rises from cracks within the crater floor 400 feet below. Across the way is the large cinder cone Puu Puai formed when cinders fell from towering lava fountains in 1959. Kilauea Iki Overlook also leads to the trailhead that descends into the crater. ✉ *Crater Rim Dr.* ✣ *3.2 miles from Kilauea Visitor Center* ☎ *808/985–6011* 🌐 *www.nps.gov/havo.*

Steam Vents and Sulphur Banks

VOLCANO | A short walk from the Kilauea Visitor Center leads to the pungent yet fascinating sulphur banks, where gases composed of hydrogen sulfide produce a smell akin to rotten eggs. Most of the rocks surrounding the vents have been dyed yellow due to constant gas exposure. Throughout the surrounding landscape, dozens of active steam vents emit white, billowing vapors that originate from groundwater heated by volcanic rocks. Located on the caldera's edge, Steaming Bluff is a short walk from a nearby parking area. **■ TIP→ The best steam vents are across the road from the main steam vent parking area; they vary in size and are scattered alongside the dirt trails.** ✉ *Crater Rim Dr.* ✣ *Within walking distance of Kilauea Visitor Center* ☎ *808/985–6101* 🌐 *www.nps.gov/havo.*

TRAILS

Devastation Trail

TRAIL | A paved pathway takes visitors across a barren lavascape strewn with chunky cinders that descended from towering lava fountains during the 1959 eruption of nearby Kilauea Iki Crater. The easy 1-mile (round-trip) hike ends at the edge of the Kilauea Iki Crater. This must-see view of the crater could yield such memorable sights as white-tailed tropic birds gliding in the breeze or a rainbow stretching above the crater's rim after a sunlit rain shower. *Easy.* ✉ *Hawaii Volcanoes National Park* ✣ *Trailhead: 4 miles from visitor center at intersection of Crater Rim Dr. and Chain of Craters Rd.* ☎ *808/985–6101* 🌐 *www.nps.gov/havo.*

Halemaumau Trail

TRAIL | This extraordinary trail, accessed just behind Volcano House, descends 425 feet down to the floor of the mighty Kilauea Caldera, passing by forested terrain and giant boulders. Since 1846, guests of Volcano House have used this historic 1.8-mile trail to hike into the Summit Caldera. From this vantage at the caldera's perimeter, one can see Halemaumau Crater in the distance. Add another mile to your journey and connect with Byron Ledge and Kilauea Iki trails leading back up to the Kilauea Iki Overlook. *Moderate.* ✉ *Crater Rim Dr.* ✣ *Trailhead: Just behind Volcano House* ☎ *808/985–6011* 🌐 *www.nps.gov/havo.*

★ Kilauea Iki Trail

TRAIL | The stunning 4-mile loop hike descends 400 feet into a massive crater via a forested nature trail. When you hike across the crater floor, you're actually walking on a solidified lava lake. Still steaming in places, the crater is dotted with baby ohia trees emerging from the cracks. Venture across the crater floor to the Puu Puai cinder cone that was formed by spatter from a towering lava fountain during the 1959 Kilauea Iki eruption. There are three different trailheads for Kilauea Iki; the main one, which takes two- or three hours, begins at the Kilauea Iki Overlook parking lot off Crater Rim Drive. You can also access the crater from Devastation Trail or Puu Puai on the other side. ■ **TIP→ Bring water, snacks, a hat, sunscreen, and hooded rain gear, as weather can change at a moment's notice.** *Easy.* ✉ *Crater Rim Dr.* ✥ *Trailhead: 3 miles from visitor center* ☎ *808/985–6011* 🌐 *www.nps.gov/havo.*

VISITOR CENTER

Kilauea Visitor Center

INFO CENTER | Rangers and volunteers greet people and answer all questions at this visitor center, located just beyond the park entrance. There are lots of educational murals and displays, maps, and guidebooks. Also check out the daily itinerary of ranger-led activities and plan to sign up for some. The gift shop operated by the Hawaii Pacific Park Association stocks plenty of excellent art, books, apparel, and more. A small theater plays documentaries about the park. ✉ *1 Crater Rim Dr.* ☎ *808/985–6011* 🌐 *www.nps.gov/havo.*

Restaurants

The Rim at Volcano House

$$ | **HAWAIIAN** | **FAMILY** | This fine-dining restaurant overlooks the rim of Kilauea Caldera and the expansive Halemaumau Crater. Featuring two bars (one of which is adjacent to a lounge) and live entertainment nightly, the restaurant highlights island-inspired cuisine and locally sourced ingredients. **Known for:** views of Halemaumau Crater; Hilo coffee–rubbed rack of lamb; well-priced Taste of Hawaii lunch special. [$] *Average main: $25* ✉ *Volcano House, 1 Crater Rim Dr.* ☎ *808/756–9625* 🌐 *www.hawaiivolcanohouse.com.*

Coffee and Quick Bites

Before you enter the park for your day of exploration, you can stop in Volcano Village (just one mile from park entrance) and get breakfast and coffee at the Lava Rock Cafe. Next door is a general store where you can also pick up snacks and coffee to go. Inside the park, Volcano House serves hot coffee in the lobby, and also offers breakfast items at the Rim Restaurant and in Uncle George's Lounge. Also located inside the park, Kilauea Military Camp (KMC) has a casual diner inside a bowling alley. KMC's Lava Lounge is the go-to place for cocktails and dinner in the evenings. KMC also has a general store stocked with snacks and beverages.

Hotels

★ Volcano House

$$ | **HOTEL** | Hawaii's oldest hotel—and the only one in Hawaii Volcanoes National Park—is committed to sustainable practices and promoting local Hawaiian culture and history through its locally sourced restaurants, artisan-crafted decor, and eco-focused guest programs. **Pros:** unbeatable location; views of crater; sense of place and history. **Cons:** basic facilities; books up quickly; some rooms have parking lot views. [$] *Rooms from: $220* ✉ *1 Crater Rim Dr.* ☎ *808/756–9625* 🌐 *www.hawaiivolcanohouse.com* *33 rooms* *No meals.*

Nightlife

After Dark in the Park

On selected Tuesdays beginning at 7 pm, the After Dark in the Park program presents educational talks by scientists, artists, rangers, or cultural experts. Co-sponsored by Friends of Hawaii Volcanoes National Park, the free presentations take place in the auditorium at Kilauea Visitor Center. ✉ *Kilauea Visitor Center, 1 Crater Rim Dr.* ☎ *808/985–6011* 🌐 *www.nps.gov/havo.*

Shopping

Volcano House presents two gift shops filled with interesting trinkets, souvenirs, apparel, art, crafts, books, and even cold-weather jackets. Inside Kilauea Visitor Center, books, trail guides and merchandise are sold in a small gift shop operated by Hawaii Pacific Parks Association. In addition to lodging (for military families only) and some recreational activities, Kilauea Military Camp has a general store and a gas station, making it the best place in the park to stop if you need supplies.

Kilauea Military Camp

COMMERCIAL CENTER | FAMILY | Located inside the park, Kilauea Military Camp, established in 1916, offers visitor accommodations to members of the military and their families but also has places open to the public, including an arcade, bowling alley, diner, buffet, general store, and gas station. In addition, the Lava Lounge cocktail bar features live music on weekends. ✉ *99-252 Crater Rim Dr.* ☎ *808/967–8333* 🌐 *www.kilaueamilitary-camp.com.*

Volcano Art Center Gallery

MUSEUM | Occupying a portion of the original Volcano House hotel built in 1877, this mesmerizing art gallery, within walking distance of the hotel across the way, has showcased works by local artists since 1974. From stained and hand-blown glass to wood crafts, paintings, sculptures, original block prints, jewelry, photographs, and more, the gallery features fine art (for sale) that depicts indigenous and cultural themes of Hawaii Island. In addition, live hula shows in the ancient style are often featured on the lawn that fronts the gallery. ✉ *Crater Rim Dr.* ✥ *Within walking distance of Kilauea Visitor Center* ☎ *808/967–8222* 🌐 *www.volcanoartcenter.org.*

Volcano House Gift Shop

STORE/MALL | More than a gift store with souvenirs, this impressive retail shop in the lobby of Volcano House also features native arts, pottery, crafts, original paintings, jewelry, and framed photographs by local artisans. ✉ *Volcano House, 1 Crater Rim Dr.* ☎ *808/756–9625* 🌐 *www.volcanohouse.com.*

Greater Park Area

22 miles from Kilauea Visitor Center to sea level; 23.7 miles to Pahala side of the park from Kilauea Visitor Center; 42 miles to Kahuku Unit from Kilauea Visitor Center; 11 miles to Mauna Loa Lookout from Hwy. 11; 31.1 miles to summit of Mauna Loa (no road beyond lookout)

Spanning landscapes from sea level to the summits of two of the most active volcanoes in the world, Hawaii Volcanoes National Park boasts a diverse landscape with rain forests, rugged coastlines, surreal lava fields, and sacred cultural sites. There's also a sense of peace and tranquility here, despite the upheavals of nature. A drive down Chain of Craters Road toward the ocean allows you to access the greater area of the park, affording opportunities for exploration beyond the summit destinations. Along the way are birding trails, backcountry hikes, two campgrounds, pit craters, and a dramatic sea arch at the coast.

GEOLOGICAL FORMATIONS

Ka'u Desert Footprints Area

ARCHAEOLOGICAL SITE | Explosive events at the summit between 1500 and 1790 sent pyroclastic "hurricanes" of volcanic ash for miles across the Ka'u Desert. In addition to the many ancient footprints preserved in the hardened ash, there are 246 cultural features in the Footprints area including habitation sites, dry-stack shelters, and basalt quarries. It's a short 20-minute walk from the trailhead to the Footprints pavilion. ✉ *Hawaii Volcanoes National Park* ✥ *Take Hwy. 11 toward Kona 8 miles from the park entrance* ☎ *808/985–6011* ⊕ *www.nps.gov/havo.*

Mauna Loa

VOLCANO | Kilauea may get all the headlines, but Mauna Loa is the largest active volcano on the planet and potentially more devastating when it erupts again. Rising 13,681 feet above sea level, Mauna Loa encompasses more than half of the entire Big Island. Its long submarine flanks descend 3 miles to the sea floor, and its sheer weight depresses the mountain into the sea floor by an additional 26,200 feet making Mauna Loa's true height 55,700 feet from base to summit. Mauna Loa has erupted 33 times since 1843; the most recent eruption happened in 1984 and came within 11 miles of Hilo Bay. It's not a question of if, but when, Mauna Loa will erupt again. ✉ *Hawaii Volcanoes National Park.*

Mauna Ulu

NATURE SITE | The vast lava fields of Mauna Ulu showcase a wealth of geological sights all in one area. Formed during the 1969–75 eruption of Mauna Ulu, the surreal landscape includes everything from lava-tree molds, spatter ramparts, and a tephra (material ejected from a volcano eruption) field, to a perched lava pond, and actual fissures (cracks) from where eruptions poured forth. It's a ¼-mile steep climb up Puu Huluhulu, a forested cinder cone that survived the vast lava flows that surround it. The top of the hill reveals views of Mauna Ulu's steaming shield, and in the distance, views of the inactive Puu Oo vent, Mauna Loa, Mauna Kea, and the ocean. ✉ *Hawaii Volcanoes National Park* ✥ *Take Chain of Craters Rd. 7.4 miles from Kilauea Visitor Center* ☎ *808/985–6011* ⊕ *www.nps.gov/havo.*

Pu'u Lea Petroglyphs and Holei Sea Arch

ARCHAEOLOGICAL SITE | A traditional Hawaiian trail through a coastal lava field leads to ancient images etched in stone. A boardwalk helps protect clusters of petroglyphs from direct foot traffic. After visiting the petroglyphs, drive a few miles to the end of Chain of Craters Road to the Holei Sea Arch. Ninety feet high and sculpted by the ocean, this interesting lava-rock formation extends from beyond the sea cliffs as though it were part of a Medieval castle. The viewing area from which to gaze at arch is located a short distance from the end of Chain of Craters Road. ✉ *Hawaii Volcanoes National Park* ✥ *Viewing station is 1000 feet past the gate at the end of Chain of Craters Rd.* ☎ *808/985–6011.*

Puu o Lokuana Cinder Cone

TRAIL | A short 0.4-mile loop hike takes visitors to the top of a hill featuring outstanding views of lower Ka'u. This cinder cone was formed by the relentless downpour of cinder from erupting lava fountains. On the way to the top there are remnants of a historic cinder quarry that reveal the actual crimson color of the cinder. During WWII, Puu o Lokuana was the site for a secret radar station. ✉ *Hawaii Volcanoes National Park* ☎ *808/985–6011* ⊕ *www.nps.gov/havo.*

SCENIC DRIVES

★ Chain of Craters Road

SCENIC DRIVE | The coastal region of Hawaii Volcanoes National Park is accessed via scenic Chain of Craters Road, which descends 18.8 miles to sea level. You could drive it without stopping, but it's well worth spending a few hours or a day exploring the various stops and trails. Winding past ancient craters and modern eruption sites, this scenic road was realigned in 1979 after parts of it were buried by the Mauna Ulu eruption.

Marked stops along the way include Lua Manu Crater, Hilina Pali Road, Pauahi Crater, the Mauna Ulu eruption site, Kealakomo Lookout, and Puu Loa Petroglyphs. As you approach the coast, panoramic ocean vistas prevail. The last marked stop features views of the striking natural Holei Sea Arch from an overlook. In recent years, many former sights along the coast have been covered in lava, including a black-sand beach and the old campground. ✉ *Hawaii Volcanoes National Park* ☎ *808/985–6101* 🌐 *www.nps.gov/havo.*

Hilina Pali Road

VIEWPOINT | This obscure 9-mile road doesn't offer the spectacular scenery of the park's two main roads, but it does take you to the very scenic Hilina Pali Overlook with views of the coast. The one-lane road meanders past native underbrush and ohia trees amid the faultline between Kilauea's east and southwest rift zones. Kulanaokuaiki Campground is located on this road, as is the Maunaiki Trailhead for the start of a 7-mile hike to the "petrified" footprints of the Ka'u Desert. ✉ *1 Crater Rim Dr.* ✣ *2/3 mile from the start of Chain of Craters Rd.* ☎ *808/985–6011* 🌐 *www.nps.gov/havo.*

SCENIC STOPS

Kealakomo Overlook

VIEWPOINT | Further down Chain of Craters Road, 13.2 miles from Kilauea Visitor Center, the Kealakomo Overlook is well worth the stop. Park in the lot and stroll across a ramp to an open wooden deck perched at the 2,000-foot elevation unveiling horizon-to-horizon views. ✉ *Hawaii Volcanoes National Park* ✣ *13.2 miles down Chain of Craters Rd. near the Kealakomo parking lot* ☎ *808/985–6011* 🌐 *www.nps.gov/havo.*

TRAILS

Ka'u Desert Trail

ARCHAEOLOGICAL SITE | **FAMILY** | In 1790, a volcanic explosion at the summit deposited layers of ash throughout a remote region of the park known as the Ka'u Desert. A group of Native Hawaiians traveling through the area left their footprints preserved in the ash, which can still be seen today along the Ka'u Desert Trail. It's an easy 0.8-mile walk to a sheltered informational exhibit about the footprints. Along the trail are informative storyboards about the historic events and archeological discoveries. You can also reach this area via a 7-mile hike from within the park proper along the remote Maunaiki Trail. *Easy.* ✉ *1 Crater Rim Dr.* ✣ *Trailhead: Off Hwy. 11 about a 15-minute drive from the park entrance* ☎ *808/985–6011* 🌐 *www.nps.gov/havo/planyourvisit/footprints.htm.*

Kipukapuaulu (Bird Park) Trail

TRAIL | **FAMILY** | This special ecological area provides a peaceful 1.2-mile loop trail through an oasis of Hawaiian forest. Showcasing a range of biological diversity, the area reveals indigenous and endemic native ferns, trees, herbs, and insect species, as well as hundreds of rare hau kuahiwi trees introduced to the forest in the 1950s to replace the lone surviving tree that died in 1930. Visitors can enjoy a picnic area with rest stop (wheelchair-accessible). *Easy.* ✉ *1 Crater Rim Dr.* ✣ *Trailhead: Approximately 5 miles from the visitor center south on Hwy. 11, and up Mauna Loa Rd. another 1½ miles* ☎ *808/985–6011* 🌐 *www.nps.gov/havo.*

★ Mauna Ulu Trail

TRAIL | The Mauna Ulu lava flow presents an incredible variety of geological attractions within a moderate, 2½-mile round-trip hike. The diverse lava landscape was created during the spectacular 1969–74 Mauna Ulu flow, which featured enormous "lavafalls" the size of Niagara Falls. Visitors can see everything from lava tree molds and fissure vents to cinder cones and portions of the old highway still exposed under the flow. Hawaiian nene geese roam the area, feeding on ripe ohelo berries.

Hike to the top of a small hill that survived the flow for an incredible view of the Puu Oo Vent in the distance. On clear days, you can see Mauna Loa, Maunakea, and the Pacific Ocean from atop this hill, known as Puu Huluhulu. **■TIP→ Purchase the Mauna Ulu trail booklet at the Kilauea Visitor Center for under $3. This excellent resource includes descriptions of trailside attractions, trail maps, history, eyewitness accounts, and photographs.** *Moderate.* ✉ *Chain of Craters Rd.* ✣ *Trailhead: 7 miles from Kilauea Visitor Center* ☎ *808/985–6101* 🌐 *www.nps.gov/havo.*

Kahuku Unit

On Hwy. 11 at the 70½ mile mark 35 miles southwest of Kilauea Visitor Center

Acquired by Hawaii Volcanoes National Park in 2003, the Kahuku Unit occupies historic ranchlands on Mauna Loa's southwest slopes spanning 116,000 acres near South Point. Nearly half the size of the entire park, the Kahuku Unit presents a pastoral landscape of woodland meadows, grassy cinder cones, and tree-lined trails. Visitors can learn about the 1868 eruption of Mauna Loa, which was preceded by a devastating 7.9-magnitude earthquake that caused massive mudslides, landslides, and a tsunami that wiped out coastal villages. Walk across some of these historic flows and see lava-tree molds, fissures, and other geological remnants of the event. Learn about the family who saw first-hand, and survived, what is considered to be the island's greatest volcanic disaster in known history. The Kahuku Unit is generally open five days a week from 9 am to 4 pm, but it's best to call ahead since staffing is limited. Ranger-led hikes are offered and entry is free.

Sights

TRAILS

Kamakapa'a Trail

TRAIL | This ½-mile loop trail traverses a grassy meadow on the way to the top of a small cinder cone. *Easy.* ✉ *Hawaii Volcanoes National Park* ✣ *Trailhead: Kahuku Rd.* ☎ *808/985–6011* 🌐 *www.nps.gov/havo.*

Palm Trail

TRAIL | The longest hike in the unit, the 2.6-mile Palm Trail presents all-encompassing views of Kahuku, as well as access to flows and fissures from the 1868 eruption of Mauna Loa. *Moderate.* ✉ *Hawaii Volcanoes National Park* ✣ *Trailhead: 1.7 miles from the parking lot* ☎ *808/985–6011* 🌐 *www.nps.gov/havo.*

Puu o Lokuana Trail

TRAIL | Shaded by trees, this 2-mile loop trail reveals such sights as lava tree molds created by the fast-flowing eruption of 1868, a portion of which can be seen along the trail. There's also a hidden pasture close by. *Moderate.* ✉ *Hawaii Volcanoes National Park* ✣ *Trailhead: 500 feet from the parking lot* ☎ *808/985–6011* 🌐 *www.nps.gov/havo.*

Activities

BIKING

BikeVolcano.com

BICYCLING | This outfitter leads three- or five-hour bike rides through Hawaii Volcanoes National Park, mostly downhill, that take in fantastic sights from rain forests to craters. The company also coordinates and leads a cool ride to the 2018 eruption site in Puna. Equipment, support van, and food are included; pickup locations are in Hilo and Volcano (and Kona by request). Cruise passengers are welcome. ✉ *Hilo* ☎ *808/934–9199, 808/934–9199* 🌐 *www.bikevolcano.com* 🎟 *From $155.*

CAMPING

If you really want to commune with the natural elements on an active volcano, camping under the stars can offer an unforgettable experience. The park has two drive-in campgrounds and eight primitive backcountry campsites. The main campground, Namakanipaio, offers the most amenities including camper cabins, bathrooms, fire pits and hot showers. Kulanaokuaiki, the park's other main campground, is a bit more primitive but equally memorable.

Namakanipaio Campground. Set amid a fragrant eucalyptus grove, this drive-in campsite has running water, bathrooms, picnic tables, and barbeque pits. Additionally, there are 10 rustic one-room cabins that can sleep four people each. Priced at $85 a night, cabins include bunkbeds, a picnic table, and an outdoor barbecue grill and firepit. The campground is located just 3 miles from the park entrance off Highway 11 and is operated by Volcano House, which handles reservations and payments. Daily camping fee is $15, but if you need to, you can even rent a tent for two for an additional $55 a night complete with air mattress, linens, lantern, chairs, blankets, pillows, and a cooler. ✉ *1 Crater Rim Dr., Hawaii Volcanoes National Park* ☎ *808/756–9625* 🌐 *www.hawaiivolcanohouse.com.*

Kulanaokuaiki Campground. With nine walk-in campsites and picnic tables, this "remote" campground is located off-the-beaten track on Hilina Pali Road 10 miles from the Kilauea Visitor Center. Campfires are not permitted (fueled camping stoves only), and there's no running water, but there is an ADA-accessible vaulted toilet. Reservations aren't required to camp here, but there is a $10 self-pay station at the campground itself. Bring of potable water with you. ✉ *1 Crater Rim Dr., Hawaii Volcanoes National Park* ☎ *808/985–6011* 🌐 *www.nps.gov/havo.*

EDUCATIONAL PROGRAMS

The park's history is inextricably linked with the myths, legends, and rich traditions passed on through generations of Native Hawaiians. Free programs invite visitors to learn about traditional Hawaiian culture and its ancient connection to the Kilauea summit at Hawaii Volcanoes National Park.

Those with a passion for geology will appreciate the plethora of educational resources available online and in the park. A division of United States Geological Survey (USGS), Hawaii Volcano Observatory (HVO) provides vast resources about current conditions, hazards, historical events, and more. Park rangers can answer most any question about the park's geology; printed trail-guide booklets are less than $3 at the Kilauea Visitor Center.

"Ike Hana Noeau" ("Experience the Skillful Work")
CULTURAL FESTIVALS | FAMILY | A volunteer organization in partnership with the park, Hawaii Pacific Parks Association offers special programs where visitors can experience authentic Hawaiian arts and crafts taught by traditional practitioners. Sessions might include anything from lei making or fiber arts to poi pounding or lauhala weaving. If your timing is right, you might even see hula performed in the ancient style on the lawn in front of Volcano Art Center. ✉ *Kilauea Visitor Center, 1 Crater Rim Dr.* ☎ *808/985–6011* 🌐 *www.nps.gov/havo.*

Volcano Art Center Classes and Workshops
ART GALLERIES—ARTS | FAMILY | Children and adults can pursue creative expression at any number of arts and writing classes presented by Big Island artisans and creative types. Workshops feature everything from papermaking and drawing to silk painting and Japanese floral arranging. Some classes may be held at the center's Niaulani Campus in nearby Volcano Village. ✉ *1 Crater Rim Dr.* ✥ *Next to Kilauea Visitor Center* ☎ *808/967–7565* 🌐 *www.volcanoart-center.com.*

HIKING

Perhaps the Big Island's premier area for hikers, the park has more than 155 miles of trails providing close-up, often jaw-dropping views of fern and rain forest environments, cinder cones, craters, steam vents, lava fields, rugged coastline, and current eruption activity. Day hikes range from easy to moderately difficult, and from one or two hours to a full day. For a bigger challenge, consider an overnight or multiday backcountry hike with a stay in a park cabin (available en route to the remote coast, in a lush forest, or atop frigid Mauna Loa). To do so, you must first obtain a permit at the backcountry office in the Visitor Emergency Operations Center. **TIP→ Daily guided hikes are led by knowledgeable, friendly park rangers.** The bulletin boards outside Kilauea Visitor Center have the day's schedule of guided hikes.

Experienced wilderness hikers will find miles of remote destinations in Hawaii Volcanoes National Park, such as a southern shoreline called Halepe, for instance, or the impressive Napau Crater, which is a 6.2-mile journey across lava fields beginning at the Mauna Ulu parking area. There are a total of eight backcountry campsites scattered throughout the far reaches of the park: Kaaha. Halape, Keauhou, Apua Point, Napau, Pepeiao Cabin, Red Hill Cabin, and Mauna Loa Cabin. Camping permits are required in addition to a $10 fee. The Backcountry Office (🌐 *808/985–6178*) provides essential information and safety guidelines for backcountry visitors.

★ KapohoKine Adventures

HIKING/WALKING | **FAMILY** | One of the largest outfitters on the island, locally owned KapohoKine Adventures offers a number of excellent hiking tours that depart from both Hilo and Kona. The epic full-day Elite Volcano Hike hits all the great spots, including now-quiet areas in Puna impacted by the 2018 eruption. Hikers will encounter a 40-foot wall of lava and follow it to the sea and an enormous black-sand beach. Also included are Kalapana, the Kaumana Caves, the Steaming Bluffs, and a tour of Hawaii Volcanoes National Park. The final stop at Volcano Winery features a wine tasting and Hawaiian barbecue dinner. Lunch is also included. ✉ *Grand Naniloa Hotel Hilo, 93 Banyan Dr., Hilo* ☎ *808/964–1000* 🌐 *www.kapohokine.com* 🎫 *From $269.*

SCENIC FLIGHTS

There's nothing quite like the aerial view of a waterfall crashing down a couple of thousand feet into cascading pools, or witnessing the surreal terrain of an active volcano from the air. You can get this bird's-eye view from a helicopter or a fixed-wing small plane. All operators pay strict attention to safety. So how to get the best experience for your money? **TIP→ Before you choose a company, be a savvy traveler and ask the right questions. What kind of aircraft do they fly? What is their safety record?**

Big Island Air Tours

FLYING/SKYDIVING/SOARING | This small charter company, in business since the 1980s, offers fixed-wing tours of the Big Island that include Kilauea Volcano and its various rift zones. Because a fixed-wing plane is allowed to fly above the altitude restrictions at Hawaii Volcanoes National Park, Big Island Air Tours can take you directly above Halemaumau Crater for rare views of the crater not available with a helicopter tour. You'll also be able to soar above such sights as the infamous Puu Oo vent, as well as the devastated areas of lower Puna inundated by lava in 2018. Tours depart from Kona International Airport. For visitors on Maui, there is a round-trip circle-island tour of the Big Island that includes Kilauea Volcano on the itinerary. ✉ *Kona International Airport, 73–103 Ulu St., Kailua-Kona* ☎ *808/329–4868* 🌐 *www.bigislandair.com* 🎫 *From $398.*

Blue Hawaiian Helicopters
FLYING/SKYDIVING/SOARING | Hawaii Island's premier aerial tour is on Blue Hawaiian's roomy Eco-Star helicopters—so smooth and quiet you hardly realize you're taking off. There are no worries about what seat you get because each has great views. Pilots are also State of Hawaii–certified tour guides, so they are knowledgeable and experienced but not overly chatty. In the breathtaking Waimanu Valley, the helicopter hovers amazingly close to 2,600-foot cliffs and cascading waterfalls. Departing from Waikoloa, the two-hour Big Island Spectacular also takes in the incredible landscapes of Hawaii Volcanoes National Park, as well as the stunning valleys; you can even choose an optional waterfall landing as part of it. Leaving from Hilo, the 50-minue Circle of Fire tour showcases Kilauea Volcano and other major sites of the Big Island. ✉ *Waikoloa Heliport, Hwy. 19, Waikoloa* ☎ *808/961–5600* 🌐 *www.bluehawaiian.com* 🎟 *From $309.*

★ **Paradise Helicopters**
FLYING/SKYDIVING/SOARING | Even when the volcano is not actively flowing, there's still plenty to see from the air, with great options from this locally owned and operated company. Departing from Kona, the "Circle Island Experience" and "Experience Hawaii" tours both fly over the Volcanoes National Park area including the summit and Puu Oo Vent. Departing from Hilo, the "Doors-Off Lava and Rainforest Adventure" offers an unforgettable excursion in a Hughes 500 helicopter for unobstructed views of Kilauea Volcano. There's also a combo tour in conjunction with Hawaii Forest & Trails that offers on-ground activities via the "Volcano By Air and Land Tour." For the ultimate customized tour, private charters are available with a world-renowned volcanologist who will land the 'copter on his own lava-covered property just outside the park where he leads on an up-close tour of various lava formations. ■ TIP→ **The only helicopter company in Hawaii certified by the Hawaii Ecotour Association, Paradise offers you the option to offset your tour's carbon footprint by having a tree planted in Hawaii for each ride you take.** ☎ *808/969–7392, 866/876–7422* 🌐 *www.paradisecopters.com* 🎟 *From $274.*

Safari Helicopters
FLYING/SKYDIVING/SOARING | Departing from the Hilo airport, Safari offers a 45-minute tour of the East Rift Zone or a 55-minute tour that includes Hawaii Volcanoes National Park plus the waterfalls. ■ TIP→ **Book online for substantial discounts.** ✉ *Hilo International Airport, 2350 Kekuanaoa St., Hilo* ☎ *808/969–1259* 🌐 *www.safarihelicopters.com* 🎟 *From $189.*

What's Nearby

No trip to Hawaii Volcanoes National Park would be complete without a visit to **Volcano Village** located just 1 mile from the park entrance. This artists' community features a number of galleries, artist studios, and boutique shops scattered throughout fern-shrouded, historic neighborhoods. Consider an overnight stay at one of the many quaint vacation accommodations in Volcano Village—everything from cottages and tree houses to historic lodges and cozy cabins. Several restaurants and cafés offer decent dining options, and there are also some worthwhile stops for shoppers in search of unique treasures. Near the Volcano Golf Course and Country Club, Volcano Winery presents tastings and tours.

Take a side trip to the town of **Pahoa** in Lower Puna to learn about the massive destruction that took place during the 2018 Kilauea eruption that decimated more than 700 homes. The Pahoa Lava Zone Museum showcases recent geological artifacts from the event, as well as exhibits on loan from the now-permanently closed Jaggar Museum at Hawaii

Volcanoes National Park. Visitors can also trek to at Mackenzie State Recreation Area to see the recently altered coastline and the new black sand beach at Pohoiki. Twelve miles from Pahoa, the coastal village of **Kalapana** reveals the desolate lava flows that engulfed portions of the area in 1990.

NATIONAL PARKS

In addition to Hawaii Volcanoes National Park, the Big Island is home to two other national parks, both of which are located on the Kona side. The Tri-Park pass provides entry to both Hawaii Volcanoes National Park and Puuhonua O Honaunau National Historical Park in south Kona. Entry is free at Kaloko-Honokohau National Historical Park, which is located near the harbor in Kailua-Kona.

Kaloko–Honokohau National Historical Park
NATIONAL/STATE PARK | FAMILY | The trails at this sheltered 1,160-acre coastal park near Honokohau Harbor, just north of Kailua-Kona, are popular with walkers and hikers. The free park is a good place to observe Hawaiian archaeological history and intact ruins, including a *heiau* (temple), house platforms, ancient fishponds, and numerous petroglyphs along a boardwalk. The park's wetlands provide refuge to waterbirds, including the endemic Hawaiian stilt and coot. Two beaches here are good for swimming, sunbathing, and sea turtle spotting: **Aiopio,** a few yards north of the harbor, is small and calm, with protected swimming areas (good for kids), while **Honokohau Beach** is a ¾-mile stretch with ruins of ancient fishponds, also north of the harbor. Of the park's three entrances, the middle one leads to a visitor center with helpful rangers and lots of information. Local docents with backgrounds in geology or other subjects give nature talks. To go directly to the beaches, take the harbor road north of the Gentry retail center, park in the gravel lot, and follow the signs. ✉ *74–425 Kealakehe Pkwy., off Hwy. 19 near airport, Kailua-Kona* ⊕ *3 miles south of Kona International Airport* ☎ *808/329–6881* 🌐 *www.nps.gov/kaho* 🎫 *Free.*

★ **Puuhonua O Honaunau National Historical Park** (*Place of Refuge*)
HISTORIC SITE | The 420-acre National Historical Park has the best preserved *puuhonua* (place of refuge) in the state. Providing a safe haven for noncombatants, *kapu* (taboo) breakers, defeated warriors, and others, the *puuhonua* offered protection and redemption for anyone who could reach its boundaries, by land or sea. The oceanfront, 960-foot stone wall still stands and is one of the park's most prominent features. A number of ceremonial temples, including the restored **Hale o Keawe Heiau** (circa 1700), have served as royal burial chambers. An aura of ancient sacredness and serenity still imbues the place. ✉ *Rte. 160, Honaunau* ⊕ *About 20 miles south of Kailua-Kona* ☎ *808/328–2288* 🌐 *www.nps.gov/puho* 🎫 *$20 per vehicle* ⏲ *Sunset times vary throughout the year; check website for closing times.*

Chapter 34

HOT SPRINGS NATIONAL PARK

Updated by
Leslie Fisher

Camping ★★★★☆

Hotels ★★★★☆

Activities ★★★★☆

Scenery ★★★★☆

Crowds ★★★☆☆

WELCOME TO HOT SPRINGS NATIONAL PARK

TOP REASONS TO GO

★ **Bathhouse Row:** Showcasing the opulence of the "Golden Age of Bathing," the eight historic bathhouses here date from 1892 to 1923. Most have been creatively repurposed, but two still operate as bathhouses, inviting soaks in the thermal waters that gave Hot Springs its name and its fame.

★ **Outdoor recreation:** In addition to having its own woods laced by trails and scenic drives, Hot Springs National Park is in the Ouachita Mountains—a playground for hikers, mountain bikers, campers, and other outdoors enthusiasts.

★ **Colorful history:** As a one-time haven for organized crime and the birthplace of spring training, America's first resort town hosted both the famous and the infamous with regular guests including Babe Ruth and Al Capone.

1 **In the Park.** Nestled in the Ouachita Mountains, this enchanting, 5,550-acre park is uniquely situated in and around the town of Hot Springs. Puffs of steam rise from the decorative water features found in the park's urban area, where Bathhouse Row runs right along the main thoroughfare, adjacent to shops, restaurants, and hotels. Simply crossing the street takes you from park property to city property. Trails and scenic drives travel directly from downtown to the park's quiet wooded areas.

2 **Elsewhere in Town.** The charming, historic downtown of this small resort city features ornate buildings from the 1880s to the 1930s. The lively community also has several top-rated contemporary attractions and thriving arts and festivals scenes.

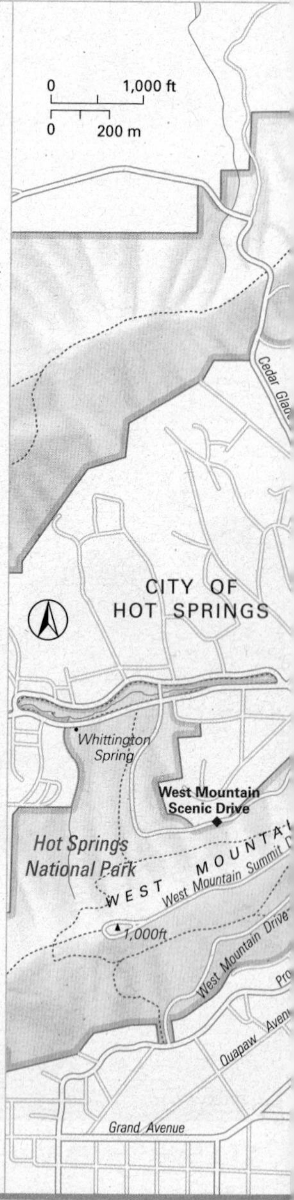

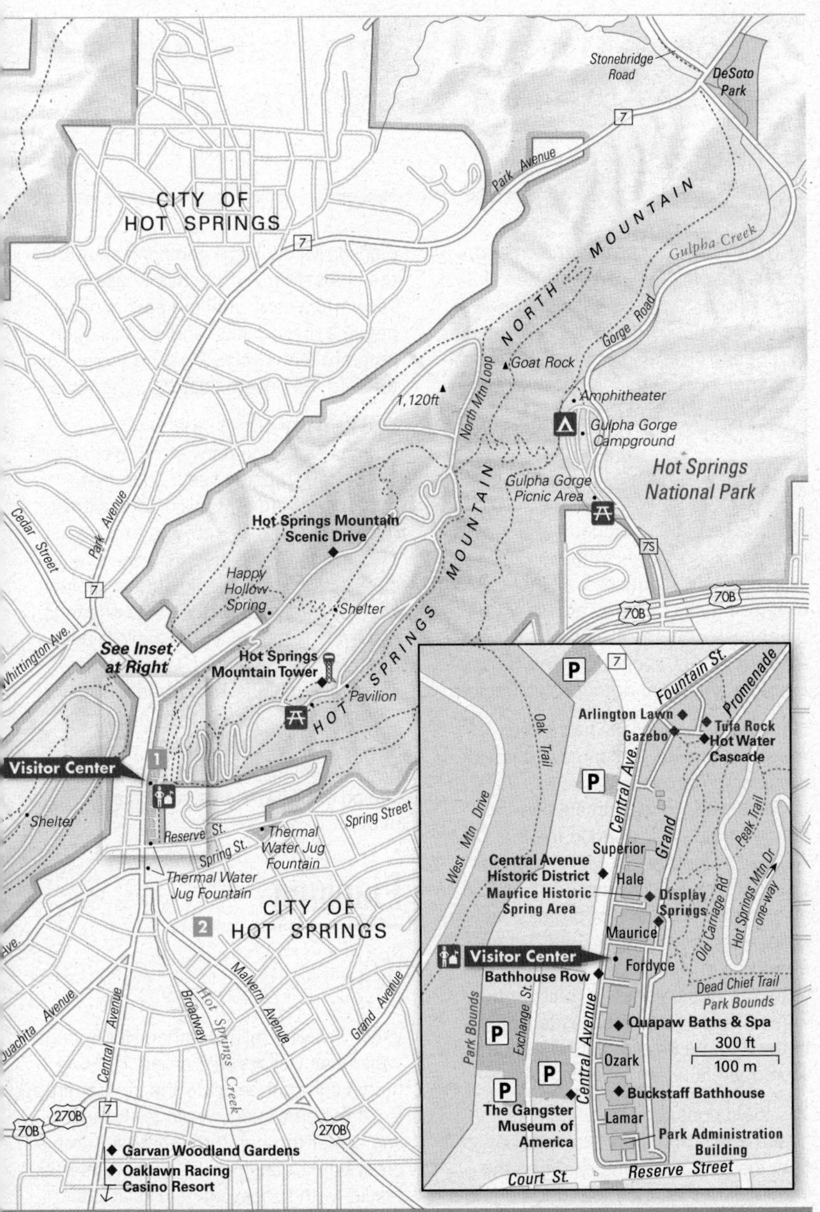
Stonebridge Road
DeSoto Park
Park Avenue
CITY OF HOT SPRINGS
NORTH MOUNTAIN
Gulpha Creek
Gorge Road
Goat Rock
1,120ft
North Mtn Loop
Amphitheater
Gulpha Gorge Campground
Hot Springs National Park
Gulpha Gorge Picnic Area
Hot Springs Mountain Scenic Drive
Happy Hollow Spring
Shelter
HOT SPRINGS MOUNTAIN
Cedar Street
Whittington Ave.
See Inset at Right
Hot Springs Mountain Tower
Pavilion
Visitor Center
Shelter
Reserve St.
Spring St.
Thermal Water Jug Fountain
Spring Street
Thermal Water Jug Fountain
CITY OF HOT SPRINGS
Malvern Avenue
Grand Avenue
Broadway
Hot Springs Creek
Central Avenue
Ouachita Avenue
70B
270B
Garvan Woodland Gardens
Oaklawn Racing Casino Resort
Oak Trail
Fountain St.
Promenade
Arlington Lawn
Gazebo
Tufa Rock
Hot Water Cascade
Central Ave.
West Mtn Drive
Peak Trail
Superior
Grand
Central Avenue Historic District
Hale
Maurice Historic Spring Area
Display Springs
Old Carriage Rd
Hot Springs Mtn Dr one-way
Maurice
Visitor Center
Fordyce
Bathhouse Row
Dead Chief Trail
Park Bounds
Exchange St.
Central Avenue
Quapaw Baths & Spa
300 ft
100 m
Ozark
Buckstaff Bathhouse
The Gangster Museum of America
Lamar
Park Administration Building
Court St.
Reserve Street

Named for springs that produce 700,000 gallons of 143-degree water daily, one of the country's smallest national parks is also one of the few in an urban setting—and one of the first to be federally protected.

In 1832—decades before the creation of the National Park System—the U.S. government signed legislation to preserve the springs for public use, creating Hot Springs Reservation. By the time of this intervention, the area was already catering to those who wanted to "take the waters," and it quickly evolved from a rough frontier town to an elegant spa, achieving national park status in 1921.

Despite its bathing industry, the town's image was less than squeaky clean, with brothels, nightclubs, and illegal casinos on city property across from the bathhouses. By the 1930s, the town was a haven for Al Capone, Charles "Lucky" Luciano, and other notorious characters.

Hot Springs historically had more reputable guests, of course, including presidents Theodore Roosevelt, Franklin D. Roosevelt, Harry Truman, and, Bill Clinton, who was raised in the Spa City. As the "birthplace" of Major League Baseball's spring training, Hot Springs also hosted hundreds of professional ballplayers, beginning in 1886, when members of the Chicago White Stockings (now the Cubs) came to "boil out the winter." Babe Ruth later made history here when he hit the first home run to fly more than 500 feet.

The town continued to flourish as a health resort and entertainment hot spot until the mid-20th century, when the bathing industry went into decline and a crackdown on illegal gambling shuttered the clubs. Many of the bathhouses sat vacant for years, until the park service began a preservation and rehabilitation program that involved leasing the structures to the private sector.

Like its national park, the town of Hot Springs has since reinvented itself. Today, it's a family-friendly destination that attracts upward of 3 million overnight guests a year. They come to experience the national park's historic sites, scenic drives; and trails; to enjoy the community's beautiful architecture, arts offerings, and lively festivals; and to explore area mountain-biking routes, lakes, state parks, and national forestlands. But Hot Springs' history is still a big part of its charm, and the past lives on: after all, nothing feels better after a day of sightseeing or hiking than a soak in a thermal bath.

Planning

When to Go

With relatively mild weather, Hot Springs welcomes visitors year round. Hot and humid summer days are the perfect time to hit the area lakes, while fall foliage and cooler temperatures make autumn a great time to explore the trails. Winter is festive with holiday lights displays, and

AVERAGE HIGH/LOW TEMPERATURES					
JAN.	**FEB.**	**MAR.**	**APR.**	**MAY**	**JUNE**
51/30	56/33	65/41	74/49	81/59	89/67
JULY	**AUG.**	**SEPT.**	**OCT.**	**NOV.**	**DEC.**
94/70	93/69	86/63	76/51	63/41	54/33

a thermal-bath soak is especially nice on a chilly day. Spring weather is perfect—unless it's raining.

FESTIVALS AND EVENTS

The Arkansas Derby. This top preparatory race for the Kentucky Derby is a grand affair all its own, with thousands of spectators, some wearing big hats and placing big bets. It's held over an April weekend in conjunction with the Racing Festival of the South at Oaklawn Racing Gaming Resort. On "Derby Day," the infield has concerts, food and drink vendors, and more. 🌐 *www.oaklawn.com.*

Hot Springs Documentary Film Festival. The oldest festival (established in 1992) of its type in North America is held over nine days in October throughout downtown and features screenings of 75 to 100 nonfiction films, panels, after parties, and opportunities to meet industry professional and celebrities. 🌐 *www.hsdfi.org.*

The World's Shortest St. Patrick's Day Parade. With celebrity guests, live music, and colorful floats, this annual event attracts thousands of spectators who transform downtown into a sea of green. The parade travels the length of Bridge Street, which, at 90 feet and 11 inches, is billed as the "world's shortest street in everyday use." 🌐 *www.shorteststpats.com.*

Getting Here and Around

AIR

The nearest major airport is in Little Rock, about 55 miles and an hour northeast of the park via I–30 and US–70.

CAR

It's a three-hour drive from Memphis to Hot Springs via I–40 W, which passes through Arkansas' capital city of Little Rock. It's almost a straight shot between Dallas and Hot Springs on I–30, a drive of about 4½ hours.

Inspiration

Written by Hot Springs native and award-winning journalist David Hill, *The Vapors: A Southern Family, the New York Mob, and the Rise and Fall of Hot Springs, America's Forgotten Capital of Vice* is the incredible true tale of Hot Springs in its gambling heyday, when gangsters flocked to the spa town to get in on the action.

Maxine: "Call Me Madam" is an autobiographical tell-all by Maxine Temple Jones, a madam who ran notorious brothel in the 1950s and '60s.

Park Essentials

ACCESSIBILITY

Bathhouse Row, a highlight of the park, is fronted by a wide sidewalk that enables all visitors to enjoy the architecture. The Fordyce Visitor Center and Museum is wheelchair accessible with a ramp, wide hallways, and an elevator to all floors. Self-guided tour books in braille are available, as are audio descriptions and closed captioning for the park's film shown in the Fordyce's first-floor theater. Although the Grand Promenade, a wide, paved walkway behind Bathhouse Row, can be accessed via ramps off Fountain Street and behind the Fordyce

Bathhouse, the ramps are somewhat steep and are not ADA-certified. The Gulpha Gorge Campground and all park bathrooms are wheelchair accessible.

PARK FEES AND PERMITS

There is no fee to enter the park or tour the Fordyce Visitor Center and Museum. Sites at Gulpha Gorge Campground are $30 per night. The only option for bathing in the thermal waters is to visit one of the bathhouses (or the Arlington Resort Hotel & Spa, outside of the national park), and fees start at $20.

PARK HOURS

Hot Springs National Park is open year round. Gated park roads are open from 8 am to 10 pm; the rest of the park is open from 5 am to 10 pm.

CELL PHONE RECEPTION

Cell phone reception is generally good—there's even a self-guided cell-phone tour of the park.

Hotels

Hot Springs National Park's one hotel offers a unique experience. Located in the historic Hale Bathhouse (the oldest structure on Bathhouse Row), Hotel Hale features large soaking tubs in each room with thermal spring water piped directly in, so you can enjoy long baths in privacy. This boutique hotel has only nine rooms (including two suites), so it may prove difficult to book during the high season, but the surrounding town of Hot Springs has hundreds of accommodations, including plush hotels, B&Bs, retro motels, rustic cabins, and privately owned vacation rentals.

Restaurants

Dining in Hot Springs National Park is limited to a few noteworthy restaurants operating inside the historic bathhouses on Bathhouse Row. The surrounding town has an array of casual and fine-dining establishments, from cafés and pizza joints to ethnic eateries to steak and seafood houses.

Hotel and restaurant reviews have been shortened. For full information visit Fodors.com. Hotel prices are the lowest cost of a standard double room in high season. Restaurant prices are the average cost of a main course at dinner, or if dinner is not served, at lunch.

What It Costs

	$	$$	$$$	$$$$
RESTAURANTS				
	under $10	$10–$20	$21–$30	over $30
HOTELS				
	under $150	$150–$200	$201–$250	over $250

Tours

Hot Springs Trolley

GUIDED TOURS | FAMILY | Hop on this air-conditioned bus—outfitted to look like a historic trolley—for a fun, informative, 90-minute ride. Tours cruise in and around downtown before traveling up West Mountain for scenic views of both the park and Hot Springs. Along the way, you'll hear tales of gangsters, baseball players, and other local characters; discover how hot the spring water gets; and find out what else there is to see and do in the area. The driver also stops at one of the park's cold-water fountains so you can fill up your complimentary jug. ✉ *Hot Springs Trolleys Gift Shop, 706 Central Ave., Hot Springs* ☎ *501/701–4410* 🌐 *www.hotspringstrolley.com* 🎫 *$18.*

Visitor Information

CONTACTS Hot Springs National Park. ✉ *369 Central Ave., Hot Springs* ☎ *501/620–6715* 🌐 *www.nps.gov/hosp.*

In the Park

55 miles southwest of Little Rock, 188 miles southwest of Memphis, 286 miles northeast of Dallas.

Situated in and around Hot Springs' historic downtown, the park includes Bathhouse Row, Arlington Lawn, and the surrounding mountains where visitors can enjoy scenic drives, 26 miles of hiking trails, and stunning views.

Sights

GEOLOGICAL FORMATIONS

Hot Water Cascade

HOT SPRINGS | FAMILY | This steamy, dreamy site in Arlington Lawn is the park's largest visible spring, with thermal water pouring freely over the mountainside into two man-made pools. Dip a finger in to feel its heat, the result of a lengthy journey through the ground to a depth of 6,000 to 8,000 feet. In total, it takes about 4,000 years for the water to travel down and back out. ✉ *Hot Springs National Park, Hot Springs* ✣ *At northern end of Bathhouse Row.*

HISTORIC SIGHTS

Bathhouse Row

HISTORIC SITE | FAMILY | Fronted by a wide sidewalk and a row of magnolia trees, Bathhouse Row consists of eight architecturally unique structures that date from 1892 to 1923 and showcase the importance of hydrotherapy prior to the advent of modern medicine. Once doctors stopped prescribing the "water cure," most of the bathhouses sat vacant until the park—in an effort to preserve and utilize the stately structures—began leasing them to the private sector. Today, all but one is occupied. Two operate as actual bathhouses (Quapaw and Buckstaff), and the others house a brewery and restaurant (Superior), a hotel and restaurant (Hale), a visitor center and museum (Fordyce), a cultural center featuring artwork from the park's Artist-in-Residence Program (Ozark), and a gift shop (Lamar). ✉ *Hot Springs National Park, Hot Springs* ✣ *From 329 Central Ave. in the north to intersection of Central Ave. and Reserve St.* 🌐 *www.nps.gov/hosp.*

Buckstaff Bathhouse

SPA—SIGHT | Immerse yourself in Hot Springs' unique history at the Buckstaff, where you can experience the hydrotherapy treatments that were in vogue at the height of the bathing industry. Built in the Greco-Roman style, with Colorado marble throughout, the Buckstaff opened in 1912. The traditional package includes a whirlpool mineral bath with a personal bath attendant to scrub you down and lead you through a series of stations featuring hot packs, a sitz bath, a steam cabinet, and a cooling needle shower. All this is followed by a 20-minute massage. ✉ *Hot Springs National Park, 509 Central Ave., Hot Springs* ☎ *501/623–2308* 🌐 *www.buckstaffbaths.com* 🕒 *Closed Sun. Dec.–Feb.*

★ **Quapaw Baths & Spa**

SPA—SIGHT | This Spanish Colonial revival–style bathhouse opened in 1922 and operated until 1984. After sitting vacant for more than 20 years, it became the first structure to be leased to the private sector under the park's rehabilitation initiative. The beautifully renovated Quapaw Baths & Spa, which opened in 2008, features original tile and marble fixtures and attractive stained-glass skylights. It has four large-capacity thermal pools, private and couples baths, and a variety of spa services, including facials and massages. ✉ *Hot Springs National Park, 413 Central Ave., Hot Springs* ☎ *501/609–9822* 🌐 *www.quapawbaths.com* 🎟 *Admission to thermal pools: $20. Spa services: from $55.* 🕒 *Closed Tues. and 1st few wks of Jan.*

Although the park extends into the surrounding mountains, it's best known for its historic downtown bathhouses.

SCENIC DRIVES

Hot Springs Mountain Scenic Drive

SCENIC DRIVE | FAMILY | Built as a carriage road in the 1880s, this historic route winds up and around Hot Springs and North mountains. At the summit is the Hot Springs Mountain Tower, which offers stunning 360-degree views. There is also a picnic area with charcoal grills and bathrooms, a pretty pagoda overlooking town, and hiking trails. Including an optional loop at the top, the route is just under 4 miles. ✉ *Hot Springs National Park, Hot Springs* ✥ *Turn right at the end of Fountain St. in downtown* ⏲ *Gate closes at 10 pm.*

West Mountain Scenic Drive

SCENIC DRIVE | FAMILY | This short scenic road travels up and over the mountain, connecting Prospect Avenue and Whittington Avenue. Enter from either end to reach the Summit Loop for sweeping views of downtown and the Ouachita Mountains. One of the three overlooks along the way has a historic shelter and a couple of picnic tables. There are also trailheads for the West Mountain and Sunset trails. The road loops around an outcrop of Arkansas novaculite at the summit before descending back into town. ✉ *Hot Springs National Park, Hot Springs* ✥ *Access is from Prospect Ave. or Whittington Ave.* ⏲ *Gated road closes at 10 pm.*

SCENIC STOPS

Hot Springs Mountain Tower

VIEWPOINT | FAMILY | Overlooking some 140 square miles, this 216-foot tall, elevator-accessible tower at the summit of its namesake mountain provides sweeping views of the park and the Ouachita Mountains. The tower is open daily and has an open-air observation deck; an enclosed, lower-level deck with exhibits on area history; and a ground-level gift shop. ✉ *Hot Springs National Park, 401 Hot Springs Mountain Dr., Hot Springs* ☎ *501/881–4020* 🌐 *www.hotspringstower.com* 🎟 *$10.*

TRAILS

★ Goat Rock Trail

TRAIL | This 1.1-mile (one-way) trail leads to a set of stone stairs that climb 240 feet to a small but scenic lookout atop massive novaculite boulders. The slight ascent from the trailhead is worth the effort for the views. Goat Rock can also be reached via connecting trails from downtown Hot Springs and the Gulpha Gorge Campground. *Easy–Moderate.* ✉ *Hot Springs National Park, Hot Springs* ✣ *Trailhead: At North Mountain Overlook.*

Grand Promenade

PROMENADE | FAMILY | This charming, red brick pathway stretches for ½ mile behind Bathhouse Row, providing views of the park and downtown Hot Springs. Along the way there's access to several trails leading up into the mountain. An elegant staircase between the Fordyce and the Maurice bathhouses leads to the promenade, but it can also be accessed via a staircase on the south end and a ramp on the north end. *Easy.* ✉ *Hot Springs National Park, Hot Springs.*

Hot Springs Mountain Trail

TRAIL | Follow this 1.7-mile loop for a jaunt around the summit of Hot Springs Mountain, with scenic views all along the way. The trail passes a shelter and crosses Hot Springs Mountain Drive three times. *Easy–Moderate.* ✉ *Hot Springs National Park, Hot Springs* ✣ *Trailhead: At pagoda on Hot Springs Mountain Dr.*

Mountain Top Trail

TRAIL | FAMILY | Traveling up and over West Mountain from Prospect Avenue to Whittington Avenue, this wooded trail is 1.5 miles one-way. Street parking is available on either end. For a longer hike, combine this route with the West Mountain North and South trails to make a loop around the summit before heading back down the same way you came up. If you end your hike on Whittington Avenue, you can refill your water bottle and quench your thirst at the cold-water filling station just west of the trailhead. *Moderate–Difficult.* ✉ *Hot Springs National Park, Hot Springs* ✣ *Trailheads: On Prospect Ave. and Whittington Ave.*

Pullman Trail

TRAIL | The national park's only hiking trail that's open to bikers travels, the nearly 1-mile Pullman connects downtown and the park to the Northwoods Trail System, a network with 26-plus miles of world-class mountain biking routes located outside of the park. *Easy–Moderate.* ✉ *Hot Springs National Park, Hot Springs* ✣ *Trailhead: At end of Pullman Ave.*

Sunset Trail

TRAIL | FAMILY | At roughly 10 miles one-way, this is the park's longest trail. It's also the park's most versatile one: it has several trailheads and parking spots, so you can hike it in shorter sections, or you can combine it with other park trails to make a 15- to 17-mile loop. The Sugarloaf Mountain section features a short spur trail leading to Balanced Rock, a scenic overlook named for the massive chunks of Arkansas novaculite that appear to have been carefully stacked there. *Moderate–Difficult.* ✉ *Hot Springs* ✣ *Trailheads: West Mountain Summit Dr., Blacksnake and Cedar Glades roads, and Gulpha Gorge Campground.*

VISITOR CENTER

Fordyce Bathhouse Visitor Center and Museum

INFO CENTER | FAMILY | Soak up Hot Springs' rich history on a free, self-guided tour of the largest and most opulent bathhouse on Bathhouse Row. The Fordyce, which operated from 1915 to 1962, is now the park's visitor center and museum, where you can pick up trail maps, speak with helpful park employees, and get an insightful glimpse into the Golden Age of bathing. Extensively restored, the Fordyce features marble throughout, beautiful stained-glass ceilings, period rooms, and hydrotherapy equipment dating from the early 20th century. A 15-minute video in the first-floor theater covers area history; a shorter video shown on the second floor details the traditional bathing regimen. ✉ *Hot Springs National Park, 369 Central Ave., Hot Springs* ☎ *501/620–6715* 🌐 *www.nps.gov/hosp.*

Restaurants

Eden

$$$ | AMERICAN | Set in the historic Hale Bathhouse, now a boutique hotel, this atrium restaurant is both casual and refined, with exposed brick, a marble bar, and a living wall of plants flourishing beneath large skylights. During the day, the upscale menu features salads and other light fare; there's a curated selection of entrées in the evening. **Known for:** exceptional weekend brunch; expansive drink menu with tasty cocktails and mimosa flights; filet mignon and shrimp served with Bordelaise. $ *Average main: $30* ✉ *Hot Springs National Park, 341 Central Ave., Hot Springs* ☎ *501/760–9010* 🌐 *www.hotelhale.com* ⊙ *Closed Mon.–Wed.*

★ Superior Bathhouse Brewery

$$ | AMERICAN | FAMILY | Located in a historic bathhouse, this one-of-a-kind brewery—the first headquartered in a U.S. national park—uses thermal spring water to create its craft beers, including the Superior Pale Ale (SPA) and the Hitchcock Spring, a Kölsch named for an area spring. The farm-to-table food is top-notch, too, with an eclectic selection of salads and elevated pub grub. **Known for:** Beez Kneez, a slightly sweet Kölsch made with local honey and basil; people-watching along Bathhouse Row; rootbeer that's also brewed in-house using spring water. $ *Average main: $10* ✉ *329 Central Ave., Hot Springs* ☎ *501/624–2337* 🌐 *www.superiorbathhouse.com.*

Coffee and Quick Bites

Quapaw Café

$ | CAFÉ | Refuel with a salad or sandwich at this little café inside the Quapaw Bathhouse. Grab a fruit smoothie or a cup of Joe to go, or stay a while and sip a beer or a glass of wine or champagne. **Known for:** delicious chicken salad sandwich; fruit smoothies, including strawberry banana and peach mango; the signature sangria. $ *Average main: $7* ✉ *Hot Springs National Park, 413 Central Ave., Hot Springs* ☎ *501/609–9822* 🌐 *www.quapawbaths.com* ⊙ *Closed Tues. and 1st few wks of Jan.*

Hotels

★ Hotel Hale

$$$$ | HOTEL | This luxury boutique hotel offers the unique experience of staying in a historic bathhouse—built in 1892—and the oldest structure on Bathhouse Row. Shuttered for several decades, the Hale was extensively remodeled and reopened in 2019, winning the Preserve Arkansas' Excellence in Preservation through Rehabilitation Award that same year. **Pros:** thermal baths in the privacy of your room; delectable breakfast and weekend brunch; chilled spring water and free coffee service to your room. **Cons:** no on-site parking; difficult to book in high season due to a limited number of rooms; one of the pricier options in town. $ *Rooms from: $270* ✉ *Hot Springs National Park, 341 Central Ave., Hot Springs* ☎ *501/760–9010* 🌐 *www.hotelhale.com* *9 rooms* *Free breakfast.*

Shopping

Bathhouse Row Emporium

GIFTS/SOUVENIRS | FAMILY | This nonprofit gift shop in the historic Lamar Bathhouse supports the park's educational programs. Gift items includes T-shirts, hiking sticks, books, locally made spa products, and glass growlers for filling up with spring water at one of the park's jug fountains. ✉ *Hot Springs National Park, 515 Central Ave., Hot Springs* ☎ *501/620–6740.*

Elsewhere in Town

55 miles southwest of Little Rock, 188 miles southwest of Memphis, 286 miles northeast of Dallas.

Home to nearly 40,000 residents, Hot Springs has quite a lot to offer for a town of its size. In addition to the national park and its namesake thermal waters, it has a bustling historic district, a thriving arts community, and a thoroughbred racetrack.

Sights

HISTORIC SIGHTS

Central Avenue Historic District

HISTORIC SITE | Stretching a little more than ½ mile, this district contains an array of commercial buildings constructed between 1886 and 1930 in a variety of styles, including Classical, Italianate, Romanesque, Victorian, and Art Deco. Among the notable structures are the impressive Arlington Resort Hotel & Spa and the Medical Arts Building, a 1929 skyscraper that was the state's tallest structure until 1960. The district was placed on the National Register of Historic Places in 1985, and today these architecturally delightful buildings house a variety of businesses including restaurants, nightclubs, and boutiques. ✉ *Hot Springs* ✣ *From the 100 block to the 700 block of Central Ave.*

The Gangster Museum of America

MUSEUM | Pull back the covers on this charming little town, and you'll discover a past rampant with crime and corruption. From the 1920s to the 1960s, Hot Springs was a hotbed of illegal activity that attracted mobsters like Al Capone, Lucky Luciano, and Owney "The Killer" Madden. This museum's guided tour, which lasts a little over an hour, takes you through a series of galleries with photos, memorabilia, and short videos that reveal how this small Southern town became America's original Sin City. ✉ *510 Central Ave., Hot Springs* ☎ *501/318–1717* 🌐 *www.tgmoa.com* 🎫 *$15.*

Oaklawn Racing Casino Resort

CASINO—SIGHT | Since it was established in 1904, Oaklawn has grown into one of the country's top thoroughbred racetracks and the state's top tourist attraction. Live racing is held from late January through early May, culminating with the Arkansas Derby. Year-round, Oaklawn offers simulcast racing and a sprawling casino with craps and blackjack tables and a dizzying array of slot machines. In 2019, a $100 million-plus development project added an expanded casino, a new restaurant, a high-rise hotel overlooking the track, and a multipurpose event center. ✉ *2705 Central Ave., Hot Springs* ☎ *501/623–4411, 800/625–5296* 🌐 *www.oaklawn.com.*

SCENIC STOPS

★ **Garvan Woodland Gardens**

GARDEN | **FAMILY** | Located on 210 acres of woodland bordering Lake Hamilton, this world-class botanical garden is a wonderland of flowers, rare shrubs, and trees, including 160 different types of azaleas, 300 varieties of Asian ornamental plants, and thousands of daffodils and tulips blooming each spring. The holiday season is just as stunning with the annual Holiday Lights display. Meandering footpaths cross stone bridges and pass trickling waterfalls, too. Architectural highlights include the towering Anthony Chapel with floor-to-ceiling glass walls and the multilevel treehouse in the Children's Adventure Garden. Note that complimentary wheelchairs and strollers are available at the welcome center on a first-come, first-served basis. ✉ *550 Arkridge Rd., Hot Springs* ☎ *501/262–9300, 800/366–4664* 🌐 *www.garvangardens.org* 🎫 *$15* 🕑 *Closed Jan.*

Restaurants

★ 501 Prime

$$$$ | **STEAKHOUSE** | Serving USDA Prime steaks cooked to perfection and delectable seafood entrées, this stylish restaurant is warm and romantic, with reclaimed wood throughout and private little dining nooks. Reservations are highly recommended. **Known for:** impeccable service; attractive oyster bar; casual upstairs Bourbon Bar with a huge whiskey selection. *Average main: $55 ✉ 215 E. Grand Ave., Hot Springs ☎ 501/623–0202 🌐 www.501prime.com ⏲ Closed Sun. and Mon.*

McClard's Bar-B-Q

$$ | **BARBECUE** | **FAMILY** | Established in 1928 and owned by four generations of the same family until 2020, the legacy lives on at this award-winning barbecue joint. McClard's is still *the* place to use up a wad of napkins while eating a plate of ribs dripping in the family's famous barbecue sauce. **Known for:** the story of the "down-and-out traveler" who paid for his board with the recipe for his barbecue sauce; the Tamale Spread; hickory-smoked pork ribs. *Average main: $12 ✉ 505 Albert Pike Rd., Hot Springs ☎ 501/624–9586 🌐 www.mcclards.com ⏲ Closed Mon.*

Steinhaus Keller

$$$ | **GERMAN** | **FAMILY** | Located in the "grotto" of Spencer's Corner, this authentic German restaurant has an old-world vibe with exposed rock and barreled ceilings. The menu features wursts, schnitzels, and other chef-made Bavarian and European delights, like *roulade* (rolled beef) and *schweinshaxe* (braised pork knuckle). **Known for:** outdoor biergarten; Arkansas' largest selection of German and European beer; live polka music on the weekends. *Average main: $22 ✉ 801 Central Ave. , Suite 15, Hot Springs ☎ 501/624–7866 🌐 www.steinhauskeller.com ⏲ Closed Sun. and Mon.*

Coffee and Quick Bites

Kollective Coffee+Tea

$$ | **CAFÉ** | **FAMILY** | This third-wave downtown coffee and teahouse could have been plucked from Portland or San Francisco. The nitro cold brew on draft and other coffee options are all made with single origin beans, and nearly everything on the menu is organic or natural and locally sourced. **Known for:** more than 50 varieties of loose-leaf tea; coffee sourced and roasted by Onyx Coffee Lab from northwest Arkansas; hosts Wednesday Night Poetry series. *Average main: $11 ✉ 110 Central Ave., Hot Springs ☎ 501/701–4000 🌐 www.kollectivecoffeetea.com.*

Red Light Roastery Coffee House

$ | **CAFÉ** | **FAMILY** | The setting in a renovated 1890s house—with an inviting front porch and a wood-burning stove—gives this neighborhood hangout a homey vibe. Hot and cold espresso drinks, locally brewed kombucha, and waffles or other gluten-free sweet treats are all on the menu. **Known for:** single-origin, freshly roasted coffee beans (also available for purchase); all tips donated to a different local nonprofit each month; also sells artisanal soaps made by one of the owners. *Average main: $5 ✉ 1003 Park Ave., Hot Springs ☎ 501/609–9357 🌐 www.redlightroastery.com ⏲ Closed Mon. and Tues.*

Hotels

Arlington Resort Hotel & Spa

$ | **HOTEL** | Looming large over downtown, this impressive Mediterranean-style landmark, one of the state's largest hotels, opened with a New Year's Eve party in 1924 and has since hosted presidents, celebrities, and gangsters, like Al Capone, who stayed in Room 443. **Pros:** rich history and beautiful architecture; in walking distance of Bathhouse Row, trails, restaurants, and shops; spa offers traditional thermal baths. **Cons:** some rooms need updating; in-room heat and a/c can't be adjusted (only turned on/off); free parking lot is off-site (fee for on-site garage and valet parking). *Rooms from: $135 239 Central Ave., Hot Springs 501/623–7771, 800/643–1502 www.arlingtonhotel.com 478 rooms No meals.*

The Waters Hotel Hot Springs, Tapestry Collection by Hilton

$ | HOTEL | Located in a beautifully and extensively renovated building from 1913, this boutique hotel combines historic charm with modern amenities and amazing views. **Pros:** in walking distance of Bathhouse Row, hiking trails, restaurants, and shops; rooftop restaurant with national park and town views; package deals available with breakfast included. **Cons:** can be noisy; no on-site parking; pets not allowed (except for service animals). *Rooms from: $139 340 Central Ave., Hot Springs 501/321–0001 www.thewatershs.com 62 rooms No meals.*

Nightlife

Maxine's Live

BARS/PUBS | Depending on the night of the week, you can sing karaoke, catch a drag show, or shake it to some live music at this cozy, dimly lit, and sometimes raucous venue. A former brothel turned bar and Italian eatery, it is named for the madam who once ran the place. *700 Central Ave., Hot Springs 501/321–0909 www.maxineslive.com.*

Ohio Club

BARS/PUBS | Opened in 1905, Arkansas' oldest bar has survived Prohibition, police raids, and fires. Although its backroom casino (a popular hangout for the likes of Al Capone and Lucky Luciano) was shuttered in 1969, the Ohio Club lives on as a bar and grill and live-music venue. *336 Central Ave., Hot Springs 501/627–0702 www.theohioclub.com.*

Shopping

All Things Arkansas

GIFTS/SOUVENIRS | The name says it all. Everything in this stylish gift shop is from Arkansas, made in Arkansas, or relates to the state, including pottery, bath products, knives, jewelry, books, wines, and quartz crystals. *610-C Central Ave., Hot Springs 501/620–3971 www.allthingsarkansas.com Closed Sun.*

Dryden Art Pottery

CERAMICS/GLASSWARE | This pottery produces collectable works of functional art in a style unique to the Dryden family, which has owned and operated the studio for three generations. You can shop a large selection of handmade vases, bowls, and mugs and see pottery-wheel demonstrations from 10 to 11 am Monday through Saturday or by request. *341 Whittington Ave., Hot Springs 501/623–4201 www.drydenpottery.com Closed Sun.*

State & Pride Provisions Company

CLOTHING | Get outfitted for a hike or find a cool souvenir at this eclectic, outdoorsy shop, carrying Arkansas-based apparel brands like Fayettechill, Arkansasocks, and Nativ, as well as clothing and gear from The North Face, KÜHL, and Fjällräven. *518 Central Ave., Hot Springs 501/627–0759 www.stateandpride.com.*

Activities

BICYCLING

Hot Springs, rated a bronze-level ride center by the International Mountain Biking Association, has three IMBA EPIC rides within an hour's drive and the Northwoods Trail System right in its backyard, with more than 26 miles of mountain bike trails accessible directly from downtown. If you prefer pavement, hit the Hot Springs Creek Greenway Trail, or take a bike tour.

Hot Springs Bicycle Touring Company
BICYCLING | This shop offers repairs, rentals ($10 an hour, $45 for three hours), and guided tours, including a popular excursion ($30) to five spring-fed jug fountains in Hot Springs National Park (water bottle included). The Greenway Art and Sculpture Garden Tour showcases local works along a pleasant, paved, waterside route. ✉ *436 Broadway St., Hot Springs* ☎ *501/276–2175* 🌐 *www.facebook.com/HotSpringsBicycleTouringCompany*.

Parkside Cycle
BICYCLING | In business since 1995, Parkside Cycle has everything you need to get out on Hot Springs' renowned mountain biking trails, whether it's a new bike, a rental, or a repair. It also carries clothing and accessories and has a friendly, knowledgeable staff. ✉ *719 Whittington Ave., Hot Springs* ☎ *501/623–6188* 🌐 *www.parksidecycle.com* 🕓 *Closed Sun.–Mon.*

Spa City Cycling
BICYCLING | A ½-mile ride from the start of the Pullman Trail that connects downtown to the Northwoods Trail System, this full-service shop carries a wide variety of bicycles and accessories and offers rentals and repairs. ✉ *873 Park Ave., Suite B, Hot Springs* ☎ *501/463–9364* 🌐 *www.spacitycycling.com* 🕓 *Closed Sun.–Mon.*

CAMPING

Gulpha Gorge Campground. Located at the base of North Mountain, this scenic campground offers trail access (you can hike to downtown) and has a nice creek flowing through it. Its 40 first-come, first-served sites accommodate tents and RVs (full hookups). There are bathrooms but no showers. ✉ *305 Gulpha Gorge Rd., Hot Springs* ☎ *501/620–6715* 🌐 *www.nps.gov/hosp.*

HIKING

In addition to having its own trails, Hot Spring National Park is nearby other protected lands, including two state parks and the expansive Ouachita National Forest. Hiking opportunities range from short jaunts through the national park to strenuous, multiday backpacking excursions in the Ouachita Mountains.

Ouachita Outdoor Outfitters
CAMPING—SPORTS-OUTDOORS | The friendly, knowledgeable staff at this outdoors store will get you fully outfitted with gear for kayaking, camping, hiking, fly-fishing, and more. Kayak and stand-up paddleboard rentals (from $40 a day) are also available. ✉ *112 Blackhawk La., Hot Springs* ☎ *501/767–1373* 🌐 *www.ouachitaoutdoors.com* 🕓 *Closed Sun.–Mon.*

Chapter 35

INDIANA DUNES NATIONAL PARK

Updated by
Eric Peterson

Camping	Hotels	Activities	Scenery	Crowds
★★☆☆☆	★☆☆☆☆	★★★☆☆	★★☆☆☆	★☆☆☆☆

WELCOME TO INDIANA DUNES NATIONAL PARK

TOP REASONS TO GO

★ **Hit the beach:** The park's 15-mile shoreline encompasses eight beaches with access to the waters of Lake Michigan. They are major regional destinations on hot summer days.

★ **Experience the dunes:** Shaped by water, wind, and time, the park's namesake dunes are in four different complexes, marked by 200-foot ridges that are separated by valleys and wetlands.

★ **Explore a rare black oak savanna:** Although oak savannas once dominated vast tracts of land from Indiana to Nebraska, most were cleared for wood in the 1800s and 1900s. Only 0.02 percent of these fertile ecosystems remain in the Midwest, and this park has several of them.

★ **Watch the birds:** With more than 350 different species of birds sighted here, Indiana Dunes ranks in the top five national parks for avian diversity. The lake, forest, and grasslands attract a variety of migratory visitors, too.

1 Lakefront. Shores on both sides of the Port of Indiana make up the heart of the park and feature beaches, dune complexes, the Great Marsh, several historic homes, a campground, and Cowles Bog.

2 Inland Areas. The park encompasses several noncontiguous segments south of the lakefront, including Pinhook Bog, the Heron Rookery, Hobart Prairie Grove, and Hoosier Prairie State Natural Preserve. These areas, which cover less than 2,000 acres, can be explored in a few hours.

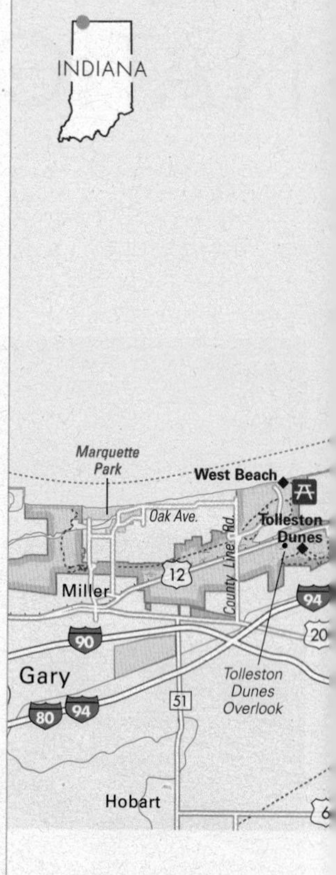

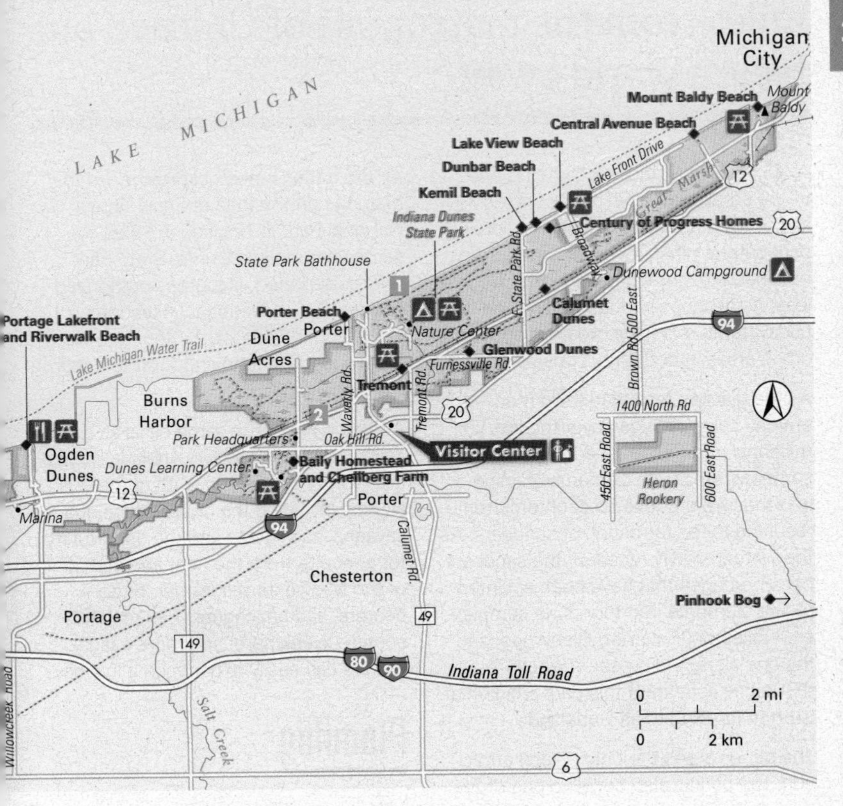
LAKE MICHIGAN
Michigan City
Mount Baldy Beach
Mount Baldy
Central Avenue Beach
Lake View Beach
Dunbar Beach
Kemil Beach
Indiana Dunes State Park
Lake Front Drive
Great Marsh
Century of Progress Homes
Broadway
E. State Park Rd.
State Park Bathhouse
Dunewood Campground
Calumet Dunes
Porter Beach
Porter
Nature Center
Portage Lakefront and Riverwalk Beach
Dune Acres
Lake Michigan Water Trail
Glenwood Dunes
Furnessville Rd.
Brown Rd 500 East
Tremont
Waverly Rd.
Tremont Rd.
Burns Harbor
1400 North Rd
Park Headquarters
Oak Hill Rd.
Visitor Center
Ogden Dunes
Baily Homestead and Chellberg Farm
Dunes Learning Center
450 East Road
600 East Road
Heron Rookery
Porter
Marina
Calumet Rd.
Chesterton
Pinhook Bog
Portage
Indiana Toll Road
Willowcreek Road
Salt Creek
0
2 mi
0
2 km
94
20
12
49
149
80
90
6
1
2

On Lake Michigan's southern shore, this park—one of the best places in the country to see dunes—is less than 50 miles from the metropolis of Chicago but feels a world away.

At 15,067 acres, Indiana Dunes is one of the smaller national parks, and some said it did not meet traditional national park criteria when it was elevated from national lakeshore status in 2019. Regardless, its beaches and fascinating inland ecosystems make it a great escape from urban areas in both directions.

As the glaciers retreated from modern-day Lake Michigan over the last 20 millennia, currents pushed sand to its southeastern shore. Streams draining into the lake produced a countercurrent, resulting in the formation of sandbars. As the waters slowly receded, the sandbars became ridges that have been sculpted by the elements into four dune complexes—Tolleston, Calumet, Glenwood, and the one along the present-day shore—that today constitute this park amid what is often referred to as Duneland.

The dunes aren't the only natural attraction. The park is also home to one of the last black oak savannas in the Midwest. Although these savannas once covered 50 million acres, only 30,000 acres of them remain in the region. The park also has swamps, prairies, and rivers within its boundaries.

The flora and fauna here are also diverse, with more than 1,100 native plants and over 600 animal species, including more than 350 different birds. Surprisingly, this makes Indiana Dunes the fourth-most biodiverse national park.

A "Save the Dunes" campaign led to hearings on the idea of Sand Dunes National Park in Chicago in 1926, the same year Indiana Dunes State Park was established. Congress authorized Indiana Dunes National Lakeshore in 1966, and Indiana's U.S. Senators were instrumental in lobbying for it to become a national park.

Although not in the same class as a Yellowstone or Yosemite, Indiana Dunes is a worthy destination with numerous allures, including the unique dune and savanna landscapes and the opportunity for a respite from the heat and humidity of the Midwestern summer. Birders, boaters, and beachgoers can readily spend a week here, and more casual visitors can easily experience it in a day.

Planning

When to Go

The lakeshore is most popular in the summer, when heat and humidity overwhelm Chicago and other nearby cities. That can also mean crowds, whereas the park sees far fewer visitors in fall and spring. Winters can be harsh on Lake Michigan, with plenty of wind, snow, and cold.

AVERAGE HIGH/LOW TEMPERATURES					
JAN.	**FEB.**	**MAR.**	**APR.**	**MAY**	**JUNE**
33/20	36/21	47/31	59/39	69/49	78/59
JULY	**AUG.**	**SEPT.**	**OCT.**	**NOV.**	**DEC.**
82/64	80/62	75/56	63/45	50/35	38/25

FESTIVALS AND EVENTS

Apple Festival. Held in late September at historic Chellberg Farm, the Apple Festival is like a master class on the uses of apples—in everything from applesauce to vinegar. There's also live music, storytelling, and the chance to feed the farm's resident animals. Check the park website for details.

Indiana Dunes Birding Festival. The park's feathered denziens are the focus of the lectures and tours held as part of this mid-May festival. 🌐 *indunesbirdingfestival.com.*

Getting Here and Around

AIR

Chicago's O'Hare and Midway international airports are 61 and 53 miles northwest of the park, respectively. The smaller Gary/Chicago International Airport is 20 miles west of the park.

CAR

The park is easily accessed via I–90, I–94, and U.S. 12 from Chicago to the west and from South Bend, Indiana, or Kalamazoo, Michigan, to the east. The park has eight parking lots of varying sizes. All have restrooms and drinking fountains, and all are free except for West Beach ($6). In summer, call ahead (☎ *219/395–1003*) to check on parking availability. There is additional parking at Indiana Dunes State Park. Note that it is illegal to drive on the beaches or dunes.

SHUTTLE

Free shuttles (dubbed "dune buggies") offer transportation from 10 am to 6 pm on summer weekends. The West End Shuttle connects the South Shore train station on East Dunes Highway in Gary with Lake Streer Beach. The East End Shuttle runs between the Dunewood Campground and Kemil Beach. Consult the park website or call (☎ *219/395–1824*) for more details.

TRAIN

Amtrak (🌐 *www.amtrak.com*) stops just east of the park in Michigan City, Indiana, and west of the park in Hammond, Indiana. You don't necessarily need a car to access the park thanks to the South Shore Line, which runs between downtown Chicago and South Bend, Indiana, with stops in Gary, Portage, Beverly Shores, and Michigan City.

CONTACTS South Shore Line. ☎ *312/836–7000 for schedules, 219/926–5744 for information weekdays 8–4* 🌐 *www.mysouthshoreline.com.*

Inspiration

Public Enemies, a 2009 movie starring Johnny Depp as John Dillinger, featured scenes shot along the beach at Indiana Dunes. The book *Diana of the Dunes: The True Story of Alice Gray,* by Janet Zenke Edwards, tells the tale of the woman who left Chicago for a simpler existence of solitude in a hut among the dunes in 1915.

Park Essentials

ACCESSIBILITY

Park visitor centers, the Portage Lakefront and Riverwalk, and the Dunewood Campground are wheelchair-accessible with assistance. Accessible parking and restrooms are located throughout the park, as are the picnic areas at West Beach, Bailly Homestead and Chellberg Farm, Tremont, Lake View Beach, and Tolleston Dunes Overlook. West Beach and Lake View Beach have limited accessibility to beach areas. The park can provide a sand-friendly wheelchair at West Beach (first-come, first-served).

PARK FEES AND PERMITS

Most areas of the park are free to enter, but there is a $6 per vehicle entrance fee for West Beach from Memorial Day weekend to Labor Day weekend.

PARK HOURS

The park entrance at West Beach is open from 7 am to 9 pm year-round. Most other areas of the park are open from 6 am to 11 pm year-round.

CELL PHONE RECEPTION

Reception is generally good throughout the park, with a few dead zones in the dunes and on the beaches.

Hotels

The only overnight option in the national park is Dunewood Campground, though the adjacent Indiana Dunes State Park also has a campground. Several private area campgrounds offer tent and RV sites as well as cabins.

Restaurants

There are no full-service restaurants in the park, but there are snack bars and concessionaires at the Portage Lakefront and Riverwalk.

Tours

★ Mount Baldy Hikes

GUIDED TOURS | At 126 feet in height, Mount Baldy is the largest active (or "living") dune in the park and one of the tallest lakefront dunes on Earth. It moves inland about 4 feet a year, but beach erosion led to an ongoing restoration project and restricted access. You can only ascend the dune for a view of the Chicago skyline during short but steep ranger-led hikes on summer weekends and occasionally at other times of the year. ✉ *Indiana Dunes National Park Visitor Center, 1100 N. Mineral Springs Rd., Porter* ☎ *219/395–1882* 🌐 *www.nps.gov/indu.*

Visitor Information

CONTACTS Indiana Dunes National Park Visitor Center. ✉ *1100 N. Mineral Springs Rd., Porter* ☎ *219/395–1882* 🌐 *www.nps.gov/indu.*

Lakefront

50 miles southeast of Chicago, 16 miles east of Gary, 50 miles west of South Bend.

This is the heart of the park, with most of its dunes, beaches, and man-made attractions. The park's eastern lakefront—separated from the western lakefront by the Port of Indiana and its steel mills and power plant—encompasses wetlands, the Calumet and Glenwood dune complexes, a campground, and a historic farm. Farther to the east, the national park surrounds Indiana Dunes State Park.

To the west, the lakefront intermingles with the streets of Gary, with Marquette Park (home to a beach, concessions, and a boat launch) and is bookended by the national park. Tolleston Dunes is on the west side of the park, as is Long Lake.

Swimming is allowed at all of the park's beaches. On the west side are Riverwalk Beach and West Beach, the main hub of activity and the only beach with an admission fee and lifeguards. The eastern lakefront's six beaches include (from west to east) Porter, Kemil, Dunbar, Lake View, Central Avenue, and Mount Baldy.

Sights

BEACHES

Central Avenue Beach

BEACH—SIGHT | **FAMILY** | With no facilities besides restrooms and two picnic tables, this stretch sees fewer visitors than other park beaches. The dunes here are prime nesting spots for swallows that come and go in spring and summer. **Amenities:** parking (no fee); toilets (seasonal). **Best for:** solitude; swimming; walking. ✉ *Indiana Dunes National Park, Central Ave., Pines* ✣ *1 mile north of the intersection of Central Ave. and U.S. Hwy. 12.*

Dunbar Beach

BEACH—SIGHT | **FAMILY** | Near the town of Beverly Shores, Dunbar Beach is just west of the 1933 Century of Progress homes and is a smelt fishing (no permit required) hot spot in spring. **Amenities:** parking (no fee); toilets (seasonal). **Best for:** swimming; walking. ✉ *Indiana Dunes National Park, Dunbar Ave. and Lake Front Dr., Beverly Shores.*

Kemil Beach

BEACH—SIGHT | **FAMILY** | Just southwest of adjacent Dunbar Beach, Kemil has good access to Dunes Ridge Trail and Indiana Dunes State Park. **Amenities:** parking (no fee); toilets. **Best for:** swimming; walking. ✉ *Indiana Dunes National Park, E. State Park Rd., Beverly Shores* ✣ *1 mile north of U.S. Hwy. 12 on E. State Park Rd.*

Lake View Beach

BEACH—SIGHT | **FAMILY** | Lake View Beach features picnic shelters (first-come, first served) with charcoal grills. The beach earns its name from the expansive views of Lake Michigan. **Amenities:** parking (no fee); toilets. **Best for:** walking; swimming. ✉ *Indiana Dunes National Park, Lake Front Dr., Beverly Shores* ✣ *1/8 mile west of Broadway St. on Lake Front Dr.*

Mount Baldy Beach

BEACH—SIGHT | **FAMILY** | Named for the 126-foot dune that's one of the tallest lakefront dunes on Earth, Mount Baldy Beach is at the far eastern end of the park's lakefront. Rangers guide hikes up Mount Baldy on summer weekends; access is otherwise restricted due to a restoration project. **Amenities:** parking (no fee); toilets. **Best for:** swimming; walking. ✉ *Indiana Dunes National Park, 101 Rice St., Michigan City.*

Portage Lakefront and Riverwalk Beach

BEACH—SIGHT | **FAMILY** | The former site of a steel mill has been reclaimed as a beach with a paved 0.9-mile trail alongside the Burns Waterway and a pavilion with restrooms and a seasonal snack bar. There are also picnic tables and fishing access. **Amenities:** food and drink; parking (no fee); toilets. **Best for:** swimming; walking. ✉ *Indiana Dunes National Park, 100 Riverwalk Dr., Portage.*

Porter Beach

BEACH—SIGHT | **FAMILY** | Just southwest of Indiana Dunes State Park and northeast of Cowles Bog, Porter Beach has limited facilities but it often draws big crowds. **Amenities:** parking (no fee); toilets (seasonal). **Best for:** swimming; walking. ✉ *Indiana Dunes National Park, Johnson Beach Rd., Porter* ✣ *Intersection of Wabash Ave. and Johnson Beach Rd.*

West Beach

BEACH—SIGHT | **FAMILY** | The most popular beach in the park is also the most developed, with lifeguards, showers, year-round restrooms, and picnic facilities. Note that this beach has a $6 per vehicle-entry fee in the summer. Three interconnected loop trails crisscross the area: Dune Succession Trail (0.9 miles, moderate), West Beach Trail (1.2 miles, easy), and Long Lake Trail (2.2 miles, moderate). Dune Succession offers some of the best dune views, while Long Lake is a prime birding destination. **Amenities:** lifeguards; showers; parking (seasonal fee); toilets. **Best for:** swimming; walking.

A boardwalk through a dune complex.

✉ *Indiana Dunes National Park, 376 N. County Line Rd., Gary.*

GEOLOGICAL FORMATIONS

Calumet Dunes

NATURE SITE | FAMILY | Calumet Dunes, which crest at 620 feet above sea level, began forming about 12,000 years ago, when Lake Michigan's water level was higher. Explore them on a paved, ½-mile trail that connects with trails to the Glenwood Dunes complex and Dunewood Campground. ✉ *Indiana Dunes National Park, 1596 N. Kemil Rd., Chesterton.*

Glenwood Dunes

NATURE SITE | FAMILY | With ridges cresting at 640 feet above sea level, the dunes in this complex are some of the park's tallest. They're also readily explorable via the Glenwood Dunes Horse and Hiking Trail, which has 13 trail junctions, so a map (available at the trailhead or visitor center) is a must. The loops range from 1 to 15 miles in length and are easy to moderate in difficulty, with routes for horseback riding (or, in winter, cross-country skiing) as well as hiking. Dunewood Trace connects the trails with Dunewood Campground. ✉ *Indiana Dunes National Park, 1475 N. Brummitt Rd., Chesterton.*

Tolleston Dunes

NATURE SITE | FAMILY | Tolleston Dunes began forming nearly 5,000 years ago when the water levels of Lake Michigan were 25 feet higher than they are today. The ridges encompass wetlands, black oak savanna, wildflowers, and cactus, with a 2.9-mile loop trail offering access to explore the area by foot. Located on the south side of U.S. Highway 12 and accessible via a 0.1-mile boardwalk, the Tolleston Dunes Marsh Overlook affords a good view of the dunes and wetlands. ✉ *Indiana Dunes National Park, 5364 U.S. Hwy. 12, Portage.*

HISTORIC SIGHTS

Bailly Homestead and Chellberg Farm

FARM/RANCH | Accessible via an easy, 2.1-mile, trail network, these two sights offer a glimpse into the agricultural history of Duneland. First settled in 1822, the Bailly Homestead is a National Historic Landmark with a striking main house, log cabins, and a family cemetery. Established by a Swedish family in 1869, Chellberg Farm is centered on an 1885 farmhouse restored to its early appearance and a barn that dates from the 1870s. Many structures at both sites are open to the public during special events and ranger-guided tours. ✉ *Indiana Dunes National Park, Mineral Springs Rd., Porter* ✣ *0.2 miles north of U.S. Hwy. 20.*

Century of Progress Homes

BUILDING | The Century of Progress Homes debuted at the 1933 World's Fair in Chicago and were then transported by barge to what is now the park. Four of the five homes showcase a futuristic vision from another era, while the Cypress House takes cues from log cabin design. Indiana Landmarks offers tours by reservation the last weekend of September. (Tickets go on sale in August and sell out almost immediately.) You can, however, walk along the street in front of the houses at other times. Be mindful of private property, though: most are residences (leased long term to people who have agreed to restore and preserve them). ✉ *Indiana Dunes National Park, 127 W. Lake Front Dr., Michigan City* ☎ *574/232–4534* 🌐 *www.indianalandmarks.org.*

SCENIC STOPS

Tremont

GHOST TOWN | FAMILY | Named for a triad of massive dunes, Tremont is the site of a ghost town (little remains today) and is also a premier birding area. There is a picnic area here with summer-only restrooms. ✉ *Indiana Dunes National Park, 25 E. U.S. Hwy. 12, Chesterton.*

TRAILS

Cowles Bog Trail

TRAIL | FAMILY | Just northeast of the Port of Indiana, this 4.7-mile loop runs through prairie, wetlands, and oak savanna and over a dune ridge to Lake Michigan. *Difficult.* ✉ *Indiana Dunes National Park, 1450 N. Mineral Springs Rd., (main trailhead parking lot), Dune Acres.*

Great Marsh Trail

TRAIL | FAMILY | This 1.3-mile trail (round-trip) accesses the largest wetland complex in the Lake Michigan watershed, making it a favored destination for bird-watchers. An observation deck is located 0.2 miles from the northern parking lot. *Easy.* ✉ *Indiana Dunes National Park, Broadway Ave., Beverly Shores* ✣ *Trailhead: 0.2 miles north of U.S. Hwy. 12 on Broadway Ave.*

Little Calumet River Trail

TRAIL | FAMILY | Following alongside its namesake river, this 1.9-mile loop navigates forest, prairie, and a ravine. It's accessed from the parking lot for the Bailly Homestead and Chellberg Farm. *Moderate.* ✉ *Indiana Dunes National Park, Mineral Springs Rd., Porter* ✣ *Trailhead: 0.2 miles north of U.S. Hwy. 20 on Mineral Springs Rd.*

Paul H. Douglas Trail

TRAIL | FAMILY | From the visitor center of the same name, this trail starts with a relatively level, 0.9-mile loop in Miller Woods, with a more rugged 1.2-mile extension (one-way) to Lake Michigan. The longer hike crosses through all of the park's major habitats: wetlands, dunes, beach, and oak savanna. *Moderate.* ✉ *Indiana Dunes National Park, 100 N. Lake St., Trailhead: Near the Paul H. Douglas Visitor Center, Gary.*

VISITOR CENTERS

Indiana Dunes Visitor Center

INFO CENTER | The park's main visitor center, also known as the Dorothy Buell Visitor Center, is open daily (8 am to 6 pm in summer and 9 am to 4 pm the rest of the year). It has displays, an activity room, a bookstore, art exhibits, and video presentations. As the center is also home to Indiana Dunes Tourism, you can get information about both the park and the surrounding communities. ✉ *Indiana Dunes National Park, 1215 N. State Rd. 49, Porter* ☎ *219/395–1882* 🌐 *www.nps.com/indu.*

Paul H. Douglas Center for Environmental Education

INFO CENTER | The park's western visitor center is open daily (8 to 6 in summer and 9 to 4 in winter) and has educational exhibits and ranger-guided hikes, lectures, and other programs, including those geared to kids. You'll also find a Nature Play Zone and the trailhead for the center's namesake route through Miller Woods. ✉ *100 N. Lake St., Gary* ☎ *219/395–1824* 🌐 *www.nps.gov/indu.*

Coffee and Quick Bites

Dig the Dunes Trail Stop

$ | AMERICAN | FAMILY | The seasonal eatery at the Portage Lakefront and Riverwalk Pavilion offers fast food, wine, and beer. **Known for:** outdoor seating; live-music performances; stellar lake views. [$] *Average main: $5* ✉ *1000 Riverwalk Dr., Portage* ☎ *219/762–1675.*

Shopping

Camp Stop General Store & Beach Stop

CONVENIENCE/GENERAL STORES | Across from the Dunewood Campground, this one-stop shop sells swimwear, firewood, groceries, and other supplies for beachgoers and campers. It also rents bikes, kayaks, and paddleboards. ✉ *2 W. Dunes Hwy., Beverly Shores* ☎ *219/878–1382.*

Inland Areas

50 miles southeast of Chicago, 16 miles east of Gary, 50 miles west of South Bend.

Several noncontiguous areas, with few facilities but no entrance fees, under the management of the National Park Service and the State of Indiana are located up to 20 miles south of the shoreline and the park visitor centers. These areas protect rare, intact ecosystems ranging from ancient bogs to some of the country's largest remaining tracts of black oak savanna.

Sights

GEOLOGICAL FORMATIONS

Pinhook Bog

NATURE SITE | FAMILY | Featuring two distinct ecosystems, this 580-acre segment of the park is atop a moraine left in the wake of glacial recession 15,000 years ago. A lush forest grows around a depression with an ancient bog, and the moss is 6 feet thick in some places. There are picnic tables near the parking lot; there's also a seasonal porta potty. ✉ *Indiana Dunes National Park, 946 N. Wozniak Rd., La Porte* ✣ *About 16 miles east of Indiana Dunes Visitor Center via I–94 or U.S. Hwy. 20.*

TRAILS

Heron Rookery Trail

TRAIL | FAMILY | The 1.6-mile (one-way) route parallels the Little Calumet River through a section of the park near the Dunewood Campground. While the namesake great herons have moved on, it remains one of the best places to go bird-watching in the Midwest. It's also known for wildflowers in spring and fishing in spring and fall during the trout and salmon spawning runs. *Easy.* ✉ *Indiana Dunes National Park, 1336 600 East, Michigan City* ✣ *Trailhead: About 5 miles south of Dunewood Campground.*

Hobart Woodland Trail

TRAIL | FAMILY | This 2.2-mile round-trip route takes you to Lake George. You can also walk on the paved Oak Savannah Bike Trail from the same trailhead for an easy 4-mile, in-and-out hike. This park segment (Hobart Prairie Grove) includes one of the largest remaining oak savannas in the Midwest and more than 300 different plant species in all. *Easy.* ✉ *Indiana Dunes National Park, 5227 S. Liverpool Rd., Hobart* ✣ *Trailhead: 19 miles southwest of Indiana Dunes Visitor Center via I–94.*

Pinhook Bog Trails

TRAIL | Two trails explore the bog and forest here: the 2.1-mile Upland Trail makes a loop through a mature maple and beech forest, and the 0.9-mile Bog Trail (round-trip) explores this area's namesake bog, a National Natural Landmark. Teeming with carnivorous plants, orchids, and ferns, this rare acidic bog is very distinct from the forest. *Moderate.* ✉ *Indiana Dunes National Park, 946 N. Wozniak Rd., La Porte* ✣ *Trailhead: About 16 miles east of Indiana Dunes Visitor Center via I–94 or U.S. Hwy. 20.*

Activities

BIKING

Most of the park's bike routes are relatively flat, and you can rent bikes at the Camp Stop General Store & Beach Stop, across from the Dunewood Campground. The Calumet Bike Trail follows railroad tracks and power lines parallel to the shoreline for 8.5 miles through the eastern and western lakefront sections. At the Hobart Prairie Grove, bikes can access the Oak Savannah Bike Trail, offering an 8.9-mile ride between the towns of Hobart and Griffith over Lake George.

Pedal Power Rentals

BICYCLING | FAMILY | This outfit offers rentals ($9 per hour or $36 per day) for adults and kids in summer and weekends in fall, as well as guided, 90-minute, Saturday, sunset bike tours ($10 per person, bikes included) to the beach at Indiana Dunes State Park. ✉ *1215 State Hwy. 49, Porter* ☎ *219/921–3085* 🌐 *www.pedalpowerrentals.com.*

BIRD-WATCHING

With more than 350 birds living in or migrating through the park, Indiana Dunes offers some of the Midwest's best bird-watching. Lake Michigan's shore, the Great Marsh, and the Heron Rookery are among the top spots. The **Indiana Audubon Society** (🌐 *indianaaudubon.org*) offers occasional field trips (typically $15) and organizes the annual Indiana Dunes Birding Festival in May.

BOATING, CANOEING, AND KAYAKING

Lake Michigan is a popular sailing and powerboating destination, but there are no marinas or boat launches in the national park. There is a boat launch at Marquette Park in Gary and a public marina in Portage. Canoeing is not recommended on Lake Michigan, but it is popular on the Little Calumet River.

The Little Calumet River also offers kayaking opportunities for a variety of skill levels. Kayakers can launch from any of the park's beaches outside of the swimming area at West Beach. The Lake Michigan Water Trail connects Chicago with New Buffalo, Michigan, on a 75-mile route along the south shore, including the waters off Indiana Dunes National Park. Note that the Camp Stop General Store & Beach Stop, across from the Dunewood Campground, rents kayaks and paddleboards.

Miller's Marine Center

BOATING | This outfit rents powerboats ($550 per day), fishing boats ($300 per day), kayaks ($20 per day), and canoes ($20 per day). ✉ *1305 State Rd. 249, Portage* ☎ *219/762–8767* 🌐 *www.mwmarina.com.*

CAMPING

Dunewood Campground. The only campground in the park offers 66 sites (13 walk-in and 4 accessible sites) for tents and RVs (no hookups) with restrooms and showers in a nicely treed area 1.5 miles south of Lake Michigan. The campground is closed November through March. ✉ *Indiana Dunes National Park, Golf Wood Rd., Porter, IN* ☎ *219/395–1882* 🌐 *www.recreation.gov.*

Indiana Dunes State Park Campground. Located between national park parcels adjacent to Lake Michigan, Indiana Dunes State Park offers another options for tent campers and RVers, with

140 sites that have electric hookups. The property, just a ½ mile from the beach by trail, features a camp store, playground, vault toilets, and showers. ✉ *Indiana Dunes State Park, 1600 N. 25 East, Chesterton, IN* ☎ *219/926–1952* 🌐 *www.in.gov.*

CROSS-COUNTRY SKIING

Winter is a serene (albeit chilly) time to explore the park. The Glenwood Dunes, Tolleston Dunes, and Paul H. Douglas trails are open to cross-country skiing in the winter. Free-use skis and snowshoes are available at the Paul H. Douglas Center for Envrionmantal Education on the west side of the park for use on the Paul H. Douglas Trail; you'll need to bring your own equipment for the other trails. A note of caution: The shelf ice on the edge of Lake Michigan is notoriously unstable. Never walk on it.

FISHING

The Little Calumet River in the Heron Rookery is a popular destination for anglers during the spring and fall salmon- and trout-spawning runs, as is Lake Michigan, one of the world's largest freshwater lakes. An Indiana state fishing license is required.

Brother Nature Fishing Adventures
FISHING | Brother Nature departs from several marinas on the south shore on five- or six-hour Lake Michigan fishing charters for one to four anglers. Rates start at $379. ✉ *Lake Michigan, Portage* ☎ *219/394–2123* 🌐 *www.brother-nature.com.*

HIKING

The park has more than 50 miles of trails, and hiking is the best way to explore its dune, oak-savanna, and prairie ecosystems. Most of the terrain is relatively flat and easy or moderate in difficulty. It's important to stay on the trails and respect closed-area signs, as the landscape here is notably fragile. Check the weather forecast before heading out, bring drinking water and insect repellent, and watch out for ticks and poison ivy.

What's Nearby

There are numerous hotels and restaurants in the surrounding communities of **Gary, Chesterton, Porter,** and **Michigan City.** The big regional draw is **Chicago.** Visitors can take the South Shore Line to Duneland from downtown Chicago and be back in time for a night of deep-dish pizza and blues music.

Chapter 36

ISLE ROYALE NATIONAL PARK

Updated by
Eric Peterson

Camping	Hotels	Activities	Scenery	Crowds
★★★★★	★★★☆☆	★★★★☆	★★★☆☆	★★★★★

WELCOME TO ISLE ROYALE NATIONAL PARK

TOP REASONS TO GO

★ **A backpacker's paradise:** With no roads and 166 miles of trails, the park offers a true wilderness experience.

★ **Exploring the waters:** Motor- and paddle-powered boats can access more than 800 square miles of the surrounding waters of Lake Superior and 450 islands beyond Isle Royale proper.

★ **See the wildlife dynamic:** Wolves prey on moose on Isle Royale, and when one population declines, the other rises. A last pair of wolves has been bolstered by transplants from Canada, giving the 2,000 strong moose in the park their only predators.

★ **Get away from it all:** Thanks to its remote location accessible only by water or air, Isle Royale is the least-visited park outside of Alaska, with about 25,000 visitors a year.

★ **Savor civilization at Rock Harbor:** With the only hotel, Rock Harbor Lodge, and full-service restaurants in the park, this is the island's main hub of visitor activity.

1 Isle Royale. There are more than 450 islands in the park, but at 45 miles long, and 9 miles at its widest point, Isle Royale is the park's largest island. Rock Harbor, located on the eastern end of the island, is the main hub of human activity, with the park's only hotel and restaurants centered on the smaller Snug Harbor, and Windigo offers a store, marina, and rental cabins on the eastern tip. The Greenstone Ridge Trail connects the two areas, with numerous camping options along the route. A number of lakes, including Lake Desor and Siskiwit Lake, the park's largest, are accessible by offshoot trails and offer camping options as well.

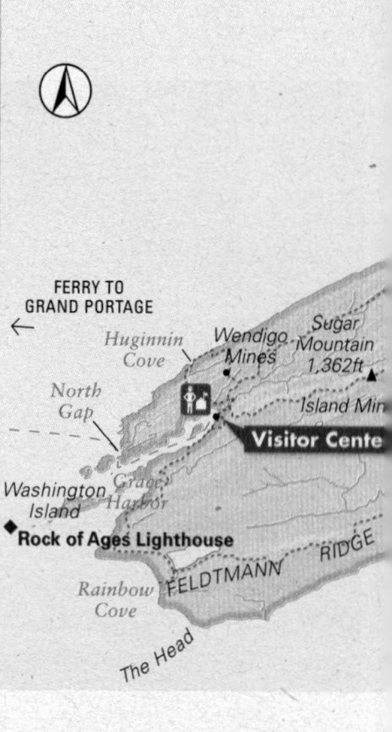

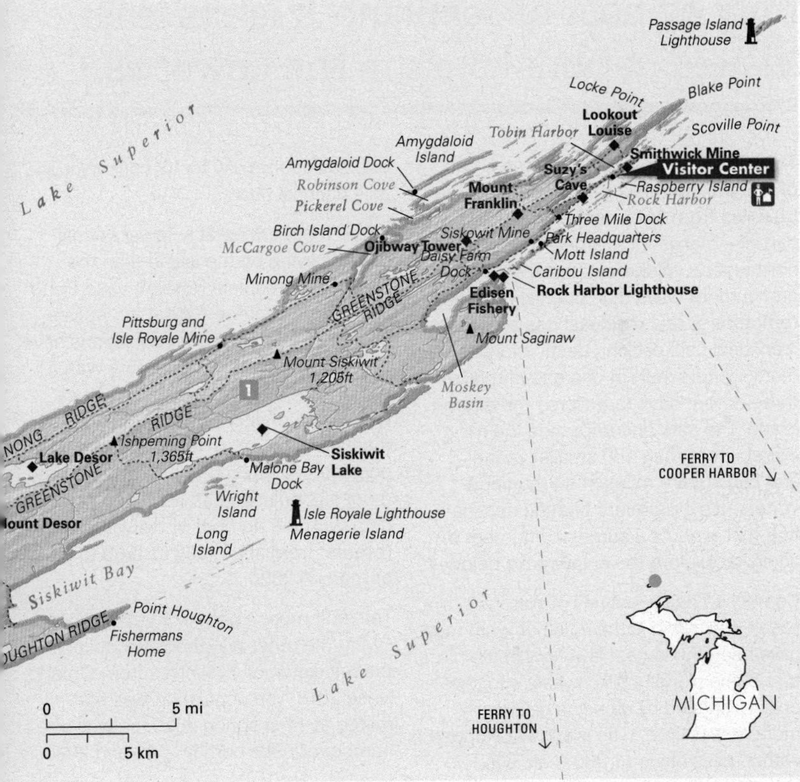

Passage Island Lighthouse
Locke Point
Blake Point
Lookout Louise
Scoville Point
Tobin Harbor
Smithwick Mine
Visitor Center
Suzy's Cave
Raspberry Island
Rock Harbor
Amygdaloid Island
Amygdaloid Dock
Robinson Cove
Pickerel Cove
Mount Franklin
Three Mile Dock
Lake Superior
Birch Island Dock
Siskowit Mine
Park Headquarters
McCargoe Cove
Ojibway Tower
Daisy Farm Dock
Mott Island
Caribou Island
Minong Mine
GREENSTONE RIDGE
Edisen Fishery
Rock Harbor Lighthouse
Pittsburg and Isle Royale Mine
Mount Saginaw
Mount Siskiwit 1,205ft
1
Moskey Basin
NONG RIDGE
RIDGE
Ishpeming Point 1,365ft
Lake Desor
Siskiwit Lake
Malone Bay Dock
GREENSTONE
FERRY TO COOPER HARBOR
Wright Island
Isle Royale Lighthouse
Menagerie Island
Mount Desor
Long Island
Siskiwit Bay
Point Houghton
HOUGHTON RIDGE
Fishermans Home
Lake Superior
MICHIGAN
0
5 mi
0
5 km
FERRY TO HOUGHTON

This rugged fin of volcanic rock is the largest island in the largest freshwater lake (Lake Superior) on Earth. Accessed only by boat or seaplane, it is the least visited national park in the Lower 48.

The isolation—15 miles from the shore of Ontario, 18 miles from Minnesota, and 56 miles from Michigan, of which it is part of—makes for a largely untouched northwoods wilderness that's off the grid in more ways than one. Isle Royale's remoteness and roadlessness also make it an ideal backpacking destination, as many visitors start at one end and take three or four days to traverse the entire island. The park encompasses the main island, more than 450 smaller islands, and 850 square miles of surrounding waters. It's a premiere boating destination that attracts a surprising number of divers to explore the shipwrecks below.

Composed nearly entirely of volcanic basalt, the island is the result of what may have been the largest lava flow in the history of the planet a billion years ago, give or take, shaped by receding glaciers in more recent time. (The island was topped with 2 miles of ice 11,000 years ago.) Copper and other minerals are in smaller supply on the island's surface. A rugged shoreline gives way to undulating and verdant hills and ridges, nestling numerous fjords, lakes, and wetlands.

The park was officially established in 1940 by an act of Congress. After a short-lived copper-mining boom in the mid-1800s, Isle Royale became a hub for the commercial fishing industry and then emerged as a tourist destination in the early 20th century, with the construction of numerous lakeside resorts. However, the Great Depression all but ended this era, paving the way for its conservation as a national park.

While there are notably fewer animal species living on the island than the nearest shores, Isle Royale's varied landscapes make prime habitat for wolves and moose. These twin populations have ebbed and flowed for a century with a singular predator-prey dynamic. There was a high of about 50 wolves living in the park in the early 1980s, but the lupine population dwindled to two by 2018. The moose population has oscillated in tandem with the number of wolves, but in reverse: from about 500 in 1980 to 2,000 or more in 2020.

The wolf-moose pendulum could soon swing the other way, however, following the relocation of 19 wolves from Ontario since 2018. The population was estimated at 14 in spring 2020, as well as a number of pups born in 2019 and 2020.

Planning

When to Go

Isle Royale and the surrounding islands are open from April 15 to October 31. Only the waters of Lake Michigan are open to boaters in the off seasons, and the islands reopen for the season on April 15. Many backpackers aim to go late in the season in hopes of an early freeze dampening the mosquito population.

AVERAGE HIGH/LOW TEMPERATURES					
JAN.	**FEB.**	**MAR.**	**APR.**	**MAY**	**JUNE**
18/-1	24/3	35/13	46/36	58/36	66/46
JULY	**AUG.**	**SEPT.**	**OCT.**	**NOV.**	**DEC.**
72/51	72/51	63/44	49/33	35/21	23/7

Getting Here and Around

The only access to Isle Royale is via ferry or seaplane.

AIR

The first step is typically flying into Houghton County Memorial Airport (CMX), Thunder Bay International Airport (YQT), or Duluth International Airport (DLH). From Houghton or Grand Marais, Minnesota (100 miles northeast of Duluth), visitors can take a seaplane with Isle Royale Seaplanes to Windigo, Rock Harbor, or a prearranged place in between the two. Round trips range from $290 to $380; it takes about 30–45 minutes to get to the park.

CONTACTS Isle Royale Seaplanes. ☎ *960/483–4991* 🌐 *isleroyaleseaplanes.com.*

CAR

Isle Royale is not accessible by car. Houghton and Copper Harbor are gateways on Michigan's Upper Peninsula on U.S. Highway 41, as well as Grand Portage and Grand Marais in Minnesota, on U.S. Highway 61.

FERRIES

If you don't have a private watercraft or a seaplane ticket, you will be taking a ferry from Houghton or Copper Harbor, Michigan, or Grand Portage, Minnesota, to Isle Royale for an overnight trip.

Visitors can travel via ferry on the *Ranger III* from Houghton (a six-hour one-way trip starts at $55) or the *Isle Royale Queen IV* from Copper Harbor, Michigan (a three-hour round-trip starts at $135), or from Grand Portage, Minnesota, on the *Voyageur II* (a two-hour one-way trip starts at $76) or *Sea Hunter III* (a day trip starts at $80). Ferries from Windigo and Rock Harbor are also available, as is water taxi service from Rock Harbor Lodge (rates start at about $60 for 1–2 people for a one-way trip). Water bus service takes visitors on a sightseeing boat to Daisy Farm or Hidden Lake (tickets range $16–$18); it's a great option for hikers looking to return to Rock Harbor on foot.

CONTACTS Isle Royale Queen IV. ☎ *906/289–4437* 🌐 *www.isleroyale.com.* **Ranger III.** ☎ *906/482–0984* 🌐 *www.nps.gov/isro/planyourvisit/ranger-iii-info.htm.* **Voyageur II.** ☎ *218/600-0765* 🌐 *www.isleroyaleboats.com.*

Park Essentials

ACCESSIBILITY

Visitor centers in Houghton and Rock Harbor have accessible restrooms and entrances. The Windigo Visitor Center has accessible restrooms near the dock; the visitor center is located up a fairly steep grade, but features an accessible entrance. Staff operates golf carts at both Rock Harbor and Windigo to help transport visitors who need it; contact the park before you arrival to make arrangements. The *Ranger III* ferry, *MV Sandy* boat tours, and Rock Harbor Lodge are all accessible, but the other ferries are not.

PARK FEES AND PERMITS

There is a $7 daily entrance fee for visitors. A season pass that covers the passholder and up to three traveling companions is $60. This includes first-come, first-served campsites in the backcountry for groups of six or fewer; groups of seven or more pay additional fees for camping. Fees can be paid online at *pay.gov* prior to arrival; print a receipt to show to the ranger.

PARK HOURS

The park is open 24 hours a day, but visitor centers, ranger stations, and other facilities have varying hours.

CELL PHONE RECEPTION

Cell phones are not reliable in Isle Royale National Park. Satellite phones are available for a fee at the Windigo and Rock Harbor visitor centers.

Hotels

The park has one hotel at Rock Harbor and a pair of rental cabins at Windigo.

Restaurants

There are two restaurants at the Rock Harbor Lodge and a general store with food and camping gear at both Windigo and Rock Harbor.

HOTEL AND RESTAURANT PRICES

Hotel and restaurant reviews have been shortened. For full information visit Fodors.com. Hotel prices are the lowest cost of a standard double room in high season. Restaurant prices are the average cost of a main course at dinner, or if dinner is not served, at lunch.

What It Costs

$	$$	$$$	$$$$
RESTAURANTS			
under $5	$5–$15	$15–$25	over $25
HOTELS			
under $60	$60–$150	$151–$250	over $250

Tours

Rangers offer a number of talks and programs; check the park website for the current schedule.

Rock Harbor Lodge operates a tour boat, *the MV Sandy,* that take visitors to Passage Island, Hidden Lake, Edisen Fishery, and other locales on and around Isle Royale. Beyond the boat cruise, the lodge's tours include such activities as guided hikes and visits to historic lighthouses.

Isle Royale Charters

ADVENTURE TOURS | Based in Grand Portage, Minnesota, this outfit specializes in five-day scuba diving excursions in the waters off Isle Royale. Charters often sell out several years in advance. *Grand Portage Marina, 41 Marina Rd., Grand Portage* *855/348–3472* *www.isleroyalecharters.com.*

Isle Royale Seaplanes

AIR EXCURSIONS | While most customers fly over for a multiday visit, Isle Royale Seaplanes also offers scenic day trips from Houghton and Grand Marais. Prices start around $300 per person. *Hancock Portage Canal, 21205 Royce Rd.* *906/483–4491* *www.isleroyaleseaplanes.com.*

Keweenaw Adventure Company

BOAT TOURS | An all-inclusive kayaking adventure offers a completely different perspective on Isle Royale. Keweenaw Adventure Company offers all-inclusive, four- to six-day tours exploring the shoreline that depart from Copper Harbor on the *Isle Royale Queen II* ferry. *155 Gratiot St., Copper Harbor* *906/289–4303* *www.keweenawadventure.com.*

***MV Sandy* Tours**

BOAT TOURS | FAMILY | Rock Harbor Lodge operates a tour boat, the *MV Sandy*, that take visitors to Passage Island, Hidden Lake, Edisen Fishery, and other locales on and around Isle Royale. Beyond the boat cruise, the tours include such activities as guided hikes and visits to historic lighthouses. ✉ *Isle Royale National Park* ✣ *Tours depart from Rock Harbor* ☎ *906/337–4993* 🌐 *rockharborlodge.com.*

Rock Harbor Lodge Fishing Charters

BOAT TOURS | Charters out of Rock Harbor primarily troll for lake trout and salmon. The Lighthouse Restaurant will cook your catch for dinner. A four-hour trip is about $450. ✉ *Rock Harbor Lodge, Isle Royale National Park* ☎ *906/337–4993* 🌐 *www.rockharborlodge.com.*

Sea Hunter III

BOAT TOURS | This is the only option to take a day trip to the park ($87 adults). The boat leaves Grand Portage, Minnesota, at 8:30 am and returns at 3:30 pm multiple times per week from early June to early September. ✉ *Grand Portage* ☎ *218/600–0765* 🌐 *www.isleroyaleboats.com.*

Timberline Hike and Bike Adventures

ADVENTURE TOURS | Timberline offers guided weeklong outings for backpackers who want a guide to accompany them on their northwoods adventure. The trips are all-inclusive and start around $4,000 for a single person. Check the website for the current schedule. ☎ *800/417–2453* 🌐 *www.timberline-adventures.com.*

Visitor Information

CONTACTS Isle Royale National Park. ☎ *906/482–0984* 🌐 *www.nps.gov/isro.*

Isle Royale

61 miles north from Houghton, Michigan.

Located in the middle of Lake Superior, Isle Royale is by far the largest of the more than 450 islands that make up the national park, it's also the only one with any visitor services. This is where you'll find lodging and dining options as well as stores for backpackers and boaters to stock up on food, gear, and fuel.

Rock Harbor is located on the eastern end of the island. Snug Harbor, the center of activity in the area, is where you'll find lodging, dining, and shops.

Sights

GEOLOGICAL FORMATIONS

Lake Desor

NATIONAL/STATE PARK | Located between the Greenstone Ridge Trail and Minong Ridge Trail, about one-third of the way from Windigo to Rock Harbor, this is one of Isle Royale's larger lakes. It's known for its fishing, and has campgrounds on the north and south sides. ✉ *Isle Royale National Park* ✣ *Accessible from the Greenstone Ridge and Minong Ridge trails.*

Mount Desor

MOUNTAIN—SIGHT | At 1,394 feet above sea level, this is Isle Royale's highest mountain. It's located in a forested area on the Greenstone Ridge Trail about 9 miles east of Windigo; because of the dense foliage, the only time you get good views is fall. ✉ *Isle Royale National Park* ✣ *On Greenstone Ridge Trail.*

Siskiwit Lake

BODY OF WATER | At 4,150 acres in surface area, Siskiwit Lake is the largest lake on Isle Royale. Home to populations of trout and perch (as well as loons, snails, mussels, and leeches), the cold, clear lake is popular for angling and canoeing. The lake has been separated from Lake Superior for roughly 5,000 years, leading to distinct species of fish evolving in its waters. There are several islands in the lake, but Ryan Island has the irresistibly odd designation of being the largest island on the largest lake on the largest island (Isle Royale) on the largest lake (Lake Superior) in the world. ✉ *Isle Royale National Park* ✣ *On the south side of Isle Royale about 8 miles southwest of Rock Harbor.*

First lit in 1856, the Rock Harbor Lighthouse was only operational for about 20 years. Today it's a museum.

Suzy's Cave

NATURE SITE | Technically not a cave but an inland sea arch, this geological anomaly is accessible by trail between Rock Harbor and Three Mile Campground on a 0.2-mile spur trail that connects the Rock Harbor Trail and Tobin Harbor Trail. Waves formed the arch about 4,000 years ago when the lake level was higher. ✉ *Isle Royale National Park* ✢ *1.8 miles west of Rock Harbor.*

HISTORIC SIGHTS

Edisen Fishery

FISH HATCHERY | The Isle Royale fishing industry was booming in the late 1800s and early 1900s. The Edisen Fishery on the south side of Rock Harbor offers a glimpse into this era as the best-preserved example of the fishing camps that once dotted the island's shores. Still operational and open to visitors, the site consists of several intact structures and outbuildings that are home to reenactors who staff it during the summer months. ✉ *Isle Royale National Park* ✢ *South side of Rock Harbor; accessible by private boat, water taxi, or MV Sandy tours.*

Rock Harbor Lighthouse

LIGHTHOUSE | First lit in 1856 to guide ships supplying the local mining and fishing industries, the Rock Harbor Lighthouse was only operational for about 20 years, projecting illumination visible for 15 miles. Today it serves as a museum that provides a look into the prepark era. ✉ *Isle Royale National Park* ✢ *South side of Rock Harbor; accessible by private boat, water taxi, or MV Sandy tours* ⏲ *Closed Nov.–mid-Apr.*

Rock of Ages Lighthouse

LIGHTHOUSE | Perched on a rocky outcropping just off the west end of Isle Royale is one of the most iconic lighthouses in the Great Lakes. Still operational, the unmanned 117-foot lighthouse was a feat of early 20th-century engineering and featured one of the most potent lenses of any lighthouse at the time. A crew lived in the 10-level structure until 1977, and a modern, solar-powered lens replaced the iconic one (now on display at the Windigo Visitor Center) in 1985. The waters around it remain popular for fishing boats and divers exploring nearby shipwrecks. ✉ *Isle Royale National Park* ⊕ *Outside Washington Harbor in Lake Superior* ⊙ *Closed Nov.–mid-Apr.*

Smithwick Mine

MINE | This vestige of the island's copper mining industry dates back to the 1840s. While it wasn't very productive and there are no tours, it is the easiest mining site to visit on Isle Royale. It consists of four shafts off the Stoll Memorial Trail from Snug Harbor. ✉ *Isle Royale National Park.*

SCENIC SPOTS

Lookout Louise

VIEWPOINT | This overlook offers one of the best panoramas on Isle Royale. On a clear day, you can see all the way to Ontario, Canada, and the islands between Isle Royale and Thunder Bay. You'll need a boat, or else transportation on *MV Sandy* to get to the trailhead for the 2-mile hike (round-trip, moderate) to the lookout. ✉ *Isle Royale National Park* ⊕ *Hidden Lake Trailhead at the east end of the Greenstone Ridge Trail.*

Mount Franklin

VIEWPOINT | The summit of this 1,074-foot mountain between Ojibway Tower and Lookout Louise on the Greenstone Ridge Trail gives hikers a panorama that spans the island interior to the Canadian mainland. It's a challenging, 10-mile round trip to hike from Rock Harbor. ✉ *Isle Royale National Park* ⊕ *On Greenstone Ridge Trail.*

Ojibway Tower

VIEWPOINT | Located atop Mount Ojibway, this lookout tower is partially open to the public for expansive views of the eastern side of Isle Royale. It's a 1.7-mile, moderate hike from Daisy Farm Campground, and can be reached on a long day hike from Rock Harbor. If you have don't have much time, you can hire a water taxi and then it's a short hike. ✉ *Isle Royale National Park* ⊕ *On Greenstone Ridge Trail.*

TRAILS

★ Greenstone Ridge Trail

TRAIL | The spine of the park, Greenstone Ridge Trail is a 42-mile trail that connects the Rock Harbor and Windigo areas on a multiday backpacking route. From Windigo, the trail rises from wetlands into forest over Mount Desor (the highest mountain in the park, peaking at 1,394 feet above sea level), then descends to Lake Desor. Farther east, an offshoot trail accesses Siskiwit Lake, then the main trail passes numerous campgrounds and lakes en route to its western terminus at Lookout Louise, one of the best scenic viewpoints in the park. Hikers heading to Rock Harbor can divert to Moskey Basin, home to an unforgettable campground, on the way to Daisy Farm. *Difficult.* ✉ *Isle Royale National Park* ⊕ *Trailhead: Western trailhead is at Windigo Ranger Station; eastern trailhead is at Hidden Lake near Tobin Harbor* ⊙ *Closed Nov.–mid-Apr.*

Rock Harbor Trail

TRAIL | FAMILY | While not exactly crowded, Rock Harbor Trail is the most-hiked trail in the park. The 10.9-mile route connects Moskey Basin and Snug Harbor, but hikers can take different forks in the trail to visit attractions like Suzy's Cave, the Mt. Ojibway Tower, and the summit of Mt. Franklin. For a 4-mile loop, take Suzy's Cave Trail to Tobin Harbor Trail and return to Snug Harbor. *Moderate.* ✉ *Isle Royale National Park* ⊕ *Trailhead: Western trailhead is at Moskey Basin; eastern trailhead is at Snug Harbor.*

★ Stoll Memorial Trail / Scoville Point Trail

TRAIL | Take this trail to the end of the earth. The 4.2-mile loop traverses Isle Royale's rugged shoreline and evergreen forest on the way to and from Scoville Point. The rocky endpoint offers a one-of-a-kind view of Lake Superior, and little else. *Moderate.* ✉ *Isle Royale National Park* ⊕ *Trailhead: At Snug Harbor.*

VISITOR CENTERS

Houghton Visitor Center

INFO CENTER | Located in the gateway city of Houghton (not on Isle Royale) on Michigan's Upper Peninsula, this visitor center is open June to mid-September. It's the home port for the *Ranger III* ferry and the place to pick up permits for private boat trips to the island. ✉ *800 E. Lakeshore Dr., Houghton.*

Rock Harbor Visitor Center

INFO CENTER | At the northeastern end of Isle Royale, this is the main point of contact with rangers in the Rock Harbor area from May to September. It's located in Snug Harbor at the ferry dock. ✉ *Isle Royale National Park.*

Windigo Visitor Center

INFO CENTER | The Windigo Visitor Center is one of just a few facilities on the west side of Isle Royale, offering information and a few exhibits on the park and its history from May to September. ✉ *Isle Royale National Park.*

Restaurants

Greenstone Grill

$$ | **PIZZA** | **FAMILY** | The casual option at Rock Harbor Lodge, Greenstone Grill's staple is pizza, but the menu also includes a range of sandwiches and pub grub for lunch and dinner, with egg dishes and flapjacks for breakfast. Craft beer and wine are available. **Known for:** relaxed atmosphere; local craft beer selection; tasty pizza. $ *Average main: $10* ✉ *Isle Royale National Park* ✣ *Rock Harbor* ☎ *906/337–4993* 🌐 *rockharborlodge.com.*

Lighthouse Restaurant

$$$$ | **SEAFOOD** | This is Rock Harbor Lodge's upscale destination for dinner; it's under the same roof as the Greenstone Grill but in a different seating area with an elevated dinner menu. The breakfasts and lunches are traditional American, with flapjacks and eggs and burgers and sandwiches, while the dinner menu includes a selection of seafood from Lake Superior, as well as pasta dishes and other entrees. **Known for:** lake trout dinners; quality ingredients; creative seafood dishes. $ *Average main: $27* ✉ *Isle Royale National Park* ✣ *Rock Harbor* ☎ *906/337–4993* 🌐 *rockharborlodge.com.*

Hotels

Rock Harbor Lodge

$$$$ | **HOTEL** | Isle Royale's sole hotel dates back to the early 1900s when it was one of several resorts on the island; the park service took over the property over post Great Depression. **Pros:** comfortable furnishings and beds; stylish decor with a old school lake resort vibe; great views of the lake from some rooms and other areas of the property. **Cons:** expensive room rates for the size and amenities; the property is difficult to get to; it requires a ferry or flight; accommodations are in high demand so you need to book early. $ *Rooms from: $260* ✉ *Isle Royale National Park* ✣ *Rock Harbor* ☎ *906/337–4993* 🌐 *rockharborlodge.com* ⏲ *Closed Nov.–mid-Apr.* *60 rooms, 20 cottages* *No meals.*

Windigo Camper Cabins

$ | **RENTAL** | **FAMILY** | The only lodging on the park's west side, this pair of spartan cabins have two bunk beds and a futon each, offering an alternative to camping in the Windigo area. **Pros:** rustic—exactly what you expect in a basic cabin in terms of decor and setting; the basic cabins are all you need for the setting; comfortable bunk beds. **Cons:** no indoor plumbing; no a/c or heat; basic and small with limited furnishings and amenities. $ *Rooms from: $52* ✉ *Isle Royale National Park* ✣ *Washington Harbor* ☎ *906/337–4993* 🌐 *rockharborlodge.com* ⏲ *Closed Nov.–mid-Apr.* *2 cabins* *No meals.*

Nightlife

Rangers give evening talks about the ecology and history of the park at the auditorium or amphitheater in Rock Harbor most nights in July and August, and on a more limited schedule in June and September. Check with the visitor center for current information.

The Dockside Store at the main dock in Rock Harbor offers groceries, beer and wine, ice, assorted outdoor gear, toiletries, and books, and fuel for backpacking stoves. On the other end of the island, the Windigo Store offers a similar selection. Both stores have coin-operated laundry and showers.

Activities

BIRD-WATCHING

About 200 species of birds call Isle Royale home for part or all of the year. The varieties of birds spotted in the park have changed over the past 200 years, and now include sandpipers, sparrows, peregrine falcons, and loons. Sandhill cranes are somewhat common in the park's drained wetlands.

BOATING AND RAFTING

Boaters must obtain a permit at the Houghton Visitor Center before any overnight trip to the island and pay entrance fees in advance online at 🌐 *www.pay.gov*. Boaters in private vessels on day trips are not required to get a permit, but it is recommended due to the unpredictable waters of Lake Superior. There are marinas at Windigo and Rock Harbor, and numerous docks around the island. Dock space is first come, first served.

Motorized boats are permitted in Lake Superior, but not on any of the inland lakes or streams. There are numerous no-wake zones, quiet periods for generators, and requirements to combat the spread of invasive aquatic species via watercraft. Check the park website or call for additional information.

Motorboat rentals are available at the Rock Harbor Marina.

Rock Harbor Marina

BOATING | The main hub of boating activity on the island, the Rock Harbor Marina rents motorboats for $105 daily, as well as canoes ($40 daily) and kayaks ($58 daily). Dockage is available for private boats up to 65 feet in length, and fuel and pump-out service are offered. ✉ *Isle Royale National Park* ☎ *906/337–4933* 🌐 *www.rockharborlodge.com*.

Windigo Marina

BOATING | Located at the harbor of the same name on the southwestern tip of Isle Royale, the marina offers watercraft rentals (motorboats $85, canoes $40, and kayaks $59 per day) as well as fuel and pump-out service. ✉ *Isle Royale National Park* ☎ *906/337–4993* 🌐 *www.rockharborlodge.com*.

CAMPING

Isle Royale has 36 campgrounds, all of which are accessible only by foot or watercraft. All offer tent sites, water, and toilets and some have enclosed shelters and picnic tables. Backpackers typically hike 6–8 miles per day and plan their trip across Isle Royale in advance. Some inland lakes have sites accessible only to kayakers and canoeists, and there are docks for private boats to moor overnight (permit required; *see Boating and Rafting above*). Campsites are first-come, first-served for parties of six or fewer (who must still obtain a free permit from a visitor center before embarking on their hike); groups of seven and larger must make advance reservations via the park website and pay a $25 fee.

Daisy Farm. Location is everything, especially when it comes to Daisy Farm Campground. Located at the intersection of the Rock Harbor and Mount Ojibway trails, the campground has access to Greenstone Ridge (2 miles on the Mount Ojibway Trail) and Rock Harbor (8 miles east) if you're using this as a base and day hiking. It's the park's largest campground, with 16 shelters and 6 tent sites, plus 3 group camping sites. ✉ *At the intersection of Daisy Farm, Rock Harbor,* *and Mount Ojibway trails* ☎ *906/482–0894* 🌐 *www.nps.gov/isro.*

Moskey Basin. At the far west end of Rock Harbor with a rocky and rugged arc of shoreline ringed by trees and dotted with a galaxy of multihued lichen, this is one of Isle Royale's most scenic campgrounds. There are six shelters, two tent sites, and two group sites. ✉ *2 miles west of Daisy Farm on Daisy Farm Trail* ☎ *906/482–0984* 🌐 *www.nps.gov/isro.*

Washington Creek Campground. On the far east end of the island, this is a good campground if you're arriving at Windigo and looking to explore from a base on that side of the park without backpacking. It includes 10 shelters, 6 tent sites, and 4 group camping sites. ✉ *0.3 miles east of Windigo Harbor* ☎ *906/482–0984* 🌐 *www.nps.gov/isro.*

CANOEING

Multiday canoe trips are a unique option for exploring the eastern end of Isle Royale. Portages between bodies of water are marked and notably strenuous.

Ferries will transport canoes for a fee. Canoe rentals are available at Rock Harbor Marina and Windigo Marina. ⇨ *See the Boating section for marina information.*

DIVING AND SNORKELING

Isle Royale has a long history of shipwrecks in the surrounding waters, making it a popular diving destination. Nine shipwrecks are buoyed for mooring by dive boats. Divers must register at a visitor center in advance for a free permit.

FISHING

Northern pike, perch, and trout are common in the lakes that dot Isle Royale, and lake trout and salmon inhabit the surrounding waters.

A license is not necessary to fish on Isle Royale's inland waters, but a Michigan state license is required for any fishing on Lake Superior.

HIKING

Isle Royale is a true hiker's paradise. With 165 miles of trails crisscrossing its 45-foot length, there are options for both day hikes from Windigo or Rock Harbor as well as multiday backpacking trips across the island. This is the best way to truly experience the wilderness in the heart of the park.

Bring drinking water, a poncho, snacks, and a first aid kit. Backpackers will need a water filter or other means of purification. Insect repellent is a must, and the rocky areas demand sturdy footwear.

KAYAKING

Experienced kayakers have their pick of seemingly endless lakes, bays, and islands to explore on and around Isle Royale. Sea kayaks are recommended for excursions on Lake Superior.

Ferries will transport kayaks for a fee. Rentals are available at Rock Harbor Marina and Windigo Marina.

What's Nearby

The two prime gateways are **Houghton, Michigan,** and **Grand Marais, Minnesota.**

Houghton, a college town on the Upper Peninsula, has a number of chain properties as well as a few historic hotels and inns. There are numerous independent restaurants downtown; the emphasis is squarely on hearty American fare.

There are a number of lakefront resorts in the **Grand Marais** area, as well as mostly independent motels in town. Restaurants tend toward local seafood and American fare.

Chapter 37

JOSHUA TREE NATIONAL PARK

Updated by Cheryl Crabtree

Camping	Hotels	Activities	Scenery	Crowds
★★★★★	★★★★☆	★★★★★	★★★★★	★★★★☆

WELCOME TO JOSHUA TREE NATIONAL PARK

TOP REASONS TO GO

★ **Rock climbing:** Joshua Tree is a world-class site with challenges for climbers of just about every skill level.

★ **Peace and quiet:** Roughly two hours from Los Angeles, this great wilderness is the ultimate escape from technology.

★ **Stargazing:** You'll be mesmerized by the Milky Way flowing across the summer sky. For spectacular natural fireworks, visit in mid-August during the Perseid meteor shower and watch shooting stars streak overhead.

★ **Wildflowers:** In spring, the hillsides explode in a patchwork of yellow, blue, pink, and white.

★ **Sunsets:** Twilight is a magical time here, especially during the winter, when the setting sun casts a golden glow on the mountains.

1 **Park Boulevard.** Drive the paved loop road between the west and north entrances to explore many of the park's main sights. Crawl between the big rocks at Hidden Valley, and you'll understand why this boulder-strewn area near the park's west entrance was once a cattle rustlers' hideout.

2 **Keys View Road.** Keys View is the park's most dramatic overlook—on clear days you can see Signal Mountain in Mexico.

3 **Highway 62.** Spot wildlife at Black Rock and Indian Cove (you might spy a desert tortoise). Near the park's north entrance, walk the nature trail around Oasis of Mara, which the first settlers, the Serrano, dubbed "the place of little springs and much grass."

4 **Pinto Basin Road.** Pull out binoculars at Cottonwood Spring, one of the best birding spots in the park. Come to Cholla Cactus Garden in the late afternoon, when the spiky stalks of the bigelow (jumping) cholla cactus are backlit against an intense blue sky.

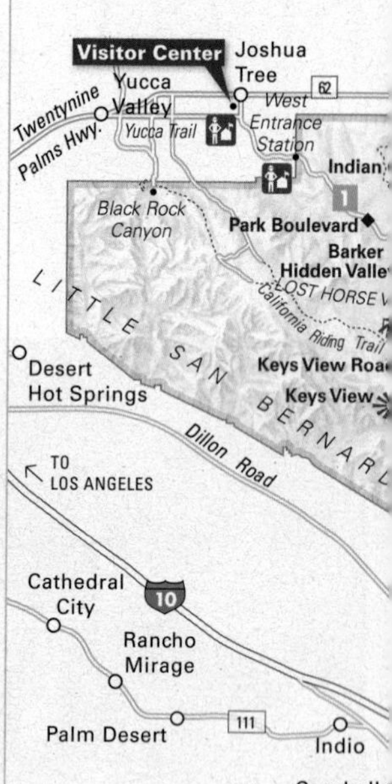

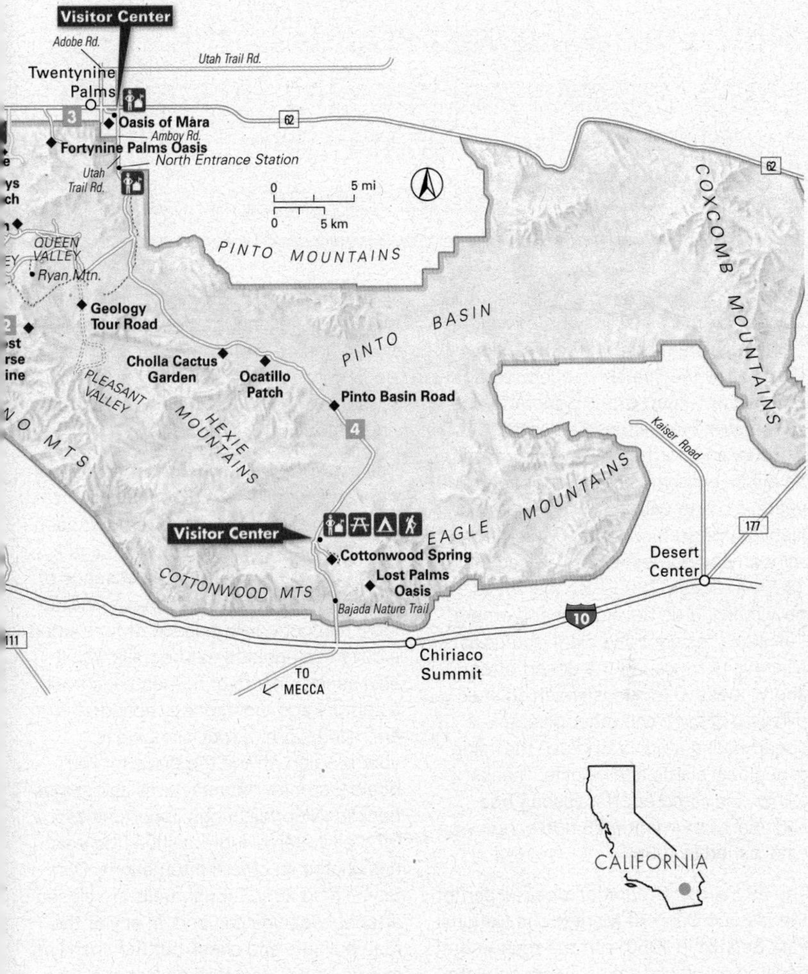

Visitor Center
Adobe Rd.
Utah Trail Rd.
Twentynine Palms
3
Oasis of Mara
Amboy Rd.
Fortynine Palms Oasis
North Entrance Station
Utah Trail Rd.
62
0 5 mi
0 5 km
PINTO MOUNTAINS
QUEEN VALLEY
Ryan Mtn.
Geology Tour Road
PINTO BASIN
COXCOMB MOUNTAINS
Cholla Cactus Garden
Ocatillo Patch
Pinto Basin Road
PLEASANT VALLEY
HEXIE MOUNTAINS
4
Kaiser Road
EAGLE MOUNTAINS
Visitor Center
Cottonwood Spring
Lost Palms Oasis
COTTONWOOD MTS
Bajada Nature Trail
177
Desert Center
10
111
Chiriaco Summit
TO MECCA

Joshua Tree teems with fascinating landscapes and life-forms, including its namesake trees. Dagger-like tufts grace the branches of the Yucca brevifolia, which grows in vast stands in the park's western reaches. Nearly 3 million people visit the park annually, but it's mysteriously quiet at dawn and dusk.

The park occupies a remote area in southeastern California, where two distinct ecosystems meet: the arid Mojave Desert and the sparsely vegetated Colorado Desert—part of the Sonoran Desert, which stretches across California, Arizona, and northern Mexico. Humans have inhabited the area for at least 5,000 years, starting with the Pinto and other Native American cultures. Cattlemen, miners, and homesteaders arrived in the 1800s and early 1900s. By the 1920s, new roads lured developers and others. Pasadena resident and plant enthusiast Minerva Hoyt visited the desert often and witnessed reckless poaching and pillaging of cacti and other plants. She spearheaded studies to prove the value of regional plants and wildlife. Thanks to her dedicated efforts, Joshua Tree National Monument (825,000 acres) was established in 1936.

The 29 Palms Corporation deeded part of the historic Oasis of Mara to the National Park Service in 1950, and the monument became an official national park on October 31, 1994. Today the park encompasses about 800,000 acres (nearly 600,000 is designated wilderness). Elevation ranges from 536 feet to the peak of 5,814-foot Quail Mountain. The diverse habitats within the park protect more than 800 plant, 250 bird, and 57 mammal species, including the desert bighorn sheep and 46 reptile species, such as the endangered desert tortoise. The park also preserves numerous archaeological sites and historic structures.

You can experience Joshua Tree National Park on several levels. Even on a short excursion along Park Boulevard between the Joshua Tree entrance station and Oasis of Mara, you'll see the essence of North American desert scenery—including a staggering abundance of flora along a dozen self-guided nature trails. You'll also see remnants of homesteads from a century ago, now mostly abandoned and wind-worn. If rock climbing is your passion, this is the place for you: boulder-strewn mountaintops and slopes beckon. Nightfall brings opportunities for stellar stargazing—Joshua Tree was designated an official International Dark Sky Park in 2017. Though trails are closed after sunset, you can park at any of the road pullouts and check out the sparkling shows above. Joshua Tree National Park is a pristine wilderness where you can enjoy a solitary stroll along a trail and commune with nature. Be sure to take some time to explore on your own and enjoy the peace and quiet.

AVERAGE HIGH/LOW TEMPERATURES					
JAN.	**FEB.**	**MAR.**	**APR.**	**MAY**	**JUNE**
62/32	65/37	72/40	80/50	90/55	100/65
JULY	**AUG.**	**SEPT.**	**OCT.**	**NOV.**	**DEC.**
105/70	101/78	96/62	85/55	72/40	62/31

Planning

When to Go

October through May, when the desert is cooler, is when most visitors arrive. Daytime temperatures range from the mid-70s in December and January to mid-90s in October and May. Lows can dip to near freezing in midwinter, and you may even encounter snow at the higher elevations. Summers can be torrid, with daytime temperatures reaching 110°F.

FESTIVALS AND EVENTS

Pioneer Days. Outhouse races, live music, and arm wrestling mark this celebration held annually, during the third full October weekend, in Twentynine Palms. The event also features a parade, carnival, chili dinner, and an old timers' gathering. 🌐 *www.visit29.org*.

Riverside County Fair & National Date Festival. Head to Indio for camel and ostrich races. 🌐 *www.datefest.org*.

Getting Here and Around

AIR

Palm Springs International Airport is the closest major air gateway to Joshua Tree National Park. It's about 45 miles from the park. The drive from Los Angeles International Airport to Joshua Tree takes about two to three hours.

CAR

An isolated island of pristine wilderness—a rarity these days—Joshua Tree National Park is within a short drive of 11 million Southern California residents. Most visitors, in fact, make the two- to three-hour drive from the Los Angeles area to enjoy a weekend of solitude in 792,726 acres of untouched desert. The urban sprawl of Palm Springs (home to the nearest airport) is 45 miles away, but gateway towns Joshua Tree, Yucca Valley, and Twentynine Palms are just north of the park. If you're staying in the Palm Springs area, you can enjoy the highlights of the park in one day, including a stop for a picnic at a scenic spot. Within the park, passenger cars are fine for paved areas, but you'll need four-wheel drive for many of the rugged backcountry roadways. At the park's most popular sites, parking is limited. Joshua Tree does not have public transportation.

■ **TIP→ If you'd prefer not to drive, most Palm Springs area hotels can arrange a half- or full-day tour that hits the highlights of Joshua Tree National Park.** But you'll need to spend two or three days camping here to truly experience the quiet beauty of the desert.

Inspiration

Keys Desert Queen Ranch, A Visual and Historical Tour, by Thomas Crochetiere, tells the history of Bill and Frances Keys' home, where they raised a family and developed what became a self-sustaining cornerstone of Joshua Tree National Park.

No Place for a Puritan: The Literature of California's Desert, edited by Ruth Nolan, is an anthology of short pieces by 80 writers, including Hunter Thompson, Joan Didion, John Hilton, and pioneer women of the 1920s and '30s.

On Foot in Joshua Tree National Monument, by Patty Furbush, lists more than 90 park trails and is a good introduction to hiking in Joshua Tree.

Wonder Valley, by Ivy Pochoa, is a thriller novel set in Twentynine Palms in 2006 that includes forays into Joshua Tree National Park and nearby towns.

Park Essentials

ACCESSIBILITY

Black Rock Canyon and Jumbo Rocks campgrounds have one accessible campsite each. Nature trails at Oasis of Mara, Bajada, Keys View, and Cap Rock are accessible. Some trails at roadside viewpoints can be negotiated by those with limited mobility.

PARK FEES AND PERMITS

Park admission is $30 per car; $15 per person on foot, bicycle, or horse; and $25 per person by motorcycle. The Joshua Tree Pass, good for one year, is $55.

PARK HOURS

The park is open every day, around the clock, but visitor centers are staffed from approximately 8 am to 5 pm. The park is in the Pacific time one.

CELL PHONE RECEPTION

Cell phones don't work in most areas of the park, and there are no telephones in its interior.

Hotels

Area lodging choices are limited to a few motels, chain hotels, vacation rentals, and several upscale establishments in the gateway towns. In general, most offer few amenities and are modestly priced. For a more extensive range of lodging options, you'll need to head to Palm Springs and the surrounding desert resort communities. Book ahead for the spring wildflower season—reservations may be difficult to obtain then.

Restaurants

Dining options in the gateway towns around the park are extremely limited—you'll mostly find fast-food outlets and a few casual eateries in Yucca Valley and Twentynine Palms. The exception is the restaurant at 29 Palms Inn, which has an interesting California-cuisine menu that features lots of veggies. For the most part, though, plan on traveling to the Palm Springs desert resort area for a fine-dining experience.

Tours

Big Wheel Tours

EXCURSIONS | Based in Palm Desert, Big Wheel Tours offers van excursions, jeep tours, and hiking trips through the park. Bicycle tours (road and mountain bike) are available outside the park boundary. Pickups are available at Palm Springs area hotels. ✉ *41625 Eclectic St., Suite O-1, Palm Desert* ☎ *760/779–1837* 🌐 *www.bwbtours.com* 🎫 *From $169.*

Joshua Tree Adventures

GUIDED TOURS | A local family operates this well-respected tour company, which offers a range of customized private outings, from hikes and scenic tours to full- and multiday hike-and-climb combinations. ✉ *61622 El Cajon Dr., Joshua Tree* ☎ *802/673–4385* 🌐 *jtreeadventures.com* 🎫 *From $70.*

★ **Keys Ranch Tour**

GUIDED TOURS | A guide takes you through the former home of a family that homesteaded here for 60 years. In addition to the ranch, a workshop, store, and schoolhouse are still standing, and the grounds are strewn with vehicles and mining equipment. The 90-minute tour, which begins at the Keys Ranch gate, tells the history of the family that built the ranch. Tickets are $10, and reservations are required. ✉ *Keys Ranch gate* ☎ *760/367–5522* 🌐 *www.nps.gov/jotr.*

Mojave Guides

SPECIAL-INTEREST | Led by resident and certified climbing instructor Seth Pettit, a team of expert guides provides customized half-, full-, and multiday technical rock-climbing courses for everyone from beginners to experts. ✉ *Joshua Tree* ☎ *760/820–2806* 🌐 *www.mojaveguides.com* 🎫 *From $100.*

Twentynine Palms Astronomy Club

SPECIAL-INTEREST | Book a private night sky experience for 2 to 10 people led by astrophotographer Steve Caron and others who have a passion for sharing the night sky. They bring high-powered telescopes and other equipment to a location of your choice in the Morongo Basin—from Morongo Valley in the west to Wonder Valley in the east, plus Pioneertown and Landers. ✉ *Twentynine Palms* ☎ *760/401–3004* 🌐 *www.29palmsastronomy.org* 🎫 *From $250 for a 2-hr session.*

Visitor Information

CONTACTS Joshua Tree National Park. ✉ *74485 National Park Dr., Twentynine Palms* ☎ *760/367–5522* 🌐 *www.nps.gov/jotr.*

Park Boulevard

Well-paved Park Boulevard—the park's main artery—loops between the west entrance near the town of Joshua Tree and the north entrance just south of Twentynine Palms. If you have time only for a short visit, driving Park Boulevard is your best choice. It traverses the most scenic portions of Joshua Tree in the park's high-desert section. Along with some sweeping desert views, you'll see jumbles of splendid boulder formations, stands of Joshua trees, and Hidden Valley and Barker Dam, remnants of the area's wild and woolly past. From the Oasis Visitor Center, drive south. After about 5 miles, the road forks; turn right and head west toward Jumbo Rocks (clearly marked with a road sign).

Sights

HISTORIC SIGHTS

Hidden Valley

NATURE SITE | **FAMILY** | This legendary cattle-rustlers' hideout is set among big boulders along a 1-mile loop trail. Kids love to scramble on and around the rocks. There are shaded picnic tables here. ✉ *Park Blvd.* ✣ *14 miles south of west entrance.*

★ **Keys Ranch**

HOUSE | This 150-acre ranch, which once belonged to William and Frances Keys and is now on the National Historic Register, illustrates one of the area's most successful attempts at homesteading. The couple raised five children under extreme desert conditions. Most of the original buildings, including the house, school, store, and workshop, have been restored to the way they were when William died in 1969. The only way to see the ranch is on one of the 90-minute walking tours, usually offered Friday–Sunday, October–May and weekends in summer; reservations are required. ✉ *Joshua Tree National Park* ✣ *2 miles north of Barker Dam Rd.* ☎ *877/444–6777* 🌐 *www.nps.gov/jotr/planyourvisit/ranchtour.htm* 🎫 *$10, reservations through recreation.gov.*

SCENIC STOPS

Barker Dam

DAM | Built around 1900 by ranchers and miners to hold water for cattle and mining operations, the dam now collects rainwater and is a good place to spot wildlife such as the elusive bighorn sheep. ✉ *Barker Dam Rd.* ✣ *Off Park Blvd., 10 miles south of west entrance.*

TRAILS

Hidden Valley Trail

TRAIL | FAMILY | Crawl through the rocks surrounding Hidden Valley to see where cattle rustlers supposedly hung out on this 1-mile loop. *Easy.* ⊠ *Joshua Tree National Park* ✣ *Trailhead: At Hidden Valley Picnic Area.*

★ Ryan Mountain Trail

TRAIL | The payoff for hiking to the top of 5,461-foot Ryan Mountain is one of the best panoramic views of Joshua Tree. From here, you can see Mt. San Jacinto, Mt. San Gorgonio, Lost Horse Valley, and the Pinto Basin. You'll need two to three hours to complete the 3-mile round-trip with 1,000-plus feet of elevation gain. *Moderate.* ⊠ *Joshua Tree National Park* ✣ *Trailhead: At Ryan Mountain parking area, 13 miles southeast of park's west entrance, or Sheep Pass, 16 miles southwest of Oasis Visitor Center.*

Skull Rock Trail

TRAIL | The 1.7-mile loop guides hikers through boulder piles, desert washes, and a rocky alley. It's named for what is perhaps the park's most famous rock formation, which resembles the eye sockets and nasal cavity of a human skull. Access the trail from within Jumbo Rocks Campground or from a small parking area on the highway just east of the campground. *Easy.* ⊠ *Joshua Tree National Park* ✣ *Trailhead: At Jumbo Rocks Campground.*

Split Rock Loop Trail

TRAIL | Experience rocks, trees, and geological wonders along this 2½-mile loop trail (including a short spur to Face Rock) through boulder fields and oak and pine woodlands up to Joshua tree stands. *Moderate.* ⊠ *Joshua Tree National Park* ✣ *Trailhead: Along dirt road off main Park Blvd. (signs point the way).*

VISITOR CENTERS

Joshua Tree Visitor Center

INFO CENTER | This visitor center has maps and interesting exhibits illustrating park geology, cultural and historic sites, and hiking and rock-climbing activities. There's also a small bookstore and café. Restrooms with flush toilets are on the premises. ⊠ *6554 Park Blvd., Joshua Tree* ☎ *760/366–1855* ⊕ *www.nps.gov/jotr.*

Keys View Road

Keys View Road travels south from Park Boulevard from Cap Rock up to Keys View, the best vista point in the park. If you plan to hike up to historic Lost Horse Mine, you'll find the trailhead along the way.

Sights

HISTORIC SIGHTS

Lost Horse Mine

MINE | This historic mine, which produced 10,000 ounces of gold and 16,000 ounces of silver between 1894 and 1931, was among Southern California's most productive mines. The 10-stamp mill is considered one of the best preserved of its type in the park system. The site is accessed via a fairly strenuous, 4-mile, round-trip hike. Mind the park warnings, and don't enter any mine in Joshua Tree. ⊠ *Keys View Rd.* ✣ *About 15 miles south of west entrance.*

SCENIC STOPS

★ Keys View

VIEWPOINT | At 5,185 feet, this point affords a sweeping view of the Santa Rosa Mountains and Coachella Valley, the San Andreas Fault, the peak of 11,500-foot Mt. San Gorgonio, the shimmering surface of Salton Sea, and—on a rare clear day—Signal Mountain in Mexico. Sunrise and sunset are magical times, when the light throws rocks and trees into high relief before bathing the hills in brilliant shades of red,

Did You Know?

Found only in Arizona, California, Nevada, and Utah, the Joshua tree (*Yucca brevifolia*) is actually a member of the agave family. Native Americans used the Joshua tree's hearty foliage like leather, forming it into everyday items like baskets and shoes. Later, early settlers used its core and limbs for building fences to contain their livestock.

orange, and gold. ✉ *Keys View Rd.* ✣ *16 miles south of park's west entrance.*

TRAILS

Cap Rock

TRAIL | This ½-mile, wheelchair-accessible loop—named after a boulder that sits atop a huge rock formation like a cap—winds through other fascinating rock formations and has signs that explain the geology of the Mojave Desert. *Easy.* ✉ *Joshua Tree National Park* ✣ *Trailhead: Keys View Rd. near junction with Park Blvd.*

Highway 62

Highway 62 stretches along the northern border of the park, from Yucca Valley in the West and Twentynine Palms in the east. Visitors can access the Black Rock, Indian Cove, Fortynine Palms, and Oasis of Mara sections of the park off this road, as well as the main visitor centers and park entrances in Joshua Tree and Twentynine Palms.

Sights

SCENIC STOPS

Fortynine Palms Oasis

NATIVE SITE | A short drive off Highway 62, this site is a bit of a preview of what the park's interior has to offer: stands of fan palms, interesting petroglyphs, and evidence of fires built by early Native Americans. Because animals frequent this area, you may spot a coyote, bobcat, or roadrunner. ✉ *End of Canyon Rd.* ✣ *4 miles west of Twentynine Palms.*

Indian Cove

RESTAURANT—SIGHT | The view from here is of rock formations that draw thousands of climbers to the park each year. This isolated area is reached via Twentynine Palms Highway. ✉ *End of Indian Cove Rd.*

TRAILS

Hi-View Nature Trail

TRAIL | This 1.3-mile loop climbs nearly to the top of 4,500-foot Summit Peak. The views of nearby Mt. San Gorgonio (snow-capped in winter) make the moderately steep journey worth the effort. You can pick up a pamphlet describing the vegetation you'll see along the way at any visitor center. *Moderate.* ✉ *Joshua Tree National Park* ✣ *Trailhead: ½ mile west of Black Rock Canyon Campground.*

Indian Cove Trail

TRAIL | Look for lizards and roadrunners along this ½-mile loop that follows a desert wash. A walk along this well-signed trail reveals signs of Native American habitation, animals, and flora such as desert willow and yucca. *Easy.* ✉ *Joshua Tree National Park* ✣ *Trailhead: At west end of Indian Cove Campground.*

Oasis of Mara Trail

TRAIL | A stroll along this short, wheelchair-accessible trail, located just outside the visitor center, reveals how early settlers took advantage of this oasis, which was first settled by the Serrano tribe. *Mara* means "place of little springs and much grass" in their language. The Serrano, who farmed the oasis until the mid-1850s, planted one palm tree for each male baby born during the first year of the settlement. *Easy.* ✉ *Joshua Tree National Park* ✣ *Trailhead: At Oasis Visitor Center.*

VISITOR CENTERS

Oasis Visitor Center

INFO CENTER | Exhibits here illustrate how Joshua Tree was formed, reveal the differences between the park's two types of desert, and demonstrate how plants and animals eke out an existence in this arid climate. Take the ½-mile nature walk through the nearby Oasis of Mara, which is alive with palm trees and mesquite shrubs. Facilities include picnic tables, restrooms, and a bookstore. ✉ *74485 National Park Dr., Twentynine Palms* ☎ *760/367–5500* 🌐 *www.nps.gov/jotr.*

Pinto Basin Road

This paved road takes you from high Mojave desert to low Colorado desert. A long, slow drive, the route runs from the main part of the park to Interstate 10; it can add as much as an hour to and from Palm Springs (round-trip), but the views and roadside exhibits make it worth the extra time. From the Oasis Visitor Center, drive south. After about 5 miles, the road forks; take a left, and continue another 9 miles to the Cholla Cactus Garden, where the sun fills the cactus needles with light. Past that is the Ocotillo Patch, filled with spindly plants bearing razor-sharp thorns and, after a rain, bright green leaves and brilliant red flowers. Side trips from this route require a 4X4.

Sights

SCENIC DRIVES

Geology Tour Road

SCENIC DRIVE | Some of the park's most fascinating landscapes can be observed from this 18-mile dirt road. Parts of the journey are rough; a 4X4 vehicle is required after mile marker 9. Sights to see include a 100-year-old stone dam called Squaw Tank, defunct mines, and a large plain with an abundance of Joshua trees. There are 16 stops along the way, so give yourself about two hours to complete the round-trip trek. ✉ *South of Park Blvd., west of Jumbo Rocks.*

SCENIC STOPS

Cholla Cactus Garden

GARDEN | This stand of bigelow cholla (sometimes called jumping cholla, because its hooked spines seem to jump at you) is best seen and photographed in late afternoon, when the backlit spiky stalks stand out against a colorful sky. ✉ *Pinto Basin Rd.* ✣ *20 miles north of Cottonwood Visitor Center.*

Cottonwood Spring

NATIVE SITE | Home to the native Cahuilla people for centuries, this spring provided water for travelers and early prospectors. The area, which supports a large stand of fan palms and cottonwood trees, is one of the best stops for bird-watching, as migrating birds (and bighorn sheep) rely on the water as well. A number of gold mines were located here, and the area still has some remains, including concrete pillars. ✉ *Cottonwood Visitor Center.*

Lost Palms Oasis

TRAIL | More than 100 fan palms comprise the largest group of the exotic plants in the park. A spring bubbles from between the rocks but disappears into the sandy, boulder-strewn canyon. The 7½-mile, round-trip hike is not for everyone, and not recommended during summer months. Bring plenty of water! ✉ *Cottonwood Visitor Center.*

Ocotillo Patch

GARDEN | Stop here for a roadside exhibit on the dramatic display made by the red-tipped succulent after even the shortest rain shower. ✉ *Pinto Basin Rd.* ✣ *About 3 miles east of Cholla Cactus Gardens.*

TRAILS

Bajada

TRAIL | Learn all about what plants do to survive in the Colorado Desert on this ¼-mile loop. *Easy.* ✉ *Joshua Tree National Park* ✣ *Trailhead: South of Cottonwood Visitor Center, ½ mile from park entrance.*

Mastodon Peak Trail

TRAIL | Some boulder scrambling is optional on this 3-mile hike that loops up to the 3,371-foot Mastodon Peak, and the journey rewards you with stunning views of the Salton Sea. The trail passes through a region where gold was mined from 1919 to 1932, so be on the lookout for open mines. The peak draws its name from a large rock formation that early miners believed looked like the head of a prehistoric behemoth. *Moderate.* ✉ *Joshua Tree National Park* ✣ *Trailhead: At Cottonwood Spring Oasis.*

VISITOR CENTERS

Cottonwood Visitor Center

INFO CENTER | The south entrance is the closest to Interstate 10, the east–west highway from Los Angeles to Phoenix. Exhibits in this small center, staffed by rangers and volunteers, illustrate the region's natural history. The center also has restrooms with flush toilets. ✉ *Cottonwood Spring, Pinto Basin Rd.* 🌐 *www.nps.gov/jotr.*

Activities

BIKING

Mountain biking is a great way to see Joshua Tree. Bikers are restricted to roads that are used by motorized vehicles, including the main park roads and a few four-wheel-drive trails. Bicycling on dirt roads is not recommended during the summer. Most scenic stops and picnic areas have bike racks.

Covington Flats

BICYCLING | This 4-mile route takes you past impressive Joshua trees as well as pinyon pines, junipers, and areas of lush desert vegetation. It's tough going toward the end, but once you reach 5,518-foot Eureka Peak you'll have great views of Palm Springs, the Morongo Basin, and the surrounding mountains. ✉ *Joshua Tree National Park* ✣ *Trailhead: at Covington Flats picnic area, La Contenta Rd., 10 miles south of Rte. 62.*

Pinkham Canyon and Thermal Canyon Roads

BICYCLING | This challenging 20-mile route begins at the Cottonwood Visitor Center and loops through the Cottonwood Mountains. The unpaved trail follows Smoke Tree Wash through Pinkham Canyon, rounds Thermal Canyon, and loops back to the beginning. Rough and narrow in places, the road travels through soft sand and rocky floodplains. ✉ *Joshua Tree National Park* ✣ *Trailhead: At Cottonwood Visitor Center.*

Queen Valley

BICYCLING | This 13.4-mile network of mostly level roads winds through one of the park's most impressive groves of Joshua trees. You can also leave your bike at one of the racks placed in the area and explore on foot. ✉ *Joshua Tree National Park* ✣ *Trailhead: At Hidden Valley Campground, and accessible opposite Geology Tour Rd. at Big Horn Pass.*

BIRD-WATCHING

Joshua Tree, located on the inland portion of the Pacific Flyway, hosts about 250 species of birds, and the park is a popular seasonal location for bird-watching. During the fall migration, which runs mid-September through mid-October, there are several reliable sighting areas. At Barker Dam you might spot white-throated swifts, several types of swallows, or red-tailed hawks. Lucy's warblers, flycatchers, and Anna's hummingbirds cruise around Cottonwood Spring, a serene palm-shaded setting; occasional ducks, herons, and egrets, as well as migrating rufous and calliope hummingbirds, wintering prairie falcons, and a resident barn owl could show up. Black Rock Canyon sees pinyon jays, while Covington Flats reliably gets mountain quail, and you may see La Conte's thrashers, ruby-crowned kinglets, and warbling vireos at either locale. Rufous hummingbirds, Pacific slope flycatchers, and various warblers are frequent visitors to Indian Cove. Lists of birds found in the park, as well as information on recent sightings, are available at visitor centers.

CAMPING

Camping is the best way to experience the stark, exquisite beauty of Joshua Tree. You'll also have a rare opportunity to sleep outside in a semi-wilderness setting. The campgrounds, set at elevations from 3,000 to 4,500 feet, have only primitive facilities; few have drinking water. Most campgrounds accept reservations up to six months in advance but only for October through Memorial Day. Campsites at Belle, Hidden Valley, and White Tank are on a first-come, first-served basis. Belle and White Tank campgrounds, and parts of Black Rock Canyon, Cottonwood, and Indian Cove campgrounds, are closed from the day after Memorial Day to September. ■ **TIP→ Campgrounds fill quickly, so reserve well in advance. Also, the park may soon require reservations at all campgrounds.**

Belle Campground. This small campground is popular with families as there are a number of boulders kids can scramble over and around. ✉ *9 miles south of Oasis of Mara* ☎ *760/367–5500* 🌐 *www.nps.gov/jotr.*

Black Rock Canyon Campground. Set among juniper bushes, cholla cacti, and other desert shrubs, Black Rock Canyon is one of the park's prettiest campgrounds. ✉ *Joshua La., south of Hwy. 62 and Hwy. 247* ☎ *877/444–6777* 🌐 *www.recreation.gov.*

Cottonwood Campground. In spring, this campground, the southernmost one in the park (and therefore often the last to fill up), is surrounded by some of the desert's finest wildflowers and is a great spot to watch the night sky. ✉ *Pinto Basin Rd., 32 miles south of North Entrance Station* ☎ *877/444–6777* 🌐 *www.nps.gov/jotr.*

Hidden Valley Campground. This campground is a favorite with rock climbers, who make their way up valley formations that have names like the Blob, Old Woman, and Chimney Rock. ✉ *Off Park Blvd., 20 miles southwest of Oasis of Mara* ☎ *760/367–5500* 🌐 *www.nps.gov/jotr.*

Indian Cove Campground. This is a sought-after spot for rock climbers, primarily because it lies among the 50 square miles of rugged terrain at the Wonderland of Rocks. ✉ *Indian Cove Rd., south of Hwy. 62* ☎ *877/444–6777* 🌐 *www.nps.gov/jotr.*

Jumbo Rocks. Each campsite at this well-regarded campground tucked among giant boulders has a bit of privacy. It's a good home base for visiting many of Joshua Tree's attractions. ✉ *Park Blvd., 11 miles from Oasis of Mara* ☎ *877/444–6777* 🌐 *www.nps.gov/jotr.*

White Tank. This small, quiet campground is popular with families because a nearby trail leads to a natural arch. ✉ *Pinto Basin Rd., 11 miles south of Oasis of Mara* ☎ *760/367–5500* 🌐 *www.nps.gov/jotr.*

EDUCATIONAL PROGRAMS

The Desert Institute at Joshua Tree National Park

COLLEGE | The nonprofit educational partner of the park offers a full schedule of lectures, classes, and hikes. Class topics include basket making, painting, and photography, while field trips include workshops on cultural history, natural science, and how to survive in the desert. ✉ *74485 National Park Dr., Twentynine Palms* ☎ *760/367–5535* 🌐 *www.joshuatree.org.*

Stargazing

COLLEGE | At Joshua Tree National Park, designated an International Dark Sky Park in 2017, you can tour the Milky Way on summer evenings using binoculars. Rangers also offer programs on some evenings when the moon isn't visible. Browse the schedule online. The park also partners with Sky's the Limit Observatory on the Utah Trail in Twentynine Palms (🌐 *www.skysthelimit29.org*); check the website for current offerings. ✉ *Cottonwood Campground Amphitheater, Oasis Visitor Center, Sky's the Limit Observatory* 🌐 *www.nps.gov/jotr/planyourvisit/calendar.htm.*

RANGER PROGRAMS

Evening Programs

TOUR—SIGHT | Rangers present 45-minute-long programs, often on Friday or Saturday evening, at Cottonwood Amphitheater, Indian Cove Amphitheater, and Jumbo Rocks Campground. Topics range from natural history to local lore. As times and days for such offerings aren't fixed, it's best to check the online schedule. ✉ *Joshua Tree National Park* 🎫 *Free.*

HIKING

There are more than 190 miles of hiking trails in Joshua Tree, ranging from ¼-mile nature trails to 35-mile treks. Some connect with each other, so you can design your own desert maze. Remember that drinking water is hard to come by—you won't find it in the park except at the entrances. Bring along at least a gallon per person for all but the shortest hikes, more if the weather is hot.

Before striking out on a hike or apparent nature trail, check out the signage. Roadside signage identifies hiking- and rock-climbing routes.

ROCK CLIMBING

With an abundance of weathered igneous boulder outcroppings, Joshua Tree is one of the nation's top winter-climbing destinations. There are more than 4,500 established routes offering a full menu of climbing experiences—from bouldering for beginners in the Wonderland of Rocks to multiple-pitch climbs at Echo Rock and Saddle Rock. The best-known climb in the park is Hidden Valley's Sports Challenge Rock. A map inside the *Joshua Tree Guide* shows locations of selected wilderness and nonwilderness climbs.

Joshua Tree Rock Climbing School
CLIMBING/MOUNTAINEERING | The school offers several programs, from one-day introductory classes to multiday programs for experienced climbers, and provides all needed equipment. Beginning classes, offered year-round on most weekends, are limited to six people age eight or older. ✉ *Joshua Tree National Park* ☎ *760/366–4745* 🌐 *www.joshuatreerockclimbing.com* 🎫 *From $195.*

Vertical Adventures Rock Climbing School
CLIMBING/MOUNTAINEERING | About 1,000 climbers each year learn the sport in Joshua Tree National Park through this school. Classes, offered September–May, meet at a designated location in the park, and all equipment is provided. ✉ *Joshua Tree National Park* ☎ *800/514–8785 office, 949/322–6108 mobile/text* 🌐 *www.vertical-adventures.com* 🎫 *From $165.*

What's Nearby

Palm Springs, about a 45-minute drive from the North Entrance Station at Joshua Tree, serves as the home base for most park visitors. This city of 46,000 has 95 golf courses, 600 tennis courts, and 50,000 swimming pools. A hideout for Hollywood stars since the 1920s, Palm Springs also offers a glittering array of shops, restaurants, and hotels. Stroll down Palm Canyon Drive, and you're sure to run into a celebrity or two.

There are four small communities in close proximity to Joshua Tree National Park. About 9 miles north of Palm Springs and closer to the park is **Desert Hot Springs,** which has more than 1,000 natural hot mineral pools and 40 health spas ranging from low-key to luxurious. **Yucca Valley** is the largest and fastest growing of the communities straddling the park's northern border. The town boasts a handful of motels, supermarkets, and a Walmart. Tiny **Joshua Tree,** the closest community to the park's west entrance, is where the serious rock climbers make their headquarters. **Twentynine Palms,** known as "two-nine" by locals, is sandwiched between the Marine Corps Air Ground Task Force Center to the north and Joshua Tree National Park to the south. Here you'll find a smattering of coffeehouses, antiques shops, and cafés.

Chapter 38

KATMAI NATIONAL PARK AND PRESERVE

Updated by
Teeka Ballas

Camping ★★★★★ | Hotels ★☆☆☆☆ | Activities ★★★☆☆ | Scenery ★★★★★ | Crowds ★☆☆☆☆

WELCOME TO KATMAI NATIONAL PARK AND PRESERVE

TOP REASONS TO GO

★ **Where salmon spawn, Katmai bears feast:** At Brooks River falls and pools and on streams throughout the park, brown bears dive, clutch, trap, steal, and catch salmon. They graze on sedge flats and dig for clams along th outer coast. Ducks fuss over nesting space alongside whistling swans, loons, grebes, gulls, and shorebirds. Bald eagles perch on rocky seaside pinnacles, and seals and Steller's sea lions hang out on rock outcroppings. The fishing is good here, too—for rainbow or lake trout, arctic grayling, and, of course, salmon. Bristol Bay's sockeye is renowned.

★ **Natural forces:** Katmai embodies the handiwork of volcanoes, earthquakes, glaciers, tides, and weather. You can see the results everywhere—in fossils, ash cliffs carved by wind and rain, colorful rocks once baked by fumerole steam, lava domes. You can fully experience the results on a visit to the Valley of Ten Thousands Smokes.

1 **King Salmon.** Located on the north bank of the Naknek River, King Salmon (population 500) offers access to numerous fly-in fishing and adventure camps and lodges; a park visitor center; and food, lodging, and travel services.

2 **Brooks Camp.** Visitor facilities and activities, including bear-viewing opportunities and excursions to the Valley of Ten Thousand Smokes, are centered in this area of the park and the western lakes. Outside this area, lodges are few, and the backcountry is immense, filling an area nearly the size of Connecticut.

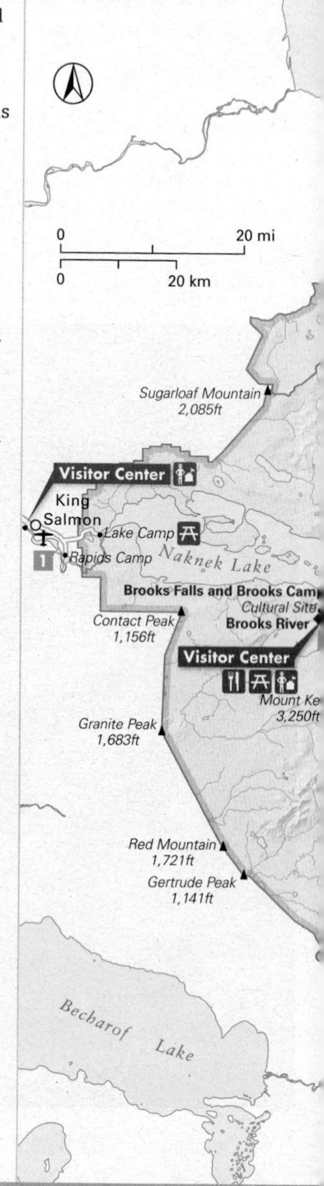

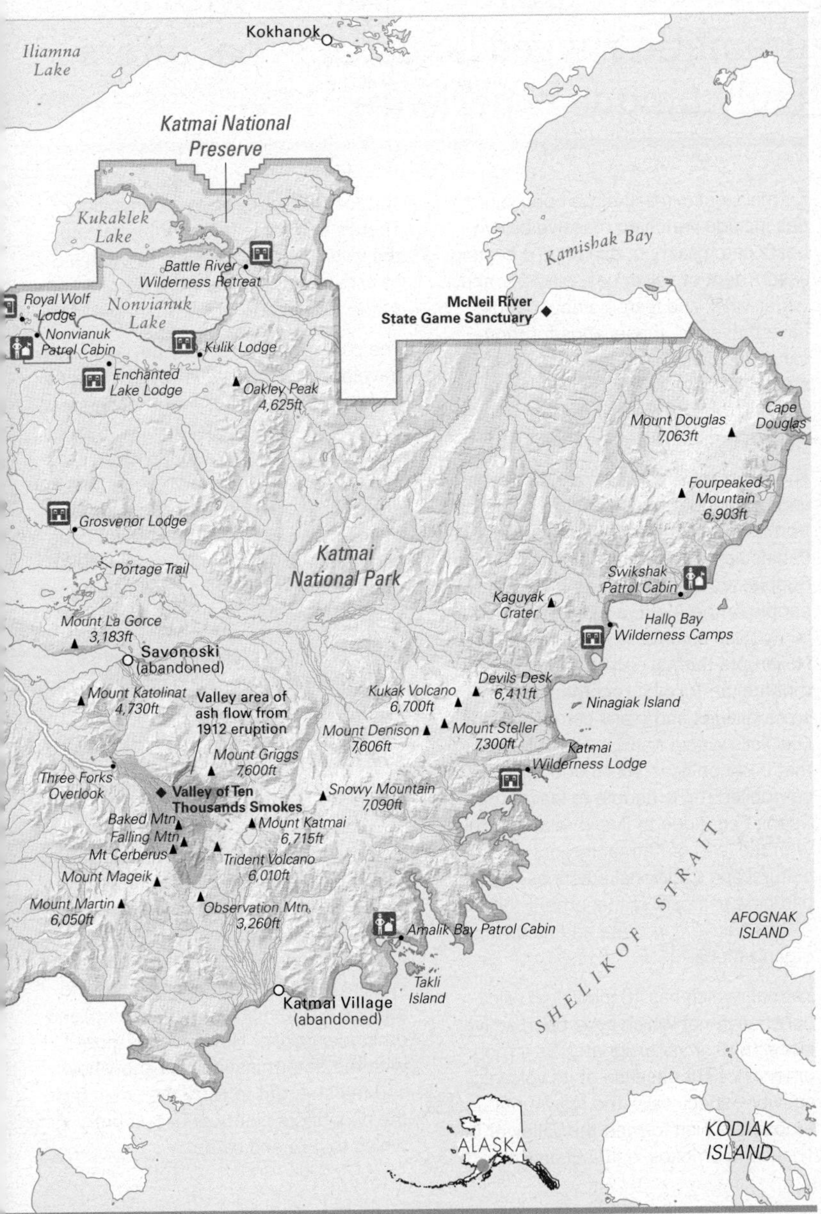

Kokhanok
Iliamna Lake
Katmai National Preserve
Kukaklek Lake
Kamishak Bay
Battle River Wilderness Retreat
Royal Wolf Lodge
Nonvianuk Lake
McNeil River State Game Sanctuary
Nonvianuk Patrol Cabin
Kulik Lodge
Enchanted Lake Lodge
Oakley Peak 4,625ft
Cape Douglas
Mount Douglas 7,063ft
Fourpeaked Mountain 6,903ft
Grosvenor Lodge
Katmai National Park
Portage Trail
Swikshak Patrol Cabin
Kaguyak Crater
Hallo Bay Wilderness Camps
Mount La Gorce 3,183ft
Savonoski (abandoned)
Devils Desk 6,411ft
Kukak Volcano 6,700ft
Mount Katolinat 4,730ft
Valley area of ash flow from 1912 eruption
Ninagiak Island
Mount Denison 7,606ft
Mount Steller 7,300ft
Mount Griggs 7,600ft
Katmai Wilderness Lodge
Three Forks Overlook
Valley of Ten Thousands Smokes
Snowy Mountain 7,090ft
Baked Mtn
Mount Katmai 6,715ft
Falling Mtn
Mt Cerberus
Trident Volcano 6,010ft
Mount Mageik
Mount Martin 6,050ft
Observation Mtn. 3,260ft
SHELIKOF STRAIT
Amalik Bay Patrol Cabin
AFOGNAK ISLAND
Takli Island
Katmai Village (abandoned)
ALASKA
KODIAK ISLAND

Remote Katmai receives very few annual visitors. Those who do make the effort, however, are richly rewarded with a dramatic, rugged landscape that offers truly unique experiences.

Katmai's once-in-a-lifetime opportunities include watching massive brown bears catch salmon; exploring a riveting assortment of volcanoes, glaciers, and waterways; and learning how people have thrived on these lands for thousands of years. Although the bears often steal the show, Katmai is also home to wolves, moose, lynx, and eagles. The salmon runs here are legendary, too.

The Sugpiat have lived in the Katmai area and throughout the coastal regions—from Prince William Sound to the Alaska Peninsula—for thousands of years. (The Sugpiat are also known as the Alutiiq people or the Aleut, a word introduced by Russian colonizers.) Before the 1912 Novarupta-Katmai eruption, one of the most powerful ever recorded, there were villages and many camps in what now falls within Katmai. Heavy ash from that eruption covered 46,000 miles and compelled many people to leave. The Sugpiat continue to live in relationship with the land of Katmai through their cultural and traditional practices, and they participate in park management through Alaska Native corporate and nonprofit organizations.

Katmai, which has 18 individual volcanoes, seven of which have been active since 1900, was designated as a monument in 1918 because of its volcanic activity—specifically, the Novarupta eruption, which formed the Valley of Ten Thousand Smokes, a 40-square-mile, 100-to-700-foot-deep pyroclastic flow. There's a 6.6 mile (round-trip) trail into the valley that's accessible through a park tour and bus ride from Brooks Camp to the trailhead.

The park remained largely unvisited by travelers until the 1950s, when the area and surrounding lands were recognized by more people for their wide variety of wildlife, including an abundance of sockeye salmon and the brown bears that are drawn to them for food. After a series of boundary expansions, the present park and preserve were established in 1980 under the Alaska National Interest Lands Conservation Act.

There are many archaeological sites throughout Katmai, including village and camp sites that were abandoned after the Novarupta eruption. The Brooks River area is both a National Historic Landmark and a National Register of Historic Places Archeological District.

Remote and expensive to reach, even by Alaska standards, the park offers limited visitor facilities beyond a single campground, a few wilderness lodges, and a few miles of maintained trails. Most visitors rely on outfitters and lodges to arrange hiking, fishing, flightseeing, and other excursions. However, for those with the determination, the know-how, and the strength to carry their own gear, the park offers plenty of backcountry in which to hike and camp.

AVERAGE HIGH/LOW TEMPERATURES IN KING SALMON					
JAN.	**FEB.**	**MAR.**	**APR.**	**MAY**	**JUNE**
24/9	27/11	32/14	42/25	53/34	60/42
JULY	**AUG.**	**SEPT.**	**OCT.**	**NOV.**	**DEC.**
64/47	63/47	56/40	42/27	31/16	26/10

Planning

When to Go

Katmai weather has been called miserable by those who show up unprepared for or just weary of the wind, cold, rain, sun, mosquitoes (seriously, they're a kind of weather system), or, really, whatever mix of conditions the day brings. The park is huge, and includes two climactic zones, continental and maritime, so temperatures and precipitation can vary dramatically from area to area.

Expect rainier, stormier weather on the Pacific (eastern) side of the park, and dryer interior conditions in the vicinity of King Salmon, home to park headquarters and Brooks Camp. Few travelers visit in winter when facilities are closed, access is more difficult, and conditions are harsh, snowy, and cold. June and July are by far the warmest and busiest months.

Getting Here and Around

AIR

You can't drive to Katmai National Park. To get here, you can fly from Anchorage (🌐 *www.alaskaair.com*)—enjoying amazing views of Cook Inlet and the lofty, snowy Alaska Range peaks—to King Salmon, near Bristol Bay. From there, you transfer to a floatplane for a 20-minute hop to Naknek Lake and Brooks Camp.

BOAT

You can also travel from King Salmon to Brooks Camp by boat. On arrival, you must check in at the park ranger station, next to Brooks Lodge, for a mandatory bear-safety talk (for the safety of both you and the bears).

Inspiration

The award-winning, well-researched, and beautifully written *Dominion of Bears*, by Sherry Simpson, who grew up and lived most of her life in Alaska, weaves in and out of Katmai's Brook's River and surrounding lands as it delves into the long, storied relationship between bears and people.

Park Essentials

ACCESSIBILITY

At Brooks Camp most of the public buildings and all of the bear-viewing platforms are ADA accessible, though assistance may be necessary to reach platforms as the trails to them are narrow, rough, and can become muddy. Entering and exiting floatplanes can be challenging for people with limited mobility. Wheelchairs and services for assisting visitors are not available around the Brooks Camp area.

PARK FEES AND PERMITS

There is no entrance fee for Katmai. The per-person camping fee at Brooks Camp is $12 a night. Although backcountry camping is free and no permits are required, it's limited to 14 days in any one location.

PARK HOURS

Katmai is open 24 hours every day, though there are some backcountry camping closures at certain times of year. Check the park website for updates.

CELL PHONE RECEPTION

There's no Wi-Fi or cell phone service in most of Katmai, although some cell service is available at the visitor center in King Salmon.

Hotels

Accommodations that are available through the park concessionaire include Brooks Lodge, at the Brooks River, and Grosvenor Lodge between Lake Coville and Lake Grosvenor. Other lodges are on inholdings (privately owned land) within the park. Lodge cabins sometimes accommodate more than two people. Rates are steep as they're often for more than one night and might include not only meals but also transportation and guided adventures. Before booking, check on what's included and on whether or not the lodge has minimum-stay requirements.

Restaurants

Food and beverages are available at Brooks Lodge and Grosvenor Lodge. Brooks Lodge allows you to choose the meals you want and dine when not a lodge guest. Other lodges offer all-inclusive rates with meals for guests only.

Tours

Alaska Alpine Adventures–Katmai

ADVENTURE TOURS | **FAMILY** | This adventure outfitter offers an array of 5- to 12-day hiking, backpacking, and multisport excursions into Katmai, with some trips geared to families. *877/525–2577* *www.alaskaalpineadventures.com* *From $3995 per person.*

Katmailand

GUIDED TOURS | This company offers sport-fishing and landscape- or wildlife-viewing packages to and within Katmai National Park, along with a day tour of the Valley of Ten Thousand Smokes. You can usually just pick up the day tour ($96 with lunch), which departs from Brooks Camp, on arrival, though it's best to book ahead during the busiest time (July). *4125 Aircraft Dr., Anchorage* *907/243–5448, 877/708–1391* *www.katmailand.com* *Packages from $950.*

Ouzel Expeditions

GUIDED TOURS | This outfitter does fishing and wildlife-viewing trips ($5,500) on American Creek in Katmai, starting at Hammersly Lake and ending at Coville lake. The trip covers 40 miles in 8 days and offers great opportunities to catch rainbow trout. *907/783–2216, 800/825–8196* *www.ouzel.com.*

Visitor Information

CONTACTS Katmai National Park and Preserve. *1000 Silver St. , Bldg. 603, King Salmon* *907/246–4250 King Salmon Visitor's Center, 907/246–3305 park headquarters* *www.nps.gov/katm.*

In the Park

Sights

King Salmon is 290 air miles southwest of Anchorage; Brooks Camp is 30 air miles southeast of King Salmon.

Katmai's volcanic landscape and rich wetlands and waterways provide vital habitats for thriving salmon runs and thousands of brown bears. Although few travelers visited the area until 50 or 60 years ago, Katmai was first established as a monument in 1918 to protect and study the 1912 eruption of Novarupta and became a national park in 1980. Now, people come to watch bears fish; hike the Valley of Ten Thousand Smokes; and explore archaeological sites, mountains, waterways, and coastline.

BEACHES

Katmai's eastern coast stretches almost 500 miles, with remote areas ranging from narrow fjords to broad coastal flats. Marshes, sedges, beaches, thickets, and mudflats nourish a range of animals such as wolves, caribou, puffins, cormorants, kittiwakes, and bald eagles, plus marine animals like sea lions, sea otters, harbor seals, and porpoise. Brown bears spend early summer foraging on coastal sedge flats; some also clam along tidal flats. When the salmon arrive, many bears move to rivers and streams to feast.

Campsites from thousands of years ago can be found on the coast, along with more recent signs of human activity, including from commercial canneries and modern-day campers and adventurers. Eastern coastal areas and beaches are accessible by plane and/or boat from Homer, Kodiak, and King Salmon, where operators take visitors on single- and multi-day trips.

GEOLOGICAL FORMATIONS

Valley of Ten Thousands Smokes

NATURE SITE | This dramatically sculpted landscape demonstrates the power of volcanic eruptions and their effect on geology, flora, and fauna. The impact of the Novarupta eruption on the park's ecosystems can be both obvious and subtle, so it's helpful to have a guide. The park concessioner offers a tour ($96, including lunch) that departs from Brooks Camp on a 46-mile (round-trip) bus ride to the valley, with an optional 3.4-mile hike to the valley floor and back. This is also the bus to take for multi-day backpacking trips up the valley to Mount Katmai or the foot of Novarupta itself. ✉ *Katmai National Park and Preserve* 🌐 *katmailand.com.*

SCENIC STOPS

Brooks Falls and Brooks Camp

BODY OF WATER | At Katmai's biggest draw, viewing platforms overlook Brook Falls, a 6-foot cascade. Here, salmon leap upriver to their spawning grounds while brown bears stand on the edge of the falls to catch them, particularly in July and September. An access trail and boardwalk are separated from the river to avoid confrontations with bears. Note, too, that the daily tour to the Valley of Ten Thousand Smokes starts from nearby Brooks Lodge, and there's camping at Brooks Camp (just $12 a night, no permit required). ✉ *Katmai National Park and Preserve* ☎ *907/246–4250 King Salmon Visitor Center, 907/246–3305 park headquarters* 🌐 *www.nps.gov/katm.*

Brooks River

BODY OF WATER | Just downstream from Brooks Falls, you can fish for salmon and rainbow trout in Brooks River. Note, though, that sometimes only fly-fishing is permitted, and there are seasonal closures to prevent contact with bears, so check locally for the latest information. ✉ *Katmai National Park and Preserve* ☎ *907/246–3305* 🌐 *www.nps.gov/katm.*

★ McNeil River State Game Sanctuary

NATURE PRESERVE | At the northern end of the Alaska Peninsula, this sanctuary protects the world's largest gathering of brown bears. During the July to mid-August chum season, when salmon return to spawn, 50, 60, or even 70 brown bears congregate daily at the McNeil River falls to fish, eat, play, nap, and nurse cubs. The action happens within 15 to 20 feet of a viewing pad, so close that you can hear these magnificent creatures breathe and catch a whiff of their wet fur. Only 10 people a day can visit the viewing sites, and staffers (armed) are on hand to ensure that everyone behaves in nonthreatening, noninstrusive ways.

Because demand is so high, the Alaska Department of Fish and Game issues permits via a mid-March lottery. Applications

Hiking in the Valley of Ten Thousand Smokes.

and a nonrefundable $30 fee must be received by March 1, and Alaska residents get preferential treatment. Those who win pay an additional fee of just over $100 to $525, depending on the type of permit and the holder's residency. Air taxis to the sanctuary fly out of Homer on the Kenai Peninsula. Once in the sanctuary, all travel is by foot and guided by state biologists. Permit holders camp on gravel pads, in a protected area near a communal cook house, and must bring all their food. ✉ *Anchorage* ☏ *907/267–2189 Alaska Dept. of Fish and Game, Wildlife Conservation* 🌐 *www.adfg.state.ak.us.*

Restaurants

Brooks Lodge

$$ | AMERICAN | FAMILY | Open to guests and nonguests, the dining room at the Brooks Lodge serves both buffets and plated meals. It also offers beer, wine, and a small selection of cocktails. **Known for:** breakfast, lunch, and dinner; buffet-style meals; dairy- or gluten-free and vegetarian options. $ *Average main: $19* ☏ *907/243–5448* 🌐 *www.katmailand.com/brooks-lodge* ⏲ *Closed Sept.–May.*

Hotels

★ **Brooks Lodge**

$$$$ | B&B/INN | At the nexus of multiple lakes, rivers, and streams, this lodge makes a good base from which to fish—for rainbow or lake trout, arctic grayling, and, of course, salmon—and to visit the bear-viewing areas and the Valley of 10,000 Smokes. **Pros:** private facilities; bear viewing at Brooks Falls; amazing access to fishing. **Cons:** expensive; requires flying or boating in; bunk beds only. $ *Rooms from: $1000* ☏ *907/243–5448, 877/708–1391* 🌐 *www.katmailand.com/brooks-lodge* ⏲ *Closed Sept.–May* 🛏 *16 cabins* 🍽 *No meals.*

Grosvenor Lodge

$$$$ | B&B/INN | This intimate in-park lodge centers on fish, wildlife, and the lake system of the western Katmai. **Pros:** great access to fishing; accessible to two spawning streams; only four to six guests at a time. **Cons:** bathhouse is outside the cabin; absolute seclusion not for everyone; often booked far in advance. *Rooms from: $3775 907/243–5448, 877/708–1391 grosvenorlodge.com Closed Sept.–May 3 cabins All meals.*

Katmai Wilderness Lodge

$$$$ | B&B/INN | This rustic but modern log-cabin lodge on Kukak Bay straddles the rugged outer coast of Katmai National Park, along the shores of the Alaska Peninsula. **Pros:** bear viewing guarantee; private rooms and bathrooms with hot showers; guide services. **Cons:** pricey; you have to get to Kodiak first; minimum three-night stay. *Rooms from: $4250 800/488–8767, 907/486–8767 in Alaska www.katmai-wilderness.com Closed Oct.–mid-May 7 cabins All-inclusive.*

Kulik Lodge

$$$$ | B&B/INN | Along the Kulik River between Nonvianuk and Kulik lakes, this remote wilderness lodge sits in the northwest quadrant of the national park, near the boundery of the preserve. **Pros:** great rainbow-trout fishing; modern facilities; complimentary drinks when telling fish stories. **Cons:** need to bring your own tackle; fishing focused; minimum stay required. *Rooms from: $4495 907/243–5448, 877/708–1391 kuliklodge.com Closed Sept.–May 12 cabins All meals.*

Activities

BIRD-WATCHING

Spring, summer, and fall bring the greatest diversity and abundance of bird life, though birds like spruce grouse and willow ptarmigan live in the park all year, as do ravens, magpies. great-horned owls, gray jays, black-capped chickadees, boreal chickadees, and common redpolls. Look for eagles, black oystercatchers, horned and tufted puffins, black-legged kittiwakes, and common murres along the coast. Find yellowlegs and Hudsonian godwits, and waterfowl-like tundra swans, many species of ducks, loons, and grebes in interior lakes, marshes, and wetlands. Thrushes, warblers, and sparrows can be found in a range of habitats. Salmon streams attract ducks and scavenger birds like eagles, ravens, and gulls.

BOATING AND RAFTING

People have used waterways to get around Katmai and to catch or gather food for millenia. Naknek Lake is the largest lake entirely contained within any U.S. national park. It's accessible by road from King Salmon. The 5-mile road ends at Lake Camp, where there's a boat ramp, parking area, picnic area, and vault toilets. Many of the park's lodges use jet boats to transport guests to fishing and bear viewing areas.

CAMPING

Brooks Campground. This National Park Service campground is a short walk from Brooks Lodge, where campers can pay to eat meals and shower. The camp includes designated cooking and eating shelters, latrines, well water, and a storage cache to protect food from the ever-present brown bears. An electric-wire fence surrounds the camping area. Sites costs $12 per night per person, and reservations are required. *907/246–3305 for info, 877/444–6777 for reservations www.recreation.gov.*

CANOEING AND KAYAKING

The many lakes in Katmai make it a fantastic, if logistically challenging, place to canoe or kayak. The Savonoski Loop is a popular multi-day canoeing and kayaking route that starts at Brooks Camp at the north arm of Naknek Lake and travels 80 miles, with one significant portage, to return via the Savanoski River and Iliuk Arm. The Brooks Lodge trading post rents canoes and kayaks by the hour or the day. American Creek, Moraine Creek, and Funnel Creek are popular with rafters. Multiple outfitters offer adventure trips on these lakes and creeks.

EDUCATIONAL PROGRAMS

Rangers take visitors on a free daily educational walking tours of the Brooks River area daily at 2 pm starting at Brooks Camp. Walks follow easy terrain and take about 45 minutes to an hour. There's also a nightly (8 pm) program in the Brooks Camp Auditorium that includes a range of topics and stories about Katmai. Both programs run every day from early June to late August or mid-September.

FISHING

The phenomenal fishing (license required) at Katmai draws people to lakes, rivers and streams throughout the park, just as it has for thousands of years. Most package trips to Katmai include fishing as a primary or optional activity. Fishing gear rentals are available at the trading post run by Brooks Lodge. Note that areas that attract large numbers of bears are sometimes closed to fishing.

HIKING

The park's few maintained trails start near Brooks River. The Brooks Falls trail is about 1.2 miles and wheelchair accessible; it basically goes from the lower Brooks River bear viewing platform to the falls. The Dumpling Mountain trail climbs 800 feet through boreal forest, subalpine meadows, and alpine tundra to an overlook above Brooks Camp with expansive views. It's about 3 miles out and back, though you can continue another 2½ miles beyond the overlook to reach the summit of the mountain.

The Valley of Ten Thousand Smokes hike starts at Brooks Camp, too. You can either walk the 23 mile road to the Robert F. Griggs Visitor Center overlooking the valley or catch the bus tour that includes an optional 3.4-mile hike to the valley floor and back. Another trail offers a multi-day backpacking adventure that includes creek crossings and walking on pumice-covered flats to the volcanoes.

SCENIC FLIGHTS

Branch River Air Service

FISHING | Branch River Air Service in King Salmon offers flightseeing, bear-viewing, and custom-charter trips around Bristol Bay and Katmai National Park, as well as charter flights to various remote locations on the Alaska Peninsula. Rates are available upon request. ✉ *King Salmon* ☎ *907/246–3437 June–Sept., 907/248–3539 Oct.–May* 🌐 *www.branchriverair.com.*

Katmai Air Services

TOUR—SPORTS | Katmai Air offers flightseeing tours to the Valley of 10,000 Smokes and other areas of the park, along with one-day bear-viewing trips and charter flights from Anchorage and King Salmon to Brooks Camp. They also travel to multiple lodges and have scheduled flights from Anchorage to King Salmon. ✉ *4125 Aircraft Dr., Anchorage* ☎ *800/544–0551 reservations, 907/243–5448 in Anchorage* 🌐 *www.katmailand.com* 🎫 *From $225.*

Northwind Aviation

TOUR—SPORTS | This Homer-based air taxi company offers charter flights to Katmai and McNeil River, with one-day trips to Brooks Falls for bear viewing and Chinitna Hallo bays for sightseeing and wildlife viewing. ✉ *1184 Lakeshore Dr., Homer* ☎ *907/235–7482* 🌐 *www.northwindak.com* 🎫 *From $725.*

What's Nearby

Although fewer than 500 people live in **King Salmon,** situated on the north bank of the Naknek River, it plays a vital role in commercial and sport-fishing, with access to numerous fly-in fishing and adventure camps and lodges on the Alaska Peninsula. In addition to a park visitor center, the town has food, lodging, and travel services. A 16-mile road runs from King Salmon to **Naknek,** where the population swells from hundreds to thousands in summer, during Bristol Bay's commercial sockeye-salmon season.

Chapter 39

KENAI FJORDS NATIONAL PARK

39

Updated by
Teeka Ballas

Camping	Hotels	Activities	Scenery	Crowds
★★☆☆☆	★☆☆☆☆	★★★★★	★★★★★	★★☆☆☆

WELCOME TO KENAI FJORDS NATIONAL PARK

TOP REASONS TO GO

★ **Boat tours:** Summer boat tours of the fjords can be a magical experience with optimal viewing of tidewater glaciers, breeching whales, backfloating otters, sun bathing sea lions, and chattering birds.

★ **Kayaking:** Kayaking Resurrection Bay is a once-in-a-lifetime experience. While not for beginners, the waters are certainly navigable with a guide.

★ **Fishing:** Great opportunities abound with both fresh water and saltwater backcountry fishing for salmon and dolly varden.

★ **Birding:** More than 200 species of marine birds reside on the outcroppings and rookeries within the fjords. Birders flock from all over the world to catch a glimpse of all these winged-delights.

★ **Flightseeing:** More than 30 glaciers in the park originate from the 700 square miles of Harding Icefield. The only way to witness all of them, as well as the sheer immensity of the icefield, is from the air. The perfect flying day may also yield glimpses of grazing goat and fishing bears.

1 Inside the Park. Kenai Fjords National Park takes up a considerable part of the eastern side of the Kenai Peninsula. It butts up against and consumes part of Resurrection Bay, which includes the port city of Seward, a fishing town 126 miles south of Anchorage. The majority of the park is comprised of ice and water. The only road access to any of the park is by means of the Herman Leirer Road to Exit Glacier, a spur road just north of Seward. You can't drive to the glacier, but it will take you close enough to hike up to the toe of the glacier. The more than 30 glaciers spawned by the 700 square miles of the Harding Ice Field, glacially carved deep fjords, and rugged terrain and coastal backcountry are only accessible by air taxi, water taxi, or chartered boat service.

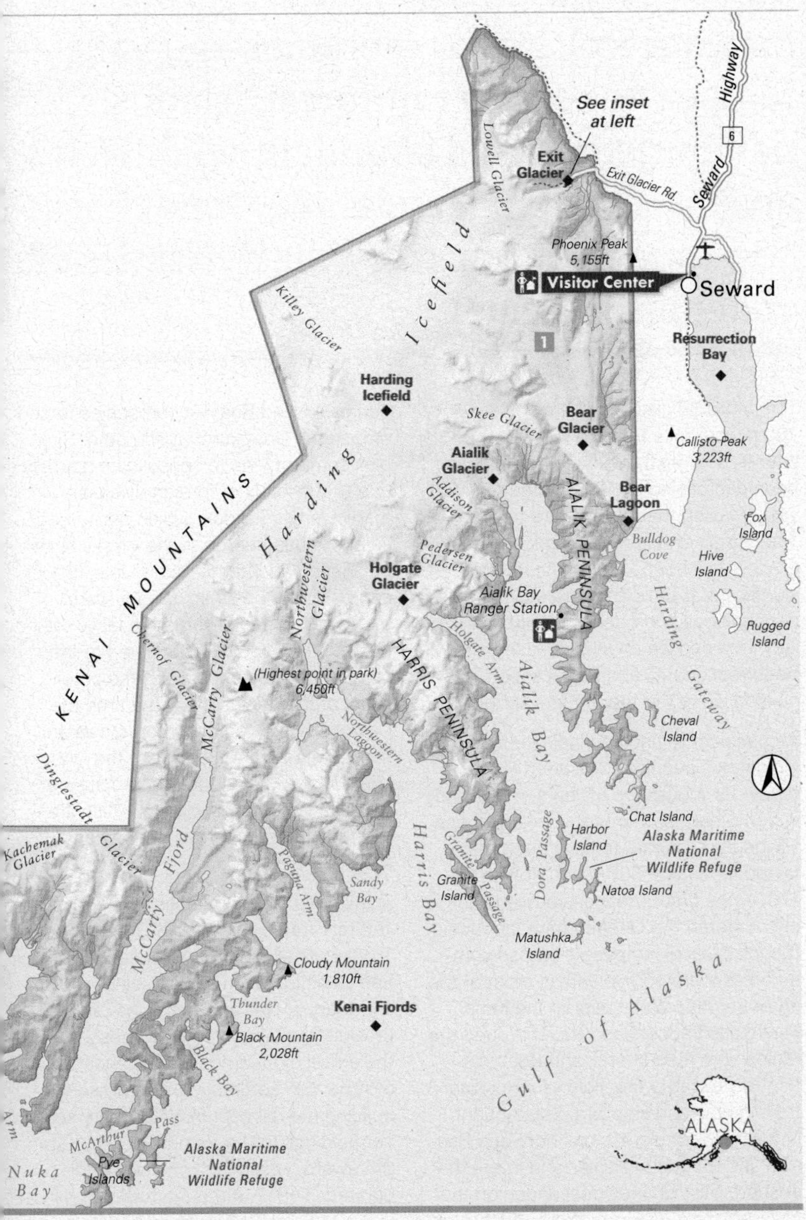

See inset at left
Exit Glacier
Exit Glacier Rd.
Seward Highway
6
Lowell Glacier
Phoenix Peak 5,155ft
Visitor Center
Seward
Killey Glacier
Harding Icefield
Resurrection Bay
Skee Glacier
Bear Glacier
Callisto Peak 3,223ft
Aialik Glacier
Addison Glacier
Bear Lagoon
AIALIK PENINSULA
Bulldog Cove
Fox Island
Hive Island
KENAI MOUNTAINS
Pedersen Glacier
Holgate Glacier
Northwestern Glacier
Aialik Bay Ranger Station
Rugged Island
Harding Gateway
Chernof Glacier
McCarty Glacier
(Highest point in park) 6,450ft
Holgate Arm
HARRIS PENINSULA
Aialik Bay
Cheval Island
Northwestern Lagoon
Dinglestadt Glacier
Chat Island
Kachemak Glacier
McCarty Fjord
Harris Bay
Granite Passage
Dora Passage
Harbor Island
Alaska Maritime National Wildlife Refuge
Paguna Arm
Sandy Bay
Granite Island
Natoa Island
Matushka Island
Cloudy Mountain 1,810ft
Kenai Fjords
Thunder Bay
Black Mountain 2,028ft
Black Bay
Gulf of Alaska
Arm
McArthur Pass
Pye Islands
Alaska Maritime National Wildlife Refuge
Nuka Bay
ALASKA

Kenai Fjords National Park is a vast, jagged masterpiece of mountains, nunateks (peaks that poke out from beneath ice), glacial moraines and valleys, temperate coastal rainforest, islands, narrow jetties, and abundant wildlife. It's an ever-changing landscape—one that's continuously shaped by the dynamics of water and glaciers.

The park's 38 glaciers all flow off the 700-square-mile Harding Icefield (the country's largest), whose elevation has been decreasing by 10 to 12 feet every year, causing the fjord waters to rise. The impact of this on the park and its glaciers has been, and continues to be, significant. It's important to stay abreast of conditions and heed warnings, particularly involving ice chunks released into Resurrection Bay and Bear Lagoon and on land along the toe of Exit Glacier.

Archaeological findings indicate that indigenous peoples have been in the region for thousands of years, many living in permanent settlements, including one village that appears to have been maintained for almost 900 years. In the mid-1700s, the first Europeans arrived and encountered the Unegkurmiut, an Alutiiq (Sugpiak)-speaking people whose communities were spread across most of the outer southeastern coast of the Kenai Peninsula. Trappers and traders found the region very resourceful, and Resurrection Bay became the sight of a Russian trading post and shipyard. Subsequent battles and transgressions between Russian and European armies and interests ensued. Missionaries descended on the peninsula, and Russian companies forced or paid the Unegkurmiut and other Sugpiak communities to consolidate. Largely due to the influx of foreign diseases (particularly smallpox, which decimated an enormous portion of the Alaska Native population during the mid- to late 1800s) and because the Unegkurmiut were either persuaded or forced to leave their homes, the population declined to the point of nonexistence along the outer coast of the peninsula by the time the City of Seward was incorporated as an American town. Ancestors of the Unegkurmiut now live in the communities of Port Graham and Nanwalek, which are located on the (inner) southwest end of the Kenai Peninsula.

The United States purchased the Alaska Territory from Russia in 1867, and about 10 years later the first American-identified inhabitants arrived including Frank and Mary Lowell and their nine children. In 1903, the Lowel family witnessed the arrival of steam ships with hoards of American settlers looking for work building the railroad. In 1906, Mary sold her holdings to the founders of the City of Seward, which was officially incorporated in 1912. Although fur trading in

AVERAGE HIGH/LOW TEMPERATURES					
JAN.	FEB.	MAR.	APR.	MAY	JUNE
26/8	28/10	35/16	45/27	56/38	62/43
JULY	AUG.	SEPT.	OCT.	NOV.	DEC.
64/49	57/39	43/27	43/27	31/15	27/11

the area was no longer viable, as the sea otter had become practically extinct from over-harvesting, the fjords became a dominant destination for the fishing industry.

Kenai Fjords became a national monument in 1978, and just two years later it became a national park. Today, the harbor town of Seward (population 3,000), on the north end of Resurrection Bay, is the gateway to Alaska's fifth most-popular national park, which has approximately 350,000 visitors per year. In addition to being the location for the park's headquarters, it's a beautiful town with excellent eateries, lodgings, and camping options.

Planning

When to Go

The ideal months to visit the Kenai Fjords National Park are June, July, and August. Although the park is open year-round, much of it is inaccessible from September through May, and visitor centers are closed. Rough waters make it nearly impossible to reach the park's coastal backcountry and too dangerous for water excursions. The Herman Leirer Road to Exit Glacier is not plowed when the snow falls and is closed to automobiles, however, the area is a great destination for winter activities like cross-country skiing, fat biking, and snowmachining.

When visiting the park in the summer months, it's important to know the only thing predictable about the weather is that it's wildly unpredictable. It is erratic; sunny moments can be rapidly lost to cool rain or even a snow flurry. The region is highly influenced by Japan's air currents, providing a relatively temperate maritime climate. Summer daytime temperatures generally range from the mid 40s to the low 70s.

Getting Here and Around

AIR

The Ted Stevens Anchorage International Airport (ANC) is the nearest major airport to the Kenai Fjords National Park, 126 miles away. Travelers can catch a 40-minute flight with Rust's Flying Service, or grab a shuttle to Lake Hood, just a mile away from the international airport, and take a flight on a float plane with Seward Air Tour. Seward has a small airport that accommodates air taxis and flightseeing outfits, the latter of which is the only way to visually grasp how massive the Harding Icefield is, and the only way to see all of the region's glaciers.

CAR

The only part of the park you can drive to is Exit Glacier, which is accessible off the Seward Highway, eight miles north of Seward, 126 miles south of Anchorage. There are a number of car rental companies located directly at the airport, but it's important to book a car in advance, as many of them are booked solid during the summer months.

TRAIN

A 4½-hour scenic railroad trip from Anchorage to Seward with Alaska Railroad is an excellent way to begin your park visit. It's a fair jaunt from the depot to the boat harbor, but there are free shuttles if you're slated to do a boat or kayaking trip.

Alaska Railroad
The "Coastal Classic" route from Anchorage to Seward is considered the most visually stunning of the railroad's trips. Only available during the summer months, this four-hour trip includes luggage service, dining services, and a shuttle. Round-trip tickets start at $224. ✉ *W. 411 1st Ave., Anchorage* ☎ *800/544–0552* 🌐 *www.alaskarailroad.com*.

Inspiration

Shot in Seward, *Sugar Mountain*, a 2016 drama thriller starring Jason Momoa, gives viewers excellent vantage points of the park and surrounding wilderness.

Winner of the 2020 National Outdoor Book Award for Outdoor Classic, *The Only Kayak: A Journey into the Heart of Alaska,* written by Kim Heacox, is a coming-of-middle-age memoir, a heartfelt and contemplative introduction to the wonders that can only be experienced rowing the Arctic waters.

For decades, poet and scientist Eva Saulitis researched and brought voice to the endangered orca wales of Prince William Sound. She presented her findings in her 2013 novel, *Into Great Silence: A Memoir of Discovery and Loss among Vanishing Orcas.* Since the Exxon Valdez oil spill of 1989, not a single calf has been born to the group in three decades.

Park Essentials

ACCESSIBILITY
Both the Kenai Fjords National Park Visitor Center in Seward and the Exit Glacier Nature Center are wheelchair-accessible. Exit Glacier has a one-mile wheelchair-accessible loop that leads to a fantastic panoramic view of the glacier; the two remote public use cabins are also wheelchair-accessible, however, assistance may be needed from the beach.

PARK FEES AND PERMITS
There are no entrance fees or camping fees within the park, however, public use cabins must be reserved in advance and are $75 a night.

PARK HOURS
Access to the park is open year-round, but the Kenai Fjords National Park Visitor's Center and the Exit Glacier Nature Center are only open June through September.

CELL PHONE RECEPTION
Once you leave Seward, cell phone service can be spotty throughout the park, though on the water it tends to be strong.

Hotels

There are no lodges or hotels within the park. There are, however, two public use cabins available during the summer season. These must booked in advance 🌐 *www.recreation.gov* and are only accessible by water. Most visitors find lodging in or around Seward or Anchorage.

Restaurants

There are no eateries within the park, but Seward—ultimately the base camp for most Kenai Fjord visitors—has an ample supply of restaurants and pubs.

Tours

Adventure 60 North
ADVENTURE TOURS | This year-round kayaking outfitter offers a number of excellent adventures that can only be had in the Kenai Fjords. Chill out while quietly gliding through the iceberg monoliths of Bear Glacier Lake, or kayak back and forth between the massive calving Aialik

and Holgate Glaciers in Aialik Bay. Spend a day, or spend a few; get heli-dropped or take a two-hour water taxi ride chock-full wildlife viewing to get to your paddle-dipping destination. ✉ *31872 Herman Leirer Rd., Seward* ☎ *907/224–2600* 🌐 *www.adventure60.com* 💴 *Day trips start at $499; multiday trips start at $799.*

Exit Glacier Guides

ADVENTURE TOURS | Single or multiday hikes and climbs, fly-in or paddle-to, Exit Glacier Guides offer small group or private guided adventures throughout the park and surrounding areas. ✉ *1013 3rd Ave., Seward* ☎ *907/224–5569* 🌐 *www.exitglacierguides.com.*

Kenai Fjords Tours

BOAT TOURS | This company offers multiple day trips through Resurrection Bay and into the park for glacier viewing, whale-watching, and evening stops for dinner at Fox Island. ✉ *Seward* ☎ *800/808–8068* 🌐 *www.alaskacollection.com.*

Northern Latitudes Adventures

BOAT TOURS | Offering small group boat tours, with a maximum of six people, eco-friendly Northern Latitudes offers day-long trips for seasonal whale-watching, animal viewing, bird-watching, and glacier marveling. ✉ *Seward* ☎ *907/422–0432* 🌐 *northernlatitudeadventures.com.*

Seward Air Tours

AIR EXCURSIONS | Land on a glacier, spy wildlife, fly to the farthest reaches of the park waters, or just get an air taxi. This outfit offers one-hour to day-long tours, and if there's something they're not offering, you can build-your-own adventure with them. ✉ *Seward Airport, 2300 Airport Rd., Seward* ☎ *907/978–3089* 🌐 *www.sewardair.com.*

Seward Ocean Excursions

BOAT TOURS | One of the few companies that offers year-round boat-based tours, Seward Ocean Excursions also provides water taxi service, custom trips, and even scuba outings. This outfitter allows visitors to see the park's many different faces that change with the season. ✉ *Seward Small Boat Harbor, Seward Harbor Slips M-3 & M-5, Seward* ☎ *907/599–0499* 🌐 *sewardoceanexcursions.com.*

Seward Wilderness Collective

GUIDED TOURS | The Collective was established to offer affordable private hiking tours that provide travelers with the opportunity to have important conversations about climate change, learn firsthand about the ways our surroundings alert us to global patterns, and discuss how we can make a difference in the climate narrative of the 21st century. They also offer guided glacier hikes as well as boating and hiking day trips. ✉ *328 3rd Ave., Seward* ☎ *907/224–3960* 🌐 *www.hikeseward.com.*

Seward Wildlife Tours

BOAT TOURS | This company offers small boat tours for 3–6 passengers into Kenai Fjords and beyond. ✉ *Small Boat Harbor, Seward* ☎ *907/491–1960* 🌐 *www.sewardwildlife.com.*

Sunny Cove Kayaking

ADVENTURE TOURS | Kayak for a day or for several, paddle to islands and glaciers, hike and camp—the opportunities are bountiful with this company. ✉ *1304 B, 4th Ave., Seward* ☎ *907/224–4426* 🌐 *www.sunnycove.com.*

Visitor Information

CONTACTS Kenai Fjords National Park. ☎ *907/422–0500* 🌐 *www.nps.gov/kefj.*

In the Park

126 miles south from Anchorage.

Resurrection Bay, the fjord that serves as Seward's harbor and a popular destination for kayakers, is the maritime entry point of the Kenai Fjords National Park. During the summer months, the

the collective fjords are exploding with glacier and wildlife sights. The marine mammals you'll likely see are the Dall porpoises, sea lions, otters, seals, dolphins and whales (orca, humpback, gray, minke, sei, and fin). In the air, on the water, and populating the many islands and outcroppings along the way are almost 200 species of birds that call this region home including falcons, eagles, and puffins. Whether kayaking along the coastline or cruising through the channels on a tour boat, there are also many mammal sightings to be had including bears, moose, mountain goats, and the gray wolf.

Sights

GEOLOGICAL FORMATIONS

Aialik Glacier

BODY OF WATER | Just 15 miles from Seward, this the largest glacier in Aialik Bay. The glacier calves mostly in May and June. It's best seen by taking a cruise from Seward or kayaking; look for seals, porpoises, and whales. ✉ *Kenai.*

Bear Glacier

BODY OF WATER | This is the park's largest glacier—the tidewater glacier is so big that it can be seen from the deck of a cruise ship departing Seward. However, local tour operators and water taxis can give you a defined experience by dropping you off with a kayak and a guide. Kayak into the Bear Glacier Lagoon, past and through the eerily silent monolithic icebergs that have calved off the glacier ✉ *Kenai Peninsula.*

Bear Lagoon

SIGHTS OVERVIEW | Bear Lagoon is a proglacier lagoon, a lake that resides between a glacier and its moraine. Its stunning blue waters are speckled with slow-floating icebergs wrought into gorgeous formations. Several boat tours and water taxis will take you to the lagoon and drop you off with a kayak or a paddleboard and a guide. ✉ *Kenai Peninsula.*

Exit Glacier

VIEWPOINT | One of the few accessible valley glaciers in the state, Exit is the only destination in the park accessible by car. Named for being a mountaineering expeditions' exit from the first recorded successful crossing of the Harding Icefield in 1968, this glacier is the park's most popular destination.

Harding Icefield

NATURE SITE | This is the largest icefield located entirely in the United States. It began forming during the Pleistocene Epoch, about 23,000 years ago, and is now comprised of a number of interconnected glaciers. As it's not possible to see through the ice, it's hard to gauge the depth of it, but radio wave studies have indicated that it's at least 1,500 feet deep in a ridge above Exit Glacier. The surface area is relatively easy to study, however, and research shows that over the past 10 years, the ice field's melt has increased, dropping it 10–12 feet in elevation every year.

Holgate Glacier

BODY OF WATER | While this is one of Aialik Bay's smallest glaciers, it's a popular spot to witness calving glaciers that can best be seen on a cruise from Seward or on a kayak. ✉ *Kenai.*

Kenai Fjords

NATURE SITE | The Kenai Fjords explode with glaciers, rainforests, and wildlife sights. The marine mammals you'll likely see are the Dall porpoises, sea lions, otters, seals, dolphins, and whales (orca, humpback, gray, minke, sei, and fin). In the air, on the water, and populating the many islands and outcroppings along the way are almost 200 species of birds that call this region home including falcons, eagles, and puffins.

Resurrection Bay

NATURE SITE | Serving as the port for the city of Seward, this 18-mile long fjord is the epic destination for kayakers from all over the world, as well as the entry point

Spire Cove in Resurrection Bay is best seen on a tour.

to the Kenai Fjords National Park. Framed by snow-tip peaks, this scenic body of water is an exciting place for viewing birds and marine life in the summer months.

TRAILS

Glacier View Loop

TRAIL | A 1-mile, wheelchair-accessible trail that offers excellent viewing angles of Exit Glacier. *Easy.* ✣ *Trailhead: The Nature Center.*

The Glacier Overlook Trail

TRAIL | Piggy-backing off the Glacier View Loop, this additional 0.6-mile hike is moderately strenuous. *Moderate.* ✣ *Trailhead: The Nature Center.*

Harding Icefield Trail

TRAIL | This 8.6-mile hike begins on the valley floor and with a gain of 1,000 feet, makes its way up through forests, then above the tree line and offers a stunning view of the Harding Icefield. This hike is considered strenuous and usually takes 6–8 hours. *Difficult.* ✣ *Trailhead: The Nature Center.*

VISITOR CENTERS

Exit Glacier Nature Center

INFO CENTER | Open daily from Memorial Day to Labor Day, the center includes a bookstore, exhibits of topographical maps, stories of explorers and adventurers, and geological and glaciological artifacts. The center is ADA compatible and has rangers on staff to answer questions and guide short tours of the immediate area. ✉ *24620 Herman Leirer Rd., Seward.*

Kenai Fjords National Park Visitor Center

INFO CENTER | Located in Seward's small boat harbor, the main visitor center is open daily from June- to mid-September. The small center has a few things for sale, issues marine tour tickets, and offers free viewings of a short two-minute film narrated from the perspective of a wilderness kayaker, a marine ecologist, and a Sugpiaq family whose ancestors hailed from the region. Park rangers are on staff to answer questions about the area. ✉ *1212 4th Ave., Seward* ☎ *907/422–0500* 🌐 *www.nps.gov/kefj* ⏲ *Closed mid-Sept.–May.*

Activities

BIRD-WATCHING

A fjords marine tour past the rookery island is a bird lover's paradise. There are almost 200 species of birds that call this region home including Kittlitz's murrelets, three types of cormorants, parakeet auklets, both the horned and tufted puffins, and a number of other winged-species that are either nearly or entirely impossible to see anywhere else but from the deck of a boat in the Kenai Fjords.

CAMPING

Because the majority of the Kenai Fjords park is only ice and water, there is just one campground in the entire park. **■TIP→ Some of the coastline within the parklands is owned by the Alaska Native-owned Port Graham Village Corporation; a permit must be obtained in order to camp on those lands.** There are several privately-owned campgrounds in Seward, and camping in the nearby Chugach National Forest. It is also important to note that

Exit Glacier Campground. There is a 12-site, walk-in, tent-only campground located along the road to the glacier. Two sites are ADA accessible. Sites are first come, first served, 14-day maximum stay, and there is no fee. Drinking water and pit toilets are available, but pets are not allowed. Bear bins are provided. ✉ *Mile 8, Herman Leirer Rd.* 🌐 *www.nps.gov/kefj/planyourvisit/campgrounds.htm.*

EDUCATIONAL PROGRAMS

There are a few ranger-led talks and walks hosted at the Exit Glacier Nature Center and the Kenai Fjords Vistor Center. Some marine tour companies include a ranger-tour guide who will point out sites and wildlife along the way.

KAYAKING

Kayaking is the primary athletic sport in the region. People come from all over the world to experience putting their paddle into Resurrection Bay, which is surrounded by snow capped peaks and abundant marine life. Traveling with a guide is strongly recommended in these waters. The fjords are exposed to the excessive rain and winds that blow in from the Gulf of Alaska, making for treacherous waters and rough surf.

SCENIC FLIGHTS

Flightseeing is the best way to grasp the magnitude and vastness of the Harding Icefield, and the only way to see all of the glaciers that flow off of it. Overflights may also provide glimpses of wildlife—salmon-choked streams, ambling brown bear, rock climbing mountain goats, and isolated nunataks (mountain peaks that project through the hundreds or thousands of feet of ice). Some flight tour operators also offer glacier and icefield landings and expeditions where you can explore ice caves, crevasses, and glacial lakes.

What's Nearby

Seward (🌐 *www.seward.com*) is the gateway to the Kenai Fjords. Travelers arrive by car, cruise ship, ferry, plane or train. It's a saltwater fishing town and in the summer months has dozens of fishing charters, kayaking and flightseeing outfits, restaurants featuring local catch, watering holes, and an array of lodgings This scenic small town is surrounded by dense woods, snowy peaks and the eco-rich bay. There are a number of privately-owned campgrounds directly in town as well as on both the north and south ends of town. Most outfitters, establishments, and campgrounds are registered on the Seward Chamber of Commerce site.

Chapter 40

LAKE CLARK NATIONAL PARK

Updated by
Teeka Ballas

Camping	Hotels	Activities	Scenery	Crowds
★★★★★	★★★☆☆	★★★★★	★★★★★	★☆☆☆☆

WELCOME TO LAKE CLARK NATIONAL PARK

TOP REASONS TO GO

★ **Land adventures:** Undeveloped wilderness and 4 million acres of solitude make this an excellent park in which to set up camp. Hiking is allowed throughout the park, including day hikes along maintained trails originating in Port Alsworth, and fat- or studded-tire bikes are great for winter explorations.

★ **Water adventures:** The paddling on rivers—including the Kvichak, Tlikakila, Newhalen—and Lake Clark and other lakes is excellent here. The fishing is good, too: this is a pristine destination for salmon anglers in summer and ice fishing for trout and greylings in winter.

★ **Bear viewing:** The heart of coastal bear country is Chinitna Bay. In June and July, you might see up to 20 bears at a time from two viewing stations set just 2 miles apart along the beach. In addition, during the July and August salmon run, the bear viewing intensifies at Silver Salmon Creek. Several aerial outfits offer bear-viewing trips.

1 Port Alsworth. On the shore of Lake Clark and home to the park visitor center, Port Alsworth is one of six communities on park lands. The others include Lime Village, Nondalton, Iliamna, Newhalen, and Pedro Bay. Land ownership and status divisions within the park are complicated. There are also homesteads (remnants from the 1862 Homestead Act), Alaska Native allotments, and village or regional Native corporation claims.

2 Tikahtnu (Cook) Inlet. The park's east side is along this inlet whose waters are often too rough for open-ocean crossings. Some tour companies do, however, offer private charters along the coast.

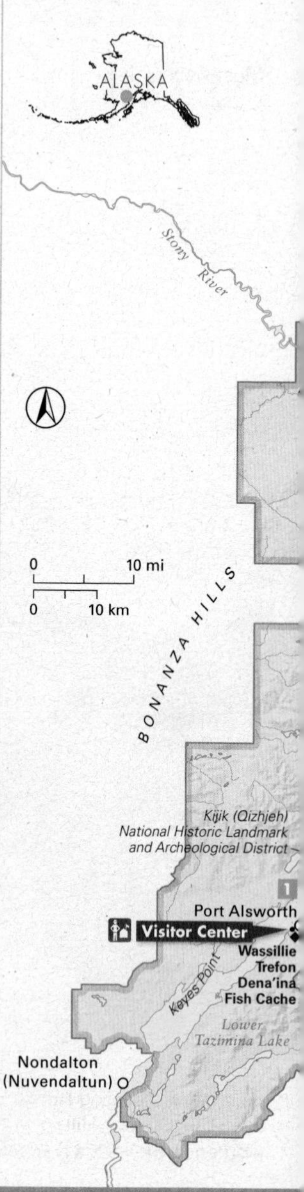

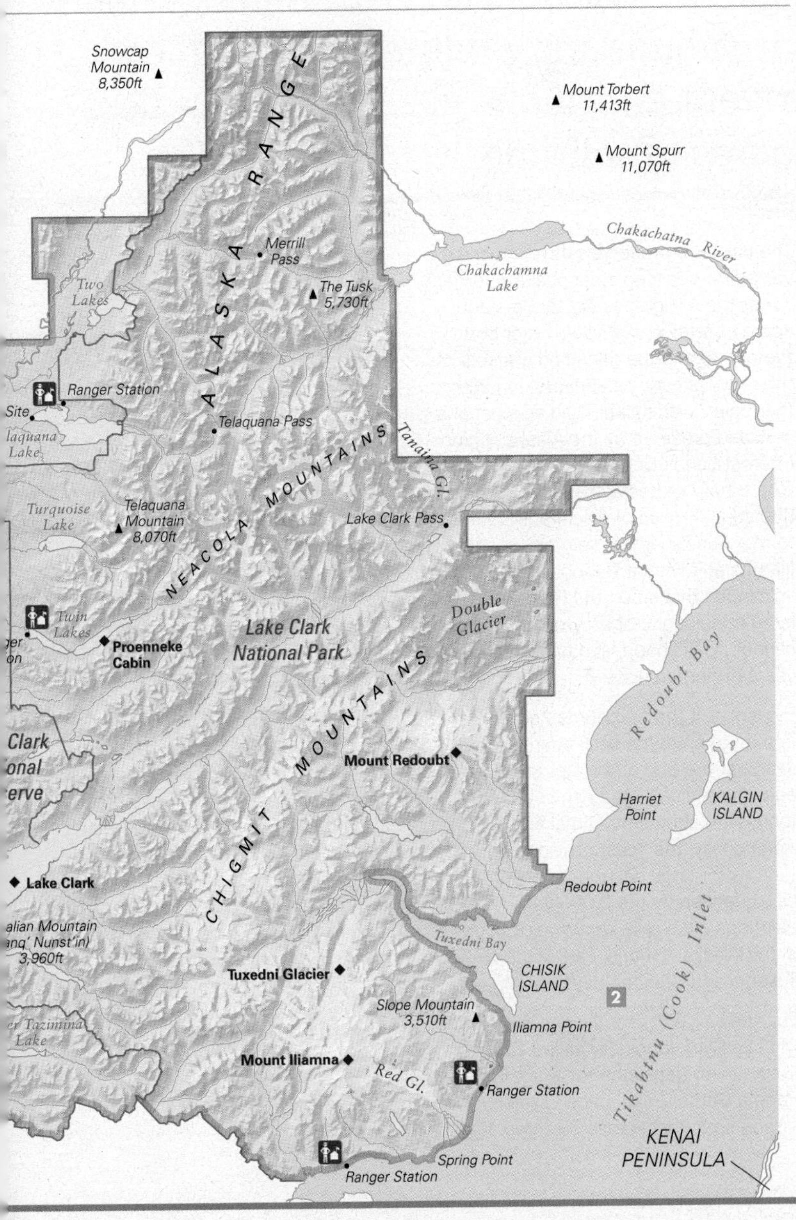
Snowcap Mountain 8,350ft
Mount Torbert 11,413ft
Mount Spurr 11,070ft
ALASKA RANGE
Merrill Pass
The Tusk 5,730ft
Chakachatna River
Chakachamna Lake
Two Lakes
Ranger Station
Site
laquana Lake
Telaquana Pass
Tanaina Gl.
NEACOLA MOUNTAINS
Turquoise Lake
Telaquana Mountain 8,070ft
Lake Clark Pass
Twin Lakes
Proenneke Cabin
Lake Clark National Park
Double Glacier
CHIGMIT MOUNTAINS
Mount Redoubt
Redoubt Bay
Harriet Point
KALGIN ISLAND
Clark
onal
erve
Lake Clark
Redoubt Point
alian Mountain
inq' Nunst'in)
3,960ft
Tuxedni Bay
Tuxedni Glacier
CHISIK ISLAND
2
Slope Mountain 3,510ft
Iliamna Point
Tikahtnu (Cook) Inlet
Lake
Mount Iliamna
Red Gl.
Ranger Station
KENAI PENINSULA
Spring Point
Ranger Station

Lake Clark might have fewer visitors than other national parks, but it's hardly short on reasons to visit. Among them are abundant wildlife, salmon-filled rivers, enormous glaciers, and endless acres of solitude.

The park and preserve's 4 million acres were first declared a national monument under the Antiquities Act by President Jimmy Carter in 1978 to protect both the nature and the ruins and artifacts of the region's early inhabitants. In 1980, the region was established as a national park and preserve by the Alaska National Interest Lands Conservation Act (ANILCA). It now protects coastal rain forest; 900 square miles of glaciers; tributaries to the world's largest salmon run; Mount Iliamna and Mount Redoubt—two active volcanoes that sit on the Ring of Fire—large populations of brown bear, moose, caribou, Dall sheep, and eagles; and years of human history.

Evidence of the first human settlers in the region dates back nearly 10,000 years, at the end of the last great ice age. The region was a rich source of food, with abundant animal and plant life. Additionally, the coast provided opportunities for large sea-mammal hunting, as evidenced by the 2,000-year-old rock paintings—the only known rock paintings in the Alaska National Park system—in Tuxedni and Chinitna Bays.

For nearly 1,000 years, along the shores of Lake Clark (originally called Qizhjeh Vena which translates to "Place Where People Gather Lake"), the Qizhjeh Village sprawled across 25 acres. It was inhabited by the Dena'ina Athabaskan, and people came from villages across the region to trade. In the late 1800s, European American settlers arrived, and in 1902, a flu–measles epidemic struck the village. By 1909, it was abandoned as the survivors fled to nearby Nondalton, and Qizhjeh, which is now a National Historical Landmark maintained by the park service. The area holds more than a dozen archeological sites, and hikers still walk the Telaquana Route, which once connected Qizhjeh to what is now the northern part of the park at Telequana Lake. This truly an outdoor explorer's backcountry route that taps into all the scout badges you earned growing up.

Lake Clark National Park and Preserve offers endless opportunities for adventure. There are no roads, there are no shops, and there are no restaurants—it's just 4 million acres of nature and a smattering of remote lodges. The most reliable means of getting there, one that doesn't risk the rough seas or require climbing mountain ranges, is by plane. Most air-taxi services that travel from Anchorage to the parklands also offer flightseeing tours and wilderness adventure drops, just as most lodges offer guided fishing, wildlife viewing, and adventure trips.

AVERAGE HIGH/LOW TEMPERATURES IN PORT ALSWORTH					
JAN.	**FEB.**	**MAR.**	**APR.**	**MAY**	**JUNE**
22/1	30/10	30/10	43/25	53/35	62/42
JULY	**AUG.**	**SEPT.**	**OCT.**	**NOV.**	**DEC.**
68/54	63/46	53/39	41/28	29/16	25/11

Planning

When to Go

Lake Clark National Park and Preserve has two primary climate zones: the coast and the interior. The weather within the interior of the park can change at a minute's notice and is largely unpredictable. It's always best to prepare for all weather when planning hiking and camping trips. The coast, being part of the 1,000 miles of temperate rain forest that stretches from the Canadian border to the Kodiak Archipelago, receives an average rainfall of 40 to 80 inches annually. This means you can anticipate fog and rain during your visit. The same weather systems that bring precipitation to the coast also bring milder winters, but the interior temperatures often drop as low as-40°F.

Frost and snow can happen throughout the park at any time but are more common between September and early June. Although the peak season is between July and August, a handful of hardy adventurers seek the visual delight of fall colors, the awe of the aurora borealis, and pressing a fat-tire tread into ice and snow during the winter months. It's important to note that the visitor center and park headquarters in Port Alsworth are closed from October to late May.

Getting Here and Around

AIR

Although the eastern shore of the Lake Clark parklands is accessible by boat, it requires a two- to four-hour crossing of rough open waters and navigating the extreme tides of Tikahtnu Inlet. Thus, flying into the park via wheeled craft or floatplane is the standard form of entry. The nearest international airport is the Ted Stevens International in Anchorage. Several air taxis depart from there, but most—especially floatplanes—depart from Lake Hood, just 2 miles down the road from the international airport.

CONTACTS Lake and Peninsula Airlines. ✉ *1740 E. 5th Ave., Anchorage* ☎ *907/345–2228* 🌐 *lakeandpenair.com.* **Regal Air.** ✉ *4506 Lakeshore Dr., Anchorage* ☎ *907/243–8535* 🌐 *regal-air.com.* **Trygg Air.** ✉ *Lake Hood Airport, Anchorage* ☎ *907/350–8675* 🌐 *tryggair.com.*

Inspiration

Alaska: A Novel by James A. Michener, is sweeping saga that encompasses the history of Alaska from its early days through the 20th century. In *Looking For Alaska* author Peter Jenkins shares the experiences he had while traveling throughout the state during the course of 18 months.

One Man's Wilderness: An Alaskan Odyssey, by Sam Keith and Richard Proenneke, documents Dick Proenneke's day-to-day world, gleaned from the journals he kept, while living in the remote cabin he built in Lake Clark.

Tales of Alaska's Bush Rat Governor: The Extraordinary Autobiography of Jay Hammond, Wilderness Guide and Reluctant Politician is an insightful and humorous account of life in contemporary Alaska.

Park Essentials

ACCESSIBILITY

There are no roads or paved trails in Lake Clark National Park and Preserve, however, the visitor center in Port Alsworth does have a wheelchair access ramp, and there are all-terrain wheelchairs available for loan at the Port Alsworth, Silver Salmon Creek, and Chinitna Bay ranger stations. Call in advance (☎ *907/781–2218*) to check on availability.

PARK FEES AND PERMITS

There are no entrance fees or permits needed for any park recreational activities, including backpacking, camping, river running, bear viewing, or visiting Dick Proenneke's cabin. There are fees for the two public-use cabins in the parklands, and online reservations are required (🌐 *www.nps.gov/lacl/public-use-cabins.htm*). Additionally, licenses and fees are needed for fishing; many outfitters provide the licensing.

PARK HOURS

Lake Clark National Park and Preserve is open 24 hours a day all year long. The Port Alsworth visitor center is only open from late May through September.

CELL PHONE RECEPTION

Because there is no cell phone service within the park, it's important that you register with the park service before embarking on any backcountry trips. Most lodges have an on-site satellite phone or landline for use in the event of an emergency.

Hotels

Although there are two rustic and remote public-use cabins, a maintained campground in Port Alsworth, and 4 million acres of primitive camping space, most visitors opt for the comfort and safety of a lodge, and there are a good number of them from which to choose. Meals are often, but not always, included in the rates; a few places also include activities or air transportation to the property, but always check on what's included before booking. Note, too, that some rates are based on multiple-night stays and are for cabins that sleep more than two people.

Restaurants

There are no restaurants or grocery stores in or near park lands. Area lodges offer dining, though not all of them include meals in their room rates, so check when you book. If you're planning on camping, check with your outfitter to make sure food is provided. If it's not, or if you're backcountry camping on your own, be sure to pack enough food, proper gear, and a water purifier before you leave Anchorage, as there is nowhere in the park to stock up on provisions.

Tours

Alaska Air Service

AIR EXCURSIONS | When it comes to Lake Clark, this air service is all about the bears. On a six- to seven-hour trip, its guides will land you on the beach of Chinitna Bay or the grasslands of Silver Salmon Creek to safely explore and watch the bears in their natural habitat. The flight home is sure to provide stunning views, too. Lunch is provided. ✉ *Merrill Field Airport , 2600 E. 5th Ave., Hangar "C" located in North Edge Airpark, Anchorage* ☎ *907/694–8687* 🌐 *flyakair.com* 🎫 *From $745 per person.*

★ **Alaska Alpine Adventures**

ADVENTURE TOURS | Whether you wan to raft, paddle, hike, or climb, this outfitter can hook you up on 4- to 10-day (or longer) guided excursions. Renowned for their expertise and experience, the guides have a thorough, safe, and extensive track record. ✉ *300 E. 76th Ave., Unit B, Anchorage* ☎ *877/525–2577* 🌐 *www.alaskaalpineadventures.com* 💵 *From $3350 per person.*

Kenai Backcountry Adventures

ADVENTURE TOURS | Heli-rafting, bear viewing, glacier hiking, fly-in fishing, backcountry skiing—this company offers all kinds of adventures lasting from just one day to a whole week. ☎ *907/331–4912* 🌐 *kenaibackcountryadventures.com* 💵 *From $995 per person.*

Smokey Bay Air

AIR EXCURSIONS | Sometimes the best way to see the extraordinary phenomena that abounds in Alaska's natural world is by flying into it. In fact, it's the only way to see the park's two volcanoes in the Ring of Fire and the best way to access the beaches where you can view the great brown bears in their natural habitat. Flights with this company originate in Homer. ✉ *2100 Kachemak Dr., Homer* ☎ *888/281–2635* 🌐 *www.smokeybayair.com* 💵 *From $490 per person.*

Trek Alaska

ADVENTURE TOURS | This outfit is all about backcountry hiking. Its rates cover the flight into Port Alsworth and the bush plane needed to drop you and your experienced guide off to embark on a once-in-a-lifetime adventure. ☎ *907/795–5252* 🌐 *www.trekalaska.com* 💵 *From $3395 per person.*

Tulchina Adventures

ADVENTURE TOURS | This company focuses entirely on Lake Clark National Park and can set you up with day trips, self-guided backpacking trips, or guided multiday kayaking and rafting trips deep into parkland. ☎ *907/782–4720* 🌐 *www.tulchinaadventures.com.*

Visitor Information

CONTACTS Lake Clark National Park and Preserve. ☎ *907/781–2218* 🌐 *www.nps.gov/lacl.*

In the Park

120 air miles southwest of Anchorage; 65 air miles northwest of Homer.

Lake Clark National Park and Preserve is a region comprised largely of fire and ice, with a seemingly endless array of exquisite sights to behold, including 900 miles of glaciers and two active volcanoes. Every turn of the head can offer another awe-inducing moment. Likewise, there is adventure—as well as potential danger—at every turn. It's important to be prepared for abrupt and extreme weather changes, as well as potential bear and moose activity.

Sights

GEOLOGICAL FORMATIONS

Lake Clark

BODY OF WATER | Centrally located, the park's namesake lake is 50 miles long and filled with nooks, crannies, coves, and islands. Port Alsworth, which is on the lake's south-central shore, is the jumping off point for hundreds of possible adventures: kayaking to a remote campsite, hiking to a public-use cabin, catching a floatplane to a hidden lakeside lodge. Although the lake is an access point for lodges and campsites, it offers sublime solitude and awe-inspiring nature. ✉ *Lake Clark National Park and Preserve.*

An Alaskan perspective: a lone (and, no doubt, big) bear is dwarfed by a vast, mountainous backdrop.

Mount Iliamna

VOLCANO | The peak of this 10,016-foot strato-volcano, which is in the southeast corner of the park, is home to 10 glaciers. Although not active, it is expected to erupt at some time in the future. It's noted as being the 25th most prominant peak in North America. ✉ *Lake Clark National Park and Preserve.*

Mount Redoubt

VOLCANO | This active volcano, located north of Tuxedni Bay on the eastern side of the park, can be seen from many different vantage points in south central Alaska, but from within Lake Clark National Park, it is a truly impressive sight. Its sister, Mount Iliamna, has blown plumes of ash and smoke but has had no recorded eruptions, unlike Redoubt, which has erupted 30 times in the past 10,000 years, including four times just in the last century. ✉ *Lake Clark National Park and Preserve.*

Tuxedni Glacier

NATURE SITE | Most of the park's glaciers are found in the Chigmit Mountains. The longest is the 19-mile Tuxedni Glacier, which is one of 10 that radiates from the Mount Iliamna volcano. ✉ *Lake Clark National Park and Preserve.*

HISTORIC SIGHTS

Proenneke Cabin

HISTORIC SITE | In 1969, naturalist and conservationist icon Richard L. Proenneke built his cabin by hand with tools he created himself. He lived there and sustained himself off the land until his death in 1999. Located on the south shore of Upper Twin Lake, this cabin is only accessed by float plane or backpacking up to it. It is maintained by nearby park service employees. ✉ *Lake Clark National Park and Preserve.*

Wassillie Trefon Dena'ina Fish Cache

HISTORIC SITE | There used to be Dena'ina and Yup'ik villages and summer fish camps all over the Lake Clark region. Fish caches, like this one in Port Alsworth, were very common, but they have now largely disappeared. This particular cache is approximately 100 years old. It is a hand-hewn, square-notched log building built by Wassillie Trefon, a Dena'ina master woodworker. The cache was constructed without nails or spikes, with a vertical stick hammered into a groove to provide the rigidity necessary to keep the logs bound. This is now a largely extinct local way preserving and securing food. ✉ *Lake Clark National Park and Preserve, Port Alsworth.*

TRAILS

There are only two maintained trail systems in Lake Clark National Park and Preserve: Tanalian Trails and Portage Creek Trail. Aside from routes that might be maintained on private property, all other hiking in the park is off-trail.

Portage Creek Trail

TRAIL | This trail originates 13 miles north–northwest of Port Alsworth at the Joe Thompson Public Use Cabin. The cabin can be accessed by floatplane, and the hike is 3¼ miles and ascends 1,850 feet,ending in the tundra. *Difficult.* ✉ *Lake Clark National Park and Preserve* ✣ *Trailhead: At Joe Thompson Public Use Cabin.*

Tanalian Trails

TRAIL | This system is comprised of four day-hike trails that begin in Port Alsworth. They range from moderate to strenuous and offer up stunning vistas, waterfalls, beaver dams, mountainous summits, lava cliffs, and serene glacier waters. *Moderate–difficult.* ✉ *Lake Clark National Park and Preserve* ✣ *Trailheads: Port Alsworth.*

VISITOR CENTERS

Port Alsworth Visitor Center

INFO CENTER | Only open in the summer months (late May through mid-September), the visitor center is a place to register for outings, learn about the area, pick up a couple of gifts, and start off on your exploration. ✉ *Lake Clark National Park and Preserve, Port Alsworth* ☎ *907/781–2117* 🌐 *www.nps.gov/lacl.*

Hotels

Alaska Backcountry Fishing Lodge

$$$$ | **ALL-INCLUSIVE** | Located on the beach of Lake Clark, this lodge organizes day trips and fishing or rafting adventures, whether you want a guide, or you prefer to head out on your own. **Pros:** close to the national park visitor center; terrific views; very friendly. **Cons:** there could be a bear outside your door; fishing license not included; must make your own travel arrangements. [$] *Rooms from: $1400* ✉ *Port Alsworth* ☎ *907/310–1165* 🌐 *www.alaskabackcountryfishing.com* *4 rooms* 🍽 *All-inclusive.*

Chulitna Lodge and Wilderness Retreat

$$$ | **ALL-INCLUSIVE** | Though large enough to accommodate a small wedding party, this remote lodge tends to keep things intimate with just five to eight guests at a time, a rugged but comfortable style, and warm hospitality. **Pros:** remote, pristine, natural experience; fantastic food; excellent guides and hospitality. **Cons:** no cell service; no Internet; dry cabins. [$] *Rooms from: $415* ✣ *Lake Clark, across from Port Alsworth* ☎ *907/781–3144* 🌐 *chulitnalodge.com* *7 cabins* 🍽 *All-inclusive.*

The Farm Lodge

$ | **ALL-INCLUSIVE** | This family-friendly lodge, replete with a playground and youth activities, has comfortable cabins along the shore of Lake Clark right in Port Alsworth. **Pros:** great meals; family-oriented; friendly and helpful service. **Cons:** rooms are basic; long flight of stairs to the main lodge; no alcohol with meals in the main house (BYOB in the cabins). [$] *Rooms from: $240* ✉ *Port Alsworth* ☎ *888/440–2281* 🌐 *www.thefarmlodge.com* *4 cabins* 🍽 *All-inclusive.*

Island Lodge–Lake Clark

$$$$ | **ALL-INCLUSIVE** | Situated on an island in Lake Clark and accessible only by floatplane, this lodge offers stays of from four to six nights in heated, bathroom-equipped cabins that sleep two to four people. **Pros:** peaceful;

includes fishing gear and guide; private bathrooms. **Cons:** no Wi-Fi, cell service, or land line; only generator-supplied electricity; remote. *Rooms from: $2400* *Lake Clark* *www.islandlodge.com* *Cabins* *All-inclusive.*

Redoubt Mountain Lodge

$$$$ | **ALL-INCLUSIVE** | The only privately owned property and lodge on the 9-mile Crescent Lake offers excellent meals, plenty of comfort, memorable adventures, and a fantastic view of Mount Redoubt—the park's volcano—8 miles away. **Pros:** arranges outdoor activities; sauna and hot tub; Internet and phone available. **Cons:** super remote; a little pricey. *Rooms from: $3300* *Crescent Lake* *866/733–3034* *redoubtlodge.com* *6 cabins* *All-inclusive.*

Tulchina Adventures

$ | **RENTAL** | Located on 40 acres near the mouth of the Tanalian River, just ½ mile outside Port Alsworth, this remote but homey property guarantees instant access to the great outdoors and pristine views of Lake Clark and the surrounding peaks from either a comfy cabin or one of three, 10x12-foot, "glamping" huts (($65 per night) with a fire pit and an outhouse. **Pros:** terrific views; kitchen amenities; phone line. **Cons:** outhouse only; no meals supplied; no Internet. *Rooms from: $225* *Port Alsworth* *907/782–4720* *www.tulchinaadventures.com* *1 cabin* *No meals.*

The Wilder B&B

$$ | **B&B/INN** | A great base camp for extraordinary adventures, this B&B offers creekside cabins that can accommodate five to six people. **Pros:** terrific hosts; right beside the airplane hangar; can set you up with adventure outfitters. **Cons:** right beside the airplane hangar; no adventure packages included; no phone service. *Rooms from: $309* *Port Alsworth* *wilderbb.wordpress.com* *3 cabins* *Free breakfast.*

Chapter 41

LASSEN VOLCANIC NATIONAL PARK

Updated by
Andrew Collins

Camping ★★★★★

Hotels ★★★☆☆

Activities ★★★★★

Scenery ★★★★☆

Crowds ★★★☆☆

WELCOME TO LASSEN VOLCANIC NATIONAL PARK

TOP REASONS TO GO

★ **Hike a volcano:** The 2½-mile trek up Lassen Peak rewards you with a spectacular view of far northern California.

★ **Spot a rare bloom:** The Lassen Smelowskia, a small white-to-pinkish flower, which grows only in the Cascade Mountains, is especially prolific on Lassen Peak.

★ **View volcano varieties:** All four types of volcanoes found in the world—shield, plug dome, cinder cone, and composite—are represented here.

★ **Listen to the Earth:** The park's thumping mud pots and venting fumaroles roil, gurgle, and belch a raucous symphony, their actions generated by heat from beneath the Earth's crust.

★ **Escape the crowds:** Lassen, in sparsely populated far northern California, is one of the lesser-known national parks.

1 **Southwest.** Hydrothermal activity is greatest in the park's most-visited area; you'll see evidence on the hike to Bumpass Hell and strolling along the sidewalks at the Sulphur Works, just beyond the Kohm Yah-mah-nee Visitor Center.

2 **Manzanita and Summit Lakes.** The northern half of Lassen Park Highway, starting around Summit Lake, winds past the forested Devastated Area and Chaos Jumbles before reaching lush, wooded Manzanita Lake, near the park's northwest entrance.

3 **Warner Valley and Juniper Lake.** In the park's southeastern quadrant, Warner Valley has dazzling hydrothermal features and the park's only lodging, historic Drakesbad Guest Ranch. Juniper Lake has relaxing hikes and nonmotorized boating fishing and boating.

4 **Butte Lake.** Located in the park's rugged and less-visited northeast corner, Butte and Snag lakes were formed by lava from a cinder cone whose summit you can hike to.

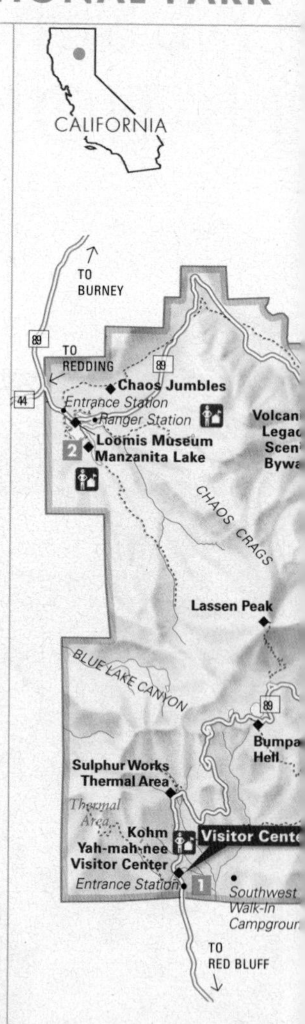

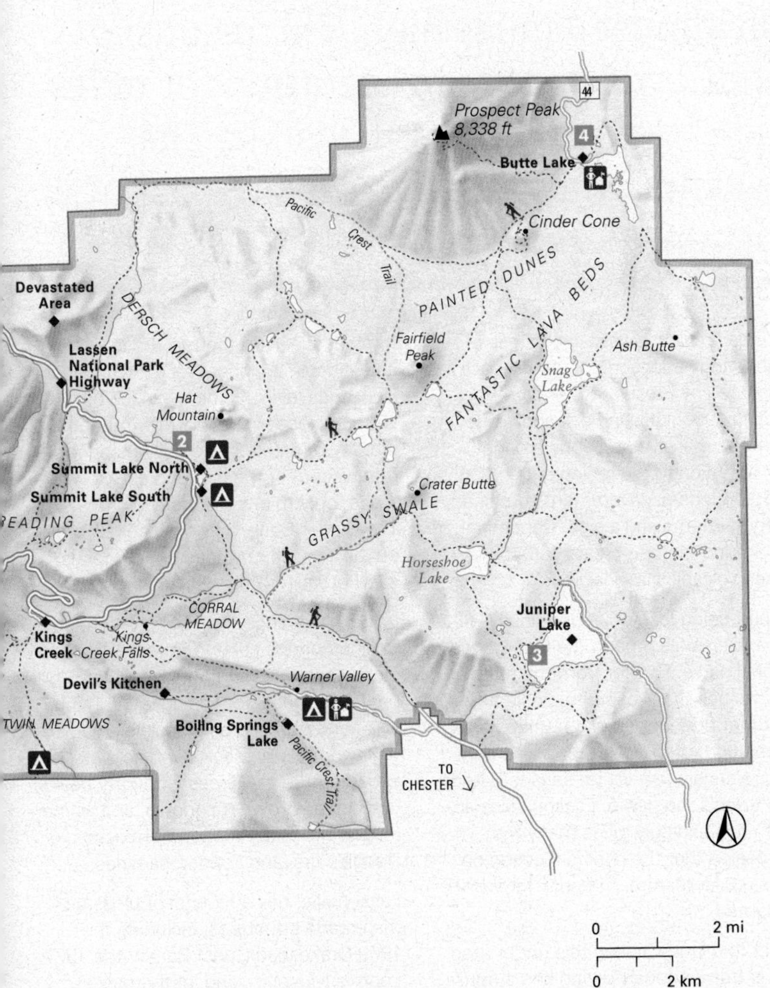
44
Prospect Peak
8,338 ft
4
Butte Lake
Pacific
Crest
Trail
Cinder Cone
PAINTED DUNES
FANTASTIC LAVA BEDS
Ash Butte
Devastated
Area
DERSCH MEADOWS
Lassen
National Park
Highway
Fairfield
Peak
Snag
Lake
Hat
Mountain
2
Summit Lake North
Summit Lake South
Crater Butte
READING PEAK
GRASSY SWALE
Horseshoe
Lake
CORRAL
MEADOW
Juniper
Lake
Kings
Creek
Kings
Creek Falls
3
Warner Valley
Devil's Kitchen
TWIN MEADOWS
Boiling Springs
Lake
Pacific Crest Trail
TO
CHESTER
0
2 mi
0
2 km

Lassen Peak, a plug dome, is the most famous feature of this 166-square-mile tract of coniferous forests and alpine meadows. Its most spectacular outburst occurred in 1915, when it blew a cloud of ash almost 6 miles high. The resulting mudflow destroyed vegetation for miles and the evidence is still visible. The volcano finally came to rest in 1921 but is not considered dormant.

The area previously contained a pair of neighboring national monuments, each designated by President Theodore Roosevelt in 1907: Lassen Peak and Cinder Cone. The massive eruptions brought such attention to the region that in August 1916, the federal government combined the monuments and a significant chunk of land around them to create 106,452-acre Lassen Volcanic National Park.

Despite being located in populous California, Lassen is among the less-visited national parks. Farther from the state's bigger cities than Yosemite, Joshua Tree, and other buzzier parks, it requires a bit of time and effort to get to. It also contains relatively few visitor services. And then there's the name, Lassen Volcanic, which misleadingly gives many the impression that the park is focused on one singular feature, the peak for which it's named.

In fact, the landscape in this underrated park is tremendously varied and surprisingly lush. The peak itself is undeniably impressive (and great fun to hike), but arguably more memorable are the three active hydrothermal areas within its shadow—Sulphur Works, Bumpass Hell, and Devils Kitchen—which delight with up-close views of frothy mudpots, steamy fumaroles, and boiling springs reminiscent of those found at Yellowstone, only minus the jostling crowds. The Cinder Cone, in the park's remote but accessible northeastern corner, is another star feature.

Lakes here range from hot and forbidding Boiling Springs Lake to refreshing, deep-blue Manzanita, Summit, Butte, and Juniper lakes—ideal for fishing, swimming, and nonmotorized boating. Well-marked trails connect these marvelous waters and hydrothermal areas with lofty peaks, wildflower-strewn meadows, and alpine forests rife with Western hemlocks, Douglas firs, and Ponderosa pines.

Lassen also has a handful of pleasant man-made structures, including the 1909 Drakesbad Guest Ranch, the 1927 Loomis Museum, and, at the park's southwestern entrance, the airy, contemporary, LEED-certified Kohm Yah-mah-nee Visitor Center.

AVERAGE HIGH/LOW TEMPERATURES					
JAN.	FEB.	MAR.	APR.	MAY	JUNE
50/13	51/13	53/16	61/23	70/29	79/34
JULY	AUG.	SEPT.	OCT.	NOV.	DEC.
84/40	85/40	78/36	69/30	56/21	50/14

Thanks to renewed interest in camping and off-the-beaten-path adventures (and to social media) Lassen's annual visitor numbers have been increasing. For now, though, one of California's greatest natural wonders still offers plenty of solitude.

Planning

When to Go

The park is open year-round, though most roads—the main exception being Lassen Park Highway up to Kohm Yah-mah-nee Visitor Center—are closed from late October to mid-June due to snow. The park's high elevation offers a cool respite in summer from California's hot central valley, while spring and fall are typically mild during the day, but you should prepare for lows below freezing at night even in June and September.

Getting Here and Around

AIR

Redding Municipal Airport (RDD), about an hour's drive west, provides the nearest commercial air service, with regular flights on United Express from San Francisco and Los Angeles. Most major airlines serve the airports in Reno, a 2½-hour drive, and Sacramento, a three-hour drive.

CAR

From the north, take the Highway 44 exit off Interstate 5 in Redding and drive east about 50 miles to the park's northwest entrance, at Highway 89. From the south, take Exit 649 off Interstate 5 and follow Highway 36 northeast 45 miles, turning left onto Highway 89 to reach the southwest (and only year-round) entrance. The 30-mile main park road, officially called Lassen National Park Highway but often called simply Lassen Park Highway, skirts around the southern, eastern, and northern sides of Lassen Peak, connecting the southwest and northwest entrances. Take Highway 36 from the southwest entrance to Chester to reach Warner Valley and Juniper Lake, in the remote southeastern side of the park, and follow Highway 44 east from Manzanita to reach the similarly secluded Butte Lake area.

Inspiration

Lassen Volcanic National Park & Vicinity, by Jeffrey P. Schaffer, is a comprehensive book about the park.

Park Essentials

ACCESSIBILITY

Kohm Yah-mah-nee Visitor Center, the Loomis Museum, and the Manzanita Camper Store are fully accessible to those with limited mobility. The Devastated Area Interpretive Trail and the Sulphur Works wayside exhibits are accessible, as are most ranger programs. Butte Lake, Manzanita Lake, and Summit Lake North have some accessible campsites.

PARK FEES AND PERMITS

From mid-April through November the fee to enter the park is $30 per car ($25 for motorcycles); the rest of the year the fee is $10 for cars and motorcycles. The fee covers seven consecutive days.

Those entering by bus, bicycle, horse, or on foot pay $15. An annual park pass costs $55. For backcountry camping, pick up a free permit at the Loomis Museum or Kohm Yah-mah-nee Visitor Center, or request an application online at 🌐 *www.nps.gov/lavo.*

PARK HOURS

The park is open 24/7 year-round. It is in the Pacific time zone.

CELL PHONE RECEPTION

Cell phones don't work in most parts of the park, although you can usually pick up a signal near the Bumpass Hell parking area and the north shore of Manzanita Lake.

Hotels

Other than the inviting camping cabins at Manzanita Lake, Drakesbad Guest Ranch is the only lodging available inside Lassen. It's rustic (no electricity, just old-fashioned kerosene lamps), expensive, and tends to book up a year or more in advance for summer stays.

Restaurants

Dining options within the park are limited to simple fare at Lassen Café & Gift in Kohm Yah-mah-nee Visitor Center and at the Manzanita Lake Camper Store, and the delicious meals at Drakesbad Guest Ranch, which does offer meals to nonguests by reservation only.

The nearest community with a good mix of mostly casual dining options is Chester, about a half-hour drive from the southwest entrance station. About an hour away, the town of Susanville and the small city of Redding have more extensive restaurant selections.

Hotel and restaurant reviews have been shortened. For full information, visit Fodors.com. Hotel prices are the lowest cost of a standard double room in high season. Restaurant prices are the average cost of a main course at dinner, or if dinner is not served, at lunch.

What It Costs

$	$$	$$$	$$$$
RESTAURANTS			
under $16	$16–$22	$22–$30	over $30
HOTELS			
under $125	$126–$175	$176–$225	over $225

Visitor Information

CONTACTS Lassen Volcanic National Park. ✉ *Kohm Yah-mah-nee Visitor Center, 21820 Lassen National Park Hwy., Mineral* ☎ *530/595–4480* 🌐 *www.nps.gov/lavo.*

Southwest

30 miles south of Manzanita Lake, 30 miles west of Chester, 52 miles east of Red Bluff.

Home to the park's only year-round entrance and visitor center, Lassen's southwest quadrant also contains the span of Lassen Park Highway that's likely to evoke the most oohs and aahs, as the road twists, turns, rises, and dips sharply to the south and then east of the soaring volcanic peak for which the park is named. You could spend a full day exploring this part of the park, with its fascinating hydrothermal features and breathtaking, though sometimes quite arduous, hiking trails. It's also the most popular and accessible part of the park in winter, a great time for snowshoeing and cross-country skiing.

Sights

SCENIC STOPS

★ Lassen Peak

NATURE SITE | When this plug dome volcano erupted in 1915, it spewed a huge mushroom cloud of debris almost 6 miles into the air. You can admire the peak from a number of points along the park road, and a fabulous panoramic view rewards those who make the strenuous 2½-mile hike to the 10,457-foot summit. ✉ *Lassen Park Hwy.* ✢ *7 miles north of southwest entrance.*

Sulphur Works Thermal Area

NATURE SITE | FAMILY | Proof of Lassen Peak's volatility becomes evident shortly after you enter the park at the southwest entrance. Sidewalks skirt boiling springs and sulfur-emitting steam vents. This area is usually the last site to close in winter, but even when the road is closed, you can access the area via a 2-mile round-trip hike through the snow. ✉ *Lassen Park Hwy.* ✢ *1 mile from southwest entrance.*

TRAILS

★ Bumpass Hell Trail

TRAIL | FAMILY | This 3-mile round-trip hike leads to arguably the park's most mesmerizing feature, a wondrous landscape of hydrothermal activity characterized by boiling springs, hissing steam vents, and roiling gray mud pots. Give yourself about two hours to complete the loop, which involves a gradual 300-foot descent into the Bumpass Hell basin, and be sure to venture to the basin's several upper viewpoints, which provide amazing views of the entire scene. Stay on trails and boardwalks near the thermal areas, as what appears to be firm ground may be only a thin crust over scalding mud. From the basin, you have the option of continuing another 1.9 miles along a scenic ridge to Cold Boiling Lake, from which you can trek farther to Kings Creek Picnic Area or Crumbaugh Lake. *Moderate.* ✉ *Lassen Park Hwy.* ✢ *Trailhead: 6 miles from southwest entrance.*

Crumbaugh Lake Trail

TRAIL | This 2.6-mile round-trip hike through meadows and forests to Cold Boiling and Crumbaugh lakes presents an excellent opportunity to view spring wildflowers, but it's quite pretty throughout summer and fall. At Cold Lake, it's possible to detour to Bumpass Hell (thereby adding 3.8 miles round-trip to your trek). *Moderate.* ✉ *Lassen Park Hwy.* ✢ *Trailhead: Kings Creek picnic area, 13 miles north of southwest entrance.*

Kings Creek Falls Trail

TRAIL | Nature photographers love this 2.3-mile loop hike through forests dotted with wildflowers. A steady 700-foot ascent leads to the spectacular falls. It can be slippery in spots, including along a stone staircase, so watch your step. *Moderate.* ✉ *Lassen Park Hwy.* ✢ *Trailhead: 3 miles south of Summit Lake.*

★ Lassen Peak Trail

TRAIL | This trail winds 2½ miles to the mountaintop. It's a tough climb—2,000 feet uphill on a steady, steep grade—but the reward is a spectacular view. At the peak you can see into the rim and view the entire park (and much of California's Far North). Give yourself about five hours to complete this climb, and bring sunscreen, water, snacks, a first-aid kit, and a jacket—it can be windy and cold at the summit. *Difficult.* ✉ *Lassen Park Hwy.* ✢ *Trailhead: 7 miles north of southwest entrance.*

Mill Creek Falls Trail

TRAIL | This 2½-hour 3.8-mile round-trip hike through forests and wildflowers takes you to where East Sulphur and Bumpass creeks merge to create the park's highest waterfall. For a longer adventure, you can continue past the falls for 2.5 miles to Crumbaugh Lake, and another 1.3 miles past Cold Boiling Lake to Kings Creek Picnic Area. *Moderate.* ✉ *Lassen Park Hwy.* ✢ *Trailhead: Southwest Walk-In Campground parking lot.*

VISITOR CENTERS

★ Kohm Yah-mah-nee Visitor Center

INFO CENTER | FAMILY | A handsome, contemporary LEED-certified structure at the southwest entrance, this helpful year-round resource is a good place to pick up maps, inquire about kids' activities and ranger programs, view an engaging park film, and check out the well-conceived interactive exhibits. There's also an excellent bookstore and a casual café. ✉ *21820 Lassen National Park Hwy.* ☎ *530/595–4480* 🌐 *www.nps.gov/lavo.*

Restaurants

Lassen Café & Gift

$ | CAFÉ | Coffee and hot cocoa, wine and beer (including local brews from Lassen Ale Works), and sandwiches, burgers, soups, salads, bagels, and pizzas are served in this casual eatery inside the park's only year-round visitor center. Indoors, there's a fireplace, but if the weather is fine, the patio with its mountain views is the place to be. **Known for:** local beers; stunning mountain views from the outdoor patio; gift shop with local art and crafts. 💲 *Average main: $9* ✉ *Kohm Yah-mah-nee Visitor Center, 21820 Lassen National Park Hwy.* ☎ *530/595–3555* 🌐 *www.lassenrecreation.com* ⏲ *Closed weekdays mid-Oct.–late May.*

Manzanita and Summit Lakes

30 miles north of southwest entrance, 50 miles east of Redding.

The most recognizable landmarks in the park's vast northwestern quadrant, Manzanita and Summit lakes are connected by the Lassen Park Highway, which continues south toward Lassen Peak and the southwest entrance. As the road passes through Devasted Area, it offers an up-close glimpse of the destruction wrought by the 1915 eruption. Both lakes are popular for swimming and boating, and Manzanita Lake is just beyond the park's northwest entrance and adjacent to its largest cluster of facilities, including Loomis Museum, tent and cabin camping, and a camper store.

Sights

HISTORIC SITES

★ Loomis Museum

MUSEUM | FAMILY | In this handsome building constructed of volcanic rock in 1927, you can view artifacts from the park's 1914 and 1915 eruptions, including dramatic original photographs taken by Benjamin Loomis, who was instrumental in the park's establishment. The museum also has a bookstore, excellent exhibits about the area's Native American heritage, and a helpful staff who can recommend hikes and points of interest on this side of the park. ✉ *Lassen Park Hwy.* ✣ *Next to Manzanita Lake* ☎ *530/595–6140* 🎟 *Free* ⏲ *Closed late Oct.–late May.*

SCENIC DRIVES

★ Lassen National Park Highway

SCENIC DRIVE | This 30-mile scenic route, the main thoroughfare through the park, passes by such prominent sites as Lassen Peak, Bumpass Hell, Sulphur Works, Kings Creek, Devastated Area, and Chaos Crags, connecting the southwest entrance with Manzanita Lake and the northwest entrance. It's often referred to simply as Lassen Park Highway. ✉ *Lassen Volcanic National Park.*

SCENIC STOPS

Chaos Jumbles

NATURE SITE | More than 350 years ago, an avalanche from the Chaos Crags lava domes scattered hundreds of thousands of rocks—many of them from 2 to 3 feet in diameter—over a couple of square miles. ✉ *Lassen Park Hwy.* ✣ *2 miles east of northwest entrance.*

Did You Know?

"I took this photo on a camping trip to Lake Manzanita in Lassen Volcanic National Park. The log in the water seemed to point towards the partly snow-covered Lassen Peak." —photo by Shyam Subramanyan, Fodors.com member

Devastated Area

NATURE SITE | FAMILY | Lassen Peak's 1915 eruptions cleared this area, which makes up a good chunk of the center of the park, of all vegetation, though after all these years the forest has gradually returned. The easy ½-mile interpretive trail loop is wheelchair accessible. ✉ *Lassen Park Hwy.* ✥ *2½ miles northwest of Summit Lake.*

Manzanita Lake

BODY OF WATER | Lassen Peak is reflected in the waters of this rippling lake, which has good catch-and-release trout fishing and a pleasant trail for exploring the area's abundant wildlife. ✉ *Lassen Park Hwy.* ✥ *Near northwest entrance station.*

Summit Lake

BODY OF WATER | The midpoint between the northern and southern entrances, Summit Lake is a good place to take an afternoon swim. A trail leads around the lakeshore, and several other trails lead east—for quite a few miles—toward a cluster of smaller lakes in the park's more remote northeastern quadrant. ✉ *Lassen Park Hwy.* ✥ *17½ miles from southwest entrance.*

TRAILS

Lily Pond Nature Trail

TRAIL | FAMILY | This ½-mile jaunt loops past a small lake and through a wooded area, ending at a pond that is filled with yellow water lilies in summer. Marked with interpretive signs, it's a good choice for families. *Easy.* ✉ *Lassen Park Hwy.* ✥ *Trailhead: Across from Loomis Museum.*

Coffee and Quick Bites

Manzanita Lake Camper Store

$ | CAFÉ | Pick up simple prepared foods, groceries, and beverages—local wines and beers among them—at the store, which has an ATM and a pay phone. **Known for:** good local craft beer selection; supplies for a picnic by the lake; hearty deli sandwiches. Ⓢ *Average main: $7* ✉ *Manzanita Lake Campground, Lassen Park Hwy.* ☎ *530/335–7557* 🌐 *www.lassenrecreation.com* ⏲ *Closed mid-Oct.–mid-June.*

Hotels

Manzanita Lake Camping Cabins

$ | RENTAL | FAMILY | This lakeside compound of 20 rustic but handsomely designed modern cabins provides the only roof-over-your-head lodgings on the main park highway, but this is a camping experience, albeit a nicely outfitted one. **Pros:** only lodgings on Lassen Park Highway; picturesque setting; guests can purchase amenity packages, including sleeping bags. **Cons:** must supply your own bedding; rustic; open only seasonally. Ⓢ *Rooms from: $76* ✉ *Manzanita Lake, Lassen Park Hwy.* ☎ *530/779–0307* 🌐 *www.lassenlodging.com* ⏲ *Closed mid-Oct.–mid-June* *20 cabins* *No meals.*

Warner Valley and Juniper Lake

18 miles northwest of Chester (to Warner Valley), 12 miles north of Chester (to Juniper Lake), 47 miles east of the park's southwest entrance.

Relatively few visitors explore the park's south-central and southeastern sections, home to the sunny meadows and impressive hydrothermal features of the Warner Valley—which also contains the park's only lodging (historic Drakesbad Guest Ranch)—and the azure waters of Juniper Lake. It takes a little effort to get to both areas, which are set along unpaved gravel roads reached by way of the small town of Chester. Although it's also possible to make your way to Warner Valley on foot from Kings Creek Trailhead in the park's Southwest area, you need to be in good shape or plan to spend a night camping if you attempt this hike that's 11 miles round-trip, not including potential side hikes to Boiling Lake or Devils Kitchen.

Sights

SCENIC STOPS

★ Juniper Lake

BODY OF WATER | The park's largest body of water, Juniper Lake is accessible only in summer and sits at an elevation of nearly 7,000 feet in the little-visited eastern section of the park, about a 90-minute drive—the last span of it on a gravel road—from the Southwest Entrance and a half-hour north of Chester. The reward for making your way here is the chance for swimming and kayaking or canoeing in a pristine lake, which is also a lovely spot for a picnic, perhaps before or after hiking up to the fire tower atop nearby Mt. Harkness. There's a small seasonal ranger station and a primitive campground here, as well. ✉ *Juniper Lake Rd.* ✢ *12 miles north of Chester* ⏲ *Road to lake closed Nov.–June.*

TRAILS

Boiling Springs Lake Trail

TRAIL | **FAMILY** | This worthwhile 3-mile loop leads from the Warner Valley Trailhead to Boiling Springs Lake, which is surrounded by high bluffs topped with incense cedar, Douglas fir, and other conifers. Vents beneath the milky gray-green lake release bubbles into it, heating it to a temperature of 125°F. Most who come all the way to Warner Valley combine this hike with one of the others that it connects with, typically either Devils Kitchen or Terminal Geyser. *Easy–Moderate.* ✉ *Warner Valley Rd.* ✢ *Trailhead: Across the street from Warner Valley Campground.*

★ Devils Kitchen Trail

TRAIL | A moderately hilly 4.2 mile round-trip hike through open meadows and conifer forest leads to the least-frequented of the park's three main hydrothermal areas, the others being Sulphur Works and Bumpass Hell. The lack of crowds makes this an especially enjoyable place to view burping mud pots, misty steam vents, hot boiling pools, and even Lassen Peak in the distance. *Moderate–Difficult.* ✉ *Warner Valley Rd.* ✢ *Trailhead: Across the street from Warner Valley Campground.*

Mount Harkness Trail

TRAIL | Because of its 1,250-foot elevation change, this is the most strenuous but also rewarding of the handful of hikes from quiet Juniper Lake. Your reward for making your way through forest groves and lupine meadows to the summit of a dormant 8,046-foot shield volcanic are panoramic views from a handsome stone-and-wood fire tower built in 1930. ✉ *Lassen Volcanic National Park* ✢ *Trailhead: Juniper Lake Ranger Station.*

Hotels

★ Drakesbad Guest Ranch

$$$$ | **B&B/INN** | With propane furnaces and kerosene lamps, everything about this century-old property in the Lassen Volcanic National Park's remote but beautiful southeastern corner harks back to a simpler time. **Pros:** back-to-nature experience; great for family adventures; only full-service lodging inside the park. **Cons:** on a remote partially paved road 45 minutes' drive from nearest town (Chester); rustic, with few in-room frills; not open year-round. $ *Rooms from: $384* ✉ *14423 Warner Valley Rd., Chester* ☎ *866/999–0914* 🌐 *www.drakesbad.com* ⏲ *Closed mid-Oct.–early June* 🛏 *19 rooms* 🍴 *All meals.*

Butte Lake

33 miles east of Manzanita Lake, 47 miles northwest of Susanville, 55 miles north of Chester.

Even more isolated and less-visited than Warner Valley, Butte Lake anchors the park's northeastern corner and is at least an hour's drive from any other parts of the park. A lot of folks don't come here until their second or third visit to Lassen, but if you're able to find the time, it's worth making the effort just to view the lake's lava-rock shoreline and, ideally, to hike to the Cinder Cone that had itself been designated a national monument prior to becoming part of Lassen Volcanic National Park. ■TIP→ **Come prepared: there are no facilities in this areas except for vault toilets and potable water, although the tent campground here is one of the park's largest.**

Sights

SCENIC STOPS

Butte Lake

BODY OF WATER | Dark, dramatic lava beds form the western shore of this peaceful body of water in the park's secluded northeastern corner. It's a great destination for kayaking and canoeing, and trails run alongside the lake's northern and eastern shores (eventually to Widow Lake), and a short loop leads to tiny, neighboring Bathtub Lake, which is nice for a quick swim on hot days. Amenities, which are open early June through mid-October, include a boat launch, campground, and ranger station. ✉ *End of Butte Lake Rd.* ✣ *6 miles from Hwy. 44.*

TRAILS

★ Cinder Cone Trail

TRAIL | Though set in the park's remote northeastern corner, this is one of its most fascinating trails, as it offers views of a dazzling variety of volcanic features, including Painted Dunes, Fantastic Lava Beds, and Prospect Peak. It's a somewhat challenging undertaking, because the 4-mile round-trip hike to the cone summit requires a steep 845-foot climb over ground that's slippery in parts with loose cinders. For a better understanding of the geology along this hike, pick up an interpretive brochure at the trailhead or visitor centers. *Moderate–Difficult.* ✉ *Boat ramp at end of Butte Lake Rd.* ✣ *Trailhead: Off Hwy. 44, 33 miles east of Manzanita Lake.*

Activities

BIKING

Biking is prohibited on trails and can be a bit nerve-racking on Lassen Park Highway because of the lack of shoulders and guardrails, and due to—on the southern half of Lassen Park Highway—some steep grades. Only experienced cyclists should attempt this drive. The gravel roads to Warner Valley and both Butte and Juniper lakes are open to cyclists and receive far less auto traffic than Lassen Park Highway. For casual cyclists, the area around Lake Almanor in Chester is quite appealing.

BOATING

People are sometimes surprised that a park named for a volcanic peak abounds with lakes. Among these, kayakers and canoers favor Manzanita, Summit, Butte, and Juniper lakes, all of which have good road access (Butte and Manzanita have actual boat launches). Motorized watercraft are not permitted anywhere in the park, and none of the park's other lakes with road access allow boating of any kind.

CAMPING

You can drive a vehicle to all seven of Lassen's campgrounds except the Southwest Walk-In, which is a short stroll from Kohm Yah-mah-nee Visitor Center. This is the only campground open year-round; the others usually open in June and close in early fall. Overnight fees range from $12 to $26. Butte Lake, Juniper, Southwest Walk-In, and Warner Valley are first-come, first-served. For reservations at the other campgrounds, visit 🌐 *www.recreation.gov* or call ☎ *877/444–6777.*

Butte Lake. Situated near the edge of a lake flanked by lava rocks, this peaceful area with 101 sites is in the secluded northeastern corner of the park. ✉ *End of Butte Lake Rd.*

Juniper Lake. On the east shore of the park's largest lake, these campsites are close to the water in a wooded area. To reach them, you have to take a rough gravel road 13 miles north of Chester to the park's southeast corner; trailers are not advised. There is no potable water here. ✉ *Chester Juniper Lake Rd.*

Manzanita Lake. The largest of Lassen campgrounds accommodates RVs up to 35 feet and has 20 rustic cabins. Many ranger programs begin here, and a trail nearby leads to the crater that holds Crags Lake. ✉ *Off Lassen Park Hwy., near park's northwest entrance.*

Southwest Walk-In. Relatively small and Lassen's only campground open year-round, Southwest lies within a conifer forest and has views of Brokeoff Peak. Snow camping is allowed, and drinking water is available at visitor center entryway. ✉ *Near southwest entrance, beside Kohm Yah-mah-nee Visitor Center.*

Summit Lake North. This completely forested campground has easy access to backcountry trails. You'll likely observe deer grazing. ✉ *Lassen Park Hwy., 17½ miles north of southwest entrance.*

Summit Lake South. Less crowded than its neighbor to the north, this campground has wet meadows where wildflowers grow in the spring. No potable water is available after mid-September. ✉ *Lassen Park Hwy., 17½ miles north of southwest entrance.*

Warner Valley. You'll find 17 sites at this quite, rustic campground near the trailhead for Boiling Lake, Devils Kitchen, and several other notable hydrothermal features in this breathtaking valley in the park's somewhat remote southeastern quadrant. ✉ *Off Warner Valley Rd., just before Drakesbad Guest Ranch.*

EDUCATIONAL PROGRAMS

If you're wondering why fumaroles fume, how lava is formed, or which critter left those tracks beside the creek, check out the array of ranger-led programs. Most groups meet outside Loomis Museum or near Manzanita Lake. See the park bulletin boards for daily topics and times.

RANGER PROGRAMS

Kids Program

TOUR—SIGHT | **FAMILY** | Junior Rangers, ages 5 to 12, meet for 45 minutes three times a week with rangers, including for talks about the role wildfires have in shaping our national parks. Kids can earn patches by completing an activity book, or joining the Chipmunk Club and earning a sticker by completing various activities. ✉ *Lassen Volcanic National Park.*

FISHING

The best place to fish is in Manzanita Lake, though it's catch and release only. Butte, Juniper, Snag, and Horseshoe lakes, along with several creeks and streams, are also popular fishing destinations within the park. Anglers will need a California freshwater fishing license, which you can obtain at most sporting-goods stores or through the California Department of Fish and Wildlife's website (🌐 *www.dfg.ca.gov*).

The Fly Shop

FISHING | Famous among fly-fishers, the Fly Shop carries tackle and equipment and offers guide services. ✉ *4140 Churn Creek Rd., Redding* ☎ *530/222–3555, 800/669–3474* 🌐 *www.flyshop.com.*

HIKING

Of the 150 miles of hiking trails within the park, 17 miles are part of the interstate Pacific Crest Trail, which accesses Warner Valley on its way through the park. Trails in Lassen offer an astounding range of scenery, some winding through coniferous forest and others across rocky alpine slopes, along meandering waterways, or through basins of dazzling hydrothermal boiling springs and steam vents.

HORSEBACK RIDING

Drakesbad Guest Ranch

HORSEBACK RIDING | **FAMILY** | This property in the park's Warner Valley offers guided rides to nonguests by reservation. Among the options is a two-hour loop to

Devils Kitchen. There's also an eight-hour five-lake loop for advanced riders. ✉ *End of Warner Valley Rd., Chester* ☎ *530/524–2841* 🌐 *www.drakesbad.com* 🎫 *From $45.*

SNOWSHOEING

You can snowshoe anywhere in the park. The gentlest places are near the northwest entrance, while more challenging terrain is in the Southwest corner of the park but is easier to access because the park road stays open here all winter. Cross-country skiing is also popular in these areas.

■ TIP→ Beware of hidden cavities in the snow. Park officials warn that heated sulfur emissions, especially in the Sulphur Works Area, can melt out dangerous snow caverns, which may be camouflaged by thin layers of fresh snow that skiers and snowshoers can easily fall through.

Bodfish Bicycles & Quiet Mountain Sports
SNOW SPORTS | You can rent snowshoes, skis, boots, and poles at this popular shop 30 miles from the park's Southwest Entrance. ✉ *149 Main St., Chester* ☎ *530/258–2338* 🌐 *www.bodfishbicycles.com.*

Lassen Mineral Lodges
SNOW SPORTS | This lodge near the park rents snowshoes as well as cross-country skis and poles. ✉ *38348 Hwy. 36, Mineral* ☎ *530/595–4422* 🌐 *www.mineralllodge.com.*

Snowshoe Walks
SNOW SPORTS | On weekend afternoons from January through March, park rangers lead two-hour snowshoe walks that explore the park's geology and winter ecology. The hikes require moderate exertion at an elevation of 7,000 feet; children under age eight are not allowed. If you don't have snowshoes you can borrow a pair; $1 donation suggested. Walks are first-come, first-served; free tickets are issued beginning at 9 am (try to arrive by 11 am to be sure to secure a spot) the day of the hike at the Kohm Yah-mah-nee Visitor Center. ✉ *21820 Lassen National Park Hwy.* ☎ *530/595–4480* 🌐 *www.nps.gov/lavo* 🎫 *Free.*

What's Nearby

Located in remote northeastern California, Lassen has few towns of any real size around it, although you will find a smattering of places to stay in unincorporated areas near the park's southwest and northwest entrances. The nearest actual town is the small logging center of **Chester,** which has a handful of eateries and lodgings and is about a 40-minute drive from the southwest entrance. You'll find more options another 35 miles east in the larger high-desert town of **Susanville.** About an hour west of the park in the northern reaches of the state's Central Valley, the small city of **Red Bluff** (population 14,300) and the area's largest metropolis, **Redding** (population 92,000), have a wide variety of restaurants and hotels. Redding, in particular, has a handful of distinctive places to stay and eat and some notable attractions—it's also a gateway for visiting beautiful **Shasta Lake,** about 10 miles north.

Chapter 42

MAMMOTH CAVE NATIONAL PARK

Updated by
Tres Seymour

Camping	Hotels	Activities	Scenery	Crowds
★★★☆☆	★★★☆☆	★★★★☆	★★★★☆	★★★★☆

WELCOME TO MAMMOTH CAVE NATIONAL PARK

TOP REASONS TO GO

★ **The world's longest cave:** At more than 400 miles of interconnected passageways (mapped so far), no other cave system on Earth comes close.

★ **Time stops here:** You lose track of time underground; on the surface, the forests seem rooted in a different age. An hour spent drifting down Green River can seem like three spent in a dream.

★ **Bountiful botany:** Within its 52,000 acres, Mammoth Cave National Park supports more than 1,100 species of wildflowers—a figure not far behind Great Smoky Mountains, a park ten times as large.

★ **Laid-back waters:** Green River has no white-water rapids or waterfalls, but it's an adventure all the same—mystery grottoes in the rock, unexpected creatures peering from the bank, islands to explore on a whim.

★ **Watchable wildlife:** The normally skittish wild turkey and white-tailed deer are often seen in Mammoth and there's great birdwatching.

1 Visitor Center Area. This is the park's gateway, a physical nexus to features both surface and subterranean, and all cave tours begin here.

2 Frontcountry. In the park's southeast sector below Green River, the sinkhole plain to the south infiltrates the Pennyroyal Plateau that rises up along its edge. Some of Mammoth Cave's principal entrances lie in this region, along with massive sinkholes and the Big Barrens and the Mammoth Cave Railroad Bike & Hike trail.

3 The Green River Valley. The lifeblood of Mammoth, Green River bisects the park with a deep valley running east to west, from above Dennison Ferry to below Houchins Ferry. Many visitors come purely for the pleasures of angling, canoeing, and kayaking.

4 The Hilly Backcountry. North of Green River, the park's landscape rises and falls into ridges and hollows networked by more than 70 miles of backcountry trails that go through diverse forest communities, from river bottomland to dry upland hardwood forests, from hemlock groves to a stand of old-growth timber.

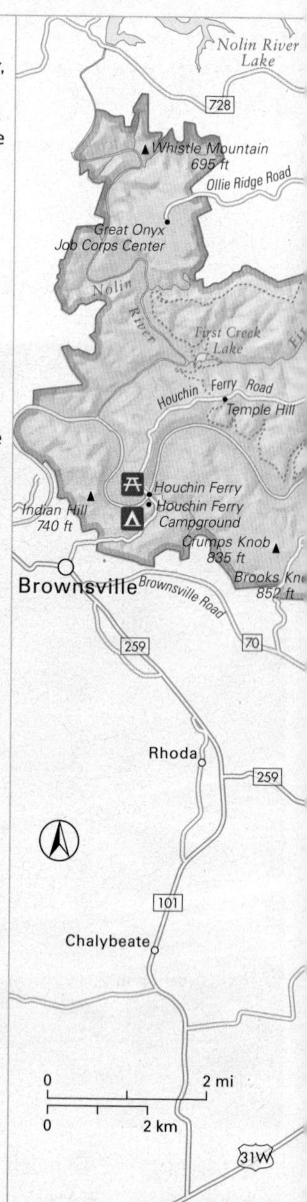

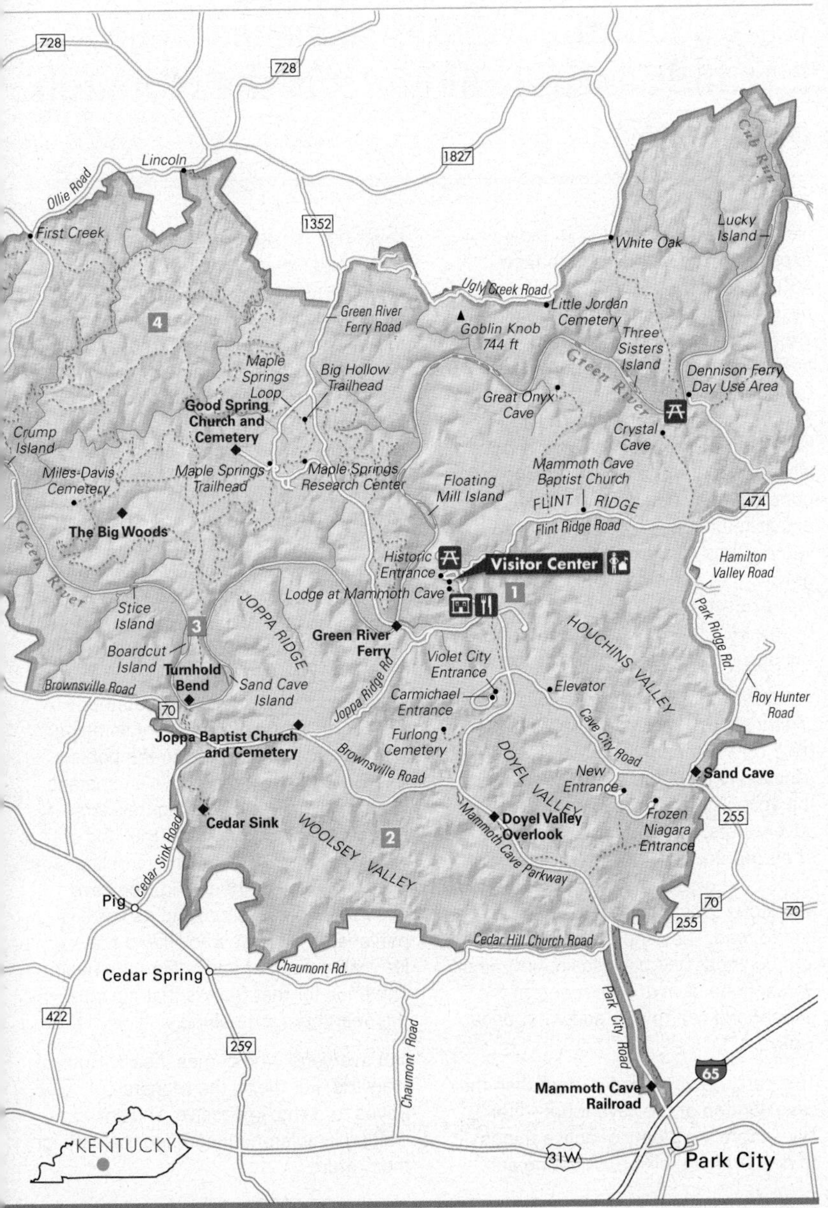
728
728
1827
1352
Lincoln
Ollie Road
First Creek
White Oak
Lucky Island
Cub Run
Ugly Creek Road
Little Jordan Cemetery
Green River Ferry Road
Goblin Knob 744 ft
Three Sisters Island
4
Maple Springs Loop
Big Hollow Trailhead
Green River
Dennison Ferry Day Use Area
Great Onyx Cave
Good Spring Church and Cemetery
Crystal Cave
Crump Island
Mammoth Cave Baptist Church
Miles-Davis Cemetery
Maple Springs Trailhead
Maple Springs Research Center
Floating Mill Island
FLINT RIDGE
474
Flint Ridge Road
The Big Woods
Green River
Historic Entrance
Visitor Center
Hamilton Valley Road
Lodge at Mammoth Cave
1
Stice Island
JOPPA RIDGE
HOUCHINS VALLEY
Park Ridge Rd.
3
Green River Ferry
Boardcut Island
Violet City Entrance
Turnhold Bend
Sand Cave Island
Brownsville Road
Carmichael Entrance
Elevator
Roy Hunter Road
Joppa Ridge Rd
70
Furlong Cemetery
Cave City Road
Joppa Baptist Church and Cemetery
Brownsville Road
DOYEL VALLEY
New Entrance
Sand Cave
255
Cedar Sink
WOOLSEY VALLEY
Doyel Valley Overlook
Frozen Niagara Entrance
Mammoth Cave Parkway
2
Cedar Sink Road
Pig
70
70
255
Cedar Hill Church Road
Cedar Spring
Chaumont Rd.
422
259
Park City Road
Chaumont Road
65
Mammoth Cave Railroad
KENTUCKY
31W
Park City

In 1844, Alexander Clark Bullitt penned the first traveler's guide to Mammoth Cave. He wrote, "In extent, in grandeur, in wild, solemn, serene, unadorned majesty, it stands entirely alone. It is the Monarch of Caves!"

He didn't know the half of it. Today, explorers have mapped more than 400 miles of interconnecting passages, making the Mammoth–Flint Ridge Cave System by far the longest known cave system on Earth. Lying twisted beneath about 25 square miles of central Kentucky countryside, Mammoth Cave is a world apart—a shadowed, silent labyrinth of earth, mud, water, and stone, punctuated by sudden airy cathedrals and exquisite beauties of natural art. There is wonder, and terror, and it draws us in like gravity, that gnawing question: *What's In There?* Each year, tens of thousands of people visit this park to find out, braving the dark on the park's several cave tours.

What they find is that the cave is a trove of stories. The stories tell of ancient people 5,000 years ago. They tell of enslaved Africans two centuries past who mined the soils. They tell of explorers, of adventurers, of scientists, of journalists, of entrepreneurs ... of travelers from across the globe. The stories tie the rock and stone to water, and to time, to river and to road. They show how light leads into darkness and back again, how, like Persephone of myth, what enters the underworld can return, and what price it pays.

This park, however, is far more than the cave. On top of the cave tours—literally—there are plenty of active things to do: camping, hiking, canoeing and kayaking, fishing, biking, and horseback riding. You can visit the museum at the visitor center, shop for books and gifts, eat a meal, and stay at the lodge. Rangers may offer programs from bird walks to the story of strange fate of caver Floyd Collins. Young people can participate in the Junior Ranger program. You can make your trip busy and active, or very laid-back.

Mammoth Cave National Park is not ostentatious—it doesn't have the visual gobsmacking quality of a Half Dome or a Grand Canyon; it doesn't hold up an icon like Lady Liberty or the Gateway Arch. The landscape is not soaring mountains, but Kentucky hill country—as seasoned and wise as a grandfather, and worth every minute spent listening to the advice of the wind in the poplars. The Green River's trickling is a constant chatter, always encouraging travelers to create their own stories, the kind of yarns that spin out long and rambling just for the joy of the telling. The cave itself speaks in silence, and its voice is perilous—a traveler who listens may learn some secret told only to the heart. The price for that truth is that a part of the heart gets left behind.

Not everyone who comes, hears. But many do. For them, the Monarch of Caves remains, impassive, ancient, waiting in solemn, unadorned majesty for their return.

AVERAGE HIGH/LOW TEMPERATURES					
JAN.	FEB.	MAR.	APR.	MAY	JUNE
44/26	49/29	59/37	70/46	78/55	86/64
JULY	AUG.	SEPT.	OCT.	NOV.	DEC.
89/68	88/66	82/59	71/47	58/37	48/30

Planning

When to Go

The cave itself doesn't care when you come—its internal climate is the same regardless of the season (the temperature remains 54°F, 12°C, year-round) and it's open every day except Christmas Day. The number and variety of tours, however, will vary by season, with the greatest being in summer and the least being in winter. The park's high season generally runs from Memorial Day to Labor Day, with crowd spikes on both ends coinciding with school spring and fall breaks. By early June, cave tours start filling up completely, with demand only dropping off when school starts again in mid-August. Weather-wise, Kentucky's summers aren't too scorching and winters aren't too bitter, but midsummer humidity can be oppressive. Winter snow and ice are infrequent, but if such conditions exist, check the park website for possible road closures or service interruptions.

Aboveground, certain other considerations apply. For canoeists and kayakers, spring and fall tend to be rainy periods, with the chance of high water on the Green River; if the water level rises too high, the park will temporarily prohibit these activities. Mammoth Cave and Maple Springs Campgrounds are unavailable December through February, though you can still camp at Houchin Ferry, or in the backcountry or on the river by permit. Winter hiking can be unusually rewarding in the hilly country as the park takes off its mantle of leaves and shows off its curves. (You, however, will want to make sure you wear layers.)

FESTIVALS AND EVENTS

In early December, the park commemorates the **Cave Sing,** a tradition begun in the mid-1800s when a group of travelers descended into the cave and sang holiday carols around a decorated tree that illuminated one of the passages. Today, the slate of performers differs each year, but usually features two or three area choirs. The free event is open to the public; check the park's website in the weeks prior to the event for an actual date and time.

Getting Here and Around

AIR

The major hubs serving Mammoth Cave National Park are Louisville Muhammad Ali International Airport (SDF) and Nashville International Airport (BNA). Both reach the park via Interstate 65, from the north and south respectively; allow approximately an hour and a half to drive to the park from either airport. Independent aviators looking for smaller regional airports may inquire at the Glasgow Regional Airport (GLW), 25 minutes from the park, or at the Warren County Regional Airport (BWG) in Bowling Green, 40 minutes from the park.

CAR

If you're coming from points north, south, or east, Interstate 65 will get you to the park. From the north, it's Exit 53 (Cave City). From the south, it's Exit 48 (Park City/Brownsville), and from the east, follow the Cumberland Parkway until it joins Interstate 65 south of Park

City. ■ TIP→ **Do not rely on your electronic GPS navigation to get you to the visitor center. Several travelers have too trustingly followed their digital pilot and found themselves in the yard of a man on the park's north boundary. (He is not amused.)**

FERRY

Access to the park's north side and backcountry may be had via the Green River Ferry which has been operating in one form or another since horse-and-buggy days. Located on Green River Ferry Road off the Mammoth Cave Parkway south of the visitor center, the ferry can shuttle a couple of vehicles across the river at a time, so you may have a short wait. The ferry operates from 6 am to 10 pm; no fee is required. Ferry operations may be interrupted due to high or low water, or if Green River Ferry Road is closed.

Inspiration

Mammoth Cave National Park has a long history of guidebooks, and possibly the most interesting is among the first, written by journalist Alexander Clark Bullitt in *Rambles in the Mammoth Cave, During the Year 1844, By a Visitor,* which includes a foldout of Stephen Bishop's map of Mammoth Cave, one of the first ever drawn.

For a poetic take on the Mammoth Cave region, try *Ultima Thule,* by Davis McCombs. Ultima Thule is the last chamber reached by explorer Max Kämper in 1809. The phrase, meaning "distant, unknown regions," describes where these poems take the reader in the cave—and the imagination.

Written by Roger Brucker, a noted authority on Mammoth Cave, *Grand, Gloomy, and Peculiar: Stephen Bishop at Mammoth Cave* is based on the life of the enslaved Bishop, whose cave explorations by lantern inspired generations of explorers to seek new passages in the world's longest cave. The story is told from the perspective of Bishop's wife, Charlotte.

Both the book *Trapped!* by Brucker and Roger Murray, and the documentary film *The Death of Floyd Collins* (2015), tell a tale intimately bound to the Mammoth Cave area and its hollow roots, where explorer Collins became trapped in Sand Cave in 1925. The rescue attempts made national headlines.

Mammoth Cave—A Way to Wonder and *Mammoth Cave—A Place Called Home,* two documentaries produced by WKYU-PBS, explore the intricacy of the natural and cultural threads that interweave to form the Mammoth Cave story. Both are available online, or on DVD.

Park Essentials

ACCESSIBILITY

The Mammoth Cave National Park Visitor Center is an accessible facility, with accessible restrooms. Designated parking is available at most locations. Although the cave itself presents insurmountable obstacles to access, one tour is fully accessible, the Mammoth Cave Access Tour. Four Trails have been designed for accessibility: Echo River Spring Trail, Heritage Trail, Sand Cave Trail, and Sloan's Crossing Pond Walk. Accessible campsites are available at the Mammoth Cave Campground, and four fully accessible rooms are offered at the Heritage Trail Rooms in The Lodge at Mammoth Cave.

PARK FEES AND PERMITS

There's no entry fee for Mammoth Cave National Park, though a fee is required to visit the cave. ⇨ *See Tours for the cost of individual cave tours.*

Camping in the backcountry and on the islands and floodplain of the Green River requires a permit. Backcountry campsites are first-come, first-served. ⇨ *See Camping.*

PARK HOURS

The park itself never closes, and there is no entrance gate. The visitor center and park services operate 9 am–5 pm, though fall and winter schedules may shift the times by half an hour so check the website before arrival. ■ TIP→ **Mammoth Cave National Park is in the Central Time Zone.** Travelers headed south cross into Central Time shortly before approaching the park, and it's very common for people to arrive only to discover that they've "gained an hour." Allow for this shift in your planning.

CELL PHONE RECEPTION

Cell phone reception in the park is a mixed bag, mainly depending on your carrier. Phones with service under Verizon or Bluegrass Cellular will generally get cell access on high ground and ridgetops around the park, though some dead zones persist in deep hollows and in the valley of the Green River. Access to other providers' service is severely limited. If planning an excursion on the river or in the backcountry, do not rely on cell service for communication or navigation. Public Wi-Fi is available locally at the Mammoth Cave Visitor Center, The Lodge at Mammoth Cave, and the Sunset Terrace.

Hotels

Mammoth Cave has a long tradition of hospitality—in one form or another, there has been a Mammoth Cave Hotel serving travelers here since the early 1800s. The current version, The Lodge at Mammoth Cave, offers both hotel-style rooms and rustic cottages. The Lodge has four Heritage Trail rooms, while the nearby Sunset Terrace has another 20 rooms available. The Woodland Cottages, adjacent to the park's main picnic area, are rustic—no heat, air-conditioning, TV, or Wi-Fi—multibedroom accommodations. The Historic Cottages, across the lawn on the south side of the Lodge, are slightly less rustic stone structures; they are air-conditioned and more comfortably furnished. ■ TIP→ **The Lodge operates a day-boarding kennel for dogs and cats, though it is not designed for small dogs.**

Restaurants

Inside The Lodge at Mammoth Cave, the **Green River Grill** serves breakfast, lunch, and dinner. The **Spelunkers Cafe & Ice Cream Parlor** is found near the visitor center, offering coffee, fast food, and confections.

HOTEL AND RESTAURANT PRICES

Hotel prices in the reviews are the lowest cost of a standard double room in high season. Restaurant prices in the reviews are the average cost of a main course at dinner, or if dinner is not served, at lunch.

What It Costs

$	$$	$$$	$$$$
RESTAURANTS			
under $10	$10–$13	$14–$28	over $28
HOTELS			
under $71	$71–$93	$94–$136	over $136

Tours

Cave Guides have been leading travelers into Mammoth Cave (and most of them back out again) since 1816. Nearly 14 miles of tunnels, chambers, and natural formations are on public display via guided or ranger-attended subterranean visits. Most tours visit three main sections of the cave: the Historic Section, the Cleveland Avenue/Grand Avenue section, and the Frozen Niagara Section. All areas feature tunnels in shapes from tubular to canyonlike, and in sizes from squeezy to echoey.

Twenty different cave tours are offered, though tour availability varies by season. All tours begin and end at the park visitor center, and range from about 1¼ to 4½ hours in duration. In the high season (mid-May to Labor Day), tours are usually snapped up well in advance, and reservations are usually necessary. So plan accordingly. 🌐 *www.recreation.gov*

Warnings: Be prepared to hike, and know your ability. Tours are rated easy, moderate, and strenuous; visitors with any sort of walking, respiratory, or cardiac issue should decline strenuous tours. If you're afraid of the dark, or get claustrophobic, consider how you'll feel underground.

Photography: Unless you are a professional photographer with mad skills shooting in dark places, you're better off not bringing your camera. Photography isn't forbidden, but flash photography, tripods, and monopods *are*.

What to Wear: Though cave temperatures vary widely near entrances, farther in the cave air settles in at 54°F (12°C) year-round, so a light, removable jacket or sweater is a good choice. Paths can be rocky, uneven, sandy, or slick, so appropriate footwear is a must; always keep to the trail. A small flashlight may also be useful for peering into nooks and crannies.

What Not to Bring: Flash cameras, tripods, and monopods; metal framed backpacks, backpacks higher than the shoulders, or child backpack carriers (front child carriers are allowed); strollers; walking sticks; firearms and other weapons; and pets.

What Not to Do: While in the cave, touch nothing you don't have to, and leave everything where you find it. Caves are delicate environments, and any damage you do is magnified by time. Even the oil from a fingerprint can stop the growth of a formation for years.

Cleaveland Avenue Tour

GUIDED TOURS | **FAMILY** | The long flight of stairs down the Carmichael Entrance rewards you with a view—the spacious open chamber known as Dismal Hollow. Almost at once, you turn away down the side tunnel of Cleaveland Avenue and everything abruptly changes. The passageway becomes an oval tube, and its walls are lined with crystals. You'll spend your walk just taking in all the different ways gypsum can take shape ... and soaking up the remarkable history of the people whose names are bound to this place. **■ TIP→ The tour takes about 2 hours and covers about 1 mile including 188 stairs.** ✉ *Mammoth Cave National Park Visitor Center, 1 Mammoth Cave Pkwy., Mammoth Cave* ☎ *270/758–2180 Park Information Line* 🌐 *www.nps.gov/maca* 🎟 *$20.*

Domes & Dripstones Tour

GUIDED TOURS | **FAMILY** | You "follow the water" on this tour, down through a sinkhole as you enter through New Entrance, down breathtaking domes and pits to emerge into long-abandoned river passages deep below. The bends, rises and falls of these tunnels lead you to the place where water works in a different way creating fascinating formations where the cave again meets the surface at Frozen Niagara Entrance. Includes the Frozen Niagara Tour route and part of the Grand Avenue Tour route. **■ TIP→ This tour takes two hours and covers ¾ mile including 500 stairs.** ✉ *Mammoth Cave National Park Visitor Center, 1 Mammoth Cave Pkwy., Mammoth Cave* ☎ *270/758–2180 Park Information Line* 🌐 *www.nps.gov/maca* 🎟 *$17.*

Frozen Niagara Tour

GUIDED TOURS | **FAMILY** | This easy walk centers on its namesake formation, Frozen Niagara, which looks like a waterfall frozen in mid-torrent. All around it are stalactites, stalagmites, soda straws, draperies, cave bacon, rimstone dams, and more, but don't touch any of it as

White-Nose Syndrome

White-nose syndrome (WNS), a disease that affects hibernating bats, gets its name from the white fuzz on bats' faces that marks the presence of the fungus *Pseudogymnoascus destructans.* The fungus grows in cold, dark and damp places where bats like to hibernate. It attacks bats' bare skin while they're hibernating and inactive. As it grows, the fungus makes bats more active than usual and burn up fat they need to survive the winter.

This deadly fungus has already killed millions of bats. In places, 90%–100% of the bat population has been lost. The fungus spreads mostly bat-to-bat, but can survive for long periods on surfaces like clothing, outdoor gear, and footwear making it easily transferable. Thankfully, the illness doesn't affect humans, but the threat to bats is serious, as the creatures consume insect pests, pollinate plants, and disperse seeds. There is no cure, but travelers can help by sanitizing all clothing and gear after any visit to a cave or mine.

Mammoth Cave, Carlsbad Caverns, Jewel Cave, and Wind Cave National Parks have all been confirmed to have the fungus. In response, all tour participants are required to walk across bio-security mats immediately after the tour ends, without exception, to help contain the spread of the disease to other areas.

a single fingerprint can damage the formations. This trip is a good choice for those who may have difficulty walking or using stairs. ■ TIP→ **A 1½ hour tour that takes visitors on an easy ¼ mile route that includes 12 stairs, plus an optional 90 at the Drapery Room.** ✉ *Mammoth Cave National Park Visitor Center, 1 Mammoth Cave Pkwy., Mammoth Cave* ☎ *270/758–2180 Park Information Line* 🌐 *www.nps.gov/maca* 🎟 *$14.*

Grand Avenue Tour

GUIDED TOURS | FAMILY | One doesn't fully appreciate the phrase "longest cave" until after finishing the Grand Avenue Tour. Although the route covers a mere 1% of the cave's total length, the trek keeps introducing new types of cave and passages change from dry to damp, from level to practically mountainous, from tubelike tunnels to snakelike canyons to airy open passageway. Though the journey is its own reward, the big payoff lies at the end in the splendors of Frozen Niagara. It's best to be frank here—this trip is not recommended if you are not reasonably physically fit or have trouble walking. ■ TIP→ **The strenuous four-hour tour covers 4 miles that include 670 stairs and steep inclines; parts of this tour are also seen on the Cleaveland Avenue, Domes & Dripstones, and Frozen Niagara Tours.** ✉ *Mammoth Cave National Park Visitor Center, 1 Mammoth Cave Pkwy., Mammoth Cave* ☎ *270/758–2180 Park Information Line* 🌐 *www.nps.gov/maca* 🎟 *$30.*

Historic Tour

GUIDED TOURS | FAMILY | If you're looking for the classic, quintessential Cave trip that will provide the best sense of the place as well as a broad sampling of different cave passages, from the canyonlike Broadway Avenue to rather tight Fat Man's Misery, this is a sure bet. Expect to hear fascinating tales of cave travelers past along the way. An extended version of this tour also includes a side trip to the site of an experimental 1840s underground tuberculosis hospital. ■ TIP→ **This two-hour tour takes visitors on a moderate 2 mile journey that involves**

540 stairs, including a 155-stair tower climb at Mammoth Dome. ✉ *Mammoth Cave National Park Visitor Center, 1 Mammoth Cave Pkwy., Mammoth Cave* ☎ *270/758–2180 Park Information Line* 🌐 *www.nps.gov/maca* 🎫 *$17.*

Mammoth Cave Discovery Tour

SELF-GUIDED | **FAMILY** | This tour, at your own pace, is good to whet your appetite for what the cave has to offer. Its short sampling of the Historic Section offers glimpses into the wealth of artifacts and geologic marvels that lie beyond the gaping Historic Entrance. Rangers are stationed at intervals to answer questions. Includes part of the Historic Tour and all of the Mammoth Passage Tour route. **■ TIP→ This easy tour takes ½ hour and covers ¾ mile, but does include 160 stairs.** ✉ *Mammoth Cave National Park Visitor Center, 1 Mammoth Cave Pkwy., Mammoth Cave* ☎ *270/758–2180 Park Information Line* 🌐 *www.nps.gov/maca* 🎫 *$6.*

Mammoth Cave Access Tour

GUIDED TOURS | **FAMILY** | Persons with mobility limitations, disabilities, or those who need to avoid stairs can get underground by way of the cave's one elevator on this tour. Visitors caravan in a private vehicle to the elevator, then descend to the Snowball Room. The route takes in a section of Cleaveland Avenue with its sparkling crystal formations and historic signatures. Wheelchairs, scooters, and other assistive devices are permitted on the tour, but must be accompanied. **■ TIP→ This is an easy ½-mile tour that usually last two hours; restrooms at this location are accessible.** ✉ *Mammoth Cave National Park Visitor Center, 1 Mammoth Cave Pkwy., Mammoth Cave* ☎ *270/758–2180 Park Information Line* 🌐 *www.nps.gov/maca* 🎫 *$20.*

Mammoth Passage Tour

GUIDED TOURS | **FAMILY** | If you want a tour that lets you see what the cave's all about without investing a lot of time, the Mammoth Passage Tour is a good option. The trip takes you into Historic Entrance and reveals why the cave is called "mammoth," before continuing to the Rotunda, the cave's sixth-largest room, the canyon-like Audubon Avenue, and the spacious Rafinesque Hall. **■ TIP→ The easy 1¼ hour, ¾ mile tour includes 160 stairs and part of the Historic Tour and all of the Mammoth Cave Discovery Tour route.** ✉ *Mammoth Cave National Park Visitor Center, 1 Mammoth Cave Pkwy., Mammoth Cave* ☎ *270/758–2180 Park Information Line* 🌐 *www.nps.gov/maca* 🎫 *$8.*

Visitor Information

CONTACTS Mammoth Cave National Park. ✉ *Mammoth Cave National Park Visitor Center, 1 Mammoth Cave Pkwy., Mammoth Cave* ☎ *270/758–2180 Park Information Line* 🌐 *www.nps.gov/maca.*

Visitor Center Area

9 miles from the park's south entrance at Park City.

The true gateway to Mammoth Cave National Park isn't at its boundary, but at its heart, in the area around its visitor center. All cave tours start and end here, but the area also contains many significant park features like trails, historic sites, and recreational activities all within walking distance, or a short drive, from the center. In fact, the cave's gaping Historic Entrance lies a short rock-tumble down the hill. All the park's lodging, dining, and shopping are also found in the visitor center area.

Travelers have gravitated to this locale for more than 200 years, and that hasn't changed much. The first cave tour was given in 1816, and ever since, millions have journeyed by horse, stagecoach, train, and automobile along these same roads.

The Kentucky Cave Wars

People have found their way up Mammoth Cave Ridge looking for the cave's entrance since tours began in 1816. But Mammoth isn't the only cave here—these hills are riddled with small caverns unconnected to the great labyrinth, most on private property.

Many "show caves" have opened over the decades, such as Diamond Caverns, Great Onyx, Great Crystal, Crystal Onyx, Mammoth Onyx, Dossey Domes, and Lost River. By the 1920s the cutthroat competition to sell a ticket became what we now call the Kentucky Cave Wars.

Back then, you might have come planning to see Mammoth Cave, but you might never have made it that far. Along the road you would have found a roadside booth with a sign reading "Official Cave Information." If you stopped, a man would tell you recent rains had flooded Mammoth Cave and closed all tours, but never fear! You could still tour another cave, just as fine, and purchase your ticket then and there. If you didn't stop at the booth, a plucky young man further on might wave you down in the road to warn you not to go any farther due to some calamity at Mammoth Cave, but to detour to another cave. Finally someone erected a sign that read: *Do Not Be Confused—No One Has The Right To Stop You On This Road.*

The Cave Wars had a casualty, Floyd Collins. His family owned and operated Great Crystal Cave, but to reach it, you had to pass the more famous destination. Floyd hoped to find a cave much closer to the town, and in 1925, he pinned his hopes on exploring a sandstone cave called Sand Cave. The cave pinned him back.

While in a narrow crawlspace, a rock fell and wedged his leg, trapping him underground. The 17-day effort to rescue him became a national sensation, making headlines across the country. His rescue was not a success, and Floyd died of exposure. Within a few years, Mammoth Cave would become a National Park, and would swallow up caves like Great Crystal and Great Onyx within its boundary. Sand Cave, too, lies within the park; you can walk the short Sand Cave Trail at the park's eastern entrance and see where history happened.

You won't be stopped roadside on your way to Mammoth Cave today, but the Cave Wars continue. The rival caves' brochures still vie for your attention from racks at hotels, restaurants, and attractions across the area, and many of these privately operated caves are well worth a visit. Each has its own history and slice of subterranean beauty.

Sights

GEOLOGICAL FORMATIONS

The Mammoth Cave/Flint Ridge cave system is mostly contained within a small handful of Kentucky ridges—Mammoth Cave Ridge, Flint Ridge, and Joppa Ridge. These ridges are predominantly Mississippian limestone that's around 325 million years old, capped by Carboniferous sandstones and shales. The most notable expressions of this *karst,* or eroded limestone, terrain in the immediate visitor center vicinity are the large open cave entrances of **Historic Entrance** and **Dixon Cave Entrance** downhill from

There are twenty different cave tours offered that help visitors get a glimpse of this massive cave system.

the visitor center; **Mammoth Dome Sink,** visible along the Sinkhole Trail branching from the Heritage Trail; the entrance to **White Cave** along the White Cave Trail; and the **River Styx** and **Echo River Spring** emerging from the cave at the level of the Green River along the Echo River Spring Trail. Along the **Green River Bluffs Trail,** take note of large, broken boulders on the upper flank of the trail; these mark the place where the ridge's **sandstone cap** gives way and exposes the limestones below to erosion.

Big Clifty Sandstone

NATURE SITE | **FAMILY** | The Big Clifty Sandstone, part of the Golconda Formation, lies atop the limestone bedrock of the Mammoth Cave region like a roof. Its cross-bedded layers of sandstone and shale form a shield impermeable to water, protecting the limestone beneath from dissolution. Only through cracks and holes in this shield can rainwater penetrate and begin undermining the caprock, flowing through the soluble limestones beneath and making caves. The Big Clifty Sandstone shows off its profile nicely at this location right off the Historic Entrance Trail nearby the visitor center. An outdoor exhibit facing the formation highlights the feature. ✉ *Mammoth Cave* ✥ *On the left, 300 feet down Historic Entrance Trail* ☎ *270/758–2180 Park Information Line* 🌐 *www.nps.gov/maca.*

Dixon Cave Entrance

CAVE | **FAMILY** | A relic of Mammoth Cave's geologic younger years, Dixon Cave Entrance lies at the end of an underground passage once connected to the rest of the cave. Now choked with stone, this dry hillside pit was at one time a mighty spring that fed Green River. Now, standing on the overlook, you peer down into darkness as though backward into time itself. ✉ *Mammoth Cave* ✥ *Follow Dixon Cave Trail ¼ mile from Historic Entrance* ☎ *270/758–2180 Park Information Line* 🌐 *www.nps.gov/maca.*

HISTORIC SIGHTS

Engine No.4

HISTORIC SITE | FAMILY | Between the Lodge at Mammoth Cave and the Caver's Camps Store, Engine No. 4 is one of the original donkey engines and passenger cars of the Mammoth Cave Railroad that brought travelers to Mammoth Cave before the turn of the 20th century. ✉ *Mammoth Cave* ✣ *Take the Engine No.4 Trail at the southeast corner of the Lodge at Mammoth Cave parking area* ☎ *270/758–2180 Park Information Line* 🌐 *www.nps.gov/maca.*

Historic Entrance

CAVE | FAMILY | This historic entrance to Mammoth Cave provides the centerpiece of historic locations in the visitor center area, a singular point to which human beings have gravitated—and into which they have descended—for 5,000 years. It's easily found at the end of the Historic Entrance Trail. ✉ *Mammoth Cave* ✣ *From the visitor center, follow the Historic Entrance Trail 0.12 miles down the hill* ☎ *270/758–2180 Park Information Line* 🌐 *www.nps.gov/maca.*

Old Guide's Cemetery

CEMETERY | FAMILY | One of about 80 cemeteries located within the park, this cemetery contains the resting place of famed Mammoth Cave Guide, Stephen Bishop. First as an enslaved guide and then as a free man, Bishop spent almost 20 years giving tours Mammoth Cave. He is considered by many to be the cave's most famous guide and explorer. Exhibits at the site help to locate his stone within the enclosure and also discuss other African American guides of Mammoth Cave as well as the old Mammoth Cave Estate. Listed on the National Register of Historic Places, the cemetery is also the final resting place to three patients from the 1842 Tuberculosis Experiment that was held within the cave. ✉ *Mammoth Cave* ✣ *From the visitor center, cross the footbridge and take the Heritage Trail on the right until the junction with the loop; the cemetery is on the left* ☎ *270/758–2180 Park Information Line* 🌐 *www.nps.gov/maca.*

Mammoth Cave Baptist Church

HISTORIC SITE | FAMILY | Two miles from the visitor center along Flint Ridge Road stands one of three churches that still stand from the time before the park was formed. In its adjacent cemetery lies the resting place of cave explorer Floyd Collins. ✉ *Mammoth Cave* ✣ *From the visitor center, follow Flint Ridge Road for 2 miles* ☎ *270/758–2180 Park Information Line* 🌐 *www.nps.gov/maca.*

SCENIC DRIVES

Flint Ridge Road

SCENIC DRIVE | FAMILY | From the visitor center, a drive out Flint Ridge Road, onto Park Ridge Road, then onto Cave City Road and then back to the visitor center via the Mammoth Cave Parkway provides a rustic excursion through peaceful forests, with a glimpse of rural Kentucky farmland along the park boundary. Along Flint Ridge Road, discover historic Mammoth Cave Baptist Church on the left, one of three remaining churches from the prepark period. **■TIP→ This loop can be especially attractive in the fall.** ✉ *Mammoth Cave* ✣ *Start at the visitor center* ☎ *270/758–2180 Park Information Line* 🌐 *www.nps.gov/maca.*

SCENIC STOPS

Green River Bluffs Overlook

BODY OF WATER | FAMILY | Located halfway along the Green River Bluffs Trail, this overlook has an excellent view up the river valley. There's also a long term air quality monitoring webcam. ✉ *Mammoth Cave* ✣ *1.3 miles along the Green River Bluffs Trail* ☎ *270/758–2180 Park Information Line* 🌐 *www.nps.gov/maca.*

Sunset Point Overlook

VIEWPOINT | FAMILY | Located along the ½ mile Heritage Trail, the overlook provides views of the Green River Valley and surrounding hills. ✉ *Mammoth Cave* ✣ *At the halfway point of the Heritage Trail* *loop* ☎ *270/758–2180 Park Information Line* 🌐 *www.nps.gov/maca.*

TRAILS

Stepping outside the visitor center puts you on the path of up to 14 miles of trail in the immediate area. These trails run from the easy and ADA-accessible Heritage Trail to hikes with steep grades and significant changes in elevation. The trails encounter river bluffs and river bottoms, cave entrances and springs, forests, and rock formations, and ample flora and fauna for the observant. You can even follow a path that shows you what part of the cave is underneath your feet. Wherever you start, you can always find your way back to the visitor center.

Amphitheater Trail

TRAIL | FAMILY | This 0.2 mile-long trail leads to the park's outdoor amphitheater, where some evening programs are offered. *Easy.* ✉ *Mammoth Cave* ✥ *Trailhead: Enter at the southeast end of the Lodge at Mammoth Cave's parking lot or from the north side of the Caver's Camp Store* ☎ *270/758–2180 Park Information Line* 🌐 *www.nps.gov/maca.*

Beneath Your Feet

TRAIL | FAMILY | This is a trail-beneath-a-trail—numbered markers along the route explain what part of Mammoth Cave lies directly beneath your feet. Fourteen locations along trails and footpaths in the area surrounding the visitor center and the Mammoth Cave Campground are marked with images and corresponding information, along with smartphone-ready QR codes linked to video content. *Easy.* ✉ *Mammoth Cave* ✥ *Trailhead: The first stop is located near the beginning of the Engine No. 4 trail, just off the southeast end of the Lodge at Mammoth Cave parking lot* ☎ *270/758–2180 Park Information Line* 🌐 *beneathyourfeet.oncell.com.*

Cabins Trail

TRAIL | FAMILY | The 0.2-mile trail leads across the open lawns south of The Lodge at Mammoth Cave to the row of Historic Cottages near the park Amphitheater. *Easy.* ✉ *Mammoth Cave* ✥ *Trailhead: The trail begins across the parking lot on the south side of The Lodge at Mammoth Cave* ☎ *270/758–2180 Park Information Line* 🌐 *www.nps.gov/maca.*

Dixon Cave Overlook Trail

TRAIL | FAMILY | Proceeding down the bluff from the park's main picnic area, this short (0.1 mile) forest trail leads to a platform overlooking the mysterious mouth of Dixon Cave, thought to have once been an ancient outlet of Mammoth Cave. Slightly further down, the trail joins Dixon Cave Trail. *Moderate.* ✉ *Mammoth Cave* ✥ *Trailhead: At the park's main picnic area, turn left, and follow the road to the cul-de-sac* ☎ *270/758–2180 Park Information Line* 🌐 *www.nps.gov/maca.*

Engine No.4 Trail

TRAIL | FAMILY | This short spur trail (0.2 miles) leads to Engine No. 4, an original donkey engine and passenger car that once conveyed travelers to Mammoth Cave along the rails of the Mammoth Cave Railroad. *Easy.* ✉ *Mammoth Cave* ✥ *Trailhead: This trail splits to the left from the Amphitheater Trail shortly after the parking lot south of the Lodge at Mammoth Cave* ☎ *270/758–1280 Park Information Line* 🌐 *www.nps.gov/maca.*

Mammoth Cave Campground Trail

TRAIL | FAMILY | This wooded connecting path (0.2 mile) links Mammoth Cave Campground with the park's outdoor amphitheater by way of the Caver's Camp Store. *Easy.* ✉ *Mammoth Cave* ✥ *Trailhead: The trail begins behind the Caver's Camp Store and emerges near the park's outdoor amphitheater* ☎ *270/758–2180 Park Information Line* 🌐 *www.nps.gov/maca.*

Old Guides Cemetery Trail

TRAIL | **FAMILY** | This short (0.1 mile) spur trail leads off the loop of the Heritage Trail into the center toward the Old Guides Cemetery. Outdoor exhibits at the end interpret the cemetery and its related history. *Easy.* ✉ *Mammoth Cave* ✥ *Trailhead: Begin this trail on the Heritage trail where the lead-in trail joins the loop* ☎ *270/758–2180 Park Information Line* 🌐 *www.nps.gov/maca.*

Old Guides Trail

TRAIL | **FAMILY** | This short (0.1 mile) connector trail is the way people historically came down to the cave entrance from the old Mammoth Cave Hotel. It can still be used that way today, following the old stone stairway. The path emerges on the Heritage Trail next to The Lodge at Mammoth Cave. At the top, turn left to get to the Lodge and the footbridge to the visitor center. *Moderate.* ✉ *Mammoth Cave* ✥ *Trailhead: Begin on Historic Entrance Trail on the right, just above the Historic Entrance* ☎ *270/758–2180 Park Information Line* 🌐 *www.nps.gov/maca.*

River Valley Trail

TRAIL | **FAMILY** | This trail (0.3 miles) connects Sinkhole Trail with Echo River Spring Trail along a direct line down the forested valley slope. An old stone water treatment structure stands not far from the southern junction. *Moderate.* ✉ *Mammoth Cave* ✥ *Trailhead: Use the Sinkhole Trail Trailhead near the Heritage Trail* ☎ *270/758–2180 Park Information Line* 🌐 *www.nps.gov/maca.*

VISITOR CENTER

Mammoth Cave Visitor Center

INFO CENTER | **FAMILY** | The visitor center, perched on the ridgetop just above the cave's renowned Historic Entrance, is the hub of all park activity. All cave tours begin and end here, as well as all other ranger-led activities. This is where you purchase and pick up tickets, shop for books and souvenirs at the bookstore and gift areas, and find the restrooms. The information desk is centrally located, with tour schedules prominently posted, and maps available. This is also the place where young people start and complete the Junior Ranger Program. The visitor center includes a large museum space with exhibits that equip visitors with an understanding of the park's complex nature, culture, and communities. ✉ *Mammoth Cave National Park Visitor Center, 1 Mammoth Cave Pkwy., Mammoth Cave* ☎ *270/758–2180 Park Information Line* 🌐 *www.nps.gov/maca.*

Restaurants

Green River Grill

$$$ | **SOUTHERN** | **FAMILY** | Inside The Lodge at Mammoth Cave, the Green River Grill serves dinner after 5 pm. The menu specializes in traditional Kentucky standards such as blackened catfish po boy sandwiches, bacon-wrapped rainbow trout, country ham, and the item the locals come for, southern fried chicken. **Known for:** southern fried chicken; fried catfish; country ham. 💲 *Average main: $14* ✉ *171 Hotel Rd., Mammoth Cave* ☎ *270/451–2283 dining inquiries* 🌐 *mammothcavelodge.com/green-river-grill/.*

Coffee and Quick Bites

Spelunkers Café and Ice Cream Parlor

$ | **CAFÉ** | **FAMILY** | A café and ice-cream parlor, Spelunkers offers coffee, breakfast and lunch sandwiches, yogurt parfaits, and burgers. Warren County's local favorite, Chaney's Dairy Barn, provides the ice cream—and they make the black cherry flavor only for Mammoth Cave. **Known for:** locally made ice cream; generous servings; to-go breakfast and lunch options. 💲 *Average main: $8* ✉ *171 Hotel Rd., Mammoth Cave* ☎ *270/451–2283 Dining Inquiries* 🌐 *mammothcavelodge.com/spelunkers-cafe/* ☞ *Dining service at the Lodge at Mammoth Cave will be located in temporary facilities at the location during renovation through their 2022 season.*

Hotels

The Lodge at Mammoth Cave–Heritage Trail Rooms

$$$ | HOTEL | FAMILY | Located inside the lodge, the four Heritage Trail rooms are fully handicap accessible; two have roll-in showers. **Pros:** inside the main lodge with shopping and dining; all rooms are ADA accessible; the visitor center is just across the footbridge. **Cons:** limited availability; the Lodge can be busy; TV channel selection is limited. *Rooms from: $136* *171 Hotel Rd., Mammoth Cave* *844/760–2283* *www.mammothcavelodge.com* *4 rooms* *No meals.*

The Lodge at Mammoth Cave–Historic Cottages

$$ | HOTEL | FAMILY | The Historic Cottages, across the lawn in a semicircle on the south side of the Lodge, are wooden cottages on stone foundations, rustic yet comfortably furnished. **Pros:** close to the visitor center; quiet location; adjacent to the park outdoor amphitheater. **Cons:** no TV or Wi-Fi; rooms are not ADA-accessible; advance reservation is recommended as rooms tend to book up quickly. *Rooms from: $93* *171 Hotel Rd., Mammoth Cave* *844/760–2283* *www.mammothcavelodge.com* *Closed Dec.–Memorial Day* *10 cottages* *No meals.*

The Lodge at Mammoth Cave–Sunset Terrace

$$$ | HOTEL | FAMILY | The Sunset Terrace consists of a row of 20 rooms close to the edge of the blufftop near the Heritage Trail, with windows providing views of the deep woodlands extending into the hollows. **Pros:** convenient to the park's visitor center; windows open directly onto nearby forest; instant access to local trail network. **Cons:** facility is not as modern as a comparable hotel outside the park; limited counter space in the bathrooms; access to the main lodge requires a 0.1 mile walk. *Rooms from: $136* *171 Hotel Rd., Mammoth Cave* *844/760–2283* *www.mammothcavelodge.com* *20 rooms* *No meals.*

The Lodge at Mammoth Cave–Woodland Cottages

$$ | HOTEL | FAMILY | The Woodland Cottages, adjacent to the park's main picnic area, are rustic one-, two-, three-, and four-bedroom cabins that provide either queen or twin beds, a shower, ceiling fans, mini-refrigerator, coffeemaker, and screened windows and doors for each room. **Pros:** next to the park's main campground; pet-friendly; very simple and rustic. **Cons:** no air-conditioning (cabins can get muggy midsummer); close to the main visitor center parking lot; cabins are not ADA-accessible. *Rooms from: $71* *171 Hotel Rd., Mammoth Cave* *844/760–2283* *www.mammothcavelodge.com* *Closed Dec.–Memorial Day* *21 cabins* *No meals.*

Shopping

America's National Parks Bookstore

BOOKS/STATIONERY | FAMILY | The bookstore sells a curated selection of park-related books, educational gifts, and souvenirs. All proceeds go to support the park's preservation and education programs. *Mammoth Cave National Park Visitor Center, 1 Mammoth Cave Pkwy., Mammoth Cave* *270/758–2180 Park Information Line* *shop.americasnationalparks.org.*

Caver's Camp Store

CONVENIENCE/GENERAL STORES | FAMILY | Located adjacent to Mammoth Cave Campground, the camp store offers basic camp staples, drinks, quick food, and souvenirs. *Mammoth Cave Pkwy., Mammoth Cave* *844/760–2283* *mammothcavelodge.com.*

Frontcountry

4 miles from the visitor center

In the park's southeast sector below Green River, the sinkhole plain to the south infiltrates the Pennyroyal Plateau that rises up along its edge. Some of Mammoth Cave's principal entrances lie in this region, along with massive sinkholes and remnants of the Big Barrens—the eastern savannahs that existed at the time of European arrival. Within the eroded ridges and hollows of this transitional environment are tucked away some of the park's least appreciated short hike destinations, as well as the Mammoth Cave Railroad Bike & Hike trail. This part of the park still has a sense of connectedness to the land and communities adjacent to the park.

Sights

GEOLOGICAL FORMATIONS

Cedar Sink

FOREST | FAMILY | This massive karst sinkhole is open for exploration via the Cedar Sink Trail. As a collapse feature, it acts as a window into geologic processes still going on deep beneath the earth. Related sinkholes are found along Turnhole Bend Nature Trail. ✉ *Cedar Sink Rd., Mammoth Cave* ☎ *270/758–2180 Park Information Line* 🌐 *www.nps.gov/maca.*

Pennyroyal Plateau

NATURE SITE | FAMILY | Strangely eroded limestone banks give way to hollows that creep into hillsides; grassy prairie-like fields yield to woodlands; sinkholes interrupt the forested landscape. You have begun climbing into the Pennyroyal Plateau from the Sinkhole Plain, but the margin between the two is ... complicated. The compromises made between rock and water, between grass and tree, between high and low, have resulted in a twisted patchwork landscape. It's covered over with a quilt of green, but as you look beneath, there's plenty to wonder at all the way to the visitor center. ✉ *Mammoth Cave* ⊕ *From the park's southern entrance at Park City, look for outcrops and sinks along Mammoth Cave Pkwy.* ☎ *270/758–2180 Park Information Line* 🌐 *www.nps.gov/maca.*

HISTORIC SIGHTS

Joppa Baptist Church and Cemetery

RELIGIOUS SITE | FAMILY | A handful of structures remain from the communities that existed before this park was established including three churches: Mammoth Cave Baptist, Good Spring, and Joppa Church. Joppa Church was established in 1862, but the present building was built around 1900. It was added to the National Register of Historic Places in 1991. An outdoor exhibit gives some of its history. ✉ *Brownsville Pkwy., Mammoth Cave* ☎ *270/758–2180 Park Information Line* 🌐 *www.nps.gov/maca.*

The Mammoth Cave Railroad

HISTORIC SITE | FAMILY | Before the age of the automobile, travelers often reached Mammoth Cave on the Mammoth Cave Railroad, a spur line of the Louisville & Nashville Railroad. The entire route is now the Mammoth Cave Railroad Bike & Hike Trail, which begins at the southern park boundary at Park City, and ends at the visitor center, where you can see one of the original engines and its passenger car. Historic stops along the way with parking are at Diamond Caverns, Locust Grove, Sloan's Crossing Pond, and Doyel Valley Overlook. Other historic points of interest accessible on foot or by mountain bike include Union City, Ferguson Cemetery, Doyel Valley Trestle, and Engine No. 4. ✉ *Mammoth Cave Pkwy., Mammoth Cave* ☎ *270/758–2180 Park Information Line* 🌐 *www.nps.gov/maca.*

Sand Cave

CAVE | FAMILY | Most of the park's caves lie within its hundreds of feet of limestone strata, but atop that limestone sits a layer of sandstone and shale. Sandstone caves can be found in this ridgetop layer, which often lead to greater limestone caverns farther down. In hope of making such a discovery, explorer Floyd Collins entered Sand Cave in 1925, but never left. His entrapment, and attempted rescue, made headlines across the nation and caused a near-carnival of activity outside the cave entrance. That entrance is visible close at hand from the overlook at the end of Sand Cave Trail. ✉ *Cave City Rd., Mammoth Cave* ☎ *270/758–2180 Park Information Line* 🌐 *www.nps.gov/maca.*

SCENIC DRIVES

From late September into early November, motorists often follow the Mammoth Cave Parkway, the Cave City Road, and the Brownsville Road/Brownsville Road to enjoy the colorful change of the leaves. Some years put on more of a show than others, but the dogwoods seldom disappoint. That's especially true in the spring, when both dogwoods and redbuds aren't bashful with their blossoms.

SCENIC STOPS

Doyel Valley Overlook

VIEWPOINT | **FAMILY** | The only overlook accessible by vehicle, here you can peer back in time across one of the frontcountry hollows. Outdoor exhibits discuss the valley's past communities and help put the view in the context of what was, what is, and what will someday be. ✉ *Mammoth Cave Pkwy., Mammoth Cave* ✣ *2.2 miles south of the visitor center* ☎ *270/758–2180 Park Information Line* 🌐 *www.nps.gov/maca.*

TRAILS

Cedar Sink Trail

TRAIL | **FAMILY** | A half-mile of forest trail leads to the brim of Cedar Sink. From there, viewing platforms along another half-mile inside the sink allow hikers a peek at the underground waters from the Sinkhole Plain as it makes its way toward Green River. This massive sinkhole creates a microclimate of its own where wildflowers often bloom slightly out-of-season. *Moderate.* ✉ *Mammoth Cave* ✣ *Trailhead: ½ mile along Cedar Sink Rd. on left* ☎ *270/758–2180 Park Information Line* 🌐 *www.nps.gov/maca.*

Mammoth Cave Railroad Bike & Hike Trail–South

TRAIL | **FAMILY** | This 5-mile trail follows the path of the original Mammoth Cave Railroad, a spur line of the Louisville and Nashville Railroad, that brought travelers to visit Mammoth Cave before the turn of the 20th century. This leg visits historic points at Diamond Caverns, Union City, and Locust Grove, ending at Sloan's Crossing Pond. The trail surface is rough gravel, suitable for mountain bikes and hikers only. Road crossing is required; be alert for oncoming traffic. *Moderate.* ✉ *Mammoth Cave* ✣ *Trailhead: The park's southern entrance along the Mammoth Cave Pkwy. near Park City* ☎ *270/758–2180 Park Information Line* 🌐 *www.nps.gov/maca.*

Sand Cave Trail

TRAIL | **FAMILY** | This accessible 0.1-mile trail through the forest leads to an overlook over the mouth of Sand Cave. In 1925, the underground entrapment of cave explorer Floyd Collins within Sand Cave made news across the nation. At that time, a "carnival atmosphere" prevailed in this location, but now only the trees stand sentinel around the cave's opening, but placards along the path tell the somber tale. *Easy.* ✉ *Mammoth Cave* ✣ *Trailhead: Parking area at the park boundary along Cave City Rd.* ☎ *270/758–2180 Park Information Line* 🌐 *www.nps.gov/maca.*

Sloan's Crossing Pond Walk

TRAIL | **FAMILY** | Sloan's Crossing Pond is an anomaly—a standing body of water in a place where most water disappears under the earth. This accessible 0.4-mile boardwalk trail encircles the pond, offering turnouts to appreciate the aquatic life of a woodland pond. A small picnic area is available. *Easy.* ✉ *Mammoth Cave* ✣ *Trailhead: Sloan's Crossing Pond parking lot along Mammoth Cave Pkwy.*

☎ *270/758–2180 Park Information Line* 🌐 *www.nps.gov/maca.*

Green River Valley

11 miles from the visitor center to the Green River Ferry.

The lifeblood of every biome of the park, Green River bisects the park with deep valley running 25 miles east to west, from above Dennison Ferry to below Houchin Ferry. The Nolin River courses 9 miles from Nolin Dam just outside the park's northwest boundary to just below Houchin Ferry.

Visitors come purely for the pleasures of angling, canoeing, kayaking, boating, or even simply watching the waters flow by.

Sights

GEOLOGICAL FORMATIONS

The mighty force of water seeking its way to Green River underground has hollowed the limestone layers in the surrounding ridges for millennia. It reaches its goal at numerous springs along the rivers, some of them notable for their size, output, and beauty. The River Styx and Echo River Springs emerge from the cave at the level of the Green River along the River Styx Spring Trail and the Echo River Spring Trail, with outlets onto Green River. It's possible to access these springs by inlet from the river, or by surface trail. Further downstream, Turnhole Spring emerges in a spring so large that steamboats once used it as a place to turn around. Other springs and seeps can be found if you're observant—water's underground journey to the river continues.

HISTORIC SIGHTS

Green River Ferry

BODY OF WATER | FAMILY | The Green River Ferry is one of the country's longest-running river ferries, the last of a group of such ferries that once shuttled traffic across the river before the area became a national park. This free ferry, which has been operating since 1941, runs daily 6 am–9:55 pm unless interrupted by high, or low, water levels. Vehicles cannot exceed 12 tons or 16 feet in length. There's an outdoor informational exhibit at the ferry dock. ✉ *Green River Ferry Rd., Mammoth Cave* ☎ *270/758–2166* 🌐 *www.nps.gov/maca.*

Turnhole Bend

BODY OF WATER | FAMILY | At Green River mile 193, you arrive at the middle of Turnhole Bend, a large bend in the river. The bend is so nearly complete that someday in the geologic future, the river will erode the neck of the bend away entirely, cutting Turnhole Bend off from the backcountry. Downstream 0.2 miles on the south side you will find Turnhole Spring, an outlet of an underground waterway. This spring creates a bluehole so large that before the turn of the 19th century, steamboats plying the Green River with passengers and cargo would use this natural "turn hole" to turn around. ✉ *Mammoth Cave* ⇔ *Follow Turnhole Bend Trail 1.8 miles to its end* ☎ *270/758–2180 Park Information Line* 🌐 *www.nps.gov/maca.*

SCENIC STOPS

The Green River Valley is more or less a continuous scenic stop, but standouts include the several islands along the way such as Cave Island below the visitor center area. Water-thirsty sycamores often hug the riverbanks; look for their bone-white upper trunks towering above you. Karst features like curiously eroded limestone outcrops will surprise you when least expected, and you can get a close look at some of the springs where the underground streams meet the river. A brief stop at Green River Ferry puts you at the Echor River Spring Trailhead, a short hike from the place where the Echo River emerges from its underground journey to join the Green River at Echo River Spring. Farther downriver, forested river bluffs tower over you as the river cuts deeper into the landscape.

Hilly Backcountry

5 miles from the visitor center via the Maple Springs Trailhead

Among the features Congress recognized in the formation of Mammoth Cave National Park is its hilly country, a characteristic of this western edge of Appalachia. North of Green River, the park's backcountry landscape rises and falls into ridges and hollows networked by more than 70 miles of trails. Many of these trails are clues to a time before this place was a national park, as they follow the old road beds and paths used by the people of the early 20th-century communities that called these hills home. The area is now covered in wildflowers, wildlife, hardwood forests, and hemlock groves, but remnants of these past communities still dot the landscape.

Sights

HISTORIC SIGHTS

Good Spring Church and Cemetery

CEMETERY | **FAMILY** | One of three original churches still standing in the park, Good Spring is a remnant of the Cade community. The adjacent cemetery contains stones with names of the families that lived here. ■ **TIP→ More information about the Cade community is available at an outdoor exhibit at Maple Springs Group Campground nearby on Maple Springs Loop Road.** ✉ *Good Spring Church Rd., Mammoth Cave* ☎ *270/758–2180 Park Information Line* 🌐 *www.nps.gov/maca.*

SCENIC STOPS

The Big Woods

FOREST | **FAMILY** | To the left of the White Oak Trail in the east of the park's backcountry lies something very uncommon—a small area of forest that has never once been cut for timber. This is The Big Woods, one of only two areas of true Old Growth forest remaining in Kentucky. White Oak Trail is not connected to the rest of the backcountry trail network, but the trip along Ugly Creek Road may be worth a chance to see forest that has never seen a saw or an axe since the world began. ✉ *Mammoth Cave* ✣ *From the White Oak Trailhead, The Big Woods begin on the left of the trail after about 0.2 miles* ☎ *270/758–2180 Park Information Line* 🌐 *www.nps.gov/maca.*

TRAILS

The park's backcountry offers more than 70 miles of backcountry trails to hikers, horseback riders, and mountain bikers. Total elevation change is around 400 feet, and some grades are steep. Interspersed along these trails are 13 backcountry campsites available by reservation; a Backcountry Use Permit is required for camping.

Big Hollow Trail

FOREST | **FAMILY** | This a designated mountain-biking and hiking trail divided into two loops joined by a connector. The Big Hollow Trail North Loop runs 5.3 miles, with a 0.1-mile shortcut, along moderately easy ascents through rolling woodlands. The Big Hollow Trail South Loop, including the connector, runs 3.7 miles through more jumbled rocky terrain, partly along the blufftop over Green River. Horses are not permitted on this trail. ■ **TIP→ There is no parking along Green River Ferry Road North or the Maple Springs Loop Road.** *Moderate.* ✉ *Mammoth Cave* ✣ *Trailhead: Junction of the Maple Springs Trail and the Mill Branch Trail* ☎ *270/758–2180 Park Information Line* 🌐 *www.nps.gov/maca.*

Buffalo Creek Trail

TRAIL | **FAMILY** | This trail cuts across the southern backcountry, following old roadbeds to the Buffalo Creek drainage, and links several trails. At 1.1 miles, Dry Prong Trail heads north and Turnhole Bend Trail heads south. At 2.4 miles, Sal Hollow Trail heads south and Dry Prong Trail reconnects. At mile 4.4, the trail ends at a junction with Collie Ridge Trail and Wet Prong Trail. Horses and hiking only. *Moderate.* ✉ *Mammoth Cave*

Trailhead: The trail begins on the west side of the road at Maple Springs Trailhead ☎ *270/758–2180 Park Information Line* 🌐 *www.nps.gov/maca.*

Collie Ridge Trail

TRAIL | FAMILY | A wide path following old roadbeds along the spine of Collie Ridge, this trail serves as an artery connecting several trails deep in the backcountry, and forms the basis for several possible hiking loops. The trail junctions with Blair Springs Hollow, Raymer Hollow, Mill Branch, Buffalo Creek, and Wet Prong Trails. Collie Ridge backcountry campsite is reached via a 0.7-mile spur extending from the end of the trail. Horses and hiking only. *Moderate.* ✉ *Mammoth Cave* *Trailhead: The trail begins at Lincoln Trailhead; from KY-728, 0.4 miles on Ollie Rd.* ☎ *270/758–2180 Park Information Line* 🌐 *www.nps.gov/maca.*

First Creek Trail

BODY OF WATER | FAMILY | This trail follows a ridgeline to the Second Creek drainage into the Nolin River valley, then descends along the Nolin to First Creek Lake before climbing upward past broken sandstone blocks to the trailhead at Temple Hill. Stream crossings, wet and muddy areas, and some rocky slopes may challenge footing. At 3 miles, the Second Creek backcountry campsite can by accessed by a short spur. At 4.2 miles, a spur leads to First Creek backcountry campsite 1. At 5.2 miles, a spur accesses First Creek backcountry campsite 2. Horses and hiking only. *Moderate.* ✉ *Mammoth Cave* *Trailhead: Take Ollie Rd. until it becomes Houchin Ferry Rd. in the park; in 2.8 miles, First Creek Trailhead will be on the right* ☎ *270/758–2180 Park Information Line* 🌐 *www.nps.gov/maca.*

Sal Hollow Trail

TRAIL | FAMILY | Several stream crossings and boulder outcrops add interest to this winding 8.6-mile trail. Turnhole Bend Trail intersects it at 3.8 miles. At 7.2 miles, Sal Hollow backcountry campsite is accessible via a short spur trail. At 8.3 miles a trail on the left leads to the Miles-Davis Cemetery. Another trail at that point leads to the Bluffs backcountry campsite 0.6 miles westward. The trail ends at a junction with Buffalo Creek Trail. Horses and hiking only. *Moderate.* ✉ *Mammoth Cave* *Trailhead: The trail begins on the west side of the road at Maple Springs Trailhead* ☎ *270/758–2180 Park Information Line* 🌐 *www.nps.gov/maca.*

Activities

BIKING

Certain areas of Mammoth Cave National Park are specially designated for mountain bikes. These include the 9-mile Mammoth Cave Railroad Bike & Hike Trail in the frontcountry and the 9-mile Big Hollow Trail in the backcountry. The Maple Springs Trail from Big Hollow Trailhead to Maple Springs Trailhead is also open to mountain bikes. All other trails in the park are closed to bicycles, and these trails are not appropriate for road bikes. For road bikes, the network of park roads is open to bicycle use, although there are no bike lanes.

The park is now a part of two recognized formal biking routes: the TransAmerica Bicycle Route, which extends from Virginia to Oregon, and the Cave Country Bicycle Route, a 109-mile route that links the TransAmerica Bicycle Route at the Tennessee Border to small towns and sites in Kentucky's Cave Region.

BIRD-WATCHING

Bird-watching is excellent throughout the park. One locale to try is Sloan's Crossing Pond Walk on the Mammoth Cave Parkway. Aquatic birds are frequently seen along the banks of Green River and at First Creek Lake.

CAMPING

Whether you like your camping hard-boiled or over-easy, you can get it either way at Mammoth Cave. Mammoth Cave and Maple Springs provide developed campsites March through November, while Houchin Ferry offers year-round primitive camping. With a free Backcountry Use Permit, available at the visitor center, campers can plant stakes at one of 13 primitive backcountry sites, or at certain places along the Green River floodplain or islands.

Mammoth Cave Campground. Less than ¼ mile from the visitor center, the campground offers 111 sites in four loops. Some sites are tent-only, while others can accommodate RVs. Restrooms are located centrally to each loop, while showers are available for a small charge at the nearby Caver's Camp Store. Fees are $25 for a single tent site, $40 for a group site, and $25 for an RV site. Access Passport holders receive a discount. ✉ *2811 Mammoth Cave Pkwy.* ☎ *270/758–2424* 🌐 *www.recreation.gov.*

Maple Springs Group Campground. Six miles from the visitor center, these eight sites make an ideal base for backcountry excursions on foot or on horseback. Four sites cater to travelers with horses and two can accommodate RVs. Each site has a fire ring and picnic tables, and potable water is available. The vault-style toilets are in the center of the ring. Fees are $50 per site. ✉ *2811 Mammoth Cave Pkwy.* ☎ *270/758–2424* 🌐 *www.recreation.gov.*

Houchin Ferry Campground. There are 12 tent-only riverside sites with drive-up access, a fire ring and picnic table, and potable water. Fees are $20 per site; Access Passport holders receive a discount. ■ **TIP→ There are no ADA accessible sites in this campground.** ✉ *Houchin Ferry Rd.* ☎ *270/758–2424* 🌐 *www.recreation.gov.*

CANOEING AND KAYAKING

The Green River might have been made expressly for the canoe. There are no dangerous whitewater or treacherous shoals, only the occasional tricky shallow, hidden sunken log, or hanging branch. Flora and wildlife are abundant, and several river islands offer opportunities to stop and rest or explore. If you don't own a canoe or kayak, there are three park approved outfitters: Cave Country Canoe, Green River Canoeing, and Mammoth Cave Canoe & Kayak. ■ **TIP→ Plan to station a vehicle at your takeout point, or arrange with one of the approved outfitters for transportation, to get back to your launch point.**

Four main options are recommended for those who want to explore these waters: Dennison Ferry to Green River Ferry; Dennison Ferry to Houchin Ferry; Green River Ferry to Houchin Ferry, and Nolin/Tailwater to Houchin Ferry. The Dennison Ferry Day-Use Area provides a canoe and kayak launch. From here, beginners can head to the Green River Ferry takeout point, which is 8 miles downstream. Those looking for a longer, or more challenging trip, can continue on to the Houchin Ferry takeout point, which is about 20 miles.

If you plan to explore the Nolin/Tailwater to Houchin Ferry 9-mile route, the put-in is above the park boundary at the U.S. Army Corps of Engineers Tailwater Recreation Area below the Nolin Lake Dam on Nolin River. From the dam's tailwaters, follow the Nolin River to its confluence with the Green River below Houchin Ferry, then paddle upstream to take out at Houchin Ferry. The Nolin is narrower than the Green, and fallen trees can present obstacles that require portage. The route can be more challenging than a float down the Green River, but the Nolin has charms of its own with its overhanging canopy of trees, its variety of rock formations, and abundant flora and fauna. ■ **TIP→ A U.S. Coast Guard–approved life preserver is required to be worn at all times while on the rivers.**

Cave Country Canoe
CANOEING/ROWING/SKULLING | FAMILY | ✉ *856 Old Mammoth Cave Rd., Cave City* ☎ *270/834–6208.*

Green River Canoeing, Inc.
CANOEING/ROWING/SKULLING | **FAMILY** | ✉ *3057 Mammoth Cave Rd., Cave City* ☎ *270/773–5712* 🌐 *mammothcavecanoe.com.*

Mammoth Cave Canoes & Kayak
CANOEING/ROWING/SKULLING | **FAMILY** | ✉ *1240 Old Mammoth Cave Rd., Cave City* ☎ *270/773–6087* 🌐 *adventuresofmammothcave.com.*

Tailwater Recreation Area
BOATING | **FAMILY** | Tailwater Recreation Area is operated by the U.S. Army Corps of Engineers–Louisville District, and lies outside the boundary of Mammoth Cave National Park. It includes a boating ramp to the tailwaters of the Nolin River at the base of the Nolin River Dam at Nolin Lake. Nolin River reaches the park boundary approximately 1 river mile below the dam. ✉ *2150 Nolin Dam Rd., Mammoth Cave* ✣ *From Brownsville, take KY-259 north to KY-728, turn right; continue to 2150 Nolin Dam Rd.* ☎ *270/286–4511* 🌐 *www.lrl.usace.army.mil/Missions/Civil-Works/Recreation/Lakes/Nolin-River-Lake* ☞ *A $5 fee is charged for boat launching at all USACE ramps.*

FISHING

Anglers have 34 miles of river in which to pit their skill against the finned ones in some of the most biologically diverse waterways in America. Largemouth, smallmouth and rock bass, walleye/sauger, crappie, bluegill, catfish, and muskellunge are all popular targets among the sunken logs, sandbars, blueholes and outcrops along the Green and Nolin Rivers. No fishing license is required in the park.

HIKING

Just stepping outside the park's visitor center sets you up for 14 miles of possible trails that cross from ridgetop to riverbottom, past mysterious cave entrances and sinkholes, splendid overlooks, and long forgotten cemeteries. One of these, the Echo River Spring Trail, is designed as a fully accessible trail for people with disabilities and features accessible exhibits. Easy access to this trail begins at the Echo River Spring Trailhead adjacent to Green River Ferry. Small, unexpected adventures await in other short frontcountry hikes such as Sand Cave Trail, Sloan's Crossing Pond Walk, Cedar Sink Trail, and Turnhole Bend Trail.

In the Backcountry, more than 70 miles of rugged footpaths follow the contours of the park's Kentucky hill country, with elevation changes of around 400 feet. Unlike trails in many parks that have a particular arrival destination, Mammoth Cave's backcountry trails are best enjoyed for the journey. They largely follow the roads and tracks of people who lived here before this was a park, and the places they were going may have disappeared along with them, but their spirit echoes in the bones of the earth and whispers in the branches.

HORSEBACK RIDING

If you don't own a horse, or would like to participate in a guided horseback outing, contact Double J Stables.

Double J Stables
CAMPING—SPORTS-OUTDOORS | ✉ *542 Lincoln School Rd., Mammoth Cave* ☎ *270/286–8167* 🌐 *www.doublejstables.com.*

SPELUNKING

So far, more than 400 miles of Mammoth Cave have been mapped and surveyed, and there is no end in sight. Exploration is ongoing, but you must be involved in an officially sanctioned research expedition as a member of the Cave Research Foundation to explore the caves in Mammoth Cave National Park. Because these natural resources are so fragile and in need of professional care, there are no opportunities for independent cave exploration. You can, however, have a spelunking experience on one of the park's spelunking tours: Trog, Introduction to Caving, or Wild Cave Tour. ⇨ *See Tours for more information.*

What's Nearby

Munfordville, 25 minutes northeast of the visitor center on I–65, offers river access into the park at the Green River Park and Arboretum, and is the location of a major Civil War battlefield at the Battle for the Bridge Historic Preserve.

The American Cave Museum/Hidden River Cave and Kentucky Down Under/ Mammoth Onyx Cave are at **Horse Cave,** 20 minutes east of the park on Interstate 65.

Cave City, 20 minutes southeast of the visitor center on KY-70, offers a choice of lodging and dining, as well as a handful of tourist-oriented attractions.

The park's southern gateway at **Park City** features nearby Diamond Caverns.

For a broader selection of dining, **Bowling Green** is 45 minutes southwest of the park on Interstate 65. It's home to the Corvette Museum, the Historic Railpark and Train Museum, and the Kentucky Museum at Western Kentucky University. It's also where you'll find the Lost River Cave, the state's only cave with a river that you can see on a boat.

Abraham Lincoln Birthplace National Historical Park is in **Hodgenville,** 44 miles north on U.S. Highway 31-E.

Chapter 43

MESA VERDE NATIONAL PARK

Updated by
Aimee Heckel

Camping	Hotels	Activities	Scenery	Crowds
★★★☆☆	★★☆☆☆	★★★★☆	★★★★★	★★★☆☆

WELCOME TO MESA VERDE NATIONAL PARK

TOP REASONS TO GO

★ **Ancient artifacts:** Mesa Verde is a time capsule for the Ancestral Pueblo culture; more than 4,000 archaeological sites and 3 million objects have been unearthed here.

★ **Bright nights:** Mesa Verde's lack of light and air pollution, along with its high elevation, make for spectacular views of the heavens.

★ **Active adventures:** Get your heart pumping outdoors with hiking, biking, and exploring on trails of varying difficulties.

★ **Cliff dwellings:** Built atop the pinyon-covered mesa tops and hidden in the park's valleys are 600 ancient dwellings, some carved directly into the sandstone cliff faces.

★ **Geological marvels:** View the unique geology that drew the Ancient Pueblo to the area: protected desert canyons, massive alcoves in the cliff walls, thick bands of sandstone, continuous seep springs, and soils that could be used for both agriculture and architecture.

1 **Morefield.** The only campground in Mesa Verde, Morefield includes a village area with a gas station and store, and is close to the main visitor center and some of the best hiking trails in the park.

2 **Far View.** Almost an hour's drive from Mesa Verde's entrance, Far View is the park's epicenter, with several restaurants and the park's only overnight lodge. The fork in the road here takes you west toward the sites at Wetherill Mesa or south toward Chapin Mesa.

3 **Chapin Mesa.** Home to the park's most famous cliff dwellings and archaeological sites, the Chapin Mesa area includes the famous 150-room Cliff Palace and Spruce Tree House dwellings and other man-made and natural wonders, as well as the Chapin Mesa Archeological Museum.

4 **Wetherill Mesa.** See Long House, Two Raven House, Kodak House, and the Badger House Community.

COLORADO

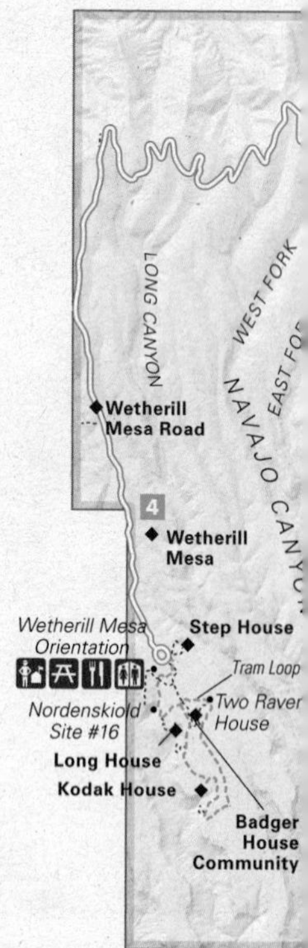

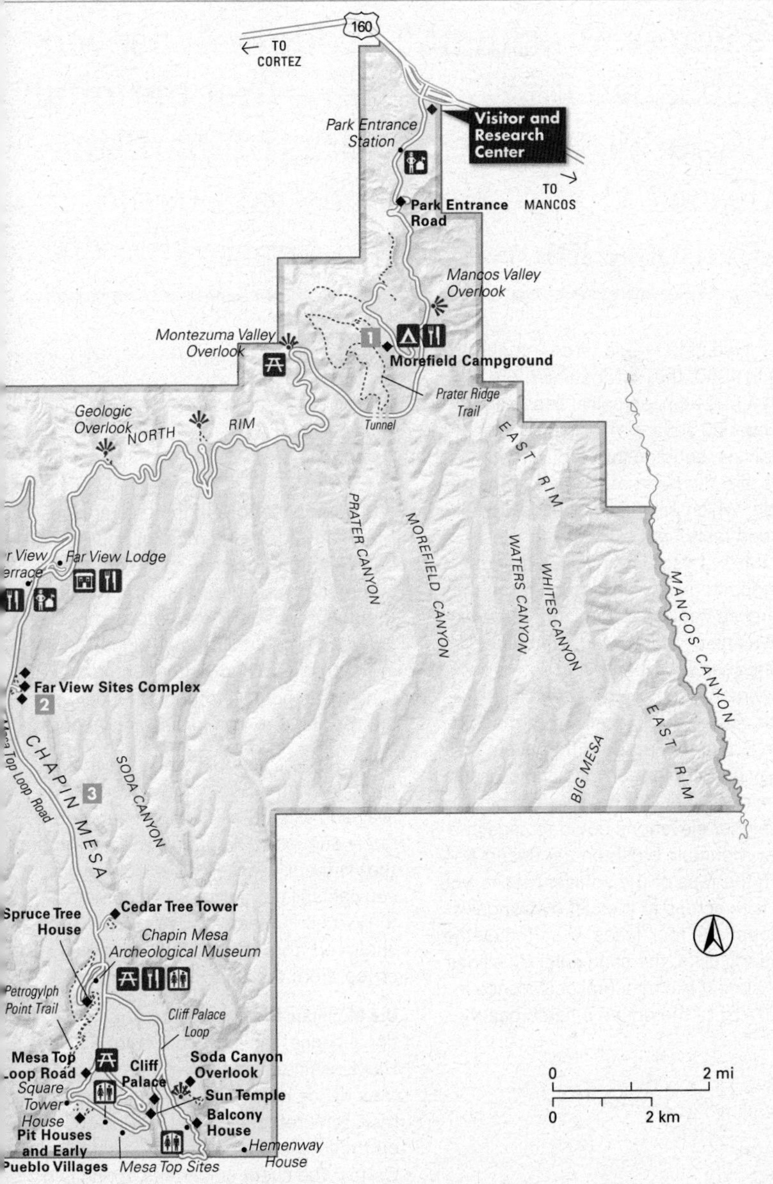
160
TO CORTEZ
Visitor and Research Center
Park Entrance Station
TO MANCOS
Park Entrance Road
Mancos Valley Overlook
Montezuma Valley Overlook
1
Morefield Campground
Prater Ridge Trail
Tunnel
Geologic Overlook
NORTH RIM
EAST RIM
PRATER CANYON
MOREFIELD CANYON
WATERS CANYON
WHITES CANYON
MANCOS CANYON
Far View Lodge
Far View Sites Complex
2
CHAPIN MESA
SODA CANYON
3
BIG MESA
EAST RIM
Cedar Tree Tower
Spruce Tree House
Chapin Mesa Archeological Museum
Petrogylph Point Trail
Cliff Palace Loop
Mesa Top Loop Road
Cliff Palace
Soda Canyon Overlook
Square Tower House
Sun Temple
Balcony House
Pit Houses and Early Pueblo Villages
Mesa Top Sites
Hemenway House
0
2 mi
0
2 km

Unlike the other national parks, Mesa Verde earned its status from its ancient cultural history rather than its geological treasures. President Theodore Roosevelt established it in 1906 as the first national park to "preserve the works of man," in this case that of the Ancestral Pueblo, previously known as the Anasazi.

They lived in the region from roughly 550 to 1300; they left behind more than 4,000 archaeological sites spread out over 80 square miles. Their ancient dwellings, set high into the sandstone cliffs, are the heart of the park. Mesa Verde (which in Spanish means, literally, "Green Table," but translates more accurately to something like "green flat-topped plateau") is much more than an archaeologist's dreamland, however. It's one of those windswept places where man's footprints and nature's paintbrush—some would say chisel—meet. Rising dramatically from the San Juan Basin, the jutting cliffs are cut by a series of complex canyons and covered in several shades of green, from pines in the higher elevations down to sage and other mountain brush on the desert floor. From the tops of the smaller mesas, you can look across to the cliff dwellings in the opposite rock faces. Dwarfed by the towering cliffs, the sand-color dwellings look almost like a natural occurrence in the midst of the desert's harsh beauty.

Planning

When to Go

The best times to visit the park are late May, early June, and most of September, when the weather is fine but the summer crowds have thinned. Mid-June through August is Mesa Verde's most crowded time. In July and August, lines at the museum and visitor center may last half an hour. Afternoon thunderstorms are common in July and August.

The park gets as much as 100 inches of snow in winter. Snow may fall as late as May and as early as October, but there's rarely enough to hamper travel. In winter, the Wetherill Mesa Road is closed, but you can still get a glimpse of some of the Wetherill Mesa sandstone dwellings, sheltered from the snow in their cliff coves, from the Chapin Mesa area.

Ute Mountain Ute Bear Dance. This traditional dance, the local version of a Sadie Hawkins (in which the women choose their dance partners—and the selected men can't refuse), is held in May or June on the Towaoc Ute reservation south of Cortez. The event celebrates spring and

AVERAGE HIGH/LOW TEMPERATURES					
JAN.	FEB.	MAR.	APR.	MAY	JUNE
37/16	41/20	49/26	57/31	67/39	79/49
JULY	AUG.	SEPT.	OCT.	NOV.	DEC.
84/55	81/53	74/46	61/36	48/25	38/18

the legacy of a mythical bear that taught the Ute people her secrets. It's part of a multiday festival that includes music, races, and softball games, and culminates with an hour-long dance that's over when only one couple remains. 🌐 *www.utemountainutetribe.com*

Durango Fiesta Days. A parade, one of the oldest rodeos in the state, barbecue, street dance, cook-offs, live music, and more come to the Durango Fairgrounds in July. 🌐 *www.downtowndurango.org*

Durango Cowboy Poetry Gathering. A parade accompanies art exhibitions, poetry readings, music, theater, and storytelling in this four-day event run by the Durango Cowboy Poetry Gathering, a nonprofit set up to preserve the traditions of the American West. It's held the first weekend in October. 🌐 *www.durangocowboypoetrygathering.org*

Getting Here and Around

AIR

The cities of Durango (36 miles east of the park entrance) and Cortez (11 miles to the west) have airports.

CAR

The park has just one entrance, off U.S. 160, between Cortez and Durango in what's known as the Four Corners area (which spans the intersection of Colorado, New Mexico, Arizona, and Utah). Most of the roads at Mesa Verde involve steep grades and hairpin turns, particularly on Wetherill Mesa. Vehicles over 8,000 pounds or 25 feet are prohibited on this road. Trailers and towed vehicles are prohibited past Morefield Campground. Check the condition of your vehicle's brakes before driving the road to Wetherill Mesa. For the latest road information, tune to 1610 AM, or call ☎ *970/529–4461*. Off-road vehicles are prohibited in the park. At less-visited Wetherill Mesa, you must leave your car behind and hike or bike to the Long House, Kodak House, and Badger House Community.

Inspiration

Mesa Verde National Park: Shadows of the Centuries, by Duane A. Smith, discusses the history and current issues facing the park.

Ancient Peoples of the American Southwest, by Stephen Plog, is an archaeologist's account of the Ancestral Pueblo people and two other cultures.

Mesa Verde: Ancient Architecture, by Jesse Walter Fewkes, tells the stories behind the park's dwellings.

Park Essentials

PARK FEES AND PERMITS

Admission is $25 per vehicle for a seven-day permit. An annual pass is $40. Ranger-led tours of Cliff Palace, Long House, and Balcony House are $5 per person. You can also take ranger-guided bus tours from the Far View Lodge, which last between 3½ and 4 hours and cost $55 ($33 for kids; under five free). Backcountry hiking and fishing are not permitted at Mesa Verde.

PARK HOURS

Mesa Verde's facilities each operate on their own schedule, but most are open daily, from Memorial Day through Labor Day, between about 8 am and sunset. The rest of the year, they open at 9. In winter, the Spruce Tree House is open only to offer a few scheduled tours each day. Wetherill Mesa (and all the sites it services) is open from May through October, weather depending. Far View Center, Far View Terrace, and Far View Lodge are open between April and October. Morefield Campground and the sites nearby are open from mid-April through mid-October (and until early November for limited camping with no services). Specific hours are subject to change, so check with the visitor center upon arrival.

CELL-PHONE RECEPTION AND INTERNET

You can get patchy cell service in the park. Best service is typically at the Morefield Campground area, which is the closest to the neighboring towns of Cortez and Mancos. Public telephones can be found at all the major visitor areas (Morefield, Far View, and Spruce Tree). You can get free Wi-Fi throughout the Far View Lodge and at the Morefield Campground store.

Restaurants

Dining options in Mesa Verde are limited inside the park, but comparatively plentiful and varied if you're staying in Cortez, Mancos, or Durango. In surrounding communities, Southwestern restaurants, farm-fresh eateries, and steak houses are common options.

Hotels

All 150 rooms of the park's Far View Lodge, open mid-April through late October, fill up quickly—so reservations are recommended, especially if you plan to visit on a weekend in summer. Options in the surrounding area include chain hotels, cabins, and bed-and-breakfast inns. Although 40 minutes away, Durango in particular has a number of hotels in fine old buildings reminiscent of the Old West.

Restaurant and hotel reviews have been shortened. For full information, visit Fodors.com. Restaurant prices are the average cost of a main course at dinner or, if dinner is not served, at lunch. Hotel reviews are the lowest cost of a standard double room in high season, excluding taxes and service charges.

What It Costs

	$	$$	$$$	$$$$
RESTAURANTS				
	under $13	$13–$18	$19–$25	over $25
HOTELS				
	under $121	$121–$170	$171–$230	over $230

Tours

BUS TOURS

Aramark Tours

GUIDED TOURS | FAMILY | If you want a well-rounded visit to Mesa Verde's most popular sites, consider a group tour. The park concessionaire provides all-day and half-day guided tours of the Chapin Mesa and Far View sites, departing in buses from either Morefield Campground or Far View Lodge. Tours are led by Aramark guides or park rangers, who share information about the park's history, geology, and excavation processes. Cold water is provided, but you'll need to bring your own snacks. Buy tickets at Far View Lodge, the Morefield Campground, or online. Tours sell out, so reserve in advance. ✉ *Far View Lodge, 1 Navajo Hill, mile marker 15, Mesa Verde National Park* ☎ *970/529–4422 Far View Lodge, 800/449–2288 Aramark* 🌐 *www.*

visitmesaverde.com *From $41* *700 Years Tour closed late Oct.–mid-Apr. Far View Explorer Tour closed mid-Aug.–late May.*

GUIDED TOURS

Ranger-Led Tours

GUIDED TOURS | The cliff dwellings known as Balcony House, Cliff Palace, and Long House can be explored only on ranger-led tours; the first two last about an hour, the third is 90 minutes. Buy tickets at the Mesa Verde Visitor and Research Center. These are active tours and may not be suitable for some children; each requires climbing ladders without handrails and squeezing through tight spaces. Be sure to bring water and sunscreen. Site schedules vary so check ahead. *Mesa Verde National Park* *970/529–4465* *www.nps.gov/meve/planyourvisit/visit-cliffdwelling.htm* *$5 per site* *Closed: Cliff Palace: Oct./Nov.–late May. Balcony House: early Oct.–late Apr. Long House: mid-Oct.–mid-May.*

Visitor Information

PARK CONTACT INFORMATION Mesa Verde National Park. *970/529–4465* *www.nps.gov/meve.*

Morefield

Sights

SCENIC DRIVES

Park Entrance Road

NATIONAL/STATE PARK | The main park road, also known as SH 10, leads you from the entrance off U.S. 160 into the park. As a break from the switchbacks, you can stop at a couple of pretty overlooks along the way, but hold out for Park Point, which, at the mesa's highest elevation (8,572 feet), gives you unobstructed, 360-degree views. Note that trailers and towed vehicles are not permitted beyond Morefield Campground. *Mesa Verde National Park.*

TRAILS

Knife Edge Trail

TRAIL | Perfect for a sunset stroll, this easy 2-mile (round-trip) walk around the north rim of the park leads to an overlook of the Montezuma Valley. If you stop at all the flora identification points that the trail pamphlet suggests, the hike takes about 1½ to 2 hours. The patches of asphalt you spot along the way are leftovers from old Knife Edge Road, built in 1914 as the main entryway into the park. *Easy.* *Mesa Verde National Park* *Trailhead: Morefield Campground, 4 miles from park entrance.*

Prater Ridge Trail

TRAIL | This 7.8-mile round-trip loop, which starts and finishes at Morefield Campground, is the longest hike you can take inside the park. It provides fine views of Morefield Canyon to the south and the San Juan Mountains to the north. About halfway through the hike, you'll see a cutoff trail that you can take, which shortens the trip to 5 miles. *Difficult.* *Mesa Verde National Park* *Trailhead: West end of Morefield Campground, 4 miles from park entrance.*

VISITOR CENTER

Mesa Verde Visitor and Research Center

INFO CENTER | **FAMILY** | The visitor center is the best place to go to sign up for tours, get the information you need to plan a successful trip, and buy tickets for the Cliff Palace, Balcony House, and Long House ranger-led tours. The sleek, energy-efficient research center is filled with more than 3 million artifacts and archives. The center features indoor and outdoor exhibits, a gift shop, picnic tables, and a museum. Find books, maps, and videos on the history of the park. *Park entrance on the left, 35853 Rd H.5, Mancos* *970/529–4465* *www.nps.gov/meve/planyourvisit/meve_vc.htm.*

Restaurants

Knife Edge Cafe
$ | CAFÉ | FAMILY | Located in the Morefield Campground, this simple restaurant in a covered outdoor terrace with picnic tables serves a hearty all-you-can-eat pancake breakfast with sausage every morning. Coffee and beverages are also available. **Known for:** lively gathering spot; breakfast burritos; large coffees with free refills all day. *Average main: $10 ✉ 4 miles south of park entrance, Mesa Verde National Park ☎ 970/565–2133 🌐 www.nps.gov/meve/planyourvisit/restaurants.htm ⏲ Closed mid-Sept.–late Apr.*

Far View

Sights

HISTORIC SITES

Far View Sites Complex
ARCHAEOLOGICAL SITE | FAMILY | This was probably one of the most densely populated areas in Mesa Verde, comprising as many as 50 villages in a ½-square-mile area at the top of Chapin Mesa. Most of the sites here were built between 900 and 1300. Begin the self-guided tour at the interpretive panels in the parking lot, then proceed down a ½-mile, level trail. *✉ Park entrance road, near the Chapin Mesa area, Mesa Verde National Park 🌐 www.nps.gov/meve Free ☞ In winter, access by parking at the gate and walking in.*

TRAILS

Farming Terrace Trail
TRAIL | FAMILY | This 30-minute, ½-mile loop begins and ends on the spur road to Cedar Tree Tower, about 1 mile north of the Chapin Mesa area. It meanders through a series of check dams, which the Ancestral Pueblo built to create farming terraces. *Easy. ✉ Mesa Verde National Park ✣ Trailhead: Park entrance road, 4 miles south of Far View Center.*

Restaurants

Far View Terrace Café
$ | AMERICAN | This full-service cafeteria offers great views, but it's nothing fancy. Grab a simple coffee here or head across the dining room to Mesa Mocha for a latte. **Known for:** beautiful views; lattes; great gift shop. *Average main: $12 ✉ Across from Far View Center, Mesa Verde National Park 🌐 www.visitmesaverde.com/lodging-camping/dining/far-view-terrace-cafe ⏲ Closed late Oct.–mid-Apr.*

Metate Room Restaurant
$$$ | AMERICAN | The park's rugged terrain contrasts with this relaxing space just off the lobby of the Far View Lodge. The well-regarded dining room is upscale, but the atmosphere remains casual. **Known for:** Native American artwork; cheese and cured meats board; great views. *Average main: $25 ✉ Far View Lodge, 1 Navajo Rd., across from Far View Center, 15 miles southwest of park entrance, Mesa Verde National Park ☎ 970/529–4422 🌐 www.visitmesaverde.com/lodging-camping/dining/metate-room-restaurant ⏲ Closed late Oct.–mid-Apr. No lunch.*

Hotels

★ Far View Lodge
$$ | HOTEL | Talk about a view—all rooms have a private balcony, from which you can admire views of the neighboring states of Arizona, Utah, and New Mexico up to 100 miles in the distance. **Pros:** close to the key sites; views are spectacular; small on-site fitness center. **Cons:** simple rooms and amenities, with no TV; walls are thin and less than soundproof; no cell-phone service. *Rooms from: $151 ✉ Across from Far View Center, 1 Navajo Rd., 15 miles southwest of park entrance, Mesa Verde National Park ☎ 800/449–2288 🌐 www.visitmesaverde.com ⏲ Closed late Oct.–mid-Apr. 150 rooms No meals.*

Shopping

Far View Terrace Shop

CLOTHING | In the same building as the Far View Terrace Café, this is the largest gift shop in the park, with gifts, souvenirs, Native American art, toys, and T-shirts galore. ✉ *Mesa Top Loop Rd., 15 miles south of park entrance, Mesa Verde National Park* ☎ *800/449–2288 Aramark.*

Chapin Mesa

Sights

HISTORIC SIGHTS

★ **Balcony House**

ARCHAEOLOGICAL SITE | The stonework of this 40-room cliff dwelling is impressive, but you're likely to be even more awed by the skill it must have taken to reach this place. Perched in a sandstone cove 600 feet above the floor of Soda Canyon, Balcony House seems suspended in space. Even with modern passageways and trails, today's visitors must climb a 32-foot ladder and crawl through a narrow tunnel. Look for the intact balcony for which the house is named. The dwelling is accessible only on a ranger-led tour. ✉ *Cliff Palace/Balcony House Rd., 10 miles south of Far View Center, Cliff Palace Loop, Mesa Verde National Park* 🌐 *www.nps.gov/meve/learn/historyculture/cd_balcony_house.htm* 🎫 *$5* 🕓 *Closed early Oct.–late Apr.*

★ **Cliff Palace**

ARCHAEOLOGICAL SITE | This was the first major Mesa Verde dwelling seen by cowboys Charlie Mason and Richard Wetherill in 1888. It is also the largest, containing about 150 rooms and 23 kivas on three levels. Getting there involves a steep downhill hike and three ladders. ■ **TIP→ You may enter Balcony House or Cliff Palace by ranger-guided tour only so purchase tickets in advance.** The 90-minute, small-group "twilight tours" at sunset present this archaeological treasure with dramatic sunset lighting. Tour tickets are only available in advance at the Visitor and Research Center, Morefield Ranger Station, Durango Welcome Center, and online at 🌐 *www.recreation.gov.* ✉ *Mesa Verde National Park* ✣ *Cliff Palace Overlook, about 2½ miles south of Chapin Mesa Archeological Museum* 🌐 *www.nps.gov/meve/learn/historyculture/cd_cliff_palace.htm* 🎫 *Regular tickets $5; twilight tours $20.* 🕓 *Closed Oct./Nov.–late May; loop closes at sunset.*

Pit Houses and Early Pueblo Villages

ARCHAEOLOGICAL SITE | Three dwellings, built on top of each other from 700 to 950, at first look like a mass of jumbled walls, but an informational panel helps identify the dwellings—and the stories behind them are fascinating. The 325-foot trail from the walking area is paved, wheelchair accessible, and near a restroom. ✉ *Mesa Top Loop Rd., about 2½ miles south of Chapin Mesa Archeological Museum, Mesa Verde National Park* 🎫 *Free.*

Spruce Tree House

ARCHAEOLOGICAL SITE | **FAMILY** | This 138-room complex is the best-preserved site in the park; however, the alcove surrounding Spruce Tree House became unstable in 2015 and was closed to visitors. Until alcove arch support is added, visitors can view but not enter this site. You can still hike down a trail that starts behind the Chapin Mesa Archeological Museum and leads you 100 feet down into the canyon to view the site from a distance. Because of its location in the heart of the Chapin Mesa area, the Spruce Tree House trail and area can resemble a crowded playground during busy periods. When allowed inside the site, tours are self-guided (allow 45 minutes to an hour), but a park ranger is on-site to answer questions. ✉ *Mesa Verde National Park* ✣ *At the Chapin Mesa Archeological Museum, 5 miles south of Far View Center* 🌐 *www.nps.gov/meve/learn/historyculture/*

With about 150 rooms, Cliff Palace is Mesa Verde's largest cliff dwelling; it can be seen on a guided ranger tour.

cd_spruce_tree_house.htm 🎫 *Free* ⏲ *Tours closed for reconstruction.*

Sun Temple

ARCHAEOLOGICAL SITE | Although researchers assume it was probably a ceremonial structure, they're unsure of the exact purpose of this complex, which has no doors or windows in most of its chambers. Because the building was not quite half finished when it was left in 1276, some researchers surmise it might have been constructed to stave off whatever disaster caused its builders—and the other inhabitants of Mesa Verde—to leave. ✉ *Mesa Top Loop Rd., about 2 miles south of Chapin Mesa Archeological Museum, Mesa Verde National Park* 🌐 *www.nps.gov/meve/historyculture/mt_sun_temple.htm* 🎫 *Free.*

SCENIC DRIVES

Mesa Top Loop Road

SCENIC DRIVE | This 6-mile drive skirts the scenic rim of Chapin Mesa and takes you to several overlooks and short, paved trails. You'll get great views of Sun Temple and Square Tower, as well as Cliff Palace, Sunset House, and several other cliff dwellings visible from the Sun Point Overlook. ✉ *Mesa Verde National Park.*

SCENIC STOPS

Cedar Tree Tower

ARCHAEOLOGICAL SITE | A self-guided tour takes you to, but not through, a tower and kiva built between 1100 and 1300 and connected by a tunnel. The tower-and-kiva combinations in the park are thought to have been either religious structures or signal towers. ✉ *Mesa Verde National Park* ✣ *Near the 4-way intersection on Chapin Mesa; park entrance road, 1½ miles north of Chapin Mesa Archeological Museum* 🌐 *www.nps.gov/meve/learn/historyculture/mt_cedar_tree_tower.htm* 🎫 *Free.*

Soda Canyon Overlook

CANYON | Get your best view of Balcony House here. You can also read interpretive panels about the site and the surrounding canyon geology. ✉ *Cliff Palace Loop Rd., about 1 mile north of Balcony House parking area, Mesa Verde National*

Park ☞ Access in winter by walking the Cliff Palace Loop.

TRAILS

★ Petroglyph Point Trail

TRAIL | Scramble along a narrow canyon wall to reach the largest and best-known petroglyphs in Mesa Verde. If you pose for a photo just right, you can manage to block out the gigantic "don't touch" sign next to the rock art. A map—available at any ranger station—points out three dozen points of interest along the trail. However, the trail is not open while Spruce Tree House is closed; check with a ranger for more information. *Moderate.* ✉ *Mesa Verde National Park* ✥ *Trailhead: At Spruce Tree House, next to Chapin Mesa Archeological Museum.*

Soda Canyon Overlook Trail

TRAIL | **FAMILY** | One of the easiest and most rewarding hikes in the park, this little trail travels 1½ miles round-trip through the forest on almost completely level ground. The overlook is an excellent point from which to photograph the Chapin Mesa–area cliff dwellings. *Easy.* ✉ *Mesa Verde National Park* ✥ *Trailhead: Cliff Palace Loop Rd., about 1 mile north of Balcony House parking area* ☞ *Access in winter via Cliff Palace Loop.*

Spruce Canyon Trail

TRAIL | While Petroglyph Point Trail takes you along the side of the canyon, this trail ventures down into its depths. It's only 2.4 miles long, but you descend about 600 feet in elevation. Remember to save your strength; what goes down must come up again. The trail is open even while Spruce Tree House is closed. Still, check with a ranger. *Moderate.* ✉ *Mesa Verde National Park* ✥ *Trailhead: At Spruce Tree House, next to Chapin Mesa Archeological Museum* ☞ *Registration required at trailhead.*

VISITOR CENTER

Chapin Mesa Archeological Museum

MUSEUM | This is an excellent first stop for an introduction to Ancestral Pueblo culture, as well as the area's development into a national park. Exhibits showcase original textiles and other artifacts, and a theater plays an informative film every 30 minutes. Rangers are available to answer your questions. The shop focuses on educational materials, but you can also find park-themed souvenirs. The museum sits at the south end of the park entrance road and overlooks Spruce Tree House. Nearby, you'll find park headquarters, a gift shop, a post office, snack bar, and bathrooms. ✉ *Park entrance road, 5 miles south of Far View Center, 20 miles from park entrance, Mesa Verde National Park* ☎ *970/529–4465 General information line* 🌐 *www.nps.gov/meve/planyourvisit/museum.htm* 🎟 *Free.*

Restaurants

Spruce Tree Terrace Café

$ | **AMERICAN** | This small cafeteria has a limited selection of hot food, coffee, salads, burgers, and sandwiches. The patio is pleasant, and it's conveniently located across the street from the museum. **Known for:** Southwest specialties; soup of the day specials; Navajo tacos. $ *Average main: $10* ✉ *Near Chapin Mesa Archeological Museum, 5 miles south of the Far View Center, Mesa Verde National Park* ☎ *970/529–4465* 🌐 *www.visitmesaverde.com/lodging-camping/dining/spruce-tree-terrace-cafe* ⏲ *No dinner in off-season.*

Shopping

Chapin Mesa Archeological Museum Shop

BOOKS/STATIONERY | Books and videos are the primary offering here, with more than 400 titles on Ancestral Pueblo and Southwestern topics. You can also find a selection of touristy T-shirts and hats. Hours vary throughout the year. ✉ *Spruce Tree Terrace, near Chapin Mesa Archeological Museum, Mesa Verde National Park* ✥ *5 miles from Far View Center* ☎ *970/529–4445* 🌐 *www.nps.gov/meve/planyourvisit/museum.htm.*

Wetherill Mesa

HISTORIC SIGHTS

Badger House Community

ARCHAEOLOGICAL SITE | A self-guided walk along paved and gravel trails takes you through a group of four mesa-top dwellings. The community, which covers nearly 7 acres, dates back to the year 650, the Basketmaker Period, and includes a primitive, semisubterranean pit house and what's left of a multistory stone pueblo. Allow about 45 minutes to see the sites. The trail is 2.4 miles round-trip. ✉ *Wetherill Mesa Rd., 12 miles from Far View Center, Mesa Verde National Park* 🌐 *www.nps.gov/meve/historyculture/mt_badger_house.htm* 🎫 *Free* ⏲ *Closed late Oct.–early May; road closes at 6 pm.*

Long House

ARCHAEOLOGICAL SITE | This Wetherill Mesa cliff dwelling is the second largest in Mesa Verde. It is believed that about 150 people lived in Long House, so named because of the size of its cliff alcove. The spring at the back of the cave is still active today. The in-depth, ranger-led tour begins a short distance from the parking lot and takes about 90 minutes. You hike about 2 miles, including two 15-foot ladders. ✉ *On Wetherill Mesa, 29 miles past the visitor center, near mile marker 15, Mesa Verde National Park* 🌐 *www.nps.gov/meve/learn/historyculture/cd_long_house.htm* 🎫 *Tours $5* ⏲ *Closed mid-Oct.–mid-May.*

Step House

ARCHAEOLOGICAL SITE | So named because of a crumbling prehistoric stairway leading up from the dwelling, Step House is reached via a paved (but steep) trail that's ¾ mile long. The house is unique in that it shows clear evidence of two separate occupations: the first around 626, the second a full 600 years later. The self-guided tour takes about 45 minutes. ✉ *Wetherill Mesa Rd., 12 miles from Far View Center, Mesa Verde National Park* 🌐 *www.nps.gov/meve/historyculture/cd_step_house.htm* 🎫 *Free* ⏲ *Closed mid-May–mid-Oct.; hrs vary seasonally.*

SCENIC DRIVES

Wetherill Mesa Road

SCENIC DRIVE | This 12-mile mountain road, stretching from the Far View Center to the Wetherill Mesa, has sharp curves and steep grades (and is restricted to vehicles less than 25 feet long and 8,000 pounds). Roadside pull-outs offer unobstructed views of the Four Corners region. At the end of the road, you can access Step House, Long House, and Badger House. ✉ *Mesa Verde National Park* ⏲ *Closed late Oct.–early May.*

SCENIC STOPS

Kodak House Overlook

VIEWPOINT | Get an impressive view into the 60-room Kodak House and its several small kivas from here. The house, closed to the public, was named for a Swedish researcher who absentmindedly left his Kodak camera behind here in 1891. ✉ *Wetherill Mesa Rd., Mesa Verde National Park* 🌐 *www.nps.gov/meve* ⏲ *Closed late Oct.–May.*

Coffee and Quick Bites

Wetherill Mesa Snack Bar

$ | AMERICAN | There's little on offer here, just chips, soft drinks, and concessions served on picnic tables under an awning, but it's the only choice on Wetherill Mesa. 💲 *Average main: $7* ✉ *12 miles southwest of the park entrance, Mesa Verde National Park* ☎ *970/529–4465* 🌐 *www.nps.gov/meve* 💳 *No credit cards* ⏲ *Closed Sept.–May.*

Activities

At Mesa Verde, outdoor activities are restricted, due to the fragile nature of the archaeological treasures here. Hiking (allowed on marked trails only) is the best option, especially as a way to view some of the Ancestral Pueblo dwellings.

BIRD-WATCHING

Turkey vultures soar between April and October, and large flocks of ravens hang around all summer. Among the park's other large birds are red-tailed hawks, great horned owls, and a few golden eagles. The Steller's jay (the male looks like a blue jay with a dark hat on) frequently pierces the pinyon-juniper forest with its cries, and hummingbirds dart from flower to flower in the summer and fall. Any visit to cliff dwellings late in the day will include frolicking white-throated swifts, which make their home in rock crevices overhead.

Pick up a copy of the park's "Checklist of the Birds" brochure or visit the National Park Service's website (🌐 *www.nps.gov/meve/planyourvisit/birdwatching.htm*) for a detailed listing of the feathered inhabitants here.

CAMPING

Morefield Campground is the only option within the park, and it's an excellent one. Reservations are accepted; it's open mid-April through mid-October, and through early November with no services. In nearby Mancos, just across the highway from the park entrance, there's a campground with full amenities (but no electrical hookups), while the San Juan National Forest offers backcountry camping.

Morefield Campground and Village. With 267 campsites, including 15 full-hookup RV sites, access to trailheads, a pet kennel, and plenty of amenities (including a gas station and a grocery store), the only campground in the park is an appealing mini-city for campers. It's a 40-minute drive to reach the park's most popular sites. Reservations are recommended, especially for RVs. ✉ *4 miles south of park entrance* ☎ *970/564–4300, 800/449–2288* 🌐 *www.visitmesaverde.com.*

EDUCATIONAL PROGRAMS

RANGER PROGRAMS

Evening Ranger Campfire Program

TOUR—SIGHT | FAMILY | Every night in summer at the Morefield Campground Amphitheater, park rangers present a different 45- to 60-minute program on topics such as stargazing, history, wildlife, and archaeology. ✉ *Morefield Campground Amphitheater, 4 miles south of park entrance, Mesa Verde National Park* ☎ *970/529–4465* 🎫 *Free* ⏲ *Closed early Sept.–late May.*

Junior Ranger Program

TOUR—SIGHT | FAMILY | Children ages 4 through 12 can earn a certificate and badge for successfully completing at least three activities in the park's Junior Ranger booklet (available at the park or online). ✉ *Mesa Verde Visitor and Research Center or Chapin Mesa Archeological Museum, Mesa Verde National Park* ☎ *970/529–4465* 🌐 *www.nps.gov/meve/forkids/beajuniorranger.htm.*

HIKING

A handful of trails lead beyond Mesa Verde's most visited sites and offer more solitude than the often-crowded cliff dwellings. The best canyon vistas can be reached if you're willing to huff and puff your way through elevation changes and switchbacks. Carry more water than you think you'll need, wear sunscreen, and bring rain gear—cloudbursts can come seemingly out of nowhere. Certain trails are open seasonally, so check with a ranger before heading out. No backcountry hiking is permitted in Mesa Verde, and pets are prohibited.

STARGAZING

There are no large cities in the Four Corners area, so there is little artificial light to detract from the stars in the night sky. Far View Lodge and Morefield Campground are great for sky watching.

What's Nearby

A onetime market center for cattle and crops, **Cortez,** 11 miles west of the park, is now the largest gateway town to Mesa Verde and a base for tourists visiting the Four Corners region. You can still see a rodeo here at least once a year. **Dolores,** steeped in a rich railroad history, is on the Dolores River, 19 miles north of Mesa Verde. Near both the San Juan National Forest and McPhee Reservoir, Dolores is a favorite of outdoor enthusiasts. East of Mesa Verde by 36 miles, **Durango,** the region's main hub, comes complete with a variety of restaurants and hotels, shopping, and outdoor-equipment shops. Durango became a town in 1881 when the Denver and Rio Grande Railroad pushed its tracks across the neighboring San Juan Mountains.

Chapter 44

MOUNT RAINIER NATIONAL PARK

Updated by
Shelley Arenas

Camping ★★★★★ | Hotels ★★★☆☆ | Activities ★★★★☆ | Scenery ★★★★★ | Crowds ★★★☆☆

WELCOME TO MOUNT RAINIER NATIONAL PARK

TOP REASONS TO GO

★ **The mountain:** Some say Mt. Rainier is the most magical mountain in America. At 14,411 feet, it is a popular peak for climbing, with more than 10,000 attempts per year—nearly half of which are successful.

★ **The glaciers:** About 35 square miles of glaciers and snowfields encircle Mt. Rainier, including Carbon Glacier and Emmons Glacier, the largest glaciers by volume and area, respectively, in the continental United States.

★ **The wildflowers:** More than 100 species of wildflowers bloom in the park's high meadows; the display dazzles from midsummer until the snow flies.

★ **Fabulous hiking:** More than 240 miles of maintained trails provide access to old-growth forest, river valleys, lakes, and rugged ridges.

★ **Unencumbered wilderness:** Under the provisions of the 1964 Wilderness Act and the National Wilderness Preservation System, 97% of the park is preserved as wilderness.

1 **Longmire.** Inside the Nisqually Gate explore Longmire historic district's museum and visitor center, ruins of the park's first hotel.

2 **Paradise.** The park's most popular destination is famous for wildflowers in summer and skiing in winter.

3 **Ohanapecosh.** Closest to the southeast entrance and the town of Packwood, the giant old-growth trees of the Grove of the Patriarchs are a must-see.

4 **Sunrise and White River.** Sunrise is the highest stretch of road in the park and a great place to take in the alpenglow—reddish light on the peak of the mountain near sunrise and sunset. Mt. Rainier's premier mountain-biking area, White River, is also the gateway to more than a dozen hiking trails.

5 **Carbon River and Mowich Lake.** Near the Carbon River Entrance Station is a swath of temperate forest, but to really get away from it all, follow the windy gravel roads to remote Mowich Lake.

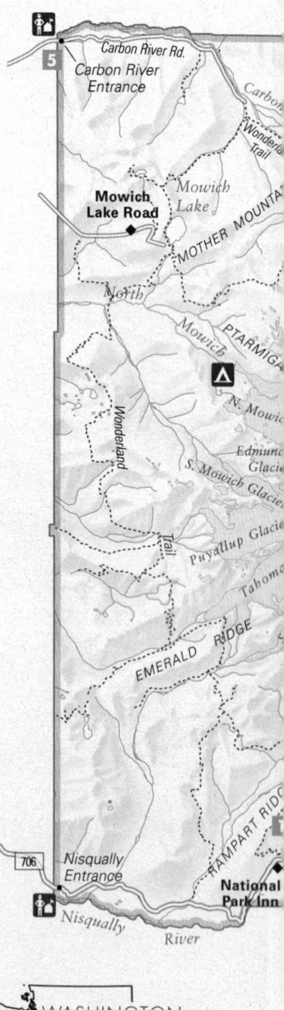

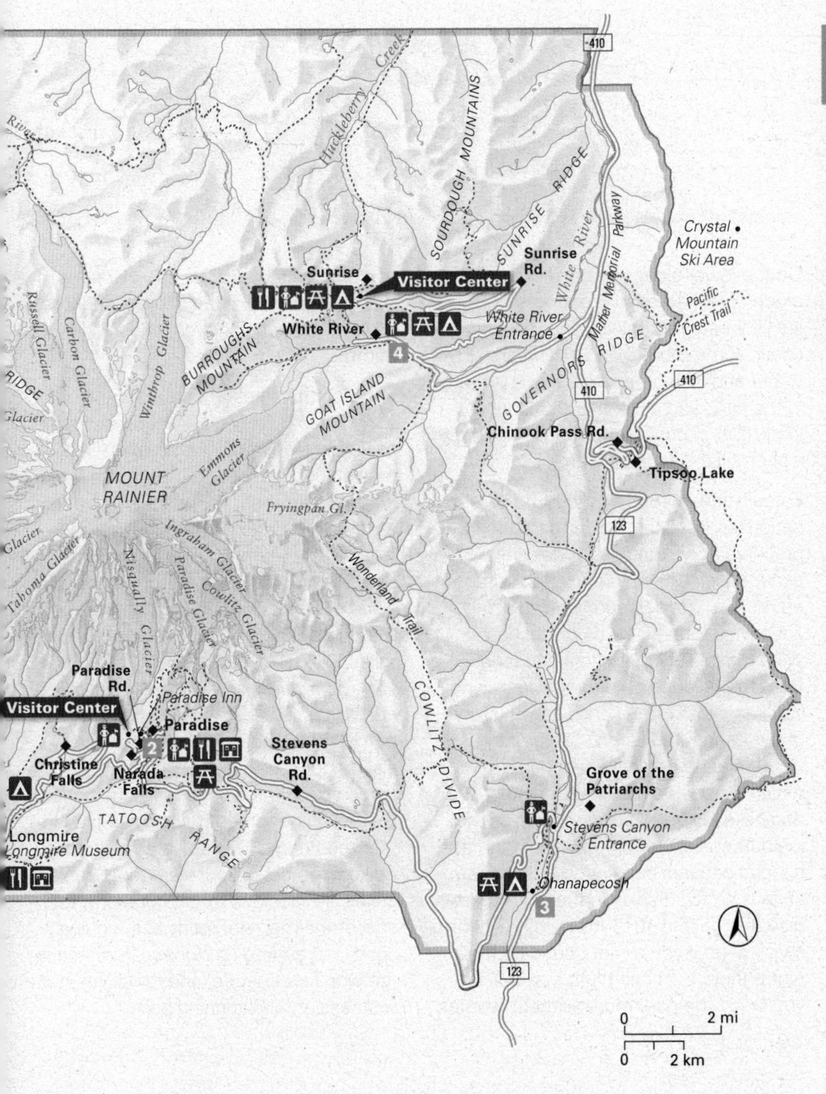

410
Huckleberry Creek
River
SOURDOUGH MOUNTAINS
SUNRISE RIDGE
White River
Mather Memorial Parkway
Crystal Mountain Ski Area
Sunrise
Visitor Center
Sunrise Rd.
Pacific Crest Trail
White River
White River Entrance
4
RIDGE
410
410
GOVERNORS
Russell Glacier
Carbon Glacier
Winthrop Glacier
BURROUGHS MOUNTAIN
GOAT ISLAND MOUNTAIN
RIDGE
Glacier
Chinook Pass Rd.
Tipsoo Lake
Emmons Glacier
MOUNT RAINIER
Fryingpan Gl.
123
Glacier
Tahoma Glacier
Nisqually Glacier
Paradise Glacier
Ingraham Glacier
Cowlitz Glacier
Wonderland Trail
Paradise Rd.
Paradise Inn
Visitor Center
Paradise
2
COWLITZ DIVIDE
Christine Falls
Narada Falls
Stevens Canyon Rd.
Grove of the Patriarchs
TATOOSH RANGE
Stevens Canyon Entrance
Longmire
Longmire Museum
Ohanapecosh
3
123
0
2 mi
0
2 km

Mt. Rainier is the centerpiece of its namesake park. The impressive volcanic peak stands at an elevation of 14,411 feet, making it the fifth-highest peak in the lower 48 states. More than 2 million visitors a year enjoy spectacular views of the mountain and return home with a lifelong memory of its image.

On the lower slopes you find silent forests made up of cathedral-like groves of Douglas fir, western hemlock, and western red cedar, some more than 1,000 years old. Water and lush greenery are everywhere in the park, and dozens of thundering waterfalls, accessible from the road or by a short hike, fill the air with mist.

Established in 1899, it's the fifth-oldest national park in the U.S., created to preserve opportunities for generations to experience nature's beauty and outdoor recreation. Conservationists including John Muir lobbied for its protection as wilderness, saving its flora and fauna from the ravages of logging and mining. You can explore the park's early history in the Longmire Historic District, the location of its original headquarters, which includes a museum in one of the original early 1900 buildings and an inn in another. Farther up the mountain, the historic national park lodge architecture style is on full display in the iconic Paradise Inn, built in 1917. It's definitely worth a visit even if you're not spending the night, though an overnight stay will let you enjoy the park more without worries of traffic or parking. The Paradise area is the park's most visited and parking lots often fill up early on weekends and in the summer.

As the fifth highest mountain in the contiguous U.S., Mt. Rainier is renowned as a premier climbing destination—more than 10,000 people attempt to reach the summit every year. Climbers are strongly encouraged to go with a guide service for at least their first climb, and mountain safety practices are important for all visitors to follow when exploring the park. And there is a lot to explore—369 square miles, 275 trails, 120 miles of roads, and 97% designated as wilderness. Stopping at a visitor center is highly recommended, both to learn more about the park and also to get helpful advice and information on current road and trail conditions. Guided ranger programs and self-guided "Citizen Ranger Quests" are fun ways to make the most of your visit, too. Scenic drives are fabulous for photography, for spur-of-the-moment stops at intriguing spots and getting up close to immerse in the wonder of nature, and for taking in the vastness of this stunning park.

AVERAGE HIGH/LOW TEMPERATURES					
JAN.	**FEB.**	**MAR.**	**APR.**	**MAY**	**JUNE**
36/24	40/26	44/28	53/32	62/37	66/43
JULY	**AUG.**	**SEPT.**	**OCT.**	**NOV.**	**DEC.**
75/47	74/47	68/43	57/38	45/31	39/28

Planning

When to Go

Rainier is the Puget Sound's weather vane: if you can see it, skies will be clear. Visitors are most likely to see the summit July through September. Crowds are heaviest in summer, too, meaning the parking lots at Paradise and Sunrise often fill before noon, campsites are reserved months in advance, and other lodgings are reserved as much as a year ahead.

True to its name, Paradise is often sunny during periods when the lowlands are under a cloud layer. The rest of the year, Rainier's summit gathers flying-saucer-like lenticular clouds whenever a Pacific storm approaches; once the peak vanishes from view, it's time to haul out rain gear. The rare periods of clear winter weather bring residents up to Paradise for cross-country skiing.

Getting Here and Around

AIR

Seattle–Tacoma International Airport, 15 miles south of downtown Seattle, is the nearest airport to the national park.

CAR

The Nisqually entrance is on Highway 706, 14 miles east of Route 7; the Ohanapecosh entrance is on Route 123, 5 miles north of U.S. 12; and the White River entrance is on Route 410, 3 miles north of the Chinook and Cayuse passes. These highways become mountain roads as they reach Rainier, winding up and down many steep slopes, so cautious driving is essential: use a lower gear, especially on downhill sections, and take care not to overheat brakes by constant use. These roads are subject to storms any time of year and are repaired in the summer from winter damage and washouts.

Side roads into the park's western slope are narrower, unpaved, and subject to flooding and washouts. All are closed by snow in winter except Highway 706 to Paradise and Carbon River Road, though the latter tends to flood near the park boundary. (Route 410 is open to the Crystal Mountain access road entrance.)

Park roads have a maximum speed of 35 mph in most places, and you have to watch for pedestrians, cyclists, and wildlife. Parking can be difficult during peak summer season, especially at Paradise, Sunrise, Grove of the Patriarchs, and at the trailheads between Longmire and Paradise; arrive early if you plan to visit these sites. All off-road-vehicle use—4X4 vehicles, ATVs, motorcycles, snowmobiles—is prohibited in Mount Rainier National Park.

Inspiration

The Ledge: An Adventure Story of Friendship and Survival on Mount Rainier, by Jim Davidson, details the ill-fated trip of two friends.

Road to Rainier Scenic Byway, by Donald M. Johnstone and the South Pierce County Historical Society and part of the Images of America Series, documents how a Native American trail became a modern scenic route. *The Road to Paradise,* by Karen Barnett, is a romance novel set in 1927 that tells the tale of a young woman who follows her naturalist inclinations to start a new life in Mt. Rainier during the early days of the National Park Service.

Tahoma and Its People: A Natural History of Mount Rainier National Park, by Jeff Antonelis-Lapp, focuses on the park's nature and environment from the perspectives of Native Americans, park rangers, archaeologists, and others.

Park Essentials

ACCESSIBILITY

The only trail in the park that is fully accessible to those with impaired mobility is Kautz Creek Trail, a ½-mile boardwalk that leads to a splendid view of the mountain. Parts of the Trail of the Shadows at Longmire and the Grove of the Patriarchs at Ohanapecosh are also accessible. Campgrounds at Cougar Rock and Ohanapecosh have several accessible sites. All main visitor centers, as well as National Park Inn at Longmire, are accessible. Wheelchairs are available at the Jackson Visitor Center for guests to use in the center.

PARK FEES AND PERMITS

The entrance fee of $30 per vehicle and $15 for those on foot, motorcycle, or bicycle is good for seven days. Annual passes are $55. Climbing permits are $51 per person per climb or glacier trek. Wilderness camping permits must be obtained for all backcountry trips, and advance reservations are highly recommended.

PARK HOURS

Mount Rainier National Park is open 24/7 year-round, but with limited access in winter. Gates at Nisqually (Longmire) are staffed year-round during the day; facilities at Paradise are open daily from late May to mid-October; and Sunrise is open daily July to early September. During off-hours you can buy passes at the gates from machines that accept credit and debit cards. Winter access to the park is limited to the Nisqually entrance, and the Jackson Memorial Visitor Center at Paradise is open on weekends and holidays in winter. The Paradise snowplay area is open when there is sufficient snow.

CELL PHONE RECEPTION

Cell phone reception is unreliable throughout much of the park, although access is clear at Paradise, Sunrise, and Crystal Mountain. Public telephones are at all park visitor centers, at the National Park Inn at Longmire, and at Paradise Inn at Paradise.

Hotels

The Mt. Rainier area is remarkably bereft of quality lodging. Rainier's two national park lodges, at Longmire and Paradise, are attractive and well maintained. They exude considerable history and charm, especially Paradise Inn, but unless you've made summer reservations a year in advance, getting a room can be a challenge. Dozens of motels, cabin complexes, and private vacation-home rentals are near the park entrances; while they can be pricey, the latter are convenient for longer stays. *Hotel reviews have been shortened. For full information, visit Fodors.com.*

Restaurants

A limited number of restaurants are inside the park, and a few worth checking out lie beyond its borders. Mt. Rainier's picnic areas are justly famous, especially in summer, when wildflowers fill the meadows. Resist the urge to feed the yellow pine chipmunks darting about. *Restaurant reviews have been shortened. For full information, visit Fodors.com.*

Park picnic areas are usually open only from late May through September.

What It Costs

$	$$	$$$	$$$$
RESTAURANTS			
under $16	$16–$22	$23–$30	over $30
HOTELS			
under $150	$150–$200	$201–$250	over $250

Visitor Information

PARK CONTACT INFORMATION Mount Rainier National Park. ✉ *55210 238th Ave. East, Ashford* ☎ *360/569–2211, 360/569–6575* 🌐 *www.nps.gov/mora.*

Longmire

12 miles east of Ashford via Hwy. 706; 6 miles east of Nisqually Entrance.

Established in 1899 as the original park headquarters, this area is designated a national historic district. One of its first buildings (from 1916) is now a museum, and the circa-1917 National Park Inn is open year-round with basic accommodations, dining, and winter recreation equipment rentals.

Sights

HISTORIC SITES

National Park Inn

BUILDING | Even if you don't plan to stay overnight, you can stop by year-round to view the architecture of this inn, built in 1917 and on the National Register of Historic Places. While you're here, relax in front of the fireplace in the lounge, stop at the gift shop, or dine at the restaurant. ✉ *Longmire Visitor Complex, Hwy. 706, 10 miles east of Nisqually entrance, Longmire* ☎ *360/569–2411* 🌐 *www.mtrainierguestservices.com/accommodations/national-park-inn.*

TRAILS

Trail of the Shadows

TRAIL | This ¾-mile loop is notable for its glimpses of meadowland ecology, its colorful soda springs (don't drink the water), James Longmire's old homestead cabin, and the foundation of the old Longmire Springs Hotel, which was destroyed by fire around 1900. *Easy.* ✉ *Mt. Rainier National Park* ✣ *Trailhead: At Hwy. 706, 10 miles east of Nisqually entrance* 🌐 *www.nps.gov/mora/planyourvisit/day-hiking-at-mount-rainier.htm.*

VISITOR CENTERS

Longmire Museum and Visitor Center

INFO CENTER | Glass cases inside this museum preserve the park's plants and animals, including a stuffed cougar. Historical photographs and geographical displays provide a worthwhile overview of the park's history. The adjacent visitor center has some perfunctory exhibits on the surrounding forest and its inhabitants, as well as pamphlets and information about park activities. ✉ *Hwy. 706, 10 miles east of Ashford, Longmire* ☎ *360/569–6575* 🌐 *www.nps.gov/mora/planyourvisit/longmire.htm.*

Restaurants

National Park Inn Dining Room

$$$ | **AMERICAN** | Photos of Mt. Rainier taken by top photographers adorn the walls of this inn's large dining room, a bonus on the many days the mountain refuses to show itself. Meals are simple but tasty: flat iron steak, bison meat loaf, rosemary grilled salmon, and blackberry cobbler à la mode. **Known for:** only restaurant open year-round in the park; hearty breakfast options; nice dessert choices. $ *Average main: $25* ✉ *Hwy. 706, Longmire* ☎ *360/569–2411* 🌐 *www.mtrainierguestservices.com.*

Hotels

National Park Inn

$$$ | B&B/INN | A large stone fireplace warms the common room of this country inn, the only one of the park's two inns that's open year-round, while rustic details such as wrought-iron lamps and antique bentwood headboards adorn the small rooms. **Pros:** classic national park lodge ambience; on-site restaurant with simple American fare; winter packages with perks like breakfast and free snowshoe use. **Cons:** jam-packed in summer; must book far in advance; some rooms have a shared bath. *Rooms from: $224* ✉ *Longmire Visitor Complex, Hwy. 706, 6 miles east of Nisqually entrance, Longmire* ☎ *360/569–2275, 855/755–2275* 🌐 *www.mtrainierguestservices.com* *43 rooms* *No meals.*

Paradise

11 miles northeast of Longmire, 18 miles from Nisqually Entrance.

The most popular area of the park has something for everyone—an impressive and informative visitor center with guided ranger programs, wildflower-filled meadows, trails that range from easy nature walks to steep hikes, and a historic national park lodge for dining and overnighting in the park. In winter there's a snowplay area open when there's enough snow; patches of snow sometimes linger well into summer.

Sights

SCENIC DRIVES

Paradise Road

SCENIC DRIVE | This 9-mile stretch of Highway 706 winds its way up the mountain's southwest flank from Longmire to Paradise, taking you from lowland forest to the ever-expanding vistas of the mountain above. Visit early on a weekday if possible, especially in peak summer months, when the road is packed with cars. The route is open year-round, though there may be some weekday closures in winter. From November through April, all vehicles must carry chains. ✉ *Mt. Rainier National Park* 🌐 *www.nps.gov/mora/planyourvisit/paradise.htm.*

SCENIC STOPS

Christine Falls

BODY OF WATER | These two-tiered falls were named in honor of Christine Louise Van Trump, who climbed to the 10,000-foot level on Mt. Rainier in 1889 at the age of nine, despite having a crippling nervous-system disorder. ✉ *Mt. Rainier National Park* ✣ *4 miles north of Longmire via Paradise Valley Road, about 2½ miles east of Cougar Rock Campground* 🌐 *www.nps.gov/mora/learn/nature/waterfalls.htm.*

Narada Falls

BODY OF WATER | A steep but short trail leads to the viewing area for these spectacular 168-foot falls, which expand to a width of 75 feet during peak flow times. In winter the frozen falls are popular with ice climbers. ✉ *Paradise Valley Rd., Mt. Rainier National Park* ✣ *1 mile west of turnoff for Paradise, 6 miles east of Cougar Rock Campground* 🌐 *www.nps.gov/mora/planyourvisit/longmire.htm.*

TRAILS

Nisqually Vista Trail

TRAIL | Equally popular in summer and winter, this trail is a 1¼-mile round-trip through subalpine meadows to an overlook point for Nisqually Glacier. The gradually sloping path is a favorite venue for cross-country skiers in winter; in summer, listen for the shrill alarm calls of the area's marmots. *Easy.* ✉ *Mt. Rainier National Park* ✣ *Trailhead: At Jackson Memorial Visitor Center, Rte. 123, 1 mile north of Ohanapecosh, at high point of Hwy. 706* 🌐 *www.nps.gov/mora/planyourvisit/day-hiking-at-mount-rainier.htm.*

★ Skyline Trail

TRAIL | This 5-mile loop, one of the highest trails in the park, beckons day-trippers with a vista of alpine ridges and, in summer, meadows filled with brilliant flowers and birds. At 6,800 feet, Panorama Point, the spine of the Cascade Range, spreads away to the east, and Nisqually Glacier tumbles downslope. *Moderate.* ✉ *Mt. Rainier National Park* ✥ *Trailhead: Jackson Memorial Visitor Center, Rte. 123, 1 mile north of Ohanapecosh at high point of Hwy. 706* 🌐 *www.nps.gov/mora/planyourvisit/skyline-trail.htm.*

Van Trump Park Trail

TRAIL | You gain an exhilarating 2,200 feet on this route while hiking through a vast expanse of meadow with views of the southern Puget Sound and Mt. Adams and Mt. St. Helens. On the way up is one of the highest waterfalls in the park, Comet Falls. The 5¾-mile track provides good footing, and the average hiker can make it up and back in five hours. *Moderate.* ✉ *Mt. Rainier National Park* ✥ *Trailhead: Hwy. 706 at Christine Falls, 4½ miles east of Longmire* 🌐 *www.nps.gov/mora/planyourvisit/comet-falls-van-trump-park-trail.htm.*

VISITOR CENTER

Jackson Memorial Visitor Center

INFO CENTER | High on the mountain's southern flank, this center houses exhibits on geology, mountaineering, glaciology, and alpine ecology. Multimedia programs are staged in the theater; there's also a snack bar and gift shop. This is the park's most popular visitor destination, and it can be quite crowded in summer. ✉ *Hwy. 706 E, 19 miles east of Nisqually park entrance, Mt. Rainier National Park* ☎ *360/569–6571* 🌐 *www.nps.gov/mora/planyourvisit/paradise.htm* ⏲ *Closed weekdays mid-Oct.–Apr.*

Restaurants

Paradise Camp Deli

$ | AMERICAN | Grilled meats, sandwiches, salads, and soft drinks are served daily from May through early October and on weekends and holidays the rest of the year. **Known for:** a quick bite to eat; family-friendly cuisine; mountain-size deli sandwiches. $ *Average main: $10* ✉ *Jackson Visitor Center, Paradise Rd. E, Paradise* ☎ *360/569–6571 visitor center, 855/755–2275 guest services* 🌐 *www.mtrainierguestservices.com* ⏲ *Closed weekdays early Oct.–Apr.*

Paradise Inn Dining Room

$$$ | AMERICAN | Tall windows in this historic timber lodge provide terrific views of Rainier, and the warm glow of native wood permeates the large dining room, where hearty Pacific Northwest fare is served. Sunday brunch is legendary and served during the summer months; on other days and during the shoulder season there's a breakfast buffet. **Known for:** locally sourced ingredients; warm liquor drinks; great Sunday brunch. $ *Average main: $27* ✉ *E. Paradise Rd., near Jackson Visitor Center, Paradise* ☎ *360/569–2275, 855/755–2275* 🌐 *www.mtrainierguestservices.com* ⏲ *Closed Oct.–mid-May.*

Hotels

★ Paradise Inn

$$$ | HOTEL | With its hand-carved Alaskan cedar logs, burnished parquet floors, stone fireplaces, and glorious mountain views, this 1917 inn is a classic example of a national park lodge. **Pros:** central to trails; pristine vistas; nature-inspired details. **Cons:** rooms are small and basic; many rooms have shared bathrooms; no elevators, air-conditioning, cell service, TV, or Wi-Fi. $ *Rooms from: $226* ✉ *E. Paradise Rd., near Jackson Visitor Center, Paradise* ☎ *360/569–2275, 855/755–2275* 🌐 *www.mtrainierguestservices.com* ⏲ *Closed mid-Oct.–mid-May* 🛏 *121 rooms* 🍴 *No meals.*

Ohanapecosh

12 miles north of Packwood, via Hwy. 123, 3 miles north of park boundary, 42 miles east of the park's Nisqually Entrance.

The Ohanapecosh River runs through this old-growth forest area in the southeastern corner of the park. It's less crowded than the Paradise and Longmire areas, so it can be a good option to visit when their parking lots fill up. The Grove of the Patriarchs is a must-see. The area is not accessible by vehicle in winter.

Sights

SCENIC DRIVES

Route 123 and Stevens Canyon Road

SCENIC DRIVE | At Chinook Pass you can pick up Route 123 and head south to its junction with Stevens Canyon Road. Take this road west to its junction with the Paradise–Nisqually entrance road, which runs west through Longmire and exits the park at Nisqually. The route winds among valley-floor rain forest and uphill slopes; vistas of Puget Sound and the Cascade Range appear at numerous points along the way. ✉ *Mt. Rainier National Park.*

SCENIC STOPS

★ Grove of the Patriarchs

TRAIL | Protected from the periodic fires that sweep through the surrounding areas, this small island of 1,000-year-old trees is one of Mount Rainier National Park's most memorable features. A 1½-mile loop trail heads through the old-growth forest of Douglas fir, cedar, and hemlock. ✉ *Rte. 123, west of the Stevens Canyon entrance, Mt. Rainier National Park* 🌐 *www.nps.gov/mora/planyourvisit/ohanapecosh.htm.*

VISITOR CENTER

Ohanapecosh Visitor Center

INFO CENTER | Learn about the region's dense old-growth forests through interpretive displays and videos at this visitor center, near the Grove of the Patriarchs. ✉ *Rte. 123, 11 miles north of Packwood, Mt. Rainier National Park* ☎ *360/569–6581* 🌐 *www.nps.gov/mora/planyourvisit/ohanapecosh.htm* ⏲ *Closed mid-Oct.–May.*

Sunrise and White River

17 miles from Ohanapecosh to the Sunrise/White River Road cutoff from Hwy. 410, 14 miles from Crystal Mountain.

This area on the northeast side of the park has a short season (generally open only July–September) yet is the second most popular part of the park. Visitors come especially for the stunning views and the thrill of being at the highest drivable point in the park, as well as access to trails and stops along Chinook Pass (Hwy. 410). Intrepid trekkers on the Wonderland Trail can start or end their 93-mile journey around the mountain here.

Sights

SCENIC DRIVES

Chinook Pass Road

SCENIC DRIVE | Route 410, the highway to Yakima, follows the eastern edge of the park to Chinook Pass, where it climbs the steep 5,432-foot pass via a series of switchbacks. At its top, take in broad views of Rainier and the east slope of the Cascades. The pass usually closes for the winter in November and reopens by late May. During that time, it's not possible to drive a loop around the park. ✉ *Mt. Rainier National Park* 🌐 *www.wsdot.wa.gov/traffic/passes/chinook-cayuse.*

Sunrise Road

SCENIC DRIVE | This popular (and often crowded) scenic road to the highest drivable point at Mt. Rainier carves its way 11 miles up Sunrise Ridge from the White River Valley on the northeast side of the park. As you top the ridge, there are sweeping views of the surrounding lowlands. The road is usually open July through September. ✉ *Mt. Rainier National Park* 🌐 *www.nps.gov/mora/planyourvisit/sunrise.htm* ⏲ *Usually closed Oct.–June.*

SCENIC STOPS

Tipsoo Lake

BODY OF WATER | FAMILY | The short, pleasant trail that circles the lake—ideal for families—provides breathtaking views. Enjoy the subalpine wildflower meadows during the summer months; in late summer to early fall there is an abundant supply of huckleberries. ✉ *Mt. Rainier National Park* ✥ *Off Cayuse Pass east on Hwy. 410* 🌐 *www.nps.gov/mora/planyourvisit/sunrise.htm.*

TRAILS

Sunrise Nature Trail

TRAIL | The 1½-mile-long loop of this self-guided trail takes you through the delicate subalpine meadows near the Sunrise Visitor Center. A gradual climb to the ridgetop yields magnificent views of Mt. Rainier and the more distant volcanic cones of Mt. Baker, Mt. Adams, and Glacier Peak. *Easy.* ✉ *Mt. Rainier National Park* ✥ *Trailhead: At Sunrise Visitor Center, Sunrise Rd., 15 miles from White River park entrance* 🌐 *www.nps.gov/mora/planyourvisit/sunrise.htm.*

★ Wonderland Trail

TRAIL | All other Mt. Rainier hikes pale in comparison to this stunning 93-mile trek, which completely encircles the mountain. The trail passes through all the major life zones of the park, from the old-growth forests of the lowlands to the alpine meadows and goat-haunted glaciers of the highlands—pick up a mountain-goat sighting card from a ranger station or visitor center if you want to help in the park's effort to learn more about these elusive animals. Wonderland is a rugged trail; elevation gains and losses totaling 3,500 feet are common in a day's hike, which averages 8 miles. Most hikers start out from Longmire or Sunrise and take 10–14 days to cover the 93-mile route. Snow lingers on the high passes well into June (sometimes July); count on rain any time of the year. Campsites are wilderness areas with pit toilets and water that must be purified before drinking. Only hardy, well-equipped, and experienced wilderness trekkers should attempt this trip, but those who do will be amply rewarded. Wilderness permits are required, and reservations are strongly recommended. *Difficult.* ✉ *Mt. Rainier National Park* ✥ *Trailheads: Longmire Visitor Center, Hwy. 706, 17 miles east of Ashford; Sunrise Visitor Center, Sunrise Rd., 15 miles west of White River park entrance* 🌐 *www.nps.gov/mora/planyourvisit/the-wonderland-trail.htm.*

VISITOR CENTER

Sunrise Visitor Center

INFO CENTER | Exhibits at this center explain the region's sparser alpine and subalpine ecology. A network of nearby loop trails leads you through alpine meadows and forest to overlooks that have broad views of the Cascades and Rainier. The visitor center has a snack bar and gift shop. ✉ *Sunrise Rd., 15 miles from White River park entrance, Mt. Rainier National Park* ☎ *360/663–2425* 🌐 *www.nps.gov/mora/planyourvisit/sunrise.htm* ⏲ *Closed mid-Sept.–June.*

Restaurants

Sunrise Day Lodge Food Service

$ | AMERICAN | FAMILY | A cafeteria and grill serve tasty hamburgers, chili, hot dogs, and soft-serve ice cream from July through September. **Known for:** only food service in this part of the park; often busy. $ *Average main: $10* ✉ *Sunrise Rd., 15 miles from White River park entrance, Mt. Rainier National Park* ☎ *360/663–2425 visitor center, 855/755–2275 guest services* 🌐 *www.mtrainierguestservices.com* ⏲ *Closed Oct.–June.*

Carbon River and Mowich Lake

24 miles from Wilkeson to park entrance, via Hwy. 165.

The northwest corner of the park has some unique features, including the Carbon Glacier, which is the lowest-elevation glacier in the continental U.S. It also has a rainforest climate and because of past floods and road damage, vehicle access is limited past the Carbon River Ranger Station, though this is the one area of the park where mountain bikes are allowed. The road to Mowich Lake, also via Highway 165, leads to the deepest and biggest lake in the park.

Sights

SCENIC DRIVES

Mowich Lake Road

SCENIC DRIVE | In the northwest corner of the park, this 24-mile mountain road begins in Wilkeson and heads up the Rainier foothills to Mowich Lake, traversing beautiful mountain meadows along the way. Mowich Lake is a pleasant spot for a picnic. The road is open mid-July to mid-October. ✉ *Mt. Rainier National Park* 🌐 *www.nps.gov/mora/planyourvisit/carbon-river-and-mowich.htm* ⏲ *Closed mid-Oct.–mid-July.*

Activities

BIRD-WATCHING

Be alert for kestrels, red-tailed hawks, and, occasionally, golden eagles on snags in the lowland forests. Also present at Rainier, but rarely seen, are great horned owls, spotted owls, and screech owls. Iridescent rufous hummingbirds flit from blossom to blossom in the drowsy summer lowlands, and sprightly water ouzels flutter in the many forest creeks. Raucous Steller's jays and gray jays scold passersby from trees, often darting boldly down to steal morsels from unguarded picnic tables. At higher elevations, look for the pure white plumage of the white-tailed ptarmigan as it hunts for seeds and insects in winter. Waxwings, vireos, nuthatches, sapsuckers, warblers, flycatchers, larks, thrushes, siskins, tanagers, and finches are common throughout the park.

CAMPING

Three drive-in campgrounds are in the park—Cougar Rock, Ohanapecosh, and White River—with almost 500 sites for tents and RVs. None has hot water or RV hookups. The nightly fee is $20. The more primitive Mowich Lake Campground has 10 walk-in sites for tents only; no fee is charged.

Cougar Rock Campground. A secluded, heavily wooded campground with an amphitheater, Cougar Rock is one of the first to fill up. Reservations are accepted for summer only. ✉ *2½ miles north of Longmire* ☎ *877/444–6777* 🌐 *www.recreation.gov* for reservations.

Ohanapecosh Campground. This lush, green campground in the park's southeast corner has an amphitheater and self-guided trail. It's one of the first campgrounds to open for the season. ✉ *Rte. 123, 1½ miles north of park boundary* ☎ *877/444–6777* 🌐 *www.recreation.gov* for reservations.

White River Campground. At an elevation of 4,400 feet, White River is one of the park's highest and least wooded campgrounds. Here you can enjoy campfire programs, self-guided trails, and partial views of Mt. Rainier's summit. ✉ *5 miles west of White River entrance* ☎ *360/569–2211.*

EDUCATIONAL OFFERINGS

RANGER PROGRAMS

Citizen Ranger Quests

NATIONAL/STATE PARK | **FAMILY** | Older kids and adults can do their own version of the Junior Ranger program by exploring the park on various learning adventures

Mt. Rainier was originally called Tahoma (or Takhoma) by native Salishan speakers, meaning "the mountain that was God." Most Puget Sound residents simply call it "the mountain."

that take from 30 minutes to two hours to complete. After doing at least four activities (from more than a dozen choices), participants earn a Citizen Ranger patch and certificate. ✉ *Mt. Rainier National Park* ☎ *360/569–2211* 🌐 *www.nps.gov/mora/planyourvisit/citizen-ranger.htm.*

Junior Ranger Program

LOCAL SPORTS | **FAMILY** | Youngsters ages 6 to 11 can pick up an activity booklet at a visitor center and fill it out as they explore the park. When they complete it, they can show it to a ranger and receive a Mount Rainier Junior Ranger badge. ✉ *Visitor centers, Mt. Rainier National Park* ☎ *360/569–2211* 🌐 *www.nps.gov/mora/planyourvisit/rangerprograms.htm* 🎟 *Free with park admission.*

Ranger Programs

LOCAL SPORTS | **FAMILY** | Park ranger-led activities include **guided snowshoe walks** in the winter (most suitable for those older than eight) as well as **evening programs** during the summer at Longmire/Cougar Rock, Ohanapecosh, and White River campgrounds, and at the Paradise Inn. Evening talks may cover subjects such as park history, its flora and fauna, or interesting facts on climbing Mt. Rainier. There are also daily guided programs that start at the Jackson Visitor Center, including meadow and vista walks, tours of the Paradise Inn, a morning ranger chat, and evening astronomy program. ✉ *Visitor centers, Mt. Rainier National Park* ☎ *360/569–2211* 🌐 *www.nps.gov/mora/planyourvisit/rangerprograms.htm* 🎟 *Free with park admission.*

HIKING

Although the mountain can seem remarkably benign on calm summer days, hiking Rainier is not a city-park stroll. Dozens of hikers and trekkers annually lose their way and must be rescued—and lives are lost on the mountain each year. Weather that approaches cyclonic levels can appear quite suddenly, any month of the year. All visitors venturing far from vehicle access points, with the possible exception of the short loop hikes listed here, should carry day packs with warm clothing, food, and other emergency supplies.

MULTISPORT OUTFITTERS

RMI Expeditions

CLIMBING/MOUNTAINEERING | Reserve a private hiking guide through this highly regarded outfitter, or take part in its one-day mountaineering classes (mid-May through late September), where participants are evaluated on their fitness for the climb and must be able to withstand a 16-mile round-trip hike with a 9,000-foot gain in elevation. The company also arranges private cross-country skiing and snowshoeing guides. ✉ *30027 Hwy. 706 E, Ashford* ☎ *888/892–5462, 360/569–2227* 🌐 *www.rmiguides.com* 💵 *From $1222 for 4-day package.*

Whittaker Mountaineering

CLIMBING/MOUNTAINEERING | You can rent hiking and climbing gear, cross-country skis, snowshoes, and other outdoor equipment at this all-purpose Rainier Base Camp outfitter, which also arranges for private cross-country skiing and hiking guides. If you forget to bring tire chains (which all vehicles are required to carry in the national park in winter), they rent those, too. ✉ *30027 SR 706 E, Ashford* ☎ *800/238–5756, 360/569–2982* 🌐 *www.whittakermountaineering.com.*

SKIING AND SNOWSHOEING

Mt. Rainier is a major Nordic ski center for cross-country and telemark skiing. Although trails are not groomed, those around Paradise are extremely popular; it's also a great place for snowshoeing.

General Store at the National Park Inn

SKIING/SNOWBOARDING | The store at the National Park Inn in Longmire rents cross-country ski equipment and snowshoes. It's open daily in winter, depending on snow conditions. ✉ *National Park Inn, Longmire* ☎ *360/569–2411* 🌐 *www.mtrainierguestservices.com/activities-and-events/winter-activities/cross-country-skiing.*

Paradise Snowplay Area and Nordic Ski Route

SKIING/SNOWBOARDING | Sledding on flexible sleds (no toboggans or runners), inner tubes, and plastic saucers is allowed only in the Paradise snowplay area adjacent to the Jackson Visitor Center. The area is open when there is sufficient snow, usually from late December through mid-March. The easy 3½-mile Paradise Valley Road Nordic ski route begins at the Paradise parking lot and follows Paradise Valley/Stevens Canyon Road to Reflection Lakes. Equipment rentals are available at Whittaker Mountaineering in Ashford or at the National Park Inn's General Store in Longmire. ✉ *Adjacent to Jackson Visitor Center at Paradise, Mt. Rainier National Park* ☎ *360/569–2211* 🌐 *www.nps.gov/mora/planyourvisit/winter-recreation.htm.*

What's Nearby

Ashford sits astride an ancient trail across the Cascades used by the Yakama tribe to trade with the coastal tribes of western Washington. The town began as a logging railway terminal; today it's the main gateway to Mt. Rainier—and the only year-round access point to the park—with lodges, restaurants, grocery stores, and gift shops. Surrounded by Cascade peaks, **Packwood** is a pretty mountain village on U.S. 12, below White Pass and less than 12 miles from the Ohanapecosh area of the national park. It's a perfect jumping-off point for exploring local wilderness areas. Near the Sunrise entrance on the northeast side of the park, the **Crystal Mountain** area provides lodging, dining, and year-round outdoor recreation options, including a popular resort for snow sports.

Chapter 45

NATIONAL PARK OF AMERICAN SAMOA

Updated by
Gary McKechnie

Camping	Hotels	Activities	Scenery	Crowds
★☆☆☆☆	★☆☆☆☆	★★★★☆	★★★★★	★★☆☆☆

WELCOME TO NATIONAL PARK OF AMERICAN SAMOA

TOP REASONS TO GO

★ **A South Pacific adventure:** Reaching the only American park located south of the equator means you'll likely land or dock in Pago Pago before setting out to hike through rain forest or swim amid colorful coral reefs. Farther afield are the Manua islands and even more distant locales.

★ **Liquid assets:** As far from land as pretty much anyplace on Earth, pristine South Seas waters and 300-plus species of fish and other marine life, ranging from whales to living corals, make this national park a great destination for water recreation.

★ **Ancient traditions:** Spend a little time on the islands, and you'll learn about Faa Samoa—the Samoan Way—an unwritten tenet that plays an important role in society here by helping to preserve the customs, beliefs, and traditions of the 3,000-year-old Samoan cultures.

1 Tutuila. The most accessible and developed of the three islands (relatively speaking) is a good base from which to explore. From Pago Pago, it's a 10-minute drive to the park entrance, your gateway to rain forests, jagged peaks, deep valleys, and miles of coastline.

2 Ofu. If reaching Tutuila seemed like taking a giant leap forward, making it to Ofu and its beautiful namesake beach requires taking one step beyond. The island is nearly 112 km (70 miles) east of Tutuila, so you'll either need to book a flight (35 minutes) or take the ferry (eight hours) to get there.

3 Tau. The easternmost and largest (44 square km [17 square miles]) of the three islands is also the least developed, featuring dramatic sea cliffs and Mount Lata, American Samoa's highest peak.

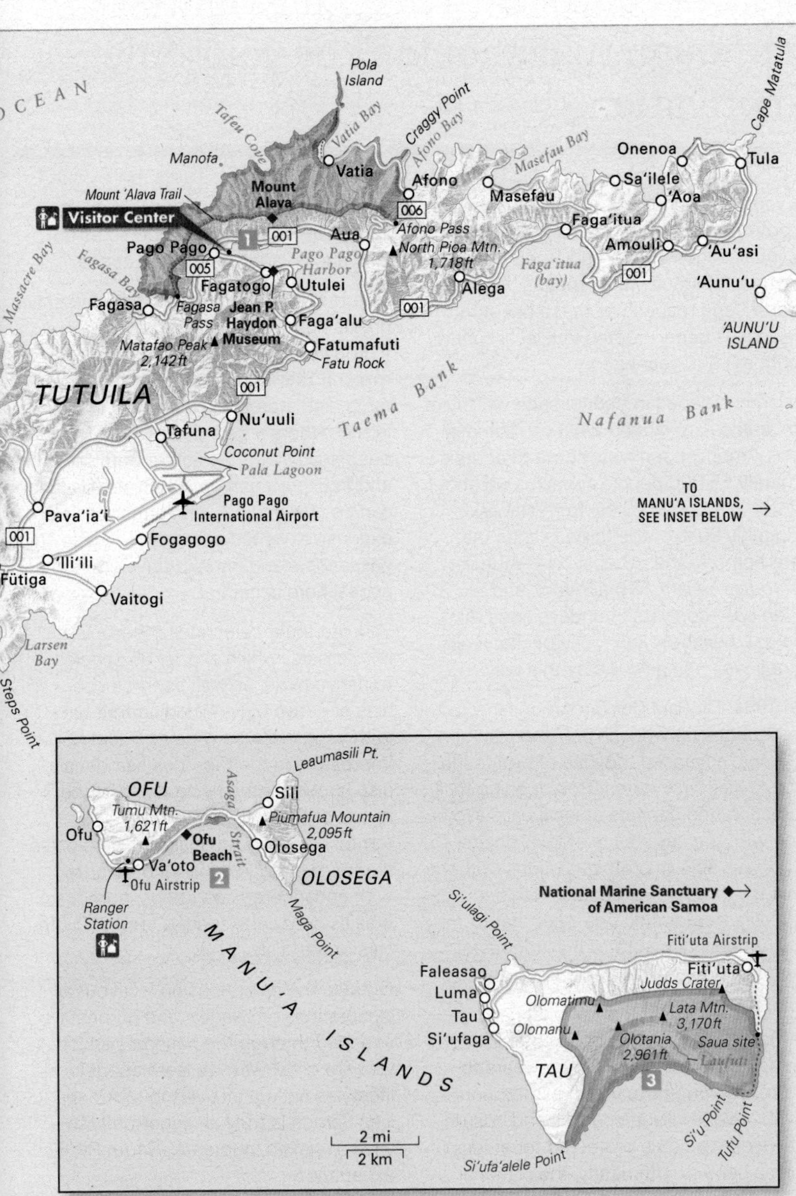
OCEAN
Pola Island
Tafeu Cove
Vatia Bay
Craggy Point
Afono Bay
Masefau Bay
Cape Matatula
Manofa
Vatia
Afono
Masefau
Onenoa
Tula
Sa'ilele
'Aoa
Mount 'Alava Trail
Mount Alava
Visitor Center
006
Afono Pass
Faga'itua
1
001
Aua
North Pioa Mtn. 1,718 ft
Amouli
'Au'asi
Massacre Bay
Fagasa Bay
Pago Pago
005
Pago Pago Harbor
Fagatogo
Utulei
Alega
Faga'itua (bay)
001
'Aunu'u
Fagasa
Fagasa Pass
Jean P. Haydon Museum
Faga'alu
001
'AUNU'U ISLAND
Matafao Peak 2,142 ft
Fatumafuti
Fatu Rock
TUTUILA
001
Taema Bank
Nafanua Bank
Nu'uuli
Tafuna
Coconut Point
Pala Lagoon
TO MANU'A ISLANDS, SEE INSET BELOW
Pago Pago International Airport
Pava'ia'i
001
Fogagogo
'Ili'ili
Fütiga
Vaitogi
Larsen Bay
Steps Point
Leaumasili Pt.
OFU
Asaga Strait
Sili
Tumu Mtn. 1,621 ft
Piumafua Mountain 2,095 ft
Ofu
Ofu Beach
Olosega
Va'oto
Ofu Airstrip
2
OLOSEGA
Ranger Station
Maga Point
National Marine Sanctuary of American Samoa
Si'ulagi Point
MANU'A ISLANDS
Fiti'uta Airstrip
Faleasao
Fiti'uta
Luma
Judds Crater
Olomatimu
Tau
Lata Mtn. 3,170 ft
Si'ufaga
Olomanu
Olotania 2,961 ft
Saua site
Laufuti
TAU
3
Si'u Point
Tufu Point
2 mi
2 km
Si'ufa'alele Point

When it comes to visiting off-the-beaten-track destinations, a trip to American Samoa comes with bragging rights—although that shouldn't be your only motivation.

Everything about this destination seems exotic, starting with the name of its captial, Pago Pago (pronounced *pongo pongo*). "Samoa" itself means "sacred earth," and respect for these beautiful islands is deeply rooted in a local culture with a 3,000-year history.

Islands steeped in tradition and worthy of reverance are indeed what you'll find in this American territory, home to approximately 55,000 people and situated about 4,200 km (2,600 miles) from Hawaii. Roughly 90% of the three islands that are home to the national park—Tutuila *(Too-too-ee-lah)*, Ofu *(Oh-foo)*, and Tau *(Tah-oo)*—consists of undeveloped rain forest, beaches, and rocky peaks. If all goes well, things will stay this way.

In 1984, Dr. Paul Cox, an American ethnobotanist working on American Samoa, advanced the idea of protecting the lowland rain forest from logging to preserve the habitats of local bats. Working with the assistance of local chiefs, Dr. Cox was able to protect portions of these islands through the Federal Fish and Wildlife Restoration Act. With that victory, the wheels began to turn a little faster, and the vision expanded a lot further.

By October 1988, the National Park of American Samoa had been established, although it took several more years to formalize long-term leasing agreements with several village councils and ensure the land would be protected for at least half a century. Ultimately, the National Park of American Samoa became the southernmost most national park, its 13,500 acres covering 9,500 acres on land and an additional 4,000 at sea.

Due to its remote location, the park only greets about 28,000 guests annually (compared to, say, Grand Canyon's 6 million). There are few hotels, restaurants, and stores, especially on smaller islands; there's a slim selection of diving, deep-sea fishing, and other outfitters; and transportation between the islands can be challenging—and either basic or expensive. Visited primarily by cruise ship passengers and intrepid travelers, the appeal here is natural.

Park literature celebrates the tropical rain forests, which shelter 35 species of native birds, as well as three species of native bats, including fruit bats with wingspans as wide as 3 feet. (So impressive is the Pteropus samoensis, also known as the flying fox, that the image of the bat is featured on the territory's American quarter.) The diverse marine system is equally noteworthy, with endangered sea turtles, humpback whales, 250 coral species, and 950 species of reef fish.

Outside the park, rides on local buses, explorations of villages, and homestays arranged through the national park service are great ways to learn about local lifestyles and culture. A trip to American Samoa is truly an opportunity to have a relaxed, authentic, South Pacific experience.

AVERAGE HIGH/LOW TEMPERATURES					
JAN.	**FEB.**	**MAR.**	**APR.**	**MAY**	**JUNE**
87/75	87/75	87/73	86/75	86/75	94/75
JULY	**AUG.**	**SEPT.**	**OCT.**	**NOV.**	**DEC.**
84/73	82/73	84/73	84/75	86/75	86/75

Planning

When to Go

During the dry or high season, which lasts from roughly mid-April to October, you can spend all day traversing the islands without fear of a downpour (a meteorological fact that's reflected in higher hotel prices). Traditionally, despite rains between December to mid-January, things can seem relatively busy as American Samoans return home from their holiday trips. What follows is a general lull until late March, and it's during this dip that you'll find better deals on lodging. From mid-April to June hotel rates begin to creep up, taking another dip before rising again in November and leading to the holidays.

Getting Here and Around

Just 33 km (21 miles) long by 5 km (3 miles) wide, the main island of Tutuila is lined by a road that roughly follows the southern coast with a few feeder roads venturing into the interior. The international airport is about 6 km (4 miles) south of Pago Pago, the captial and commercial hub of American Samoa. Most sites on Tutuila can be explored in a day by car. Venturing to the neighboring Manua islands—112 km (70 miles) east of Tutuila—requires a long ferry ride or short (but more expensive) flight on a small plane. If you opt for the latter, Ofu and Tau make lovely day trips.

AIR

It's a 35-minute flight to Pago Pago from Apia, the capital of Samoa, but Hawaiian Airlines offers direct flights (5½ hours) to Tutuila's Pago Pago International Airport from Honolulu. From there Samoa Airways (🌐 *www.samoaairways.com*) flies a 19-seat Otter aircraft to Ofu Airport (35 minutes) and Tau's Fiti'uta Airport (39 minutes); the fare is about $200 each way.

BOAT

Most visitors arrive aboard cruise ships, which dock at Pago Pago Harbor. Passengers then explore the island on prearranged shore excursions.

BUS

You can't miss American Samoa's colorful local buses, known as *agia,* or family buses. They converge on downtown Pago Pago from both sides of the island. Music blares from them, they bear names such as "Miracle of God" or "Queen Sophia," and they're festooned with flowers on days when ships are in port. Stops are found throughout the island, although you can wave down a driver anytime they pass—just be sure they're heading to your destination. The aiga operate weekdays between 9 am and 5 pm, with reduced scheduled on weekends when traveling by taxi or rental car is the way to go. One-way fares (paid upon boarding) range from $2 to $14, depending on the destination.

CAR

Although the main island of Tutuila is small, the most efficient way to sightsee is by rental car. The main road runs along the island's southern shore while a few feeder roads venture into the interior.

FERRY

A weekly ferry, the MV *Lady Naomi,* makes the seven-hour journey between Samoa and American Samoa. Linking Tutuila with the Manua islands of Ofu and Tau, the Manuatele ferry's MV *Sili* has a hit-or-miss schedule. It generally departs on its eight-hour trip every other Thursday, sailing out in the morning, reaching the Manua islands that afternoon, and returning to Pago Pago the following morning. Keep in mind that the ship is primarily for freight, the run east is rather rough due to prevailing winds, and if the ship can't make it into the harbor you'll have to wait for small boats to take you to shore. The rate is about $35 one-way.

Inspiration

Alchemies of Distance, an acclaimed book of poetry that questions Samoan identity, was penned by notable American Samoan writer Caroline Sinavaiana-Gabbard. In *Nafanua: Saving the Samoan Rain Forest,* ethnobotanist Paul Alan Cox documents the events leading to the creation of the National Park of American Samoa. The 1920s short story, *Rain* (aka *Miss Thompson*), by British novelist W. Somerset Maugham, inspired numerous films, including 1953's *Miss Sadie Thompson,* starring Rita Hayworth.

Park Essentials

ACCESSIBILITY

Aside from the visitor center and restrooms, there's relatively little modified access provided for people with mobility issues. The Lower Sauma Ridge on Tutuila is an overlook that is accessible with assistance.

PARK FEES AND PERMITS

Entrance to the only U.S. national park south of the equator is absolutely free.

PARK HOURS

Park headquarters and its visitor center in Pago Pago are open weekdays from 8 am to 4:30 pm.

CELL PHONE RECEPTION

Cell phone service on the islands is scant. In Pago Pago, you'll have to look for free Wi-Fi connections, mobile hot spots, or Internet cafés. Some travelers purchase a BlueSky SIM card to connect.

Hotels

Although there is no lodging (not even camping) within the national park, the park service facilitates the popular Homestay program (🌐 *www.nps.gov/npsa/learn/historyculture/homestay.htm*) in which travelers can stay the night (or longer) in the home of a local family. Note that a homestay is the only option when on an overnight in Tau.

Restaurants

Your only dining options are in area towns and villages, with Pago Pago offering the greatest variety. You can tip if you'd like although, officially, it's not required in American Samoa. Note, too, that the currency here is the U.S. dollar, and prices are on par with or slightly cheaper than those on the mainland.

Tours

Pago Pago Marine Charters
EXCURSIONS | This company arranges deep-sea fishing, diving, snorkeling, and coastal excursions. 🌐 *pagopagomarine-charters.com.*

Ranger-Led Hikes
WALKING TOURS | On Saturdays from late June through mid-September, rangers lead guided hikes on various park trails, including Lower Sauma Trail, Mount Alava Trail, and World War II Heritage Trail. Since space is limited to 28 hikers, participants

must sign up in advance by phone or email (npsa_info@nps.gov). ✉ *National Park of American Samoa* ☎ *684/633–7082* 🌐 *www.nps.gov/experiences/ranger-led-saturday-hikes.htm.*

Tour American Samoa

SPECIAL-INTEREST | This outfit's guides offer group excursions, mainly for cruise-ship pasengers, as well as customized private tours (for a higher fee). Options include a scenic bus tour, visiting a village, heading out on a canoe trip, or exploring the World War II Heritage Trail. 🌐 *www.touramericansamoa.com.*

Visitor Information

CONTACTS National Park of American Samoa. ✉ *Tutuila Island, Pago Pago* ☎ *684/ 633–7082* 🌐 *www.nps.gov/npsa.*

Tutuila

4,200 km (2,600 miles) southwest of Honolulu, Hawaii.

On the main island of Tutuila, the national park stretches northeast from Pago Pago, both along and inland from the north coast. Although the island's main road doesn't travel in the park or along the shore here, in-park trails lead to overlooks where cliffs plunge down to the sea. Be on the lookout for native geckos and skinks as well as flowering plants and ferns that traveled over the seas from Southeast Asia. The park is also home to a variety of birds, as well as three bat species, including a massive fruit bat known as the "flying fox."

Elsewhere, the main road skirts the shoreline in several places, providing access to the National Marine Sanctuary of American Samoa. While driving along the southern coast, you'll see volcanic ridges overlooking the ocean. The Afono Pass between Rainmaker Mountain and Maugaloa Ridge opens to panoramic, photo-worthy views.

GEOLOGICAL FORMATIONS

Mount Alava

MOUNTAIN—SIGHT | Within the national park on Tutuila are several named summits including 490-meter (1,610-foot) Mount Alava. Outside the park, is iconic Rainmaker Mountain. Often shrouded in clouds, it's one of three volcanic peaks ranging in height from 493 meters (1,619 feet) to 524 meters (1,718 feet) and loom over Pago Pago Harbor. For a closeup view, drive up Rainmaker Pass. ✉ *National Park of American Samoa.*

HISTORIC SIGHTS

Jean P. Haydon Museum

MUSEUM | Before or after a visit to the national park, stop by this museum to learn about American Samoa's customs and history. Occupying a former naval commissary and garage buildings, the museum features cultural exhibits, books, and performances. A small *fale* (house) in front of the museum often hosts arts and crafts demonstrations. An unusual exhibit shows the American Samoan flag that was taken to the moon by astronauts on four Apollo moon missions from 1969 to 1971, along with a collection of moon rocks gathered on the missions and gifted to the territory by President Nixon. ✉ *Main Road, Fagatogo* ☎ *684/699–1026* 🎫 *Free.*

UNDERWATER SIGHTS

National Marine Sanctuary of American Samoa

NATURE PRESERVE | A visit to this pristine bay, within an eroded volcanic crater on the south side of Tutuila, nicely complements a visit to the national park. Beneath the waters are beautiful corals, hundreds of fish, and many turtles as well as sharks and—at certain times of the year—whales. The bay and nearby walking trails are on land belonging to the Fuimaono family,

South Pacific scenery, sun, and solitude are abundant on the beaches here.

who have lived here for about 1,000 years. Visitors are allowed to hike the trails, swim, and snorkel but must first register their names in a book at a gate. To reach Fagatele Bay, drive or take a local bus to Futiga Village, about 11 km (7 miles) southwest of Pago Pago, and turn left at the US Mart. Follow the small feeder road past a landfill area to the locked gate. After registering, it's a 1½-km (1-mile) walk to the first interpretative sign and another mile to the beach. Visitors can also hire a boat to get here. ■ TIP→ **Take water for the hike, and dress in a modest style when walking and swimming (no bikinis).** ✉ *Off Main Road, Futiga Village* ☎ *684/633–5155* 🌐 *americansamoa.noaa.gov.*

VISITOR CENTERS

National Park of American Samoa Visitor Center

INFO CENTER | Unlike at many national parks, the visitor center is not at the entrance but rather on the second floor of the MHJ Building in Pago Pago. ✉ *Pago Pago* ☎ *684/ 633–7082* 🌐 *www.nps.gov/npsa.*

Ofu

112 kilometers (70 miles or 60 nautical miles) east of Tutuila.

While much of this island is preserved within the park, it's arguably the famed Ofu Beach, considered one of the world's most beautiful, that holds the most appeal to travelers. Gaze across the endless seas from its shores, or take to the waters and explore its marine life. Athough the Tumu Mountain Trail is outside the park, it will take you to Ofu's highest point (494 meters [1,621feet]). From the top, it's just a short distance to an outcropping that opens to views of three Manua islands and the park's coral lagoons. Getting here from Tutuila involves a ferry ride (eight hours and about $35 each way) or a flight in a small plane (roughly $200 each way).

Sights

BEACHES

Ofu Beach

BEACH—SIGHT | Although this milelong crescent is far and away the most popular attraction on Ofu, don't be surprised if the only footprints in the white sands are yours. You can laze in the shade of a palm tree and wade into the warm, crystal-clear waters to explore the colorful, 350-acre coral reef, the perfect place to snorkel (bring your own gear) amid sea turtles, fish, and starfish. Indeed, the waters around Ofu contain more than 950 species of fish and over 250 species of corals. If you'd like to dive deeper, it's best to arrange a tour on Pago Pago as there are no vendors here. ✉ *National Park of American Samoa.*

Tau

128 kilometers (80 miles or 70 nautical miles) east of Tutuila.

As with Ofu, a ferry or flight is the only way to reach the island. Flights from Pago Pago land at Tau's Fitiuta Airport, which is a 39-minute one-way trip; count on eight hours via the ferry. There's only one road on the north side of the island, and no car rental places, so hiking and taxis are the only ways to get around.

The highest peak in American Samoa is Lata Mountain on Tau, although you may not see it. Even at 966 meters (3,170 feet), it's often concealed by clouds draped over the thick layer of forest vegetation and tree ferns.

Sights

TRAILS

Siu Point Trail

TRAIL | On Tau Island, the sole path suggested by the national park service is this 9-km (5.7-mile) round-trip route. It leads south from the airport along an old road past coastal forest to the sacred Saua site where Tagaloa, Samoa's supreme ruler and creator of the Universe, is said to have created the first humans who departed Tau to populate Polynesia. A small structure marks the site and is a good place to contemplate the origins of Oceania before continuing on to the island's southeastern tip. ✉ *National Park of American Samoa* ✥ *Trailhead: Near the airport.*

Activities

DIVING AND SNORKELING

The National Marine Sanctuary of American Samoa (🌐 *americansamoa.noaa.gov*) consists of six sanctuary management areas. Its visitor center features free exhibits and tours highlighting the biodiversity of island waters and marine sites such as deep-water reefs, hydrothermal vent communities, islands, bays, and atolls. You can arrange snorkeling and diving excursions with operators in Pago Pago. The reef on the south side of Tutuila is a popular site for exploring beautiful corals teeming with schools of fish and gentle sea turtles. The waters off Ofu also have stellar reefs.

HIKING

More than a dozen hiking trails lace Tutuila and the Manua islands, the easiest being the 650-foot Pola Island Trail and the most challenging being a round-trip to the summit of Mount Alava for fantastic views over Pago Pago Harbor, a trek that will take about three hours. The park service offers an overview of trails (🌐 *www.nps.gov/npsa/planyourvisit/upload/Day-Hikes-SB_NPSA_high-res.pdf*) leading through rain forest, along dramatic stretches of shore, and up volacanic peaks. Some routes access the archaeological site of an ancient star mound, the marine sanctuary, and historic World War II gun emplacements. The best way to explore such trails is on an organized hike led by rangers or local guides.

What's Nearby

Most people base themselves on the island of Tutuila, usually in or near the capital city of **Pago Pago,** which has several hotels with on-site dining options, including Sadie's by the Sea, the Sadie Thompson Inn, and the Tradewinds Hotel. In addition, Tisa's Barefoot Bar is a B&B and casual beachside restaurant with a patio where you can dine and sip piña coladas as the sun sets and the moon rises.

Before exploring the park on Tutuila, stock up on picnic items in Pago Pago at KS Mart, a popular grocery store with baked goods, canned foods, produce, coffee, cold drinks, and prepared meals. Another good bet is Steven & Son, which sells fresh, ready-to-go Samoan dishes featuring fish or meat often served with papaya, banana, and coconut milk.

On the island of **Ofu,** near the harbor and only a short walk to Ofu Beach, the Vaoto Lodge is a cash-only, family-owned hotel on a sandy stretch beneath Mt. Tumutumu. The homestays arranged through the national park service's program are your only lodging options on neighboring **Tau Island.**

Chapter 46

NEW RIVER GORGE NATIONAL PARK AND PRESERVE

Updated by
Erin Gifford

Camping	Hotels	Activities	Scenery	Crowds
★☆☆☆☆	★☆☆☆☆	★★★★★	★★★★★	★★★☆☆

WELCOME TO NEW RIVER GORGE NATIONAL PARK AND PRESERVE

TOP REASONS TO GO

★ **Hiking:** Lace up your hiking boots to tackle scenic trails across the park that range from less than ¼-mile to more than 7 miles.

★ **White-water rafting:** Strap on your helmet and grab a paddle for the thrill of a lifetime as you raft along the free-flowing New River.

★ **Fishing:** Fishing is one of the most popular activities at this national park. Drop in a line to catch a smallmouth bass, walleye, bluegill, or carp.

★ **The bridge:** Plan to take in the views of the New River Gorge Bridge from all angles, including from the overlook at the Canyon Rim Visitor Center and from below on Fayette Station Road.

1 **New River Gorge Bridge.** See the western hemisphere's longest steel arch bridge in all its glory from the overlook behind the Canyon Rim Visitor Center.

2 **Sandstone Falls.** The largest waterfall on the New River plunges 15 to 25 feet and spans more than 1,500 feet. A boardwalk trail allows for exquisite views.

3 **Fayette Station.** This 100-year-old road was once the only way to cross the New River Gorge. Today, the 40-minute drive awes with eye-pleasing bridge views.

4 **Historic Thurmond.** This once-booming coal town was among the busiest railway towns in the early-1900s. A self-guided walking tour springs this ghost town back to life.

5 **Kaymoor Mines.** Once one of the largest coal operations in the New River Gorge, abandoned structures, like coke ovens and coal conveyors, tell the mine's story.

6 **Grandview.** Soak in unparalleled east-facing views of the winding New River from Main Overlook, a large platform that sits 1,400 feet above the dramatic gorge.

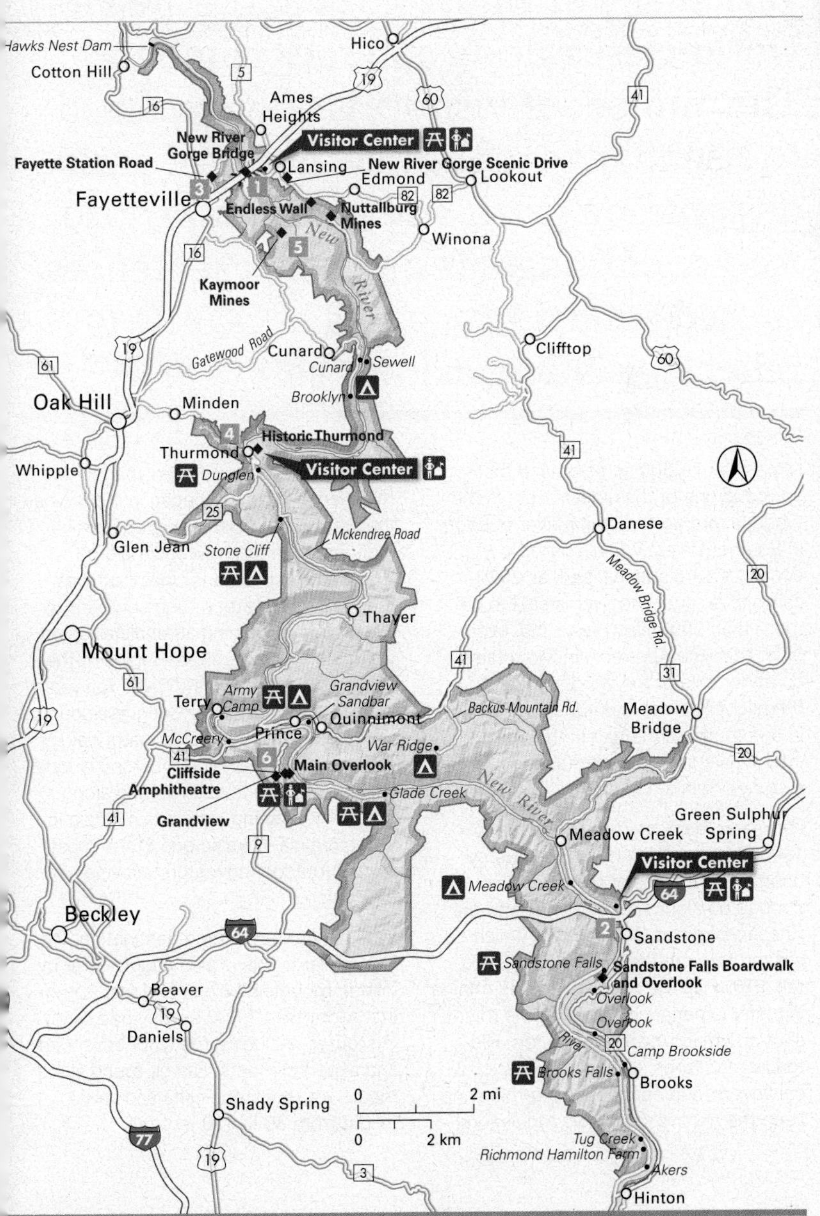
Hawks Nest Dam
Cotton Hill
Hico
Ames Heights
New River Gorge Bridge
Visitor Center
Fayette Station Road
Lansing
New River Gorge Scenic Drive
Edmond
Lookout
Fayetteville
Endless Wall
Nuttallburg Mines
Winona
New River
Kaymoor Mines
Gatewood Road
Cunard
Sewell
Clifftop
Brooklyn
Oak Hill
Minden
Historic Thurmond
Thurmond
Visitor Center
Whipple
Dunglen
Danese
Glen Jean
Stone Cliff
Mckendree Road
Meadow Bridge Rd.
Thayer
Mount Hope
Army Camp
Terry
Grandview Sandbar
Quinnimont
Prince
Backus Mountain Rd.
Meadow Bridge
McCreery
War Ridge
Main Overlook
Cliffside Amphitheatre
Glade Creek
Grandview
New River
Green Sulphur Spring
Meadow Creek
Visitor Center
Meadow Creek
Beckley
Sandstone
Sandstone Falls
Sandstone Falls Boardwalk and Overlook
Overlook
Overlook
Beaver
Daniels
River
Camp Brookside
Brooks Falls
Brooks
Shady Spring
0
2 mi
0
2 km
Tug Creek
Richmond Hamilton Farm
Akers
Hinton

The New River Gorge region brings in more than one million visitors each year, many of whom flock to the area for world-class rafting and rock climbing. The number of visitors is only expected to rise thanks to the new national park designation given on December 27, 2020. An Act of Congress, and a few sentences tucked amidst 2,124 pages of COVID-19 relief legislation, made it so.

More than 70,000 acres of land that surround one of the oldest rivers in the world (a rare north-flowing river to boot) in Southern West Virginia became the country's 63rd national park as 2020 came to an end. The river is said to be more than 300 million years old, even older than the Appalachian Mountains on either side of the winding river. The 53-mile stretch of park runs from Hinton in the south to Anstead in the north, interweaving rugged natural beauty with a storied mining history.

For many years, starting in the late-1800s, the coal-rich New River Gorge boomed as dozens of mining towns popped up alongside coalfields and the Chesapeake and Ohio railway, which passed through the mining camps. By the 1950s, as the once-flourishing mining industry experienced decline, the mines shut down and were abandoned. Historical structures, like coke ovens, coal conveyors, and headhouses, remain and keep the mining story alive for visitors.

As nature began to reclaim abandoned mine lands, a rebirth began in 1968 when the first commercial rafting operations cropped up in the New River Gorge. Wildwater Expeditions Unlimited was the first whitewater rafting company in West Virginia, guiding adrenaline-fueled visitors along the frenzied rapids of the wild and wondrous New River. Ten years later, in 1978, an Act of Congress sought to preserve this venerable waterway by decreeing the New River Gorge National River. Today, whitewater rafting along these free-flowing waters is a staple in West Virginia. It's also one of the most popular outdoor adventure activities in the region.

While a first-rate rafting destination, the New River Gorge is also sought-after by hikers, mountain bikers, and rock climbers. More than 1,600 established climbing routes, including many for advanced and expert climbers, can be found along the park's sandstone cliffs and vary in height from 30 to 120 feet tall.

AVERAGE HIGH/LOW TEMPERATURES					
JAN.	FEB.	MAR.	APR.	MAY	JUNE
40/21	44/23	54/30	66/39	73/49	79/57
JULY	AUG.	SEPT.	OCT.	NOV.	DEC.
81/60	82/60	76/54	65/42	55/32	44/25

Planning

When to Go

Summer is a popular time to cool off on whitewater rafting trips along the New and Gauley Rivers, where Class II to V rapids draw enthusiasts of all levels. Fall is the most predictable season, with temps in the 60s and generally dry days. The park is quiet in winter, with a range of cold conditions, but it's the perfect season for peaceful hikes. Spring can be wet, but it still charms visitors with mild temperatures and colorful wildflowers. Rhododendrons, the state flower, pop in late-spring with fragrant pink, purple, or white blooms.

FESTIVALS AND EVENTS

Bridge Day. October's Bridge Day draws adrenaline junkies eager to base jump or rappel from the New River Gorge Bridge. Other activities include a 5K and a food festival. 🌐 *officialbridgeday.com*

Getting Here and Around

AIR

The nearest major airport is Yeager Airport (CRW) in Charleston, West Virginia. It's a 75-minute drive southeast to the park's Canyon Rim Visitor Center.

CAR

New River Gorge's Canyon Rim Visitor Center in the north end of the park is 61 miles southeast of Charleston via Interstate 64, but it's another 61 miles from here to Sandstone Falls in the south end of the park via State Routes 20 and 26. From Roanoke, Virginia, it's a two-hour drive to the Sandstone Visitor Center in the park's south end. Drive north on Interstate 81, then west on Interstate 64. From this visitor center, it's a 35-minute drive south to Sandstone Falls.

TRAIN

Amtrak's *Cardinal,* which runs between Chicago and New York, stops in Hinton and Prince. Thurmond serves as a flag stop for ticketed passengers.

Inspiration

Thurmond and Ghost Towns of the New River Gorge, by Melody Bragg, delves into the history of all but forgotten ghost towns in the New River Gorge, including Thurmond.

New River Gorge, by J. Scott Legg, shares the history of a region turned upside down by coal barons, then brought back to life as nature began to reclaim the gorge.

Park Essentials

ACCESSIBILITY

All four visitor centers, including restrooms, are accessible to wheelchairs. Assistive listening devices are available at the Canyon Rim Visitor Center for the park film. The Canyon Rim Boardwalk has an accessible ramp to the first overlook for scenic views of the New River Gorge Bridge. At Sandstone Falls, an accessible wooden boardwalk traverses two bridges and leads to islands and overlooks. The first ¼-mile of the Long Point Trail and Glade Creek Trail is also accessible and leads to viewing areas. A wheelchair-accessible fishing area is at Glade Creek Campground.

PARK FEES AND PERMITS

There is no entrance fee to access this national park. There are also no fees to camp at any of the six primitive family campgrounds in the park. All visitors 15 and older must hold a valid state fishing license to fish in the park.

PARK HOURS

New River Gorge National Park and Preserve is open all day, every day. The park's two primary visitor centers, Canyon Rim and Sandstone, are open daily from 9 am to 5 pm (except major holidays). The satellite visitor centers at Grandview and Thurmond Depot are open daily from June to August and weekends in September and October (Thurmond Depot only). The park is in the Eastern time zone.

CELL PHONE RECEPTION

There's a moderate signal throughout the park. Free Wi-Fi is available at the Canyon Rim and Sandstone visitor centers.

Hotels

There are no hotels, motels, or lodges within the park. There are two hotels in Fayetteville, less than a 10-minute drive from the Canyon Rim Visitor Center, and many in Beckley, which is less than a 30-minute drive from both the Canyon Rim and Sandstone visitor centers. For mountain cabins that range from rustic to luxe, as well as tent and RV sites, Adventures on the Gorge is a five-minute drive from Canyon Rim Visitor Center.

Restaurants

There are no restaurants or food concessions inside the park. The nearest restaurants are in Fayetteville, which is less than a 10-minute drive from the Canyon Rim Visitor Center.

Tours

African-American Heritage Auto Tour
DRIVING TOURS | This self-driving audio tour shares the stories of black laborers, including coal miners and railroad workers, who played a significant role in shaping the region. The narrated tour includes 17 points of interest across Nicholas, Fayette, Summers, and Raleigh counties and can be found within the free National Park Service app.

Bridge Walk
GUIDED TOURS | Steps from Canyon Rim Visitor Center, Bridge Walk offers guided tours—including Full Moon and Sunset tours—of the New River Gorge Bridge from a 2-foot-wide metal catwalk underneath the famed bridge. Tours can run two to three hours and offer unparalleled views of the New River and New River Gorge as you walk the 3,030 foot long bridge. ✉ *57 Fayette Mine Rd., Lansing* ☎ *304/574–1300* 🌐 *bridgewalk.com* 🎫 *From $59.*

Visitor Information

CONTACTS New River Gorge National Park and Preserve. ☎ *304/465–0508* 🌐 *www.nps.gov/neri.*

Inside the Park

61 miles southeast of Charleston via Interstate 64.

Encompassing more than 70,000 acres of land along the 53-mile-long New River, the park and preserve stretches roughly from the New River Gorge Bridge in the northwest to the Sandstone/Brooks Falls areas, just north of the town of Hinton, in the southeast.

Main Overlook at Grandview offers amazing New River panoramas.

Sights

GEOLOGICAL FORMATIONS

Endless Wall

NATURE SITE | FAMILY | For many rock climbers, Endless Wall is the crown jewel in the New River Gorge region thanks to nearly 3 miles of unbroken sandstone cliffs and spectacular views of the dramatic gorge. The 3.2-mile round-trip Endless Wall Trail is equally popular thanks to far-reaching gorge views from Diamond Point. ✉ *New River Gorge National Park* ✣ *Lansing-Edmond Rd.*

HISTORIC SIGHTS

Cliffside Amphitheatre

ARTS VENUE | FAMILY | The Grandview section of the park is home to an outdoor theatre for seasonal productions put on by Theatre West Virginia. Founded in 1955, performances aim to share the culture of West Virginia, including such musical productions as *Hatfields and McCoys* and *Honey in the Rock*. ✉ *Grandview.*

Historic Thurmond

HISTORIC SITE | This once-flourishing coal town along the Chesapeake and Ohio rail line is now little more than a memory, but restored buildings, including a post office and bank, allow your imagination to bring this town to life. Start at the Thurmond Depot (now a seasonal visitor center), then stroll the once-bustling commercial district, which met its demise when the swanky Lafayette Hotel burned down in 1963. ✉ *Thurmond.*

Kaymoor Mines

MINE | At its peak, the Kaymoor One mining operation employed more than 800 coal workers, making the mine one of the largest coal producers in the New River Gorge. In the boom years, the mining complex had a tennis court and movie theater, even a company baseball team. Operations ceased by 1962, leaving behind historic structures, like coke ovens, a coal processing plant, and a power station. ✉ *Kaymoor Rd., Fayetteville.*

New River Gorge Bridge

BRIDGE/TUNNEL | This 3,030-foot-long steel arch bridge crosses the New River Gorge. As you drive onto the bridge, a sign proclaims that it's the "Western Hemisphere's Longest Arch Bridge." Completed in 1977, this impressive steel span structure reduced the drive between Fayetteville and Lansing, the towns on either side of the bridge, from 40 minutes to less than one minute. ✉ *Grandview.*

Nuttalburg Mines

MINE | At one time, nearly 50 coal towns sprung up along the New River Gorge, including Nuttallburg. This prosperous community was founded by John Nuttall who saw the lucrative potential of this coal-rich region. Long-abandoned mining structures remain today, including the headhouse, coal conveyor, coke ovens, coal tipple, and the mine entrance. ✉ *Beauty Mountain Rd., Fayetteville* ✥ *Park in Short Creek lot.*

SCENIC DRIVES

Fayette Station Road

SCENIC DRIVE | Go back in time as you motor along the one hundred-year-old road that was once the only way to cross the gorge on one- and two-way roads, including hairpin turns. Stop to revel in cascades at Wolf Creek Falls and Marr Branch Falls, or to watch paddlers disembark from rafts under the dramatic steel span bridge. Allow at least 40 minutes for the scenic drive with many eye-catching bridge views. ✉ *Fayette Station Rd., Lansing.*

New River Gorge Scenic Drive

SCENIC DRIVE | This three-hour, 83-mile driving route encircles the park, allowing visitors a look at former mines, historic districts, tumbling waterfalls, and far-reaching overlooks. The self-guided tour begins and ends on the rim of the gorge, at Canyon Rim Visitor Center, where an overlook enchants with vistas of the spectacular single-span bridge. ✉ *New River Gorge National Park.*

SCENIC STOPS

Main Overlook

VIEWPOINT | At 1,400 feet over the gorge, Main Overlook at Grandview delights with sensational views of the meandering New River and surrounding mountains. A short hike along the Grandview Rim Trail leads to North Overlook and Turkey Spur Rock for even more far-reaching panoramas of the awe-inspiring gorge. ✉ *Grandview.*

New River Gorge Bridge Overlook

VIEWPOINT | A wheelchair-accessible observation deck steps from Canyon Rim Visitor Center allows for endless views of the New River Gorge Bridge. For a closer look, continue along a wooden boardwalk and descend 178 steps to a second overlook. ✉ *Canyon Rim Visitor Center, New River Gorge National Park.*

Sandstone Falls Overlook and Boardwalk

BODY OF WATER | The largest waterfall on the New River is a sight to behold thanks to tumbling cascades. Stroll the boardwalk or walk the Island Loop Trail, which encircles the largest island near the falls. ✉ *New River Gorge National Park* ✥ *At the end of River Rd. (State Rte 26).*

TRAILS

Brooks and Sandstone Trails

TRAIL | FAMILY | There are four area trails with views of the rushing New River at it leads on to tumbling Sandstone Falls. The easy 0.4-mile round-trip walk along the Sandstone Falls Boardwalk is a popular pick to get up close to the falls. On the way to the trails, stop at the scenic overlook that sits 600 feet above the falls. Sandstone Falls is 20 miles from the Sandstone Visitor Center. ✉ *New River Gorge National Park.*

Grandview Trails

TRAIL | FAMILY | There are seven area trails that expose visitors to wildly scenic panoramas of the New River Gorge. Take in the views from Main Overlook, then hike north on the Grandview Rim Trail, making stops at North Overlook and Turkey Spur Rock on this moderate 3.2-mile round-trip hike. This hike begins steps from Grandview Visitor Center (seasonal). ✉ *New River Gorge National Park.*

Lansing and Fayetteville Trails

TRAIL | FAMILY | There are 12 trails in this area that provide a solid overview of the national park, offering scenic views of the New River Gorge Bridge and deep dives into the once-booming Kaymoor Mines. The easy 3.2-mile round-trip Long Point Trail begins 5 miles south of the Canyon Rim Visitor Center, rewarding with a rocky bridge overlook. The strenuous 2-mile round-trip Kaymoor Miners Trail descends a forested trail, past a flowing waterfall, then down 821 steps to remains of coke ovens and coal processing plants. ✉ *New River Gorge National Park.*

Nuttalburg Trails

TRAIL | FAMILY | There are seven trails in this area that allow visitors a look into the once-thriving coal mining town of Nuttallburg. A best bet is the moderate 1.4-mile round-trip hike on the Headhouse Trail, which is 3½ miles southeast of the Canyon Rim Visitor Center. Here you'll see the 1920s era coal mine and historic headhouse used for moving coal. ✉ *New River Gorge National Park.*

VISITOR CENTERS

Canyon Rim Visitor Center

INFO CENTER | This is the primary visitor center in the park's north section with rotating park films on how the bridge was constructed and how the natural gorge was created. There is also a book store and an exhibit area with historic photographs and exhibits, as well as a bridge overlook. ✉ *162 Visitor Center Rd., Lansing* ☎ *304/574–2115.*

Grandview Visitor Center

INFO CENTER | Grandview Visitor Center is a small, seasonal visitor center that serves as a touchpoint for visitors with questions. It's steps away from scenic hiking trails, as well as Main Overlook for jaw-dropping views of the dramatic New River Gorge. ✉ *Grandview Rd., Beaver* ☎ *304/763–3715.*

Sandstone Visitor Center

INFO CENTER | Sandstone Visitor Center is a full-service visitor center in the south section that features a short video on the New River and a native garden, as well as a book store. ✉ *330 Meadow Creek Rd., Meadow Bridge* ☎ *304/466–0417.*

Thurmond Depot Visitor Center

INFO CENTER | Thurmond Depot Visitor Center is a seasonal visitor center located inside a historic train depot. It's steps from the historic district, which includes a restored post office and a bank. ✉ *Thurmond* ☎ *304/469–9138.*

Activities

BIKING

New River Gorge is a sought-after destination for mountain bikers thanks to a variety of terrain and loop trails for all levels of riders. The Arrowhead Trails include four moderate to challenging mountain bike loops, including the Clovis, Adena, Dalton, and LeCroy Trails. There are also short trails open to mountain bikes in the Nuttallburg area, as well as near the historic Thurmond Depot.

BOATING AND RAFTING

As the leading outdoor activity in the New River Gorge region, whitewater rafting is a must-do in warm-weather months on the New and Gauley Rivers. Whitewater rafting trips range from family trips on mild whitewater of the Upper New River to adrenaline-pumping overnight trips on the Gauley River and Lower New River. Local outfitters like Adventures on the Gorge and Ace Adventure Resort offer multiple whitewater options for all skill levels.

Ace Adventure Resort

WHITE-WATER RAFTING | Half-day, full-day, or overnight rafting trips for all levels are available. The outfitter offers plenty of land-based adventures too, like ziplining, rappelling, ATV tours, and paintball. There is also a 5-acre waterpark on a spring-fed lake. Stay in a cabin or book a site for your tent or RV. 🌐 *aceraft.com.*

Adventures on the Gorge

WHITE-WATER RAFTING | This local outfitter runs multiple whitewater rafting trips that range from half-day family floats to multi-day high-adrenaline adventures along the New River and Gauley River. Beyond rafting, the company also offers adventures that range from treetop canopy tours and ziplining to mountain biking and rock climbing. Stay on-site in a cabin or glamping tent. A 35-acre campground has sites for RVs and tents. 🌐 *adventuresonthegorge.com.*

Wildwater Expeditions

WHITE-WATER RAFTING | Since 1968, Wildwater Expeditions has been offering whitewater rafting trips on the New and Gauley Rivers. Off-river adventures include mountain biking, horseback riding, paintball, and climbing. ☎ *800/982–7238* 🌐 *www.wvaraft.com.*

CAMPING

New River Gorge National Park and Preserve has six primitive campgrounds that range in size from 3 to 18 sites. The Brooklyn campground is for tents-only. All sites are available on a first-come, first-served basis. Backcountry camping is allowed at least 100 feet from developed trails. No permits are required.

FISHING

The warm waters of the north-flowing New River make this national park a popular spot to fish for bluegill, walleye, carp, crappie, catfish, and bass. Public river access points can be found throughout the park, including at Tug Creek Beach, Mill Creek, Grandview Sandbar, and Stone Cliff. All visitors 15 and older must hold a valid state fishing license to fish in the park.

HIKING

There are more than 100 miles of trails that criss-cross New River Gorge National Park and Preserve for hiking, biking, and horseback riding. There are seven distinct trail systems, including Nuttallburg Trails and Grandview Trails, across this 53-mile long park. There are trails for all levels, from easy boardwalk trails to rugged hikes that lead to historic mines and wildly scenic views. More than 20 trails range in length from 1/10 mile to over eight miles. Most are in the easy to moderate range, though there are some strenuous trails in the park.

ROCK CLIMBING

Known to rock climbers as simply "The New," the New River Gorge region has become one of the preeminent climbing destinations the country thanks to more than 1,600 established climbing routes. The majority of the routes are for advanced and expert climbers. Popular areas with multiple routes include Endless Wall and Bubba City.

What's Nearby

On the other side of the New River Gorge Bridge from the Canyon Rim Visitor Center in Lansing is **Fayetteville.** Park-goers have quick and easy access to a wide range of supplies, meals, and lodging options like the Quality Inn or Comfort Inn. You'll also find quick-service meal options, like Dunkin' and Taco Bell, as well as local sit-down favorites, like **Pie & Pints** and **Firecreek BBQ & Steaks.**

Chapter 47

NORTH CASCADES NATIONAL PARK

Updated by
Shelley Arenas

Camping ★★★★★

Hotels ★★★☆☆

Activities ★★★★☆

Scenery ★★★★★

Crowds ★☆☆☆☆

WELCOME TO NORTH CASCADES NATIONAL PARK

TOP REASONS TO GO

★ **Pure wilderness:** Spot bald eagles, deer, elk, and other wildlife on nearly 400 miles of mountain and meadow hiking trails.

★ **Majestic glaciers:** The North Cascades are home to several hundred moving ice masses, more than half of the glaciers in the United States.

★ **Splendid flora:** A bright palette of flowers blankets the hillsides in midsummer, while October's colors paint the landscape in vibrant autumn hues.

★ **Thrilling boat rides:** Lake Chelan, Ross Lake, and the Stehekin River are the starting points for kayaking, white-water rafting, and ferry trips.

★ **19th-century history:** Delve into the state's farming, lumber, and logging pasts in clapboard towns and homesteads around the park.

1 North Cascades Scenic Highway and Ross Lake National Recreation Area. The North Cascades Scenic Highway (State Highway 20), which runs west–east between the park's North and South units, is dotted with scenic viewpoints, trailheads, and towns that have visitor centers and other amenities. The route also runs through the Ross Lake National Recreation Area, whose eastern end stretches north toward British Columbia and whose placid lake is edged with pretty bays that draw summer swimmers and boaters.

2 Lake Chelan National Recreation Area. Ferries cruise between small waterfront villages along this pristine waterway, while kayakers and hikers follow quiet trails along its edges. This is one of the Northwest's most popular summer escapes, with nature-bound activities and rustic accommodations.

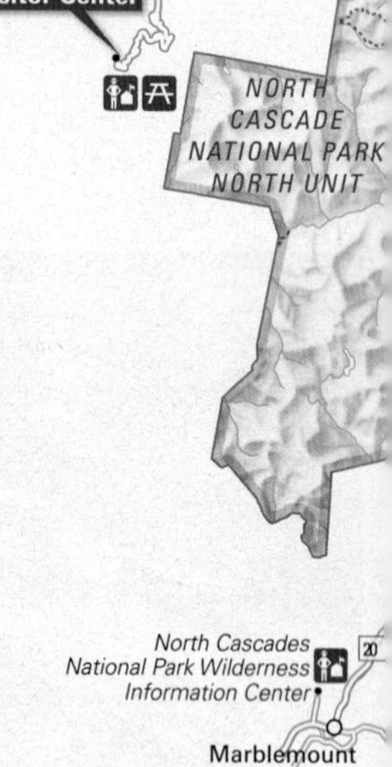

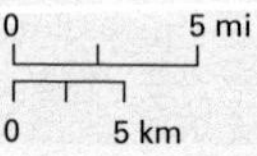

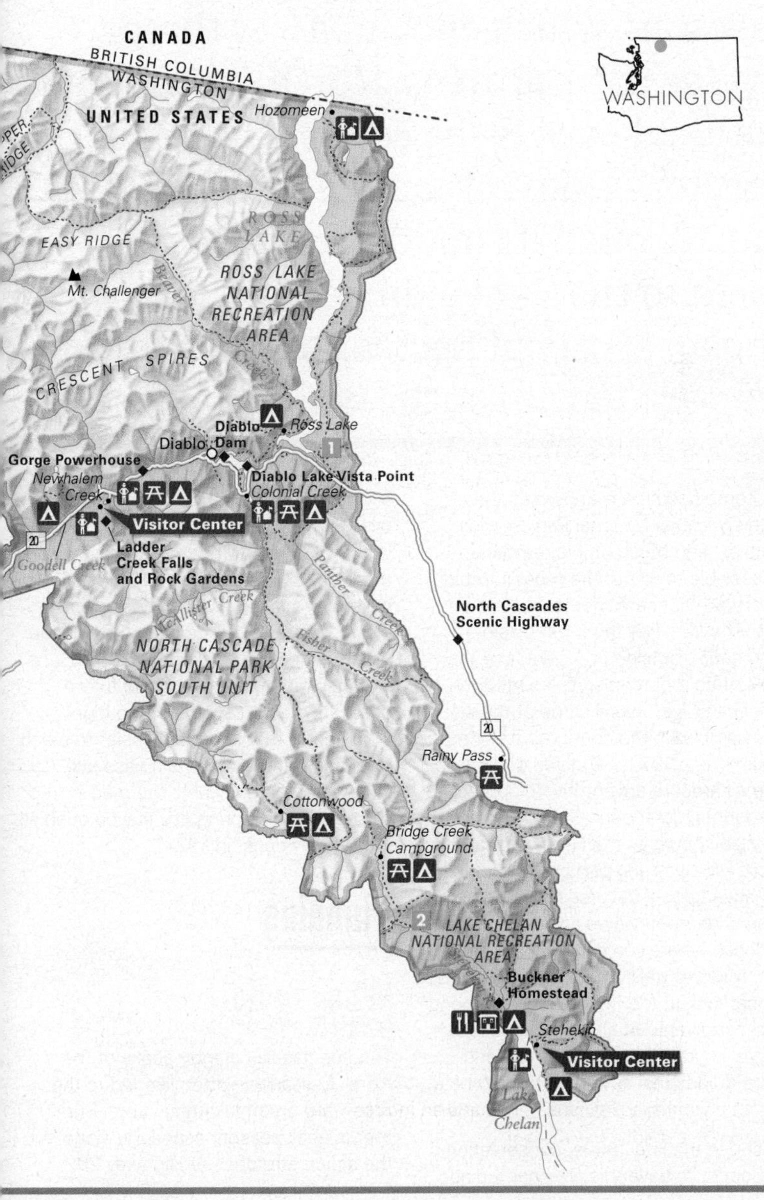
CANADA
BRITISH COLUMBIA
WASHINGTON
UNITED STATES
Hozomeen
WASHINGTON
ROSS LAKE
EASY RIDGE
Mt. Challenger
Beaver
ROSS LAKE NATIONAL RECREATION AREA
CRESCENT SPIRES
Creek
Diablo Dam
Diablo
Ross Lake
1
Gorge Powerhouse
Newhalem Creek
Diablo Lake Vista Point
Colonial Creek
Visitor Center
20
Ladder Creek Falls and Rock Gardens
Goodell Creek
Panther Creek
McAllister Creek
North Cascades Scenic Highway
NORTH CASCADE NATIONAL PARK SOUTH UNIT
Fisher Creek
20
Rainy Pass
Cottonwood
Bridge Creek Campground
2
LAKE CHELAN NATIONAL RECREATION AREA
Buckner Homestead
Stehekin
Visitor Center
Lake
Chelan

Countless snow-clad mountain spires dwarf narrow glacial valleys in this 684,000-acre expanse of the North Cascades, which encompasses three diverse natural areas. North Cascades National Park is the core of the region. The Ross Lake National Recreation Area cuts through its middle and also runs north to the Canadian border; Lake Chelan National Recreation Area flanks the park to the south.

This combined area is known as the North Cascades National Park Service Complex, and much of it is remote and inaccessible to all but the most intrepid explorers—just as wilderness is meant to be. The park has the most glaciers in the nation outside of Alaska, and the peaks of its mountains, nicknamed the "American Alps," were some of the last to be climbed in the contiguous United States (in the 1970s). But you don't have to be a hardcore adventurer to appreciate the mountain grandeur: State Highway 20—also known as the North Cascades Scenic Highway and part of the greater Cascades Loop—traverses the park, providing wide-open views and well-placed overlooks where you can stop to take it all in. Miles of trails offer more vistas and a closer look at the flora, which is among the most diverse of all the national parks. Wildlife is prevalent, too; rangers and nature guides can advise on how to best interact if you have a surprise encounter.

Starting in the late 1800s, conservationists sought to have this area named as a national park. Despite many efforts over the decades, this didn't happen until 1968, when Congress designated the park to preserve "certain majestic mountain scenery, snowfields, glaciers, alpine meadows, lakes and other unique glaciated features ... for the benefit, use and inspiration of present and future generations." Expansion of the highway in the early 1970s made it easier to reach the park, but the mountain pass still closes from late fall until the road is free of snow in mid-spring (it's stayed open all winter only once, in 1976).

Planning

When to Go

The spectacular, craggy peaks of the North Cascades—often likened to the Alps—are breathtaking anytime. Summer is peak season, especially along the alpine stretches of Highway 20;

AVERAGE HIGH/LOW TEMPERATURES					
JAN.	FEB.	MAR.	APR.	MAY	JUNE
39/30	43/32	49/34	56/38	64/43	70/49
JULY	AUG.	SEPT.	OCT.	NOV.	DEC.
76/52	76/53	69/49	57/42	45/36	39/31

weekends and holidays can be crowded. Summer is short and glorious in the high country, extending from snowmelt (late May to July) to early September.

The North Cascades Scenic Highway is a popular drive in September and October, when the changing leaves put on a colorful show. The lowland forest areas, such as the complex around Newhalem, can be visited almost any time of year. These are wonderfully quiet in early spring or late autumn on mild rainy days. Snow closes the North Cascades Scenic Highway from mid-November through mid-April, and sometimes longer.

Getting Here and Around

AIR

The closest airports to the western gateway town of Sedro-Woolley are Bellingham International Airport, 31 miles to the northwest; Paine Field Airport in Everett, 52 miles to the south; and Seattle-Tacoma International Airport, 87 miles to the south—all via Interstate 5. On the eastern side of park, Pangborn Memorial Airport in Wenatchee is 45 miles south of Chelan via US 97.

BOAT

If you're not up for a lengthy hike, you can reach Stehekin and other remote spots along Lake Chelan by boat.

Lake Chelan Boat Co

The *Lady of the Lake II* makes journeys from May to October, departing Chelan at 8:30 and returning at 6 ($45 round-trip). The *Lady Express,* a speedy catamaran, runs between Stehekin, Holden Village, the national park, and Lake Chelan year-round; schedules vary with the seasons, with daily trips during summer and three to five trips weekly the rest of the year. Tickets are $68 round-trip May to October and $45 round-trip the rest of the year. The vessels also can drop off and pick up at lakeshore trailheads. ✉ *1418 Woodin Ave., Chelan* ☎ *509/682–4584, 888/682–4584* 🌐 *ladyofthelake.com.*

CAR

Highway 20, the North Cascades Scenic Highway, splits the park's North and South units. It runs through the park's Ross Lake National Recreation Area, connecting towns like Sedro-Woolley, Newhalem, and Marblemount in the west with (in warmer months) Mazama, Winthrop, and Twisp in the east. This route is part of a greater Cascades Loop (www.cascadeloop.com), which continues to Chelan (via Methow, along WA 153 and U.S. 97) and loops south and west again (along U.S. 97 and Route 2).

The gravel Cascade River Road, which runs southeast from Marblemount, peels off Highway 20, and Sibley Creek/Hidden Lake Road (USFS 1540) turns off Cascade River Road to the Cascade Pass trailhead. Thornton Creek Road is another rough four-wheel-drive track. For the northern reaches of Ross Lake, the unpaved Hozomeen Road (Silver–Skagit Road) provides access between Hope, British Columbia, and Silver Lake and Skagit Valley provincial parks. From Stehekin, the Stehekin Valley Road continues to High Bridge and Car Wash Falls—although seasonal floods may cause washouts. Note that roads are narrow and some are closed seasonally, many sights are off the beaten path, and the scenery is so spectacular that you'll want to make more than a day trip.

Inspiration

Crown Jewel Wilderness: Creating North Cascades National Park, by Laura Danner, offers an in-depth look at how this national park came to be and highlights the tireless efforts of conservationists.

Hiking Naked: A Quaker Woman's Search for Balance, by Iris Graville, is a memoir about the author and her family's choice to leave city life behind and move to the remote village of Stehekin.

The North Cascades: Finding Beauty and Renewal in the Wild Nearby, by William Dietrich, is filled with stunning photos from 20 photographers and park essays by the author and others.

Park Essentials

ACCESSIBILITY

Visitor centers along North Cascades Scenic Highway are accessible by wheelchair. Hikes include Sterling Munro, Skagit River Loop, and Rock Shelter, three short trails into lowland old-growth forest, all at mile 120 along Highway 20 near Newhalem, and the Happy Creek Forest Trail at mile 134.

PARK FEES AND PERMITS

There are no entrance fees to the national park and no parking fees at trailheads on park land. A Northwest Forest Pass, required for parking at Forest Service trailheads, is $5 per vehicle for a calendar day or $30 for a year. A free wilderness permit is required for all overnight stays in the backcountry; these are available in person only. Dock permits for boat-in campgrounds are $5 per day. Car camping is $10 per night at Gorge Lake Campground and $16 per night at Colonial Creek, Goodell Creek, and Newhalem Creek campgrounds during the summer and free off-season; the primitive Hozomeen Campground is free all year.

PARK HOURS

The park never closes, but access is limited by snow in winter. Highway 20 (North Cascades Scenic Highway), the major access to the park, is partially closed from mid-November to mid-April, depending on snow levels.

CELL PHONE RECEPTION

Cell reception in the park is unreliable. Public telephones are found at the North Cascades Visitor Center and Skagit Information Center in Newhalem and the Golden West Visitor Center and North Cascades Lodge in Stehekin.

Hotels

Accommodations in North Cascades range from remote inns and homey cabin rentals to spartan campgrounds. Expect to pay roughly $50 to $200 per night, depending on the rental size and the season. Book at least three months in advance, or even a year for popular accommodations in summer.

Restaurants

There are no formal restaurants in North Cascades National Park, just a lakeside café at the North Cascades Environmental Learning Center. Stehekin has three options: the Stehekin Valley Ranch dining room, North Cascades Lodge, or the Stehekin Pastry Company; all serve simple, hearty, country-style meals and sweets.

Hotel and restaurant reviews have been shortened. For full information visit Fodors.com. Hotel prices are the lowest cost of a standard double room in high season. Restaurant prices are the average cost of a main course at dinner, or if dinner is not served, at lunch.

What It Costs in U.S. Dollars

	$	$$	$$$	$$$$
RESTAURANTS				
	under $12	$12–$20	$21–$30	over $30
HOTELS				
	under $100	$100–$150	$151–$200	over $200

Tours

★ **North Cascades Environmental Learning Center**
ECOTOURISM | FAMILY | This is the spot for information on hiking, wildlife watching, horseback riding, climbing, boat rentals, and fishing in the park, as well as classroom education and hands-on nature experiences. Guided tours from the center include lake and dam visits, mountain climbs, pack-train excursions, and guided canoe trips on Diablo Lake. Other choices range from forest ecology and backpacking trips to writing and art retreats. Family getaway weekends in summer are a fun way to unplug from technology and introduce kids to nature. There's also a research library, a dock on Diablo Lake, an amphitheater, and overnight lodging. The center is operated by the North Cascades Institute in partnership with the National Park Service and Seattle City Light. ✉ *1940 Diablo Dam Rd., Diablo* ☎ *360/854–2599 headquarters, 206/526–2599 environmental learning center* 🌐 *www.ncascades.org* 🎫 *Day programs from $110; overnight lodging (including meals) from $256 per couple* ⏲ *Closed during winter months.*

Visitor Information

PARK CONTACT INFORMATION North Cascades National Park. ✉ *810 Rte. 20, Sedro-Woolley* ☎ *360/854–7200* 🌐 *www.nps.gov/noca.* **Glacier Public Service Center.** ✉ *10091 Mt. Baker Hwy., Glacier* ☎ *360/599–2714* 🌐 *www.nps.gov/noca/planyourvisit/visitorcenters.htm.*

North Cascades Scenic Highway and Ross Lake National Recreation Area

Entrance to national recreation area is about 50 miles east of Sedro-Woolley and 40 miles west of Mazama via the 140-mile North Cascades Scenic Highway (Highway 20).

Perhaps the easiest way to experience the park's breathtaking scenery (and, perhaps, just a bit of its wilderness) is on a drive along North Cascades Scenic Highway (Highway 20), which traverses the national park's Ross Lake National Recreation Area from west to east—or vice versa if you prefer. North and west of the Ross Lake NRA is the national park's North Unit. Inaccessible by roads, this unit's seemingly endless landscape of pine-topped peaks and ridges centers on snowy Mt. Challenger and stretches over the Picket Range toward the Canadian border.

On the other side of the highway, the national park's South Unit—with its lake-filled mountain foothills and flower-filled meadows—is rife with waterfalls and wildlife. Like its northern sibling, the unit doesn't have any services, but it does offer scenic outlooks and trailheads near the highway, some of which are just outside the park and and accessed via side roads.

In addition to running the length of the North Cascades Scenic Highway, Ross Lake National Recreation Area also runs along the Skagit River north to the U.S.–Canada border, encompassing the three lake reservoirs created by the power projects on the river. The largest reservoir, Ross Lake, is popular for on-the-water recreation. A water taxi shuttles hikers to remote trails in the north end of the park.

HISTORIC SIGHTS

Diablo Dam

DAM | The Diablo Dam is one of three in the area that collectively produce hydroelectric power for Seattle City Light. Although its powerhouse can only be visited on bus tours that are sometimes offered (check at the Skagit Information Center), the experience of driving across a dam makes the short detour off Highway 20 worthwhile. To see the dam from the water, continue a mile farther east along Diablo Dam Road to the North Cascades Environmental Learning Center, which offers Diablo Lake boat tours. Guides share the secret of how the lake gets its vibrant turquoise color as you cruise past Diablo Dam and then north to Ross Dam, where guides can sometimes take visitors into the powerhouse for a closer look. ✉ *Diablo Dam Rd., Diablo* ✣ *Turnoff is off North Cascades Scenic Hwy. (Hwy. 20), 7 miles northeast of Newhalem.*

SCENIC DRIVES

North Cascades Scenic Highway

SCENIC DRIVE | Also known as Highway 20, this classic scenic route, part of the greater Cascades Loop, runs roughly 140 miles between Sedro-Woolley and Twisp. Heading west to east, the highway first winds through the green pastures and woods of the upper Skagit Valley, with mountains looming in the distance. Beyond Concrete, a former cement-manufacturing town, the highway climbs into the mountains, passes the Diablo and Ross dams, and traverses the park's Ross Lake National Recreation Area. Here several pull-outs offer great views of the lake and the surrounding snow-capped peaks. From June to September, the meadows are covered with wildflowers, and from late September through October, the mountain slopes glow with fall foliage. The pinnacle of this stretch is 5,477-foot-high Washington Pass: look east, to where the road descends quickly into a series of hairpin curves between Early Winters Creek and the Methow Valley. Remember, this section of the highway is closed from roughly November to April, depending on snowfall, and sometimes closes temporarily during the busy summer season due to mudslides from storms. From the Methow Valley, Highway 153 travels along the Methow River's apple, nectarine, and peach orchards to Pateros, on the Columbia River; from here, you can continue east to Grand Coulee or south to Lake Chelan. 🌐 *www.cascadeloop.com.*

SCENIC STOPS

Diablo Lake Vista Point

VIEWPOINT | FAMILY | This is a must-stop photo op: indeed, countless photos of the gorgeous lake have been taken from here over the decades. ✉ *North Cascades Scenic Hwy. (Hwy. 20)* ✣ *11 miles east of Newhalem.*

Ladder Creek Falls and Rock Gardens

TOUR—SIGHT | The rock gardens overlooking Ladder Creek Falls, 7 miles west of Diablo, are beautiful and inspiring. In summer, a slide show about the powerhouse and the area's history is offered at 8 pm on Thursday and Friday evening in Currier Hall in Newhalem, followed by a free guided walk to the falls; visitors can reserve in advance for a chicken dinner at 7 pm. Skagit Information Center has maps for a self-guided walk. ✉ *North Cascades Hwy., Newhalem* ✣ *2 miles east of North Cascades Visitor Center* ☎ *360/854–2589* 🌐 *www.seattle.gov/light/tours/skagit* 🎫 *$19/dinner; walking tour free* ⏲ *Closed Oct.–Apr.*

TRAILS

★ Cascade Pass

TRAIL | This extremely popular, 3¾-mile, four-hour trail is known for stunning panoramas from the great mountain divide. Dozens of peaks line the horizon as you make your way up the fairly flat, hairpin-turn track, the scene fronted by a blanket of alpine wildflowers from July to mid-August. Arrive before noon if you want a parking spot at the trailhead. If you're feeling fit (and ambitious), a much longer hike (23 miles) goes all the way to High Bridge, where you can catch a shuttle to Stehekin in the Lake Chelan National Recreation Area. *Moderate.* ✉ *North Cascades National Park* ✣ *Trailhead: At end of Cascade River Rd., 14 miles from Marblemount off Hwy. 20* 🌐 *www.nps.gov/noca/planyourvisit/cascade-pass-trail.htm.*

Diablo Lake Trail

TRAIL | Explore nearly 4 miles of waterside terrain on this route, which is accessed from the Sourdough Creek parking lot. An excellent alternative for parties with young hikers is to take the Seattle City Light Ferry one-way. *Moderate.* ✉ *North Cascades National Park* ✣ *Trailhead: At milepost 135, Hwy. 20* 🌐 *www.nps.gov/noca.*

Happy Creek Forest Walk

TRAIL | **FAMILY** | Old-growth forests are the focus of this kid-friendly boardwalk route, a ½-mile loop through the trees off the North Cascades Scenic Highway. Interpretive signs provide details about flora along the way. *Easy.* ✉ *North Cascades National Park* ✣ *Trailhead: At milepost 135, North Cascades Scenic Hwy.* 🌐 *www.nps.gov/noca.*

Rainy Lake Trail

TRAIL | An easy, accessible, 1-mile paved trail leads to Rainy Lake, a waterfall, and a glacier-view platform. *Easy.* ✉ *North Cascades National Park* ✣ *Trailhead: Off Hwy. 20, 35 miles west of Winthrop* 🌐 *www.fs.usda.gov/recarea/okawen/recarea/?recid=59385.*

River Loop Trail

TRAIL | Take this flat and easy, 1¾-mile, wheelchair-accessible trail through stands of huge old-growth firs and cedars toward the Skagit River. *Easy.* ✉ *North Cascades National Park* ✣ *Trailhead: Near North Cascades Visitor Center* 🌐 *www.nps.gov/noca/planyourvisit/newhalem-area-trails.htm.*

Rock Shelter Trail

TRAIL | This short trail—partly boardwalk—leads to a campsite used 1,400 years ago by Native Americans; interpretive signs tell the history of human presence in the region. *Easy.* ✉ *North Cascades National Park* ✣ *Trailhead: Off Hwy. 20 near Newhalem Creek Campground* 🌐 *www.nps.gov/noca/planyourvisit/newhalem-area-trails.htm.*

Sterling Munro Trail

TRAIL | Starting from the North Cascades Visitor Center, this popular introductory stroll follows a short 300-foot path over a boardwalk to a lookout above the forested Picket Range peaks. *Easy.* ✉ *North Cascades National Park* ✣ *Trailhead: Milepost 120, near Newhalem Creek Campground* 🌐 *www.nps.gov/noca/planyourvisit/newhalem-area-trails.htm.*

Trail of the Cedars

TRAIL | Less than a ½ mile long, this trail winds its way through one of the finest surviving stands of old-growth western red cedar in Washington. Some of the trees along the path are more than 1,000 years old. *Easy.* ✉ *Newhalem* ✣ *Trailhead: Near North Cascades Visitor Center, milepost 120, Hwy. 20* 🌐 *www.nps.gov/noca/planyourvisit/newhalem-area-trails.htm.*

VISITOR CENTERS

North Cascades Visitor Center

INFO CENTER | The main visitor facility for the park has extensive displays on the surrounding landscape. Learn about the history and value of old-growth trees, the many creatures that depend on the rain-forest ecology, and the effects of human activity on the ecosystem. Check bulletin boards for special programs with park rangers. ✉ *Milepost 120, North Cascades Hwy., Newhalem* ☎ *206/386–4495* 🌐 *www.nps.gov/noca/planyourvisit/visitorcenters.htm* 🕒 *Closed Oct.–mid-May.*

Snowy, misty peaks and alpine wildflowers along the Cascade Pass Trail.

Skagit Information Center

INFO CENTER | This center is operated by Seattle City Light, North Cascades Institute, and the national park. It's the gathering point for various tours run by Seattle City Light and has exhibits about the utility's hydroelectric projects in the North Cascades. Pick up a map to a self-guided walking tour of historic Newhalem, as well as other park information. ✉ *Hwy. 20 and Main St., Newhalem* ☎ *360/854–2589* ⏲ *Closed Oct.–mid-May.*

Hotels

Ross Lake Resort

$$$$ | **HOTEL** | Remote and unique, it's not easy to snag a booking at the only lodging in the Ross Lake area, but it's worth the effort for a chance to immerse yourself in nature in a lakefront cabin. **Pros:** spectacular setting; plenty of recreational equipment to rent; worth a day visit if you can't get lodging. **Cons:** not accessible by road; short season and books up fast; no food services but cabins have kitchens.

$ *Rooms from: $220* ✉ *Ross Lake Resort, 503 Diablo St.* ☎ *206/486–3751* 🌐 *www.rosslakeresort.com* ⏲ *Closed Nov.–June* 15 units 🍽 *No meals.*

Lake Chelan National Recreation Area

Accessed via boat from Chelan to Stehekin.

This area includes the north end of Lake Chelan and the Stehekin Valley and river. Access from the north is by trail (on foot or horseback). The small village of Stehekin is a favorite tourist stop for its peaceful isolation; without road connections, your easiest option for getting there is a scenic boat ride on one of the vessels that runs regularly between Chelan and Stehekin. (In the past, a seaplane company provided faster service and a fun adventure, but it is temporarily closed.)

Sights

HISTORIC SITES

Buckner Homestead

FESTIVAL | Dating from 1889, this restored pioneer farm includes an apple orchard, farmhouse, barn, and many ranch buildings. You can pick up a self-guided tour booklet from the drop box. Feel free to enjoy apples from the trees in season. A harvest festival is held in October. ✉ *Stehekin Valley Rd., 3½ miles northwest of Stehekin Landing, Stehekin* 🌐 *www.bucknerhomestead.org.*

VISITOR CENTERS

Chelan Ranger Station

INFO CENTER | The base for the Chelan National Recreation Area and Wenatchee National Forest has an information desk and a shop selling regional maps and books. ✉ *428 W. Woodin Ave., Chelan* ☎ *509/682–4900* 🌐 *www.fs.usda.gov/detail/okawen/about-forest/offices* ⏲ *Closed weekends.*

Golden West Visitor Center

INFO CENTER | Maps and concise displays at this visitor center explain the layered ecology of the valley, which encompasses virtually every ecosystem in the Northwest. Rangers offer guidance on hiking, camping, and other activities and arrange bike tours. There is also an arts-and-crafts gallery and audiovisual and children's programs. Campers can pick up free backcountry permits. Note that access to Stehekin is by boat or trail only. ✉ *Stehekin Valley Rd., Stehekin* ✥ *¼ mile north of Stehekin Landing* ☎ *509/699–2080* 🌐 *www.nps.gov/noca/planyourvisit/visitorcenters.htm* ⏲ *Closed Oct.–mid-May.*

Restaurants

Restaurant at Stehekin Valley Ranch

$$ | **AMERICAN** | **FAMILY** | Meals in the rustic log ranch house, served at polished wood tables, include buffet dinners of steak, ribs, hamburgers, fish, salad, beans, and dessert. Note that breakfast is served 7 to 9, lunch is noon to 1, and dinner is 5:30 to 7; show up later than that, and you'll find the kitchen is closed. **Known for:** hearty meals; fresh berries, fruit, and produce; communal dining. [$] *Average main: $20* ✉ *Stehekin Valley Rd., 9 miles north of Stehekin Landing, Stehekin* ☎ *509/682–4677* 🌐 *www.stehekinvalleyranch.com* ⏲ *Closed Oct.–mid-June.*

Coffee and Quick Bites

Stehekin Pastry Company

$ | **BAKERY** | As you enter this lawn-framed timber chalet, you're immersed in the tantalizing aromas of a European bakery. Glassed-in display cases are filled with trays of homemade baked goods, and the pungent espresso is eye-opening. **Known for:** fruit pie; amazing pastries; hearty lunch food. [$] *Average main: $9* ✉ *Stehekin Valley Rd., Stehekin* ✥ *About 2 miles north of Stehekin Landing* ☎ *509/682–7742* 🌐 *www.stehekinpastry.com* ⏲ *Closed mid-Oct.–mid-May.*

Hotels

North Cascades Lodge at Stehekin

$$$ | **HOTEL** | Crackling fires and Lake Chelan views are provided both in standard rooms in the Alpine House, with its shared lounge and lakeside deck, and in larger rooms in the Swiss Mont building, with its private decks overlooking the water. **Pros:** on the water; recreation center with pool table; kayak and canoe rentals. **Cons:** no air-conditioning; TV is available only in the recreation building; limited Internet service and no cell phone service. *Rooms from: $154* *955 Stehekin Valley Rd., Stehekin* *509/699–2056, 855/685–4167 reservations* *www.lodgeatstehekin.com* *Closed Nov.–Jan.* *29 units* *No meals.*

Stehekin Valley Ranch

$$$$ | ALL-INCLUSIVE | FAMILY | Alongside pretty meadows at the edge of pine forest, this rustic ranch is a center for hikers and horseback riders, who stay in barnlike cabins with cedar paneling, tile floors, and a private bath or in canvas-roof tent cabins with bunk beds, kerosene lamps, and shared bathrooms. **Pros:** easy access to recreation; playground and outdoor game fields; hearty meals included. **Cons:** no bathrooms in tent cabins; many repeat guests so book early; short opening season. *Rooms from: $290* *Stehekin Valley Rd., Stehekin* *9 miles north of Stehekin Landing* *509/682–4677* *stehekinvalleyranch.com* *Closed Oct.–mid-June* *15 cabins* *All meals.*

Activities

BIKING

Mountain bikes are permitted on highways, unpaved back roads, and a few designated tracks around the park; however, there is no biking on footpaths. It's $31 round-trip to bring a bike on the Lake Chelan ferry to Stehekin.

Discovery Bikes

BICYCLING | You can rent mountain bikes and helmets by the hour at a self-serve rack in front of the Stehekin Log office in Stehekin. For a longer excursion, meet up at 8 am for a van ride and narrated tour to the Stehekin Valley Ranch. After enjoying a full breakfast, hop on a bike to explore the trails and sites. *Stehekin Valley Rd., Stehekin* *5-min walk from boat landing* *www.stehekindiscoverybikes.com* *From $5 per hr; $38 for ranch breakfast ride.*

BOATING AND RAFTING

North Cascades River Expeditions

WHITE-WATER RAFTING | From April to September, North Cascades River Expeditions offers white-water rafting on the Upper Skagit and other area rivers. November to early March, you can take an easy paddle through the Skagit River Bald Eagle Natural Area for great opportunities to photograph these majestic birds in their habitat. *800/634–8433* *www.riverexpeditions.com* *From $60.*

Orion River Expeditions

WHITE-WATER RAFTING | FAMILY | Family-oriented floats are offered in August on the Skagit River for ages six and up. More lively white-water tours run on other area rivers April to September. *509/548–1401, 509/881–9556* *www.orionexp.com* *From $90.*

Ross Lake Resort

BOATING | From mid-June through October, the resort rents motorboats, kayaks, and canoes. It also operates a water taxi taking hikers to and from eight trailheads. The taxi is available by reservation and can accommodate up to six passengers. *503 Diablo St., Rockport* *206/486–3751* *www.rosslakeresort.com.*

CAMPING

Lake Chelan National Recreation Area. Many backcountry camping areas are accessible via park shuttles or boat. All require a free backcountry permit. Purple Point, the most popular campground due to its quick access to Stehekin Landing, has six tent sites, bear boxes, and nearby road access. *Stehekin Landing, Stehekin* *509/699–2080.*

Ross Lake National Recreation Area. The National Park Service maintains three upper Skagit Valley campgrounds; some are open fully or partially year round, with the rest open mid-May through mid-October. You can make reservations for the seasonal Newhalem Creek Campground, which has 107 sites (some suitable for RVs of up to 45 feet), drinking water, and flush toilets but not showers or hookups. Ten of the 93 sites in the South Loop of the Colonial Creek Campground are open year-round. Reservations are accepted here but not at the campground's North Loop, which has 42 seasonal sites. Both sections can accommodate tents and small RVs (no hookups or showers) and have flush toilets and drinking water. The main Goodell Creek Campground is open year round and has 19 sites (some suitable for small RVs, though no hookups or showers), pit toilets, and drinking water (seasonal). Aside from a few group sites, camping here is first-come, first-served. ✉ *North Cascades National Park* ☎ *877/444–6700* 🌐 *recreation.gov.*

EDUCATIONAL OFFERINGS

Seattle City Light Information and Tour Center

TOUR—SIGHT | Based at a history museum that has exhibits about the introduction of electric power through the Cascade ranges, Seattle's public electric company offers tours and programs during summer. Several trails start at the building, and the group offers sightseeing excursions on Diablo Lake during the summer in partnership with the North Cascades Institute, Thursday through Monday lunch cruises by advance reservation, and afternoon cruises Friday through Sunday. The boat tour includes a visit to the Diablo Dam. Other tours include a visit to the powerhouse (with picnic lunch) on weekends, and an evening dinner and guided walk to Ladder Creek Falls on Thursday and Friday. Free 45-minute walking tours through the historic town of Newhalem are offered daily from July through Labor Day. ✉ *Milepost 120, North Cascades Hwy., Newhalem* ☎ *360/854–2589* 🌐 *www.skagittours.com* 🎟 *Walking tour free, other tours from $19* ⏲ *Closed Oct.–Apr.*

HORSEBACK RIDING

Many hiking trails and backwoods paths are also popular horseback-riding routes, particularly around the park's southern fringes.

Stehekin Outfitters

HORSEBACK RIDING | Since 1947, the Courtney family has been guiding adventures in the Stehekin Valley. Departing from Stehekin Valley Ranch, 2½-hour horseback trips head to Howard Lake, while full-day rides (lunch included) take you to Bridge Creek. Stehekin Outfitters also offers tent rentals at two local campgrounds and multiday hiking adventures from June to mid-September. ✉ *North Cascades National Park* ☎ *509/682–7742* 🌐 *stehekinoutfitters.com* 🎟 *From $95.*

KAYAKING

Ross Lake Resort

BOATING | The resort, open mid-June to October, rents kayaks, motor boats, canoes, and fishing equipment, and offers a water taxi and portage service for exploring Ross Lake. The resort is not accessible by road. ✉ *503 Diablo St., Rockport* ☎ *206/486–3751* 🌐 *www.rosslakeresort.com.*

Stehekin Valley Ranch

KAYAKING | Kayak tours of the upper estuary of Lake Chelan are offered every morning during the summer. ✉ *Stehekin Valley Rd., Stehekin* ✥ *3½ miles from Stehekin Landing* ☎ *509/682–4677* 🌐 *www.stehekinvalleyranch.com* 🎟 *$50.*

SKIING

Mt. Baker, just off the park's far northwest corner, is one of the Northwest's premier skiing, snowboarding, and snowshoeing regions—the area set a world record for most snow in a single season during the winter of 1998–99 (1,140 inches).

Stehekin is another base for winter sports. The Stehekin Valley alone has 20 miles of trails; some of the most popular are around Buckner Orchard, Coon Lake, and the Courtney Ranch (Cascade Corrals).

Mt. Baker Ski Area

SNOW SPORTS | This is the closest winter-sports area, with facilities for downhill and cross-country skiing, snowboarding, and other recreational ventures. The main base is the town of Glacier, 17 miles west of the slopes, where lodging is available. Equipment rental and food service are onsite. **Facilities:** 38 trails; 1,000 acres; 1,500-foot vertical drop; 10 lifts (8 quad chairs, 2 rope tows). ✉ *Hwy. 542, Glacier* ✥ *52 miles east of Bellingham* ☎ *360/734–6771, 360/671–0211 for snow reports* 🌐 *www.mtbaker.us* 🎫 *Lift ticket: weekdays $62, weekends and holidays $69.*

What's Nearby

Heading into North Cascades National Park from Seattle on Interstate 5 to Highway 2, **Sedro-Woolley** (pronounced "*see*-droh *wool*-lee") is the first main town you encounter. A former logging and steel-mill base settled by North Carolina pioneers, the settlement still has a 19th-century ambience throughout its rustic downtown area. It's also home to the North Cascades National Park Headquarters. From here, it's about 40 miles to the park's western edges. Along the way, you can stop for supplies in tiny Concrete, about 20 miles from the park along Highway 20. **Marblemount** is 10 miles farther east, about 12 miles west of the North Cascades Visitor Center. It's another atmospheric former timber settlement nestled in the mountain foothills, and its growing collection of motels, cafés, and tour outfitters draws outdoors enthusiasts each summer.

The village of **Mazama,** in the Methow Valley, is the closest town to the park's eastern entrance and the first place you can stop for gas and food when coming down the mountain from the west. It's about 24 miles from Washington Pass. **Winthrop,** a relaxed, riverside, rodeo town—complete with clapboard cafés and five-and-dime charm—is about 20 minutes east of Mazama. This is also an outdoor-recreation base. Less than 10 miles southeast of Winthrop, the tiny town of **Twisp** is settled in the farmlands and orchards, its streets lined with a few small lodgings and eateries. The resort town of **Chelan,** nestled around its serene namesake lake, lies about 60 miles due south of Winthrop along Highway 153.

Chapter 48

OLYMPIC NATIONAL PARK

48

Updated by
Shelly Arenas

Camping ★★★★★

Hotels ★★★★★

Activities ★★★★★

Scenery ★★★★★

Crowds ★★★☆☆

WELCOME TO OLYMPIC NATIONAL PARK

TOP REASONS TO GO

★ **Exotic rain forest:** A rain forest in the Pacific Northwest? Indeed, Olympic National Park is one of the few places in the world with this unique temperate landscape.

★ **Beachcombing:** Miles of rugged, spectacular coastline hemmed with sea stacks and tidal pools edge the driftwood-strewn shores of the Olympic Peninsula.

★ **Nature's hot tubs:** A dip in Sol Duc's natural geothermal mineral pools offers a secluded spa experience in the wooded heart of the park.

★ **Lofty vistas:** The hardy can hike up meadowed foothill trails or climb the frosty peaks throughout the Olympics—or just drive up to Hurricane Ridge for endless views.

★ **A sense of history:** Native American history is key to this region, where eight tribes have traditional ties to the park lands—there's 12,000 years of history to explore.

1 Coastal Olympic. The ocean has carved some of the park's most memorable scenes into the rugged coastline, and provided the beaches and tide pools with sea stars, crabs, and anemones.

2 Rain Forests. Centered on the Hoh, Queets, and Quinault river valleys, this is the region's most unique landscape: Douglas firs and Sitka spruces coexist with fern- and moss-draped cedars, maples, and alders.

3 Lake Crescent and Sol Duc Valley. At the park's northern flank, old-growth forests frame stunning Lake Crescent, the state's second-deepest lake. Nearby, the Sol Duc Valley beckons with waterfalls, hot springs, the salmon-filled Sol Duc River, and hiking trails.

4 Mountains. Craggy gray peaks and snow-covered summits dominate the skyline, while low-level foliage and wildflower meadows make for excellent plateau hiking, but temperatures can be brisk; some roads are closed in winter.

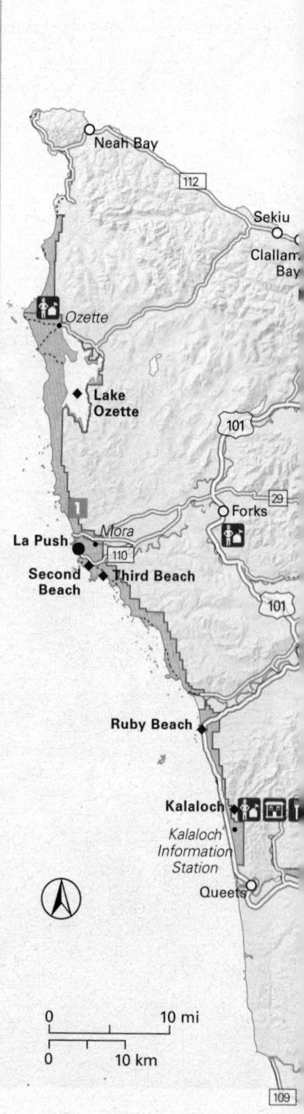

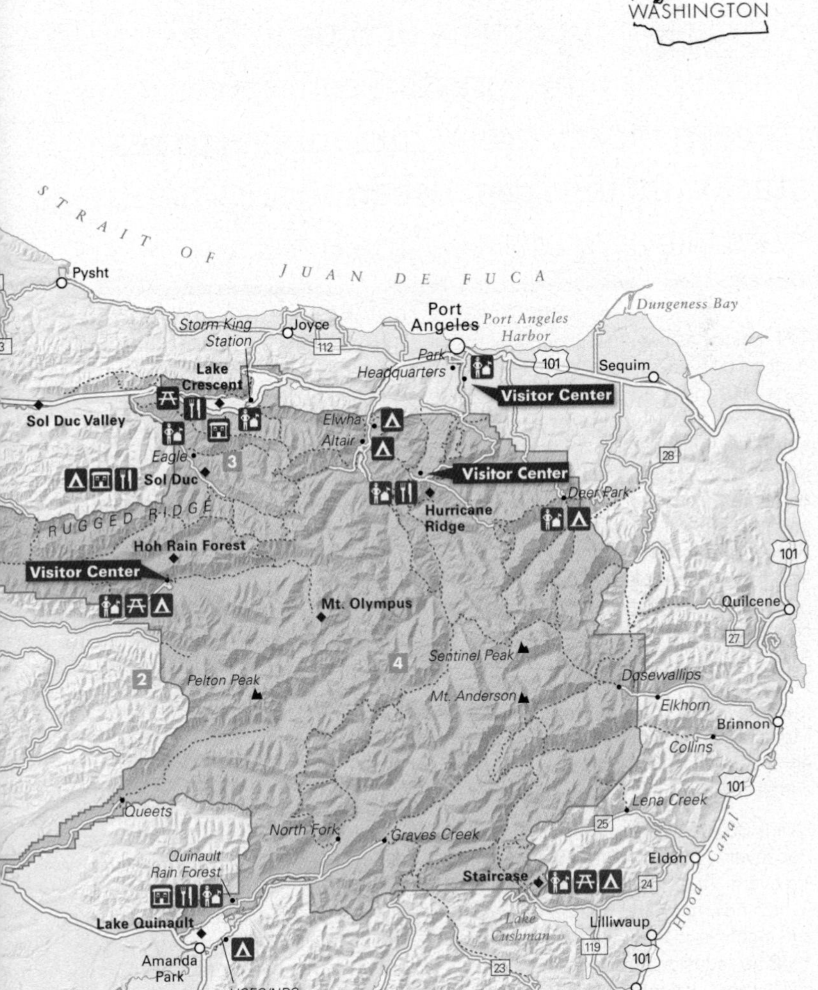
WASHINGTON
STRAIT OF JUAN DE FUCA
Pysht
Storm King Station
Joyce
112
Port Angeles
Port Angeles Harbor
Dungeness Bay
Park Headquarters
101
Sequim
Visitor Center
Lake Crescent
Sol Duc Valley
Elwha
Altair
Eagle
3
Sol Duc
Visitor Center
28
Hurricane Ridge
Deer Park
RUGGED RIDGE
Hoh Rain Forest
Visitor Center
101
Mt. Olympus
Quilcene
27
Sentinel Peak
4
2
Pelton Peak
Dosewallips
Mt. Anderson
Elkhorn
Brinnon
Collins
101
Lena Creek
Queets
25
North Fork
Graves Creek
Quinault Rain Forest
Eldon
Staircase
24
Hood Canal
Lake Quinault
Lake Cushman
Lilliwaup
119
101
Amanda Park
23
USFS/NPS Information Station
Hoodsport
101

Edged on all sides by water, the forested landscape is remote and pristine, and works its way around the sharpened ridges of the snowcapped Olympic Mountains. Big lakes cut pockets of blue in the rugged blanket of pine forests. From towering trees in mossy green rain forests to sea stacks jutting from ocean shores, nature puts the awe in awesome here.

The region has been described as magical by many a visitor for more than a century, and appreciated by the Native Americans that lived here for centuries before. In the late 1800s efforts began to preserve this unique area of mountains, rain forest, coast, and the diverse flora and fauna that thrive in its environment. Responding to conservationist John Muir's encouragement to save the old growth forests, President Cleveland created the Olympic Forest Reserve in his final days in office in 1897. In 1909 President Theodore Roosevelt designated the area as the Mount Olympus National Monument, in part to protect the native elk that were later renamed in his honor and still roam in the Hoh Rain Forest.

Nearly 30 years later, another President Roosevelt (Franklin) visited the area, staying overnight at the Lake Crescent Lodge (which now has cabins named after him) and lunching at the Lake Quinault Inn. In 1938 he redesignated the federal lands as Olympic National Park. Some years later, a coastal section was added.

The park gets more than 3 million visitors annually and covers a lot of area—nearly 1,500 square miles. There are more than 600 miles of trails, 168 miles of roads, 73 miles of shoreline... in other words, a lot to see and do! Most of the park's attractions are found either off U.S. Highway 101 or down trails that require hikes of 15 minutes or longer. The coastal beaches are linked to the highway by downhill tracks; the number of cars parked alongside the road at the start of the paths indicates how crowded the beach will be.

Five in-park lodging options—including two historic lodges on sparkling lakes and one perched above the Pacific Ocean—make it possible to take your time and really immerse yourself in this wondrous place, while gazing out at the same views that have been inspiring awe for generations. It can be an exercise in patience to try and book a room during the high season at these very popular lodges, where some families return every year. Plan ahead, visit midweek, or consider a spring or fall stay (especially fun if you like storm-watching).

AVERAGE HIGH/LOW TEMPERATURES					
JAN.	**FEB.**	**MAR.**	**APR.**	**MAY**	**JUNE**
45/33	48/35	51/36	55/39	60/44	65/48
JULY	**AUG.**	**SEPT.**	**OCT.**	**NOV.**	**DEC.**
68/50	69/51	66/48	58/42	50/37	45/34

Planning

When to Go

Summer, with its long stretches of sun-filled days, is prime touring time for Olympic National Park. June through September are the peak months; Hurricane Ridge, the Hoh Rain Forest, Lake Crescent, and Ruby Beach are bustling by 10 am.

Late spring and early autumn are also good bets for clear weather; anytime between April and October, you'll have a good chance of fair skies. Between Thanksgiving and Easter, it's a toss-up as to which days will turn out fair; prepare for heavy clouds, rain showers, and chilly temperatures, then hope for the best.

Winter is a great time to visit if you enjoy isolation. Locals are usually the only hardy souls here during this time, except for weekend skiers heading to the snowfields around Hurricane Ridge. Many visitor facilities have limited hours or are closed from October to April, and some of the park lodgings close for the winter, too.

Getting Here and Around

You can enter the park at a number of points, but because the park is 95% wilderness, access roads do not penetrate far. The best way to get around and to see many of the park's top sights is on foot.

AIR

Seattle–Tacoma International Airport is the nearest airport to Olympic National Park. It's roughly a two-hour drive from the park.

BOAT

Ferries provide another unique (though indirect) link to the Olympic area from Seattle; contact **Washington State Ferries** (☎ *888/808–7977, 206/464–6400* 🌐 *www.wsdot.wa.gov/ferries*) for information.

BUS

Grays Harbor Transit runs buses Monday through Saturday from Aberdeen and Hoquiam to Amanda Park, on the west end of Lake Quinault. Jefferson Transit operates a Forks–Amanda Park route Monday through Saturday.

BUS CONTACTS Grays Harbor Transit. ☎ *360/532–2770, 800/562–9730* 🌐 *www.ghtransit.com.* **Jefferson Transit.** ☎ *800/371–0497, 360/385–4777* 🌐 *www.jeffersontransit.com.*

CAR

U.S. 101 essentially encircles the main section of Olympic National Park, and a number of roads lead from the highway into the park's mountains and toward its beaches. You can reach U.S. 101 via Interstate 5 at Olympia, via Route 12 at Aberdeen, or via Route 104 from the Washington state ferry terminals at Bainbridge or Kingston.

Inspiration

Craig Romano's *Day Hiking Olympic Peninsula: National Park/Coastal Beaches/Southwest Washington* is a detailed guide to day hikes in and around the national park.

Rob Sandelin and Stephen Whitney's *A Field Guide to the Cascades and Olympics* is an excellent trailside reference, covering more than 500 plant and animal species found in the park.

Park Essentials

ACCESSIBILITY

There are wheelchair-accessible facilities—including trails, campgrounds, and visitor centers—throughout the park; contact visitor centers for information.

PARK FEES AND PERMITS

Seven-day vehicle admission is $30; an annual pass is $50. Individuals arriving on foot, bike, or motorcycle pay $15. An overnight wilderness permit, available at visitor centers and ranger stations, is $8 per person per night plus a $6 per night reservation fee. An annual wilderness camping permit costs $45. Fishing in freshwater streams and lakes within Olympic National Park does not require a Washington state fishing license; however, anglers must acquire a salmon-steelhead catch record card when fishing for those species. Ocean fishing and harvesting shellfish require licenses, which are available at sporting-goods and outdoor-supply stores.

PARK HOURS

Six park entrances are open 24/7; gate kiosk hours (for buying passes) vary according to season and location, but most are staffed during daylight hours. Olympic National Park is in the Pacific time zone.

CELL PHONE RECEPTION

Note that cell reception is sketchy in wilderness areas. There are public telephones at the Olympic National Park Visitor Center, Hoh Rain Forest Visitor Center, and lodging properties within the park—Lake Crescent, Kalaloch, and Sol Duc Hot Springs. Fairholme General Store also has a phone.

Hotels

Major park resorts run from good to terrific, with generally comfortable rooms, excellent facilities, and easy access to trails, beaches, and activity centers. Midsize accommodations, like Sol Duc Hot Springs Resort, are often shockingly rustic—but remember, you're here for the park, not for the rooms.

Restaurants

The major resorts are your best bets for eating out in the park. Each has a main restaurant, café, and/or kiosk, as well as casually upscale dinner service, with regional seafood, meat, and produce complemented by a range of microbrews and good Washington and international wines. Reservations are either recommended or required.

Hotel and restaurant reviews have been shortened. For full information visit Fodors.com. Hotel prices are the lowest cost of a standard double room in high season. Restaurant prices are the average cost of a main course at dinner, or if dinner is not served, at lunch.

What It Costs

	$	$$	$$$	$$$$
RESTAURANTS	under $16	$16–$22	$23–$30	over $30
HOTELS	under $150	$150–$200	$201–$250	over $250

Visitor Information

PARK CONTACT INFORMATION Olympic National Park. ✉ *Olympic National Park Visitor Center, 3002 Mt. Angeles Rd., Port Angeles* ☎ *360/565–3130* 🌐 *www.nps.gov/olym.*

Coastal Olympic

15 miles from Forks.

Olympic National Park's coastal region showcases the powerful Pacific Ocean coastline and the unique geology created over centuries where the sea meets the shore. Some beaches are as close as a walk from a (sometimes crowded) parking lot, while others are reached via longer trails. Sea life is abundant, in tide pools and offshore. The area is also rich in history from the Native American tribes that have lived off these lands for generations.

Sights

HISTORIC SITES

La Push

BEACH—SIGHT | At the mouth of Quileute River, La Push is the tribal center of the Quileute people. In fact, the town's name is a variation on the French *la bouche,* which means "the mouth." Offshore rock spires known as sea stacks dot the coast here, and you may catch a glimpse of bald eagles nesting in the nearby cliffs. ✉ *Rte. 110, La Push* ✣ *14 miles west of Forks* 🌐 *www.nps.gov/olym/planyourvisit/upload/mora.pdf.*

SCENIC STOPS

Kalaloch

BEACH—SIGHT | With a lodge and restaurant, a huge campground, miles of coastline, and easy access from the highway, this is a popular spot. Keen-eyed beachcombers may spot sea otters just offshore. ✉ *Hwy. 101, Kalaloch* ✣ *43 miles southwest of Forks* ☎ *360/565–3130 visitor center, 360/962–2283 ranger station* 🌐 *www.nps.gov/olym/planyourvisit/visiting-kalaloch-and-ruby-beach.htm.*

Lake Ozette

BEACH—SIGHT | The third-largest glacial impoundment in Washington anchors the coastal strip of Olympic National Park at its north end. The small town of Ozette, home to a coastal tribe, is the trailhead for two of the park's better one-day hikes. Both 3-mile trails lead over boardwalks through swampy wetland and coastal old-growth forest to the ocean shore and uncrowded beaches. ✉ *Ozette* ✣ *At end of Hoko-Ozette Rd., 26 miles southwest of Hwy. 112 near Sekiu* ☎ *360/565–3130* 🌐 *www.nps.gov/olym/planyourvisit/visiting-ozette.htm.*

★ Ruby Beach

BEACH—SIGHT | The northernmost and arguably the most breathtaking of Olympic National Park's Kalaloch area beaches, this wild and windswept swath of shoreline is named for the rosy fragments of garnet that color its sands. From an evergreen-shaded bluff, a short trail winds down to the wave-beaten sands where Cedar Creek meets the ocean, and you may spy sea otters along with bald eagles, oystercatchers, cormorants, and other birdlife. Driftwood separates the woods from the sand—it's a good spot to set up a picnic blanket and watch the sun fall over the pounding surf. Up and down the coast, dramatic sea stacks and rock cairns frame the beach, which is a favorite place for beachcombers, artists, and photographers. **Amenities:**

toilets. **Best for:** sunset; walking. ✉ *U.S. 101, Kalaloch* ⊕ *28 miles southwest of Forks* 🌐 *www.nps.gov/olym.*

Second and Third Beaches

BEACH—SIGHT | During low tide these flat, driftwood-strewn expanses are perfect for long afternoon strolls. Second Beach, accessed via an easy forest trail through Quileute lands, opens to a vista of the Pacific Ocean and sea stacks. Third Beach offers a 1¼-mile forest hike for a warm-up before reaching the sands. ✉ *Hwy. 101* ⊕ *14 miles west of Forks* ☎ *360/565–3130* 🌐 *www.nps.gov/olym.*

TRAILS

Cape Alava Trail

TRAIL | Beginning at Ozette, this 3-mile boardwalk trail leads from the forest to wave-tossed headlands. *Moderate.* ✉ *Ozette* ⊕ *Trailhead: End of Hoko-Ozette Rd., 26 miles south of Hwy. 112, west of Sekiu* 🌐 *www.nps.gov/olym/planyourvisit/lake-ozette-area-brochure.htm.*

Restaurants

Creekside Restaurant

$$$ | **AMERICAN** | A tranquil country setting and ocean views at Kalaloch Lodge's restaurant create the perfect backdrop for savoring Pacific Northwest dinner specialties like grilled salmon, fresh shellfish, and elk burgers. Tempting seasonal desserts include local fruit tarts and cobblers in summer and organic winter-squash bread pudding in winter; flourless chocolate torte is enjoyed year-round. **Known for:** locally sourced food; Washington wines; stunning setting. $ *Average main: $28* ✉ *157151 Hwy. 101, Forks* ☎ *866/662–9928, 360/962–2271* 🌐 *www.thekalalochlodge.com/dine-and-shop/creekside-restaurant.*

Hotels

★ Kalaloch Lodge

$$$$ | **HOTEL** | **FAMILY** | Overlooking the Pacific, Kalaloch has cozy lodge rooms with sea views and separate cabins along the bluff. **Pros:** ranger tours; clam digging; supreme storm-watching in winter. **Cons:** no Wi-Fi and most units don't have TVs; some rooms are two blocks from main lodge; limited cell phone service. $ *Rooms from: $251* ✉ *157151 U.S. 101, Forks* ☎ *360/962–2271, 866/662–9928* 🌐 *www.thekalalochlodge.com* *64 rooms* *No meals.*

Rain Forests

Hoh Rain Forest is 31 miles south of Forks via Hwy. 101.

The National Park is best known as the home to one of the few temperate rain forest ecosystems in the U.S. There are actually four rain forests here; most people go to the Hoh, which has a visitor center and trails that are filled in summer with visitors from around the world. For the most serene experience, visit during the shoulder season or as early in the day as you can.

Sights

SCENIC STOPS

★ Hoh Rain Forest

FOREST | South of Forks, an 18-mile spur road links Highway 101 with this unique temperate rain forest, where spruce and hemlock trees soar to heights of more than 200 feet. Alders and big-leaf maples are so densely covered with mosses they look more like shaggy prehistoric animals than trees, and elk browse in shaded glens. Be prepared for precipitation: the region receives 140 inches or more each year. ✉ *Upper Hoh Rd.* ☎ *360/374–6925* 🌐 *www.nps.gov/olym/planyourvisit/visiting-the-hoh.htm.*

Did You Know?

Encompassing more than 70 miles of beachfront, Olympic is one of the few national parks of the West with an ocean beach (Redwood, Channel Islands, and some of the Alaskan parks are the others). The park is therefore home to many marine animals, including sea otters, whales, sea lions, and seals.

Lake Quinault

BODY OF WATER | This glimmering lake, 4½ miles long and 300 feet deep, is the first landmark you'll reach when driving the west-side loop of U.S. 101. The rain forest is thickest here, with moss-draped maples and alders, and towering spruce, fir, and hemlock. Enchanted Valley, high up near the Quinault River's source, is a deeply glaciated valley that's closer to the Hood Canal than to the Pacific Ocean. A scenic loop drive circles the lake and travels around a section of the Quinault River. ✉ *Hwy. 101* ✣ *38 miles north of Hoquiam* ☎ *360/565–3131 Quinault Rain Forest ranger station* 🌐 *www.nps.gov/olym/planyourvisit/visiting-quinault.htm.*

TRAILS

★ Hoh River Trail

TRAIL | FAMILY | From the Hoh Visitor Center, this rain-forest jaunt takes you into the Hoh Valley, wending its way for 17½ miles alongside the river, through moss-draped maple and alder trees and past open meadows where elk roam in winter. *Easy.* ✉ *Olympic National Park* ✣ *Trailhead: Hoh Visitor Center, 18 miles east of U.S. 101* 🌐 *www.nps.gov/olym/planyourvisit/hoh-river-trail.htm.*

VISITOR CENTERS

Hoh Rain Forest Visitor Center

INFO CENTER | Pick up park maps and pamphlets, permits, and activities lists in this busy, woodsy chalet; there's also a shop and exhibits on natural history. Several short interpretive trails and longer wilderness treks start from here. ✉ *Hoh Valley Rd., Forks* ✣ *31 miles south of Forks* ☎ *360/374–6925* 🌐 *www.nps.gov/olym/planyourvisit/visitorcenters.htm* ⏲ *Closed Jan. and Feb., and Mon.–Thurs. off-season.*

South Shore Quinault Ranger Station

INFO CENTER | The National Forest Service's ranger station near the Lake Quinault Lodge has maps, campground information, and program listings. ✉ *353 S. Shore Rd., Quinault* ☎ *360/288–2525* 🌐 *www.fs.usda.gov/main/olympic/home* ⏲ *Closed weekends after Labor Day until Memorial Day weekend.*

Hotels

Lake Quinault Lodge

$$$ | HOTEL | On a lovely glacial lake in Olympic National Forest, this beautiful early-20th-century lodge complex is within walking distance of the lakeshore and hiking trails in the spectacular old-growth forest. **Pros:** boat tours of the lake are interesting; family-friendly ambience; year-round pool and sauna. **Cons:** no TV in some rooms; some units are noisy and not very private; Wi-Fi is expensive after first 30 minutes free. $ *Rooms from: $215* ✉ *345 S. Shore Rd., Quinault* ☎ *360/288–2900, 888/896–3818* 🌐 *www.olympicnationalparks.com/lodging/lake-quinault-lodge/* *92 rooms* *No meals.*

Lake Crescent and Sol Duc Valley

Lake Crescent is 22 miles west of Port Angeles via Hwy. 101; Sol Duc Valley is about 20 miles south of Lake Crescent via Sol Duc-Hot Springs Road.

North of the rain forest region, the sparkling blue waters of Lake Crescent and the verdant Sol Duc Valley abound with water activities and hiking trails. Historic and rustic accommodations make overnight stays in the sprawling national park convenient and memorable.

Sights

SCENIC STOPS

Lake Crescent

BODY OF WATER | Visitors see Lake Crescent as Highway 101 winds along its southern shore, giving way to gorgeous views of teal waters rippling in a basin formed by Tuscan-like hills. In the evening, low bands of clouds caught between the surrounding mountains often linger over its reflective surface. ✉ *Hwy. 101* ✣ *16 miles west of Port Angeles and 28 miles northeast of Forks* ☎ *360/565–3130 visitor center* 🌐 *www.nps.gov/olym/planyourvisit/visiting-lake-crescent.htm.*

Sol Duc Valley

BODY OF WATER | Sol Duc Valley is one of those magical places where all the Northwest's virtues seem at hand: lush lowland forests, sparkling river scenes, salmon runs, and serene hiking trails. Here, the popular Sol Duc Hot Springs area includes three attractive sulfuric pools ranging in temperature from 98°F to 104°F (admission to the pools costs $15). ✉ *Sol Duc Rd.* ✣ *South of U.S. 101, 12 miles past west end of Lake Crescent* ☎ *360/565–3130* 🌐 *www.nps.gov/olym/planyourvisit/visiting-the-sol-duc-valley.htm.*

TRAILS

Graves Creek Trail

TRAIL | This 6-mile-long moderately strenuous trail climbs from lowland rain forest to alpine territory at Sundown Pass. Due to spring floods, a fjord halfway up is often impassable in May and June. *Moderate.* ✉ *Olympic National Park* ✣ *Trailhead: End of S. Shore Rd., 23 miles east of U.S. 101* 🌐 *www.nps.gov/olym.*

★ **Sol Duc River Trail**

TRAIL | FAMILY | The 1½-mile gravel path off Sol Duc Road winds through thick Douglas fir forests toward the thundering, three-chute Sol Duc Falls. Just off the road, below a wooden platform over the Sol Duc River, you'll come across the 70-foot Salmon Cascades. In late summer and autumn, thousands of salmon negotiate 50 miles or more of treacherous waters to reach the cascades and the tamer pools near Sol Duc Hot Springs. The popular 6-mile **Lovers Lane Loop Trail** links the Sol Duc falls with the hot springs. You can continue up from the falls 5 miles to the **Appleton Pass Trail,** at 3,100 feet. From there you can hike on to the 8½-mile mark, where views at the High Divide are from 5,050 feet. *Moderate.* ✉ *Olympic National Park* ✣ *Trailhead: Sol Duc Rd., 12 miles south of U.S. 101* 🌐 *www.nps.gov/olym/planyourvisit/sol-duc-river-trail.htm.*

Restaurants

Lake Crescent Lodge

$$$ | AMERICAN | Part of the original 1916 lodge, the fir-paneled dining room overlooks the lake; you won't find a better spot for sunset views. Dinner entrées include wild salmon, brown butter–basted halibut, grilled steak, and roasted chicken breast; the lunch menu features elk cheeseburgers, inventive salads, and a variety of sandwiches. **Known for:** award-winning Pacific Northwest wine list; house-made lavender lemonade; lovely setting. $ *Average main: $29* ✉ *416 Lake Crescent Rd., Port Angeles* ☎ *360/928–3211* 🌐 *www.olympicnationalparks.com/lodging/dining/lake-crescent-lodge/* ⏲ *Closed Jan.–Apr.*

The Springs Restaurant

$$$ | AMERICAN | The main Sol Duc Hot Springs Resort restaurant is a rustic, fir-and-cedar-paneled dining room surrounded by trees. In summer big breakfasts are turned out daily—hikers can fill up on biscuits and sage-pork-sausage gravy, bananas foster French toast, and omelets before hitting the trails; for lighter fare, there's steel cut oatmeal and yogurt and granola parfaits. **Known for:** three breakfast mimosa choices; boxed lunches. $ *Average main: $24* ✉ *12076 Sol Duc Rd. , at U.S. 101, Port Angeles* ☎ *360/327–3583* 🌐 *www.olympicnationalparks.com/dining/sol-duc-hot-springs-resort/* ⏲ *Closed Nov.–late Mar.*

Hotels

Lake Crescent Lodge

$$$ | HOTEL | Deep in the forest at the foot of Mt. Storm King, this 1916 lodge has a variety of comfortable accommodations, from basic rooms with shared baths to spacious two-bedroom fireplace cottages. **Pros:** gorgeous setting; free wireless access in the lobby; lots of opportunities for off-the-grid fun outdoors. **Cons:** no laundry; Roosevelt Cottages often are booked a year in advance for summer stays; crowded with nonguest visitors. *Rooms from: $218* *416 Lake Crescent Rd., Port Angeles* *360/928–3211, 888/896–3818* *www.olympicnationalparks.com/lodging/lake-crescent-lodge/* *Closed Jan.–Apr., except Roosevelt fireplace cabins open weekends* *52 rooms* *No meals.*

Log Cabin Resort

$$$ | **HOTEL** | **FAMILY** | This rustic resort has an idyllic setting at the northeast end of Lake Crescent with lodging choices that include A-frame chalet units, standard cabins, small camper cabins, motel units, and RV sites with full hookups. **Pros:** boat rentals available on-site; convenient general store; pets allowed in some cabins. **Cons:** cabins are extremely rustic; no plumbing in the camper cabins; no TVs. *Rooms from: $161* *3183 E. Beach Rd., Port Angeles* *888/896–3818, 360/928–3325* *www.olympicnationalparks.com* *Closed Oct.–late May* *24 rooms* *No meals.*

Sol Duc Hot Springs Resort

$$$$ | **HOTEL** | Deep in the brooding forest along the Sol Duc River and surrounded by 5,000-foot-tall mountains, the main draw of this remote 1910 resort is the pool area, with soothing mineral baths and a freshwater swimming pool. **Pros:** nearby trails; peaceful setting; some units are pet-friendly. **Cons:** units are dated and very basic; no air-conditioning, TV, or Wi-Fi; pools get crowded. *Rooms from: $230* *12076 Sol Duc Hot Springs Rd.* *888/896–3818, 360/327–3583* *www.olympicnationalparks.com/lodging/sol-duc-hot-springs-resort/* *Closed Oct.–late May* *33 rooms* *No meals.*

The Mountains

Hurricane Ridge is 17 miles north of Port Angeles.

Providing a stunning backdrop for sunsets visible from the Seattle area, the Olympic Mountain range encompasses more than a dozen mountains within Olympic National Park and adjacent Olympic National Forest. Hurricane Ridge is the most accessible by car and offers views of other mountains that can't easily be seen from elsewhere, including the highest peak in the range, Mt. Olympus. On winter weekends, snow sports are often an option at Hurricane Ridge, too.

Sights

SCENIC DRIVES

★ Port Angeles Visitor Center to Hurricane Ridge

VIEWPOINT | The premier scenic drive in Olympic National Park is a steep ribbon of curves that climbs from thickly forested foothills and subalpine meadows into the upper stretches of pine-swathed peaks. At the top, the visitor center at Hurricane Ridge has some spectacular views over the heart of the peninsula and across the Strait of Juan de Fuca. A mile past the visitor center, there are picnic tables in open meadows with photo-worthy views of the mountains to the east. Hurricane Ridge also has an uncommonly fine display of wildflowers in spring and summer. In winter, vehicles must carry chains, and the road is usually open Friday to Sunday only (call first to check conditions). *Olympic National Park* *www.nps.gov/olym.*

SCENIC STOPS

★ Hurricane Ridge

MOUNTAIN—SIGHT | The panoramic view from this 5,200-foot-high ridge encompasses the Olympic range, the Strait of Juan de Fuca, and Vancouver Island. Guided tours from the visitor center are given in summer along the many paved and unpaved trails, where wildflowers and wildlife such as deer and marmots flourish. ✉ *Hurricane Ridge Rd.* ✣ *17 miles south of Port Angeles* ☎ *360/565–3130* 🌐 *www.nps.gov/olym/planyourvisit/visiting-hurricane-ridge.htm* ⏲ *Closed when road is closed.*

Mt. Olympus

MOUNTAIN—SIGHT | The highest peak in the Olympic Mountain range, Mt. Olympus towers over the park at 7,980 feet. It gets 50–70 feet of snow every year, supporting several glaciers including Blue Glacier, which has been one of the most-studied glaciers in the world. That glacier and others in the mountain range have been retreating rapidly in recent decades due to climate change. Because of its location in the park, the best view of Mt. Olympus is from Hurricane Ridge. Unlike other major mountains in Washington state, it can't be seen from major cities or even nearby towns. ✉ *Olympic National Park* 🌐 *www.nps.gov/olym.*

TRAILS

High Divide Trail

TRAIL | A 9-mile hike in the park's high country defines this trail, which includes some strenuous climbing on its last 4 miles before topping out at a small alpine lake. A return loop along High Divide wends its way an extra mile through alpine territory, with sensational views of Olympic peaks. This trail is only for dedicated, properly equipped hikers who are in good shape. *Difficult.* ✉ *Olympic National Park* ✣ *Trailhead: End of Sol Duc River Rd., 13 miles south of U.S. 101* 🌐 *www.nps.gov/olym/planyourvisit/high-divide-loop.htm.*

Hurricane Ridge Meadow Trail

TRAIL | A ¼-mile alpine loop, most of it wheelchair accessible, leads through wildflower meadows overlooking numerous vistas of the interior Olympic peaks to the south and a panorama of the Strait of Juan de Fuca to the north. *Easy.* ✉ *Olympic National Park* ✣ *Trailhead: Hurricane Ridge Rd., 17 miles south of Port Angeles* 🌐 *www.nps.gov/olym/planyourvisit/visiting-hurricane-ridge.htm.*

VISITOR CENTERS

Hurricane Ridge Visitor Center

INFO CENTER | The upper level of this visitor center has exhibits and nice views; the lower level has a gift shop and snack bar. Guided walks and programs start in late June. In winter, find details on the surrounding ski and sledding slopes and take guided snowshoe walks. ✉ *Hurricane Ridge Rd.* ☎ *360/565–3131 for road conditions* 🌐 *www.nps.gov/olym/planyourvisit/visitorcenters.htm* ⏲ *Operating hrs/days vary off-season.*

Olympic National Park Visitor Center

INFO CENTER | This modern, well-organized facility, staffed by park rangers, provides everything: maps, trail brochures, campground advice, weather forecasts, listings of wildlife sightings, educational programs and exhibits, information on road and trail closures, and a gift shop. ✉ *3002 Mount Angeles Rd., Port Angeles* ☎ *360/565–3130* 🌐 *www.nps.gov/olym/planyourvisit/visitorcenters.htm.*

Wilderness Information Center (WIC)

INFO CENTER | Located behind Olympic National Park Visitor Center, this facility provides all the information you'll need for a trip in the park, including trail conditions, safety tips, and weather bulletins. The office also issues camping permits, takes campground reservations, and loans bear-proof food canisters. ✉ *3002 Mount Angeles Rd., Port Angeles* ☎ *360/565–3100* 🌐 *www.nps.gov/olym/planyourvisit/wic.htm* ⏲ *Hrs vary during off-season.*

Activities

BIKING

Ben's Bikes

BICYCLING | This bike, gear, and repair shop is a great resource for advice on routes around the Olympic Peninsula, including the Olympic Discovery Trail. They can deliver bikes to local lodgings and to the ferry docks in Port Angeles and Port Townsend. They rent a variety of different styles, with rentals starting at $30 per day and $110 per week. ✉ *1251 W. Washington St., Sequim* ☎ *360/683–2666* 🌐 *www.bensbikessequim.com.*

Sound Bike & Kayak

BICYCLING | This sports outfitter rents and sells bikes, and sells kayaks, climbing gear, and related equipment. They offer several guided mountain climbs, day hikes, and custom trips, and a climbing wall to practice skills. Bike rentals start at $10 per hour and $45 per day. ✉ *120 E. Front St., Port Angeles* ☎ *360/457–1240* 🌐 *www.soundbikeskayaks.com.*

CAMPING

Note that only a few places take reservations; if you can't book in advance, you'll have to arrive early to get a place. Each site usually has a picnic table and grill or firepit, and most campgrounds have water, toilets, and garbage containers; for hookups, showers, and laundry facilities, you'll have to head into the towns or stay at a privately owned campground. Firewood is available from camp concessions, but if there's no store, you can collect dead wood within 1 mile of your campsite. Dogs are allowed in campgrounds, but not on most trails or in the backcountry. Trailers should be 21 feet long or less (15 feet or less at Queets Campground), though a few campgrounds can accommodate up to 35 feet. There's a camping limit of two weeks. Nightly rates run $15–$22 per site.

If you have a backcountry pass, you can camp virtually anywhere throughout the park's forests and shores. Overnight wilderness permits are $8 per person per night and are available at visitor centers and ranger stations. Note that when you camp in the backcountry, you must choose a site at least ½ mile inside the park boundary.

Kalaloch Campground. Kalaloch is the biggest and most popular Olympic campground, and it's open all year. Its vantage of the Pacific is unmatched on the park's coastal stretch. ✉ *U.S. 101, ½ mile north of Kalaloch Information Station, Olympic National Park* ☎ *877/444–6777* or 🌐 *www.recreation.gov* for reservations.

Lake Quinault Rain Forest Resort Village Campground. Stretching along the south shore of Lake Quinault, this RV campground has many recreation facilities, including beaches, canoes, ball fields, and horseshoe pits. The 31 RV sites, which rent for $45 per night, are open year-round, but bathrooms are closed in winter. The resort also rents motel rooms and cabins. ✉ *3½ miles east of U.S. 101, S. Shore Rd., Lake Quinault* ☎ *360/288–2535, 800/255–6936* 🌐 *www.rainforestresort.com.*

Mora Campground. Along the Quillayute estuary, this campground doubles as a popular staging point for hikes northward along the coast's wilderness stretch. ✉ *Rte. 110, 13 miles west of Forks* ☎ *No phone.*

Ozette Campground. Hikers heading to Cape Alava, a scenic promontory that is the westernmost point in the lower 48 states, use this lakeshore campground as a jumping-off point. ✉ *Hoko-Ozette Rd., 26 miles south of Hwy. 112* ☎ *No phone.*

Sol Duc Campground. Sol Duc resembles virtually all Olympic campgrounds save one distinguishing feature—the famed hot springs are a short walk away. ✉ *Sol Duc Rd., 11 miles south of U.S. 101* ☎ *877/444–6777* 🌐 *www.recreation.gov.*

Staircase Campground. In deep woods away from the river, this campground is a popular jumping-off point for hikes into the Skokomish River Valley and the Olympic high country. ✉ *Rte. 119, 16 miles northwest of U.S. 101* ☎ *No phone.*

EDUCATIONAL OFFERINGS

CLASSES AND SEMINARS

NatureBridge

COLLEGE | FAMILY | This rustic educational facility offers talks and excursions focusing on park ecology and history. Trips range from canoe trips to camping excursions, with a strong emphasis on family programs. ✉ *111 Barnes Point Rd., Port Angeles* ☎ *360/928–3720* 🌐 *www.naturebridge.org/olympic.*

RANGER PROGRAMS

Junior Ranger Program

TOUR—SIGHT | FAMILY | Anyone can pick up the booklet at visitor centers and ranger stations and follow this fun program, which includes assignments to discover park flora and fauna, ocean life, and Native American lore. Kids get a badge when they turn in the finished work. Kids can also earn an "Ocean Steward" badge by doing activities in another booklet that teaches about the park's coastal ecosystem. ✉ *Olympic National Park* ☎ *360/565–3130* 🌐 *www.nps.gov/olym/learn/kidsyouth/beajuniorranger.htm.*

FISHING

There are numerous fishing possibilities throughout the park. Lake Crescent is home to cutthroat and rainbow trout, as well as petite kokanee salmon; lakes Cushman, Quinault, and Ozette have trout, salmon, and steelhead. As for rivers, the Bogachiel and Queets have steelhead salmon in season. The glacier-fed Hoh River is home to Chinook salmon April to November, and coho salmon from August through November; the Sol Duc River offers all five species of salmon. The Elwha River has been undergoing restoration since two dams were removed; strong salmon and steelhead runs have returned, although a fishing moratorium has been in place for several years. Other places to go after salmon and trout include the Dosewallips, Duckabush, Quillayute, Quinault, Salmon, and Skokomish rivers. A Washington state punch card is required during salmon-spawning months; fishing regulations vary throughout the park, and some areas are for catch and release only. Punch cards are available from sporting-goods and outdoor-supply stores.

Piscatorial Pursuits

FISHING | This company, based in Forks, offers salmon and steelhead fishing trips around the Olympic Peninsula from October through mid-May. ✉ *Forks* ☎ *866/347–4232* 🌐 *www.piscatorialpursuits.com* 💵 *From $225 (rate per person for parties of 2 or more).*

HIKING

Know your tides, or you might be trapped by high water. Pick up tide tables at a visitor center or ranger stations. Remember: wilderness permits are required for overnight backcountry visits.

KAYAKING AND CANOEING

Lake Crescent, a serene expanse of teal-color waters surrounded by deep-green pine forests, is one of the park's best boating areas. Note that the west end is for swimming only; no speedboats are allowed here.

Lake Quinault has boating access from a gravel ramp on the north shore. From U.S. 101, take a right on North Shore Road, another right on Hemlock Way, and a left on Lakeview Drive. There are plank ramps at Falls Creek and Willoughby campgrounds on South Shore Drive, 0.1 mile and 0.2 mile past the Quinault Ranger Station, respectively.

Lake Ozette, with just one access road, is a good place for overnight trips. Only experienced canoe and kayak handlers should travel far from the put-in, since fierce storms occasionally strike—even in summer.

Adventures Through Kayaking

KAYAKING | FAMILY | This outfitter offers lake kayak rentals (from $64/day), two-hour sea kayaking tours along the Whale Trail (from $79), and three-hour kayak tours on Lake Crescent (from

$79). Children as young as four years old can participate. ✉ *2358 Hwy. 101, Port Angeles* ☎ *360/417–3015* 🌐 *www.atkayaking.com.*

Fairholme General Store

CANOEING/ROWING/SKULLING | Kayaks and canoes on Lake Crescent are available to rent from $20 per hour to $60 for eight hours. The store is at the lake's west end, 27 miles west of Port Angeles. ✉ *221121 U.S. 101, Port Angeles* ☎ *360/928–3020* 🌐 *www.olympicnationalparks.com* ⏲ *Closed after Labor Day until Memorial Day weekend.*

Lake Crescent Lodge

CANOEING/ROWING/SKULLING | You can rent kayaks and paddleboards here for $25 per hour and $60 for a half day; canoes are $35/hour, $70/half day. ✉ *416 Lake Crescent Rd.* ☎ *360/928–3211* 🌐 *www.olympicnationalparks.com* ⏲ *Closed Jan.–Apr.*

Log Cabin Resort

CANOEING/ROWING/SKULLING | This resort, 17 miles west of Port Angeles, has paddleboat, kayak, canoe, and paddleboard rentals for $20 per hour and $60 per day. The dock provides easy access to Lake Crescent's northeast section. ✉ *3183 E. Beach Rd., Port Angeles* ☎ *360/928–3325* 🌐 *www.olympicnationalparks.com* ⏲ *Closed Oct.–mid-May.*

RAFTING

Olympic has excellent rafting rivers, with Class II to Class V rapids. The Elwha River is a popular place to paddle, with some exciting turns. The Hoh is better for those who like a smooth, easy float.

Hoh River Rafters

WHITE-WATER RAFTING | Local guides lead Class II rafting trips down the Hoh. The three-hour trips run twice daily from March through August and cost $75. All equipment is provided and no experience is needed. ✉ *4883 Upper Hoh Rd., Forks* ☎ *360/683–9867* 🌐 *www.hohriverrafters.com.*

Nearby Towns

Although most Olympic Peninsula towns have evolved from their exclusive reliance on timber, **Forks,** outside the national park's northwest tip, remains one of the region's logging capitals. Washington state's wettest town (100 inches or more of rain a year), it's a small, friendly place with just over 3,800 residents and a modicum of visitor facilities. South of Forks and Lake Quinault, Washington's newest beach community (established in 2004), **Seabrook,** near the tiny village of **Pacific Beach,** is 25 miles from the southwest corner of the national park via the Moclips Highway. Created as a planned community mainly for vacationers, it's convenient for visiting both the park and the state's ocean beaches to the south. **Port Angeles,** a city of around 20,000, focuses on its status as the main gateway to Olympic National Park and Victoria, British Columbia. Set below the Strait of Juan de Fuca and looking north to Vancouver Island, it's an enviably scenic settlement filled with attractive, Craftsman-style homes.

The Pacific Northwest has its very own "Banana Belt" in the waterfront community of **Sequim,** 17 miles east of Port Angeles along U.S. 101. The town of 7,500 is in the rain shadow of the Olympics and receives only 16 inches of rain per year (compared with the 140 to 170 inches that drench the Hoh Rain Forest just 40 miles away). The Victorian-era town of **Port Towsend,** in the northeast corner of the Olympic Peninsula, has around 9,700 residents. It's a popular destination for day trips, romantic getaways to the many historic B&Bs, families exploring the old military forts and aquatic learning centers, and anyone looking for an interesting detour before or after a trip to the national park.

Chapter 49

PETRIFIED FOREST NATIONAL PARK

Updated by
Elise Riley

Camping ★☆☆☆☆ | Hotels ★☆☆☆☆ | Activities ★★☆☆☆ | Scenery ★★★★★ | Crowds ★★☆☆☆

WELCOME TO PETRIFIED FOREST NATIONAL PARK

TOP REASONS TO GO

★ **Terrific timber:** Be mesmerized by the clusters of petrified (fossilized) wood. The trees look like they're made of colorful stone.

★ **Walls with words:** Don't scratch the surface, but see how others did. Ancestors of the Hopi, Zuni, and Navajo left their mark in petroglyphs cut, scratched, or carved into stone.

★ **Route 66 kicks:** A section of the fabled road is preserved in the park, the only section of the highway protected in a national park.

★ **Triassic treasures:** Find an oasis of water in the desert, or at least evidence that it once existed. Clam fossils in the park indicate that waterways once prevailed where sand, stone, and trees now define the land.

★ **Corps creations:** The Painted Desert Inn, a National Historic Landmark, was modernized by the Civilian Conservation Corps (CCC) during the throes of the Great Depression. It is now a museum and bookstore.

1 **Petrified Forest National Park.** In the park's northern section, its main area, the Painted Desert is where the park headquarters, the Painted Desert Inn National Historic Landmark, and Route 66 are located. It's also the best place for hiking. The 28-mile park road begins here, off Interstate 40. In the heart of the Painted Desert, the 1-mile Blue Mesa trail begins off a loop road accessed from the park road. Petrified trees lie among hills of bluish bentonite clay. Get a trail guide at the Rainbow Forest Museum for the short Giant Logs Trail located behind the museum, and keep an eye out for Old Faithful, a log almost 10 feet wide. The southern terminus for the park road is here.

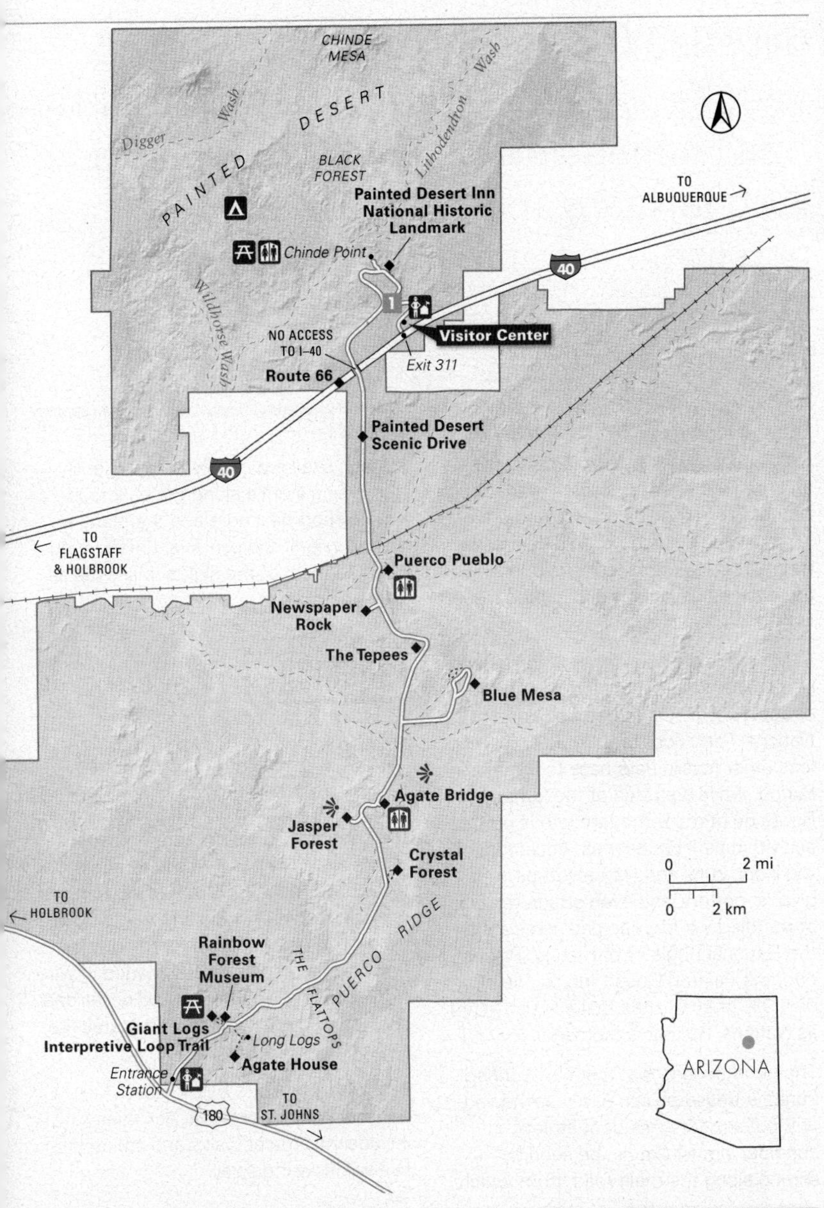
CHINDE MESA
PAINTED DESERT
Digger Wash
Lithodendron Wash
BLACK FOREST
Painted Desert Inn National Historic Landmark
Chinde Point
TO ALBUQUERQUE
40
1
Visitor Center
Wildhorse Wash
NO ACCESS TO I-40
Exit 311
Route 66
Painted Desert Scenic Drive
40
TO FLAGSTAFF & HOLBROOK
Puerco Pueblo
Newspaper Rock
The Tepees
Blue Mesa
Agate Bridge
Jasper Forest
Crystal Forest
0 2 mi
0 2 km
TO HOLBROOK
Rainbow Forest Museum
THE FLATTOPS
PUERCO RIDGE
Giant Logs Interpretive Loop Trail
Long Logs
Agate House
Entrance Station
180
TO ST. JOHNS
ARIZONA

Petrified Forest National Park's 221,390 acres, which include portions of the Painted Desert, are covered with petrified tree trunks whose wood cells were fossilized over centuries by brightly hued mineral deposits—silica, iron oxide, carbon, manganese, aluminum, copper, and lithium. Remnants of humans and their artifacts have been recovered at more than 500 sites in the park.

Only about 1½ hours from Show Low and the lush, verdant forests of the White Mountains, Arizona's diverse and dramatic landscape changes from pine-crested mountains to sun-baked terrain. Inside the lunar landscape of the Painted Desert is the Petrified Forest.

There are few places where the span of geologic and human history is as wide or apparent as it is at Petrified Forest National Park. Fossilized trees and countless other fossils date back to the Triassic Period, while a stretch of the famed Route 66 of more modern lore is protected within park boundaries. Ancestors of the Hopi, Zuni, and Navajo left petroglyphs, pottery, and even structures built of petrified wood. Nine park sites are on the National Register of Historic Places; one, the Painted Desert Inn, is one of only 3% of such sites that are also listed as National Historic Landmarks.

The good thing is that most of Petrified Forest's treasures can easily be viewed without a great amount of athletic conditioning. Much can be seen by driving along the main road, from which historic sites are readily accessible. By combining a drive along the park road with a short hike here and there and a visit to one of the park's landmarks, you can see most of the sights in as little as half a day.

Planning

When to Go

The park is rarely crowded. Weatherwise, the best time to visit is autumn, when nights are chilly but daytime temperatures hover near 70°F. Half of all yearly rain falls between June and August, so it's a good time to spot blooming wildflowers. The park is least crowded in winter because of cold winds and occasional snow, though daytime temperatures are in the 50s and 60s.

FESTIVALS AND EVENTS

National Wildflower Week. Activities include wildflower walks and an interactive wildflower display.

AVERAGE HIGH/LOW TEMPERATURES					
JAN.	**FEB.**	**MAR.**	**APR.**	**MAY**	**JUNE**
48/21	54/25	60/29	70/35	79/43	89/52
JULY	**AUG.**	**SEPT.**	**OCT.**	**NOV.**	**DEC.**
92/60	89/59	84/52	72/40	59/28	48/22

Petrified Forest Park Anniversary. A national monument since 1906 and a national park since 1962, Petrified Forest throws a party for its birthday, with homemade cider, cookies, and cultural demonstrations.

Getting Here and Around

AIR

The nearest major airports are in Phoenix, Arizona (259 miles away via U.S. 17 and U.S. 40), and Albuquerque, New Mexico (204 miles via U.S. 40).

CAR

Holbrook, the nearest large town with services such as gas or food, is on U.S. 40, 27 miles from the park's north entrance and 18 miles from its south entrance.

Parking is free, and there's ample space at all trailheads, as well as at the visitor center and the museum. The main park road extends 28 miles from the Painted Desert Visitor Center (north entrance) to the Rainbow Forest Museum (south entrance). For park road conditions, call ☎ *928/524–6228.*

Inspiration

When Wood Turns to Stone: The Story of the Arizona National Petrified Forest, by K.S. Tankersley, explains the science behind petrified wood, as well as the park's origin.

While not a story about the national park itself, *The Petrified Forest,* a 1936 film starring Bette Davis, Leslie Howard, and Humphrey Bogart tells the story of a drifter, a waitress, and a gangster who cross paths in the Petrified Forest area.

Park Essentials

ACCESSIBILITY

The visitor center, museum, and overlooks on the scenic drive are wheelchair accessible. All trails are paved, although they are uneven, rough, and sometimes steep. Check the park website (🌐 *nps.gov/pefo*) for information on accessibility. The park's visitor centers, as well as some picnic areas, have accessible restrooms.

PARK FEES AND PERMITS

Entrance fees are $25 per car for seven consecutive days or $15 per person on foot or bicycle, or $20 per motorcycle. Backcountry hiking and camping permits are free (15-day limit) at the Painted Desert Visitor Center or the Rainbow Forest Museum before 4 pm.

PARK HOURS

It's a good idea to call ahead or check the website, because the park's hours vary so much; as a rule of thumb, the park is open daily from sunrise to sunset or approximately 8 am–5 pm. Keep in mind that the area does not observe daylight saving time.

Hotels

There is no lodging within Petrified Forest. Outside the park, lodging choices include modern resorts, rustic cabins, and small bed-and-breakfasts. Note that air-conditioning is not a standard amenity in the mountains, where the nights are cool enough for a blanket even in summer. Closer to the Navajo and Hopi reservations many establishments are run by Native Americans, tribal enterprises intent on offering first-class service and hospitality. Nearby Holbrook offers some national chain motels and comfortable accommodations.

Restaurants

Dining in the park is limited to a cafeteria in the Painted Desert Visitor Center and snacks in the Rainbow Forest Museum. In and around the Navajo and Hopi reservations, be sure to sample Indian tacos, an authentic treat made with scrumptious fry bread, beans, and chilies. If you're searching for burger-and-fries fare, Holbrook is your best bet.

Visitor Information

PARK CONTACT INFORMATION Petrified Forest National Park. ✉ *1 Park Rd.* ☎ *928/524–6228* 🌐 *www.nps.gov/pefo.*

In the Park

Sights

Though named for its famous fossilized trees, Petrified Forest has something to see for history buffs of all stripes, from a segment of Route 66 to ancient dwellings to even more ancient fossils. And the good thing is that most of Petrified Forest's treasures can easily be viewed without a great amount of athletic conditioning. Much can be seen by driving along the main road, from which historic sites are readily accessible. By combining a drive along the park road with a short hike here and there and a visit to one of the park's landmarks, you can see most of the sights in as little as half a day.

Touch—But Don't Take

One of the most commonly asked questions about the Petrified Forest is, "Can I touch the wood?" Yes! Feel comfortable to touch anything, pick it up, inspect it . . . just make sure you put it back where you found it. It's illegal to remove even a small sliver of fossilized wood from the park.

HISTORIC SITES

Agate House

ARCHAEOLOGICAL SITE | This eight-room pueblo is thought to have been built entirely of petrified wood 700 years ago. Researchers believe it might have been used as a temporary dwelling by seasonal farmers or traders from one of the area tribes. ✉ *Rainbow Forest Museum parking area.*

Newspaper Rock

ARCHAEOLOGICAL SITE | See huge boulders covered with petroglyphs believed to have been carved by the Pueblo people more than 500 years ago. **■ TIP→ Look through the binoculars that are provided here—you'll be surprised at what the naked eye misses.** ✉ *Main park road* ✣ *6 miles south of Painted Desert Visitor Center.*

Painted Desert Inn National Historic Landmark

MUSEUM | A nice place to stop and rest in the shade, this site offers vast views of the Painted Desert from several lookouts. Inside, cultural history exhibits, murals, and Native American crafts are on display. ✉ *Main park road* ✣ *2 miles north of Painted Desert Visitor Center.*

Puerco Pueblo

ARCHAEOLOGICAL SITE | This is a 100-room pueblo, built before 1400 and said to have housed Ancestral Pueblo people. Many visitors come to see the petroglyphs, as well as a solar calendar. ✉ *Main park road* ✣ *10 miles south of Painted Desert Visitor Center.*

SCENIC DRIVES

Painted Desert Scenic Drive

SCENIC DRIVE | A 28-mile scenic drive takes you through the park from one entrance to the other. If you begin at the north end, the first 5 miles take you along the edge of a high mesa, with spectacular views of the Painted Desert. Beyond lies the desolate Painted Desert Wilderness Area. After the 5-mile point, the road crosses Interstate 40, then swings south toward the Puerco River across a landscape covered with sagebrush, saltbrush, sunflowers, and Apache plume. Past the river, the road climbs onto a narrow mesa leading to Newspaper Rock, a panel of Pueblo rock art. Then the road bends southeast, enters a barren stretch, and passes tepee-shape buttes in the distance. Next you come to Blue Mesa, roughly the park's midpoint and a good place to stop for views of petrified logs. The next stop on the drive is Agate Bridge, really a 100-foot log over a wide wash. The remaining overlooks are Jasper and Crystal forests, where you can get further glimpses of the accumulated petrified wood. On your way out of the park, stop at the Rainbow Forest Museum for a rest and to shop for a memento. ✉ *Begins at Painted Desert Visitor Center.*

SCENIC STOPS

Agate Bridge

NATURE SITE | Here you'll see a 100-foot log spanning a 40-foot-wide wash. ✉ *Main park road* ✣ *19 miles south of Painted Desert Visitor Center.*

Crystal Forest

NATURE SITE | The fragments of petrified wood strewn here once held clear quartz and amethyst crystals. ✉ *Main park road* ✣ *20 miles south of Painted Desert Visitor Center.*

Giant Logs Interpretive Loop Trail

NATURE SITE | A short walk leads you past the park's largest log, known as Old Faithful. It's considered the largest because of its diameter (9 feet 9 inches), as well as how tall it once was. ✉ *Main park road* ✣ *28 miles south of Painted Desert Visitor Center.*

Jasper Forest

VIEWPOINT | More of an overlook than a forest, this spot has a large concentration of petrified trees in jasper or red. ✉ *Main park road* ✣ *17 miles south of Painted Desert Visitor Center.*

The Tepees

NATURE SITE | Witness the effects of time on these cone-shape rock formations colored by iron, manganese, and other minerals. ✉ *Main park road* ✣ *8 miles south of Painted Desert Visitor Center.*

TRAILS

Agate House

TRAIL | A fairly flat 1-mile trip takes you to an eight-room pueblo sitting high on a knoll. *Moderate.* ✉ *Petrified Forest National Park* ✣ *Trailhead: 26 miles south of Painted Desert Visitor Center.*

★ Blue Mesa

TRAIL | Although it's only 1 mile long and significantly steeper than the rest, this trail at the park's midway point is one of the most popular and worth the effort. *Moderate.* ✉ *Petrified Forest National Park* ✣ *Trailhead: 14 miles south of Painted Desert Visitor Center.*

Crystal Forest Trail

TRAIL | This easy ¾-mile loop leads you past petrified wood that once held quartz crystals and amethyst chips. *Easy.* ✉ *Petrified Forest National Park* ✣ *Trailhead: 20 miles south of Painted Desert Visitor Center.*

Giant Logs Trail

TRAIL | At 0.4 mile, Giant Logs is the park's shortest trail. The loop leads you to Old Faithful, the park's largest petrified log—9 feet, 9 inches at its base, weighing an estimated 44 tons. *Easy.*

Different minerals in different concentrations cause the rich colors in petrified wood and in the Painted Desert.

✉ *Petrified Forest National Park* ⊕ *Trailhead: Directly behind Rainbow Forest Museum, 28 miles south of Painted Desert Visitor Center.*

Kachina Point

TRAIL | This is the trailhead for wilderness hiking at Petrified Forest National Park. A 1-mile trail leads to the Wilderness Area, but from there you're on your own. There are no developed trails, so hiking here is cross-country style. Expect to see strange formations, beautifully colored landscapes, and maybe, just maybe, a pronghorn antelope. *Difficult.* ✉ *Petrified Forest National Park* ⊕ *Trailhead: On northwest side of Painted Desert Inn National Historic Landmark.*

Long Logs Trail

TRAIL | Although barren, this easy 1.6-mile loop passes the largest concentration of wood in the park. *Easy.* ✉ *Petrified Forest National Park* ⊕ *Trailhead: 26 miles south of Painted Desert Visitor Center.*

Painted Desert Rim

TRAIL | The 1-mile trail is at its best in early morning or late afternoon, when the sun accentuates the brilliant red, blue, purple, and other hues of the desert and petrified forest landscape. *Moderate.* ✉ *Petrified Forest National Park* ⊕ *Trail runs between Tawa Point and Kachina Point, 1 mile north of Painted Desert Visitor Center; drive to either point from visitor center.*

Puerco Pueblo Trail

TRAIL | **FAMILY** | A relatively flat and interesting 0.3-mile trail takes you past remains of a home of the Ancestral Pueblo people, built before 1400. The trail is paved and wheelchair accessible. *Easy.* ✉ *Petrified Forest National Park* ⊕ *Trailhead: 10 miles south of Painted Desert Visitor Center.*

VISITOR CENTERS

Painted Desert Inn National Historic Landmark

INFO CENTER | This visitor center isn't as large as the other two, but here you can get information as well as view cultural history exhibits. ✉ *Main park road* ⊕ *2*

Petroglyphs: The Writing on the Wall

The rock art of early Native Americans is carved or painted on basalt boulders, on canyon walls, and on the underside of overhangs throughout the area. No one knows the exact meaning of these signs, and interpretations vary; they've been seen as elements in shamanistic or hunting rituals, as clan signs, maps, or even indications of visits by extraterrestrials.

Where to Find Them

Susceptible to (and often already damaged by) vandalism, many rock-art sites aren't open to the public. Two good petroglyphs to check out at **Petrified Forest National Park** are Newspaper Rock, an overlook near mile marker 12, and Puerco Pueblo, near mile marker 11. Other sites in Arizona include **Hieroglyphic Point** in Salt River Canyon and **Deer Valley Petroglyph Preserve** north of Phoenix.

Determining Its Age

It's just as difficult to date a "glyph" as it is to understand it. Archaeologists try to determine a general time frame by judging the style, the date of the ruins and pottery in the vicinity, the amount of patination (formation of minerals) on the design, or the superimposition of newer images on top of older ones. Most of Eastern Arizona's rock art is estimated to be at least 1,000 years old, and many of the glyphs were created even earlier.

Varied Images

Some glyphs depict animals like bighorn sheep, deer, bear, and mountain lions; others are geometric patterns. The most unusual are the anthropomorphs, strange humanlike figures with elaborate headdresses. Concentric circles are a common design. A few of these circles served as solstice signs, indicating the summer and winter solstices and other important dates. At the solstice, when the angle of the sun is just right, a shaft of light shines through a crack in a nearby rock, illuminating the center of the circle. Archaeologists believe that these solar calendars helped determine the time for ceremonies and planting.

Many solstice signs are in remote regions, but you can visit Petrified Forest National Park around June 20 to see a concentric circle illuminated during the summer solstice. The glyph, reached by a paved trail just a few hundred yards from the parking area, is visible year-round, but light shines directly in the center during the week of the solstice. The phenomenon occurs at 9 am.

■ TIP→ **Do not touch petroglyphs or pictographs—the oil from your hands can damage the images.**

miles north of Painted Desert Visitor Center ☎ *928/524–6228.*

Painted Desert Visitor Center

INFO CENTER | This is the place to go for general park information and an informative 20-minute film. Proceeds from books purchased here will fund continued research and interpretive activities for the park. ✉ *North entrance* ✣ *Off I–40, 27 miles east of Holbrook* ☎ *928/524–6228.*

Rainbow Forest Museum and Visitor Center

INFO CENTER | View displays of prehistoric animals, watch an orientation video, and—perhaps most important—use the restroom facilities at this visitor center at the southern end of the park. ✉ *South* *entrance* ✥ *Off U.S. 180, 18 miles southeast of Holbrook* ☎ *928/524–6228.*

Restaurants

Dining in the park is limited to a cafeteria in the Painted Desert Visitor Center and snacks in the Rainbow Forest Museum. You may want to pack a lunch and eat at one of the park's picnic areas.

Painted Desert Visitor Center Cafeteria
$ | **AMERICAN** | Serving standard (but pretty decent) cafeteria fare, this is the only place in the park where you can get a full meal. **Known for:** closest restaurant to the park; gift shop; excellent lamb stew and Navajo tacos. $ *Average main: $7* ✉ *North entrance* ☎ *928/524–6228.*

Activities

Because the park goes to great pains to maintain the integrity of the fossil- and artifact-strewn landscape, sports and outdoor options in the park are limited to on-trail hiking.

CAMPING

There are no campgrounds in the park. Backpacking or minimal-impact camping is allowed in a designated zone north of Lithodendron Wash in the Wilderness Area; a free permit must be obtained (pick up at the visitor center or museum), and group size is limited to eight. RVs are not allowed. There are no fire pits or designated sites, nor is any shade available. Note that if it rains, that pretty Painted Desert formation turns to sticky clay.

EDUCATIONAL OFFERINGS

Ask at either park visitor center for the availability of special ranger-led tours, such as the after-hours lantern tour of the Painted Desert Inn Museum.

Junior Ranger
TOUR—SIGHT | **FAMILY** | Children 12 and younger can learn more about the park's extensive human, animal, and geologic history as they train to become a Junior Ranger. ✉ *Petrified Forest National Park.*

Ranger Walks and Talks
TOUR—SIGHT | Park rangers lead regular programs along the Great Logs Trail, inside the Painted Desert Inn Museum, and to the Puerco Pueblo. You can view which ranger programs are currently being offered at the visitor centers or online at *www.nps.gov/pefo.* ✉ *Petrified Forest National Park.*

HIKING

All trails begin off the main road, with restrooms at or near the trailheads. Most maintained trails are relatively short, paved, clearly marked, and, with a few exceptions, easy to moderate in difficulty. Hikers with greater stamina can make their own trails in the wilderness area, located just north of the Painted Desert Visitor Center. Watch your step for rattlesnakes, which are common in the park—if left alone and given a wide berth, they're passed easily enough.

What's Nearby

Located in eastern Arizona just off Interstate 40, Petrified Forest National Park is set in an area of grasslands, overlooked by mountains in the distance. At nearly an hour from **American Indian Nations,** nearly two hours from **Flagstaff,** and three hours from the **Grand Canyon,** the park is relatively remote and separated from many comforts of travel. Just a half hour away, **Holbrook,** the nearest town, is the best place to grab a quick bite to eat or take a brief rest.

Chapter 50

PINNACLES NATIONAL PARK

Updated by
Andrew Collins

Camping	Hotels	Activities	Scenery	Crowds
★★★☆☆	★★☆☆☆	★★★☆☆	★★★★☆	★★★☆☆

WELCOME TO PINNACLES NATIONAL PARK

TOP REASONS TO GO

★ **Condor encounters:** This is one of the few places to potentially view these critically endangered birds flying overhead; of the few hundred California condors alive in the wild today, about 65 have been released or hatched in Pinnacles or nearby along the coast.

★ **Cave exploring:** The park contains two talus caves—a unique type of cave formed when boulders fall into narrow canyons, creating ceilings, passageways, and small chambers.

★ **Hiking the pinnacles:** The best way to see the otherworldly rock formations of the ancient volcano at the park's center is to hike the more than 30 miles of trails.

★ **Climbing sans crowds:** Pinnacles receives relatively few visitors because of its out-of-the-way location, leaving the hundreds of rock-climbing routes crowd-free.

★ **Star appeal:** Far from cities, the park is a popular stargazing destination, especially during the annual Perseid meteor shower.

1 **East Side.** Of the park's two entrances to Pinnacles, the East Side is best for families and first-time visitors. It has the park's only visitor center and campground—which includes a modest grocery store and a small swimming pool that's especially inviting on hot days. This entrance also offers the best access to both easy and more challenging hikes, including the highly popular trek to Bear Gulch Cave.

2 **West Side.** The park's quieter side has fewer amenities, but entering here and driving to the Chaparral Parking Area provides the best way to sneak a glimpse of the high-peak formations without having to walk anywhere. Hikers, however, will find some of the park's most rugged and exciting trails, including treks to Balconies Cave and up into the High Peaks.

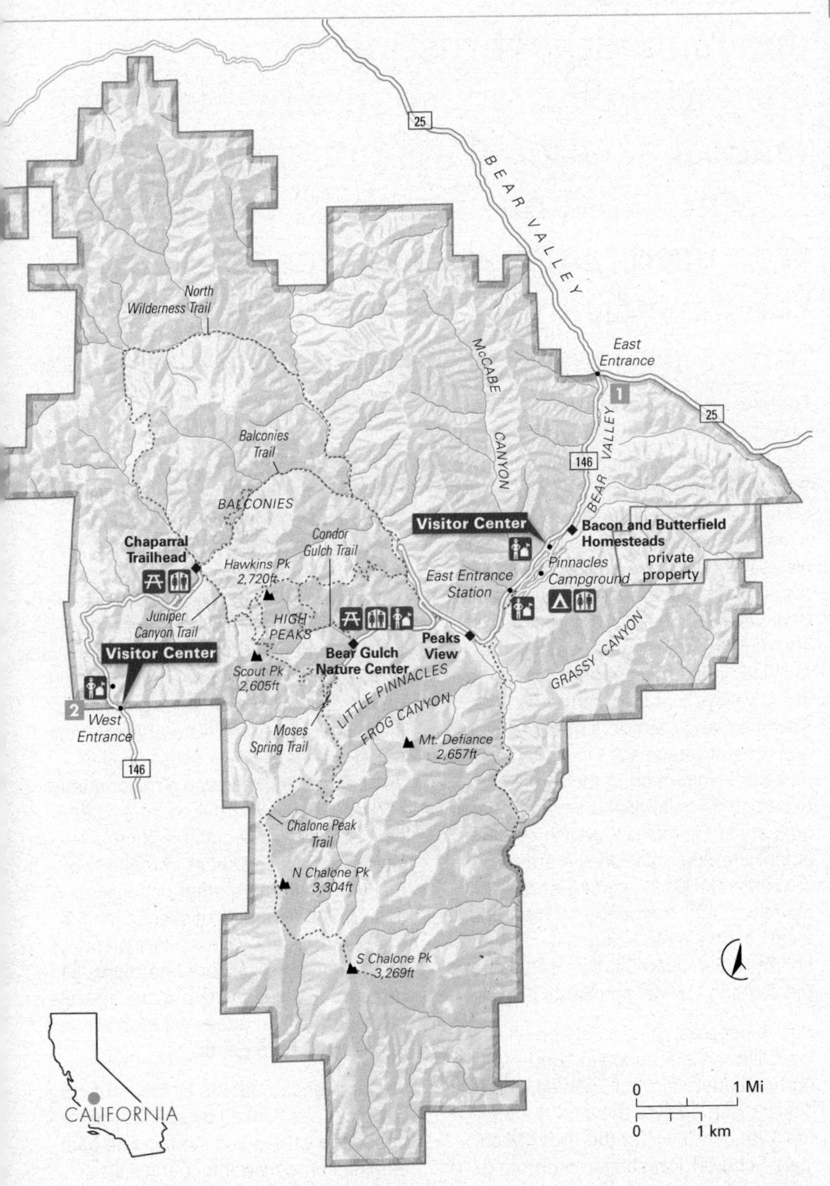

25
BEAR VALLEY
East Entrance
1
25
McCABE CANYON
146
BEAR VALLEY
North Wilderness Trail
Balconies Trail
BALCONIES
Condor Gulch Trail
Visitor Center
Bacon and Butterfield Homesteads
private property
Pinnacles Campground
East Entrance Station
Chaparral Trailhead
Hawkins Pk 2,720ft
HIGH PEAKS
Juniper Canyon Trail
Peaks View
Visitor Center
Bear Gulch Nature Center
GRASSY CANYON
Scout Pk 2,605ft
LITTLE PINNACLES
FROG CANYON
2
West Entrance
Moses Spring Trail
Mt. Defiance 2,657ft
146
Chalone Peak Trail
N Chalone Pk 3,304ft
S Chalone Pk 3,269ft
CALIFORNIA
0
1 Mi
0
1 km

President Theodore Roosevelt recognized the uniqueness of the Pinnacles Volcanic Formation—its jagged spires and monoliths thrusting upward from chaparral-covered mountains—when he made it a national monument in 1908. Legends abound of robbers and banditos who used talus caves as hideouts, though the most famous denizens of the park today are the California condors.

The Pinnacles volcanic field formed some 23 million years ago and has slowly shifted to the northwest nearly 200 miles as a result of tectonic shifting of the Pacific plate. The peaks rise beside the San Andreas Rift Zone, which slices through Bear Valley just east of the park boundary. Highway 25 roughly parallels the faultline. Indigenous people have lived in the valleys that bracket the park for centuries, and members of the Chalon and Amah Matsun still work closely with park staff, volunteering their time and expertise on cultural and environmental projects at Pinnacles. Spanish settlers established the mission system through the region in 1769—settlements and churches from the period still stand just west of the park in Soledad as well as nearby in San Juan Bautista and out on the coast in Carmel and Santa Cruz.

Native peoples, Spaniards, and—following California statehood in 1850—white homesteaders farmed, worked, and occasionally battled over the land throughout the 19th century. A settler from Michigan, Schuyler Hain began promoting the beauty of Pinnacles around the turn of the 20th century, leading visitors on hikes up into talus caves in Bear Valley. Word spread, which led to the park's national monument designation. In the 1930s, the federal government hired hundreds of CCC (Civilian Conservation Corps) workers to further develop the monument—they carved out many miles of the trails that still extend through the park today, along with several buildings, including Bear Gulch Nature Center and the stone restroom at Scout Peak. In 2013, Pinnacles received a major status upgrade, becoming the country's 59th national park. Although it lacks the singular thrills and sheer immensity of many of California's other national parks, this 26,000-acre park (it's less than 1% the size of Death Valley) offers plenty of wonder and magnificent photo ops, all of them contained within a manageable package that's at once secluded yet relatively easy to get to.

The park encompasses a cluster of craggy volcanoes flanked by scenic, sparsely populated valleys and contains no park lodgings or restaurants, but it's also within day-tripping distance of Monterey

AVERAGE HIGH/LOW TEMPERATURES					
JAN.	FEB.	MAR.	APR.	MAY	JUNE
62/27	63/30	67/32	72/33	80/37	88/41
JULY	AUG.	SEPT.	OCT.	NOV.	DEC.
95/45	95/45	90/42	81/36	69/31	61/27

Bay, San Francisco, and San Luis Obispo County. If it's your first time visiting the park, however, consider spending the night somewhere relatively near the park, such as King City, Salinas, or Hollister, or overnighting in the park's picturesque campground. Local options are neither fancy nor distinctive, but this strategy will allow you to explore each side of the park at a leisurely pace.

What's remarkable about visiting Pinnacles from anywhere on the coast is the chance to experience such a strikingly different landscape within about 35 miles of the ocean. The park's soaring golden peaks and rocky spires and comparatively arid, sunny climate look and feel a world away. The signature attractions are the high peaks and the intriguing caves, which are in the middle of the park and can be hiked to in a half-day from either side. However you approach Pinnacles, you'll find opportunities to spy rare California condors flying overhead and to soak up a breathtaking landscape.

Planning

When to Go

Triple-digit temperatures are not uncommon in summer; luckily this means fewer crowds, especially on weekdays. Spring, particularly March and April, is the most popular season—a prime time to view spectacular displays of lupine, poppies, and other wildflowers. October through December is a great time to visit if you want to enjoy cooler temperatures and smaller crowds. Winters are cold by California standards, but this is an opportune time to hike, especially the High Peaks, where most of the trails are in the sun. Just keep in mind that temperatures in the deeply shaded areas such as the Balconies Trail can reach below freezing.

Note that Bear Gulch Cave is hugely popular but also home to a large colony of Townsend's big-eared bats. This protected species raises its young in late spring and summer, so the cave is closed from about mid-May to mid-July. Check the park website for the latest information on closures.

Getting Here and Around

AIR

It's about a 90-minute drive north to reach the nearest major airport in San Jose, and about two hours to the airports in San Francisco and Oakland. Pleasantly compact Monterey Regional Airport is about a 75-minute drive west and is served by Alaska, Allegiant, American, and United.

CAR

One of the first things you need to decide when visiting Pinnacles is whether to arrive through the east or west entrance. There is no road through the park, although it's possible to hike across the park in an hour or two and to reach the key attractions—the High Peaks and two talus caves—from either side. If you've never been to the park, entering the east side is a good strategy as it contains the main visitor center and a convenience store as well as access to more trailheads. On the other hand, if you're making just a short visit while driving up

U.S. 101 or looking for the quickest hiking access to the High Peaks, the west entrance makes sense. It takes roughly the same amount of time to reach each entrance, whether you approach from San Jose, the coast, or San Luis Obispo. The east side is accessed via Highway 146 from rural and scenic Highway 25, and the west side is reached from a different—narrow, hilly, and one-way in places—section of Highway 146 from the town of Soledad, just off the U.S. 101 freeway. RVs and trailers are advised not to use the west entrance.

Inspiration

The landscape around Pinnacles and the adjacent farming town of Soledad figured prominently in the writings of the great American novelist John Steinbeck. His 1937 novella *Of Mice and Men* took place in Soledad, but it's his epic 1952 novel *East of Eden* that most poignantly describes Pinnacles' majestic, mountainous landscape.

Shirlaine Baldwin's lushly photographed 2016 book *California Condors: A Day at Pinnacles National Park* offers a beautiful and informative look at these huge birds that had become extinct in the wild by the early 1980s but that are slowly making a comeback in the skies above the park.

Park Essentials

PARK FEES AND PERMITS

Park admission—good for seven days—is $30 per car, $25 for motorcycles, $15 per person on foot or bicycle.

PARK HOURS

The east entrance is always open. The west entrance is open daily 7:30 am–8 pm, but cars can exit the park through an automatic gate anytime after closing time.

CELL PHONE RECEPTION

The closer you get to Pinnacles, the less reliable the cell phone service; it's nearly nonexistent within the park. There's a pay phone at the visitor center at the east entrance, and here you can also purchase Wi-Fi from the visitor center.

Hotels

Although there aren't any lodgings in the park, the Pinnacles Campground is right by the east entrance and offers everything from primitive tent sites to newer tent cabins with electricity.

Restaurants

The park has no restaurants—just a tiny convenience store (with bags of ice and basic snacks) next to the visitor center on the east side. So plan accordingly, and pack a cooler if you plan on picnicking or camping. The nearest communities with grocery stores and a limited selection of restaurants are Hollister to the north, King City to the south, and Soledad just outside the western entrance.

Visitor Information

CONTACTS Pinnacles National Park. ✉ *5000 Hwy. 146, Paicines* ☎ *831/389–4486* 🌐 *www.nps.gov/pinn.*

East Side

31 miles southeast of Hollister, 31 miles north of King City.

The larger of the park's two sides has a visitor center, campground, and convenience store. It also has a bit more infrastructure and roadway to explore, including the Bear Gulch Day Use Area, which has a small nature center, one of the best picnic spots in the park, and access to many of the park's top trails.

The hike to Bear Gulch Cave is popular with families.

Sights

HISTORIC SITES

Bacon and Butterfield Homesteads

HISTORIC SITE | On the park's eastern side, these two preserved homesteads are in the heart of the 331-acre Ben Bacon Ranch Historic District, which the park acquired in 2006. A walk along the former road through this section illustrates what subsistence farming in the area looked like from 1865 to 1941, before large-scale agriculture and ranching became the norm. You reach the area by way of the gravel road that starts just east of the Pinnacles Visitor Center; it then continues north about 1.3 miles by the old homesteads. ✉ *Off Hwy. 146.*

Bear Gulch Nature Center

MUSEUM | **FAMILY** | This small stone building constructed by the CCC (Civilian Conservation Corps) in the 1930s makes for a short but engaging stop while hiking from or picnicking in the Bear Gulch Day Use Area. Inside you can watch a film and view interpretive displays about the park, and the rangers can offer advice about nearby trails and talus caves. ✉ *Bear Gulch Day Use Area, Paicines* ☎ *831/389–4486.*

TRAILS

★ **Bear Gulch Cave–Moses Spring–Rim Trail Loop**

TRAIL | **FAMILY** | Perhaps the most popular hike at Pinnacles, this relatively short (2.2-mile) loop trail is fun for kids and adults. It leads to the Bear Gulch cave system, and if your timing is right, you'll pass by several seasonal waterfalls inside the caves (flashlights are required). If it's been raining, check with a ranger, as the caves can flood. The upper side of the cave is usually closed in spring and early summer to protect the Townsend's big-ear bats and their pups. *Easy.* ✣ *Trailhead: Bear Gulch Day Use Area.*

★ **Condor Gulch Trail**

TRAIL | The trailhead starts at the Bear Gulch Day Use area, and it's a short but somewhat strenuous 1-mile hike uphill to the Condor Gulch Overlook, where you can get a good view of the High Peaks above. You can turn back the same way you came, or continue another 0.7 mile up to the High Peaks Trail (a total elevation gain of 1,100 feet)—and extend your hike by following it in either direction. If you're feeling ambitious, continue into the park's west side, to the Balconies Cliffs Trail, returning back via the level Old Pinnacles Trail. *Moderate–Difficult.* ✉ *Pinnacles National Park* ✣ *Trailhead: Bear Gulch Day Use Area.*

Pinnacles Visitor Center to Bear Gulch Day Use Area

TRAIL | This 4.6-mile round-trip hike (allow about three hours) follows the Chalone and Bear creeks first along the level Bench Trail for about 1½ miles, where it meets up with the Sycamore Trail, which ascends gradually through a tree-shaded ravine on its way to Bear Gulch. Purchase an interpretive map at the visitor center and keep your eyes open for signs pointing out where you might be able to spot the rare red-legged frog or the native three-spined stickleback fish. *Moderate.* ✉ *Pinnacles National Park* ✣ *Trailhead: Pinnacles Visitor Center.*

Pinnacles Visitor Center to South Wilderness Trail

TRAIL | This 6½-mile round-trip hike with no elevation gain is an easy if somewhat long stroll, first on the Bench Trail and then alongside the Chalone River to the park's southeastern boundary. A favorite of wildlife-watching enthusiasts, it's a lovely trail for listening to birds sing along the creek, and it leads through magnificent groves of valley oaks. *Easy–Moderate.* ✉ *Pinnacles National Park* ✣ *Trailhead: Pinnacles Visitor Center.*

VISITOR CENTERS

Pinnacles Visitor Center

INFO CENTER | At the park's main visitor center, near the eastern entrance, you'll find a helpful selection of maps, books, and gifts. The adjacent campground store sells light snacks. ✉ *5000 Hwy. 146, Paicines* ☎ *831/389–4485* 🌐 *www.nps.gov/pinn.*

West Side

10 miles east of Soledad, 25 miles north of King City,

Although more accessible from the coast and bigger highways and towns, the west side of Pinnacles is actually the quieter and more secluded of the two halves. You enter it via a beautiful, winding country road, and once inside the park you'll find the contact ranger station and a parking area that serves as the trailhead to several outstanding hikes.

Sights

TRAILS

★ **Balconies Cliffs–Cave Loop**

TRAIL | **FAMILY** | Grab your flashlight before heading out from the Chaparral Trailhead parking lot for this 2.4-mile loop that takes you through the Balconies Caves. This trail is especially beautiful in spring, when wildflowers carpet the canyon floor. About 0.6 mile from the start of the trail, turn left to begin ascending the Balconies Cliffs Trail, where you'll be rewarded with close-up views of Machete Ridge and other steep, vertical formations; you may run across rock climbers testing their skills before rounding the loop and descending back through the cave. *Easy–Moderate.* ✉ *Pinnacles National Park* ✣ *Trailhead: Chaparral Parking Area.*

★ **Juniper Canyon Loop**

TRAIL | This steep 4.3-mile loop climbs into the heart of the dramatic High Peaks with a 1,215-foot elevation gain. Summer temps can soar, so bring plenty of water. From the trailhead follow the switchbacks up for 1.2 miles, where the trail veers right; stop at Scout Peak, where you'll find restrooms and fantastic views in all directions—keep an eye out for the occasional California condor in flight. Follow the High Peaks Trail north through a steep and narrow section, where you hug the side of rock faces until reaching a short, nearly vertical staircase that has a railing to help you up. Then pick up the Tunnel Trail to complete your loop back to the trailhead via the Juniper Canyon Trail. *Difficult.* ✉ *Pinnacles National Park* ✣ *Trailhead: Chaparral Parking Area.*

Prewett Point to Jawbone Trail

TRAIL | **FAMILY** | You can hike these two connected trails, starting with the 0.9-mile wheelchair-accessible Prewett Point hike, from the West Pinnacles Visitor Contact Station. It leads to an impressive overlook and offers panoramic views of the High Peaks, Balconies Cliffs, and Hain Wilderness. It's mostly exposed, however, so avoid it during midday in summer. The easy-to-moderate Jawbone Trail extends from Prewett Point, descending 1.2 miles through the hills to the Jawbone Parking Area, which is another 0.3 miles to Chaparral Parking Area. Allow about 45 minutes to hike to Prewett Point and back, and up to two hours round-trip if you tackle both trails. *Easy–Moderate.* ✉ *Pinnacles National Park* ✣ *Trailhead: West Pinnacles Visitor Contact Station.*

VISITOR CENTERS

West Pinnacles Visitor Contact Station

INFO CENTER | This small ranger station is just past the park's western entrance, about 10 miles east of Soledad. Here you can get maps and information, watch a 13-minute film about Pinnacles, and view interpretive exhibits. No food or drink is available here. ✉ *Hwy. 146, Soledad* ☎ *831/389–4427* 🌐 *www.nps.gov/pinn.*

Activities

BIRD-WATCHING

You're most likely to see a condor in the early morning or in the early evening in the relatively remote High Peaks area, on the Balconies Cliff Trail as you look toward Machete Ridge, or just southeast of the campground. There are two spotting scopes in the campground that may help you get a closer look. Do not under any circumstances approach these federally protected birds—you can be fined for doing so.

The High Peaks are a good place to spot other raptors, such as prairie and peregrine falcons, golden eagles, red-tailed hawks, and American kestrels.

CAMPING

Pinnacles Campground. Set under a canopy of live oaks that provides welcome shade over most of its 134 sites, this year-round campground has flush toilets and showers and a seasonal swimming pool and camp store. Each tent ($35), RV ($45), and glamping-style tent cabin ($115–$125) has a picnic table and a fire ring. ☎ *877/444–6777* 🌐 *www.visitpinnacles.com.*

EDUCATIONAL PROGRAMS

Illustrated Ranger Talks

COLLEGE | On some weekend evenings, rangers give free presentations at the east entrance's campground amphitheater. The topics depend on the ranger's particular interests but always relate to the park's main stories and its geology, plants, or wildlife. Times vary, so check the Pinnacles website or the Activity Boards at the east or west entrances or the Bear Gulch Nature Center. ✉ *5000 Hwy. 146* ☎ *831/389–4486* 🌐 *www.nps.gov/pinn/planyourvisit/programs.htm.*

Junior Ranger Program

LOCAL INTEREST | **FAMILY** | Kids can pick up a free Junior Ranger booklet at Bear Nature Center and the park visitor centers and earn a badge for completing a series of fun educational activities. ✉ *Pinnacles National Park.*

HIKING

Hiking is by far the park's most popular activity, and the only way to get between its east and west sides, as no roads traverse the Pinnacles. There are some 30 miles of trails, most of them starting from the west side's Chaparral Parking Area and the east side's Bear Gulch Day Use Area. The best hikes across the park are either the flat and easy 3-mile Old Pinnacles Trail or by climbing up and through the High Peaks, which can entail anything from a 5- to 8-mile trek and some serious elevation gains. In summer when it can get very hot in the park, try to tackle the steeper, more arduous trails in the morning or early evening.

Flashlights are required in the Bear Gulch and Balconies cave systems—you won't be able to get through the caves without one. Penlights won't do the job; the best choice is a hands-free, head-mounted light. Also, although the hikes to the caves themselves are easy and short, getting through the caves requires much scrambling, ducking, climbing, and squeezing. Make sure you have suitable, closed-toe shoes.

GUIDED HIKES

★ Ranger-Guided Hikes and Activities
Ranger programs and guided hikes, including occasional and very popular full-moon night hikes, are offered on weekends, fall–spring. For details, check activity boards or talk with staff at the visitor centers. ✉ *Pinnacles National Park.*

STARGAZING

Despite its proximity to the populous Bay Area, Pinnacles remains nearly untouched by light pollution, making it an outstanding place to watch meteor showers, stars, or the full moon. It's popular with astronomy clubs, whose members occasionally set up their telescopes for public use. Park rangers sometimes lead nighttime activities (reservations required; call or check the park website a few days ahead), usually on the weekends, that include dark-sky and full-moon hikes and "star parties" to watch meteor showers and other celestial phenomena.

Nearby Towns

The small town of **Soledad,** just outside the park's western entrance, is most famous as the setting of John Steinbeck's *Of Mice and Men,* but it's also in the heart of the Monterey County wine region and has some excellent wineries with tasting rooms, though few amenities beyond these. A short drive south, the similarly agricultural community of **King City** has a few modest lodgings and good restaurants—it's a good base for visiting either park entrance.

To the north, you'll find a larger though still mostly chain-oriented selection of hotels and eateries in **Salinas,** a once-gritty city of about 155,000 that's lately begun undergoing a downtown renaissance and is home to the famed National Steinbeck Center, and **Hollister,** a farming town and bedroom community with some good wineries in the countryside; the historic neighboring hamlet of San Juan Bautista has plenty of charm.

The famous Pacific coastal communities of the **Monterey Peninsula,** including Carmel Valley and Monterey, as well as **Santa Cruz** at the top of Monterey Bay, are just a 60- to 90-minute drive, yet feel like a world away, with world-class beaches, golf course, winery tasting rooms, boutiques, and distinctive dining and lodging options.

Chapter 51

REDWOOD NATIONAL AND STATE PARKS

Updated by
Andrew Collins

Camping ★★★☆☆

Hotels ★★★★☆

Activities ★★★★☆

Scenery ★★★★★

Crowds ★★★★☆

WELCOME TO REDWOOD NATIONAL AND STATE PARKS

TOP REASONS TO GO

★ **Giant trees:** These mature coastal redwoods, which you can hike beneath in numerous groves throughout the park, are the tallest trees in the world.

★ **Hiking along the sea:** The park offers many miles of ocean access, including the Coastal Trail, which runs along the western edge of the park.

★ **Rare wildlife:** Mighty Roosevelt elk favor the park's flat prairie and open lands; seldom-seen black bears roam the backcountry; trout and salmon leap through streams; and Pacific gray whales swim along the coast during their spring and fall migrations.

★ **Stepping back in time:** Hike mossy and mysterious Fern Canyon Trail and explore a prehistoric scene of lush vegetation and giant ferns—a memorable scene in *Jurassic Park 2* was shot here.

★ **Getting off-the-grid:** Amid the majestic redwoods you're usually out of cell phone range and often free from crowds, offering a rare opportunity to disconnect.

1 **South.** The highlights of the parks' southern section are the hikes and scenic driving along Bald Hills Road, including the Lady Bird Johnson Grove, and the beautiful coastal scenery at Thomas H. Kuchel Visitor Center and the estuarial lagoons to the south. This section encompasses much of the original Redwood National Park and is where you'll find the small village of Orick, which has a gas station and a few other basic services.

2 **Middle.** Here in the span of park that extends from north of Orick to the Yurok tribal community of Klamath, you'll find some of the most magnificent and accessible stands of old-growth redwoods. Start your adventures at Prairie Creek Redwoods State Park's visitor center, from which several trails emanate. Also set aside time to explore the meadows inhabited by Roosevelt elk, the trail to Fern Canyon from Gold Bluffs Beach, and the gorgeous drives along Newton B. Drury Scenic Parkway and Klamath's Coastal Drive Loop

3 **North.** Anchored by the region's largest community, Crescent City, the park's northern third encompasses the rugged, pristine forests of Jedediah Smith Redwoods State Park, which is slightly inland, and Del Norte Coast Redwoods State Park, which also offers visitors the chance to visit stretches of windswept beaches, steep sea cliffs, and forested ridges. On a clear day it's postcard-perfect; with fog, it's mysterious and mesmerizing.

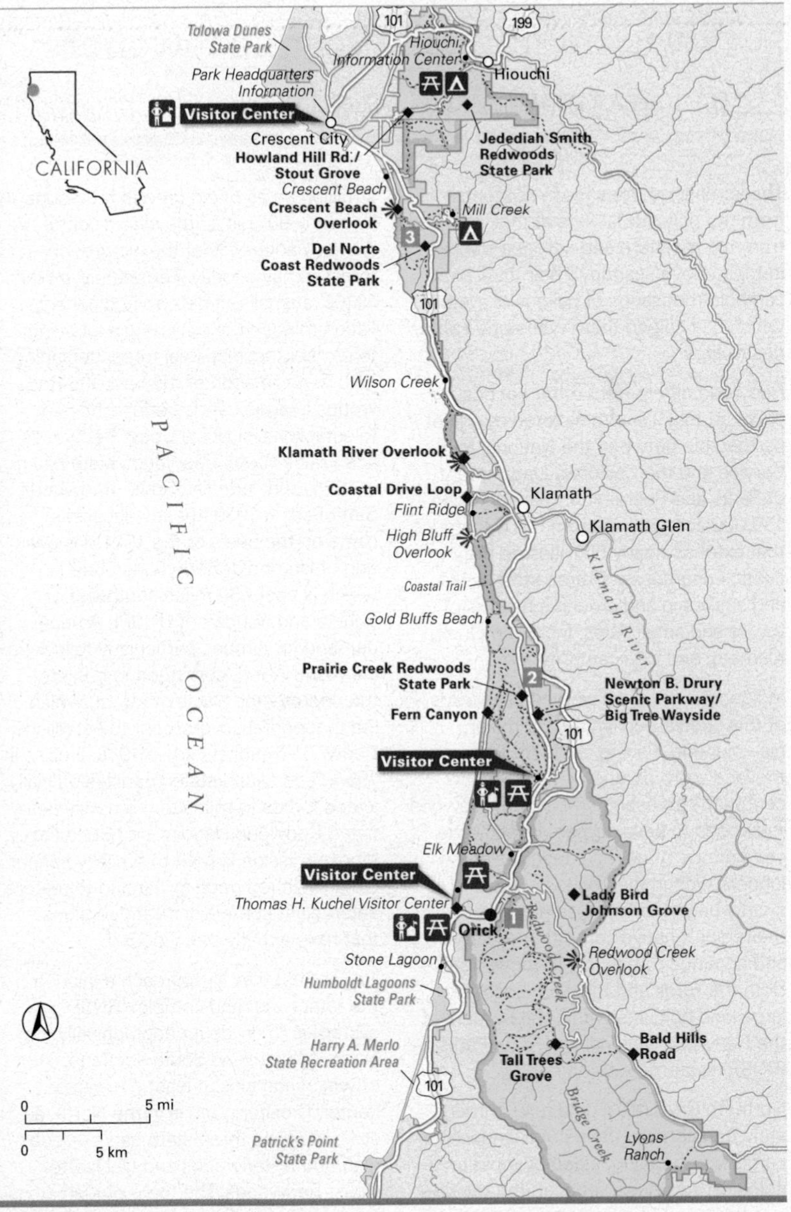

Tolowa Dunes State Park
101
199
Hiouchi Information Center
Hiouchi
Park Headquarters Information
Visitor Center
Crescent City
Howland Hill Rd./ Stout Grove
Jedediah Smith Redwoods State Park
CALIFORNIA
Crescent Beach
Crescent Beach Overlook
Mill Creek
Del Norte Coast Redwoods State Park
Wilson Creek
PACIFIC OCEAN
Klamath River Overlook
Coastal Drive Loop
Klamath
Flint Ridge
Klamath Glen
High Bluff Overlook
Klamath River
Coastal Trail
Gold Bluffs Beach
Prairie Creek Redwoods State Park
Newton B. Drury Scenic Parkway/ Big Tree Wayside
Fern Canyon
Visitor Center
Elk Meadow
Visitor Center
Lady Bird Johnson Grove
Thomas H. Kuchel Visitor Center
Orick
Redwood Creek
Redwood Creek Overlook
Stone Lagoon
Humboldt Lagoons State Park
Bald Hills Road
Tall Trees Grove
Harry A. Merlo State Recreation Area
Bridge Creek
0
5 mi
0
5 km
Patrick's Point State Park
Lyons Ranch

Soaring more than 375 feet high, California's coastal redwoods are miracles of efficiency—some have survived hundreds of years, a few more than two millennia.

These massive trees glean nutrients from the rich alluvial flats at their feet and from the moisture and nitrogen trapped in their uneven canopy. Their thick bark can hold thousands of gallons of water, which has helped them withstand centuries of fires.

Redwood differs from other national parks, in that it's administered by a joint partnership between the National Park Service and the California Department of Parks and Recreation. This sprawling 139,000-acre park system has a footprint that extends nearly 50 miles up the coast, encompasses three state parks, and snakes in and around a handful of towns and small cities, including Orick, Klamath, and Crescent City.

Indigenous people have been stewards of this special ecosystem for millennia—hunting, fishing, and foraging the land early on, and in more recent centuries harvesting timber from downed redwoods to build homes. Despite the cruel efforts of gold prospectors and loggers who in the 1850s arrived and swiftly began trying to eradicate them, the region's native communities survived and continue to this day to thrive here. Both the Yurok and Tolowa tribes have large land holdings within the borders of the Redwood National and State Parks (RNSP) system.

Northern California's gold rush immediately transformed the natural landscape. Large-scale logging, aided by rapid technological advances, reduced the region's 2 million acres of old-growth redwoods by nearly 90% in a little over a century—only about 5% of the old-growth forest remains today. Fortunately, by the 1910s, a small but determined conservation-minded minority began lobbying to protect these special trees, beginning with the formation of the Save-the-Redwoods League, whose efforts helped to establish Del Norte Coast Redwoods and Prairie Creek Redwoods state parks in 1925, and Jedediah Smith Redwoods State Park in 1939 (these successes came on the heels of the 1921 designation of Humboldt Redwoods State Park, which is about 30 miles southeast of Eureka and not part of RNSP). A huge demand for lumber, particularly following World War II, continued to deplete the unprotected tracts of forest, which led the federal government to establish Redwood National Park in 1968. Finally, in 1994, federal and state agencies officially joined forces to manage the newly designated Redwood National and State Parks, whose mission is both to preserve uncut old-growth redwood forest and to restore and replant some significant sections that have already been logged.

The easiest way to approach exploring the rather vast and complex RNSP system is to divide it geographically into North, Middle, and South sections, each of which contains at least one visitor center. Crescent City is in the North, as are two of the three state parks—Jedediah Smith Redwoods and Del Norte Coast Redwoods. The town of Klamath is

AVERAGE HIGH/LOW TEMPERATURES					
JAN.	FEB.	MAR.	APR.	MAY	JUNE
54/39	56/41	57/41	59/42	62/45	65/48
JULY	AUG.	SEPT.	OCT.	NOV.	DEC.
67/51	67/51	68/49	64/46	58/43	55/40

in the Middle section, as is Prairie Creek Redwoods State Park. And the village of Orick is in the South, which also contains much of the original national park, although you'll find other sections of it in the Middle and North sections, too. Additionally, there are four coastal parks just south of RNSP: Humboldt Lagoons State Park, Harry A. Merlo State Recreation Area, Big Lagoon Beach and County Park, and Patrick's Point State Park. U.S. 101 is the main north–south route through the park, but the northern section is also bisected by a short stretch of U.S. 199 east of Crescent City.

Some park attractions, scenic drives, and trails are in the national park, and others are in state parks, but as you explore, it's difficult—and not particularly important—to know which section you're in. Just adhere to the excellent map in the free park brochure and visitor guide newspaper, and you'll easily figure out where you're going and how to get around this magnificent preserve that aims to protect one of the world's oldest and largest living things.

Planning

When to Go

Campers and hikers flock to the park from mid-June to early September. The crowds disappear in winter, but you'll have to contend with frequent rains and nasty potholes and even occasional closures on side roads. Temperatures fluctuate widely: the foggy coastal lowland is much cooler than the higher-altitude interior.

The average annual rainfall is between 60 and 80 inches, most of it falling between November and April. During the dry summer, thick fog rolling in from the Pacific can veil the forests, providing the redwoods a large portion of their moisture intake.

Getting Here and Around

AIR

United Airlines flies a few times daily between San Francisco and the most practical gateway, California Redwood Coast–Humboldt County Airport, between Trinidad and Arcata, about 16 miles north of Eureka. The regional carrier Contour offers daily service from Oakland to Del Norte County Regional Airport in Crescent City. Another option is Oregon's Rogue Valley International Medford Airport, which is served by Alaska, Allegiant, American, Delta, and United, and is about a two-hour drive from the northern end of the park in Crescent City.

CAR

U.S. 101 runs north–south nearly the entire length of the park. You can access all the main park roads via U.S. 101 and U.S. 199, which runs east–west through the park's northern portion. Many roads within the park aren't paved, and winter rains can turn them into obstacle courses; sometimes they're closed completely. Motor homes/RVs and trailers aren't permitted on some routes. The drive from San Francisco to the park's southern end takes about six hours via U.S. 101. From Portland it takes roughly the same amount of time to reach the park's northern section via Interstate 5 to

U.S. 199. ■**TIP→ Don't rely solely on GPS, which is inaccurate in parts of the park; closely consult official park maps.**

Inspiration

Richard Preston's *The Wild Trees: A Story of Passion and Daring* chronicles the redwood-climbing exploits of several botanists fiercely passionate about the endangered tall trees and the ecosystem that supports them.

The parks' larger-than-life landscapes have made their way into a handful of movies. Most famously, in 1997, Steven Spielberg filmed portions of *The Lost World: Jurassic Park* amid the verdant rainforest foliage of Fern Canyon. Perhaps he was inspired by his friend George Lucas's decision 15 years earlier to film in a grove of redwoods just outside Jedediah Smith Redwoods State Park in the famed Ewoks chase scene in *Return of the Jedi*.

Park Essentials

PARK FEES AND PERMITS

Admission to Redwood National Park is free; a few areas in the state parks collect day-use fees of $8, including the Gold Bluffs Beach and Fern Canyon sections of Prairie Creek Redwoods State Park, and the day-use areas accessed via the campground entrances in Jedediah Smith and Del Norte Coast state parks (the fee for camping overnight is $35). To visit the popular Tall Trees Grove, you must get a free permit at the Kuchel Visitor Center in Orick. Free permits, available at the Kuchel, Crescent City, and (summer only) Hiouchi visitor centers, are needed to stay at all designated backcountry camps.

PARK HOURS

The park is open year-round, 24 hours a day.

CELL PHONE RECEPTION

It's difficult to pick up a signal in much of the park, especially in the camping areas and on many hiking trails. The Prairie Creek and Jedediah Smith visitor centers have pay phones.

Hotels

The only lodgings within park grounds are the Elk Meadow Cabins, near Prairie Creek Redwoods Visitor Center. Orick, to the south of Elk Meadow, and Klamath, to the north, have basic motels, and in Klamath there's also the charming and historic Requa Inn. Elegant Victorian inns, seaside motels, and fully equipped vacation rentals are among the options in Crescent City to the north, and Eureka and to a more limited extent Trinidad and Arcata to the south. In summer, try to book at least a week ahead at lodgings near the park.

Restaurants

The park has no restaurants, but Eureka and Arcata have diverse dining establishments—everything from hip oyster bars to some surprisingly good ethnic restaurants. The dining options are more limited, though decent, in Crescent City and Trinidad, and there are just a couple of very basic options in Klamath and tiny Orick. Most small-town restaurants close early, around 7:30 or 8 pm.

Hotel and restaurant reviews have been shortened. For full information visit Fodors.com. Hotel prices are the lowest cost of a standard double room in high season. Restaurant prices are the average cost of a main course at dinner, or if dinner is not served, at lunch

What It Costs

$	$$	$$$	$$$$
RESTAURANTS			
under $16	$16–$22	$23–$30	over $30
HOTELS			
under $125	$125–$175	$176–$225	over $225

Visitor Information

CONTACTS Redwood National and State Parks Headquarters. ✉ *1111 2nd St., Crescent City* ☎ *707/465–7306* 🌐 *www.nps.gov/redw.*

South

19 miles north of Trinidad, 8 miles south of Prairie Creek Visitor Center, 44 miles south of Crescent City.

This is the section of the park system that you'll reach if driving up the coast from Eureka and Trinidad, and it's home to one of the largest visitor information resources, the beachfront Thomas H. Kuchel Visitor Center, which is on U.S. 101 shortly after you enter the park. For the purposes of this chapter, this section includes the town of Orick and everything else south of the turnoff onto Bald Hills Road, which leads to some of the largest stands of redwoods in the park, including the Lady Bird Johnson and Tall Trees groves.

Sights

SCENIC DRIVES

Bald Hills Road

SCENIC DRIVE | A winding, steep, and dramatic road that stretches into the park's southernmost section and highest elevations, Bald Hills Road accesses some great hikes—Lady Bird Johnson Grove and Lyons Ranch among them—as well as the access road to the Tall Trees Grove. But it's also wondrously scenic route all on its own, passing through sometimes misty patch of redwoods before entering a stretch of open meadows with wildflowers in spring and the chance to see Roosevelt elk and bears any time of year. Do stop at Redwood Creek Overlook, a 2,100-foot elevation pullout at mile 6.6. Bald Hills Road is paved for the first 13 miles. It continues another 4 miles unpaved to the park's southern boundary, and it's then possible to continue another 20 miles or so to the small village of Weitchpec and then onward inland toward Redding or Yreka. ✉ *Off U.S. 101, Orick.*

TRAILS

★ Lady Bird Johnson Grove Trail

TRAIL | One of the park's most accessible spots to view big trees, this impressive grove just a short drive northeast of Orick was dedicated by, and named for, the former first lady. A level 1.4-mile nature loop crosses a neat old wooden footbridge and follows an old logging road through this often mist-shrouded forest of redwoods. *Easy.* ✉ *Orick* ✣ *Trailhead: Bald Hills Rd., 2 miles east of U.S. 101.*

Lyons Ranch Trail

TRAIL | You won't see redwoods on this open upper-elevation 3.7-mile round-trip trail, but on summer days when the coast is socked in with rain or fog, an adventure to this typically sunny prairie at the park's southeastern boundary is highly rewarding, as is the steep—but slow—17-mile drive on Bald Hills Road. The trail leads hikers to a former sheep and cattle ranch with a few interesting old outbuildings that date to the turn-of-the-20th-century. *Moderate.* ✉ *Redwood National Park* ✣ *Trailhead: Off Bald Hills Rd., 17 miles south of U.S. 101.*

Tall Trees Trail

TRAIL | Although every bit as beautiful as the other stands of old-growth redwood in the park, getting to this roughly 30-acre grove requires a steep and windy 14-mile drive, followed by a somewhat rigorous 4-mile round-trip hike that involves an 800-foot descent into the Redwood Creek flood plain. Additionally, you must obtain a free permit at the Kuchel Visitor Center to access the unpaved road off of Bald Hills Road. Rangers dispense a limited number per day, first come, first served. No trailers or RVs. Given the effort required, if you don't have a lot of time, it's best to save this one for your second or third visit. *Moderate.* ✉ *Orick* ✣ *Trailhead: Tall Trees Access Rd., off Bald Hills Rd., 7 miles from U.S. 101, then 6½ miles to trailhead.*

VISITOR CENTER

★ Thomas H. Kuchel Visitor Center

INFO CENTER | **FAMILY** | The park's southern section contains this largest and best of the Redwoods visitor centers. Rangers here dispense brochures, advice, and free permits to drive up the access road to Tall Trees Grove. Whale-watchers find the center's deck an excellent observation point, and bird-watchers enjoy the nearby Freshwater Lagoon, a popular layover for migrating waterfowl. Many of the center's exhibits are hands-on and kid-friendly. ✉ *U.S. 101, Orick* ✣ *Redwood Creek Beach County Park* ☎ *707/465–7765* 🌐 *www.nps.gov/redw.*

Middle

8 miles north of Thomas H. Kuchel Visitor Center, 34 miles south of Crescent City.

Encompassing a relatively narrow band of coastal forest that extends north of Orick (starting around Elk Meadow) to north of Klamath (up to Requa Road), the park's middle section is home to one of the most magical places to stroll through a redwood forest, Prairie Creek State Park, which is laced with both easy and challenging trails and traversed by the stunning Newton B. Drury Scenic Parkway. Near the visitor center and in nearby Elk Meadow, you can often view herds of Roosevelt elk. The state park extends west to famously spectacular Gold Bluffs Beach and Fern Canyon on the coast. The middle section's other highlight are the sections of the park along both sides of the Klamath River, including Coastal Drive and Klamath River Overlook.

Sights

SCENIC DRIVES

★ Coastal Drive Loop

SCENIC DRIVE | The 9-mile, narrow, and partially unpaved Coastal Drive Loop takes about 45 minutes to traverse. Weaving through stands of redwoods, the road yields close-up views of the Klamath River and expansive panoramas of the Pacific. Recurring landslides have closed sections of the original road; this loop, closed to trailers and RVs, is all that remains. Hikers access the Flint Ridge section of the Coastal Trail off the drive. ✉ *Klamath* ✣ *Off Klamath Beach Rd. exit from U.S. 101.*

★ Newton B. Drury Scenic Parkway

SCENIC DRIVE | This paved 10-mile route threads through Prairie Creek Redwoods State Park and old-growth redwoods. It's open to all noncommercial vehicles. Great stops along the route include the 0.8-mile walk to Big Tree Wayside and observing Roosevelt elk in the prairie—both of these are near the Prairie Creek Visitor Center. ✉ *Orick* ✣ *Entrances off U.S. 101 about 5 miles south of Klamath and 5 miles north of Orick.*

SCENIC STOPS

★ Fern Canyon

CANYON | Enter another world and be surrounded by 50-foot canyon walls covered with sword, deer, and five-finger ferns. Allow an hour to explore the ¼-mile-long vertical garden along a 0.7-mile loop. From the northern end of Gold Bluffs Beach it's an easy walk, although you'll have to wade across or scamper along planks that traverse a small stream several times (in addition to driving across

Fern Canyon lives up to its name.

a couple of streams on the way to the parking area). But the lush, otherworldly surroundings, which appeared in *Jurassic Park 2,* are a must-see when creeks aren't running too high. Motor homes/RVs and all trailers are prohibited. You can also hike to the canyon from Prairie Creek Visitor Center along the challenging West Ridge–Friendship Ridge–James Irvine Loop, 12½ miles round-trip. ✉ *Orick* ✣ *2¾ miles north of Orick, take Davison Rd. northwest off U.S. 101 and follow signs to Gold Bluffs Beach.*

Klamath River Overlook

VIEWPOINT | This grassy, windswept bluff rises 650 feet above the confluence of the Klamath River and the Pacific. It's one of the best spots in the park for spying migratory whales in early winter and late spring, and it accesses a section of the Coastal Trail. Warm days are ideal for picnicking at one of the tables. ✉ *End of Requa Rd., Klamath* ✣ *2¼ miles west of U.S. 101.*

TRAILS

★ Coastal Trail

TRAIL | This gorgeous 70-mile trail, much of it along dramatic bluffs high above the crashing surf, can be tackled in both short, relatively easy sections and longer, strenuous spans that entail backcountry overnight camping. Here are some of the most alluring smaller sections, listed in order from north to south, which are accessible at well-marked trailheads. The moderate-to-difficult **DeMartin section** (accessed from mile marker 15.6 on U.S. 101) leads south past 6 miles of old-growth redwoods and through sweeping prairie. It connects with the moderate 5½-mile-long **Klamath section,** which proceeds south from Wilson Creek Picnic Area to Klamath River Overlook, with a short detour to Hidden Beach and its tide pools, providing coastal views and whale-watching opportunities. If you're up for a real workout, hike the brutally difficult but stunning **Flint Ridge section** (accessed from the Old Douglas Memorial Bridge Site on Klamath Beach Rd.), with its 4½ miles of steep grades and numerous switchbacks past Marshall Pond and through stands of old-growth redwoods. There are additional spans at the northern and southern ends of the park. *Moderate.* ✉ *Klamath.*

★ Prairie Creek–Big Tree–Cathedral Trees Loop

TRAIL | **FAMILY** | This flat, well-maintained 3½-mile loop starts and ends at the Prairie Creek Visitor Center and passes beneath some of the most awe-inspiring redwoods in the park. The 1-mile section along the Prairie Creek Trail fringes a babbling brook; you then cross Newton B. Drury Scenic Parkway, turn south onto the Cathedral Trees Trail and make a short detour along the 0.3-mile Big Tree Loop before meandering south and west through yet more gorgeous old-growth forest. Options for extending your hike include walking 1½ miles up Cal-Barrel Road (an old, unpaved logging route), and then looping back 2 miles on the Rhododendron Trail to rejoin Cathedral Trees. *Easy–Moderate.* ✉ *Orick* ✣ *Trailhead: Prairie Creek Visitor Center.*

Trillium Falls Trail

TRAIL | **FAMILY** | On this lush trek through a mix of old-growth redwoods, ferns, smaller deciduous trees, and some clusters of trillium flowers, you'll encounter the pretty cascades that give the hike its name after the first ½ mile. It's worth continuing on, though, and making the full 2.8-mile loop, as the southern end of the hike offers the best views of soaring redwoods. Herds of elk sometimes roam in the meadow by the trailhead. *Easy–Moderate.* ✉ *Orick* ✣ *Trailhead: Elk Meadow parking lot, Davison Rd., just west of U.S. 101.*

VISITOR CENTER

★ Prairie Creek Visitor Center

INFO CENTER | **FAMILY** | A massive stone fireplace anchors this small redwood lodge with wildlife displays that include a section of a tree a young elk died beside. Because of the peculiar way the redwood grew around the elk's skull, the tree appears to have antlers. The center has information about interpretive programs as well as a gift shop, a picnic area, restrooms, and exhibits on flora and fauna. Roosevelt elk often roam the vast field adjacent to the center, and several trailheads begin nearby. Stretch your legs with an easy stroll along **Revelation Trail,** a short loop that starts behind the lodge. ✉ *Prairie Creek Rd., Orick* ✣ *Off southern end of Newton B. Drury Scenic Pkwy.* ☎ *707/488–2039* 🌐 *www.nps.gov/redw.*

Hotels

★ Elk Meadow Cabins

$$$$ | **B&B/INN** | **FAMILY** | From the porches of these beautifully restored 1,200-square-foot former mill workers' cottages, guests often see Roosevelt elk meandering in the meadows—or even their backyards. **Pros:** elks frequently congregate on the grounds; perfect for groups or families; adjacent to stunning Prairie Creek State Park. **Cons:** a bit of a drive from most area restaurants; expensive for just two occupants, though reasonable for families or groups; furnishings are comfortable but plain. $ *Rooms from: $314* ✉ *7 Valley Green Camp Rd., off U.S. 101 north of Davison Rd., Orick* ☎ *707/488–2222, 866/733–9637* 🌐 *www.elkmeadowcabins.com* *9 cabins* *No meals.*

North

34 miles north of Prairie Creek Redwoods State Park, 84 miles north of Eureka, 73 miles south of Grants Pass, OR, 133 miles south of Coos Bay, OR.

Home to the small city of Crescent City, which is also where you'll find the Redwood National and State Parks headquarters, the North is home to two state parks: Del Norte Redwoods and Jedediah Smith Redwoods. Del Norte lies 5 miles south of Crescent City on U.S. 101 and contains 15 memorial redwood groves and 8 miles of pristine coastline, which you can most easily access at Crescent Beach and Wilson Beach. Jedediah Smith is 5 miles east of Crescent City on U.S. 199 and is home to the legendary Stout Memorial Grove, along with some 20 miles of hiking and nature trails. The park is named after a trapper who in 1826 became the first white man to explore Northern California's interior. If coming from interior Oregon, this is your first chance to drive and hike among stands of soaring redwoods.

Sights

SCENIC DRIVES

★ Howland Hill Road through Stout Grove

SCENIC DRIVE | Take your time as you drive this 10-mile route along Mill Creek, which meanders within inches of the hulking trunks of old-growth redwoods and past the Smith River. Trailers and RVs are prohibited on this route, which is unpaved but well maintained for the roughly 7 miles that pass through Jedediah Smith Redwoods State Park. There are several pull-outs along the route, including the trailheads for the Stout Grove and Boy Scout Tree trails. You can enter either from downtown Crescent Road or off U.S. 199, via South Fork and Douglas Park Roads. ✣ *Western access from Elk Valley Rd. in Crescent City.*

SCENIC STOPS

Crescent Beach Overlook

VIEWPOINT | The scenery here includes views of the ocean and, in the distance, Crescent City and its working harbor. In balmy weather this is a great place for a picnic. You may spot migrating gray whales between November and April. ✉ *Enderts Beach Rd.* ✣ *4½ miles south of Crescent City.*

TRAILS

★ Boy Scout Tree Trail

TRAIL | This is the most challenging but also the most rewarding of the hikes along Howland Hill Road. Give yourself about three hours to complete this 5.6-mile round-trip trek to verdant Fern Falls, as the old-growth redwoods along this tranquil trek are absolutely magnificent. If you don't have as much time, the easy ½-mile-loop Stout Grove Trail is a good alternative along this route. *Moderate.* ✉ *Crescent City* ✣ *Trailhead: Howland Hill Rd., 3.7 miles east of Elk Valley Rd.*

Simpson-Reed Trail

TRAIL | **FAMILY** | Of the redwood hikes in Jedediah Smith Redwoods State Park, this flat and easy 1-mile loop through an incredibly dense forest is the best fit if you have only an hour or so. The trailhead is a short hop off U.S. 199 between Crescent City and Hiouchi, and interpretative signs tell a bit about the diverse flora—you'll encounter hemlocks, huckleberries, and lots and lots of ferns along this route. *Easy.* ✉ *Crescent City* ✣ *Trailhead: Walker Rd., off U.S. 199, 2.5 miles east of U.S. 101.*

Yurok Loop Trail

BEACH—SIGHT | **FAMILY** | Providing a lovely opportunity to stretch your legs and breathe in the fresh sea air, this 1.2-mile loop starts at the Lagoon Creek Picnic Area on U.S. 101, at the very southern end of Del Norte Coast Redwoods State Park, and follows a short stretch of the California Coastal Trail. It then forks off toward False Klamath Cove, providing sweeping views of the ocean—keep an eye out for shore birds and migrating whales. Just to the north of False Klamath Cove, there's great beachcombing to be had along Wilson Creek Beach. *Easy.* ✉ *Klamath* ✣ *Trailhead: Lagoon Creek Picnic Area on U.S. 101, 6.5 miles north of Klamath.*

VISITOR CENTERS

Crescent City Information Center

INFO CENTER | At the park's headquarters, this downtown Redding visitor center with a gift shop and picnic area is the main information stop if you're approaching the Redwoods from the north. ✉ *1111 2nd St., Crescent City* ☎ *707/465–7335* 🌐 *www.nps.gov/redw* ⏲ *Closed Tues. and Wed. in Nov.–Mar.*

Hiouchi Information Center

INFO CENTER | This small center at Jedediah Smith Redwoods State Park has exhibits about the area flora and fauna and screens a 12-minute park film. A starting point for ranger programs, the center has restrooms and a picnic area. ✉ *U.S. 199* ✣ *Opposite Jedediah Smith Campground, 9 miles east of Crescent City* ☎ *707/458–3294* 🌐 *www.nps.gov/redw.*

Jedediah Smith Visitor Center

INFO CENTER | Adjacent to the Jedediah Smith Redwoods State Park main campground, this seasonal center has information about ranger-led walks and evening campfire programs. Also here are nature and history exhibits, a gift shop, and a picnic area. ✉ *U.S. 199, Hiouchi* ✣ *At Jedediah Smith Campground* ☎ *707/458–3496* 🌐 *www.nps.gov/redw* ⏲ *Closed Oct.–May.*

Activities

BIKING

Besides the roadways, you can bike on several trails, many of them along former logging roads. Best bets include the 11-mile Lost Man Creek Trail, which begins 3 miles north of Orick; the 12-mile round-trip Coastal Trail (Last Chance Section), which starts at the southern end of Enderts Beach Road and becomes steep and narrow as it travels through dense slopes of foggy redwood forests; and the 19-mile, single-track Ossagon Trail Loop in Prairie Creek Redwoods State Park, on which you're likely to see elk as you cruise through redwoods before coasting ocean side toward the end. ■ **TIP→ You can rent electric bikes, which are especially nice for riding the hilly Lost Man Creek Trail, from Redwood Adventures** **(see Hiking).**

BIRD-WATCHING

Many rare and striking winged specimens inhabit the area, including chestnut-backed chickadees, brown pelicans, great blue herons, pileated woodpeckers, northern spotted owls, and marbled murrelets. By 2022, California condors are planned to be reintroduced to the park.

CAMPING

Within a 30-minute drive of Redwood National and State parks, you'll find roughly 60 public and private camping facilities. None of the primitive or backcountry areas in Redwood—DeMartin, Elam Creek, Flint Ridge, 44 Camp, Little Bald Hills, or Redwood Creek—is a drive-in site, although Flint Ridge is just a ¼-mile from the road. You must obtain a free permit from the Kuchel or Hiouchi visitor centers before camping in these areas; all are first come, first served. Bring your own drinking water—there are no sources at the sites.

Redwood has four developed, drive-in campgrounds—Elk Prairie, Gold Bluffs Beach, Jedediah Smith, and Mill Creek, all of them within the state-park boundaries. None has RV hookups, but Jedediah Smith and Mill Creek have dump stations. Fees are $35 nightly. For reservations, contact ☎ *800/444–7275* or 🌐 *www.reserveamerica.com.*

DEVELOPED CAMPGROUNDS

Elk Prairie Campground. Roosevelt elk frequent this popular campground adjacent to a prairie and old-growth redwoods. ✉ *Newton B. Drury Scenic Pkwy., Prairie Creek Redwoods State Park.*

Gold Bluffs Beach Campground. You can camp in tents right on the beach at this Prairie Creek Redwoods State Park campground near Fern Canyon. ✉ *End of Davison Rd., off U.S. 101.*

Jedediah Smith Campground. This is one of the few places to camp—in tents or RVs—within groves of old-growth redwood forest. ✉ *9 miles east of Crescent City on U.S. 199.*

Mill Creek Campground. Redwoods tower over large Mill Creek, in the remote and quiet interior of Del Norte Coast Redwoods State Park. Open mid-May–September. ✉ *U.S. 101, 7 miles southeast of Crescent City.*

EDUCATIONAL PROGRAMS

RANGER PROGRAMS

All summer long, ranger-led programs explore the mysteries of both the redwoods and the sea. Topics include how the trees grow from fleck-size seeds to towering giants, what causes those weird fungi on old stumps, why the ocean fog is so important to redwoods, and exactly what those green-tentacled creatures are that float in tide pools. Campfire programs can include slide shows, storytelling, music, and games. Check with visitor centers for offerings and times.

Junior Ranger Program

LOCAL SPORTS | FAMILY | Kids earn a badge by completing activity books, which are available from visitor centers. Additionally, rangers lead programs for kids throughout the summer, including nature walks and lessons in bird identification and outdoor survival.

Ranger Talks

LOCAL SPORTS | From mid-May through mid-September, state park rangers regularly lead discussions on the redwoods, tide pools, geology, and Native American culture. Check schedules at the visitor centers.

Redwood EdVentures

TOUR—SIGHT | FAMILY | Fun and engaging Redwood EdVentures nature scavenger hunts for kids, called Quests, include ones in the park. Visit the website for "treasure map" PDFs detailing the Quests, which typically take no more than an hour. Participants receive a patch upon completion. 🌐 *www.redwood-edventures.org.*

FISHING

Deep-sea and freshwater fishing are popular here. Anglers often stake out sections of the Klamath and Smith rivers seeking salmon and trout. A single state license (🌐 *www.wildlife.ca.gov/licensing/fishing*) covers both ocean and river fishing. A two-day license costs about $27. You can go crabbing and clamming on the coast, but check the tides carefully: rip currents and sneaker waves can be deadly. No license is needed to fish from the long B Street Pier in Crescent City.

HIKING

The park has miles of trails, including quite a few short, level treks just off the main roads and easily managed even if you have limited experience. Avid hikers will find plenty of fantastic rambles with serious elevation gains and thrilling flora and fauna. Note that some of the park's most delightful treks don't actually pass any big trees but rather hug Northern California's pristine and wild shoreline. Most famous is the Coastal Trail, which runs for about 70 miles from the northern to southern ends of the park.

★ Redwood Adventures

HIKING/WALKING | Operated by and run out of the office of Elk Meadow Cabins, this small agency with a highly knowledgeable, passionate staff offers half- and full-day hikes through some of the park's most stunning stands of redwoods, as well as adventures exploring coastal tidepools and Fern Canyon. Backpacking with overnight camping options are also available, as are electric-bike rentals, which are great for touring around the park, especially the Lost Man Creek Trail. ✉ *7 Valley Green Camp Rd., Orick* ☎ *866/733–9637* 🌐 *www.redwoodadventures.com.*

KAYAKING

With many miles of often shallow rivers, streams, and estuarial lagoons, kayaking is a popular pastime in the park, especially in the southern end of the park near Kuchel Visitor Center, on Arcata and Humboldt bays near Eureka, up north along the Klamath and Smith rivers, and on the ocean in Crescent City.

Humboats Kayak Adventures

KAYAKING | You can rent kayaks and book kayaking tours that from December to June include whale-watching trips. Half-day river kayaking trips pass beneath massive redwoods; the whale-watching outings get you close enough for good photos. ✉ *Woodley Island Marina, 601 Startare Dr., Dock A, Eureka* ☎ *707/443–5157* 🌐 *www.humboats.com* 💳 *From $30 rentals, $55 tours.*

★ **Kayak Trinidad**

KAYAKING | This respected outfitter rents kayaks and stand-up paddleboards, good for touring the beautiful estuarial and freshwater lagoons of Humboldt Lagoons State Park or sea kayaking out at sea. You can also book guided half-day paddles around Big Lagoon and Stone Lagoon, and along Trinidad Bay. The lagoons are stunning. Herds of Roosevelt elk sometimes traipse along the shoreline of Big Lagoon; raptors, herons, and waterfowl abound in both lagoons; and you can paddle across Stone Lagoon to a spectacular secluded Pacific-view beach. ✉ *Trinidad* ☎ *707/329–0085* 🌐 *www.kayaktrinidad.com.*

WHALE-WATCHING

Good vantage points for whale-watching include Crescent Beach Overlook, the Kuchel Visitor Center in Orick, points along the Coastal Trail, Klamath Beach Road, and Klamath River Overlook. From late November through January is the best time to see their southward migrations; from February through April the whales return, usually passing closer to shore.

Nearby Towns

The North Coast's largest city is **Eureka,** population 27,000 and the Humboldt County seat. Its Old Town has an alluring waterfront boardwalk, several excellent restaurants and shops, and the region's largest selection of lodgings. It borders and forms a small metro area with the progressive college town of **Arcata,** just to the north, which has a handsome little downtown and a bevy of hip cafés and bars. Both Eureka and Arcata make good practical bases for touring the South and Middle portions of Redwood National and State Park, especially if you want to stay someplace with plenty of other diversions. A quieter and absolutely stunning little gem of a town that's 15 miles closer to the park than Arcata, **Trinidad** has a cove harbor that attracts fishermen and photographers and a few notable dining and lodging options.

Once you enter the park, as you continue north up U.S. 101 you'll come first to tiny Orick, which has but 300 residents and just a few businesses, and then to slightly larger **Klamath,** where you'll discover a handful of worthwhile places to stay and eat as well as a modern casino resort operated by the local Yurok tribe.

Crescent City, close to its Del Norte Redwoods and Jedediah Smith Redwoods state parks, is the largest town (population about 6,800) up north and home to the Redwood National and State parks headquarters as well as a good supply of restaurant and lodging options. Though it curves around a beautiful stretch of ocean, rain and bone-chilling fog often prevail.

Chapter 52

ROCKY MOUNTAIN NATIONAL PARK

52

Updated by
Lindsey Galloway

Camping ★★★☆☆ | Hotels ★★☆☆☆ | Activities ★★★★☆ | Scenery ★★★★★ | Crowds ★★★★★

WELCOME TO ROCKY MOUNTAIN NATIONAL PARK

TOP REASONS TO GO

★ **Awesome ascents:** Seasoned climbers can trek to the summit of 14,259-foot Longs Peak or attack the rounded granite domes of Lumpy Ridge. Novices can summit Twin Sisters Peaks or Mount Ida, both reaching more than 11,000 feet.

★ **Continental Divide:** Straddle this great divide, which cuts through the western part of the park, separating water's flow to either the Pacific or Atlantic Ocean.

★ **Gorgeous scenery:** Peer out over more than 100 lakes, gaze up at majestic mountain peaks, and soak in the splendor of lush wetlands, pine-scented woods, forests of spruce and fir, and alpine tundra in the park's four distinct ecosystems.

★ **More than 355 miles of trails:** Hike on dozens of marked trails, from easy lakeside strolls to strenuous mountain climbs.

★ **Wildlife viewing:** Spot elk and bighorn sheep, along with moose, otters, and more than 280 species of birds.

1 **Moraine Park.** This area offers easy access to several trailheads, the park's largest campground, and the Beaver Meadows Visitor Center near the east side entrance.

2 **Bear Lake.** One of the park's most photographed places is the hub for many trailheads and a stop on the park's shuttle service.

3 **Longs Peak.** The park's highest (and toughest to climb) peak, this Fourteener pops up in many park vistas. A round-trip summit trek takes 10 to 15 hours; most visitors opt for a (still spectacular) partial journey.

4 **Trail Ridge Road.** Alpine tundra is the highlight here, as the road—the nation's highest continuous highway—climbs to over 12,000 feet (almost 700 feet above timberline).

5 **Timber Creek.** The park's far western area is much less crowded than other sections, though it has evening programs, 98 camping sites, and a visitor center.

6 **Wild Basin Area.** Far from the crowds, this southeastern quadrant has lovely subalpine forest punctuated by streams and lakes.

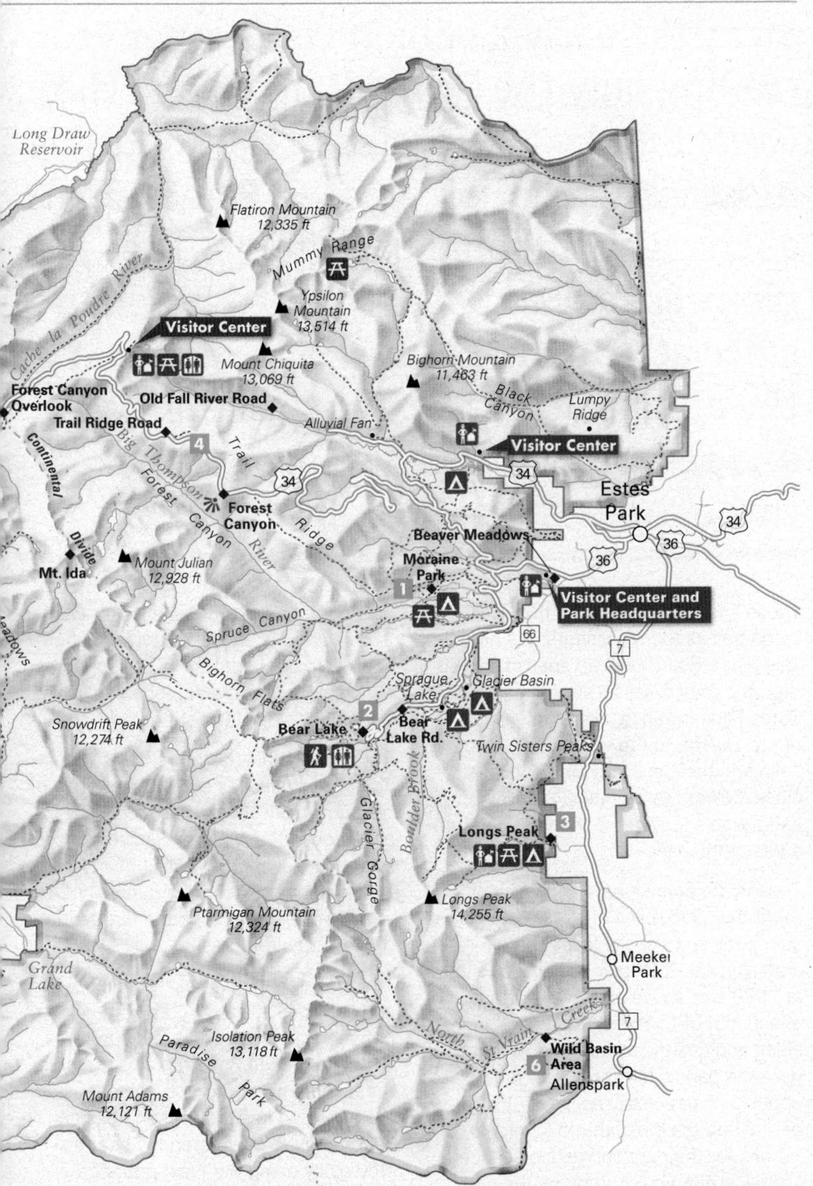

Long Draw Reservoir
Flatiron Mountain 12,335 ft
Mummy Range
Cache la Poudre River
Ypsilon Mountain 13,514 ft
Visitor Center
Mount Chiquita 13,069 ft
Bighorn Mountain 11,463 ft
Forest Canyon Overlook
Old Fall River Road
Black Canyon
Lumpy Ridge
Trail Ridge Road
Alluvial Fan
Visitor Center
Continental Divide
Big Thompson
Trail Ridge
34
Forest Canyon
Estes Park
Forest Canyon River
Beaver Meadows
34
36
Mt. Ida
Mount Julian 12,928 ft
Moraine Park
36
Visitor Center and Park Headquarters
Spruce Canyon
66
7
Bighorn Flats
Sprague Lake
Glacier Basin
Snowdrift Peak 12,274 ft
Bear Lake
Bear Lake Rd.
Twin Sisters Peaks
Glacier Gorge
Boulder Brook
Longs Peak
Ptarmigan Mountain 12,324 ft
Longs Peak 14,255 ft
Grand Lake
Meeker Park
North St. Vrain Creek
7
Isolation Peak 13,118 ft
Paradise Park
Wild Basin Area
Allenspark
Mount Adams 12,121 ft

With its towering mountains, active and abundant wildlife, and crystal clear lakes and rivers, Rocky Mountain attracts nearly 5 million visitors per year, trailing only the Grand Canyon and the Great Smoky Mountains in the country's most visited national parks. Established as the 10th national park in 1915, the picturesque land has attracted humans since at least 11,000 years ago, based on the archaeological artifacts like shelters and speartips that have been found throughout the park.

These ancient people used the very same trail as today's visitors: the 48-mile Trail Ridge Road. With an apex of 12,183 feet, the road travels from the east side Estes Park entrance, across the Continental Divide, to the west side Grand Lake entrance, giving even nonhikers a close look at the montane, subalpine, and alpine ecosystems found at different areas of the park.

Those who do hike have their pick of more than 355 miles of trails, with paths suited for every ability level. The park's high altitude—the lowest elevation starts at 7,000 feet above sea level—often affects out-of-towners, but a good night's sleep and healthy hydration go a long way. The park is famous for its robust elk population, especially active in "Elk-to-ber" when the elk come to lower elevations for their annual mating season. Moose are more common on the west side near the Kawuneeche Visitor Center and near rivers and lakes, while bighorn sheep are best spotted in late spring and early summer at the appropriately named Sheeps Lake in Horseshoe Park.

Rocky Mountain has more than 1,000 archaeological sites and 150 buildings of historic significance; 47 of the buildings are listed in the National Register of Historic Places. Most buildings at Rocky Mountain are done in the rustic style, which strives to incorporate nature into man-made structures.

Though the park has year-round access and activities, most visitors come between late spring and mid-autumn when Trail Ridge Road remains open. In the high summer months, the east side entrance and lower elevation trails can become quite congested, so beat the crowds by using the west entrance or

AVERAGE HIGH/LOW TEMPERATURES					
JAN.	**FEB.**	**MAR.**	**APR.**	**MAY**	**JUNE**
39/16	41/17	45/21	53/27	62/34	73/41
JULY	**AUG.**	**SEPT.**	**OCT.**	**NOV.**	**DEC.**
78/46	76/45	70/38	60/30	46/23	40/18

arriving before 8 am. *In 2020, a pair of devastating fires swept across approximately 30,000 acres, around 9% of the park, primarily in the west and far north part of the park, so check the latest conditions and closures on the park's website before setting off.*

Planning

When to Go

More than 80% of the park's annual 4.7 million visitors come in summer and fall. For thinner high-season crowds, come in early June or September. But there is a good reason to put up with summer crowds: only from late May to mid-October will you get the chance to make the unforgettable drive over Trail Ridge Road (note that the road may still be closed during those months if the weather turns bad).

Spring is capricious—75°F one day and a blizzard the next (March sees the most snow). June can range from hot and sunny to cool and rainy. July typically ushers in high summer, which can last through September. Up on Trail Ridge Road, it can be 15°F–20°F cooler than at the park's lower elevations. Wildlife viewing and fishing is best in any season but winter. In early fall, the trees blaze with brilliant foliage. Winter, when backcountry snow can be 4 feet deep, is the time for cross-country skiing, snowshoeing, and ice fishing.

FESTIVALS AND EVENTS

Elk Fest. In early autumn, the calls of bulls fill the forest as elk head down from the mountains for mating season. Estes Park celebrates with elk bugle contests, live music, and elk educational seminars. 🌐 *www.visitestespark.com/events-calendar/special-events/elk-fest.*

Longs Peak Scottish-Irish Highland Festival. A traditional tattoo (drum- and bugle-filled parade) kicks off this fair of ancient Scottish athletic competitions. There's also Celtic music, Irish dancing, and events for dogs of the British Isles (such as terrier racing and sheepdog demonstrations). 🌐 *www.scotfest.com.*

Rooftop Rodeo. Consistently ranked one of the top small rodeos in the country (and a tradition since 1908), this six-day event features a parade and nightly rodeo events, such as barrel racing and saddle bronc riding. 🌐 *www.rooftoprodeo.com.*

Getting Here and Around

AIR

The closest commercial airport is **Denver International Airport** (DEN). Its **Ground Transportation Information Center** (☎ *800/247–2336 or 303/342–4059* 🌐 *www.flydenver.com*) assists visitors with car rentals, door-to-door shuttles, and limousine services. From the airport, the eastern entrance of the park is 80 miles (about two hours). **Estes Park Shuttle** (☎ *970/586–5151* 🌐 *www.estesparkshuttle.com*; reservations essential) serves Estes Park and Rocky Mountain from both Denver International Airport and Longmont/Boulder.

BUS

Rocky Mountain has limited parking, but offers three free shuttle buses, which operate daily from 7 am to 8 pm, late May to early October. All three shuttles can be accessed from a large Park & Ride located within the park, 7 miles from the Beaver Meadows entrance. Visitors who don't want to drive into the park at all can hop on the Hiker Shuttle at the Estes Park Visitor Center. The shuttle, which runs every half hour during peak times, makes stops at the Beaver Meadows Visitor Center and the Park & Ride, where visitors can switch to one of the other two shuttles, which head to various trailheads. The Moraine Park Route shuttle runs every 30 minutes and stops at the Moraine Park Visitor Center and then continues on to the Fern Lake Trailhead. The Bear Lake Route shuttle runs every 10 to 15 minutes from the Park & Ride to the Bear Lake Trailhead.

CAR

Estes Park and Grand Lake are the Rocky Mountains' gateway communities; from these you can enter the park via U.S. 34 or 36 (Estes Park) or U.S. 34 (Grand Lake). U.S. 36 runs from Denver through Boulder, Lyons, and Estes Park to the park; the portion between Boulder and Estes Park is heavily traveled—especially on summer weekends. Though less direct, Colorado Routes 119, 72, and 7 have much less traffic (and better scenery). If you're driving directly to Rocky Mountain from the airport, take the E–470 tollway from Peña Boulevard to Interstate 25.

The **Colorado Department of Transportation** (for road conditions ☎ *303/639–1111* 🌐 *www.cotrip.org*) plows roads efficiently, but winter snowstorms can slow traffic and create wet or icy conditions. In summer, the roads into both Grand Lake and Estes Park can see heavy traffic, especially on weekends.

WITHIN THE PARK

The main thoroughfare in the park is Trail Ridge Road (U.S. 34); in winter, it's closed from the first storm in the fall (typically in October) through the spring (depending on snowpack, this could be at any time between May and June). During that time, it's plowed only up to Many Parks Curve on the east side and the Colorado River trailhead on the west side. (For current road information: ☎ *970/586–1222* 🌐 *www.codot.gov.*)

The spectacular Old Fall River Road runs one way between the Endovalley Picnic Area on the eastern edge of the park and the Alpine Visitor Center at the summit of Trail Ridge Road, on the western side. It is typically open from July to September, depending on snowfall. It's a steep, narrow road (no wider than 14 feet), and trailers and vehicles longer than 25 feet are prohibited, but a trip on this 100-year-old thoroughfare is well worth the effort. For information on road closures, contact the park: ☎ *970/586–1206* 🌐 *www.nps.gov/romo*.

Inspiration

A Lady's Life in the Rocky Mountains, by Isabella L. Bird, has long been a favorite with Colorado residents and visitors to the park.

Hiking Rocky Mountain National Park: The Essential Guide, by Erik Stensland, matches your hiking ability and time allotted to find the perfect trail.

The Magnificent Mountain Women, by Janet Robertson, gives historical accounts of early pioneers.

Park Essentials

ACCESSIBILITY

All visitor centers are accessible to wheelchair users. The Sprague Lake, Coyote Valley, Lily Lake, and Bear Lake trails are all accessible loops of hard-packed gravel, ½ to 1 mile long. The Bear Lake trail is not entirely flat and is considered the most challenging of the accessible trails. A backcountry campsite at Sprague Lake accommodates up to 12 campers, including six in wheelchairs. The Moraine Park and Timber Creek campgrounds also offer some accessible sites and restroom facilities. All in-park shuttles and bus stops are wheelchair-accessible.

PARK FEES AND PERMITS

Entrance fees are $25 per automobile for a one-day pass or $35 for a seven-day pass. Those who enter via foot or bicycle can get a seven-day pass for $20. Motorcyclists can get a seven-day pass for $30. An annual pass to Rocky Mountain costs $70, while the National Parks' America The Beautiful pass costs $80 and grants admission to more than 2,000 sites across the United States.

Wilderness camping requires a permit that's $30 per party from May through October, and free the rest of the year. Visit 🌐 *www.nps.gov/romo/planyourvisit/wilderness-camping.htm* before you go for a planning guide to backcountry camping. You can get your permit online, by phone (☎ *970/586–1242*), or in person. In person, you can get a day-of-trip permit year-round at one of the park's two backcountry offices, located next to the Beaver Meadows Visitor Center and in the Kawuneeche Visitor Center.

PARK HOURS

The park is open 24/7 year-round; some roads close in winter. It is in the Mountain time zone.

CELL PHONE RECEPTION

Cell phones work in some sections of the park, and free Wi-Fi can be accessed in and around the Beaver Meadows Visitor Center, Fall River, and the Kawuneeche Visitor Center.

Hotels

Bed-and-breakfasts and small inns in north central Colorado vary from old-fashioned fluffy cottages to sleek, modern buildings with understated lodge themes. If you want some pampering, guest ranches and spas will fit the bill.

In Estes Park, Grand Lake, and other nearby towns, the elevation keeps the climate cool, and you'll scarcely need (and you'll have a tough time finding) air-conditioned lodging. For a historic spot, try the Stanley Hotel in Estes Park, which dates to 1909. The park itself has no hotels or lodges.

Restaurants

Restaurants in north central Colorado run the gamut from simple diners with tasty, homey basics to elegant establishments with extensive wine lists. Some restaurants take reservations, but many—particularly midrange spots—seat on a first-come, first-served basis. In the park itself, the Trail Ridge Store next to the Alpine Visitor Center has a café and coffee bar open from late May to October. The park also has a handful of scenic picnic areas, all with tables and pit or flush toilets.

Tours

Green Jeep Tours

ADVENTURE TOURS | FAMILY | From the back of an open-air, neon-green Jeep on these tours, you can enjoy the majestic scenery while your experienced guide points out wildlife along the way. Green Jeep Tours also offers a three-hour tour in September and October that focuses on finding elk. Admission includes the cost of the one-day pass into the park. ✉ *157 Moraine Ave., Estes Park* ☎ *970/577–0034* 🎟 *From $90.*

Wildside 4x4 Tours

DRIVING TOURS | This company's most popular tour, the "Top of the World," takes visitors in an open-top vehicle all the way to Old Fall River Road and back down Trail Ridge. A waterfall tour and sunset valley tour offer great wildlife spottings at lower elevations. ✉ *212 E. Elkhorn Ave., Estes Park* ☎ *970/586–8687* 🌐 *www.wildside4x4tours.com* 🎫 *From $80.*

★ **Yellow Wood Guiding**

ADVENTURE TOURS | Guided photo safaris, offered year-round, ensure visitors leave the Rocky Mountain National Park with more than just memories. Customized for either beginners or experts, the tours offer the use of professional digital cameras for visitors who don't have their own. ✉ *404 Driftwood Ave., Estes Park* ☎ *303/775–5484* 🌐 *www.ywguiding.com* 🎫 *From $175.*

Visitor Information

CONTACTS Rocky Mountain National Park. ✉ *1000 U.S. 36, Estes Park* ☎ *970/586–1206* 🌐 *www.nps.gov/romo.*

Moraine Park

3 miles from Estes Park.

The starting point for most first-timers, the easternmost part of the park is easy to access via car or park shuttle. A number of popular trailheads originate here, particularly suited for half-day hikes, and a large campground accommodates those who want to stay overnight. It's also where you'll find the Beaver Meadows Visitor Center.

Sights

TRAILS

Cub Lake Trail

TRAIL | This 4.6-mile, three-hour (round-trip) hike takes you through meadows and stands of aspen trees and up 540 feet in elevation to a lake with water lilies. *Moderate.* ✉ *Rocky Mountain National Park* ✥ *Trailhead: At Cub Lake, about 1¾ miles from Moraine Park Campground.*

Deer Mountain Trail

TRAIL | This 6-mile round-trip trek to the top of 10,083-foot Deer Mountain is a great way for hikers who don't mind a bit of a climb to enjoy the views from the summit of a more manageable peak. You'll gain more than 1,000 feet in elevation as you follow the switchbacking trail through ponderosa pine, aspen, and fir trees. The reward at the top is a panoramic view of the park's eastern mountains. *Difficult.* ✉ *Rocky Mountain National Park* ✥ *Trailhead: At Deer Ridge Junction, about 4 miles west of Moraine Park Visitor Center, U.S. 34 at U.S. 36.*

Fern Lake Trail

TRAIL | Heading to Odessa Lake from the north involves a steep hike, but on most days you'll encounter fewer other hikers than if you had begun the trip at Bear Lake. Along the way, you'll come to the Arch Rocks; the Pool, an eroded formation in the Big Thompson River; two waterfalls; and Fern Lake (3.8 miles from your starting point). Less than a mile farther, Odessa Lake itself lies at the foot of Tourmaline Gorge, below the craggy summits of Gabletop Mountain, Little Matterhorn, Knobtop Mountain, and Notchtop Mountain. For a full day of spectacular scenery, continue past Odessa to Bear Lake (9 miles total), where you can pick up the shuttle back to the Fern Lake Trailhead. *Moderate.* ✉ *Rocky Mountain National Park* ✥ *Trailhead: Off Fern Lake Rd., about 2½ miles south of Moraine Park Visitor Center.*

Sprague Lake

TRAIL | With virtually no elevation gain, this ½-mile, pine-lined looped path near a popular backcountry campground is wheelchair accessible and provides views of Hallet Peak and Flattop Mountain. *Easy.* ✉ *Rocky Mountain National*

Park ✣ Trailhead: At Sprague Lake, Bear Lake Rd., 4½ miles southwest of Moraine Park Visitor Center.*

VISITOR CENTERS

Alpine Visitor Center

INFO CENTER | At 11,796 feet above sea level, this is the highest visitor center in the National Park Service. Open only when Trail Ridge Road is navigable, the center also houses the park's only gift shop and snack bar. ✉ *Fall River Pass, at junction of Trail Ridge and Old Fall River Rds., 22 miles from Beaver Meadows entrance* ☎ *970/586–1206.*

Beaver Meadows Visitor Center

INFO CENTER | Housing the park headquarters, this visitor center was designed by students of the Frank Lloyd Wright School of Architecture at Taliesin West using the park's popular rustic style. The center has a terrific 20-minute orientation film and a large relief map of the park. ✉ *U.S. 36, 3 miles west of Estes Park and 1 mile east of Beaver Meadows Entrance Station* ☎ *970/586–1206.*

Restaurants

Café at Trail Ridge

$ | AMERICAN | The park's only source for food, this small café offers snacks, sandwiches, hot dogs, and soups. A coffee bar also serves fair-trade coffee, espresso drinks, and tea, plus water, juice, and salads. **Known for:** quick bite; fair-trade coffee; no-frills food. *Ⓢ Average main: $7* ✉ *Trail Ridge Rd., at Alpine Visitor Center* ☎ *970/586–3097* 🌐 *www.trailridgegiftstore.com* ⏲ *Closed mid-Oct.–late-May. No dinner.*

Trail Ridge Store

CLOTHING | This is the park's only official store (though you'll find a small selection of park souvenirs and books at the visitor centers). Trail Ridge stocks sweatshirts and jackets, postcards, and assorted craft items. ✉ *Trail Ridge Rd., adjacent to Alpine Visitor Center* 🌐 *www.trailridgegiftstore.com.*

Bear Lake

7 miles southwest of Moraine Park Visitor Center.

Thanks to its picturesque location, easy accessibility, and the good hiking trails nearby, this small lake below Flattop Mountain and Hallett Peak is one of the park's most popular destinations.

Sights

SCENIC DRIVES

Bear Lake Road

SCENIC DRIVE | This 23-mile round-trip drive offers superlative views of Longs Peak (14,259-foot summit) and the glaciers surrounding Bear Lake, winding past shimmering waterfalls shrouded with rainbows. You can either drive the road yourself (open year-round) or hop on one of the park's free shuttle buses. ✉ *Runs from the Beaver Meadow Entrance Station to Bear Lake.*

SCENIC STOPS

Farview Curve Overlook

VIEWPOINT | At an elevation of 10,120 feet, this lookout affords a panoramic view of the Colorado River near its origin and the Grand Ditch, a water diversion project dating from 1890 that's still in use today. You can also see the once-volcanic peaks of Never Summer Range along the park's western boundary. ✉ *Trail Ridge Rd., about 14 miles north of Kawuneeche Visitor Center.*

Forest Canyon Overlook

VIEWPOINT | Park at a dedicated lot to disembark on a wildflower-rich, 0.2-mile trail. Easy to access for all skill levels, this glacial valley overlook offers views of ice-blue pools (the Gorge Lakes) framed by ragged peaks. ✉ *Trail Ridge Rd., 6 miles east of Alpine Visitor Center.*

TRAILS

Bear Lake Trail

TRAIL | The virtually flat nature trail around Bear Lake is an easy, 0.6-mile loop that's wheelchair and stroller accessible. Sharing the route with you will likely be plenty of other hikers as well as songbirds and chipmunks. *Easy.* ✉ *Rocky Mountain National Park* ✥ *Trailhead: At Bear Lake, Bear Lake Rd.*

★ Bear Lake to Emerald Lake

TRAIL | This scenic, calorie-burning hike begins with a moderately level, ½-mile journey to **Nymph Lake.** From here, the trail gets steeper, with a 425-foot elevation gain, as it winds around for 0.6 miles to **Dream Lake.** The last stretch is the most arduous part of the hike, an almost all-uphill 0.7-mile trek to lovely **Emerald Lake,** where you can perch on a boulder and enjoy the view. All told, the hike is 3.6 miles, with an elevation gain of 605 feet. Allow two hours or more. *Moderate.* ✉ *Rocky Mountain National Park* ✥ *Trailhead: At Bear Lake, off Bear Lake Rd., 8 miles southwest of the Moraine Park Visitor Center.*

★ Glacier Gorge Trail

TRAIL | The 2.8-mile hike to **Mills Lake** can be crowded, but the reward is one of the park's prettiest lakes, set against the breathtaking backdrop of Longs Peak, Pagoda Mountain, and the Keyboard of the Winds. There's a modest elevation gain of 750 feet. On the way, about 1 mile in, you pass **Alberta Falls,** a popular destination in and of itself. The hike travels along Glacier Creek, under the shade of a subalpine forest. Give yourself at least four hours for hiking and lingering. *Easy.* ✉ *Rocky Mountain National Park* ✥ *Trailhead: Off Bear Lake Rd., about 1 mile southeast of Bear Lake.*

Mills Lake

TRAIL | From this popular spot, you can admire the Keyboard of the Winds, a jagged ridge connecting Pagoda and Longs Peaks that looks like the top of a spiny reptile's back. The 5.6-mile hike gains 750 feet in elevation as it takes you past Alberta Falls and Glacier Falls en route to the shimmering lake at the mouth of Glacier Gorge. *Moderate.* ✉ *Rocky Mountain National Park* ✥ *Trailhead: At Glacier Gorge Junction, about 1 mile from Bear Lake.*

Longs Peak

10.5 miles from Estes Park; trailhead at Longs Peak Ranger Station.

At 14,259 feet above sea level, Longs Peak has long fascinated explorers to the region. Longs Peak is the northernmost of the Fourteeners—the 53 mountains in Colorado that reach above the 14,000-foot mark—and one of more than 114 named mountains in the park that are higher than 10,000 feet. The peak, in the park's southeast quadrant, has a distinctive flat-topped, rectangular summit that is visible from many spots on the park's east side and on Trail Ridge Road.

Explorer and author Isabella L. Bird wrote of it: "It is one of the noblest of mountains, but in one's imagination it grows to be much more than a mountain. It becomes invested with a personality." It was named after Major Stephen H. Long, who led an expedition in 1820 up the Platte River to the base of the Rockies. Long never ascended the mountain—in fact, he didn't even get within 40 miles of it—but a few decades later, in 1868, the one-armed Civil War veteran John Wesley Powell climbed to its summit.

The ambitious climb to Longs summit is recommended only for those who are strong climbers and well acclimated to the altitude. If you're up for the 10- to 15-hour climb, begin before dawn so that you're down from the summit prior to typical afternoon thunderstorms.

Sights

TRAILS

Chasm Lake Trail

TRAIL | Nestled in the shadow of Longs Peak and Mount Meeker, Chasm Lake offers one of Colorado's most impressive backdrops, which also means you can expect to encounter plenty of other hikers on the way. The 4.2-mile Chasm Lake Trail, reached via the Longs Peak Trail, has a 2,360-foot elevation gain. Just before the lake, you'll need to climb a small rock ledge, which can be a bit of a challenge for the less sure-footed; follow the cairns for the most straightforward route. Once atop the ledge, you'll catch your first memorable view of the lake. *Difficult.* ✉ *Rocky Mountain National Park* ✣ *Trailhead: At Longs Peak Ranger Station, off Rte. 7, 10 miles from the Beaver Meadows Visitor Center.*

Longs Peak Trail

TRAIL | Climbing this 14,259-foot mountain (one of 53 "Fourteeners" in Colorado) is an ambitious goal for almost anyone—but only those who are very fit and acclimated to the altitude should attempt it. The 16-mile round-trip climb requires a predawn start (3 am is ideal), so that you're off the summit before the typical summer afternoon thunderstorm hits. Also, the last 2 miles or so of the trail are very exposed—you have to traverse narrow ledges with vertigo-inducing drop-offs. That said, summiting Longs can be one of the most rewarding experiences you'll ever have. The Keyhole route is the most popular means of ascent, and the number of people going up it on a summer day can be astounding, given the rigors of the climb. Though just as scenic, the Loft route, between Longs and Mount Meeker from Chasm Lake, is less crowded but not as clearly marked and therefore more difficult to navigate. *Difficult.* ✉ *Rocky Mountain National Park* ✣ *Trailhead: At Longs Peak Ranger Station, off Rte. 7, 10 miles from Beaver Meadows Visitor Center.*

Trail Ridge Road

Also known as U.S. 34 runs between Estes Park and Grand Lake.

The park's star attraction and the world's highest continuous paved highway (topping out at 12,183 feet), this 48-mile road connects the park's gateways of Estes Park and Grand Lake. The views around each bend—of moraines and glaciers, and craggy hills framing emerald meadows carpeted with columbine—are truly awesome. As it passes through three ecosystems—montane, subalpine, and arctic tundra—the road climbs 4,300 feet. You can complete a one-way trip across the park on Trail Ridge Road in two hours, but it's best to give yourself three or four hours to allow for leisurely breaks at the overlooks. Note that the middle part of the road closes with the first big snow (typically by mid-October) and most often reopens around Memorial Day, though you can still drive up about 10 miles from the west and 8 miles from the east.

Sights

HISTORIC SIGHTS

Lulu City

ARCHAEOLOGICAL SITE | The remains of a few cabins are all that's left of this onetime silver-mining town, established around 1880. Reach it by hiking the 3.6-mile Colorado River Trail. Look for wagon ruts from the old Stewart Toll Road and mine tailings in nearby Shipler Park (this is also a good place to spot moose). ✉ *Off Trail Ridge Rd., 9½ miles north of Grand Lake Entrance Station.*

SCENIC DRIVES

Old Fall River Road

SCENIC DRIVE | More than 100 years old and never more than 14 feet wide, this road stretches from the park's east side to the Fall River Pass (11,796 feet above sea level) on the west. The drive provides a few white-knuckle moments, as the road is steep, serpentine, and lacking in guardrails. Start at West Horseshoe Park, which has the park's largest concentrations of sheep and elk, and head up the gravel road, passing Chasm Falls. ✉ *Runs north of and roughly parallel to Trail Ridge Road, starting near Endovalley Campground (on east) and ending at Fall River Pass/Alpine Visitor Center (on west).*

TRAILS

Chapin Pass

TRAIL | This is a tough hike, but it comes with great views of the park's eastern lower valleys. It's about 3½ miles one way, including a 2,874-foot gain in elevation to the summit of Ypsilon Mountain (elevation 13,514 feet); you pass the summits of Mount Chapin and Mount Chiquita on the way. From the trailhead, the path heads downhill to Chapin Creek. For a short distance after leaving the trailhead, keep a sharp eye out to the right for a less obvious trail that heads uphill to the tree line and disappears. From here head up along the steep ridge to the summit of Mount Chapin. Chiquita and Ypsilon are to the left, and the distance between each peak is about 1 mile and involves a descent of about 400 feet to the saddle and an ascent of 1,000 feet along the ridge to Chiquita. From Ypsilon's summit you'll look down 2,000 feet at Spectacle Lakes. You may wish to bring a topo map and compass. *Difficult.* ✉ *Rocky Mountain National Park* ✣ *Trailhead: At Chapin Pass, off Old Fall River Rd., about 6½ miles from the Endovalley Picnic Area.*

VISITOR CENTER

Fall River Visitor Center

INFO CENTER | FAMILY | The Discovery Room, which houses everything from old ranger outfits to elk antlers, coyote pelts, and bighorn sheep skulls for hands-on exploration, is a favorite with kids at this visitor center. ✉ *U.S. 34, at the Fall River Entrance Station* ☎ *970/586–1206.*

Timber Creek

10 miles north of Grand Lake.

Located along the Colorado River, the west part of the park attracts fewer people and more wildlife in its valleys, especially moose. The towering mountain vistas are fewer here than in the east, but the expansive meadows, rivers, and lakes offer their own peaceful beauty. Unfortunately, wildfires in 2020 destroyed many acres of forest and damaged trails here, so check conditions and closures before setting off.

Sights

HISTORIC SIGHTS

Holzwarth Historic Site

ARCHAEOLOGICAL SITE | FAMILY | A scenic ½-mile interpretive trail leads you over the Colorado River to the original dude ranch that the Holzwarth family, some of the park's original homesteaders, ran between the 1920s and 1950s. Allow about an hour to view the buildings—including a dozen small guest cabins—and chat with a ranger. Though the site is open year-round, the inside of the buildings can be seen only June through early September. ✉ *Off U.S. 34, about 8 miles north of Kawuneeche Visitor Center, Estes Park.*

TRAILS

Colorado River Trail

TRAIL | This walk to the ghost town of Lulu City on the west side of the park is excellent for looking for the bighorn sheep, elk, and moose that reside in the area. Part of the former stagecoach route that went from Granby to Walden, the 3.7-mile trail parallels the infant Colorado River to the meadow where Lulu City once stood. The elevation gain is 350 feet. *Moderate.* ✉ *Rocky Mountain National Park* ✣ *Trailhead: At Colorado River, off Trail Ridge Rd., 1¾ miles north of the Timber Creek Campground.*

Continental Divide National Scenic Trail

TRAIL | This 3,100-mile corridor, which extends from Montana's Canadian border to the southern edge of New Mexico, enters Rocky Mountain National Park in two places, at trailheads only about 4 miles apart and located on either side of the Kawuneeche Visitor Center on Trail Ridge Road, at the park's southwestern end. Within the park, it covers about 30 miles of spectacular montane and subalpine terrain and follows the existing Green Mountain, Tonahutu Creek, North Inlet, and East Shore Trails. *Moderate.* ✉ *Rocky Mountain National Park* ✣ *Trailheads: At Harbison Meadows Picnic Area, off Trail Ridge Rd., about 1 mile inside park from Grand Lake Entrance, and at East Shore Trailhead, just south of Grand Lake.*

East Inlet Trail

TRAIL | An easy hike of 0.3 miles from East Inlet trailhead, just outside the park in Grand Lake, will get you to **Adams Falls** in about 15 minutes. The area around the falls is often packed with visitors, so if you have time, continue east to enjoy more solitude, see wildlife, and catch views of **Mount Craig** from near the East Meadow campground. Note, however, that the trail beyond the falls has an elevation gain of between 1,500 and 1,900 feet, making it a more challenging hike. *Easy.* ✉ *Grand Lake* ✣ *Trailhead: At East Inlet, end of W. Portal Rd. (CO 278) in Grand Lake.*

VISITOR CENTER

Kawuneeche Visitor Center

INFO CENTER | FAMILY | The only visitor center on the park's far west side, Kawuneeche has exhibits on the plant and animal life of the area, as well as a large three-dimensional map of the park and an orientation film. ✉ *U.S. 34, 1 mile north of Grand Lake and ½ mile south of Grand Lake Entrance Station* ☎ *970/586–1206.*

Elk Bugling

In September and October, there are traffic jams in the park as people drive up to listen to the elk bugling. Rangers and park volunteers keep track of where the elk are and direct visitors to the mating spots. The bugling is high-pitched, and if it's light enough, you can see the elk put their heads in the air.

Wild Basin

13 miles south of Estes Park, off Rte 7.

This section in the southeast region of the park consists of lovely expanses of subalpine forest punctuated by streams and lakes. The area's high peaks, along the Continental Divide, are not as easily accessible as those in the vicinity of Bear Lake; hiking to the base of the divide and back makes for a long day. Nonetheless, a visit here is worth the drive south from Estes Park, and because the Wild Basin trailhead is set apart from the park hub, crowding isn't a problem.

Sights

TRAILS

Bluebird Lake Trail

TRAIL | The 6-mile climb from the Wild Basin trailhead to Bluebird Lake (2,478-foot elevation gain) is especially scenic. You pass Copeland Falls, Calypso Cascades, and Ouzel Falls, plus an area that was burned in a lightning-instigated fire in 1978—today it's a mix of bright pink fireweed and charred tree trunks. *Difficult.* ✉ *Rocky Mountain National Park* ✣ *Trailhead: At Wild Basin Ranger Station, about 2 miles west of Wild Basin Entrance Station off Rte. 7, 12¾ miles south of Estes Park.*

Copeland Falls

TRAIL | FAMILY | The 0.3-mile hike to these Wild Basin Area falls is a good option for families, as the terrain is relatively flat (there's only a 15-foot elevation gain). *Easy.* ✉ *Rocky Mountain National Park* ✥ *Trailhead: At Wild Basin Ranger Station.*

Activities

BIKING

There are no bike paths in the park, and bikes are not allowed on trails. Bicyclists are permitted on Trail Ridge Road, but it's too strenuous for most people due to its enormous changes in elevation. Those who have an extra lung or two to spare, however, might tackle a ride up the gravel 9-mile Old Fall River Road, then a ride down Trail Ridge Road.

BIRD-WATCHING

Spring and summer, early in the morning, are the best times for bird-watching in the park. **Lumpy Ridge** is a nesting ground for several kinds of birds of prey. Migratory songbirds from South America have summer breeding grounds near the **Endovalley Picnic Area.** The **alpine tundra** is habitat for white-tailed ptarmigan. The **Alluvial Fan** is the place for viewing broad-tailed hummingbirds, hairy woodpeckers, ouzels, and the occasional raptor.

CAMPING

The park's five campgrounds accommodate campers looking to stay in a tent, trailer, or RV (only three campgrounds accept reservations—up to six months in advance at 🌐 *www.recreation.gov* or 🌐 *www.reserveamerica.com*; the others fill up on a first-come, first-served basis).

Aspenglen Campground. This quiet, east-side spot near the north entrance is set in open pine woodland along Fall River. There are a few excellent walk-in sites for those who want to pitch a tent away from the crowds but still be close to the car. Reservations are recommended in summer. ✉ *Drive past Fall River Visitor Center on U.S. 34 and turn left at the campground road.*

Glacier Basin Campground. This spot offers expansive views of the Continental Divide, easy access to the free summer shuttles to Bear Lake and Estes Park, and ranger-led evening programs in the summer. Reservations are essential. ✉ *Drive 5 miles south on Bear Lake Rd. from U.S. 36* ☎ *877/444–6777.*

Longs Peak Campground. Open May to November, this campground is only a short walk from the Longs Peak trailhead, making it a favorite among hikers looking to get an early start there. The tent-only sites, which are first come, first served, are limited to eight people; firewood, lighting fluid, and charcoal are sold in summer. ✉ *9 miles south of Estes Park on Rte. 7.*

Moraine Park Campground. The only campground in Rocky Mountain open year-round, this spot connects to many hiking trails and has easy access to the free summer shuttles. Rangers lead evening programs in the summer. You'll hear elk bugling if you camp here in September or October. Reservations are essential from mid-May to late September. ✉ *Drive south on Bear Lake Rd. from U.S. 36, 1 mile to campground entrance.*

Timber Creek Campground. Anglers love this spot on the Colorado River, 10 miles from Grand Lake village and the only east-side campground. In the evening you can sit in on ranger-led campfire programs. The 98 campsites are first-come, first-served. ✉ *1 Trail Ridge Rd., 2 miles west of Alpine Visitor Center.*

EDUCATIONAL PROGRAMS

RANGER PROGRAMS

Junior Ranger Program

TOUR—SIGHT | FAMILY | Stop by the Junior Ranger Headquarters at Hidden Valley off Trail Ridge Road for ranger-led talks during the summer months. You can also pick up a Junior Ranger activity book (in

English or Spanish) at any visitor center in the park, or download it from the park's website in advance. With different activity books aimed at children of different ages, the material focuses on environmental education, identifying birds and wildlife, and outdoor safety skills. Once a child has completed all of the activities in the book, a ranger will look over his or her work and award a Junior Ranger badge. ✉ *Rocky Mountain National Park* ☎ *970/586–1206* 🌐 *www.nps.gov/romo/forkids* 🎫 *Free.*

Ranger Programs
TOUR—SIGHT | FAMILY | Join in on free hikes, talks, and activities about wildlife, geology, vegetation, and park history. In the evening, rangers lead twilight hikes, stargazing sessions, and storytelling around the campfire. Look for the extensive program schedule in the park's newspaper available at the main entrances. ✉ *Rocky Mountain National Park* ☎ *970/586–1206* 🎫 *Free.*

FISHING

Rocky Mountain is a wonderful place to fish, especially for trout—German brown, brook, rainbow, cutthroat, and greenback cutthroat—but check at a visitor center about regulations and closures. No fishing is allowed at Bear Lake. To avoid the crowds, rangers recommend angling in the more-remote backcountry. To fish in the park, anyone 16 and older must have a valid Colorado fishing license, which you can obtain at local sporting-goods stores. See 🌐 *www.cpw.state.co.us* for details.

Estes Angler
FISHING | This popular fishing guide arranges fly-fishing trips from two to eight hours into the park's quieter regions, year-round. The best times for fishing are generally from April to mid-November. Equipment is also available for rent. ✉ *338 W. Riverside Dr., Estes Park* ☎ *970/586–2110, 800/586–2110* 🌐 *www.estesangler.com* 🎫 *From $149.*

Kirks Fly Shop
CAMPING—SPORTS-OUTDOORS | This Estes Park outfitter offers various guided fly-fishing trips, as well as backpacking, horseback, and llama pack trips. The store also carries fishing and backpacking gear. ✉ *230 E. Elkhorn Ave., Estes Park* ☎ *970/577–0790, 877/669–1859* 🌐 *www.kirksflyshop.com* 🎫 *From $149.*

Scot's Sporting Goods
FISHING | This shop rents and sells fishing gear, and provides instruction trips daily from May through mid-October. Clinics, geared toward first-timers, focus on casting, reading the water, identifying insects for flies, and properly presenting natural and artificial flies to the fish. ✉ *870 Moraine Ave., Estes Park* ☎ *970/586–2877 May–Sept., 970/443–4932 Oct.–Apr.* 🌐 *www.scotssportinggoods.com* 🎫 *From $220.*

HIKING

Rocky Mountain National Park contains more than 355 miles of hiking trails, so you could theoretically wander the park for weeks. Most visitors explore just a small portion of these trails—those that are closest to the roads and visitor centers—which means that some of the park's most accessible and scenic paths can resemble a backcountry highway on busy summer days. The high-alpine terrain around Bear Lake is the park's most popular hiking area, and although it's well worth exploring, you'll get a more frontierlike experience by hiking one of the trails in the less-explored sections of the park, such as the far northern end or in the Wild Basin area to the south.

Keep in mind that trails at higher elevations may have some snow on them, even in late summer. And because of afternoon thunderstorms on most summer days, an early morning start is highly recommended: the last place you want to be when a storm approaches is on a peak or anywhere above the tree line.

Did You Know?

A pine beetle epidemic that is affecting forests nationwide has caused some of the Rocky Mountain National Park's trees to turn a reddish color and eventually die. The mitigation efforts of the park service are to remove hazard trees and protect "high value" trees near campgrounds, picnic areas, and visitor centers.

HORSEBACK RIDING

Horses and riders can access 260 miles of trails in Rocky Mountain National Park.

Glacier Creek Stable

HORSEBACK RIDING | FAMILY | Located within the park near Sprague Lake, Glacier Creek Stable offers 2- to 10-hour rides to Glacier Basin, Odessa Lake, and Storm Pass. ✉ *Glacier Creek Campground, off Bear Lake Rd. near Sprague Lake* ☎ *970/586–3244 stables, 970/586–4577 off-season reservations* 🌐 *sombrero.com* 🎫 *From $70.*

Moraine Park Stable

HORSEBACK RIDING | FAMILY | Located inside the park just before the Cub Lake Trailhead, Moraine Park Stable offers two- to eight-hour trips to Beaver Meadows, Fern Lake, and Tourmaline Gorge. ✉ *549 Fern Lake Rd.* ☎ *970/586–2327 stables, 970/586–4577 off-season reservations* 🌐 *www.sombrero.com* 🎫 *From $70.*

National Park Gateway Stables

HORSEBACK RIDING | FAMILY | Guided trips into the national park range from two-hour rides to Little Horseshoe Park to half-day rides to Endo Valley and Fall River. The six-hour ride to the summit of Deer Mountain is a favorite. Preschool-aged children can take a 10- or 30-minute pony ride on nearby trails. ✉ *4600 Fall River Rd., Estes Park* ☎ *970/586–5269* 🌐 *www.skhorses.com* 🎫 *From $80.*

ROCK CLIMBING

Experts as well as novices can try hundreds of classic and big-wall climbs here (there's also ample opportunity for bouldering and mountaineering). The burgeoning sport of ice climbing also thrives in the park. The Diamond, Lumpy Ridge, and Petit Grepon are the places for serious rock climbing, while well-known ice-climbing spots include Hidden Falls, Loch Vale, and Emerald and Black lakes.

★ Colorado Mountain School

CLIMBING/MOUNTAINEERING | FAMILY | Guiding climbers since 1877, Colorado Mountain School is the park's only official provider of technical climbing services. They can teach you rock climbing, mountaineering, ice climbing, avalanche survival, and many other skills. Take introductory half-day and one- to five-day courses on climbing and rappelling technique, or sign up for guided introductory trips, full-day climbs, and longer expeditions. Make reservations a month in advance for summer climbs. ✉ *341 Moraine Ave., Estes Park* ☎ *720/387–8944, 303/447–2804* 🌐 *coloradomountainschool.com* 🎫 *From $199.*

WINTER ACTIVITIES

Each winter, the popularity of snowshoeing in the park increases. It's a wonderful way to experience Rocky Mountain's majestic winter side, when the jagged peaks are softened with a blanket of snow and the summer hordes are nonexistent. You can snowshoe any of the summer hiking trails that are accessible by road; many of them also become well-traveled cross-country ski trails. Two trails to try are Tonahutu Creek Trail (near Kawuneeche Visitor Center) and the Colorado River Trail to Lulu City (start at the Timber Creek Campground).

Estes Park Mountain Shop

CLIMBING/MOUNTAINEERING | You can rent or buy snowshoes and skis here, as well as fishing, hiking, and climbing equipment. The store is open year-round and gives four-, six-, and eight-hour guided snowshoeing, fly-fishing, and climbing trips to areas in and around Rocky Mountain National Park. ✉ *2050 Big Thompson Ave., Estes Park* ☎ *970/586–6548, 866/303–6548* 🌐 *www.estesparkmountainshop.com* 🎫 *From $95.*

Never Summer Mountain Products
CAMPING—SPORTS-OUTDOORS | This well-stocked shop sells and rents all sorts of outdoor equipment, including cross-country skis, hiking gear, kayaks, and camping supplies. ✉ *919 Grand Ave., Grand Lake* ☎ *970/627–3642* 🌐 *www.neversummermtn.com.*

What's Nearby

Location is just one reason why **Estes Park** is the most popular RMNP gateway (both the Beaver Meadow and Fall River entrances are 4 miles away). The town is also very family oriented, with lots of stores selling Western-theme trinkets and sweets. Many of the mom-and-pop businesses lining its streets have been passed down through several generations.

Estes Park's smaller cousin, **Grand Lake,** 1½ miles outside the park's west entrance, gets busy in summer, but has a low-key, quintessentially Western graciousness. Even with its wooden boardwalks and Old West–style storefronts, Grand Lake seems less spoiled than many other resorts.

At the park's southwestern entrance are the Arapaho and Roosevelt national forests, the Arapaho National Recreation Area, and the small town of **Granby,** the place to go for golf, mountain biking, and skiing.

Chapter 53

SAGUARO NATIONAL PARK

Updated by
Elise Riley

Camping ★★★☆☆

Hotels ★★★☆☆

Activities ★★☆☆☆

Scenery ★★★★☆

Crowds ★☆☆☆☆

WELCOME TO SAGUARO NATIONAL PARK

TOP REASONS TO GO

★ **Saguaro sightseeing:** Hike, bike, or drive through dense saguaro stands for an up-close look at this king of all cacti.

★ **Wildlife-watching:** Diverse wildlife roams through the park, including such ground dwellers as javelinas, coyotes, and rattlesnakes, and winged residents ranging from the migratory lesser long-nosed bat to the diminutive elf owl.

★ **Ancient artwork:** Get a glimpse into the past at the numerous petroglyph rock-art sites where ancient peoples etched into the stones as far back as 5000 BC.

★ **Desert hiking:** Take a trek through the undisturbed and magical Sonoran Desert, and discover that it's more than cacti.

★ **Two districts, one park:** Split into two districts, the park offers a duo of separate experiences on opposite sides of Tucson.

1 **Saguaro East.** This area, known as the Rincon Mountain District, encompasses 57,930 acres of designated wilderness area, an easily accessible scenic loop drive, several easy and intermediate trails through the cactus forest, and opportunities for adventure and backcountry camping at six rustic campgrounds.

2 **Saguaro West.** Also called the Tucson Mountain District, this is the park's smaller, more-visited section. At the visitor center is a video about saguaros; also in the park's western part are hiking trails, an ancient Hohokam petroglyph site at Signal Hill, and a scenic drive through the park's densest desert growth. This section is near the Arizona–Sonora Desert Museum in Tucson's Westside, and many visitors combine these sights.

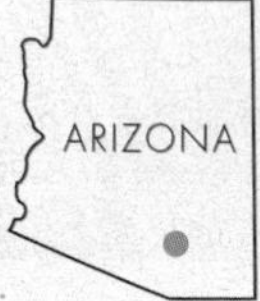

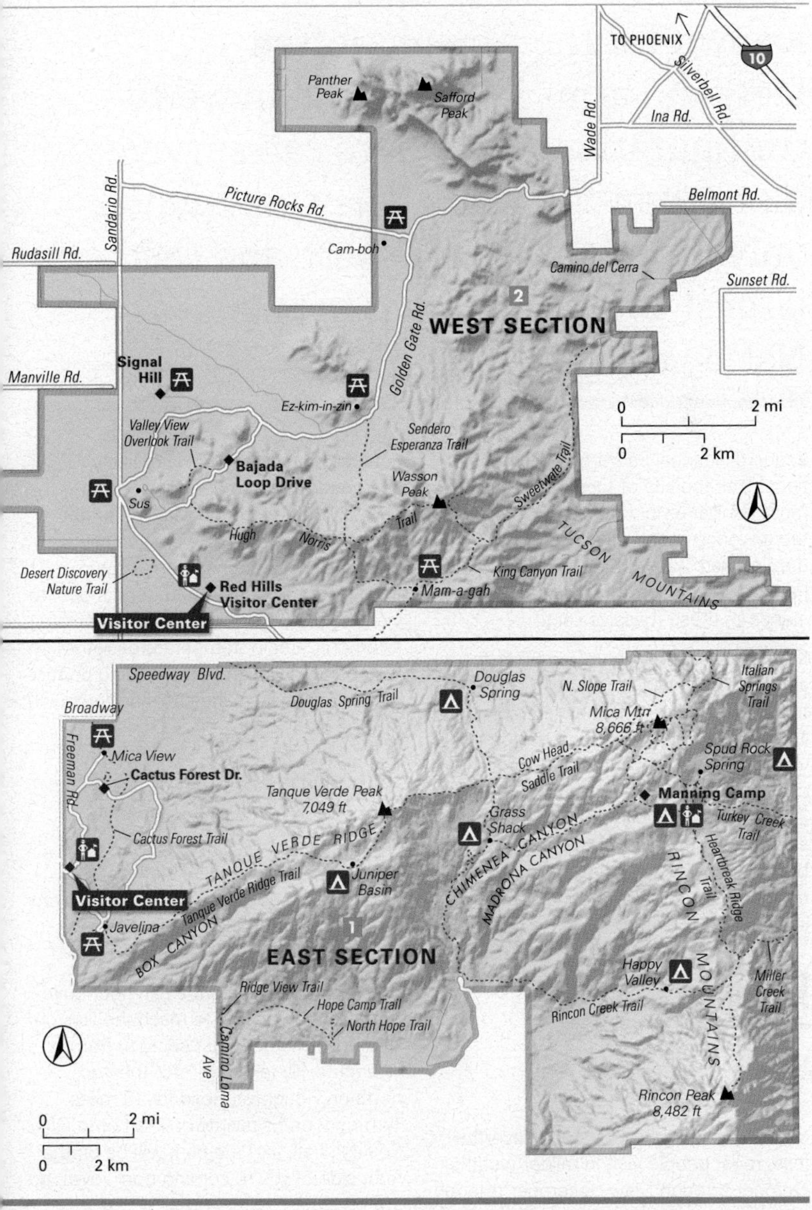

TO PHOENIX
10
Silverbell Rd.
Ina Rd.
Wade Rd.
Belmont Rd.
Panther Peak
Safford Peak
Picture Rocks Rd.
Sandario Rd.
Rudasill Rd.
Cam-boh
Camino del Cerra
Sunset Rd.
2
WEST SECTION
Golden Gate Rd.
Signal Hill
Manville Rd.
Ez-kim-in-zin
0 2 mi
0 2 km
Valley View Overlook Trail
Bajada Loop Drive
Sendero Esperanza Trail
Wasson Peak
Sus
Trail
Sweetwater Trail
Hugh Norris
TUCSON MOUNTAINS
Desert Discovery Nature Trail
King Canyon Trail
Red Hills Visitor Center
Mam-a-gah
Visitor Center
Speedway Blvd.
Douglas Spring
Italian Springs Trail
N. Slope Trail
Douglas Spring Trail
Broadway
Mica Mtn 8,666 ft
Freeman Rd.
Mica View
Cactus Forest Dr.
Cow Head Saddle Trail
Spud Rock Spring
Tanque Verde Peak 7,049 ft
Manning Camp
Grass Shack
Turkey Creek Trail
Cactus Forest Trail
TANQUE VERDE RIDGE
CHIMENEA CANYON
MADRONA CANYON
Heartbreak Ridge Trail
RINCON MOUNTAINS
Tanque Verde Ridge Trail
Juniper Basin
Visitor Center
Javelina
BOX CANYON
1
EAST SECTION
Happy Valley
Miller Creek Trail
Ridge View Trail
Hope Camp Trail
Rincon Creek Trail
North Hope Trail
Camino Loma Ave
Rincon Peak 8,482 ft
0 2 mi
0 2 km

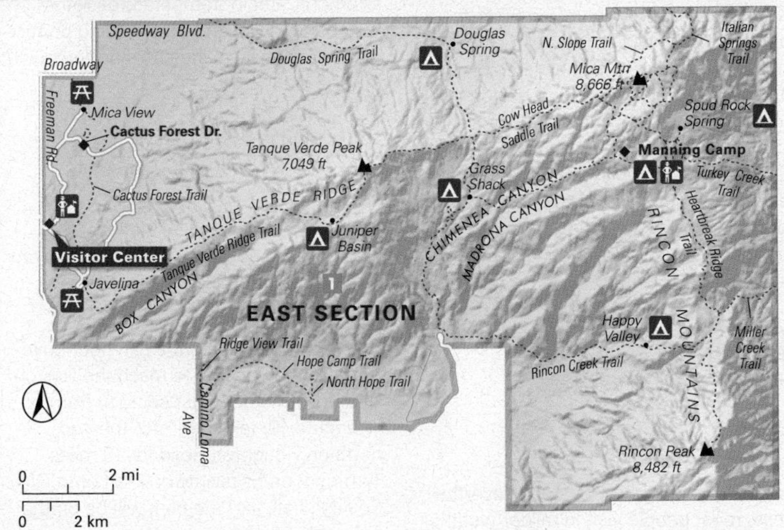

Standing sentinel in the desert, the towering saguaro is perhaps the most familiar emblem of the Southwest. Known for their height (often 50 feet) and arms reaching out in weird configurations, a saguaro can survive more than 200 years. They are found only in the Sonoran Desert, and the largest concentration is in Saguaro National Park.

Saguaro National Park's two distinct sections flank the city of Tucson. Perhaps the most familiar emblem of the Southwest, the towering saguaros are found only in the Sonoran Desert. Saguaro National Park preserves some of the densest stands of these massive cacti.

Known for their height (often 50 feet) and arms reaching out in weird configurations, these slow-growing giants can take 15 years to grow a foot high and up to 75 years to grow their first arm. The cacti can live up to 200 years and weigh up to 2 tons. In late spring (usually May), the succulent's top is covered with tiny white blooms—the Arizona state flower. The cacti are protected by state and federal laws, so don't disturb them.

Planning

When to Go

Saguaro never gets crowded. Nevertheless, most people visit in milder weather, October through May. December through February can be cool and are likely to see gentle rain showers. The spring days of March through May are bright and sunny with wildflowers and cacti in bloom. Because of high temperatures, from June through September it's best to visit the park in the early morning or late afternoon. Cooler temperatures return in October and November, providing perfect weather for hiking and camping throughout the park.

Getting Here and Around

AIR

Both districts of Saguaro National Park are approximately a 30-minute drive from the Tucson International Airport.

CAR

Both districts are about a half-hour drive from Central Tucson. To reach the Rincon Mountain District (East section) from Interstate 10, take Exit 275, then go north on Houghton Road for 10 miles. Turn right on Escalante and left onto Old Spanish Trail, and the park will be on the right side. If you're coming from town, go

AVERAGE HIGH/LOW TEMPERATURES					
JAN.	**FEB.**	**MAR.**	**APR.**	**MAY**	**JUNE**
63/38	66/40	72/44	80/50	89/57	98/67
JULY	**AUG.**	**SEPT.**	**OCT.**	**NOV.**	**DEC.**
98/73	96/72	93/67	84/57	72/45	65/39

east on Speedway Boulevard to Houghton Road. Turn right on Houghton and left onto Old Spanish Trail.

To reach the Tucson Mountain District (West section) from Interstate 10, take Exit 242 or Exit 257, then go west on Speedway Boulevard (the name will change to Gates Pass Road), follow it to Kinney Road, and turn right.

As there's no public transportation to or within Saguaro, a car is a necessity. In the western section, Bajada Loop Drive takes you through the park and to various trailheads; Cactus Forest Drive does the same for the eastern section.

Inspiration

The *Tucson Hiking Guide*, by Betty Leavengood, is a useful and entertaining book with day hikes in the park.

Books that give a general introduction to the park include *Saguaro National Park*, by Doris Evans, and *Sonoran Desert: The Story Behind the Scenery*, by Christopher L. Helms.

All About Saguaros, by Carle Hodge and published by Arizona Highways Books, includes fabulous color photos of the cactus.

For a poetic take by a naturalist, try Gary Nabhan's *Saguaro: A View of Saguaro National Monument and the Tucson Basin*.

Park Essentials

ACCESSIBILITY

In the western section, the Red Hills Visitor Center and two nearby nature trails are wheelchair accessible. The eastern district's visitor center is accessible, as are the paved Desert Ecology and Cactus Garden Trails.

PARK FEES AND PERMITS

Admission to Saguaro is $25 per vehicle and $15 for individuals on foot or bicycle; it's good for seven days from purchase at both park districts. Annual passes cost $45. For hike-in camping at one of the primitive campsites in the eastern district (the closest campsite is 6 miles from the trailhead), obtain a required backcountry permit ($8 per night) up to three months in advance. 🌐 *www.recreation.gov*

PARK HOURS

The park opens at sunrise and closes at sunset every day but Christmas day. It's in the Mountain time zone. Arizona (excluding the Navajo Nation) does not observe daylight saving time. The visitor center is open daily from 9 to 5.

CELL PHONE RECEPTION

Cell phone reception is generally good in the eastern district but is unreliable in the western district. The visitor centers have pay phones.

Hotels

Although there are no hotels within the park, its immediate proximity to Tucson makes finding a place to stay easy. A couple of B&Bs are a short drive from the park. Some ranches and smaller accommodations close during the hottest months of summer, but many inexpensive B&Bs and hotels are open year-round, and offer significantly lower rates from late May through August.

Restaurants

At Saguaro, you won't find more than a sampling of Southwest jams, hot sauces, and candy bars at the two visitor centers' gift shops. Vending machines outside sell bottled water and soda, but pack some lunch for a picnic if you don't want to drive all the way back into town. Five picnic areas in the west district, and two in the east, offer scenery and shade. However, the city of Tucson, sandwiched neatly between the two park districts, offers some of the best Mexican cuisine in the country. A genuine college town, Tucson also has excellent upscale Southwestern cuisine, as well as good sushi, Thai, Italian, and Ethiopian food.

Visitor Information

PARK CONTACT INFORMATION Saguaro National Park. ✉ *3693 S. Old Spanish Trail, Tucson* ☎ *520/733–5158 for Saguaro West, 520/733–5153 for Saguaro East* 🌐 *www.nps.gov/sagu.*

Saguaro East

12 miles east of Central Tucson.

In the Rincon Mountains, Saguaro East encompasses nearly 60,000 acres of designated wilderness area, an easily accessible scenic loop drive, several easy and intermediate trails through the cactus forest, and opportunities for adventure and backcountry camping at six rustic campgrounds.

Sights

HISTORIC SITES

Manning Camp

HOUSE | The summer home of Levi Manning, onetime Tucson mayor, was a popular gathering spot for the city's elite in the early 1900s. The cabin can be reached only on foot or horseback via one of several challenging high-country trails: Douglas Spring Trail to Cow Head Saddle Trail (12 miles), Turkey Creek Trail (7.5 miles), or Tanque Verde Ridge Trail (15.4 miles). The cabin itself is not open for viewing. ✉ *Saguaro East* ✣ *Douglas Spring Trail (6 miles) to Cow Head Saddle Trail (6 miles).*

SCENIC DRIVES

★ Cactus Forest Drive

SCENIC DRIVE | This paved 8-mile drive provides a great overview of all Saguaro East has to offer. The one-way road, which circles clockwise, has several turnouts with roadside displays that make it easy to pull over and admire the scenery; you can also stop at two picnic areas and three easy nature trails. This is a good bicycling route, but watch out for snakes and javelinas crossing in front of you. ✉ *Cactus Forest Dr., Saguaro East.*

TRAILS

Cactus Forest Trail

TRAIL | This 2½-mile one-way loop is a moderately easy walk along a dirt path that passes historic lime kilns and a wide variety of Sonoran Desert vegetation. It's one of the only off-road trails for bicyclists. *Moderate.* ✉ *Saguaro East* ✣ *Trailhead: 2 miles south of Rincon Mountain Visitor Center, off Cactus Forest Dr.*

Desert Ecology Trail

TRAIL | **FAMILY** | Exhibits on this ¼-mile loop near the Mica View picnic area explain how local plants and animals subsist on limited water. Dogs on leash are permitted. *Easy.* ✉ *Saguaro East* ✣ *Trailhead: 2 miles north of Rincon Mountain Visitor Center.*

Freeman Homestead Trail

TRAIL | Learn a bit about the history of homesteading in the region on this 1-mile loop. Look for owls living in the cliffs above as you make your way through the lowland vegetation. *Easy.* ✉ *Saguaro East* ✣ *Trailhead: Next to Javelina picnic area, 2 miles south of Rincon Mountain Visitor Center.*

★ **Hope Camp Trail**

TRAIL | Well worth the 5-mile round-trip trek, this Rincon Valley route rewards hikers with gorgeous views of the Tanque Verde Ridge and Rincon Peak. The trail is also open to mountain bicyclists. *Moderate.* ✉ *Saguaro East* ✣ *Trailhead: From Camino Loma Alta trailhead to Hope Camp.*

Tanque Verde Ridge Trail

TRAIL | Be rewarded with spectacular scenery on this 18-mile round-trip trail that takes you through desert scrub, oak, alligator juniper, and pinyon pine at the 6,000-foot peak, where views of the surrounding mountain ranges from both sides of the ridge delight. *Difficult.* ✉ *Saguaro East* ✣ *Trailhead: Javelina picnic area, 2 miles south of Red Hills Visitor Center.*

VISITOR CENTER

Rincon Mountain Visitor Center

INFO CENTER | Stop here to pick up free maps and printed materials on various aspects of the park, including maps of hiking trails and backcountry camping permits. Exhibits at the center are comprehensive, and a relief map of the park lays out the complexities of this protected landscape. Two 20-minute slide shows explain the botanical and cultural history of the region, and there is a short self-guided nature walk along the paved Cactus Garden Trail. A select variety of books and other gift items, along with energy bars, beef jerky, and refillable water bottles, are sold here. ✉ *3693 S. Old Spanish Trail, Saguaro East* ☎ *520/733–5153* 🌐 *www.nps.gov/sagu.*

Saguaro West

14 miles west of Central Tucson.

This popular district makes up less than one-third of the park. Here you'll find a native American video orientation to saguaros at the visitor center, hiking trails, an ancient Hohokam petroglyph site at Signal Hill, and a scenic drive through the park's densest desert growth.

Sights

SCENIC DRIVES

★ **Bajada Loop Drive**

SCENIC DRIVE | This 6-mile drive winds through thick stands of saguaros and past two picnic areas and trailheads to a few short hikes, including one to a petroglyph site. Although the road is unpaved and somewhat bumpy, it's a worthwhile trade-off for access to some of the park's densest desert growth. It's one-way between Hugh Norris Trail and Golden Gate Road, so if you want to make the complete circuit, travel counterclockwise. The road is susceptible to flash floods during the monsoon season (July and August), so check road conditions at the visitor center before proceeding. This loop route is also popular among bicyclists, and dogs on leash are permitted along the road. ✉ *Saguaro West.*

SCENIC STOPS

Signal Hill

ARCHAEOLOGICAL SITE | **FAMILY** | The most impressive petroglyphs, and the only ones with explanatory signs, are on the Bajada Loop Drive in Saguaro West. An easy five-minute stroll from the signposted parking area takes you to one of the largest concentrations of rock carvings in the Southwest. You'll have a close-up view of the designs left by the Hohokam people between AD 900 and 1200, including large spirals some believe are astronomical markers. ✉ *Bajada Loop Dr., Saguaro West* ⊕ *4½ miles north of visitor center.*

TRAILS

Desert Discovery Trail

TRAIL | **FAMILY** | Learn about plants and animals native to the region on this paved path in Saguaro West. The ½-mile loop is wheelchair accessible, and has resting benches and ramadas (wooden shelters that supply shade). Dogs on leash are permitted here. *Easy.* ✉ *Saguaro West* ⊕ *Trailhead: 1 mile north of Red Hills Visitor Center.*

★ Hugh Norris Trail

TRAIL | This 10-mile trail through the Tucson Mountains is one of the most impressive in the Southwest. It's full of switchbacks, and some sections are moderately steep, but the top of 4,687-foot Wasson Peak treats you to views of the saguaro forest spread across the *bajada* (the gently rolling hills at the base of taller mountains). *Difficult.* ✉ *Saguaro West* ⊕ *Trailhead: 2½ miles north of Red Hills Visitor Center on Bajada Loop Dr.*

★ Signal Hill Trail

TRAIL | **FAMILY** | This ¼-mile trail in Saguaro West is a simple, rewarding ascent to ancient petroglyphs carved a millennium ago by the Hohokam people. *Easy.* ✉ *Saguaro West* ⊕ *Trailhead: 4½ miles north of Red Hills Visitor Center on Bajada Loop Dr.*

Sweetwater Trail

TRAIL | Though technically within Saguaro West, this trail is on the eastern edge of the district, and affords access to Wasson Peak from the eastern side of the Tucson Mountains. After gradually climbing 3.4 miles, it ends at King Canyon Trail (which would then take you on a fairly steep 1.2-mile climb to Wasson Peak). Long and meandering, this little-used trail allows more privacy to enjoy the natural surroundings than some of the more frequently used trails. *Moderate.* ✉ *Saguaro West* ⊕ *Trailhead: Western end of El Camino del Cerro Rd.*

★ Valley View Overlook Trail

TRAIL | On clear days you can spot the distinctive slope of Picacho Peak from this relatively easy 1½-mile trail with a gentle ascent in Saguaro West. There are splendid vistas of Avra Valley and signs describing the flora along the way. *Moderate.* ✉ *Saguaro West* ⊕ *Trailhead: 3 miles north of Red Hills Visitor Center on Bajada Loop Dr.*

VISITOR CENTER

Red Hills Visitor Center

INFO CENTER | Take in gorgeous views of nearby mountains and the surrounding desert from the center's large windows and shaded outdoor terrace. A spacious gallery is filled with educational exhibits, and a lifelike display simulates the flora and fauna of the region. A 15-minute slide show, "Voices of the Desert," provides a poetic, Native American perspective on the Saguaro. Park rangers and volunteers hand out maps and suggest hikes to suit your interests. The bookstore sells books, trinkets, a few local items like honey and prickly pear jellies, and reusable water bottles that you can fill at water stations outside. ✉ *2700 N. Kinney Rd., Saguaro West* ☎ *520/733–5158* 🌐 *www.nps.gov/sagu.*

Activities

BIKING

Scenic drives in the park—Bajada Loop in the West and Cactus Forest Drive in the East section—are popular among cyclists, though you'll have to share the roads with cars. Bajada Loop Drive is a gravel and dirt road, so it's quite bumpy and only suitable for mountain bikers; Cactus Forest Drive is paved. In the East section, Cactus Forest Trail (2.5 miles) is a great unpaved path for both beginning and experienced mountain bikers who don't mind sharing the trail with hikers

A saguaro grows under the protection of another tree, such as a paloverde or mesquite, before superseding it.

and the occasional horse; Hope Camp Trail is also open to mountain bikes.

Fair Wheel Bikes

BICYCLING | Mountain bikes and road bikes can be rented by the day or week here. The company also organizes group rides of varying difficulty. ✉ *1110 E. 6th St., University* ☎ *520/884–9018* 🌐 *fair-wheelbikes.com.*

BIRD-WATCHING

To check out the more than 200 species of birds living in or migrating through the park, begin by focusing your binoculars on the limbs of the saguaros, where many birds make their home. In general, early morning and early evening are the best times for sightings. In winter and spring, volunteer-led birding hikes begin at the visitor centers.

The finest areas to flock to in Saguaro East (the Rincon Mountain District) are the Desert Ecology Trail, where you may find rufous-winged sparrows, verdins, and Cooper's hawks along the washes, and the Javelina picnic area, where you'll most likely spot canyon wrens and black-chinned sparrows. At Saguaro West (the Tucson Mountain District), sit down on one of the visitor center benches and look for ash-throated flycatchers, Say's phoebes, curve-billed thrashers, and Gila woodpeckers. During the cooler months, keep a lookout for wintering neotropical migrants such as hummingbirds, swallows, orioles, and warblers.

Wild Bird Store

BIRD WATCHING | This shop is an excellent resource for birding information, feeders, books, and trail guides. Free bird walks are offered most Sundays October–May. ✉ *3160 E. Fort Lowell Rd., Central* ☎ *520/322–9466* 🌐 *www.wildbirdsonline.com.*

CAMPING

There's no drive-up camping in the park. All six primitive campgrounds are in the eastern district and require a hike to reach—the shortest hikes are to Douglas Spring Campground (6 miles) and to Happy Valley (5 miles). All are open year-round. Pick up your backcountry camping permit ($6 per night) at the Rincon Mountain Visitor Center. Before choosing a camping destination, look over the relief map of hiking trails and the book of wilderness campground photos taken by park rangers. You can camp in the backcountry for a maximum of 14 days. Each site can accommodate up to six people. Reservations can be made via mail or in person up to two months in advance. Hikers are encouraged to set out before noon. If you haven't the time or the inclination to hike in, several more camping opportunities exist within a few miles of the park.

EDUCATIONAL OFFERINGS

Junior Ranger Program

TOUR—SIGHT | **FAMILY** | In the Junior Ranger Discovery program, young visitors can pick up an activity pack any time of the year at either visitor center and complete it within an hour or two. During June, there also are daylong camps for kids ages 5 through 12 in the East district. ✉ *Rincon Mountain and Red Hills visitor centers, Saguaro National Park* ☎ *520/733–5153* 🌐 *nps.gov/sagu.*

Orientation Programs

TOUR—SIGHT | Daily programs at both park districts introduce visitors to the desert. You might find presentations on bats, birds, or desert blooms, and naturalist-led hikes (including moonlight hikes). Check online or call for the current week's activities. ✉ *Rincon Mountain and Red Hills visitor centers, Saguaro National Park* ☎ *520/733–5100* 🌐 *nps.gov/sagu* 🎫 *Free.*

Ranger Talks

TOUR—SIGHT | The assortment of talks by national park rangers are a great way to hear about wildlife, geology, and archaeology. ✉ *Rincon Mountain and Red Hills visitor centers, Saguaro National Park* ☎ *520/733–5100* 🎫 *Free.*

HIKING

The park has more than 100 miles of trails. The shorter hikes, such as the **Desert Discovery** and **Desert Ecology** trails, are perfect for those looking to learn about the desert ecosystem without expending too much energy. The **Hope Camp Trail**, **Hugh Norris Trail**, and **Signal Hill Trail** are also excellent for hiking. For more information see the trail listings under ⇨ *Sights.*

■ TIP→ Rattlesnakes are commonly seen on trails; so are coyotes, javelinas, roadrunners, Gambel's quail, and desert spiny lizards. Hikers should keep their distance from all wildlife.

What's Nearby

Saguaro stands as a protected desert oasis, with metropolitan **Tucson,** Arizona's second-largest city, lying between the two park sections. Spread over 227 miles, and with a population of nearly a half million, Tucson averages 340 days of sunshine a year.

Chapter 54

SEQUOIA AND KINGS CANYON NATIONAL PARKS

Updated by
Cheryl Crabtree

Camping	Hotels	Activities	Scenery	Crowds
★★★★☆	★★★★☆	★★★★☆	★★★★★	★★★☆☆

WELCOME TO SEQUOIA AND KINGS CANYON NATIONAL PARKS

TOP REASONS TO GO

★ **Gentle giants:** You'll feel small—in a good way—walking among some of the world's largest living things in Sequoia's Giant Forest and Kings Canyon's Grant Grove.

★ **Because it's there:** You can't even glimpse it from the main part of Sequoia, but the sight of majestic Mt. Whitney is worth the trip to the eastern face of the High Sierra.

★ **Underground exploration:** Far older even than the giant sequoias, the gleaming limestone formations in Crystal Cave will draw you along dark, marble passages.

★ **A grander-than-Grand Canyon:** Drive the twisting Kings Canyon Scenic Byway down into the jagged, granite Kings River canyon, deeper in parts than the Grand Canyon.

★ **Regal solitude:** To spend a day or two hiking in a subalpine world of your own, pick one of the many trailheads at Mineral King.

1 **Giant Forest–Lodgepole Village.** One of Sequoia's most visited areas has major sights such as Giant Forest, General Sherman Tree, Crystal Cave, and Moro Rock.

2 **Grant Grove Village–Redwood Canyon.** The "thumb" of Kings Canyon is its busiest section, where Grant Grove, General Grant Tree, Panoramic Point, and Big Stump are the main draws.

3 **Cedar Grove.** The drive through the high-country of Kings Canyon to Cedar Grove Village, on the canyon floor, reveals magnificent granite formations of varied hues. Rock meets river in breathtaking fashion at Zumwalt Meadow.

4 **Mineral King.** In Sequoia's southeast section, the highest road-accessible part of the park is a good place to hike, camp, and soak up the grandeur of the Sierra Nevada.

5 **Mt. Whitney.** The highest peak in the Lower 48 stands on the eastern edge of Sequoia; to get there from Giant Forest you must either backpack eight days through the mountains or drive nearly 300 miles around the park to its other side.

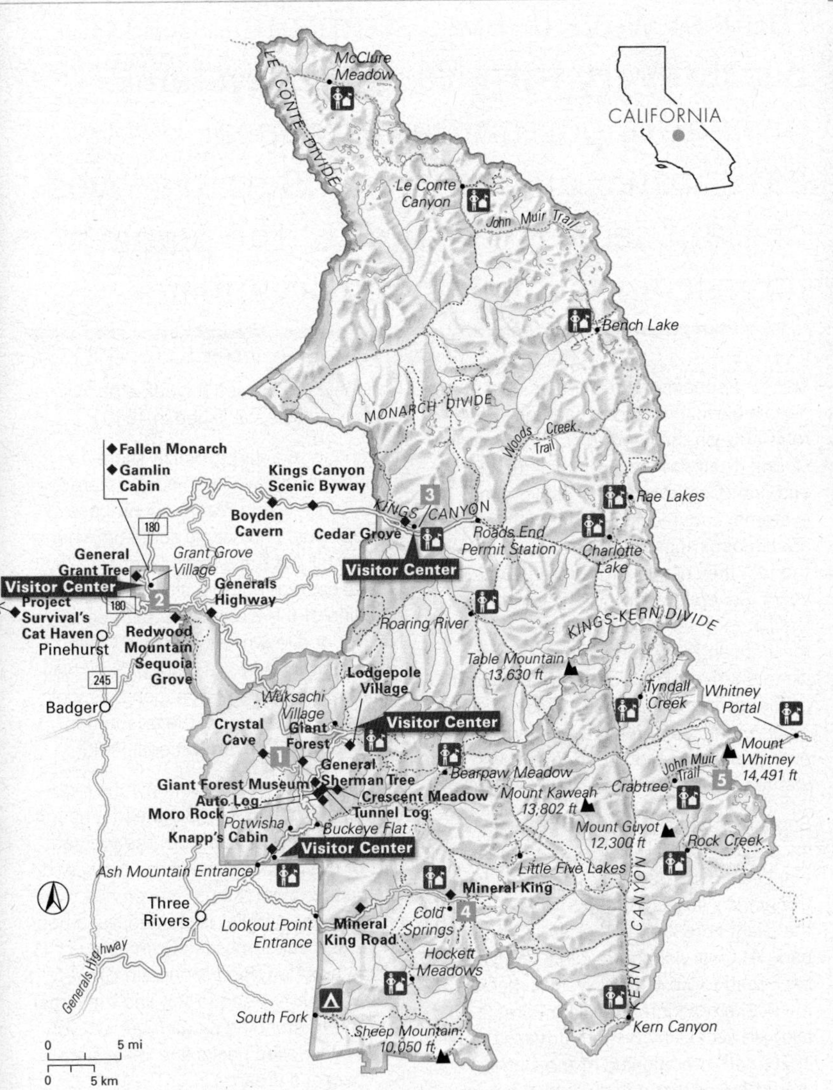
CALIFORNIA
McClure Meadow
LE CONTE DIVIDE
Le Conte Canyon
John Muir Trail
Bench Lake
MONARCH DIVIDE
Woods Creek Trail
Fallen Monarch
Gamlin Cabin
Kings Canyon Scenic Byway
Boyden Cavern
KINGS CANYON
Cedar Grove
Roads End Permit Station
Rae Lakes
Charlotte Lake
180
General Grant Tree
Grant Grove Village
Visitor Center
Generals Highway
Project Survival's Cat Haven
Pinehurst
Redwood Mountain Sequoia Grove
Roaring River
KINGS-KERN DIVIDE
Table Mountain 13,630 ft
245
Badger
Lodgepole Village
Wuksachi Village
Crystal Cave
Giant Forest
Tyndall Creek
Whitney Portal
Mount Whitney 14,491 ft
General Sherman Tree
Giant Forest Museum
Auto Log
Moro Rock
Crescent Meadow
Tunnel Log
Bearpaw Meadow
Mount Kaweah 13,802 ft
Crabtree
Potwisha
Buckeye Flat
Knapp's Cabin
Mount Guyot 12,300 ft
Rock Creek
Ash Mountain Entrance
Little Five Lakes
Mineral King
Three Rivers
Lookout Point Entrance
Mineral King Road
Cold Springs
KERN CANYON
Hockett Meadows
Generals Highway
South Fork
Sheep Mountain 10,050 ft
Kern Canyon
0 5 mi
0 5 km

The word "exceptional" best describes these two parks, which offer some of the nation's greatest escapes. Drives along their byways deliver stunning vistas at nearly every turn. Varied ecosystems provide opportunities for repeat adventures, among them hikes to groves of giant sequoias—some of the planet's largest, and oldest, living organisms.

This rare species of tree grows only at certain elevations and in particular environments on the Central Sierra's western slopes. Their monstrously thick trunks and branches, remarkably shallow root systems, and neck-craning heights really are almost impossible to believe, as is the fact they can live for more than 2,500 years. Several Native American groups lived among these magnificent trees for thousands of years before modern visitors arrived. By the late 1800s, word of the giant sequoias (*Sequoiadendron giganteum*) had spread, attracting logging enterprises and mobilizing those who wanted to protect these living treasures.

Sequoia National Park—the nation's second oldest after Yellowstone—was established in 1890, officially preserving the world's largest sequoia groves in the Giant Forest and other areas of the park. At first, visitors traveled along a pack road to view the towering marvels. In 1903, a road into the Giant Forest allowed access by wagon. It wasn't until 1926, with the opening of the General's Highway, that autos could chug up the mountain. Kings Canyon National Park, which included the General Grant National Park formed a week after Sequoia, was established in 1940.

Today, the two parks, which share a boundary and have been administered jointly since World War II, encompass 865,964 wild and scenic acres between the foothills of California's Central Valley and its eastern borders along the craggy ridgeline of the Sierra's highest peaks. Next to or a few miles off the 46-mile Generals Highway are most of Sequoia National Park's main attractions, as well as Grant Grove Village, the orientation hub for Kings Canyon National Park.

Sequoia includes Mt. Whitney, the highest point in the lower 48 states (although it is impossible to see from the western part of the park and is a chore to ascend from either side). Kings Canyon has two portions: the smaller is shaped like a bent finger and encompasses Grant Grove Village and Redwood Mountain Grove (both with many sequoias), and the larger is home to stunning Kings River Canyon, where unspoiled peaks and valleys are a backpacker's dream.

AVERAGE HIGH/LOW TEMPERATURES (MID-LEVEL ELEVATIONS)					
JAN.	FEB.	MAR.	APR.	MAY	JUNE
42/24	44/25	46/26	51/30	58/36	68/44
JULY	AUG.	SEPT.	OCT.	NOV.	DEC.
76/51	76/50	71/45	61/38	50/31	44/27

Planning

When to Go

The best times to visit are spring and fall, when temperatures are moderate and crowds thin. Summertime can draw hordes of tourists to see the giant sequoias, and the few, narrow roads mean congestion at peak holiday times. If you must visit in summer, go during the week. By contrast, in wintertime you may feel as though you have the parks all to yourself. But because of heavy snows, sections of the main park roads can be closed without warning, and low-hanging clouds can move in and obscure mountains and valleys for days. From early October to late April, check road and weather conditions before venturing out. ■ **TIP→ Even in summer, you can escape hordes of people just walking ¼ to ½ mile off the beaten path on a less-used trail.**

FESTIVALS AND EVENTS

Annual Trek to the Tree. On the second Sunday of December, visitors and carolers gather at the base of General Grant Tree for a nondemoninational celebration that has taken place for nearly a century.

Three Rivers Jazzaffair. On the second weekend of April, a festival of mostly traditional jazz takes place at several venues just south of the parks. 🌐 *www.threeriversjazzaffair.com*

Getting Here and Around

AIR

The closest airport to Sequoia and Kings Canyon national parks is Fresno Yosemite International Airport (FAT).

AIRPORT CONTACTS Fresno Yosemite International Airport. *(FAT)* ✉ *5175 E. Clinton Way, Fresno* ☎ *800/244–2359 automated info, 559/621–4500* 🌐 *www.flyfresno.com.*

CAR

Sequoia is 36 miles east of Visalia on Route 198; Grant Grove Village in Kings Canyon is 56 miles east of Fresno on Route 180. There is no automobile entrance on the eastern side of the Sierra. Routes 198 and 180 are connected by Generals Highway, a paved two-lane road (also signed as Highway 198) that sometimes sees delays at peak times due to ongoing improvements. The road is extremely narrow and steep from Route 198 to Giant Forest, so keep an eye on your engine temperature gauge, as the incline and congestion can cause vehicles to overheat; to avoid overheated brakes, use low gears on downgrades.

If you are traveling in an RV or with a trailer, study the restrictions on these vehicles. Do not travel beyond Potwisha Campground on Generals Highway (Route 198) with an RV longer than 22 feet; take straighter, easier Route 180 through the Kings Canyon park entrance instead. Maximum vehicle length on Generals Highway is 40 feet, or 50 feet combined length for vehicles with trailers. For current road and weather conditions, call ☎ *559/565–3341* or visit the park website: 🌐 *www.nps.gov/seki.*

Inspiration

King Sequoia: The Tree That Inspired a Nation, Created Our National Park System, and Changed the Way We Think about Nature, by naturalist and former park ranger William C. Tweed, dives deep into the story of human discovery and connection with giant sequoias.

The Overstory: A Novel, by Richard Powers, includes tales rooted around timber wars and characters who become champions of the natural world. The book won the 2019 Pulitzer Prize in fiction.

Park Essentials

ACCESSIBILITY

All the visitor centers, the Giant Forest Museum, and Big Trees Trail are wheelchair accessible, as are some short ranger-led walks and talks. General Sherman Tree can be reached via a paved, level trail near a parking area. None of the caves is accessible, and wilderness areas must be reached by horseback or on foot. Some picnic tables are extended to accommodate wheelchairs. Many of the major sites are in the 6,000-foot range, and thin air at high elevations can cause respiratory distress for people with breathing difficulties. Carry oxygen if necessary. Contact the park's main number for more information.

PARK FEES AND PERMITS

The admission fee is $35 per vehicle, $30 per motorcycle, and $20 per person for those who enter by bus, on foot, bicycle, horse, or any other mode of transportation; it is valid for seven days in both parks. U.S. residents over the age of 62 pay $80 for a lifetime pass, and permanently disabled U.S. residents are admitted free.

If you plan to camp in the backcountry, you need a permit, which costs $15 for hikers or $30 for stock users (e.g., horseback riders). One permit covers the group. Availability of permits depends upon trailhead quotas. Reservations are accepted by mail or email for a $15 processing fee, beginning March 1, and must be made at least 14 days in advance (☎ *559/565–3766*). Without a reservation, you may still get a permit on a first-come, first-served basis starting at 1 pm the day before you plan to hike. For more information on backcountry camping or travel with pack animals (horses, mules, burros, or llamas), contact the Wilderness Permit Office (☎ *530/565–3766*).

PARK HOURS

The parks are open 24/7 year-round. They are in the Pacific time zone.

CELL PHONE RECEPTION

Cell phone reception is poor to nonexistent in the higher elevations and spotty even on portions of Generals Highway, where you can (on rare clear days) see the Central Valley. Public telephones may be found at the visitor centers, ranger stations, some trailheads, and at all restaurants and lodging facilities in the park.

Hotels

Hotel accommodations in Sequoia and Kings Canyon are limited, and, although they are clean and comfortable, they tend to lack much in-room character. Keep in mind, however, that the extra money you spend on lodging here is offset by the time you'll save by being inside the parks. You won't be faced with a 60- to 90-minute commute from the less-expensive motels in Three Rivers (by far the most charming option), Visalia, or Fresno. Reserve as far in advance as you can, especially for summertime stays.

Restaurants

In Sequoia and Kings Canyon national parks, you can treat yourself (and the family) to a high-quality meal in a wonderful setting in the Peaks restaurant at Wuksachi Lodge, but otherwise you should keep your expectations modest. You can grab bread, spreads, drinks, and fresh produce at one of several small grocery stores for a picnic, or get takeout food from the Grant Grove Restaurant, the Cedar Grove Grill, or one of the two small Lodgepole eateries.

Hotel and restaurant reviews have been shortened. For full information visit Fodors.com. Hotel prices are the lowest cost of a standard double room in high season. Restaurant prices are the average cost of a main course at dinner, or if dinner is not served, at lunch.

What It Costs

$	$$	$$$	$$$$
RESTAURANTS			
under $12	$12–$20	$21–$30	over $30
HOTELS			
under $100	$100–$150	$151–$200	over $200

Tours

★ **Sequoia Parks Conservancy Field Institute**
SPECIAL-INTEREST | The Sequoia Parks Conservancy's highly regarded educational division conducts half-, single-, and multiday tours that include backpacking hikes, natural-history walks, astronomy programs, snowshoe treks, and custom adventures. ✉ *47050 Generals Hwy., Unit 10, Three Rivers* ☎ *559/565–4251* 🌐 *www.sequoiaparksconservancy.org* 🎫 *From $150 for 2-hr guided tour.*

Sequoia Sightseeing Tours
GUIDED TOURS | This locally owned operator's friendly, knowledgeable guides conduct daily interpretive sightseeing tours in Sequoia and Kings Canyon. Reservations are essential. The company also offers private tours. ✉ *Three Rivers* ☎ *559/561–4189* 🌐 *www.sequoiatours.com* 🎫 *From $79 tour of Sequoia; from $169 tour of Kings Canyon.*

Visitor Information

NATIONAL PARK SERVICE Foothills Visitor Center. ✉ *47050 Generals Hwy., Rte. 198, 1 mile north of Ash Mountain entrance, Sequoia National Park* ☎ *559/565–3341.*
Sequoia and Kings Canyon National Parks. ✉ *47050 Generals Hwy. (Rte. 198), Three Rivers* ☎ *559/565–3341* 🌐 *nps.gov/seki.*

Sequoia National Park

Sequoia National Park is all about the trees, and to understand the scale of these giants you must walk among them. If you do nothing else, get out of the car for a short stroll through one of the groves. But there is much more to the park than the trees. Try to access one of the vista points that provide a panoramic view over the forested mountains. Generals Highway (which connects Routes 198 and 180) will be your route to most of the park's sights. A few short spur roads lead from the highway to some sights, and Mineral King Road branches off Route 198 to enter the park at Lookout Point, winding east from there to the park's southernmost section.

Giant Forest—Lodgepole Village

Giant Forest is 16 miles from the Sequoia National Park Visitor Center.

The Sequoia National Park entrance at Ash Mountain is the main gateway to the Giant Forest and many of the park's major sights. From there, the narrow, twisty General's Highway snakes up the mountain from a 1,700-foot elevation through the Giant Forest (a 45-minute drive from the entrance) up to 6,720 feet at Lodgepole Village.

Sights

HISTORIC SIGHTS

Giant Forest Museum

MUSEUM | Well-imagined and interactive displays at this worthwhile stop provide the basics about sequoias, of which there are 2,161 with diameters exceeding 10 feet in the approximately 2,000-acre Giant Forest. ✉ *Sequoia National Park* ✣ *Generals Hwy., 4 miles south of Lodgepole Visitor Center* ☎ *559/565–4436* 💵 *Free* ☞ *Shuttle: Giant Forest or Moro Rock–Crescent Meadow.*

SCENIC DRIVES

★ Generals Highway

SCENIC DRIVE | One of California's most scenic drives, this 46-mile road (also signed as Route 198) is the main asphalt artery between Sequoia and Kings Canyon national parks. Named after the landmark Grant and Sherman trees that leave so many visitors awestruck, Generals Highway runs from Sequoia's Foothills Visitor Center north to Kings Canyon's Grant Grove Village. Along the way, it passes the turnoff to Crystal Cave, the Giant Forest Museum, Lodgepole Village, and other popular attractions. The lower portion, from Hospital Rock to the Giant Forest, is especially steep and winding. If your vehicle is 22 feet or longer, avoid that stretch by entering the parks via Route 180 (from Fresno) rather than Route 198 (from Visalia or Three Rivers). Take your time on this road—there's a lot to see, and wildlife can scamper across at any time. ✉ *Sequoia National Park.*

SCENIC STOPS

Auto Log

FOREST | Before its wood showed signs of severe rot, cars drove right on top of this giant fallen sequoia. Now it's a great place to pose for pictures or shoot a video. ✉ *Sequoia National Park* ✣ *Moro Rock–Crescent Meadow Rd., 1 mile south of Giant Forest.*

Crescent Meadow

TRAIL | A sea of ferns signals your arrival at what John Muir called the "gem of the Sierra." Walk around for an hour or two, and you might decide that the Scotland-born naturalist was exaggerating a bit, but the verdant meadow is quite pleasant, and you just might see a bear. Wildflowers bloom here throughout the summer. ✉ *Sequoia National Park* ✣ *End of Moro Rock–Crescent Meadow Rd., 2.6 miles east off Generals Hwy.* ☞ *Shuttle: Moro Rock–Crescent Meadow.*

★ Crystal Cave

CAVE | One of more than 200 caves in Sequoia and Kings Canyon, Crystal Cave is composed largely of marble, the result of limestone being hardened under heat and pressure. It contains several eye-popping formations. There used to be more, but some were damaged or obliterated by early-20th-century dynamite blasting. You can see the cave only on a tour. The Daily Tour ($17), a great overview, takes about 50 minutes. To immerse yourself in the cave experience—at times you'll be crawling on your belly—book the exhilarating Wild Cave Tour ($140). Availability is limited—reserve tickets at least 48 hours in advance at 🌐 *www.recreation.gov* or stop by either the Foothills or Lodgepole visitor center first thing in the morning to try to nab a same-day ticket; they're not sold at the cave itself. ✉ *Crystal Cave Rd., off Generals Hwy.* ☎ *877/444–6777*

🌐 www.sequoiaparksconservancy.org/crystalcave.html 🎫 $17 🕓 Closed Oct.–late May.

★ General Sherman Tree

LOCAL INTEREST | The 274.9-foot-tall General Sherman is one of the world's tallest and oldest sequoias, and it ranks No. 1 in volume, adding the equivalent of a 60-foot-tall tree every year to its approximately 52,500 cubic feet of mass. The tree doesn't grow taller, though—it's dead at the top. A short, wheelchair-accessible trail leads to the tree from Generals Highway, but the main trail (½ mile) winds down from a parking lot off Wolverton Road. The walk back up the main trail is steep, but benches along the way provide rest for the short of breath. ✉ *Sequoia National Park* ✥ *Main trail Wolverton Rd. off Generals Hwy. (Rte. 198)* ☞ *Shuttle: Giant Forest or Wolverton–Sherman Tree.*

★ Moro Rock

NATURE SITE | This sight offers panoramic views to those fit and determined enough to mount its 350 or so steps. In a case where the journey rivals the destination, Moro's stone stairway is so impressive in its twisty inventiveness that it's on the National Register of Historic Places. The rock's 6,725-foot summit overlooks the Middle Fork Canyon, sculpted by the Kaweah River and approaching the depth of Arizona's Grand Canyon, although smoggy, hazy air often compromises the view. ✉ *Sequoia National Park* ✥ *Moro Rock–Crescent Meadow Rd., 2 miles east off Generals Hwy. (Rte. 198) to parking area* ☞ *Shuttle: Moro Rock–Crescent Meadow.*

Tunnel Log

LOCAL INTEREST | This 275-foot tree fell in 1937, and soon a 17-foot-wide, 8-foot-high hole was cut through it for vehicular passage (not to mention the irresistible photograph) that continues today. Large vehicles take the nearby bypass. ✉ *Sequoia National Park* ✥ *Moro Rock–Crescent Meadow Rd., 2 miles east of Generals Hwy. (Rte. 198)* ☞ *Shuttle: Moro Rock–Crescent Meadow.*

TRAILS

★ Big Trees Trail

TRAIL | The 0.7-mile, wheelchair-accessible portion of this path is a must, as it does not take long, and the setting is spectacular: beautiful Round Meadow, surrounded by many mature sequoias. Well-thought-out interpretive signs along the way explain the ecology on display. Parking at the trailhead lot off Generals Highway is for cars with handicap placards only. The full, round-trip loop from the Giant Forest Museum is about a mile long. *Easy.* ✉ *Sequoia National Park* ✥ *Trailhead: Off Generals Hwy. (Rte. 198), near the Giant Forest Museum* ☞ *Shuttle: Giant Forest.*

★ Congress Trail

TRAIL | This 2-mile trail, arguably the best hike in the parks in terms of natural beauty, is a paved loop that begins near General Sherman Tree. You'll get close-up views of more big trees here than on any other Sequoia hike. Watch for the clusters known as the House and Senate. The President Tree, also on the trail, supplanted the General Grant Tree in 2012 as the world's second largest in volume (behind the General Sherman). An offshoot of the Congress Trail leads to Crescent Meadow, where, in summer, you can catch a free shuttle back to the Sherman parking lot. *Easy.* ✉ *Sequoia National Park* ✥ *Trailhead: Off Generals Hwy. (Rte. 198), 2 miles north of Giant Forest* ☞ *Shuttle: Giant Forest.*

Crescent Meadow Trails

TRAIL | A 1-mile trail loops around lush Crescent Meadow to Tharp's Log, a cabin built from a fire-hollowed sequoia. From there you can embark on a 60-mile trek to Mt. Whitney, if you're prepared and have the time. Brilliant wildflowers bloom here in midsummer. *Easy.* ✉ *Sequoia National Park* ✥ *Trailhead: The end of Moro Rock–Crescent Meadow Rd., 2.6 miles east* *off Generals Hwy. (Rte. 198)* ☞ *Shuttle: Moro Rock–Crescent Meadow.*

Little Baldy Trail

TRAIL | Climbing 700 vertical feet in 1¾ miles of switchbacking, this trail ends at a granite dome with a great view of the peaks of the Mineral King area and the Great Western Divide. The walk to the summit and back takes about four hours. *Moderate.* ⊠ *Sequoia National Park* ✣ *Trailhead: Little Baldy Saddle, Generals Hwy. (Rte. 198), 9 miles north of General Sherman Tree* ☞ *Shuttle: Lodgepole-Wuksachi-Dorst.*

Marble Falls Trail

TRAIL | The 3.7-mile trail to Marble Falls crosses through the rugged foothills before reaching the cascading water. Plan on three to four hours one-way. *Moderate.* ⊠ *Sequoia National Park* ✣ *Trailhead: Off dirt road across from concrete ditch near site 17 at Potwisha Campground, off Generals Hwy. (Rte. 198).*

Muir Grove Trail

TRAIL | You will attain solitude and possibly see a bear or two on this unheralded gem of a hike, a 4-mile round-trip from the Dorst Creek Campground. The remote grove is small but lovely, its soundtrack provided solely by nature. The trailhead is subtly marked. In summer, park in the amphitheater lot and walk down toward the group campsite area. *Easy.* ⊠ *Sequoia National Park* ✣ *Trailhead: Dorst Creek Campground, Generals Hwy. (Rte. 198), 8 miles north of Lodgepole Visitor Center* ☞ *Shuttle: Lodgepole-Wuksachi-Dorst.*

Tokopah Falls Trail

TRAIL | This trail with a 500-foot elevation gain follows the Marble Fork of the Kaweah River for 1¾ miles one-way and dead-ends below the impressive granite cliffs and cascading waterfall of Tokopah Canyon. The trail passes through a mixed-conifer forest. It takes 2½ to 4 hours to make the round-trip journey. *Moderate.* ⊠ *Sequoia National Park* ✣ *Trailhead: Off Generals Hwy. (Rte. 198), ¼ mile north of Lodgepole Campground* ☞ *Shuttle: Lodgepole-Wuksachi-Dorst.*

VISITOR CENTERS

Lodgepole Visitor Center

INFO CENTER | Along with exhibits on the area's history, geology, and wildlife, the center screens an outstanding 22-minute film about bears. You can buy books, maps, wilderness permits, and tickets to cave tours here. ⊠ *Sequoia National Park* ✣ *Generals Hwy. (Rte. 198), 21 miles north of Ash Mountain entrance* ☎ *559/565–3341* ⏲ *Closed Oct.–Apr.* ☞ *Shuttle: Giant Forest or Wuksachi-Lodgepole-Dorst.*

Restaurants

Lodgepole Market and Café

$$ | **CAFÉ** | The choices here run the gamut from simple to very simple, with several counters only a few strides apart in a central eating complex. The café also sells fresh and prepackaged salads, sandwiches, and wraps. **Known for:** quick and convenient dining; many healthful options; grab-and-go items for picnics. $ *Average main: $12* ⊠ *Next to Lodgepole Visitor Center* ☎ *559/565–3301* 🌐 *www.visitsequoia.com/dine/lodgepole-dining.*

The Peaks

$$$ | **MODERN AMERICAN** | Huge windows run the length of the Wuksachi Lodge's high-ceilinged dining room, and a large fireplace on the far wall warms both body and soul. The diverse dinner menu—by far the best at both parks—reflects a commitment to locally sourced and sustainable products. **Known for:** seasonal menus with fresh local ingredients; great views of sequoia grove; box lunches. $ *Average main: $28* ⊠ *Wuksachi Lodge, 64740 Wuksachi Way, Wuksachi Village* ☎ *559/625–7700* 🌐 *www.visitsequoia.com/dine/the-peaks-restaurant.*

Hotels

★ Wuksachi Lodge

$$$$ | HOTEL | The striking cedar-and-stone main building is a fine example of how a structure can blend effectively with lovely mountain scenery. **Pros:** best place to stay in the parks; lots of wildlife; easy access to hiking and snowshoe/ski trails. **Cons:** rooms can be small; main lodge is a few-minutes' walk from guest rooms; slow Wi-Fi. *$ Rooms from: $229 ✉ 64740 Wuksachi Way, Wuksachi Village ☎ 559/625–7700, 888/252–5757 reservations 🌐 www.visitsequoia.com/lodging/wuksachi-lodge ⇨ 102 rooms 🍴 No meals.*

Mineral King

25 miles east of Generals Hwy. (Rte. 198) via Mineral King Rd.

A subalpine valley of fir, pine, and sequoia trees with myriad lakes and hiking trails, Mineral King sits at 7,500 feet at the end of a steep, winding road. This is the highest point to which you can drive in the park. It is open only from Memorial Day through late October.

Sights

SCENIC DRIVES

Mineral King Road

SCENIC DRIVE | Vehicles longer than 22 feet are prohibited on this side road into southern Sequoia National Park, and for good reason: it's smaller than a regular two-lane road, some sections are unpaved, and it contains 589 twists and turns. Anticipating an average speed of 20 mph is optimistic. The scenery is splendid as you climb nearly 6,000 feet from Three Rivers to the Mineral King Area. In addition to maneuvering the blind curves and narrow stretches, you might find yourself sharing the pavement with bears, rattlesnakes, and even soft-ball-size spiders. Allow 90 minutes each way. *✉ Sequoia National Forest ⊕ East off Sierra Dr. (Rte. 198), 3 ½ miles northeast of Three Rivers ⏲ Road typically closed Nov.–late May.*

TRAILS

Mineral King Trails

TRAIL | Many trails to the high country begin at Mineral King. Two popular day hikes are Eagle Lake (6.8 miles round-trip) and Timber Gap (4.4 miles round-trip). At the Mineral King Ranger Station (☎ *559/565–3768*) you can pick up maps and check about conditions from late May to late September. *Difficult. ✉ Sequoia National Park ⊕ Trailheads: At end of Mineral King Rd., 25 miles east of Generals Hwy. (Rte. 198).*

VISITOR CENTERS

Mineral King Ranger Station

INFO CENTER | The station's small visitor center has exhibits on area history. Wilderness permits and some books and maps are available. *✉ Sequoia National Park ⊕ Mineral King Rd., 24 miles east of Rte. 198 ☎ 559/565–3341 ☞ Typically closed mid-Sept.–mid-May.*

Hotels

Silver City Mountain Resort

$$$ | RESORT | High on Mineral King Road, this privately owned resort has rustic cabins and deluxe chalets—all with a stove, refrigerator, and sink—plus three hotel rooms with private baths. **Pros:** rustic setting; friendly staff; great location for hikers. **Cons:** long, winding road is not for everybody; not much entertainment except hiking; some units have shared baths. *$ Rooms from: $170 ✉ Sequoia National Park ⊕ Mineral King Rd., 21 miles southeast of Rte. 198 ☎ 559/242–3510, 559/561–1322 reservations 🌐 www.silvercityresort.com ⏲ Closed Nov.–late May ⇨ 16 units 🍴 No meals.*

Mt. Whitney

276 miles by car from Sequoia National Park/Foothills Visitor Center (looping around the Sierra Nevada) on U.S. 395, 60 miles on foot (an 8-day trek) along Mt. Whitney Trail.

At 14,494 feet, Mt. Whitney is the highest point in the contiguous United States and the crown jewel of Sequoia National Park's wild eastern side. The peak looms high above the tiny, high-mountain desert community of Lone Pine, where numerous Hollywood Westerns have been filmed. The high mountain ranges, arid landscape, and scrubby brush of the eastern Sierra are beautiful in their vastness and austerity.

Despite the mountain's scale, you can't see it from the more traveled west side of the park because it is hidden behind the Great Western Divide. The only way to access Mt. Whitney from the main part of the park is to circumnavigate the Sierra Nevada via a 10-hour, nearly 400-mile drive outside the park. No road ascends the peak; the best vantage point from which to catch a glimpse of the mountain is at the end of Whitney Portal Road. The 13 miles of winding road leads from U.S. 395 at Lone Pine to the trailhead for the hiking route to the top of the mountain. Whitney Portal Road is closed in winter.

TRAILS

Mt. Whitney Trail

TRAIL | The most popular route to the summit, the Mt. Whitney Trail can be conquered by very fit and experienced hikers. If there's snow on the mountain, this is a challenge for expert mountaineers only. All overnighters must have a permit, as must day hikers on the trail beyond Lone Pine Lake, about 2½ miles from the trailhead. From May through October, permits are distributed via a lottery run each February by *recreation.gov*. The Eastern Sierra Interagency Visitor Center (*760/876–6200*), on Route 136 at U.S. 395 about a mile south of Lone Pine, is a good resource for information about permits and hiking. *Kings Canyon National Park 760/873–2483 trail reservations www.fs.usda.gov/inyo.*

Activities

BIKING

Steep, winding roads and shoulders that are either narrow or nonexistent make bicycling here more of a danger than a pleasure. Outside of campgrounds, you are not allowed to pedal on unpaved roads.

BIRD-WATCHING

More than 200 species of birds inhabit Sequoia and Kings Canyon national parks. Not seen in most parts of the United States, the white-headed woodpecker and the pileated woodpecker are common in most mid-elevation areas here. There are also many hawks and owls, including the renowned spotted owl. Due to the changes in elevation, both parks have diverse species ranging from warblers, kingbirds, thrushes, and sparrows in the foothills to goshawk, blue grouse, red-breasted nuthatch, and brown creeper at the highest elevations. The Sequoia Parks Conservancy (*559/565–4251 www.sequoiaparksconservancy.org*) has information about bird-watching in the southern Sierra.

CAMPING

Some campgrounds are open year-round, others only seasonally. Except for Bearpaw (around $350 a night including meals), fees at the campgrounds range from $22 to $45, depending on location and size. There are no RV hookups at any of the campgrounds. Expect a table and a fire ring with a grill at standard sites. You can make reservations (book as far ahead as possible) at Bearpaw, Dorst Creek, Lodgepole, and Potwisha. The rest are first-come, first-served. The Lodgepole and Dorst Creek campgrounds can be quite busy in the summer and are popular with families. Black bears are prevalent in these areas; carefully follow all posted instructions about food storage. Bear-proof metal containers are provided at many campgrounds.

Atwell Mill Campground. At 6,650 feet, this peaceful, tent-only campground is just south of the Western Divide. ✉ *Mineral King Rd., 20 miles east of Rte. 198* ☎ *559/565–3341.*

Bearpaw High Sierra Camp. Classy camping is the order of the day at this tent hotel and restaurant. Make reservations starting on January 2. ✉ *High Sierra Trail, 11.5 miles from Lodgepole Village* ☎ *866/807–3598* 🌐 *www.visitsequoia.com.*

Buckeye Flat Campground. This tents-only campground at the southern end of Sequoia National Park is smaller—and consequently quieter—than campgrounds elsewhere in the park. Because of its low elevation (2,800 feet), it's hot in summer. ✉ *Generals Hwy., 6 miles north of Foothills Visitor Center* ☎ *559/784–1500.*

Dorst Creek Campground. Wildlife sightings are common at this large campground at elevation 6,700 feet. ✉ *Generals Hwy., 8 miles north of Lodgepole Visitor Center* ☎ *559/565–3341, 877/444–6777.*

Lodgepole Campground. The largest Lodgepole-area campground is also the noisiest, though things quiet down at night. ✉ *Off Generals Hwy. beyond Lodgepole Village* ☎ *559/565–3341, 877/444–6777.*

Potwisha Campground. On the Marble Fork of the Kaweah River, this midsize, year-round campground at an elevation of 2,100 feet gets no snow in winter and can be hot in summer. ✉ *Generals Hwy., 4 miles north of Foothills Visitor Center* ☎ *559/565–3341, 877/444–6777.*

CROSS-COUNTRY SKIING

For a one-of-a-kind experience, cut through the groves of mammoth sequoias in Giant Forest. Some of the Crescent Meadow trails are suitable for skiing as well; none of the trails is groomed. You can park at Giant Forest. Note that roads can be precarious in bad weather. Some advanced trails begin at Wolverton.

Alta Market and Ski Shop

SKIING/SNOWBOARDING | Rent cross-country skis and snowshoes here. Depending on snowfall amounts, instruction may also be available. Reservations are recommended. Marked trails cut through Giant Forest, about 5 miles south of Wuksachi Lodge. ✉ *Sequoia National Park* ✥ *At Lodgepole, off Generals Hwy. (Rte. 198)* ☎ *559/565–3301* ☞ *Shuttle: Wuksachi-Lodgepole-Dorst.*

EDUCATIONAL PROGRAMS

Educational programs at the parks include museum-style exhibits, ranger- and naturalist-led talks and walks, film screenings, and sightseeing tours, most of them conducted by either the park service or the nonprofit Sequoia Parks Conservancy. Exhibits at the visitor centers and the Giant Forest Museum focus on different aspects of the park: its history, wildlife, geology, climate, and vegetation—most notably the giant sequoias. Weekly notices about programs are posted at the visitor centers and elsewhere.

Grant Grove Visitor Center at Kings Canyon National Park has maps of self-guided park tours. Ranger-led walks and programs take place throughout the year in Grant Grove. Cedar Grove and Forest Service campgrounds have activities from Memorial Day to Labor Day. Check bulletin boards or visitor centers for schedules.

Free Nature Programs

WILDLIFE-WATCHING | Almost any summer day, ½-hour to 1½-hour ranger talks and walks explore subjects such as the life of the sequoia, the geology of the park,

Did You Know?

Sequoias once grew throughout the northern hemisphere, until they were almost wiped out by glaciers. Some of the fossils in Arizona's Petrified Forest National Park are extinct sequoia species.

and the habits of bears. Giant Forest Museum, Lodgepole Visitor Center, and Wuksachi Village are frequent starting points. Look for less frequent tours in the winter from Grant Grove. Check bulletin boards throughout the park for the week's offerings. *www.sequoiaparks-conservancy.org.*

Junior Ranger Program

HIKING/WALKING | **FAMILY** | Children over age five can earn a patch upon completion of a fun set of age-appropriate tasks outlined in the Junior Ranger booklet. Pick one up at any visitor center. *559/565–3341.*

Sequoia Parks Conservancy Evening Programs

HIKING/WALKING | The Sequoia Parks Conservancy offers hikes and evening lectures during the summer and winter. The popular Wonders of the Night Sky programs celebrate the often stunning views of the heavens experienced at both parks year-round. *Sequoia National Park* *559/565–4251* *www.sequoiaparksconservancy.org.*

Sequoia Parks Conservancy Seminars

WILDLIFE-WATCHING | Expert naturalists lead seminars on a range of topics, including birds, wildflowers, geology, botany, photography, park history, backpacking, and pathfinding. Reservations are required. Information about times and prices is available at the visitor centers or through the Sequoia Parks Conservancy. *Sequoia National Park* *559/565–4251* *www.sequoiaparksconservancy.org.*

FISHING

There's limited trout fishing in the creeks and rivers from late April to mid-November. The Kaweah River is a popular spot; check at visitor centers for open and closed waters. Some of the park's secluded backcountry lakes have good fishing. A California fishing license, required for persons 16 and older, costs about $16 for one day, $24 for two days, and $48 for 10 days (discounts are available for state residents and others). For park regulations, closures, and restrictions, call the parks at *559/565–3341* or stop at a visitor center. Licenses and fishing tackle are usually available at Hume Lake.

California Department of Fish and Game

FISHING | The department supplies fishing licenses and provides a full listing of regulations. *916/928–5805* *www.wildlife.ca.gov.*

HIKING

The best way to see the park is to hike it. The grandeur and majesty of the Sierra is best seen up close. Carry a hiking map and plenty of water. Visitor center gift shops sell maps and trail books and pamphlets. Check with rangers for current trail conditions, and be aware of rapidly changing weather. As a rule of thumb, plan on covering about a mile per hour.

HORSEBACK RIDING

Grant Grove Stables

HORSEBACK RIDING | Grant Grove Stables isn't too far from parts of Sequoia National Park and is perfect for short rides from June to September. Reservations are recommended. *559/335–9292 summer* *www.nps.gov/seki/planyourvisit/horseride.htm* *From $50.*

Horse Corral Packers

HORSEBACK RIDING | One- and two-hour trips through Sequoia are available for beginning and advanced riders. *Big Meadow Rd., 12 miles east of Generals Hwy. (Rte. 198) between Sequoia and Kings Canyon national parks* *559/565–3404 summer, 559/565–6429 off-season,* *hcpacker.com* *From $50.*

SLEDDING AND SNOWSHOEING

The Wolverton area, on Generals Highway (Route 198) near Giant Forest, is a popular sledding spot, where sleds, inner tubes, and platters are allowed. You can buy sleds and saucers, with prices starting at $15, at the Alta Market and Ski Shop (*559/565–3301*) at the Lodgepole Visitor Center. The shop also rents snowshoes ($18–$24). Naturalists lead snowshoe walks around Giant Forest and Wuksachi Lodge, conditions permitting, on Saturday and holidays. Make reservations and check schedules at Giant Forest Museum (☎ *559/565–3341*) or Wuksachi Lodge.

Kings Canyon National Park

Kings Canyon National Park consists of two sections that adjoin the northern boundary of Sequoia National Park. The western portion, covered with sequoia and pine forest, contains the park's most visited sights, such as Grant Grove. The vast eastern portion is remote high country, slashed across half its southern breadth by the deep, rugged Kings River canyon. Separating the two is Sequoia National Forest, which encompasses Giant Sequoia National Monument. The Kings Canyon Scenic Byway (Route 180) links the major sights within and between the park's two sections.

Grant Grove Village—Redwood Canyon

56 miles east of Fresno on Rte. 180, 26 miles north of Lodgepole Village in Sequoia National Park.

Grant Grove Village, home to the Kings Canyon Visitor Center, Grant Grove Cabins, John Muir Lodge, a market, and two restaurants, anchors the northwestern section of the park. Nearby attractions include the General Grant Tree and Redwood Canyon sequia grove. The Kings Canyon Scenic Byway begins here and travels 30 miles down to the Kings River Canyon and Cedar Grove.

HISTORIC SIGHTS

Fallen Monarch

TOUR—SIGHT | This toppled sequoia's hollow base was used in the second half of the 19th century as a home for settlers, a saloon, and even a U.S. Cavalry stable. As you walk through it (assuming entry is permitted, which is not always the case), notice how little the wood has decayed, and imagine yourself tucked safely inside, sheltered from a storm or protected from the searing heat. ✉ *Kings Canyon National Park* ✣ *Grant Grove Trail, 1 mile north of Kings Canyon Park Visitor Center.*

Gamlin Cabin

BUILDING | Despite being listed on the National Register of Historic Places, this replica of a modest 1872 pioneer cabin is only borderline historical. The structure, which was moved and rebuilt several times over the years, once served as U.S. Cavalry storage space and, in the early 20th century, a ranger station. ✉ *Grant Grove Trail.*

SCENIC DRIVES

★ **Kings Canyon Scenic Byway**

SCENIC DRIVE | The 30-mile stretch of Route 180 between Grant Grove Village and Zumwalt Meadow delivers eye-popping scenery—granite cliffs, a roaring river, waterfalls, and Kings River canyon itself—much of which you can experience at vista points or on easy walks. The canyon comes into view about 10 miles east of the village at **Junction View.** Five miles beyond, at **Yucca Point,** the canyon is thousands of feet deeper than the more famous Grand Canyon. **Canyon View,** a special spot 1 mile east of the Cedar Grove Village turnoff, showcases evidence of the area's glacial history. Here, perhaps more than anywhere else, you'll understand why John Muir compared Kings Canyon vistas with those in Yosemite. ■ **TIP→ Note that this byway is a dead-end road—you have to turn around and head back the way you came.**

The drive takes about an hour each way without stops. ✉ *Kings Canyon National Park* ✣ *Rte. 180 north and east of Grant Grove village.*

SCENIC STOPS

Boyden Cavern

NATURE SITE | The Kings River has carved out hundreds of caverns, including Boyden, which brims with stalagmite, stalactite, drapery, flowstone, and other formations. In summer, the Bat Grotto shelters a slew of bats. If you can't make it to Crystal Cave in Sequoia, Boyden is a reasonable substitute. Regular tours take about 45 minutes and start with a steep walk uphill. ✉ *Sequoia National Forest, 74101 E. Kings Canyon Rd. (Rte. 180), between Grant Grove and Cedar Grove* ☎ *888/965–8243* 🌐 *boydencavern.com* 🎫 *$16.*

General Grant Tree

LOCAL INTEREST | President Coolidge proclaimed this to be the "nation's Christmas tree," and, 30 years later, President Eisenhower designated it as a living shrine to all Americans who have died in wars. Bigger at its base than the General Sherman Tree, it tapers more quickly. It's estimated to be the world's third-largest sequoia by volume. A spur trail winds behind the tree, where scars from a long-ago fire remain visible. ✉ *Kings Canyon National Park* ✣ *Trailhead: 1 mile north of Grant Grove Visitor Center.*

Project Survival's Cat Haven

ZOO | Take the rare opportunity to glimpse a Siberian lynx, a clouded leopard, a Bengal tiger, and other endangered wild cats at this conservation facility that shelters more than 30 big cats. A guided hour-long tour along a ¼-mile walkway leads to fenced habitat areas shaded by trees and overlooking the Central Valley. ✉ *38257 E. Kings Canyon Rd. (Rte. 180), 15 miles west of Kings Canyon National Park, Dunlap* ☎ *559/338–3216* 🌐 *cathaven.com* 🎫 *$15* ⏲ *Closed Tues. May–Sept. Closed Tues. and Wed. Oct.–Apr.*

Redwood Mountain Sequoia Grove

FOREST | One of the world's largest sequoia groves, Redwood contains within its 2,078 acres nearly 2,200 specimens whose diameters exceed 10 feet. You can view the grove from afar at an overlook or hike 6 to 10 miles via moderate loop trails down into the richest regions, which include two of the world's 25 heaviest trees. ✉ *Kings Canyon National Park* ✣ *Drive 6 miles south of Grant Grove on Generals Hwy. (Rte. 198), then turn right at Quail Flat; follow it 2 miles to the Redwood Canyon trailhead.*

TRAILS

Big Baldy Trail

TRAIL | This hike climbs 600 feet and 2 miles up to the 8,209-foot summit of Big Baldy. Your reward is the view of Redwood Canyon. Round-trip, the hike is 4 miles. *Moderate.* ✉ *Kings Canyon National Park* ✣ *Trailhead: 8 miles south of Grant Grove on Generals Hwy. (Rte. 198).*

Big Stump Trail

TRAIL | From 1883 until 1890, logging was done here, complete with a mill. The 1-mile loop trail, whose unmarked beginning is a few yards west of the Big Stump entrance, passes by many enormous stumps. *Easy.* ✉ *Kings Canyon National Park* ✣ *Trailhead: Near Big Stump Entrance, Generals Hwy. (Rte. 180).*

Buena Vista Peak Trail

TRAIL | For a 360-degree view of Redwood Canyon and the High Sierra, make the 2-mile ascent to Buena Vista. *Difficult.* ✉ *Kings Canyon National Park* ✣ *Trailhead: Off Generals Hwy. (Rte. 198), south of Kings Canyon Overlook, 7 miles southeast of Grant Grove.*

★ Grant Grove Trail

TRAIL | Grant Grove is only 128 acres, but it's a big deal. More than 120 sequoias here have a base diameter that exceeds 10 feet, and the **General Grant Tree** is the world's third-largest sequoia by volume. Nearby, the Confederacy is represented by the **Robert E. Lee Tree,** recognized as the world's 11th-largest sequoia. Also along the easy-to-walk trail are the **Fallen Monarch** and the **Gamlin Cabin,** built by 19th-century pioneers. *Easy.* ✉ *Kings Canyon National Park* ✣ *Trailhead: Off Generals Hwy. (Rte. 180), 1 mile north of Kings Canyon Park Visitor Center.*

Panoramic Point Trail

TRAIL | You'll get a nice view of whale-shape Hume Lake from the top of this Grant Grove path, which is paved and only 300 feet long. It's fairly steep—strollers might work here, but not wheelchairs. Trailers and RVs are not permitted on the steep and narrow road that leads to the trailhead parking lot. *Moderate.* ✉ *Kings Canyon National Park* ✣ *Trailhead: At end of Panoramic Point Rd., 2.3 miles from Grant Grove Village.*

Redwood Canyon Trails

TRAIL | Two main trails lead into Redwood Canyon grove, the world's largest sequoia grove. The 6.5-mile **Hart Tree and Fallen Goliath Loop** passes by a 19th-century logging site, pristine Hart Meadow, and the hollowed-out Tunnel Tree before accessing a side trail to the grove's largest sequoia, the 277.9-foot-tall Hart Tree. The 6.4-mile **Sugar Bowl Loop** provides views of Redwood Mountain and Big Baldy before winding down into its namesake, a thick grove of mature and young sequoias. *Moderate.* ✉ *Kings Canyon National Park* ✣ *Trailhead: Off Quail Flat. Drive 5 miles south of Grant Grove on Generals Hwy. (Rte. 198), turn right at Quail Flat and proceed 1½ miles to trailhead.*

VISITOR CENTERS

Kings Canyon Visitor Center

INFO CENTER | The center's 15-minute film and various exhibits provide an overview of the park's canyon, sequoias, and human history. Books, maps, and weather advice are dispensed here, as are (if available) $15 wilderness permits. ✉ *Kings Canyon National Park* ✣ *Grant Grove Village, Generals Hwy. (Rte. 198), 3 miles northeast of Rte. 180, Kings Canyon National Park entrance at Big Stump* ☎ *559/565–3341.*

Restaurants

Grant Grove Restaurant

$$ | **AMERICAN** | Gaze at giant sequoias and a verdant meadow while enjoying a meal in this eco-friendly restaurant's spacious dining room with a fireplace or on its expansive deck. The menu centers around locally sourced natural and organic ingredients and offers standard American fare. **Known for:** takeout service year-round; walk-up window for pizza, sandwiches, coffee, ice cream; picnic tables on outdoor deck. $ *Average main: $16* ✉ *Grant Grove Village* ☎ *559/335–5500.*

Hotels

Grant Grove Cabins

$$ | **HOTEL** | Some of the wood-panel cabins here have heaters, electric lights, and private baths, but most have woodstoves, battery lamps, and shared baths. **Pros:** warm, woodsy feel; clean; walk to Grant Grove Restaurant. **Cons:** can be difficult to walk up to if you're not in decent physical shape; costly for what you get; only basic amenities. $ *Rooms from: $135* ✉ *Kings Canyon Scenic Byway in Grant Grove Village* ☎ *866/807–3598* 🌐 *www.visitsequoia.com/Grant-Grove-Cabins.aspx* *50 units* *No meals.*

John Muir Lodge

$$$$ | **HOTEL** | In a wooded area in the hills above Grant Grove Village, this modern, timber-sided lodge has rooms and suites with queen- or king-size beds and private baths. **Pros:** open year-round; common room stays warm; quiet. **Cons:** check-in is down in the village; spotty Wi-Fi; remote location. $ *Rooms from: $210* ✉ *Kings Canyon Scenic Byway, ¼ mile north of Grant Grove Village, 86728 Hwy. 180* ☎ *866/807–3598* 🌐 *www.*

visitsequoia.com/john-muir-lodge.aspx *36 rooms* *No meals.*

Montecito-Sequoia Lodge
$$$$ | HOTEL | FAMILY | Outdoor activities are what this year-round family resort is all about, including many that are geared toward teenagers and small children. **Pros:** friendly staff; great for kids; lots of fresh air and planned activities. **Cons:** can be noisy with all the activity; no TVs or phones in rooms; not within national park. *Rooms from: $229* *63410 Generals Hwy., 11 miles south of Grant Grove, Sequoia National Forest* *559/565–3388, 800/227–9900* *www.mslodge.com* *Closed 1st 2 wks of Dec.* *52 rooms* *All meals.*

Cedar Grove

35 miles east of Grant Grove Village.

The Cedar Grove section of Kings Canyon National Park bears many similarities to Yosemite Valley: a mighty river flowing through a verdant valley, ringed by massive glacier-hewn granite cliffs that loom several thousand feet above. Drive along the Kings Canyon Scenic Byway to access this relatively uncrowded wonderland, where you can hike excellent backcountry trails, stroll around lush Zumwalt Meadows, and take a break in Cedar Grove Village.

Sights

HISTORIC SIGHTS

Knapp's Cabin
BUILDING | Stop here not so much for the cabin itself, but as an excuse to ogle the scenery. George Knapp, a Santa Barbara businessman, stored gear in this small wooden structure when he commissioned fishing trips into the canyon in the 1920s. *Kings Canyon National Park* *Kings Canyon Scenic Byway, 2 miles east of Cedar Grove Village turnoff.*

TRAILS

Hotel Creek Trail
TRAIL | For gorgeous canyon views, take this trail from Cedar Grove up a series of switchbacks until it splits. Follow the route left through chaparral to the forested ridge and rocky outcrop known as Cedar Grove Overlook, where you can see the Kings River canyon stretching below. This strenuous, 5-mile round-trip hike gains 1,200 feet and takes three to four hours to complete. *Difficult.* *Kings Canyon National Park* *Trailhead: At Cedar Grove Pack Station, 1 mile east of Cedar Grove Village.*

Mist Falls Trail
TRAIL | This sandy trail follows the glaciated South Fork Canyon through forest and chaparral, past several rapids and cascades, to one of the largest waterfalls in the two parks. Nine miles round-trip, the hike is relatively flat, but climbs 600 feet in the last 2 miles. It takes from four to five hours to complete. *Moderate.* *Kings Canyon National Park* *Trailhead: At end of Kings Canyon Scenic Byway, 5½ miles east of Cedar Grove Village.*

Roaring River Falls Walk
TRAIL | Take a shady five-minute walk to this forceful waterfall that rushes through a narrow granite chute. The trail is paved and mostly accessible. *Easy.* *Kings Canyon National Park* *Trailhead: 3 miles east of Cedar Grove Village turnoff from Kings Canyon Scenic Byway.*

★ **Zumwalt Meadow Trail**
TRAIL | Rangers say this is the best (and most popular) day hike in the Cedar Grove area. Just 1½ miles long, it offers three visual treats: the South Fork of the Kings River, the lush meadow, and the high granite walls above, including those of Grand Sentinel and North Dome. *Easy.* *Kings Canyon National Park* *Trailhead: 4½ miles east of Cedar Grove Village turnoff from Kings Canyon Scenic Byway.*

VISITOR CENTERS

Cedar Grove Visitor Center

INFO CENTER | Off the main road and behind the Sentinel Campground, this small ranger station has books and maps, plus information about hikes and other activities. ✉ *Kings Canyon National Park* ✣ *Kings Canyon Scenic Byway, 30 miles east of Rte. 180/198 junction* ☎ *559/565–3341* ⏲ *Closed mid-Sept.–mid-May.*

Restaurants

Cedar Grove Grill

$$ | **AMERICAN** | The menu here is surprisingly extensive, with dinner entrées such as pasta, pork chops, trout, and steak. For breakfast, try the egg burrito, French toast, or pancakes; sandwiches, wraps, burgers (including vegetarian patties) and hot dogs dominate the lunch choices. **Known for:** scenic river views; extensive options; alfresco dining on balcony overlooking the Kings River. $ *Average main: $16* ✉ *Cedar Grove Village* ☎ *886/807–3598* 🌐 *www.visitsequoia.com/dine/cedar-grove-grill* ⏲ *Closed Oct.–May.*

Hotels

Cedar Grove Lodge

$$ | **HOTEL** | Backpackers like to stay here on the eve of long treks into the High Sierra wilderness, so bedtimes tend to be early. **Pros:** a definite step up from camping in terms of comfort; great base camp for outdoor adventures; on-site snack bar. **Cons:** impersonal; not everybody agrees it's clean enough; remote location. $ *Rooms from: $147* ✉ *Kings Canyon Scenic Byway* ☎ *866/807–3598* 🌐 *www.visitsequoia.com/lodging/cedar-grove-lodge* ⏲ *Closed mid-Oct.–mid-May* *21 rooms* *No meals.*

Activities

BIKING

Bicycles are allowed only on the paved roads in Kings Canyon. Cyclists should be extremely cautious along the steep highways and narrow shoulders.

CAMPING

Campgrounds in Kings Canyon occupy wonderful settings, with lots of shade and nearby hiking trails. All are first-come, first-served, and the campgrounds around Grant Grove get busy in summer with vacationing families. Keep in mind that this is black-bear country and carefully follow posted instructions about storing food. Bear-proof metal containers are provided at many campgrounds.

Azalea Campground. Of the three campgrounds in the Grant Grove area, Azalea is the only one open year-round. It sits at 6,500 feet amid giant sequoias. ✉ *Kings Canyon Scenic Byway, ¼ mile north of Grant Grove Village* ☎ *559/565–3341.*

Canyon View Campground. The smallest and most primitive of four campgrounds near Cedar Grove, this one is near the start of the Don Cecil Trail, which leads to Lookout Point. The elevation of the camp is 4,600 feet along the Kings River. There are no wheelchair-accessible sites. ✉ *Off Kings Canyon Scenic Byway, ½-mile east of Cedar Grove Village* ☎ *No phone.*

Crystal Springs Campground. Near the Grant Grove Village and the towering sequoias, this camp is at 6,500 feet. There are accessible sites here. ✉ *Off Generals Hwy. (Rte. 198), ¼ mile north of Grant Grove Visitor Center* ☎ *No phone.*

Sentinel Campground. At 4,600 feet and within walking distance of Cedar Grove Village, Sentinel fills up fast in summer. ✉ *Kings Canyon Scenic Byway, ¼ mile west of Cedar Grove Village* ☎ *559/565–3341.*

Sheep Creek Campground. Of the overflow campgrounds, this is one of the prettiest. ✉ *Off Kings Canyon Scenic Byway, 1 mile west of Cedar Grove Village* ☎ *No phone.*

Sunset Campground. Many of the easiest trails through Grant Grove are adjacent to this large camp, near the giant sequoias at 6,500 feet. ✉ *Off Generals Hwy., near Grant Grove Visitor Center* ☎ *No phone.*

CROSS-COUNTRY SKIING

Roads to Grant Grove are accessible even during heavy snowfall, making the trails here a good choice over Sequoia's Giant Forest when harsh weather hits.

Grant Grove Ski Touring Center

SKIING/SNOWBOARDING | The Grant Grove Market doubles as the ski-touring center, where you can rent cross-country skis or snowshoes in winter. This is a good starting point for a number of marked trails, including the Panoramic Point Trail and the General Grant Tree Trail. ✉ *Grant Grove Market, Generals Hwy. (Rte. 198), 3 miles northeast of Rte. 180, Big Stump entrance* ☎ *559/335–5500* 🌐 *www.visitsequoia.com/cross-country-skiing.aspx* 🎫 *From $15.*

FISHING

There is limited trout fishing in the park from late April to mid-November, and catches are minor. Still, Kings River is a popular spot. Some of the park's secluded backcountry lakes have good fishing. Licenses are available, along with fishing tackle, in Grant Grove and Cedar Grove. *See Activities, in Sequoia National Park for more information about licenses.*

HIKING

You can enjoy many of Kings Canyon's sights from your car, but the giant gorge of the Kings River canyon and the sweeping vistas of some of the highest mountains in the United States are best seen on foot. Carry a hiking map—available at any visitor center—and plenty of water. Check with rangers for current trail conditions, and be aware of rapidly changing weather. Except for one trail to Mt. Whitney, permits are not required for day hikes.

Roads End Permit Station

INFO CENTER | You can obtain wilderness permits, maps, and information about the backcountry at this station, where bear canisters, a must for campers, can be rented or purchased. When the station is closed (typically October–mid-May), complete a self-service permit form. ✉ *Kings Canyon National Park* ✣ *Eastern end of Kings Canyon Scenic Byway, 6 miles east of Cedar Grove Visitor Center.*

HORSEBACK RIDING

One-day destinations by horseback out of Cedar Grove include Mist Falls and Upper Bubb's Creek. In the backcountry, many equestrians head for Volcanic Lakes or Granite Basin, ascending trails that reach elevations of 10,000 feet. Costs per person range from $40 for a one-hour guided ride to around $300 per day for fully guided trips for which the packers do all the cooking and camp chores.

Cedar Grove Pack Station

HORSEBACK RIDING | Take a day ride or plan a multiday adventure along the Kings River canyon with Cedar Grove Pack Station. Popular routes include the Rae Lakes Loop and Monarch Divide. Closed early September–late May. ✉ *Kings Canyon National Park* ✣ *Kings Canyon Scenic Byway, 1 mile east of Cedar Grove Village* ☎ *559/565–3464 summer, 559/337–2413 off-season* 🌐 *www.nps.gov/seki/planyourvisit/horseride.htm* 🎫 *From $50 per hr or $90 per day.*

Grant Grove Stables

HORSEBACK RIDING | A one- or two-hour trip through Grant Grove leaving from the stables provides a taste of horseback riding in Kings Canyon. The stables are closed October–early June. ✉ *Kings Canyon National Park* ✣ *Rte. 180, ½ mile north of Grant Grove Visitor Center* ☎ *559/335–9292* 🌐 *www.nps.gov/seki/planyourvisit/horseride.htm* 🎫 *From $50 per hr, $90 for 2 hrs.*

SLEDDING AND SNOWSHOEING

In winter, Kings Canyon has a few great places to play in the snow. Sleds, inner tubes, and platters are allowed at both the Azalea Campground area on Grant Tree Road, ¼ mile north of Grant Grove Visitor Center, and at the Big Stump picnic area, 2 miles north of the lower Route 180 entrance to the park.

Snowshoeing is good around Grant Grove, where you can take occasional naturalist-guided snowshoe walks from mid-December through mid-March as conditions permit. Grant Grove Market rents sleds and snowshoes.

What's Nearby

Numerous towns and cities tout themselves as "gateways" to the parks, with some more deserving of the title than others. One that certainly merits the name is **Three Rivers,** a Sierra foothills hamlet (population 2,200) that's along the Kaweah River and close to Sequoia's Ash Mountain and Lookout Point entrances.

Visalia, a Central Valley city of about 128,000 people, lies 58 miles southwest of Sequoia's Wuksachi Village and 56 miles southwest of the Kings Canyon Park Visitor Center. Its vibrant downtown contains several good restaurants. If you're into Victorian and other old houses, drop by the visitor center and pick up a free map of them. A clear day's view of the Sierra from Main Street is spectacular, and even Sunday night can find the streets bustling with pedestrians. Visalia provides easy access to grand Sequoia National Park and the serene Kaweah Oaks Preserve.

Closest to Kings Canyon's Big Stump entrance, **Fresno,** the main gateway to the southern Sierra region, is about 55 miles west of Kings Canyon and about 85 miles northwest of Wuksachi Village. This Central Valley city of nearly a half-million people is sprawling and unglamorous, but it has all the cultural and other amenities you'd expect of a major crossroads.

Chapter 55

SHENANDOAH NATIONAL PARK

Updated by
Erin Gifford

Camping	Hotels	Activities	Scenery	Crowds
★★★★☆	★★★★☆	★★★☆☆	★★★★★	★★★★☆

WELCOME TO SHENANDOAH NATIONAL PARK

TOP REASONS TO GO

★ **Scenic drives:** Motor along famed Skyline Drive for scenic pull-offs, like Range View Overlook (milepost 17.1) and Spitler Knoll Overlook (milepost 48.0), for sweeping views across the majestic Shenandoah Valley.

★ **Hiking:** More than 500 miles of forested hiking trails crisscross Shenandoah National Park, including 101 miles of the iconic white-blazed Appalachian Trail.

★ **Amazing vistas:** Savor far-reaching vistas aplenty from atop high points at leading park destinations, like Bearfence Mountain and Mary's Rock.

★ **History:** Historical remains, like family cemeteries and homestead ruins, can be found across the park, as can restored structures like President Herbert Hoover's former summer retreat, Rapidan Camp.

★ **Wildlife:** It's not uncommon to see a black bear in the woods just off a hiking trail. The park is also known for white-tailed deer and fox squirrels, as well as the rare Shenandoah Salamander.

1 North District. Many visitors race through this quiet section to reach the more popular Central District, but slow down for historic cemeteries and homesteads, as well as the tallest waterfall in the park, Overall Run Falls.

2 Central District. The bustling Central District is home to the park's only lodges and restaurants, as well as two campgrounds and four picnic grounds. You'll also find horseback trail rides and spectacular hikes, like Old Rag and Little Stony Man Cliffs.

3 South District. The mountainous South District has few services, allowing for a greater sense of peace and tranquillity across the quiet hiking trails. Still, you'll find tumbling waterfalls and far-reaching views from Blackrock Summit.

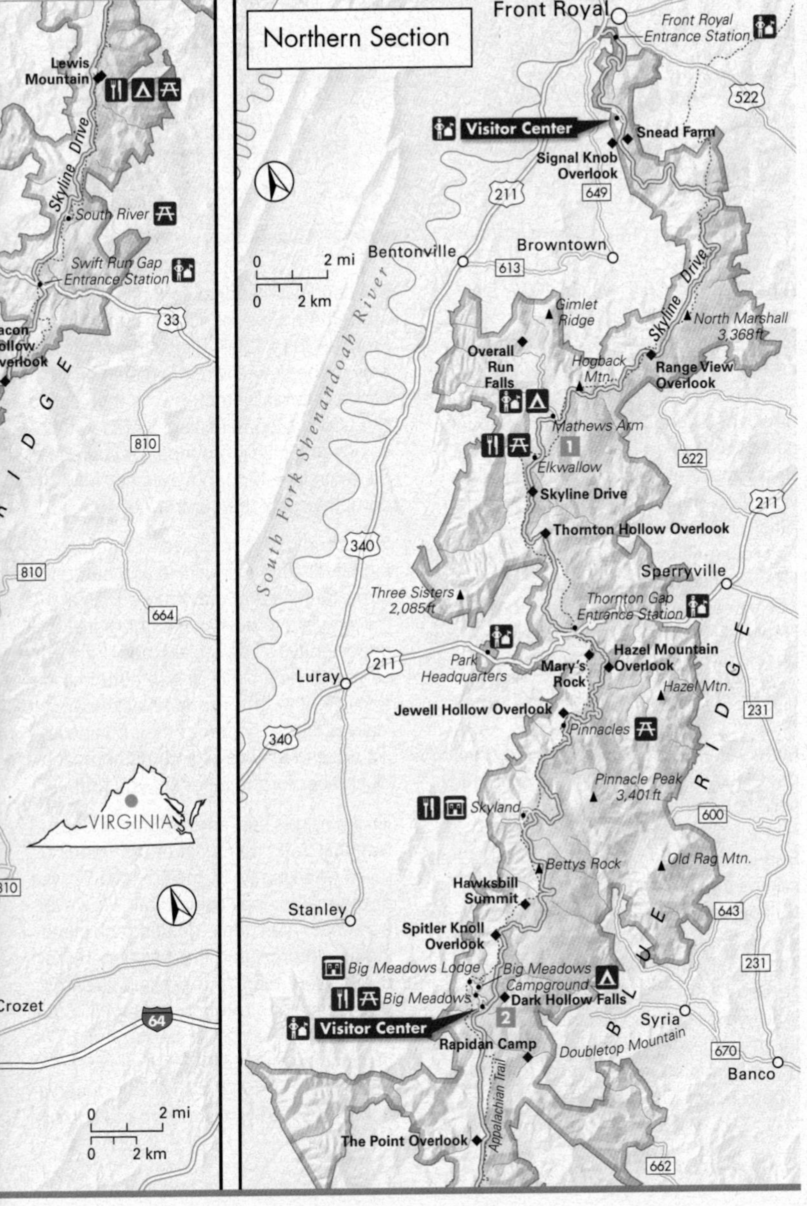
Northern Section
Front Royal
Front Royal Entrance Station
522
Visitor Center
Snead Farm
Signal Knob Overlook
649
211
Bentonville
Browntown
613
0 2 mi
0 2 km
South Fork Shenandoah River
Gimlet Ridge
North Marshall 3,368 ft
Skyline Drive
Overall Run Falls
Hogback Mtn.
Range View Overlook
Mathews Arm
1
Elkwallow
622
Skyline Drive
211
Thornton Hollow Overlook
340
Sperryville
Three Sisters 2,085 ft
Thornton Gap Entrance Station
Park Headquarters
211
Luray
Mary's Rock
Hazel Mountain Overlook
Hazel Mtn.
Jewell Hollow Overlook
231
Pinnacles
340
Pinnacle Peak 3,401 ft
Skyland
600
Bettys Rock
Old Rag Mtn.
Hawksbill Summit
Stanley
643
Spitler Knoll Overlook
Big Meadows Lodge
Big Meadows Campground
231
Big Meadows
Dark Hollow Falls
2
Visitor Center
Syria
Rapidan Camp
Doubletop Mountain
670
Banco
Appalachian Trail
The Point Overlook
662
BLUE RIDGE
Lewis Mountain
Skyline Drive
South River
Swift Run Gap Entrance Station
33
Bacon Hollow Overlook
RIDGE
810
810
664
VIRGINIA
810
Crozet
64
0 2 mi
0 2 km

Perched between the majestic Shenandoah Valley and the lush rolling hills of Virginia's Piedmont region, visitors to Shenandoah National Park are transported into breathtaking hollows, ridges, meadows, peaks, and farmland across this 197,439-acre national park.

Authorized by Congress in 1926, Shenandoah National Park officially came to be on December 26, 1935, in part to create more parks east of the Mississippi River. Before the first visitors arrived, however, Shenandoah National Park served as a one-time summer home to 31st President Herbert Hoover and his wife, Lou Henry Hoover. Upon leaving office, Hoover donated the 164-acre hemlock-enclosed retreat to the National Park Service for incorporation into the soon-to-be-established Shenandoah National Park. In 1988, Camp Hoover was designated a National Historic Landmark.

Located in Virginia's Blue Ridge Mountains, this long, narrow park has a storied history that extends well beyond President Hoover. Native Americans hunted and gathered on the land long before the first European settlers arrived. The name Shenandoah even has Native American origins and is said to mean either "beautiful daughter of the stars" or "spruce river" as it refers to the flowing Shenandoah River. By the 1930s, the land was well settled by some 400 homestead families who were later nudged into resettlement communities set up by Rural Resettlement Administration in order to further create this national park.

Shenandoah National Park has a long and storied African-American history, too. From 1939 to 1950, Blacks were allowed only in the Lewis Mountain section of park's Central District. It was then called the Lewis Mountain Negro Area with cabins and picnic grounds. Desegration began in late-1945, but was not fully complete until the summer of 1950.

While the park does have an interesting history, it's the wildlife and nature opportunities that draw more than a million visitors every year. For many, the opportunity to see a black bear lumbering across Skyline Drive or a forested hiking trail is a highlight. Though black bears typically prefer to go about their business, it's wise to stay calm and not approach a black bear for the safety of you both.

Hiking reigns supreme at Shenandoah National Park, thanks to more than 500 miles of hiking trails, including 101 miles of the iconic Appalachian Trail. However, horseback trail rides, guided rock climbing adventures, and trout fishing in the park's more than 70 mountain streams provide lifelong memories as well. But a leisurely drive along famed Skyline Drive, a scenic byway built by the young men of the Depression-era Civilian Conservation Corps, wows visitors young and old,

AVERAGE HIGH/LOW TEMPERATURES					
JAN.	**FEB.**	**MAR.**	**APR.**	**MAY**	**JUNE**
35/17	38/20	46/26	56/36	64/45	72/53
JULY	**AUG.**	**SEPT.**	**OCT.**	**NOV.**	**DEC.**
75/57	74/56	68/50	58/39	48/31	39/22

especially in October when the foliage is bursting with vibrant ambers and golds.

Planning

When to Go

Shenandoah National Park is visited by some 1.5 million visitors each year, many of whom come in October to see the brilliant foliage. If you can, go early in the day or on weekdays to avoid inching along Skyline Drive, the park's famed scenic byway. The other seasons charm visitors, too. In spring and summer, the park is teeming with wildflowers, like violets, trillium, azaleas, and mountain laurel. Goldenrods and asters reign in late-summer and welcome visitors into fall. In winter, the park enchants with frozen waterfalls and wildlife tracks on freshly-fallen snow. Skyline Drive can be disagreeable, often closed in winter due to ice, snow, even fallen tree branches. Before you leave for the park, call the park's phone line at ☎ *540/999–3500* to confirm the current status.

FESTIVALS AND EVENTS

Night Sky Festival. The wildly popular Night Sky Festival takes place across three nights in mid-August, allowing visitors an opportunity for pure unadulterated stargazing. Park rangers are on hand with super-size telescopes for ranger chats, kids' activities and presentations on such topics as weather in space and the future of space exploration. Kids ages 5–12 can become earn special Junior Ranger Night Explorer status by completing an activity book available at visitor centers.

Getting Here and Around

There are four entrances to the park, with the northernmost at Front Royal off I–66 and Route 340 and the southernmost at Rockfish Gap, off I–64 and Route 250. Rockfish Gap is also the northernmost entrance to the Blue Ridge Parkway. In between, you can access the park at Thornton Gap via Route 211 and Swift Run Gap via Route 33. Mileposts begin at 0.0 at the Front Royal entrance and continue to 105 at the southern end. If you're traveling with an RV, camping trailer, or horse trailer, you'll have to shift into low gear frequently and make sure you can clear Mary's Rock Tunnel (12 feet 8 inches), south of Thornton Gap.

AIR

The nearest major airport is Washington Dulles International Airport (IAD) in Loudoun County, Virginia. It's a one-hour drive to the park's Front Royal entrance.

CAR

It can take three hours to drive the length of Skyline Drive, the 105-mile road that stretches from the top of the park at the Front Royal entrance, to the bottom of the park at the Rockfish Gap entrance. **■ TIP→ The speed limit within the park is 35 mph; and if you get a speeding ticket from park police, it's a federal offense.** There are more than 75 scenic overlooks along Skyline Drive that offer dramatic and far-reaching vistas.

Shenandoah's North District is 70 miles from Washington, DC via U.S. Route 66, accessible by way of the Front Royal entrance. From Richmond, it's a 93-mile drive along State Route 64 to enter the park's South District at the Rockfish Gap entrance.

Two park entrances in the Central District enable visitors to drive into the park from the east and west. On State Route 211, the park's Thornton Gap entrance is 10 miles east of Luray and 8 miles west of Sperryville. Further south, drive 25 miles east from Harrisonburg on State Route 33 to enter by way of the park's Swift Run Gap entrance.

SHUTTLE

There are no authorized shuttle providers in the park.

Park Essentials

ACCESSIBILITY

All visitor centers, restrooms, and park buildings are accessible, as are some sites at all campgrounds and picnic grounds. Accessible lodging is available at Big Meadows Lodge, Skyland, and Lewis Mountain. The Limberlost Trail is the only fully accessible trail in the park. Portable assistive listening devices are available at visitor centers for ranger-led programs and park films.

PARK FEES AND PERMITS

The entrance fee is $30 per private vehicle and is valid for seven days from the date of entry. Entry by motorcycle is $25; walk-up entry on foot or bicycle is $15. Mandatory backcountry camping permits are free and are good for up to 14 consecutive nights. Apply for a permit online at 🌐 *nps.gov/shen* or self-register for a permit at entrance stations, Appalachian Trail entry points, the Old Rag parking area, or Loft Mountain Wayside. All state residents 16 and older must hold a valid state fishing license to fish in the park.

PARK HOURS

Shenandoah National Park is open all day, every day. However, all or portions of Skyline Drive may close in winter due to inclement driving conditions. Most in-park facilities, including visitor centers, campgrounds, lodging, and food services begin to open in March and close for the season by late-November. The park is in the Eastern time zone.

CELL PHONE RECEPTION

Cell phone reception is largely non-existent in the park's North and Central Districts, and spotty at best in the South District. There is potential to achieve a bar or two of cell service at the summits of higher-elevation trails.

Hotels

There are two full-service historic lodges located in the park's Central District. Skyland sits at the top of Skyline Drive at milepost 41.7, while Big Meadows Lodge is at milepost 51. Both offer traditional mountain lodge rooms and detached small cabins, including pet-friendly rooms.

Restaurants

Restaurants are located at both lodges in the park. At Skyland, Pollock Dining Room and Mountain Taproom are both inside the lodge. Spottswood Dining Room and New Market Taproom are a short walk from Big Meadows Lodge.

There are also three quick-serve food stops for grab-and-go sandwiches, salads and snacks, including Elkwallow Wayside (milepost 24.1), Big Meadows Wayside (milepost 51), and Loft Mountain Wayside (milepost 79.5).

HOTEL AND RESTAURANT PRICES

Hotel prices in the reviews are the lowest cost of a standard double room in high season. Restaurant prices in the reviews are the average cost of a main course at dinner, or if dinner is not served, at lunch.

What It Costs

	$	$$	$$$	$$$$
RESTAURANTS				
	under $16	$16–$22	$23–$30	over $30
HOTELS				
	under $120	$120–$180	$181–$240	over $240

Tours

Rapidan Camp Tour

GUIDED TOURS | From late-spring through late-fall, Shenandoah National Park offers 2.5-hour ranger-led tours of Rapidan Camp, the beloved 164-acre summer retreat of President Herbert Hoover and First Lady Lou Henry Hoover. The ranger tour includes an inside look at the president's personal cabin, Brown House, and Prime Minister's Cabin. Both have been historically restored. Tours are offered twice-daily four days a week (Thursday to Sunday). Tickets must be booked online. ✉ *Skyline Drive milepost 53* 🌐 *www.recreation.gov.*

Visitor Information

CONTACTS Shenandoah National Park. ✉ *3655 U.S. Hwy 211 E, Luray* ☎ *540/999–3500* 🌐 *www.nps.gov/shen.*

North District

70 miles west of Washington, DC via U.S. Rte. 66; Big Meadows Lodge is 50 miles south of this entrance.

The North District begins where Skyline Drive meets U.S. Route 340 in Front Royal. Enter the park through the Front Royal entrance at milepost 0.6. This quiet section of the park runs to the Thornton Gap entrance at milepost 31.5. In the North District, you'll find Overall Run Falls, the tallest waterfall in the park, and remains of historic homesteads and cemeteries along the Fox Hollow Trail and at Snead Farm.

Sights

HISTORIC SIGHTS

Historic sights are bountiful at Shenandoah National Park, and range from family cemeteries to farmsteads kept up by families well before this national park came to be in 1935. Take a look at the crumbling gravestones at the Fox family cemetery on the Fox Hollow Trail and imagine farm life at Snead Farm a bit further down Skyline Drive.

Snead Farm

HISTORIC SITE | FAMILY | From Skyline Drive, a hike of less than 1 mile leads to Snead Farm, a small farm once owned by a family living on the park land. There is a white family barn, as well as a root cellar and the stone foundation remains of the family home. ✉ *Skyline Drive milepost 5.1, Shenandoah National Park.*

SCENIC DRIVES

★ Skyline Drive

SCENIC DRIVE | Alternating between wide-open vistas and forest-hemmed stretches, Skyline Drive offers 105 miles of easily accessible wilderness. Designated as a National Historic Landmark, the winding two-lane scenic byway runs from Front Royal in the north to Waynesboro in the south. On weekends and holidays, in particular, a 35-mph speed limit, rubber-necking leaf-lookers, small overlook pull-offs, and the occasional black bear sighting can cause cars to inch along Skyline Drive. It's best to choose a weekday and give yourself a full day to explore; you may want to spend an hour or two simply savoring the views from a roadside boulder. ✉ *Luray* 🌐 *nps.gov/shen/planyourvisit/driving-skyline-drive.htm* ⏲ *Closed during inclement weather in winter.*

SCENIC STOPS

Overall Run Falls

BODY OF WATER | The park's tallest waterfall can only be seen by hiking the 6½-mile Ocerall Run Falls loop. The 93-foot-tall falls are best viewed in spring or fall when there's a gushing waterfall, rather than a trickle, which can be the case in summer. ✉ *Shenandoah National Park.*

Range View Overlook

VIEWPOINT | The inspiring overlook has far-reaching vistas along the length of the rugged Blue Ridge Mountains. Direct your gaze southward for Stony Man Mountain, Gimlet Ridge, and Massanutten Mountain. ✉ *Skyline Drive milepost 17.1, Shenandoah National Park.*

Signal Knob Overlook

VIEWPOINT | Just north of Dickey Ridge Visitor Center is the west-facing Signal Knob Overlook. Revel in the flowing Shenandoah River and the northern peak of Massanutten Mountain, which was used as a Civil War lookout point during the Battle of Cedar Creek in 1864. ✉ *Skyline Drive milepost 5.5, Shenandoah National Park.*

Thornton Hollow Overlook

VIEWPOINT | This overlook enjoys an elevation of nearly 2,500 feet. Peer out into Thornton Hollow, then re-focus for expansive views of rolling mountains, including Fork Mountain, Mt. Marshall, and Overtop Mountain. Captivating east-facing panoramas make this a crowd-pleasing destination for sunrise-seekers. ✉ *Skyline Drive milepost 27.5, Shenandoah National Park.*

TRAILS

Compton Gap

TRAIL | FAMILY | This moderately difficult 2½-mile hike guides visitors east- and west-facing viewpoints with distinctly different rewards. A gentle ascent along the iconic white-blazed Appalachian Trail first leads to a concrete trail marker. A short westbound spur trail reveals a rocky outcrop at Compton Peak for spectacular views of Dickey Ridge and Massanutten Mountain. An eastbound spur trail delivers visitors to a curious hexagonal-patterned geological feature made of greenstone lava and basalt called a columnar jointing. Settle in on a log to ogle this wondrous natural formation. Hiking time is about two hours. *Moderate.* ✥ *Trailhead: Skyline Drive milepost 10.4, west of the Compton Gap parking area* 🌐 *nps.gov/places/000/compton-gap-trailhead.htm.*

Fox Hollow Trail

TRAIL | FAMILY | This historic 1¼-mile loop trail begins across Skyline Drive from the Dickey Ridge Visitor Center, allowing visitors a peek into rural mountain life by stepping foot onto what was once a family farm. Stroll past carefully placed rock walls, periwinkle vines, and a family cemetery filled with grave sites of the Fox family, one of more than 400 families that lived on the land before Shenandoah National Park was established in 1935. Hiking time is less than one hour. No pets allowed on this trail. *Easy.* ✥ *Trailhead: Skyline Drive milepost 4.6, east of the visitor center* 🌐 *nps.gov/thingstodo/fox-hollow-trail.htm.*

Overall Run Falls

TRAIL | FAMILY | Sensational views of 93-foot-tall Overall Run Falls, the park's tallest waterfall, are yours when you embark on this moderately challenging 6½-mile loop hike. Beyond the falls, eye-pleasing views of the dramatic Shenandoah Valley and Massanutten Mountain from well-placed rock ledges reward resolute hikers. The falls are best viewed in spring or fall when you're more likely to reach a gushing waterfall, rather than a trickle, which can be the case in summer. An elevation gain of 1,600-feet can challenge hikers on this steep and rocky circuit hike, but the cascades over the rocks make it worth every step. Hiking time is about four hours. *Moderate.* ✥ *Trailhead: Skyline Drive milepost 21.1, from the parking area south of Hogback Overlook.*

VISITOR CENTER

Dickey Ridge Visitor Center

INFO CENTER | Explore nature-oriented exhibits and a large topographical map of the park, watch a short orientation film, or wander the bookstore for souvenirs. Park rangers can suggest hiking trails and help you navigate the park. Pick up a Junior Ranger activity booklet for kids ages 7–12 to complete to be sworn in as a Junior Ranger and earn a badge. Savor the views from a west-facing landing behind the visitor center that attracts plein air painters on clear days when you can see for miles. Restrooms are located in a separate building adjacent to the visitor center. ✉ *Skyline Drive milepost 4.6* ☏ *540/999–3500* 🌐 *nps.gov/shen/planyourvisit/visitorcenters.htm.*

Restaurants

There are no restaurants in the North District, but there is a seasonal stop for snacks, supplies, and souvenirs on Skyline Drive called Elkwallow Wayside at milepost 24.1.

Central District

Shenandoah National Park's most popular section is the Central District, which runs from the Thornton Gap entrance at Skyline Drive milepost 31.5 to the Swift Run Gap entrance at Skyline Drive milepost 65.7. In the Central District, you'll find the park's two lodges, Skyland and Big Meadows Lodge, as well as Big Meadows Campground and Lewis Mountain Campground. Hike to Hawksbill Summit, the highest point in the park, or revel in the beauty of the tumbling cascades at Dark Hollow Falls.

Sights

GEOLOGICAL FORMATIONS

Hawksbill Summit

MOUNTAIN—SIGHT | At 4,050 feet, Hawksbill Summit reigns as the highest point in the park, rewarding visitors with far-reaching 270-degree views, including Massanutten Mountain to the west and Old Rag Mountain to the northeast. ✉ *Skyline Drive milepost 45.6.*

Mary's Rock

MOUNTAIN—SIGHT | This 3,514-foot tall mountain sits just south of the Thornton Gap Entrance on Skyline Drive. View-seekers can hike one of two routes along the Appalachian Trail to reach the summit of the park's eighth highest peak. ✉ *Skyline Drive milepost 31.6.*

HISTORIC SIGHTS

The Central District is teeming with history, especially if you keep your eyes open as you casually hike the trails. You may see an old stone fireplace from a former homestead family on the way to Mary's Rock or more prominently, a summer retreat once used by our 31st president Herbert Hoover. At Camp Hoover (also known as Rapidan Camp), three historic structures have been fully restored to their 1929 appearances.

Rapidan Camp

HISTORIC SITE | Between 1929 and 1932, President Herbert Hoover used this part of the park, also known as Camp Hoover, as his summer retreat. Hoover and his wife, Lou Henry, hosted celebrities, dignitaries, and foreign leaders. When he left office, Hoover donated the 164-acre retreat to the National Park Service to be used in the creation of the Shenandoah National Park. In 1988, Camp Hoover was designated a National Historic Landmark. Three original structures have been restored to their 1929 appearances, including the President's Cabin ("Brown House"), the Prime Minister's Cabin, and the Creel Cabin. ■ **TIP→ Ranger-led tours of Rapidan Camp are offered from**

late-spring to late-fall, taking visitors inside two of the cabins. An exhibit inside the Prime Minister's Cabin has various historical photos and artifacts on display. ✉ *Skyline Drive milepost 53.*

SCENIC DRIVES

Skyline Drive runs the length of the Central District from the Thornton Gap entrance at milepost 31.5 to the Swift Run Gap entrance at milepost 65.7.

SCENIC STOPS

Dark Hollow Falls

BODY OF WATER | The scenic 70-foot waterfall is among the most popular in the park thanks to multiple drops and close proximity to the main park road. ✉ *Skyline Drive milepost 50.7* ✣ *Along Dark Hollow Falls Trail.*

Hazel Mountain Overlook

VIEWPOINT | A sizeable granodiorite rock formation provides a first-rate vantage point to savor views of Hazel Mountain and Buck Ridge in the distance. With southeast-facing views, it's also tops for a vibrant sunrise. ✉ *Skyline Drive milepost 33.*

Jewell Hollow Overlook

VIEWPOINT | This overlook has it all, including scenic views of Morning Star Lake, Jewell Hollow, and Neighbor Mountain in the distance. The large overlook has a generous green space and lots of room to move. ✉ *Skyline Drive milepost 36.4.*

The Point Overlook

VIEWPOINT | This Skyline Drive overlook is all about mountains as far as the eye can see, including Powell, Green, and Grindstone Mountains. You may even be able to see the small town of Elkton. A secret rocky outcrop only reachable by a short but steep trail from the parking area leads to The Point. ✉ *Skyline Drive milepost 55.5.*

Spitler Knoll Overlook

VIEWPOINT | A wide-open grassy field where cattle once grazed takes center stage as Dovel Mountain and Dog Slaughter Ridge hang back in the distance. Northwest-facing views make this a top spot on Skyline Drive for a colorful sunset. A short spur trail from the overlook connects to the Appalachian Trail. ✉ *Skyline Drive milepost 48.*

TRAILS

Dark Hollow Falls Trail

TRAIL | FAMILY | This rocky 1½-mile hike guides visitors parallel to a flowing stream all the way to the tumbling cascades of Dark Hollow Falls. It's all uphill on the return, so plan accordingly. Hiking time is under two hours. No pets allowed on this trail. *Moderate.* ✣ *Trailhead: Skyline Drive milepost 50.7* 🌐 *nps.gov/thingstodo/dark-hollow-falls.htm.*

Hawksbill Summit

TRAIL | FAMILY | There is more than one route to reach Hawksbill Summit, the highest point in the park at an elevation of 4,051 feet. The most popular is the 1½-mile out-and-back hike under a dense forest canopy that leads to Byrds Nest Shelter #2, a day-use shelter with a picnic table, then on to a stone viewing platform for 270-degree views of the Shenandoah Valley, as well as craggy Massanutten and Old Rag Mountains. Hiking time is 90 minutes. *Moderate.* ✣ *Trailhead: Skyline Drive milepost 45.5* 🌐 *nps.gov/thingstodo/hawksbill-summit.htm.*

Limberlost Trail

TRAIL | FAMILY | This mostly flat, crushed greenstone walkway winds visitors along a forested 1¼-mile loop trail through ancient hemlocks, then over wooden boardwalk and foot bridges. Well-placed benches allow for a break on this stroller-friendly trail. Cross over gentle Whiteoak Canyon Run, then pause for a columnar jointing (a geological structure formed by basalt lava flows). Hiking time is one hour. No pets allowed on this trail. For more steps, turn right onto the Crescent Rock Trail near the ½-mile mark to reach sweeping mountain views from the Crescent Rock Overlook. *Easy.*

⊕ *Trailhead: Skyline Drive milepost 43* 🌐 *nps.gov/thingstodo/limberlost.htm.*

★ Old Rag

TRAIL | The hike to reach 360-degree panoramas from high atop Old Rag is wildly popular, frequently ranking among the top hikes in the world (not just in Virginia). This 10-mile loop hike begins with a switchback-laden ascent before reaching a challenging rock scramble. From here, it's a solid mile of climbing, gripping, pulling, and scrambling. Plan to navigate narrow spaces and strategize paths up, over, and around rocks and boulders to earn the spoils at the top. Hiking time is six to seven hours. No pets allowed on this trail. *Difficult.* ⊕ *Trailhead: Near the end of Nethers Rd. (State Rte 600) in Sperryville.*

★ Rapidan Camp

TRAIL | This 3¾-mile out-and-back historic hike leads visitors alongside rolling Mill Prong and past Big Rock Falls on the Mill Prong Trail to Rapidan Camp (also known as Camp Hoover), President Herbert Hoover's summer retreat. Here you'll find three original structures that have since been restored to their 1929 appearances, including the President's Cabin ("Brown House"), the Prime Minister's Cabin, and the Creel Cabin. *Moderate.* ⊕ *Trailhead: Skyline Drive milepost 52.8, west of the Milam Gap parking area.*

VISITOR CENTER

Harry F. Byrd, Sr. Visitor Center

INFO CENTER | Situated near the center of the park, Byrd Visitor Center is a stone's throw from Big Meadows Lodge and Big Meadows Campground. On the way in, admire the "Iron Mike" statue dedicated to the Civilian Conservation Corps, the men who created much of the park during the Great Depression. Inside, a U-shaped exhibit hall tells the story of the park's establishment and development through historic photos and artifacts. Watch *Shenandoah: The Gift,* a 14-minute video on the creation of this national park. You'll also find restrooms and a park bookstore. From the back porch, take in the sweeping views across Big Meadows. ✉ *Skyline Drive milepost 51* 🌐 *nps.gov/shen/planyourvisit/visitorcenters.htm.*

 Restaurants

Mountain Taproom

$ | AMERICAN | FAMILY | This no-frills bar and grill serves favorites, like chicken wings, soups, salads, burgers, and sandwiches. You can order a slice of the signature blackberry ice cream pie here, too. **Known for:** lighter fare; late-afternoon bites; nightly entertainment. $ *Average main: $14* ✉ *Skyland, Skyline Drive milepost 41.7* ⏲ *Closed late-Nov.–late-Mar.*

New Market Taproom

$ | AMERICAN | FAMILY | Enjoy casual fare, like personal pizzas and green salads, as well as specialty drinks and local beers and wines. Nightly entertainment is a fun way to cap off an active day in the park. **Known for:** lighter fare; late-afternoon bites; nightly entertainment. $ *Average main: $14* ✉ *Big Meadows Lodge, Skyline Drive milepost 51* ⏲ *Closed early-Nov.–late-Apr.*

Pollock Dining Room

$$ | AMERICAN | FAMILY | Gaze out an elegant wall of windows into the Shenandoah Valley while dining on elevated entrees, like pan-seared trout and sweet potato poutine, as well as comfort favorites, like burgers and pulled pork sandwiches. A "Junior Ranger" menu for kids 10 and under includes grilled-cheese sandwiches and junior burgers. **Known for:** farm-to-fork flavors; regional specialties; blackberry ice-cream pie; central location. $ *Average main: $22* ✉ *Skyland, Skyline Drive milepost 41.7* ⏲ *Closed late-Nov.–late-Mar.*

Spottswood Dining Room

$$ | AMERICAN | FAMILY | Savor regional and thematic dishes, like the New Deal roast turkey plate or Roosevelt's roasted chicken; there's also Virginia grilled cheese and peanut soup. The "Junior

Ranger" menu for kids 10 and under has options like mac & cheese and a turkey dinner, and there's a "Yappy Hour" menu available for four-legged friends on the terrace. **Known for:** Virginia specialties; elevated fare; central location; outdoor seating. *Average main: $19* *Big Meadows Lodge, Skyline Drive milepost 51* *Closed early-Nov.–late-Apr.*

Coffee and Quick Bites

Big Meadows Wayside

$ | **AMERICAN** | **FAMILY** | For sundries and supplies, even grab-and-go sandwiches and a made-to-order grill for burgers and fries, look to Big Meadows Wayside. Here you'll find restrooms, camping supplies, and park souvenirs. **Known for:** grab-and-go bites; camping supplies; restrooms. *Average main: $8* *Skyline Drive milepost 51* *Closed mid-Nov.–late-Mar.*

Elkwallow Wayside

$ | **AMERICAN** | For camping supplies and quick bites in the North District, make a stop at Elkwallow Wayside. This stop-and-shop is a resource for day visitors and overnight campers at nearby Mathews Arm Campground in need of snacks and sundries. **Known for:** grab-and-go bites. *Average main: $8* *Skyline Drive milepost 24.1* *Closed mid-Nov.–early-Apr.*

Hotels

Big Meadows Lodge

$ | **RESORT** | Located 1 mile from the large grassy meadow of the same name, you'll find a main lodge with satellite buildings and detached historic cabins. **Pros:** central location; scenic views; close to visitor center. **Cons:** no in-room Wi-Fi; no televisions or telephones in guest rooms; no cell reception. *Rooms from: $118* *Skyline Drive milepost 51* *Closed early-Nov.–late-Apr.* *101 units* *No meals.*

Skyland

$ | **RESORT** | With an array of accommodation options (guest rooms, rustic-chic cabins, and modern suites), this lodge sits atop the highest point on Skyline Drive and is the park's largest lodge. **Pros:** great views; on-site restaurant; nightly entertainment. **Cons:** limited Wi-Fi in dining room; no televisions, telephones, Wi-Fi in rooms; no cell reception. *Rooms from: $113* *Skyline Drive milepost 41.7* *Closed late-Nov.–late-Mar.* *179 units* *No meals.*

Performing Arts

Skyland Amphitheater

READINGS/LECTURES | **FAMILY** | Just steps from lodging at Skyland is the Skyland Amphitheater for ranger-led talks and programs from late-spring to fall. The program schedule can be found on a bulletin board at the entrance to the amphitheater. *Skyline Drive milepost 41.7.*

South District

Southern entrance is 18 miles west of Charlottesville via I–81.

Much like the North District, Shenandoah National Park's South District is relatively quiet and serene, though decidedly more rugged and mountainous. This section begins where Skyline Drive meets U.S. Route 64 in Waynesboro. Here you can enter the park through the Rockfish Gap entrance at milepost 105.4; this entrance is more easily accessible for visitors coming from Charlottesville, Richmond and Roanoke. This mellow section of the park runs to the district's other entrance, Swift Run Gap, at Skyline Drive milepost 65.7. In the South District, you'll find tumbling waterfalls, like Jones Run Falls, as well as easy-to-reach mountain views, like Blackrock Summit. Loft Mountain Campground, one of four campgrounds, is also in the South District, as is Dundo

A "not-to-miss-moment": Seeing the sun rise over the Blue Ridge Mountains from Blackrock Summit.

Group Campground, the park's only campground for large groups.

Sights

HISTORIC SIGHTS

Enjoy a hands-on history lesson in the park's South District where you'll find Lewis Mountain, which was once a segregated area for black park-goers who were not allowed to visit any other areas of Shenandoah National Park. Today, Lewis Mountain is home to a small campground and rustic-chic cabins. You'll also find ruins of homes and communities left behind by several hundred mountain-side residents.

Lewis Mountain

MOUNTAIN—SIGHT | This was a segregated area for black park-goers who were not allowed to visit any other areas of Shenandoah National Park from 1939 to 1950. In this time before the Civil Rights era, the area was operated under the widely excercised "separate but equal" principle. The park was fully integrated by the summer of 1950 and today Lewis Mountain is home to a small campground, rustic cabins, and picnic grounds. ✉ *Skyline Drive milepost 57.5.*

SCENIC DRIVES

Skyline Drive runs the length of the South District from the Switft Run Gap entrance at milepost 65.7 to the Rockfish Gap entrance at milepost 105.4.

SCENIC STOPS

Bacon Hollow Overlook

VIEWPOINT | Looking southward, visitors can take in the views of low-lying Bacon Hollow, which sits squarely in the frame of view. In the fall, prepare for a never-ending sea of amber, crimson, and gold leaves. ✉ *Skyline Drive milepost 69.*

Rockytop Overlook

VIEWPOINT | This west-facing scenic overlook allows you to savor the views of cascading mountains, one right behind the next in the more rugged South District. Rocktop Mountain is the pointy one right in the middle, flanked on either side by Lewis Mountain and Loft Mountain. ✉ *Skyline Drive milepost 78.*

Turk Mountain Overlook

VIEWPOINT | From this west-facing overlook, you're looking directly at Turk Mountain, a quartzite-covered peak. Turk Mountain got its name from the family that lived here before the establishment of the national park. To the right, you can peer out into the Shenandoah Valley. ✉ *Skyline Drive milepost 93.5.*

TRAILS

★ Blackrock Summit

TRAIL | This relaxing 1-mile loop hike hugs the mountain following along the Appalachian Trail. The forested trail guides visitors to a boulder field with expansive views across the Shenandoah Valley and Massanutten Mountain. Hiking time is less than one hour. *Easy. ✣ Trailhead: Skyline Drive milepost 84.4, at the back of the parking area ⊕ nps.gov/thingstodo/blackrock-summit.htm.*

Doyles River Falls

TRAIL | **FAMILY** | This 3½-mile hike pulls out all the stops with crystal-clear, flowing streams, water crossings, and two cascading waterfalls, including 28-foot-tall Upper Doyles Falls and 63-foot-tall Lower Doyles Falls. You'll walk alongside Doyles River nearly the entire hike, but be prepared for an elevation gain of nearly 1,200 feet before the hike is done. Hiking time is three hours. *Moderate. ✣ Trailhead: Skyline Drive milepost 81.1, at the back of the Doyles River parking area ⊕ nps.gov/thingstodo/doyles-river-falls.htm.*

Jones Run Falls

TRAIL | **FAMILY** | A dreamy 2-mile hike through the forest leads to 42-foot-tall cascading Jones Run Falls. As you close in on the falls, the trail rubs up against Jones Run. Continue past the main falls to reach smaller falls and cascades. As you proceed, you'll spy several swimming holes for a refreshing splash on a warm day. Retrace your steps to the parking area, but take it slow, it will be all uphill on the return. Hiking time is three hours. *Moderate. ✣ Trailhead: Skyline Drive milepost 84.1, at the back of the Jones Run parking area.*

Loft Mountain Loop

TRAIL | **FAMILY** | This 2-mile hike pairs the easy-going Frazier Discovery Trail with the Appalachian Trail for an eye-pleasing hike with rock scrambles, creek crossings, and far-reaching views. Take this loop counter-clockwise and you'll reach a show-stopping vista just past the midway point that's perfect for spotting the sunrise. Continue on to connect with the Blue Spring Trail and pass the Ivy Creek maintenance hut before the conclusion of this hike. Hiking time is two hours. *Easy. ✣ Trailhead: Skyline Drive milepost 79.5, across from Loft Mountain Wayside.*

★ Riprap Trail

TRAIL | There are spectacular views to savor along this 9½-mile loop that takes hikers past a mysterious wonderland of gigantic rocks at Calvary Rocks and then to a panoramic viewpoint filled with cool, flat top rocks along the ridge of Rocks Mountain at Chimney Rock. From here, drop down into Cold Spring Hollow, then cross a stream to Riprap Shelter and a large swimming hole. Hiking time is less than five hours. *Difficult. ✣ Trailhead: Skyline Drive milepost 90, at the front of the Riprap Trail parking area.*

VISITOR CENTER

There is no brick-and-mortar Visitor Center in the South District. However, an award-winning Mobile Visitor Center patrols the mountainous district of the park. Park rangers on board provide trip advice, answer questions, and provide park maps.

Coffee and Quick Bites

Loft Mountain Wayside

$ | **AMERICAN** | For camping supplies and souvenirs in the South District, stop in Loft Mountain Wayside. It's just across Skyline Drive from pouplar Loft Mountain

Campground. **Known for:** grab-and-go bites; camping supplies; flush toliets. [$] *Average main: $5* ✉ *Skyline Drive milepost 79.5* ⏲ *Closed early-Nov.–late-Apr.*

Activities

BIKING

Cycling is allowed along Skyline Drive and on paved roads in the park. Cycling is not allowed on any hiking trails, unpaved fire roads, or grassy sections in the park. Headlights and taillights are required to cycle within the park. Be prepared for steep climbs, narrow shoulders, and potentially distracted motorists (ogling far-reaching mountain views).

CAMPING

Big Meadows Campground. Open from late-March to early-November, this campground is just north of the Swift Run Gap entrance. It's also the park's largest campground. There are 221 sites, 51 of which are tent-only; 168 sites can be reserved online. The remaining sites are first-come, first-served. All individual RV and tent sites are $20/night. Two group campsites allow up to 15 people at a rate of $45/night. All campsites are nonelectric with no hook-ups. The campground is an easy walk to a large picnic area, as well as the full-service Big Meadows Lodge. ✉ *Skyline Drive milepost 51.2* 🌐 *www.recreation.gov.*

Dundo Group Campground. Open from May to October, the only group campground is a stone's throw from Loft Mountain. Each of the three nonelectric sites can accommodate up to 20 people. Sites can be booked online up to one-year in advance at a rate of $45/night. All check-ins take place just north on Skyline Drive at Loft Mountain Campground. The Appalachian Trail rubs up against the south side of this campground. From here, it's an easy hike to Blackrock Summit. ✉ *Skyline Drive milepost 83.7* 🌐 *www.recreation.gov.*

Lewis Mountain Campground. This campground is closest to the Swift Run Gap entrance and is open from late-March to October; it's also an easy 6-mile drive south of Big Meadows. With just 30 first-come, first-served only sites, this is the park's smallest campground, but there are also 15 mountain cabins available for rent from mid-June to late-November. Cabins start at $45/night. All individual RV and tent sites are $15/night. All campsites are nonelectric with no hook-ups. ✉ *Skyline Drive milepost 57.5.*

Loft Mountain Campground. Open from May to October, this large campground sits squarely atop Big Flat Mountain. There are 207 sites, including 55 sites that can be reserved online, and 50 that are tent-only. All individual RV and tent sites are $15/night. Campsites are nonelectric with no hook-ups. An on-site camp store is open from mid-May to October. ✉ *Skyline Drive milepost 79.5* 🌐 *www.recreation.gov.*

Mathews Arm Campground. Open from May to October, it's a cinch to reach Mathews Arm Campground from both the Front Royal and Thornton Gap entrances. There are 166 sites, including 47 sites that can be reserved online. All individual sites are $15/night and are open to both tents and RVs. There are three group campsites for up to 25 people at a rate of $50/night. All campsites are nonelectric with no hook-ups. There are no showers at this campground. The easy-going 1¾-mile Traces Trail loops around the wooded campground. ✉ *Skyline Drive milepost 22.1* 🌐 *www.recreation.gov.*

FISHING

The park's more than 70 mountain streams afford numerous opportunities to fish for more than 40 species of fish, including rainbow trout and brook trout. All Virginia residents ages 16 and up must have a valid state fishing in their possession. A five-day license costs $14 for residents and $21 for nonresidents. You can purchase them online at 🌐 *gooutdoorsvirginia.com.*

HIKING

Hiking is the primary way to enjoy the park, particularly in the easy-going North District. Several dozen hiking trails originate in this section of the park. Many are short and sweet, but it's wise to carry a day pack stocked with plenty of water, energy-boosting trail snacks, and first-aid supplies, like bandages and antibiotic ointment.

HORSEBACK RIDING

Skyland Stables

HORSEBACK RIDING | Trail rides leave from the park's Skyland Stables several times daily Monday through Thursday, and once daily Friday and Saturday, from April through mid-November. The route takes riders along leafy trails through an apple orchard and an old growth forest in the Limberlost area. You can choose a one-hour ride or a 2½-hour ride. Reservations are required. ✉ *Skyline Drive milepost 42.5, Luray* ☎ *877/847–1919* 🎫 *$50 1-hr ride; $110 2½-hr ride.*

ROCK CLIMBING

The rock outcrops and faces of Shenandoah National Park attracts rock climbers and rappelers from all across the region. An updated list of permanent and temporary mountain closures can be found at 🌐 *nps.gov/shen/learn/nature/romp.htm.*

Shenandoah Mountain Guides

CLIMBING/MOUNTAINEERING | Introductory to intermediate rock climbing sessions are available from April to November. Instructors take visitors to Little Stony Man Cliffs for full-day climbing outings that include a boxed lunch. Minimum age is 8 years old. Fee is $150 per person and reservations are required. ✉ *Skyline Drive milepost 42* ☎ *877/847–1919.*

What's Nearby

Historic **Front Royal** sits just minutes from Skyline Drive, enabling park-goers easy access to a wide range of supplies, meals, and lodging. You'll find multiple fast food restaurants, as well as sit-down restaurants, like Front Royal Brewing Company and L'Dees Pancake House. There are a handful of budget motels in Front Royal, including Super 8 and Hampton Inn. For groceries, medicines and supplies, there is a Martin's Food, CVS and Family Dollar. Mountain Trails, an outdoor outfitter, sells tents, trekking poles, and backpacks. Look for the colorful Appalachian Trail mural just outside the entrance.

Harrisonburg, a bustling college town that's home to James Madison University, is a 25-mile drive west of the Swift Run Gap entrance on State Route 33. Whatever you need can likely be found on Market Street including fast-food joints as well as sit-down restaurants, like Rocktown Kitchen and Food.Bar. Food. For no-frills fun, you can't miss with Grilled Cheese Mania. Catch a snooze and resupply thanks to Quality Inn, Courtyard by Marriott, Food Lion, and Family Dollar. Alternatively, **Luray** is a 10-mile drive west of the Thornton Gap entrance on State Route 211. If time allows, take a tour of Luray Caverns, an underground labyrinth of stalactites and stalagmites with names like Totem Poles and Titania's Veil. Luray is the Cabin Capital of Virginia, you know. On VRBO alone, you'll find more than 200 cabin listings, including log cabins and historic cottages with sensational views to boot.

Waynesboro is an easy 5-mile drive from the Rockfish Gap entrance, enabling park visitors to access a wider variety of services. There are budget motels, and plenty of fast food restaurants along Main Street; there are also popular sit-down restaurants, like Tailgate Grill and The Fishin' Pig. For groceries, medicine and supplies, there's a CVS, Family Dollar, and Walmart. Basic City Beer Co. on Main Street is where to go for local craft brews and comfort eats.

Chapter 56

THEODORE ROOSEVELT NATIONAL PARK

Updated by
Carson Walker

Camping ★★★☆☆ | Hotels ★★★★☆ | Activities ★★★☆☆ | Scenery ★★★★★ | Crowds ★★★★★

WELCOME TO THEODORE ROOSEVELT NATIONAL PARK

TOP REASONS TO GO

★ **The "Granddaddy Trail":** Hike the Maah Daah Hey Trail, which means "grandfather" or "been here long." It's one of the most popular and well-maintained trails in western North Dakota.

★ **Views from above:** Get an encompassing 360-degree view of the badlands from Buck Hill.

★ **History lessons from the frontier:** View Maltese Cross Ranch Cabin, which once belonged to Theodore Roosevelt.

★ **Badlands Broadway:** Come experience a theatrical tribute to the history and personalities that make up the Old West at the Medora Musical, located in the town, not the park.

★ **Great clubbing—golf, that is:** Perfect your swing at Bully Pulpit Golf Course in Medora, one of America's premier courses near the national park.

★ **Away from it all:** As this is not a heavily visited park, you'll likely encounter more wild horses than people here.

1 **North Unit.** Visitors looking to enjoy the great outdoors should be sure to travel along the 14-mile scenic drive and stop at one of the many hiking trailheads along the way. These trailheads give easy access to the backcountry of the North Unit.

2 **South Unit.** Often considered the main unit of Theodore Roosevelt National Park and adjacent to the famous town of Medora, the South Unit is home to some of the former president's personal artifacts, as well as his cabin, the Maltese Cross Ranch Cabin, and the 218-acre Elkhorn, which started it all.

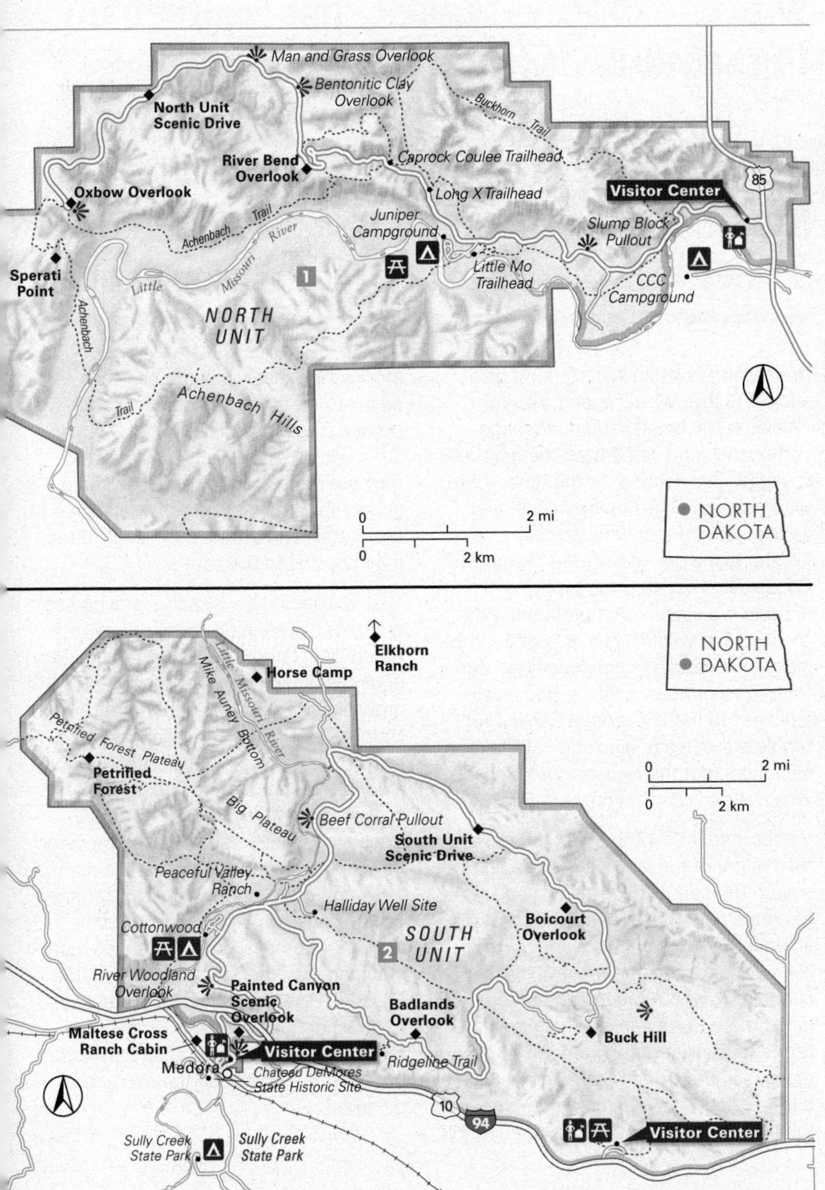
Man and Grass Overlook
Bentonitic Clay Overlook
North Unit Scenic Drive
Buckhorn Trail
River Bend Overlook
Caprock Coulee Trailhead
Oxbow Overlook
Long X Trailhead
Visitor Center
85
Achenbach Trail
Juniper Campground
Slump Block Pullout
Missouri River
Sperati Point
1
Little
Little Mo Trailhead
CCC Campground
NORTH UNIT
Achenbach
Achenbach Hills
Trail
0
2 mi
0
2 km
NORTH DAKOTA
Elkhorn Ranch
Horse Camp
Little Missouri River
Mike Auney Bottom
NORTH DAKOTA
Petrified Forest Plateau
Petrified Forest
Big Plateau
0
2 mi
0
2 km
Beef Corral Pullout
South Unit Scenic Drive
Peaceful Valley Ranch
Halliday Well Site
Boicourt Overlook
Cottonwood
SOUTH UNIT
2
River Woodland Overlook
Painted Canyon Scenic Overlook
Badlands Overlook
Maltese Cross Ranch Cabin
Buck Hill
Visitor Center
Ridgeline Trail
Medora
Chateau DeMores State Historic Site
10
94
Sully Creek State Park
Sully Creek State Park
Visitor Center

The solitude that a young Theodore Roosevelt sought after the deaths of his wife and mother is also what draws many of the 750,000 visitors to this rugged swath of North Dakota every year. The 110-square-mile national park, named in honor of the former president, lacks something plentiful at other parks: people.

Roosevelt arrived in 1883 to hunt bison and fell in love with the land. Within weeks, he invested in an open range cattle ranch and came back the next year to establish a second. At the time, there were no fence lines in the prairie, and as the influx of settlers brought more livestock, the prairie became overgrazed. Roosevelt advocated for grazing and hunting regulations that protected both the land and wildlife, giving the park the nickname "cradle of conservation." Contrary to what many believe, Roosevelt established the U.S. Forest Service to regulate the use of land and wildlife (conservation), not the National Park Service, which is dedicated to preservation.

Established in 1947, the park preserves the history of the land's influence on Roosevelt. The park service also has plans to create new museum exhibits that tell an equally important story: that of the Native Americans, the region's original caretakers, who foraged and hunted here long before European settlers arrived. Some of the last untouched mixed prairie grasses in the United States grow wild here, protected by the craggy ravines, tablelands and gorges of the otherworldly moonscape that made the badlands unsuited for crops but ideal for cattle grazing. The badlands of North Dakota are twice as old as South Dakota's, so they are more rounded and less sharp geographically, have more vegetation on the buttes, and attract more wildlife than their cousins to the south.

That wildlife (bison, elk, and feral horses) is one of the main draws of the park's South Unit, largely thanks to the prairie dogs that keep the grass short and growing, which is also good for grazing. Unfortunately, erosion washed away part of the roadway that created a loop around the unit, but the park still offers a very worthwhile out-and-back drive. Roosevelt's North Unit is best known for its scenery and its solitude, and a day trekking its backcountry trails or remote gravel roads can be uninterrupted by any other humans. The area is also more stunning than the South Unit. The Little Missouri River, one of a few waterways to flow north, creates a true riparian forest with cottonwood trees that regenerate naturally because the river isn't dammed.

AVERAGE HIGH/LOW TEMPERATURES					
JAN.	**FEB.**	**MAR.**	**APR.**	**MAY**	**JUNE**
27/1	34/8	43/18	58/30	71/40	79/50
JULY	**AUG.**	**SEPT.**	**OCT.**	**NOV.**	**DEC.**
87/55	87/52	75/41	62/30	43/17	32/7

Planning

When to Go

The park is open year-round, but North Dakota winters can be extremely cold and windy. Portions of some roads close during winter months, depending on snowfall. Rangers discontinue their outdoor programs when autumn comes, and they recommend that only experienced hikers do any winter explorations. Check the park's website for current conditions.

■ TIP→ **Although July and August tend to be the busiest months, the park is rarely crowded.** About 750,000 people visit each year, with the South Unit receiving the greatest number of visitors. The best times to see wildlife and hike comfortably are May through October. The park is all but desolate December through February, but it's a beautiful time to see the wildlife—also, winter sunsets can be very vivid as the colors reflect off the snow and ice. The park gets an average of 30 inches of snow per year.

Dakota Nights Astronomy Festival. Without light pollution from nearby towns, Theodore Roosevelt National Park is ideal for astronomical observation any cloudless night of the year. To enjoy the stars with others, come during the annual Dakota Nights Astronomy Festival in September (dates vary). Check the park website for a current schedule, which includes day and evening activities in the park and in the town of Medora. 🌐 *www.nps.gov/thro*

Getting Here and Around

AIR

Planes fly into Bismarck, North Dakota (147 miles east of park's South Unit along Interstate 94), and Billings, Montana (295 miles west). There's also some service to even smaller airports in the North Dakota towns of Dickinson (50 miles east) and Williston (60 miles north of North Unit, 140 miles north of South Unit).

CAR

Despite its somewhat remote location, getting to and from the park is relatively easy. The South Unit entrance and visitor center is just off Interstate 94 in the tiny but lively town of Medora at Exits 24 and 27. The Painted Canyon Visitor Center is 7 miles east of Medora on Interstate 94 at Exit 32. The North Unit entrance is south of Williston and Watford City on U.S. 85 and Interstate 94.

There's ample parking space at all trailheads, and parking is free. Some roads are closed in winter. You may encounter bison and other wildlife on the roadway.

Inspiration

Leave It as It Is: A Journey Through Theodore Roosevelt's American Wilderness, by David Gessner, documents the intrepid president's experiences in the badlands and other wild American places.

The Wilderness Warrior: Theodore Roosevelt and the Crusade for America, by best-selling historian David Brinkley, is an epic, compelling biography of the "naturalist president."

Park Essentials

ACCESSIBILITY

The visitor centers, campgrounds, and historic sites such as Roosevelt's cabin, are all wheelchair accessible, and the film at the South Unit Visitor Center is captioned. The first part of the Little Mo Nature Trail in the North Unit and the ¼-mile Skyline Vista Trail in the South Unit are both paved.

PARK FEES AND PERMITS

The entrance pass is $30 per vehicle, $25 per motorcycle, and $15 for an individual, good for seven days. A variety of annual passes are available. A backcountry permit, free from the visitor centers, is required for overnight camping away from campgrounds.

PARK HOURS

The park is open year-round. The North Unit is in the Central time zone. The South Unit and the Painted Canyon Visitor Center are in the Mountain time zone. Keep the locale in mind when checking schedules for park programs, which reflect these time differences. The South Unit Visitor Center is open year-round. The North Unit Contact Station is open daily April through October, and Thursday through Sunday the rest of the year; the Painted Canyon Visitor Center operates from early May through late October. Check the park website for current operating hours.

CELL PHONE RECEPTION

Cell phone reception occurs in some areas of the park, but many places receive no signal. Public telephones can be found at the South Unit's Cottonwood Campground and at the Painted Canyon Visitor Center.

Hotels

If you're set on sleeping within the park, be sure to pack your tent. Outside the park are mostly small chain hotels catering to interstate travelers—largely retired couples in RVs and young families in minivans. However, there is a handful of historic properties and working ranches that offer guests a truly Western experience.

Restaurants

One does not visit Theodore Roosevelt National Park for the fine dining. In fact, the only venues within the park are the picnic areas, and provided you're prepared, this can be a perfectly simple and satisfying way to experience the open spaces and natural wonder of the badlands. In the towns near the park you'll find casual, down-to-earth family establishments that largely cater to the locals. Expect steak and potatoes, and lots of them. Fortunately, the beef here is among the best in the country.

Visitor Information

PARK CONTACT INFORMATION Theodore Roosevelt National Park. ☎ *701/623–4466 South Unit* 🌐 *www.nps.gov/thro.*

North Unit

69 miles north of the South Unit via Hwy. 85 and I–94, 11 miles south of Watford City vis Hwy. 85.

Fewer people visit the North Unit (rather than the South Unit) because it's more than an hour's drive off Interstate 94, but that's changing. Visitation has increased from about 10% to 15% of the park's total because more people are searching for a true wilderness experience. The unit's isolated hiking trails offer otherworldly views of stunning buttes, which are also visible along the 28-mile-roundtrip scenic drive. One stop along the drive, the River Bend Overlook, provides expansive views of the Little Missouri floodplain. The Oxbow Overlook, at the halfway point, shows the bend where the river turns to the east.

Most of the park's petrified wood is found in the South Unit's west end, which is accessible via the Petrified Forest Loop Trail.

Sights

SCENIC DRIVES

North Unit Scenic Drive

SCENIC DRIVE | The 14-mile, two-way drive follows rugged terrain above spectacular views of the canyons, and is flanked by more than a dozen turnouts with interpretive signs. Notice the slump blocks, massive segments of rock that have slipped down the cliff walls over time. Farther along pass through badlands coulees, deep-water clefts that are now dry. There's a good chance of meeting bison, mule deer, and bighorn sheep along the way, also keep an eye out for longhorn steers, just like the ones you would see in Texas. ✉ *From unit entrance to Oxbow Overlook, North Unit.*

SCENIC STOPS

Oxbow Overlook

VIEWPOINT | The view from this spot at the end of the North Unit drive looks over the unit's westerly badlands and the Little Missouri River, where it takes a sharp turn east. This is the place to come for stargazing. ✉ *Theodore Roosevelt National Park* ✥ *14 miles west of North Unit Visitor Center.*

River Bend Overlook

VIEWPOINT | The National Park Service calls this the North Unit's most iconic view. Take the short walk off the parking area to see the Little Missouri River floodplain and a 1930s stone shelter. ✉ *Theodore Roosevelt National Park* ✥ *Midway through the 28-mile scenic drive.*

Sperati Point

VIEWPOINT | For a great view of the Missouri River's 90-degree angle, hike a 1½-mile round-trip stretch of the much longer Achenbach Trail to this spot 430 feet above the riverbed. ✉ *Theodore Roosevelt National Park* ✥ *14 miles west of North Unit Visitor Center.*

TRAILS

Achenbach Trail

TRAIL | This 18-mile round-trip trail climbs through the Achenbach Hills, descends to the river, and ends at Oxbow Overlook. Check with rangers about river-fording conditions. For a shorter (6-mile) hike to Oxbow, begin at the River Bend Overlook. This is an all-day trail. *Moderate–Difficult.* ✉ *Theodore Roosevelt National Park* ✣ *Trailhead: Juniper Campground in the North Unit.*

Buckhorn Trail

TRAIL | FAMILY | A thriving prairie-dog town is just 1 mile from the trailhead of this 11.4-mile round-trip North Unit trail. It travels over level grasslands, then it loops back along the banks of Squaw Creek. If you're an experienced hiker, you'll complete the entire trail in about half a day. Novices or families might want to plan on a whole day, however. *Moderate–Difficult.* ✉ *Theodore Roosevelt National Park* ✣ *Trailhead: Caprock Coulee Nature Trail, 1½ miles west of Juniper Campground.*

Little Mo Nature Trail

TRAIL | FAMILY | The unpaved but flat outer loop of this 1.1-mile trail passes through badlands and woodlands to the river's edge. The trail's paved 0.7-mile inner loop is wheelchair-accessible. It's a great way to see the park's diverse terrain and wildlife, and because it shouldn't take you longer than an hour, it's a great trail for families with children. *Easy.* ✉ *Theodore Roosevelt National Park* ✣ *Trailhead: Juniper Campground in the North Unit.*

Upper Caprock Coulee Trail

TRAIL | The first ¾-mile of this 4.3-mile round-trip trail takes you along a nature trail. It then loops around the pockmarked lower-badlands coulees. There's a slow incline that takes you up 300 feet. Portions of the trail are slippery. Beginners should plan a half day for this hike. *Moderate–Difficult.* ✉ *Theodore Roosevelt National Park* ✣ *Trailhead: 8 miles west of North Unit Visitor Center.*

VISITOR CENTER

North Unit Contact Station

INFO CENTER | While planning for a new visitor center facility is underway, this unit is being housed in temporary trailers. It still offers park information and a park film. Amenities include restrooms and a gift shop. It's open daily between April and October and Friday through Monday the rest of the year. ✉ *North Unit entrance, off U.S. 85, North Unit* ☎ *701/623-4466* 🌐 *www.nps.gov/thro* 🎫 *Free.*

South Unit

69 miles south of the North Unit via Hwy. 85 and I–94.

Visitors who have limited time to spend in Roosevelt should consider visiting only the South Unit because it offers a taste of the park's unique landscapes, wildlife, and rich history. Part of the park's main road closed in 2019 because of erosion and won't reopen for the foreseeable future because major repairs are needed, but it's still possible to see much of the park. The full trip out and back is still 24 miles one way, so it takes about two hours. If you can't afford that amount of time, a must-see stop is the Wind Canyon Trail, 11 miles into the unit. It's a short hike that offers gorgeous views of the river corridor from the top of a butte, a well-known sunset-viewing location, as well as wildlife along the way. The main entrance into the South Unit is on the northwest end of Medora, where the visitors center and Roosevelt's original cabin, the Maltese Cross, are also located.

HISTORIC SIGHTS

Elkhorn Ranch

NATURE PRESERVE | This remote unit of the park is composed of the 218 acres of ranchland where Theodore Roosevelt ran cattle on the open range. Today there are no buildings, but foundation blocks outline the original structures. **■ TIP→ Visitors who have two to three days in the park or are diehard "Rooseveltians" should make this trek, and then only when it hasn't been raining because most of the**

route is on unpaved roads; check with visitor center staff about road conditions. This area truly encapsulates the spirit of why this is called Roosevelt National Park. ✉ *Theodore Roosevelt National Park* ✣ *35 miles north of South Unit Visitor Center* ☎ *701/623–4466 South Unit* 🎫 *Free.*

Maltese Cross Ranch Cabin

BUILDING | About 7 miles from its original site in the river bottom sits the cabin Theodore Roosevelt commissioned to be built on his Dakota Territory property. Inside is Roosevelt's travel trunk. Interpretive tours are scheduled every day May through August. ✉ *South Unit entrance, Exits 24 and 27 off I–94* ☎ *701/623–4466 South Unit* 🎫 *Free.*

SCENIC DRIVES

South Unit Scenic Drive

SCENIC DRIVE | A 24-mile, one-way scenic loop takes you past prairie-dog towns, coal veins, trailheads, and panoramic views of the badlands. Information on the park's natural history is posted at the various overlooks—stop at all of the interpretive signs to learn about the park's natural and historical phenomena. Some of the best views can be seen from Boicourt Overlook, Badlands Overlook, Skyline Vista Trail, and Buck Hill. If you hit the road at dusk, be prepared to get caught in a bison jam, as the huge creatures sometimes block the road and aren't in any hurry to move. Don't get out of your car or honk at them—they don't like it. ✉ *Begins at South Unit Visitor Center in Medora.*

SCENIC STOPS

Badlands Overlook

VIEWPOINT | This stop is a great place to spend time taking in the panoramic view looking north. It's also where the park's main road was closed in 2019 because of erosion, so you'll have to turn around for the 24-mile return trip to the visitor center. ✉ *Theodore Roosevelt National Park* ✣ *End of the main park road, 24 miles from South Unit Visitor Center.*

Boicourt Overlook

VIEWPOINT | This stop is on the northeast end of the South Unit, so it looks south onto one of the best views of the badlands. There's an easy 15-minute hike, and it's a great place to watch the sunset over the South Unit. ✉ *Theodore Roosevelt National Park* ✣ *Northeast side of South Unit road.*

★ **Buck Hill**

VIEWPOINT | At 2,855 feet, this is one of the highest points in the park and provides a spectacular 360-degree view of the badlands. Come here for the sunset. ✉ *Theodore Roosevelt National Park* ✣ *17 miles east of South Unit Visitor Center.*

Painted Canyon Scenic Overlook

VIEWPOINT | Catch your first glimpse of badlands majesty here—the South Unit canyon's colors change dramatically with the movement of the sun across the sky. ✉ *South Unit* ✣ *Exit 32 off I–94.*

Petrified Forest

NATURE SITE | Although bits of petrified wood have been found all over the park, the densest collection is in the South Unit's west end, accessible via the Petrified Forest Loop Trail from Peaceful Valley Ranch (10 miles round-trip) or from the park's west boundary (3 miles round-trip), which is the most recommended route ✉ *Theodore Roosevelt National Park* ✣ *Trailheads: Peaceful Valley Ranch, 7 miles north of South Unit Visitor Center; west boundary, 10 miles north of Exit 23 off I–94/U.S. 10.*

TRAILS

Jones Creek Trail

TRAIL | This out-and-back 7-mile trail runs east-west across the South Unit's Jones Creek with close-up views of the vegetation on the badlands floor. For a longer trek, head south on the Lower Talkington and Lower Paddock Creek trails, which loop back to the park road on the west. *Moderate.* ✉ *Theodore Roosevelt National Park* ✣ *Accessible from the west or east side of the park road.*

Lower Paddock Creek Trail

TRAIL | Trail access is located on the west end of the park at one of the South Unit's few public restrooms. The 3½-mile trail runs along Paddock Creek and provides access to a couple of other good hikes. Take the Upper Paddock Creek Trail to the far southeast corner of the South Unit, or head north on the Badlands Spur and Lower Talkington trails and connect with Jones Creek Trail, which loops you back to the west. *Moderate.* ✉ *Theodore Roosevelt National Park* ✣ *Trailhead is near the restrooms south of Peaceful Valley Ranch.*

★ Maah Daah Hey Trail

TRAIL | **FAMILY** | Traversing the full length of the 144-mile Maah Daah Hey Trail is a true multiday wilderness adventure. A popular and well-maintained route, it runs through private and public lands—including the Little Missouri Grasslands and both the North and South units of the national park—with several access points and numerous campgrounds. Maps are available at the park visitor centers and through the U.S. Forest Service and the Maah Daah Hey Trail Association. The 7.1-mile one-way segment that runs through the park's South Unit will take you three or four hours; plan on a full day out and back. *Moderate–Difficult.* ✉ *Theodore Roosevelt National Park* ✣ *Trailhead: Sully Creek State Park, 3 miles south of South Unit Visitor Center* 🌐 *mdhta.com.*

Ridgeline Nature Trail

TRAIL | Before heading out along this short (0.6-mile) loop pick up the accompanying map and brochure with information designed to enlighten you on the ecology of the badlands. The first few yards are steep and difficult, and there's a steep descent at the end, but otherwise the trail is even. You'll complete this trail in about a half hour. *Moderate.* ✉ *Theodore Roosevelt National Park* ✣ *Trailhead at River Bend Overlook.*

Skyline Vista Trail

TRAIL | This short, wheelchair-accessible trail is one of the first stops on the South Unit's main road after you leave the visitor center. It's on top of a plateau that overlooks the Little Missouri River valley. *Easy.* ✉ *Theodore Roosevelt National Park* ✣ *West side of the park road near the visitor center entrance.*

Wind Canyon Trail

TRAIL | This short hike is one of the must-see stops in the South Unit because of the views it offers of the Little Missouri River as well as canyons shaped by the wind. It's also one of the best places to watch a sunset. *Easy.* ✉ *Theodore Roosevelt National Park* ✣ *About 11 miles north of the visitor center.*

VISITOR CENTERS

Painted Canyon Visitor Center

INFO CENTER | Easily reached off Interstate 94, this South Unit Visitor Center has an information desk, exhibits, a Theodore Roosevelt Nature and History Association bookstore, a picnic area, restrooms, vending machines, water fountains, and public phones. ✉ *South Unit* ✣ *Exit 32 off I–94* ☎ *701/575–4020* 🌐 *www.nps.gov/thro* 🎫 *Free* ⏲ *Closed late Oct.–early May.*

South Unit Visitor Center

INFO CENTER | This building houses a large auditorium screening the 17-minute film *Refuge of the American Spirit.* There's also an excellent exhibit on Theodore Roosevelt's life with artifacts such as the clothing he wore while ranching in the Dakota Territory, his firearms, and several writings in his own hand reflecting his thoughts on the nation's environmental resources. Be sure to stop in the Theodore Roosevelt Nature and History Association bookstore. Restrooms and a drinking fountain are also available. ✉ *Theodore Roosevelt National Park* ✣ *South Unit entrance, Exits 24 and 27 off I–94* ☎ *701/623–4466* 🌐 *www.nps.gov/thro* 🎫 *Free.*

Activities

BIRD-WATCHING

Theodore Roosevelt has a recorded 185 observed species of birds and 22 species that are suspected to be in the park but have yet to be observed. Bird-watchers are asked to report to park officials if they spot a bird that is new to the list.

CAMPING

For the adventurous traveler, camping in Theodore Roosevelt is well worth the effort. The unadulterated isolation, epic views, and relationship with nature afforded by the Spartan campgrounds within the park create an experience you'll be hard-pressed to find elsewhere in the United States. Just remember that the park's campgrounds are relatively undeveloped—you'll have to pack in everything you need. If you pick a campsite in the surrounding wilderness, you must obtain a backcountry camping permit (available free) from a visitor center first.

Cottonwood Campground. Nestled under juniper and cottonwood trees on the bank of the Little Missouri River, this is a wonderful place to watch buffalo, elk, and other wildlife drink from the river at sunrise and just before sunset. ✉ *½ mile north of South Unit Visitor Center* ☎ *701/623–4466.*

Juniper Campground. The sites here are surrounded by junipers, hence the name. Don't be surprised if you see a bison herd wander through on its way to the Little Missouri River. ✉ *5 miles west of North Unit Visitor Center* ☎ *701/842–2333.*

EDUCATIONAL OFFERINGS

RANGER PROGRAMS

Evening Programs

LOCAL SPORTS | FAMILY | Rangers host a variety of 15- to 45-minute presentations and discussions on such subjects as park history, astronomy, fires, and wildlife. Also check to see if your visit coincides with one of the park's Full Moon hikes, held several evenings each summer. Look for times and subjects posted at park campgrounds and visitor centers. ✉ *Cottonwood Campground, South Unit; Juniper Campground, North Unit* ☎ *701/623–4466* 🌐 *www.nps.gov/thro.*

Junior Ranger Adventure

HIKING/WALKING | On Saturday from May through August, rangers lead a short hike (just under a mile). Kids also get an activity book and can earn a badge. Bring water; as the route is dusty, wear closed-toe shoes. ✉ *South Unit Visitor Center* ☎ *701/623–4466* 🌐 *www.nps.gov/thro* 🎫 *Free.*

Ranger-Led Talks and Walks

HIKING/WALKING | FAMILY | Rangers take visitors on the trails of both units, discussing such subjects as geology, paleontology, wildlife, and natural history. There are also tours of Roosevelt's Maltese Cross Cabin, Geology Talks, and special Bison Chats. Check at campground entrances or at the visitor centers for times, topics, departure points, and destinations. ✉ *Theodore Roosevelt National Park* ☎ *701/623–4466* 🌐 *www.nps.gov/thro* 🎫 *Free.*

FISHING

Catfish, northern pikes, and saugers are among the underwater inhabitants of the Little Missouri River. If you wish to fish in the park or elsewhere in the state and are over age 16, you must obtain a North Dakota fishing license. For out-of-state residents, a three-day permit is $28, a 10-day permit is $38, and a one-year permit is $48. For in-state residents, a one-year permit is $18.

HIKING

During the summer months, the park is best seen by hiking its many trails. Particularly in the South Unit, there are numerous opportunities to jump on a trail right from the park road. The North and South units are connected by the 144-mile Maah Daah Hey Trail. Backcountry hiking is allowed, but you need a permit (free from any visitor center) to camp in the wild. Park maps are available at all three visitor centers. If you plan to camp overnight, let several people know about where you plan to pitch your tent, and inquire about river conditions, maps, regulations, trail updates, and additional water sources before setting out.

What's Nearby

Medora is the gateway to the park's South Unit and it has plenty of restaurants and places to stay. Roughly 50 miles to the east is **Dickinson** (population 28,000), the largest town near the national park. North of Dickinson and about 35 miles east of the park's North Unit, **Killdeer** (pop. about 825) is known for its Roundup Rodeo—North Dakota's oldest—and its gorgeous scenery. Killdeer is the place to fill your tank, because there isn't another gas station around for 40 miles. **Williston** (pop. about 30,000) is 60 miles north of the North Unit (141 miles from the South Unit), just over the Missouri River. The Amtrak stop nearest to the national park is here.

Chapter 57

VIRGIN ISLANDS NATIONAL PARK

Updated by
Carol Bareuther

Camping ★★☆☆☆ | Hotels ★☆☆☆☆ | Activities ★★★★☆ | Scenery ★★★★★ | Crowds ★★★☆☆

WELCOME TO VIRGIN ISLANDS NATIONAL PARK

TOP REASONS TO GO

★ **Postcard-perfect beaches:** White-sand stretches sandwiched between tropical palms and turquoise seas at Hawksnest, Trunk, Cinnamon, and Maho bays on the north shore are among the world's most camera-worthy spots.

★ **Walk back in time:** Stonework ruins of Danish colonial forts, sugar mills, and estate walls throughout the park offer a peek into a bygone time.

★ **Hike on the wild side:** More than 20 well-marked hiking trails lace the park—from sea to tree level and beyond.

★ **Snorkel a trail:** Gear up in a mask and snorkel to swim the Underwater Trail at Trunk Bay. Submerged plaques guide the way and discuss the sealife.

1 Cruz Bay and the North Shore. The 7-mile (11-km) drive along St. John's north shore, starting in Cruz Bay, home to the park visitor center, and ending at the Annaberg Plantation by Leinster Bay, travels along iconic park beaches. Overlooks provide bird's-eye vantage points for photos of these palm-lined sands bordering the Atlantic. Parking and other facilities make each beach user-friendly.

2 East End and South Shore. Compared with those on the north shore, trails and beaches here are more off the beaten track, making them perfect for sampling the park's back-to-nature vibe. The best known sites are Salt Pond Bay, with its nearby trail to Ram Head Point, and the Reef Bay Trail, just west of Lameshur Bay.

3 Hassel Island. Located in St. Thomas Harbor, about 11½ miles (18½ km) west of St. John, nearly all of this 136-acre island is park land. Focal points here are an 18th-century fort, signal tower, and marine railway.

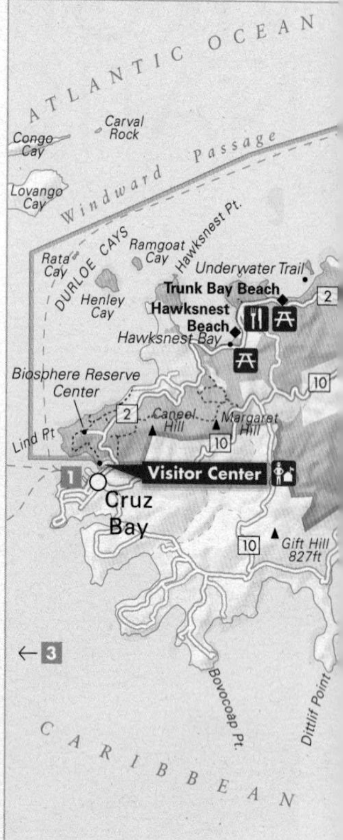

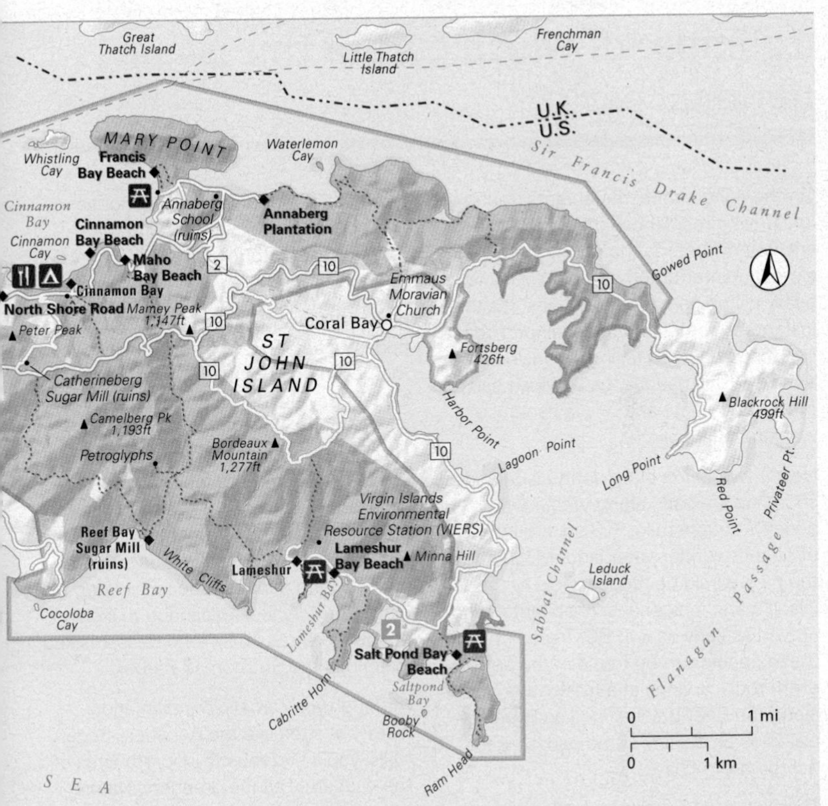
Great Thatch Island
Little Thatch Island
Frenchman Cay
U.K.
U.S.
Sir Francis Drake Channel
MARY POINT
Whistling Cay
Francis Bay Beach
Waterlemon Cay
Annaberg School (ruins)
Annaberg Plantation
Cinnamon Bay
Cinnamon Bay Beach
Cinnamon Cay
Maho Bay Beach
Cinnamon Bay
North Shore Road
Mamey Peak 1,147ft
Emmaus Moravian Church
Coral Bay
Gowed Point
Peter Peak
ST JOHN ISLAND
Fortsberg 426ft
Catherineberg Sugar Mill (ruins)
Camelberg Pk 1,193ft
Petroglyphs
Bordeaux Mountain 1,277ft
Harbor Point
Blackrock Hill 499ft
Lagoon Point
Long Point
Red Point
Privateer Pt.
Virgin Islands Environmental Resource Station (VIERS)
Reef Bay Sugar Mill (ruins)
Lameshur Bay Beach
Minna Hill
White Cliffs
Lameshur
Reef Bay
Sabbat Channel
Leduck Island
Passage
Cocoloba Cay
Lameshur Bay
Salt Pond Bay Beach
Flanagan
Saltpond Bay
Cabritte Horn
Booby Rock
Ram Head
SEA
0 1 mi
0 1 km

There's only one way to reach St. John—by boat. On the short ferry ride from St. Thomas's east end to Cruz Bay, you get a glimpse of which part of this island is national park.

On the right, shops, restaurants, resorts, and private residences mark the town and its environs. To the north, there's almost uninterrupted greenery, save for a few hilltop park-ranger houses. It's the lush green forest and undeveloped coastline that are key to telling when you've arrived at this national park, which has no formal entry gate and only a handful of welcome signs.

Nearly two-thirds of St. John's land and shoreline are park, along with another nearly 9 square miles (23 square km) of offshore underwater land. Much of the park would be recognizable to the island's first indigenous inhabitants, who arrived as early as 840 BC. Traces of these people can be found in the petroglyph rock carvings at a freshwater pool along the Reef Bay Trail and archaeological finds on display at the park's visitor center in Cruz Bay.

The history of European settlement begins with the Danes, who planted their homeland's flag on St. John—as well as on the other U.S. Virgin Islands of St. Thomas and St. Croix—in the late 17th century. (Although the British claimed St. John in 1684, at roughly the same time as the Danes did, they never built a settlement on the island. By 1792, England had stopped asserting ownership, and St. John officially came under Danish rule.) Sugar production once dominated the economy here, and the ruins of plantations, great houses and boundary walls are among the park's most historic sights.

The United States bought the Danish Virgins in 1917, and, by the 1950s, tourism began to take root. American businessman Laurence Rockefeller, who built his Caneel Bay Resort on St. John, was an avid conservationist and philanthropist. He ultimately purchased nearly all of today's park land through his nonprofit Jackson Hole Preserve and then deeded it to the federal government. In 1956, the Virgin Islands National Park became the nation's 29th park. Two decades later, the park's territory was expanded to include about 120 acres on historic Hassel Island, located in the St. Thomas Harbor.

Although you can explore plantation history at sites like the Annaberg Sugar Mills, you'll find mostly just remnants of the past amid all the greenery. Nature is everything in this national park. At Francis Bay, there's a boardwalk through the mangroves where birds are plentiful. Salt Pond Bay offers pleasant snorkeling. More than 20 trails lace the north and south shores, with guided hikes along the most popular routes. A full-day trip to Reef Bay is a must; it's an easy hike through lush and dry forest, past the ruins of an old plantation, and to a sugar factory adjacent to the beach.

AVERAGE HIGH/LOW TEMPERATURES					
JAN.	**FEB.**	**MAR.**	**APR.**	**MAY**	**JUNE**
84/70	84/70	84/70	85/72	86/74	88/76
JULY	**AUG.**	**SEPT.**	**OCT.**	**NOV.**	**DEC.**
89/76	89/76	89/75	88/74	87/73	85/71

Planning

When to Go

Late November through May, when it's cold in more northerly climates, is the park's peak season, when parking spots can be scarce at park beaches and when, three to four days a week, a hundred or more cruise ship passengers day-trip to Trunk Bay, making it busy between 10 am and 2 pm. Peak season offers advantages, though, such as ranger-led hikes and educational seminars led by the nonprofit Friends of the Virgin Islands National Park. These activities happen less often during the off season (June through October), which is also hurricane season.

FESTIVALS AND EVENTS

Folk Life Festival. Local customs and traditions come to life in music, food, and craft demonstrations the last weekend in February to commemorate Black History Month. There's also storytelling and appearances by Mocko Jumbies (costumed, masked stilt walkers named after the West Indian term for spirits/ghosts). Festivities alternate in location between the ball field adjacent to the park's visitor's center in Cruz Bay and the Annaberg Plantation.

Getting Here and Around

AIR

St. John does not have an airport, so you will need to fly into the Cyril E. King Airport on the western side of St. Thomas and then take a ferry over. American, Delta, Frontier, JetBlue, Spirit, Sun Country, and United fly direct from major U.S. cities.

BOAT

Inter Island Boat Services operates a ferry between the Crown Bay Marina, about 1 mile (1½ km) east of Cyril E. King Airport on St. Thomas, and Cruz Bay, St. John, departing each afternoon at 3:30 pm and 5:30 pm. (Note that this ferry uses the dock by the Virgin Island National Park visitor's center, *not* St. John's main Cruz Bay ferry dock.) Return service to St. Thomas is at 11 am and 4:15 pm daily. The fare is $20 per person each way, and trips takes 35 minutes.

Other companies, such as Varlack Ventures, offer ferry service to Cruz Bay, St. John, departing on the hour from Red Hook, St. Thomas—an $11- to $15-per-person, 30- to 40-minute (longer during rush hour) taxi ride across the island from the Cyril E. King Airport. The fare for these ferries is $8.15 per person each way, and trips lasts 15 to 20 minutes. Although there's car-ferry service from Red Hook to Cruz Bay, most St. Thomas rental companies will not allow you to take a car to St. John, so if you need one, it's best to rent it on arrival there.

Virgin Islands ferry schedules are published on the websites of the visitor magazine, *Virgin Islands This Week* (🌐 *virginislandsthisweek.com*) and the *Virgin Islands Vacation Guide and Community* (🌐 *www.vinow.com*). Schedules do change, so confirm times on these sites and/or directly with the ferry companies.

The St. Thomas Historical Trust (☎ *340/774–5541*) offers tours of and boat transportation to Hassel Island, as does the Virgin Islands National Park (check with the visitor center). On request, the captain of the Water Island Ferry can also take visitors to

Hassel Island ($10 per person round-trip). In addition, Virgin Island Ecotours runs kayak trips from Frenchtown, St. Thomas, to Hassel Island.

BOAT INFORMATION Inter Island Boat Services. ☎ *340/776–6597* 🌐 *www.inter-islandboatservices.com.* **Varlack Ventures.** ☎ *340/693–9933* 🌐 *www.varlack-ventures.com.* **Water Island Ferry.** ☎ *340/690–4159* 🌐 *waterislandferry.com.*

CAR

If you're only interested in a day trip to the park from St. Thomas, there's no need to rent a vehicle. Taxis are available at the ferry dock in Cruz Bay for either island tours or trips to and from any of the north shore beaches. Rates are set rather than metered. Approximate, per-person fares for two-plus passengers from Cruz Bay are $5 to Caneel or Hawksnest, $6 to Trunk Bay, $7 to Maho and Cinnamon bays, and $9 to Francis and Coral bays.

For overnight and longer visits, especially if you're staying at a villa or in Coral Bay, a vehicle is a must for getting around. The terrain on St. John is very hilly, the roads are winding, and the blind curves are numerous. Major roads are well paved, but once you get off a specific route, dirt roads filled with potholes are common. For such driving, a four-wheel-drive vehicle is your best bet. Jeep rentals run from about $85 to $100 per day in winter and spring. Rates drop to $75 to $95 per day in the summer and fall off seasons. ⚠ **You can't bring all rental cars to St. John from St. Thomas. Even if you find a rental agency that allows it, there isn't always space on the car ferry.**

Inspiration

Pam Gaffin's *Feet, Fins and Four Wheel Drives* details a variety of ways to see all of St. John, from its most popular places to its off-the-beaten-track spots. *St. John Backtime,* by Ruth Hull Low and Rafael Valls, presents fascinating eye-witness accounts of life on St. John from 1718 to 1956.

Park Essentials

ACCESSIBILITY

Bathrooms at Trunk Bay are wheel-chair accessible. Some beaches, like Hawksnest, have ramps from concrete walkways down to the sand. All beaches have designated accessible parking spots. Portions of the trail at Francis Bay and the Cinnamon Bay Loop Trail are boardwalk, making them wheel-chair friendly.

PARK FEES AND PERMITS

There is no park entrance, but a $5 per day fee at Trunk Bay covers the use of facilities such as restrooms and showers. Those on boats pay $26 per night for a mooring. Floating mooring-fee stations are at Leinster, Francis, and Caneel bays; land-based mooring-fee stations are at the park's Cruz Bay visitor center, Salt Pond Beach, and on the VIERS (Virgin Islands Environmental Research Station) dock in Lameshur Bay.

PARK HOURS

The park is open 24/7, though the Cruz Bay visitor center's hours are 8:30 am to 4:30 pm daily (closed on July 4 and Thanksgiving and Christmas days). Trunk Bay's snack bar and souvenir shops are open from 10 am to 4 pm.

CELL PHONE RECEPTION

There is cell phone service throughout the park, although some carriers have better coverage than others. AT&T has the best reception except for at many of the north shore beaches. Verizon, T-Mobile, and Sprint work fairly well in Cruz Bay but not other parts of the island. ⚠ **Be aware of international roaming charges especially near Coral Bay on the park's eastern side, where you're likely to pick up a cell-tower signal from the neighboring British Virgin Islands.**

Hotels

There are no hotels within Virgin Islands National Park, but St. John has options in many price ranges, though most of the island's accommodations are in private villas. The Cinnamon Bay Resort & Campground is expected to open in December 2021 after an extensive rebuild following hurricanes in 2017.

Restaurants

There are casual places to eat at Trunk Bay and at the Cinnamon Bay Resort & Campground. Elsewhere on the island, the dining options vary in terms of offerings and prices.

Tours

St. John taxi drivers offer island tours with stops at various sites, including Trunk Bay and Annaberg Plantation. A three-hour tour for two or more passengers is about $35 per person. Rangers at the park visitor center conduct several on- and offshore tours, some of which require reservations. The Friends of the Virgin Islands National Park also has a number of seasonal offerings.

Friends of Virgin Islands National Park
SPECIAL-INTEREST | This nonprofit offers tours or seminars each month between December and May. Options might include exploring the traditional uses for local plants, guided paddles of Maho Bay to learn about turtles, and hikes on more challenging trails like those to Ram Head and at Brown Bay. Friends' seminars are free to members ($30 a year) or $30 per person for nonmembers. ☎ *340/779–4940* 🌐 *friendsvinp.org.*

Visitor Information

CONTACTS Virgin Islands National Park. ✉ *North Shore Rd., at creek, Cruz Bay* ☎ *340/776–6201* 🌐 *www.nps.gov/viis.*

St. John

6½ miles (10½ km) east via ferry from Red Hook on St. Thomas to Cruz Bay on St. John.

About twice as long as it is wide, St. John has a "spine" of barely inhabited, 1,000-foot (305-km) peaks running along its center. Two main settlements outside park boundaries cap both ends of the island: Cruz Bay, home to the park visitor center, is to the west, and Coral Bay is to the east. Drives between things here are short. On the east end, you'll find park beaches and trails about 2 miles (3¼ km) east of Coral Bay and 10 miles (16 km) east of Cruz Bay. From Cruz Bay, south shore attractions include the Reef Bay Trailhead (5½ miles [9 km]) and Salt Pond Bay (12 miles [19¼ km]).

BEACHES

Cinnamon Bay Beach
BEACH—SIGHT | **FAMILY** | This long, sandy beach faces beautiful cays. There's excellent snorkeling off the point to the right; look for the big angelfish and large schools of purple triggerfish. Afternoons on Cinnamon Bay can be windy—a boon for windsurfers but an annoyance for sunbathers—so arrive early to beat the gusts. The Cinnamon Bay hiking trail begins across the road from the beach parking lot; ruins mark the trailhead. There are actually two paths here: a level nature trail (with signs to identify flora) that loops through the woods and passes an old Danish cemetery and a steep trail that starts where the road bends past the ruins and heads straight up to

Route 10. **Amenities:** parking; toilets. **Best for:** snorkeling; swimming; walking; windsurfing. ✉ *North Shore Rd., Rte. 20, Cinnamon Bay* ✣ *About 4 miles (6 km) east of Cruz Bay* 🌐 *www.nps.gov/viis.*

Francis Bay Beach

BEACH—SIGHT | Because there's little shade, this beach gets toasty in the afternoon, when the sun comes around to the west, but the rest of the day it's a delightful stretch of white sand. The only facilities are a few picnic tables tucked among the trees and a portable restroom, but folks come here to watch the birds that live in the swampy area behind the beach. There's a boardwalk here for bird-watching. The park offers bird-watching hikes here on Friday morning; sign up at the visitor center in Cruz Bay. To get here, turn left at the Annaberg intersection. **Amenities:** parking; toilets. **Best for:** snorkeling; swimming; walking. ✉ *North Shore Rd., Rte. 20, Francis Bay* ✣ *¼ mile (½ km) from Annaberg intersection* 🌐 *www.nps.gov/viis.*

Hawksnest Beach

BEACH—SIGHT | Seagrapes and waving palm trees line this narrow beach, and there are portable toilets, cooking grills, and a covered shed for picnicking. It's the closest drivable beach to Cruz Bay, so it's often crowded with locals and visitors. A patchy reef just offshore means snorkeling is an easy swim away, but the best underwater views are reserved for ambitious snorkelers who head farther to the east along the bay's fringes. Watch out for boat traffic: although a channel of buoys marks where dinghies or other small vessels can come up onto the sand to drop off or pick up passengers, the occasional boater strays into the swim area. **Amenities:** parking; toilets. **Best for:** snorkeling; swimming. ✉ *North Shore Rd., Rte. 20, Estate Hawksnest* ✣ *About 2 miles (3 km) east of Cruz Bay* 🌐 *www.nps.gov/viis.*

Lameshur Bay Beach

BEACH—SIGHT | This seagrape-fringed beach is toward the end of a partially paved, rut-strewn road (don't attempt it without a four-wheel-drive vehicle) on the southeast coast. The reward for your bumpy drive is good snorkeling and a chance to spy on some pelicans. The beach has a couple of picnic tables, rusting barbecue grills, and a portable restroom. The ruins of the old plantation are a five-minute walk down the road past the beach. The area has good hiking trails, including a trek (nearly 2 miles [3 km]) up Bordeaux Mountain before an easy walk to Yawzi Point. **Amenities:** parking; toilets. **Best for:** snorkeling; swimming; walking. ✉ *Off Rte. 107, Lameshur Bay* ✣ *About 1½ miles (2½ km) from Salt Pond* 🌐 *www.nps.gov/viis.*

Maho Bay Beach

BEACH—SIGHT | Maho Bay Beach is a gorgeous strip of sand that sits right along the North Shore Road. It's a popular place, particularly on weekends, when locals come out in droves to party at the picnic tables on the south end of the beach. The snorkeling along the rocky edges is good, but the center is mostly sea grass. If you're lucky, you'll cross paths with turtles. There are portable toilets at the end of the beach, and a food truck, bar, and a couple of shops across from the beach. **Amenities:** food and drink; parking; toilets. **Best for:** snorkeling; swimming. ✉ *North Shore Rd., Rte. 20, Estate Maho Bay* 🌐 *www.nps.gov/viis.*

Salt Pond Bay Beach

BEACH—SIGHT | If you're adventurous, this rocky beach on the scenic southeastern coast—next to rugged Drunk Bay—is worth exploring. It's a short hike down a hill from the parking lot, and the only facilities are a portable toilet and a few picnic tables scattered about. Tide pools are filled with all sorts of marine creatures, and the snorkeling is good, particularly along the bay's edges. A short walk takes you to a pond where salt crystals collect around the edges. Hike farther uphill past cactus gardens to Ram Head for see-forever views. Leave nothing valuable in your car, as thefts are common. **Amenities:** parking; toilets. **Best for:** snorkeling; swimming; walking. ✉ *Rte. 107, about 3 miles (5 km) south of Coral Bay, Concordia* 🌐 *www.nps.gov/viis.*

★ Trunk Bay Beach

BEACH—SIGHT | St. John's most photographed beach is also the preferred spot for beginning snorkelers because of its underwater trail. (Cruise-ship passengers interested in snorkeling for a day flock here, so if you're looking for seclusion, arrive early or later in the day.) Crowded or not, this stunning beach is one of the island's most beautiful. There are changing rooms with showers, bathrooms, a food concession, picnic tables, a gift shop, phones, lockers, and snorkeling-equipment rentals. The parking lot often overflows, but you can park along the road as long as the tires are off the pavement. **Amenities:** food and drink; lifeguards; parking; showers; toilets; water sports. **Best for:** snorkeling; swimming; windsurfing. ✉ *North Shore Rd., Rte. 20, Estate Trunk Bay* ✣ *About 2½ miles (4 km) east of Cruz Bay* 🌐 *www.nps.gov/viis* 🎫 *$5.*

HISTORIC SIGHTS

★ Annaberg Plantation

HISTORIC SITE | In the 18th century, sugar plantations dotted the steep hills of this island. Slaves and free Danes and Dutchmen toiled to harvest the cane that was used to create sugar, molasses, and rum for export. Built in the 1780s, the partially restored plantation at Leinster Bay was once an important sugar mill. Although there are no official visiting hours, the National Park Service has regular tours, and some well-informed taxi drivers will show you around. Occasionally you may see a living-history demonstration—someone making johnnycakes or weaving baskets. For information on tours and cultural events, contact the national park visitor center. ✉ *Leinster Bay Rd., Annaberg* ☎ *340/776–6201* 🌐 *www.nps.gov/viis.*

SCENIC DRIVES

North Shore Road

SCENIC DRIVE | Start at the national park visitor center, and head east along North Shore Road (aka Route 20). The nearly 7-mile (11-km) stretch passes some of the park's most iconic beaches and scenic stops. 🌐 *www.nps.gov/viis.*

SCENIC STOPS

Caneel Bay Overlook

VIEWPOINT | The first pullover on the North Shore Road driving east from Cruz Bay overlooks the former Caneel Resort. Hurricanes in 2017 damaged the property, but the beach view is as beautiful as ever. ✉ *North Shore Rd., Rte. 20, Estate Caneel Bay* ✣ *1½ miles (2½ km) east of Cruz Bay* 🌐 *www.nps.gov/viis.*

Coral Bay Overlook

VIEWPOINT | Just west of Coral Bay, this overlook offers sweeping views of its namesake bay and the harbor. ✉ *Centerline Rd., Rte. 10, Coral Bay* ✣ *About 2 miles (3¼ km) west of Coral Bay, 7 miles (11¼ km) east of Cruz Bay* 🌐 *www.nps.gov/viis.*

Cruz Bay Overlook

VIEWPOINT | Slightly east of the national park visitor center on North Shore Road, this viewpoint offers a bird's-eye look at Cruz Bay and the east end of St. Thomas to the west. ✉ *North Shore Rd., Rte. 20, Estate Caneel Bay* ✣ *¼ mile (½ km) east of Cruz Bay* 🌐 *www.nps.gov/viis.*

Maho Bay Overlook

VIEWPOINT | On a sunny day, stands of sea grass are visible beneath the bay's clear turquoise waters from this vantage point. It's this grass that attracts sea turtles (and the snorkelers to see the turtles). ✉ *North Shore Rd., Rte. 20, Estate Maho Bay* ✣ *5½ miles (9 km) east of Cruz Bay* 🌐 *www.nps.gov/viis.*

The park service offers tours of the 18th-century Annaberg sugar plantation.

Trunk Bay Overlook

VIEWPOINT | Just east of the Caneel Bay Overlook, this roadside pullout offers a similar hillside view down on Trunk Bay Beach. If you look closely, or with binoculars, you can see snorkelers looking down at the submerged plaques along an underwater trail. ✉ *North Shore Rd., Rte. 20, Estate Trunk Bay* ✣ *3 miles (5 km) east of Caneel Bay* 🌐 *www.nps.gov/viis.*

TRAILS

Cinnamon Bay Loop Trail & Cinnamon Bay Trail

TRAIL | An easy, self-guided, ½-mile (1-km) loop trail takes you on a leisurely tour of the former Cinnamon Bay Plantation grounds. Numerous stone ruins, fragrant bay rum trees, and even tombs of the former 19th-century owners are here. Placards point out the sights and narrate the history. For those up to a more ambitious hike, the Cinnamon Bay Trail starts just east of the loop trail's entrance. It's a 1-mile (1½-km) hike uphill to where the trail ends at Centerline Road. At the 1/3-mile mark, a spur trail leads to the great house ruins at America Hill. *Easy–Moderate.* ✉ *North Shore Rd., Rte. 20, Cinnamon Bay* ✣ *Trailhead: About 4 miles (6 km) east of Cruz Bay* 🌐 *www.nps.gov/viis.*

Lind Point Trail

TRAIL | Starting from the national park visitor center, this 1.1-mile (1¾-km) trail connects Cruz Bay and Honeymoon Beach at Caneel. Along the way are scenic views of Cruz Bay and an abundance of flora and fauna, including cactus and hermit crabs. At the ¾-mile point, a spur trail runs down to Salomon Beach, reachable only on foot or by boat. A beach bar and restaurant at Honeymoon Beach sells food and drink and offers water-sports and beach-chair rentals. *Easy.* ✉ *North Shore Rd., Rte. 20, Cruz Bay* ✣ *Trailhead: At the Creek in Cruz Bay* 🌐 *www.nps.gov/viis.*

★ Reef Bay Trail

TRAIL | This is one of the most interesting hikes on St. John, but unless you're a rugged individualist who wants a physical challenge (and that describes a lot of people who stay on St. John), you can probably get the most out of the trip if you join a hike led by a park service ranger. A ranger can identify the trees and plants on the hike down, fill you in on the history of the Reef Bay Plantation, and tell you about the petroglyphs on the rocks at the bottom of the trail. A side trail takes you to the plantation's great house, a gutted but mostly intact structure with vestiges of its former beauty.. Take the safari bus from the park's visitor center. A boat takes you from the beach at Reef Bay back to the visitor center, saving you the uphill climb. It's a good idea to make reservations for this trip, especially during the winter season. They can be made at the Friends of the Park store, in Mongoose Junction. *Difficult.* ✉ *Rte. 10, Reef Bay* ☎ *340/779–4940 for reservations* 🌐 *www.nps.gov/viis or friendsvinp.org* 🎫 *$60 includes a safari bus ride to the trailhead, a guided tour, and a boat ride back to the visitor center.*

UNDERWATER SIGHTS

Trunk Bay Underwater Trail

TRAIL | This 650-foot round-trip snorkel trail starts just off the beach, follows the west side of Trunk Bay Cay, then turns back towards shore. Underwater plaques narrate what you see along the way as well as trail directions. Hard corals, soft corals, and parrotfish are a few of the topics. ✉ *North Shore Rd., Rte. 20, Estate Trunk Bay* ✣ *About 2½ miles (4 km) east of Cruz Bay* 🌐 *www.nps.gov/viis.*

VISITOR CENTERS

V.I. National Park Visitors Center

INFO CENTER | To pick up a useful guide to St. John's hiking trails, see various large maps of the island, and find out about current park service programs, including guided walks and cultural demonstrations, stop by the visitor center. ✉ *North Shore Rd., near creek, Cruz Bay* ☎ *340/776–6201* 🌐 *www.nps.gov/viis.*

Coffee and Quick Bites

Snack Shack

$ | **AMERICAN** | Burgers, hot dogs, pulled-pork nachos, fries, chips, and ice cream are among the menu items at this concession situated up under the trees near Trunk Bay Beach. **Known for:** takeout treats; shady beach-area locale; beer and blender drinks. 💲 *Average main: $11* ✉ *Trunk Bay , North Shore Rd., Rte. 20, Estate Trunk Bay* ✣ *About 2½ miles (4 km) east of Cruz Bay* 🌐 *www.nps.gov/viis.*

Shopping

★ **Friends of the Park Store**

ART GALLERIES | Find books and locally made beachwear, such as flip-flops made of coconut husks and recycled rubber, at this store run by the nonprofit group that raises money for Virgin Islands National Park. It's a great spot to buy educational materials for kids and books about the island. It's also the place to make reservations for a guided hike along Reef Bay Trail. ✉ *Mongoose Junction Shopping Center, North Shore Rd., Cruz Bay* ☎ *340/779–4940* 🌐 *www.friendsvinp.org.*

National Park Headquarters Bookstore

BOOKS/STATIONERY | The bookshop at Virgin Islands National Park Visitor Center sells several good histories of St. John. ✉ *Visitor Center, North Shore Rd., Rte. 20, Cruz Bay* ☎ *340/776-6201* 🌐 *www.nps.gov/viis.*

Hassel Island

11½ miles (18½ km) west of Cruz Bay, St. John, in the St. Thomas Harbor.

Hassel Island, which has a couple historic sites, is accessible only by the Water Island Ferry, on a kayak tour, private boat, or as part of a tour led by the Virgin Islands National Park or the St. Thomas Historical Trust.

Cruz Bay, home to the national park visitor center, is a good base from which to explore.

Sights

HISTORIC SIGHTS

Creque Marine Railway

HISTORIC SITE | The epicenter of ship repair in the Virgin Islands in the 1800s sat at this marine railway, which could handle vessels of up to 1,200 tons. You can still see remnants of the rails that led into the water, the cradle on which vessels sat, and the winch that helped to hoist them so that shipwrights could perform repairs. ⊕ *In St. Thomas' Charlotte Amalie Harbor* 🌐 *www.nps.gov/viis.*

Shipley's Battery

HISTORIC SITE | Established by the Danes in the late 1700s to guard the entrance to the St. Thomas Harbor, this site was occupied by the British in the early 1800s during the Napoleonic Wars. Today, you can walk the ruins and see the remnants of a guard house. ⊕ *In St. Thomas' Charlotte Amalie Harbor* 🌐 *www.nps.gov/viis.*

Activities

BIRD-WATCHING

Some 144 bird species either live on or visit the island during the year. The 1-mile (1½-km) boardwalk trail at Francis Bay is a prime spot for sighting shore birds. Species here and nearby vary depending on the time of year and include hummingbirds, doves, cuckoos, thrashers, and stilts. The park visitor center in Cruz Bay offers free birding lists, which you can also download (🌐 *www.nps.gov/viis/learn/nature/upload/virginislandsbirdlist.pdf*).

BOATING AND RAFTING

Love City Excursions

BOATING | **FAMILY** | Half- and full-day charters make swimming and snorkeling stops at park beaches, quiet anchorages, and offshore cays. The company operates three powerboats, two of which are catamarans that offer great stability for family trips. The per-person cost for snorkel trips is between $90 (half day) and $140 (full day). Powerboat trips for up to eight people cost between $750 (half day) and $1,000 (full day), including captain, fuel, towels, and cold drinks. ✉ *Cruz Bay, Cruz Bay* ✢ *Across from national park visitor center* ☏ *340/998–7604* 🌐 *www.lovecity-excursions.com.*

CAMPING

Cinnamon Bay Campground & Resort. This camping resort sits right on the beach in the heart of Virgin Islands National Park. It was damaged during the 2017 hurricane and slated to reopen in December of 2021 featuring 31 platform bare sites with picnic tables and charcoal grills; 55 eco-tents, with queen-size beds or a queen and set of bunks, along with linens, electricity, fans, picnic tables, charcoal grills, and cooking and dining supplies; and 40 cottages with the same assortment of amenities as the eco-tents. Showers and flush toilets, as well as a small store and a cafeteria-style restaurant serving three meals a day, are a short walk from the campsites. The area can be buggy, and there can be some traffic noise, but the beachfront location is nice as is the concession that rents single and double kayaks, stand-up paddleboards, snorkel gear, and beach chairs. There are hiking trails and other activities close by, too. Reservations are essential in the winter and recommended at other times. ✉ *North Shore Rd., Rte. 20, Cinnamon Bay* ☏ *340/776–6201* 🌐 *www.cinnamonbayresort.com.*

DIVING AND SNORKELING

Although just about every beach has nice snorkeling—Trunk Bay, Cinnamon Bay, and Waterlemon Cay at Leinster Bay get the most praise—you need a boat (sign on with any of the island's water-sports operators) to reach the more remote snorkeling locations and the best scuba spots. Top places between St. John and St. Thomas include the tunnels at **Thatch Cay,** the ledges at **Congo Cay,** and the wreck of the ***General Rogers.*** Dive off St. John at **Stephens Cay,** a short boat ride out of Cruz Bay, where fish swim around the reefs as you float downward. At **Devers Bay,** on St. John's south shore, fish dart about in colorful schools. **Carval Rock,** shaped like an old-time ship, has gorgeous rock formations, coral gardens, and lots of fish. It can be too rough here in winter, though.

Count on paying $120 for a one-tank dive and $145 for a two-tank dive. Rates include equipment and a tour. If you've never dived before, try an introductory resort course. If scuba certification is in your vacation plans, island dive shops can help you get your card.

Cruz Bay Watersports

SCUBA DIVING | Regular reef, wreck, and night dives, as well as USVI and BVI snorkel tours, are among this operator's offerings. It has a second location at the Ritz Carlton, St. Thomas, on St. Thomas. ✉ *The Westin St. John, 300 Chocolate Hole, Cruz Bay* ☏ *844/359–5457* 🌐 *www.cruzbaywatersports.com.*

Low Key Watersports

SCUBA DIVING | This PADI Five Star training facility offers two-tank dives and specialty courses. ✉ *1 Bay St., Cruz Bay* ☏ *340/693–8999* 🌐 *www.divelowkey.com.*

EDUCATIONAL PROGRAMS

Throughout the year, park rangers conduct several weekly talks and guided tours. Schedules are available at the visitor center in Cruz Bay. From December to May, the nonprofit Friends of Virgin Islands National Park offers enlightening seminars or outings.

FISHING

Just Fish St. John

FISHING | Captain Josh offers four-, six-, and eight-hour charters. Half-day (four-hour) inshore trips are usually in park waters. Catch bonito, rainbow runner, and the occasional tuna that makes it way closer to shore. Charters, which include bait, tackle, beer, and soft drinks, start at $650 for a half day. ✉ *Cruz Bay, Cruz Bay* ✥ *At the Creek in front of the park visitor center* ☎ *340/244–9633* 🌐 *www.justfishstjohn.com.*

HIKING

Although it's fun to go on guided hikes, don't be afraid to head out on your own. Stop by the visitor center in Cruz Bay, and pick up the free guide detailing points of interest, trail lengths, and estimated hiking times, as well as any dangers you might encounter. Although the park staff recommends long pants to protect against thorns and insects, most people hike in shorts because it can get very hot. Wear sturdy shoes or boots even if you're hiking to the beach. Don't forget to bring water and insect repellent.

KAYAKING AND PADDLEBOARDING

Guided kayak and stand-up paddleboard (SUP) tours are offered several times weekly by private companies that operate within park waters. Outfitters like Arawak Adventures rent sit-atop kayaks for $50 a day or $200 a week.

Arawak Expeditions

KAYAKING | FAMILY | In addition to half-day kayak and SUP tours of the park's east end, near Hurricane Hole, this operator offers instruction and rentals. Expect to pay from $75 per person for a half-day kayak tour and $95 for a half-day SUP tour. You can rent kayaks ($50) and SUPs ($75) by the day or by the week (from $200). ✉ *North Shore Rd., Rte. 20, at Mongoose Junction Shopping Center next to Sun Dog Cafe, Cruz Bay* ☎ *340/693–8912* 🌐 *arawakexp.com.*

Crabby's Watersports

KAYAKING | FAMILY | Crabby's rents kayaks ($50) and SUPs ($75) by the day and offers guided tours of Hurricane Hole. ✉ *Rte. 107, Coral Bay* ✥ *At the Coco Lobo Plaza, Coral Bay* ☎ *970/ 817–8817* 🌐 *www.crabbyswatersports.com.*

★ **Virgin Islands Ecotours**

KAYAKING | FAMILY | Learn about natural history on three- or five-hour guided kayak trips, with free snorkel instruction, to St. John's Honeymoon Bay, Hassel Island, and St. Thomas's Mangrove Lagoon (there's also a one-hour stand-up paddleboard tour of the lagoon), as well as on excursions to Henley and Patricia cays. The Hassel Island tour features a visit to historic forts, a short hike to a breathtaking vista, and a swim off a deserted beach. Three-hour trips include snacks; five-hour trips include lunch. ✉ *Mangrove Lagoon, Rte. 32, 2 miles (3 km) east of the intersection of Rtes. 32 and 30, Nadir* ☎ *340/779–2155, 877/845–2925* 🌐 *www.viecotours.com* 💵 *From $69 per person; 1-hr SUP tour $39.*

Nearby Towns

St. John's towns, **Cruz Bay** on the west end and **Coral Bay** to the east, are the two oases where there's several many services and amenities. Cruz Bay is by far the bigger of the two towns and has major resorts, condo complexes, and guesthouses; restaurants that range from open-air beach bars to white tablecloth establishments; and shops that sell everything from diamonds to batik beachwear. There are also supermarkets, banks, churches, pharmacies, car rentals, a taxi stand, and gas stations. The inter-island ferry dock is also here.

Coral Bay—really more of a settlement than a town—is home to a few restaurants and bars, a supermarket, and watersports rentals. Villa rentals, built on small, non-park-land inholdings, are available all over the island.

Chapter 58

VOYAGEURS NATIONAL PARK

Updated by
Eric Peterson

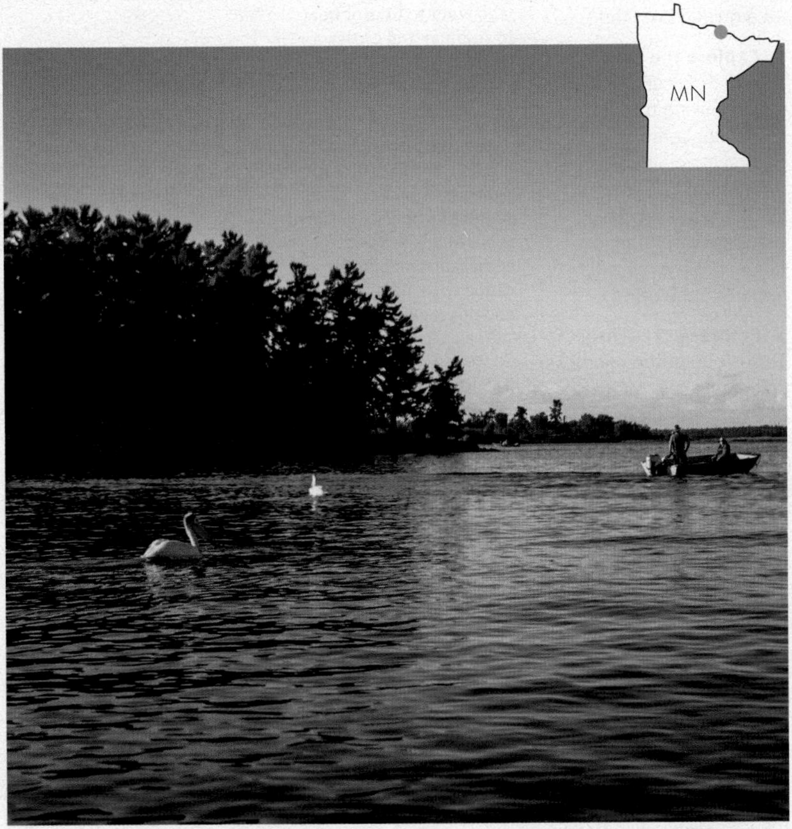

MN

WELCOME TO VOYAGEURS NATIONAL PARK

TOP REASONS TO GO

★ **Explore the waters:** You can follow in the ripples left by trappers and anglers from a bygone at this park, much of which is only accessible by water. Bring a vessel—motorized or not—or reserve a spot on a guided boat tour.

★ **Explore the North Woods:** You can reach several hiking trails from the visitor centers without embarking on a boat trip. Accessing trailheads for longer routes typically requires water transportation, but the rewards are worth the effort.

★ **Embrace the winter:** This is one of the country's coldest places, but that doesn't deter cross-country skiers, snowshoers, and snowmobilers from visiting when the lakes are topped with ice. Indeed, ice roads on the lakes make the park more car-friendly in the winter than it is in the summer.

★ **Find solitude:** Although about a ¼ million people visit each year, the heart of the park remains peaceful, with the calls of loons and howls of wolves replacing the sounds of civilization.

1 Rainy Lake. East of International Falls, Minnesota, the region's largest body of water is on the northwest side of Voyageurs. The southeastern corner of this lake lies within park boundaries, and its eponymous visitor center, which is accessible by car, is the primary hub for those who want to hike or boat in summer and cross-country-ski or drive ice roads in winter.

2 Kabetogama Lake. Also accessible by car, this lake is southeast of Rainy Lake. Its namesake visitor center sits on its southern shore and is a major embarkation point for canoe trips, boat tours, and other excursions. To the east, Ash Point Visitor Center also sits on Kabetogama's edge and is a good starting point for backcountry canoe trips to Namakan and Sand Point lakes.

3 Namakan Lake. Just east of Kabetogama and inaccessible by car, the lake has the park's only hotel on its north shore at Kettle Falls.

4 Sand Point Lake. The smallest of the park's major lakes is southeast of Namakan and is also inaccessible by car.

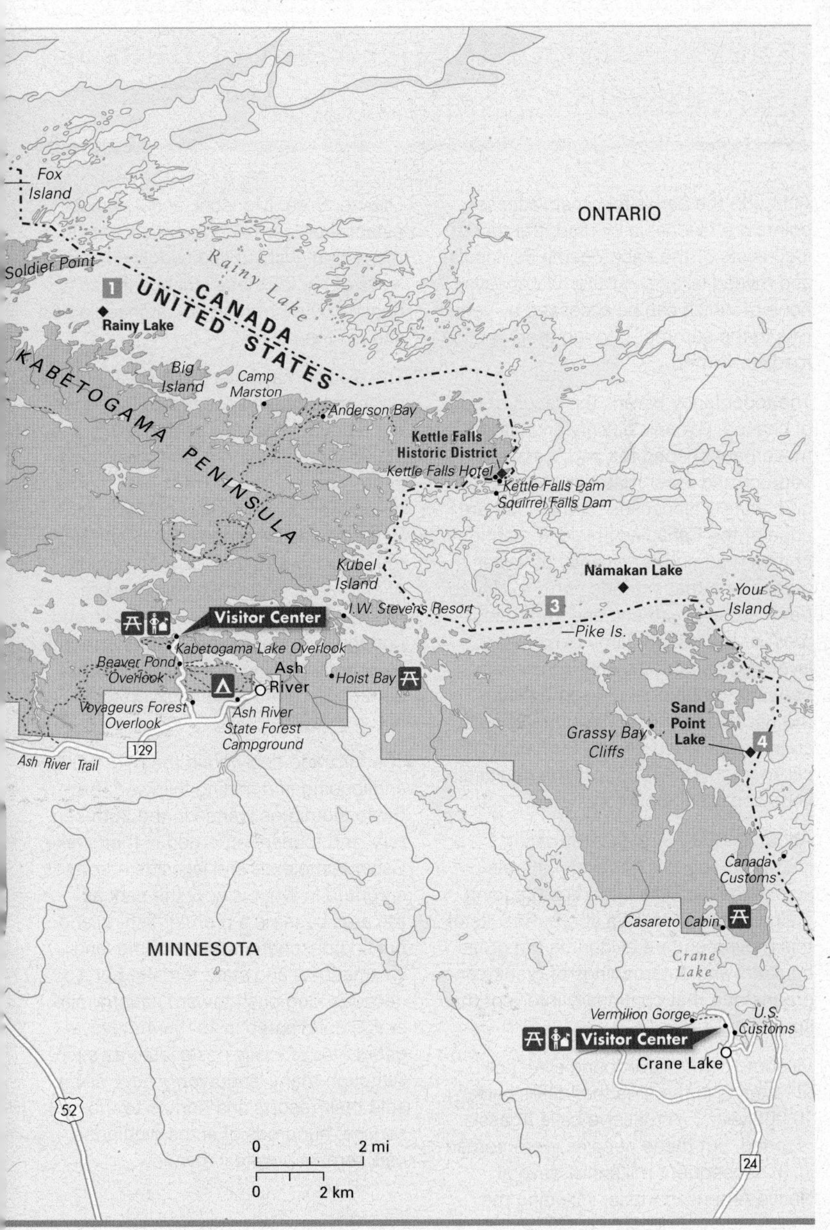

ONTARIO
Fox Island
Soldier Point
Rainy Lake
1
Rainy Lake
CANADA
UNITED STATES
KABETOGAMA PENINSULA
Big Island
Camp Marston
Anderson Bay
Kettle Falls Historic District
Kettle Falls Hotel
Kettle Falls Dam
Squirrel Falls Dam
Kubel Island
Namakan Lake
3
Your Island
I.W. Stevens Resort
Pike Is.
Visitor Center
Kabetogama Lake Overlook
Beaver Pond Overlook
Ash River
Hoist Bay
Voyageurs Forest Overlook
Ash River State Forest Campground
129
Ash River Trail
Grassy Bay Cliffs
Sand Point Lake
4
Canada Customs
Casareto Cabin
Crane Lake
MINNESOTA
Vermilion Gorge
U.S. Customs
Visitor Center
Crane Lake
52
24
0
2 mi
0
2 km

You must rent, borrow, or own a watercraft to access most of this untouched wilderness, located along 55 miles of the border between Minnesota and Ontario, Canada.

Although the park's four main access points are reachable by road, the rest of it consists of the Kabetogama Peninsula and myriad lakes and other waterways, none of which can be accessed by vehicles in the summer (though there are ice roads in winter).

The topography here is the result of eons of change. Volcanic activity and glacial movement shaped the park's ancient bedrock and other material into this rugged, watery landscape on the southern edge of the Canadian Shield, a mantle of rock made predominantly of volcanic greenstone that extends north to Hudson Bay. Farther south and encompassing most of the Kabetogama Peninsula, a layer of granite and biotite schist lies beneath the bedrock. In some places, the two types of rock have intermingled, creating a swirled-striped formation called migmatite. South of the peninsula, vermilion granite predominates.

About 11,000 years ago, retreating glaciers dragged rocks and minerals across the land like fingertips dragging grains of sand across a shore. Results of this movement are evident in the great boulders and outcroppings of granite and greenstone that continually interrupt the soil line.

Paleontologists have found evidence of humans in the area that dates back 10,000 years, as massive Lake Agassiz receded, but these peoples were nomadic. In subsequent millennia, several Native American tribes, including the Ojibwe, Cree, Monsoni, and Assiniboin, established permanent settlements in the region. Fishing and paddling were ways of life for these inhabitants, as evidenced by more than 200 archaeological sites in the park.

The glacier may have given Voyageurs its ancient, rumpled appearance, but it was the hardy fur trappers of the 1700s and 1800s who gave the park its evocative, contemporary name. The most colorful of these men were the French Canadians who traveled by canoe from Montréal to far northwestern Canada in pursuit of animal pelts. *Les voyageurs* were renowned for their ability to paddle and portage with near super-human strength, reportedly making one powerful stroke per second and traveling for up to 16 hours a day.

The fur trade declined in the mid-1800s, and logging and mining followed. But those industries waned in the 20th-century, and tourism emerged in their wake. Cabin complexes and lakeside resorts sprouted in what is now the park as the area became a premier fishing and boating destination. Most of the land was national and state forests, but a decades-long push toward national park status culminated in 1975 when Voyageurs was officially designated as such. Although many landowners have since sold their resorts and homes to the park service, hundreds of acres within the park remain privately owned.

AVERAGE HIGH/LOW TEMPERATURES					
JAN.	FEB.	MAR.	APR.	MAY	JUNE
16/-5	23/-2	35/12	52/27	65/39	73/49
JULY	AUG.	SEPT.	OCT.	NOV.	DEC.
77/54	76/52	66/43	51/32	34/19	20/2

Planning

When to Go

If you're a snowmobiler, cross-country skier, or ice fisher, January and February visits are best, though snow often lasts well into March. Early spring isn't the best time to visit: it's too humid, and the mosquitoes and black flies are ferocious. If you're coming up for warm-weather fishing, you'll do best in late May and June or September and October. Summer is when the park is most crowded—with both people and bugs! Late summer and early fall are great seasons for hiking and boating.

Getting Here and Around

AIR

The nearest major airport is Minneapolis–St. Paul International, about 300 miles south of Voyageurs. From there, you can take a connecting flight to the airport in International Falls, 12 miles west of the park's Rainy Lake Visitor Center.

BOAT

Though you can get to its entrances by car, actually driving into this watery park is another matter. You need a boat for most adventures. Although the park allows motorboats to be used everywhere, it's not allowed to rent them itself, as part of a deal made (when establishing the park) between landowners and the government. Concessionaires and lakeside resort owners supply rentals and "water taxi" services to visitors who haven't brought their own vessels.

CAR

From the Twin Cities, take I–35 to Route 33; then follow Route 33 for 17 miles north to U.S. 53. Take U.S. 53 north about 130 miles to Route 122, turn right, and follow the signs to Voyageurs' Kabetogama Visitor Center. If you're coming from International Falls, take U.S. 53 south 25 miles to Kabetogama or Route 11 roughly 12 miles east to Rainy Lake. Once you arrive, you'll need to park; there are no roads in the park, with the notable exception of ice roads on the frozen surfaces of Kabetogama and Rainy lakes in winter.

Inspiration

Grace Lee Nute's 1951 tome, *The Voyageur,* offers perhaps the most definitive history of the colorful fur traders to whom the park owes its name.

Park Essentials

ACCESSIBILITY

All three visitor centers (and their restrooms) are accessible to visitors with disabilities. Two short trails, the Oberholtzer and the Kabetogama Lake Overlook, are accessible, as are vessels used for park service tours; boat launches at Kabetogama and Rainy lakes; and campsites at Rainy, Kabetogama, and Namakan lakes.

PARK FEES AND PERMITS

There are no fees to enter the park. However, boats must be licensed, and overnight trips require a campsite permit ($15 to $25 per night plus $10 one-time reservation fee). Some park tours also have fees.

PARK HOURS

Voyageurs is open 24 hours daily, although services are limited after visitor centers close for the night at 4 or 5 pm.

CELL PHONE RECEPTION

Cell phone reception is spotty throughout the park, especially in the backcountry.

Hotels

There's only one property, the Kettle Falls Hotel, in Voyageurs, and it's only accessible by water. There are, however, numerous area lakeside resorts and cabin complexes outside park boundaries.

Restaurants

The Kettle Falls Hotel is home to the park's only dining room, as well as a legendary watering hole. Reaching the hotel requires a boat ride, though. You'll find more dining options (as well as grocery stores) in International Falls, other area communities, and at lakeside resorts outside Voyageurs' boundaries.

Hotel and restaurant reviews have been shortened. For full information visit Fodors.com. Hotel prices are the lowest cost of a standard double room in high season. Restaurant prices are the average cost of a main course at dinner, or if dinner is not served, at lunch.

What It Costs

$	$$	$$$	$$$$
RESTAURANTS			
under $10	$10–$20	$21–$30	over $30
HOTELS			
under $70	$70–$90	$91–$200	over $200

Tours

Border Guide Service

BOAT TOURS | This outfitter offers narrated boat tours, including a sunset cruise on Kabetogama Lake; outings to Kettle Falls; and a full-day tour of Rainy, Kabetogama, Namakan, Sand Point, and Crane. Rates range from $40 to $200. Fishing, overnight, and customized tours are also available, as is water taxi service ($60). ✉ *9910 Gappa Rd., Kabetogama* ☎ *218/324–2430* 🌐 *www.voyageursnationalparktours.com.*

Voyageurs National Park Tour Boats

BOAT TOURS | Park boat tours travel from Rainy and Kabetogama lakes to Kettle Falls and beyond. If you're interested in wildlife, look into the Grand Tour or Life on the Lake excursion. Rates range from $25 to $45. Once a week in July and August, the park offers a free, 1½-hour North Canoe Voyage (from Rainy Lake) aboard a 26-foot canoe like those used by the original *voyageurs.* ✉ *Voyageurs National Park, 360 Hwy. 11 E, International Falls* ☎ *800/444–6777 for reservations, 218/286–5258 for information* 🌐 *www.recreation.gov.*

Voyageurs Outfitters

BOAT TOURS | Kayak or canoe trips and overnight "glamping" adventures are among this outfitter's park offerings. Per-person rates start at $50 or $100 for two-hour trips and run to $300 or $600 for up to six people on six-hour private outings. The company also offers water taxi services and rents camping gear, as well as canoes, stand-up paddleboards, sailboats, and cabin cruisers. Nonmotorized watercraft rentals are $40 a day; gear rentals and taxi fares vary. ✉ *3485 Spruce St., Ranier* ☎ *218/244–6506* 🌐 *www.voyageursoutfitters.com.*

The Ellsworth Rock Gardens are a great place to picnic.

Visitor Information

CONTACTS Voyageurs National Park. ✉ *360 Hwy. 11 E, International Falls* ☎ *218/283–6600.*

In the Park

International Falls is 12 miles west of Rainy Lake Visitor Center.

More than a third of the surface of Voyageurs National Park is water, with four major lakes accounting for most of it. From the west, the lakes are Rainy, Kabetogama, Namakan, and Sand Point. South of Sand Point and just outside the park's southeastern boundary, Crane Lake is a prime jumping-off point for trips to Sand Point Lake. The Kabetogama Peninsula separates the lake of the same name from Rainy Lake to the north.

Sights

GEOLOGICAL FORMATIONS

Kabetogama Lake

BODY OF WATER | In the heart of the park, this 25,000-acre lake is known for abundant walleye, 100 verdant miles of shoreline, and countless beautiful islands. It's the only lake in Voyageurs that's entirely within U.S. boundaries, though it's connected to other park lakes via waterways that travel into Canada. ✉ *Voyageurs National Park* ✣ *North of U.S. 53 via Gamma and Gappa roads.*

Namakan Lake

BODY OF WATER | Roughly the same size as Kabetogama Lake, this body of water is a premier fishing destination that's known not only for walleye and northern pike but also bluegill, lake sturgeon, and bullhead. It's only accessibly by boat, typically from the Ash River Visitor Center on the park's south side. ✉ *Voyageurs National Park* ✣ *South side of the park.*

Rainy Lake

BODY OF WATER | With a surface area of more than 227,000 acres, Rainy is one of the larger lakes (aside from the Great Lakes) straddling the Minnesota–Ontario border. A major destination for camping as well as boating and fishing, it's most easily accessed from the Rainy Lake Visitor Center. ✉ *Voyageurs National Park* ✣ *East of International Falls via Hwy. 11.*

Sand Point Lake

BODY OF WATER | The smallest of the four major lakes in Voyageurs takes its name from a sandy point on its Canadian shore. It's only accessible by boat (most trips start at the ranger station at Crane Lake to the south) and is popular for its fishing, camping, and snowmobiling opportunities. ✣ *North of Crane Lake via U.S. 53 and Hwys. 23 and 24.*

HISTORIC SIGHTS

Ellsworth Rock Gardens

GARDEN | Starting in the 1940s, Jack Ellsworth used native materials to craft terraced flower beds and abstract sculptures at his summer home on the north shore of Kabetogama Lake. The National Park Service acquired the property in the late 1970s and restored Ellsworth's creations—which range from figures to tables to gateways—in the process creating the park's most popular day-use area (it's a great spot for a picnic). The easiest way to get here is on a boat tour. ✉ *Voyageurs National Park* ✣ *On the north shore of Kabetogama Lake.*

TRAILS

Blind Ash Bay Trail

TRAIL | **FAMILY** | This is the best trail in Voyageurs that doesn't require a boat to reach the trailhead. Starting near the Ash River Visitor Center on the south side of Kabetogama Lake, the 2½-mile loop navigates rocky terrain through a boreal forest with superlative scenery. *Moderate.* ✉ *Vayageurs National Park, 9899 Mead Wood Rd., Orr* ✣ *Trailhead: At Kabetogama Lake Overlook near the Ash River Visitor Center.*

★ Cruiser Lake Trail

TRAIL | You need a boat to reach this route's trailhead, but it's worth it. The best hiking trail in Voyageurs is also the longest, running about 9 miles from Lost Bay on Kabetogama Lake to Rainy Lake, but there are several side loops you can take if you want a longer adventure. It's a good way to see the variety of the park's terrain, from spruce bogs to rocky ridges to tranquil lakes. Along this trail you'll also find campsites. Many are on small, tree-lined lakes, which means great views, a source of water (just be sure to filter or boil it), and an excellent chance that loons will serenade you to sleep. *Difficult.* ✉ *Voyageurs National Park* ✣ *Trailhead: On the northeastern side of Kabetogama Lake.*

Oberholtzer Trail

TRAIL | One of a few Voyageurs trails that can be reached without a boat, this 1.7-mile round-trip loop provides access to forest and wetland environments. It also has two scenic overlooks. *Easy.* ✉ *1797 Ut-342, International Falls* ✣ *Trailhead: At the Rainy Lake Visitor Center.*

VISITOR CENTERS

Ash River Visitor Center

INFO CENTER | Situated in the historic Meadwood Lodge, the Ash River Visitor Center overlooks Kabetogama Lake and features an accessible picnic area, a bookstore, exhibits, and an information desk. It's open from 9 am to 5 pm in the summer and is closed from late September to late May. ✉ *Voyageurs National Park, 9899 Mead Wood Rd., Orr* ☎ *218/374–3221* 🌐 *www.nps.gov/voya.*

Kabetogama Lake Visitor Center

INFO CENTER | On the southwest shoreline of its namesake lake and open 9 am to 5 pm from late May to late September, this visitor center has interactive exhibits, a bookstore, a boarding dock for ranger-led tours, and a free public boat launch. There's also separate access for paddle-powered craft. ✉ *Voyageurs National Park, 9940 Cedar La., Kabetogama* ☎ *218/875–2111* 🌐 *www.nps.gov/voya.*

Rainy Lake Visitor Center
INFO CENTER | On the south shore of Black Bay, 12 miles east of International Falls, this is the main access point for the north part of the park. It's also the only year-round visitor center, with a bookstore, exhibits, and a free public boat launch. In winter, it serves as the gateway to the Rainy Lake Ice Road. ✉ *Voyageurs National Park, 1797 Ut-342, International Falls* ☎ *218/286–5258* 🌐 *www.nps.gov/voya.*

Restaurants

Kettle Falls Hotel Dining Room
$$ | **AMERICAN** | The setting is rustic, and the food is traditional Minnesotan (chicken, burgers, and, of course, walleye) at the park's only restaurant, which is accessible only by boat or seaplane and serves three meals a day to guests and nonguests. Dinners are all-you-can-eat affairs, with two main-course options, and the bar (aka The Lumberjack Saloon at the Tiltin' Hilton), is a thing of legend, with a hardwood floor that's not only sloped but also full of divots left by loggers who walked on it in their spiky boots. **Known for:** hearty meals; convivial atmosphere; authentic historical setting. $ *Average main: $20* ✉ *Mailing address, 10518 Gamma Rd., Kabetogama* ✣ *In the Kettle Hotel on the north shore of the junction of Rainy and Namakan lakes* ☎ *218/240–1726, 218/875–2070 off-season information* 🌐 *www.kettlefallshotel.com* ⏲ *Closed Oct.–Apr.*

Hotels

★ **Kettle Falls Hotel**
$$ | **RESORT** | Opened in 1913 and renovated in 1987, the park's only hotel is trim, tidy, and remote (15 miles from the nearest road and less than ½ mile from Canada); it also has a colorful history that begins with its initial proprietress, Madame Nellie Bly, who, as the story goes, sold it to a bootlegger in 1918 for $1,000 and four bottles of whiskey. **Pros:** has the national park's only restaurant; picture-perfect veranda with great sunset views; comfortable, peaceful, and historically interesting. **Cons:** remote (only accessible by boat or seaplane); basic amenities; rooms in main building are small. $ *Rooms from: $90* ✉ *10518 Gamma Rd., Kabetogama* ✣ *On the north shore of the junction of Rainy and Namakan lakes* ☎ *218/240–1726, 218/875–2070 off-season information* 🌐 *www.kettlefallshotel.com* ⏲ *Closed Oct.–Apr.* *18 units* *No meals.*

Activities

BOATING, CANOEING, AND KAYAKING

Boating, canoeing, and kayaking—for fishing, to reach trailheads and camping spots, or just for pleasure—is the chief summer pastime at Voyageurs. There are boat launches at all the park visitor centers and private docks at most lakeside resorts outside park boundaries. Many resorts also rent boats (fees vary). For most visitors, though, a guided excursion is the best way to explore these waters. The park maintains a list of authorized outfitters.

Although the park service leaves most boat rentals to the resorts, it does offer canoes for day use and overnight trips on various inland lakes, including Locator, Cruiser, Ek, Loiten, Shoepack, and Little Shoepack. Though same-day canoes might be available, it's best to reserve at least week in advance (🌐 *recreation.gov*). The canoes are locked up at shorelines; you pick up the keys at visitor centers. Several area boat-tour companies also rent canoes, as well as kayaks, stand-up paddleboards, and motorized vessels.

There is yet another boating option here during the May-to-October season: houseboating. Large double-decker craft, which have sleeping quarters and kitchens, in most cases, combine recreation with lodging. Depending on the number of people in your party and the size of the boat, rates range from $300 to $1,500 per day, with the per-day cost dropping if you rent by the week.

Northern Lights Resort & Outfitting
BOATING | FAMILY | This well-established cabin resort on Kabetogama Lake offers a range of boat rentals, including motorized fishing boats, canoes, and kayaks. Motorboats typically start at $165 per day; canoes and kayaks are $35 to $50 a day. ✉ *10179 Bay Club Dr., Kabetogama* ☎ *218/875–2591* 🌐 *www.nlro.com.*

Voyagaire Lodge & Houseboats
BOATING | Set on Crane Lake, the southeastern gateway to Voyageurs, this slick resort has all the trappings. It also rents houseboats (about $2,000–$7,000 a week) as well as motorized fishing boats ($125–$225 a day) and canoes and kayaks ($25–$40 a day). ✉ *7576 Gold Coast Rd., Crane Lake* ☎ *218/993–2266* 🌐 *www.voyagaire.com.*

CAMPING

The park has are more than 130 developed, tent-only campsites, which typically have two tent pads, a fire grate, a picnic table, a pit toilet, and, in some cases, bear-proof storage lockers. Most sites are on the big lakes and accessible only by boat; a few are on their own tiny islands or peninsulas. All require a permit, with fees of about $15 to $35 per night (plus a $10 one-time reservation fee). Reservations are available via the park website and 🌐 *recreation.gov.*

EDUCATIONAL PROGRAMS

Voyageurs maintains a summer (usually mid-June to late August) schedule of naturalist-guided activities, including day and evening programs such as cruises. The area is also a prime spot to see the aurora borealis (aka the Northern Lights), so keep your eyes on the night sky.

FISHING

Fishing was a draw here even before Voyageurs became a national park. It's best between May and June or September and October. The most common fish are walleye and northern pike, but the "big lakes" (Rainy, Kabetogama, Namakan, and Sand Point) also have black crappie, rock bass, and smallmouth bass. A few inland lakes also have largemouth bass, lake trout, and even the occasional muskie. In winter, several of the large lakes are popular ice-fishing spots.

All visitors wishing to sink a line in park lakes must obtain a Minnesota fishing license. For more information, contact the Minnesota Department of Natural Resources (☎ *651/296–6157* 🌐 *dnr.state.mn.us*).

Minnesota Fishing Pros
FISHING | This local guide service will take you out on the lakes in and around Voyageurs National Park in pursuit of northern pike and walleye. Rates are $400–$500 per day for one to three anglers; half-day trips are also available. ✉ *Deer River* ☎ *218/246–2159* 🌐 *mnfishingpros.com.*

What's Nearby

Just 12 miles west of the Rainy Lake Visitor Center is **International Falls,** the area's largest community, which has a good selection of chain and independent restaurants, motels, and hotels. You'll also find numerous lakefront resorts (which often have restaurants) and cabin complexes on all sides of Voyageurs, in and around the communities of **Orr, Crane Lake,** and **Kabetogama.**

Chapter 59

WHITE SANDS NATIONAL PARK

Updated by
Andrew Collins

Camping ★★★☆☆

Hotels ★★☆☆☆

Activities ★★☆☆☆

Scenery ★★★★★

Crowds ★★★★☆

WELCOME TO WHITE SANDS NATIONAL PARK

TOP REASONS TO GO

★ **Wander the dunes:** Slip off your shoes and walk—or run—barefoot up and down snow-white-color gypsum dunes, some as high as 60 feet.

★ **Walk with a ranger:** The best way to understand this peculiar landscape and its amazing geology is by taking one of the park's popular ranger-led hikes—the nightly sunset strolls are especially fun.

★ **Hit the boardwalk:** Lined with fascinating interpretative signs, the short and scenic Interdune Boardwalk Trail is fully accessible for wheelchairs and strollers.

★ **Lunch with a view:** Enjoy lunch at one of the dozens of covered mid-century-modern-style shelters with tables and grills, set among three dune-side picnic areas along the park's main drive.

★ **Go sledding:** Buy a plastic sled from the park gift shop and hit the slopes—you'll get the hang of sledding down these soaring dunes in no time.

1 **Dunes Drive.** An attraction in its own right, this 8-mile loop route—part of it with a hard-packed white-sand surface—also accesses all of the park's sites and attractions, starting with the visitor center and continuing past all of the picnic areas and trailheads.

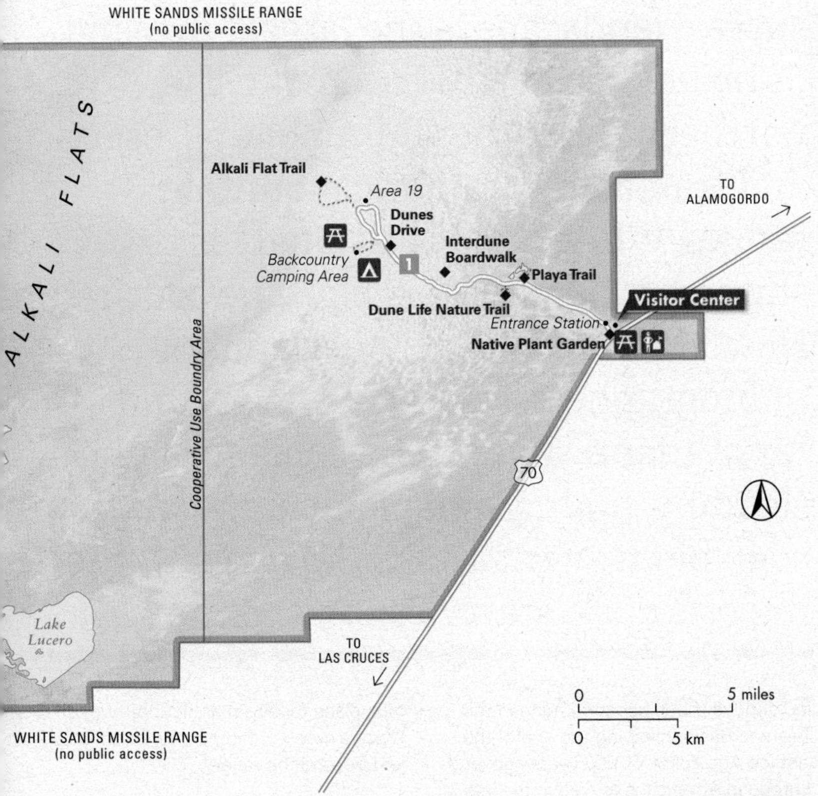
WHITE SANDS MISSILE RANGE
(no public access)
ALKALI FLATS
Alkali Flat Trail
Area 19
Dunes
Drive
Interdune
Boardwalk
Backcountry
Camping Area
1
Playa Trail
Visitor Center
Dune Life Nature Trail
Entrance Station
Native Plant Garden
TO
ALAMOGORDO
Cooperative Use Boundry Area
70
Lake
Lucero
TO
LAS CRUCES
0
5 miles
0
5 km
WHITE SANDS MISSILE RANGE
(no public access)

Stretching across a 275-square-mile swath of the Tularosa Basin, half of it protected within the national park, this surreal landscape is the largest gypsum dune field on earth. Located in the northern tip of the Chihuahuan Desert and framed by dramatic mountain ranges, White Sands National Park shimmers beneath the big, blue southern New Mexico sky. A wonderland for photographers, it's also a playground for outdoors lovers who come for dune-sledding, hiking, and picnicking—you can even pitch a tent and camp beneath the region's dark, starry canopy.

Indigenous tribes began farming in the Tularosa Basin following the end of the last Ice Age some 11,000 years ago, and European Americans arrived in the late 19th century. By the 1940s, the U.S. military had discovered a new use for this isolated landscape: testing weapons. On July 16, 1945, scientists from New Mexico's Los Alamos National Laboratory detonated the first atomic bomb in a lonely, arid patch of desert about 75 miles north of the park, now known as the Trinity Site. The site is part of the vast White Sands Missile Range, which forms the park's western border and still conducts missile tests that result in the temporary closure of both the park and a stretch of U.S. 70—these pauses usually take place for about an hour or two, up to twice a week. Holloman Air Force Base is just beyond the range.

As the region's military importance grew, so too did the reputation of its astounding white dunes, which began to draw tourists from far and near. The dunes also drew commercial interest, as mining companies saw the potential value in extracting the vast stores of gypsum sand, the primary ingredient in plaster and wallboard. Conservationists ultimately convinced the federal government of the need to protect this unique natural resource, and in 1933, President Herbert Hoover designed White Sands National Monument. In December 2019, White Sands achieved full national park status.

AVERAGE HIGH/LOW TEMPERATURES

JAN.	FEB.	MAR.	APR.	MAY	JUNE
57/22	63/27	71/32	79/40	88/50	97/59
JULY	**AUG.**	**SEPT.**	**OCT.**	**NOV.**	**DEC.**
97/64	94/62	89/55	79/41	67/28	57/21

Visitors who spend even a couple of hours exploring the undulating white-sand dunes often come away transformed by the experience. Beyond the sheer grandeur of the endless dunes, one of the park's most amazing attributes is that it supports a habitat of plants and animals that can be found only here. These flora and fauna have thrived through ingenious adaptation—sand verbena that spread its seeds quickly, shrubs with dense root systems that take hold in the sand, and lizards and mice whose light coloring both camouflage and cool them down amid the shifting white dunes. As enormous as it is, White Sands is a relatively straightforward park to visit, as the portion of it accessible to the public is relatively small and can be fully experienced in a full day. A single 8-mile park road leads through the heart of the park, which has only a handful of marked trails and no lodgings or restaurants—just a gift shop that also sells a few snacks. You will find an impressive visitor center, however, that's noteworthy both for its historic Pueblo Revival design and the engaging exhibits in its museum.

Planning

When to Go

White Sands National Park is a year-round destination, but summer can be uncomfortably hot at midday, when temperatures can climb into the 90s and 100s. Try to plan your mid-June–mid-September visits for morning or late afternoon, keeping in mind that thunderstorms are common late in the day in summer. Days are temperate and sunny throughout the winter, but from December to February nights are often below freezing, and it does snow here occasionally—usually not more than an inch or two, once or twice a year. Seeing snow over the white sand adds an extra layer of surrealness.

Getting Here and Around

AIR

The nearest major airport to the park is in El Paso, about 100 miles south, and it's served by all major airlines and car rental companies. Another option is Albuquerque, 225 miles north.

CAR

The entrance to White Sands is along a well-traveled four-lane highway, U.S. 70, about an hour's drive northeast of Las Cruces and a 20-minute drive southwest of Alamogordo, which is also where you'll find the nearest gas stations and other services.

Inspiration

Among the several photo books that have been produced about the park, *Into The Great White Sands*, by Craig Varjabedian, is particularly impressive.

The Geology of Southern New Mexico's Parks, Monuments, and Public Lands (GSNM), published by the New Mexico Bureau of Geology and Mineral Resources, conveys a thorough understanding of how White Sands formed and came to look as it does today. It's also a great resource for learning about the many other remarkable parks and natural attractions in the southern half of the state.

The singularly surreal landscape of White Sands has appeared in countless films, fashion shoots, and music videos (Solange's 2016 "Cranes in the Sky" video is but one memorable example of the latter). You can see the park in the 1950 adventure film *King Solomon's Mines,* which one a Best Color Cinematography Oscar, as well as in 2007's *Transformers,* but its most striking and inventive use is its appearance as the distant home planet of Thomas Newton (played by David Bowie), in Nicolas Roeg's 1976 sci-fi yarn, *The Man Who Fell to Earth.*

Park Essentials

ACCESSIBILITY

The park's gift shop and visitor center are fully accessible for wheelchairs, and there are several accessible tables and vault toilets at the three designated picnic areas. Most importantly, the outstanding Interdune Boardwalk Trail is fully accessible and provides an up-close view of some of the park's biggest dunes.

PARK FEES AND PERMITS

The park fee of $25 per vehicle, $20 per motorcycle, and $15 per pedestrian or cyclist is good for one week and payable at the entrance station to Dunes Drive; there's no fee just to enter the visitor center and see its exhibits. Backcountry camping is $3 nightly per person.

PARK HOURS

The park is open year-round except on Christmas Day, and the gate opens each morning at 7. It closes in the evening generally between 6 and 9 pm, depending on the season (later in summer, earlier in winter). Visitor center hours are 9–5 most of the year, but until 6 pm from Memorial Day to early September. The park is in the Mountain time zone.

CELL PHONE RECEPTION

Cell coverage is generally good around the visitor center and the first few miles of Dunes Drive, but the signal fades a bit the farther into the park you go, depending on your carrier.

Hotels

There are no hotels or RV/car camping sites within White Sands National Park. The nearest accommodations are 20 minutes away in Alamogordo, but an hour away in Las Cruces you'll find many more options.

Restaurants

The park has no restaurants or markets, just a gift shop with a very limited selection of packaged snacks. It's a 20-minute drive to the nearest dining options and grocery stores in Alamogordo.

Visitor Information

CONTACTS White Sands National Park. ✉ *19955 U.S. 70 W, Alamogordo* ☎ *575/479–6124* 🌐 *www.nps.gov/whsa.*

Dunes Drive

16 miles southwest of Alamogordo, 52 miles northeast of Las Cruces.

This 8-mile loop drive provides access to all of the park's attractions, from the visitor center at the start of the road to several hiking trails and three picnic areas. Just making your way along this road, which has a hard-packed white-sand surface along the section in the heart of the park, is great fun and yields astonishing views.

Sights

SCENIC DRIVES

★ Dunes Drive

SCENIC DRIVE | FAMILY | This gorgeous drive through the heart of White Sands accesses virtually every part of the park that's accessible to visitors, including all of the trails and picnic areas. It's an 8-mile drive from the visitor center and entrance gate to the one-way loop at the end. The first 5 miles are paved, and as you make your way from the park entrance, the landscape becomes steadily more dominated by higher and whiter dunes, until you reach the final 3 miles, which are unpaved along smooth, hard-packed gypsum. This is where the experience starts to feel truly surreal, as it's easy to feel as though you're driving through a winter wonderland—the gypsum really does look like snow (which feels particularly odd if you're driving this route on a hot summer day). You'll come to the Primrose and Roadrunner picnic areas, on the right, as you enter the one-way loop portion of Dunes Drive, and you'll come to several larger parking areas that access some of the park's biggest dunes as the road curves back around at the Alkali Flat Trailhead. It takes only about 45 minutes to drive the entire route, round-trip, but you'll want to stop and explore the dunes on foot. Part of the fun is watching park visitors, especially kids, riding sleds down the dunes. Groups of friends and families also regularly come and set up tents and umbrellas on the dunes nearest the parking areas and bask in the sun all day. It's quite a sight. Do obey speed limits, which are 45 mph as you enter but drop to 15 mph along the unpaved loop in areas with lots of pedestrian traffic. It may look tempting to zip around, but the sand can get slippery, and the road curves in places, limiting visibility. ✉ *Alamogordo.*

SCENIC STOPS

Native Plant Garden

GARDEN | FAMILY | Located in front of the park visitor center, which is outside the entrance station (and thus free of charge), this small garden that's especially colorful and fragrant from mid-March through November (even more so after it rains) provides an up-close look at plant life—including soaptree yucca, ocotillos, myriad wildflowers, and cottonwood trees (which have beautiful foliage in autumn)—that's native to the Chihuahuan Desert. You can download a plant guide from the park website or pick one up in the visitor center. ✉ *White Sands Visitor Center, Alamogordo* ☎ *505/479–6124.*

TRAILS

★ Alkali Flat Trail

TRAIL | The park's most ambitious trail is arguably its most rewarding, too, as it crosses an ancient lakebed now piled high with dunes, and once you're about a mile into it, it can feel as though you're on another planet, as you'll see almost nothing but white sand. Despite the name, it's actually an undulating 5-mile round-trip route over sometimes quite steep dunes. It's not the distance that makes it challenging but those hills, and that walking on dunes is slower going, and more taxing—especially in summer—than over conventional terrain. Along the way, you'll cross ridges and pinnacles, and see some of the biggest dunes in the park. Pack lots of water, hike with at least one buddy, and keep an eye out for the bright red trail markers—it can be easy to get disoriented if there's a lot of wind (common in spring), which can greatly reduce visibility. *Difficult.* ✉ *Alamogordo* ✥ *Trailhead: Just past the 8-mile mark of Dunes Dr.*

★ Dune Life Nature Trail

TRAIL | FAMILY | Give yourself about an hour to complete this 1-mile self-guided loop trail that, while short, does climb over a couple of pretty tall dunes. This hike offers an interesting contrast with

The Interdune Boardwalk is the park's only trail that's fully accessible to wheelchairs and strollers.

other parts of the park, as there's quite a lot of flora along it—you can really learn about the unusual plants that thrive in this harsh environment. Keep an eye out for the series of 14 interpretive signs that discuss the foxes, birds, reptiles, and other wildlife that live in the park. *Easy–Moderate.* ✉ *Alamogordo* ✣ *Trailhead: 2.3 miles north of entrance station on Dunes Dr.*

★ Interdune Boardwalk

TRAIL | **FAMILY** | Along this easy 0.4-mile boardwalk trail, the only one in the park fully accessible to wheelchairs and strollers, you can read about the park's fascinating geology and ecosystem at 10 different signed interpretive stations along the route. The trail provides a fun and simple way to observe the dunes up close without having to walk through the sand itself. *Easy.* ✉ *Alamogordo* ✣ *Trailhead: Just before the end of the paved section of Dune Dr.*

Playa Trail

TRAIL | **FAMILY** | This short and level ½-mile round-trip ramble is the first one you'll come to along Dunes Drive after passing through the entrance station. It's not as exciting as some of the other park trails, although it is interesting in summer when the otherwise dry lake bed it leads to usually fills with rain water. *Easy.* ✉ *Alamogordo* ✣ *Trailhead: About 2 miles past entrance station on Dunes Dr.*

VISITOR CENTERS

★ White Sands Visitor Center

BUILDING | **FAMILY** | The centerpiece of the small White Sands Historic District, a complex of park buildings constructed by the WPA in New Mexico's distinctive Spanish–Pueblo Revival style in the mid-1930s, the park's only visitor center is built of thick adobe (mud and straw) bricks and has a traditional *viga* (beam) and *savina* (also called latilla) aspen-pole ceiling and architectural details typical of the period and style, like punched-tin light fixtures and hand-carved wooden benches. Inside you'll find an info desk and an array of excellent, modern, interactive exhibits as well as a small theater that shows a short film about the dunes. Walk out back to reach the park gift shop, which has books, souvenirs, water, a very limited assortment of snacks, and sleds with which to careen down the park's dunes. The district's other seven buildings include a visitor restroom, ranger residences, and various utility buildings. ✉ *19955 U.S. 70W, Alamogordo* ☎ *575/479–6124* 🌐 *www.nps.gov/whsa*.

Activities

BIKING

Cyclists are welcome on Dunes Drive, and this flat loop route is pretty easy to manage on two wheels, even the unpaved portion, as the white-sand surface is hard-packed. That said, because drifting sand can be an issue, especially during the windy spring months, and the road can be bumpy after rainy periods, a mountain bike or a bike with fat tires (such as a beach cruiser) is ideal. Biking on the dunes or anywhere off-road is strictly prohibited, and violators will be fined.

CAMPING

Although there are no campgrounds inside the park, you can set up a tent at one of the primitive sites along the short backcountry camping loop trail just off Dunes Drive (about 6 miles from the entrance station). You must obtain a permit—the cost is $3 per person per night—at the entrance station.

EDUCATIONAL PROGRAMS

★ Full Moon Hikes

TOUR—SIGHT | FAMILY | Once a month from April through October, the park offers ranger-led full-moon hikes along the Dune Life Nature Trail. These nocturnal adventures are fun for the whole family and show the landscape in a fascinating, luminous perspective. Tickets are required and can be purchased online for $8; it's a good idea to book at least a week ahead, as space is limited. ✉ *Alamogordo* ☎ *877/444–6777* 🌐 *www.recreation.gov*.

Lake Lucero Tours

NATURE SITE | Just once a month, and only from November through April, the park offers up to 50 participants the chance to visit Lake Lucero, in the southwest corner of the park. This generally dry lake bed is fascinating because of what it shows us about how the park formed—a story that rangers tell during these tours, which cost $8 per person and must be booked in advance (up to 30 days ahead). The lake bed is filled with selenite crystals, which over time erode and break, forming ever smaller fragments and eventually forming the bright white dunes for which the park is famous. Tours begin at the White Sands Missile Range "Small Missile" Gate at mile marker 174 on U.S. 70, about 25 miles southwest of the park entrance. ✉ *Alamogordo* ☎ *877/444–6777* 🌐 *www.recreation.gov*.

★ Sunset Stroll

TRAIL | FAMILY | One of the most enjoyable ways to get to know the park is to take a 45-minute to 1-hour ranger-guided sunset stroll, which takes place nightly year-round and departs from the signed parking area along Dunes Drive 4.7 miles past the park's entrance station. The exact departure times vary according to, drum roll please, the time the sun sets, which you can find out each day at the visitor center, but plan to get to the departure point about an hour before sunset. Along this leisurely 1-mile trek, you'll see dunes similar to those on the Alkali Flat Trail but with a local expert to fill you in on the plants, animals, and geology you encounter. ✉ *Dunes Dr., Alamogordo*.

HIKING

Although there are only a few marked trails in the park, you can easily hike short distances over any dune field adjoining the several parking areas along Dunes Drive. Traipsing through this strangely gorgeous landscape can take some getting used to, however, and despite the fact that the park's gently rolling dunes look about as threatening as a big sandbox, this terrain is deceptively dangerous, and you should take its potential hazards seriously. Because the dunes shift constantly and are sometimes buffeted by high winds (especially in spring), which can severely reduce visibility, it's relatively easy to get lost. Take it slow, bring lots of water, and always have a compass and a charged cell phone with you (cell service is a little uneven but it generally works on and near Dunes Drive). Although the park is in a broad basin, it's still at a lofty elevation of 4,235 feet. It's also completely unshaded, and temperatures can exceed 100 degrees in summer—it's rare, but visitors have been injured and even died from heat exhaustion after becoming disoriented. Unless you're on a marked trail, always stay within view of Dunes Drive, or at the very least other people. The good news: you don't have to scamper far from Dunes Drive to encounter mesmerizing views of seemingly endless dunes framed against majestic mountain peaks. Also, the white gypsum sand is cool to the touch, which makes it pleasant to walk barefoot through even on hot days. However, if hiking more than a few hundred feet, and especially on the longer Alkali Flat Trail, wear hiking boots, as your feet will appreciate the extra support after a mile or so of trekking over sometimes steep dunes.

SLEDDING

Further contributing to the sensation at times that you've entered an enormous landscape of snow rather than white sand, as you make your way along Dunes Drive into the heart of the park, you'll see kids and adults sledding down the dunes on plastic sleds, or snow saucers, which—if you don't have your own—you can buy at the gift shop attached to the visitor center for about $20, plus a couple of bucks for wax, which you'll need to coat your sled for it to work on the sand. Used sleds cost less but aren't always available; you can also return your new sled for $5 when you're finished. Park staffers are great with tips on how to sled on gypsum sand and also the best areas to do it, but a good place to start is the dunes adjacent either to the Interdune Boardwalk or beside the Alkali Flat Trailhead parking lot. There's also a good "how to" video on the park website.

What's Nearby

Because White Sands National Park has no dining or lodging facilities, most visitors stay in one of three nearby communities. The military town of **Alamogordo** is closest, just 15 miles away, but it's also a somewhat prosaic, suburban community with mostly middle-of-the-road chain hotel and restaurant options. Far more charming and just 20 miles farther away (up a spectacular scenic highway), tiny **Cloudcroft** is situated high in the cool and crisp-aired Sacramento Mountains and is home to a famous old hotel, the Lodge Resort, plus a bunch of vacation-rental cabins and bungalows. Although it's nearly an hour west of the park, **Las Cruces** is actually the most popular base for visiting. It's big, located at the junction of two big interstate freeways, has plenty of hotels (although again, most are chains) and an increasingly noteworthy dining and nightlife scene, and is home to another remarkable constituent of the federal park system, Organ Mountains–Desert Peaks National Monument. One other possible option is **El Paso, Texas,** which is an easy 90-minute drive south of White Sands and has much to offer in the way of services and attractions.

Chapter 60

WIND CAVE NATIONAL PARK

60

Updated by
Carson Walker

Camping ★★★☆☆ | Hotels ★★★★★ | Activities ★★★★★ | Scenery ★★★★★ | Crowds ★★★★☆

WELCOME TO WIND CAVE NATIONAL PARK

TOP REASONS TO GO

★ **Underground exploring:** Wind Cave offers visitors the chance to get their hands and feet dirty on guided tours through long and complex caves.

★ **The call of the wild:** Wind Cave National Park boasts a wide variety of animals: bison, coyote, deer, antelope, elk, and prairie dogs.

★ **Education by candlelight:** Wind Cave offers numerous educational and interpretive programs, including the Candlelight Cave Tour, which allows guests to explore the cave by candlelight only.

★ **Historic cave:** On January 9, 1903, President Theodore Roosevelt signed a bill that made Wind Cave the first cave in the United States to be named a national park.

★ **Noteworthy neighbors:** With its proximity to national parks, state parks, and other monuments, Wind Cave is situated perfectly to explore some of America's greatest national treasures.

1 **Wind Cave.** With an explored maze of caverns of more than 150 miles, Wind Cave is considered one of the world's longest caves. Notably, scientists estimate that only 10% of the cave has been explored to date. Most of the world's known boxwork formations are found here, which means that visitors are treated to some of the rarest geological features on the planet. The cave lies at the confluence of western mountains and central plains, which blesses the park with a unique landscape. A series of established trails weave in and out of forested hillsides and grassy prairies, providing treks of varying difficulty.

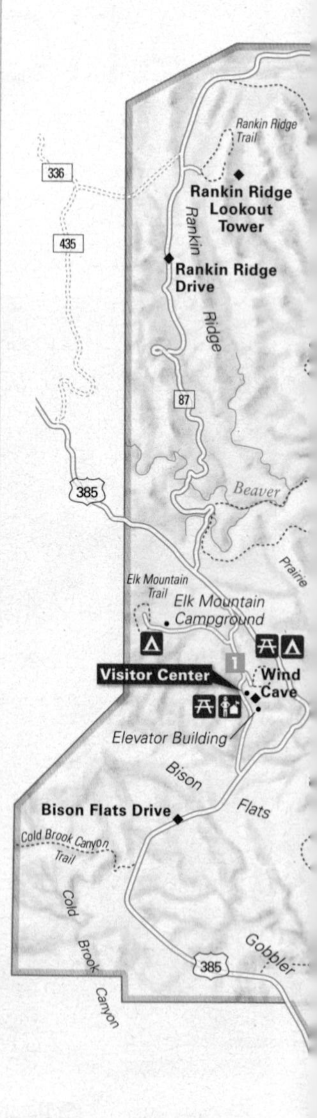

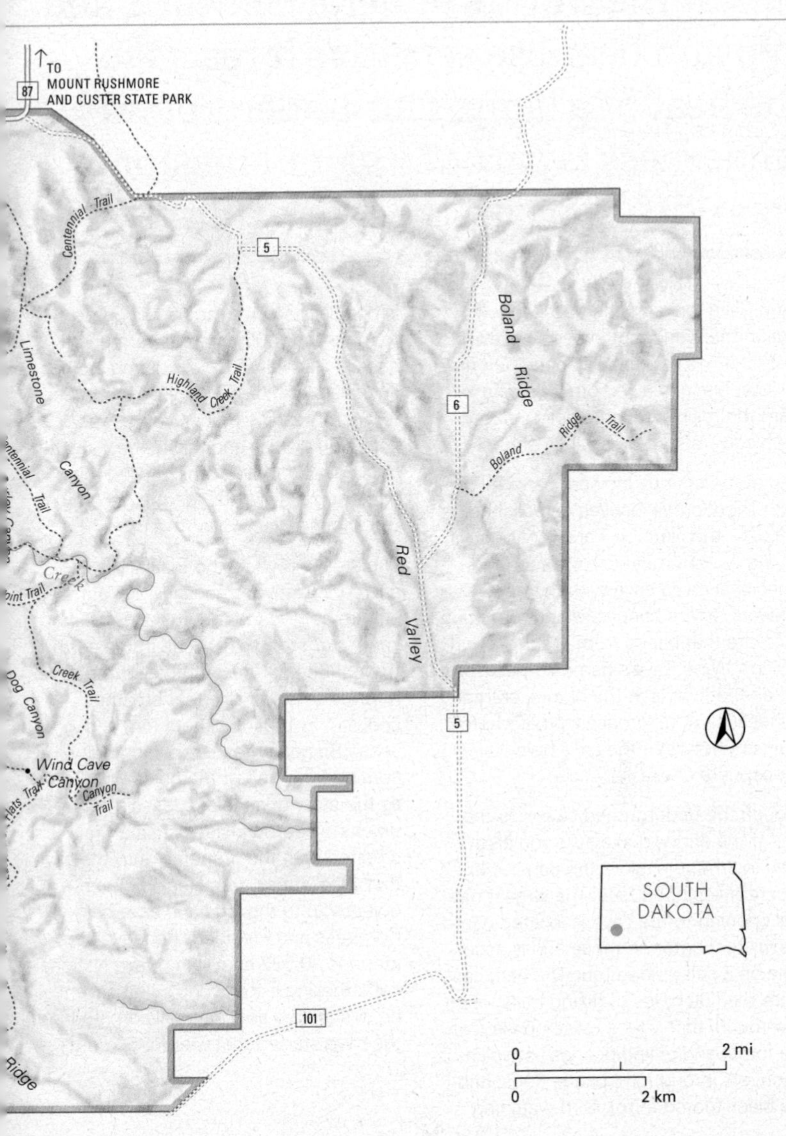
TO
MOUNT RUSHMORE
AND CUSTER STATE PARK
87
Centennial Trail
5
Highland Creek Trail
Limestone
Canyon
Boland
Ridge
6
Boland Ridge Trail
Red
Valley
Creek
Creek Trail
Dog Canyon
Wind Cave
Canyon
Canyon
Trail
5
101
Ridge
SOUTH
DAKOTA
0
2 mi
0
2 km

Wind Cave has 148 miles of underground passageways. Cave formations include 95% of the world's mineral boxwork, and gypsum beard so sensitive it reacts to the heat of a lamp. This underground wilderness is part of a giant limestone labyrinth beneath the Black Hills.

Wind Cave ranks as the sixth-longest cave in the world, but experts believe 90% of it has yet to be mapped. On the surface, bison, elk and other wildlife roam the rolling hills that demonstrate the biodiversity of grasslands and forest.

One of the country's oldest parks—President Theodore Roosevelt established it in 1903—the National Park Service says it's the world's most complex three-dimensional maze cave with the best boxwork, a rare honeycombed formation of calcite that hangs from the walls and ceilings. Wind Cave's name comes from the air that howls at the natural entrances because of differences in barometric pressure between the cave below and atmosphere above.

Though the underground cavern is the star of the show, make sure you also build in time to explore the park's 44 square miles of surface. The largest natural opening to the cave is located near the visitor center entrance and is accessible on a self-guided tour. The park has more than 30 miles of hiking trails, open year-round, that offer a close-up view of the forest and rolling prairies as well as bison, elk, pronghorn, prairie dogs, and the black-footed ferret. Bird-watching is popular because the park is home to more than 100 different permanent species as well as others during spring and fall migration. If you visit in mid-September to early October, you'll see fall colors on display and maybe hear the elk bugling. A 20-mile scenic driving tour is a another great way to see the geology of the pristine Black Hills.

The area known as the Black Hills is sacred to Native Americans. Lakota culture believes that humans and bison came from the spirit world in the earth through the natural entrance of the cave, referred to as a "hole that breathes cool air." In 1881, brothers Tom and Jesse Bingham heard the sound of wind coming from one of the holes which, as the story goes, blew Jesse's hat off when he peered inside. Charlie Crary is credited with the first entry into the cave that year. After several legal fights over ownership to the land and cave below, Congress and President Roosevelt created the 10,522-acre Wind Cave National Park, making it the world's first cave to be designated as a national park. Tours of the cave started that year for 50 cents.

AVERAGE HIGH/LOW TEMPERATURES					
JAN.	FEB.	MAR.	APR.	MAY	JUNE
37/8	41/14	49/21	58/30	67/40	77/49
JULY	AUG.	SEPT.	OCT.	NOV.	DEC.
84/55	84/53	76/44	63/32	46/20	39/12

Planning

When to Go

The biggest crowds come to Wind Cave from June to September, but the park and surrounding Black Hills are large enough to diffuse the masses. Neither the cave nor grounds above are ever uncomfortably packed, although on busy summer days tours sometimes sell out over an hour ahead of time, so come early in the day and reserve your spot. Park officials contend it's actually less busy during the first full week in August, when the Sturgis Motorcycle Rally brings roughly a half-million bikers to the region, clogging highways for miles around. Most hotels within a 100-mile radius are booked up to a year in advance.

The colder months are the least crowded, though you can still explore underground, thanks to the cave's constant 54°F temperature. The shoulder seasons are also quieter, though autumn is a perfect time to visit. The days are warm, the nights are cool, and in late September/early October the park's canyons and coulees display incredible colors.

FESTIVALS AND EVENTS

Crazy Horse Volksmarch. This 6.2-mile hike up the mountain where the massive Crazy Horse Memorial is being carved is the largest event of its kind and gives hikers the opportunity to stand on the Lakota leader's outstretched arm. It's held the first full weekend in June. Another one-day Volksmarch is held in late September, timed to coincide with the Custer State Park Buffalo Roundup. 🌐 *crazyhorsememorial.org.*

Custer State Park Buffalo Roundup & Arts Festival. The nation's largest buffalo roundup is one of South Dakota's most exciting events. Early on a Friday morning in late September, cowboys, cowgirls, and rangers saddle up to corral and vaccinate the park's 1,300 head of bison. You'll hear the thunder of more than 5,000 hooves before you even see the bison. Before, during, and after the roundup, a three-day festival showcases works by South Dakota artists and artisans. 🌐 *gfp.sd.gov/parks/detail/custer-state-park.*

Days of '76. This outdoor, award-winning, Professional Rodeo Cowboys Association (PRCA) event includes the usual riding, roping, and bull riding, as well as two parades with vintage carriages and coaches and Western arts and crafts. This five-day affair is one of the state's most popular, featuring the top cowboys and cowgirls in the sport. 🌐 *daysof76.com.*

Deadwood Jam. A quarter-century strong and still filling the streets of Deadwood with live music, the Black Hills' premier music festival showcases an eclectic collection of country, rock, and blues for two days in mid-September. 🌐 *www.deadwood.com/event/deadwood-jam.*

Gold Discovery Days. A parade, carnival, car show, stick-horse rodeo, hot-air-balloon rally, hunt for gold nuggets, and bed races are all part of the fun at this three-day event in late July in Custer. 🌐 *www.visitcuster.com/gold-discovery-days.*

Sturgis Motorcycle Rally. This 10-day event held in early August regularly draws more than 500,000 bikers and nonbikers alike who pack the Black Hills town's streets. It features a variety of food, music, T-shirt stands and, of course, motorcycles of all varieties. 🌐 *www.sturgismotorcyclerally.com.*

Getting Here and Around

AIR

The nearest commercial airport is in Rapid City.

BUS

Bus lines serve Rapid City and Wall.

CAR

Wind Cave is 56 miles from Rapid City, via U.S. 16 and Highway 87, which runs through the park, and 73 miles southwest of Badlands National Park.

U.S. 385 and Highway 87 travel the length of the park on the west side. Additionally, two unpaved roads, NPS Roads 5 and 6, traverse the northeastern part of Wind Cave. NPS Road 5 joins Highway 87 at the park's north border.

Inspiration

Wind Cave National Park is one of the featured destinations in the 2001 IMAX movie *Journey Into Amazing Caves.* Narrated by Liam Neeson, with music by The Moody Blues, the immersive film follows scientists into unique underground worlds.

Wind Cave National Park: The First 100 Years includes more than 200 historic images as well as history and stories about the cave and park.

Wind Cave: The Story Behind the Scenery provides good photos and information about the park; it can be purchased at the visitor center.

Park Essentials

ACCESSIBILITY

The visitor center is entirely wheelchair accessible, but only a few areas of the cave itself are navigable by those with limited mobility. Arrangements can be made in advance for a special ranger-assisted tour for a small fee. The Elk Mountain Campground has two accessible sites.

PARK FEES AND PERMITS

There's no fee to enter the park; cave tours cost $10–$30. The requisite backcountry camping and horseback-riding permits are both free from the visitor center. Rates at Elk Mountain Campground are $18 a night per site early spring through late fall (when the water is turned on in the restroom facility); $9 a night per site the rest of the year.

PARK HOURS

The park is open year-round, though visitor center hours and tour schedules vary seasonally. It is in the Mountain time zone.

CELL PHONE RECEPTION

Cell phone reception is hit and miss in the park. You will find a public phone outside the visitor center.

Hotels

Wind Cave has only one campground, and you'll have to look outside park boundaries if you want to bed down in something more substantial than a tent. New chain hotels with modern amenities are plentiful in the Black Hills, but when booking accommodations consider a stay at one of the area's historic properties. From grand brick downtown hotels to intimate Queen Anne homes converted to bed-and-breakfasts, historic lodgings are easy to locate. Other distinctive lodging choices include the region's mountain lodges and forest retreats.

It may be difficult to obtain quality accommodations during summer—and downright impossible during the Sturgis Motorcycle Rally, held the first full week of August every year—so plan ahead and make reservations (three or four months out is a good rule of thumb) if you're going to travel during peak season. To find the best value, choose a hotel far from Interstate 90. *Hotel reviews have been shortened. For full information, visit Fodors.com.*

What It Costs			
$	$$	$$$	$$$$
RESTAURANTS			
under $13	$13–$20	$21–$30	over $30
HOTELS			
under $101	$101–$150	$151–$200	over $200

Restaurants

If you're determined to dine in Wind Cave National Park, be sure to pack your own meal, because other than vending machines, the only dining venues inside park boundaries are the two picnic areas, one near the visitor center and the other at Elk Mountain Campground. The towns beyond the park offer additional options. Deadwood claims some of the best-ranked restaurants in South Dakota. Buffalo, pheasant, and elk are relatively common ingredients in the Black Hills. No matter where you go, beef is king. *Restaurant reviews have been shortened. For full information, visit Fodors.com.*

Tours

Candlelight Cave Tour

GUIDED TOURS | Available once or twice daily, mid-June through Labor Day, this tour goes into a section of the cave with no paved walks or lighting. Everyone on the tour carries a lantern similar to those used in expeditions in the 1890s. The tour lasts two hours, covers 2/3 mile, and is limited to 10 people, so reservations are essential. Children younger than eight are not admitted. *Moderate.* ✉ *26611 U.S. 385, Wind Cave National Park* ✣ *Starts at visitor center* 🌐 *www.nps.gov/wica* 🎟 *$12.*

Fairgrounds Cave Tour

GUIDED TOURS | View examples of nearly every type of calcite formation found in the cave on this 1½-hour, 2/3-mile tour, available at the visitor center from early June through mid-August. There are some 450 steps, leading up and down. *Moderate.* ✉ *26611 U.S. 385, Wind Cave National Park* ✣ *Off U.S. 385, 3 miles north of the park's southern boundary* 🌐 *www.nps.gov/wica/planyourvisit/tour-fairgrounds.htm* 🎟 *$12.*

Fort Hays and Mount Rushmore Tours

SPECIAL-INTEREST | **FAMILY** | This nine-hour tour amid the Black Hills begins at Fort Hays on the *Dances with Wolves* film set and visits Mount Rushmore, Custer State Park, and the Crazy Horse Memorial. Guests are responsible for their own lunches at the State Game Lodge; a pre-trip breakfast and a post-trip cowboy dinner show are add-on options. ✉ *2255 Fort Hayes Dr., Rapid City* ☎ *605/343–3113* 🌐 *www.mountrushmoretours.com* 🎟 *From $90.*

Garden of Eden Cave Tour

GUIDED TOURS | You don't need to go far to see boxwork, popcorn, and flowstone formations. Just take the relatively easy, one-hour tour, which covers 1/3 mile and 150 stairs. It's available one to four times daily in summer. *Easy.* ⊠ *26611 U.S. 385, Wind Cave National Park* ✣ *3 miles north of park's southern border* ⊕ *www.nps.gov/wica/planyourvisit/tour-garden-of-eden.htm* 🎟 *$10.*

Natural Entrance Cave Tour

GUIDED TOURS | This 1¼-hour tour takes you 2/3 miles into the cave, onto more than 300 stairs (most heading down), and out an elevator exit. Along the way are some significant boxwork deposits on the middle level. The tour leaves several times daily year-round. *Easy.* ⊠ *26611 U.S. 385, Wind Cave National Park* ✣ *Off U.S. 385, 3 miles north of park's southern border* ⊕ *www.nps.gov/wica/planyourvisit/tour-natural-entrance.htm* 🎟 *$12.*

Visitor Information

PARK CONTACT INFORMATION Wind Cave National Park. ⊠ *26611 U.S. 385, Hot Springs* ☎ *605/745–4600* ⊕ *www.nps.gov/wica.*

In The Park

Sights

SCENIC DRIVES

Bison Flats Drive (South Entrance)

SCENIC DRIVE | Entering the park from the south on U.S. 385 takes you past Gobbler Ridge and into the hills commonly found in the southern Black Hills region. After a couple of miles, the landscape gently levels onto the Bison Flats, one of the mixed-grass prairies on which the park prides itself. You might see a herd of grazing buffalo (the park has roughly 400 of them) between here and the visitor center. You can also catch panoramic views of the parklands, surrounding hills, and limestone bluffs. ⊠ *Hwy. 385, Wind Cave National Park.*

★ Rankin Ridge Drive (North Entrance)

SCENIC DRIVE | Entering the park across the north border via Highway 87 is perhaps the most beautiful drive into the park. As you leave behind the grasslands and granite spires of Custer State Park and enter Wind Cave, you see the prairie, forest, and wetland habitats of the backcountry and some of the oldest rock in the Black Hills. The silvery twinkle of mica, quartz, and feldspar crystals dots Rankin Ridge east of Highway 87, and gradually gives way to limestone and sandstone formations. ⊠ *Hwy. 87, Wind Cave National Park.*

SCENIC STOPS

Rankin Ridge Lookout Tower

VIEWPOINT | Although some of the best panoramic views of the park and surrounding hills can be seen from this 5,013-foot tower, it's typically not staffed or open to the public. Still, if you want to stretch your legs on a car ride along Rankin Ridge Drive, consider following the 1-mile Rankin Ridge loop to the tower and back. ⊠ *Wind Cave National Park* ✣ *6 miles north of the visitor center on Hwy. 87.*

★ Wind Cave

CAVE | Known to Native Americans for centuries, Wind Cave was named for the strong air currents that alternately blow in and out of its entrances. The cave's winds are related to the difference in atmospheric pressure between the cave and the surface. When the atmospheric pressure is higher outside than inside, the air blows in, and vice versa. With more than 150 miles of known passageway divided into three different levels, Wind Cave ranks among the longest in the world. It's host to an incredibly diverse collection of geologic formations, including more boxwork than any other known cave, plus a series of underground lakes, though they are located in the deepest parts of the cave not seen on any tours. All tours are led by National Park Service rangers and leave from the visitor center. These tours allow you to see the unusual and beautiful formations with names such as popcorn, frostwork, and boxwork. The cave remains a steady 54°F year-round, so wear closed-toe shoes and bring along a jacket or sweater. Tickets are sold at the visitor center and typically sell out two hours before each tour during summer, so plan accordingly. Check out the park website for the different tours, times, and pricing. ✉ *Wind Cave National Park* ✣ *U.S. 385 to Wind Cave Visitor Center* 🌐 *www.nps.gov/wica/planyourvisit/guidedtours.htm.*

TRAILS

Boland Ridge Trail

TRAIL | Get away from the crowds for a half day via this strenuous, 2.6-mile (one way) hike. The panorama from the top is well worth it, especially at night. *Difficult.* ✉ *Wind Cave National Park* ✣ *Trailhead: off Park Service Rd. 6, 1 mile north of junction with Park Service Rd. 5.*

Centennial Trail

TRAIL | Constructed to celebrate South Dakota's centennial in 1989, this trail bisects the Black Hills, covering 111 miles from north to south, from Bear Butte State Park through Black Hills National Forest, Black Elk Wilderness, Custer State Park, and into Wind Cave National Park. Designed for bikers, hikers, and horses, the trail is rugged but accommodating (note, however, that bicycling on the trail is not allowed within park boundaries). It will take you at least a half day to cover the 6-mile Wind Cave segment. *Moderate.* ✉ *Wind Cave National Park* ✣ *Trailhead: off Hwy. 87, 2 miles north of visitor center.*

Cold Brook Canyon Trail

TRAIL | **FAMILY** | Starting on the west side of U.S. 385, 2 miles south of the visitor center, this 1.4-mile (one way), mildly strenuous hike runs past a former prairie-dog town, the edge of an area burned by a controlled fire in 1986, and through Cold Brook Canyon to the park boundary fence. Experienced hikers can conquer this trail and return to the trailhead in an hour or less, but more leisurely visitors will probably need more time. *Moderate.* ✉ *Wind Cave National Park* ✣ *Trailhead: west side of U.S. 385, 2 miles south of visitor center.*

Highland Creek Trail

TRAIL | This difficult, roughly 8.6-mile (one way) trail is the longest and most diverse trail within the park, traversing mixed-grass prairies, ponderosa pine forests, and the riparian habitats of Highland Creek, Beaver Creek, and Wind Cave Canyon. Even those in good shape will need a full day to cover this trail round-trip. *Difficult.* ✉ *Wind Cave National Park* ✣ *Southern trailhead stems from Wind Cave Canyon trail 1 mile east of U.S. 385. Northern trailhead on Forest Service Rd. 5.*

Wind Cave Canyon Trail

TRAIL | This easy 1.8-mile (one way) trail follows Wind Cave Canyon to the park boundary fence. The canyon, with its steep limestone walls and dead trees, provides the best opportunity in the park for bird-watching. Be especially vigilant for cliff swallows, great horned owls, and red-headed and Lewis woodpeckers. Deer, least chipmunks, and other small animals also are attracted to the sheltered environment of the canyon. Even though you could probably do a round-trip tour of this trail in less than an hour and a half, be sure to spend more time here to observe the wildlife. *Easy.* ✉ *Wind Cave National Park* ✣ *Trailhead: east side of Hwy. 385, 1 mile north of southern access road to visitor center.*

VISITOR CENTERS

Wind Cave Visitor Center

INFO CENTER | The park's sole visitor center is the primary place to get park information and embark on cave tours. Located on top of the cave, it has three exhibit rooms, with displays on cave exploration, Native American culture, and prairie management. The center also hosts ranger programs and has an auditorium

Wind Cave is the world's sixth longest cave and includes delicate and unique boxwork.

that presents the film, *Wind Cave, Two Worlds*. Other than vending machines, there's no coffee or snacks here or elsewhere in the park. ✉ *26611 U.S. 385, Hot Springs* ✥ *Off U.S. 385, 3 miles north of park's southern border* ☎ *605/745–4600* 🌐 *www.nps.gov/wica* 🎟 *Free.*

Activities

Many visitors come to Wind Cave solely to descend into the park's underground passages. While there are great ranger-led tours for casual visitors—and more daring explorations for experienced cavers—the prairie and forest above the cave shouldn't be neglected.

EDUCATIONAL OFFERINGS

Adventures in Nature

TOUR—SIGHT | Although annual themes and individual program topics vary, nature is always the focus on these seasonally offered adventures held at the visitor center. They're open to children ages 3 to 12, who are divided into groups that participate in age-appropriate activities. ✉ *26611 Hwy. 385, Wind Cave National Park* ☎ *605/745–4600* 🌐 *www.nps.gov/wica.*

Junior Ranger Program

TOUR—SIGHT | **FAMILY** | Kids 12 and younger (and adults too) can earn a Junior Ranger badge by completing activities that teach them about the park's ecosystems, the cave, the animals, and protecting the environment. Pick up the Junior Ranger guidebook for free at the Wind Cave Visitor Center. ✉ *Wind Cave National Park, 26611 Hwy. 385, Wind Cave National Park* ☎ *605/745–4600.*

BIKING

Bikes are prohibited on all of the park's trails and in the backcountry. Cyclists may ride on designated roads, and on the 111-mile Centennial Trail, once it passes the park's northern border.

Two Wheeler Dealer Cycle and Fitness

BICYCLING | Family-owned and-operated Two Wheeler Dealer Cycle and Fitness, based in Spearfish, stocks bicycles for

Common Cave Terms

Sound like a serious spelunker with this cavemen cheat sheet for various *speleothems* (cave formations).

Boxwork: Composed of interconnecting thin blades that were left in relief on cave walls when the bedrock was dissolved away.

Cave balloons: Thin-walled formations resembling partially deflated balloons, usually composed of hydromagnesite.

Flowstone: Consists of thin layers of a mineral deposited on a sloping surface by flowing or seeping water.

Frostwork: Sprays of needles that radiate from a central point that are usually made of aragonite.

Gypsum beard: Composed of bundles of gypsum fibers that resemble a human beard.

Logomites: Consist of popcorn and superficially resemble hollowed-out stalagmites.

Pool Fingers: Deposited underneath water around organic filaments.

Stalactites: Carrot-shape formations formed from dripping water that hang down from a cave ceiling.

Stalagmites: Mineral deposits from dripping water built up on a cave floor.

sale and rent. The store is also a great place to pick up advice on where and how to explore the area's trails by bike. ✉ *305 Main St., Spearfish* ☎ *605/642–7545* 🌐 *www.twowheelerdealer.com.*

BIRD-WATCHING

Rankin Ridge

BIRD WATCHING | See large birds of prey here, including turkey vultures, hawks, and golden eagles. ✉ *Wind Cave National Park* ✥ *6 miles north of the visitor center on Hwy. 87.*

★ Wind Cave Canyon

BIRD WATCHING | Here's one of the best birding areas in the park. The limestone walls of the canyon are ideal nesting grounds for cliff swallows and great horned owls, while the standing dead trees on the canyon floor attract red-headed and Lewis woodpeckers. As you hike down the trail, the steep-sided canyon widens to a panoramic view east across the prairies. ✉ *Wind Cave National Park* ✥ *About ½ mile east of visitor center* 🌐 *www.nps.gov/wica.*

CAMPING

Camping is one of this region's strengths. While there is only one primitive campground within the park, there are countless campgrounds in the Black Hills. The public campgrounds in the national forest are accessible by road but otherwise secluded and undeveloped; private campgrounds typically have more amenities, as do some of those in Custer State Park, which has numerous options.

Elk Mountain Campground. If you prefer a relatively developed campsite and relative proximity to civilization, Elk Mountain is an excellent choice. You can experience the peaceful pine forests and wild creatures of the park without straying too far from the safety of the beaten path. ✉ *½ mile north of visitor center* ☎ *605/745–4600.*

HIKING

There are more than 30 miles of hiking trails within the boundaries of Wind Cave National Park, covering ponderosa forest and mixed-grass prairie. The landscape has changed little over the past century,

The colossal Mount Rushmore is one of the United States' most famous monuments.

so a hike through the park is as much a historical snapshot of pioneer life in the 1890s as it is exercise. Be sure to hit the Wind Cave Canyon Trail, where limestone cliffs attract birds like cliff swallows and great horned owls, and the Cold Brook Canyon Trail, a short but fun trip past a prairie-dog town to the park's edge. Besides birds and small animals such as squirrels, you're apt to see deer and pronghorn while hiking, and probably some bison.

Hiking into the wild, untouched backcountry is perfectly safe, provided you have a map (available from the visitor center) and a good sense of direction. Don't expect any amenities, however; bathrooms and a water-bottle filling station are available only at the visitor center, and the trails are dirt or gravel. There are no easily accessible sources along the trails, and water from backcountry sources must be treated, so pack your own.

MULTISPORT OUTFITTERS

Granite Sports

TOUR—SPORTS | Several miles north of Wind Cave Park in Hill City, Granite Sports sells a wide range of hiking, climbing, and camping apparel and accessories; they also know the best local guides. ✉ *201 Main St., Hill City* ☎ *605/574–2121* 🌐 *www.granite-sports.com.*

SPELUNKING

You may not explore the depths of Wind Cave on your own, but you can choose from five ranger-led cave tours, available from June through August; the rest of the year, only one or two tours are available. On each tour you pass incredibly beautiful cave formations, including extremely well-developed boxwork. The least crowded times to visit in summer are mornings and weekends.

The cave is 54°F year-round, so bring a sweater. Note that the uneven passages are often wet and slippery. Rangers discourage those with heart conditions and physical limitations from taking the organized tours. However, with some advance warning (and for a nominal fee) park rangers can arrange private, limited tours for those with physical disabilities. To prevent the spread of white-nose syndrome, a disease that is deadly to bats, don't wear any clothes or shoes or bring any equipment that you might have used to explore other caves (with the exception of the nearby Jewel Cave National Monument).

Tours depart from the visitor center. A schedule can be found online at 🌐 *www.nps.gov/wica.* To make a reservation, call ☎ *605/745–4600.*

What's Nearby

Wind Cave is part of South Dakota's Black Hills, a diverse region of alpine meadows, ponderosa pine forests, and creek-carved, granite-walled canyons covering 2 million acres in the state's southwest quadrant. This mountain range contrasts sharply with the sheer cliffs and dramatic buttes of the Badlands to the north and east, and the wide, wind-swept plains of most of the state. Though anchored by Rapid City—the largest city for 350 miles in any direction—the Black Hills' crown jewel is Mount Rushmore National Memorial, visited by nearly 3 million people each year. U.S. 385 is the backbone of the Black Hills.

Known as the Mother City of the Black Hills, **Custer** is a great place to stay if you can spend a few days in the southern Black Hills. It's a short drive to world-class attractions like Mount Rushmore, Crazy Horse, Wind Cave National Park, Jewel Cave National Monument, and Custer National Park. With all the lodging, food and shopping options, you can explore all day and still find time to relax at your hotel or cabin.

Founded in the 1880s by prospectors searching for gold deposits, the small town of **Keystone** has an abundance of restaurants, shops, and attractions. To serve the millions of visitors passing through the area, there are more than 900 hotel rooms—that's about three times the town's number of permanent residents.

★ Crazy Horse Memorial

MEMORIAL | Designed to be the world's largest work of art (the face alone is 87 feet tall), this tribute to the spirit of the North American Native people depicts Crazy Horse, the legendary Lakota leader who helped defeat General Custer at Little Bighorn. A work in progress, thus far the warrior's head has been carved from the mountain, and the colossal head of his horse is beginning to emerge. Self-taught sculptor Korczak Ziolkowski started this memorial in 1948. After his death in 1982, his family carried on the project. Near the work site stands an exceptional orientation center, the Indian Museum of North America, and Ziolkowski's home and workshop. If you're visiting in summer, consider arriving in the evening, and stick around for the spectacular laser-light show, held nightly from Memorial Day through late September. ✉ *12151 Ave. of the Chiefs, Crazy Horse Memorial* ✣ *Hwy. 385, 5 miles north of Custer* ☎ *605/673–4681* 🌐 *crazyhorsememorial.org* 🎫 *$15.*

Custer State Park

NATIONAL/STATE PARK | This 71,000-acre park is considered the crown jewel of South Dakota's state park system. Elk, antelope, mountain goats, bighorn sheep, mountain lions, wild turkey, prairie dogs, and the second-largest (behind Yellowstone National Park) publicly owned herd of bison in the world roam this pristine landscape. Scenic drives roll past fingerlike granite spires and panoramic views (try the Needles Highway). Take the 18-mile Wildlife Loop Road to see prairies teeming with animals and some of the beautiful backdrops for countless Western films. Accommodations here are outstanding, too, with numerous campgrounds and a resort network that includes five amenities-filled lodges and seven well-appointed vacation cabins. ■ **TIP→ The park is open year-round, but some amenities are closed over winter.** ✉ *13329 U.S. 16A, Custer ✈ 4 miles east of Custer ☎ 605/255–4515 🌐 gfp.sd.gov/parks/detail/custer-state-park 🎟 From $20 per vehicle.*

Jewel Cave National Monument

CAVE | Jewel Cave's more than 200 miles of surveyed passages made it the third-longest cave in the world as of 2020, while exploration continued. But for tourists who aren't cavers, it's the rare crystalline formations that abound in the cave's passages—not the cave's size—that are the main draw. Take one of the paid, year-round, ranger-led tours, and you'll be rewarded with the sight of tiny crystal Christmas trees, hydromagnesite balloons, and delicate calcite deposits dubbed "cave popcorn." Plan to arrive early in the morning, because summertime tours fill up fast and start at prescheduled intervals. While you wait, scenic surface trails and exhibits in the visitor center can be explored for free. ✉ *11149 U.S. 16, Custer ✈ 15 miles west of Custer ☎ 605/673–8300 🌐 www.nps.gov/jeca 🎟 Tours from $12.*

★ **Mount Rushmore National Memorial**

MEMORIAL | Abraham Lincoln was tall in real life—6 feet, 4 inches, though add a few more for his hat. But at one of the nation's most iconic sights, Honest Abe, along with presidents George Washington, Thomas Jefferson, and Theodore Roosevelt, towers over the Black Hills in a 60-foot-high likeness. The four images look especially spectacular at night, when they're always illuminated. Follow the Presidential Trail through the forest to gain excellent views of the colossal sculpture, or stroll the Avenue of Flags for a different perspective. Also on-site are an impressive museum, an indoor theater where an introductory film is shown, an outdoor amphitheater for live performances, an award-winning audio tour, and concession facilities. The nightly ranger program and special memorial lighting ceremony (June through mid-September) is reportedly the most popular interpretive program in all of the National Park Service system. Be sure to see the Avenue of Flags, running from the entrance of the memorial to the museum and amphitheater at the base of the mountain. This avenue has the flag of each state, commonwealth, district, and territory—arranged alphabetically—of the United States. At the Youth Exploration Area, along the Presidential Trail beneath the towering visage of George Washington, rangers present interactive programs for youngsters. ✉ *13000 Hwy. 244, Mount Rushmore ☎ 605/574–2523 🌐 www.nps.gov/moru 🎟 Free; parking from $10 per vehicle.*

Chapter 61

WRANGELL–ST. ELIAS NATIONAL PARK AND PRESERVE

Updated by
Teeka Ballas

Camping	Hotels	Activities	Scenery	Crowds
★★★★☆	★★☆☆☆	★★★★☆	★★★★★	★☆☆☆☆

WELCOME TO WRANGELL–ST. ELIAS NATIONAL PARK AND PRESERVE

TOP REASONS TO GO

★ **Amazing drives:** Wrangell–St. Elias is one of the few national parks in Alaskan that you can drive to—and into. Whether you merely travel along the park's western edge on state highways or you go the distance on the park's rough but scenic Nabesna or McCarthy roads, you earn bragging rights.

★ **Breathtaking scenery:** However you arrive at and traverse this park—by land, air, or water—its glacial and mountain scenery will take your breath away.

★ **Authentic Alaska:** In terms of authenticity, it's hard to beat the opportunity to hike to (and onto) a glacier. But the park's sites and area towns also enable you to immerse yourself in the cultures, history, and contemporary everyday life of the region.

1 Nabesna Road. One of the park's two "roads less traveled" is rough but scenic. Trailheads, rest areas, and primitive camping sites dot this 45-mile route, which starts near the village of Slana and travels into the park's northern foothills.

2 Copper Center. Situated along AK–4 (aka the Richardson Highway), a little more than midway between Slana and Chitina, this small community is home to the park's main visitor center.

3 McCarthy Road. The most popular of the two scenic routes into the park is a bumpy, 60-mile, 2½-hour drive that starts near the town of Chitina and ends at the Kennicott River, just outside the town of McCarthy. A bit farther up the road from there is the historic Kennecott Mill Town site.

4 The Southern Coast. Accessible only by plane or boat (in summer, Alaska State Ferry System vessels travel here), the park's southern reaches attract fewer visitors, most of them avid outdoor enthusiasts, particularly those who want to fish.

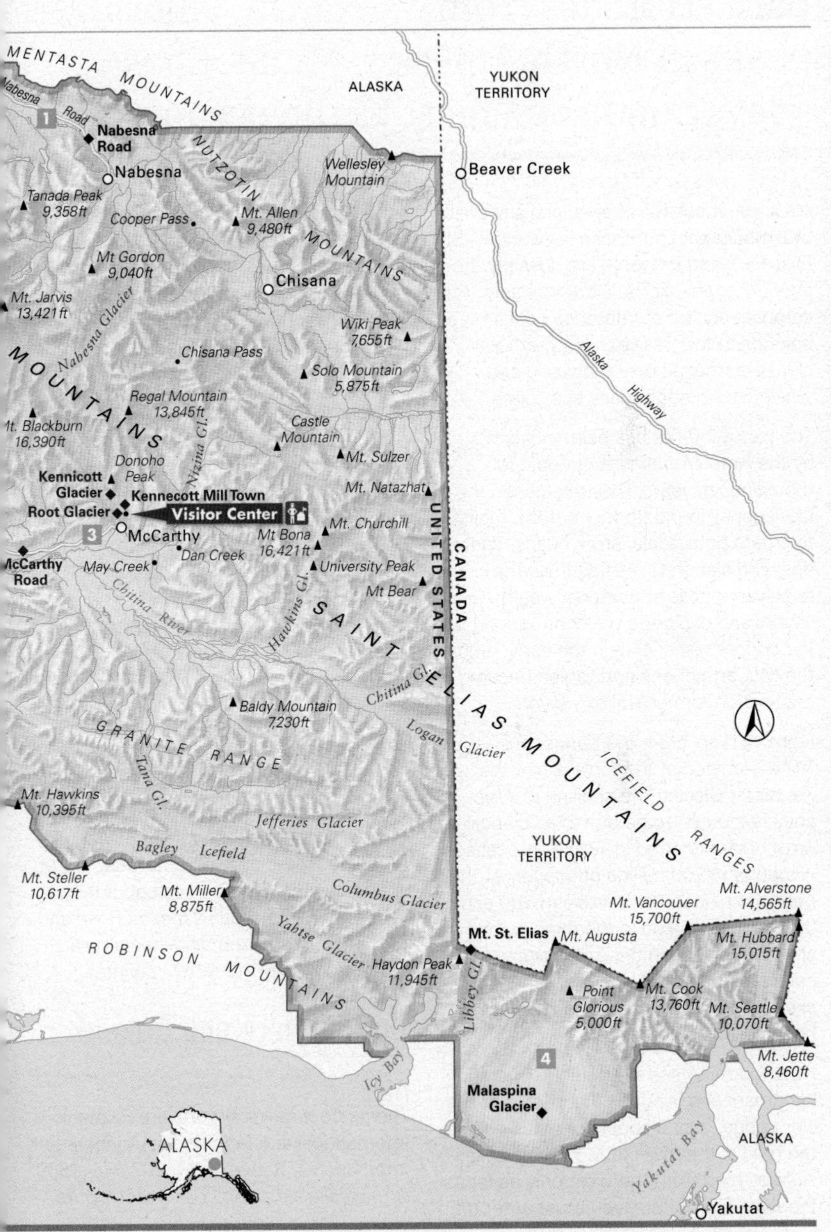
MENTASTA MOUNTAINS
Nabesna Road
1
Nabesna Road
Nabesna
NUTZOTIN MOUNTAINS
ALASKA
YUKON TERRITORY
Beaver Creek
Wellesley Mountain
Tanada Peak 9,358ft
Cooper Pass
Mt. Allen 9,480ft
Mt Gordon 9,040ft
Chisana
Mt. Jarvis 13,421ft
Nabesna Glacier
Wiki Peak 7,655ft
Chisana Pass
Alaska Highway
Solo Mountain 5,875ft
Regal Mountain 13,845ft
Mt. Blackburn 16,390ft
Castle Mountain
Nizina Gl.
Mt. Sulzer
Donoho Peak
Kennicott Glacier
Mt. Natazhat
Kennecott Mill Town
Root Glacier
Visitor Center
UNITED STATES
CANADA
Mt. Churchill
3
McCarthy
Mt Bona 16,421ft
Dan Creek
McCarthy Road
May Creek
University Peak
Mt Bear
Chitina River
Hawkins Gl.
SAINT ELIAS MOUNTAINS
Chitina Gl.
Baldy Mountain 7,230ft
Logan Glacier
GRANITE RANGE
Tana Gl.
ICEFIELD RANGES
Mt. Hawkins 10,395ft
Jefferies Glacier
Bagley Icefield
YUKON TERRITORY
Mt. Steller 10,617ft
Mt. Miller 8,875ft
Columbus Glacier
Mt. Alverstone 14,565ft
Mt. Vancouver 15,700ft
Yahtse Glacier
Mt. St. Elias
Mt. Augusta
Mt. Hubbard 15,015ft
ROBINSON MOUNTAINS
Haydon Peak 11,945ft
Libbey Gl.
Point Glorious 5,000ft
Mt. Cook 13,760ft
Mt. Seattle 10,070ft
Mt. Jette 8,460ft
4
Icy Bay
Malaspina Glacier
ALASKA
ALASKA
Yakutat Bay
Yakutat

Encompassing 13.2 million acres (it's nearly the size of West Virginia), this park stretches from one of the tallest peaks in North America, Mt. St. Elias (elevation 18,009 feet), to the ocean.

Alaska is chock full of spectacularly beautiful mountains, but those in Wrangell–St. Elias Park and Preserve are possibly the finest of them all. The extraordinarily compact cluster of immense peaks here belongs to four ranges, which attract climbers from all over the world and which rise through many eco-zones.

The park's interior has been inhabited by the Ahtna Athabascan people for thousands of years. They once used the raw copper found throughout the region to create pots, tools, arrowheads, spear tips, and elaborate shields that were largely symbolic of personal wealth. Surveyors and explorers were introduced to the copper veins, and, in the early 1900s, the McCarthy/Kennicott region became a destination for mineral extraction.

From 1911 to 1934, the Kennecott Mine—located at the terminus of the Kennicott Glacier (the spelling discrepancy is thought to be due to a "clerical error" that occurred in 1899)—processed more than $200 million of copper. At the peak of its operation, between 200 and 300 people worked in the mine camp, and 300 resided in the mill town, which consisted of a general store, school, skating rink, tennis court, recreation hall, hospital, and cow dairy.

Now the mine site is a National Historic Landmark and includes the Kennicott Glacier Lodge. Just a couple of miles down the road is the town of McCarthy, accessible by road from the west only as far as the river. From there, you must enter on foot. Much of the character from the early 1900s is still present today. There are a couple of eateries, two places to board, and one bar. During the summer months, musicians amble into town, and several guide operations set up shop.

You don't have to be a backcountry camper to experience this park—it's possible to stay in comfortable lodgings in Kennecott or McCarthy, hike to massive glaciers, and go on a flightseeing tour or a guided rafting trip—for a day or a week.

Planning

When to Go

Although it's the time of year that travelers need to be especially on their guard against bears and mosquitoes, summer—from mid-May to mid-September—is the best season to visit Wrangell–St. Elias. By the end of September, there is often snow, and services become severely limited. Both Nabesna Road and McCarthy Road are maintained all year, but not with any regularity in winter.

Getting Here and Around

AIR

The nearest major airports are Fairbanks International and Ted Stevens Anchorage International. Reeve Air (☎ *907/646–0538* 🌐 *reeveairalaska.com*) has direct flights

AVERAGE HIGH/LOW TEMPERATURES

JAN.	FEB.	MAR.	APR.	MAY	JUNE
6/-25	20/-10	32/6	45/23	58/36	67/44
JULY	**AUG.**	**SEPT.**	**OCT.**	**NOV.**	**DEC.**
70/50	65/40	55/34	38/22	17/3	10/-15

from Anchorage to Glennallen, connecting to McCarthy, year round; it also flies direct to McCarthy from May through September. Copper Valley Air Service (☎ *907/822–4200* 🌐 *www.coppervalleyairservice.com*) flies direct from Anchorage to McCarthy. Alaska Airlines offers flights direct from Anchorage to Yakutat along the park's southern edge. Floatplanes to many of the region's remote lodges usually depart from either Anchorage or Glennallen. If you want to spend time in the town of McCarthy without driving the unpaved road to it, consider flying in from the Chitina Airport with the flightseeing operator, Wrangell Air. The flight takes about 30 minutes, and you'll see glaciers along the way.

CAR

From Fairbanks, 260 miles northwest of the park, take AK–2 east to AK–1 (Glenn Highway) and follow it south to the Tok Cutoff and the village of Slana (which has no services), gateway for the scenic Nabesna Road. Alternatively, follow AK–4 (Richardson Highway) south for 258 miles from Fairbanks to the community of Copper Center, home to the park's main visitor center. From Anchorage, AK–1 travels 196 miles northeast to Copper Center. From here, Chitina, gateway to the scenic McCarthy Road, is 52 miles south via AK–4 and AK–10 (Edgerton Highway). Because the scenic roads are quite narrow in places, they're best suited to small RVs and high-clearance 4WD vehicles.

Note that some car rental companies will not allow you to drive into Wrangell–St. Elias on either scenic road due to the wear and tear it puts on the vehicle.

■ TIP→ **Potholes and old railroad ties or spikes along Nabesna and McCarthy roads may cause tire damage; to avoid being stranded, make sure your vehicle has a working jack and a properly inflated, full-size spare before heading out.**

Inspiration

One of renowned mystery writer Dana Stabanow's books, *A Cold Day for Murder,* is set in Wrangell–St. Elias. The Discovery Channel's 2014 reality show, *Edge of Alaska,* documents two men who have opposing visions for the town of McCarthy.

Park Essentials

ACCESSIBILITY

The Copper Center Visitor Center Complex is wheelchair-accessible. People with mobility impairments should contact the park ahead of time about visiting the Kennecott Mill Town: although the visitor center and some amenities and sights are wheelchair accessible, not everything is ADA compliant.

PARK FEES AND PERMITS

There is no fee to enter or camp in Wrangell–St. Elias National Park and Preserve, however, private-land campgrounds along McCarthy Road do charge fees. If you're fishing with an outfitter, be sure to inquire about any necessary licenses or permits.

PARK HOURS

The park is open 24/7 year-round, but many of its services are seasonal, and, even during peak season, you should call ahead to confirm hours. In general, the main Copper Center Visitor Center and Slana and Chitina ranger stations are open daily 9–5 from mid-May through mid-September. The Kennecott Visitor Center is open from Memorial Day through Labor Day; daily operating hours and services vary. Note, too, that the Nabesna and McCarthy roads into the park are often impassable in winter.

CELL PHONE RECEPTION

As most cell phone service providers in the Lower 48 have limited or no reception here, prepare to be without service for much of your trip. There can be intermittent Verizon and AT&T coverage along and off the state highways edging the park's northern areas and in Yakutat to the far south, but there is no cell reception with outside cell phone carriers anywhere within the parklands. In summer, the visitor center in Copper Center and the Slana and Chitina ranger stations offer free public Wi-Fi.

Hotels

You'll find a handful of in-park hotels in the McCarthy/Kennecott area. All are open only seasonally—generally May to September. A few free, primitive, public-use cabins require reservations and are only accessible by foot or float plane. Nabesa Road has a free primitive camping sites and one free maintained park campground; McCathy Road has a of couple private campgrounds.

Restaurants

Most park restaurants are in the McCarthy and Kennecott–area lodges, though there's a quick-stop coffee and pastry place on the McCarthy Road, and the town itself also has a food truck and a small free-standing restaurant that was formerly a food truck. All are open only seasonally (May to September). Chitina has a café in its lodge, and Yukatat has a couple of eateries as well. In peak season, you can pick up basic foodstuffs at a store in McCarthy, but if you're camping, it's best to stock up on food and supplies in either Anchorage or Glennallen

Restaurant and hotel reviews have been shortened. For full information, visit Fodors.com. Restaurant prices are the average cost of a main course at dinner or, if dinner is not served, at lunch. Hotel prices are the lowest cost of a standard double room in high season

What It Costs

$	$$	$$$	$$$$
RESTAURANTS			
under $14	$14–$22	$23–$32	over $32
HOTELS			
under $100	$100–$200	$201–$300	over $300

Tours

★ **St. Elias Alpine Guides**

EXCURSIONS | FAMILY | With more than three decades of experience, this is the go-to company not only for tours of historic Kennecott (including *into* historic mine buildings) but also half- or full-day hikes and longer, more adventurous outings on land or water. Reservations are essential for the two-hour Kennecott Mill Town Tours ($28 per person; three tours daily in summer) to see a mining community and operations that were abandoned in 1938.Guides share the tales of the men and women who lived, loved, toiled, and died in the quest for copper here. Don't miss the chance to explore Root Glacier on guided 5- to 6-mile half-day or 8- to 10-mile full-day hikes ($95 or $130 per person). Other short or long hikes, mountaineering lessons, ice climbs, multiday backpacking expeditions, and custom trips are also available. ✉ *Wrangell St. Elias National*

Park, Motherlode Powerhouse, McCarthy ☎ *888/933–5427 toll free, 907/554–4445 local, 907/231–6395 cell* 🌐 *www.stelias-guides.com.*

Visitor Information

CONTACTS Wrangell–St. Elias National Park. ☎ *907/822–5234* 🌐 *www.nps.gov/wrst.*

In the Park

Copper Center is 196 miles northeast of Anchorage and 260 miles southeast of Fairbanks.

When driving in Alaska, the rule of thumb is to fill up at every gas station you see, as it might be the last one (or the last one that's open) for a while. Glennallen and Copper Center have stations; Chitina and Slana do not, though Posty's Sinoa Creek Trading Post in Chistochina, 20 miles southwest of Slana, sells gas. Grocery and convenience stores are also limited in and near the park, so stock up on supplies in Anchorage, Fairbanks, or Glennallen, and pack plenty of toiletries, bear spray, and insect repellent. Be sure, too, that your car is road ready and has both a sturdy jack and a full-size spare tire. As cell service is limited, bring a road atlas, maps, and printouts of reservation confirmations or itineraries.

GEOLOGICAL FORMATIONS

Kennicott Glacier

NATURE SITE | A now-historic mine, businesses, and an entire town were built along this glacier's edge, making it one of the most visible and visited large glaciers in the state. Its stunning point of origin is the 16,390-foot Mount Blackburn, the state's fifth largest peak. The glacier's 4-mile-wide terminus moraine fills the valley immediately west of the Kennecott Mine, flowing 5 miles until is spills into Kennicott River in McCarthy. The moraine is a captivating site: enormous mounds of silt and rock, intriguing land formations, and exposed fins and patches of ice. ✉ *Wrangell-St. Elias National Park.*

Malaspina Glacier

NATURE SITE | Wrangell–St. Elias's coastal mountains are often wreathed in snow-filled clouds, their massive height making a giant wall that contains the great storms brewed in the Gulf of Alaska. As a result, they bear some of the continent's largest ice fields, with more than 100 glaciers radiating from them. One of these, the Malaspina Glacier, is 1,500 square miles—larger than the state of Rhode Island. This tidewater glacier has an incredible pattern of black-and-white stripes made by the other glaciers that coalesced to form it. If you fly between Juneau and Anchorage, look for Malaspina Glacier on the coast north of Yakutat. ✉ *Wrangell-St. Elias National Park.*

Mt. St. Elias

MOUNTAIN—SIGHT | The white-iced spire of Mt. St. Elias, in the range of the same name, reaches more than 18,000 feet. It's the second-highest peak on the North American continent and the crown of the planet's highest coastal range. It also has the world's longest ski descent. ✉ *Wrangell-St. Elias National Park.*

Root Glacier

NATURE SITE | The main road of Kennecott Mine turns into a well-groomed 2-mile hike that travels alongside the moraines of the Kennicott and Root Glaciers and then turns into a moderate 7.25-mile, single-track trail. Root Glacier is the most accessible and easily traversable of glaciers in the region. It begins with a stunning phenomenon: the Stairway Icefall, a 7,000-foot vertical wall of ice atop Regal Mountain, which can be seen from several vantage points along this trail. The glacier itself is a popular destination for glacier cave and lake hikes. ✉ *Wrangell-St. Elias National Park.*

Wrangell Mountains

MOUNTAIN—SIGHT | Covering a 100-by-70-mile area, the Wrangells tower over the 2,500-foot-high Copper River Plateau, with the peaks of mounts Jarvis, Drum, Blackburn, Sanford, and Wrangell rising from 15,000 feet to 16,000 feet above sea level. ✉ *Wrangell-St. Elias National Park.*

HISTORIC SIGHTS

Kennecott Mill Town

HISTORIC SITE | The Ahtnu and Upper Tanana Athabascan peoples who inhabited the Copper River Region for thousands of years used and traded copper found in the region. These ore deposits were noted by European surveyors in the late 1800s, and, by the early 1900s, prospectors began staking claims in the mountains above the Kennicott Glacier. The Kennecott Copper Corporation soon built a mine, a railway (now the McCarthy Road), and a company town and camp for about 300 workers.

By 1935, however, the copper ore was depleted, and the company ceased operations, leaving behind equipment, facilities, and debris. Today, the abandoned mine is one of Wrangell–St. Elias National Park and Preserve's main attractions, and restoration works have been an ongoing effort for more than a decade. The best way to see the mine is on a tour with one of the area operators, though only St. Elias Alpine Guides is authorized to take you into some of the restored buildings.

While exploring the area, it's hard not to notice the different spellings of the mine and the glacier, which was named after Robert Kennicott, a geologist who surveyed the area in 1899. Believed to have been caused by a clerical error, the discrepancy can be confusing, unless you look at it as a way to differentiate the man-made landmarks from the natural ones. ✉ *Wrangell-St. Elias National Park.*

SCENIC DRIVES

McCarthy Road

SCENIC DRIVE | The better-known of the two scenic routes into the park travels for 60 bumpy miles (fill the tank and the cooler ahead of time) along an old railroad bed from Chitina to the Kennicott River, a drive of at least 2½ hours. Just past Chitina, as you cross over the Copper River, keep an eye out for floating metal and wood contraptions that look like steampunk rafts. These are salmon fishwheels, which can only be used by Alaska residents. All along this road you will come across numerous relics of the region's mining past and countless opportunities to have your breath stolen away by glorious park vistas. At the end of the road, you must park and walk across the bridge—only residents of McCarthy are allowed to drive across it—to reach the town and the Kennecott site beyond. It's about a 15-minute walk into town; most outfitters and lodgings offer shuttles. ✉ *Wrangell-St. Elias National Park.*

Nabesna Road

SCENIC DRIVE | The bumpy, gravel, potholed Nabesna Road travels 45 miles into the park's northern foothills. There are no towns, services, or amenities anywhere along the wat, so gas up (and stock up) in Glennallen, Copper Center, or Chistochina (note that the station here is not open 24 hours), just south of Slana. Nabesna is known for its remoteness, wildlife encounters, and extraordinary views of the Wrangell, Mentasta, and Nutzotin mountains. There are a number of hiking and camping opportunities along the way. ✉ *Wrangell-St. Elias National Park.*

TRAILS

Root Glacier/Erie Mine Trail

TRAIL | The road that starts in McCarthy and goes right through the Kennicott Mill Town turns into the 4-mile round-trip Root Glacier Trail. The relatively level route winds alongside the Kennicott and Root Glaciers and offers tremendous views of Mt. Blackburn, Regal Mountain, and

Kennecott Copper Corporation's mine, railway, and workers' camp were abandoned in the mid-1930s.

Donaho Peak. If you're up for a longer trek (8 miles round trip), you can continue past Root Glacier itself along the Eerie Mine Trail. *Easy–Moderate.* ✉ *Wrangell–St. Elias National Park and Preserve, Kennicott* ⊕ *Trailhead: Kennecott Mill Town.*

VISITOR CENTERS

Copper Center Complex Visitor Center

INFO CENTER | FAMILY | Situated in the community of Copper Center near the town of Glennallen and 87 miles south of Slana (gateway for the Nabesna Road) and 52 miles north of Chitina (gateway for the McCarthy Road), the main visitor center is an excellent place learn about the park's geography and natural and cultural history. The complex includes an exhibit hall, a theater and amphitheater, and the Ahtna Cultural Center with displays on Native American peoples. It also restrooms, a picnic shelter and tables, and a bookstore that sells crafts as well as titles by local authors. It's open daily 9 to 5 between May and September (exact opening and closing dates vary). ✉ *Wrangell–St. Elias National Park, Mile 106.8, Richardson Hwy., Copper Center* ☎ *907/822–7250* 🌐 *www.nps.gov/wrst.*

Kennecott Visitor Center

INFO CENTER | FAMILY | Set in the historic Blackburn Schoolhouse at the center of the Kennecott Mill Town historic site, this is a great place to pick up trail maps, book a trip, or take a history or nature tour with a park ranger. It's open from Memorial Day through Labor Day, but hours and offerings vary, so check ahead. ✉ *Kennecott Mill Town, Wrangell-St. Elias National Park* ☎ *907/205–7106* 🌐 *www.nps.gov/wrst.*

Restaurants

Meatza Wagon

$$ | AMERICAN | This food truck is like no other: not only is everything made from scratch, but because it's situated so far from the main road system, the chef has no choice but to rely heavily on locally sourced ingredients. Be sure to try the Copper River salmon cakes and the slow-cooked Kenny Lake pork tacos. **Known for:** fantastic pork tacos; grab-and-go meals;

vegetarian and gluten-free options. *Average main: $15* *McCarthy* *www.meatzawagon.com.*

The Potato

$ | **AMERICAN** | What started as a food truck with an indoor-order bar, is now a full-blown restaurant. This is where locals come for tasty comfort food, live music, and a super laid-back vibe. **Known for:** fries, fries, and more fries; fun and relaxed ambience; live-music venue. *Average main: $10* *McCarthy* *907/554–4405* *www.theroadsidepotatohead.com* *Closed Oct.–Apr.*

★ **The Salmon & Bear Restaurant**

$$$$ | **AMERICAN** | A remote town with only 50 year-round residents seems an unlikely place to find a five-star meal, but that's exactly what the chefs here deliver, creatively assembling dishes using ingredients grown, caught, and raised in the region. The changing menu might include local yak, red angus, Kenny Lake pork, or Copper River salmon—all paired with fantastic wines. **Known for:** fine dining where you'd least expect it; seared local duck; romantic ambience. *Average main: $40* *Ma Johnson's Historical Hotel, 101 Kennicott Ave., McCarthy* *907/554–4402* *majohnsonshotel.com* *No lunch. Closed Oct.–Apr.*

Coffee and Quick Bites

Chokosna Trading Post

$ | **AMERICAN** | This roadside wood cabin is great place to stop and grab a cup of coffee and a pastry or sandwich. **Known for:** coffee; snacks; organic toiletry items. *Average main: $10* *Mile 26.5 McCarthy Road, Chitina* .

Hotels

Aspen Meadows of McCarthy B&B

$$ | **B&B/INN** | Three miles before the Kennicott River footbridge to McCarthy, this bed-and-breakfast offers rustic-but-comfortable cabins with cozy beds and an Alaskan-wilderness feel. **Pros:** breakfast includes freshly baked rolls; welcoming hosts; peaceful. **Cons:** bare-bones amenities; only two cabins have running water and bathrooms; driving directions are a little complicated. *Rooms from: $150* *McCarthy No. 42, Wrangell-St. Elias National Park* *907/554–4454, 866/487–7657* *wsen.net* *No credit cards* *Closed Sept.–May* *4 cabins* *Free breakfast.*

Kennicott Glacier Lodge

$$$ | **HOTEL** | At the top of the 10-mile gravel road from McCarthy is an astounding site: a red-and-white lodge with manicured lawns set amid the aged and worn Kennecott Mine and a receding glacier—all with a backdrop of snow-crested peaks. **Pros:** lots of character and delicious food; shuttle service to/from McCarthy; outdoor activities can be arranged for a fee. **Cons:** some rooms have shared bath; no air-conditioning; family-style dinner not for everyone. *Rooms from: $210* *15 Kennicott Millsite, Kennicott* *5 miles north of McCarthy* *800/582–5128* *www.kennicottlodge.com* *Closed mid-Sept.–mid-May* *35 rooms* *All meals.*

Lancaster's Hotel

$ | **HOTEL** | Located right on the main street in McCarthy, this backpacker hotel is comfortable and very pleasant. **Pros:** beautiful surroundings; great location; friendly service. **Cons:** shared bathrooms; no kitchen area; small rooms. *Rooms from: $70* *McCarthy* *907/554–4402* *wp.mccarthylodge.com/accommodations/lancasters-hotel* *Closed Oct.–Apr.* *10 rooms* *No meals.*

Ma Johnson's Hotel

$$$ | **B&B/INN** | A restored boarding house from McCarthy's early-1900s mining heyday is now a characterful B&B decorated with antiques and artifacts. **Pros:** cute, historical property; pickup and drop-off at the airport or foot bridge included; fantastic restaurant. **Cons:** very small rooms; no electrical outlets in rooms (charge

devices in the lobby); shared bathrooms. $ *Rooms from: $249* ✉ *McCarthy* ☎ *907/554–4402* 🌐 *majohnsonshotel.com* ⏲ *Closed Oct.–Apr.* 🛏 *20 rooms* 🍽 *Free breakfast.*

Nightlife

Golden Saloon

BARS/PUBS | Hang out with locals and seasonal guides at the only bar in town, right on the main drag. Thursday is open mic night featuring old-favorite sing-along songs and tall tale spoken-word performances. On weekend nights, there's sure to be live music outside on the grass. ✉ *McCarthy* ☎ *907/554–4402* 🌐 *wp.mccarthylodge.com.*

Shopping

McCarthy Center Store

CONVENIENCE/GENERAL STORES | **FAMILY** | This seasonal local store—the only one for miles and miles—sells fresh produce, baked goods, prepared foods, and a wide selection of organic, gluten free, and healthy items, as well as conventional groceries, basic necessities, and hardware. ✉ *McCarthy* ☎ *907/554–4402* 🌐 *wp.mccarthylodge.com/food-drink-amenities/mccarthy-center* ⏲ *Closed Oct.–Apr.*

Activities

BIKING

The dirt road up to the Kennecott Mill Town site is popular with mountain bikers. In fact, all the old mining roads in the McCarthy/Kennecott area are ideal for the sport. One such challenging route is the Nugget Creek Trail, a 30-mile round-trip that starts at mile 14.5 along the McCarthy Road and leads to a park service cabin. If you're hoping to rest there for the night, book the cabin in advance. 🌐 *www.nps.gov/wrst/planyourvisit/nugget-creek-cabin.htm*

CAMPING

Most campgrounds within Wrangell–St. Elias National Park and Preserve are privately owned and charge fees, particularly in the McCarthy area. Along the Nabesna Road, you'll find the park's free Kendesnii Campground and five primitive camping spots at rest areas.

Base Camp Kennicott. You can pitch a tent ($25 per day) at this commercial campsite at the end of McCarthy Road. That said, the rocky region is a better place to park a car ($5–$10 per day) or set up an RV (small rigs only as the road here is rough; no hookups or dump stations; $40 per night) before crossing the river to McCarthy. ✉ *Mile 59.2 McCarthy Rd.* 🌐 *www.basecampkennicott.com.*

Glacier View Campground. This private campground is an inviting place to lay out your spread and get your bearings. You can park your vehicle here for the day (free, though overnight parking is $15) before crossing the Kennicott River en route to McCarthy, or you can park a small RV or your car, pitch a tent, and stay for the night ($20 per night including vehicle and one tent; $10 for each additional tent). There's also a small camp store and cabins (from $95 per night). ✉ *McCarthy Rd.* 🌐 *glacierviewcampground.com.*

Kendesnii Campground. The only park-service-maintained camping area in Wrangell–St. Elias has 10 sites with picnic tables, fire rings, trails, and restrooms. It's a great place to fish and view wildlife. A ½-mile hike takes you to Jack Lake and more beautiful views of the Wrangell Mountains. Sites are free and don't require reservations. As the road here is best suited to passenger vehicles, this campground is geared to tents rather than RVs. ✉ *Mile 27.8, Nabesna Rd.* 🌐 *www.recreation.gov.*

FISHING

Yakutat Charters

FISHING | With five different boats and knowledgeable local captains, this company can help you reel in salmon, halibut, and black cod—and provide you with fresh filets and recipes for cooking them, too! The full-day rate for a minimum of four people is $350 per person. The company also offers boat tours to Hubbard Glacier ($900). ✉ *Yakutat* ☎ *907/784–3976* 🌐 *yakutatcharters.com.*

HIKING

There are only a few short trails along McCarthy Road, though Kotsina Trail traverses a couple of miles before reaching a network of impressive backcountry trails. Along Nabesna Road, five primary trails range from easy day hikes to strenuous overnighters. Be sure to check in with the Slana Ranger Station (🌐 *www.nps.gov/wrst/planyourvisit/slana-ranger-station.htm*) before trekking in this area.

There are no maintained trails within the parklands, and Alaska's outdoors can deadly. Before heading out on any hike, you must prepare for extreme weather, rough trail conditions, water crossings, and dangerous wildlife. You must also be equipped with maps, bear spray, bear barrels, and food.

RAFTING AND KAYAKING

Copper Oar

BOATING | FAMILY | The sister company of the well-established St. Elias Guides offers single- and multiday rafting adventures geared to different levels of experience and fitness. Some options include flightseeing, too. Per person rates range from $335 for the one-day Nizina Fly, Raft & Hike trip to $5,785 for a 15-day Source to the Sea expedition. The Two-Day Adventure package ticks all the right Wrangell–St. Elias activity boxes, is geared to all skill levels, and is a pretty good deal ($430). ✉ *McCarthy* ☎ *800/523–4453* 🌐 *www.copperoar.com.*

McCarthy Alaska River Tours and Outfitters

WHITE-WATER RAFTING | This outfitter has a variety of Wrangell–St. Elias offerings, including half-day Kennicott Glacier Lake rafting, stand-up paddlboarding, or kayaking trips ($300 or $420 per person); overnight float-and-fly outings ($715); and multiday river expeditions (from $1,075). The company also rents inflatable kayaks and stand-up paddleboards (from $55 per day) and offers custom Root Glacier hikes ($420). ✉ *McCarthy* ☎ *907/302–0688* 🌐 *raftthewrangells.com.*

SCENIC FLIGHTS

Wrangell Mountain Air

FLYING/SKYDIVING/SOARING | In addition to various flightseeing tours (from $250), glacier-hiking day trips, and backcountry-camping adventures, this company offers 30-minute direct flights between Chitina and McCarthy three times a day between mid-May and mid-September for $165 (per person each way). ✉ *Chitina Airstrip, Chitina* ☎ *800/478–1160, 907/554–4411* 🌐 *www.wrangellmountainair.com.*

What's Nearby

In the park's northwestern reaches, there are few amenities in the village of **Slana,** the gateway to the scenic Nabesna Road. On the park's western fringes, towns with hotels and restaurants (which are often in the hotels) include **Copper Center,** home to the park's main visitor center and the Copper River Princess Wilderness Lodge; **Glennallen,** on the highway from Anchorage and 16 miles northwest of Copper Center; and **Chitina,** near the McCarthy Road and home to Gilpatrick's Hotel and Restaurant.

The park's southern coastal area is accessible only by boat or plane. The gateway community of **Yakutat** has a couple of basic lodges.

Chapter 62

YELLOWSTONE NATIONAL PARK

Updated by
Andrew Collins

Camping	Hotels	Activities	Scenery	Crowds
★★★★★	★★★★★	★★★★☆	★★★★★	★★★★★

WELCOME TO YELLOWSTONE NATIONAL PARK

TOP REASONS TO GO

★ **Hot spots:** Thinner-than-normal crust depth and a huge magma chamber beneath the park explain Yellowstone's abundant geysers, steaming pools, hissing fumaroles, and bubbling mudpots.

★ **Bison sightings:** They're just one of many species that roam freely here (watch for moose and wolves, too). Seemingly docile, the bison make your heart race if you catch them stampeding across Lamar Valley.

★ **Hike for days:** Yellowstone has more than 900 miles of trails, along which you can summit a 10,000-foot peak, follow a trout-filled creek, or descend into the Grand Canyon of the Yellowstone.

★ **Lakefront leisure:** Here you can fish, boat, kayak, stargaze, bird-watch on black obsidian beaches, and stay in a grand historic hotel—just don't stray too far into the frigid water.

★ **Canyon adventures:** The Yellowstone River runs through the park, creating a deep yellow-tinged canyon with two impressive waterfalls.

1 **Mammoth Hot Springs.** This full-service area has an inn, restaurants, campsites, a visitor center, and general stores.

2 **Norris.** This is the hottest and most changeable part of Yellowstone National Park.

3 **Madison.** Here the Madison River is formed by the joining of the Gibbon and Firehole rivers. Anglers will find healthy stocks of brown and rainbow trout and mountain whitefish.

4 **Old Faithful.** Old Faithful erupts every 90 minutes or so. The geyser site is a full-service area with inns, restaurants, and general stores.

5 **Grant Village and West Thumb.** Named for President Ulysses S. Grant, Grant Village is on the western edge of Yellowstone Lake.

6 **Yellowstone Lake.** This is the largest body of water within the park. This is a full-service area.

7 **Canyon.** The Yellowstone River runs through the canyon, exposing geothermally altered rock.

8 **Tower-Roosevelt.** The least-visited area of the park is the place to go for horseback riding and animal sightings.

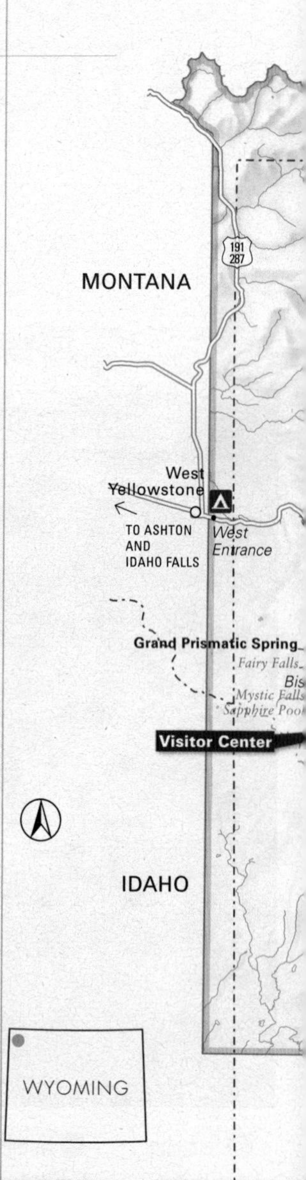

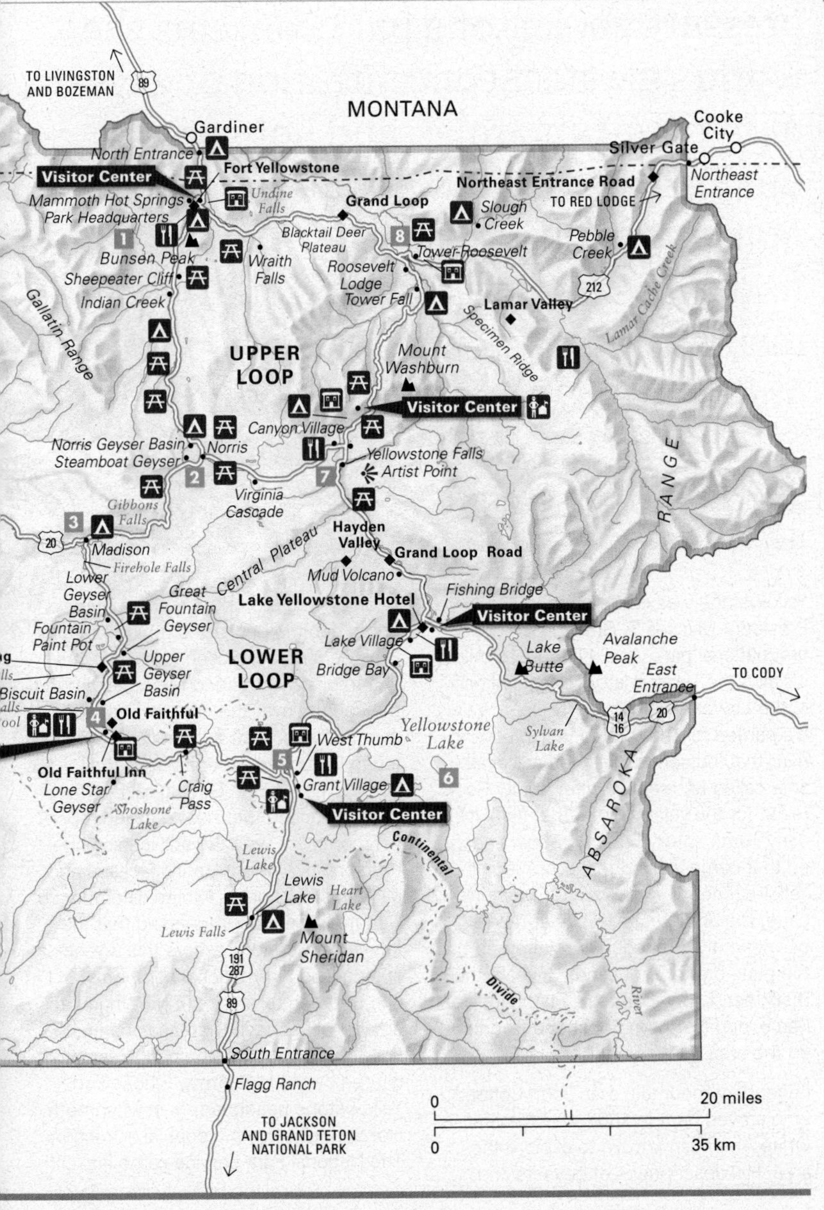
TO LIVINGSTON AND BOZEMAN
89
MONTANA
Gardiner
North Entrance
Fort Yellowstone
Visitor Center
Mammoth Hot Springs
Park Headquarters
Undine Falls
Grand Loop
Slough Creek
Northeast Entrance Road
TO RED LODGE
Cooke City
Silver Gate
Northeast Entrance
1
Bunsen Peak
Blacktail Deer Plateau
8
Tower-Roosevelt
Pebble Creek
Sheepeater Cliff
Wraith Falls
Roosevelt Lodge
212
Indian Creek
Tower Fall
Lamar Valley
Gallatin Range
Specimen Ridge
Lamar Cache Creek
UPPER LOOP
Mount Washburn
Visitor Center
Canyon Village
Norris Geyser Basin
Norris
Steamboat Geyser
Yellowstone Falls
Artist Point
2
7
Virginia Cascade
RANGE
Gibbons Falls
3
20
Madison
Hayden Valley
Firehole Falls
Great Central Plateau
Grand Loop Road
Mud Volcano
Lower Geyser Basin
Fountain Geyser
Lake Yellowstone Hotel
Fishing Bridge
Visitor Center
Fountain Paint Pot
Lake Village
Avalanche Peak
Upper Geyser Basin
LOWER LOOP
Lake Butte
Bridge Bay
East Entrance
TO CODY
Biscuit Basin
4
Old Faithful
Yellowstone Lake
14
16
20
West Thumb
Sylvan Lake
Old Faithful Inn
5
6
Lone Star Geyser
Craig Pass
Grant Village
Shoshone Lake
Visitor Center
ABSAROKA
Continental
Lewis Lake
Lewis Lake
Heart Lake
Lewis Falls
Mount Sheridan
191
287
89
Divide
River
South Entrance
Flagg Ranch
TO JACKSON AND GRAND TETON NATIONAL PARK
0
20 miles
0
35 km

A landscape of astonishing beauty that's captured the imagination of visitors for many generations, this magma-filled pressure cooker of a park contains the world's greatest concentration of geysers, mud pots, fumaroles, and hot springs. But Yellowstone's unparalleled diversity makes it truly special—here you'll also find a massive river canyon, meadows teeming with bison and wolves, a huge and pristine alpine lake, and some of the country's most striking national park architecture.

Yellowstone was established in 1872 by President Ulysses S. Grant as America's first national park. At 3,472 square miles, it's also the second largest national park in the Lower 48, trailing only Death Valley. It's named for the roaring, north-flowing river that indigenous Minnetaree inhabitants called Mi tse a-da-zi, or Yellow Rock River, for the yellow bluffs that flank it—early-19th-century French trappers adapted that name, calling the entire region Yellowstone. Only one small Shoshone band, the Sheepeaters, ever settled permanently on the land now framed by the park, but for thousands of years the Blackfeet, Crow, Bannock, Flathead, Nez Perce, and Northern Shoshone frequented the area for its plentiful wildlife.

Legendary mountain man John Colter, who arrived here in 1807, was the first white American known to explore the area. His descriptions of geysers and boiling rivers prompted some mapmakers to dub the uncharted region Colter's Hell. Reports by subsequent explorers and trappers continued to spread around the country over the next few decades, eventually spurring both privately and federally funded expeditions in the 1860s. The Hayden Geological Survey of 1871 produced the most detailed report yet, complete with the still-iconic photographs by William Henry Jackson and paintings by Thomas Moran. Members of Congress were so impressed that they felt compelled to preserve this awe-inspiring land as a national park, most of it in the then territory of Wyoming (with smaller sections in Montana and Idaho). For its first 45 years, the park was administered by the U.S. Army, whose Fort Yellowstone headquarters in Mammoth Hot Springs remain a popular attraction. The National Park Service came into

AVERAGE HIGH/LOW TEMPERATURES					
JAN.	FEB.	MAR.	APR.	MAY	JUNE
30/10	33/12	42/17	49/28	60/32	71/41
JULY	AUG.	SEPT.	OCT.	NOV.	DEC.
81/45	79/45	67/37	56/30	38/22	30/12

existence in 1916 and has been overseeing the park ever since.

Although enormous, Yellowstone National Park has been developed with a visitor-friendly logic that makes it surprisingly easy to explore. The five different entrances access 310 miles of picturesque paved roads, including the Grand Loop Road, which connects the park's most popular features. A network of historic villages with lodgings, restaurants, services, and well-maintained trails provides the opportunity for overnight stays in different sections of the park. And if you get an early start, it's possible to cover quite a lot of ground each day, especially during the longer days of summer.

That said, because there's so much to see, park lodgings book months in advance, and it can take two or three hours to travel between park entrances, it's wise to prepare a strategy before visiting. The park's geothermal features—including the geyser basins around Old Faithful and Norris and the western half of Yellowstone Lake—are a must, and they're mostly situated within or adjacent to Yellowstone Caldera, the still very active supervolcano whose three massive eruptions over the past 2.1 million years created the otherworldly landscape that makes the park so famous today. You can see much of the caldera in one long day, and each subsequent day in the park will allow you to enjoy other key attractions and activities: the Grand Canyon of the Yellowstone, Mammoth Hot Springs, Lamar Valley, and the many opportunities for viewing unusual geological features and mesmerizing wildlife, from lake cruises to snowcoach tours to both easy and rugged hikes.

Planning

When to Go

There are two major seasons in Yellowstone: summer (May–October), the only time when most of the park's roads are open to cars; and winter (mid-December–February), when over-snow travel—on snowmobiles, snowcoaches, and skis—delivers a fraction of the number of summer visitors to a frigid, bucolic sanctuary. Except for services at park headquarters at Mammoth Hot Springs, the park closes from mid-October to mid-December and from March to late April or early May.

You'll find the biggest crowds in July and August. If planning to visit at this time, book hotel accommodations inside or even near the park months in advance, and prepare for heavy traffic on park roads and parking areas. There are fewer people in the park the month or two before and after this peak season, but there are also fewer facilities open. In spring, there's also more rain, especially at lower elevations. Except for holiday weekends, there are few visitors in winter. Snow is possible year-round at high elevations.

FESTIVALS AND EVENTS

Cody Stampede Rodeo. The "Rodeo Capital of the World" has hosted the Stampede, one of the most important stops on the rodeo circuit, since 1919. The main event takes place at Cody Rodeo Grounds for several days around the July 4 holiday, and there are nightly performances at the Cody Nite Rodeo. 🌐 *www.codystampederodeo.com.*

Livingston Roundup Rodeo. Since the 1920s, the lively Montana town of Livingston has celebrated July 4 with riding, roping, bull-dogging, and barrel racing at the Roundup Rodeo. The revelry includes a parade, a three-day art show, and the crowning of the rodeo queen. 🌐 *www.livingstonroundup.com*.

Rendezvous Royale. Thomas Molesworth and his renowned Western furniture helped put Cody on the map when he moved here in the 1930s. This multiday festival held in late September celebrates his legacy with an art show, auctions, a quick-draw competition, and a major furniture exhibition. 🌐 *www.rendezvous-royale.org*.

Getting Here and Around

AIR

The closest airports to Yellowstone National Park served by most major airlines are in Cody, Wyoming, an hour from the East Entrance; Jackson, Wyoming, an hour from the South Entrance; and Bozeman, Montana, 90 minutes from the North and West entrances. Additionally, the tiny airport in West Yellowstone, Montana, just outside the park's west gate, has summer-only service on Delta from Salt Lake City.

CAR

Yellowstone is well away from the interstates—the nearest is Interstate 90, which passes through Livingston, Montana just 53 miles north of the park's North Entrance. You generally make your way here on scenic two-lane highways. Yellowstone has five road entrances. Many visitors arrive through the South Entrance, 57 miles north of Jackson and just 7 miles north of Grand Teton National Park. Other entrances are the East Entrance, 53 miles from Cody, Wyoming; the West Entrance at West Yellowstone, Montana (90 miles south of Bozeman), the North Entrance at Gardiner, Montana (80 miles south of Bozeman); and the Northeast Entrance at Cooke City, Montana, which can be reached from either Cody, Wyoming, via the Chief Joseph Scenic Highway (81 miles), or from Red Lodge, Montana, over the Beartooth Pass (67 miles). ■ **TIP→ You'll find gas stations at most of the main villages inside the park, although it's not a bad idea to fill your tank whenever you're outside Yellowstone, and gas is often cheaper in these areas.**

■ **TIP→ The best way to keep your bearings in Yellowstone is to remember that the major roads form a figure eight, known as the Grand Loop, which all entrance roads feed into. It doesn't matter at which point you begin, as you can hit most of the major attractions if you follow the entire route.**

The 466 miles of public roads in the park (310 miles of them paved) used to be riddled with potholes and hemmed in by narrow shoulders. But the park greatly upgraded its roads, and most are now smooth, if still narrow. Roadwork is likely every summer in some portion of the park. Remember, snow is possible at any time of year in almost all areas of the park. Also, never—under any circumstances—stop your car on the road any place that isn't designated. Instances of drivers blocking traffic and potentially causing accidents are rampant on park roads. Don't be a part of this problem.

Inspiration

The Yellowstone Story, by Aubrey L. Haines, is a classic, providing an illuminating and thorough history of the park, from prehistory to the present.

Decade of the Wolf, by Douglas Smith and Gary Ferguson, is the most comprehensive and gripping account of the reintroduction of wolves into the park in the 1990s.

A book that does a terrific job explaining the park's geological processes is Robert B. Smith and Lee J. Siegel's *Windows into the Earth: The Geologic Story of Yellowstone and Grand Teton National Parks*.

Lost in My Own Backyard, by Tim Cahill, is a hilarious account of one person's experiences in the park over more than 25 years.

Alston Chase's controversial *Playing God in Yellowstone* chronicles a century of government mismanagement in asserting that the National Park Service has ultimately damaged the park's ecosystem in its efforts to protect it.

Park Essentials

ACCESSIBILITY

Yellowstone has long been a National Park Service leader in providing access to visitors with disabilities. Restrooms with sinks and flush toilets designed for those in wheelchairs are in all developed areas except West Thumb, whose facilities are quite rustic. Accessible campsites and restrooms are at every park campground except Fishing Bridge RV Park. An accessible fishing platform is about 3½ miles west of Madison at Mt. Haynes Overlook. For more information, pick up a free copy of the *Visitor Guide to Accessible Features in Yellowstone National Park* at any visitor center.

PARK FEES AND PERMITS

Entrance fees of $35 per vehicle, $30 per motorcycle or snowmobile, or $20 per visitor 16 and older entering by foot, bike, ski, and so on, are good for seven days. See Activities for details on boating, camping, fishing, and horseback permits and fees.

PARK HOURS

At least some part of Yellowstone is open year-round, with 24-hour access. But many areas and entrances are closed in winter or during fall and spring shoulder seasons, and the exact times can vary depending on the weather, so it's important to check the park website for the latest details if you're planning to visit anytime from mid-October to early May. Conventional vehicles can always access the North Entrance at Gardiner, Montana, to Mammoth Hot Springs, and from Mammoth Hot Springs to the Northeast Entrance and the town of Cooke City (with no through-travel beyond Cooke City). Only over-snow vehicles can travel other parts of the park in winter. The park is in the Mountain time zone.

CELL PHONE RECEPTION

Most of the park's developed villages have (sometimes spotty) cell service, including Mammoth Hot Springs, West Yellowstone, Old Faithful, Grand Village, Lake Village, and Mt. Washburn. However, especially in the summer, crowds can overwhelm cellular capacity and greatly slow things down. Don't expect cell service on roads between these main developed areas or in the backcountry. There are public phones near visitor centers.

Hotels

Accommodations in the park continue to undergo significant upgrades, and overall, Yellowstone's lodgings are above average in quality and with rates that are comparable to many other national parks. Options range from a pair of magnificent historic hotels—the Old Faithful Inn and Lake Yellowstone Hotel—to simple cabins and utilitarian modern motels. Make reservations at least four months ahead for all park lodgings in July and August, although if planning a trip on shorter notice, it's still worth a try, as cancellations do happen. Old Faithful Snow Lodge and Mammoth Hot Springs Hotel are the only accommodations open in winter; rates are the same as in summer. There are no TVs in any park hotels. *Hotel reviews have been shortened. For full information, visit Fodors.com.*

Restaurants

The park's main developed areas all have at least one cafeteria or casual restaurant and typically a convenience store with limited groceries and deli items, but distances between these places can be considerable, and crowds during busy periods can result in long wait times for a table. For more flexibility and to be able to take advantage of the huge supply of park picnic areas, it's a good idea to fill a cooler with groceries in one of the larger towns outside the park. In addition to standard comfort fare—soups, salads, burgers, sandwiches, pizzas, ice cream—available in the park's casual eateries, you'll also encounter increasingly more sophisticated regional cuisine—with a focus on elk, bison, trout, and other game and seafood—at several more upscale restaurants, including the Old Faithful Inn, Lake Yellowstone Hotel, Grant Village Old Faithful Snow Lodge, and Mammoth Hotel dining rooms; reservations are advised, particularly in summer, at these venues. Given the park's remote location, prices at park restaurants can be a bit steep. *Restaurant reviews have been shortened. For full information, visit Fodors.com.*

PICNIC AREAS

You'll find more than 50 designated picnic areas in the park, ranging from secluded spots with a couple of tables to more popular stops with a dozen or more tables. ■ TIP→ **Keep an eye out for wildlife.** You never know when a herd of bison might decide to march through. If this happens, it's best to leave your food and move a safe distance away from them.

What It Costs

	$	$$	$$$	$$$$
RESTAURANTS				
	under $16	$16–$22	$22–$30	over $30
HOTELS				
	under $150	$151–$225	$226–$300	over $300

Tours

★ Historic Yellow Bus Tours

BUS TOURS | FAMILY | Tours by park concessionaire Xanterra on restored bright-yellow buses from as far back as the 1930s offer more than a dozen itineraries throughout Yellowstone. It's an elegant way to learn about the park, and on warm days, the driver–tour narrator rolls back the convertible top. The tour lineup includes Evening Wildlife Encounters, Picture Perfect Photo Safari, and Wake Up to Wildlife, all longtime crowd-pleasers. Other tours, including some all-day ones that efficiently cover huge swaths of the park, are on newer buses. Tours depart from several park hotels. Xanterra also gives a variety of bus, boat, stagecoach, and other tours. ☎ *307/344–7311* 🌐 *www.yellowstonenationalparklodges.com* 🎫 *From $42.*

See Yellowstone

ADVENTURE TOURS | In summer this company conducts tours that might include day hiking in the backcountry, fly-fishing in Yellowstone, and horseback riding across wildflower meadows. The company also offers snowmobile and snowcoach excursions to Old Faithful and Lower Geyser Basin as well as cross-country skiing, snowshoeing, and dogsledding adventures. ✉ *211 Yellowstone Ave., West Yellowstone* ☎ *800/221–1151* 🌐 *www.seeyellowstone.com* 🎫 *From $95.*

Visitor Information

PARK CONTACT INFORMATION Yellowstone National Park. ☎ *307/344–7381* 🌐 *www.nps.gov/yell.*

Mammoth Hot Springs

6 miles south of Gardiner, 51 miles north of Old Faithful.

This park's northernmost community—which is just south of the North Entrance in Gardiner, Montana—is known for its massive natural travertine terraces, where mineral water flows continuously, building an ever-changing display. The entire complex of terraces, which is laced with boardwalks and pathways, is within walking distance of the area's historic village, which contains some charming mid-priced (by Yellowstone standards) lodging and dining options as well as the historic buildings of Fort Yellowstone, which are lovely to walk by. You will often see elk grazing in the village.

Sights

HISTORIC SIGHTS

★ Fort Yellowstone

MILITARY SITE | The oldest buildings here served as Fort Yellowstone from 1891 to 1918, when the U.S. Army managed the park. The redbrick buildings cluster around an open area reminiscent of a frontier-era parade ground. Pick up a self-guided tour map of the area from the Albright Visitors Center on Officers Row, and start your walking tour there. ✉ *Mammoth Hot Springs.*

SCENIC DRIVES

Upper Terrace Drive

SCENIC DRIVE | This popular 1½-mile drive at the top of the Mammoth Terraces will take you back into the woods, where you can see some impressive thermal features, among them White Elephant Back and Orange Spring Mound, that aren't visible from the main road. Park at the top of the Terraces for views of Fort Yellowstone, a short walk along the boardwalk to Canary Springs, or hike down into the Lower Terraces Area. RVs aren't permitted along this drive. ✉ *Grand Loop Rd., Yellowstone National Park* ⏲ *Closed Dec.–Apr.*

SCENIC STOPS

★ Mammoth Hot Springs Terraces

BODY OF WATER | **FAMILY** | Multicolor travertine terraces formed by slowly escaping hot mineral water mark this unusual geological formation, one of the most remarkable sights in the park. You can explore the terraces via an elaborate network of boardwalks, the best of which is the Lower Terrace Interpretive Trail. If you head uphill from Liberty Cap, near the lower parking area, in a half-hour you'll pass bright and ornately terraced Minerva Spring, and in an hour you can make your way up to the Main Terrace Overlook and the side trail to Canary Spring. Along the way you might spot elk grazing nearby. Alternatively, you can drive up to the Main Terrace Overlook on Upper Terrace Drive and hike down to the Lower Terrace. Distances are fairly short amid these terraces, but give yourself at least a couple of hours to thoroughly explore them—especially if you enjoy taking lots of pictures. ✉ *Grand Loop Rd., Yellowstone National Park.*

TRAILS

Beaver Ponds Loop Trail

TRAIL | This 2½-hour, 5-mile loop starts at Liberty Cap in the busy Lower Terrace of Mammoth Hot Springs. Within minutes you'll find yourself amid the park's dense backcountry as you climb 400 feet through spruce and fir, passing several ponds and dams, as well as a glacier-carved moraine, before emerging on a windswept plain overlooking the Montana–Wyoming border. Look up to see Everts Peak to the east, Bunsen Peak to the south, and Sepulcher Mountain to the west. Your final descent into Mammoth Springs has great views of Mammoth Springs. *Moderate.* ✉ *Mammoth Hot Springs* ✣ *Trailhead: Lower Terrace parking area.*

★ **Bunsen Peak Trail**

TRAIL | Past the entrance to Bunsen Peak Road, this moderately challenging 4.4-mile round-trip trek climbs 1,280 feet to 8,527-foot Bunsen Peak for a dramatic panoramic view of Blacktail Plateau, Mammoth Hot Springs, the Gallatin Mountains, and the Yellowstone River valley. Allow about three hours. *Moderate–Difficult.* ✉ *Yellowstone National Park* ✣ *Trailhead: Grand Loop Rd., 1½ miles south of Mammoth Hot Springs.*

VISITOR CENTERS

Albright Visitor Center

INFO CENTER | **FAMILY** | Bachelor quarters for U.S. Army cavalry officers from 1909 to 1918, the carefully renovated red-roof visitor center is a great source for maps, advice, permits, and free Wi-Fi. This hefty stone structure also contains a bookstore and exhibits about the park's history, flora, and fauna, including displays of bears and wolves that kids love. ✉ *Grand Loop Rd., Mammoth Hot Springs* ☎ *307/344–2263* 🌐 *www.nps.gov/yell.*

Restaurants

Mammoth Hotel Dining Room

$$$ | **AMERICAN** | A wall of windows in the handsome art deco–style restaurant overlooks an expanse of green that was once a military parade and drill field. While enjoying breakfast, lunch, or dinner you might catch a glimpse of elk grazing on the lawn. **Known for:** bison burgers; creative appetizers; views of roaming elk. $ *Average main: $24* ✉ *305A Albright Ave., Mammoth Hot Springs* ☎ *307/344–7311, 866/439–7375* 🌐 *www.yellowstonenationalparklodges.com* ⊙ *Closed mid-Oct.–mid-Dec. and Mar.–late Apr.*

Mammoth Terrace Grill

$ | **AMERICAN** | **FAMILY** | Although the exterior looks rather elegant, this is actually the casual option at Mammoth Hot Springs, a good bet for simple fare like hot dogs, hamburgers, and chicken tenders. Continental breakfast is offered all day. **Known for:** biscuits and gravy in the morning; smoked-bison bratwurst sandwiches; pretty good beer and wine selection. $ *Average main: $9* ✉ *305B Albright Ave., Mammoth Hot Springs* ☎ *307/344–7311* 🌐 *www.yellowstonenationalparklodges.com* ⊙ *Closed mid-Oct.–late Apr.*

Hotels

★ **Mammoth Hot Springs Hotel and Cabins**

$$ | **HOTEL** | The rooms at this 1936 lodge are smaller and simpler than those at the park's other historic hotels, but this one is less expensive; the surrounding cabins look like tiny, genteel summer homes. **Pros:** good rates for a historic property; wake up to an elk bugling outside your window; cabins are among the park's nicest. **Cons:** least expensive rooms lack bathrooms; in one of the busier parts of the park; Wi-Fi is spotty. $ *Rooms from: $197* ✉ *2 Mammoth Hotel Ave., Yellowstone National Park* ☎ *307/344–7311* 🌐 *www.yellowstonenationalparklodges.com* ⊙ *Closed mid-Oct.–mid Dec. and early Mar.–late Apr.* *216 rooms* *No meals.*

Norris

21 miles south of Mammoth Hot Springs, 13 miles west of Canyon Village.

The area at the western junction of the Upper and Lower Loops has the most active geyser basin in the park. The underground plumbing occasionally reaches such high temperatures—the ground itself has heated up in areas to nearly 200°F—that a portion of the basin is periodically closed for safety reasons. There are limited visitor services: two small museums, a bookstore, and a picnic area. The 21-mile span of Grand Loop Drive from Mammoth Hot Springs to Norris is quite dramatic, passing groves of aspens that explode with fall color just south from Upper Terrace Drive and traversing a hillside of giant boulders through the Golden Gate section.

■ **TIP→ Ask rangers at the Norris Geyser Basin Museum when different geysers are expected to erupt and plan your walk accordingly.**

SCENIC STOPS

Museum of the National Park Ranger

MUSEUM | FAMILY | This historic ranger station housed soldiers from 1908 to 1918. The six-room log building is now an engaging museum where you can watch a movie telling the history of the National Park Service and visit with the retired rangers who volunteer here. Other exhibits relate to Army service in Yellowstone and early park rangers. ✉ *Norris Campground Rd., Yellowstone National Park* ⏲ *Closed late Sept.–late May.*

Norris Geyser Basin

NATURE SITE | FAMILY | From the 1930 Norris Ranger Station, which houses a small museum that helps to explain the basin's geothermal activity, you can stroll a network of short boardwalk trails—some of them suitable for wheelchairs—to Porcelain Basin, Back Basin, and several geysers and other interesting and constantly evolving thermal features. ✉ *Grand Loop Rd. at Norris Canyon Rd., Yellowstone National Park* 🌐 *www.nps.gov/yell* ⏲ *Ranger station closed mid-Oct.–mid-May.*

TRAILS

Back Basin–Porcelain Basin Loops

TRAIL | You can hike these two easy loops, which both leave from the Norris Ranger Station, in under two hours. The 1½-mile Back Basin loop passes Emerald Spring, Steamboat Geyser, Cistern Spring, and Echinus Geyser. The latter was long known as Norris's most dependable big geyser, but its schedule has become much more erratic. The ¾-mile Porcelain Basin loop leads past whitish geyserite stone and extremely active Whirligig and other small geysers. *Easy.* ✉ *Norris* ✣ *Trailhead: at Grand Loop Rd. at Norris Canyon Rd.*

Madison

14 miles southwest of Norris, 15 miles east of West Yellowstone, Montana.

The area around the junction of the West Entrance Road and the Lower Loop is a good place to take a break as you travel through the park, because you will almost always see bison grazing along the Madison River, and elk are often in the area, too. The only visitor services in Madison are a small information station.

SCENIC DRIVES

★ **Firehole Canyon Drive**

SCENIC DRIVE | FAMILY | The 2-mile narrow asphalt road twists through a deep canyon of curving lava-rock formations and passes the 40-foot Firehole Falls, which are most scenic in the morning when you're not looking into the afternoon sun. In summer look for a sign marking a pullout and swimming hole. This is one of only two places in the park (Boiling River on the North Entrance Road is the other) where you can safely and legally swim in the thermally heated waters. Look for osprey and other raptors. ✉ *Yellowstone National Park* ✣ *1 mile south of Madison junction, off Grand Loop Rd.* ⏲ *Closed early Nov.–early Apr.*

SCENIC STOPS

Gibbon Falls

BODY OF WATER | FAMILY | The water of this 84-foot fall on the Gibbon River rushes over the caldera rim. Driving east from Madison to Norris, you can see it on your right, but the angle is even better from the paved trail adjacent to the canyon's edge. ✉ *Yellowstone National Park* ✣ *Grand Loop Rd., 4 miles east of Madison.*

VISITOR CENTERS

Madison Information Station and Trailside Museum

INFO CENTER | FAMILY | In this handsome 1930s stone-and-timber structure, knowledgeable rangers share space with a store that sells books, maps, and learning aids, and a museum with exhibits on the thermal features in the vicinity. Spotting scopes are sometimes set up for viewing eagles, bison, and elk out the rear window. You can pick up backcountry camping and fishing permits, too. Picnic tables, toilets, and an amphitheater for summer-evening ranger programs are shared with the nearby campground. ✉ *Grand Loop Rd. at West Entrance Rd., Yellowstone National Park* ☎ *307/344–2876* 🌐 *www.nps.gov/yell* ⏲ *Closed early Oct.–early June.*

Old Faithful

17 miles south of Madison, 40 miles west of Fishing Bridge Village.

The world's most famous geyser is the centerpiece of this area that includes one of the largest villages in the park and three prominent geyser basins: Upper, Midway, and Lower. The 1-square-mile Upper Geyser Basin is arguably the park's most famous draw, home to Old Faithful as well as 140 different geysers—one-fifth of the known geysers in the world. It's an excellent place to spend a day or more exploring, with a complex system of boardwalks and trails—some of them suitable for bikes—and equally extensive visitor services, including several lodging and dining choices, and a very fine visitor center. In winter you can dine and stay in this area and cross-country ski or snowshoe through the geyser basin. The smaller Midway and Lower geyser basins each have their own must-see features, including Grand Prismatic Spring and Fountain Paint Pots.

Sights

HISTORIC SIGHTS

★ Old Faithful Inn

HOTEL—SIGHT | FAMILY | It's hard to imagine how any work could be accomplished with snow and ice blanketing the region, but this truly iconic hotel was constructed over the course of a single winter. Completed in 1904, what's believed to be the world's largest log structure is one of the most recognizable, and impressive, buildings in the national park system. Even if you don't spend the night, walk through or take the free 45-minute guided tour to admire its massive open-beam lobby and rock fireplace. There are antique writing desks on the second-floor balcony. You can watch Old Faithful geyser from two second-floor decks. ✉ *3200 Old Faithful Inn Rd., Old Faithful* ☎ *307/344–7311* 🌐 *www.yellowstonenationalparklodges.com* ⏲ *Closed early Oct.–early May.*

SCENIC DRIVES

Firehole Lake Drive

SCENIC DRIVE | This one-way, 3-mile-long road takes you past Great Fountain Geyser, which shoots out jets of water reaching as high as 200 feet about twice a day. Rangers' predictions provide a two-hour window of opportunity. Should you witness an eruption, you'll see waves of water cascading down the terraces that form the geyser's edges. ✉ *Firehole Lake Dr., Old Faithful* ⏲ *Closed early Nov.–early Apr.*

SCENIC STOPS

Biscuit Basin

NATURE SITE | A short drive north of Old Faithful and accessed via an easy ⅔-mile loop stroll, this basin is also the trailhead for the Mystic Falls Trail. The namesake "biscuit" formations were reduced to crumbs when Sapphire Pool erupted after the 1959 Hebgen Lake earthquake. Now, Sapphire is a calm, beautiful blue pool again, but that could change at any moment. ✉ *Grand Loop Rd., Old Faithful.*

Black Sand Basin

NATURE SITE | **FAMILY** | There are a dozen hot springs and geysers nearly opposite the cloverleaf entrance from Grand Loop Road to Old Faithful. Emerald Pool is one of the prettiest. It's an easy 1½-mile walk, ski, or bike ride from the Old Faithful area, or you can drive and park right in the middle of the basin. ✉ *Grand Loop Rd., Old Faithful.*

Geyser Hill Loop

TRAIL | **FAMILY** | Along the easy 1.3-mile Geyser Hill Loop boardwalk, accessed from the Old Faithful Boardwalk, you'll see active thermal features such as violent Giantess Geyser. Erupting only a few times each year (but sometimes going quiet for several years), Giantess spouts from 100 to 250 feet in the air for five to eight minutes once or twice hourly for a few to as long as 48 hours. Nearby Doublet Pool's two adjacent springs have complex ledges and deep blue waters that are highly photogenic. Starting as a gentle pool, Anemone Geyser overflows, bubbles, and finally erupts 10 feet or more, every three to eight minutes. The loop boardwalk brings you close to the action, making it especially fun for kids. ✉ *Old Faithful* ✧ *Trailhead: Old Faithful Visitor Center.*

★ **Grand Prismatic Spring**

NATURE SITE | **FAMILY** | You can reach Yellowstone's largest hot spring, 370 feet in diameter and arguably an even more dazzling sight than Old Faithful, by following a ⅓-mile boardwalk loop. The spring, in the Midway Geyser Basin, is deep blue in color, with yellow and orange rings formed by bacteria that give it the effect of a prism. For a stunning perspective, view it from the overlook along the Fairy Falls Trail. ✉ *Midway Geyser Basin, Grand Loop Rd., Yellowstone National Park.*

Lower Geyser Basin

NATURE SITE | With its mighty blasts of water shooting as high as 200 feet, the Great Fountain Geyser is this basin's superstar. When it spews, waves cascade down the terraces that form its edge. Check at the Old Faithful Visitor Center for predicted eruption times. Less impressive but more regular is White Dome Geyser, which shoots from a 20-foot-tall cone. You'll also find pink mudpots and blue pools at the basin's Fountain Paint Pots, a unique spot because visitors encounter all four of Yellowstone's hydrothermal features: fumaroles, mudpots, hot springs, and geysers. ✉ *Grand Loop Rd., Yellowstone National Park.*

Midway Geyser Basin

NATURE SITE | Called "Hell's Half Acre" by writer Rudyard Kipling, Midway Geyser Basin contains the breathtaking Grand Prismatic Spring and is an even more interesting stop than Lower Geyser Basin. Boardwalks wind their way to the Excelsior Geyser, which deposits 4,000 gallons of vivid blue water per minute into the Firehole River. ✉ *Grand Loop Rd., Yellowstone National Park.*

Morning Glory Pool

NATURE SITE | Shaped somewhat like a morning glory, this pool once was a deep blue, but the color is no longer as striking as before due to tourists dropping coins and other debris into the hole. To reach the pool, follow the boardwalk past Geyser Hill Loop and stately Castle Geyser, which has the biggest cone in Yellowstone. Morning Glory is the inspiration for popular children's author Jan Brett's story *Hedgie Blasts Off,* in which a hedgehog travels to another planet to unclog a geyser damaged by space tourists' debris. ✉ *Yellowstone National Park* ✧ *North end of Upper Geyser Basin.*

★ **Old Faithful**

NATURE SITE | **FAMILY** | Almost every park visitor makes it a point to view the world's most famous geyser, at least once. Yellowstone's most predictable big geyser—although neither its largest nor most regular—sometimes shoots as high as 180 feet, but it averages 130 feet. The eruptions take place every 50–120 minutes, the average is around 94 minutes. Check the park website, visitor center, or the lobbies of the Old Faithful hotels for predicted times. You can view the eruption from a bench just yards away, from the dining room at the lodge cafeteria, or the second-floor deck of the Old Faithful Inn. The 1.6-mile loop hike to Observation Point yields yet another view—from above—of the geyser and the surrounding basin. ✉ *Grand Loop Rd., Yellowstone National Park.*

TRAILS

★ Fairy Falls Trail

TRAIL | Rewarding trekkers with the chance to view Grand Prismatic Spring from high up on a bluff and to gaze up at 200-foot-tall Fairy Falls cascade from a pool of mist down below, this mostly level 5.4-mile round-trip hike is one of the highlights of the Midway Geyser Basin. *Easy.* ✉ *Old Faithful* ✣ *Trailhead: Fairy Falls Trail parking lot, Midway Geyser Basin.*

Fountain Paint Pots Nature Trail

TRAIL | FAMILY | Take the ½-mile loop boardwalk to see the fumaroles (steam vents), blue pools, pink mudpots, and mini-geysers in this thermal area. The trail is popular, and sometimes a bit overcrowded, in summer and winter because it's so accessible. *Easy.* ✉ *Yellowstone National Park* ✣ *Trailhead: at Lower Geyser Basin.*

Lone Star Geyser

TRAIL | FAMILY | A little longer, at 4.8 miles round-trip, than many of the other trails in the vicinity of Upper Geyser Basin, this enjoyable ramble along a level, partially paved trail that parallels the Firehole River leads to an overlook where you can watch Lone Star Geyser erupt up to 45 feet into the sky. Eruptions take place every three hours or so,and the trail is also popular with cyclists. *Easy–Moderate.* ✣ *Trailhead: Just south of Kepler Cascades parking area, 3½ miles south of Old Faithful.*

Mystic Falls Trail

TRAIL | From the west end of Biscuit Basin boardwalk, this 2.4-mile round-trip trail climbs gently for a mile through heavily burned forest to the lava-rock base of 70-foot Mystic Falls. It then switchbacks up Madison Plateau to a lookout with the park's least-crowded view of Old Faithful and the Upper Geyser Basin. *Easy–Moderate.* ✉ *Old Faithful* ✣ *Trailhead: Biscuit Basin.*

★ Observation Point Loop

TRAIL | A 2-mile round-trip route leaves Geyser Hill Loop boardwalk and becomes a trail shortly after the Firehole River; it circles a picturesque overview of Geyser Hill with Old Faithful Inn as a backdrop. You may also see Castle Geyser erupting. Even when 1,000-plus people are crowded on the boardwalk to watch Old Faithful, expect to find fewer than a dozen here. *Easy–Moderate.* ✉ *Old Faithful* ✣ *Trailhead: Old Faithful Visitor Center.*

VISITOR CENTERS

★ Old Faithful Visitor Education Center

INFO CENTER | FAMILY | At this impressive, contemporary, LEED-certified visitor center that's a jewel of the national park system, you can check out the interactive exhibits and children's area, read the latest geyser-eruption predictions, and find out the schedules for ranger-led walks and talks. Backcountry and fishing permits are dispensed at the ranger station adjacent to the Old Faithful Snow Lodge, across the street. ✉ *Old Faithful Bypass Rd., Yellowstone National Park* ☎ *307/344–2751* 🌐 *www.nps.gov/yell* ⏲ *Closed mid-Nov.–mid-Dec. and mid-Mar.–mid-Apr.*

Restaurants

Bear Paw Deli

$ | AMERICAN | FAMILY | You can grab a quick bite and not miss a geyser eruption at this snack shop in the Old Faithful Inn. Salmon, black-bean, and beef burgers as well as several sandwiches are available throughout the day, as is hand-dipped ice cream. **Known for:** inexpensive, no-frills meals; opens early, closes late (by park standards); great location by geyser. *Average main: $9 3200 Old Faithful Inn Rd., Old Faithful 307/344–7311 www.yellowstonenationalparklodges.com Closed early Oct.–early May.*

★ Old Faithful Inn Dining Room

$$$ | AMERICAN | The Old Faithful Inn's original dining room—designed by Robert Reamer in 1903 and expanded by him in 1927—has lodgepole-pine walls and ceiling beams and a giant volcanic rock fireplace. Note the whimsical etched-glass panels that separate the dining room from the Bear Pit Lounge; the images of partying animals were commissioned by Reamer in 1933 to celebrate the end of Prohibition. **Known for:** gorgeous interior; buffet options offered at every meal; extensive wine list. *Average main: $24 3200 Old Faithful Inn Rd., Old Faithful 307/344–7311 www.yellowstonenationalparklodges.com Closed early Oct.–early May.*

Old Faithful Snow Lodge Obsidian Dining Room

$$$ | MODERN AMERICAN | From the wood-and-leather chairs etched with animal figures to the intricate lighting fixtures that resemble snowcapped trees, there's ample Western atmosphere at this relatively intimate dining room inside the Old Faithful Snow Lodge. The huge windows give you a view of the Old Faithful area, and you can sometimes see the famous geyser as it erupts. **Known for:** hearty regional wild game dishes; open in winter; lounge offering microbrews and lighter fare. *Average main: $26 2051 Snow Lodge Ave., Yellowstone National Park 307/344–7311 www.yellowstonenationalparklodges.com Closed late-Oct.–mid-Dec. and Mar.–late Apr.*

Hotels

★ Old Faithful Inn

$$$ | HOTEL | FAMILY | Easily earning its National Historic Landmark status, this jewel of the national park system has been a favorite since the original Old House section opened in 1904—it's worth a visit whether or not you stay here. **Pros:** a one-of-a-kind property; rooms at a range of price points; incredible location near geyser. **Cons:** thin walls; waves of tourists in the lobby; least expensive rooms lack private baths. *Rooms from: $272 3200 Old Faithful Inn Rd., Old Faithful 307/344–7311 www.yellowstonenationalparklodges.com Closed mid-Oct.–early May 329 rooms No meals.*

Old Faithful Lodge Cabins

$$$ | HOTEL | There are no rooms inside the Old Faithful Lodge, but close to 100 rustic cabins can be found at the village's northeastern end. **Pros:** affordable; stone's throw from Old Faithful; services within walking distance. **Cons:** some cabins lack private bathrooms; pretty basic; few views from cabins. *Rooms from: $183 725 Old Faithful Lodge Rd., Yellowstone National Park 307/344–7311 www.yellowstonenationalparklodges.com Closed early Oct.–mid-May 96 cabins No meals.*

Old Faithful Snow Lodge

$$$$ | HOTEL | This large, contemporary lodge brings back the grand tradition of park lodges by making good use of heavy timber beams and wrought-iron accents in its distinctive facade, guest rooms that combine traditional style with up-to-date amenities. **Pros:** the park's most modern hotel; inviting common spaces; open in both summer and winter. **Cons:** pricey, but you're paying for location; rooms don't have a ton of character; busy part of the park. *Rooms from: $324 2051 Snow Lodge Ave., Old Faithful 307/344–7311 www.yellowstonenationalparklodges.com Closed late*

Oct.–mid-Dec. and mid-Mar.–late Apr. *100 rooms* *No meals.*

Old Faithful Snow Lodge Cabins
$$$ | **HOTEL** | **FAMILY** | Just yards from Old Faithful, the Western Cabins feature bright interiors and a modern motel ambience, while the Frontier Cabins are simple pine structures. **Pros:** reasonably priced; close to geyser; open during winter. **Cons:** no amenities beyond the basics; small rooms; very rustic. *Rooms from: $233* *2051 Snow Lodge Ave., Old Faithful* *307/344–7311* *www.yellowstonenationalparklodges.com* *Closed late Oct.–mid-Dec., early Mar.–late Apr.* *34 cabins* *No meals.*

Shopping

Old Faithful Basin Store
FOOD/CANDY | **FAMILY** | Recognizable by the wooden "Hamilton's Store" sign over the entrance, this shop dates to 1897 and is the second-oldest building in the park. The old-fashioned soda fountain serves up all your ice-cream favorites, including beloved huckleberry shakes. *1 Old Faithful Loop Rd., Yellowstone National Park* *307/545–7282* *www.yellowstonevacations.com.*

Grant Village and West Thumb

22 miles southeast of Old Faithful, 78 miles north of Jackson.

Along the western edge of Yellowstone Lake, called the West Thumb, Grant Village is the first community you encounter if entering the park from the South Entrance. It has some basic lodging and dining facilities and other services, but the real draw here is the geothermal activity in the West Thumb Geyser Basin.

Sights

SCENIC DRIVES

South Entrance Road
SCENIC DRIVE | The sheer black lava walls and boulder-strewn landscape of the deep Lewis River canyon make this somewhat underrated drive toward Grand Teton National Park highly memorable. Turn into the parking area at the highway bridge for a close-up view of the spectacular Lewis River Falls, one of the park's most photographed sights. There are several pull-outs along the shore of Lewis Lake that are ideal for a picnic or just to stretch your legs. *Yellowstone National Park.*

SCENIC STOPS

★ West Thumb Geyser Basin
NATURE SITE | **FAMILY** | The primary Yellowstone caldera was created by one massive volcanic eruption, but a later eruption formed the West Thumb, an unusual and particularly photogenic geyser basin because its active geothermal features are on the shore of Yellowstone Lake. Two boardwalks loop through the basin and showcase a number of sites, including the stunning blue-green Abyss Pool and Fishing Cone, where fishermen used to drop their freshly caught fish straight into boiling water without ever taking it off the hook. This area is popular in winter, when you can take advantage of the nearby warming hut and stroll around the geyser basin before continuing your trip via snowcoach or snowmobile. *Grand Loop Rd., West Thumb.*

VISITOR CENTERS

Grant Village Visitor Center
INFO CENTER | **FAMILY** | Exhibits at each visitor center describe a small piece of Yellowstone's history—the ones here provide details about the 1988 fire that burned more than a third of the park's total acreage and forced multiple federal agencies to reevaluate their fire-control policies. Watch an informative video, and learn about the 25,000 firefighters from across

A magical sunset at West Thumb Geyser Basin.

the United States who battled the blaze. Bathrooms and a backcountry office are here. ✉ *2 Grant Village Loop Rd., Grant Village* ☎ *307/242–2650* 🌐 *www.nps.gov/yell* 🕓 *Closed early Oct.–late May.*

West Thumb Information Station

INFO CENTER | This 1925 log cabin houses a bookstore and doubles as a warming hut in winter. There are restrooms in the parking area. In summer, check for informal ranger-led discussions beneath the old sequoia tree. ✉ *West Thumb Basin, West Thumb* ☎ *307/344–2650* 🌐 *www.nps.gov/yell* 🕓 *Closed early Oct.–late May.*

Restaurants

Grant Village Dining Room

$$$ | **AMERICAN** | Although the passable food here isn't the main event, the floor-to-ceiling windows of this waterfront restaurant provide dazzling views of Yellowstone Lake through the thick stand of pines. The pine-beam ceilings, cedar-shake walls, and contemporary decor lend the place a homey feel. **Known for:** sweeping water views; reliable breakfast fare; vanilla bean crème brûlée cheesecake. $ *Average main: $25* ✉ *550 Sculpin La., Grant Village* ☎ *307/344–7311* 🌐 *www.yellowstonenationalparklodges.com* 🕓 *Closed Oct.–late May.*

Hotels

Grant Village Lodge

$$$ | **HOTEL** | Grant Village is an excellent location for touring the southern half of the park, but this 1980s lodge itself feels like a bit dormlike, its rooms furnished like their counterparts at a big-city motel, with beds, nightstands, and tables, and not much else. **Pros:** near Lake Yellowstone; many facilities nearby; closest Yellowstone lodge to Grand Teton. **Cons:** expensive for what you get; small rooms without character; spotty Wi-Fi. $ *Rooms from: $291* ✉ *24 Rainbow Loop, Yellowstone National Park* ☎ *307/344–7311* 🌐 *www.yellowstonenationalparklodges.com* 🕓 *Closed late Sept.–late May* *300 rooms* *No meals.*

Lake Yellowstone

22 miles northeast of West Thumb and Grant Village, 80 miles west of Cody.

In the park's southeastern quadrant, this section is closest to the East Entrance and is dominated by the tranquil beauty of massive Yellowstone Lake. One of the world's largest alpine bodies of water, the 132-square-mile Yellowstone Lake was formed when the glaciers that once covered the region melted and filled a caldera—a crater formed by a volcano. The lake has 141 miles of shoreline, along which you will often see moose, elk, waterfowl, and other wildlife. In winter you can sometimes see otters and coyotes stepping gingerly onto the ice at the lake's edge. Many visitors head here for the excellent fishing—streams flowing into the lake provide an abundant supply of trout. There are also three small villages near the northern tip of the lake: Fishing Bridge, which has a visitor center and the park's largest campground (you may see grizzly bears hunt for fish spawning or swimming near the lake's outlet to the Yellowstone River); Lake Village, home to the striking Lake Yellowstone Hotel and the more modest Lake Lodge; and Bridge Bay, which has a marina and boat launch.

Sights

HISTORIC SIGHTS

Lake Yellowstone Hotel

HOTEL—SIGHT | Completed in 1891 and meticulously restored in recent years, the oldest lodging in Yellowstone National Park is a splendid wedding cake of a building with a gorgeous setting on the water. Casual daytime visitors can lounge in white wicker chairs in the sunroom and watch the waters of Yellowstone Lake through massive windows. Robert Reamer, the architect of the Old Faithful Inn, added a columned entrance in 1903 to enhance the original facade of the hotel. ✉ *235 Yellowstone Lake Rd., Lake Village* ☎ *307/344–7901* 🌐 *www.yellowstonenationalparklodges.com* ⏲ *Closed late Sept.–mid-May.*

SCENIC DRIVES

★ Hayden Valley on Grand Loop Road

SCENIC DRIVE | Bison, bears, coyotes, wolves, and birds of prey all call Hayden Valley home almost year-round. Once part of Yellowstone Lake, the broad valley now contains peaceful meadows, rolling hills, and a serene stretch of the Yellowstone River. There are multiple turnouts and picnic areas on this 16-mile drive. Ask a ranger about "Grizzly Overlook," an unofficial site where wildlife watchers, including NPS rangers with spotting scopes for the public to use, congregate in summer. North of Mud Volcano are 11 unsigned turnouts. Look for the telltale timber railings, and be prepared to get caught in a traffic-stopping "bison jam" along the way. ✉ *Grand Loop Rd. between Canyon and Fishing Bridge, Yellowstone National Park* ⏲ *Closed early Nov.–early Apr.*

SCENIC STOPS

LeHardy Rapids

BODY OF WATER | Witness one of nature's epic battles as cutthroat trout migrate upstream by catapulting themselves out of the water to get over and around obstacles in the Yellowstone River. The ¼-mile forested loop takes you to the river's edge. Look for waterfowl and bears, which feed on the trout. ✉ *Fishing Bridge* ✣ *3 miles north of Fishing Bridge.*

TRAILS

★ Avalanche Peak Trail

TRAIL | On a busy day in summer, only a handful of parties will fill out the trail register at the Avalanche Peak trailhead, so if you're seeking solitude, this is your hike. Starting across from a parking area on the East Entrance Road, this rigorous 4.2-mile, four-hour round-trip climbs 2,150 feet to the peak's 10,566-foot summit, from which you'll see the rugged Absaroka Mountains running north and south. Look around the talus and tundra near the top of Avalanche Peak for alpine wildflowers and butterflies. From early September to late June, the trail is often impassable due to snow, and fall also can see grizzly bear activity. Stick to summer. *Difficult.* ✉ *Fishing Bridge* ✢ *Trailhead: 2 miles east of Sylvan Lake on north side of East Entrance Rd.*

Storm Point Trail

TRAIL | **FAMILY** | Well marked and mostly flat, this 2.3-mile loop leaves the south side of the road for a perfect beginner's hike out to Yellowstone Lake, particularly with a setting sun. The trail rounds the western edge of Indian Pond, then passes moose habitat on its way to Yellowstone Lake's Storm Point, named for its frequent afternoon windstorms and crashing waves. Heading west along the shore, you're likely to hear the shrill chirping of yellow-bellied marmots. Also look for ducks, pelicans, trumpeter swans, and bison. You'll pass several small beaches that kids enjoy exploring. *Easy.* ✉ *Fishing Bridge* ✢ *Trailhead: 3 miles east of Lake Junction on East Entrance Rd.*

VISITOR CENTERS

Fishing Bridge Visitor Center

INFO CENTER | **FAMILY** | If you can't distinguish between a Clark's nuthatch and an ermine (one's a bird, the other a weasel), check out the exhibits about the park's smaller wildlife at this distinctive stone-and-log building, built in 1931. Step out the back door to find yourself on one of the beautiful black obsidian beaches of Yellowstone Lake. Adjacent is one of the park's larger amphitheaters. Ranger presentations take place here nightly in summer. ✉ *East Entrance Rd., Yellowstone National Park* ☎ *307/242–2450* 🌐 *www.nps.gov/yell* ⏲ *Closed early Sept.–late May.*

Restaurants

★ **Lake Hotel Dining Room**

$$$$ | **MODERN AMERICAN** | Opened in 1891, this double-colonnaded dining room off the lobby of the Lake Yellowstone Hotel is the park's most elegant dining spot, and with a menu that focuses on regional ingredients. Arrive early and enjoy a beverage and the view in the airy Reamer Lounge, which debuted as a sunroom in 1928. **Known for:** elegant, old-world ambience; the park's most sophisticated and creative cuisine; excellent wine list. $ *Average main: $31* ✉ *235 Yellowstone Lake Rd., Lake Village* ☎ *307/344–7311* 🌐 *www.yellowstonenationalparklodges.com* ⏲ *Closed early Oct.–early May.*

Wylie's Canteen at Lake Lodge

$ | **AMERICAN** | **FAMILY** | The former Lake Lodge Cafeteria was upgraded and rebranded as Wylie's Canteen in 2019 and still offers quick and casual bites with awe-inspiring Lake Yellowstone views, but the quality of food has improved. Try the breakfast burritos and breakfast sandwiches in the morning, or build-your-own burgers (bison, beef, chicken, Beyond Meat, or salmon), fried chicken, and salads later in the day. **Known for:** casual and affordable; wide variety of burgers; lake and meadow views. $ *Average main: $12* ✉ *459 Lake Village Rd., Yellowstone National Park* ☎ *307/344–7311* 🌐 *www.yellowstonenationalparklodges.com* ⏲ *Closed Oct.–early June.*

Hotels

Lake Lodge Cabins

$$ | **HOTEL** | **FAMILY** | Located just up the lake shoreline from the grand Lake Yellowstone Hotel, this 1920 lodge is one of the park's homey, hidden treasures. **Pros:** lovely lakeside location; great lobby; good for families. **Cons:** no Wi-Fi in cabins (only in main lodge); few amenities; Pioneer cabins are particularly bare bones. $ *Rooms from: $170* ✉ *459 Lake*

Village Rd., Lake Village ☎ *307/344–7311* 🌐 *www.yellowstonenationalparklodges.com* ⏲ *Closed late Sept.–early June* 🛏 *186 cabins* 🍽 *No meals.*

★ **Lake Yellowstone Hotel**

$$$ | HOTEL | Dating from 1891, the park's oldest lodge maintains an air of old-world refinement; just off the lobby, the spacious sun room offers priceless views of Yellowstone Lake at sunrise or sunset. **Pros:** relaxing atmosphere; the best views of any park lodging; charming old-world vibe. **Cons:** top rooms can be quite expensive; wired Internet, but no Wi-Fi; often books up months ahead. [$] *Rooms from: $242* ✉ *235 Yellowstone Lake Rd., Lake Village* ☎ *307/344–7311* 🌐 *www.yellowstonenationalparklodges.com* ⏲ *Closed late Sept.–mid-May* 🛏 *194 rooms* 🍽 *No meals.*

Canyon

18 miles north of Lake Yellowstone Village, 33 miles southeast of Mammoth Hot Springs.

You'll find one of Yellowstone's largest villages—with myriad lodging, dining, and other services—in this area near the geographical center of the park, which is home to the justly famous Grand Canyon of the Yellowstone, through which the Yellowstone River has formed one of the most spectacular gorges in the world, with its steep canyon walls and waterfalls. The river's source is in the Absaroka Mountains, in the park's southeastern corner. From there it winds its way north through the heart of the park, entering Yellowstone Lake, then continuing northward under Fishing Ridge and through Hayden Valley. The stunning canyon is 23 miles long; most visitors clog the north and south rims to see its dramatic Upper and Lower Falls. The red-and-ocher canyon walls are topped by emerald-green forest. It's a feast of color. Keep an eye peeled for osprey, which nest in the canyon's spires and precarious trees.

Sights

SCENIC STOPS

★ **Artist Point**

BODY OF WATER | An impressive view of the Lower Falls of the Yellowstone River can be had from this famous perch, which has two observation platforms, one accessible to wheelchairs. Rangers often give short talks on the lower platform. You can also access the South Rim Trail from here. ✉ *End of South Rim Rd., Yellowstone National Park.*

Lookout Point

BODY OF WATER | Midway on the North Rim Trail—also accessible via the one-way North Rim Drive—Lookout Point provides a view of the Grand Canyon of the Yellowstone. Follow the right-hand fork in the path to descend a steep trail, with an approximately 500-foot elevation change, for an eye-to-eye view of the falls from a ½ mile downstream. The best time to hike the trail is early morning, when sunlight reflects off the mist from the falls to create a rainbow. ✉ *Off North Rim Dr., Yellowstone National Park.*

TRAILS

Brink of the Lower Falls Trail

TRAIL | Especially scenic, this short but steep jaunt branches off of the North Rim Trail and can be accessed from either the Brink of the Upper Falls or Brink of the Lower Falls parking areas. The ½-mile one-way trail switchbacks 600 feet down to within a few yards of the top of the Yellowstone River's 308-foot Lower Falls. *Moderate.* ✉ *Yellowstone National Park* ✣ *Trailhead: North Rim Dr., just past junction with Grand Loop Rd.*

Mt. Washburn Trail

TRAIL | One of Yellowstone's most rewarding alpine hikes, the ascent to 10,259-foot Mt. Washburn can be approached from either the south leaving from the Dunraven Pass Trailhead or the north from the Chittenden Road Trailhead. The latter approach is a bit shorter (5.6 miles round-trip) but slightly steeper with a nearly 1,500-foot elevation gain, while from Dunraven Pass the hike switchbacks through bighorn sheep habitat and is about 6 miles round-trip, with a gain of just under 1,400 feet. Either way you'll be treated to panoramic views, and you can read interpretive exhibits in the small shelter at the summit (at the base of the fire tower). *Moderate–Difficult.* ✉ *Canyon Village* ✣ *Trailhead: Grand Loop Rd. at Dunraven Pass or Chittenden Rd.*

Mud Volcano Trail

TRAIL | **FAMILY** | This 0.6-mile loop hike in Hayden Valley curves gently around seething, sulfuric mudpots with such names as Sizzling Basin and Black Dragon's Cauldron, and around Mud Volcano itself. *Easy.* ✉ *Canyon* ✣ *Trailhead: Grand Loop Rd., 10 miles south of Canyon Village.*

North Rim Trail

TRAIL | **FAMILY** | Offering great views of the Grand Canyon of the Yellowstone, the 3-mile (each way) North Rim Trail runs from Inspiration Point to Chittenden Bridge. Particularly fetching is the ½-mile section of the North Rim Trail from the Brink of the Upper Falls parking area to Chittenden Bridge that hugs the rushing Yellowstone River as it approaches the canyon. This trail is paved and fully accessible between Lookout Point and Grand View, and it can be accessed at numerous points along North Rim Drive. *Moderate.* ✉ *Yellowstone National Park* ✣ *Trailhead: west side of Chittenden Bridge or Inspiration Point.*

Seven Mile Hole Trail

TRAIL | Give yourself the better part of a day (at least five hours) to tackle this challenging but generally uncrowded and peaceful 9.7-mile round-trip hike that begins near the North Rim's Inspiration Point, runs east for a while along the rim and then descends more than 1,000 feet to the banks of the roaring Yellowstone River. *Difficult.* ✉ *Yellowstone National Park* ✣ *Trailhead: Glacier Boulder pullout on road to Inspiration Point.*

Caution: A Wild Place

As you explore the park, keep this thought in mind: Yellowstone is not an amusement park. It is a wild place. The animals may seem docile or tame, but they are wild, and every year careless visitors are injured—sometimes even killed—when they venture too close. Particularly dangerous are female animals with their young, and bison, which can turn and charge in an instant. With bison, watch their tails: if standing up or crooked like a question mark, the animal is agitated.

★ South Rim Trail

TRAIL | **FAMILY** | Partly paved and fairly flat, this 1¾-mile trail along the south rim of the Grand Canyon of the Yellowstone affords impressive views and photo opportunities of the canyon and falls of the Yellowstone River. It starts at Chittenden Bridge, passes by magnificent Upper Falls View and Uncle Tom's Trail, and ends at Artist Point. Beyond Artist Point, you can continue your adventures for another 1.3 miles along a less-traveled and stunning trail to Point Sublime, or cut inland through high mountain meadows along the Clear Lake–Ribbon Lake Loop. You'll see fewer humans and possibly more wildlife in this more rugged backcountry, so carry bear spray. *Moderate.* ✉ *Canyon* ✣ *Trailhead: east side of Chittenden Bridge, off South Rim Dr.*

Uncle Tom's Trail

TRAIL | Accessed by the South Rim Drive, this spectacular and strenuous 700-step trail ½ mile east of Chittenden Bridge descends 500 feet from the parking area to the roaring base of the Lower Falls of the Yellowstone. Much of this walk is on steel sheeting, which can have a film of ice during early summer mornings or anytime in spring and fall. *Moderate–Difficult.* ✉ *Yellowstone National Park* ✣ *Trailhead: at South Rim Dr.*

VISITOR CENTERS

Canyon Visitor Center

INFO CENTER | FAMILY | This gleaming visitor center contains elaborate interactive exhibits for adults and kids. The focus here is on volcanoes and earthquakes and includes a room-size relief model of the park that illustrates eruptions, glaciers, and seismic activity. There are also exhibits about Native Americans and wildlife, including bison and wolves. The adjacent bookstore contains hundreds of books on the park, its history, and related science. ✉ *Canyon Village, Yellowstone National Park* ☎ *307/242–2550* 🌐 *www.nps.gov/yell* ⏲ *Closed mid-fall–late spring.*

Restaurants

Canyon Lodge Eatery

$ | ECLECTIC | FAMILY | Diners pack this mid-century-modern–inspired restaurant for casual breakfasts, as well as lunches and dinners that deviate from your standard national park fare. Design your own wok meal with veggies, meat, and toppings, or choose a protein and sauce on a three-item combo plate. **Known for:** more interesting than typical cafeteria-style fare; Asian-inspired wok stir-fries; lemon layer cake. $ *Average main: $15* ✉ *83B Lupine Ct., Yellowstone National Park* ☎ *307/344–7311* 🌐 *www.yellowstonenationalparklodges.com* ⏲ *Closed mid-Oct.–late May.*

Hotels

Canyon Lodge & Cabins

$$ | HOTEL | FAMILY | You can choose from several different types of accommodations at this large, sprawling property near the Grand Canyon of the Yellowstone, which includes a modern and attractive lodge with smartly designed and sustainable rooms, the renovated pine-frame Western Cabins, and nicely updated rooms in the historic Dunraven and Cascade Lodge buildings. **Pros:** central to different parts of the park; eco-conscious design; pretty surroundings. **Cons:** spotty Wi-Fi; a bit pricey because of location; not much dining nearby. $ *Rooms from: $214* ✉ *41 Clover La., Canyon Village* ☎ *307/344–7311* 🌐 *www.yellowstonenationalparklodges.com* ⏲ *Closed mid-Oct.–mid-May* 🛏 *590 units* 🍴 *No meals.*

Tower-Roosevelt

20 miles north of Canyon Village, 33 miles west of Cooke City–Silver Gate.

The northeastern region of Yellowstone is the least visited part of the park, making it a great place to explore without running into as many people. Packs of wolves and herds of bison can often be spotted along the majestic drive through Lamar Valley.

Sights

SCENIC DRIVES

★ **Northeast Entrance Road through Lamar Valley**

SCENIC DRIVE | This 29-mile road has the richest landscape diversity of the five entrance roads. Just after you enter the park from Cooke City, Montana, you cut between 10,928-foot Abiathar Peak and the 10,404-foot Barronette Peak. Lamar Valley is home to hundreds of bison, and the rugged peaks and ridges adjacent to it shelter some of Yellowstone's most famous wolf packs. (Wolves were reintroduced to the park in the mid-1990s.) This is the park's best place for wolf- and bison-watching, especially in the early morning and early evening. As you exit Lamar Valley, the road crosses the Yellowstone River before leading you to the rustic Roosevelt Lodge. ✉ *Yellowstone National Park.*

Northeastern Grand Loop

SCENIC DRIVE | Commonly called Dunraven Pass, this 19-mile segment of Grand Loop Road climbs to nearly 9,000 feet as it passes some of the park's finest scenery, including views of backcountry hot springs and abundant wildflowers. Near Tower Falls, the road twists beneath a series of leaning basalt columns from 40 to 50 feet high. That behemoth to the east is 10,243-foot Mt. Washburn. ✉ *Between Canyon Junction and Tower Falls, Yellowstone National Park* ⏲ *Closed early Nov.–early Apr.*

SCENIC STOPS

Tower Fall

BODY OF WATER | **FAMILY** | This is one of the easiest waterfalls to see from the roadside; you can also view volcanic pinnacles here. Tower Creek plunges 132 feet at this waterfall to join the Yellowstone River. While a trail that used to go to the base of the falls has washed out, it will take trekkers down to the river. ✉ *Grand Loop Rd., Yellowstone National Park.*

TRAILS

Slough Creek Trail

TRAIL | Starting at Slough Creek Campground, this trail climbs steeply along a historic wagon trail for 1½ miles before reaching expansive meadows and prime fishing spots, where moose are common and grizzlies occasionally wander. Allow two or three hours for the full 3.4-mile round-trip hike. *Moderate.* ✉ *Yellowstone National Park* ✣ *Trailhead: Northeast Entrance Rd. at Slough Creek Campground.*

Trout Lake Trail

TRAIL | It takes just an hour or two to enjoy this slightly elevated but generally tame 1.2-mile round-trip hike in Lamar Valley that leads through meadows and stands of Douglas fir trees and then circumnavigates pretty Trout Lake, a favorite spot for fishing. *Easy.* ✉ *Yellowstone National Park* ✣ *Trailhead: Northeast Entrance Rd., just south of Pebble Creek Campground.*

Restaurants

Roosevelt Lodge Dining Room

$$ | **AMERICAN** | **FAMILY** | The menu at this atmospheric log cabin in a pine forest includes appropriately rustic options like skirt steak, mesquite-smoked chicken, and blackened ruby red trout, but you'll also find simpler comfort fare, like carnitas nachos and fried-green tomatoes. For a real adventure, make a reservation for the Roosevelt Old West Dinner Cookout, which includes a horseback trail ride or a stagecoach ride. **Known for:** updated cowboy cuisine; wild-game chili; rustic setting. [$] *Average main: $21* ✉ *100 Roosevelt Lodge Rd., Tower Junction* ☎ *307/344–7311* 🌐 *www.yellowstonenationalparklodges.com* ⏲ *Closed early Sept.–early June.*

Hotels

Roosevelt Lodge Cabins

$$ | **HOTEL** | Near the beautiful Lamar Valley in the park's north-central reaches, this simple lodge in a pine forest dates from the 1920s and surpasses some of the park's more expensive options when it comes to rustic tranquility. **Pros:** closest cabins to Lamar Valley and its world-famous wildlife; authentic western ranch feel; some cabins are quite affordable. **Cons:** cabins are very close together; most cabins lack private bathrooms; cabins can be chilly at night. [$] *Rooms from: $209* ✉ *100 Roosevelt Lodge Rd., Tower Junction* ☎ *307/344–7901* 🌐 *www.*

YellowstoneNationalParkLodges.com ⏲ *Closed early Sept.–early June* 80 *cabins* *No meals.*

Activities

In summer, hiking, boating, and fishing are the best ways to get out and enjoy the park. During the quieter winter seasons, snowmobiling and cross-country skiing are the activities of choice.

BOATING

Motorized boats are allowed only on Lewis Lake and Yellowstone Lake. Kayaking and canoeing are allowed on all lakes except Sylvan Lake, Eleanor Lake, Twin Lakes, and Beach Springs Lagoon. Most lakes are inaccessible by car, though, so accessing them requires long portages. Boating is not allowed on any river except the Lewis between Lewis Lake and Shoshone Lake, where nonmotorized boats are permitted.

You must purchase a permit for all boats—these are available at several points in the park, including Bridge Bay Ranger Station, Grant Village Backcountry Office, and Lewis Lake Ranger Station. The cost is $5 for a week, $10 for the season, for nonmotorized boats and floatables; and $10 for a week, $20 for the season, for all others. Boat permits issued in Grand Teton National Park are honored in Yellowstone, but owners must register their vessel in Yellowstone and obtain a no-charge Yellowstone validation sticker from a permit-issuing station. Rangers inspect all boats for aquatic invasive species before issuing a permit.

Bridge Bay Marina

BOATING | Watercraft, from rowboats to powerboats, can be rented for trips on Yellowstone Lake at this well-outfitted marina, which also provides shuttle boat rides to the backcountry and dock slip rentals. Additionally, you can rent 22-foot cabin cruisers with a guide. ✉ *Grand Loop Rd., Bridge Bay* ☎ *307/344–7311* 🌐 *www.yellowstonenationalparklodges.com.*

Yellowstone Lake Scenic Cruises

BOATING | **FAMILY** | On one-hour cruises aboard the *Lake Queen II*, you'll learn about the park and the lake's history and have the chance to observe eagles, ospreys, and some of the park's big mammals along the shoreline. The vessel travels from Bridge Bay to Stevenson Island and back. Reservations are recommended. ✉ *Bridge Bay Marina, Bridge Bay* ☎ *307/344–7311* 🌐 *www.yellowstonenationalparklodges.com* *$20.*

CAMPING

Yellowstone has a dozen frontcountry campgrounds—with more than 2,000 sites—throughout the park, in addition to more than 200 backcountry sites. Most campgrounds have flush toilets; some have coin-operated showers and laundry facilities. The campgrounds run by Yellowstone National Park Lodges—Bridge Bay, Canyon, Fishing Bridge RV Park, Grant Village, and Madison—accept bookings in advance (☎ *307/344–7311* 🌐 *www.yellowstonenationalparklodges.com*); nightly rates are $27 to $32 at most of these sites, except for Fishing Bridge RV Park, which costs $79 nightly. The rest of Yellowstone's campgrounds, operated by the National Park Service, are available on a first-come, first-served basis and have rates of $15 to $20. All camping outside designated campgrounds requires a backcountry permit. For trip dates between late May (Memorial Day) and September 10, the fee is $3 per person per night; there's no charge the rest of the year.

Bridge Bay Campground. The park's largest campground, Bridge Bay rests in a wooded grove above Yellowstone Lake and adjacent to the park's major marina—the views of the water and distant Absaroka Mountains are magnificent. ✉ *Grand Loop Rd., 3 miles southwest of Lake Village.*

Canyon Campground. A large campground with nearly 300 sites, Canyon Campground accommodates everyone from hiker/biker tent campers to large RVs. ✉ *North Rim Dr., Canyon Village.*

Fishing Bridge RV Park. It's more of a parking lot than a campground, but services like tank filling and emptying and full hookups make this a popular—though pricey—option among RVers. ✉ *Grand Loop Rd., 3 miles southwest of Lake Village.*

Grant Village Campground. The park's second-largest campground, with 430 sites, Grant Village has some sites with great views of Yellowstone Lake and is close to restaurants and other services. ✉ *South Entrance Rd., Grant Village.*

Indian Creek Campground. In a picturesque setting next to a creek, this campground is in the middle of a prime wildlife-viewing area. ✉ *Grand Loop Rd., 8 miles south of Mammoth Hot Springs.*

Lewis Lake Campground. Popular with visitors from Grand Teton, this nearest campground to the South Entrance is set among old pine trees on a bluff above beautiful and relatively uncrowded Lewis Lake. It's a quiet setting, and it has a boat launch. ✉ *South Entrance Rd., 6 miles south of Grant Village.*

Madison Campground. The largest National Park Service–operated campground, Madison has eight loops and nearly 300 sites. It's a good central location, handy for visiting the geysers in Norris and Old Faithful. ✉ *Grand Loop Rd., Madison.*

Mammoth Hot Springs Campground. At the base of a sagebrush-covered hillside, this campground can be crowded and noisy in the summer, but it's close to restaurants and some great attractions, and you may see bison, mule deer, and elk roaming the area. ✉ *North Entrance Rd., Mammoth Hot Springs.*

Norris Campground. Straddling the Gibbon River, this is a quiet, popular campground. A few of its walk-in sites rank among the most desirable in the park. ✉ *Grand Loop Rd., Norris.*

Pebble Creek. Beneath multiple 10,000-foot peaks (Thunderer, Barronette Peak, and Mt. Norris) the park's easternmost campground is set creekside in a forested canopy and is also close to the fun little hike to Trout Lake. ✉ *Northeast Entrance Rd., 22 miles east of Tower-Roosevelt Junction.*

Slough Creek. Down the park's most rewarding 2 miles of dirt road, Slough Creek is a gem. Nearly every site is adjacent to the creek, which is prized by anglers. ✉ *Northeast Entrance Rd., 10 miles east of Tower-Roosevelt Junction.*

Tower Falls. It's within hiking distance of the roaring waterfall, so this modest-size campground gets a lot of foot traffic but is in a somewhat remote part of the park. ✉ *Grand Loop Rd., 3 miles southeast of Tower-Roosevelt.*

EDUCATIONAL PROGRAMS

CLASSES AND SEMINARS

Yellowstone Forever

COLLEGE | FAMILY | Learn about the park's ecology, geology, history, and wildlife from park experts, including well-known geologists, biologists, and photographers. Classes generally take place on the north side of the park, around Mammoth Hot Springs, and last from a few hours to a few days, and rates are reasonable. Some programs are designed specifically for young people and families. ✉ *Gardiner* ☎ *406/848–2400* 🌐 *www.yellowstone.org.*

RANGER PROGRAMS

Yellowstone offers a busy schedule of guided hikes, talks, and campfire programs. For dates and times, check the park's *Yellowstone Today* newsletter, available at all entrances and visitor centers.

Daytime Walks and Talks

NATURE PRESERVE | FAMILY | Ranger-led walks are held at various locations throughout the summer. Winter programs and some walks are held at West Yellowstone, Old Faithful, and Mammoth. Check the website or park newspaper for details. 🌐 *www.nps.gov/yell.*

Evening Programs

TOUR—SIGHT | FAMILY | Gather around to hear tales about Yellowstone's fascinating history, with hour-long programs on topics ranging from the return of the bison to 19th-century photographers. Every major area hosts programs during the summer; check visitor centers or campground bulletin boards for updates. Winter programs are held at Mammoth and Old Faithful. 🌐 *www.nps.gov/yell.*

Junior Ranger Program

TOUR—SIGHT | FAMILY | Children ages 4 to 12 are eligible to earn patches and become Junior Rangers. Pick up a booklet at any visitor center for $3 and start the entertaining self-guided curriculum, or download it for free online. Kids five and older can also participate in the Young Scientist Program. Purchase a self-guiding booklet for $5 at the Canyon or Old Faithful visitor centers and solve a science mystery. 🌐 *www.nps.gov/yell.*

FISHING

Fishing season begins in late May on the Saturday of Memorial Day weekend and ends in November, and it's a highly popular activity in the park's many pristine lakes and rivers. Native cutthroat trout are among the prize catches, but four other varieties—brown, brook, lake, and rainbow—along with grayling and mountain whitefish inhabit Yellowstone's waters. Popular sportfishing opportunities include the Gardner and Yellowstone rivers as well as Soda Butte Creek, but the top fishing area is Madison River.

Yellowstone fishing permits cost $18 for three days, $25 for seven days, and $40 for the season. Anglers ages 15 and younger must have a (no-fee) permit or fish under direct supervision of an adult with a permit, which can be purchased at all ranger stations, visitor centers, and Yellowstone general stores. A state license is not needed to fish in the park.

Bridge Bay Marina Fishing Charters

FISHING | The park's largest concessionaire operates Yellowstone Lake fishing charters that can last from two to 12 hours, for up to six passengers. The fee includes gear. ✉ *Bridge Bay Marina, Bridge Bay* ☎ *307/344–7311* 🌐 *www.yellowstonenationalparklodges.com* 🎫 *From $103/hr.*

HIKING

Your most memorable Yellowstone moments will likely take place along a hiking trail. Encountering a gang of elk in the woods is unquestionably more exciting than watching them graze on the grasses of Mammoth Hot Springs Hotel. Hearing the creak of lodgepole pines on a breezy afternoon feels more authentic than listening to tourists chatter as you jockey for the best view of Old Faithful. Even a one-day visitor to Yellowstone can—and should—get off the roads and into the "wilderness." Because the park is a wild place, however, even a ½-mile walk on a trail puts you at the mercy of nature, so be sure to prepare yourself accordingly. As a guide on an Old Yellow Bus Tour said, "You don't have to fear the animals—just respect them."

No matter how short the hike, the following items are essential, not discretionary, especially if you're venturing into the backcountry and away from developed areas:

Bear spray. At $50 a can and sold in the park, it's not cheap, but it's a critical deterrent if you run into one. Learn how to use it, too.

Food and water. Your "meal" can be as simple as a protein bar and a bottle of water if you're hiking only a mile or two, but for hikes of an hour or longer, it's critical to head out with an ample supply of drinking water and a variety of snacks.

Appropriate clothing. Watch the forecast closely (available at every lodging office and visitor center). Bring a layer of clothing for the opposite extreme if you're hiking at least half the day. Yellowstone is known for fierce afternoon storms, so be ready with gloves, hat, and waterproof clothing.

Altitude awareness. Much of Yellowstone lies more than 7,500 feet above sea level. The most frequent incidents requiring medical attention are respiratory problems, not animal attacks. Be aware of your physical limitations—as well as those of your young children or elderly companions.

HORSEBACK RIDING

Reservations are recommended for horseback riding in the park. Don't worry about experience, as rangers estimate 90% of riders have not been on a horse in at least 10 years.

About 50 area outfitters lead horse-packing trips and trail rides into Yellowstone. Expect to pay from $250 to $400 per day for a backcountry trip, including meals, accommodations, and guides. A guide must accompany all horseback-riding trips.

Private stock can be brought into the park. Horses are not allowed in front-country campgrounds but are permitted in certain backcountry campsites. Day-use horseback riding does not require a permit, but overnight trips with stock are $5 per person per night with no cap.

★ Wilderness Pack Trips

HORSEBACK RIDING | FAMILY | Mike and Erin Thompson at Wilderness Pack Trips have led small group trips exclusively in Yellowstone National Park for many years. Popular destinations include the spectacular remote waterfalls and wildlife-rich regions often closed to the general public. Families are welcome for these excursions. Backcountry fishing trips and other day and overnight adventures can also be arranged. ✉ *172 E. River Rd., Emigrant* ☎ *406/581–5021* 🌐 *www.yellowstonepacktrips.com* 🎫 *From $375.*

Yellowstone National Park Lodges

HORSEBACK RIDING | FAMILY | The park's largest concessionaire offers one-hour horseback rides at Mammoth, and one- and two-hour rides at Tower-Roosevelt and Canyon Village. You can also book an Old West Dinner Cookout, which includes a ride. ☎ *307/344–7311* 🌐 *www.yellowstonenationalparklodges.com* 🎫 *From $55.*

SKIING, SNOWSHOEING, AND SNOWMOBILING

Yellowstone can be the coldest place in the continental United States in winter, with temperatures of –30°F not uncommon. Still, winter-sports enthusiasts flock here when the park opens for its winter season during the last week of December. Until early March, the roads teem with over-snow vehicles like snowmobiles and snowcoaches, and trails bristle with cross-country skiers and snowshoers. The Lone Star Geyser Trail near Old Faithful Village is a good one for skiing.

Snowmobiling is an exhilarating way to experience Yellowstone. It's also controversial: there's heated debate about the pollution and disruption to animal habitats. The number of riders per day is limited, and you must have a reservation, a guide, and a four-stroke engine, which are less polluting than the more common two-stroke variety. About a dozen companies are authorized to lead snowmobile excursions. Prices vary, as do itineraries and inclusions: ask about insurance, guides, taxes, park entrance fees, clothing, helmets, and meals.

Bear Den Ski Shops

SKIING/SNOWBOARDING | FAMILY | At Mammoth Hot Springs Hotel and Old Faithful Snow Lodge, these shops rent skis, gear, and snowshoes. Lessons, guided tours, and shuttles to trails are also available. ✉ *Mammoth Hot Springs, 1 Grand Loop Rd., Yellowstone National Park* ☎ *307/344–7311* 🌐 *www.yellowstonenationalparklodges.com.*

Free Heel and Wheel

SKIING/SNOWBOARDING | This cross-country boutique outside the West Yellowstone entrance gate rents skis and other equipment and is a source for winter gear, sleds, snowshoes, and advice. Ski lessons and pull sleds for toting children are available. It also rents and repairs bicycles, and has an espresso bar to boot. ✉ *33 Yellowstone Ave., West Yellowstone* ☎ *406/646–7744* 🌐 *www.freeheelandwheel.com.*

What's Nearby

Yellowstone National Park is itself a destination, and with its considerable size and wealth of lodging and dining options, it's easily possible—and sometimes the most enjoyable strategy—to spend nearly your entire visit within the park. That said, especially if visiting in summer without having made reservations far in advance, you may find it easier and less expensive to stay in one of the several nearby communities, which range from small villages with basic services to larger towns with swanky hotels, trendy restaurants, and the area's largest airports (which are in Cody, Jackson, and Bozeman).

In Montana, nearest to the North Entrance, are the small and bustling towns of **Gardiner,** just a short drive from Mammoth Hot Springs, and **Livingston,** a charmingly historic enclave about 53 miles north at the junction with Interstate 90. Just 25 miles west of Livingston via the interstate, the youthful and hip college town of **Bozeman** is one of the fastest-growing communities in the Rockies and a hub of art, shopping, dining, and outdoor attractions. Another popular Montana gateway, particularly in winter, is **West Yellowstone,** near the park's West Entrance. It's a small town without a ton of curb appeal, but there is a wealth of lodging and dining options. It's 50 miles south of the renowned ski resort community of **Big Sky.**

In Wyoming, because of its airport and its proximity to both Grand Teton and Yellowstone national parks, **Jackson**—the closest town to Yellowstone's South Entrance—is the region's busiest community in summer and has the widest selection of dining and lodging options (⇨ *see Grand Teton National Park for more information*). The Wild West town of **Cody** lies just an hour's drive from the East Entrance and is home to one of the best museums in the Rockies as well as a number of hotels, inns, and dude ranches.

Montana is again your best bet when entering through the park's Northeast Entrance. With both Yellowstone and the Absaroka-Beartooth Wilderness at its back door, the neighboring villages of **Cooke City–Silver Gate** are good places for hiking, horseback riding, mountain climbing, and other outdoor activities. Some 50 miles to the east of Cooke City and 60 miles southeast of Billings, the small resort town of **Red Lodge** is nestled against the foot of the pine-draped Absaroka-Beartooth Wilderness and popular with skiers, anglers, golfers, and horseback riders—it has more options for dining and lodging than Cooke City.

Chapter 63

YOSEMITE NATIONAL PARK

Updated by
Cheryl Crabtree

Camping	Hotels	Activities	Scenery	Crowds
★★★★★	★★★★☆	★★★★★	★★★★★	★★★★☆

WELCOME TO YOSEMITE NATIONAL PARK

TOP REASONS TO GO

★ **Scenic falls:** An easy stroll brings you to the base of Lower Yosemite Fall, where roaring springtime waters make for misty lens caps and lasting memories.

★ **Tunnel vision:** Approaching Yosemite Valley, Wawona Road passes through a mountainside and emerges before one of the park's most heart-stopping vistas.

★ **Inhale the beauty:** Pause to take in the light, pristine air as you travel about the High Sierra's Tioga Pass and Tuolumne Meadows, where 10,000-foot granite peaks just might take your breath away.

★ **Walk away:** Leave the crowds behind—but do bring along a buddy—and take a hike somewhere along Yosemite's 800 miles of trails.

★ **Winter wonder:** Observe the snowflakes and stillness of winter in the park.

1 **Yosemite Valley.** At an elevation of 4,000 feet, in roughly the center of the park, beats Yosemite's heart. This is where you'll find the park's most famous sights and biggest crowds.

2 **Wawona.** The park's southern tip holds Wawona, with its grand old hotel and pioneer history center, and the Mariposa Grove of Giant Sequoias. These are closest to the south entrance, 35 miles (a one-hour drive) south of Yosemite Village.

3 **Tuolumne Meadows.** The highlight of east-central Yosemite is this wildflower-strewn valley that's laced with hiking trails and nestled among sharp, rocky peaks. It's a 1½-hour drive northeast of Yosemite Valley along Tioga Road (closed mid-October–late May).

4 **Hetch Hetchy.** The most remote, least visited part of Yosemite accessible by automobile, this glacial valley is dominated by a reservoir and veined with wilderness trails. It's near the park's western boundary, about a half-hour drive north of the Big Oak Flat entrance.

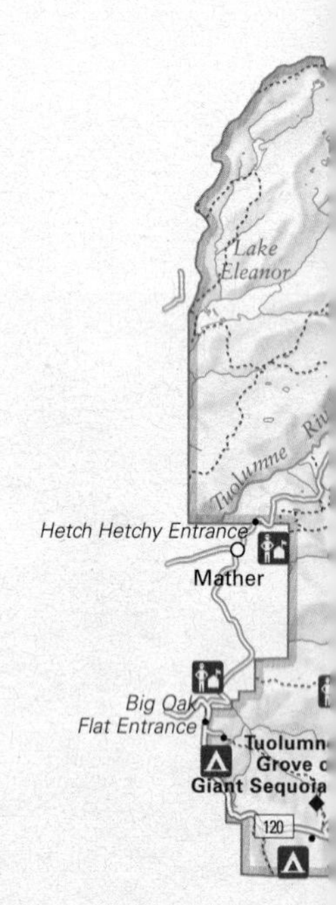

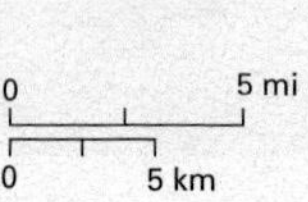

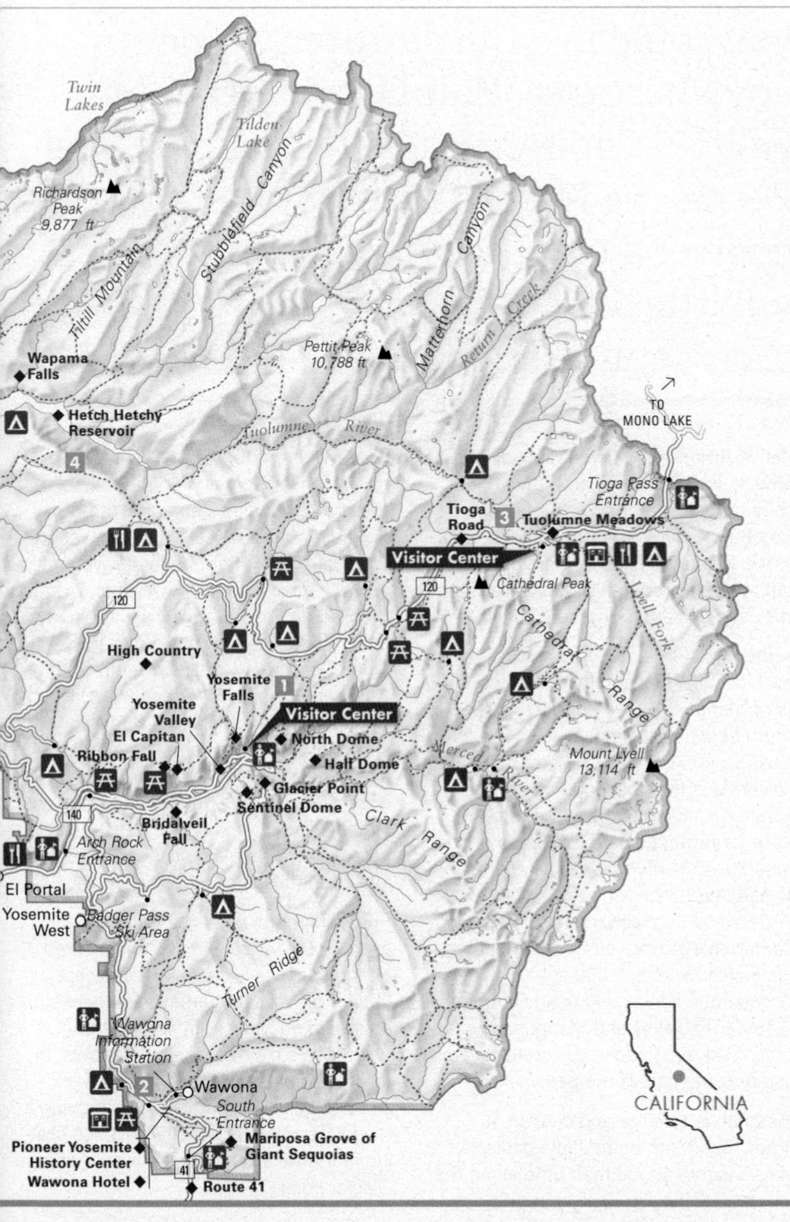
Twin Lakes
Tilden Lake
Richardson Peak 9,877 ft
Stubblefield Canyon
Tiltill Mountain
Matterhorn Canyon
Return Creek
Pettit Peak 10,788 ft
Wapama Falls
Hetch Hetchy Reservoir
Tuolumne River
TO MONO LAKE
4
Tioga Pass Entrance
Tioga Road
3
Tuolumne Meadows
Visitor Center
120
Cathedral Peak
Cathedral Range
Lyell Fork
High Country
Yosemite Falls
1
Yosemite Valley
Visitor Center
El Capitan
North Dome
Ribbon Fall
Half Dome
Glacier Point
Sentinel Dome
Merced River
Mount Lyell 13,114 ft
Clark Range
140
Bridalveil Fall
Arch Rock Entrance
El Portal
Yosemite West
Badger Pass Ski Area
Turner Ridge
Wawona Information Station
2
Wawona
South Entrance
Mariposa Grove of Giant Sequoias
Pioneer Yosemite History Center
Wawona Hotel
41
Route 41
CALIFORNIA

By merely standing in Yosemite Valley and turning in a circle, you can see more natural wonders in a minute than you could in a full day pretty much anywhere else. Half Dome, Yosemite Falls, El Capitan, Bridalveil Fall, Sentinel Dome, the Merced River, white-flowering dogwood trees, maybe even bears ripping into the bark of fallen trees or sticking their snouts into beehives—it's all here.

Native American nations—including the Miwok, Paiute, Mono, and Ahwahneechee tribes—roamed this wonderland long before other cultures. Indeed, some of the footpaths used by Native Americans to cross mountains and valleys are still used as park hiking trails today.

In the mid-1800s, the valley's special geologic qualities and the giant sequoias of Mariposa Grove 30 miles to the south began attracting visitors. The two areas so impressed a group of influential Californians that they lobbied President Abraham Lincoln to grant them to the state for protection, which he did on June 30, 1864. Further lobbying efforts by naturalist John Muir and Robert Underwood Johnson, editor of *The Century Magazine,* led Congress to set aside an additional 1,500 square miles for Yosemite National Park on October 1, 1890. The valley and Mariposa Grove, which had remained under state control, also became part of the park in 1906.

Yosemite is so large and diverse, it almost seems to be multiple parks. Many visitors spend their time along the southwestern border, between Wawona, which is open all year and is where the giant sequoias stand, and the Big Oak Flat entrance. Also very popular are Yosemite Valley, famous for its waterfalls and cliffs and also open year round, and the Badger Pass Ski Area, a winter-only destination. The seasonal, east–west Tioga Road spans the park north of the valley and bisects Tuolumne Meadows, the subalpine high country that's open for summer hiking and camping; in winter, it's accessible only via cross-country skis or snowshoes. The northwestern Hetch Hetchy district, home of less-used backcountry trails, is most accessible from late spring through early fall.

Photographers, hikers, and nature enthusiasts visit again and again, lured by the seasonally changing landscapes. In spring, waterfalls are robust thanks to abundant snowmelt. In early summer, wildflowers blanket alpine meadows. In fall, the trees showcase glorious explosions of color. In winter, snows provide a magical setting for activities like ice skating in the valley or cross-country skiing to Glacier Point.

AVERAGE HIGH/LOW TEMPERATURES					
JAN.	FEB.	MAR.	APR.	MAY	JUNE
48/29	53/30	55/32	61/36	69/43	78/49
JULY	AUG.	SEPT.	OCT.	NOV.	DEC.
85/55	84/55	79/49	70/42	56/34	47/29

Planning

When to Go

During extremely busy periods—such as weekends and holidays throughout the year—you will experience delays at the entrance gates. For smaller crowds, visit midweek. Or come January through March, when the park is a bit less busy, and the days usually are sunny and clear.

Summer rainfall is rare. In winter, heavy snows occasionally cause road closures, and tire chains or four-wheel drive may be required on the routes that remain open. The road to Glacier Point beyond the turnoff for the Badger Pass Ski Area is closed after the first major snowfall. Tioga Road is closed from late October through May or mid-June. Mariposa Grove Road is typically closed for a shorter period in winter.

FESTIVALS AND EVENTS

The Bracebridge Dinner at Yosemite. Held at The Ahwahnee hotel in Yosemite Village every Christmas since 1928, this 17th-century-theme, madrigal dinner is so popular that most seats are booked months in advance. There are also lodging packages (again, book as soon as you can). 🌐 *www.travelyosemite.com*

Chefs' Holidays. Celebrated chefs present cooking demonstrations and multicourse meals at The Ahwahnee hotel in Yosemite Village from mid-January to early February. You can get dinner or a dinner/room package, but space is limited. 🌐 *www.travelyosemite.com*

Mammoth Jazzfest. This mid-July weekend festival funded by the town of Mammoth Lakes features free jazz performances at The Village at Mammoth. 🌐 *www.mammothjazzfest.org*

Vintners' Holidays. Some of California's most prestigious vintners hold two- and three-day midweek seminars in the Great Room of The Ahwahnee hotel in Yosemite Village. The event culminates with an elegant—albeit pricey—banquet dinner. Arrive early for seats; book early for the dinner or lodging and dining packages. 🌐 *www.travelyosemite.com*

Getting Here and Around

AIR

The closest airport to the south and west entrances is Fresno Yosemite International Airport (FAT). Mammoth Yosemite Airport (MMH) is closest to the east entrance. Sacramento International Airport (SMF) is also close to the north and west entrances.

BUS AND TRAIN

Amtrak's daily *San Joaquins* train stops in Merced and connects with YARTS buses that travel to Yosemite Valley along Highway 140 from there. Seasonal YARTS buses (typically mid-May to late September) also travel along Highway 41 from Fresno, Highway 120 from Sonora, and Highway 395 and Tioga Road from Mammoth Lakes with scheduled stops at towns along the way. Once you're in Yosemite Valley, you can take advantage of the free shuttle buses, which operate on low emissions, have 21 stops, and run from 7 am to 10 pm year-round. Buses run about every 10 minutes in summer, a bit less frequently in winter. A separate (but also free) summer-only shuttle runs out to El Capitan. Also in summer, you can pay to take the "hikers' bus" from Yosemite Valley to Tuolumne or to ride a tour bus up to Glacier Point. During the snow season, buses run regularly between Yosemite Valley and Badger Pass Ski Area.

CAR

Roughly 200 miles from San Francisco, 300 miles from Los Angeles, and 500 miles from Las Vegas, Yosemite takes a while to reach—and its many sites and attractions merit much more time than what rangers say is the average visit: four hours.

Of the park's four entrances, Arch Rock is the closest to Yosemite Valley. The road that goes through it, Route 140 from Merced and Mariposa, is a scenic western approach that snakes alongside the boulder-packed Merced River. Route 41, through Wawona, is the way to come from Los Angeles (or Fresno, if you've flown in and rented a car). Route 120, through Crane Flat, is the most direct route from San Francisco. The only way in from the east is Tioga Road, which may be the best route in terms of scenery—though due to snow accumulation it's open for a frustratingly short amount of time each year (typically early June through mid-October). Once you enter Yosemite Valley, park your car in one of the two main day-parking areas, at Yosemite Village and Yosemite Falls, then visit the sights via the free shuttle bus system. Or walk or bike along the valley's 12 miles of paved paths.

There are few gas stations within Yosemite (Crane Flat and Wawona, none in the valley), so fuel up before you reach the park. From late fall until early spring, the weather is especially unpredictable, and driving can be treacherous. You should carry chains during this period as they are required when roads are icy and when it snows.

Inspiration

The Photographer's Guide to Yosemite, by Michael Frye, is an insider's guide to the park, with maps for shutterbugs looking to capture perfect images.

Sierra Nevada Wildflowers, by Karen Wiese, is perfect for budding botanists, identifying more than 230 kinds of flora growing in the Sierra Nevada region.

Yosemite: Art of an American Icon, by Amy Scott, has insightful essays accompanying museum-quality artwork.

Yosemite and the High Sierra, edited by Andrea G. Stillman and John Szarkowski, features beautiful reproductions of landmark photographs by Ansel Adams, accompanied by excerpts from the photographer's journals written when he traveled in Yosemite National Park in the early 20th century.

Park Essentials

ACCESSIBILITY

Yosemite's facilities are continually being upgraded to make them more accessible. Many of the valley floor trails—particularly at Lower Yosemite Fall, Bridalveil Fall, and Mirror Lake—are wheelchair accessible, though some assistance may be required. The Valley Visitor Center is fully accessible, as are the park shuttle buses. A sign-language interpreter is available for ranger programs. Visitors with respiratory difficulties should take note of the park's high elevations—the valley floor is approximately 4,000 feet above sea level, but Tuolumne Meadows and parts of the high country hover around 10,000 feet.

PARK FEES AND PERMITS

The admission fee, valid for seven days, is $35 per vehicle, $30 per motorcycle, or $20 per individual.

If you plan to camp in the backcountry or climb Half Dome, you must have a wilderness permit. Availability of permits depends upon trailhead quotas. It's best to make a reservation, especially if you will be visiting May through September. You can reserve two days to 24 weeks in advance by phone, mail, or fax (preferred method) (✉ *Box 545, Yosemite, CA* ☎ *209/372–0826*); you'll pay $5 per person plus $5 per reservation if and when your reservations are confirmed. You can apply online via the park website (🌐 *www.nps.gov/yose/planyourvisit/backpacking.htm*). Without a reservation, you may still get a free permit on a first-come, first-served basis at wilderness permit offices at Big Oak Flat, Hetch Hetchy, Tuolumne Meadows, Wawona, the Wilderness Center in Yosemite Village, and Yosemite Valley in summer. From fall to spring, visit the Valley Visitor Center.

PARK HOURS

The park is open 24/7 year-round. All entrances are open at all hours, except for the Hetch Hetchy entrance, which is open roughly dawn to dusk. Yosemite is in the Pacific Time Zone.

CELL PHONE RECEPTION

Cell phone reception can be hit or miss everywhere in the park. There are public telephones at entrance stations, visitor centers, all park restaurants and lodging facilities, gas stations, and in Yosemite Village.

Hotels

Indoor lodging options inside the park appear more expensive than initially seems warranted, but that premium pays off big-time in terms of the time you'll save—unless you are bunking within a few miles of a Yosemite entrance, you will face long commutes to the park when you stay outside its borders (though the Yosemite View Lodge, on Route 140, is within a reasonable half-hour's drive of Yosemite Valley).

Because of the park's immense popularity—not just with tourists from around the world but with Northern Californians who make weekend trips here—reservations are all but mandatory. Book up to one year ahead. **■ TIP→ If you're not set on a specific hotel or camp but just want to stay somewhere inside the park, call the main reservation number to check for availability and reserve (888/413–8869 or 602/278–8888 international). Park lodgings have a seven-day cancellation policy, so you may be able to snag last-minute reservations.** *Hotel reviews have been shortened. For full information, visit Fodors.com.*

Restaurants

Yosemite National Park has a couple of moderately priced restaurants in lovely (which almost goes without saying) settings: the Mountain Room at Yosemite Valley Lodge and the dining room at the Wawona Hotel. The Ahwahnee hotel provides one of the finest dining experiences in the country.

Otherwise, food service is geared toward satisfying the masses as efficiently as possible. Yosemite Valley Lodge's Base Camp Eatery is the valley's best lower-cost, hot-food option, with Italian, classic American, and world-cuisine counter options. In Curry Village, the offerings at Seven Tents are overpriced and usually fairly bland, but you can get decent pizzas on the adjacent outdoor deck. In Yosemite Valley Village, the Village Grill whips up burgers and fries, Degnan's Kitchen has made-to-order sandwiches, and The Loft at Degnan's has an open, chaletlike dining area in which to enjoy barbecue meals and appetizers.

The White Wolf Lodge and Tuolumne Meadows Lodge—both off Tioga Road and therefore guaranteed open only from early June through September—have small restaurants where meals are competently prepared. Tuolumne Meadows also has a grill, and the gift shop at Glacier Point sells premade sandwiches, snacks, and hot dogs. During ski season, you'll also find one at the Badger Pass Ski Area, off Glacier Point Road. *Restaurant reviews have been shortened. For full information, visit Fodors.com.*

What It Costs

	$	$$	$$$	$$$$
RESTAURANTS	under $12	$12–$20	$21–$30	over $30
HOTELS	under $100	$100–$150	$151–$200	over $200

Tours

★ Ansel Adams Camera Walks

SPECIAL-INTEREST | Photography enthusiasts shouldn't miss these guided, 90-minute walks offered four mornings (Monday, Tuesday, Thursday, and Saturday) each week by professional photographers. All are free, but participation is limited to 15 people so reservations are essential. Meeting points vary. ✉ *Yosemite National Park* ☎ *209/372–4413* 🌐 *www.anseladams.com* 🎟 *Free.*

Discover Yosemite

GUIDED TOURS | This outfit operates daily tours to Yosemite Valley, Mariposa Grove, and Glacier Point in 14- and 29-passenger vehicles. The tour travels along Highway 41 with stops in Bass Lake, Oakhurst, and Fish Camp; rates include lunch. Sunset tours to Sentinel Dome are additional summer options. ☎ *559/642–4400* 🌐 *discoveryosemite.com* 🎟 *From $158.*

Glacier Point Tour

GUIDED TOURS | This four-hour trip takes you from Yosemite Valley to the Glacier Point vista, 3,214 feet above the valley floor. Some people buy a $29 one-way ticket and hike down. Shuttles depart from the Yosemite Valley Lodge three times a day. ✉ *Yosemite National Park* ☎ *888/413–8869* 🌐 *www.travelyosemite.com* 🎟 *From $57* ⏲ *Closed Nov.–late May* ✍ *Reservations essential.*

Grand Tour

GUIDED TOURS | For a full-day tour of Yosemite Valley, the Mariposa Grove of Giant Sequoias, and Glacier Point, try the Grand Tour, which departs from the Yosemite Valley Lodge in the valley. The tour stops for a picnic lunch (included) at the historic Wawona Hotel. ✉ *Yosemite National Park* ☎ *209/372–1240* 🌐 *www.travelyosemite.com* 🎟 *$110* ✍ *Reservations essential.*

Moonlight Tour

GUIDED TOURS | This after-dark version of the Valley Floor Tour takes place on moonlit nights from June through September, depending on weather conditions. ✉ *Yosemite National Park* ☎ *209/372–4386* 🌐 *www.travelyosemite.com* 🎟 *$38.*

Tuolumne Meadows Hikers Bus

BUS TOURS | For a full day's outing to the high country, opt for this ride up Tioga Road to Tuolumne Meadows. You'll stop at several overlooks, and you can connect with another shuttle at Tuolumne Lodge. This service is mostly for hikers and backpackers who want to reach high-country trailheads, but everyone is welcome. ✉ *Yosemite National Park* ☎ *209/372–1240* 🌐 *www.travelyosemite.com* 🎟 *$15 one-way, $23 round-trip* ⏲ *Closed Labor Day–mid-June* ✍ *Reservations essential.*

Valley Floor Tour

GUIDED TOURS | Take a two-hour tour of Yosemite Valley's highlights, complete with narration on the area's history, geology, and flora and fauna. Tours (offered year round) are either in trams or enclosed motor coaches, depending on weather conditions. ✉ *Yosemite National Park* ☎ *209/372–1240, 888/413–8869 reservations* 🌐 *www.travelyosemite.com* 🎟 *From $38.*

Visitor Information

PARK CONTACT INFORMATION Yosemite National Park. ☎ *209/372–0200* 🌐 *www.nps.gov/yose.*

Yosemite Valley

Yosemite Valley Visitor Center is 11.5 miles from the Arch Rock entrance and 15 miles east of El Portal.

The glacier-carved Yosemite Valley stretches nearly 8 miles along the Merced River. It holds many of the park's major sights, including El Capitan, Half Dome, Glacier Point, and famous waterfalls. The valley is accessible year-round. Park your car at Yosemite Village (home of the visitor center, museum, market, and other services), Curry Village, or near Yosemite Falls. Free shuttle buses loop through the eastern and western sections of the valley.

Sights

HISTORIC SITES

The Ahwahnee

HOTEL—SIGHT | Gilbert Stanley Underwood, architect of the Grand Canyon Lodge, also designed The Ahwahnee hotel. Opened in 1927, it is generally considered his best work. You can stay here (for about $500 a night), or simply explore the first-floor shops and perhaps have breakfast or lunch in the bustling and beautiful Dining Room or more casual bar. The Great Lounge, 77 feet long with magnificent 24-foot-high ceilings and all manner of artwork on display, beckons with big, comfortable chairs and relative calm. ✉ *Yosemite Valley, Ahwahnee Rd., Yosemite Village* ✣ *About ¾ mile east of Yosemite Valley Visitor Center* ☎ *209/372–1489* 🌐 *www.travelyosemite.com/lodging/the-ahwahnee.*

Curry Village

HOTEL—SIGHT | A couple of schoolteachers from Indiana founded Camp Curry in 1899 as a low-cost option for staying in the valley, which it remains today. Curry Village's 400-plus lodging options, many of them tent cabins, are spread over a large chunk of the valley's southeastern side. This is one family-friendly place, but it's more functional than attractive. ✉ *Southside Dr.* ✣ *About ½ mile east of Yosemite Village.*

Indian Village of Ahwahnee

MUSEUM VILLAGE | This solemn smattering of structures, accessed by a short loop trail behind the Yosemite Valley Visitor Center, offers a look at what Native American life might have been like in the 1870s. One interpretive sign points out that the Miwok people referred to the 19th-century newcomers as "Yohemite" or "Yohometuk," which have been translated as meaning "some of them are killers." ✉ *Northside Dr., Yosemite Village* 🎫 *Free.*

Yosemite Museum

MUSEUM | This small museum consists of a permanent exhibit that focuses on the history of the area and the people who once lived here. An adjacent gallery promotes contemporary and historic Yosemite art in revolving gallery exhibits. A docent demonstrates traditional Native American basket-weaving techniques a few days a week. ✉ *Yosemite Village* ☎ *209/372–0299* 🎫 *Free.*

SCENIC STOPS

Bridalveil Fall

BODY OF WATER | This 620-foot waterfall is often diverted dozens of feet one way or the other by the breeze. It is the first marvelous site you will see up close when you drive into Yosemite Valley. ✉ *Yosemite Valley, access from parking area off Wawona Rd.*

El Capitan

NATURE SITE | Rising 3,593 feet—more than 350 stories—above the valley, El Capitan is the largest exposed-granite monolith in the world. Since 1958, people

Did You Know?

In mid- to late February, when the conditions are right in the evenings (clear sky, flowing falls), Horsetail Fall, on the eastern edge of El Capitan, experiences Firefall—it looks like the falls are on fire.

have been climbing its entire face, including the famous "nose." You can spot adventurers with your binoculars by scanning the smooth and nearly vertical cliff for specks of color. ✉ *Yosemite National Park* ✣ *Off Northside Dr., about 4 miles west of Valley Visitor Center.*

★ Glacier Point

VIEWPOINT | If you lack the time, desire, or stamina to hike more than 3,200 feet up to Glacier Point from the Yosemite Valley floor, you can drive here—or take a bus from the valley—for a bird's-eye view. You are likely to encounter a lot of day-trippers on the short, paved trail that leads from the parking lot to the main overlook. Take a moment to veer off a few yards to the Geology Hut, which succinctly explains and illustrates what the valley looked like 10 million, 3 million, and 20,000 years ago. ✉ *Yosemite National Park* ✣ *Glacier Point Rd., 16 miles northeast of Rte. 41* ☎ *209/372–0200* ⏲ *Closed late Oct.–mid-May.*

★ Half Dome

NATURE SITE | Visitors' eyes are continually drawn to this remarkable granite formation that tops out at more than 4,700 feet above the valley floor. Despite its name, the dome is actually about three-quarters intact. You can hike to the top of it on an 8½-mile (one-way) trail whose last 400 feet must be ascended while holding onto a steel cable. Permits, available only by lottery, are required and are checked on the trail. Call ☎ *877/444–6777* or visit 🌐 *www.recreation.gov* well in advance of your trip for details. Back down in the valley, see Half Dome reflected in the Merced River by heading to Sentinel Bridge just before sundown. The brilliant orange light on Half Dome is a stunning sight. ✉ *Yosemite National Park* 🌐 *www.nps.gov/yose/planyourvisit/halfdome.htm.*

Nevada Fall

BODY OF WATER | Climb Mist Trail from Happy Isles for an up-close view of this 594-foot cascading beauty. If you don't want to hike (the trail's final approach is quite taxing), you can see it—albeit distantly—from Glacier Point. Stay safely on the trail, as there have been fatalities in recent years after visitors have fallen and been swept away by the water. ✉ *Yosemite Valley, access via Mist Trail from Nature Center at Happy Isles.*

Ribbon Fall

BODY OF WATER | At 1,612 feet, this is the highest single fall in North America. It's also the first waterfall to dry up in summer; the rainwater and melted snow that create the slender fall evaporate quickly at this height. Look just west of El Capitan for the best view of the fall from the base of Bridalveil Fall. ✉ *Yosemite Valley, west of El Capitan Meadow.*

Sentinel Dome

VIEWPOINT | The view from here is similar to that from Glacier Point, except you can't see the valley floor. A moderately steep, 1.1-mile path climbs to the viewpoint from the parking lot. Topping out at an elevation of 8,122 feet, Sentinel is more than 900 feet higher than Glacier Point. ✉ *Glacier Point Rd., off Rte. 41.*

Vernal Fall

BODY OF WATER | Fern-covered black rocks frame this 317-foot fall, and rainbows play in the spray at its base. You can get a distant view from Glacier Point, or hike to see it close up. You'll get wet, but the view is worth it. ✉ *Yosemite Valley, access via Mist Trail from Nature Center at Happy Isles.*

★ Yosemite Falls

BODY OF WATER | Actually three falls, they together constitute the highest combined waterfall in North America and the fifth highest in the world. The water from the top descends a total of 2,425 feet, and when the falls run hard, you can hear them thunder across the valley. If they dry up—that sometimes happens in late summer—the valley seems naked without the wavering tower of spray. If you hike the mile-long loop trail (partially paved) to the base of the Lower Fall in spring, prepare to get wet. You can get a good full-length view of the falls from the lawn of Yosemite Chapel, off Southside Drive. ✉ *Yosemite Valley, access from Yosemite Valley Lodge or trail parking area.*

TRAILS

Cook's Meadow Loop

TRAIL | FAMILY | Take this 1-mile, wheelchair-accessible, looped path around Cook's Meadow to see and learn the basics about Yosemite Valley's past, present, and future. A trail guide (available at a kiosk just outside the entrance) explains how to tell oaks, cedars, and pines apart; how fires help keep the forest floor healthy; and how pollution poses significant challenges to the park's inhabitants. *Easy.* ✉ *Yosemite National Park* ✣ *Trailhead: Across from Valley Visitor Center.*

Four-Mile Trail

TRAIL | If you decide to hike up Four-Mile Trail and back down again, allow about six hours for the challenging, 9½-mile round-trip. (The original 4-mile-long trail, Yosemite's first, has been lengthened to make it less steep.) The trailhead is on Southside Drive near Sentinel Beach, and the elevation change is 3,220 feet. For a considerably less strenuous experience, you can take a morning tour bus up to Glacier Point and enjoy a one-way downhill hike. *Difficult.* ✉ *Yosemite National Park* ✣ *Trailheads: At Glacier Point and on Southside Dr.*

★ John Muir Trail to Half Dome

TRAIL | Ardent and courageous trekkers continue on from Nevada Fall to the top of Half Dome. Some hikers attempt this entire 10- to 12-hour, 16¾-mile round-trip trek in one day; if you're planning to do this, remember that the 4,800-foot elevation gain and the 8,842-foot altitude will cause shortness of breath. Another option is to hike to a campground in Little Yosemite Valley near the top of Nevada Fall the first day, then climb to the top of Half Dome and hike out the next day. Get your wilderness permit (required for a one-day hike to Half Dome, too) at least a month in advance. Be sure to wear hiking boots and bring gloves. The last pitch up the back of Half Dome is very steep—the only way to climb this sheer rock face is to pull yourself up using the steel cable handrails, which are in place only from late spring to early fall. Those who brave the ascent will be rewarded with an unbeatable view of Yosemite Valley below and the high country beyond. Only 300 hikers per day are allowed atop Half Dome, and they all must have permits, which are distributed by lottery, one in the spring before the season starts and another two days before the climb. Contact 🌐 *www.recreation.gov* for details. *Difficult.* ✉ *Yosemite National Park* ✣ *Trailhead: At Happy Isles* 🌐 *www.nps.gov/yose/planyourvisit/halfdome.htm.*

Mirror Lake Trail

TRAIL | FAMILY | Along this trail, you'll look up at Half Dome directly from its base and also take in Tenaya Canyon, Mt. Watkins, and Washington Column. The way is paved for a mile to Mirror Lake itself (total of 2 miles out and back). The trail that loops around the lake continues from there (for a total of 5 miles). Interpretive exhibits provide insight on the area's natural and cultural history. *Easy–Moderate.* ✉ *Yosemite Village* ✣ *Trailhead: Shuttle bus stop #17 on the Happy Isles Loop.*

Mist Trail

TRAIL | Except for Lower Yosemite Fall, more visitors take this trail (or portions of it) than any other in the park. The trek up to and back from Vernal Fall is 3 miles. Add another 4 miles total by continuing up to 594-foot Nevada Fall; the trail becomes quite steep and slippery in its final stages. The elevation gain to Vernal Fall is 1,000 feet, and to Nevada Fall an additional 1,000 feet. The Merced River tumbles down both falls on its way to a tranquil flow through the valley. *Moderate.* ✉ *Yosemite National Park* ✣ *Trailhead: At Happy Isles.*

★ **Panorama Trail**

TRAIL | Few hikes come with the visual punch that this 8½-mile trail provides. It starts from Glacier Point and descends to Yosemite Valley. The star attraction is Half Dome, visible from many intriguing angles, but you also see three waterfalls up close and walk through a manzanita grove. *Moderate.* ✉ *Yosemite National Park* ✥ *Trailhead: At Glacier Point.*

★ **Yosemite Falls Trail**

TRAIL | Yosemite Falls is the highest waterfall in North America. The upper fall (1,430 feet), the middle cascades (675 feet), and the lower fall (320 feet) combine for a total of 2,425 feet, and when viewed from the valley appear as a single waterfall. The ¼-mile trail leads from the parking lot to the base of the falls. Upper Yosemite Fall Trail, a strenuous 7.2-mile round-trip climb rising 2,700 feet, takes you above the top of the falls. Lower trail: *Easy.* Upper trail: *Difficult.* ✉ *Yosemite National Park* ✥ *Trailhead: Off Camp 4, north of Northside Dr.*

VISITOR CENTERS

Valley Visitor Center

INFO CENTER | Learn about Yosemite Valley's geology, vegetation, and human inhabitants at this visitor center, which is also staffed with helpful rangers and contains a bookstore with a wide selection of books and maps. Two films, including one by Ken Burns, alternate on the half hour in the theater behind the visitor center. ✉ *Yosemite Village* ☎ *209/372–0200* 🌐 *www.nps.gov/yose.*

Yosemite Conservation Heritage Center

INFO CENTER | This small but striking National Historic Landmark (formerly Le Conte Memorial Lodge), with its granite walls and steeply pitched shingle roof, is Yosemite's first permanent public information center. Step inside to see the cathedral-like interior, which contains a library and environmental exhibits. To find out about evening programs, check the kiosk out front. ✉ *Southside Dr., about ½ mile west of Half Dome Village* 🌐 *sierraclub.org/yosemite-heritage-center* ⏲ *Closed Mon., Tues., and Oct.–Apr.*

Restaurants

★ **The Ahwahnee Dining Room**

$$$$ | **EUROPEAN** | Rave reviews about The Ahwahnee hotel's dining room's appearance are fully justified—it features towering windows, a 34-foot-high ceiling with interlaced sugar-pine beams, and massive chandeliers. Reservations are always advised, and the attire is "resort casual." **Known for:** lavish $56 Sunday brunch; finest dining in the park; bar menu with lighter lunch and dinner fare at more affordable prices. Ⓢ *Average main: $39* ✉ *The Ahwahnee, Ahwahnee Rd., about ¾ mile east of Yosemite Valley Visitor Center, Yosemite Village* ☎ *209/372–1489* 🌐 *www.travelyosemite.com.*

Base Camp Eatery

$$ | **AMERICAN** | The design of this modern food court, open for breakfast, lunch, and dinner, honors the history of rock climbing in Yosemite. Choose from a wide range of menu options, from hamburgers, salads, and pizzas, to rice and noodle bowls. **Known for:** grab-and-go selections; best casual dining venue in the park; automated ordering kiosks to speed up service. Ⓢ *Average main: $12* ✉ *Yosemite Valley Lodge, about ¾ mile west of visitor center, Yosemite Village* ☎ *209/372–1265* 🌐 *www.travelyosemite.com.*

Curry Village Seven Tents

$$ | **AMERICAN** | Formerly Curry Village Pavilion, this cafeteria-style eatery serves everything from roasted meats and salads to pastas, burritos, and beyond. Alternatively, order a pizza from the stand on the deck, and take in the views of the valley's granite walls. **Known for:** convenient eats; cocktails at Bar 1899; additional venues (Meadow Grill, Pizza Patio, Coffee Corner). Ⓢ *Average main: $18* ✉ *Curry Village* ☎ *209/372–8303* ⏲ *Closed mid-Oct.–mid-Apr. No lunch.*

★ Mountain Room

$$$ | **AMERICAN** | Gaze at Yosemite Falls through this dining room's wall of windows—almost every table has a view—as you nosh on steaks, seafood, and classic California salads and desserts. The Mountain Room Lounge, a few steps away in the Yosemite Valley Lodge complex, has about 10 beers on tap. **Known for:** locally sourced, organic ingredients; usually there is a wait for a table (no reservations); vegetarian and vegan options. *Average main: $29 Yosemite Valley Lodge, Northside Dr., about ¾ mile west of visitor center, Yosemite Village 209/372–1403 www.travelyosemite.com No lunch except Sun. brunch.*

Village Grill Deck

$$ | **FAST FOOD** | If a burger joint is what you've been missing, head to this bustling eatery in Yosemite Village that serves veggie, salmon, and a few other burger varieties in addition to the usual beef patties. Order at the counter, then take your tray out to the deck, and enjoy your meal under the trees. **Known for:** burgers, sandwiches, and hot dogs; crowds; outdoor seating on expansive deck. *Average main: $12 Yosemite Village 100 yards east of Yosemite Valley Visitor Center 209/372–1207 www.travelyosemite.com Closed Oct.–Apr. No dinner.*

Hotels

★ The Ahwahnee

$$$$ | **HOTEL** | This National Historic Landmark is constructed of sugar-pine logs and features Native American design motifs; public spaces are enlivened with art-deco flourishes, Persian rugs, and elaborate iron- and woodwork. **Pros:** best lodge in Yosemite; helpful concierge; in the historic heart of the valley. **Cons:** expensive rates; some reports that service has slipped in recent years; slow or nonexistent Wi-Fi in some hotel areas. *Rooms from: $581 Ahwahnee Rd., about ¾ mile east of Yosemite Valley Visitor Center, Yosemite Village 801/559–4884 www.travelyosemite.com 125 rooms No meals.*

Curry Village

$$ | **HOTEL** | Opened in 1899 as a place for budget-conscious travelers, Curry Village has plain accommodations: standard motel rooms, simple cabins with either private or shared baths, and tent cabins with shared baths. **Pros:** close to many activities; family-friendly atmosphere; surrounded by iconic valley views. **Cons:** community bathrooms need updating; can be crowded; sometimes a bit noisy. *Rooms from: $143 South side of Southside Dr. 888/413–8869, 602/278–8888 international www.travelyosemite.com 583 units No meals.*

Yosemite Valley Lodge

$$$$ | **HOTEL** | This 1915 lodge near Yosemite Falls is a collection of numerous two-story, glass-and-wood structures tucked beneath the trees. **Pros:** centrally located; dependably clean rooms; lots of tours leave from out front. **Cons:** can feel impersonal; high prices; no in-room a/c. *Rooms from: $260 9006 Yosemite Valley Lodge Dr., Yosemite Village 888/413–8869 www.travelyosemite.com 245 rooms No meals.*

Performing Arts

Yosemite Theater

THEATER | Various theater and music programs are held throughout the year, and one of the best loved is Lee Stetson's portrayal of John Muir in *Conversation with a Tramp* and other Muir-theme shows. Purchase tickets in advance at the Conservancy Store at the Valley Visitor Center or the Tour and Activity Desk at Yosemite Valley Lodge. Unsold seats are available at the door at performance time, 7 pm. *Valley Visitor Center, Yosemite Village 209/372–0299 $10.*

Wawona

27 miles from Yosemite Valley Visitor Center, 7½ miles north of Fish Camp.

Wawona is a small village (elevation 4,000 feet) about an hours' drive south of Yosemite Valley. It's rich in pioneer history (visit the Pioneer Yosemite History Center to learn more) and is home to the Victorian-era Wawona Hotel. The park's famous Mariposa Grove of Giant Sequoias is a few miles down the road.

Sights

HISTORIC SIGHTS

Pioneer Yosemite History Center

MUSEUM | FAMILY | These historic buildings reflect different eras of Yosemite's history, from the 1850s through the early 1900s. They were moved to Wawona (the largest stage stop in Yosemite in the late 1800s) from various areas of Yosemite in the '50s and '60s. There is a self-guided-tour pamphlet available for 50 cents. Weekends and some weekdays in the summer, costumed docents conduct free blacksmithing and "wet-plate" photography demonstrations, and for a small fee you can take a stagecoach ride. ✉ *Rte. 41, Wawona* ☎ *209/375–9531* 🌐 *www.nps.gov/yose/planyourvisit/waw.htm* 🎫 *Free* 🕒 *Closed Mon., Tues., and mid-Sept.–early June.*

Wawona Hotel

HOTEL—SIGHT | Imagine a white-bearded Mark Twain relaxing in a rocking chair on one of the broad verandas of one of the park's first lodges, a whitewashed series of two-story buildings from the Victorian era. Plop down in one of the dozens of white Adirondack chairs on the sprawling lawn, and look across the road at the area's only golf course, one of the few links in the world that does not employ fertilizers or other chemicals. ✉ *Rte. 41, Wawona* ☎ *209/375–1425* 🌐 *www.travelyosemite.com/lodging/wawona-hotel* 🕒 *Closed Dec.–Mar. except 2 wks around Christmas and New Year's.*

SCENIC DRIVES

Route 41

SCENIC DRIVE | Entering Yosemite National Park via this road, which follows an ultimately curvy course 55 miles from Fresno through the Yosemite gateway towns of Oakhurst and Fish Camp, presents you with an immediate, important choice: turn right to visit the Mariposa Grove of Giant Sequoias 4 miles to the east, or turn left to travel via Wawona to Yosemite Valley, 31 miles away. Try to do both. (You can get by with an hour in Mariposa Grove if you're really pressed for time.) As you approach the valley, you will want to pull into the Tunnel View parking lot (it's on the east side of the mile-long tunnel) and marvel at what lies ahead: from left to right, El Capitan, Half Dome, and Bridalveil Fall. From here, the valley is another 5 miles. The drive time on Wawona Road alone is about an hour. Make a full day of it by adding Glacier Point to the itinerary; get there via a 16-mile seasonal road that shoots east from Route 41 and passes the Badger Pass Ski Area. ✉ *Yosemite National Park.*

SCENIC STOPS

Mariposa Grove of Giant Sequoias

FOREST | Of Yosemite's three sequoia groves—the others being Merced and Tuolumne, both near Crane Flat and Hetch Hetchy well to the north—Mariposa is by far the largest and easiest to walk around. Grizzly Giant, whose base measures 96 feet around, has been estimated to be one of the world's largest. Perhaps more astoundingly, it's about 1,800 years old. Park at the grove's welcome plaza, and ride the free shuttle (required most of the year). Summer weekends are crowded. ✉ *Yosemite National Park* ✣ *Rte. 41, 2 miles north of south entrance station* 🌐 *www.nps.gov/yose/planyourvisit/mg.htm.*

TRAILS

Chilnualna Falls Trail

TRAIL | This Wawona-area trail runs 4 miles one-way to the top of the falls, then leads into the backcountry, connecting with other trails. This is one of the park's most inspiring and secluded—albeit strenuous—trails. Past the tumbling cascade, and up through forests, you'll emerge before a panorama at the top. *Difficult.* ✉ *Wawona* ✣ *Trailhead: At Chilnualna Falls Rd., off Rte. 41.*

Restaurants

Wawona Hotel Dining Room

$$$ | **AMERICAN** | Watch deer graze in the meadow while you dine in the romantic, candlelit dining room of the whitewashed Wawona Hotel, which dates from the late 1800s. The American-style cuisine favors fresh ingredients and flavors; trout and flatiron steaks are menu staples. **Known for:** Saturday-night barbecues on the lawn; historic ambience; Mother's Day and other Sunday holiday brunches. [$] *Average main: $28* ✉ *8308 Wawona Rd., Wawona* ☎ *209/375–1425* ⏲ *Closed most of Dec., Jan., Feb., and Mar.*

Hotels

Redwoods in Yosemite

$$$$ | **RENTAL** | This collection of more than 125 homes in the Wawona area is a great alternative to the overcrowded valley. **Pros:** sense of privacy; peaceful setting; full kitchens. **Cons:** 45-minute drive from the valley; some units have no a/c; cell phone service can be spotty. [$] *Rooms from: $260* ✉ *8038 Chilnualna Falls Rd., off Rte. 41, Wawona* ☎ *209/375–6666 international, 844/355–0039* 🌐 *www.redwoodsinyosemite.com* ⇄ *125 units* 🍴 *No meals.*

Wawona Hotel

$$$ | **HOTEL** | This 1879 National Historic Landmark at Yosemite's southern end is a Victorian-era mountain resort, with whitewashed buildings, wraparound verandas, and pleasant, no-frills rooms decorated with period pieces. **Pros:** lovely building; peaceful atmosphere; historic photos in public areas. **Cons:** few modern amenities, such as phones and TVs; an hour's drive from Yosemite Valley; shared bathrooms in half the rooms. [$] *Rooms from: $157* ✉ *8308 Wawona Rd., Wawona* ☎ *888/413–8869* 🌐 *www.travelyosemite.com* ⏲ *Closed Dec.–Mar., except mid-Dec.–Jan. 2* ⇄ *104 rooms, 50 with bath* 🍴 *Free breakfast.*

Tuolumne Meadows

56 miles from Yosemite Valley, 21 miles west of Lee Vining via Tioga Rd.

The largest subalpine meadow in the Sierra (at 8,600 feet) is a popular way station for backpack trips along the Pacific Crest and John Muir trails. The setting is not as dramatic as Yosemite Valley, 56 miles away, but the almost perfectly flat basin, about 2½ miles long, is intriguing, and in July it's resplendent with wildflowers. The most popular day hike is to Lembert Dome, atop which you'll have breathtaking views of the basin below. Note that Tioga Road rarely opens before June and usually closes by November.

Sights

SCENIC DRIVES

Tioga Road

SCENIC DRIVE | Few mountain drives can compare with this 59-mile road, especially its eastern half between Lee Vining and Olmstead Point. As you climb 3,200 feet to the 9,945-foot summit of Tioga Pass (Yosemite's sole eastern entrance for cars), you'll encounter broad vistas of the granite-splotched High Sierra and its craggy but hearty trees and shrubs. Past the bustling scene at Tuolumne Meadows, you'll see picturesque Tenaya Lake and then Olmsted Point, where you'll get your first peek at Half Dome. Driving Tioga Road one way takes approximately 1½ hours. Wildflowers bloom here in July and August. By November, the high-altitude road closes for the winter;

it sometimes doesn't reopen until early June. ✉ *Yosemite National Park.*

SCENIC STOPS

High Country

NATURE PRESERVE | The high-alpine region east of the valley—a land of alpenglow and top-of-the-world vistas—is often missed by crowds who come to gawk at the more publicized splendors. Summer wildflowers, which pop up mid-July through August, carpet the meadows and mountainsides with pink, purple, blue, red, yellow, and orange. On foot or on horseback are the only ways to get here. For information on trails and backcountry permits, check with the visitor center. ✉ *Yosemite National Park.*

Restaurants

Tuolumne Meadows Grill

$ | FAST FOOD | Serving throughout the day until 5 or 6 pm, this fast-food eatery cooks up basic breakfast, lunch, and snacks. It's possible that ice cream tastes better at this altitude. **Known for:** soft-serve ice cream; crowds; fresh local ingredients. [$] *Average main: $8* ✉ *Tioga Rd. (Rte. 120), 1½ miles east of Tuolumne Meadows Visitor Center* ☎ *209/372–8426* 🌐 *www.travelyosemite.com* 🕒 *Closed Oct.–Memorial Day. No dinner.*

Tuolumne Meadows Lodge Restaurant

$$$ | AMERICAN | In a central dining tent beside the Tuolumne River, this restaurant serves a menu of hearty American fare at breakfast and dinner. The red-and-white-checkered tablecloths and a handful of communal tables give it the feeling of an old-fashioned summer camp. **Known for:** box lunches; communal tables; small menu. [$] *Average main: $24* ✉ *Tioga Rd. (Rte. 120)* ☎ *209/372–8413* 🌐 *www.travelyosemite.com* 🕒 *Closed late Sept.–mid-June. No lunch.*

White Wolf Lodge Restaurant

$$$ | AMERICAN | Those fueling up for a day on the trail or famished after a high-country hike will appreciate the all-you-can-eat, family-style breakfasts and dinners in this tiny dining room. Mashed potatoes, big pots of curried vegetables, and heaps of pasta often grace the tables in this cozy out-of-the-way place. **Known for:** all you can eat; box lunches available; rustic vibe. [$] *Average main: $24* ✉ *Yosemite National Park* ✥ *Tioga Rd. (Rte. 120), 25 miles west of Tuolumne Meadows and 15 miles east of Crane Flat* ☎ *209/372–8416* 🌐 *www.travelyosemite.com* 🕒 *Closed mid-Sept.–mid-June. No lunch.*

Hotels

White Wolf Lodge

$$ | HOTEL | Set in a subalpine meadow, the White Wolf Lodge has rustic accommodations and makes an excellent base camp for hiking the backcountry. **Pros:** quiet location; near some of Yosemite's most beautiful, less crowded hikes; good restaurant. **Cons:** far from the valley; tent cabins share bathhouse; remote setting. [$] *Rooms from: $138* ✉ *Yosemite National Park* ✥ *Off Tioga Rd. (Rte. 120), 25 miles west of Tuolumne Meadows and 15 miles east of Crane Flat* ☎ *801/559–4884* 🕒 *Closed mid-Sept.–mid-June* *28 cabins* 🍽 *No meals.*

Hetch Hetchy

18 miles from the Big Oak Flat entrance station, 43 miles north of El Portal via Hwy. 120 and Evergreen Rd.

This glacier-carved valley (now filled with water) and surrounding peaks anchor the northwestern section of the park. Drive about 2 miles west of the Big Oak Flat entrance station and turn right on Evergreen Road, which leads down to the Hetch Hetchy entrance and trails along the dam and into the mountains. Two groves of giant sequoia trees—Merced and Tuolumne—grow near Crane Flat, a tiny collection of services south of Big

Oak Flat at the intersection of Highway 120 and Tioga Road.

Sights

SCENIC STOPS

Hetch Hetchy Reservoir

BODY OF WATER | When Congress approved the O'Shaughnessy Dam in 1913, pragmatism triumphed over aestheticism. Some 2.5 million residents of the San Francisco Bay Area continue to get their water from this 117-billion-gallon reservoir. Although spirited efforts are being made to restore the Hetch Hetchy Valley to its former, pristine glory, three-quarters of San Francisco voters in 2012 ultimately opposed a measure to even consider draining the reservoir. Eight miles long, the reservoir is Yosemite's largest body of water, and one that can be seen up close from several trails. ✉ *Hetch Hetchy Rd., about 15 miles north of Big Oak Flat entrance station.*

Tuolomne Grove of Giant Sequoias

FOREST | About two dozen mature giant sequoias stand in Tuolumne Grove in the park's northwestern region, just east of Crane Flat and south of the Big Oak Flat entrance. Park at the trailhead and walk about a mile to see them. The trail descends about 500 feet down to the grove, so it's a relatively steep hike back up. Be sure to bring plenty of drinking water. ✉ *On Tioga Rd., just east of Crane Flat, about a 45-minute drive from Yosemite Valley.*

TRAILS

Merced Grove of Giant Sequoias

FOREST | Hike 1½ miles (3 miles round-trip, 500-foot elevation drop and gain) to the small and scenic Merced Grove and its approximately two dozen mature giant sequoias. The setting here is typically uncrowded and serene. Note that you can also park here and hike about 2 miles round-trip to the Tuolumne Grove. Bring plenty of water for either outing. *Moderate.* ✉ *Big Oak Flat Rd.* ⊕ *East of the Big Oak Flat entrance, about 6 miles west of Crane Flat and a 45-minute drive from Yosemite Valley.*

Hotels

Evergreen Lodge at Yosemite

$$$$ | **RESORT** | **FAMILY** | Amid the trees near Yosemite National Park's Hetch Hetchy entrance, this sprawling property is perfect for families. **Pros:** cabin complex includes amphitheater, pool, and more; guided tours available; great roadhouse-style restaurant. **Cons:** no in-room TVs; long, winding access road; spotty cell service. $ *Rooms from: $280* ✉ *33160 Evergreen Rd., 30 miles east of town of Groveland, Groveland* ☎ *209/379–2606* 🌐 *www.evergreenlodge.com* *88 cabins* 🍽 *No meals.*

★ **Rush Creek Lodge**

$$$$ | **RESORT** | **FAMILY** | Occupying 20 acres on a wooded hillside, this sleek, nature-inspired complex has a saltwater pool and hot tubs, a restaurant and tavern with indoor and outdoor seating, a guided recreation program, a spa and wellness program, a general store, nature trails, and outdoor play areas that include a zip line and a giant slide. **Pros:** close to Yosemite's Big Oak Flat entrance; YARTS bus stops here and connects with Yosemite Valley and Sonora spring–fall; year-round evening s'mores. **Cons:** no in-room TVs; pricey in high season; spotty cell service. $ *Rooms from: $410* ✉ *34001 Hwy. 120, Groveland* ⊕ *25 miles east of Groveland, 23 miles north of Yosemite Valley* ☎ *209/379–2373* 🌐 *www.rushcreeklodge.com* *143 rooms* 🍽 *No meals.*

Winter in Yosemite can be magical, especially if you like playing in the snow or solitude.

Activities

BIKING

One enjoyable way to see Yosemite Valley is to ride a bike beneath its lofty granite monoliths. The eastern valley has 12 miles of paved, flat bicycle paths across meadows and through woods, with bike racks at convenient stopping points. For a greater challenge, you can ride on 196 miles of paved park roads elsewhere. Note, though, that bicycles are not allowed on hiking trails or in the backcountry, and kids under 18 must wear a helmet.

Yosemite bike rentals

BICYCLING | You can arrange rentals ($12 per hour or $36 per day) at Yosemite Valley Lodge and Curry Village bike stands. Bikes with child trailers, baby-jogger strollers, and wheelchairs are also available. ✉ *Yosemite Valley Lodge or Curry Village* ☎ *209/372–4386* 🌐 *www.travelyosemite.com.*

BIRD-WATCHING

More than 250 bird species have been spotted in the park, including the sage sparrow, pygmy owl, blue grouse, and mountain bluebird. Park rangers lead free bird-watching walks in Yosemite Valley a few days each week in summer; check at a visitor center or information station for times and locations. Binoculars sometimes are available for loan.

Birding seminars

BIRD WATCHING | The Yosemite Conservancy organizes day- and weekend-long seminars for beginner and intermediate birders, as well as bird walks a few times a week. They can also arrange private naturalist-led walks any time of year. ✉ *Yosemite National Park* 🌐 *www.yosemite.org* 🎫 *From $99.*

CAMPING

If you are going to concentrate solely on valley sites and activities, you should endeavor to stay in one of the "Pines" campgrounds, which are clustered near Curry Village and within an easy stroll from that busy complex's many facilities. For a more primitive and quiet experience, and to be near many backcountry hikes, try one of the Tioga Road campgrounds.

RESERVATIONS

National Park Service Reservations Office
Reservations are required at many of Yosemite's campgrounds. You can book a site up to five months in advance, starting on the 15th of the month. Unless otherwise noted, book your site through the central National Park Service Reservations Office. If you don't have reservations when you arrive, many sites, especially those outside Yosemite Valley, are available on a first-come, first-served basis. ☎ *877/444–6777 reservations, 518/885–3639 international, 888/448–1474 customer service* 🌐 *www.recreation.gov.*

RECOMMENDED CAMPGROUNDS

YOSEMITE VALLEY

Camp 4. Formerly known as Sunnyside Walk-In, this is the only valley campground available on a walk-in basis—and the only one west of Yosemite Lodge. Open year-round, it's favored by rock climbers and solo campers. From mid-September to mid-May, the camp operates on a first-come, first-served basis; it typically fills early in the morning except in winter. From mid-May to mid-September, campsites are available only by daily lottery (one day in advance via Recreation.gov from midnight to 4 pm Pacific Time) for up to 12 people per application, 6 people per campsite. This is a tents-only campground with 36 sites. ✉ *Base of Yosemite Falls Trail, just west of Yosemite Valley Lodge on Northside Dr., Yosemite Village.*

Housekeeping Camp. Each of the 266 units here consists of three walls (usually concrete) that are covered with two layers of canvas; the open-air side can be closed off with a heavy, white-canvas curtain. Inside, typically, are bunk beds and a full-size bed (dirty mattresses included); outside is a covered patio, fire ring, picnic table, and bear box. You rent "bedpacks," consisting of blankets, sheets, and other comforts in the main building, which also has a small grocery. Lots of guests take advantage of the adjacent Merced River. ✉ *Southside Dr., ½ mile west of Curry Village.*

Lower Pines. This moderate-size campground with 60 small tent/RV sites sits directly along the Merced River; it's a short walk to the trailheads for the Mirror Lake and Mist trails. Expect lots of people. ✉ *At east end of valley.*

Upper Pines. One of the valley's largest campgrounds, with 238 tent and RV sites, is also the closest one to the trailheads. Expect large crowds in the summer—and little privacy. ✉ *At east end of valley, near Curry Village.*

CRANE FLAT

Crane Flat. This 166-site camp for tents and RVs is on Yosemite's western boundary, south of Hodgdon Meadow and just 17 miles from the valley but far from its bustle. A small grove of sequoias is nearby. ✉ *From Big Oak Flat entrance on Rte. 120, drive 10 miles east to campground entrance on right.*

WAWONA

Bridalveil Creek. This campground sits among lodgepole pines at 7,200 feet, above the valley on Glacier Point Road. From here, you can easily drive to Glacier Point's magnificent valley views. Fall evenings can be cold. The 74 sites can accommodate tents and RVs. ✉ *From Rte. 41 in Wawona, go north to Glacier Point Rd. and turn right; entrance to campground is 25 miles ahead on right side.*

Wawona. Near the Mariposa Grove, just downstream from a popular fishing spot, this year-round campground's 93 sites for tents and RVs are larger and less densely packed than those at campgrounds in Yosemite Valley. The downside? It's an hour's drive to the valley's attractions. ✉ *Rte. 41, 1 mile north of Wawona.*

TUOLUMNE MEADOWS

Porcupine Flat. Sixteen miles west of Tuolumne Meadows, this campground sits at 8,100 feet. Sites are close together, but if you want to be in the high country and Tuolumne Meadows is full, this is a good bet. There is no water available. The campground's 52 sites for tents and RVs can't accommodate rigs of 35 feet or longer. ✉ *Rte. 120, 16 miles west of Tuolumne Meadows.*

Tuolumne Meadows. In a wooded area at 8,600 feet, just south of its namesake meadow, this is one of the most spectacular and sought-after campgrounds in Yosemite. Hot showers can be used at the Tuolumne Meadows Lodge—though only at certain times. Half the 314 tent and RV sites are first-come, first-served, so arrive early, or make reservations. The campground is open July–September. ✉ *Rte. 120, 46 miles east of Big Oak Flat entrance station.*

White Wolf. Set in the beautiful high country at 8,000 feet, this is a prime spot for hikers from early July to mid-September. There are 87 tent and RV sites; rigs of up to 27 feet long are permitted. ✉ *Tioga Rd., 15 miles east of Big Oak Flat entrance.*

EDUCATIONAL OFFERINGS

CLASSES AND SEMINARS

Art Classes

LOCAL SPORTS | Professional artists conduct workshops in watercolor, etching, drawing, and other media. Bring your own materials, or purchase the basics at the Happy Isles Art and Nature Center. Children under 12 must be accompanied by an adult. The center also offers beginner art workshops and children's art and family craft programs ($20–$40 per person). ✉ *Happy Isles Art and Nature Center* 🌐 *www.yosemite.org* 🎫 *$20* ⏲ *No classes Sun. Closed Dec.–Feb.*

Happy Isles Art and Nature Center

LOCAL SPORTS | **FAMILY** | This family-focused center has a rotating selection of kid-friendly activities and hands-on exhibits that teach tykes and their parents about the park's ecosystem. Books, toys, and T-shirts are stocked in the small gift shop. ✉ *Yosemite National Park* ✣ *Off Southside Dr., about ¾ mile east of Curry Village* 🎫 *Free* ⏲ *Closed Oct.–Apr.*

Yosemite Outdoor Adventures

LOCAL SPORTS | Naturalists, scientists, and park rangers lead multihour to multiday outings on topics from woodpeckers to fire management to day hikes and bird-watching. Most sessions take place spring through fall with just a few in winter. ✉ *Yosemite National Park* 🌐 *www.yosemite.org* 🎫 *From $99.*

RANGER PROGRAMS

Junior Ranger Program

LOCAL SPORTS | **FAMILY** | Children ages 3 to 13 can participate in the informal, self-guided Junior Ranger program. Park activity handbooks ($3.50 for ages 7 to 13 and $3 for Junior Cubs ages 3 to 6) are available at the Valley Visitor Center, the Happy Isles Art and Nature Center, the Tuolumne Visitor Center, and the Wawona Visitor Center. Once kids complete the book, rangers present them with a badge and, in some cases, a certificate. ✉ *Valley Visitor Center or the Happy Isles Art & Nature Center* ☎ *209/372–0299.*

Ranger-Led Programs

LOCAL SPORTS | Rangers lead entertaining walks and give informative talks several times a day from spring to fall. The schedule is more limited in winter, but most days you can find a program somewhere in the park. In the evenings at Yosemite Valley Lodge and Curry Village, lectures, slide shows, and documentary films present unique perspectives on Yosemite. On summer weekends, campgrounds at Curry Village and Tuolumne Meadows host sing-along campfire programs. Schedules and locations are posted on bulletin boards throughout the park as well as in the indispensable *Yosemite Guide,* which is distributed to visitors as they arrive at the park. ✉ *Yosemite National Park* 🌐 *nps.gov/yose.*

Wee Wild Ones

LOCAL SPORTS | FAMILY | Designed for kids under 10, this 45-minute program includes naturalist-led games, songs, stories, and crafts about Yosemite wildlife, plants, and geology. The event is held outdoors before the regular Yosemite Valley Lodge evening programs in summer and fall. All children must be accompanied by an adult. ✉ *Yosemite National Park* ☎ *209/372–1153* 🌐 *www.travelyosemite.com* 🎫 *Free.*

FISHING

The waters in Yosemite are not stocked; trout, mostly brown and rainbow, live here but are not plentiful. Yosemite's fishing season begins on the last Saturday in April and ends on November 15. Some waterways are off-limits at certain times; be sure to inquire at the visitor center about regulations.

A California fishing license is required; licenses cost around $17 for one day, $26.50 for two days, and $53 for 10 days. Full-season licenses cost $53 for state residents and $142 for nonresidents (costs fluctuate year to year). Buy your license in season at **Yosemite Mountain Shop in Curry Village** (☎ *209/372–1286*) or at the **Wawona Store** (☎ *209/375–6574*).

HIKING

Wilderness Center

HIKING/WALKING | This facility provides free wilderness permits, which are required for overnight camping (advance reservations are available for $5 per person plus $5 per reservation and are highly recommended for popular trailheads in summer and on weekends). The staff here also provides maps and advice to hikers heading into the backcountry. If you don't have your own bear-resistant canisters, which are required, you can buy or rent them here. ✉ *Between Ansel Adams Gallery and post office, Yosemite Village* ☎ *209/372–0308.*

Yosemite Mountaineering School and Guide Service

HIKING/WALKING | From April to November, you can rent gear, hire a guide, or join a two-hour to full-day trek with Yosemite Mountaineering School. They also lead backpacking and overnight excursions. Reservations are recommended. In winter, cross-country ski programs are available at Badger Pass Ski Area. ✉ *Yosemite Mountain Shop, Curry Village* ☎ *209/372–8344* 🌐 *yosemitemountaineering.com.*

HORSEBACK RIDING

Reservations for guided trail rides must be made in advance at hotel tour desks or by phone. Scenic trail rides range from two hours to a half day. Four- and six-day High Sierra saddle trips are also available.

Wawona Stable

HORSEBACK RIDING | Two-hour rides at this stable start at $70, and a challenging full-day ride to the Mariposa Grove of Giant Sequoias (for experienced riders in good physical condition only) costs $144. Reservations are recommended. ✉ *Rte. 41, Wawona* ☎ *209/375–6502* 🌐 *www.travelyosemite.com/things-to-do/horseback-mule-riding.*

ICE-SKATING

Curry Village Ice Skating Rink

ICE SKATING | Winter visitors have skated at this outdoor rink for decades, and there's no mystery why: it's a kick to glide across the ice while soaking up views of Half Dome and Glacier Point. ✉ *South side of Southside Dr., Curry Village* ☎ *209/372–8319* 🌐 *www.travelyosemite.com* 🎫 *$11 per session, $5 skate rental.*

RAFTING

Rafting is permitted only on designated areas of the Middle and South forks of the Merced River. Check with the Valley Visitor Center for closures and other restrictions.

Curry Village Recreation Center

WHITE-WATER RAFTING | The per-person rental fee at Curry Village Recreation Center covers the four- to six-person raft, two paddles, and life jackets, plus a return shuttle after your trip. ✉ *South side of Southside Dr., Curry Village* ☎ *209/372–4386* 🌐 *www.travelyosemite.com/things-to-do/rafting* 🎫 *From $33.*

ROCK CLIMBING

The granite canyon walls of Yosemite Valley are world renowned for rock climbing. El Capitan, with its 3,593-foot vertical face, is the most famous, but there are many other options here for all skill levels.

Yosemite Mountain Shop

SPECIALTY STORES | A comprehensive selection of camping, hiking, backpacking, and climbing equipment, along with experts who can answer all your questions, make this store a valuable resource for outdoors enthusiasts. This is the best place to ask about climbing conditions and restrictions around the park, as well as purchase almost any kind of climbing gear. ✉ *Curry Village* ☎ *209/372–8436.*

Yosemite Mountaineering School and Guide Service

CLIMBING/MOUNTAINEERING | The one-day basic lesson offered by this outfit includes some bouldering and rappelling and three or four 60-foot climbs. Climbers must be at least 10 years old and in reasonably good physical condition. Intermediate and advanced classes include instruction in first aid; anchor building; and multipitch, summer-snow, and big-wall climbing. There's a Nordic program in the winter. ✉ *Yosemite Mountain Shop, Curry Village* ☎ *209/372–8444* 🌐 *www.travelyosemite.com* 🎫 *From $172.*

SKIING AND SNOWSHOEING

The beauty of Yosemite under a blanket of snow has long inspired poets and artists, as well as ordinary folks. Skiing and snowshoeing activities in the park center on Badger Pass Ski Area, California's oldest snow-sports resort, which is about 40 minutes away from the valley on Glacier Point Road. Here you can rent equipment, take a lesson, have lunch, and join a guided excursion.

Badger Pass Ski Area

SKIING/SNOWBOARDING | California's first ski resort has 10 downhill runs and 90 miles of groomed cross-country trails. Lessons, backcountry guiding, and cross-country and snowshoeing tours are also available. You can rent downhill, telemark, and cross-country skis, as well as snowshoes and snowboards. Note that shuttle buses run twice daily between the valley and the ski area. **Facilities:** 10 trails; 90 acres; 800-foot vertical drop; 5 lifts. ✉ *Yosemite National Park* ✥ *Badger Pass Rd., off Glacier Point Rd., 18 miles from Yosemite Valley* ☎ *209/372–8430* 🌐 *www.travelyosemite.com/winter/badger-pass-ski-area* 🎫 *Lift ticket: from $62.*

Badger Pass Ski Area School

SKIING/SNOWBOARDING | The gentle slopes of Badger Pass Ski Area make the ski school an ideal spot for children and beginners to learn downhill skiing or snowboarding for as little as $75 for a group lesson. ☎ *209/372–8430* 🌐 *www.travelyosemite.com.*

Badger Pass Ski Area Sport Shop

SKIING/SNOWBOARDING | Stop here to gear (and bundle!) up for downhill and cross-country skiing, snowboarding, and snowshoeing adventures. ✉ *Yosemite National Park* ✥ *Yosemite Ski & Snowboard Area, Badger Pass Rd., off Glacier Point Rd., 18 miles from Yosemite Valley* ☎ *209/372–8444* 🌐 *www.travelyosemite.com/winter/badger-pass-ski-area.*

Yosemite Cross-Country Ski School
SKIING/SNOWBOARDING | The highlight of Yosemite's cross-country skiing center is a 21-mile loop from Badger Pass Ski Area to Glacier Point. You can rent cross-country skis for $28 per day at the Cross-Country Ski School, which also rents snowshoes ($26.50 per day) and telemarking equipment ($36). ☎ *209/372–8444* 🌐 *www.travelyosemite.com.*

Yosemite Mountaineering School
SKIING/SNOWBOARDING | This branch of the Yosemite Mountaineering School, open at the Badger Pass Ski Area during ski season only, conducts snowshoeing, cross-country skiing, telemarking, and skate-skiing classes starting at $44. ✉ *Badger Pass Ski Area* ☎ *209/372–8444* 🌐 *www.travelyosemite.com.*

SWIMMING

Several swimming holes with small sandy beaches can be found in midsummer along the Merced River at the eastern end of Yosemite Valley. Find gentle waters to swim; currents are often stronger than they appear, and temperatures are chilling. To conserve riparian habitats, step into the river at sandy beaches and other obvious entry points. ■ TIP→ **Do not attempt to swim above or near waterfalls or rapids; people have died trying.**

What's Nearby

Marking the southern end of the Sierra's gold-bearing mother lode, **Mariposa** is the last town before you enter Yosemite on Route 140 to the west of the park. In addition to a fine mining museum, Mariposa has numerous shops, restaurants, and service stations.

Motels and restaurants dot both sides of Route 41 as it cuts through the town of **Oakhurst,** a boomtown during the gold rush that is now an important regional refueling station in every sense of the word, including organic foods and a full range of lodging options. Oakhurst has a population of about 3,000 and sits 15 miles south of the park.

Almost surrounded by the Sierra National Forest, **Bass Lake** is a warm-water reservoir whose waters can reach 80°F in summer. Created by a dam on a tributary of the San Joaquin River, the lake is owned by Pacific Gas and Electric Company and is used to generate electricity as well as for recreation.

As you climb in elevation along Highway 41 northbound, you see nothing but trees until you get to **Fish Camp,** where there's a post office and general store, but no gasoline. (For gas, head 7 miles north to Wawona, in Yosemite, or 14 miles south to Oakhurst.)

Near the park's eastern entrance, the tiny town of **Lee Vining** is home to the eerily beautiful, salty Mono Lake, where millions of migratory birds nest. Visit **Mammoth Lakes,** about 40 miles southeast of Yosemite's Tioga Pass entrance, for excellent skiing and snowboarding in winter, with fishing, mountain biking, hiking, and horseback riding in summer. Nine deep-blue lakes form the Mammoth Lakes Basin, and another hundred dot the surrounding countryside. Devils Postpile National Monument sits at the base of Mammoth Mountain.

Chapter 64

ZION NATIONAL PARK

Updated by
Shelley Arenas

Camping ★★★★☆ | Hotels ★★★★☆ | Activities ★★★★☆ | Scenery ★★★★★ | Crowds ★★★★★

WELCOME TO ZION NATIONAL PARK

TOP REASONS TO GO

★ **Eye candy:** Pick just about any trail in the park and it's all but guaranteed to culminate in an astounding viewpoint full of pink, orange, and crimson rock formations.

★ **Peace and quiet:** From February through November, cars are generally not allowed on Zion Canyon Scenic Drive, allowing this section of the park to remain relatively quiet and peaceful.

★ **Botanical wonderland:** Zion Canyon is home to more than 1,000 species of plants, more than anywhere else in Utah.

★ **Animal tracks:** Zion has expansive hinterlands where furry, scaly, and feathered residents are common. Hike long enough and you'll encounter deer, elk, rare lizards, birds of prey, and other zoological treats.

★ **Unforgettable canyoneering:** Zion's array of rugged slot canyons is the richest place on Earth for scrambling, rappelling, climbing, and descending.

1 **Zion Canyon.** This area defines Zion National Park for most people. Free shuttle buses are the only vehicles allowed February through November, the busiest months in the park. The backcountry is accessible via the West Rim Trail and the Narrows, and 2,000-foot cliffs rise all around.

2 **Kolob Canyons.** The northwestern corner of Zion is a secluded 30,000-acre wonderland that can be reached only via a special entrance. Don't miss the West Temple and the Kolob Arch, and keep looking up to spot Horse Ranch Mountain, the park's highest point.

UTAH

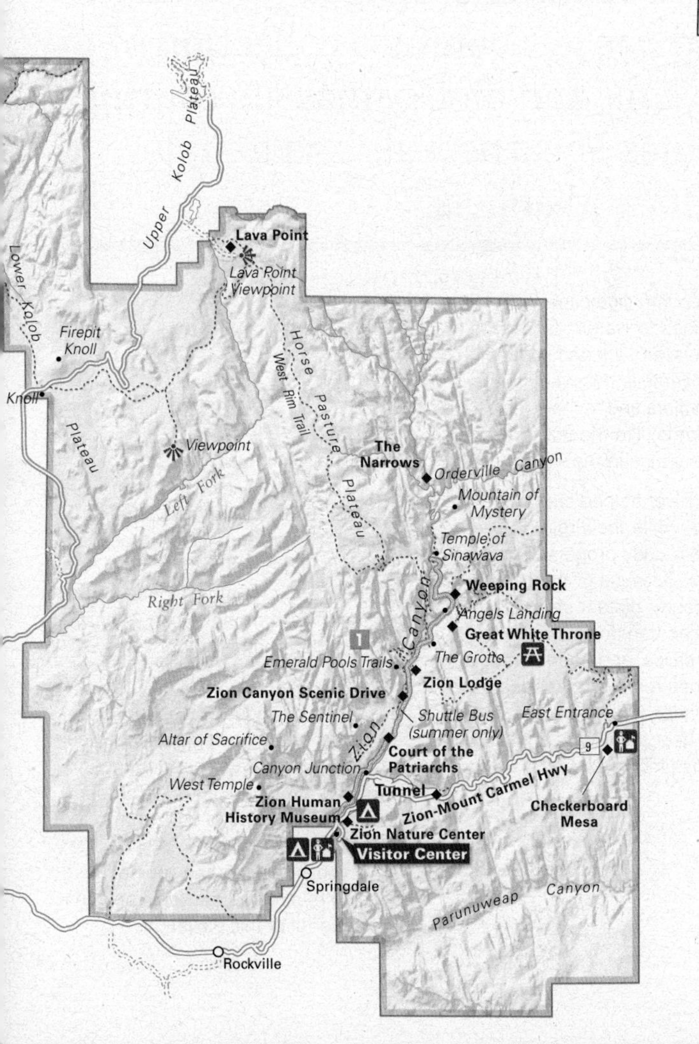
Upper Kolob Plateau
Lower Kolob Plateau
Lava Point
Lava Point Viewpoint
Firepit Knoll
Knoll
Horse Pasture Plateau
West Rim Trail
Viewpoint
Left Fork
Right Fork
The Narrows
Orderville Canyon
Mountain of Mystery
Temple of Sinawava
Weeping Rock
Angels Landing
Great White Throne
Zion Canyon
The Grotto
Emerald Pools Trails
Zion Lodge
Zion Canyon Scenic Drive
The Sentinel
Shuttle Bus (summer only)
East Entrance
Altar of Sacrifice
Court of the Patriarchs
9
Canyon Junction
West Temple
Tunnel
Zion-Mount Carmel Hwy
Checkerboard Mesa
Zion Human History Museum
Zion Nature Center
Visitor Center
Springdale
Parunuweap Canyon
Rockville

The walls of Zion Canyon soar more than 2,000 feet above the valley. Bands of limestone, sandstone, and lava in the strata point to the distant past. Greenery high in the cliff walls indicate the presence of water seepage or a spring. Erosion has left behind a collection of domes, fins, and blocky massifs bearing the names of cathedrals and temples, prophets and angels.

Trails lead deep into side canyons and up narrow ledges to waterfalls, serene spring-fed pools, and shaded spots of solitude. So diverse is this place that 85% of Utah's flora and fauna species are found here. Some, like the tiny Zion snail, appear nowhere else in the world.

The Colorado River helped create the Grand Canyon, while the Virgin River—the Colorado's muddy progeny—carved Zion's features. Because of the park's unique topography, distant storms and spring runoff can transform a tranquil slot canyon into a sluice, and flood damage does sometimes result in extended trail closures, as happened in summer 2018 to three trails near the Grotto and Zion Lodge sections of Zion Canyon.

Planning

When to Go

Zion is the most heavily visited national park in Utah, receiving 4.5 million visitors each year. Locals used to call the spring and fall the shoulder seasons because traffic would drop off from the highly visited summer months. Not so much anymore. These days the park is busy from March through November.

Summer in the park is hot and dry, punctuated by sudden cloudbursts that can create flash flooding and spectacular waterfalls. Expect afternoon thunderstorms between July and September. Whether the day starts out sunny or not, wear sunscreen and drink lots of water, even if you aren't exerting yourself or spending much time outside. The sun is very powerful at this elevation.

AVERAGE HIGH/LOW TEMPERATURES					
JAN.	**FEB.**	**MAR.**	**APR.**	**MAY**	**JUNE**
52/29	57/31	63/36	73/43	83/52	93/60
JULY	**AUG.**	**SEPT.**	**OCT.**	**NOV.**	**DEC.**
100/68	97/66	91/60	78/49	63/37	53/30

Winters are mild at lower desert elevations. You can expect to encounter winter driving conditions from November to mid-March, and although most park programs are suspended in winter, it is a wonderful and solitary time to see the canyons.

■ TIP→ **The temperature in Zion often exceeds 100°F in July and August.**

Getting Here and Around

AIR

The nearest commercial airport, with direct flights from a number of western U.S. hubs, is an hour away in St. George, Utah. It's about a three-hour drive to the nearest major airport, McCarran in Las Vegas, Nevada, and a 4½-hour drive from Salt Lake City's airport.

CAR

Zion National Park lies east of Interstate 15 in southwestern Utah. From the interstate, head east on Highway 9. After 21 miles you'll reach Springdale, which abuts the main entrance.

From February through November, you can drive on Zion Canyon Scenic Drive only if you have reservations at the Zion Lodge. Otherwise, you must park your car in Springdale or at the Zion Canyon Visitor Center and take the shuttle. There are no car restrictions in December and January.

The Zion Canyon Visitor Center parking lot fills up quickly. You can avoid parking heartburn by leaving your car in Springdale and riding the shuttle to the park entrance. Shuttles are accessible for people with disabilities and have plenty of room for gear. Consult the print park guide or check online at 🌐 *www.nps.gov/zion/planyourvisit/shuttle-system.htm* for the town shuttle schedule.

Inspiration

Towers of Stone, by J. L. Crawford, summarizes the essence of Zion National Park, its landscape, plants, animals, and human history.

Zion: Canyoneering, by Tom Jones, shows you how to explore the park's most dramatic landscapes.

An Introduction to the Geology of Zion, by Al Warneke, is a good pick for information on Zion's geology.

The Zion Tunnel, from Slickrock to Switchback, by Donald T. Garate, tells the fascinating story of the construction of the mile-long Zion Tunnel in the 1920s.

Zion National Park: Sanctuary in the Desert, by Nicky Leach, provides a photographic overview and a narrative journey through the park.

Park Essentials

ACCESSIBILITY

Both visitor centers, all shuttle buses, and Zion Lodge are fully accessible to people in wheelchairs. Several campsites (sites A24 and A25 at Watchman Campground and sites 103, 114, and 115 at South Campground) are reserved for people with disabilities, and two trails—Riverside Walk and Pa'rus Trail—are accessible with some assistance.

PARK FEES AND PERMITS

Entrance to Zion National Park costs $35 per vehicle for a seven-day pass. People entering on foot or by bicycle pay $20 per person for a seven-day pass; those on motorcycle pay $30.

Permits are required for backcountry camping and overnight hikes. Depending on which parts of the trails you intend to explore, you'll need a special permit for the Narrows and Kolob Creek or the Subway slot canyon. Climbing and canyoneering parties need a permit before using technical equipment.

Zion National Park limits the total number of overnight and canyoneering permits issued per day and has a reservation system with most of the permits now issued in an online lottery to apportion them fairly. Permits to the Subway, Mystery Canyon, the Narrows through-hikes, and West Rim are in short supply during high season. The maximum size of a group hiking into the backcountry is 12 people. Permits cost $15 for one or two people; $20 for three to seven; and $25 for eight or more. Permits are available at the visitor centers.

PARK HOURS

The park, open daily year-round, 24 hours a day, is in the Mountain time zone.

AUTOMOBILE SERVICE STATIONS

Just outside the park and in nearby Kanab and Springdale, you can fuel up, get your tires and oil changed, and have auto repairs done.

CELL PHONE RECEPTION

Cell phone reception is good in Springdale but spotty in the park. Public telephones can be found at Zion Canyon Visitor Center, Zion Lodge, and Zion Human History Museum.

EMERGENCIES

In the event of an emergency, dial 911, report to a visitor center, or contact a park ranger at ☎ *435/772–3322*. The nearest hospitals are in St. George, Cedar City, and Kanab.

Hotels

The Zion Lodge is rustic, designed in 1920s period style, and comfortable. Most lodging is located outside the park. Springdale has dozens of lodging options, from quaint bed-and-breakfasts to modest motels to chain hotels with riverside rooms, and farther west you'll find more options (and usually better values) in Hurricane and St. George. To the east and north, you'll find a smaller number of hotels and motels, from Kanab up to Panguitch, both of which are good bases if you're continuing on to Bryce or, in the case of Kanab, the Grand Canyon.

Restaurants

Only one full-service restaurant operates within the park, at the famed Zion Lodge, but in Springdale, just outside the park's South Entrance, you'll find a growing number of both casual and sophisticated eateries. To the east, options are limited, but there is a handful of options within an hour's drive.

Hotel and restaurant reviews have been shortened. For full information visit Fodors.com. Hotel prices are the lowest cost of a standard double room in high season. Restaurant prices are the average cost of a main course at dinner, or if dinner is not served, at lunch.

What It Costs

$	$$	$$$	$$$$
RESTAURANTS			
under $16	$16–$22	$23–$30	over $30
HOTELS			
under $125	$125–$175	$176–$225	over $225

Visitor Information

PARK CONTACT INFORMATION Zion National Park. ✉ *Hwy. 9, Springdale* ☎ *435/772–3256* 🌐 *www.nps.gov/zion.*

Zion Canyon

Sights

GEOLOGICAL LANDMARKS

★ The Narrows

NATURE SITE | This sinuous, 16-mile crack in the earth where the Virgin River flows over gravel and boulders is one of the world's most stunning gorges. If you hike through it, you'll find yourself surrounded—sometimes nearly boxed in—by smooth walls stretching high into the heavens. Plan to get wet, and beware that flash floods can occur here, especially in spring and summer. Check on the weather before you enter. ✉ *Zion National Park* ✣ *Begins at Riverside Walk.*

HISTORIC SIGHTS

Zion Human History Museum

MUSEUM | This informative museum tells the park's story from the perspective of its human inhabitants, among them Ancestral Puebloans and early Mormon settlers. Permanent exhibits illustrate how humans have dealt with wildlife, plants, and natural forces. Temporary exhibits have touched on everything from vintage park-employee photography to the history of Union Pacific Railroad hotels. Don't miss the incredible view of Towers of the Virgin from the back patio. ✉ *Zion Canyon Scenic Dr., ½ mile north of south entrance, Zion National Park* ☎ *435/772–3256* 🌐 *www.nps.gov/zion* 🎫 *Free.*

PICNIC AREAS

The Grotto

LOCAL INTEREST | **FAMILY** | Get your food to go at Zion Lodge, take a short walk to this scenic retreat, and dine beneath a shady oak. Amenities include drinking water, picnic tables, and restrooms, but there are no fire grates. A trail from here leads to the Emerald Pools. ✉ *Off Zion Canyon Scenic Dr., at Grotto, Zion National Park.*

Zion Nature Center

LOCAL INTEREST | **FAMILY** | In summer, rangers present family programs at this center next to South Campground. There's a nice picnic area where you can feed your kids. When the center is closed, use the restrooms at the campground. ✉ *Zion National Park* ✣ *Near entrance to South Campground, ½ mile north of south entrance.*

SCENIC DRIVES

★ Zion Canyon Scenic Drive

SCENIC DRIVE | Vividly colored cliffs tower 2,000 feet above the road that meanders north from Springdale along the floor of Zion Canyon. As you roll through the narrow, steep canyon, you'll pass the Court of the Patriarchs, the Sentinel, and the Great White Throne, among other imposing rock formations. From February through November, unless you're staying at the lodge, Zion Canyon Scenic Drive is accessed only by park shuttle. You can drive it yourself at other times. ✉ *Off Hwy. 9, Zion National Park.*

Zion–Mt. Carmel Highway and Tunnels

SCENIC DRIVE | Two narrow tunnels as old as the park itself lie between the east entrance and Zion Canyon on this breathtaking 12-mile stretch of Highway 9. One was once the longest man-made tunnel in the world. As you travel the (1.1-mile) passage through solid rock, five arched portals along one side provide fleeting glimpses of cliffs and canyons. When you emerge you'll find that the landscape has changed dramatically. Large vehicles require traffic control and a $15 permit, available at the park entrance, and have restricted hours of travel. This includes nearly all RVs, trailers, dual-wheel trucks, and campers. The Canyon Overlook Trail starts from a parking area between the tunnels. ✉ *Hwy. 9, 5 miles east of*

Canyon Junction, Zion National Park 🌐 *www.nps.gov/zion/planyourvisit/the-zion-mount-carmel-tunnel.htm.*

SCENIC STOPS

Checkerboard Mesa

NATURE SITE | It's well worth stopping at the pull-out 1 mile west of Zion's east entrance to observe the distinctive waffle patterns on this huge white mound of sandstone. The stunning crosshatch effect visible today is the result of eons of freeze-and-thaw cycles that caused vertical fractures, combined with erosion that produced horizontal bedding planes. ✉ *Zion–Mt. Carmel Hwy., Zion National Park.*

Court of the Patriarchs

NATURE SITE | This trio of peaks bears the names of, from left to right, Abraham, Isaac, and Jacob. Mount Moroni is the reddish peak on the far right that partially blocks the view of Jacob. Hike the trail that leaves from the Court of the Patriarchs Viewpoint, 1½ miles north of Canyon Junction, to get a much better view of the sandstone prophets. ✉ *Zion Canyon Scenic Dr., Zion National Park.*

Great White Throne

NATURE SITE | Dominating the Grotto picnic area near Zion Lodge, this massive Navajo sandstone peak juts 2,000 feet above the valley floor. The popular formation lies about 3 miles north of Canyon Junction. ✉ *Zion Canyon Scenic Dr., Zion National Park.*

Weeping Rock

NATURE SITE | Surface water from the rim of Echo Canyon spends several thousand years seeping down through the porous sandstone before exiting at this picturesque alcove 4½ miles north of Canyon Junction. A paved walkway climbs ¼ mile to this flowing rock face where wildflowers and delicate ferns grow. In fall, the maples and cottonwoods burst with color, and lizards point the way down the path, which is too steep for wheelchairs or strollers. A major rockslide closed the Weeping Rock Trail in summer 2019; check with the visitor center to see if it has reopened. ✉ *Zion Canyon Scenic Dr., Zion National Park.*

TRAILS

★ Angels Landing Trail

TRAIL | As much a trial as a trail, this path beneath the Great White Throne, which you access from the Lower West Rim Trail, is one of the park's most challenging hikes. Early on, you work your way through Walter's Wiggles, a series of 21 switchbacks built out of sandstone blocks. From there you traverse sheer cliffs that have chains bolted into the rock face to serve as handrails in some (but not all) places. In spite of its hair-raising nature, this trail is popular. Allow 2½ hours round trip if you stop at Scout's Lookout (2 miles), and 4 hours if you keep going to where the angels (and birds of prey) play. The trail is 5 miles round trip and is not appropriate for children or those who are uneasy about heights. *Difficult.* ✉ *Zion National Park* ✥ *Trailhead: Off Zion Canyon Scenic Dr. at the Grotto.*

★ Canyon Overlook Trail

TRAIL | **FAMILY** | The parking area just east of Zion–Mt. Carmel Tunnel leads to this popular trail, which is about 1 mile round trip and takes about an hour to finish. From the breathtaking overlook at the trail's end, you can see the West and East temples, the Towers of the Virgin, the Streaked Wall, and other Zion Canyon cliffs and peaks. The elevation change is 160 feet. There's no shuttle to this trail, and the parking area often fills up—try to come very early or late in the day to avoid crowds. *Moderate.* ✉ *Zion National Park* ✥ *Trailhead: Off Hwy. 9 just east of Zion–Mt. Carmel Tunnel.*

Emerald Pools Trail

TRAIL | **FAMILY** | Multiple waterfalls cascade (or drip, in dry weather) into algae-filled pools along this trail, about 3 miles north of Canyon Junction. The path leading to the lower pool is paved and appropriate for strollers and wheelchairs. If you've

The views along Angels Landing Trail are truly heavenly.

got any energy left, keep going past the lower pool. The ¼ mile from there to the middle pool becomes rocky and somewhat steep but offers increasingly scenic views. A less crowded and exceptionally enjoyable return route follows the Kayenta Trail, connecting to the Grotto Trail. Allow 50 minutes for the 1¼-mile round-trip hike to the lower pool, and an hour more each round trip to the middle (2 miles) and upper pools (3 miles). *Lower, easy. Upper, moderate.* ✉ *Zion National Park* ✣ *Trailhead: Off Zion Canyon Scenic Dr., at Zion Lodge or the Grotto.*

Grotto Trail

TRAIL | **FAMILY** | This flat trail takes you from Zion Lodge, about 3 miles north of Canyon Junction, to the Grotto picnic area, traveling for the most part along the park road. Allow 20 minutes or less for the walk along the ½-mile trail. If you are up for a longer hike and have two or three hours, connect with the Kayenta Trail after you cross the footbridge, and head for the Emerald Pools. You will begin gaining elevation, and it's a steady, steep climb to the pools, which you will begin to see after about 1 mile. *Easy.* ✉ *Zion National Park* ✣ *Trailhead: Off Zion Canyon Scenic Dr. at the Grotto.*

Hidden Canyon Trail

TRAIL | This steep, 2-mile round-trip hike takes you up 850 feet in elevation. Not too crowded, the trail is paved all the way to Hidden Canyon. Allow about three hours for the round-trip hike. A massive rockfall in summer 2019 resulted in the closure of this trail—check with the visitor center for updates. *Moderate–Difficult.* ✉ *Zion National Park* ✣ *Trailhead: Off Zion Canyon Scenic Dr. at Weeping Rock.*

★ The Narrows Trail

TRAIL | After leaving the paved ease of the Gateway to the Narrows trail behind, walk on the riverbed itself. You'll find a pebbly shingle or dry sandbar path, but when the walls of the canyon close in, you'll be forced into the chilly waters of the Virgin River. A walking stick and good shoes are a must. Be prepared to swim, as chest-deep holes may occur even when water levels are low. Check with park rangers about the likelihood of flash floods. A day trip up the lower section of the Narrows is 6 miles one-way to the turnaround point. Allow at least five hours round-trip. *Difficult.* ✉ *Zion National Park* ✣ *Trailhead: Off Zion Canyon Scenic Dr., at the end of Riverside Walk.*

Pa'rus Trail

TRAIL | **FAMILY** | An approximately 1¾-mile, relatively flat, paved walking and biking path, Pa'rus parallels and occasionally crosses the Virgin River. Starting at South Campground, ½ mile north of the South Entrance, the walk proceeds north along the river to the beginning of Zion Canyon Scenic Drive. Along the way you'll take in great views of the Watchman, the Sentinel, the East and West temples, and the Towers of the Virgin. Leashed dogs are allowed on this trail. Wheelchair users may need assistance. *Easy.* ✉ *Zion National Park* ✣ *Trailhead: At Canyon Junction.*

Riverside Walk

TRAIL | **FAMILY** | This 2.2-mile round-trip hike shadows the Virgin River. In spring, wildflowers bloom on the opposite canyon wall in lovely hanging gardens. The trail, which begins 6½ miles north of Canyon Junction at the end of Zion Canyon Scenic Drive, is the park's most visited, so be prepared for crowds in high season. Riverside Walk is paved and suitable for strollers and wheelchairs, though some wheelchair users may need assistance. Round-trip it takes about 90 minutes. At the end, the much more challenging Narrows Trail begins. *Easy.* ✉ *Zion National Park* ✣ *Trailhead: Off Zion Canyon Scenic Dr. at the Temple of Sinawava.*

Watchman Trail

TRAIL | For a dramatic view of Springdale and a look at lower Zion Creek Canyon and Towers of the Virgin, this strenuous hike begins on a service road east of Watchman Campground. Some springs seep out of the sandstone, nourishing the hanging gardens and attracting wildlife. There are a few sheer cliff edges, so supervise children carefully. Plan on two hours for this 3.3-mile round-trip hike that has a 368-foot elevation change. *Moderate.* ✉ *Zion National Park* ✣ *Trailhead: At Zion Canyon Visitor Center.*

VISITOR CENTERS

Zion Canyon Visitor Center

INFO CENTER | Learn about the area's geology, flora, and fauna at an outdoor exhibit next to a gurgling stream. Inside, a large shop sells everything from field guides to souvenirs. Zion Canyon shuttle buses leave regularly from the center and make several stops along the canyon's beautiful Scenic Drive; ranger-guided shuttle tours depart once a day from Memorial Day to late September. ✉ *Zion Park Blvd. at south entrance, Springdale* ☎ *435/772–3256* 🌐 *www.nps.gov/zion.*

Restaurants

Castle Dome Café & Snack Bar

$ | **CAFÉ** | Next to the shuttle stop at Zion Lodge, this small, convenient, fast-food restaurant has a lovely shaded patio. You can grab a banana, burger, smoothie, or salad to go, order local brews from the Beer Garden cart, or enjoy a dish of ice cream while soaking up the views of the surrounding geological formations. **Known for:** quick bites; gorgeous views; nice beer selection. 💲 *Average main: $6* ✉ *Zion Lodge, Zion Canyon Scenic Dr., Zion National Park* ☎ *435/772–7700* 🌐 *www.zionlodge.com/dining/castle-dome-cafe* ⏲ *Closed Dec.–Feb.*

Red Rock Grill

$$ | **AMERICAN** | The dinner fare at this restaurant in Zion Lodge includes steaks, seafood, and Western specialties, such as pecan-encrusted trout and jalapeño-topped bison cheeseburgers; salads, sandwiches, and hearty burgers are lunch highlights; and, for breakfast, you can partake of the plentiful buffet or order off the menu. Photos showcasing the surrounding landscape adorn the walls of the spacious dining room; enormous windows and a large patio take in the actual landscape. **Known for:** dinner reservations necessary in summer; astounding views inside and out; only full-service restaurant in the park. $ *Average main: $19* ✉ *Zion Lodge, Zion Canyon Scenic Dr., Zion National Park* ☎ *435/772–7760* 🌐 *www.zionlodge.com/dining/red-rock-grill.*

Hotels

★ Zion Lodge

$$$$ | HOTEL | For a dramatic location inside the park, you'd be hard-pressed to improve on a stay at the historic Zion Lodge: the canyon's jaw-dropping beauty surrounds you, access to trailheads is easy, and guests can drive their cars on the lower half of Zion Park Scenic Drive year-round. **Pros:** handsome hotel in the tradition of historic park properties; incredible views; bike rentals on-site. **Cons:** pathways are dimly lit (bring a flashlight); spotty Wi-Fi, poor cell service; books up months ahead. $ *Rooms from: $229* ✉ *Zion Canyon Scenic Dr., Zion National Park* ☎ *888/297–2757 reservations only, 435/772–7700* 🌐 *www.zionlodge.com* *122 rooms* *No meals.*

Kolob Canyons

Sights

SCENIC DRIVES

Kolob Canyons Road

SCENIC DRIVE | Kolob Canyons Road is a 5-mile immersion into red rock canyons that extend east-to-west along three forks of Taylor Creek and La Verkin Creek. The beauty starts modestly at the junction with Interstate 15, but as you move along this 5-mile road, the red walls of the Kolob finger canyons rise suddenly and spectacularly. With the crowds left behind at Zion Canyon, this drive offers the chance to take in incredible vistas at your leisure. Trails include the short but rugged Middle Fork of Taylor Creek Trail, which passes two 1930s homestead cabins, culminating 2¾ miles later in the Double Arch Alcove. At the end of the drive, take the short hike to the Kolob Canyons Viewpoint to see Nagunt Mesa, Shuntavi Butte, and Gregory Butte, each rising to nearly 8,000 feet above sea level. During heavy snowfall Kolob Canyons Road may be closed. ✉ *I–15, Exit 40, Zion National Park.*

Kolob Terrace Road

SCENIC DRIVE | Hundreds of miles of scenic desert roads crisscross the Southwest, and Kolob Terrace Road will remind you of many of them. Sprawling as much as 4,000 feet above the floor of Zion Canyon, and without the benefit of the canyon's breezes and shade, the landscape along it is arid—browns and grays and ambers—but not without rugged beauty. The 21-mile stretch begins 15 miles west of Springdale at Virgin and winds north. As you travel along, peaks and knolls emerge from the high plateau, birds circle overhead, and you might not see more than a half-dozen cars. The drive meanders in and out of the park boundaries, crossing several important trailheads, all the while overlooking the cliffs of North Creek. A popular day-use trail (permit required) leads past fossilized dinosaur tracks to the Subway, a stretch of the stream where the walls of the slot canyon close in so tightly as to form a near tunnel. Farther along the road is the Wildcat Canyon trailhead, which connects to the path overlooking the North Guardian Angel. The road terminates at the Kolob Reservoir, beneath 8,933-foot Kolob Peak. Although paved, this narrow, twisting road is not recommended for RVs. Because of limited winter plowing, the road is closed from November or December through April or May. ✉ *Zion National Park* ✥ *Begins in Virgin at Hwy. 9.*

SCENIC STOPS

Lava Point

VIEWPOINT | Infrequently visited, this area has a primitive campground and two nearby reservoirs that offer the only significant fishing opportunities in the park. Lava Point Overlook, one of the park's highest viewpoints, provides vistas of Zion Canyon from the north. The higher elevation here makes it much cooler than the Zion Canyon area. Park visitors looking for a respite from crowds and heat find the campground a nice change of pace, though the six sites fill up quickly and are only open May through September. ✉ *Zion National Park* ✣ *Kolob Terrace Rd. to Lava Point Rd., then turn right.*

Kolob Canyons Viewpoint

LOCAL INTEREST | **FAMILY** | Nearly 100% of travelers along Interstate 15 from Las Vegas to Salt Lake overlook this short drive a few hundred yards from the highway. The reward is a beautiful view of Kolob's "finger" canyons from about six picnic tables spread out beneath the trees. The parking lot has plenty of space, a pit toilet, and an overlook with a display pointing out canyon features. Restrooms and drinking water are available 5 miles away at the Kolob Canyons Visitor Center. ✉ *Zion National Park* ✣ *On Timber Creek Trail at the end of Kolob Canyons Rd.*

TRAILS

Taylor Creek Trail

TRAIL | This trail in the Kolob Canyons area descends parallel to Taylor Creek, sometimes crossing it, sometimes shortcutting benches beside it. The historic Larson Cabin precedes the entrance to the canyon of the Middle Fork, where the trail becomes rougher. After the old Fife Cabin, the canyon bends to the right into Double Arch Alcove, a large, colorful grotto with a high blind arch (or arch "embryo") towering above. To Double Arch it's 2½ miles one-way—about four hours round-trip. The elevation change is 450 feet. *Moderate.* ✉ *Zion National Park* ✣ *Trailhead: At Kolob Canyons Rd., about 1½ miles east of Kolob Canyons Visitor Center.*

VISITOR CENTERS

Kolob Canyons Visitor Center

INFO CENTER | Make this your first stop as you enter this remote section of the park. There are books and maps, a small gift shop, and clean restrooms here, and rangers are on hand to answer questions about Kolob Canyons exploration. ✉ *3752 E. Kolob Canyons Rd., Exit 40 off I–15, Zion National Park* ☎ *435/772–3256* 🌐 *www.nps.gov/zion.*

Activities

BIKING

Zion Cycles

BICYCLING | This shop just outside the park rents bikes by the hour or longer, sells parts, and has a full-time mechanic on duty. You can pick up trail tips and other advice from the staff here. They also offer guided road-biking treks in the park and mountain-biking excursions elsewhere in southern Utah. ✉ *868 Zion Park Blvd., Springdale* ☎ *435/772–0400* 🌐 *www.zioncycles.com* 🎫 *Guided tours from $175; bike rentals from $40/day.*

CAMPING

South Campground. All the sites here are under big cottonwood trees that provide some relief from the summer sun. The campground operates on a reservation system. ✉ *Hwy. 9, ½ mile north of south entrance* ☎ *435/772–3256, 877/444–6777* 🌐 *www.recreation.gov.*

Watchman Campground. This large campground on the Virgin River operates on a reservation system between March and November, but you do not get to choose your site. ✉ *Access road off Zion Canyon Visitor Center parking lot* ☎ *435/772–3256, 877/444–6777* 🌐 *www.recreation.gov.*

EDUCATIONAL PROGRAMS

CLASSES AND SEMINARS

★ Zion Natl Park Forever Project

TOUR—SIGHT | Formerly known as the Zion Natural History Association, this organization conducts in-park workshops on natural and cultural history. Topics can include edible plants, bat biology, river geology, photography, and bird-watching. Most workshops include a hike. For a glimpse of Zion's inner workings, volunteer to assist with one of their ongoing service projects. ✉ *Zion National Park* ☎ *435/772–3264* 🌐 *www.zionpark.org* 🎫 *From $45.*

RANGER PROGRAMS

Evening Programs

TOUR—SIGHT | Held each evening May through September in Watchman Campground and at Zion Lodge, these 45-minute ranger-led talks cover geology, biology, and history. You might learn about coyote calls, the night sky, animal hideouts, or observing nature with all your senses. Slide shows and audience participation are often part of the proceedings. Check the visitor center for schedules. ✉ *Zion National Park* 🌐 *www.nps.gov/zion/planyourvisit/ranger-led-activities.htm.*

★ Expert Talks

TOUR—SIGHT | Informal lectures take place on the Zion Human History Museum patio. Past topics have included wildlife, geology, and the stories of early settlers. Talks usually last from 20 to 30 minutes, though some run longer. Check park bulletin boards or the visitor center for schedules. ✉ *Zion National Park* 🌐 *www.nps.gov/zion/planyourvisit/ranger-led-activities.htm.*

Junior Ranger Program

TOUR—SIGHT | **FAMILY** | Educational activities aimed at younger visitors include the chance to earn a Junior Ranger badge. Kids do so by attending at least one nature program and completing the free *Junior Ranger Handbook,* available at visitor centers. ✉ *Zion National Park* 🌐 *www.nps.gov/zion/learn/kidsyouth/beajuniorranger.htm.*

★ Ranger-Led Hikes

TOUR—SIGHT | **FAMILY** | In summer, daily guided hikes along the 1.7-mile Pa'rus Trail provide an overview of the park's geology and natural and other history. Groups meet at 2 pm at the Zion Canyon Visitor Center. Wear sturdy footgear and bring a hat, sunglasses, sunscreen, and water. Wheelchairs are welcome on this paved trail but may need assistance. ✉ *Zion Canyon Visitor Center, Zion National Park* 🌐 *www.nps.gov/zion/planyourvisit/ranger-led-activities.htm* 🎫 *Free.*

★ Ride with a Ranger Shuttle Tours

TOUR—SIGHT | **FAMILY** | Once a day, from Memorial Day through September, rangers conduct shuttle tours of points of interest along Zion Canyon Scenic Drive. In addition to learning about the canyon's geology, ecology, and history, you'll be treated to some great photo-ops. The two-hour tour takes place in the morning and departs from the Zion Canyon Visitor Center. Make reservations in person at the visitor center up to three days in advance for up to eight people in your group. ✉ *Zion Canyon Visitor Center, Zion National Park* 🌐 *www.nps.gov/zion/planyourvisit/ranger-led-activities.htm* 🎫 *Free* ⏲ *Closed Oct.–late May.*

HORSEBACK RIDING

Canyon Trail Rides

HORSEBACK RIDING | **FAMILY** | Easygoing, one-hour and half-day guided rides are available (minimum age 7 and 10 years, respectively). These friendly folks have been around for years and are the only outfitter for trail rides inside the park. Reservations are recommended and can be made online. The maximum weight is 220 pounds, and the season runs from March through October. ✉ *Across from Zion Lodge, Zion National Park* ☎ *435/679–8665* 🌐 *www.canyonrides.com* 🎫 *From $45.*

What's Nearby

Hotels, restaurants, and shops thrive in steadily growing **Springdale,** population 581, on the southern boundary of Zion National Park, yet the town still manages to maintain its small-town charm. There are plenty of dining and lodging options, and if you take the time to stroll the main drag you can pick up souvenirs. A free shuttle carries you through town and to the park's South Entrance (which is within walking distance of the visitor center), and you can rent bikes in town.

If you have time to explore, there's always **Virgin, La Verkin,** and the ghost town of **Grafton,** which you might recognize from *Butch Cassidy and the Sundance Kid* and other films. Today there's a stone school, a dusty cemetery, and a few other restored buildings. **Hurricane,** population about 16,200, has experienced much growth since 2000 and keeps sprouting new restaurants and lodgings (many of them chains). (Locals emphasize the first syllable, barely uttering the last.) There are historical sites, a world-class golf course, and the Hurricane Canal, dug by hand and used for 80 years to irrigate fields around town. It's just up Interstate 15 from the largest city in southern Utah, **St. George** (population 82,400), a prosperous and attractive small metropolis with a dramatic red-rock setting.

Heading east from Zion is **Mount Carmel Junction,** an intersection offering a couple of funky small-town lodgings and the studio of American West artist Maynard Dixon. It's a 20-minute drive south from here to funky Kanab, a growing hub of recreation with a handful of excellent restaurants and hotels—it's an excellent base if you'll also be visiting Bryce Canyon, the Grand Canyon, and Grand Staircase–Escalante National Monument.

Index

E

H

N

O

P

S

U

V

W

X

Y

Z

Photo Credits

Front Cover: Chad M. Connell [Description: View of White Oak Canyon at Shenandoah National Park.]. **Back cover, from left to right:** Gary C. Tognoni/Shutterstock, BlueBarronPhoto/Shutterstock, silky/Shutterstock. **Spine:** Francesco R. Iacomino/Shutterstock. **Interior, from left to right:** Evan Spiler (1). Henner Damke/Shutterstock (2). **Chapter 1: Experience the National Parks of the USA:** Jeff Vanuga (14-15). cadlikai/Shutterstock (16). Tashka | Dreamstime.com (17). Anton Foltin/Shutterstock (17). DnDavis/Shutterstock (18). Ken Wolter/Shutterstock (18). Zack Frank/Shutterstock (18). Oscity/Shutterstock (18). Sean Pavone/Shutterstock (19). sumikophoto/Shutterstock (19). Jill Krueger (19). kan_khampanya/Shutterstock (19). Mike Brake/Shutterstock (20). Matthew Connolly/Shutterstock (20). Linda Moon/Shutterstock (20). Benkrut | Dreamstime.com (20). Swdesertlover | Dreamstime.com (21). Antonel | Dreamstime.com (21). Charles Haire/Shutterstock (21). Anton Foltin/Shutterstock (21). Sergey Yechikov/Shutterstock (22). neelsky/Shutterstock (22). Nina B/Shutterstock (22). kavram/Shutterstock (22). kojihirano/Shutterstock (23). Laurens Hoddenbagh/Shutterstock (23). Americanspirit | Dreamstime.com (23). Sebastien Burel/Shutterstock (23). Kelly vanDellen/Shutterstock (24). Thomas Barrat/Shutterstock (24). Ca2hill | Dreamstime.com (24). Wilsilver77 | Dreamstime.com (24). inEthos Design/Shutterstock (25). Raymona Pooler/Shutterstock (25). Jonathan A. Mauer/Shutterstock (25). Pierre Leclerc/Shutterstock (25). Kelly vanDellen/Shutterstock (26). K.E.K/Shutterstock (26). David_Pastyka/Shutterstock (27). Richard Herron/iStockphoto (28). Pierre Leclerc/Shutterstock (28). lembi/Shutterstock (28). Daniel Korzeniewski/Shutterstock (28). Anna Westman/Shutterstock (29). NPS photo/Western Arctic National Parklands/Flickr, [CC BY 2.0] (29). Rick Grainger/Shutterstock (29). Andriy Blokhin/shutterstock (29). Wildnerdpix/iStockphoto (30). Danita Delimont/Shutterstock (30). Gilles Baechler/Shutterstock (30). Ryan Schrader/Shutterstock (30). Steve Heap/Shutterstock (31). Jnjphotos/Shutterstock (31). Zack Frank/Shutterstock (31). rukawajung/Shutterstock (31). Checubus/Shutterstock (32). Gestalt Imagery/Shutterstock (32). Anton Foltin/Shutterstock (32). Isu83boo | Dreamstime.com (32). Kris Wiktor/Shutterstock (33). F11photo | Dreamstime.com (34). Lorcel/Shutterstock (34). YayaErnst/iStockphoto (34). Hale Kell/Shutterstock (35). Michel Verdure (38). Courtesy of Grand Teton Lodge Company (38). Roman Khomlyak/Shutterstock (38). Delaware North (39). Kitleong | Dreamstime.com (39). David Davis/Shutterstock (40). Dan King (40). Dan King (40). Stephen Fadem (40). Erica L. Wainer (40). Roger Bravo (41). BostonGal (41). Debbie Bowles (41). Darklich14/Wikimedia Commons (41). Bill Perry/Shutterstock (41). Danita Delimont/Shutterstock (42). slowmotiongli/Shutterstock (42). Wynianjt | Dreamstime.com (42). Chasedekker | Dreamstime.com (42). Mikaelmales | Dreamstime.com (42). Williamwise1 | Dreamstime.com (43). Shedd Aquarium/Brenna Hernandez (43). Animals_Landscape/Shutterstock. (43). Nastya81 | Dreamstime.com (43). Bruce Raynor/Shutterstock (43). Life Atlas Photography/Shutterstock (44). Hannator92 | Dreamstime.com (45). **Chapter 2: Planning Your Visit:** Lorcel/Shutterstock (47). **Chapter 3: Great Itineraries:** Som Vembar (59). **Chapter 4: Acadia:** Try Media/iStockphoto (71). f11photo/Shutterstock. (85). **Chapter 5: Arches:** Evan Spiler (91). Lukas Urwyler/Shutterstock (99). **Chapter 6: Badlands:** JOECHO-16 (103). Virrage Images/Shutterstock (110). **Chapter 7: Big Bend:** Eric Foltz/iStockphoto (115). Mike Norton/Shutterstock (125). **Chapter 8: Biscayne:** kyletperry/iStockphoto (131). Francisco Blanco/Shutterstock (137). **Chapter 9: Black Canyon of the Gunnison:** Tom Till / Alamy (141). Jim Parkin/Shutterstock (151). **Chapter 10: Bryce Canyon:** Chris Christensen (http://AmateurTraveler.com) (153). Inc/Shutterstock (164). **Chapter 11: Canyonlands:** Bryan Brazil/Shutterstock (167). Danita Delimont/Shutterstock (174). **Chapter 12: Capitol Reef:** Luca Moi/Shutterstock (179). Anton Foltin/Shutterstock (185). **Chapter 13: Carlsbad Caverns:** Nphoto | Dreamstime.com (191). Doug Meek/Shutterstock (200). **Chapter 14: Channel Islands:** Christopher Russell/iStockphoto (203). Americanspirit | Dreamstime.com (210). **Chapter 15: Congaree:** Serge Skiba/Shutterstock (215). Pierre Leclerc/Shutterstock (223). **Chapter 16: Crater Lake:** William A. McConnell (225). zschnepf/Shutterstock (234). **Chapter 17: Cuyahoga Valley:** Kenneth Keifer/Shutterstock (237). Shriram Patki/Shutterstock (244). **Chapter 18: Death Valley:** Bryan Brazil/Shutterstock (253). Evan Spiler, Fodors.com member (261). **Chapter 19: Denali:** Tyler Westhoff (267). Bingoye1 | Dreamstime.com (279). **Chapter 20: Dry Tortugas:** Mia2you/Shutterstock (285). Sandra Foyt/Shutterstock (291). Craig Hinton/Shutterstock (293). **Chapter 21: Everglades:** Brian Lasenby/Shutterstock (295). Mia2you/Shutterstock (303 & 308). **Chapter 22: Gates of the Arctic and Kobuk Valley:** West Coast Scapes/Shutterstock (313 & 320). Western Arctic National Parklands Follow/NPS photo/Flickr, [CC BY 2.0] (322). **Chapter 23: Gateway Arch:** Patricia Elaine Thomas/Shutterstock (325). RozenskiP/Shutterstock (333). **Chapter 24: Glacier and Waterton Lakes:** BGSmith/Shutterstock (337). chip phillips/iStockphoto (347). **Chapter 25: Glacier Bay:** Maridav/Shutterstock (357). Nickolas warner/Shutterstock (364). **Chapter 26: Grand Canyon:** NPS (369). Kerrick James (386). **Chapter 27: Grand Teton:** Patrick Tr/Shutterstock (393). Kenneth Keifer/Shutterstock (400). **Chapter 28: Great Basin:** Dennis Frates / Alamy (411). Heeb Christian / age fotostock (418). **Chapter 29: Great Sand Dunes:** J.C. Leacock/CTO (423). Austin Hawley/Shutterstock (429). **Chapter 30: Great Smoky Mountains:** jo Crebbin / Shutterstock (431). Paul Tessier / Shutterstock (439). **Chapter 31: Guadalupe Mountains:** Zack Frank/Shutterstock (457). Michael J Thompson/Shutterstock (467). **Chapter 32: Haleakala:** MarcPo/iStockphoto (469). Robert Michaud/iStockphoto (475). **Chapter 33: Hawaii Volcanoes:** espiegle/iStockphoto (483). Andre Nantel/Shutterstock (492). **Chapter 34: Hot Springs:** Niwat panket/Shutterstock (503). Zrfphoto | Dreamstime.com (510). **Chapter 35: Indiana Dunes:** ehrlif/Shutterstock (517). Jon Lauriat/Shutterstock (524). **Chapter 36: Isle Royale:** Mark Baldwin/Shutterstock (529). Steven Schremp/Shutterstock (536). **Chapter 37: Joshua Tree:** Eric Foltz/iStockphoto (541). Pixelite/Shutterstock (549). **Chapter 38: Katmai:** Danita Delimont/Shutterstock (555). CSNafzger/Shutterstock (562). **Chapter 39: Kenai Fjords:** Sean Lema/Shutterstock (565). Tomasz Wozniak/Shutterstock (573). **Chapter 40: Lake Clark:** Jim David/Shutterstock (575). Danita Delimont/Shutterstock (582). **Chapter 41: Lassen Volcanic:** Zack Frank/Shutterstock (585). Shyam Subramanyan (593). **Chapter 42: Mammoth Cave:** zrfphoto/iStockphoto (599). Jiawangkun | Dreamstime.com (610). **Chapter 43: Mesa Verde:** Rob Crandall/Shutterstock (623). Kerrick James (632). **Chapter 44: Mount Rainier:** chinana, Fodors.com member (637). zschnepf/Shutterstock (649). **Chapter 45: National Park of American Samoa:** Danita Delimont/Shutterstock (651). U.S. Department of the Interior/Flickr, [CC BY 2.0] (658). **Chapter 46: New River Gorge:** Steveheap | Dreamstime.com (661). Zack Frank/Shutterstock. (667). **Chapter 47: North Cascades:** LoweStock / Getty Images (671). Tobin Akehurst/Shutterstock (680). **Chapter 48: Olympic:** Rita Bellanca (685). Lindsay Douglas/Shutterstock (693). **Chapter 49: Petrified Forest:** Kerrick James (701). Clara/Shutterstock (708). **Chapter 50: Pinnacles:** yhelfman/Shutterstock (711 & 717). **Chapter 51: Redwood:** iStockphoto (721). Galyna Andrushko/Shutterstock (729). **Chapter 52: Rocky Mountain:** Stock Connection Distribution / Alamy (735). Harold R. Stinnette Stock Photography / Alamy (750). **Chapter 53: Saguaro:** Johnny Stockshooter (753). Sasha Buzko/Shutterstock (761). **Chapter 54: Sequoia and Kings Canyon:** Robert Holmes (763). urosr/Shutterstock (776). **Chapter 55: Shenandoah:** Vladimir Grablev/Shutterstock (785). Jon Bilous/Shutterstock (797). **Chapter 56: Theodore Roosevelt:** North Dakota Tourism (801). ZakZeinert/Shutterstock (807). **Chapter 57: Virgin Islands:** BlueOrange Studio/Shutterstock (813). Wangkun Jia/Shutterstock (822). ESB Professional/Shutterstock (824). **Chapter 58: Voyageurs:** Jon Lauriat/Shutterstock (827 & 833). **Chapter 59: White Sands:** sunsinger/Shutterstock (837). Michael Rosebrock/Shutterstock (844). **Chapter 60: Wind Cave:** South Dakota Tourism (847). South Dakota Tourism (856). Alex Pix/Shutterstock (858). **Chapter 61: Wrangell–St. Elias:** Jeltown | Dreamstime.com (861). Emma Rogers/Shutterstock (869). **Chapter 62: Yellowstone:** funtravlr (873). Paul Stoloff (889). **Chapter 63: Yosemite:** Jill Krueger (901). DTM Media/Shutterstock. (910). Pung/Shutterstock (919). **Chapter 64: Zion:** John Vaccarelli (925). My Good Images/Shutterstock (933).

*Every effort has been made to trace the copyright holders, and we apologize in advance for any accidental errors. We would be happy to apply the corrections in the following edition of this publication.

Fodor's THE COMPLETE GUIDE TO THE NATIONAL PARKS OF THE USA

Publisher: Stephen Horowitz, *General Manager*

Editorial: Douglas Stallings, *Editorial Director*, Jill Fergus, Amanda Sadlowski, Caroline Trefler, *Senior Editors*; Kayla Becker, Alexis Kelly, *Editors*

Design: Tina Malaney, *Director of Design and Production*; Jessica Gonzalez, *Graphic Designer;* Mariana Tabares, *Design & Production Intern*

Production: Jennifer DePrima, *Editorial Production Manager*, Elyse Rozelle, *Senior Production Editor;* Monica White, Production Editor

Maps: Rebecca Baer, *Senior Map Editor*, Mark Stroud (Moon Street Cartography), *Cartographer*

Photography: Viviane Teles, *Senior Photo Editor;* Namrata Aggarwal, Ashok Kumar, Rebecca Rimmer, *Photo Editors*

Business and Operations: Chuck Hoover, *Chief Marketing Officer*, Robert Ames, *Group General Manager*, Devin Duckworth, *Director of Print Publishing*; Amber Zhou, *Business Analyst*

Public Relations and Marketing: Joe Ewaskiw, *Senior Director of Communications & Public Relations*

Fodors.com: Jeremy Tarr, *Editorial Director;* Rachael Levitt, *Managing Editor*

Technology: Jon Atkinson, *Director of Technology;* Rudresh Teotia, *Lead Developer*, Jacob Ashpis, *Content Operations Manager*

Writers: Karen Anderson, Lehia Apana, Shelly Arenas, Teeka Ballas, Carol M. Bareuther, John Blodgett, Whitney Bryen, David Cannamore, Andrew Collins, Cheryl Crabtree, Leslie Fisher, Lindsey Galloway, Erin Gifford, Aimee Heckel, Kellee Katagi, Stratton Lawrence, Mara Levin, Mary McHugh, Gary McKechnie, Debbie Olson, Eric Peterson, Elise Riley, Cameron Roberts, Kristan Schiller, Tres Seymour, Stina Sieg, Dawnell Smith, Carson Walker

Editors: Alexis Kelly, Laura M. Kidder

Production Editors: Jennifer DePrima, Elyse Rozelle

1st edition

ISBN 978-1-64097-454-8

ISSN 2767–9152

All details in this book are based on information supplied to us at press time. Always confirm information when it matters, especially if you're making a detour to visit a specific place. Fodor's expressly disclaims any liability, loss, or risk, personal or otherwise, that is incurred as a consequence of the use of any of the contents of this book.

SPECIAL SALES

This book is available at special discounts for bulk purchases for sales promotions or premiums. For more information, e-mail SpecialMarkets@fodors.com.

PRINTED IN THE UNITED STATES OF AMERICA

10 9 8 7 6 5 4 3 2 1

About Our Writers

Karen Anderson resides in Kona, Hawaii, and works as a freelance journalist, managing editor, and professional photographer. For 13 consecutive years, she has been the managing editor of *At Home, Living with Style in West Hawaii.* She also writes for a variety of publications including *West Hawaii Today; Hawaii Island Midweek; Hawaii Luxury Magazine; Ke Ola Magazine; Hawaii Drive Magazine; Edible Hawaiian Islands Magazine*; and *USA Today Travel Tips.* She is the author of *The Hawaii Home Book, Practical Tips for Tropical Living,* which reached #1 on the Honolulu Advertiser's bestsellers nonfiction list and received the Award of Excellence from the Hawaii Book Publishers Association. Her monthly editor's column and chef/restaurant profiles are known throughout the Big Island. She updated the Hawaii Volcanoes chapter.

Born and raised on Maui, **Lehia Apana** is an island girl with a wandering spirit. She has lived in Chicago, Rome, and Sydney, but always finds her way back home. Lehia has been writing about Maui for 15 years, beginning as a reporter for *The Maui News,* and most recently as the managing editor at *Maui Nō Ka Oi Magazine.* These days, when she's not clicking away at the keyboard, she can be found working on her regenerative farm along Maui's northern coast. She developed the Haleakala chapter. Find her at @ PolipoliFarms or 🌐 *PolipoliFarms.com.*

Shelley Arenas grew up in eastern Washington and has lived in the Seattle area since college. She's been a regular contributor to Fodor's guidebooks for more than a decade, along with co-authoring a book about Seattle for families and writing for several regional publishers. She updated the Bryce, Capitol Reef, Mt. Rainier, North Cascades, and Zion chapters for this edition.

A seeker of adventure, laughter, and ridiculousness, **Teeka Ballas** works hard to avoid all things maudlin and monotonous. She has traveled to several corners of the arguably flat, seemingly square Earth, and has called Anchorage home for 16 years. After a varied past of careers, she is now a high school language arts teacher, and the co-owner of The Writer's Block Bookstore and Cafe. Teeka developed the Kenai Fjords, Lake Clark, and Wrangell–St. Elias chapters.

Carol M. Bareuther is a 30-plus-year Virgin Islands resident who met her husband while hiking the Johnny Horn Trail in St. John's Virgin Islands National Park (VINP). Since then, she has written for *Cooking Light, Produce Business, Cruising World, Marlin, Southern Boating,* and *SAIL,* often illustrated by her husband's photography. She also authored *Virgin Islands Cooking* and *Sports Fishing in the Virgin Islands.* Carol, a registered dietitian by first profession, is the mother of a Coast Guard officer, Olympic sailor, and Virgin Islands–based engineer, as well as two four-footed children: Wolfie the dachshund and Jesse a rescue, who both enjoy walking VINP trails on their requisite leashes.

Editor, writer, and photojournalist **John Blodgett** is a "boomerang"—someone, according to *Live and Work in Maine,* who grew up in Maine and moved away only to eventually return; he has contributed to numerous Fodor's Travel guides since the early aughts including the recent edition of Fodor's New England. He considers himself a native Mainiac despite being born, through no fault of his own, in Massachusetts. He lives in Scarborough and is addicted to needhams, a traditional Maine candy made with potatoes. Follow his work at 🌐 *johnmblodgett.com.* He updated the Acadia chapter.

About Our Writers

Whitney Bryen has been a journalist since 2010. She worked at the *Boulder Daily Camera* and *Longmont Times-Call* until 2016 when she took a year off to travel. From a 1968 Silver Streak trailer, Bryen explored national, state, and local parks across the country documenting her experiences in stories and photographs. Bryen returned to the workforce as an investigative reporter and continues to write about food, drinks, and travel as a freelancer. Follow @whitneywanders on Instagram. Whitney updated the Great Sand Dunes chapter.

After several years guiding and caretaking in British Columbia, **David Cannamore**—who worked on the Glacier Bay and Denali chapters—his wife Brittney, and their two cats now call Gustavus, Alaska, home. In addition to freelance writing, David passes the time as a kayak guide in nearby Glacier Bay National Park and the Tongass National Forest.

Former Fodor's staff editor **Andrew Collins** is based in both Mexico City and a small village in New Hampshire's Lake Sunapee region, but he spends much of his time traveling throughout the United States. He updated the Big Bend, Carlsbad Caverns, Crater Lake, Grand Teton, Guadalupe Mountains, Lassen Volcanic, Pinnacles, Redwood, White Sands, and Yellowstone chapters, as well as Experience, Planning Your Visit, and Great Itineraries. A long-time contributor to more than 200 Fodor's guidebooks, including Pacific Northwest, Utah, Santa Fe, Inside Mexico City, and New England, he's also written for dozens of mainstream and LGBTQ publications—*Travel + Leisure, New Mexico Magazine, AAA Living, The Advocate,* and *Canadian Traveller* among them. Additionally, Collins teaches travel writing and food writing for New York City's Gotham Writers Workshop. You can find more of his work at 🌐 *AndrewsTraveling.com*, and follow him on Instagram @ TravelAndrew.

Native Californian **Cheryl Crabtree**—who updated the Yosemite, Sequoia and Kings Canyon, Channel Islands, Death Valley, and Joshua Tree chapters—has worked as a freelance writer since 1987. She also contributes regularly to Fodor's California and Oahu guidebooks. Cheryl is editor of *Montecito Magazine*. She co-authors *The California Directory of Fine Wineries* hardcover book series (Napa•Sonoma and Central Coast editions). Her articles have appeared in numerous regional and national publications, and she has also authored travel apps for mobile devices and content for travel websites.

Leslie Fisher is a media professional working across multiple platforms as a writer and graphic designer. She wrote the chapter on Hot Springs, an area she has covered extensively for various publications and for the city's tourism bureau. While living in an RV, she wrote for a travel website she and her husband developed. Leslie has also written for *Trailer Life* and *All About Beer,* and was a producer for the television series *Mineral Explorers*.

Lindsey Galloway lives in Boulder, Colorado, and has covered travel for 15 years, including the Living In column for *BBC Travel*. She loves taking new Colorado visitors to Estes Park, especially The Stanley for its Stephen King connection. She is the founder and editor of 🌐 *TravelPretty.com,* tweets too often at @ savvylindz, and sometimes TikToks at @ travelpretty. Lindsey updated the Rocky Mountain National Park chapter for this edition.

About Our Writers

Erin Gifford is a Northern Virginia–based travel and outdoor writer. She has written about family travel, road trips, national parks and outdoor recreation for such outlets as the *Washington Post, Chicago Tribune, Parents,* and *Family Circle.* When not seeking out new outdoor adventures, like hiking, biking, camping and backpacking, she is crossing off the next state in her quest to run a half-marathon in all 50 states. She developed the Shenandoah chapter and wrote the New River Gorge chapter for this guide. Find her at 🌐 *www.eringifford.com.*

Aimee Heckel is honored to have been a part of the Fodor's Colorado guide books since 2013. She also published her own book, *Colorado Day Trips by Theme,* in 2020. She has more than two decades of journalism experience and has edited or contributed to more than 50 books. As a travel expert, Heckel has covered Colorado as a regular contributor for *USA Today,* 10Best.com, Culture Trip, SpaTravelGal.com, TripSavvy, Travel Boulder, and more. For this edition, she updated the Mesa Verde chapter. Visit 🌐 *AimeeHeckel.com*

Kellee Katagi has lived in eight U.S. states, but her present home of Colorado is her favorite. A former managing editor of *SKI magazine,* Katagi is now a freelance writer/editor specializing in travel, sports, fitness, health, and food in all its marvelous forms. When not at her desk, she enjoys playing in the Colorado mountains with her husband, their three teenage explorers, and their trusty raft, dubbed K-5 Shark. Katagi updated the Black Canyon of the Gunnison chapter.

Stratton Lawrence's idea of fun is to load his two toddlers into the truck, strap bikes, skis, and boards to the roof, and head west without a firm return date. When he's not pulling over every 20 minutes for bathroom breaks, he's on the beach in Charleston, SC, writing about adventures past and still to come. He's a contributing author to several books in the Fodor's catalog. He developed the Congaree chapter for this guide. You can follow his adventures on Instagram @ strattonlawrence or 🌐 *www.strattonlawrence.com.*

Saguaro and Grand Canyon updater **Mara Levin** divides her time between travel writing, traveling, and social work. A native of California, Mara now lives in Tucson, where the grass may not be greener, but the mountains, tranquillity, and slower pace of desert life have their own appeal.

Mary McHugh is a freelance writer and public relations professional who has an extensive background in the areas of content creation and strategy, including interviewing and reporting about unique people, places, and events for articles, blogs, advertorial copy, social platforms, and more. The St. Louis native, who has traveled extensively, especially enjoys writing about the cool, imaginative nook-and-cranny hot spots—including Gateway Arch National Park—in her hometown.

A two-time winner of the Lowell Thomas Travel Journalism Award, **Gary McKechnie** is the author of the nation's best-selling motorcycle guidebook, *Great American Motorcycle Tours,* and National Geographic's *USA 101* and *Ten Best of Everything: National Parks.* He has also written for Walt Disney World, Rand McNally, *People, National Geographic Traveler, Washington Post,* Harley-Davidson, *Orlando* and *Florida* magazines, *Chicago Tribune, Atlanta Constitution, Orlando Sentinel,* and *Miami Herald.* For this book, Gary developed the American Samoa, Biscayne, Dry Tortugas, and Everglades chapters.